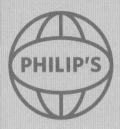

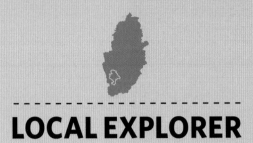

PHILIP'S

LOCAL EXPLORER

NOTTINGHAMSHIRE

www.philips-maps.co.uk

Published by Philip's, a division of
Octopus Publishing Group Ltd
www.octopusbooks.co.uk
Carmelite House, 50 Victoria Embankment,
London EC4Y 0DZ
An Hachette UK Company
www.hachette.co.uk

First edition 2023
First impression 2023
NOTFA

ISBN 978-1-84907-642-5

© Philip's 2023

This product
includes mapping
data licensed from
Ordnance Survey®
with the permission
of the Controller of His Majesty's Stationery
Office. © Crown copyright 2023. All rights
reserved. Licence number 100011710.

Photographic acknowledgements:
Alamy Stock Photo: /darren ball II top; /Terry
Mathews II bottom right; /Transportimage
Picture Library III; /travellinglight front cover.
Dreamstime.com: /Krzysztof Nahlik II
bottom left.

Printed in China

CONTENTS

II Best places to visit

IV Key to map pages

VI Route planning

X Key to map symbols

1 Street maps at 3½ inches to 1 mile

221 Approach map of Nottingham

222 Street map of Nottingham city centre at 7 inches to 1 mile

224 Index of towns, villages, streets, hospitals, industrial estates, railway stations, schools, shopping centres,

Best places to visit

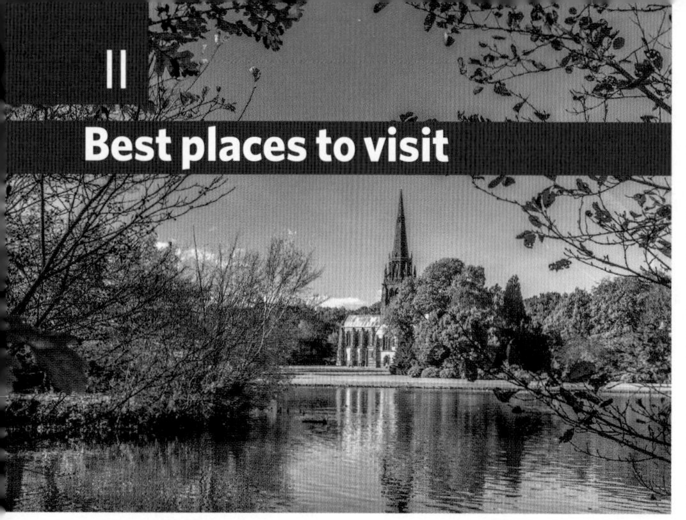

Outdoors

Attenborough Nature Reserve
Nature reserve comprising a network of flooded former gravel pits and islands. It is known particularly for its bird life, especially kingfishers and some unusual duck species, but is also important for its wide variety of plants, and is a good place to spot otters. There are bird hides, themed nature trails and a visitor centre. Frequent events include exhibitions and talks. *Nottingham* 🖥 www.nottinghamshirewildlife.org **183 E1**

Budby South Forest Area of historic heathland and other increasingly rare habitats important to wildlife, immediately north of Sherwood Forest. It is noted for its invertebrates, in particular unusual bees, wasps and beetles, as well as birds and bats. Although part of the RSPB-managed Sherwood Forest National Nature Reserve, it is deliberately 'wilder', with no waymarked trails. There is a public bridleway and footpath crossing the reserve. *Edwinstowe* 🖥 www.rspb.org.uk • 🖥 www.visitsherwood.co.uk **75 E7**

Clumber Park Large area of parkland and woodland, formerly the private estate of the Dukes of Newcastle. Clumber House has been demolished, but the imposing Gothic Revival Chapel of St Mary the Virgin can still be visited. The large walled kitchen garden is noted for its rhubarb and apple collections, its unusually long glasshouse and year-round colour. There are walking routes by the lake and in the surrounding parkland and woods, as

▲ *Sherwood Forest*

well as cycling trails, children's activities and play areas, and a Discovery Centre. *Worksop* 🖥 www.nationaltrust.org.uk **48 B3**

Creswell Crags Archaeological park, centred on a dramatic limestone gorge dotted with caves on the border between Nottinghamshire and Derbyshire. The caves, first excavated in the 19th century, were lived in by early humans during the Ice Age. Tools have been discovered as well as the earliest cave art in the UK, plus bones from woolly mammoths, bears and reindeer. The museum has an important collection of finds from here and elsewhere in the UK. There are walking trails in the woodland and by the lake. *Creswell* 🖥 www.creswell-crags.org.uk **45 B1**

Idle Valley Nature Reserve Large nature reserve, an area of lakes and wetlands surrounded by grassland and scrub, where rare-breed cattle and sheep graze. There are walking routes, a visitor centre and a play area. The reserve is mainly known for its birdlife, primarily waterfowl and wading birds, but it is also home to beavers as part of a project to reintroduce the animals to Nottinghamshire. *Retford* 🖥 www.nottinghamshirewildlife.org **29 B2**

Rufford Abbey Country park surrounding the ruins of Rufford Abbey, which was founded in the 12th century and later transformed into a grand manor house. Only the abbey's undercroft and

a Jacobean wing of the house remain. Surrounding the ruins are formal gardens and lawns, and a large area of woodland, a haven for woodland animals and wildflowers. Activities within the park include an adventure playground, mini golf, archery and boating on the lake. *Ollerton* 🖥 www.english-heritage.org.uk **91 F6**

Sherwood Forest Large area of ancient woodland, formerly a vast royal hunting ground, closely associated with the legend of Robin Hood. The RSPB-managed Sherwood National Nature Reserve covers almost 1,000 acres and is particularly well known for its ancient oaks, including the Major Oak, said to be 1,000 years old. It is a site of Special Scientific Interest for its oak-birch woodland, and is home to a huge variety of animal life, especially birds and insects. There are walking and cycling trails, guided walks, special events and a visitor centre. *Edwinstowe* 🖥 www.visitsherwood.co.uk **76 A4**

Sherwood Pines Forest park to the south of the Sherwood Forest National Nature Reserve, with plenty of outdoor activities. There are cycling trails of varying difficulty, walking routes, children's trails, play areas, special events and a café. *Clipstone* 🖥 www.forestryengland.uk/sherwood-pines **90 E3**

Thoresby Park Large area of parkland and woodland surrounding the grand country house Thoresby Hall, now a hotel. The varied woodland is known for its ancient oak trees, pines and redwood and plentiful wildlife. Signposted walks lead around the estate, and bike hire is available. The Royal Lancers and Nottinghamshire Yeomanry Museum, in the Victorian courtyard, tells the story of British cavalry up to the present day. Within the estate, although separate, is a falconry centre, which provides opportunities to fly various birds of prey. *Worksop* 🖥 http://whatsonatthoresby.co.uk **62 C3**

Towns & villages

Newark-on-Trent Historic market town on the River Trent, believed to have been settled in Roman times and for many centuries a centre of the cotton and wool trades. At its heart is a Georgian market square with a Palladian-style town hall, which houses a museum of fine art,

◄ *Newark Castle*
▼ *Nottingham*

ceramics and furniture. The 18th-century Assembly Room and Council Chamber can be visited. Just off the square is the 16th-century Governor's House, so called because it was the home of the Castle Governor during the Civil War. **Newark Castle** dates from the 12th century. It held an important role during the Civil War, when the town was a Royalist stronghold, but it is thanks to this role that it was virtually demolished afterwards. Its impressive walls and gatehouse were later restored and stand prominently on the banks of the river within gardens. The **National Civil War Centre** relates the causes and consequences of the war, and the effects of the conflict on the lives of ordinary people. There are interactive exhibits, digital displays, changing exhibitions and frequent events and activities. Nearby is **St Mary Magdalene Church**, which mainly dates from the 14th and 15th centuries, although there was a Saxon church on the site. It is unusually large, with some interesting painted panels and brasses. There is a hole in the spire, believed to have been made by a cannonball during the Civil War. A short distance outside the town is **Newark Air Museum**, located on a former World War 2 airfield and training base. It displays a large number of historic aircraft, as well as engines and a variety of aviation artefacts. On special event days visitors can access some of the cockpits. **140 C7**

Nottingham City on the River Trent, the county town of Nottinghamshire. It grew from an Anglo-Saxon settlement in the 6th century, played a prominent role in the Civil War in the 17th century, and was a centre for textile making, notably lace, from the 17th century onwards. The **Old Market Square** is at the heart of the city. A large pedestrianised square, it is dominated by **Nottingham Council House**, which dates from the 1920s and has a large dome. There are occasional tours of the elaborately decorated interior. Nearby is the historic **Lace Market** area, which dates mainly from the heyday of lace production in the 19th century. The typically Victorian streets are lined with warehouses. **St Mary's Church**, in the Lace Market, is the largest medieval building in Nottingham. The main body of the church was completed in 1475, but there have been interesting alterations and additions since then. The nave is notably spacious, and there are beautiful stained glass windows and a massive tower. **Nottingham Castle** has a long

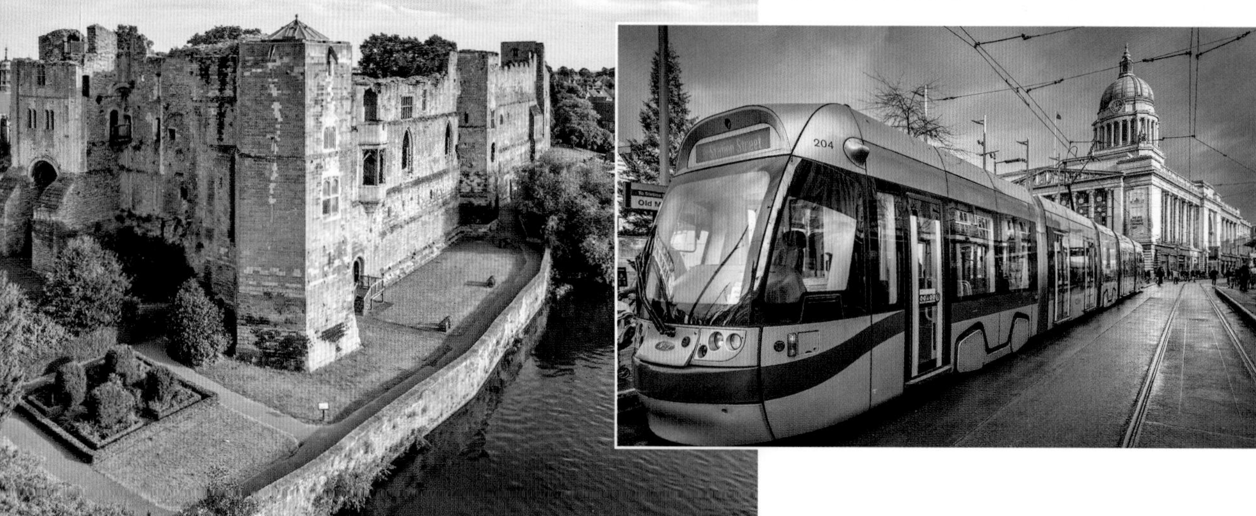

history, having been home to royalty and nobles and having played an important role during the English Civil War. What remains now, however, is a 19th-century restoration of a 17th-century mansion built on the site. Of the older castle, only the medieval gatehouse survives, and the caves and passageways in Castle Rock. The mansion houses Nottingham's fine collection of art and archaeology, alabaster carvings, stoneware and lace. The Castle has long been associated with the legend of Robin Hood. **Brewhouse Yard**, at the foot of Castle Rock, is a row of 17th-century houses where textile workers lived and worked for centuries. They back on to rock caves, a small proportion of the over 800 sandstone caves which are a feature of the city. The **Robin Hood Experience** is a family attraction, where each room brings a scene from Robin Hood's adventures to life, with interactive exhibits and activities. At the **City of Caves**, visitors can explore a large number of Nottingham's underground passageways and learn about their various uses, from a medieval tannery to air raid shelters during World War 2. The **National Justice Museum** is housed in the old Shire Hall and County Gaol. Actors bring the Victorian courtroom, the dungeons and prison cells to life, and there are exhibitions on modern justice, as well as frequent special events. Nearby is **Nottingham Contemporary**, a centre for international contemporary art. It has frequently changing exhibitions and an active programme of events, courses and performances. **Nottingham Arboretum** is the closest park to the city centre. It was opened in 1852, laid out in a naturalist style with winding paths among the lawns and trees. In addition to the more than 800 trees, representing some 220 different species and varieties, there is an aviary, Chinese pagoda and bandstand. There are tree and heritage trails. **173 B3**

Southwell Attractive historic town known mainly for its medieval minster, but also for its role in the Civil War. **Southwell Minster** has imposing twin towers, a large Norman nave and much-admired naturalistic stone carvings (the 'Leaves of Southwell') on its 13th-century Chapter House. The partially ruined **Archbishop's Palace** lies in sensory gardens next to the minster. There has been a palace on the site since the 11th century, but the ruins visible today date from the 14th century. Cardinal Wolsey lived at the palace in the 16th century, and Charles I spent time here during the Civil War. The Great Hall has been restored and can be visited. Just outside the town centre is **Southwell Workhouse**, one of the best-preserved workhouses in the country. Visitors can learn about the austere regime and the individual people who lived there. Next door is the Firbeck Infirmary, where wards have been recreated to show how they looked at different points in the building's history. There are hands-on and family activities. **121 C1**

Buildings

Green's Windmill Restored 19th-century tower windmill owned in the 1800s by the eminent mathematician and physicist George Green. Visitors can learn how the grain is ground into flour and climb the tower for excellent views

▶ *Papplewick Pumping Station*

over Nottingham. There are interactive activities in the science centre next door as well as information about Green's life and discoveries in the fields of electricity and magnetism. *Nottingham* 💻 www.greensmill.org.uk **173 F4**

Mr Straw's House Modest Edwardian semi-detached house, home to the Straw family from 1923 until 1990. William Straw was a grocer, and after his death in 1923, and that of his wife a few years later, their children neither disturbed their parents' possessions nor changed the original furnishings, decoration and contents. Visitors can explore the house and gain an insight into life in the 1920s and 1930s. The garden and orchard have also been carefully preserved. *Worksop* 💻 www.nationaltrust.org.uk **36 A5**

Newstead Abbey Historic house and former abbey, surrounded by formal gardens and parkland. The abbey's medieval cloisters remain as does the 13th-century façade, but the rest of house has been built and altered since. The poet Lord Byron lived at Newstead in the early 19th century, and visitors can see his apartments and some personal possessions. An interesting collection of paintings, maps and photographs are on display. Within the grounds are lakes, ponds and a variety of themed gardens. There are family trails. *Mansfield* 💻 www.newsteadabbey.org.uk **131 C8**

Papplewick Pumping Station Fully restored Victorian pumping station, built in the 1880s to provide the growing population of Nottingham with clean water. The Engine House has an unexpectedly ornate interior and houses the original James Watt twin beam engines. The Boiler House contains six Lancashire boilers. On steam days, visitors can see the engines and boilers in action and visit the underground reservoir. The station is set within landscaped grounds. *Nottingham* 💻 www.papplewickpumpingstation. org.uk **132 E5**

Welbeck Abbey Former monastery, founded in the 12th century, later the country seat of the Dukes of Portland. Little of the monastery remains, and the few state rooms that can occasionally be visited date from the 18th century. The Welbeck Estate, a large area of countryside surrounding the house, can be explored on a variety of walking trails. On the estate are the **Harley Gallery** and the **Portland Collection Museum**. The latter houses an important collection of fine art and decorative items gathered over centuries by the Dukes of Portland, with highlights including paintings by George Stubbs and John Singer Sargent and a drawing by Michelangelo. The Harley Gallery hosts changing exhibitions of contemporary art. There are frequent talks and workshops for all ages. *Worksop* 💻 www.harleygallery.co.uk **46 A1**

Wollaton Hall Elizabethan mansion, home to Nottingham's **Natural History Museum**. The house was built in the 1580s and owned by the aristocratic Willoughby family until the late 19th century. Visitors can see the Tudor kitchens and the Prospect Room, from which there is a lovely view. The museum has an extensive collection, ranging from shells and eggs

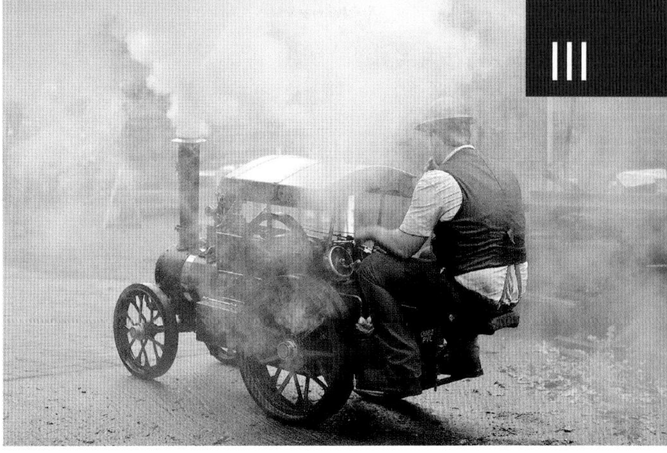

to taxidermy and fossils. Within the grounds are a deer park, lake and formal gardens, with family trails, playgrounds and outdoor activities. *Nottingham* 💻 https://wollatonhall.org.uk **172 A3**

Museums & galleries

Bassetlaw Museum Museum within a Georgian townhouse in the pretty market town of Retford. Its displays encompass the history, art and archaeology of the area, with highlights ranging from an Anglo-Saxon longboat to a 1940s kitchen. There is a Rural Heritage Centre and a gallery devoted to the area's links with the Mayflower Pilgrims. There are frequent workshops, events and family activities. *Retford* 💻 http://bassetlawmuseum. org.uk **39 F7**

Bilsthorpe Heritage Museum Small museum in the former mining village of Bilsthorpe, dedicated to the preservation of the area's mining heritage. Its collection centres on artefacts – both industrial and social – from the local mine, which began to operate in 1927 and closed in 1997. *Mansfield* 💻 http://bilsthorpemuseum. co.uk/ **105 F6**

DH Lawrence Birthplace Museum Miner's cottage where the author DH Lawrence was born in 1885. The rooms have been recreated as they would have been when the family lived here, giving an insight not only into the author but also into family life in a Victorian mining community. There is a children's trail and changing exhibitions. Other points of interest in the town relating to the author can be found using the Blue Line Trail. *Eastwood* 💻 www.broxtowe.gov.uk **143 F3**

Framework Knitters Museum Restored 19th-century framework knitters' yard, where families employed in the knitting trade lived and worked. Displays relate the history of framework knitting, encompassing the industrial revolution, the Luddite riots and the development of Nottingham's lace industry. There are original knitting machines in full working order, with frequent demonstrations and hands-on opportunities, as well as workshops and family activities. *Ruddington* 💻 https:// frameworkknittersmuseum.org.uk/ **196 C6**

Mansfield Museum Family-friendly museum, with galleries displaying paintings and ceramics by influential local artists, mainly from the 20th century onwards, as well as artefacts from Mansfield's industrial past. It has an environmental gallery full of hands-on

interactive exhibits. There are frequently changing temporary exhibitions. *Mansfield* 💻 www.mansfield.gov.uk/ museum **102 C7**

National Holocaust Centre and Museum Museum, education centre and memorial devoted to those who lost their lives in the Holocaust. The main exhibition, for older children and adults, details the experiences of Jewish people in Europe before, during and after World War 2. There is also an exhibition aimed at younger children. Both have an emphasis on the experiences of individuals. There are frequent talks by survivors. The museum is surrounded by a rose-filled memorial garden. 💻 www.holocaust.org.uk **78 E3**

Family activities

Holme Pierrepont Country Park Park and activity centre alongside the National Water Sports Centre. In addition to athletes' facilities, the centre offers outdoor and water-based activities for all ages, ranging from kayaking, rafting and water obstacle courses, to high rope trails, mini golf and archery. There are walking and cycling routes within the country park, and a play area and café. *Nottingham* 💻 www.nwscnotts.com/hpcp/ country-park **174 F3**

Sherwood Forest Railway Narrow-gauge steam railway, created as a proper steam railway in miniature, with a tunnel, level crossings and signals. There are frequent train rides along a short route through attractive countryside; driving experiences can be booked. There is a children's playground. *Mansfield* 💻 www. sherwoodforestrailway.com **89 F7**

Sundown Adventureland Family theme park aimed at children under the age of 10. There are a large number of adventure playgrounds and interactive play areas, both indoors and outdoors, with some specifically for toddlers, as well as tractor and train rides. *Retford* 💻 https://sundownadventureland.co.uk **42 E3**

White Post Farm Family farm park, with a large number of animals, both familiar and less familiar. Visitors can walk around the fields and the barn to see cows, alpacas, sheep and wallabies, among others. There are also meerkats, porcupines, rodents and a reptile house. The falconry area has a variety of birds of prey, and offers flying displays. Activities include adventure playgrounds, indoor play and opportunities to feed and handle some of the animals. *Mansfield* 💻 www.whitepostfarm.co.uk **119 B7**

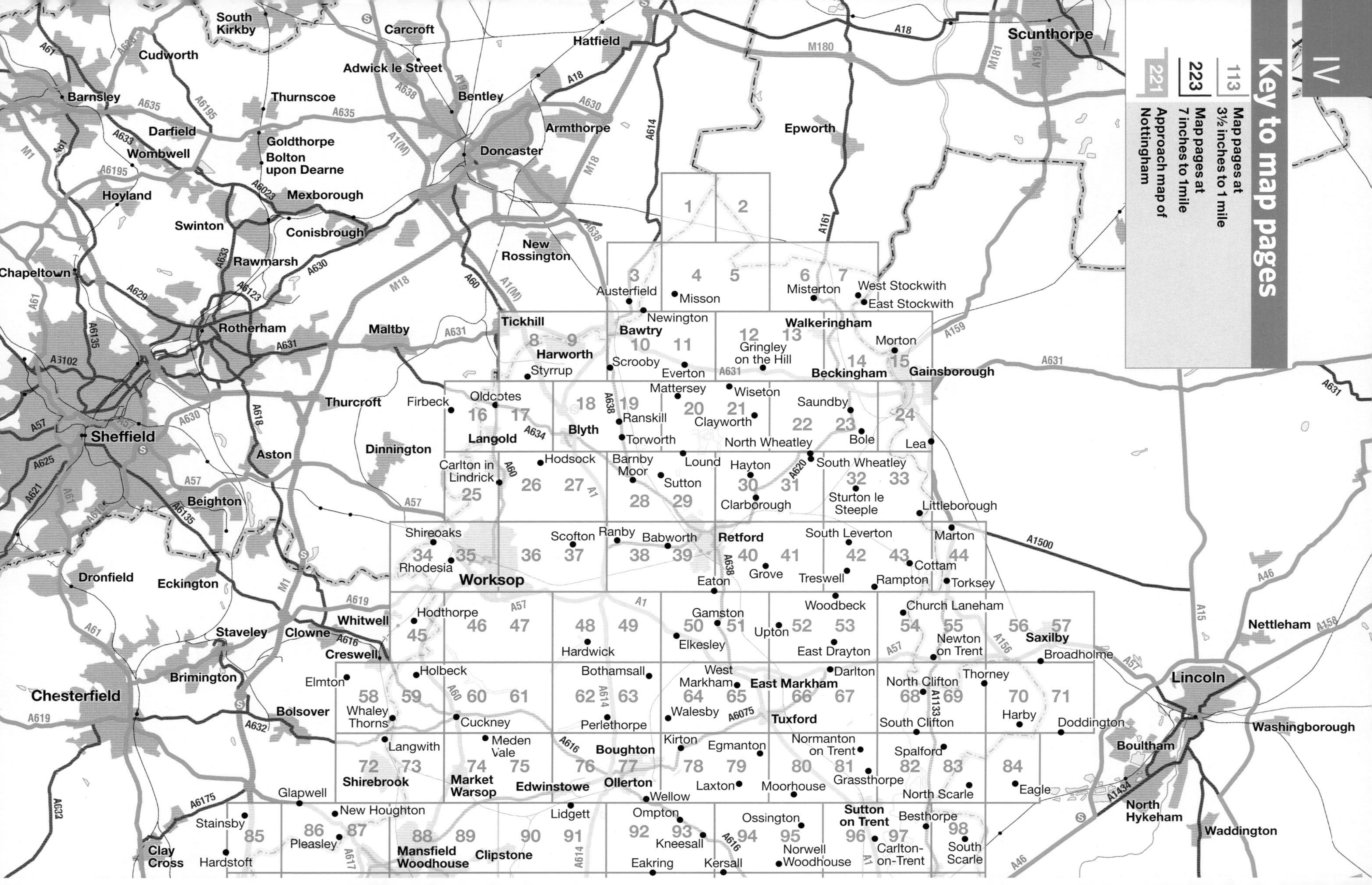

IV

Key to map pages

113	Map pages at 3½ inches to 1 mile
223	Map pages at 7 inches to 1mile
221	Approach map of Nottingham

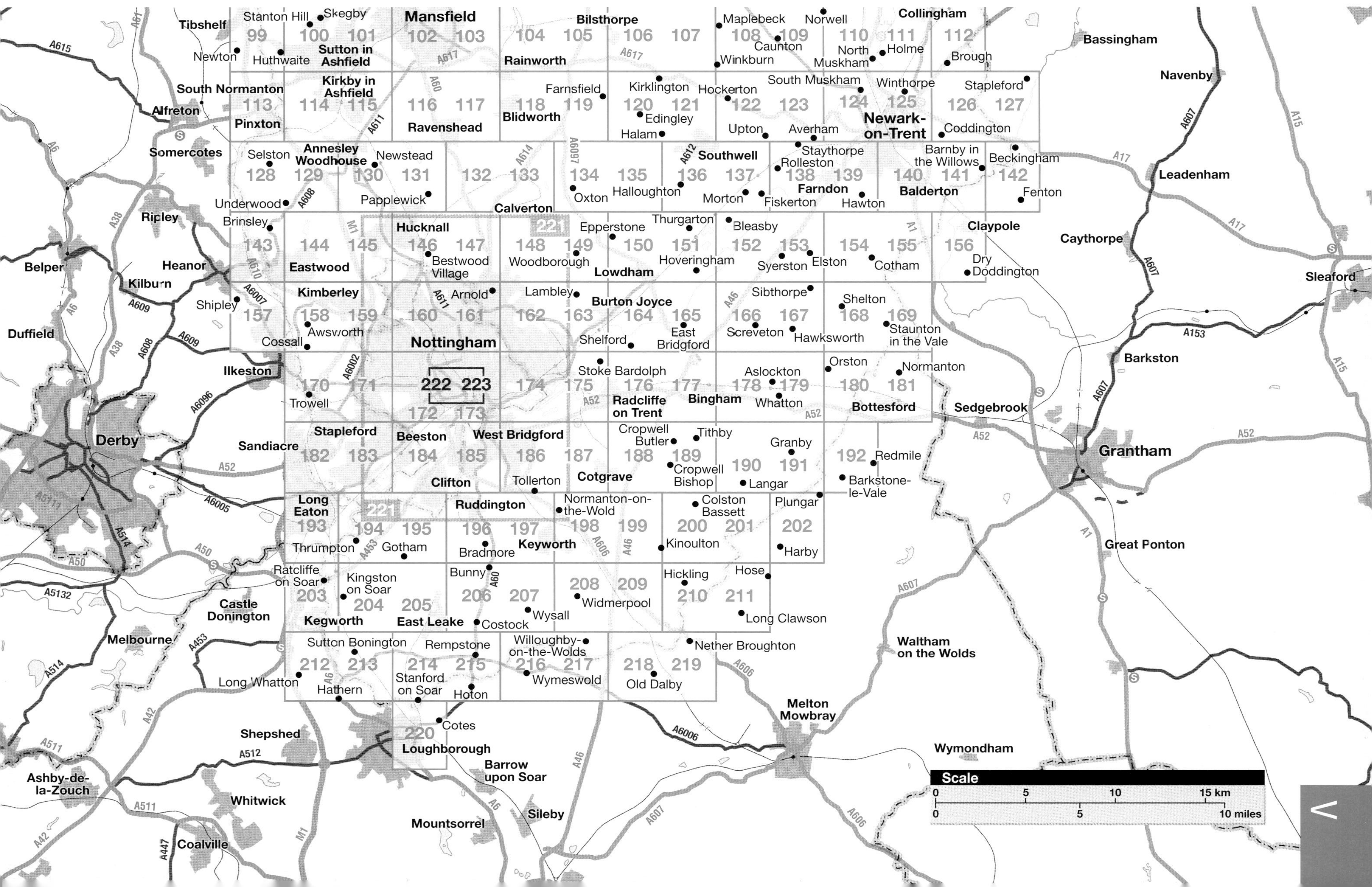

V

Scale

0   5   10   15 km
0   5   10 miles

Sleaford
Leadenham
Navenby
Bassingham
Barkston
Caythorpe
Grantham
Great Ponton
Wymondham
Waltham on the Wolds
Melton Mowbray

Collingham 112
112 Brough
Stapleford 126 127
126 127 Beckingham
Coddington 125 Fenton 142
Newark-on-Trent 141 Balderton
Barnby in the Willows 140
Claypole 156
Sedgebrook
Normanton 181
Staunton in the Vale 155
Cotham 154
Shelton 168 169
Redmile 192
Bottesford 180 Barkstone-le-Vale
Collingham 111
Holme 110
North Muskham 124
Winthorpe 125
Staythorpe 138 139
Rolleston Farndon
Hawton
Syerston Elston 153
Sibthorpe 167
Hawksworth
Aslockton 178 179
Granby 191
Plungar 202
Harby
Long Clawson
Nether Broughton
Norwell 109
Caunton 108
Winkburn 122 123
Upton 122
Southwell 137
Morton 136
Fiskerton
Bleasby 152
Hoveringham 151
East Bridgford 165
Whatton Bingham 177
Tithby 190
Cropwell Bishop 189
Langar
Colston Bassett 201
Hose 211
Hickling 210
Maplebeck 108
Norwell 109
Kirklington 120 121
Edingley 121
Halam
Oxton Halloughton 135
Thurgarton 150
Epperstone 149
Lowdham 150
Burton Joyce 164
Shelford
Stoke Bardolph 176
Radcliffe on Trent 188
Cropwell Butler 189
Kinoulton 200
Hickling 210
Widmerpool 209
Bilsthorpe 105
Rainworth 104
Farnsfield 119
Blidworth 118
Calverton 221
Woodborough 148
Lambley 163
Burton Joyce 162
Cotgrave 187
Tollerton 187
Normanton-on-the-Wold 198
Keyworth 199
Wysall 207
Willoughby-on-the-Wolds 216 217
Wymeswold
Old Dalby 218 219
Mansfield 102 103
Ravenshead 116 117
Ravenshead 132
Hucknall 146 147
Arnold 161
Bestwood Village 160
Nottingham 222 223
West Bridgford 185 186
Clifton 184
Ruddington 196 197
Bradmore 206
Bunny 206
East Leake 205
Costock 207
Rempstone 215
Hoton 215
Cotes
Loughborough 220
Barrow upon Soar
Sileby
Stanton Hill 99 100 101
Skegby
Sutton in Ashfield 114 115
Kirkby in Ashfield 115
Annesley Woodhouse 129 130
Newstead 131
Papplewick 131
Bestwood Village 145
Stapleford 183
Beeston 184
172 173
Long Eaton 193
Thrumpton 195
Gotham 195
Kingston on Soar 204
Kegworth 212 213
Stanford on Soar 214 215
Tibshelf
South Normanton 113
Pinxton 113
Selston 128
Underwood
Brinsley 143
Eastwood 144
Kimberley 158 159
Awsworth 170 171
Trowell 170
Cossall
Sandiacre 182
Ratcliffe on Soar 203
Sutton Bonington 212
Long Whatton
Hathern 212
Shepshed
Whitwick
Coalville
Ashby-de-la-Zouch
Alfreton
Somercotes
Ripley
Heanor
Kilburn
Ilkeston
Shipley
Belper
Duffield
Derby
Melbourne
Castle Donington
Mountsorrel

Route planning

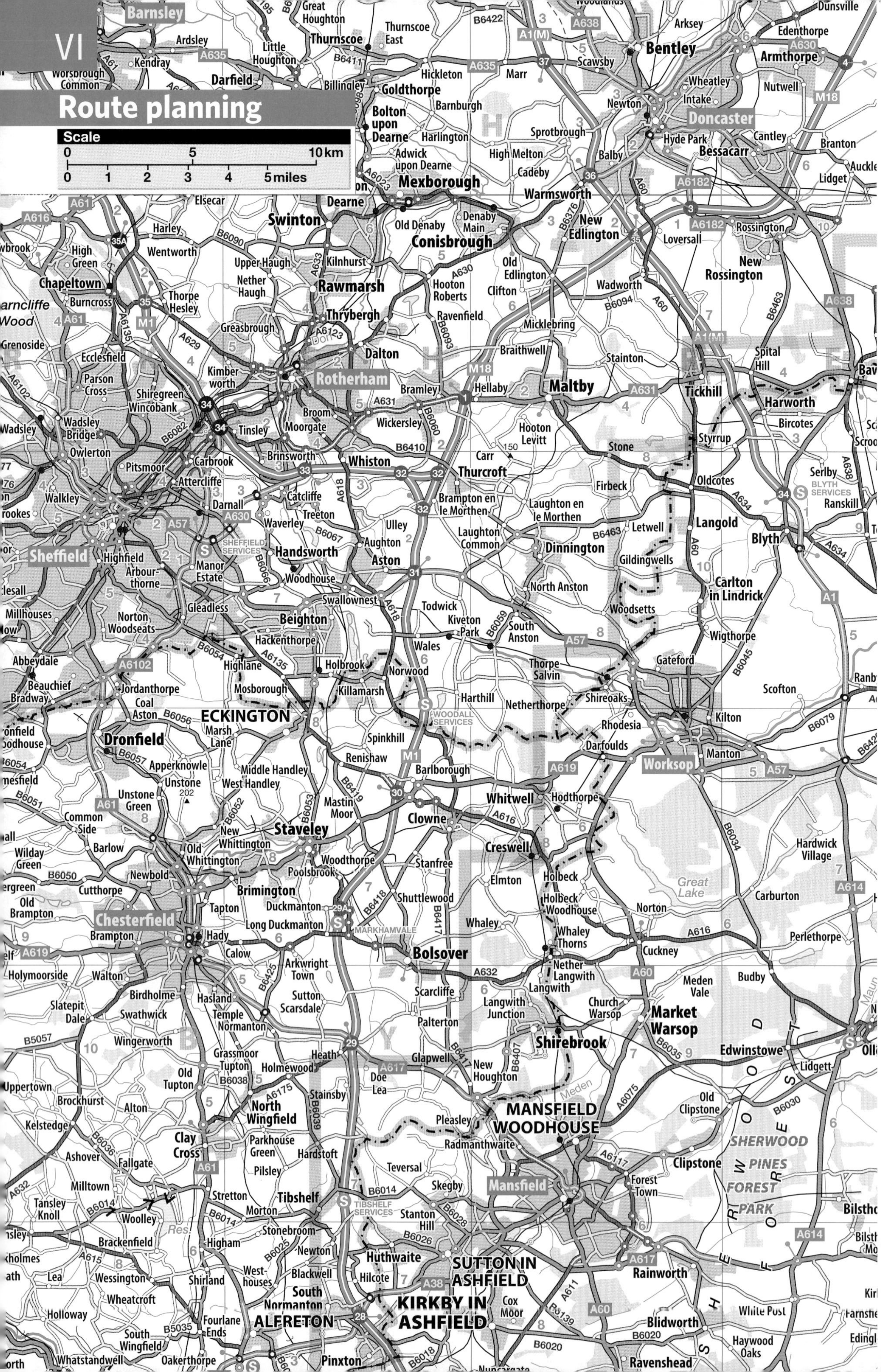
Scale
0 5 10 km
0 1 2 3 4 5 miles
Barnsley
Great Houghton
Thurnscoe
Thurnscoe East
Dunsville
Arksey
Edenthorpe
Bentley
Armthorpe
Ardsley
Kendray
Little Houghton
Darfield
Worsbrough Common
Hickleton
Marr
Scawsby
Nutwell
Wheatley
Intake
Billingley
Goldthorpe
Barnburgh
Newton
Doncaster
Bolton upon Dearne
Harlington
Sprotbrough
Hyde Park
Cantley
Branton
Adwick upon Dearne
High Melton
Balby
Bessacarr
Cadeby
Lidget
Mexborough
Warmsworth
Elsecar
Dearne
Swinton
Old Denaby
Denaby Main
New Edlington
Loversall
Rossington
Conisbrough
Harley
Wentworth
High Green
Upper Haugh
Kilnhurst
Old Edlington
New Rossington
Chapeltown
Nether Haugh
Rawmarsh
Hooton Roberts
Clifton
Wadworth
Burncross
Thorpe Hesley
Thrybergh
Ravenfield
Grenoside
Greasbrough
Micklebring
Ecclesfield
Kimberworth
Dalton
Braithwell
Stainton
Spital Hill
Parson Cross
Rotherham
Bramley
Hellaby
Maltby
Tickhill
Harworth
Shiregreen
Wincobank
Broom
Wickersley
Hooton Levitt
Bircotes
Wadsley
Wadsley Bridge
Tinsley
Moorgate
Stone
Styrrup
Owlerton
Brinsworth
Carr
Pitsmoor
Carbrook
Whiston
Thurcroft
Oldcotes
Serlby
Attercliffe
Firbeck
Blyth Services
Ranskill
Walkley
Darnall
Catcliffe
Brampton en le Morthen
Laughton en le Morthen
Treeton
Waverley
Letwell
Langold
Blyth
Sheffield
Sheffield Services
Ulley
Laughton Common
Handsworth
Aughton
Dinnington
Gildingwells
Highfield
Manor Estate
Aston
Carlton in Lindrick
Arbourthorne
Woodhouse
North Anston
Swallownest
Gleadless
Todwick
Woodsetts
Millhouses
Beighton
Kiveton Park
South Anston
Norton Woodseats
Hackenthorpe
Wales
Wigthorpe
Abbeydale
Highlane
Holbrook
Norwood
Thorpe Salvin
Gateford
Beauchief
Jordanthorpe
Mosborough
Killamarsh
Harthill
Netherthorpe
Shireoaks
Scofton
Bradway
Coal Aston
ECKINGTON
Woodall Services
Rhodesia
Kilton
Dronfield
Marsh Lane
Spinkhill
Darfoulds
Renishaw
Manton
Apperknowle
Middle Handley
Barlborough
Worksop
Unstone
West Handley
Unstone Green
Mastin Moor
Whitwell
Hodthorpe
Common Side
New Whittington
Staveley
Clowne
Barlow
Old Whittington
Woodthorpe
Creswell
Hardwick Village
Wilday Green
Poolsbrook
Stanfree
Elmton
Holbeck
Newbold
Great Lake
Holbeck Woodhouse
Cutthorpe
Brimington
Shuttlewood
Carburton
Norton
Old Brampton
Tapton
Duckmanton
Whaley
Whaley Thorns
Perlethorpe
Chesterfield
Long Duckmanton
Markham Vale
Brampton
Hady
Cuckney
Bolsover
Calow
Nether Langwith
Holymoorside
Walton
Arkwright Town
Meden Vale
Budby
Langwith
Birdholme
Hasland
Sutton Scarsdale
Scarcliffe
Langwith Junction
Church Warsop
Market Warsop
Slatepit Dale
Swathwick
Temple Normanton
Palterton
Shirebrook
Edwinstowe
Wingerworth
Grassmoor
Heath
Glapwell
Lidgett
Tupton
Holmewood
New Houghton
Old Tupton
Doe Lea
Meden
Uppertown
Old Clipstone
Brockhurst
Alton
Stainsby
MANSFIELD WOODHOUSE
North Wingfield
Pleasley
Kelstedge
Radmanthwaite
Clay Cross
Parkhouse Green
Sherwood Pines Forest Park
Ashover
Fallgate
Hardstoft
Teversal
Clipstone
Pilsley
Milltown
Forest Town
Skegby
Mansfield
Tansley Knoll
Stretton
Tibshelf
Tibshelf Services
Woolley
Morton
Stanton Hill
Bilsthorpe
Res.
Stonebroom
Higham
Brackenfield
Newton
Huthwaite
Rainworth
Shirland
Blackwell
Wessington
Lea
West-houses
Hilcote
SUTTON IN ASHFIELD
South Normanton
Wheatcroft
KIRKBY IN ASHFIELD
Cox Moor
Holloway
Fourlane Ends
ALFRETON
Blidworth
White Post
South Wingfield
Haywood Oaks
Whatstandwell
Oakerthorpe
Pinxton
Ravenshead
Sherwood Forest

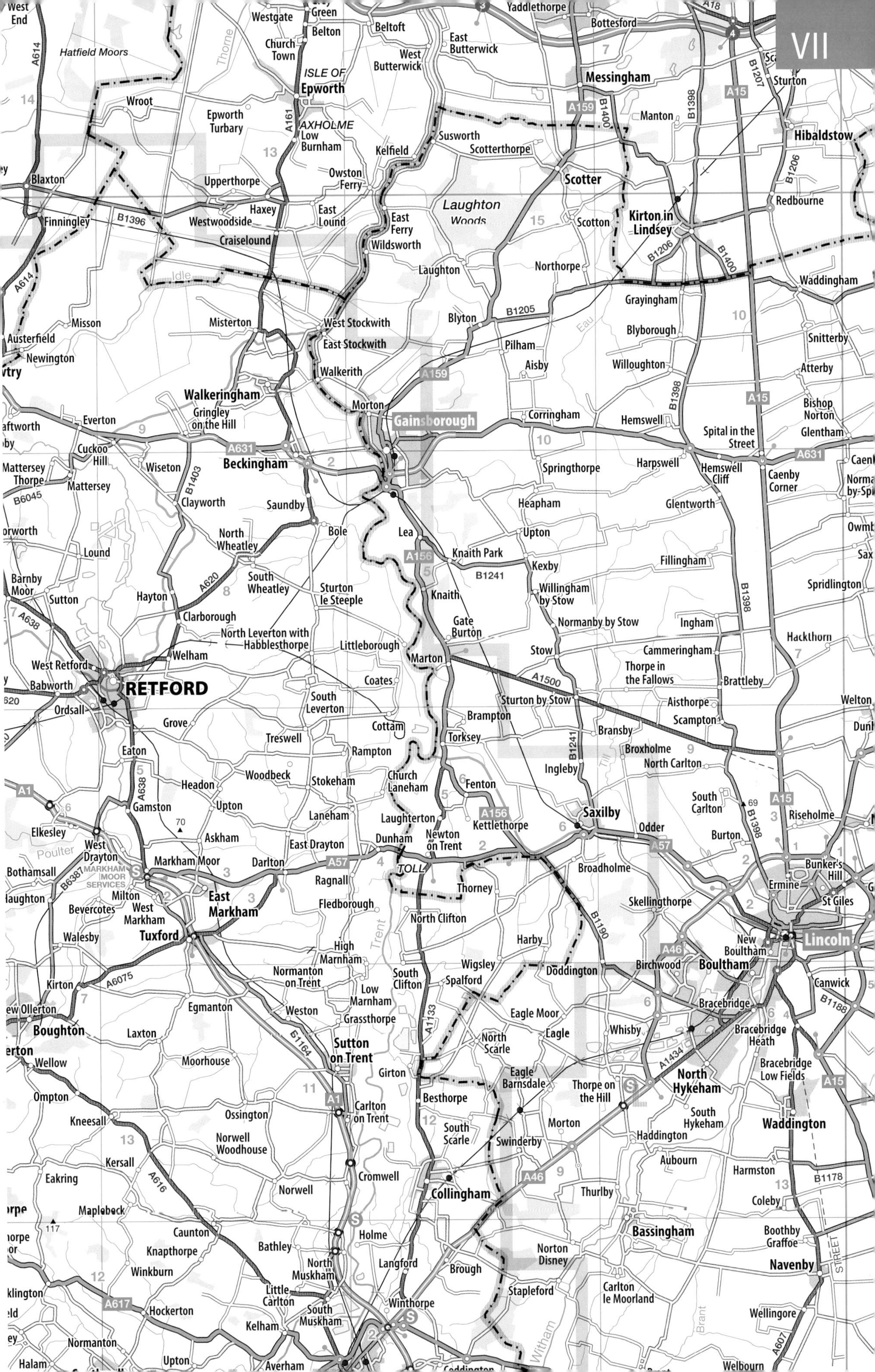
West End
Westgate
Green
Belton
Beltoft
Yaddlethorpe
Bottesford
A18
East Butterwick
West Butterwick
Church Town
Hatfield Moors
A614
Thorne
ISLE OF
Epworth
AXHOLME
Messingham
Scawby
Sturton
Wroot
Epworth Turbary
A161
Low Burnham
Kelfield
Susworth
Scotterthorpe
A159
B1400
Manton
B1398
A15
B1207
Hibaldstow
Blaxton
Upperthorpe
Owston Ferry
Scotter
B1206
Redbourne
Finningley
B1396
Haxey
Westwoodside
East Lound
East Ferry
Laughton
Woods
Scotton
Kirton in Lindsey
Craiselound
Wildsworth
Idle
Laughton
Northorpe
Waddingham
Grayingham
B1205
Blyton
Misson
Misterton
West Stockwith
Eau
Blyborough
Snitterby
Austerfield
East Stockwith
Pilham
Newington
Walkerith
Aisby
Willoughton
Atterby
Bishop Norton
Glentham
Walkeringham
Gringley on the Hill
Morton
Gainsborough
Corringham
Hemswell
Spital in the Street
Everton
A631
Cuckoo Hill
Wiseton
Beckingham
Springthorpe
Harpswell
Hemswell Cliff
Caenby Corner
Mattersey Thorpe
Mattersey
B1403
Clayworth
Saundby
Heapham
Glentworth
B6045
Bole
Lea
Upton
North Wheatley
Lound
A156
Knaith Park
Kexby
Fillingham
B1241
Barnby Moor
South Wheatley
Sturton le Steeple
Willingham by Stow
Spridlington
Sutton
Hayton
A620
Knaith
Normanby by Stow
Ingham
A638
Clarborough
Gate Burton
North Leverton with Habblesthorpe
Littleborough
Marton
Stow
Cammeringham
Hackthorn
West Retford
Welham
Thorpe in the Fallows
Brattleby
Babworth
RETFORD
Coates
A1500
Ordsall
South Leverton
Sturton by Stow
Aisthorpe
Welton
Grove
Brampton
Scampton
Cottam
Bransby
Treswell
Torksey
Eaton
Rampton
Broxholme
North Carlton
Headon
Woodbeck
Ingleby
Church Laneham
Fenton
South Carlton
A1
Gamston
Stokeham
B1398
Upton
Laneham
Laughterton
Kettlethorpe
Saxilby
Riseholme
Elkesley
Askham
Newton on Trent
Odder
Burton
West Drayton
Dunham
East Drayton
A57
Poulter
Markham Moor
Darlton
TOLL
Broadholme
Bunker's Hill
Bothamsall
MARKHAM MOOR SERVICES
Ragnall
Thorney
Ermine
B6387
Milton
East Markham
Skellingthorpe
St Giles
Bevercotes
West Markham
Fledborough
North Clifton
B1190
Walesby
Tuxford
Trent
Harby
High Marnham
New Boultham
Lincoln
Normanton on Trent
South Clifton
Wigsley
Doddington
A46
Birchwood
Boultham
Kirton
A6075
Spalford
Canwick
Low Marnham
Bracebridge
Ollerton
Egmanton
Weston
Grassthorpe
Eagle Moor
B1188
A1133
Boughton
Laxton
Whisby
Bracebridge Heath
Eagle
North Scarle
B1164
Sutton on Trent
Moorhouse
Wellow
A1434
Girton
Eagle Barnsdale
Thorpe on the Hill
North Hykeham
Bracebridge Low Fields
Ompton
Carlton on Trent
Besthorpe
South Hykeham
Waddington
Ossington
Kneesall
Morton
Haddington
South Scarle
Swinderby
Norwell Woodhouse
Aubourn
Kersall
Harmston
A616
Cromwell
A46
Thurlby
B1178
Eakring
Norwell
Collingham
Coleby
Mapleback
Caunton
Holme
Bassingham
Boothby Graffoe
Knapthorpe
Bathley
Norton Disney
North Muskham
Langford
STREET
Navenby
Winkburn
Brough
Little Carlton
Carlton le Moorland
Stapleford
A617
Hockerton
South Muskham
Winthorpe
Brant
Wellingore
Kelham
Witham
A607
Normanton
Halam
Upton
Averham
Welbourn

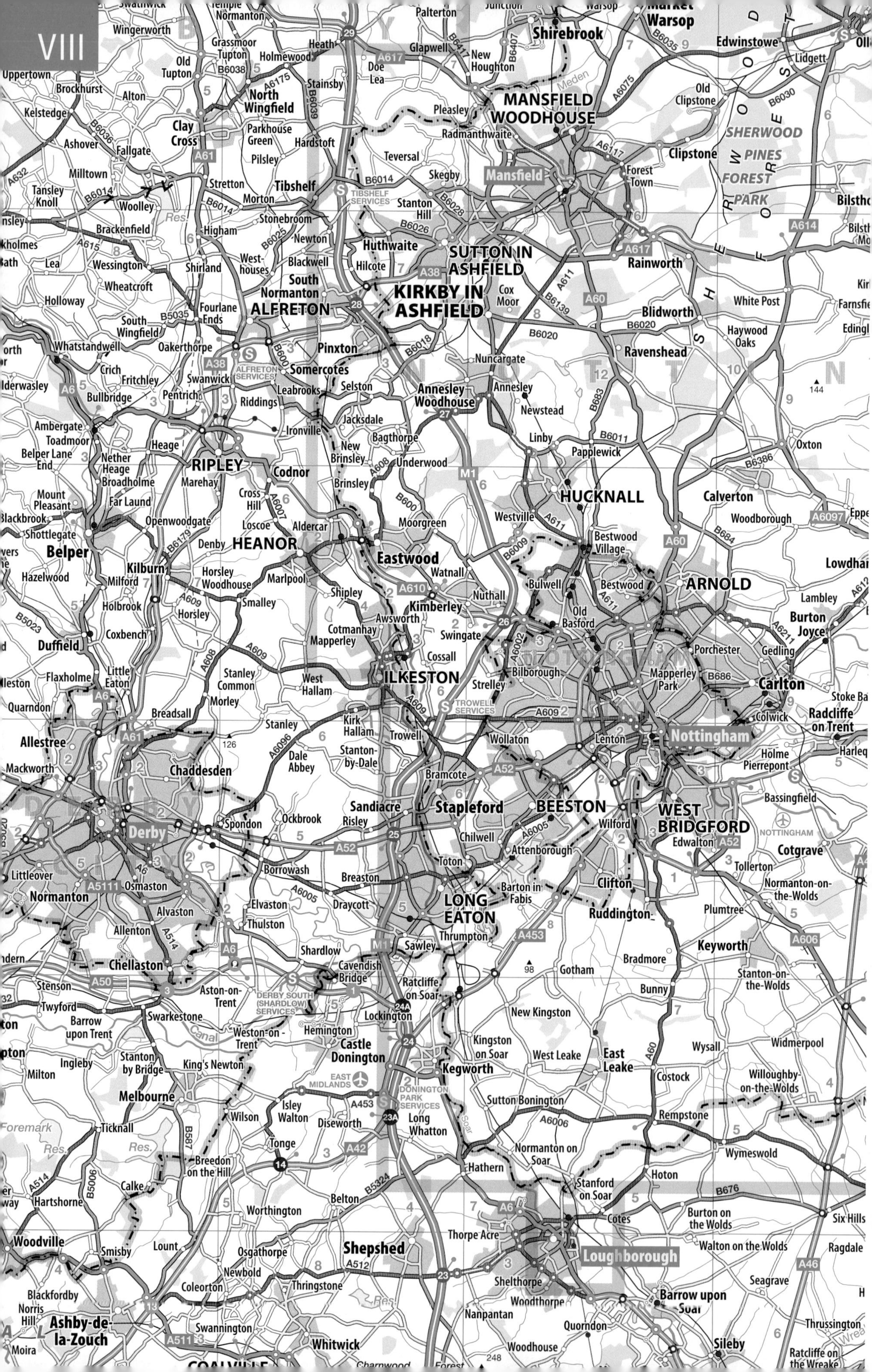

Wingerworth
Grassmoor
Tupton
Old Tupton
Uppertown
Heath
Holmewood
Palterton
Glapwell
Doe Lea
Shirebrook
Market Warsop
Edwinstowe
Lidgett
New Houghton
Brockhurst
Alton
North Wingfield
Stainsby
Kelstedge
Clay Cross
Parkhouse Green
Hardstoft
Pleasley
MANSFIELD WOODHOUSE
Old Clipstone
Ashover
Fallgate
Pilsley
Radmanthwaite
SHERWOOD PINES FOREST PARK
Clipstone
Milltown
Teversal
Skegby
Forest Town
Tansley Knoll
Stretton
Tibshelf
Mansfield
Woolley
Morton
TIBSHELF SERVICES
Stanton Hill
Stonebroom
Brackenfield
Higham
Newton
Huthwaite
SUTTON IN ASHFIELD
Rainworth
Lea
Wessington
Shirland
West-houses
Blackwell
Hilcote
Wheatcroft
South Normanton
KIRKBY IN ASHFIELD
Cox Moor
White Post
Holloway
Fourlane Ends
ALFRETON
Blidworth
South Wingfield
Oakerthorpe
Pinxton
Haywood Oaks
Ravenshead
Whatstandwell
Crich
Fritchley
Swanwick
ALFRETON SERVICES
Somercotes
Nuncargate
Bullbridge
Pentrich
Leabrooks
Selston
Annesley Woodhouse
Annesley
Newstead
Riddings
Jacksdale
Ambergate
Toadmoor
Ironville
Bagthorpe
Linby
Belper Lane End
Nether Heage
Heage
New Brinsley
Underwood
Papplewick
Oxton
RIPLEY
Codnor
Marehay
Broadholme
Brinsley
HUCKNALL
Calverton
Mount Pleasant
Far Laund
Cross Hill
Moorgreen
Woodborough
Blackbrook
Openwoodgate
Loscoe
Aldercar
Westville
Shottlegate
Denby
HEANOR
Bestwood Village
Belper
Eastwood
Kilburn
Watnall
Bulwell
Bestwood
ARNOLD
Hazelwood
Milford
Horsley Woodhouse
Marlpool
Lowdham
Shipley
Kimberley
Nuthall
Holbrook
Smalley
Horsley
Lambley
Awsworth
Old Basford
Burton Joyce
Duffield
Coxbench
Cotmanhay
Mapperley
Swingate
Porchester
Gedling
Cossall
Little Eaton
Stanley Common
Flaxholme
West Hallam
ILKESTON
NOTTINGHAM
Bilborough
Strelley
Mapperley Park
Carlton
Quarndon
Morley
TROWELL SERVICES
Colwick
Radcliffe on Trent
Breadsall
Stanley
Kirk Hallam
Trowell
Allestree
Wollaton
Lenton
Nottingham
Stanton-by-Dale
Holme Pierrepont
Dale Abbey
Mackworth
Chaddesden
Bramcote
Bassingfield
Sandiacre
Stapleford
BEESTON
WEST BRIDGFORD
Spondon
Ockbrook
Risley
Wilford
NOTTINGHAM
DERBY
Derby
Chilwell
Edwalton
Attenborough
Cotgrave
Toton
Littleover
Borrowash
Breaston
Tollerton
Osmaston
Normanton
LONG EATON
Clifton
Normanton-on-the-Wolds
Barton in Fabis
Alvaston
Elvaston
Draycott
Ruddington
Plumtree
Thulston
Allenton
Shardlow
Thrumpton
Sawley
Keyworth
Chellaston
Cavendish Bridge
Gotham
Bradmore
Stenson
Aston-on-Trent
DERBY SOUTH (SHARDLOW) SERVICES
Ratcliffe on Soar
Stanton-on-the-Wolds
Bunny
Twyford
Barrow upon Trent
Swarkestone
Lockington
New Kingston
Hemington
Weston-on-Trent
Castle Donington
Kingston on Soar
West Leake
East Leake
Wysall
Widmerpool
Milton
Ingleby
Stanton by Bridge
King's Newton
Kegworth
Costock
Melbourne
EAST MIDLANDS
DONINGTON PARK SERVICES
Willoughby-on-the-Wolds
Sutton Bonington
Isley Walton
Wilson
Long Whatton
Rempstone
Diseworth
Foremark Res.
Ticknall
Tonge
Normanton on Soar
Wymeswold
Breedon on the Hill
Hathern
Calke
Stanford on Soar
Hoton
Hartshorne
Belton
Worthington
Cotes
Burton on the Wolds
Six Hills
Thorpe Acre
Woodville
Smisby
Lount
Shepshed
Loughborough
Walton on the Wolds
Ragdale
Osgathorpe
Newbold
Shelthorpe
Seagrave
Blackfordby
Coleorton
Thringstone
Woodthorpe
Barrow upon Soar
Norris Hill
Ashby-de-la-Zouch
Swannington
Nanpantan
Quorndon
Thrussington
Moira
Whitwick
Woodhouse
Sileby
Ratcliffe on the Wreake
COALVILLE
Charnwood Forest

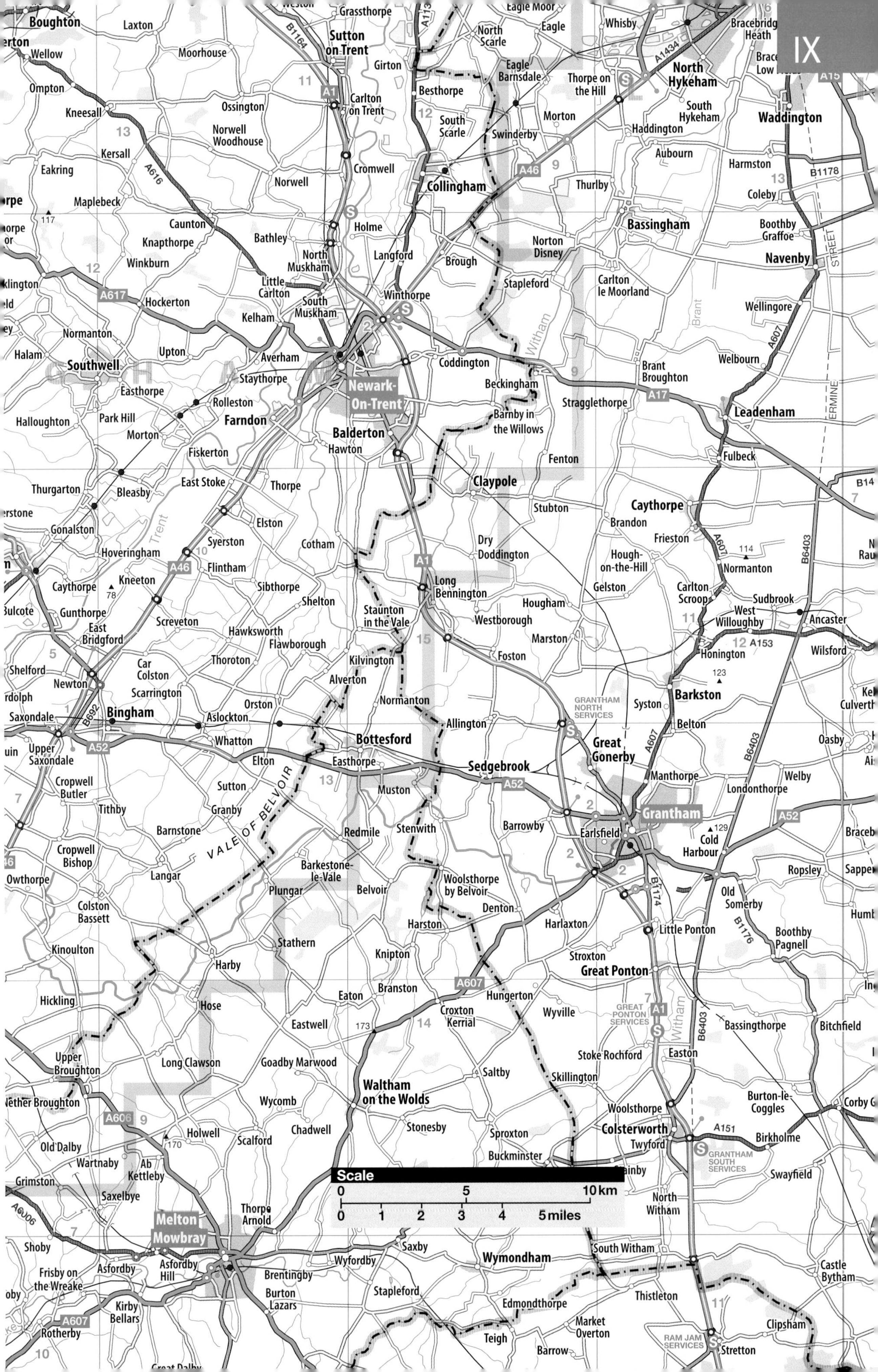

IX
Boughton
Laxton
Grassthorpe
Sutton on Trent
Eagle Moor
North Scarle
Eagle
Whisby
Bracebridge Heath
Wellow
Moorhouse
Girton
Eagle Barnsdale
Thorpe on the Hill
North Hykeham
Ompton
Kneesall
Ossington
Carlton on Trent
Besthorpe
South Hykeham
Waddington
Norwell Woodhouse
South Scarle
Swinderby
Morton
Haddington
Kersall
Eakring
Cromwell
Collingham
Thurlby
Aubourn
Harmston
Norwell
Coleby
Maplebeck
Caunton
Holme
Bassingham
Boothby Graffoe
Knapthorpe
Bathley
North Muskham
Langford
Brough
Norton Disney
Navenby
Winkburn
Little Carlton
Stapleford
Carlton le Moorland
Hockerton
South Muskham
Winthorpe
Wellingore
Kelham
Normanton
Halam
Southwell
Upton
Averham
Coddington
Welbourn
Staythorpe
Newark-On-Trent
Beckingham
Brant Broughton
Easthorpe
Rolleston
Barnby in the Willows
Stragglethorpe
Leadenham
Halloughton
Park Hill
Farndon
Balderton
Morton
Hawton
Fiskerton
Fenton
Fulbeck
East Stoke
Thorpe
Claypole
Thurgarton
Bleasby
Stubton
Caythorpe
Gonalston
Elston
Brandon
Frieston
Syerston
Cotham
Dry Doddington
Hoveringham
Flintham
Hough-on-the-Hill
Normanton
Kneeton
Sibthorpe
Gelston
Caythorpe
Shelton
Long Bennington
Carlton Scroop
Sudbrook
Gunthorpe
Staunton in the Vale
Hougham
West Willoughby
Ancaster
Screveton
Westborough
East Bridgford
Hawksworth
Flawborough
Marston
Honington
Wilsford
Thoroton
Kilvington
Foston
Shelford
Car Colston
Alverton
Newton
Scarrington
Normanton
Barkston
Syston
Saxondale
Bingham
Orston
Aslockton
Allington
Belton
Great Gonerby
Oasby
Upper Saxondale
Whatton
Bottesford
Elton
Easthorpe
Sedgebrook
Manthorpe
Londonthorpe
Welby
Cropwell Butler
Sutton
Muston
Tithby
Granby
Grantham
Barrowby
Earlsfield
Cold Harbour
Barnstone
Redmile
Stenwith
Cropwell Bishop
VALE OF BELVOIR
Ropsley
Langar
Barkestone-le-Vale
Woolsthorpe by Belvoir
Owthorpe
Plungar
Belvoir
Old Somerby
Colston Bassett
Denton
Harston
Harlaxton
Little Ponton
Boothby Pagnell
Stathern
Kinoulton
Harby
Knipton
Stroxton
Great Ponton
Hickling
Hose
Eaton
Branston
Hungerton
Wyville
Croxton Kerrial
Eastwell
Bassingthorpe
Bitchfield
Upper Broughton
Long Clawson
Goadby Marwood
Saltby
Stoke Rochford
Easton
Waltham on the Wolds
Skillington
Burton-le-Coggles
Nether Broughton
Wycomb
Woolsthorpe
Chadwell
Stonesby
Colsterworth
Holwell
Sproxton
Twyford
Birkholme
Old Dalby
Scalford
Wartnaby
Ab Kettleby
Buckminster
Swayfield
Grimston
Saxelbye
North Witham
Thorpe Arnold
Melton Mowbray
Shoby
Saxby
Wymondham
South Witham
Asfordby
Wyfordby
Frisby on the Wreake
Asfordby Hill
Brentingby
Castle Bytham
Burton Lazars
Thistleton
Kirby Bellars
Stapleford
Edmondthorpe
Rotherby
Market Overton
Clipsham
Teigh
Barrow
Stretton
RAM JAM SERVICES
GRANTHAM NORTH SERVICES
GREAT PONTON SERVICES
GRANTHAM SOUTH SERVICES
Witham
Trent
Brant
ERMINE STREET
A1
A46
A17
A52
A607
A617
A616
A1434
A153
A151
A606
B1164
B1178
B692
B1174
B1176
B6403
Scale
0 5 10 km
0 1 2 3 4 5 miles

Key to map symbols

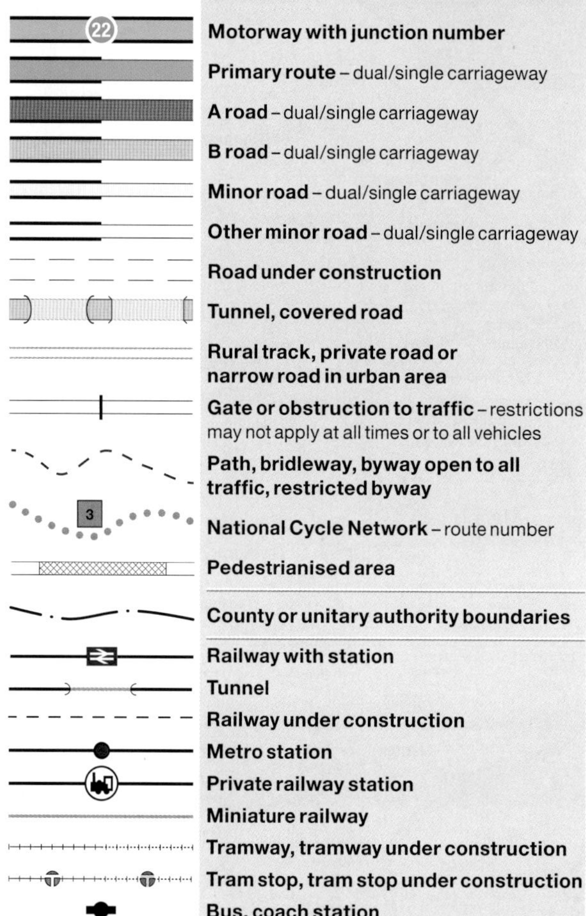

Motorway with junction number

Primary route – dual/single carriageway

A road – dual/single carriageway

B road – dual/single carriageway

Minor road – dual/single carriageway

Other minor road – dual/single carriageway

Road under construction

Tunnel, covered road

Rural track, private road or narrow road in urban area

Gate or obstruction to traffic – restrictions may not apply at all times or to all vehicles

Path, bridleway, byway open to all traffic, restricted byway

National Cycle Network – route number

Pedestrianised area

County or unitary authority boundaries

Railway with station

Tunnel

Railway under construction

Metro station

Private railway station

Miniature railway

Tramway, tramway under construction

Tram stop, tram stop under construction

Bus, coach station

Ambulance station

Coastguard station

Fire station

Police station

Accident and Emergency entrance to hospital

Hospital

Place of worship

Information centre

Shopping centre, parking

Park and Ride, Post Office

Camping site, caravan site

Golf course, picnic site

Church   ROMAN FORT   **Non-Roman antiquity, Roman antiquity**

Univ   **Important buildings, schools, colleges, universities and hospitals**

Woods, built-up area

River Medway   **Water name**

River, weir

Stream

Canal, lock, tunnel

Water

Tidal water

Adjoining page indicators and overlap bands – the colour of the arrow and band indicates the scale of the adjoining or overlapping page (see scales below)

The dark grey border on the inside edge of some pages indicates that the mapping does not continue onto the adjacent page

The small numbers around the edges of the maps identify the 1-kilometre National Grid lines

Abbreviations

Acad	**Academy**	Meml	**Memorial**
Allot Gdns	**Allotments**	Mon	**Monument**
Cemy	**Cemetery**	Mus	**Museum**
C Ctr	**Civic centre**	Obsy	**Observatory**
CH	**Club house**	Pal	**Royal palace**
Coll	**College**	PH	**Public house**
Crem	**Crematorium**	Recn Gd	**Recreation ground**
Ent	**Enterprise**		
Ex H	**Exhibition hall**	Resr	**Reservoir**
Ind Est	**Industrial Estate**	Ret Pk	**Retail park**
IRB Sta	**Inshore rescue boat station**	Sch	**School**
		Sh Ctr	**Shopping centre**
Inst	**Institute**	TH	**Town hall / house**
Ct	**Law court**	Trad Est	**Trading estate**
L Ctr	**Leisure centre**	Univ	**University**
LC	**Level crossing**	W Twr	**Water tower**
Liby	**Library**	Wks	**Works**
Mkt	**Market**	YH	**Youth hostel**

Enlarged maps only

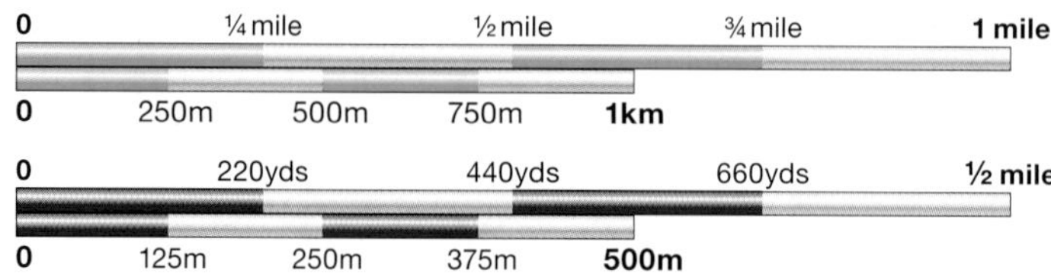

Railway or bus station building

Place of interest

Parkland

The map scale on the pages numbered in blue is 3½ inches to 1 mile
5.52 cm to 1 km • 1:18 103

0	¼ mile	½ mile	¾ mile	1 mile
0	250m	500m	750m	1km

The map scale on the pages numbered in red is 7 inches to 1 mile
11.04 cm to 1 km • 1:9051

0	220yds	440yds	660yds	½ mile
0	125m	250m	375m	500m

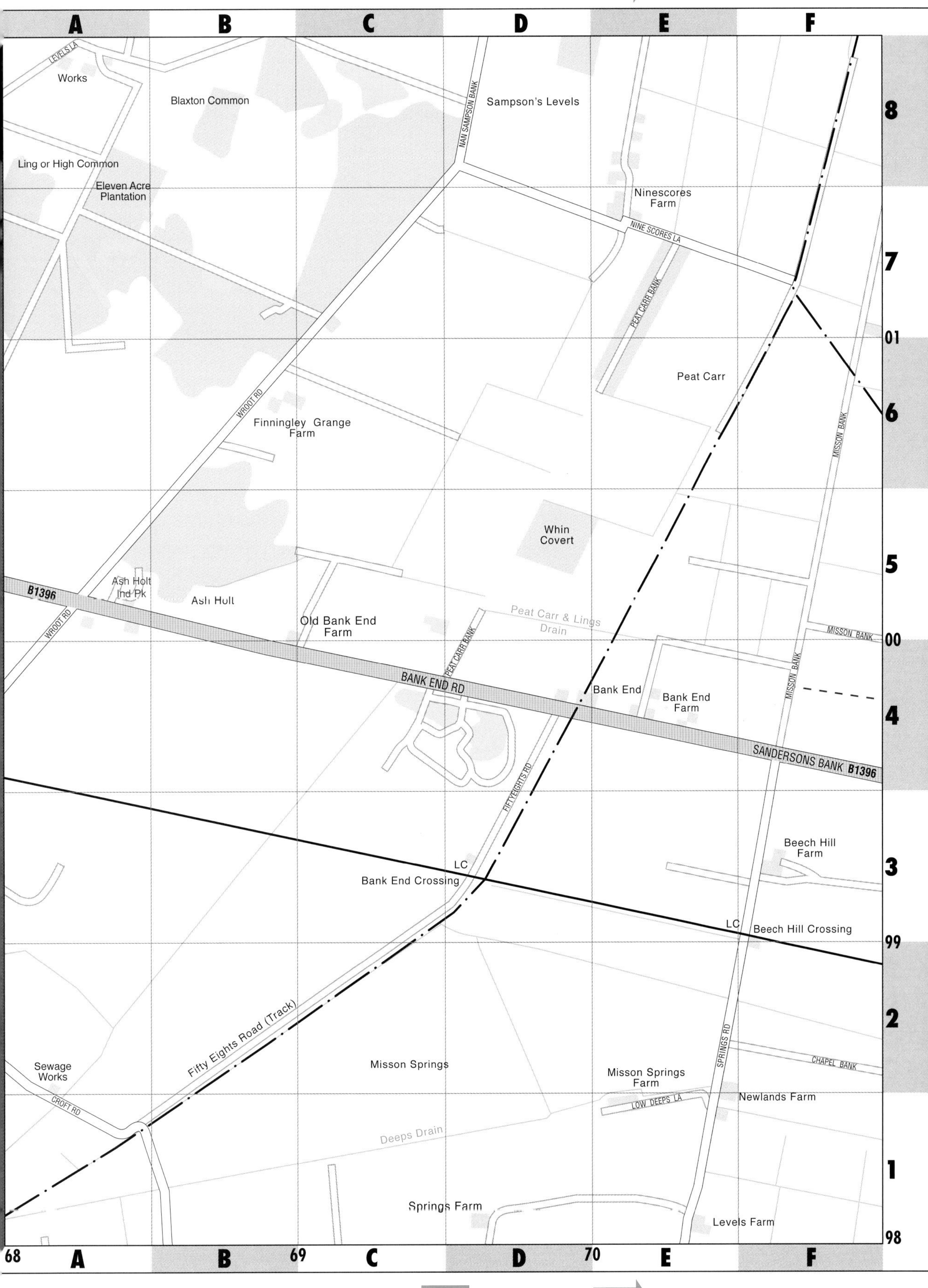

A   B   C   D   E   F

8

Works

Blaxton Common

Sampson's Levels

NAN SAMPSON BANK

Ninescores
Farm

Ling or High Common

NINE SCORES LA

7

Eleven Acre
Plantation

PEAT CARR BANK

01

WROOT RD

Peat Carr

6

Finningley Grange
Farm

MISSON BANK

Whin
Covert

5

Ash Holt
Ind Pk

B1396

Ash Holt

Peat Carr & Lings
Drain

Old Bank End
Farm

MISSON BANK

00

WROOT RD

PEAT CARR BANK

Bank End

MISSON BANK

4

Bank End
Farm

BANK END RD

SANDERSONS BANK B1396

Beech Hill
Farm

HETYEIGHTS RD

3

LC

Bank End Crossing

LC   Beech Hill Crossing

99

2

Fifty Eights Road (Track)

SPRINGS RD

CHAPEL BANK

Sewage
Works

Misson Springs

Misson Springs
Farm

Newlands Farm

CROFT RD

LOW DEEPS LA

Deeps Drain

1

Springs Farm

Levels Farm

98

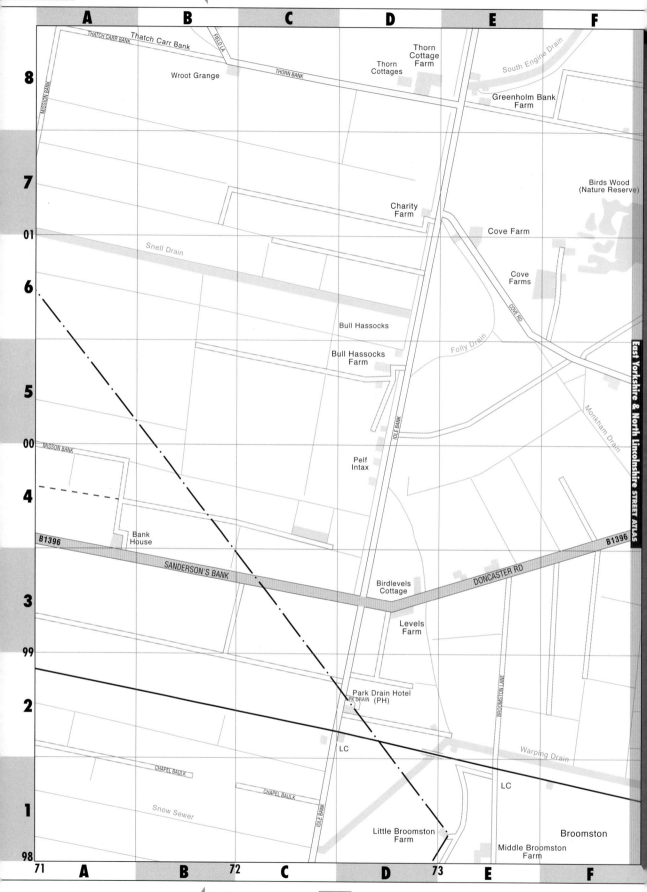

East Yorkshire & North Lincolnshire STREET ATLAS

Thatch Carr Bank

THATCH CARR BANK

Thatch Carr Bank

FIELD LA

THORN BANK

MISSION BANK

Wroot Grange

Thorn Cottages

Thorn Cottage Farm

South Engine Drain

Greenholm Bank Farm

Birds Wood (Nature Reserve)

Charity Farm

Cove Farm

Snell Drain

Cove Farms

COVE RD

Bull Hassocks

Bull Hassocks Farm

Folly Drain

Monkham Drain

MISSON BANK

Pelf Intax

IDLE BANK

B1396

Bank House

B1396

SANDERSON'S BANK

Birdlevels Cottage

DONCASTER RD

Levels Farm

BROOMSTON LANE

Park Drain Hotel (PH)

PK DRAIN

Warping Drain

LC

LC

CHAPEL BAULK

CHAPEL BAULK

IDLE BANK

Snow Sewer

Little Broomston Farm

Broomston

Middle Broomston Farm

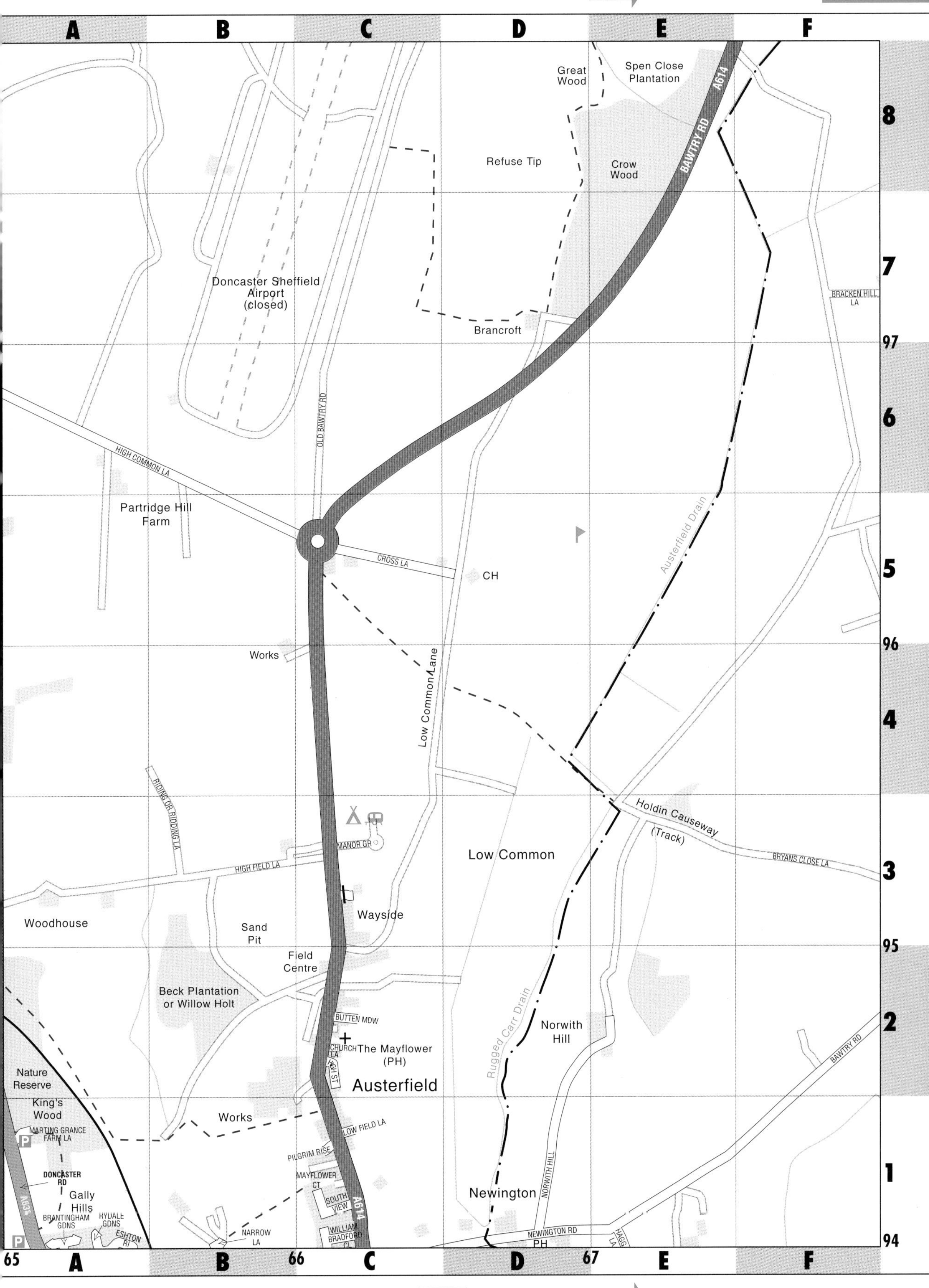
4
A
B
C
D
E
F
8
7
97
6
5
96
4
3
95
2
1
94
65
66
67
10
4
Great Wood
Spen Close Plantation
A614
BAWTRY RD
Refuse Tip
Crow Wood
Doncaster Sheffield Airport (closed)
Brancroft
BRACKEN HILL LA
OLD BAWTRY RD
HIGH COMMON LA
Partridge Hill Farm
CROSS LA
CH
Austerfield Drain
Works
Low Common Lane
RIDING OR RIDDING LA
MANOR GR
HIGH FIELD LA
Low Common
Holdin Causeway (Track)
BRYANS CLOSE LA
Woodhouse
Sand Pit
Wayside
Field Centre
Beck Plantation or Willow Holt
BUTTEN MDW
CHURCH LA
The Mayflower (PH)
HIGH ST
Austerfield
Rugged Carr Drain
Norwith Hill
BAWTRY RD
Nature Reserve
King's Wood
MARTING GRANCE FARM LA
DONCASTER RD
A638
Gally Hills
BRANTINGHAM GDNS
RYDALE GDNS
ESHTON RI
Works
LOW FIELD LA
PILGRIM RISE
MAYFLOWER CT
SOUTH VIEW
A614
WILLIAM BRADFORD CL
NARROW LA
Newington
NORWITH HILL
NEWINGTON RD
PH
HAGG LA

3
1

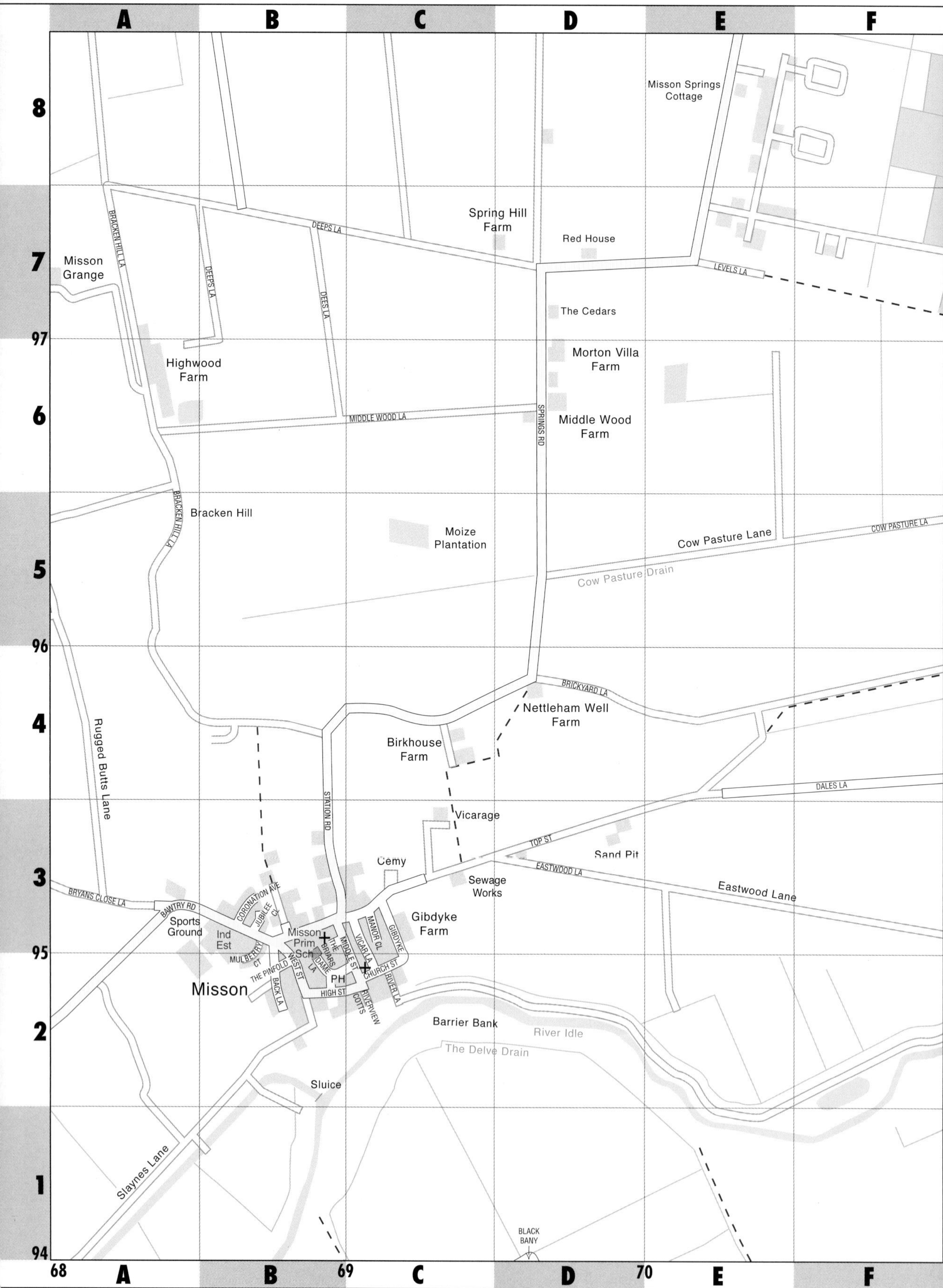
A
B
C
D
E
F
8
7
97
6
5
96
4
3
95
2
1
94
68
69
70
Misson Springs Cottage
Spring Hill Farm
Red House
DEEPS LA
BRACKEN HILL LA
Misson Grange
DEEPS LA
DEES LA
LEVELS LA
The Cedars
Morton Villa Farm
Highwood Farm
MIDDLE WOOD LA
SPRINGS RD
Middle Wood Farm
BRACKEN HILL LA
Bracken Hill
Moize Plantation
Cow Pasture Lane
COW PASTURE LA
Cow Pasture Drain
BRICKYARD LA
Nettleham Well Farm
Rugged Butts Lane
Birkhouse Farm
STATION RD
DALES LA
Vicarage
TOP ST
Sand Pit
Cemy
EASTWOOD LA
Sewage Works
Eastwood Lane
BRYANS CLOSE LA
BAWTRY RD
CORONATION AVE
JUBILEE CL
Sports Ground
Ind Est
Misson Prim Sch
THE BRIARS
DAME LA
MIDDLE ST
VICAR LA
MANOR CL
GIBDYKE
Gibdyke Farm
MULBERRY CT
THE PINFOLD
WEST ST
BACK LA
PH
CHURCH ST
RIVER LA
Misson
HIGH ST
RIVERVIEW COTTS
Barrier Bank
River Idle
The Delve Drain
Sluice
Slaynes Lane
BLACK BANY
68
A
B
69
C
D
70
E
F

3
11

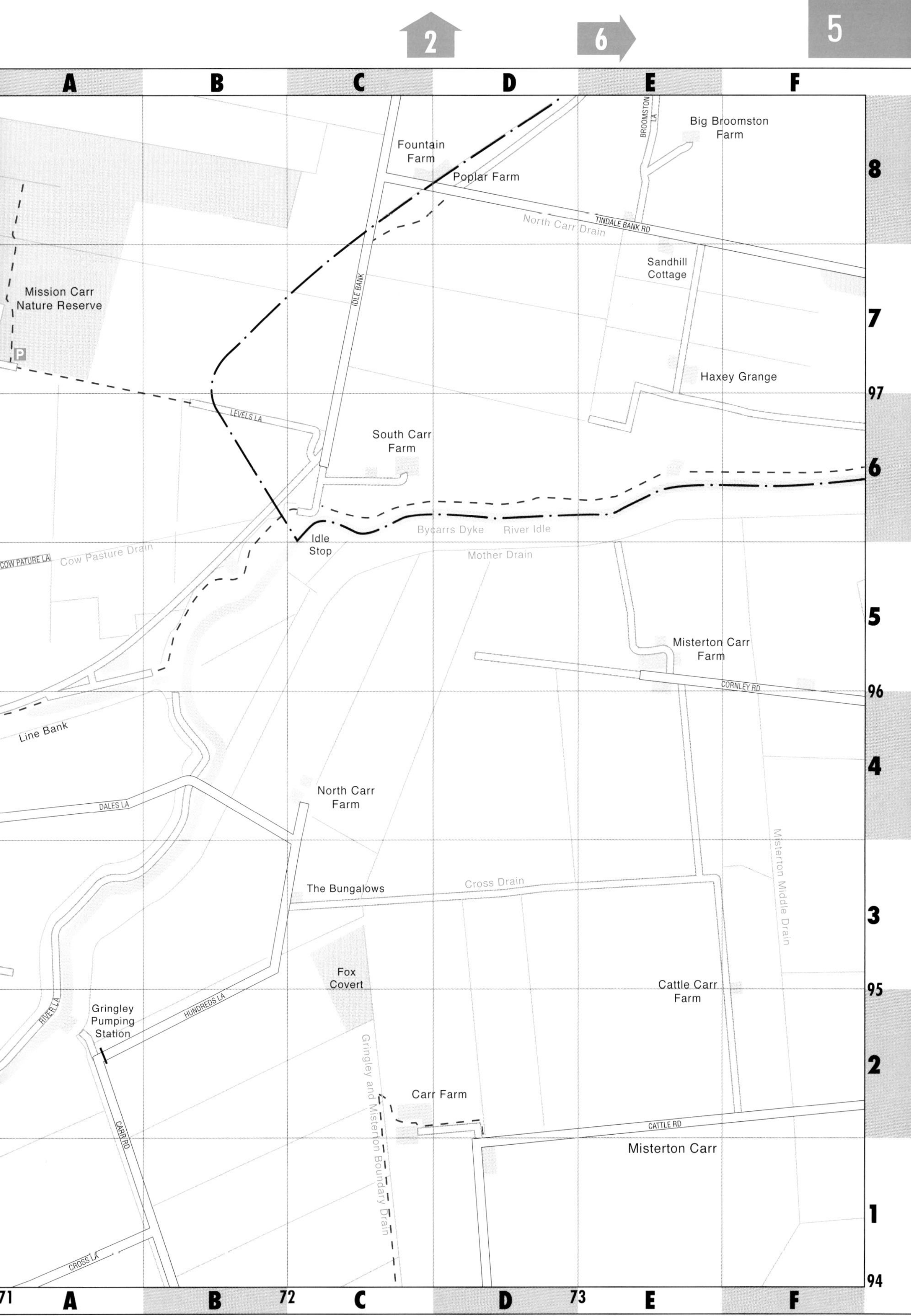

A B C D E F

8

7

97

6

5

96

4

3

95

2

1

94

71 A B 72 C D 73 E F

Mission Carr
Nature Reserve

P

Fountain
Farm

Poplar Farm

BROOMSTON LA

Big Broomston
Farm

TINDALE BANK RD

North Carr Drain

Sandhill
Cottage

Haxey Grange

IDLE BANK

LEVELS LA

South Carr
Farm

Bycarrs Dyke   River Idle

Idle
Stop

COW PATURE LA   Cow Pasture Drain

Mother Drain

Misterton Carr
Farm

CORNLEY RD

Line Bank

DALES LA

North Carr
Farm

Misterton Middle Drain

The Bungalows

Cross Drain

Fox
Covert

Cattle Carr
Farm

RIVER LA

Gringley
Pumping
Station

HUNDREDS LA

CARR RD

Gringley and Misterton Boundary Drain

Carr Farm

CATTLE RD

Misterton Carr

CROSS LA

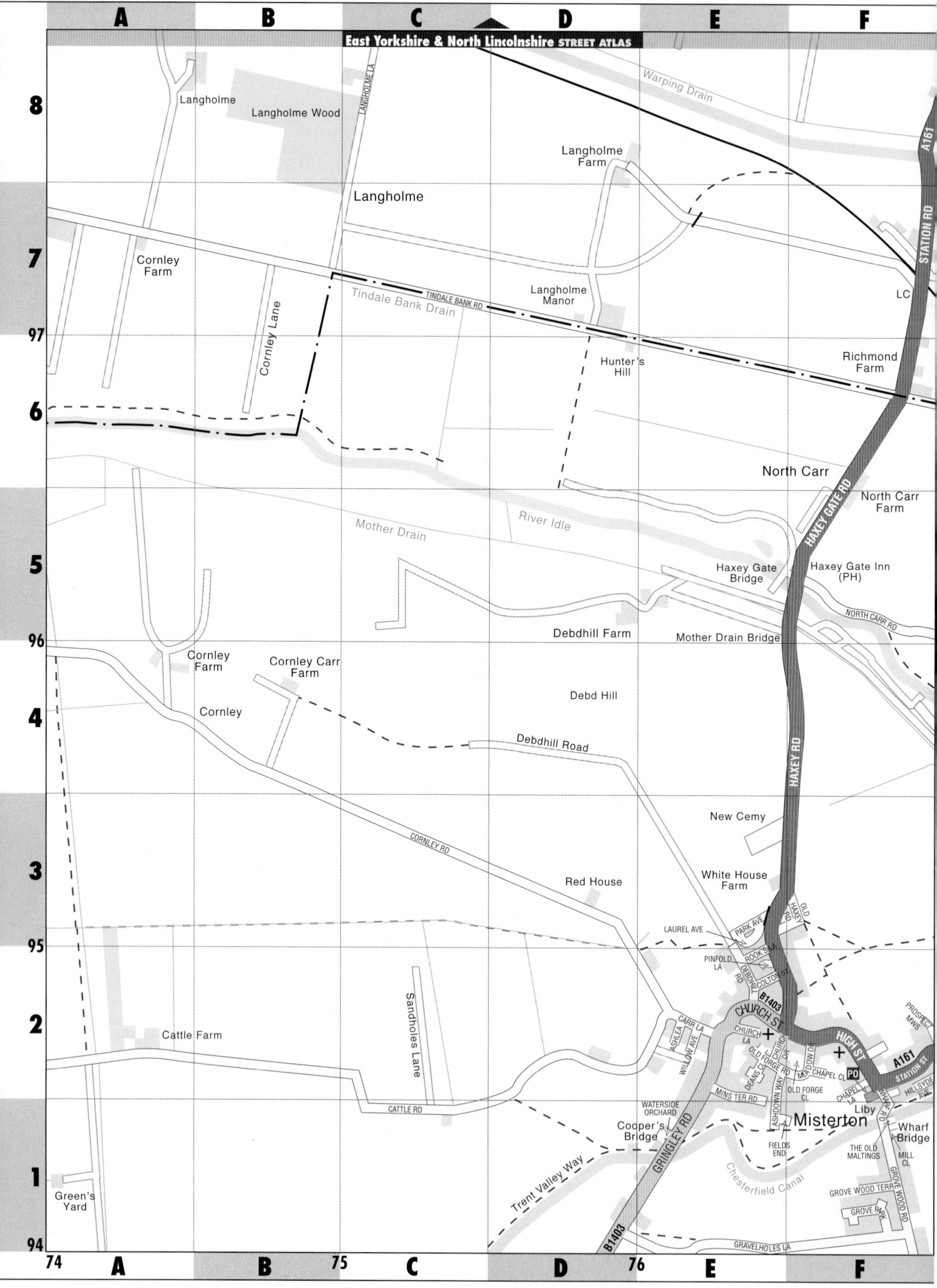

East Yorkshire & North Lincolnshire STREET ATLAS

A   B   C   D   E   F

8

Langholme
Langholme Wood
Langholme
Langholme Farm
Warping Drain

7

Cornley Farm
Cornley Lane
Tindale Bank Drain
TINDALE BANK RD
Langholme Manor
LC

97

Hunter's Hill
Richmond Farm

6

Mother Drain
River Idle
North Carr
HAXEY GATE RD
North Carr Farm

5

Haxey Gate Bridge
Debdhill Farm
Mother Drain Bridge
Haxey Gate Inn (PH)
NORTH CARR RD

96

Cornley Farm
Cornley Carr Farm
Cornley
Debd Hill

4

Debdhill Road
HAXEY RD

CORNLEY RD
Red House
New Cemy
White House Farm

3

LAUREL AVE
PARK AVE
OLD HAXEY RD

95

PINFOLD LA
ROOK'S LA
COLTON RD

2

Cattle Farm
Sandholes Lane
CARR LA
ASHLEA
WILLOW AVE
CHURCH ST
CHURCH LA
OLD FORGE RD
DEANS RD
MAY CHAPEL CL
OLD FORGE CL
MINSTER RD
B1403
HIGH ST
CHAPEL
A161
STATION ST
PO
Liby
PROSPECT MWS

CATTLE RD
WATERSIDE ORCHARD
GRINGLEY RD
Cooper's Bridge
FIELDS END
Misterton
The Old Maltings
Wharf Bridge
MILL CL
GROVE WOOD TERRE
GROVE WOOD RD

1

Green's Yard
Trent Valley Way
Chesterfield Canal
B1403
GROVE BANK

94

74   A   B   75   C   D   76   E   F

STATION RD
A161

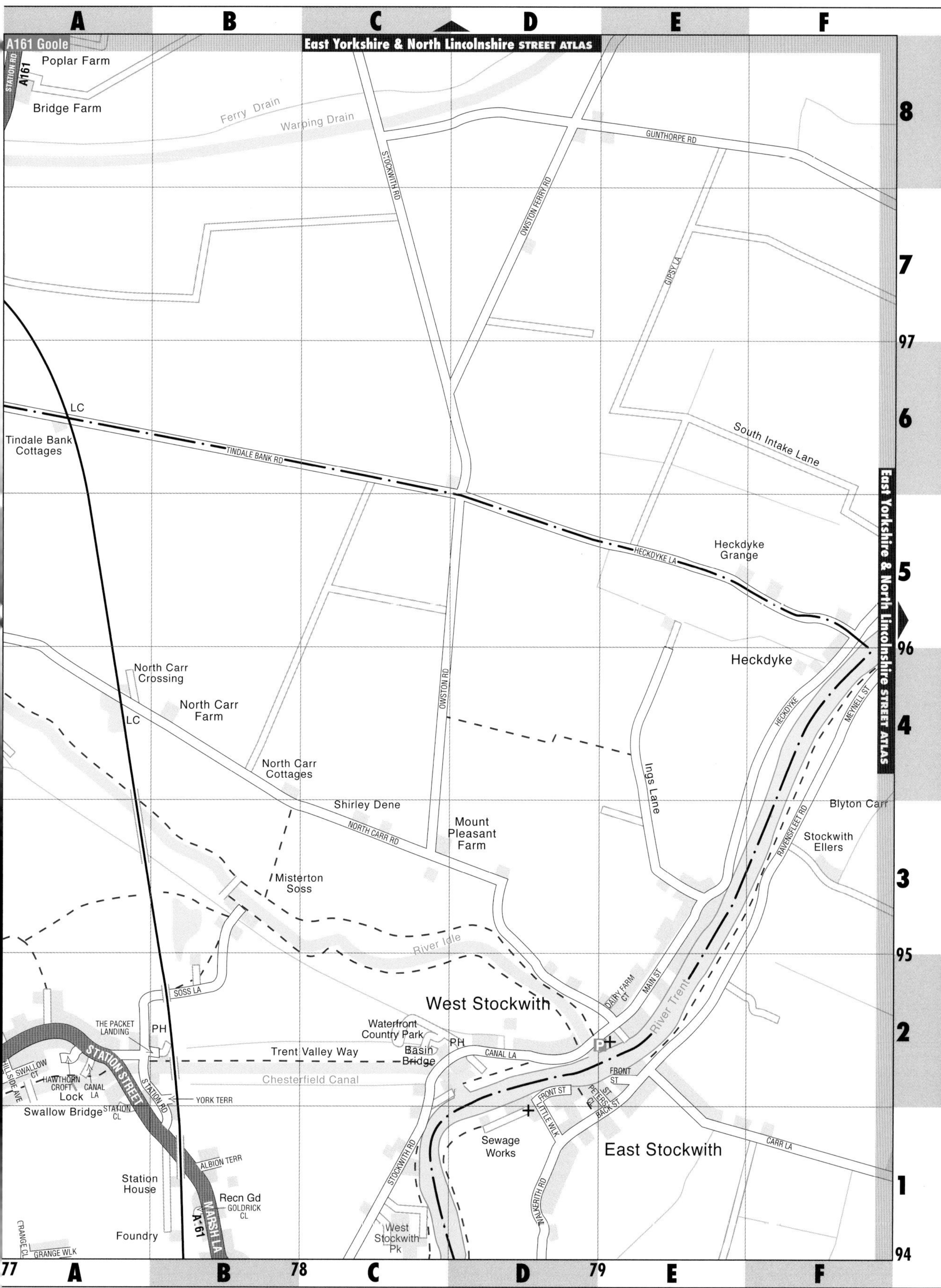

East Yorkshire & North Lincolnshire STREET ATLAS

A **B** **C** **D** **E** **F**

8

7

97

6

Poplar Farm

Bridge Farm

Ferry Drain

Warping Drain

GUNTHORPE RD

STOCKWITH RD

OWSTON FERRY RD

GIPSY LA

LC

Tindale Bank
Cottages

TINDALE BANK RD

South Intake Lane

HECKDYKE LA

Heckdyke
Grange

5

96

Heckdyke

North Carr
Crossing

LC

North Carr
Farm

North Carr
Cottages

OWSTON RD

Ings Lane

HECKDYKE

RAVENSFLEET RD

MEYNELL ST

Blyton Carr

Stockwith
Ellers

4

Shirley Dene

NORTH CARR RD

Mount
Pleasant
Farm

3

Misterton
Soss

River Idle

95

DAIRY FARM CT

MAIN ST

River Trent

SOSS LA

West Stockwith

THE PACKET
LANDING

PH

Waterfront
Country Park

PH

Basin
Bridge

CANAL LA

P

2

STATION STREET

Trent Valley Way

Chesterfield Canal

FRONT
ST

SWALLOW
CT

HAWTHORN
CROFT

CANAL
LA

STATION RD

York Terr

STOCKWITH RD

FRONT ST

PETERS
ST

BACK ST

HILLSIDE
AVE

Lock

STATION
CL

Swallow Bridge

Sewage
Works

LITTLE WLK

East Stockwith

CARR LA

Station
House

ALBION TERR

MARSH LA

A-61

Recn Gd

GOLDRICK
CL

WAXERITH RD

1

GRANGE
CL

GRANGE WLK

Foundry

West
Stockwith
Pk

94

East Yorkshire & North Lincolnshire STREET ATLAS

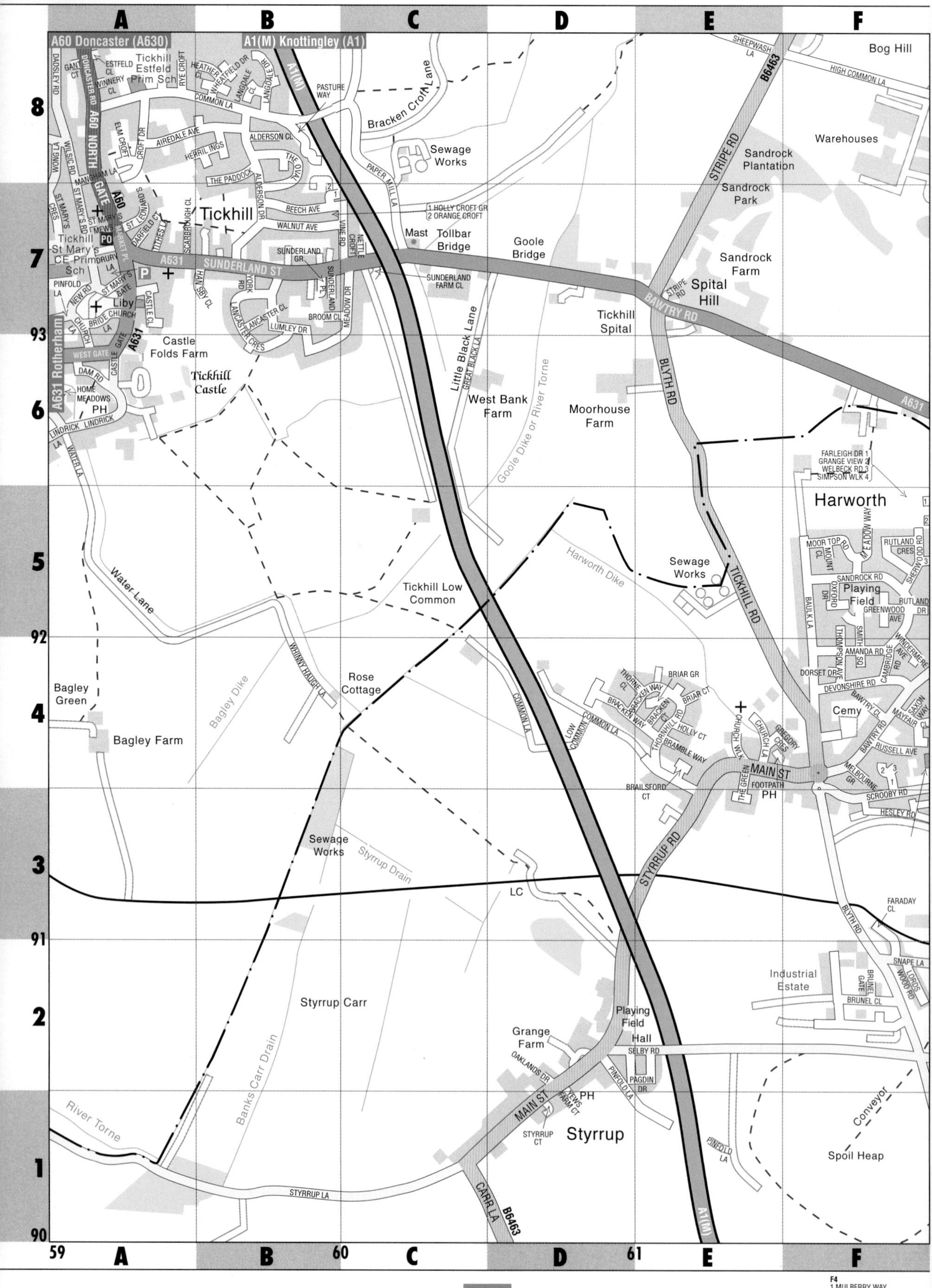

A60 Doncaster (A630)
A1(M) Knottingley (A1)

Tickhill

Spital Hill

Harworth

Styrrup

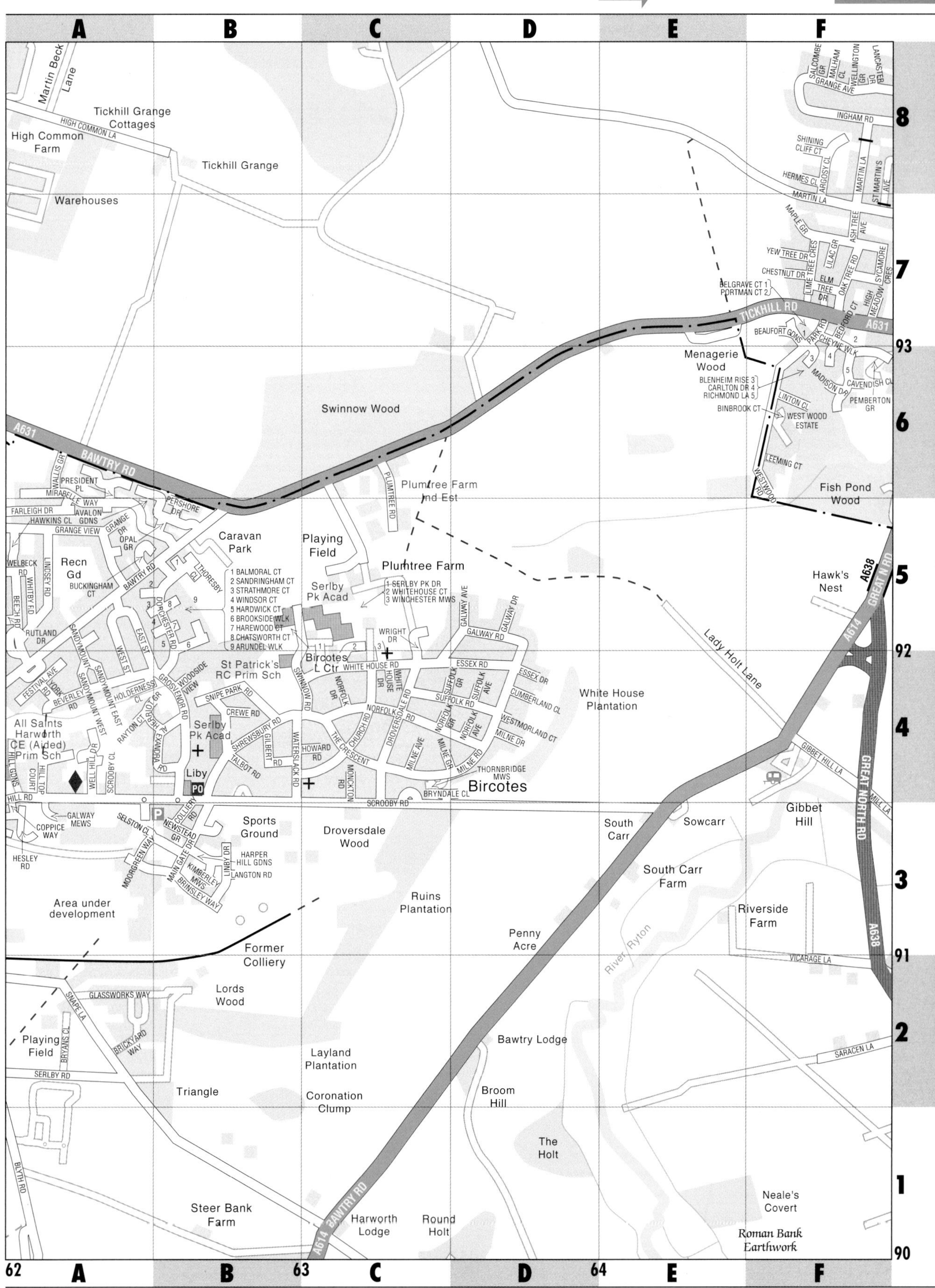
A B C D E F
8 7 93 6 5 92 4 3 91 2 1 90
62 63 64
Martin Beck Lane
High Common Farm
HIGH COMMON LA
Tickhill Grange Cottages
Tickhill Grange
Warehouses
Swinnow Wood
A631
BAWTRY RD
TICKHILL RD
Menagerie Wood
BLENHEIM RISE 3
CARLTON DR 4
RICHMOND LA 5
BINBROOK CT
WEST WOOD ESTATE
LEEMING CT
WESTWOOD RD
Fish Pond Wood
SALCOMBE GR
MALHAM CL
WELLINGTON GR
LANCASTER DR
GRANGE AVE
INGHAM RD
SHINING CLIFF CT
ARGOSY CL
HERMES CL
MARTIN LA
ST MARTIN'S AVE
MAPLE GR
ASH TREE AVE
YEW TREE DR
LILAC GR
CHESTNUT DR
LIME TREE CRES
ELM TREE DR
OAK TREE RD
SYCAMORE CRES
HIGH MEADOW
BELGRAVE CT 1
PORTMAN CT 2
BEAUFORT GDNS
PARK RD
BEDFORD CT
CHEYNE WLK
MADISON DR
CAVENDISH CL
LINTON CL
PEMBERTON GR
Plumtree Farm Ind Est
PLUMTREE RD
Plumtree Farm
1 SERLBY PK DR
2 WHITEHOUSE CT
3 WINCHESTER MWS
Playing Field
Caravan Park
Serlby Pk Acad
1 BALMORAL CT
2 SANDRINGHAM CT
3 STRATHMORE CT
4 WINDSOR CT
5 HARDWICK CT
6 BROOKSIDE WLK
7 HAREWOOD CT
8 CHATSWORTH CT
9 ARUNDEL WLK
THORESBY CL
PERSHORE DR
WALLIS GR
PRESIDENT PL
MIRABELLE WAY
FARLEIGH DR
AVALON GDNS
HAWKINS CL
GRANGE VIEW
GRANGE DR
OPAL GR
Recn Gd
WELBECK RD
LINDSEY RD
WHITBY RD
BEECH RD
BUCKINGHAM CT
BAWTRY RD
DORCHESTER RD
EAST ST
WEST ST
RUTLAND DR
SANDYMOUNT
SANDYMOUNT EAST
SANDYMOUNT WEST
FESTIVAL AVE
YORK RD
BEVERLEY RD
HOLDERNESS CL
GROSVENOR RD
WOODSIDE VIEW
RAYTON CT
ALEXANDRA RD
St Patrick's RC Prim Sch
Bircotes L Ctr
SWINNOW RD
WRIGHT DR
WHITE HOUSE RD
WHITE HOUSE DR
GALWAY AVE
GALWAY DR
GALWAY RD
ESSEX RD
ESSEX DR
NORFOLK DR
SUFFOLK GR
SUFFOLK AVE
SUFFOLK RD
CUMBERLAND CL
WESTMORLAND CT
MILNE DR
NORFOLK GR
NORFOLK AVE
NORFOLK RD
DROVERSDALE RD
CHURCH RD
THE CRESCENT
MILNE AVE
MILNE GR
MILNE RD
THORNBRIDGE MWS
BRYNDALE CL
Bircotes
SNIPE PARK RD
CREWE RD
SHREWSBURY RD
GILBERT RD
WATERSLACK RD
HOWARD RD
MONCKTON RD
TALBOT RD
All Saints Harworth CE (Aided) Prim Sch
HILL TOP
COURT
HILL GDNS
HILL RD
WELL HILL DR
SCROOBY CL
Serlby Pk Acad
Liby
PO
P
SCROOBY RD
GALWAY MEWS
COPPICE WAY
SELSTON CL
COLLIERY RD
NEWSTEAD GR
HESLEY RD
MOORGREEN WAY
MAIN GATE
KIMBERLEY MWS
BRINSLEY WAY
LINBY DR
HARPER HILL GDNS
LANGTON RD
Sports Ground
Droversdale Wood
Lady Holt Lane
White House Plantation
A638
GREAT N RD
A614
Hawk's Nest
GIBBET HILL LA
MILL LA
Gibbet Hill
South Carr
Sowcarr
South Carr Farm
Riverside Farm
GREAT NORTH RD
A638
Ruins Plantation
Penny Acre
River Ryton
VICARAGE LA
Area under development
Former Colliery
Lords Wood
GLASSWORKS WAY
SNAPE LA
BRICKYARD WAY
BRYANS CL
Playing Field
SERLBY RD
Layland Plantation
Coronation Clump
Bawtry Lodge
Broom Hill
SARACEN LA
Triangle
The Holt
BLYTH RD
Steer Bank Farm
A614 BAWTRY RD
Harworth Lodge
Round Holt
Neale's Covert
Roman Bank Earthwork

9
3

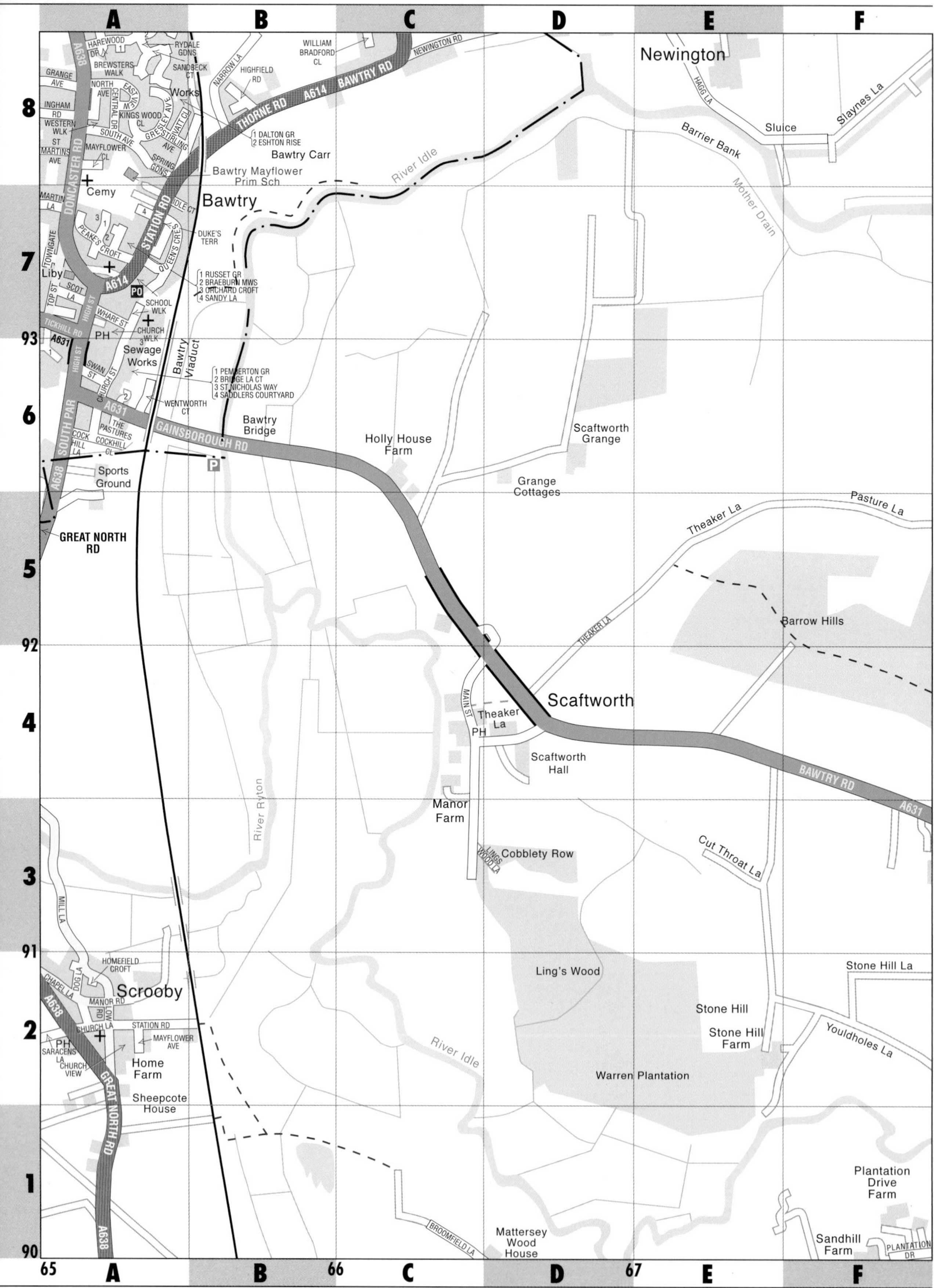
A
B
C
D
E
F
8
7
93
6
5
92
4
3
91
2
1
90
65
66
67
Newington
Hagg La
Sluice
Slaynes La
Barrier Bank
Mother Drain
River Idle
Newington Rd
William Bradford Cl
Highfield Rd
Narrow La
Thorne Rd
A614
Bawtry Rd
1 Dalton Gr
2 Eshton Rise
Bawtry Carr
Bawtry Mayflower Prim Sch
Bawtry
Harewood Dr
Rydale Gdns
Brewsters Walk
Sandbeck Ct
Grange Ave
North Ave
Eastview
Works
Ingham Rd
Central Dr
Kings Wood Cl
Gresley Ave
Western Wlk
South Ave
Stirling Ave
Tait Cl
St Martins Ave
Mayflower Cl
Spring Gdns
Doncaster Rd
A638
Cemy
Martin La
Idle Ct
Station Rd
Duke's Terr
Peake's Croft
Queen's Cres
Towngate
Liby
Scot La
Top St
1 Russet Gr
2 Braeburn Mws
3 Orchard Croft
4 Sandy La
PO
School Wlk
Wharf St
High St
Tickhill Rd
A631
PH
Church Wlk
Sewage Works
Bawtry Viaduct
Swan St
Church St
1 Pemberton Gr
2 Bridge La Ct
3 St Nicholas Way
4 Saddlers Courtyard
Wentworth Ct
South Par
The Pastures
Cock Hill La
Cockhill Cl
Gainsborough Rd
Bawtry Bridge
P
Sports Ground
Great North Rd
Holly House Farm
Scaftworth Grange
Grange Cottages
Theaker La
Pasture La
Barrow Hills
Scaftworth
Main St
Theaker La
PH
Scaftworth Hall
Bawtry Rd
Manor Farm
River Ryton
Cut Throat La
Cobblety Row
Lings Wood La
Mill La
Homefield Croft
Chapel La
Dog La
Scrooby
Manor Rd
Low Rd
Station Rd
Church La
Mayflower Ave
Saracens La
Church View
Home Farm
Sheepcote House
Ling's Wood
Stone Hill La
Stone Hill
Stone Hill Farm
Youldholes La
River Idle
Warren Plantation
Plantation Drive Farm
Broomfield La
Mattersey Wood House
Sandhill Farm
Plantation Dr

9
19

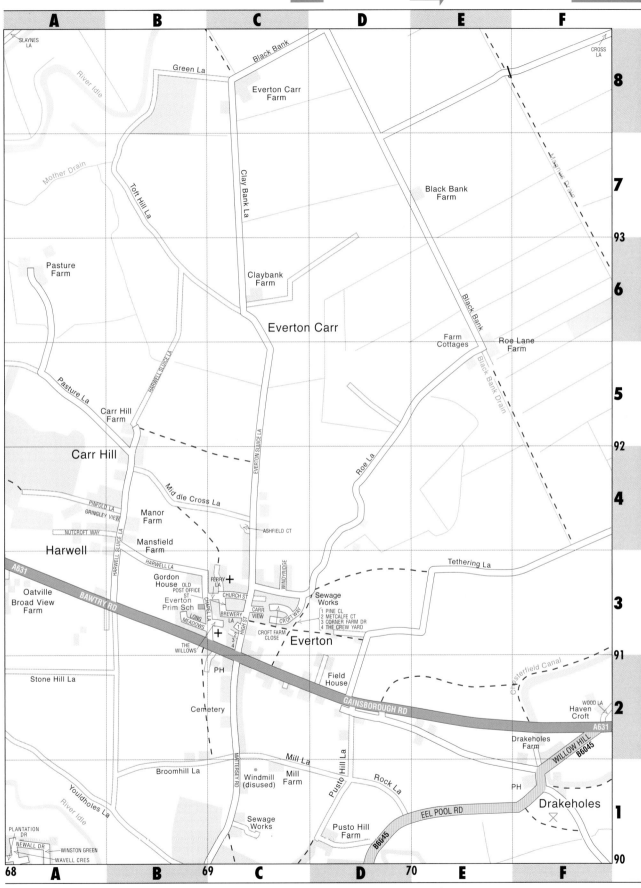
4
12

A B C D E F

SLAYNES LA
River Idle
Green La
Black Bank
Everton Carr Farm
CROSS LA
8
Mother Drain
Toft Hill La
Clay Bank La
Black Bank Farm
Magnus Drain
7
93
Pasture Farm
Claybank Farm
6
Everton Carr
Black Bank
Farm Cottages
Roe Lane Farm
Black Bank Drain
Pasture La
HARWELL SLUICE LA
Carr Hill Farm
EVERTON SLUICE LA
5
92
Carr Hill
Roe La
Mid dle Cross La
4
PINFOLD LA
GRINGLEY VIEW
Manor Farm
NUTCROFT WAY
ASHFIELD CT
Mansfield Farm
Harwell
HARWELL SLUICE LA
HARWELL LA
WINDYRIDGE
Tethering La
A631
Gordon House
FERRY LA
OLD POST OFFICE ST
CHURCH ST
Oatville
Broad View Farm
BAWTRY RD
Everton Prim Sch
CHAPEL LA
BREWERY LA
CARR VIEW
CROFT WAY
Sewage Works
1 PINE CL
2 METCALFE CT
3 CORNER FARM DR
4 THE CREW YARD
3
LONG MEADOWS
HIGH ST
CROFT FARM CLOSE
Everton
THE WILLOWS
91
PH
Field House
Chesterfield Canal
Stone Hill La
GAINSBOROUGH RD
WOOD LA
Haven Croft
2
Cemetery
A631
Drakeholes Farm
WILLOW HILL
B6045
Mill La
Broomhill La
MATTERSEY RD
Windmill (disused)
Mill Farm
Pusto Hill La
Rock La
PH
Youldholes La
River Idle
EEL POOL RD
Drakeholes
1
Sewage Works
Pusto Hill Farm
PLANTATION DR
NEWALL DR
WINSTON GREEN
WAVELL CRES
B6045
90

68 A B 69 C D 70 E F

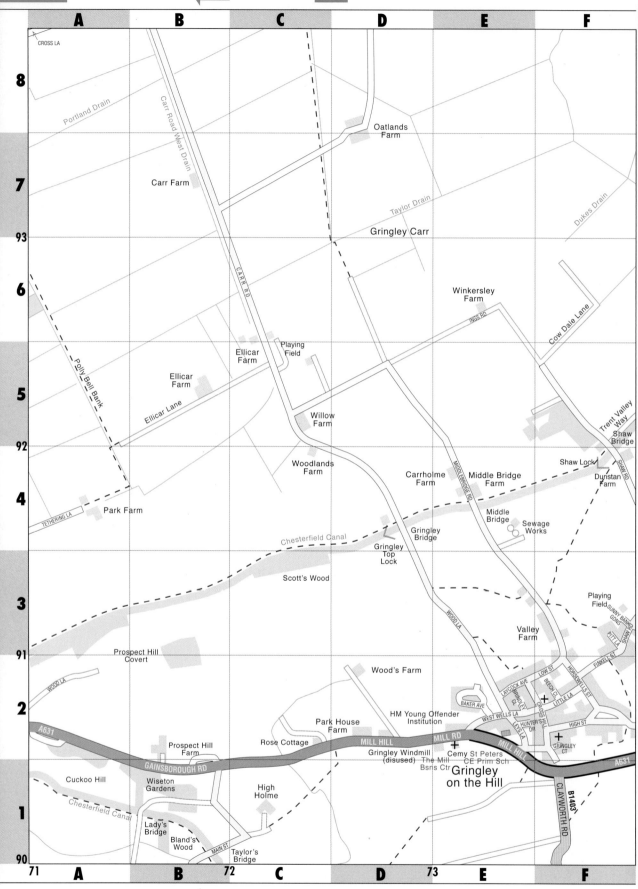
11

5

A B C D E F

8

CROSS LA

Portland Drain

Carr Road West Drain

Oatlands Farm

7

Carr Farm

Taylor Drain

Dukes Drain

93

Gringley Carr

6

CARR RD

Winkersley Farm

INGS RD

Cow Dale Lane

Playing Field

Ellicar Farm

Ellicar Farm

Polly Bell Bank

5

Ellicar Lane

Willow Farm

Trent Valley Way

Shaw Bridge

92

Shaw Lock

Woodlands Farm

Carrholme Farm

MIDDLEBRIDGE RD

Middle Bridge Farm

Dunstan Farm

SHAW RD

4

Park Farm

TETHERING LA

Middle Bridge

Sewage Works

Gringley Bridge

Chesterfield Canal

Gringley Top Lock

Scott's Wood

3

WOOD LA

Playing Field

SUNNY BANK GDNS

Valley Farm

PITT LA

SHAW RD

91

Prospect Hill Covert

FINKELL ST

Wood's Farm

WOOD LA

LOW ST

HORSEWELLS ST

LAYCOCK AVE

BEECH CL

BRINDLEY CL

2

BAKER AVE

LITTLE LA

HM Young Offender Institution

WEST WELLS LA

CROSS HILL

Park House Farm

HUNTER'S DR

HIGH ST

LEYS LA

A631

MILL RD

MILL HILL

MILL HILL

GRINGLEY CT

Prospect Hill Farm

Rose Cottage

Gringley Windmill (disused)

The Mill Bsns Ctr

Cemy

St Peters CE Prim Sch

GAINSBOROUGH RD

A631

Gringley on the Hill

Cuckoo Hill

Wiseton Gardens

High Holme

CLAYWORTH RD

B1403

1

Chesterfield Canal

Lady's Bridge

Bland's Wood

MAIN ST

Taylor's Bridge

90

71 A B 72 C D 73 E F

11

21

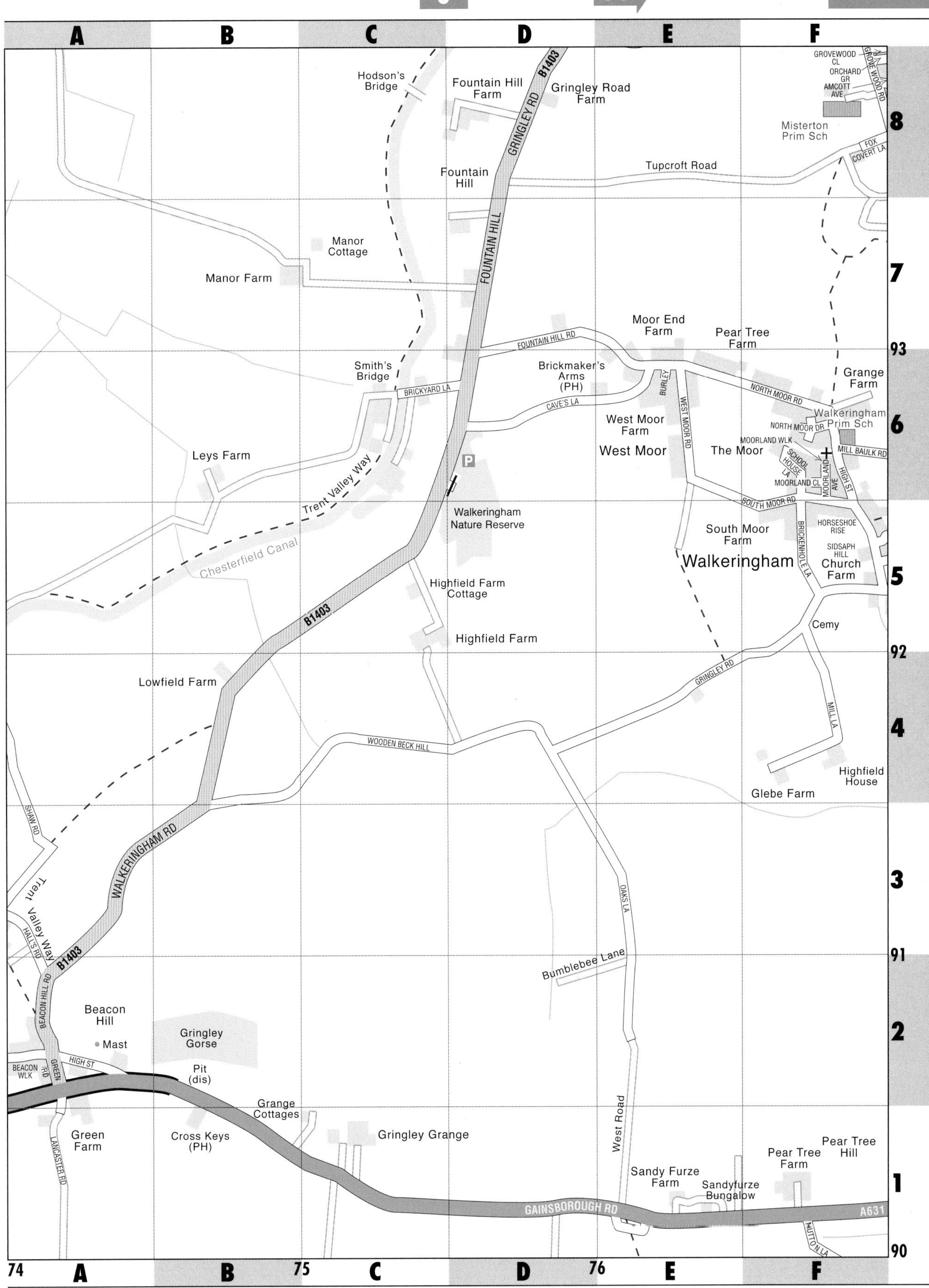
6
14
Hodson's Bridge
Fountain Hill Farm
Gringley Road Farm
B1403
GRINGLEY RD
Misterton Prim Sch
GROVEWOOD CL
ORCHARD GR
AMCOTT AVE
GROVE WOOD RD
FOX COVERT LA
Fountain Hill
Tupcroft Road
Manor Cottage
Manor Farm
FOUNTAIN HILL
Moor End Farm
Pear Tree Farm
FOUNTAIN HILL RD
Smith's Bridge
BRICKYARD LA
Brickmaker's Arms (PH)
CAVE'S LA
BURLEY
WEST MOOR RD
Grange Farm
NORTH MOOR RD
Walkeringham Prim Sch
NORTH MOOR DR
MOORLAND WLK
West Moor Farm
West Moor
The Moor
MILL BAULK RD
SCHOOL HOUSE LA
MOORLAND CL
MOORLAND AVE
HIGH ST
Leys Farm
Trent Valley Way
Walkeringham Nature Reserve
SOUTH MOOR RD
South Moor Farm
HORSESHOE RISE
SIDSAPH HILL
Chesterfield Canal
Walkeringham
BRICKENHOLE LA
Church Farm
Highfield Farm Cottage
Highfield Farm
Cemy
Lowfield Farm
GRINGLEY RD
MILL LA
WOODEN BECK HILL
Glebe Farm
Highfield House
SHAW RD
WALKERINGHAM RD
OAKS LA
Trent Valley Way
HALL'S RD
Bumblebee Lane
BEACON HILL RD
Beacon Hill
Mast
Gringley Gorse
BEACON WLK
RD
GREEN
HIGH ST
Pit (dis)
Grange Cottages
Green Farm
Cross Keys (PH)
Gringley Grange
West Road
Pear Tree Hill
Pear Tree Farm
LANCASTER RD
Sandy Furze Farm
Sandyfurze Bungalow
GAINSBOROUGH RD
A631
MUTTON LA
A B C D E F
8 7 93 6 5 92 4 3 91 2 1 90
74 75 76
22
14

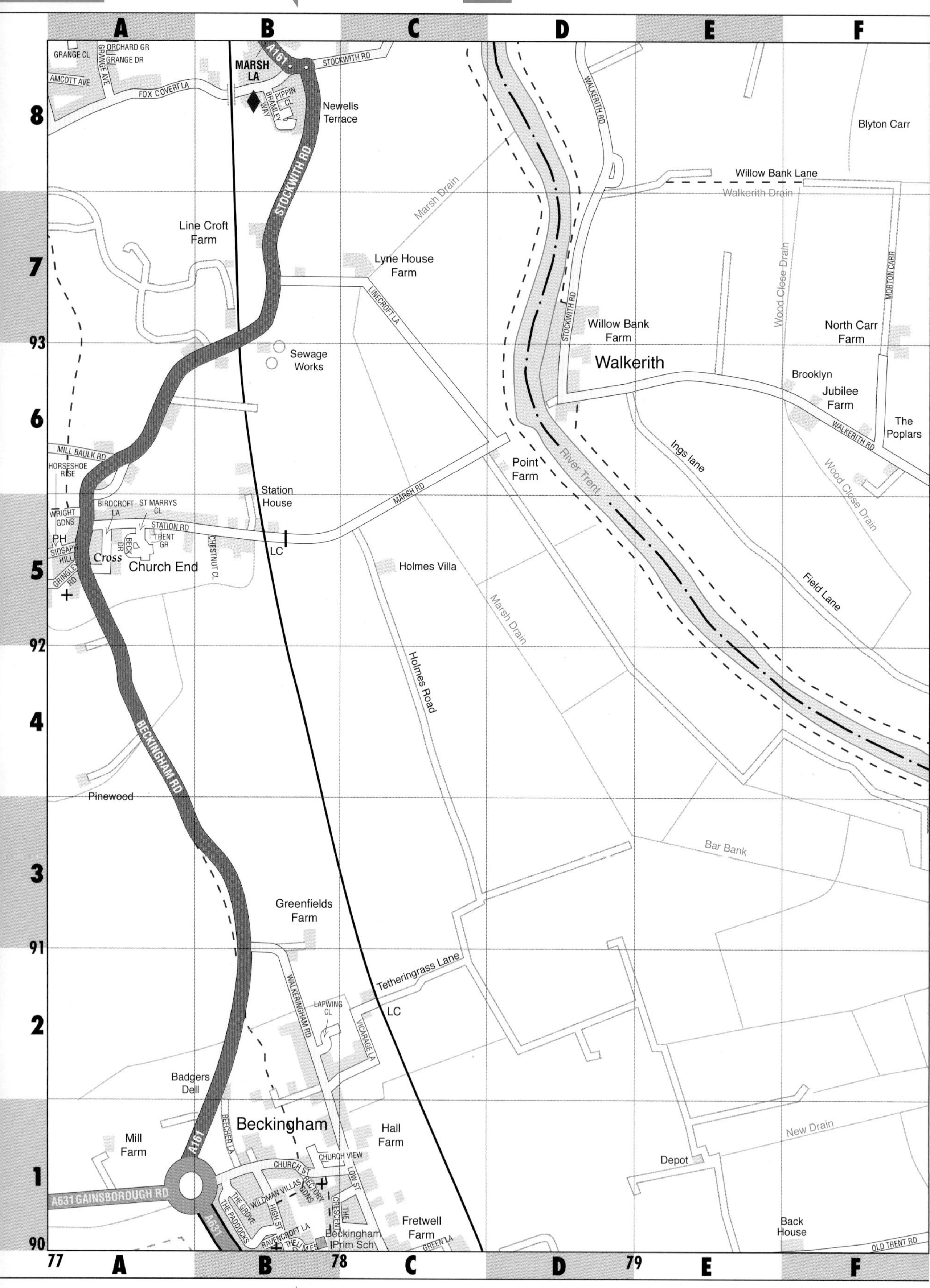
13
7
A
B
C
D
E
F
8
7
93
6
5
92
4
3
91
2
1
90
77
78
79
GRANGE CL
ORCHARD GR
GRANGE DR
GRANGE AVE
AMCOTT AVE
FOX COVERT LA
MARSH LA
A161
STOCKWITH RD
PIPPIN CL
BRAMLEY WAY
Newells Terrace
Blyton Carr
WALKERITH RD
Willow Bank Lane
Walkerith Drain
Marsh Drain
Line Croft Farm
Lyne House Farm
LINECROFT LA
Wood Close Drain
MORTON CARR
Willow Bank Farm
North Carr Farm
Walkerith
Sewage Works
Brooklyn
Jubilee Farm
The Poplars
MILL BAULK RD
HORSESHOE RISE
Point Farm
River Trent
Ings lane
Station House
MARSH RD
BIRDCROFT LA
ST MARRYS CL
WRIGHT GDNS
STATION RD
TRENT GR
PH
SIDSAPH HILL
BECK DR
CHESTNUT CL
LC
Cross
Church End
GRINGLEY RD
Holmes Villa
Field Lane
Holmes Road
BECKINGHAM RD
Pinewood
Bar Bank
Greenfields Farm
Tetheringrass Lane
LAPWING CL
WALKERINGHAM RD
VICARAGE LA
Badgers Dell
Beckingham
Hall Farm
New Drain
Mill Farm
BEECHER LA
CHURCH VIEW
Depot
CHURCH ST
RECTORY GDNS
LOW ST
A631 GAINSBOROUGH RD
A631
THE GROVE
WILDMAN VILLAS
HIGH ST
THE CRESCENT
THE PADDOCKS
RAVENCROFT LA
THE LIMES
Beckingham Prim Sch
GREEN LA
Fretwell Farm
Back House
OLD TRENT RD
13
23

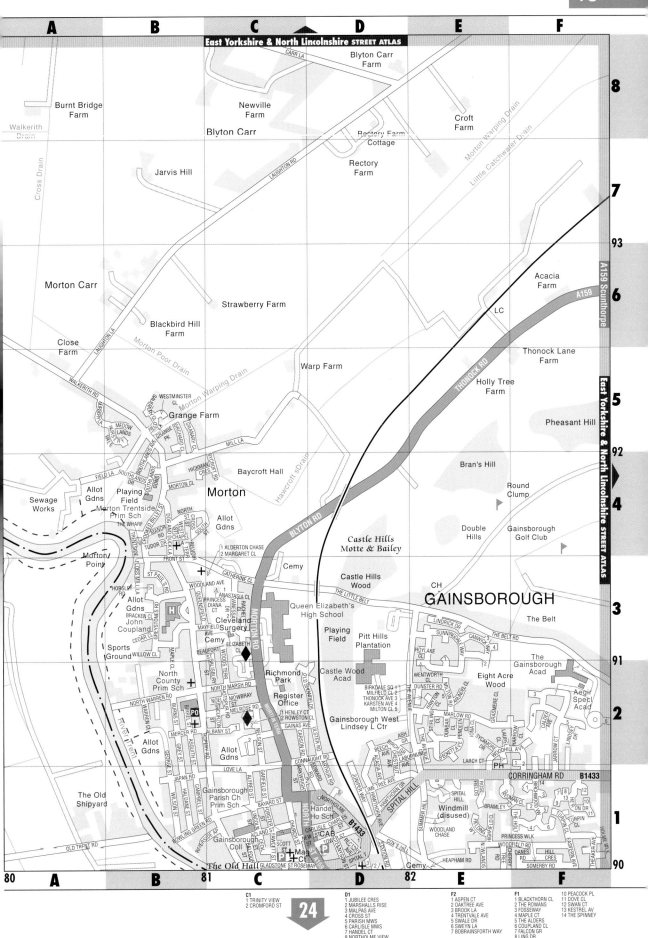

East Yorkshire & North Lincolnshire STREET ATLAS

A159 Scunthorpe

East Yorkshire & North Lincolnshire STREET ATLAS

8

93

7

6

92

5

4

91

3

2

1

90

Burnt Bridge Farm

Walkerith Drain

Cross Drain

Newville Farm

Blyton Carr Farm

Blyton Carr

Rectory Farm Cottage

Croft Farm

Morton Warping Drain

Little Catchwater Drain

Jarvis Hill

LAUGHTON RD

Rectory Farm

Morton Carr

Strawberry Farm

Blackbird Hill Farm

Close Farm

LAUGHTON LA

Morton Poor Drain

Warp Farm

Morton Warping Drain

Acacia Farm

A159

LC

Thonock Lane Farm

WALKERITH RD

WESTMINSTER CL

MEDOW LANDS

Grange Farm

MILL LA

Hawcroft s Drain

Holly Tree Farm

THONOCK RD

Pheasant Hill

FIELD LA

SOUTHLANDS DR

SOUTHLANDS

HICKMAN CRES

BYCROFT RD

MORTON CL

Baycroft Hall

Bran's Hill

Round Clump

Sewage Works

Allot Gdns

Playing Field

Morton Trentside Prim Sch

THE WHARF

Morton

Allot Gdns

Double Hills

Gainsborough Golf Club

DOG AND DUCK LA

NORTH CROSS ST

CHAPEL ST

SOUTH ST

BELVOIR TERR

BLYTON RD

Castle Hills Motte & Bailey

CH

Morton Point

TUDOR DR

FRONT ST

1 ALDERTON CHASE
2 MARGARET CL

Cemy

Castle Hills Wood

GAINSBOROUGH

The Belt

ST PAUL'S RD

HORSLEY RD

E COSS MILL LA

THE RISINGS

CROMWELL BULLEY ST

WOODLAND AVE

CATHERINE CL

1 ANASTASIA CL
PRINCESS DIANA CT

THE LITTLE BELT

LINDRICK DR

CANWICK WAY

SUNNINGDALE WAY

THE BELT RD

Allot Gdns

John Coupland

BRACKEN CL

CEDAR PL

GREYSTONES RD

H

MAYFIELD AVE

ELIZABETH CL

RACHEL CL

QUEENSFIELD

Cleveland Surgery

Cemy

Queen Elizabeth's High School

Playing Field

Pitt Hills Plantation

HOYLAKE CL

THE AVENUE

The Gainsborough Acad

Sports Ground

WILLOW CL

MAPLE CL

BEAUFORT ST

SALISBURY ST

WOODS TERR

MORTON RD

Richmond Park

Castle Wood Acad

WENTWORTH CL

DUNSTER RD

Eight Acre Wood

91

North County Prim Sch

NORTH MARSH RD

NOEL ST

SPUR RD

MELROSE RD

Register Office

BIRKDALE SQ 1
MILFIELD CL 2
THONOCK AVE 3
KARSTEN AVE 4
MILTON CL 5

STIRLING CL

HAMPTON CL

MARLOW RD

PENDER CL

GRASMERE CL

The Gainsborough Acad

BIRKBECK CL

Aegir Specl Acad

JARROW CT

LINDSEY DR

MAPLE CT

BIRHEL ST

ASQUITH ST

UPPER RD

1 HENLEY CT
2 ROWSTON CL

GAINAS AVE

Gainsborough West Lindsey L Ctr

ASH GR

DUNBAR CL

SYCAMORE DR

HARROW CT

LAUREL CT

WOODHILL AVE

CALDER AVE

PO

MERCER RD

GREY ST

CURZON ST

ALBANY ST

NELSON ST

CONNAUGHT RD

BIRCH GR

BECKETT AVE

BEECH AVE

ACACIA AVE

CHESTNUT AVE

LARCH CT

PH

Allot Gdns

MAPLE RD

BURNS ST

NORTH WARREN RD

WARREN RD

LOVE LA

ALFRED ST

GARFIELD ST

LABURNUM CL

CORRINGHAM RD

B1433

River Trent

WILSON ST

GEORGE ST

JAPAN ST

HALDANE ST

CAMPBELL ST

BAYARD ST

ACLAND ST

LINCOLN ST

FIRST ST

JUNIPER WAY

LIME TREE AVE

HAWTHORN CL

SPITAL HILL

14

ROSES FIELDS

SPITAL HILL

THE HOLT

BRAMLEY

The Old Shipyard

Gainsborough Parish Ch Prim Sch

Handel Ho Sch

NORTHOLME

CHARLES

B1433

Windmill (disused)

WOODLAND CHASE

SUMMER HILL

CHERRY TREE

WOODFIELD CT

PRINCESS WLK

HILL CRES

HETON

TURPIN CL

HOLME LA

THEAKER AVE

Gainsborough Coll

BALFOUR ST

SCOTT ST

GLADSTONE ST

Mag Ct

CAB

NEW ST

SPITAL T

COX'S HILL

Cemy

HEAPHAM RD

SOMERBY RD

DANES CL

EASEDALE AVE

The Old Hall

P

P

OLD TRENT RD

RIVERSIDE RD

BOWLING GREEN LA

Roseway

NORTH TERR

80

81

82

90

A

B

C

D

E

F

C1
1 TRINITY VIEW
2 CROMFORD ST

24

D1
1 JUBILEE CRES
2 MARSHALLS RISE
3 MALPAS AVE
4 CROSS ST
5 PARISH MWS
6 CARLISLE MWS
7 HANDEL CT
8 NORTHOLME VIEW

F2
1 ASPEN CT
2 OAKTREE AVE
3 BROOK LA
4 TRENTVALE AVE
5 SWALE DR
6 SWEYN LA
7 BOBRAINSFORTH WAY

F1
1 BLACKTHORN CL
2 THE ROWANS
3 FOSSEWAY
4 MAPLE CT
5 THE ALDERS
6 COUPLAND CL
7 FALCON GR
8 LING DR
9 HEATHER CL

10 PEACOCK PL
11 DOVE CL
12 SWAN CT
13 KESTREL AV
14 THE SPINNEY

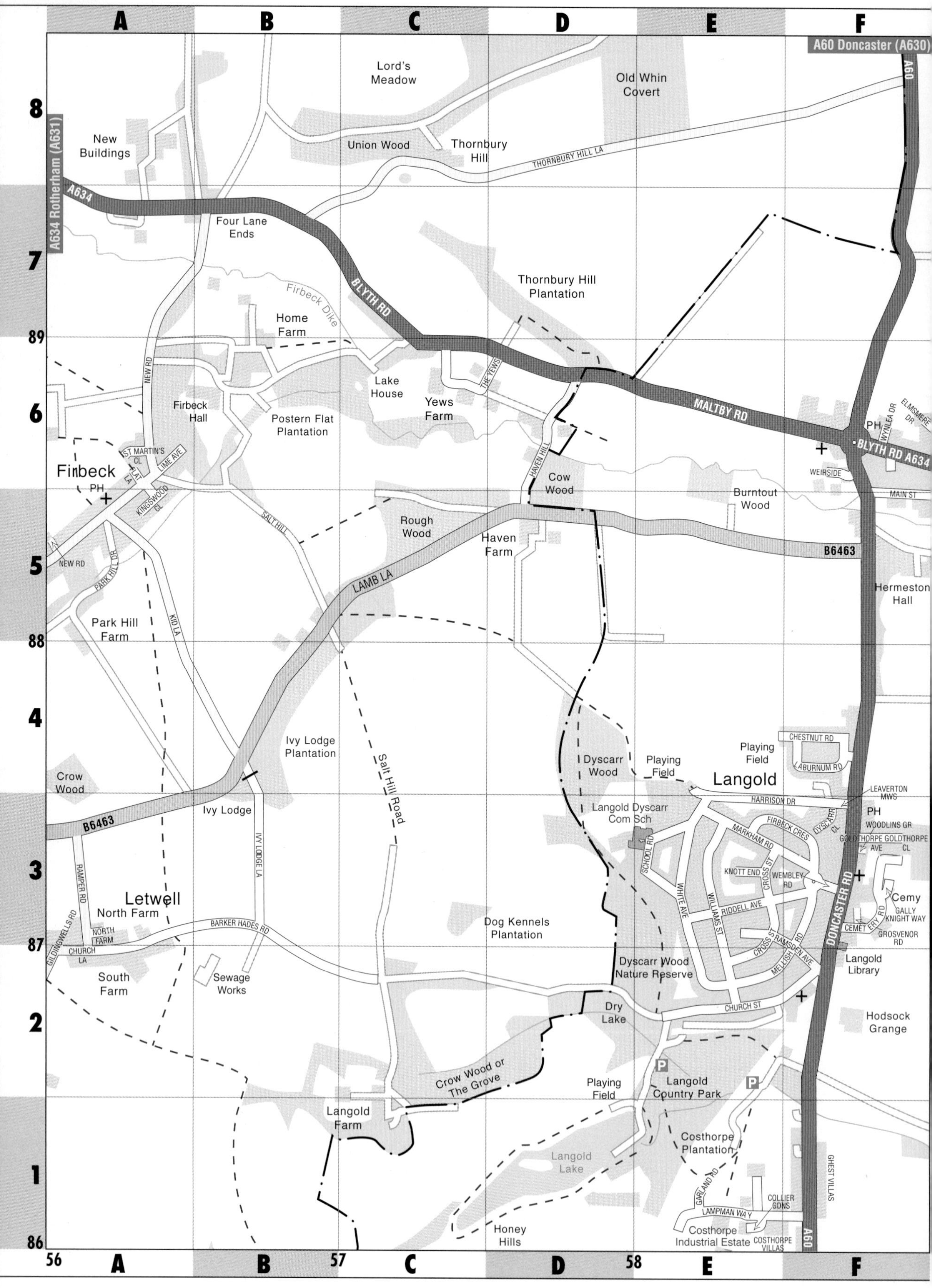

8

7

89

6

Finbeck
PH

5

New Rd

88

4

Crow
Wood

B6463

3

Letwell
North Farm

NORTH
FARM
CHURCH
LA

South
Farm

87

2

86

A   B   C   D   E   F

New Buildings

A634 Rotherham (A631)

Lord's Meadow

Union Wood

Thornbury Hill

Old Whin Covert

Thornbury Hill La

Four Lane Ends

BLYTH RD

Firbeck Dike

Home Farm

Thornbury Hill Plantation

Lake House

Yews Farm

THE YEWS

MALTBY RD

Firbeck Hall

Postern Flat Plantation

HAVEN HILL

Cow Wood

Burntout Wood

BLYTH RD A634

WEIRSIDE

MAIN ST

ST MARTIN'S CL

LIME AVE

NEW RD

SALT HILL

Rough Wood

Haven Farm

B6463

Hermeston Hall

KINGSMOOD CL

PARK HILL RD

KID LA

LAMB LA

Park Hill Farm

Ivy Lodge Plantation

Salt Hill Road

Dyscarr Wood

Playing Field

CHESTNUT RD

Playing Field

Langold

LABURNUM RD

LEAVERTON MWS

Ivy Lodge

IVY LODGE LA

Langold Dyscarr Com Sch

HARRISON DR

FIRBECK CRES

DYSCARR CL

PH
WOODLINS GR

GOLDTHORPE AVE   GOLDTHORPE CL

RAMPER RD

GILDINGWELLS RD

BARKER HADES RD

Dog Kennels Plantation

SCHOOL RD

WHITE AVE

MARKHAM RD

KNOTT END AV

CROSS ST

WEMBLEY RD

RIDDELL AVE

WILLIAMS ST

RAMSDEN AVE

CROSS ST

MELLISH RD

DONCASTER RD

Cemy

GALLY KNIGHT WAY

GROSVENOR RD

Langold Library

Sewage Works

Dyscarr Wood Nature Reserve

CHURCH ST

Hodsock Grange

Dry Lake

Crow Wood or The Grove

P

Playing Field

Langold Country Park

P

Costhorpe Plantation

GHEST VILLAS

Langold Farm

Langold Lake

GARLAND RD

COLLIER GDNS

LAMPMAN WAY

Honey Hills

Costhorpe Industrial Estate

COSTHORPE VILLAS

A60

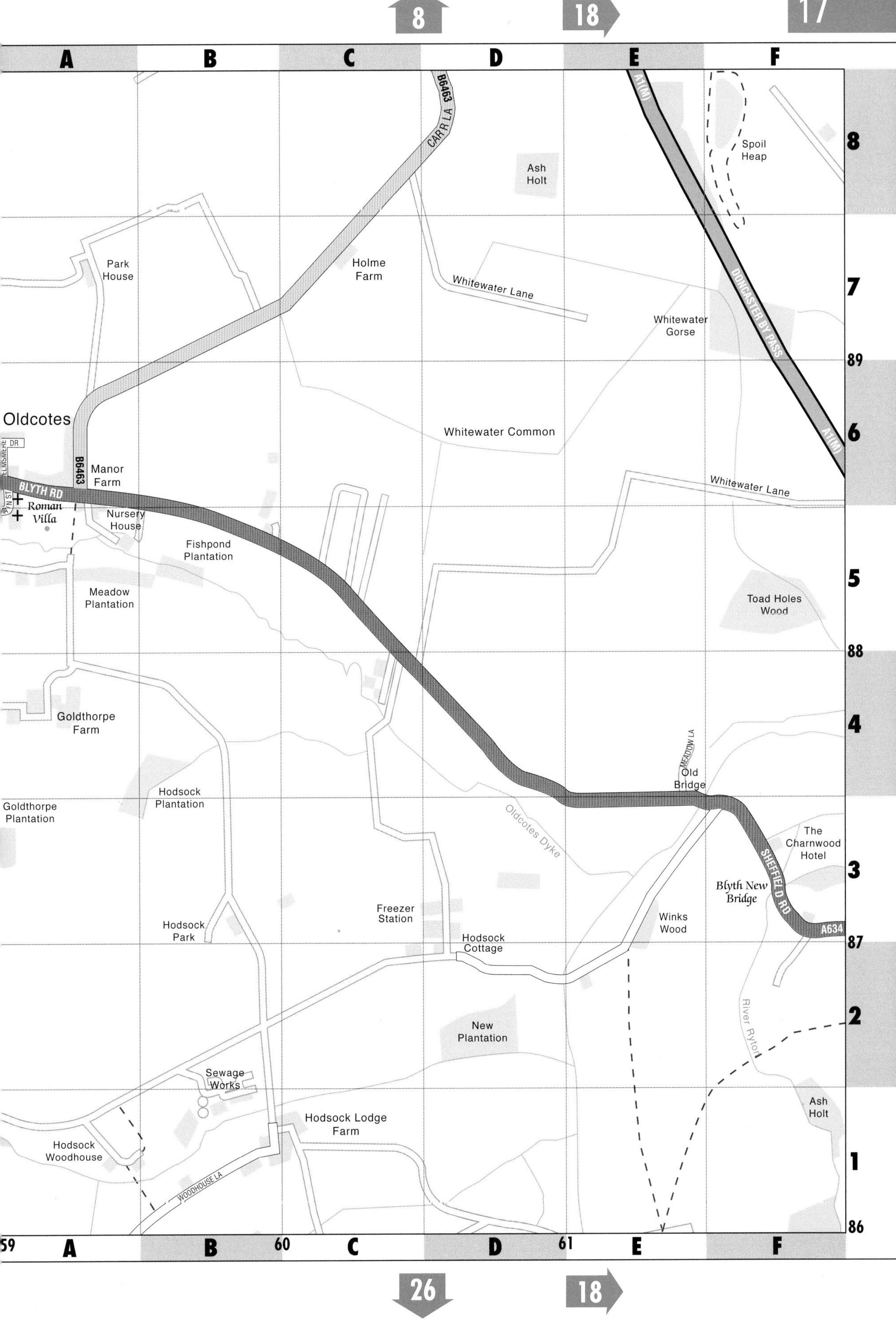

A B C D E F

8
7
89
6
5
88
4
88
3
87
2
1
86

Oldcotes

Park House

Holme Farm

Ash Holt

Spoil Heap

CARR LA

B6463

Whitewater Lane

Whitewater Gorse

DONCASTER BY PASS

A1(M)

A1(M)

Whitewater Common

Whitewater Lane

BLYTH RD

B6463

Manor Farm

Roman Villa

Nursery House

ELMS ST

DR

FIR ST

Fishpond Plantation

Meadow Plantation

Toad Holes Wood

Goldthorpe Farm

Goldthorpe Plantation

Hodsock Plantation

Oldcotes Dyke

MEADOW LA

Old Bridge

The Charnwood Hotel

Blyth New Bridge

SHEFFIELD RD

A634

Winks Wood

River Ryton

Hodsock Park

Freezer Station

Hodsock Cottage

New Plantation

Ash Holt

Sewage Works

Hodsock Lodge Farm

Hodsock Woodhouse

WOODHOUSE LA

17 9

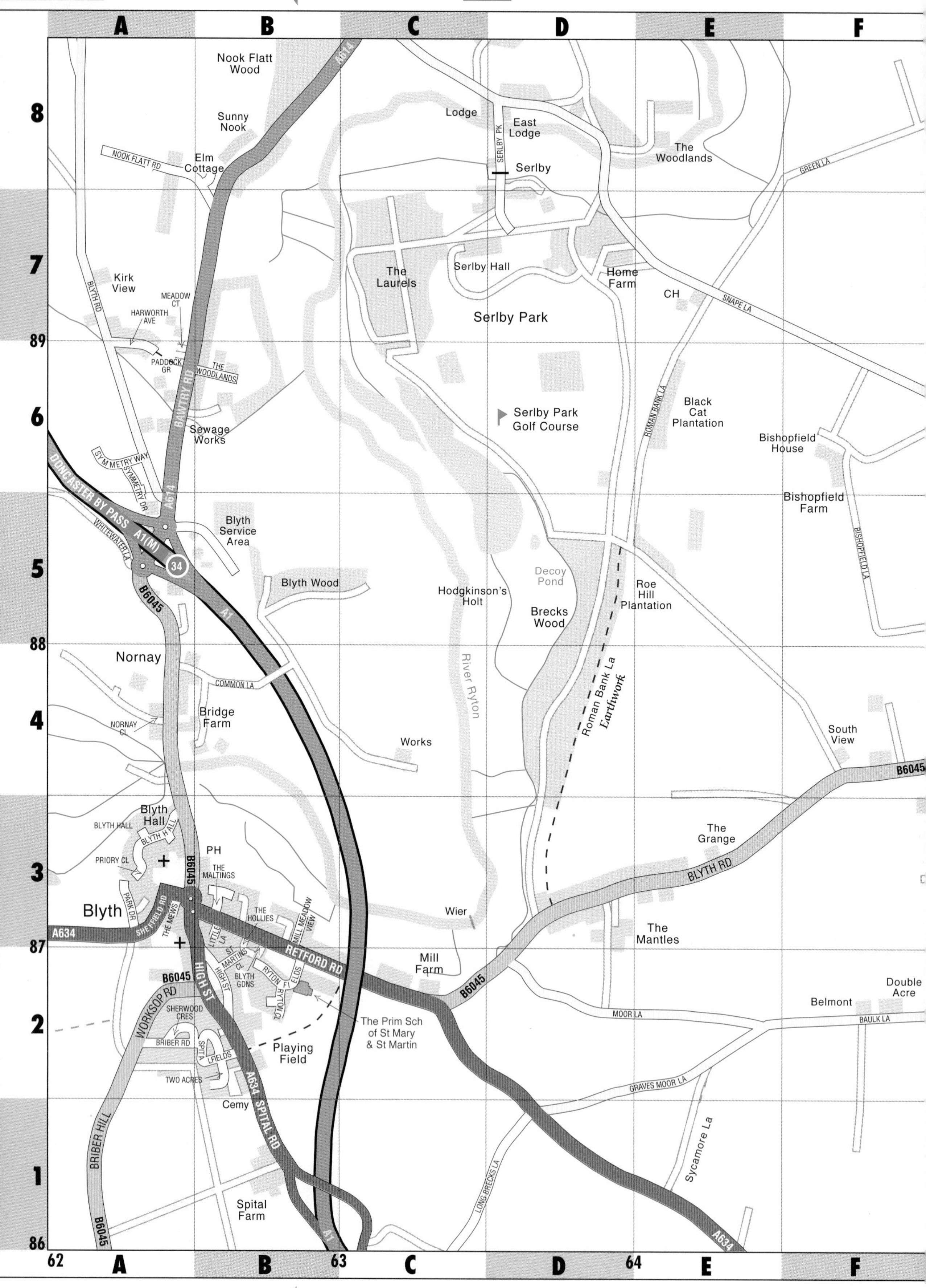
A
B
C
D
E
F
8
7
89
6
5
88
4
3
87
2
1
86
62
63
64
Nook Flatt Wood
Sunny Nook
NOOK FLATT RD
Elm Cottage
A614
Lodge
East Lodge
SERLBY PK
Serlby
The Woodlands
GREEN LA
The Laurels
Serlby Hall
Home Farm
CH
SNAPE LA
Serlby Park
Kirk View
BLYTH RD
MEADOW CT
HARWORTH AVE
PADDOCK GR
THE WOODLANDS
BAWTRY RD
Sewage Works
SYMMETRY WAY
SYMMETRY DR
ROMAN BANK LA
Black Cat Plantation
Serlby Park Golf Course
Bishopfield House
Bishopfield Farm
BISHOPFIELD LA
DONCASTER BY PASS
A1(M)
WHITEWATER LA
Blyth Service Area
34
B6045
Blyth Wood
Hodgkinson's Holt
Decoy Pond
Brecks Wood
Roe Hill Plantation
A1
Nornay
COMMON LA
River Ryton
Roman Bank La
Earthwork
NORNAY CL
Bridge Farm
Works
South View
B6045
Blyth Hall
BLYTH HALL
PH
The Grange
PRIORY CL
THE MALTINGS
BLYTH RD
PARK DR
Blyth
SHEFFIELD RD
THE MEWS
THE HOLLIES
LITTLE LA
MILL MEADOW VIEW
Wier
The Mantles
A634
RETFORD RD
ST MARTINS CL
HIGH ST
BLYTH GDNS
RYTON FIELDS
RYTON CL
Mill Farm
B6045
Double Acre
Belmont
WORKSOP RD
SHERWOOD CRES
HIGH ST
The Prim Sch of St Mary & St Martin
MOOR LA
BAULK LA
BRIBER RD
SPITAL FIELDS
Playing Field
TWO ACRES
A634
GRAVES MOOR LA
Cemy
SPITAL RD
BRIBER HILL
Sycamore La
LONG BRECKS LA
Spital Farm
A634

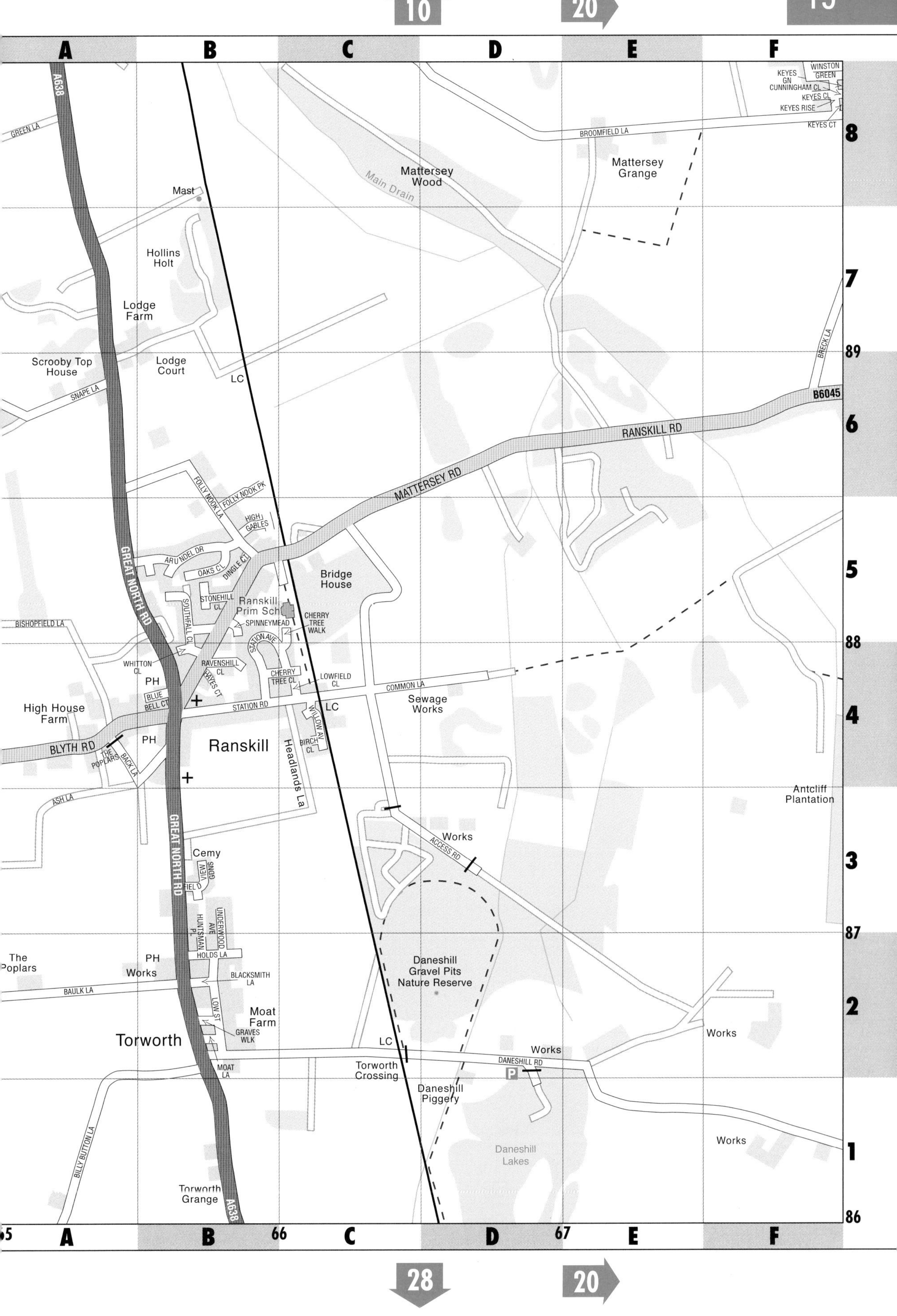

A B C D E F

KEYES GN
WINSTON GREEN
CUNNINGHAM CL
KEYES CL
KEYES RISE
KEYES CT
8

BROOMFIELD LA

GREEN LA

Mattersey Wood

Mattersey Grange

Main Drain

Mast

7

Hollins Holt

Lodge Farm

BRECK LA

89

Scrooby Top House

Lodge Court

LC

B6045

6

SNAPE LA

RANSKILL RD

FOLLY NOOK LA
FOLLY NOOK PK

MATTERSEY RD

HIGH GABLES

GREAT NORTH RD

ARUNDEL DR

DINGLE CT

OAKS CL

Bridge House

5

STONEHILL CL

Ranskill Prim Sch

SOUTHFALL CL

SPINNEYMEAD

CHERRY TREE WALK

BISHOPFIELD LA

88

RAVENSHILL CL

CHERRY TREE CL

LOWFIELD CL

KEYES CT

STATION AVE

WHITTON CL

COMMON LA

PH

BLUE BELL CT

STATION RD

LC

Sewage Works

4

High House Farm

PH

Ranskill

Headlands La

BIRCH CL

WILLOW AV

BLYTH RD

THE POPLARS

BACK LA

ASH LA

Antcliff Plantation

Cemy

Works

ACCESS RD

3

VISTA

SNDG

FIELD

87

UNDERWOOD AVE

HUNTSMAN PL

The Poplars

PH
Works

HOLDS LA

Daneshill Gravel Pits Nature Reserve

Works

2

BAULK LA

BLACKSMITH LA

LOW ST

Moat Farm

GRAVES WLK

Works

Torworth

MOAT LA

LC

Works

BILLY BUTTON LA

Torworth Crossing

DANESHILL RD

P

Daneshill Piggery

Torworth Grange

A638

Daneshill Lakes

Works

1

86

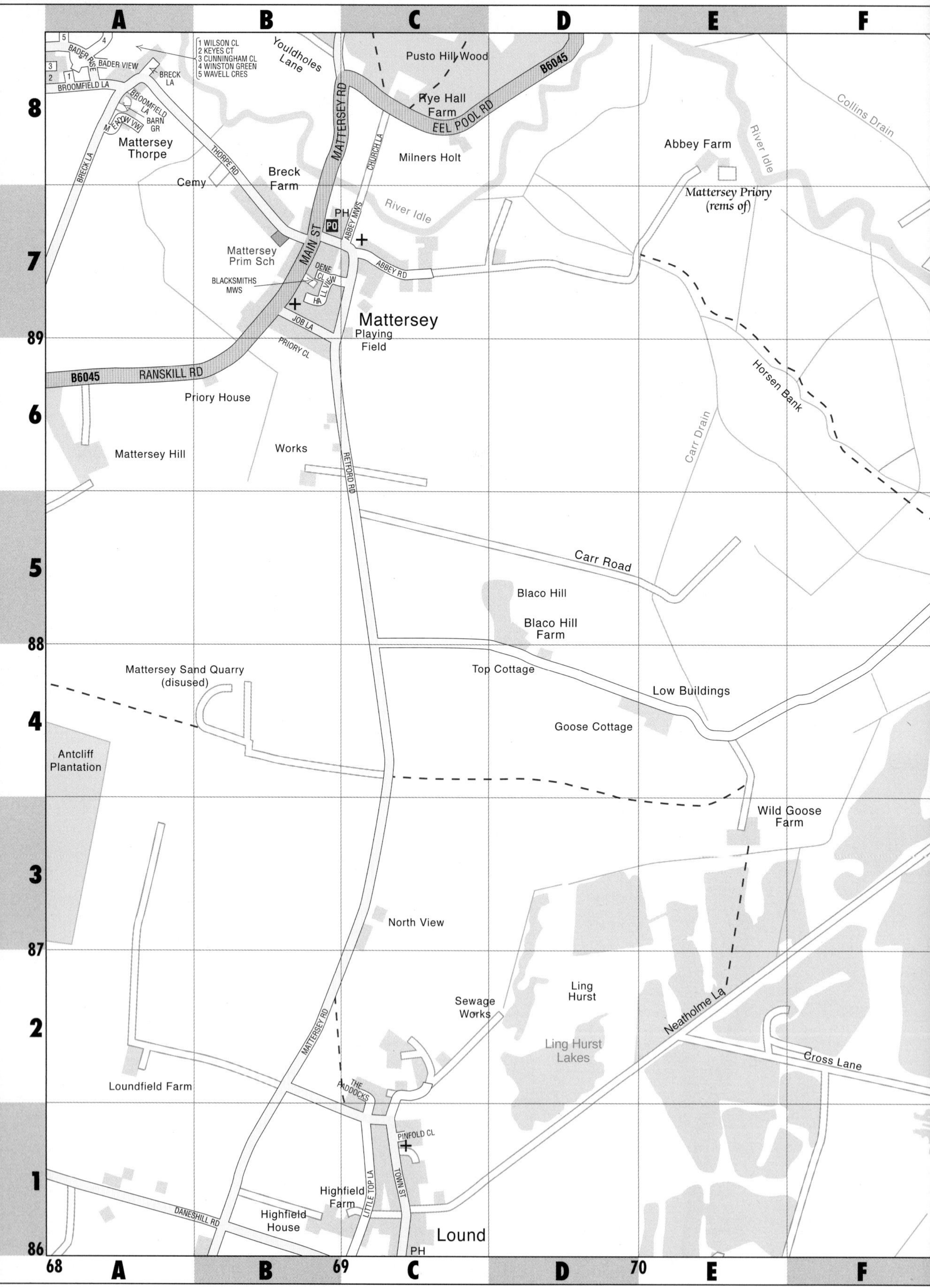

| | A | B | C | D | E | F |

8

Bader View
BROOMFIELD LA
Broomfield La
1 WILSON CL
2 KEYES CT
3 CUNNINGHAM CL
4 WINSTON GREEN
5 WAVELL CRES
Youldholes Lane
Pusto Hill Wood
B6045
Rye Hall Farm
EEL POOL RD
Collins Drain
BRECK LA
MEADOW VW
Mattersey Thorpe
BARN GR
THORPE RD
Cemy
Breck Farm
MATTERSEY RD
CHURCH LA
Milners Holt
River Idle
Abbey Farm
River Idle

7

MAIN ST
DENE
CL
LN
HA
ABBEY MWS
PH
PO
Mattersey Prim Sch
BLACKSMITHS MWS
JOB LA
ABBEY RD
Mattersey
Mattersey Priory (rems of)

89

PRIORY CL
Playing Field
B6045
RANSKILL RD
Priory House
Horsen Bank

6

Mattersey Hill
Works
RETFORD RD
Carr Drain

5

Carr Road
Blaco Hill

88

Mattersey Sand Quarry (disused)
Blaco Hill Farm
Top Cottage
Low Buildings

4

Antcliff Plantation
Goose Cottage
Wild Goose Farm

3

North View

87

MATTERSEY RD
Sewage Works
Ling Hurst
Neatholme La

2

Ling Hurst Lakes
Cross Lane
Loundfield Farm
THE PADDOCKS

1

PINFOLD CL
Highfield Farm
LITTLE TOP LA
TOWN ST
DANESHILL RD
Highfield House
Lound

86

PH

| 68 | A | | B | 69 | C | | D | 70 | E | | F |

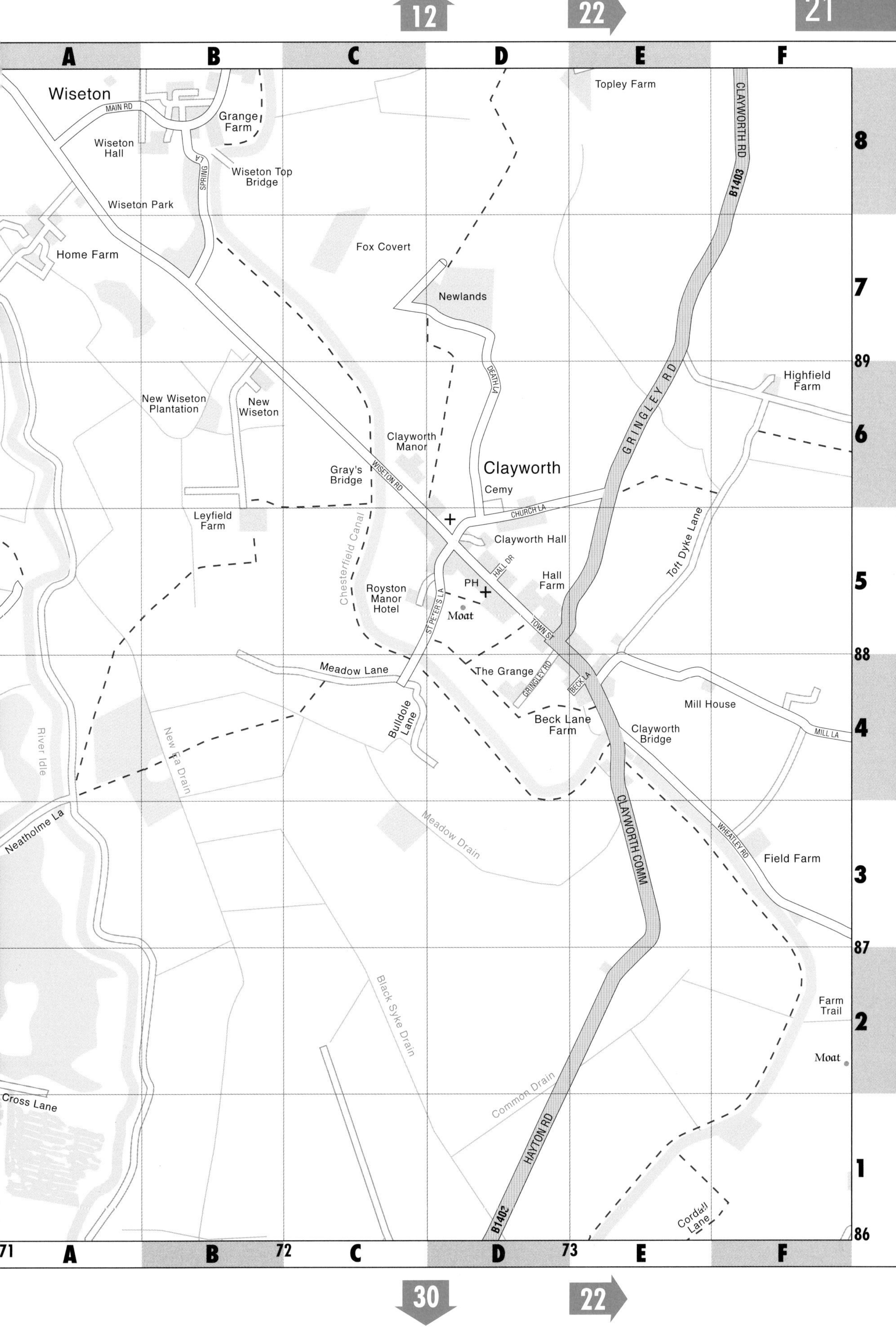
A
B
C
D
E
F
Wiseton
MAIN RD
Grange Farm
Wiseton Hall
SPRING LA
Wiseton Top Bridge
Wiseton Park
Topley Farm
CLAYWORTH RD
B1403
Home Farm
Fox Covert
Newlands
DEATH LA
GRINGLEY RD
Highfield Farm
New Wiseton Plantation
New Wiseton
Clayworth Manor
Clayworth
Gray's Bridge
WISETON RD
Cemy
CHURCH LA
Leyfield Farm
Chesterfield Canal
Clayworth Hall
Toft Dyke Lane
HALL DR
Royston Manor Hotel
PH
Hall Farm
Moat
ST PETER'S LA
TOWN ST
Meadow Lane
The Grange
GRINGLEY RD
BECK LA
Mill House
Bulldole Lane
Beck Lane Farm
Clayworth Bridge
MILL LA
River Idle
New Eau Drain
CLAYWORTH COMM
Neatholme La
Meadow Drain
WHEATLEY RD
Field Farm
Black Syke Drain
Farm Trail
Moat
Common Drain
Cross Lane
HAYTON RD
B1402
Cordall Lane
8
7
89
6
5
88
4
3
87
2
1
86
71
72
73

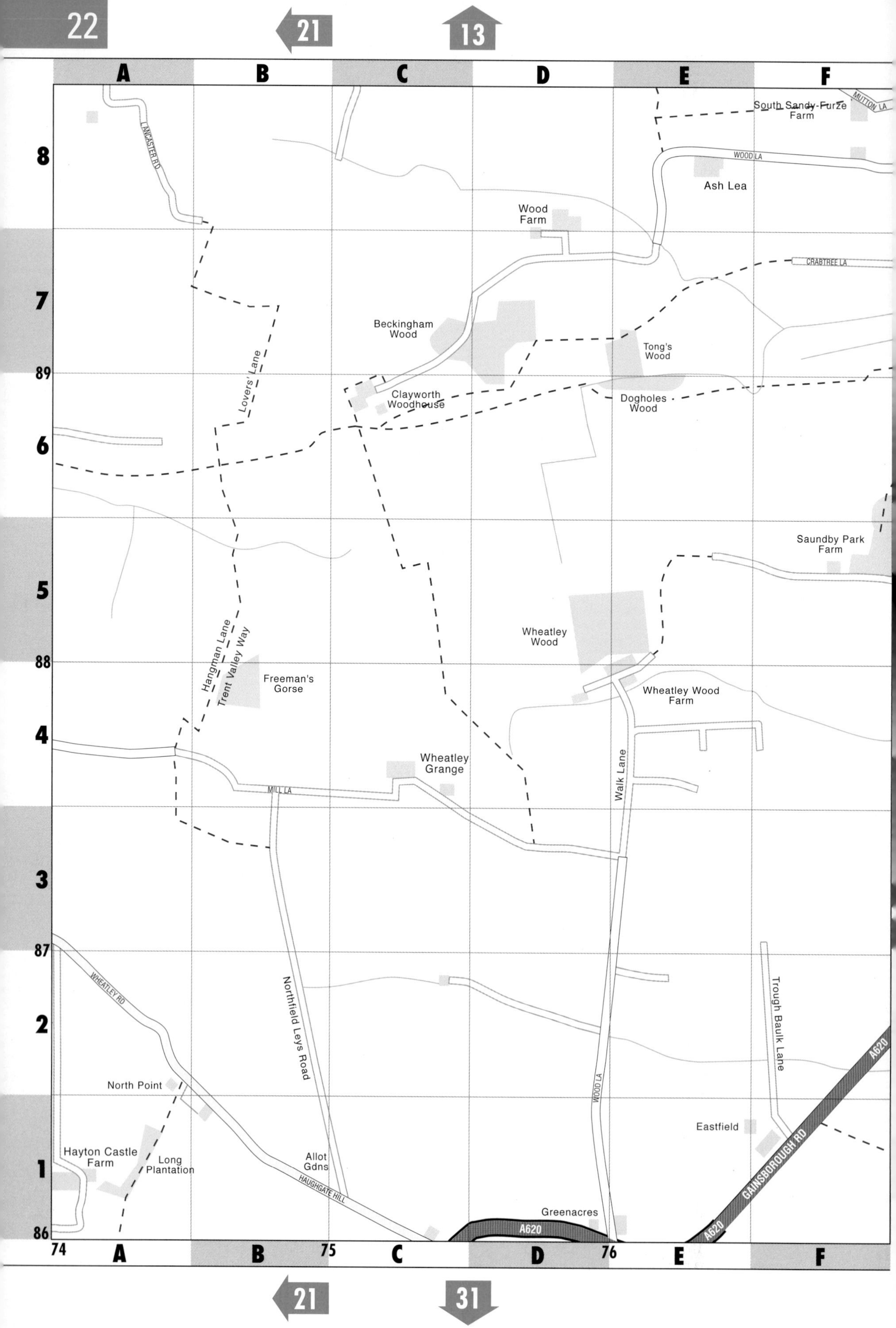

A B C D E F

8

7

89

6

5

88

4

3

87

2

1

86

74 A B 75 C D 76 E F

LANCASTER RD

South Sandy-Furze Farm

MUTTON LA

WOOD LA

Ash Lea

Wood Farm

CRABTREE LA

Beckingham Wood

Tong's Wood

Lovers' Lane

Clayworth Woodhouse

Dogholes Wood

Saundby Park Farm

Hangman Lane

Trent Valley Way

Freeman's Gorse

Wheatley Wood

Wheatley Wood Farm

Walk Lane

MILL LA

Wheatley Grange

WHEATLEY RD

Northfield Leys Road

WOOD LA

Trough Baulk Lane

A620

North Point

Hayton Castle Farm

Long Plantation

Allot Gdns

HAUGHGATE HILL

Eastfield

GAINSBOROUGH RD

Greenacres

A620

A620

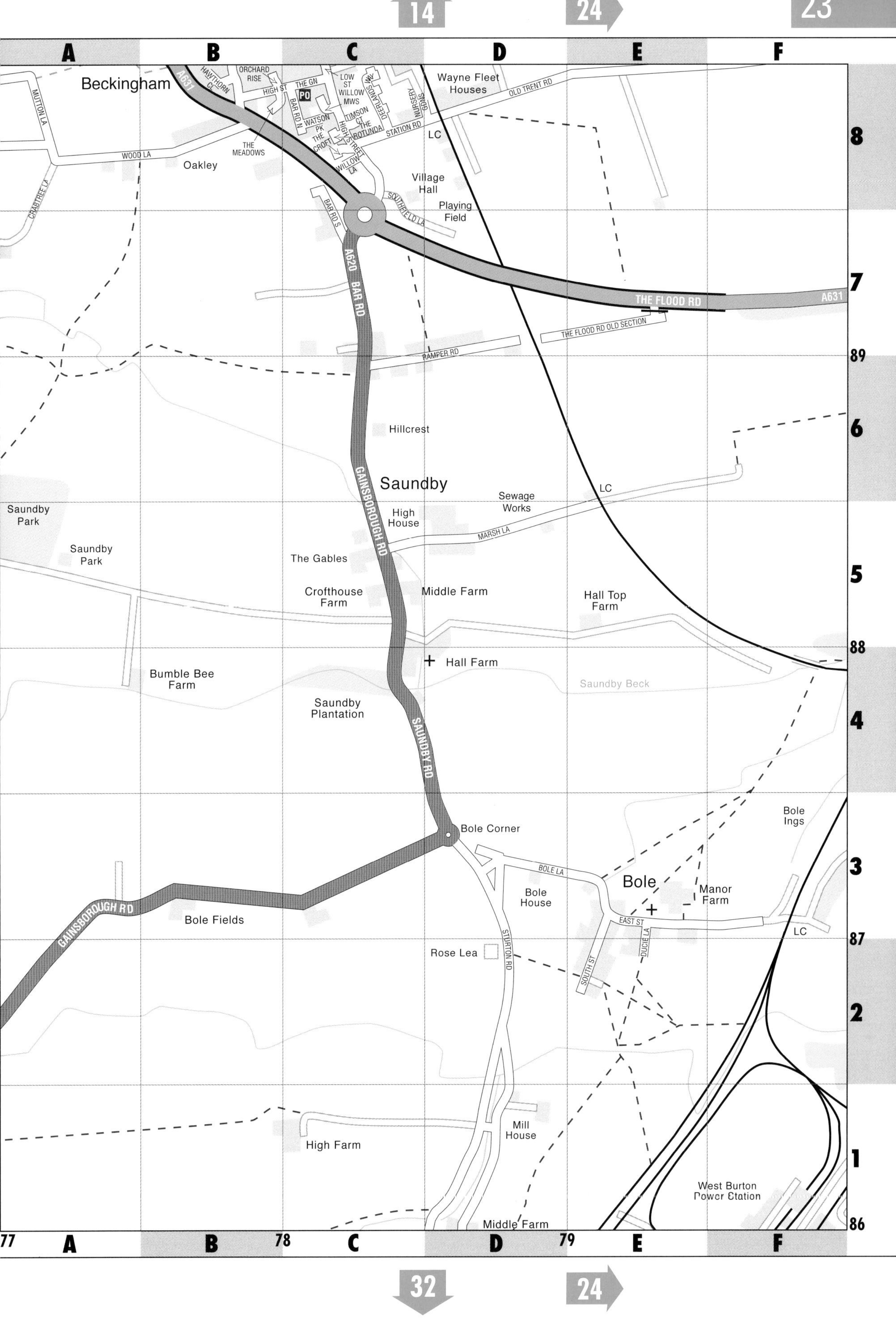
A
B
C
D
E
F
Beckingham
MUTTON LA
A631
HAWTHORN CL
ORCHARD RISE
HIGH ST
THE GN
PO
LOW ST
WILLOW MWS
DEERLANDS
WY
NURSERY GDNS
Wayne Fleet Houses
OLD TRENT RD
BAR RD N
WATSON PK
THE CROFT
TIMSON CT
THE ROTUNDA
HIGH STREET
STATION RD
LC
THE MEADOWS
WOOD LA
Oakley
WILLOW LA
Village Hall
CRABTREE LA
BAR RD S
SOUTHFIELD LA
Playing Field
A620
BAR RD
THE FLOOD RD
A631
THE FLOOD RD OLD SECTION
RAMPER RD
Hillcrest
Saundby
LC
Sewage Works
High House
MARSH LA
GAINSBOROUGH RD
Saundby Park
Saundby Park
The Gables
Crofthouse Farm
Middle Farm
Hall Top Farm
Hall Farm
Bumble Bee Farm
Saundby Beck
Saundby Plantation
SAUNDBY RD
Bole Ings
Bole Corner
BOLE LA
Bole
Manor Farm
Bole House
EAST ST
GAINSBOROUGH RD
Bole Fields
LC
Rose Lea
STURTON RD
DUCIE LA
SOUTH ST
Mill House
High Farm
West Burton Power Station
Middle Farm
8
7
89
6
5
88
4
3
87
2
1
86
77
78
79

24   ◄ 23   ▲ 15

F8
1 NEWTON CL
2 HALTHAM GN
3 HEAPHAM CRES
4 DANES RD
5 WHITE'S WOOD LA

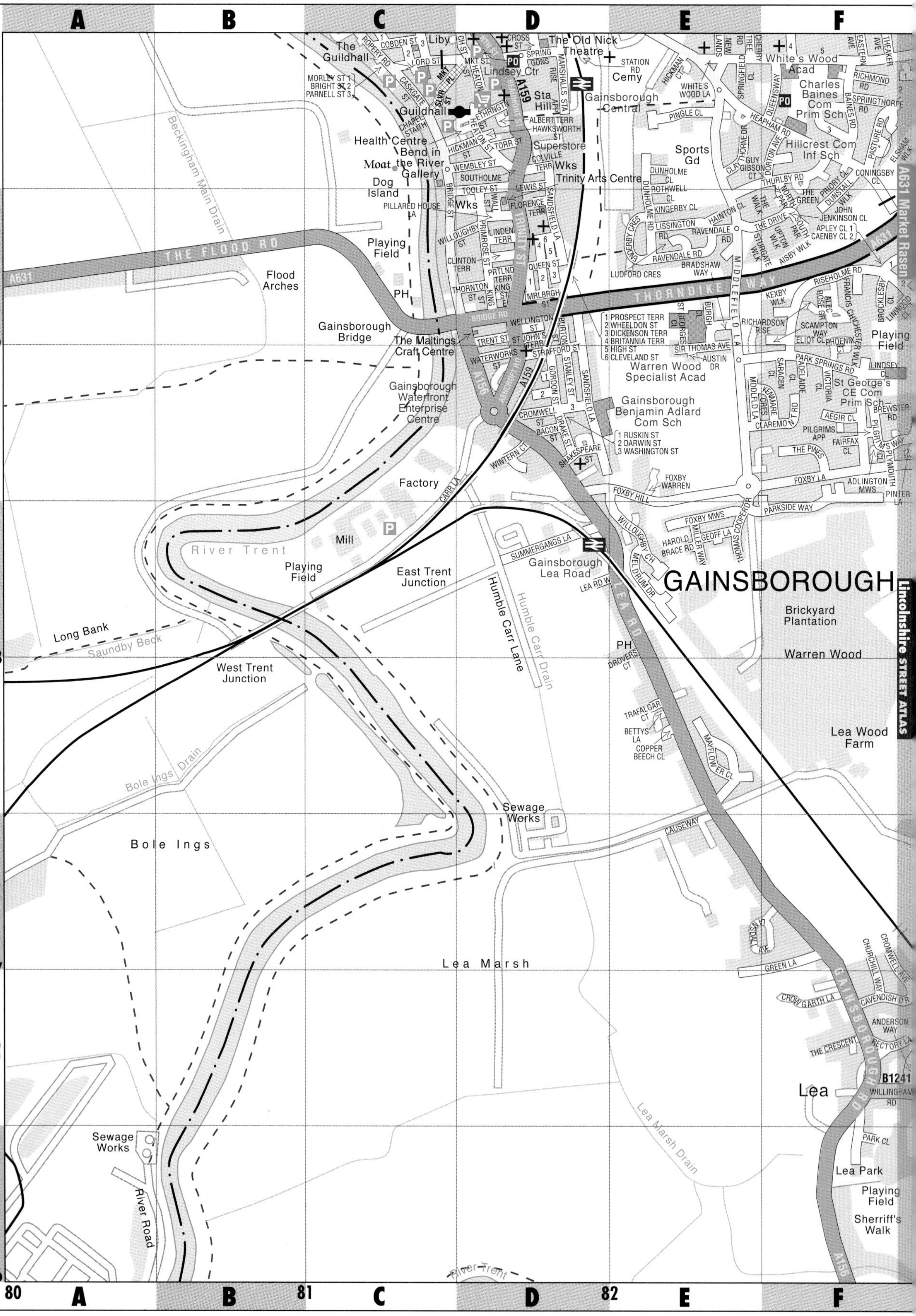

A   B   C   D   E   F

GAINSBOROUGH

Beckingham Main Drain

THE FLOOD RD

A631

Flood Arches

The Guildhall
Guildhall
MORLEY ST 1
BRIGHT ST 2
PARNELL ST 3
Health Centre
Bend in the River
Moat
Dog Island
Gallery
PILLARED HOUSE
Wks

The Maltings Craft Centre
Gainsborough Bridge
Playing Field
PH

Gainsborough Waterfront Enterprise Centre

Liby
Lindsey Ctr
Superstore
Sta Hill
PO
Cemy

The Old Nick Theatre
STATION RD
Gainsborough Central

White's Wood Acad
Charles Baines Com Prim Sch
WHITE'S WOOD LA
Hillcrest Com Inf Sch

Sports Gd

Trinity Arts Centre

Warren Wood Specialist Acad

Gainsborough Benjamin Adlard Com Sch
1 RUSKIN ST
2 DARWIN ST
3 WASHINGTON ST

THORNDIKE WAY

1 PROSPECT TERR
2 WHEELDON ST
3 DICKENSON TERR
4 BRITANNIA TERR
5 HIGH ST
6 CLEVELAND ST

Playing Field

Factory

River Trent
Mill
Playing Field
East Trent Junction

West Trent Junction
Long Bank
Saundby Beck

Bole Ings Drain

Bole Ings

Summergangs La
Gainsborough Lea Road
LEA RD

Humble Carr Lane
Humble Carr Drain

Sewage Works

PH
DROVERS CT

GAINSBOROUGH

Brickyard Plantation
Warren Wood

Lea Wood Farm

TRAFALGAR CT
BETTYS LA
COPPER BEECH CL

CAUSEWAY

Lea Marsh

Lea Marsh Drain

GAINSBOROUGH RD

Lea
B1241
Lea Park
Playing Field
Sherriff's Walk

Sewage Works
River Road

River Trent

A156

Lincolnshire STREET ATLAS
A631 Market Rasen

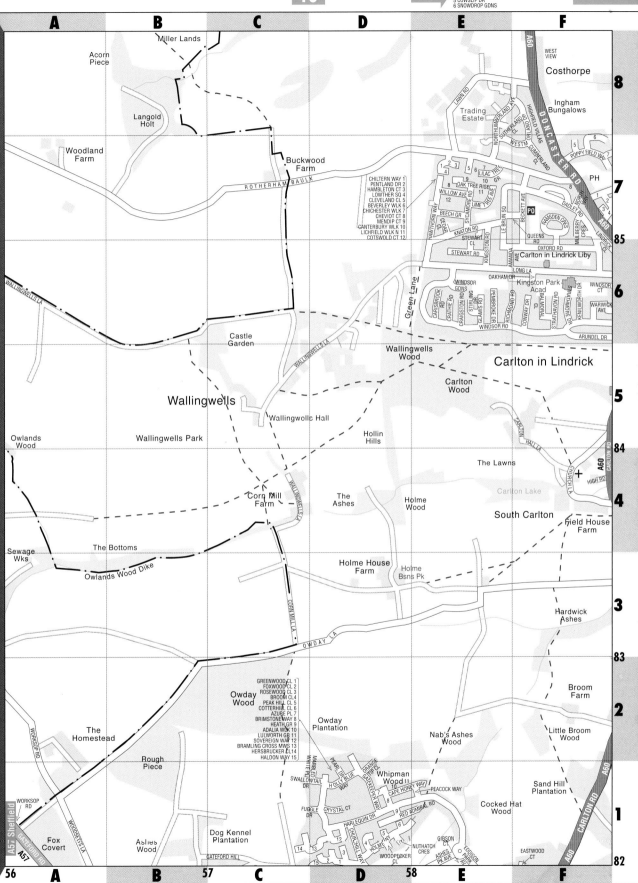
F7
1 PINFOLD DR
2 GREENFIELD WAY
3 HARVEST CL
4 PLOUGH DR
5 COWSLIP DR
6 SNOWDROP GDNS
7 BLUEBELL CL
8 REDHOLME CL

A B C D E F
Miller Lands
Acorn Piece
Langold Holt
Woodland Farm
Buckwood Farm
ROTHERHAM BAULK
CHILTERN WAY 1
PENTLAND DR 2
HAMBLETON CT 3
LOWTHER SQ 4
CLEVELAND CL 5
BEVERLEY WLK 6
CHICHESTER WLK 7
CHEVIOT CT 8
MENDIP CT 9
CANTERBURY WLK 10
LICHFIELD WLK N 11
COTSWOLD CT 12
Trading Estate
LAWN RD
NORTHUMBERLAND AVE
SUTHERLAND CL
WESTM
ORLAND DR
HIGHFIELD VILLAS
CUMBERLAND CL
DONCASTER RD
A60
WEST VIEW
Costhorpe
Ingham Bungalows
POPPY FIELD WAY
PH
LILAC TREE GR
OAK TREE RISE
WILLOW AVE
LIME TREE AVE
SYCAMORE RD
BEECH GR
CEDAR CL
HAWTHORN WAY
KNATON RD
STEWART CL
STEWART RD
KINGSTON RD
LE BRUN SQ
BECKETT AVE
PO
RAMSDEN CRES
QUEENS RD
MULBERRY CRES
DADLEY RD
NORTH WAY
LINDRICK CL
OXFORD RD
AMANDA AVE
Carlton in Lindrick Liby
LONG LA
OAKHAM DR
Kingston Park Acad
WINDSOR CT
WARWICK AVE
WINDSOR GDNS
CARISBROOK RD
CRATHIE RD
CRAIGSTON RD
STIRLING DR
GLAMIS RD
PEMBROKE DR
RICHMOND RD
CONWAY DR
BALMORAL CL
STRATHAVON RD
STRATHMORE DR
KENILWORTH DR
WINDSOR RD
ARUNDEL DR
Green Lane
WALLINGWELLS LA
Castle Garden
Wallingwells Wood
Carlton in Lindrick
Carlton Wood
Wallingwells
Wallingwells Hall
Hollin Hills
CARLTON HALL LA
Owlands Wood
Wallingwells Park
The Lawns
CHURCH LA
A60
CARLTON RD
HIGH RD
Corn Mill Farm
The Ashes
Holme Wood
Carlton Lake
South Carlton
Field House Farm
Sewage Wks
The Bottoms
Owlands Wood Dike
Holme House Farm
Holme Bsns Pk
CORN MILL LA
Hardwick Ashes
OWDAY LA
GREENWOOD CL 1
FOXWOOD CL 2
ROSEWOOD CL 3
BROOM CL 4
PEAK HILL CL 5
COTTERHILL CL 6
AZURE PL 7
BRIMSTONE WAY 8
HEATH GR 9
ADALIA WLK 10
LULWORTH GR 11
SOVEREIGN WAY 12
BRAMLING CROSS MWS 13
HERSBRUCKER CL 14
HALDON WAY 15
Owday Wood
Owday Plantation
Nab's Ashes Wood
Broom Farm
Little Broom Wood
The Homestead
WORKSOP RD
Rough Piece
MARBLED WHITE PL
PEARL DR
HOLLY BLUE WAY
ORANGE TIP CL
GATEKEEPER WAY
Whipman Wood
SWALLOWTAIL DR
CAPE HONEY WAY
PEACOCK WAY
Sand Hill Plantation
CRYSTAL CT
FUGGLE DR
RED ADMIRAL RD
HARLEQUIN DR
CHURCHILL WAY
HOLME WAY
NUTHATCH CRES
GIBSON CT
ASHES PK AVE
EDDISON PARK AV
WOODPECKER CL
Cocked Hat Wood
EASTWOOD CT
CARLTON RD
A60
WORKSOP RD
A57 Sheffield
GATEFORD RD
A57
Fox Covert
WOODSETTS LA
Ashes Wood
Dog Kennel Plantation
GATEFORD HILL
8 7 85 6 5 84 4 3 83 2 1 82
56 57 58

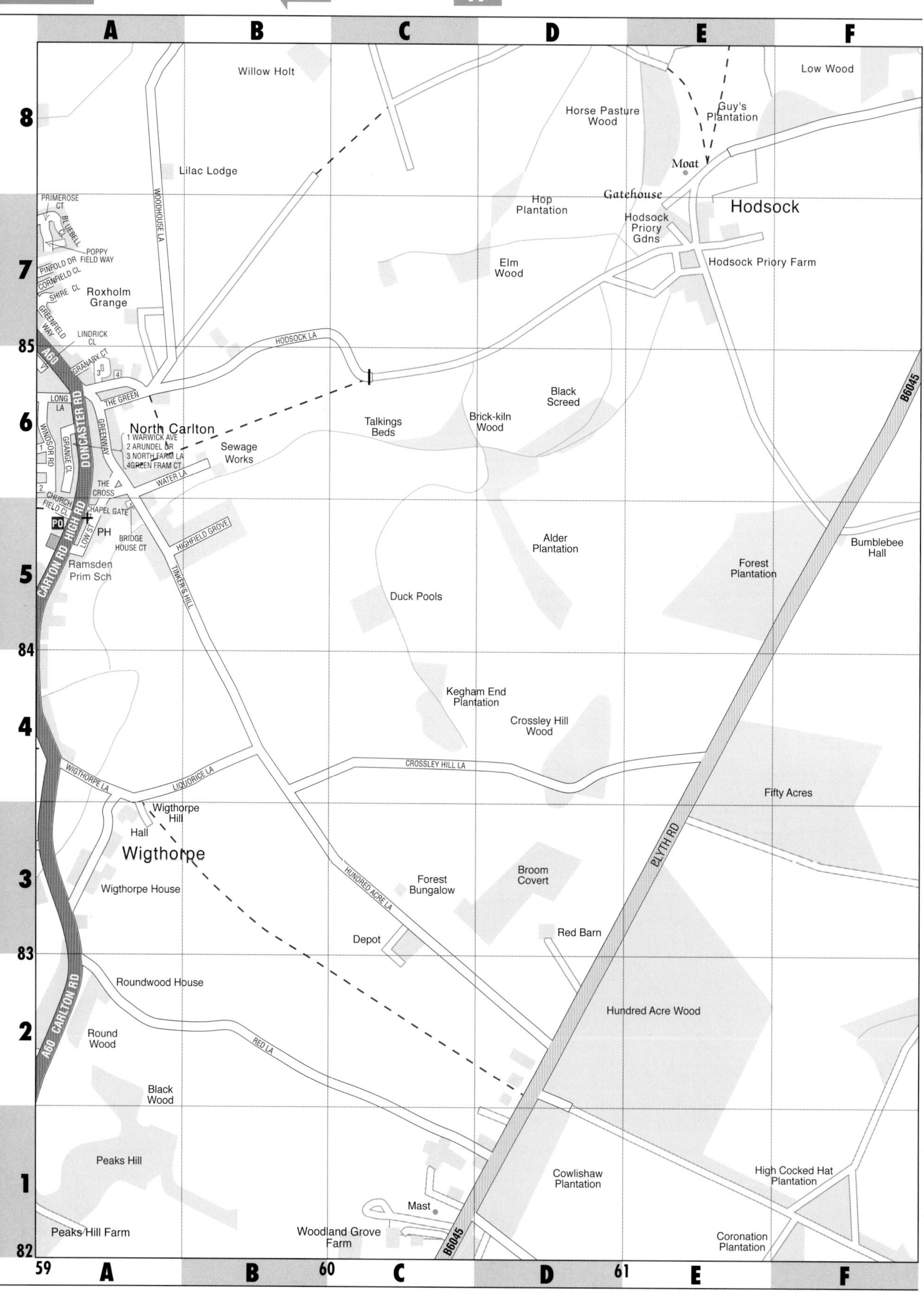

A B C D E F

8

Willow Holt

Horse Pasture
Wood

Guy's
Plantation

Low Wood

Lilac Lodge

Moat

Gatehouse

Hodsock

WOODHOUSE LA

Hop
Plantation

Hodsock
Priory
Gdns

7

PRIMROSE
CT

BLUEBELL
CL

POPPY
FIELD WAY

PINFOLD DR

CORNFIELD CL

SHIRE CL

Roxholm
Grange

Elm
Wood

Hodsock Priory Farm

GREENFIELD
WAY

LINDRICK
CL

HODSOCK LA

85

A60

GRANARY CT

4

Black
Screed

B6045

6

LONG
LA

THE GREEN

North Carlton

Talkings
Beds

Brick-kiln
Wood

DONCASTER RD

WINDSOR RD

GRANGE CL

GREENWAY

1 WARWICK AVE
2 ARUNDEL DR
3 NORTH FARM LA
4 GREEN FRAM CT

Sewage
Works

WATER LA

THE
CROSS

CHAPEL GATE

Alder
Plantation

Forest
Plantation

Bumblebee
Hall

CHURCH
FIELD CL

HIGH RD

LOW ST

PO

PH

HIGHFIELD GROVE

BRIDGE
HOUSE CT

5

CARLTON RD

Ramsden
Prim Sch

TIMKER'S HILL

Duck Pools

84

4

Kegham End
Plantation

Crossley Hill
Wood

WIGTHORPE LA

LIQUORICE LA

CROSSLEY HILL LA

Fifty Acres

Wigthorpe
Hill

BLYTH RD

Hall

3

Wigthorpe

Wigthorpe House

HUNDRED ACRE LA

Forest
Bungalow

Broom
Covert

Red Barn

83

Roundwood House

Depot

2

A60 CARLTON RD

Round
Wood

RED LA

Hundred Acre Wood

Black
Wood

1

Peaks Hill

Cowlishaw
Plantation

High Cocked Hat
Plantation

82

Peaks Hill Farm

Woodland Grove
Farm

Mast

B6045

Coronation
Plantation

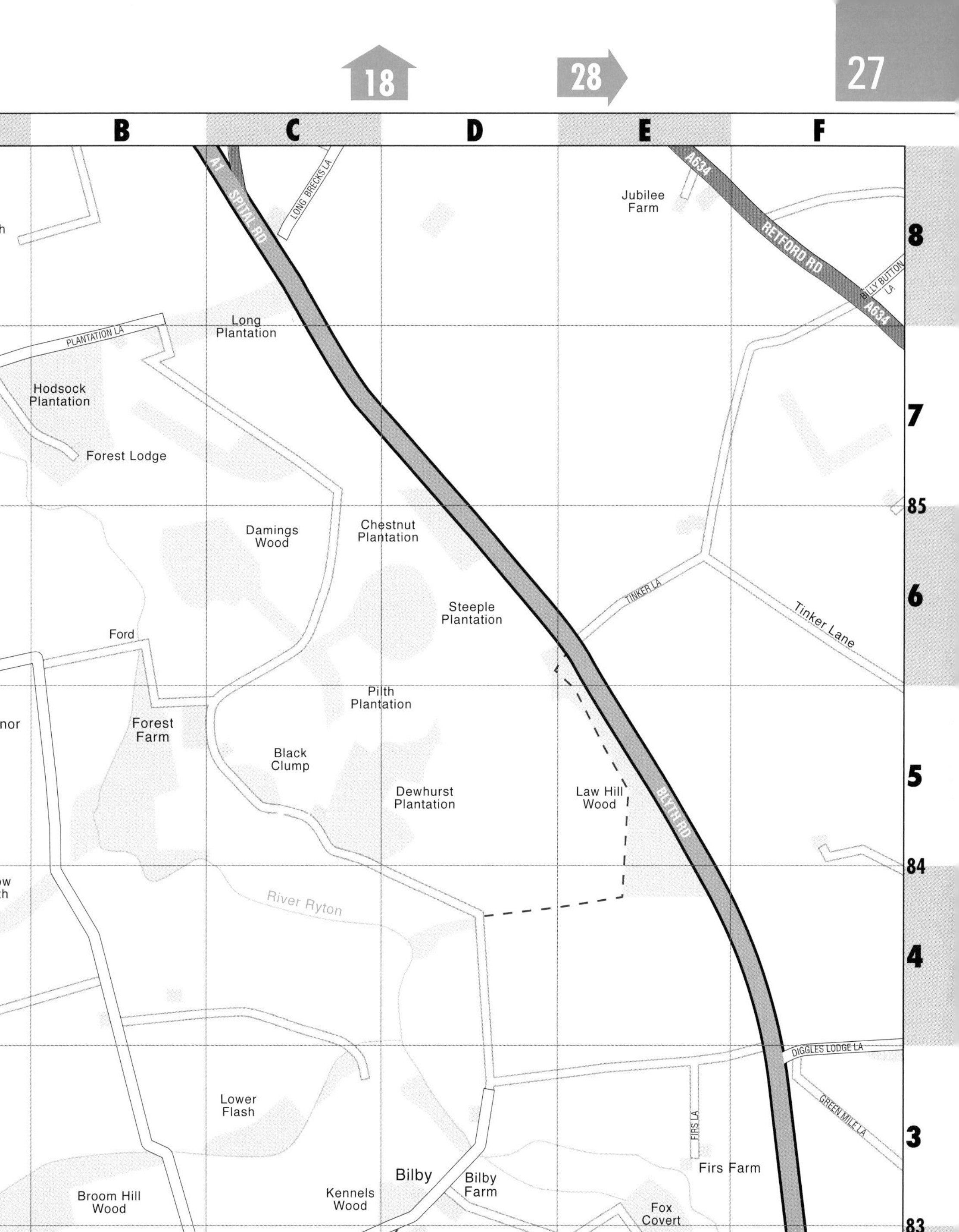
8

B6045
HODSOCK LA
SPITAL RD
A1
LONG BRECKS LA
RETFORD RD
A634
BILLY BUTTON LA
A634

Woodleigh

Ash
Holt

Jubilee
Farm

BRIBER HILL

Hodsock
Red Bridge

PLANTATION LA

Long
Plantation

7

BLYTH RD

Hodsock
Plantation

Forest Lodge

85

Damings
Wood

Chestnut
Plantation

6

Steeple
Plantation

TINKER LA

Tinker Lane

Ford

BUMBLEBEE LA

Pilth
Plantation

Hodsock Manor
Farm

Forest
Farm

Black
Clump

Dewhurst
Plantation

Law Hill
Wood

BLYTH RD

5

Willow
Garth

84

River Ryton

4

Lower
Flash

DIGGLES LODGE LA

GREEN MILE LA

3

FIRS LA

Firs Farm

Broom Hill
Wood

Kennels
Wood

Bilby

Bilby
Farm

Fox
Covert

83

Upper
Flash

2

Church
Clump

Whin
Hill

Sewage
Works

The Barracks

OLD BLYTH RD

A1

1

82

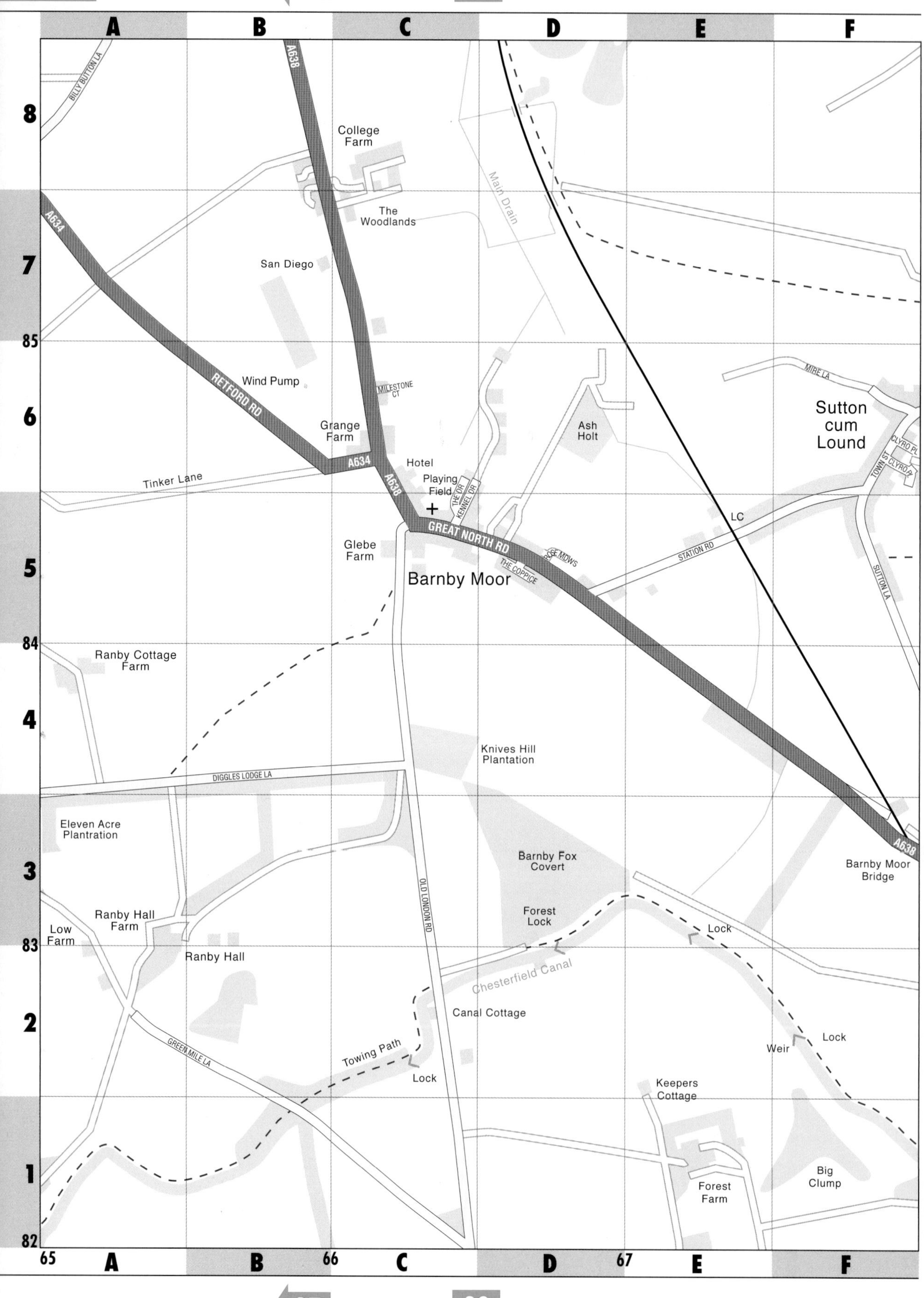

BILLY BUTTON LA

A638

College Farm

The Woodlands

San Diego

A634

RETFORD RD

Wind Pump

MILESTONE CT

Grange Farm

A634

A638

Tinker Lane

Hotel

Playing Field

THE DR

KENNEL DR

Main Drain

Ash Holt

Sutton cum Lound

MIRE LA

CLYRO PL

ST CLYRO

TOWN ST

GREAT NORTH RD

Glebe Farm

Barnby Moor

ROSE MDWS

THE COPPICE

STATION RD

LC

SUTTON LA

Ranby Cottage Farm

DIGGLES LODGE LA

Knives Hill Plantation

Eleven Acre Plantration

Barnby Fox Covert

Barnby Moor Bridge

A638

Low Farm

Ranby Hall Farm

OLD LONDON RD

Forest Lock

Lock

Ranby Hall

Chesterfield Canal

GREEN MILE LA

Canal Cottage

Weir

Lock

Towing Path

Lock

Keepers Cottage

Big Clump

Forest Farm

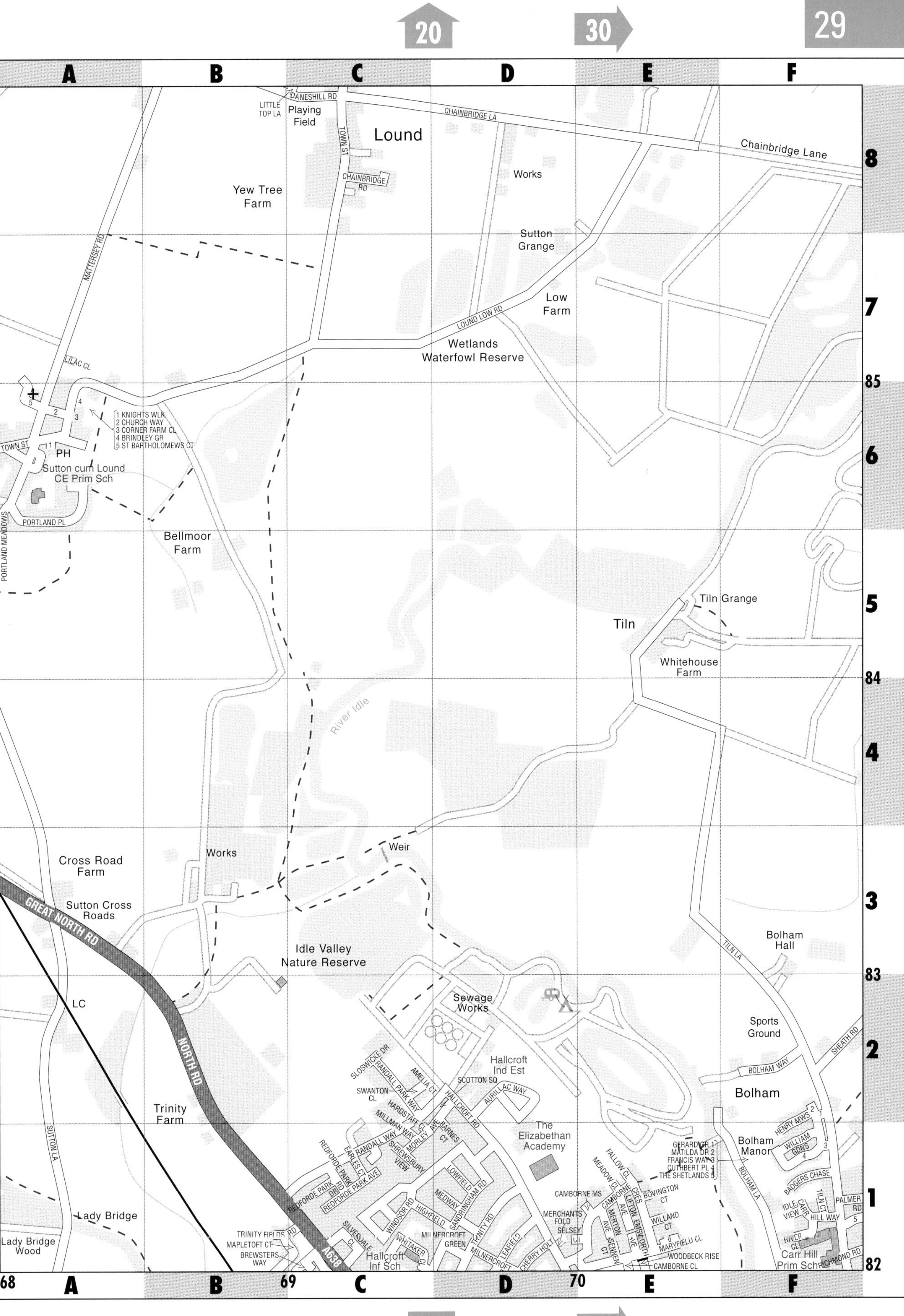

A B C D E F

8
Chainbridge Lane
7
85
6
5
84
4
83
2
1
82

LITTLE TOP LA
DANESHILL RD
Playing Field
Lound
CHAINBRIDGE LA
Works
Yew Tree Farm
TOWN ST
CHAINBRIDGE RD
Sutton Grange
MATTERSEY RD
Low Farm
LOUND LOW RD
Wetlands Waterfowl Reserve
LILAC CL
1 KNIGHTS WLK
2 CHURCH WAY
3 CORNER FARM CL
4 BRINDLEY GR
5 ST BARTHOLOMEWS CT
TOWN ST
PH
Sutton cum Lound CE Prim Sch
PORTLAND MEADOWS
PORTLAND PL
Bellmoor Farm
Tiln Grange
Tiln
Whitehouse Farm
River Idle
Cross Road Farm
Works
Weir
Sutton Cross Roads
GREAT NORTH RD
Idle Valley Nature Reserve
Bolham Hall
TILN LA
LC
Sewage Works
Hallcroft Ind Est
Sports Ground
NORTH RD
SUTTON LA
Trinity Farm
SLOSWICKE DR
RANDALL PARK WAY
AMELIA CT
SWANTON CL
HARDSTAFF CL
HALLCROFT RD
SCOTTON SQ
AURILAC WAY
BOLHAM WAY
Bolham
SHEATH RD
MILLMAN WAY
MORLEY
BARNES CT
The Elizabethan Academy
FALLOW CL
MEADOW CL
CAMBORNE CL
COPES WAY
MERTON ENF
BOLHAM LA
GERARD CR 1
MATILDA DR 2
FRANCIS WAY 3
CUTHBERT PL 4
THE SHETLANDS 5
HENRY MWS 2
WILLIAM GDNS
Bolham Manor
BADGERS CHASE
REDFORDE PARK DR
EARLES CT
RANDALL WAY
SHREWSBURY
REDFORDE PARK AVE
HIGHFIELD
LOWFIELD
SANDRINGHAM RD
CAMBORNE MS
MERCHANTS FOLD
SELSEY
WILLAND CT
CAMBORNE AVE
MERTON AVE
SEYMON CT
IDLE CL VIEW
TILN CL
CARR HILL WAY
PALMER RD
Lady Bridge
Lady Bridge Wood
TRINITY FIELDS
MAPLETOFT CT
BREWSTERS WAY
A638
SILVERDALE CL
WINDSOR RD
WHITMAKER
Hallcroft Inf Sch
HIGHFIELD
MEDWAY
MILNERCROFT GREEN
MILNERCROFT
TRINITY RD
LEAFIELD
CHERRY HOLT
WOODBECK RISE
CAMBORNE CL
MARYFIELD CL
HVCP
Carr Hill Prim Sch
RICHMOND RD

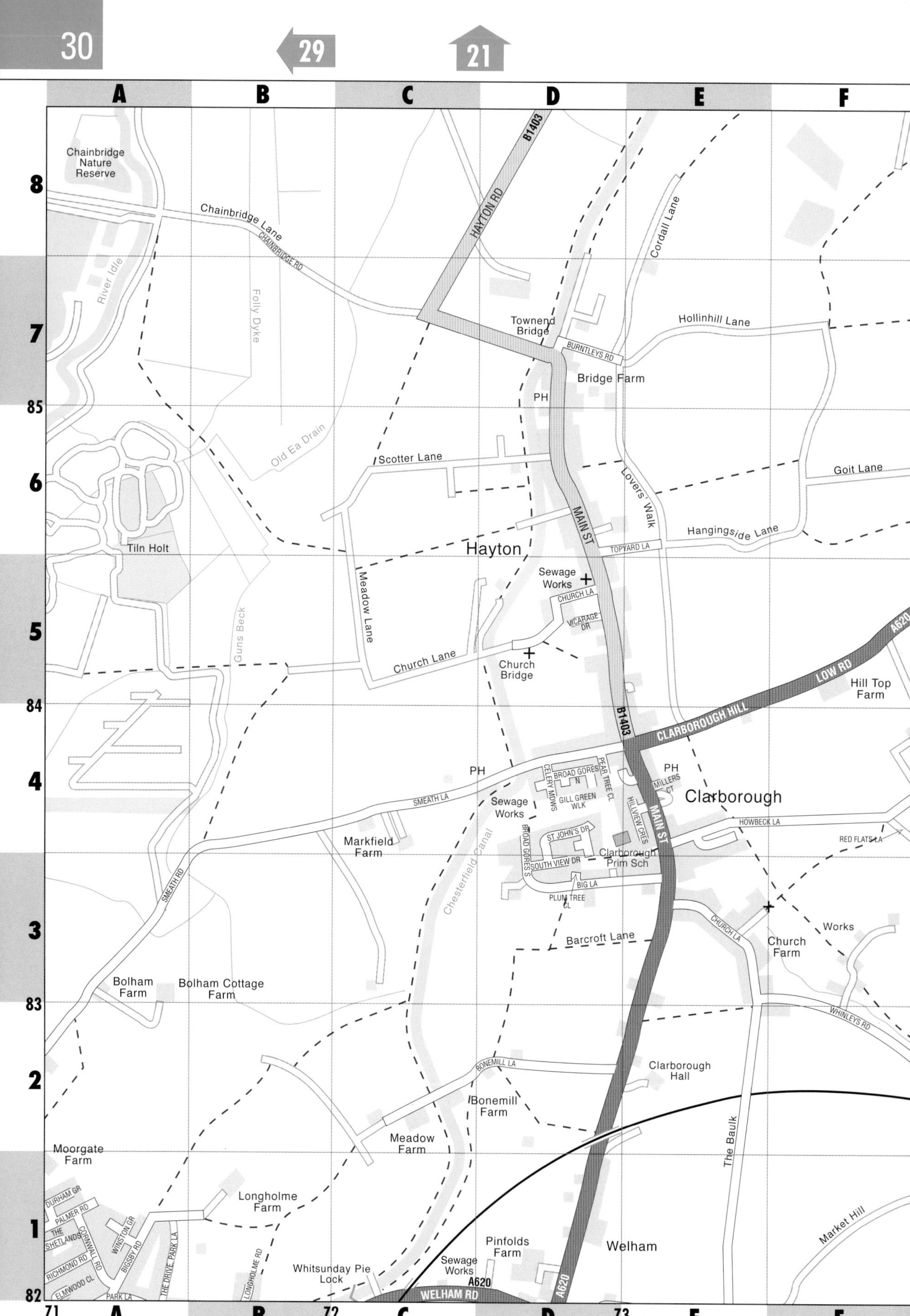

A B C D E F

8

Chainbridge Nature Reserve

Chainbridge Lane

CHAINBRIDGE RD

River Idle

Folly Dyke

HAYTON RD

B1403

Townend Bridge

BURNTLEYS RD

Bridge Farm

Cordall Lane

Hollinhill Lane

7

85

PH

Old Ea Drain

Scotter Lane

Hayton

MAIN ST

Lovers' Walk

Goit Lane

6

Tiln Holt

Meadow Lane

Guns Beck

Hangingside Lane

TOPYARD LA

Sewage Works

CHURCH LA

VICARAGE DR

5

Church Lane

Church Bridge

B1403

A620

LOW RD

CLARBOROUGH HILL

Hill Top Farm

84

PH

SMEATH LA

Sewage Works

BROAD GORES N

CELERY MDWS

PEAR TREE CL

GILL GREEN WLK

PH

MILLERS CT

Clarborough

HOWBECK LA

RED FLATS LA

4

SMEATH RD

Markfield Farm

St JOHN'S DR

BROAD GORES S

SOUTH VIEW DR

Clarborough Prim Sch

HILLVIEW CRES

MAIN ST

CHURCH LA

Works

Church Farm

3

Chesterfield Canal

BIG LA

PLUM TREE CL

Barcroft Lane

WHINLEYS RD

Bolham Farm

Bolham Cottage Farm

83

BONEMILL LA

Clarborough Hall

2

Bonemill Farm

Meadow Farm

The Baulk

Moorgate Farm

Longholme Farm

Market Hill

1

DURHAM GR

PALMER RD

THE SHETLANDS

CORNHILL RD

WINSTON GR

BIGSBY RD

RICHMOND RD

ELMWOOD CL

THE DRIVE

PARK LA

LONGHOLME RD

Whitsunday Pie Lock

Sewage Works

Pinfolds Farm

Welham

A620

A620

82

71 A B 72 C D 73 E F

WELHAM RD

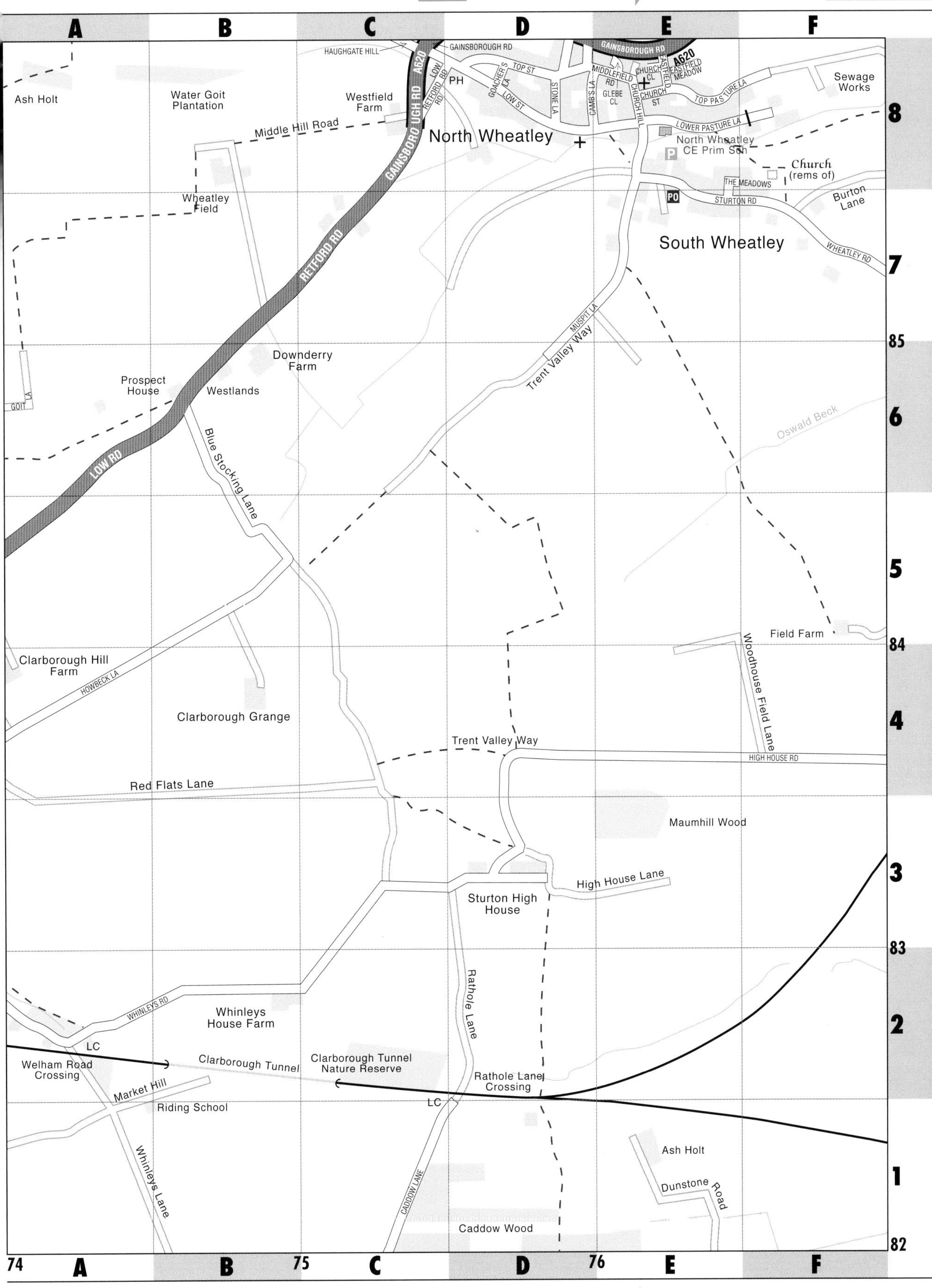

A B C D E F

Ash Holt

Water Goit Plantation

HAUGHGATE HILL

Westfield Farm

Middle Hill Road

GAINSBOROUGH RD

TOP ST

STONE LA

PH

RETFORD RD

LOW RD

GLOACHERS LA

LOW ST

GAINSBOROUGH RD

MIDDLEFIELD RD

CAMBS LA

GLEBE CL

CHURCH ST

CHURCH CL

EASTFIELD

A620

EASTFIELD MEADOW

Sewage Works

TOP PASTURE LA

LOWER PASTURE LA

8

North Wheatley

North Wheatley CE Prim Sch

Church (rems of)

Burton Lane

Wheatley Field

PO

STURTON RD

South Wheatley

WHEATLEY RD

7

GAINSBORO UGH RD A620

RETFORD RD

85

Downderry Farm

MUSPIT LA

Trent Valley Way

Oswald Beck

6

Prospect House

Westlands

Blue Stocking Lane

LOW RD

GOIT

Clarborough Hill Farm

HOWBECK LA

5

Woodhouse Field Lane

Field Farm

84

Clarborough Grange

4

Red Flats Lane

Trent Valley Way

HIGH HOUSE RD

Maumhill Wood

High House Lane

3

Sturton High House

Rathole Lane

83

Whinleys Rd

Whinleys House Farm

Clarborough Tunnel

Clarborough Tunnel Nature Reserve

Rathole Lane Crossing

2

LC

Welham Road Crossing

Market Hill

LC

Ash Holt

Riding School

Whinleys Lane

CADDOW LANE

Dunstone Road

1

Caddow Wood

82

74 A 75 B C 76 D E F

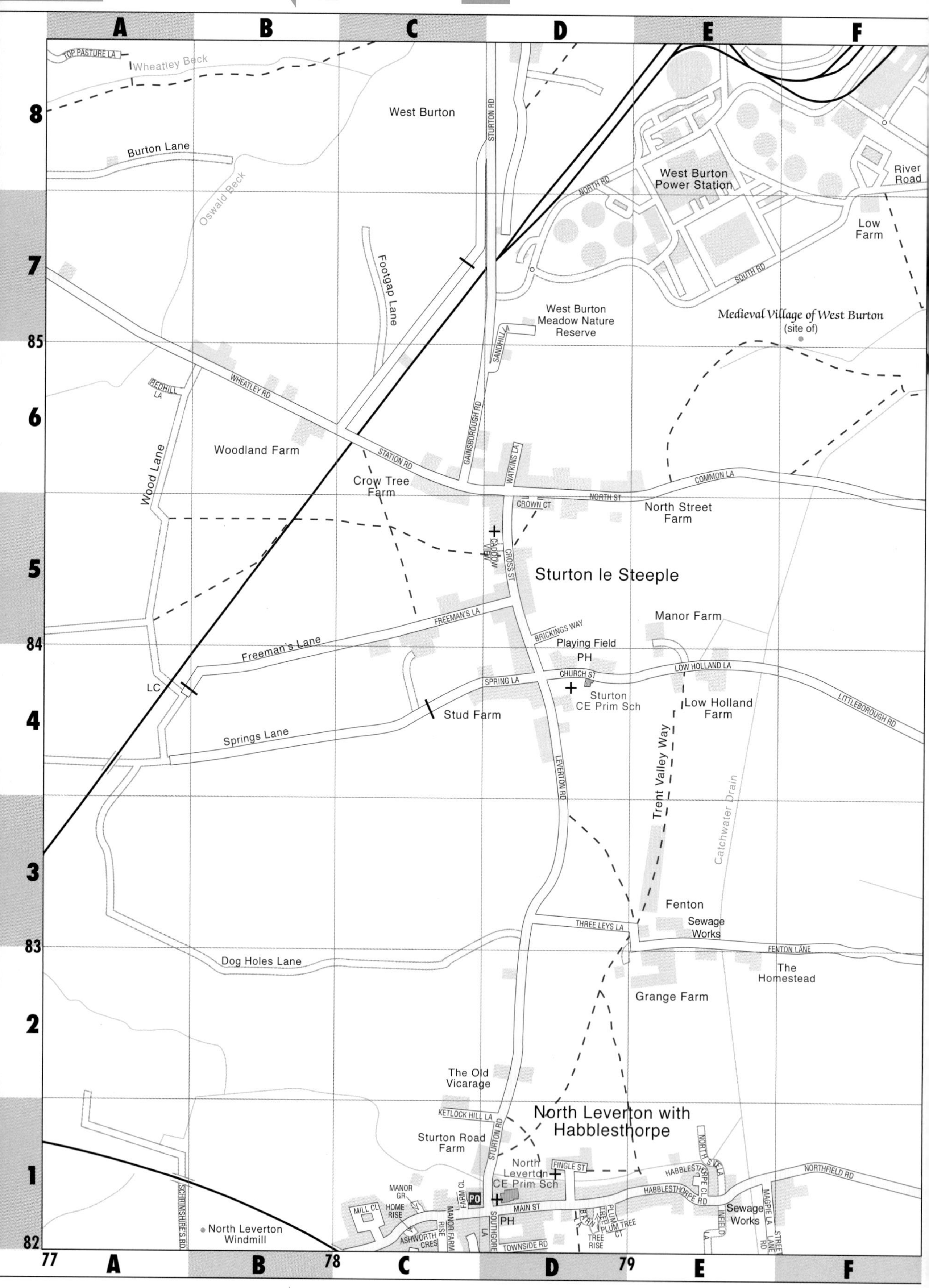

A   B   C   D   E   F

8   West Burton

Top Pasture La
Wheatley Beck
Burton Lane
Oswald Beck

West Burton Power Station

River Road

Low Farm

7

Footgap Lane
Sturton Rd
North Rd
South Rd

West Burton Meadow Nature Reserve

Medieval Village of West Burton (site of)

85

Redhill La
Wheatley Rd
Woodland Farm
Wood Lane
Station Rd

Gainsborough Rd

Common La

6

Crow Tree Farm
Watkins La
North St
North Street Farm

Crown Ct

Cross St
Caddow Vw

Sturton le Steeple

5

Manor Farm

84

Freeman's La
Brickings Way
Playing Field
PH

Freeman's Lane
Low Holland La
Littleborough Rd

LC
Spring La
Church St
Low Holland Farm

Stud Farm
Sturton CE Prim Sch

4

Springs Lane
Leverton Rd
Trent Valley Way
Catchwater Drain

3

Fenton
Sewage Works

83

Dog Holes Lane
Three Leys La
Fenton Lane

The Homestead

Grange Farm

2

The Old Vicarage

Ketlock Hill La
North Leverton with Habblesthorpe

Sturton Road Farm

Sturton Rd

North Leverton CE Prim Sch

Fingle St

Habblesthorpe Cl
North St
Northfield Rd

1

Scrimshire's Rd
Mill Cl
Manor Gr
Home Rise
Manor Farm
PO
Main St
PH
Habblesthorpe Rd
Sewage Works
Magpie La

North Leverton Windmill
Ashworth Cres
Southgore La
Plum Tree Barn
Plum Tree Ct
Tree Rise
Townside Rd
Plum Tree Rise
Infield
Street Lane Rd

82

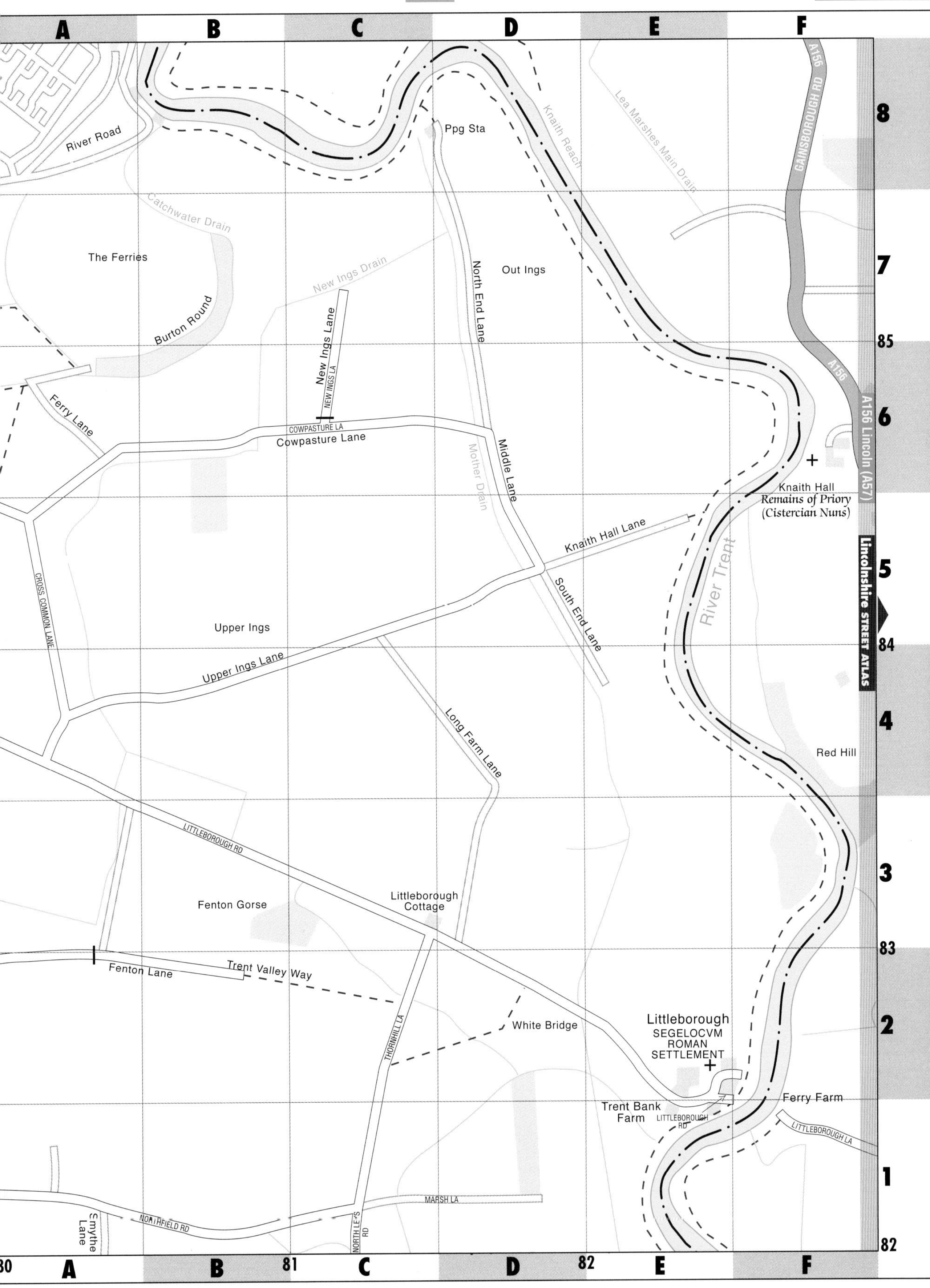

River Road

The Ferries

Burton Round

Catchwater Drain

Ferry Lane

New Ings Drain

New Ings Lane

NEW INGS LA

COWPASTURE LA
Cowpasture Lane

CROSS COMMON LANE

North End Lane

Ppg Sta

Out Ings

Knaith Reach

Lea Marshes Main Drain

GAINSBOROUGH RD

A156

A156

A156 Lincoln (A57)

Lincolnshire STREET ATLAS

Mother Drain

Middle Lane

Knaith Hall Lane

South End Lane

Knaith Hall
Remains of Priory
(Cistercian Nuns)

River Trent

Upper Ings

Upper Ings Lane

Long Farm Lane

Red Hill

LITTLEBOROUGH RD

Fenton Gorse

Littleborough
Cottage

Fenton Lane

Trent Valley Way

THORNHILL LA

White Bridge

Littleborough
SEGELOCVM
ROMAN
SETTLEMENT

Trent Bank
Farm

LITTLEBOROUGH
RD

Ferry Farm

LITTLEBOROUGH LA

Smythe
Lane

NORTHFIELD RD

NORTHLE'S RD

MARSH LA

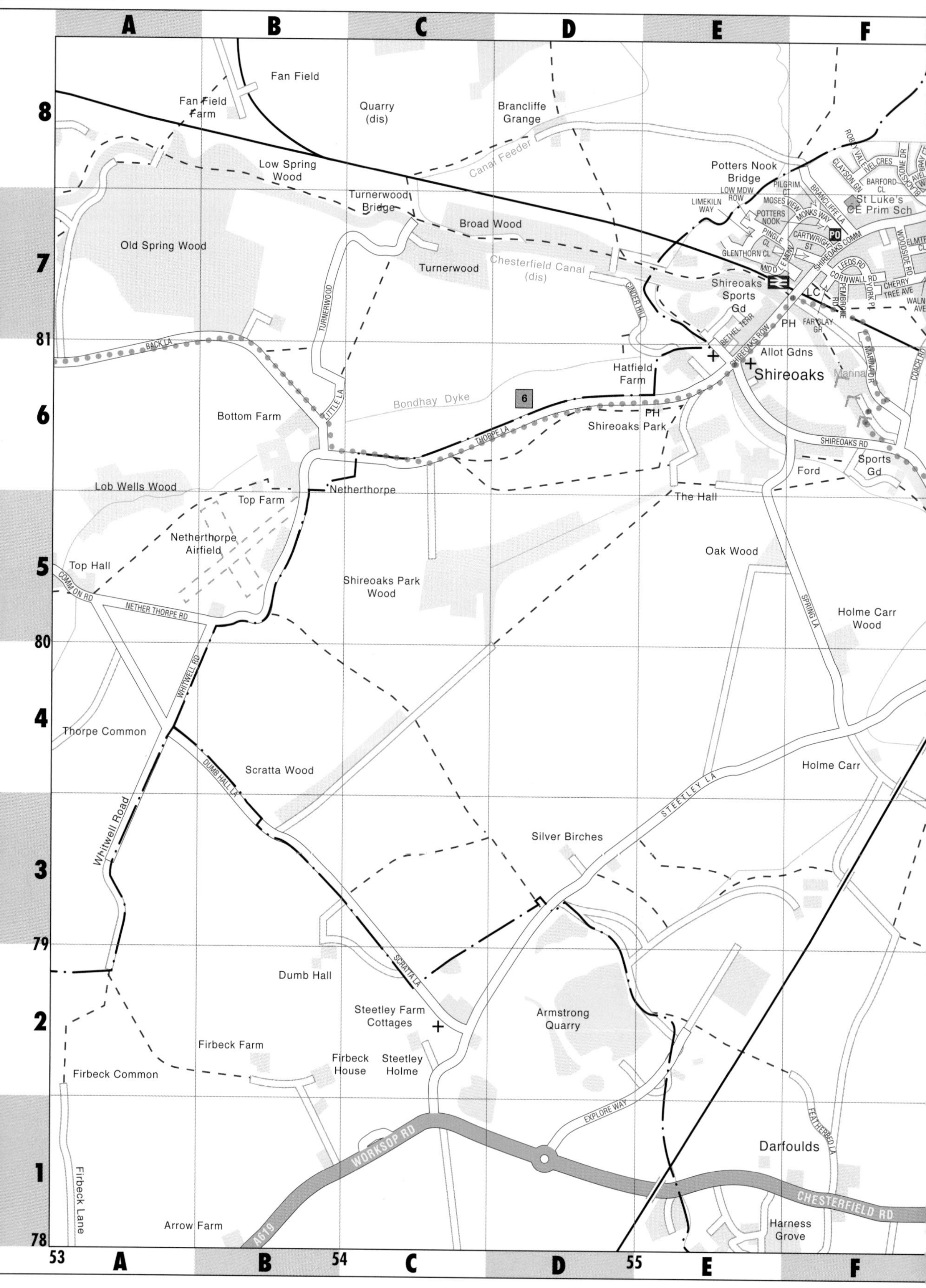
A
B
C
D
E
F
8
7
81
6
5
80
4
3
79
2
1
78
53
54
55
Fan Field
Fan Field Farm
Quarry (dis)
Brancliffe Grange
Low Spring Wood
Canal Feeder
Turnerwood Bridge
Broad Wood
Old Spring Wood
Turnerwood
Chesterfield Canal (dis)
Potters Nook Bridge
St Luke's CE Prim Sch
Shireoaks Sports Gd
Allot Gdns
Shireoaks
Marina
Hatfield Farm
Shireoaks Park
PH
Bondhay Dyke
Bottom Farm
BACK LA
TURNERWOOD
LITTLE LA
THORPE LA
CINDER HILL
BETHEL TERR
SHIREOAKS ROW
SHIREOAKS RD
Sports Gd
Ford
Lob Wells Wood
Top Farm
Netherthorpe
The Hall
Netherthorpe Airfield
Oak Wood
Top Hall
COMMON RD
NETHER THORPE RD
Shireoaks Park Wood
SPRING LA
Holme Carr Wood
WHITWELL RD
Thorpe Common
Holme Carr
Scratta Wood
DUMB HALL LA
STEETLEY LA
Whitwell Road
Silver Birches
SCRATTA LA
Dumb Hall
Steetley Farm Cottages
Armstrong Quarry
Firbeck Farm
Firbeck House
Steetley Holme
Firbeck Common
EXPLORE WAY
WORKSOP RD
Darfoulds
FEATHERBED LA
CHESTERFIELD RD
Firbeck Lane
Arrow Farm
A619
Harness Grove

45

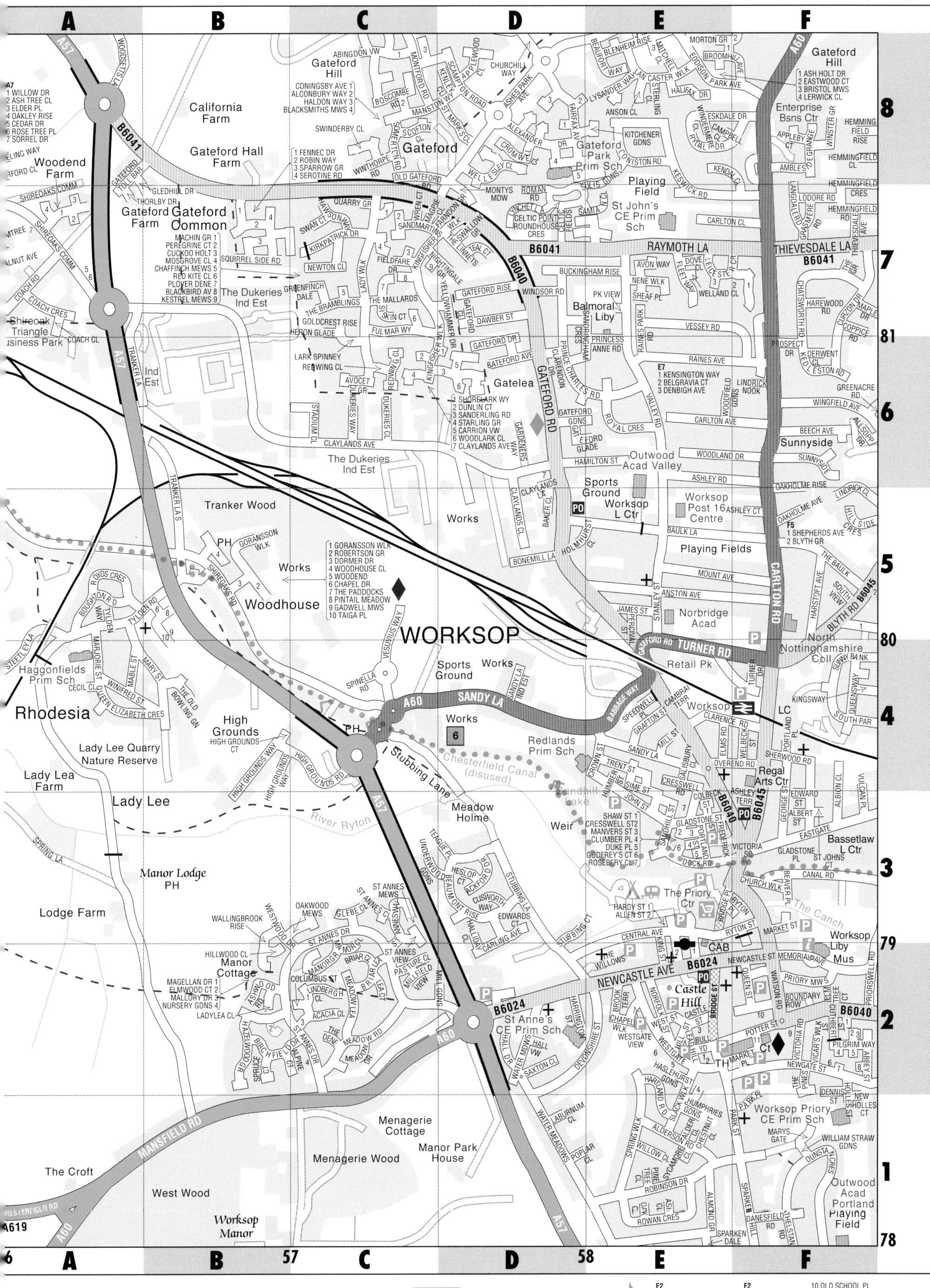

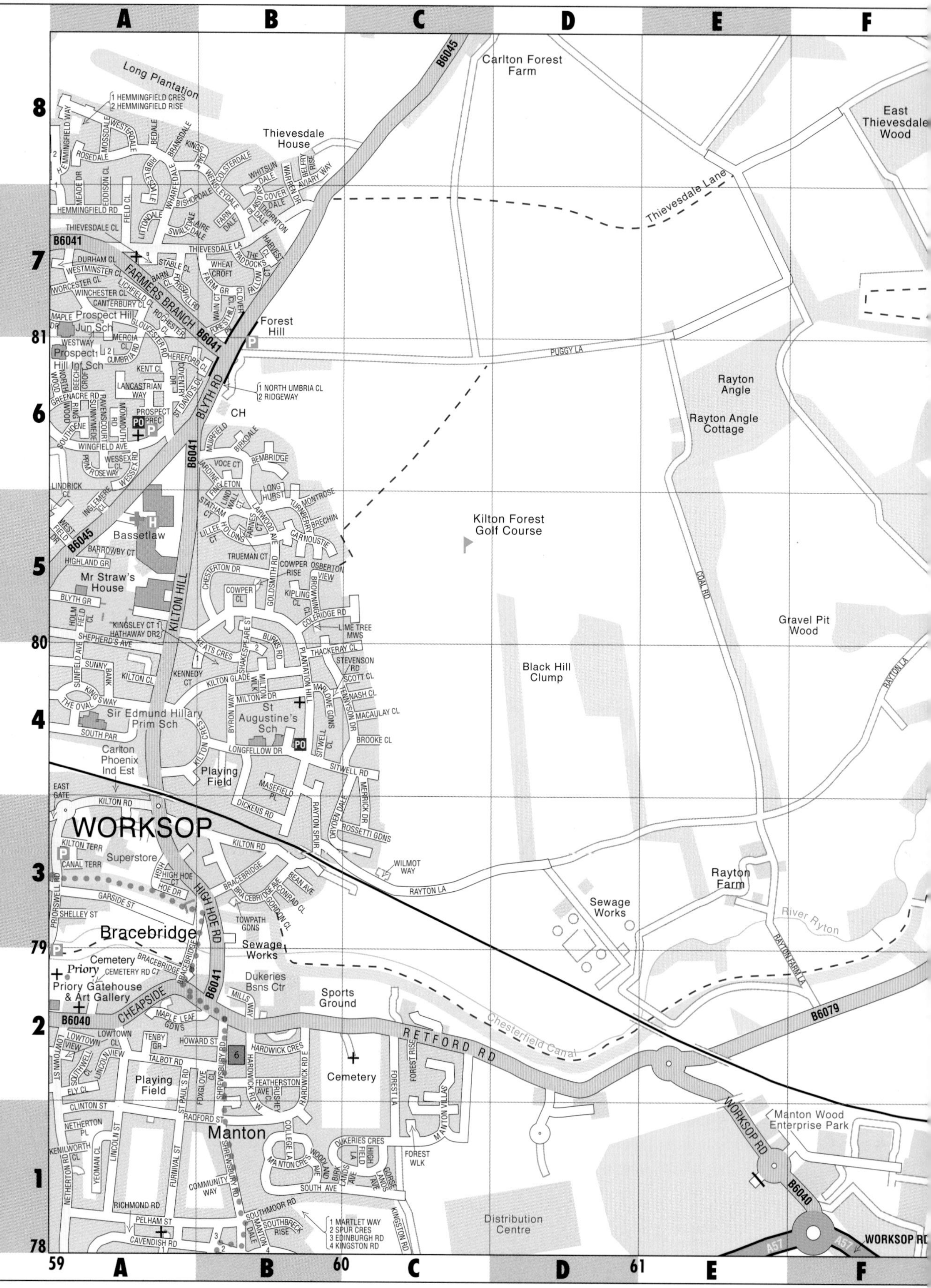

A B C D E F

8
7
81
6
5
80
4
3
79
2
1
78

59
60
61

Long Plantation
1 HEMMINGFIELD CRES
2 HEMMINGFIELD RISE

Carlton Forest
Farm

East
Thievesdale
Wood

Thievesdale
House

Thievesdale Lane

B6041

HEMMINGFIELD RD

THIEVESDALE CL
DURHAM CL
WESTMINSTER CL
WORCESTER CL
WINCHESTER CL
CANTERBURY CL
MAPLE
Prospect Hill
Jun Sch
Prospect
Hill Inf Sch

FARMERS BRANCH

Forest
Hill

Puggy La

PUGGY LA

Rayton
Angle

Rayton Angle
Cottage

1 NORTH UMBRIA CL
2 RIDGEWAY

CH

LANCASTRIAN
WAY

Kilton Forest
Golf Course

BLYTH RD

B6041

Bassetlaw
Mr Straw's
House

KILTON HILL

Gravel Pit
Wood

Black Hill
Clump

B6045

LIME TREE
MWS

St
Augustine's
Sch

COAL RD

RAYTON RD

Sir Edmund Hillary
Prim Sch

Carlton
Phoenix
Ind Est

Playing
Field

WORKSOP

Superstore
Bracebridge

KILTON RD

KILTON RD

HIGH HOE RD

B6041

Wilmot
Way

RAYTON LA

Rayton
Farm

Sewage
Works

River Ryton

Cemetery
Priory
Priory Gatehouse
& Art Gallery
B6040
CHEAPSIDE

Dukeries
Bsns Ctr

Sewage
Works

Sports
Ground

Chesterfield Canal

B6079

RETFORD RD

Manton Villas

WORKSOP RD

Manton Wood
Enterprise Park

Playing
Field

Cemetery

Manton

Forest
Wlk

Distribution
Centre

B6040

WORKSOP RD

A57

A57

1 MARTLET WAY
2 SPUR CRES
3 EDINBURGH RD
4 KINGSTON RD

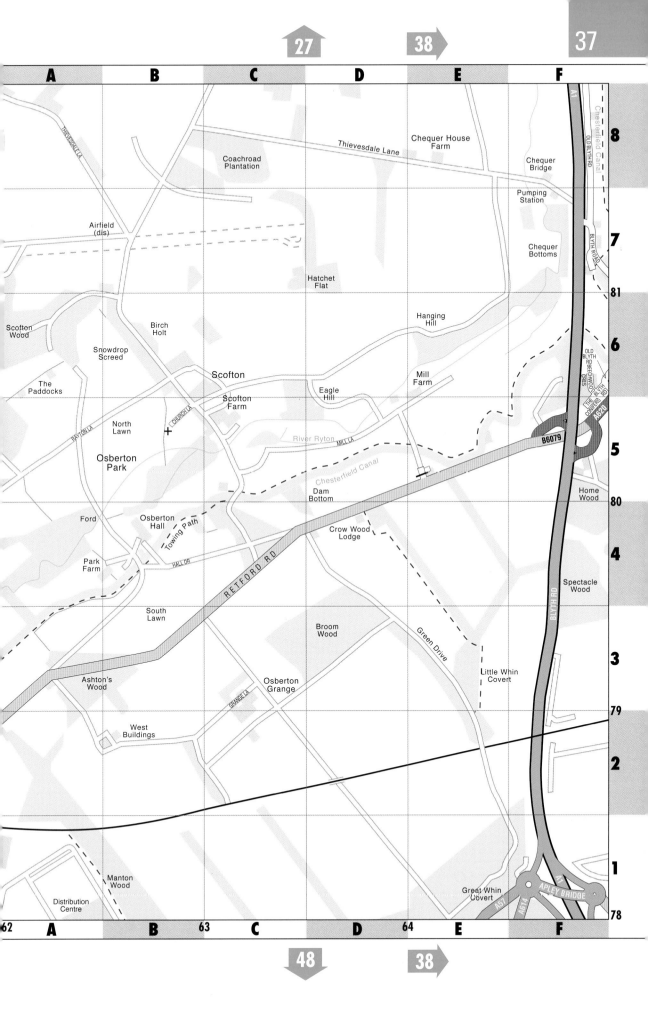
27
38

A B C D E F

8
7
81
6
5
80
4
3
79
2
1
78

Thievesdale La
Thievesdale Lane
Chequer House Farm
Coachroad Plantation
Chequer Bridge
Pumping Station
Chesterfield Canal
Old Blyth Rd
A1
Airfield (dis)
Blyth Road
Chequer Bottoms
Hatchet Flat
Hanging Hill
Scofton Wood
Birch Holt
Snowdrop Screed
Old Blyth Rd
Beechwood Cres
Blyth Rd
The Conifers
Scofton
Mill Farm
The Paddocks
Eagle Hill
Scofton Farm
Church La
A620
North Lawn
Rayton La
River Ryton
Mill La
B6079
Osberton Park
Chesterfield Canal
Dam Bottom
Home Wood
Ford
Osberton Hall
Towing Path
Crow Wood Lodge
Park Farm
Hall Dr
Retford Rd
Spectacle Wood
Blyth Rd
South Lawn
Broom Wood
Green Drive
Ashton's Wood
Little Whin Covert
Osberton Grange
Grange La
West Buildings
Manton Wood
Distribution Centre
Great Whin Covert
A57
A614
A1
Apley Bridge

62 A B 63 C D 64 E F

48
38

37
28

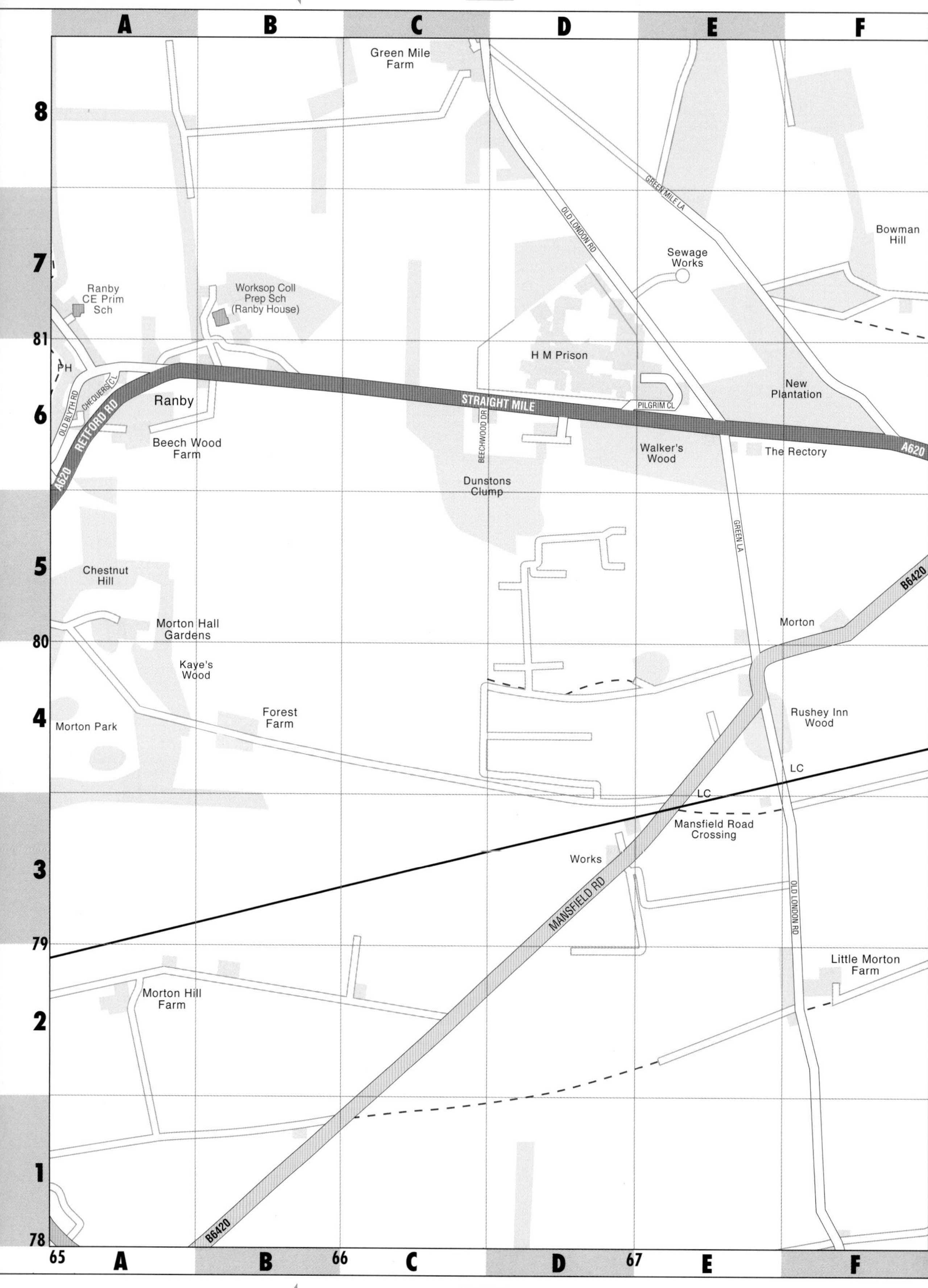
A
B
C
D
E
F
8
7
81
6
5
80
4
3
79
2
1
78
65
66
67
Green Mile Farm
Bowman Hill
Sewage Works
GREEN MILE LA
OLD LONDON RD
Ranby CE Prim Sch
Worksop Coll Prep Sch (Ranby House)
H M Prison
PH
New Plantation
Ranby
STRAIGHT MILE
PILGRIM CL
CHEQUERS CL
OLD BLYTH RD
RETFORD RD
A620
Beech Wood Farm
BEECHWOOD DR
Walker's Wood
The Rectory
Dunstons Clump
GREEN LA
Chestnut Hill
B6420
Morton Hall Gardens
Morton
Kaye's Wood
Forest Farm
Rushey Inn Wood
Morton Park
LC
Mansfield Road Crossing
Works
MANSFIELD RD
Little Morton Farm
Morton Hill Farm
B6420

37
49

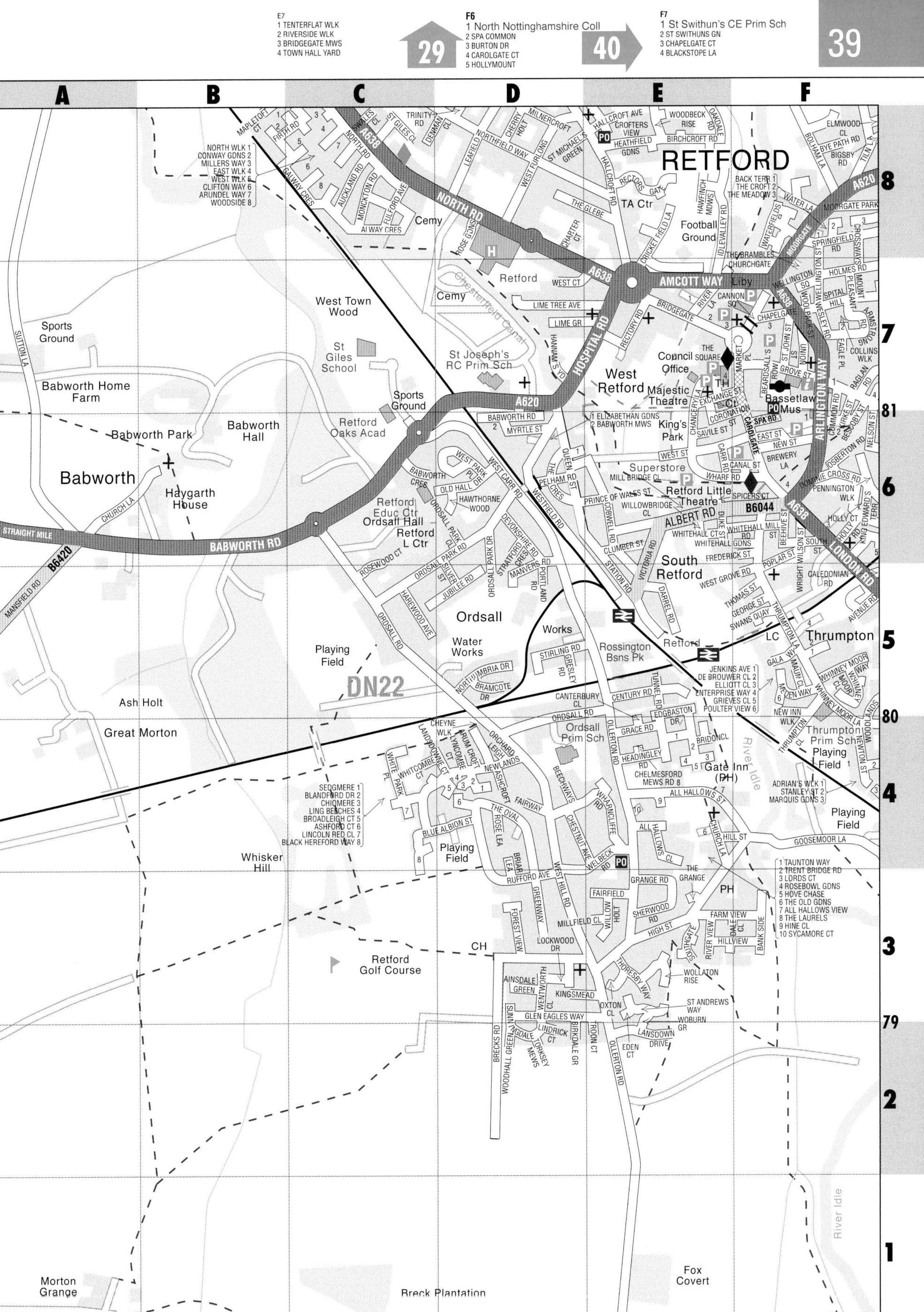

E7
1 TENTERFLAT WLK
2 RIVERSIDE WLK
3 BRIDGEGATE MWS
4 TOWN HALL YARD

29

F6
1 North Nottinghamshire Coll
2 SPA COMMON
3 BURTON DR
4 CAROLGATE CT
5 HOLLYMOUNT

40

F7
1 St Swithun's CE Prim Sch
2 ST SWITHUNS GN
3 CHAPELGATE CT
4 BLACKSTOPE LA

39

RETFORD

Street and place labels

NORTH WLK 1
CONWAY GDNS 2
MILLERS WAY 3
EAST WLK 4
WEST WLK 5
CLIFTON WAY 6
ARUNDEL WAY 7
WOODSIDE 8

West Town Wood

St Giles School

Babworth Home Farm

Babworth Park

Babworth Hall

Babworth

Haygarth House

Retford Oaks Acad

Sports Ground

St Joseph's RC Prim Sch

West Retford

Council Office

Majestic Theatre

King's Park

1 ELIZABETHAN GDNS
2 BABWORTH MWS

Superstore

Retford Little Theatre

ALBERT RD

South Retford

Bassetlaw PO Mus

Thrumpton

Retford Educ Ctr
Ordsall Hall
Retford L Ctr

Ordsall

Water Works

Works

Rossington Bsns Pk

SEDGMERE 1
BLANDFORD DR 2
CHIDMERE 3
LING BEECHES 4
BROADLEIGH CT 5
ASHFORD CT 6
LINCOLN RED CL 7
BLACK HEREFORD WAY 8

Playing Field

Ordsall Prim Sch

JENKINS AVE 1
DE BROUWER CL 2
ELLIOTT CL 3
ENTERPRISE WAY 4
GRIEVES CL 5
POULTER VIEW 6

Thrumpton Prim Sch
Playing Field

ADRIAN'S WLK 1
STANLEY ST 2
MARQUIS GDNS 3

Gate Inn (PH)

Playing Field

Whisker Hill

Ash Holt

Great Morton

DN22

1 TAUNTON WAY
2 TRENT BRIDGE RD
3 LORDS CT
4 ROSEBOWL GDNS
5 HOVE CHASE
6 THE OLD GDNS
7 ALL HALLOWS VIEW
8 THE LAURELS
9 HINE CL
10 SYCAMORE CT

Retford Golf Course

Kingsmead

Morton Grange

Breck Plantation

Fox Covert

River Idle

Babworth Rd
Straight Mile
Mansfield Rd
Amcott Way
North Rd
Hospital Rd
London Rd
Arlington Way

39
30

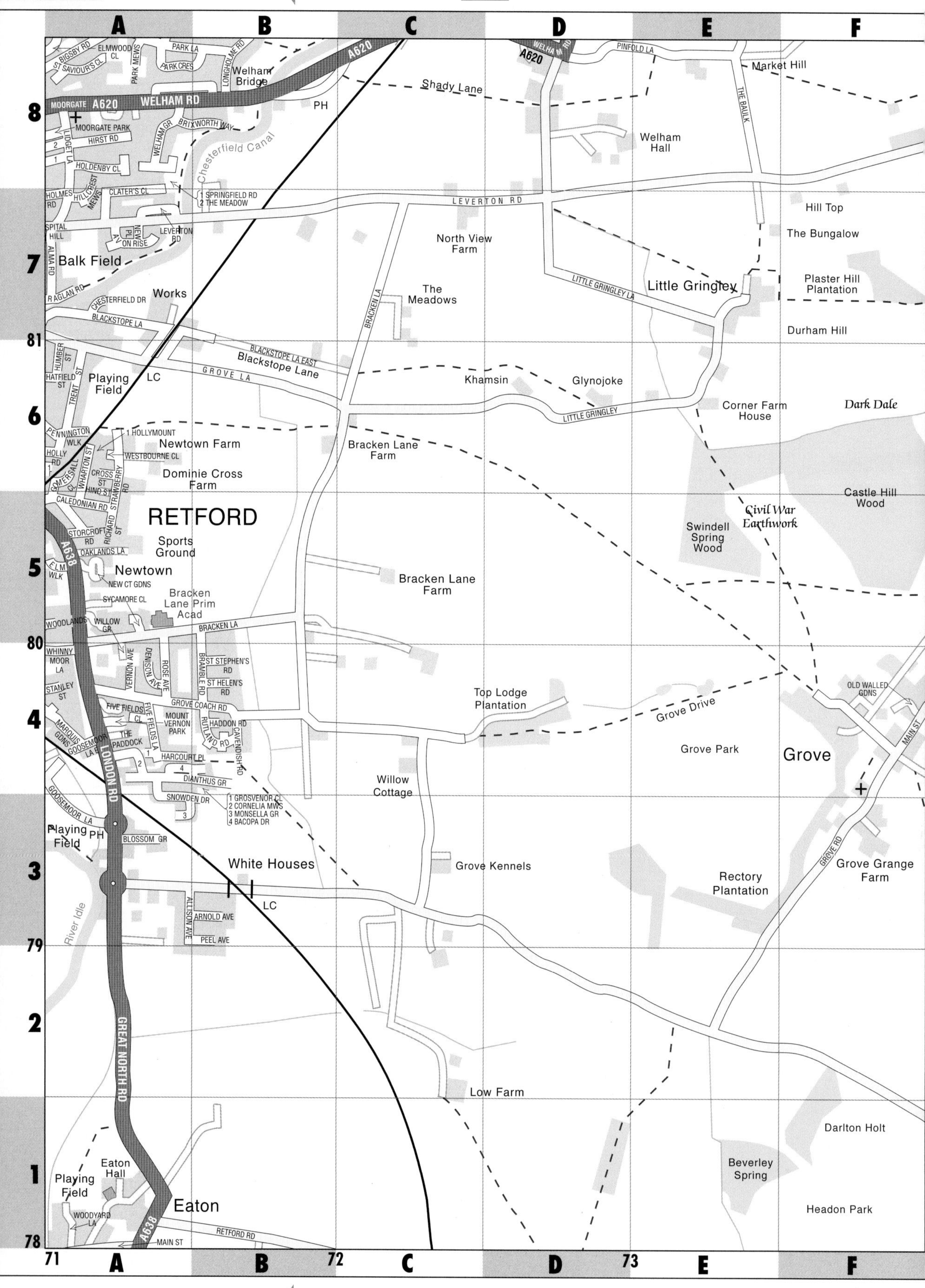
A
B
C
D
E
F
8
7
81
6
5
80
4
3
79
2
1
78
71
72
73
RETFORD
Welham Bridge
WELHAM RD
MOORGATE A620
A620
Shady Lane
Market Hill
PINFOLD LA
THE BAULK
Welham Hall
Chesterfield Canal
LEVERTON RD
Hill Top
The Bungalow
North View Farm
Balk Field
Works
The Meadows
Little Gringley
LITTLE GRINGLEY LA
Plaster Hill Plantation
Durham Hill
BLACKSTOPE LA
BLACKSTOPE LA EAST
Blackstope Lane
GROVE LA
BRACKEN LA
Playing Field
Khamsin
Glynojoke
LITTLE GRINGLEY
Corner Farm House
Dark Dale
Newtown Farm
Bracken Lane Farm
Dominie Cross Farm
Castle Hill Wood
Civil War Earthwork
Swindell Spring Wood
Sports Ground
Newtown
Bracken Lane Farm
Bracken Lane Prim Acad
Top Lodge Plantation
Grove Drive
OLD WALLED GDNS
Grove Park
Grove
MAIN ST
Willow Cottage
LONDON RD
A638
White Houses
Grove Kennels
Rectory Plantation
Grove Grange Farm
GROVE RD
LC
River Idle
GREAT NORTH RD
Low Farm
Darlton Holt
Eaton Hall
Playing Field
Eaton
Beverley Spring
Headon Park
RETFORD RD
MAIN ST
WOODYARD LA
1 SPRINGFIELD RD
2 THE MEADOW
1 HOLLYMOUNT
1 GROSVENOR CL
2 CORNELIA MWS
3 MONSELLA GR
4 BACOPA DR
PH

39
51

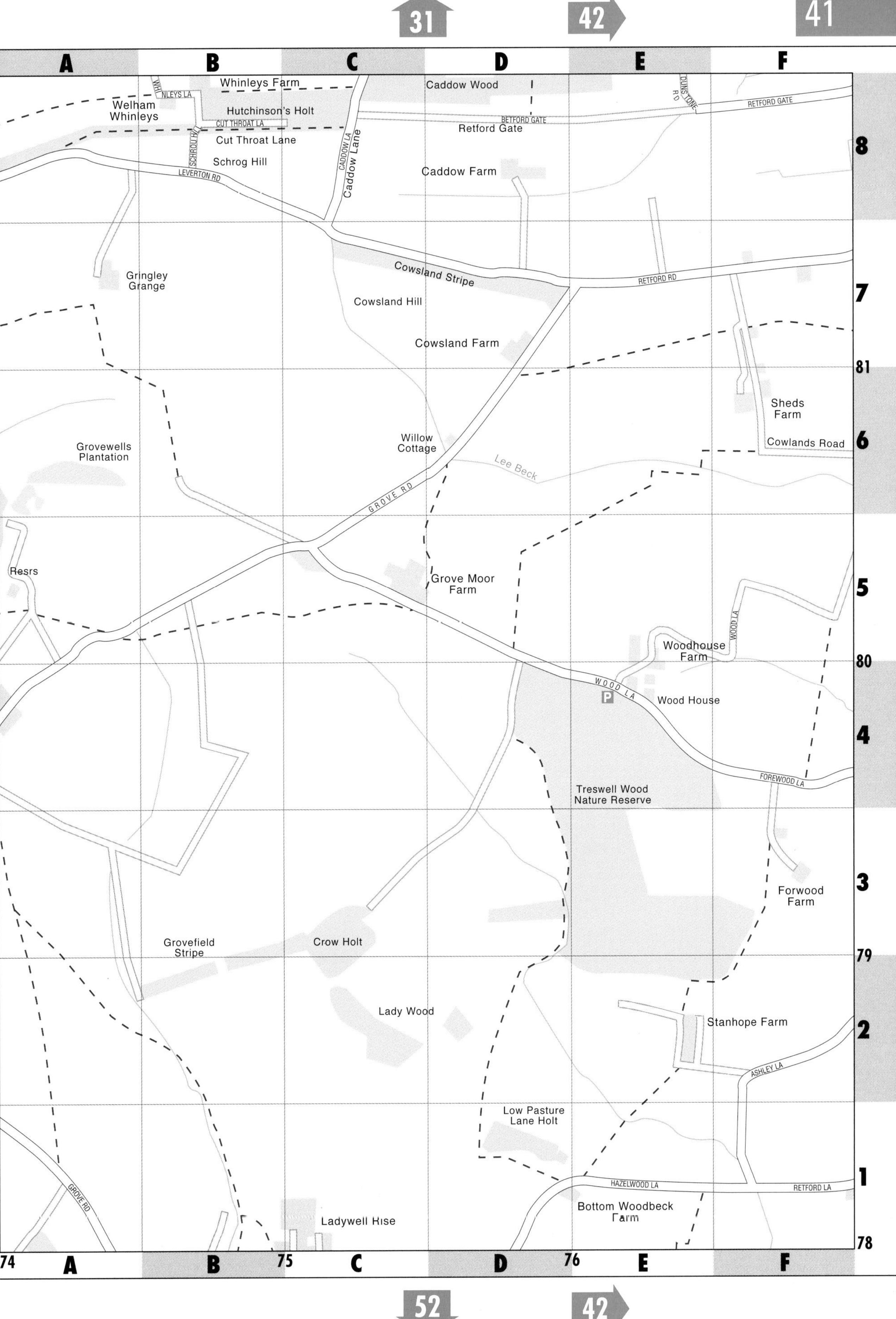

Whinleys Farm
Caddow Wood
Welham
Whinleys
Hutchinson's Holt
RETFORD GATE
WHINLEYS LA
CUT THROAT LA
BETFORD GATE
DUBS TONE RD
Cut Throat Lane
Retford Gate
SCHROG HILL
CADDOW LA
Caddow Lane
Caddow Farm
Schrog Hill
LEVERTON RD

Gringley
Grange
Cowsland Stripe
RETFORD RD

Cowsland Hill
7

Cowsland Farm
81

Grovewells
Plantation
Willow
Cottage
Sheds
Farm
Cowlands Road
6

Lee Beck
GROVE RD

Resrs
Grove Moor
Farm
5

WOOD LA
Woodhouse
Farm
80

WOOD LA
P
Wood House
4

Treswell Wood
Nature Reserve
FOREWOOD LA

Grovefield
Stripe
Crow Holt
Forwood
Farm
3

79

Lady Wood
Stanhope Farm
2

ASHLEY LA

Low Pasture
Lane Holt
1

GROVE RD
HAZELWOOD LA
RETFORD LA
78

Ladywell Rise
Bottom Woodbeck
Farm

41
32

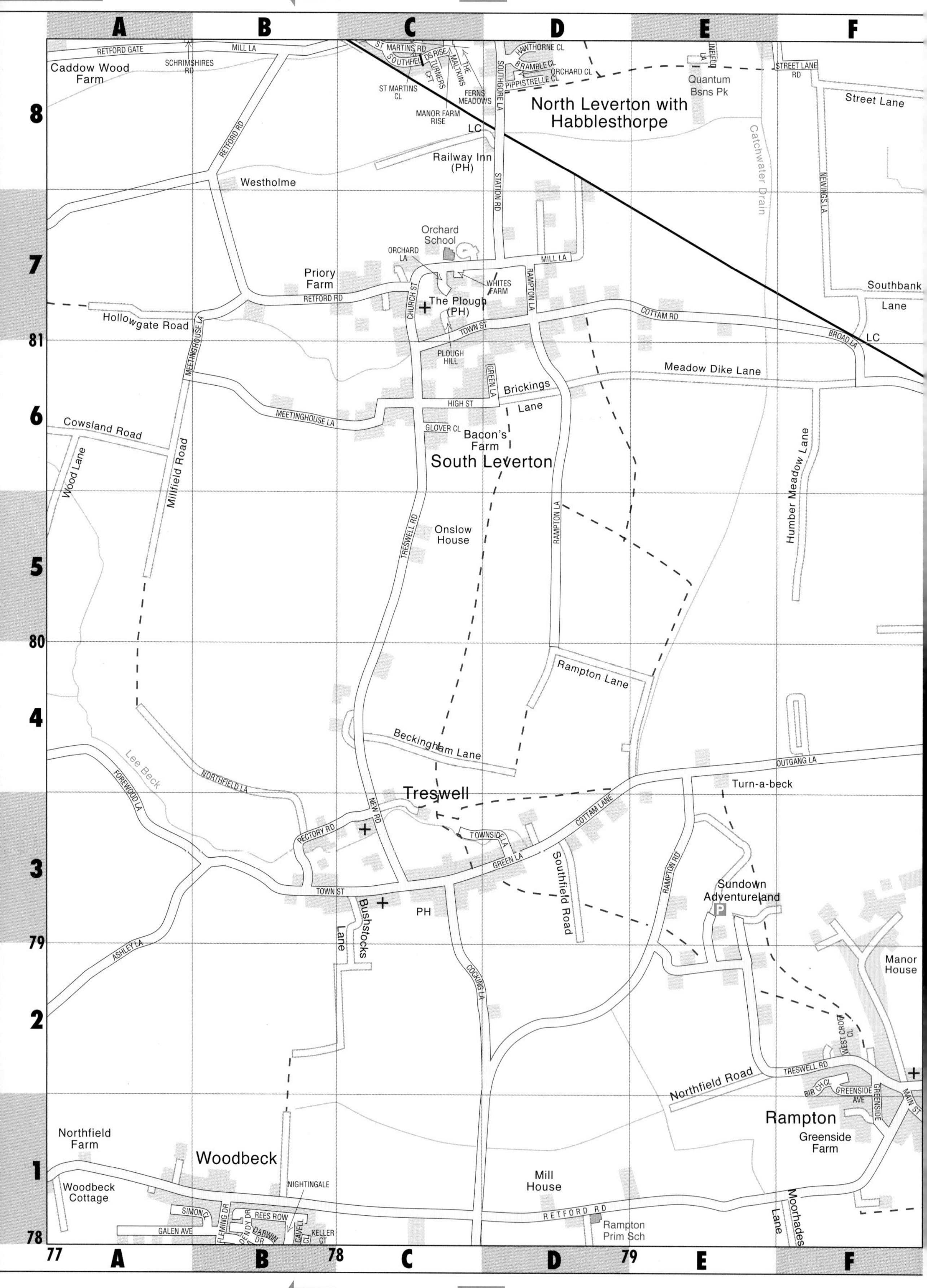
Caddow Wood Farm
RETFORD GATE
MILL LA
SCHRIMSHIRES RD
RETFORD RD
Westholme
ST MARTINS RD
SOUTHFIELD
ST MARTINS CL
TURNERS CFT
MALTKINS
THE
FERNS MEADOWS
MANOR FARM RISE
HAWTHORNE CL
BRAMBLE CL
ORCHARD CL
PIPPISTRELLE CL
SOUTHGORE LA
North Leverton with Habblesthorpe
Quantum Bsns Pk
STREET LANE RD
Street Lane
LC
Railway Inn (PH)
STATION RD
Catchwater Drain
NEWINGS LA
Orchard School
ORCHARD LA
MILL LA
Priory Farm
RETFORD RD
CHURCH ST
WHITES FARM
RAMPTON LA
The Plough (PH)
TOWN ST
COTTAM RD
Southbank Lane
BROAD LA
LC
Hollowgate Road
MEETINGHOUSE LA
PLOUGH HILL
GREEN LA
Meadow Dike Lane
Brickings Lane
HIGH ST
MEETINGHOUSE LA
GLOVER CL
Bacon's Farm
Cowsland Road
South Leverton
Wood Lane
Millfield Road
Humber Meadow Lane
TRESWELL RD
Onslow House
RAMPTON LA
Rampton Lane
Beckingham Lane
Lee Beck
FOREWOOD LA
NORTHFIELD LA
OUTGANG LA
Turn-a-beck
Treswell
NEW RD
RECTORY RD
TOWNSIDE LA
COTTAM LANE
GREEN LA
Southfield Road
RAMPTON RD
TOWN ST
Bushstocks Lane
PH
Sundown Adventureland
P
Manor House
ASHLEY LA
COCKING LA
WEST CROFT CL
Northfield Road
TRESWELL RD
BIRCH CL
GREENSIDE AVE
GREENSIDE
MAIN ST
Rampton
Greenside Farm
Northfield Farm
Woodbeck
Woodbeck Cottage
NIGHTINGALE
Mill House
RETFORD RD
Moorhades Lane
SIMON CL
GALEN AVE
FLEMING DR
DENDY DR
REES ROW
DARWIN DR
CAVELL CL
KELLER CT
Rampton Prim Sch
A B C D E F
8
7
81
6
5
80
4
3
79
2
1
78
77
78
79

41
53

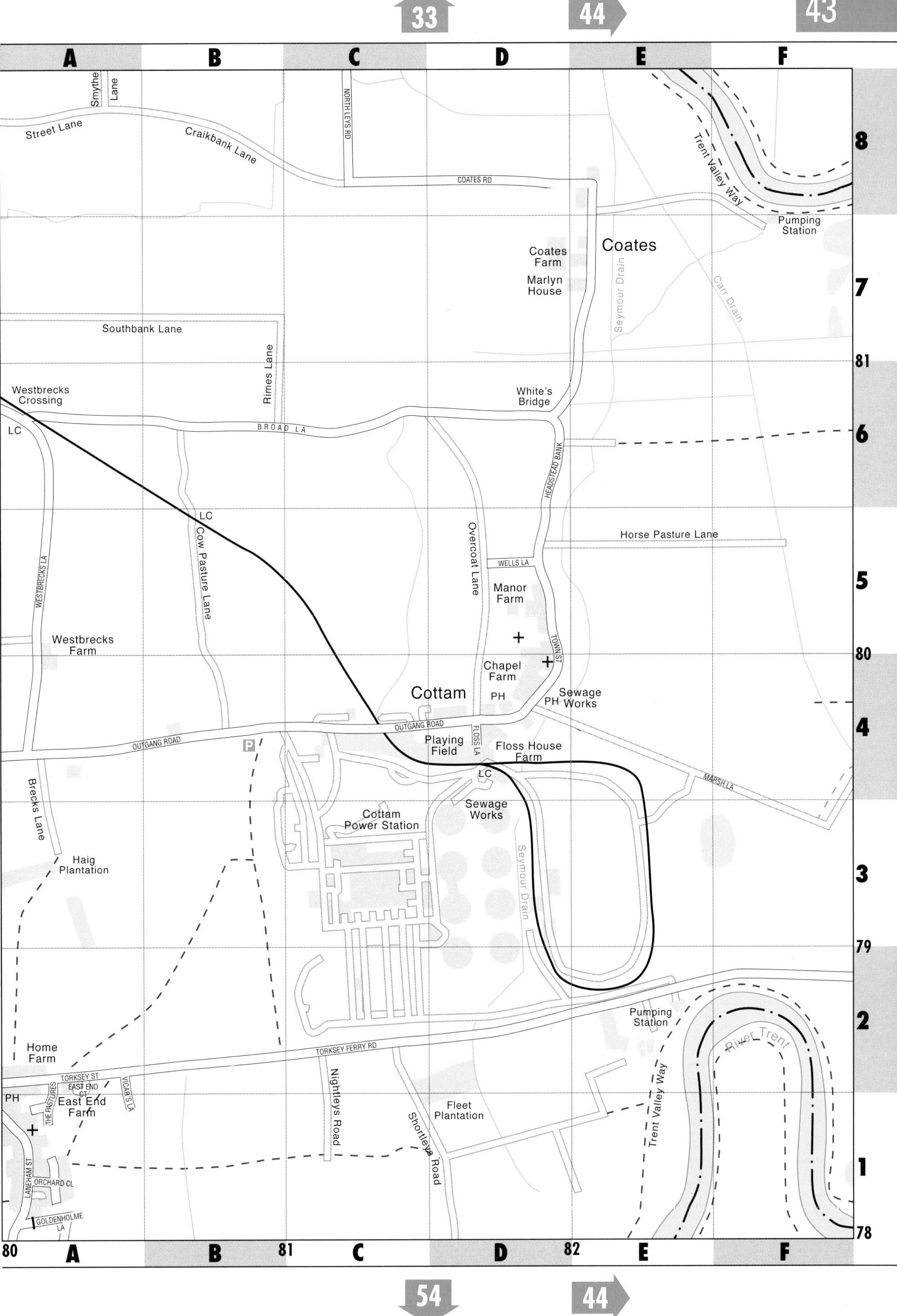

A B C D E F

Smythe Lane

Street Lane

Craikbank Lane

COATES RD

NORTH LEYS RD

8

Coates Farm

Marlyn House

Coates

Trent Valley Way

Pumping Station

Southbank Lane

Rimes Lane

7

Seymour Drain

Carr Drain

81

Westbrecks Crossing

LC

B R O A D L A

White's Bridge

HEADSTEAD BANK

6

LC

Cow Pasture Lane

WESTBRECKS LA

Overcoat Lane

Horse Pasture Lane

WELLS LA

Manor Farm

TRENT ST

5

Westbrecks Farm

+

Chapel Farm

+

80

Cottam

PH

PH

Sewage Works

OUTGANG ROAD

Playing Field

FLOSS LA

Floss House Farm

4

Outgang Road

P

LC

Sewage Works

MARSH LA

Brecks Lane

Haig Plantation

Cottam Power Station

Seymour Drain

3

79

Home Farm

Torksey Ferry Rd

Pumping Station

2

Trent Valley Way

River Trent

PH

Torksey St

EAST END CT.

VICAR'S LA

THE PASTURES

East End Farm

Nightleys Road

Shortleys Road

Fleet Plantation

1

LANEHAM ST

+

ORCHARD CL

GOLDENHOLME LA

78

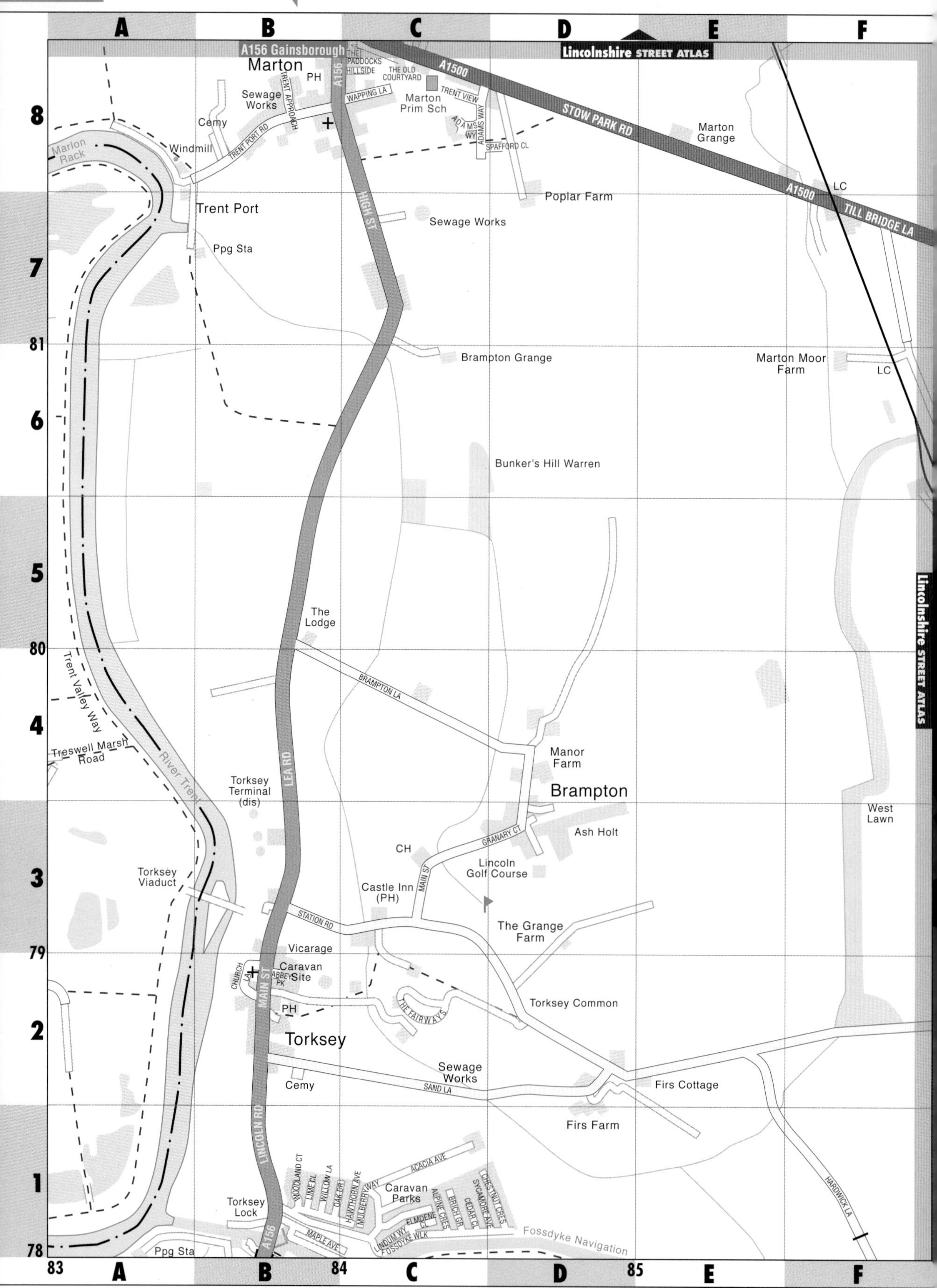

A · B · C · D · E · F

8

A156 Gainsborough
Marton
THE PADDOCKS
HILLSIDE
THE OLD COURTYARD
A1500
PH
WAPPING LA
Marton Prim Sch
TRENT VIEW
ADA MS WAY
Stow Park Rd
Marton Grange

Sewage Works
Cemy
Windmill

Marlon Rack

Trent Port
HIGH ST
Ppg Sta

A156
A1500
LC
Till Bridge La

7

81

Sewage Works
Poplar Farm

Brampton Grange
Marton Moor Farm
LC

6

Bunker's Hill Warren

5

The Lodge

80

Trent Valley Way
River Trent

BRAMPTON LA

4

Treswell Marsh Road
LEA RD
Manor Farm
Brampton
West Lawn

Torksey Terminal (dis)
GRANARY CT
Ash Holt

3

Torksey Viaduct
CH
Lincoln Golf Course

STATION RD
Castle Inn (PH)
MAIN ST
The Grange Farm

79

Vicarage
CHURCH LA
ABBEY PK
MAIN ST
Caravan Site
THE FAIRWAYS
Torksey Common

2

PH
Torksey
Cemy
Sewage Works
SAND LA
Firs Cottage
Firs Farm

LINCOLN RD

WOODLAND CT
LIME DL
WILLOW LA
OAK DRI
HAWTHORN LA
ELDERBERRY WAY
ACACIA AVE
CHESTNUT DES
SYCAMORE AVE
ALPINE CRES
CEDAR GR
BIRCH DR
HARDWICK LA

1

Torksey Lock
A156
MAPLE AVE
Caravan Parks
ELMDENE
LINDUM VW
FOSSDYKE WLK
Fossdyke Navigation

78

Ppg Sta

83 · A · B · 84 · C · D · 85 · E · F

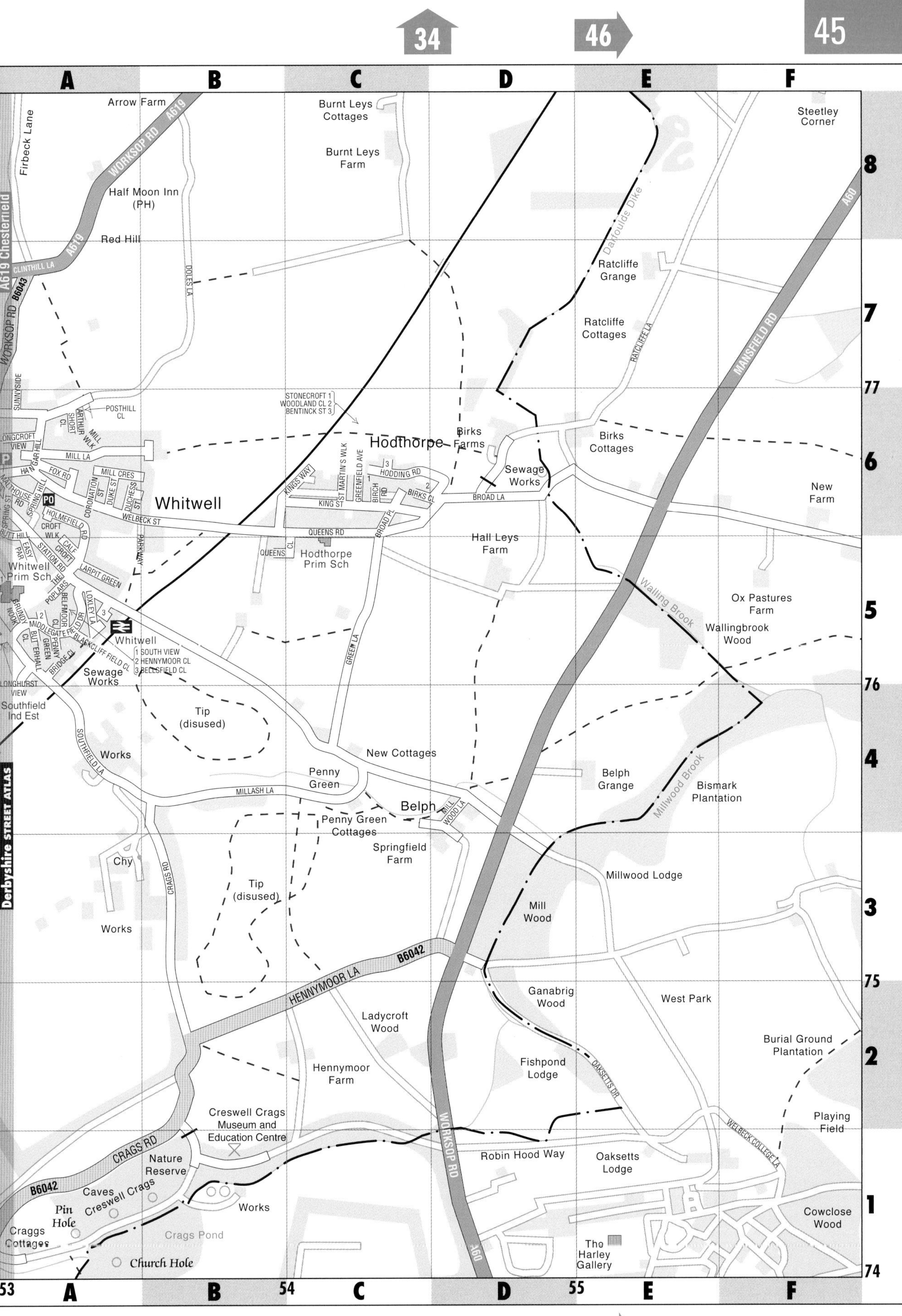

A B C D E F

8
7
77
6
5
76
4
3
75
2
1
74

Firbeck Lane
Arrow Farm
WORKSOP RD A619
Burnt Leys Cottages
Burnt Leys Farm
Steetley Corner

A619 Chesterfield
CLINTHILL LA
B6043
Half Moon Inn (PH)
Red Hill
DOLES LA
Ratcliffe Grange
Dartoulde Dike
A60

WORKSOP RD
SUNNYSIDE
POSTHILL CL
SHORT CL
ARTHUR WLK
MILL WLK
MILL LA
STONECROFT 1
WOODLAND CL 2
BENTINCK ST 3
Ratcliffe Cottages
RATCLIFFE LA
MANSFIELD RD
77

LONGCROFT VIEW
FOX RD
MILL CRES
KINGS WAY
ST MARTIN'S WLK
GREENFIELD AVE
HODDING RD
Hodthorpe
Birks Farms
Birks Cottages
New Farm
6

MATHOUSE RD
SPRING HILL
HAM RD
CORONATION ST
DUKE ST
CROSS ST
KING ST
BIRCH PL
BIRKS CL
Whitwell
WELBECK ST
QUEENS RD
Hodthorpe Prim Sch
BROAD PL
BROAD LA
Sewage Works

PO
HOLMEFIELD
CROFT
CALL CROFT
PARKWAY
QUEENS
Hall Leys Farm
Ox Pastures Farm
Wallingbrook Wood
Walling Brook
5

Whitwell Prim Sch
POPLAR
BELMOOR
LOXLEY PL
BLACKCLIFF FIELD CL
Whitwell
1 SOUTH VIEW
2 HENNYMOOR CL
3 BELLSFIELD CL
GREEN LA
76

BRUNS MOOR
MIDDLEGATE GREEN
COLLEGATE PL
PENNY
BRIDGE PL
BUTTERHALL
LONGHURST VIEW
Sewage Works
Southfield Ind Est
Tip (disused)
Belph Grange
Bismark Plantation
Millwood Brook
4

SOUTHFIELD LA
Works
MILLASH LA
CRAGS RD
Penny Green
New Cottages
Penny Green Cottages
Belph
Springfield Farm
Mill Wood
MILL WOOD LA
Millwood Lodge
3

Derbyshire STREET ATLAS
Chy
Works
Tip (disused)
HENNYMOOR LA
B6042
Ladycroft Wood
Ganabrig Wood
OAKSETTS DR
West Park
75

Hennymoor Farm
Fishpond Lodge
Burial Ground Plantation
WELBECK COLLEGE LA
2

Creswell Crags Museum and Education Centre
Nature Reserve
WORKSOP RD
Robin Hood Way
Oaksetts Lodge
Playing Field

CRAGS RD
Caves Creswell Crags
B6042
Pin Hole
Works
A60
Cowclose Wood
1

Craggs Cottages
Crags Pond
Church Hole
The Harley Gallery
74

45
35

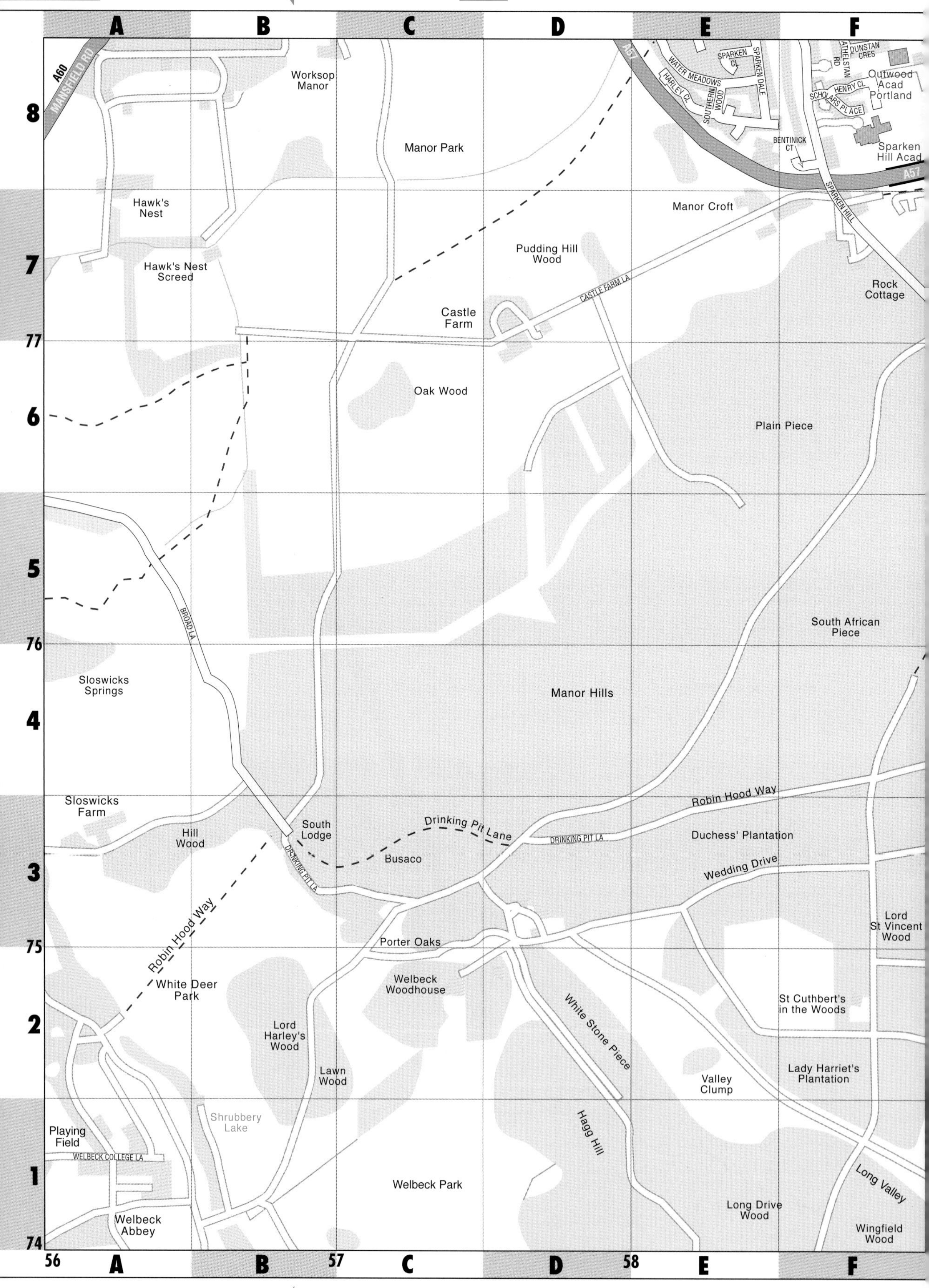
A
B
C
D
E
F
8
7
77
6
5
76
4
3
75
2
1
74
56
57
58
A60
MANSFIELD RD
Worksop Manor
Manor Park
A57
WATER MEADOWS
HARLEY CL
SPARKEN CL
SPARKEN DALE
SOUTHERN WOOD
ATHELSTAN RD
DUNSTAN CRES
Outwood Acad Portland
HENRY CL
SCHOLARS PLACE
BENTINICK CT
Sparken Hill Acad
SPARKEN HILL
Hawk's Nest
Manor Croft
Pudding Hill Wood
Hawk's Nest Screed
Castle Farm
CASTLE FARM LA
Rock Cottage
Oak Wood
Plain Piece
BROAD LA
South African Piece
Sloswicks Springs
Manor Hills
Sloswicks Farm
Robin Hood Way
Hill Wood
South Lodge
Drinking Pit Lane
DRINKING PIT LA
Duchess' Plantation
Busaco
Wedding Drive
Lord St Vincent Wood
Porter Oaks
Robin Hood Way
Welbeck Woodhouse
White Deer Park
St Cuthbert's in the Woods
White Stone Piece
Lord Harley's Wood
Lawn Wood
Lady Harriet's Plantation
Valley Clump
Shrubbery Lake
Hagg Hill
Playing Field
WELBECK COLLEGE LA
Welbeck Park
Long Valley
Long Drive Wood
Welbeck Abbey
Wingfield Wood

45
60

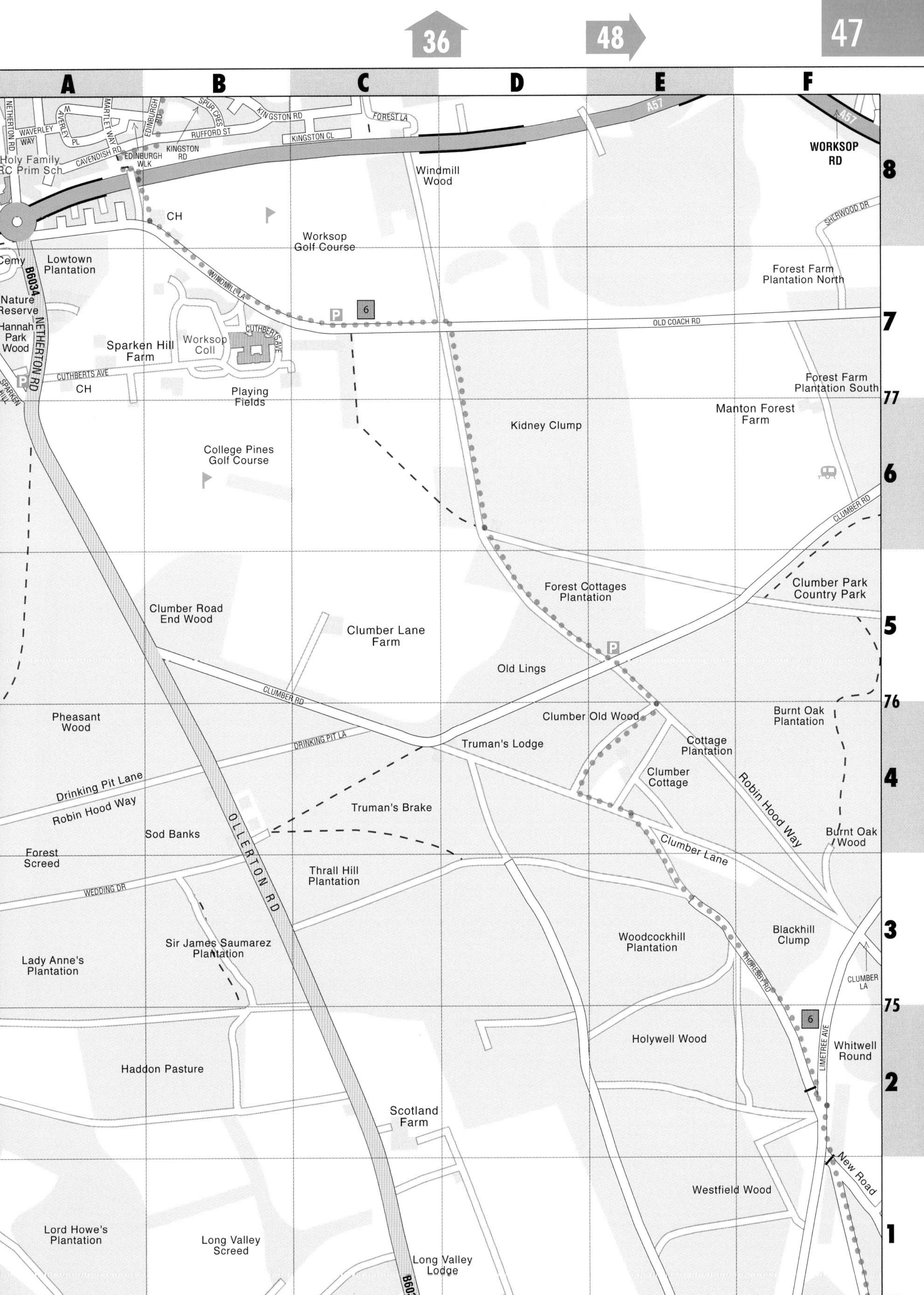

A   B   C   D   E   F

WORKSOP
RD

8

Holy Family
RC Prim Sch

Netherton Way
Waverley Way
Martley Way
Cavendish Rd
Edinburgh Rd
Edinburgh WLK
Kingston RD
Kingston RD
Spur Cres
Rufford St
Kingston CL
Forest LA

Windmill
Wood

SHERWOOD DR

A57

A57

Cemy
Lowtown
Plantation

Worksop
Golf Course

Forest Farm
Plantation North

CH

7

Nature
Reserve

Hannah
Park
Wood

Sparken Hill
Farm

Worksop
Coll

Cuthberts Ave

CH

P   6

Old Coach Rd

Forest Farm
Plantation South   77

Windmill La

Cuthberts Ave

B6034

Netherton Rd

Sparken Hill

P

CH

Playing
Fields

Kidney Clump

Manton Forest
Farm

6

College Pines
Golf Course

Clumber Rd

Clumber Road
End Wood

Clumber Lane
Farm

Forest Cottages
Plantation

Clumber Park
Country Park

5

Old Lings

Clumber Rd

Pheasant
Wood

P

Burnt Oak
Plantation   76

Drinking Pit La

Clumber Old Wood

Cottage
Plantation

Drinking Pit Lane

Truman's Lodge

Clumber
Cottage

Robin Hood Way

4

Robin Hood Way

Truman's Brake

Ollerton Rd

Forest
Screed

Sod Banks

Burnt Oak
Wood

Clumber Lane

Wedding Dr

Thrall Hill
Plantation

Woodcockhill
Plantation

Thoresby Rd

Blackhill
Clump   3

Lady Anne's
Plantation

Sir James Saumarez
Plantation

Clumber
LA   75

Limetree Ave

6

Whitwell
Round   2

Haddon Pasture

Holywell Wood

New Road

Scotland
Farm

B6034

Lord Howe's
Plantation

Long Valley
Screed

Long Valley
Lodge

Westfield Wood

1

74

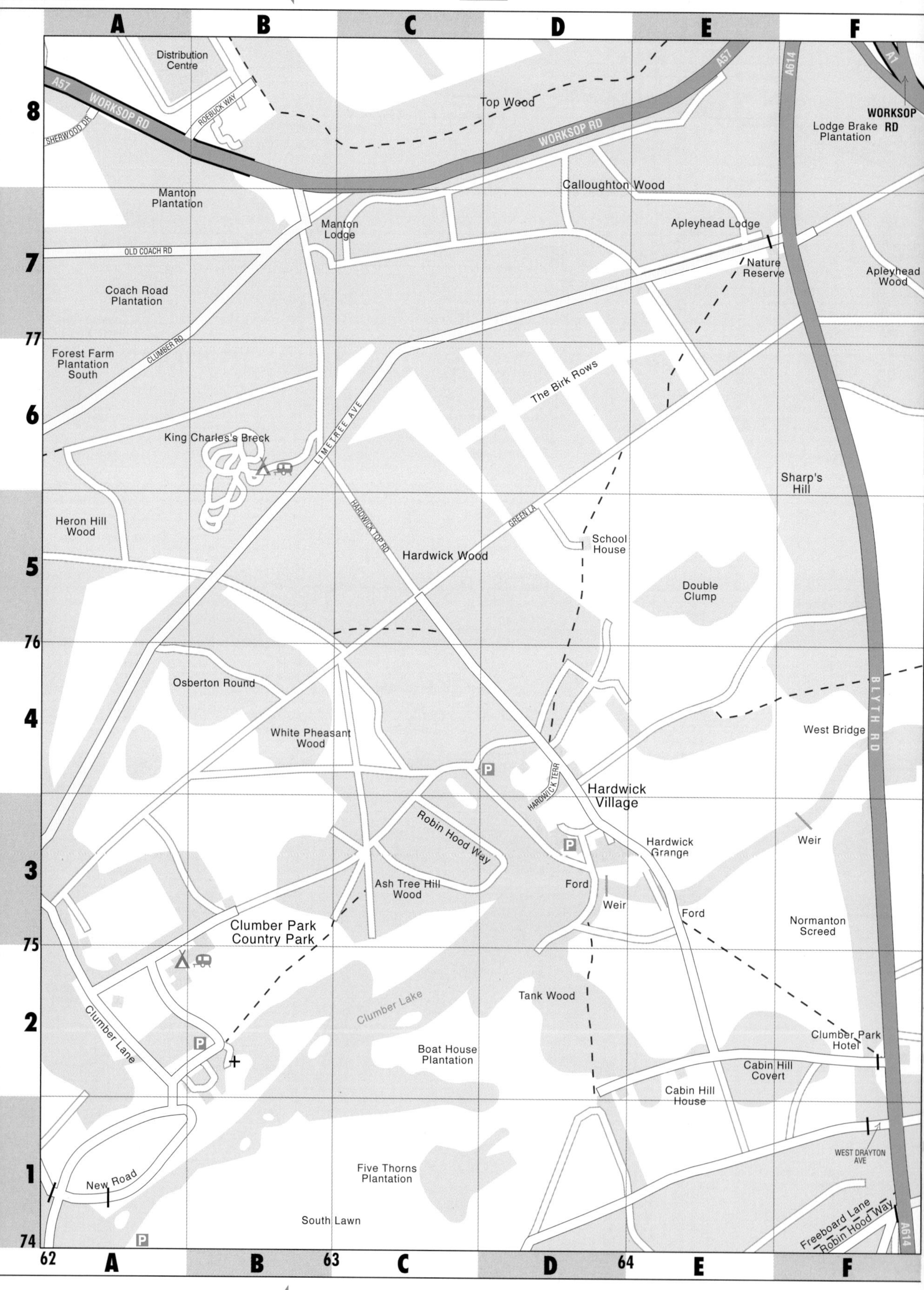

A B C D E F

8

Distribution
Centre

SHERWOOD DR

A57 WORKSOP RD

ROEBUCK WAY

Top Wood

WORKSOP RD

A57

A614

R1

WORKSOP
RD

Lodge Brake
Plantation

Manton
Plantation

Calloughton Wood

7

OLD COACH RD

Manton
Lodge

Apleyhead Lodge

Nature
Reserve

Apleyhead
Wood

Coach Road
Plantation

CLUMBER RD

77

Forest Farm
Plantation
South

The Birk Rows

6

King Charles's Breck

LIME TREE AVE

Sharp's
Hill

Heron Hill
Wood

HARDWICK TOP RD

GREEN LA

School
House

5

Hardwick Wood

Double
Clump

76

Osberton Round

BLYTH RD

4

White Pheasant
Wood

West Bridge

P

Hardwick
Village

Hardwick
Grange

Weir

3

Robin Hood Way

HARDWICK TERR

P

Ash Tree Hill
Wood

Ford

Weir

Ford

Normanton
Screed

Clumber Park
Country Park

75

Clumber Lane

Tank Wood

Clumber Park
Hotel

2

P

Clumber Lake

Boat House
Plantation

Cabin Hill
Covert

Cabin Hill
House

WEST DRAYTON
AVE

1

New Road

Five Thorns
Plantation

Freeboard Lane
Robin Hood Way

A614

74

P

South Lawn

B

D

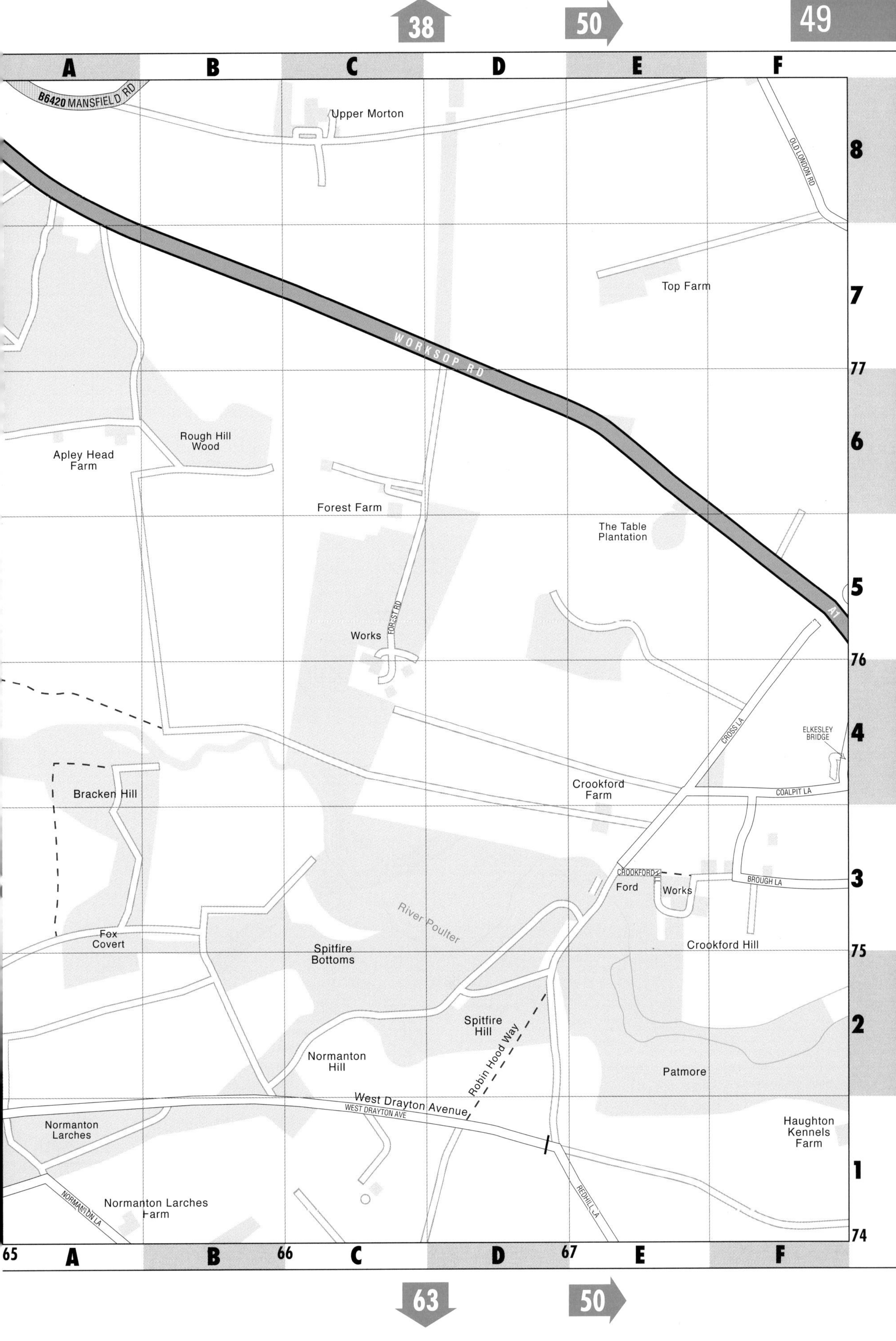

A   B   C   D   E   F

B6420 MANSFIELD RD

Upper Morton

8

Top Farm

7

WORKSOP RD

77

Rough Hill Wood

Apley Head Farm

6

Forest Farm

The Table Plantation

FOREST RD

5

A1

Works

76

CROSS LA

ELKESLEY BRIDGE

4

Bracken Hill

Crookford Farm

COALPIT LA

CROOKFORD

Ford   Works

BROUGH LA

3

River Poulter

Fox Covert

Spitfire Bottoms

Crookford Hill

75

Spitfire Hill

2

Robin Hood Way

Patmore

Normanton Hill

West Drayton Avenue
WEST DRAYTON AVE

Haughton Kennels Farm

Normanton Larches

1

REDHILL LA

NORMANTON LA

Normanton Larches Farm

74

65   A   B   66   C   D   67   E   F

49
39

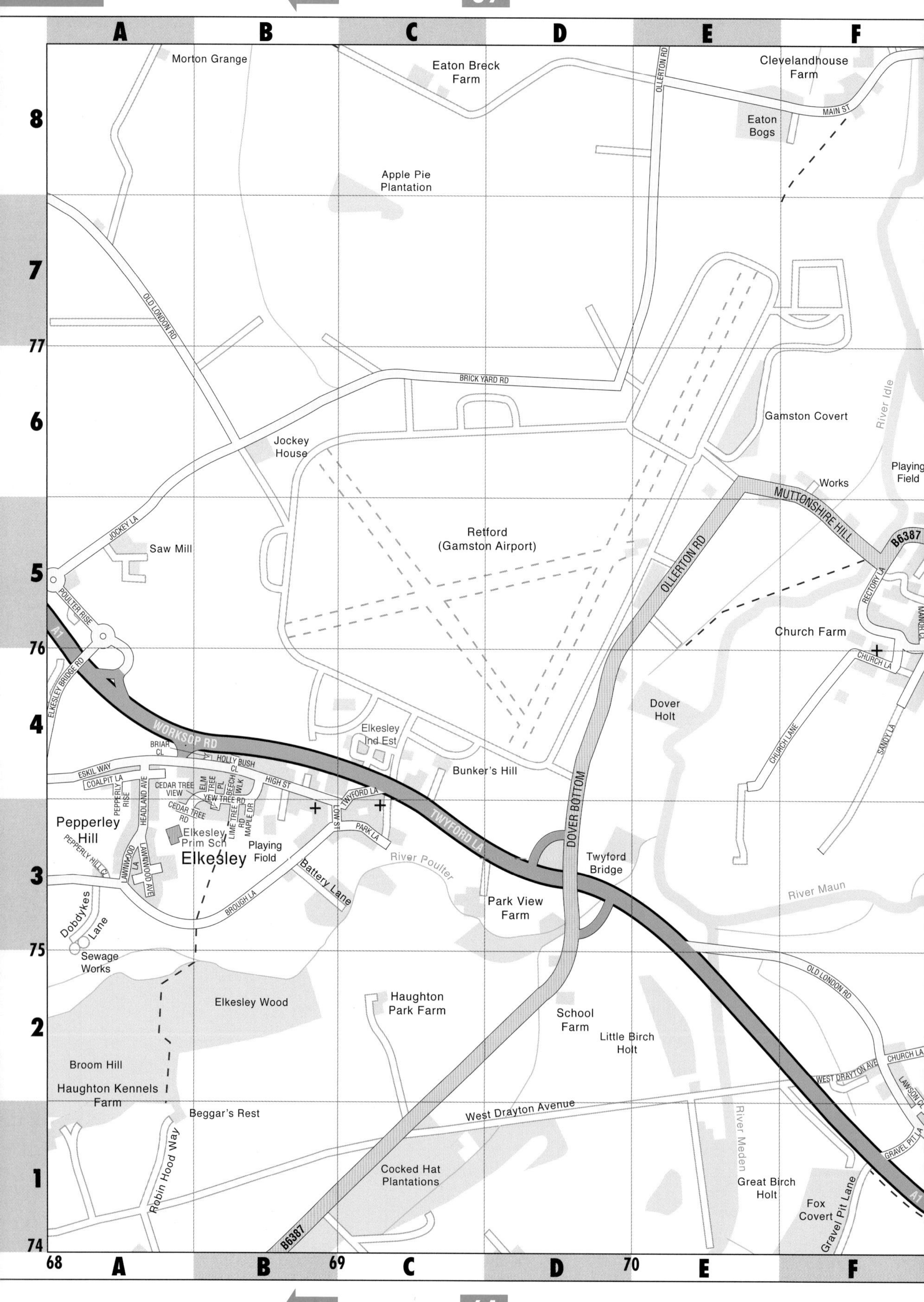
Morton Grange
Eaton Breck Farm
Clevelandhouse Farm
Eaton Bogs
MAIN ST
OLLERTON RD
Apple Pie Plantation
OLD LONDON RD
BRICK YARD RD
River Idle
Gamston Covert
Jockey House
Works
Playing Field
MUTTONSHIRE HILL
JOCKEY LA
Saw Mill
Retford (Gamston Airport)
OLLERTON RD
B6387
POULTER RISE
RECTORY LA
MANOR CL
Church Farm
A1
CHURCH LA
ELKESLEY BRIDGE RD
Dover Holt
WORKSOP RD
Elkesley Ind Est
BRIAR CL
HOLLY BUSH CL
Bunker's Hill
ESKIL WAY
COALPIT LA
HIGH ST
CHURCH LANE
SANDY LA
PEPPERLY RISE
HEADLAND AVE
CEDAR TREE VIEW
ELM TREE PL
BEECH WLK
YEW TREE RD
TWYFORD LA
CEDAR TREE RD
LIME TREE RD
MAPLE DR
LOW ST
DOVER BOTTOM
Pepperley Hill
Elkesley Prim Sch
Playing Field
PARK LA
TWYFORD LA
PEPPERLY HILL CL
LAWNWOOD LA
LAWNWOOD AVE
Elkesley
River Poulter
Twyford Bridge
Battery Lane
River Maun
Dobdykes Lane
BROUGH LA
Park View Farm
Sewage Works
OLD LONDON RD
Elkesley Wood
Haughton Park Farm
School Farm
Little Birch Holt
CHURCH LA
Broom Hill
WEST DRAYTON AVE
LAWSON CL
Haughton Kennels Farm
Beggar's Rest
West Drayton Avenue
River Meden
GRAVEL PIT LA
Robin Hood Way
Cocked Hat Plantations
Great Birch Holt
Fox Covert
Gravel Pit Lane
B6387
A1
A B C D E F
8 7 77 6 5 76 4 3 75 2 1 74
68 69 70

49
64

40
52

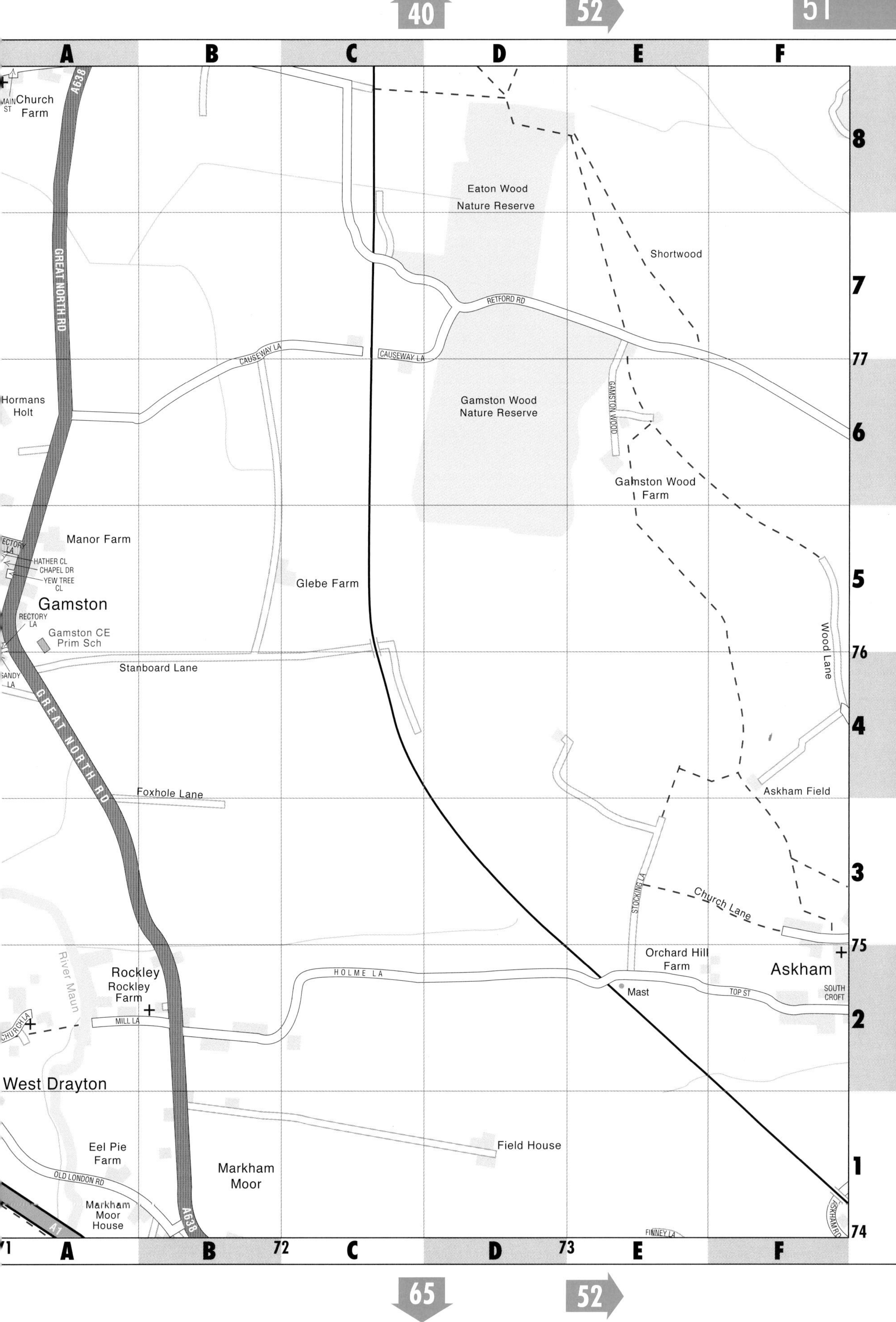
A B C D E F
8
7
77
6
5
76
4
3
75
2
1
74
71 72 73
Church Farm
MAIN ST
A638
GREAT NORTH RD
Eaton Wood Nature Reserve
Shortwood
RETFORD RD
CAUSEWAY LA
Hormans Holt
Gamston Wood Nature Reserve
GAMSTON WOOD
Gamston Wood Farm
Manor Farm
RECTORY LA
HATHER CL
CHAPEL DR
YEW TREE CL
Glebe Farm
Gamston
Gamston CE Prim Sch
Wood Lane
Stanboard Lane
SANDY LA
Foxhole Lane
Askham Field
STOCKING LA
Church Lane
Orchard Hill Farm
Askham
Rockley
Rockley Farm
River Maun
HOLME LA
Mast
TOP ST
SOUTH CROFT
CHURCH LA
MILL LA
West Drayton
Eel Pie Farm
Field House
Markham Moor
OLD LONDON RD
Markham Moor House
A1
FINNEY LA
ASKHAM RD

65
52

51
41

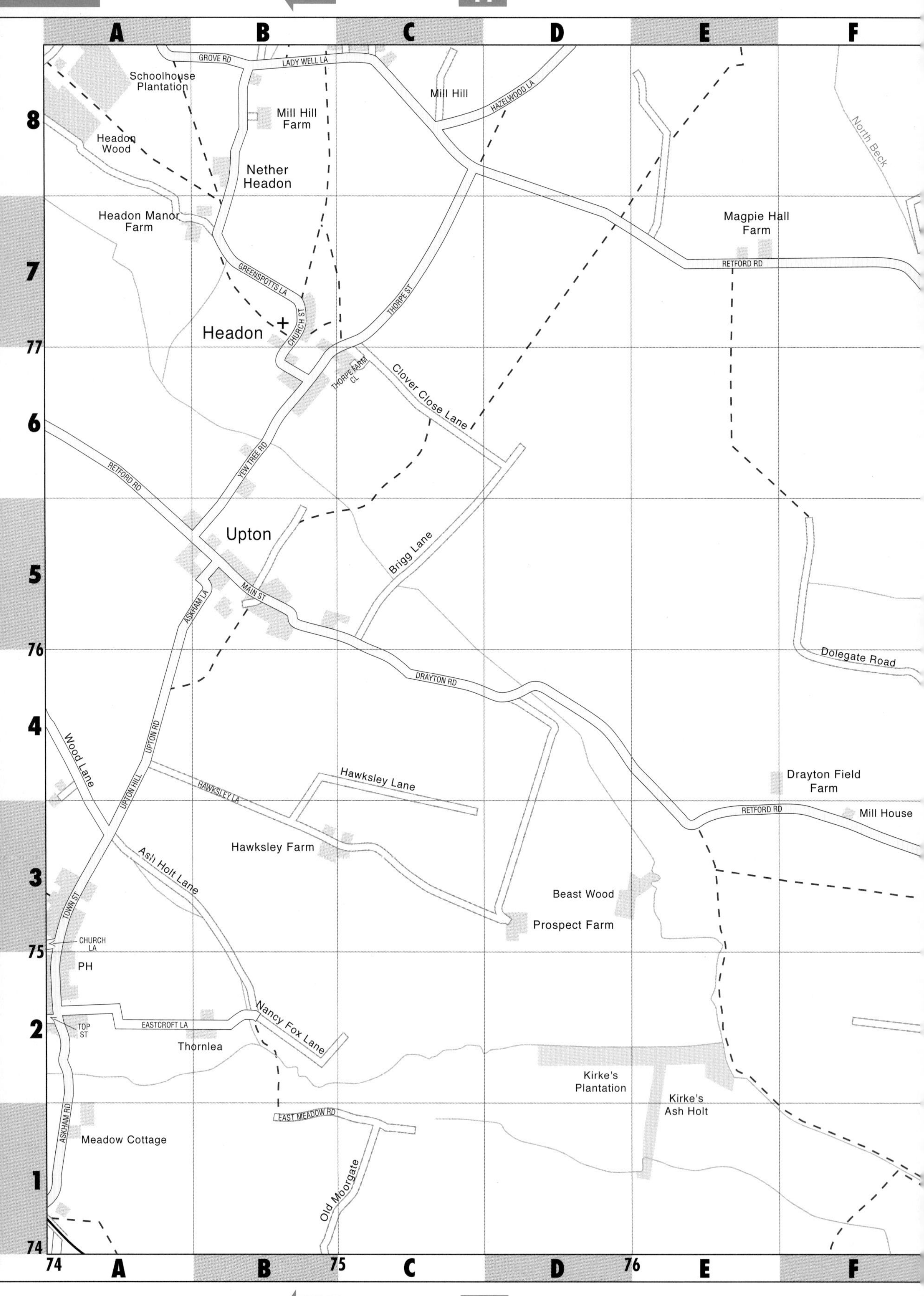
A
B
C
D
E
F
8
7
77
6
5
76
4
3
75
2
1
74
Schoolhouse Plantation
GROVE RD
LADY WELL LA
Mill Hill
HAZELWOOD LA
Mill Hill Farm
North Beck
Headon Wood
Nether Headon
Headon Manor Farm
Magpie Hall Farm
RETFORD RD
GREENSPOTTS LA
THORPE ST
CHURCH ST
Headon
THORPE FARM CL
Clover Close Lane
YEW TREE RD
RETFORD RD
Upton
Brigg Lane
MAIN ST
ASKHAM LA
Dolegate Road
DRAYTON RD
Wood Lane
UPTON RD
Hawksley Lane
HAWKSLEY LA
UPTON HILL
Drayton Field Farm
RETFORD RD
Mill House
Hawksley Farm
Ash Holt Lane
Beast Wood
Prospect Farm
TOWN ST
CHURCH LA
PH
Nancy Fox Lane
EASTCROFT LA
TOP ST
Thornlea
Kirke's Plantation
Kirke's Ash Holt
EAST MEADOW RD
ASKHAM RD
Meadow Cottage
Old Moorgate
74
A
B
75
C
D
76
E
F

51
66

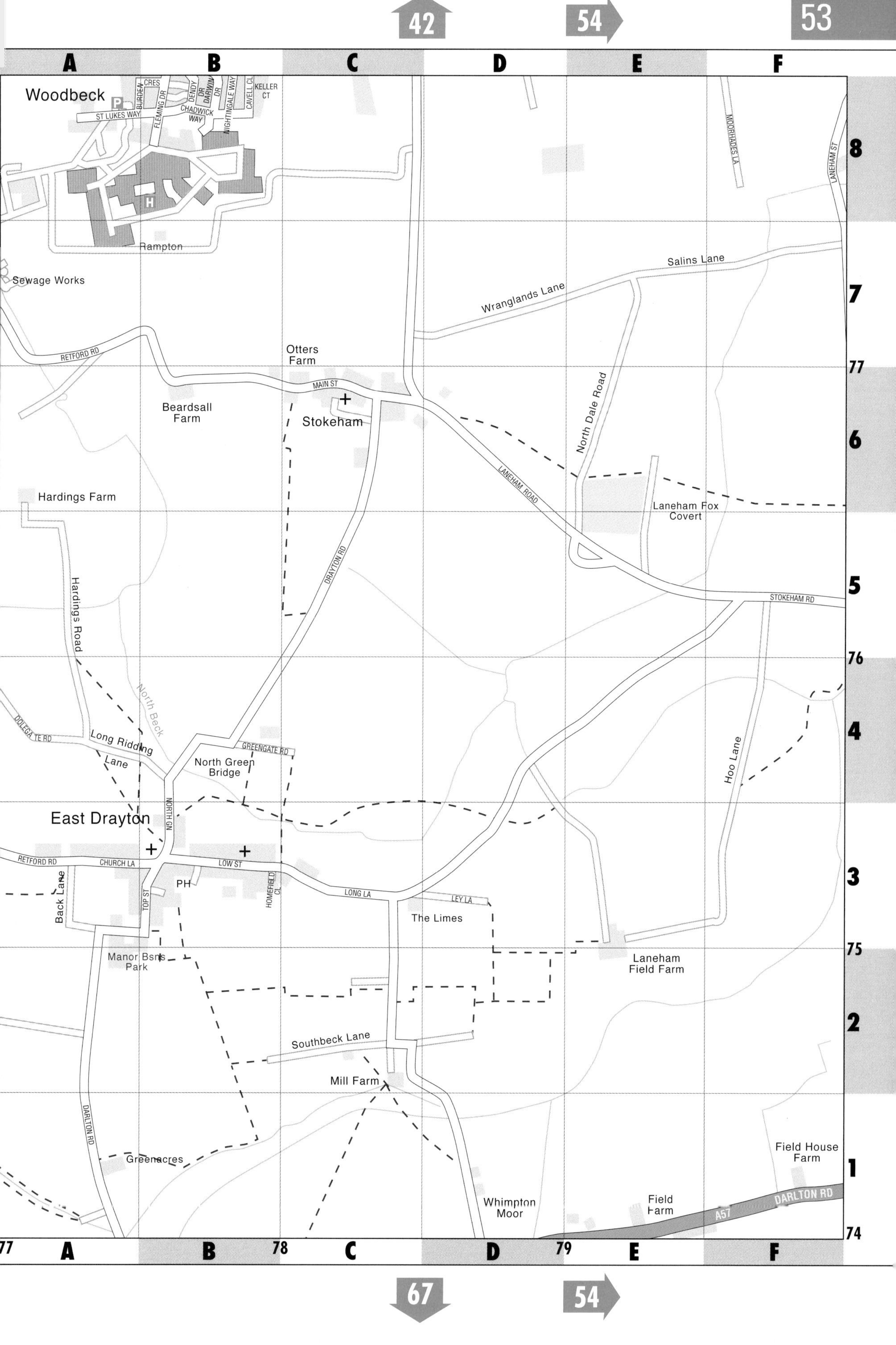

A   B   C   D   E   F

8

Woodbeck

St Lukes Way
BURDEN CRES
FLEMING DR
DENBY DR
DARWIN DR
CHADWICK WAY
NIGHTINGALE WAY
CAVELL CL
KELLER CT

H

Rampton

Sewage Works

7

Salins Lane

Wranglands Lane

77

Retford Rd

Otters Farm

Main St

Beardsall Farm

Stokeham

North Dale Road

6

Hardings Farm

Laneham Fox Covert

Drayton Rd

Laneham Road

5

Stokeham Rd

Hardings Road

North Beck

76

Dolega Te Rd

Long Ridding Lane

Greengate Rd

North Gn

North Green Bridge

Hoo Lane

4

East Drayton

Retford Rd
Church La
Low St
Long La
Ley La
The Limes

75

Back Lane

Top St

PH

Homefield Cl

Laneham Field Farm

Manor Bsns Park

3

Southbeck Lane

2

Mill Farm

Darlton Rd

Greenacres

Field House Farm

1

Whimpton Moor

Field Farm

A57   Darlton Rd

74

A   B   C   D   E   F

8

Sewage Works

LANEHAM ST

GOLDENHOLME LA

HELENSHIP LA

SHORTLEYS RD

MARSH LANE

Trentfield Farm

7

Broading Farm

Maltkilns

FIR VIEW

CLAYHOUGH LANE

Rushmoor Farm

Manor House

RAMPTON RD

BROADINGS LA

77

Holly Folly Farm

Moor Lane

Ferry Boat Inn (PH)

Laughterton Marsh

River Trent

6

Laneham

Church Laneham

MANOR FARM DR

Manor Farm

5

PH

MAIN ST

BUTCHERS MWS

Sewage Works

Ring O'Bells

STOKEHAM RD

DUNHAM RD

76

Mill House

Trent Valley Way

MARSH LANE

4

Chequers Lane

Marsh Lane

Dunham Rack

3

75

DUNHAM RD

Manor Farm

CHEQUERS LA

Dunham on Trent

2

COCKETTS HILL

Hall

White Swan (PH)

ST OSWALDS

Playing Field

Bridge Inn (PH)

CHURCH WLK

LOW ST

UPPER ROW

ASH

LINCON RD

Dunham Bridge Toll

Pumping Sta

CARTWRIGHT CL

Flears Farm

THE HAWTHORNES

THE GREEN

TALL GABLES

LEACH CL

THORNE LA

The Green

Green Lane

DUNHAM RD

TRENT LA

LANEHAM RD

DARLTON RD

Dunham-on-Trent CE Prim Sch

1

A57

MAIN ST

74

ROBERTS CL

80   **A**   81   **B**   **C**   82   **D**   **E**   **F**

44
56

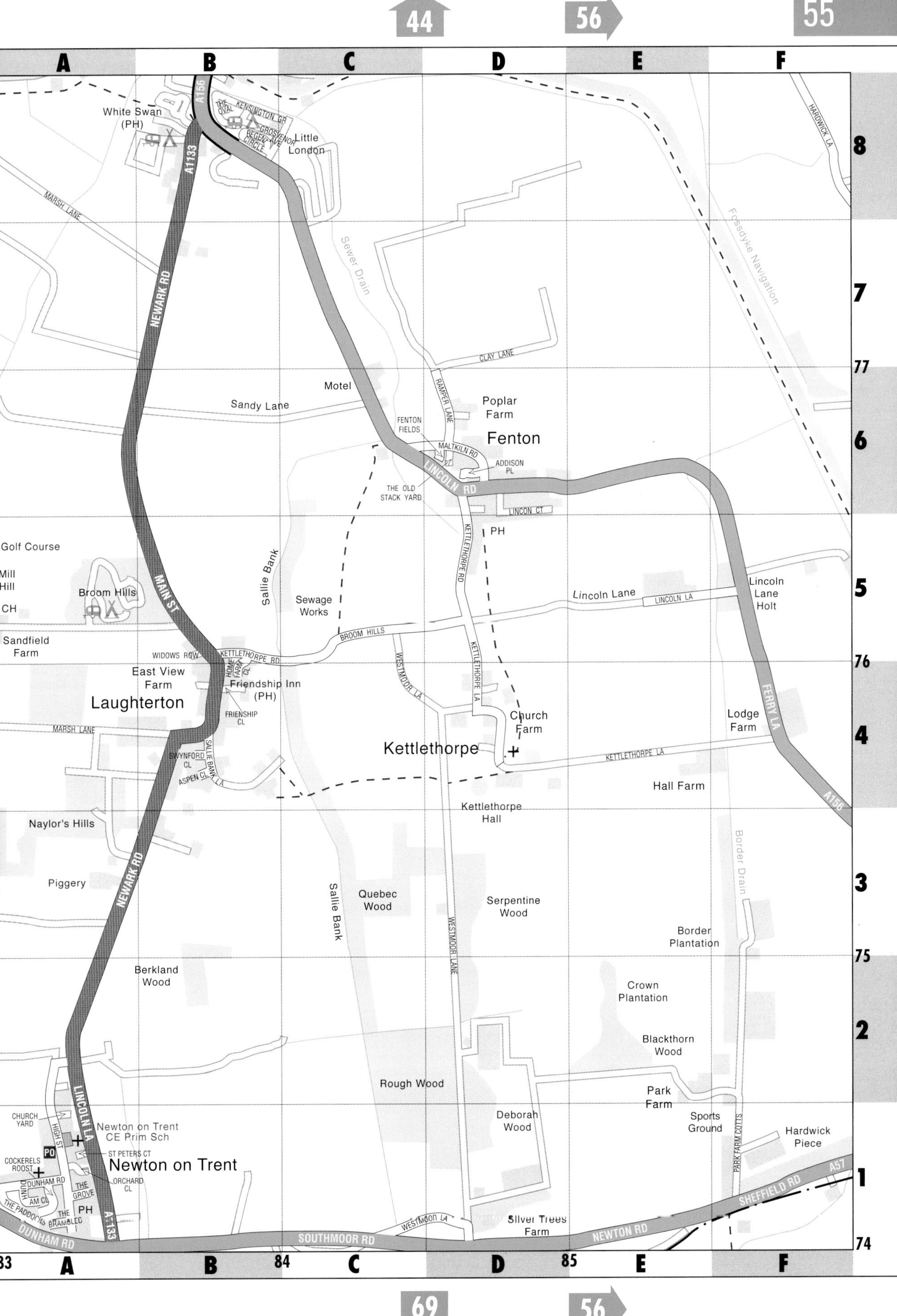
A
B
C
D
E
F
White Swan
(PH)
A156
THE OVAL
KENSINGTON GR
GROSVENOR
REGENT AVE
CIRCLE
Little
London
A1133
HARDWICK LA
8
MARSH LANE
Sewer Drain
Fossdyke Navigation
NEWARK RD
7
CLAY LANE
77
Motel
Sandy Lane
RAMPER LANE
Poplar
Farm
FENTON
FIELDS
Fenton
MALTKILN RD
ADDISON
PL
6
LINCOLN RD
THE OLD
STACK YARD
LINCON CT
PH
KETTLETHORPE RD
Golf Course
Mill
Hill
Broom Hills
Sallie Bank
Sewage
Works
Lincoln Lane
LINCOLN LA
Lincoln
Lane
Holt
5
CH
MAIN ST
BROOM HILLS
Sandfield
Farm
WIDOWS ROW
KETTLETHORPE RD
HOME FARM CL
76
East View
Farm
Friendship Inn
(PH)
WESTMOOR LA
KETTLETHORPE LA
Laughterton
FRIENSHIP
CL
Church
Farm
Lodge
Farm
FERRY LA
MARSH LANE
SWYNFORD
CL
SALLIE BANK LA
Kettlethorpe
4
ASPEN CL
KETTLETHORPE LA
Hall Farm
A156
Naylor's Hills
Kettlethorpe
Hall
Border Drain
NEWARK RD
Piggery
Sallie Bank
Quebec
Wood
Serpentine
Wood
3
WESTMOOR LANE
Border
Plantation
75
Berkland
Wood
Crown
Plantation
2
Blackthorn
Wood
LINCOLN LA
Rough Wood
Park
Farm
CHURCH
YARD
Newton on Trent
CE Prim Sch
Deborah
Wood
Sports
Ground
PARK FARM COTTS
Hardwick
Piece
HIGH ST
PO
ST PETERS CT
COCKERELS
ROOST
Newton on Trent
A57
1
DUNHAM RD
ORCHARD
CL
SHEFFIELD RD
THE
GROVE
AM CL
PH
THE PADDOCKS
THE
BRAMBLES
A1133
WESTMOOR LA
Silver Trees
Farm
DUNHAM RD
SOUTHMOOR RD
NEWTON RD
74
83
A
B
84
C
D
85
E
F

69
56

55

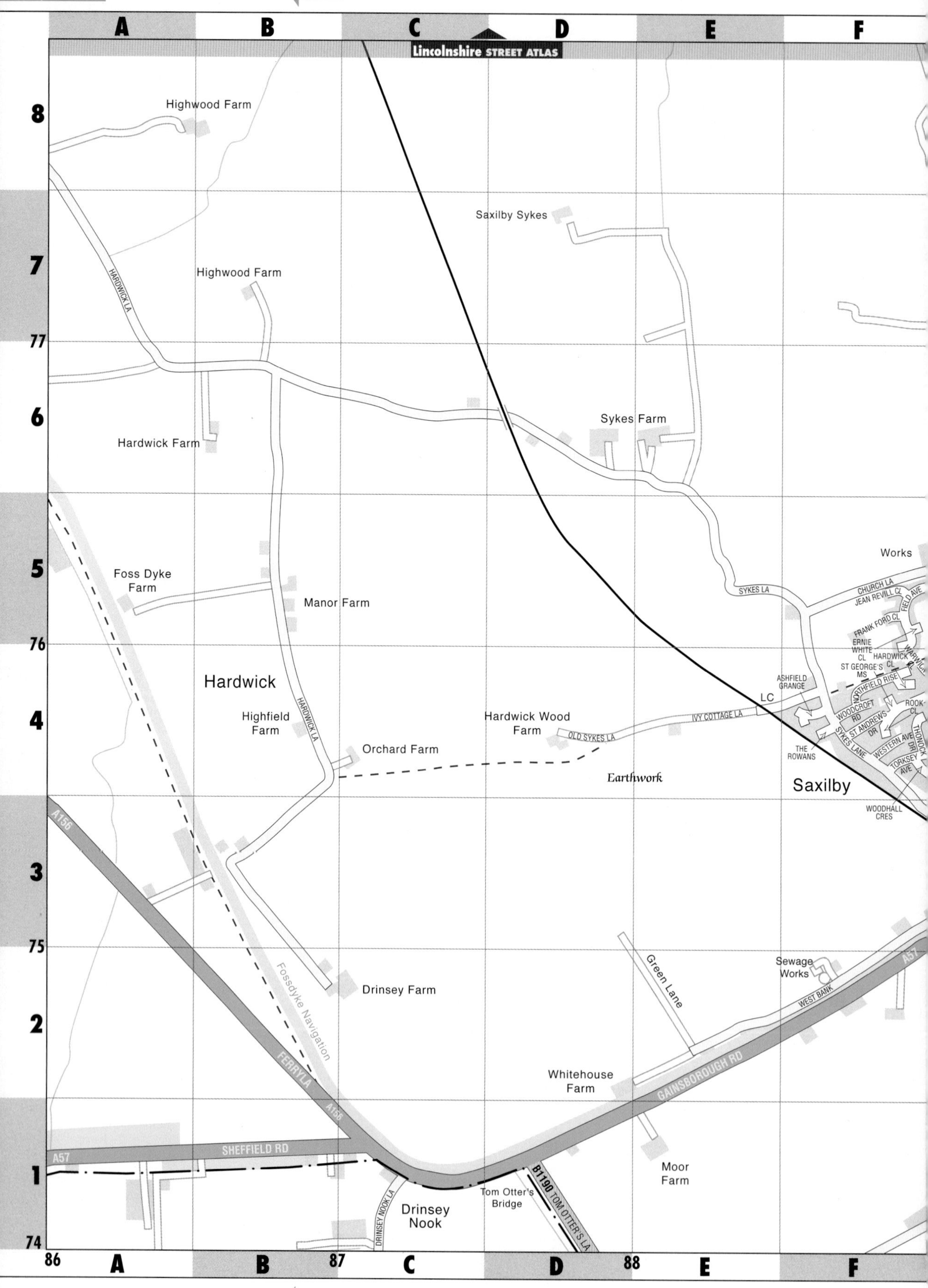

Lincolnshire STREET ATLAS

Highwood Farm

Saxilby Sykes

Highwood Farm

HARDWICK LA

Sykes Farm

Hardwick Farm

Foss Dyke Farm

Manor Farm

Works

SYKES LA

CHURCH LA
JEAN REVILL CL
FIELD AVE
FRANK FORD CL
ERNIE WHITE CL
HARDWICK CL
ST GEORGE'S MS
MYTHFIELD RISE
WARWICK

Hardwick

HARDWICK LA

ASHFIELD GRANGE

LC

WOODCROFT RD
ST ANDREWS
SYKES LANE
ROOK CL
WESTERN AVE
THORNDON DR

Highfield Farm

Orchard Farm

Hardwick Wood Farm

OLD SYKES LA

IVY COTTAGE LA

THE ROWANS
TORKSEY AVE

Earthwork

Saxilby

WOODHALL CRES

A156

Fossdyke Navigation

75

Drinsey Farm

Green Lane

Sewage Works

WEST BANK

A57

FERRY LA

A156

Whitehouse Farm

GAINSBOROUGH RD

SHEFFIELD RD

A57

DRINSEY NOOK LA

Drinsey Nook

Tom Otter's Bridge

B1190 TOM OTTER'S LA

Moor Farm

55   70

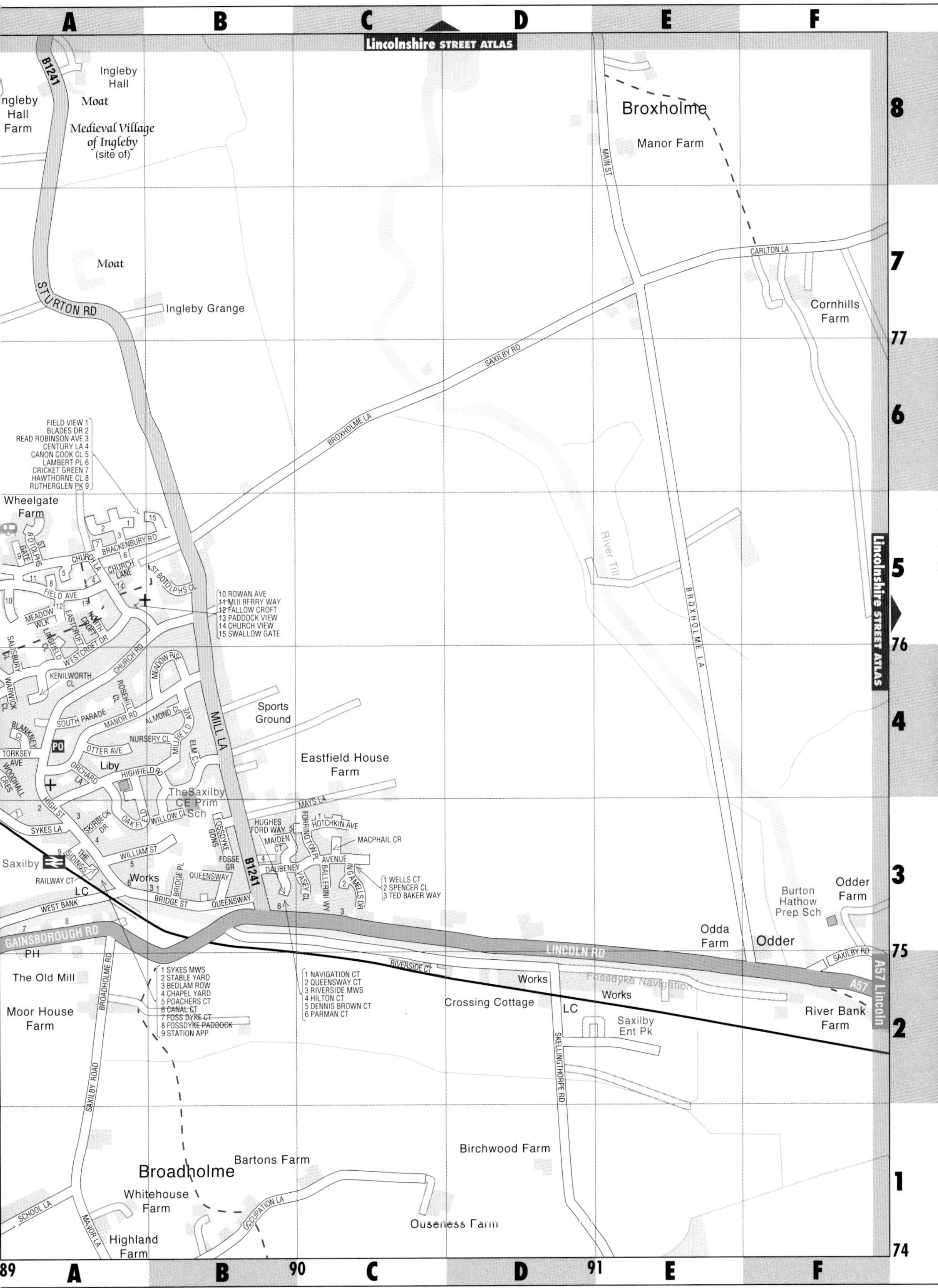

8

Broxholme

Ingleby Hall

Moat

Medieval Village of Ingleby (site of)

Ingleby Hall Farm

Manor Farm

7

Moat

STURTON RD

Ingleby Grange

CARLTON LA

Cornhills Farm

77

SAXILBY RD

6

BROXHOLME LA

FIELD VIEW 1
BLADES DR 2
READ ROBINSON AVE 3
CENTURY LA 4
CANON COOK CL 5
LAMBERT PL 6
CRICKET GREEN 7
HAWTHORNE CL 8
RUTHERGLEN PK 9

River Till

Wheelgate Farm

BRACKENBURY RD

CHURCH LANE
CHURCH CL
ST BOTOLPHS CL

5

BROXHOLME LA

FIELD AVE

10 ROWAN AVE
11 MILL RERRY WAY
12 FALLOW CROFT
13 PADDOCK VIEW
14 CHURCH VIEW
15 SWALLOW GATE

MEADOW WLK
EASTCROFT
NORTH CROFT
WESTCROFT DR
CHURCH RD
SALISBURY CL
WARWICK CL
KENILWORTH CL
MEADOW RD
MANOR RD
NURSERY CL
ALMOND CL
ELM CL

76

4

SOUTH PARADE

Sports Ground

BLANKNEY CL
TORKSEY AVE
WOODHALL CRES

PO
Liby

OTTER AVE
ORCHARD
HIGHFIELD CL
HIGH ST
SKIRBECK DR
OAK FLD
WILLOW CL

Eastfield House Farm

MILL LA

FOSSDYKE GDNS

3

Saxilby

The Saxilby CE Prim Sch

MAYS LA

HUGHES FORD WAY
MAIDEN CT
FOSSDYKE GDNS
FOSSE GR
FOSSE PL
WILLIAM ST
DAUBENEY

FORRINGTON CL
BALLERINI WY
MACPHAIL CR
HOTCHKIN AVE
AVENUE
NELSDR

1 WELLS CT
2 SPENCER CL
3 TED BAKER WAY

Burton Hathow Prep Sch

Odder Farm

RAILWAY CT
WEST BANK
B1241

Works

QUEENSWAY
BRIDGE ST
QUEENSWAY

Odda Farm

Odder

3

GAINSBOROUGH RD

PH

The Old Mill

1 SYKES MWS
2 STABLE YARD
3 BEDLAM ROW
4 CHAPEL YARD
5 POACHERS CT
6 CANAL CT
7 FOSS DYKE CT
8 FOSSDYKE PADDOCK
9 STATION APP

RIVERSIDE CT

1 NAVIGATION CT
2 QUEENSWAY CT
3 RIVERSIDE MWS
4 HILTON CT
5 DENNIS BROWN CT
6 PARMAN CT

Works

Crossing Cottage

LINCOLN RD

Fossdyke Navigation

Works

LC

SAXILBY RD

A57 Lincoln

75

Moor House Farm

BROADHOLME RD

SKELLINGTHORPE RD

Saxilby Ent Pk

River Bank Farm

2

SAXILBY ROAD

Birchwood Farm

Broadholme

Bartons Farm

1

SCHOOL LA

MANOR LA

Whitehouse Farm

OCCUPATION LA

Ouseness Farm

Highland Farm

74

89   A   B   90   C   D   91   E   F

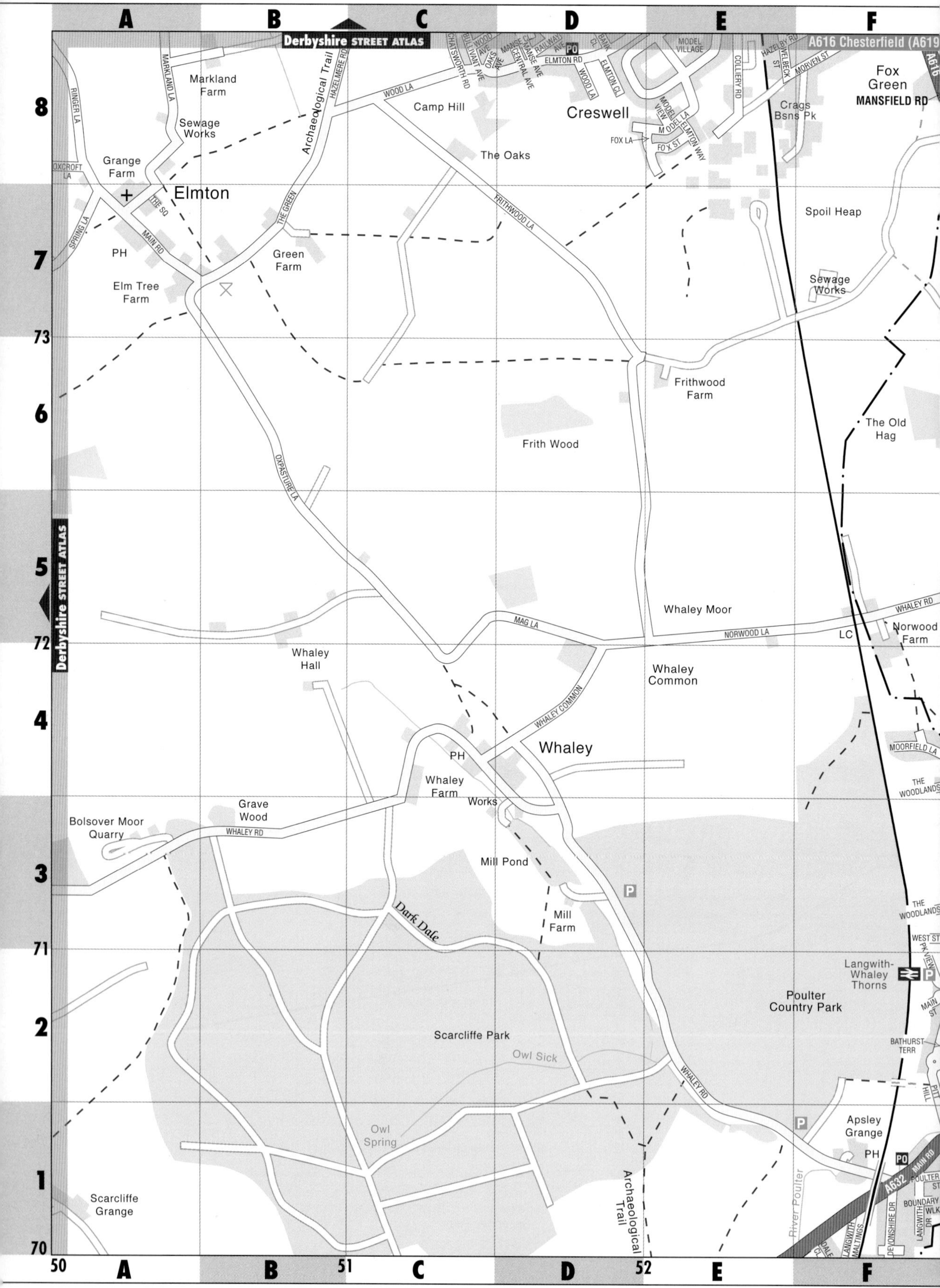

A B C D E F

58

8

7

73

6

5

72

4

3

71

2

1

70

50 A B 51 C D 52 E F

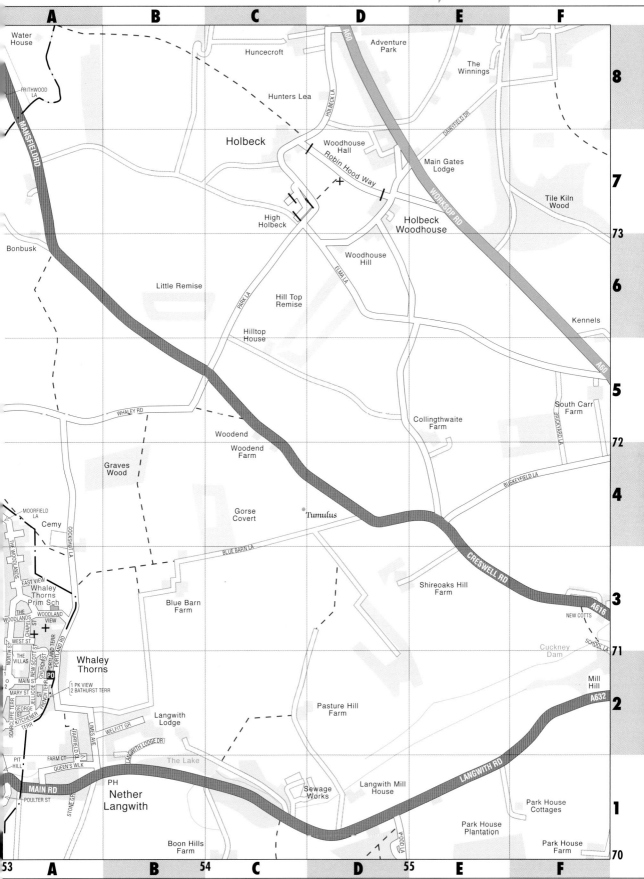
45
60

A B C D E F

Water House
FRITHWOOD LA
Huncecroft
A60
Adventure Park
The Winnings
8
Hunters Lea
HOLBECK LA
MANSFIELD RD
DARYFIELD DR
Holbeck
Woodhouse Hall
Main Gates Lodge
Robin Hood Way
7
Tile Kiln Wood
WORKSOP RD
High Holbeck
Holbeck Woodhouse
73
Bonbusk
Woodhouse Hill
ELMA LA
6
Little Remise
PARK LA
Hill Top Remise
Kennels
Hilltop House
A60
5
WHALEY RD
South Carr Farm
Collingthwaite Farm
BRICKYARD LA
Woodend
72
Woodend Farm
Graves Wood
BUSKEYFIELD LA
4
MOORFIELD LA
Gorse Covert
Tumulus
Cemy
COCKSHUT LA
THE WOODLANDS
BLUE BARN LA
CRESWELL RD
EAST VIEW
Whaley Thorns Prim Sch
Shireoaks Hill Farm
3
Blue Barn Farm
A616
THE WOODLANDS
WOODLAND VIEW
NEW COTTS
CHAPEL ST
WEST ST
PORTLAND TERR
PORTLAND RD
SCHOOL LA
71
NORTH ST
THE VILLAS
NEW SCOTT ST
CHURCH ST
Whaley Thorns
Cuckney Dam
PO
MAIN ST
1 PK VIEW
2 BATHURST TERR
Mill Hill
MARY ST
JELLICOE ST
FRENCH TERR
Pasture Hill Farm
A632
2
SCARCLIFFE TERR
GEORGE ST
KITCHENER TERR
Langwith Lodge
WELFITT GR
LIMES AVE
FAIRFIELD CL
LANGWITH LODGE DR
LANGWITH RD
FARM CT
The Lake
PIT HILL
QUEEN'S WLK
PH
MAIN RD
Nether Langwith
Sewage Works
Langwith Mill House
Park House Cottages
POULTER ST
STONE GR
1
Park House Plantation
POOL LA
Boon Hills Farm
Park House Farm
70

53 A B 54 C D 55 E F

73
60

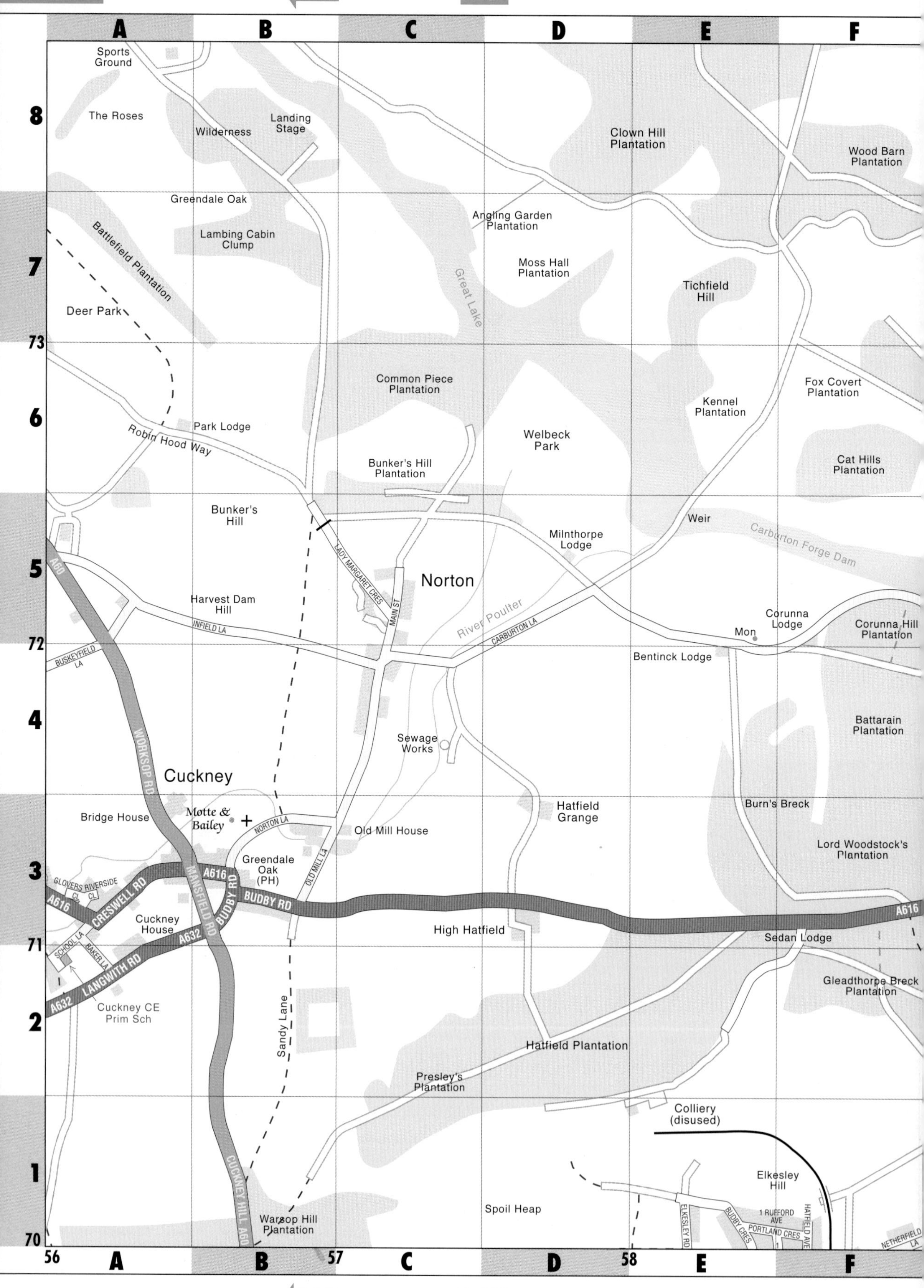

A   B   C   D   E   F

8

Sports Ground
The Roses
Wilderness
Landing Stage
Clown Hill Plantation
Wood Barn Plantation

Greendale Oak
Lambing Cabin Clump
Angling Garden Plantation
Moss Hall Plantation
Tichfield Hill

7

Battlefield Plantation
Deer Park
Great Lake
Kennel Plantation
Fox Covert Plantation

73

Robin Hood Way
Park Lodge
Common Piece Plantation
Welbeck Park
Cat Hills Plantation

6

Bunker's Hill Plantation
Milnthorpe Lodge
Weir
Carburton Forge Dam

Bunker's Hill
Norton
Corunna Lodge
Corunna Hill Plantation

5

A60
Harvest Dam Hill
INFIELD LA
LADY MARGARET CRES
MAIN ST
River Poulter
CARBURTON LA
Mon

72

BUSKEYFIELD LA
Bentinck Lodge
Battarain Plantation

4

WORKSOP RD
Sewage Works
Hatfield Grange
Burn's Breck

Cuckney

Bridge House
Motte & Bailey
Old Mill House
Lord Woodstock's Plantation

3

GLOVERS RIVERSIDE CL
CRESWELL RD
A616
MANSFIELD RD
BUDBY RD
Greendale Oak (PH)
NORTON LA
OLD MILL LA
BUDBY RD
High Hatfield
Sedan Lodge
A616

A616

71

SCHOOL LA
BAKER LA
A632
Cuckney House
Gleadthorpe Breck Plantation

2

A632
LANGWITH RD
Cuckney CE Prim Sch
Sandy Lane
Hatfield Plantation

Presley's Plantation

Colliery (disused)

1

CUCKNEY HILL A60
Elkesley Hill
1 RUFFORD AVE
PORTLAND CRES
ELKESLEY RD
BUDBY CRES
HATFIELD AVE

Warsop Hill Plantation
Spoil Heap
NETHERFIELD RD

70

47
62

A B C D E F

8
7
73
6
5
72
4
3
71
2
1
70

Long Valley
Rough Breck
Piper Lane
Lodges
B6034
Nursery
Wood
Carburton
Hills
LIMETREE AVE
Clumber Park
Country Park
Clumber Lake
Carburton Bridge
PIPER LA
Manor Farm
Carburton
Pitiful Hill
Plantation
Lake View
Cottages
LAKE VIEW
River Poulter
LIMETREE AVE
OLLERTON RD
Carburton Border
Fasque Plantation
Fasque
Screed
Nightingale
Plantation
Carburton Dam
Thompson's Covert
OLLERTON RD
Weir
Works
Gibraltar
Lodge
Gravelhole Breck
Corunna Hill
Plantation
Duncanwood Plantation
Gibraltar
Plantation
Sadler's Breck
Duncanwood
Lodge
Duncan
Wood
Hazel Gap
Wood
Robin Hood Way
Hazel
Gap
Kitchener
Plantation
Hazel Gap
Farm
Kingstand Lodge
A616
BUDBY RD
CUCKNEY RD
Budby North Forest
Gleadthorpe Breck
Plantation
Robin Hood Way
Budby Drive
Fanny's
Grove
B6034
NETHERFIELD LA
NORTH FARM LA
Gleadthorpe Screed
Gleadthorpe
Plantation
NETHERFIELD LA WEST
River Meden
North
Farm
WORKSOP RD
Works
Budby Carr
Hanger Hill Drive
Meadow
Bank
Gleadthorpe
Grange
Budby
A616

59 A B 60 C D 61 E F

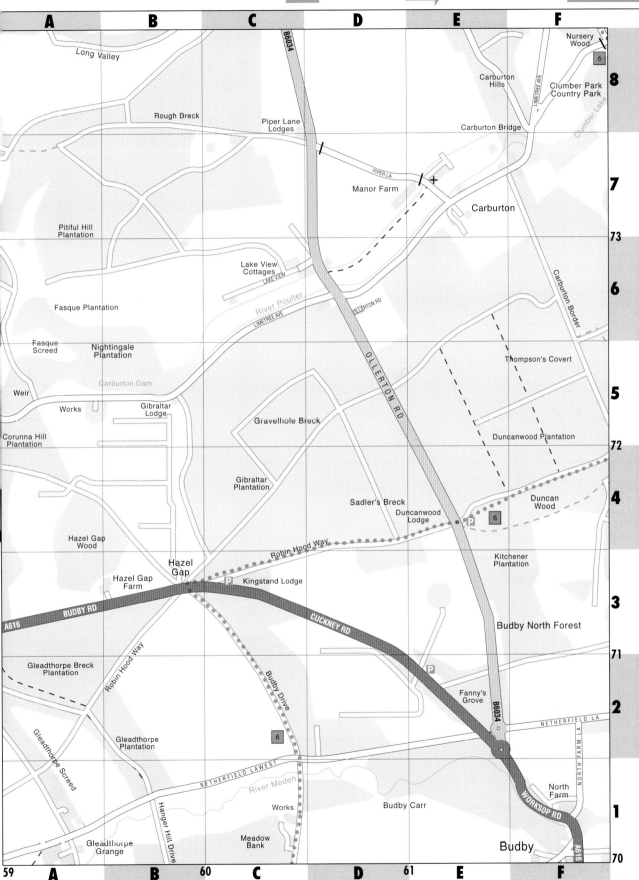

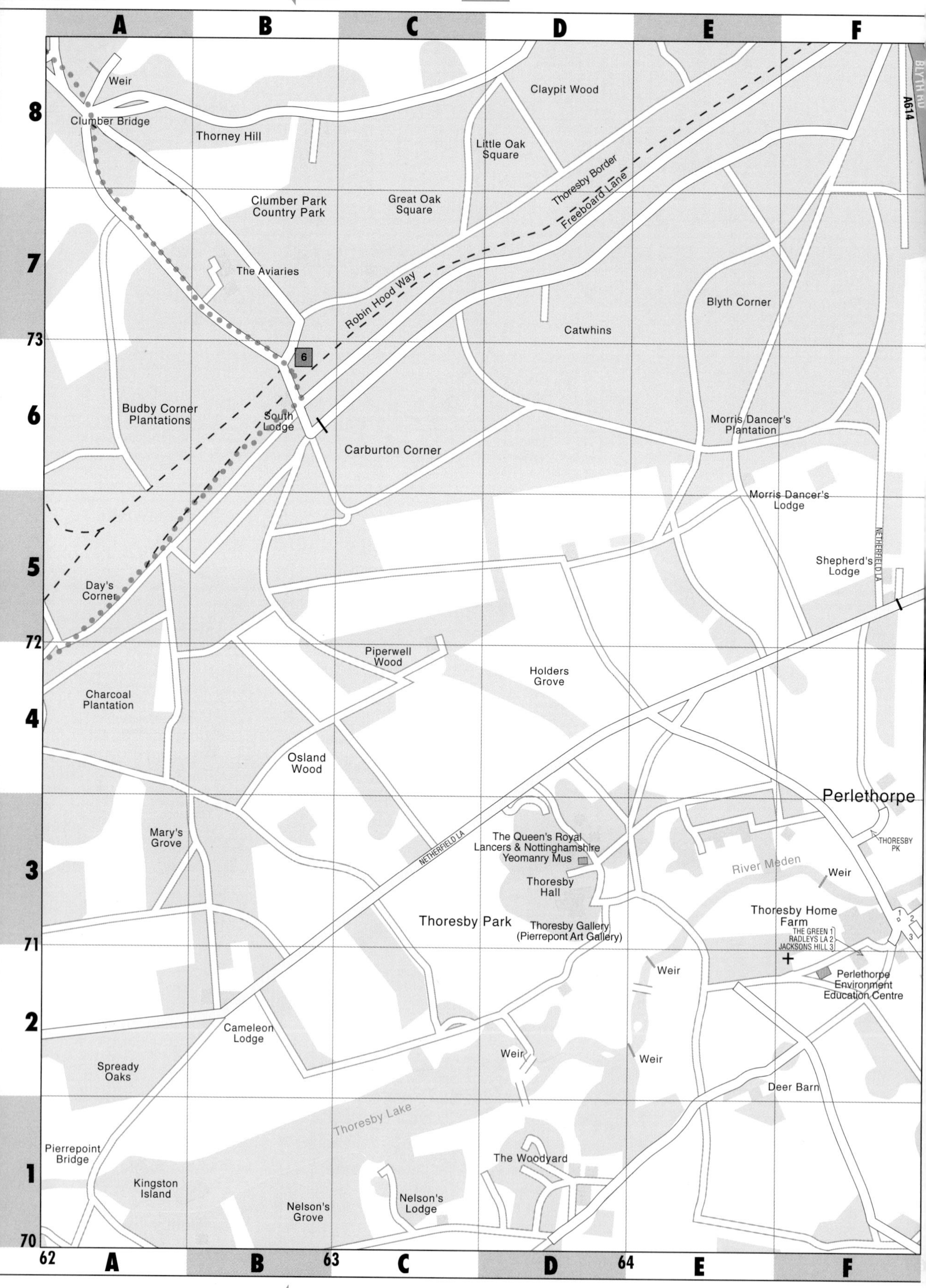

Weir

Clumber Bridge

Thorney Hill

Claypit Wood

Little Oak Square

Clumber Park Country Park

Great Oak Square

Thoresby Border

Freeboard Lane

The Aviaries

Robin Hood Way

Blyth Corner

Catwhins

6

Budby Corner Plantations

South Lodge

Carburton Corner

Morris Dancer's Plantation

Morris Dancer's Lodge

Day's Corner

Shepherd's Lodge

NETHERFIELD LA

Piperwell Wood

Holders Grove

Charcoal Plantation

Osland Wood

Perlethorpe

Mary's Grove

THORESBY PK

NETHERFIELD LA

The Queen's Royal Lancers & Nottinghamshire Yeomanry Mus

River Meden

Weir

Thoresby Hall

Thoresby Home Farm

Thoresby Park

Thoresby Gallery (Pierrepont Art Gallery)

THE GREEN 1
RADLEYS LA 2
JACKSONS HILL 3

Weir

Perlethorpe Environment Education Centre

Cameleon Lodge

Weir

Weir

Spready Oaks

Deer Barn

Thoresby Lake

Pierrepoint Bridge

Kingston Island

The Woodyard

Nelson's Grove

Nelson's Lodge

BLYTH RD   A614

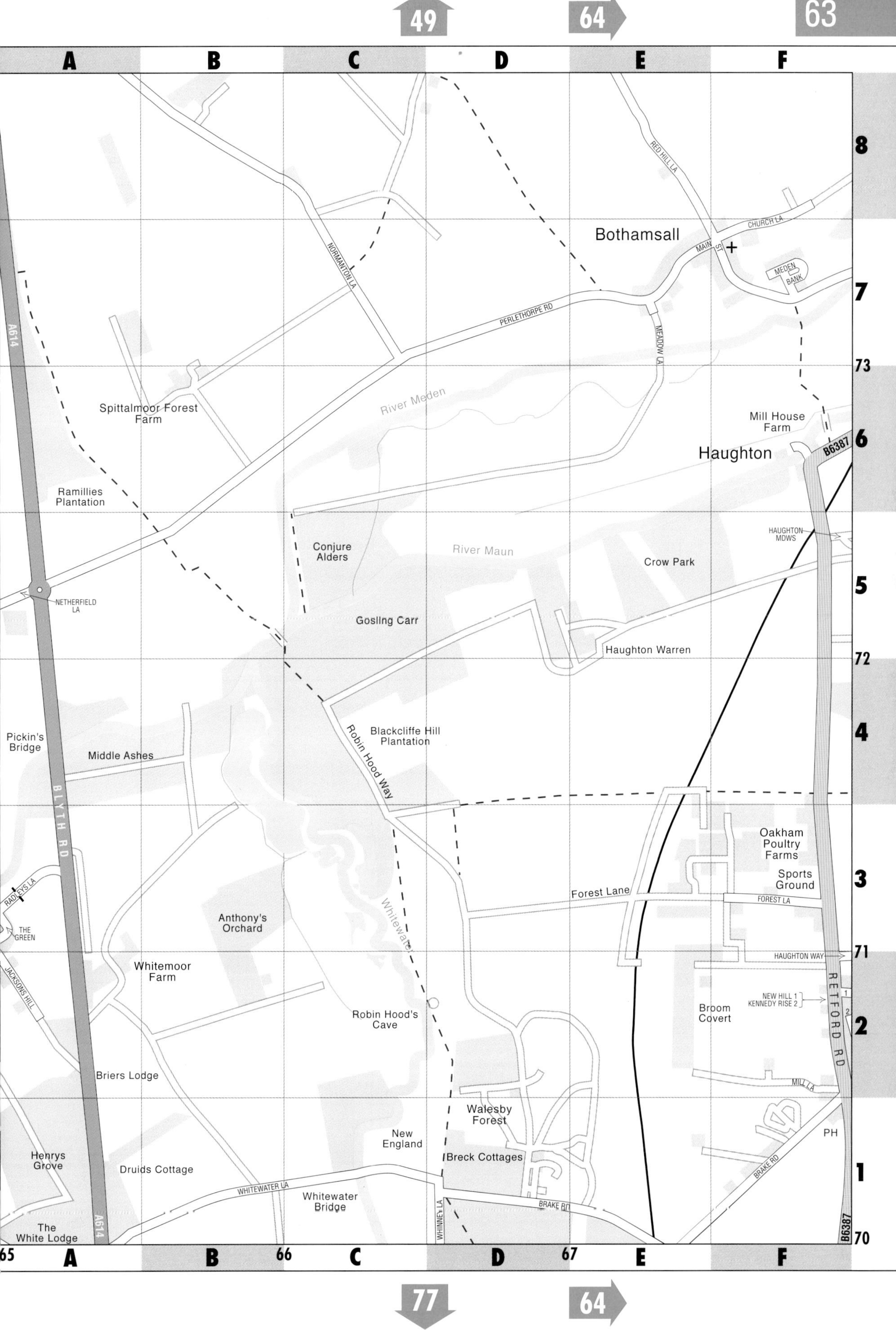
49
64
A
B
C
D
E
F
8
7
73
6
5
72
4
3
71
2
1
70
65
66
67
77
64
RED HILL LA
CHURCH LA
Bothamsall
MAIN ST
MEDEN BANK
NORMANTON LA
PERLETHORPE RD
MEADOW LA
A614
Spittalmoor Forest Farm
River Meden
Mill House Farm
Haughton
B6387
Ramillies Plantation
Conjure Alders
River Maun
HAUGHTON MDWS
Crow Park
NETHERFIELD LA
Gosling Carr
Haughton Warren
Pickin's Bridge
Middle Ashes
Blackcliffe Hill Plantation
Robin Hood Way
BLYTH RD
Oakham Poultry Farms
Sports Ground
RADLEYS LA
Forest Lane
FOREST LA
THE GREEN
Anthony's Orchard
Whitewater
HAUGHTON WAY
JACKSONS HILL
Whitemoor Farm
RETFORD RD
NEW HILL 1
KENNEDY RISE 2
Broom Covert
Robin Hood's Cave
Briers Lodge
MILL LA
Walesby Forest
PH
New England
Henrys Grove
Druids Cottage
Breck Cottages
BRAKE RD
WHITEWATER LA
Whitewater Bridge
WHINNEY LA
The White Lodge

A   B   C   D   E   F

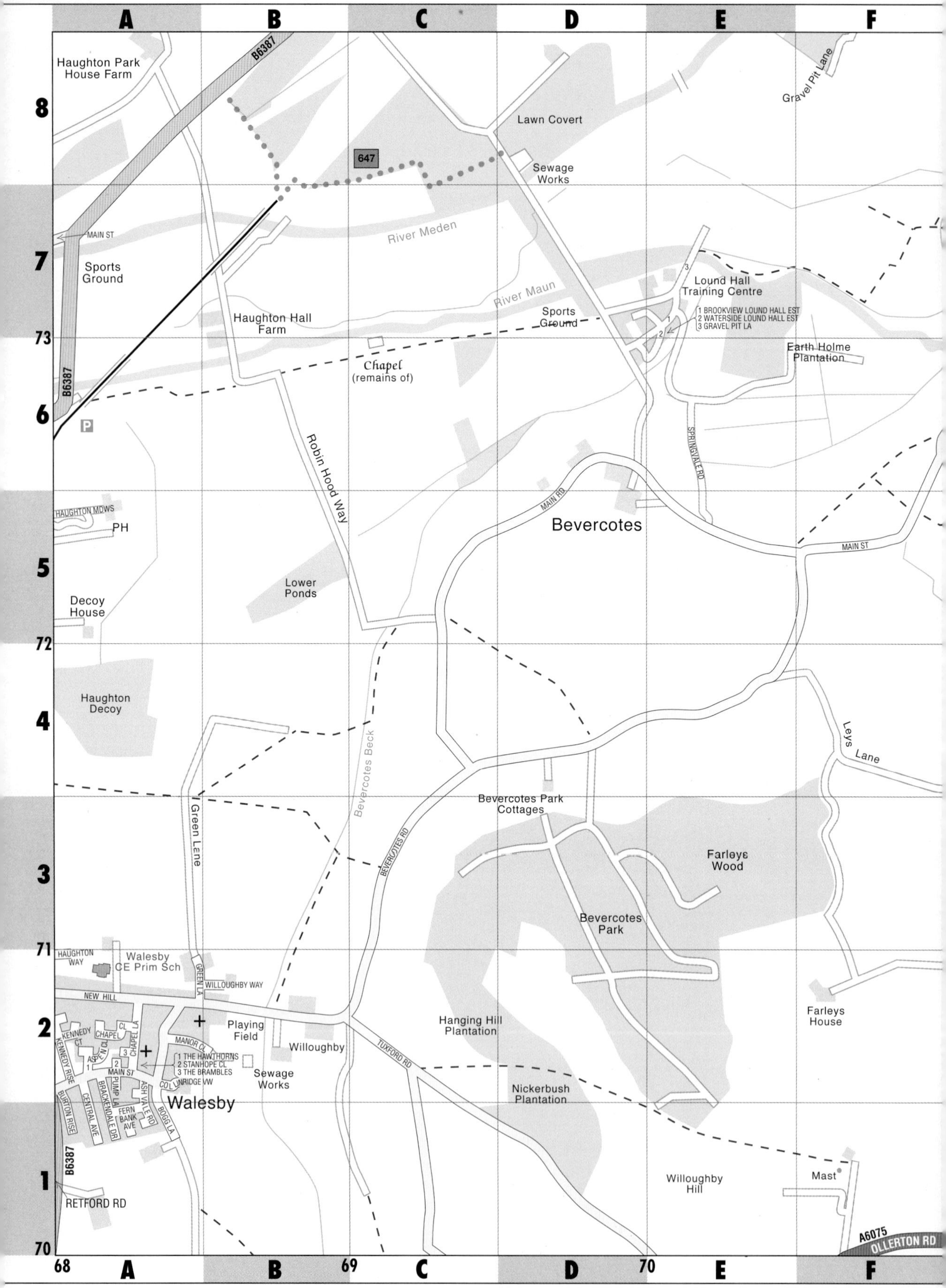

Haughton Park
House Farm

B6387

8

Lawn Covert

647

Sewage
Works

MAIN ST

7

Sports
Ground

River Meden

Lound Hall
Training Centre

River Maun

1 BROOKVIEW LOUND HALL EST
2 WATERSIDE LOUND HALL EST
3 GRAVEL PIT LA

Gravel Pit Lane

Haughton Hall
Farm

Sports
Ground

1

2

Earth Holme
Plantation

73

Chapel
(remains of)

B6387

6

P

Robin Hood Way

Bevercotes

SPRINGVALE RD

MAIN RD

MAIN ST

HAUGHTON MDWS

PH

5

Lower
Ponds

Decoy
House

72

Haughton
Decoy

4

Bevercotes Beck

Bevercotes Park
Cottages

Leys Lane

Farleys
Wood

3

Green Lane

BEVERCOTES RD

Bevercotes
Park

71

Haughton
Way

Walesby
CE Prim Sch

GREEN LA

WILLOUGHBY WAY

Farleys
House

NEW HILL

2

KENNEDY
C1

CHAPEL

CL

MANOR CL

Playing
Field

Hanging Hill
Plantation

TUXFORD RD

Willoughby

1 THE HAWTHORNS
2 STANHOPE CL
3 THE BRAMBLES

Sewage
Works

KENNEDY RISE

ASH
3
2
1

CL

PUMP LA

MAIN ST

ASH VALE RD

COLONRIDGE VW

BURTON RISE

CENTRAL AVE

BRACKENDALE DR

FERN
BANK
AVE

BUGG LA

Walesby

Nickerbush
Plantation

B6387

1

RETFORD RD

Willoughby
Hill

Mast

A6075   OLLERTON RD

70

68   A   69   B   C   70   D   E   F

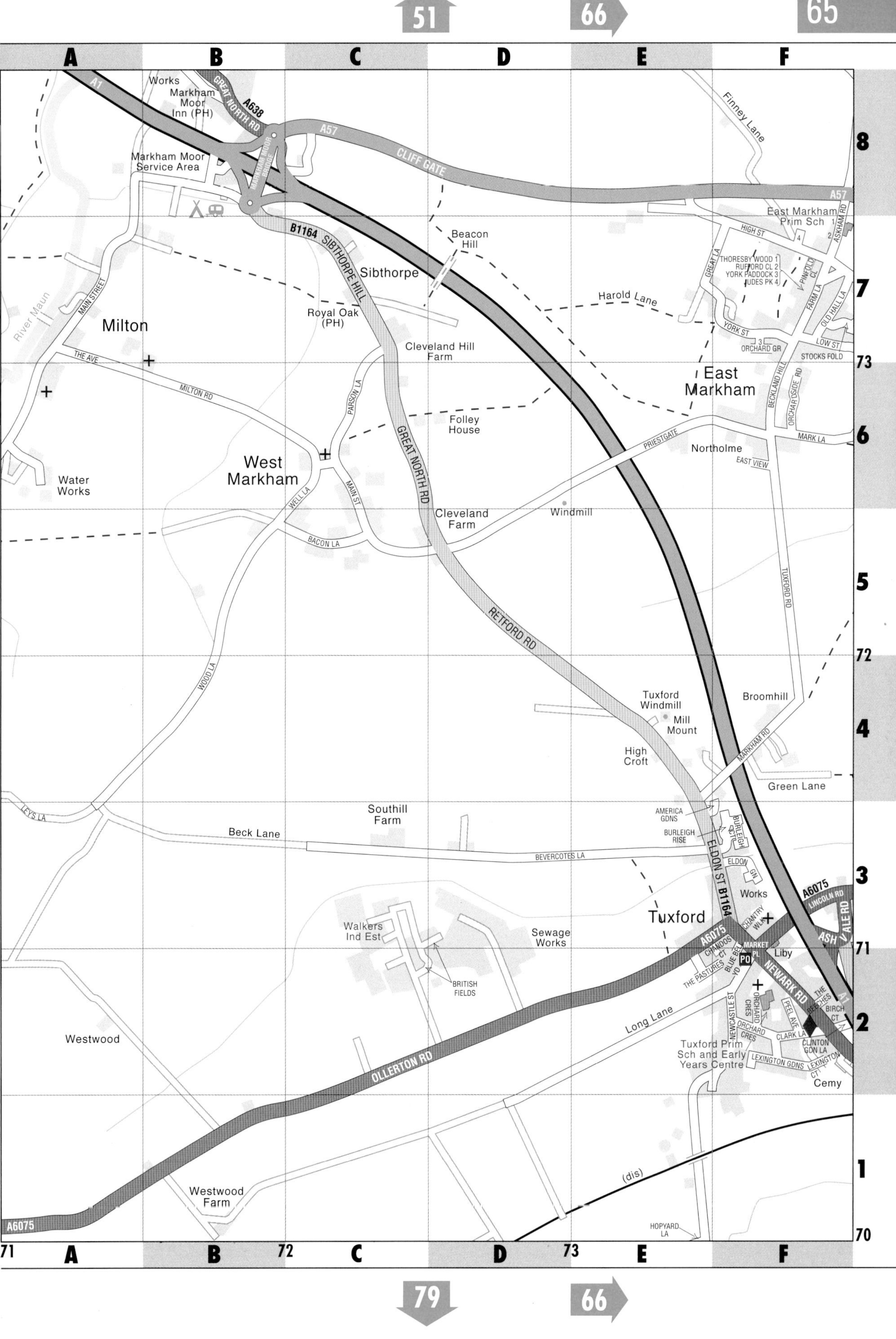
A
B
C
D
E
F
A1
Works
Markham Moor Inn (PH)
GREAT NORTH RD
A638
A57
CLIFF GATE
Finney Lane
Markham Moor Service Area
MARKHAM MOOR BRIDGE
B1164 SIBTHORPE HILL
Beacon Hill
Sibthorpe
East Markham Prim Sch
ASKHAM RD
HIGH ST
GREAT LA
THORESBY WOOD 1
RUFFORD CL 2
YORK PADDOCK 3
JUDES PK 4
PINFOLD CL
FARM LA
OLD HALL LA
Harold Lane
River Maun
MAIN STREET
Milton
Royal Oak (PH)
YORK ST
ORCHARD GR
LOW ST
STOCKS FOLD
Cleveland Hill Farm
THE AVE
MILTON RD
PARSON LA
East Markham
BECKLAND HILL
ORCHARDSIDE RD
Folley House
PRIESTGATE
MARK LA
Northolme
EAST VIEW
West Markham
Water Works
WELL LA
MAIN ST
GREAT NORTH RD
Cleveland Farm
Windmill
BACON LA
TUXFORD RD
RETFORD RD
WOOD LA
Tuxford Windmill
Mill Mount
Broomhill
High Croft
MARKHAM RD
Green Lane
LEYS LA
Southill Farm
AMERICA GDNS
BURLEIGH RISE
BURLEIGH CT
Beck Lane
BEVERCOTES LA
ELDON ST B1164
ELDON GN
Works
A6075
LINCOLN RD
Tuxford
CHANTRY WLK
Walkers Ind Est
Sewage Works
ASH VALE RD
MARKET PL
Liby
CHANDOS CT
BLUE BELL YD
PO
THE PASTURES
BRITISH FIELDS
NEWARK RD
NEWCASTLE ST
ORCHARD CRES
PEEL AVE
THE BEECHES
BIRCH CT
Westwood
Long Lane
CLARK LA
CLINTON GDN LA
Tuxford Prim Sch and Early Years Centre
LEXINGTON GDNS
LEXINGTON CT
Cemy
OLLERTON RD
(dis)
Westwood Farm
A6075
HOPYARD LA
8
7
73
6
5
72
4
3
71
2
1
70
71
72
73

65
52

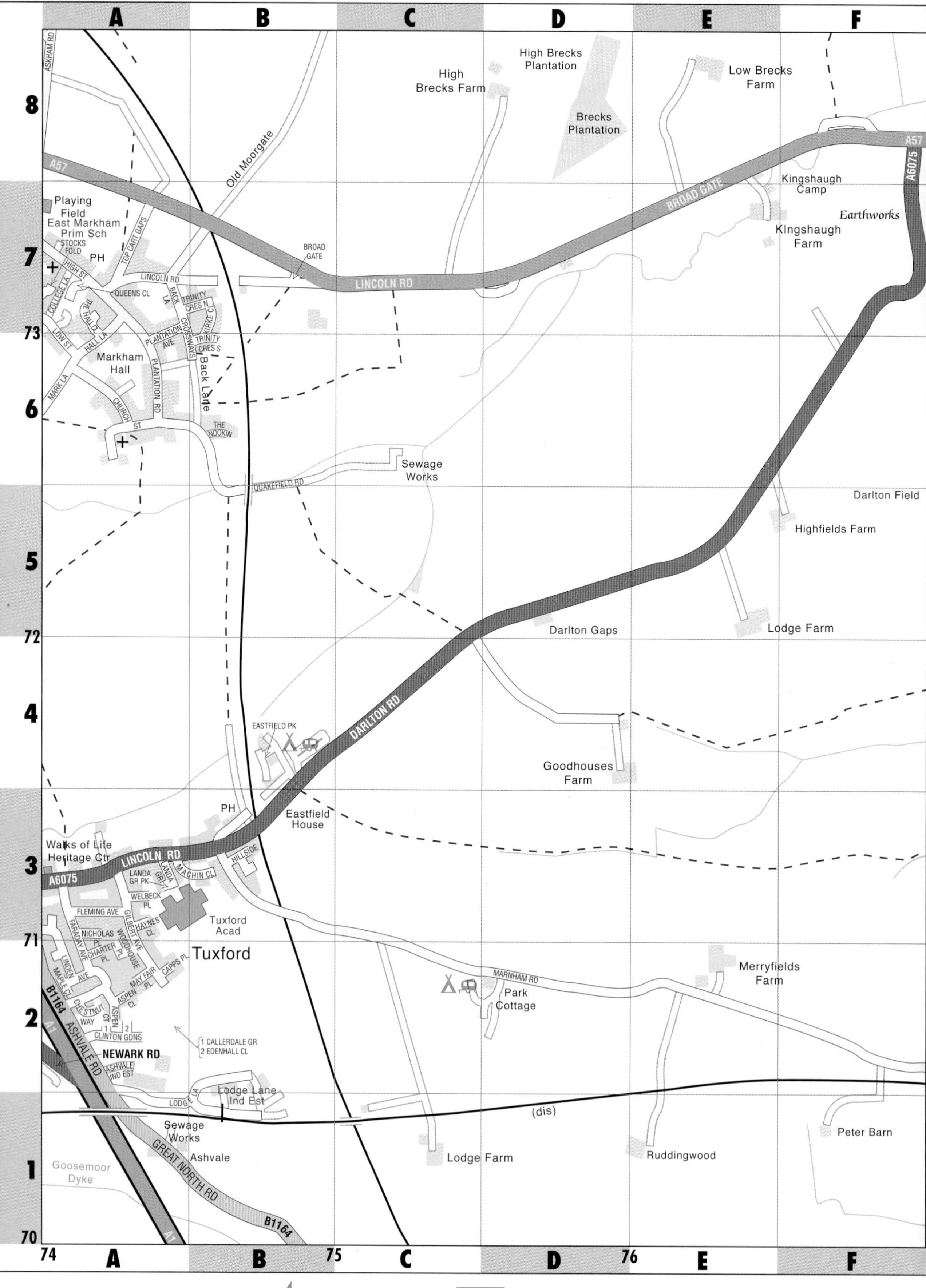
A
B
C
D
E
F
8
7
73
6
5
72
4
3
71
2
1
70
74
75
76
High Brecks Plantation
High Brecks Farm
Low Brecks Farm
Brecks Plantation
A57
A6075
Old Moorgate
BROAD GATE
Kingshaugh Camp
Earthworks
Kingshaugh Farm
Playing Field
East Markham Prim Sch
STOCKS FOLD
PH
HIGH ST
TOP CART GAPS
LINCOLN RD
QUEENS CL
COLLEGE LA
LOW ST
HALL LA
Markham Hall
MARK LA
CHURCH ST
PLANTATION AVE
PLANTATION RD
Back Lane
THE NOOKIN
TRINITY CRES N
TRINITY CRES S
CROSSWAYS
KIRKE CL
BACK LA
ASKHAM RD
QUAKEFIELD RD
Sewage Works
Darlton Field
Highfields Farm
Lodge Farm
Darlton Gaps
DARLTON RD
EASTFIELD PK
Goodhouses Farm
Eastfield House
PH
Walks of Life Heritage Ctr
LINCOLN RD
A6075
LANDA GR PK
LANDA GR
MACHIN CL
HILLSIDE
WELBECK PL
FLEMING AVE
GILBERT AVE
HAYNES CL
Tuxford Acad
Tuxford
NICHOLAS PL
FARADAY AVE
CHARTER PL
WOODHOUSE PL
CAPPS PL
MAY FAIR PL
LINDEN AVE
MAPLE CL
ASPEN CL
CHESTNUT WAY
CLINTON GDNS
1 CALLERDALE GR
2 EDENHALL CL
NEWARK RD
ASHVALE IND EST
B1164
ASHVALE RD
A1
MARNHAM RD
Park Cottage
Merryfields Farm
Lodge Lane Ind Est
LODGE LA
(dis)
Sewage Works
Ashvale
GREAT NORTH RD
Goosemoor Dyke
Lodge Farm
Ruddingwood
Peter Barn

65
80

53
68

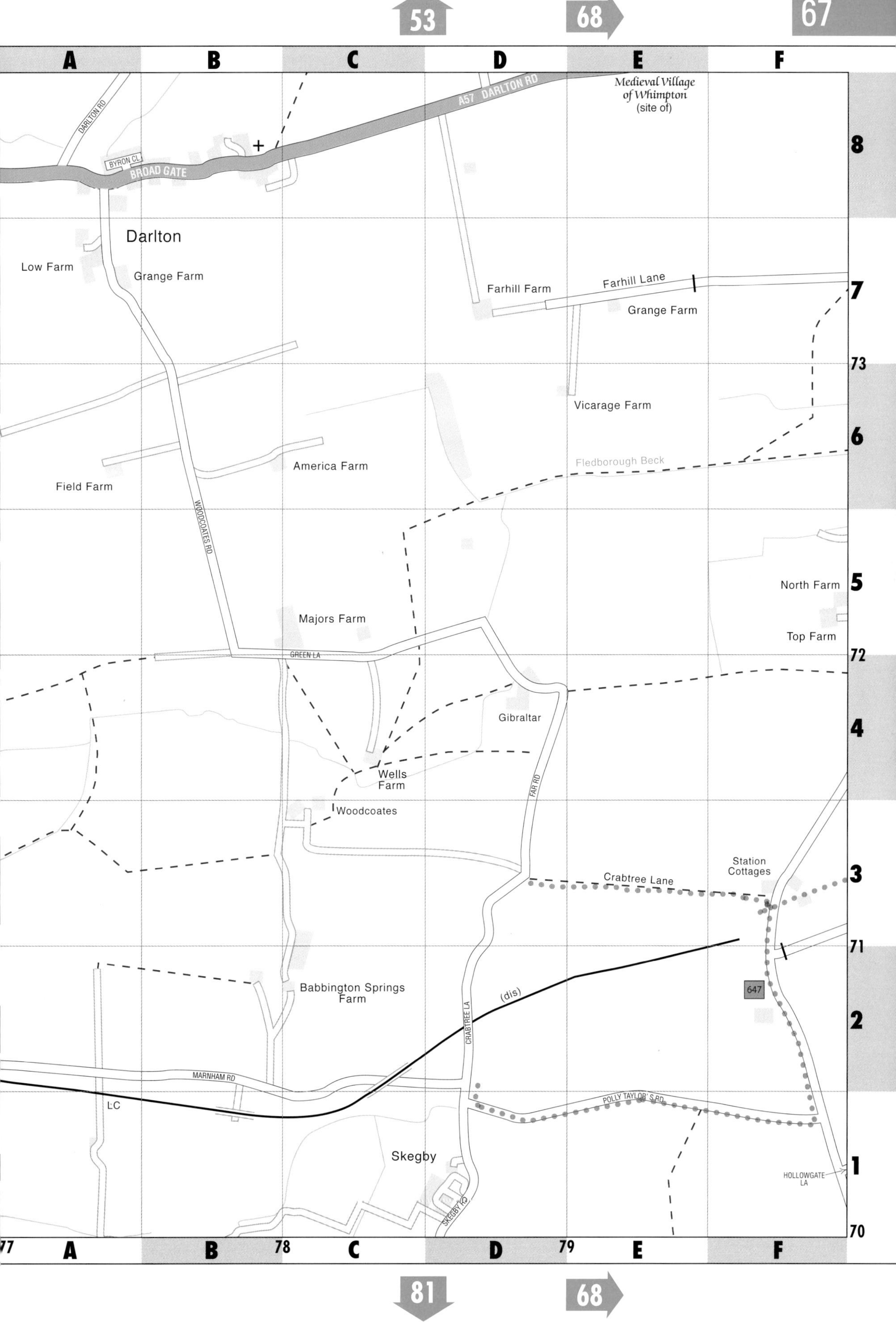
A
B
C
D
E
F
Medieval Village of Whimpton (site of)
A57 DARLTON RD
DARLTON RD
BYRON CL
BROAD GATE
8
Darlton
Low Farm
Grange Farm
Farhill Farm
Farhill Lane
Grange Farm
7
73
Vicarage Farm
6
America Farm
Fledborough Beck
Field Farm
WOODCOATES RD
5
North Farm
Majors Farm
Top Farm
GREEN LA
72
Gibraltar
4
Wells Farm
FAR RD
Woodcoates
Station Cottages
3
Crabtree Lane
71
647
Babbington Springs Farm
(dis)
2
CRABTREE LA
MARNHAM RD
POLLY TAYLOR'S RD
LC
Skegby
1
HOLLOWGATE LA
SKEGBY RD
70
77
78
79

81
68

67
54

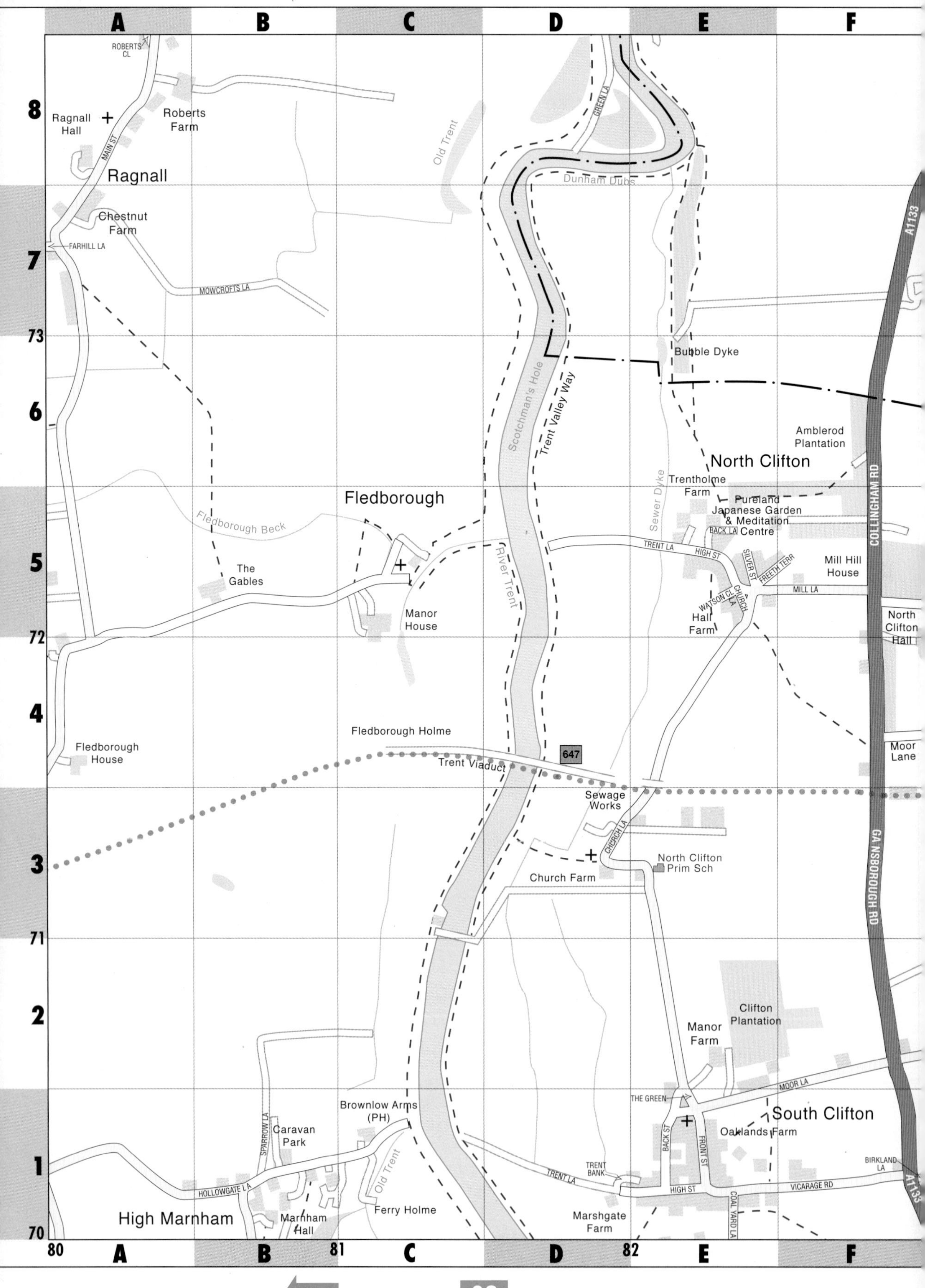
A
B
C
D
E
F
8
7
73
6
5
72
4
3
71
2
1
70
80
81
82
ROBERTS CL
Ragnall Hall
Roberts Farm
MAIN ST
Ragnall
Chestnut Farm
FARHILL LA
MOWCROFTS LA
Old Trent
GREEN LA
Dunham Dubs
Bubble Dyke
A1133
Scotchman's Hole
Trent Valley Way
Amblerod Plantation
North Clifton
Trentholme Farm
Sewer Dyke
Fledborough
Fledborough Beck
Pureland Japanese Garden & Meditation Centre
BACK LA
COLLINGHAM RD
TRENT LA
HIGH ST
SILVER ST
FREETH TERR
Mill Hill House
The Gables
River Trent
Manor House
WATSON CL
CHURCH LA
MILL LA
Hall Farm
North Clifton Hall
Fledborough Holme
647
Trent Viaduct
Fledborough House
Moor Lane
Sewage Works
CHURCH LA
North Clifton Prim Sch
Church Farm
GAINSBOROUGH RD
Manor Farm
Clifton Plantation
THE GREEN
MOOR LA
Brownlow Arms (PH)
South Clifton
SPARROW LA
Caravan Park
BACK ST
FRONT ST
Oaklands Farm
Old Trent
TRENT BANK
TRENT LA
BIRKLAND LA
HOLLOWGATE LA
HIGH ST
VICARAGE RD
High Marnham
Marnham Hall
Ferry Holme
Marshgate Farm
COAL YARD LA

67
82

55
70

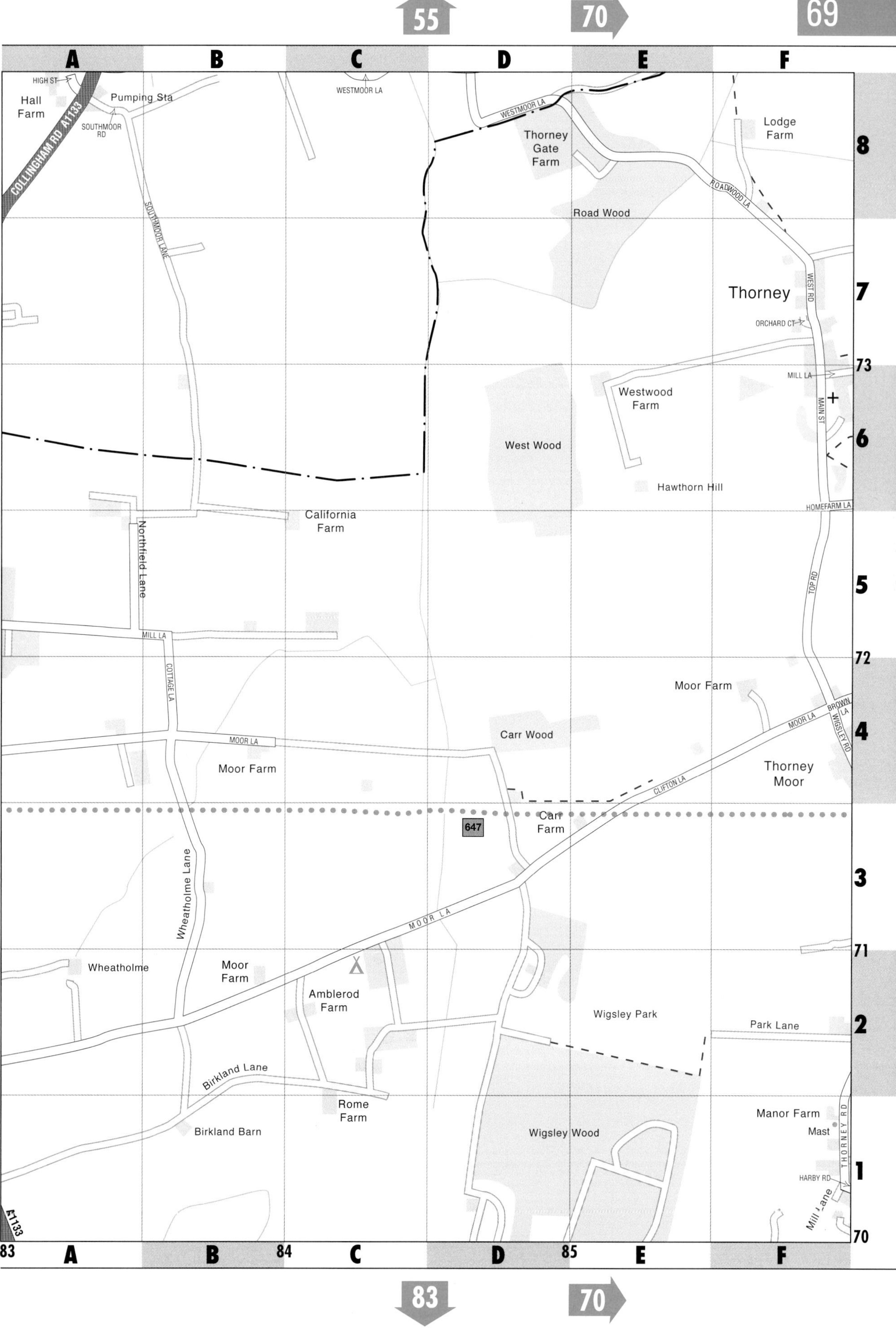
A
B
C
D
E
F
HIGH ST
Hall Farm
Pumping Sta
COLLINGHAM RD A1133
SOUTHMOOR RD
WESTMOOR LA
WESTMOOR LA
Thorney Gate Farm
Lodge Farm
8
ROADWOOD LA
Road Wood
SOUTHMOOR LANE
WEST RD
Thorney
7
ORCHARD CT
73
MILL LA
Westwood Farm
MAIN ST
6
West Wood
Hawthorn Hill
HOMEFARM LA
California Farm
Northfield Lane
5
TOP RD
MILL LA
COTTAGE LA
72
Moor Farm
BROWN LA
MOOR LA
WIGSLEY RD
4
Carr Wood
MOOR LA
Moor Farm
CLIFTON LA
Thorney Moor
Carr Farm
647
3
Wheatholme Lane
MOOR LA
71
Wheatholme
Moor Farm
Amblerod Farm
Wigsley Park
2
Park Lane
Birkland Lane
Rome Farm
Manor Farm
Mast
Birkland Barn
Wigsley Wood
THORNEY RD
1
HARBY RD
Mill Lane
A1133
70
83
84
85

83
70

A B C D E F
8
7
73
6
5
72
4
3
71
2
1
70
86 A B 87 C D 88 E F
B1190
SCHOOL LA
SAND LA
Spring Wood
Gibbet Wood
TOM OTTER'S LA
Saxilby Moor
Springwood Farm
DRINSEY NOOK LA
Gibbetwood Farm
The Ring
HARBY LA
Gibbet Lane Cottages
Glover's Wood
Five Lane Ends
Castle Farm
Crow Wood
BROWN WOOD LA
Saxilby Moor Farm
Ox Pasture Drain
CARR LA
Lee Nook Farm
HOMEFARM LA
B1190
Plot Farm
North Harby
Grange Farm
Half Moon Plantation
BROWN LA
Fir Tree Farm
Manor Farm
Wallrudding Farm
Thorney Brown
Station Farm
Lodge's Farm
WIGSLEY RD
64
647
Manterfield Farm
STATION RD
Clay Lane
Harby Queen Eleanor County Prim Sch
Plot Wood
Wigsley Drain
Ox Pasture Drain
ENFIELD CT
Windmill
LOW ST
HIGH ST
Bottle and Glass (PH)
THORNEY RD
MILL FIELD CL
PK LA
WIGSLEY RD
Harby
CROSS LA
DARBYSHIRE CL
Sewage Works
Moat
64
Wigsley
Playing Field
CHURCH RD
HARBY RD
NORTH SCARLE RD
HARBY LA
Grange Farm

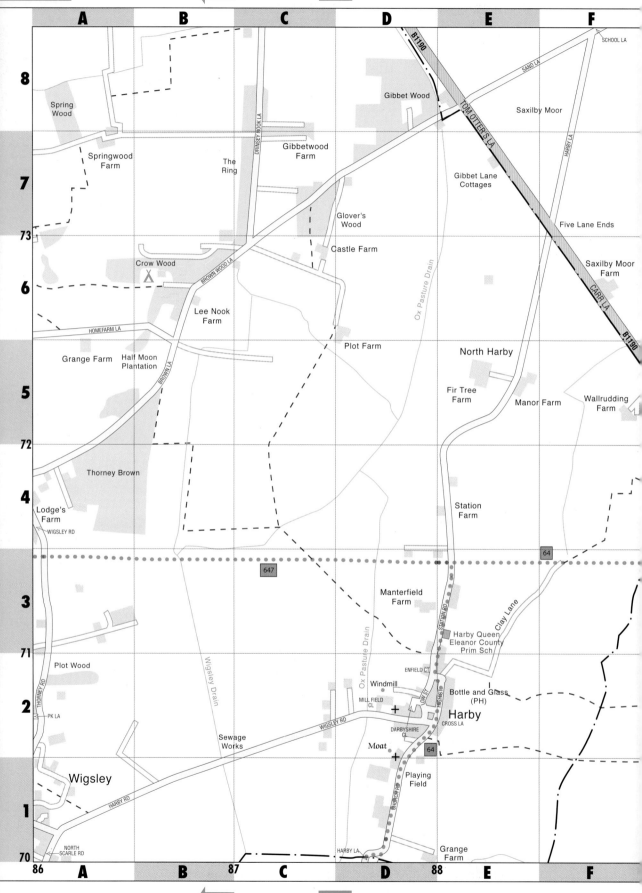

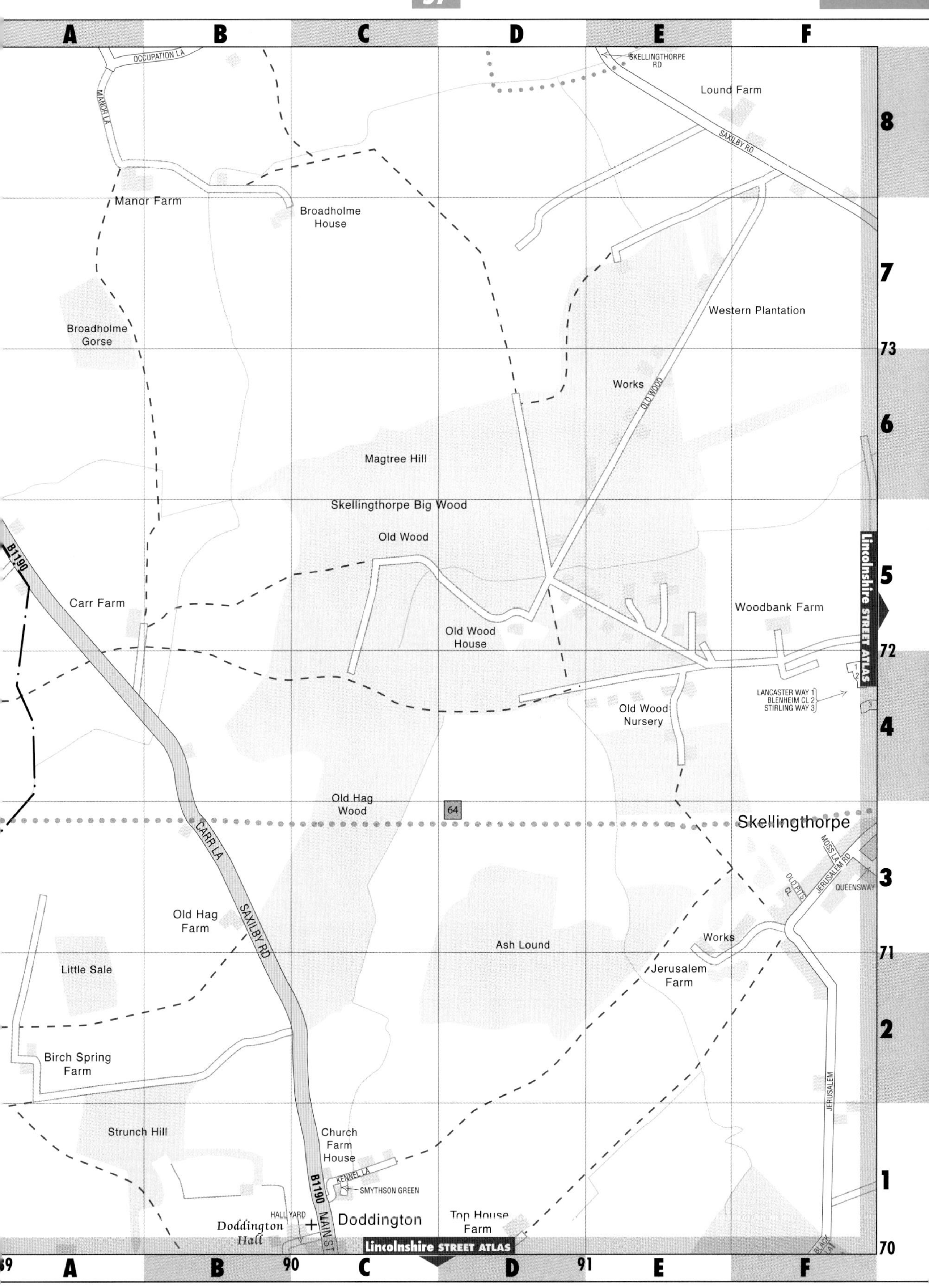

A B C D E F

8
7
73
6
5
72
4
3
71
2
1
70

OCCUPATION LA

MANOR LA

Manor Farm

Broadholme
House

SKELLINGTHORPE
RD

Lound Farm

SAXILBY RD

Broadholme
Gorse

Western Plantation

Works

OLD WOOD

Magtree Hill

Skellingthorpe Big Wood

Old Wood

Lincolnshire STREET ATLAS

B1190

Carr Farm

Old Wood
House

Woodbank Farm

72

LANCASTER WAY 1
BLENHEIM CL 2
STIRLING WAY 3

Old Wood
Nursery

Old Hag
Wood

64

Skellingthorpe

MOSS LA

JERUSALEM RD

OLD STH LA

QUEENSWAY

CARR LA

SAXILBY RD

Old Hag
Farm

Ash Lound

Works

Jerusalem
Farm

Little Sale

Birch Spring
Farm

JERUSALEM

Strunch Hill

Church
Farm
House

KENNEL LA

SMYTHSON GREEN

Top House
Farm

B1190

HALL YARD

MAIN ST

Doddington
Hall

Doddington

BLACK LA

89 A B 90 C D 91 E F

58

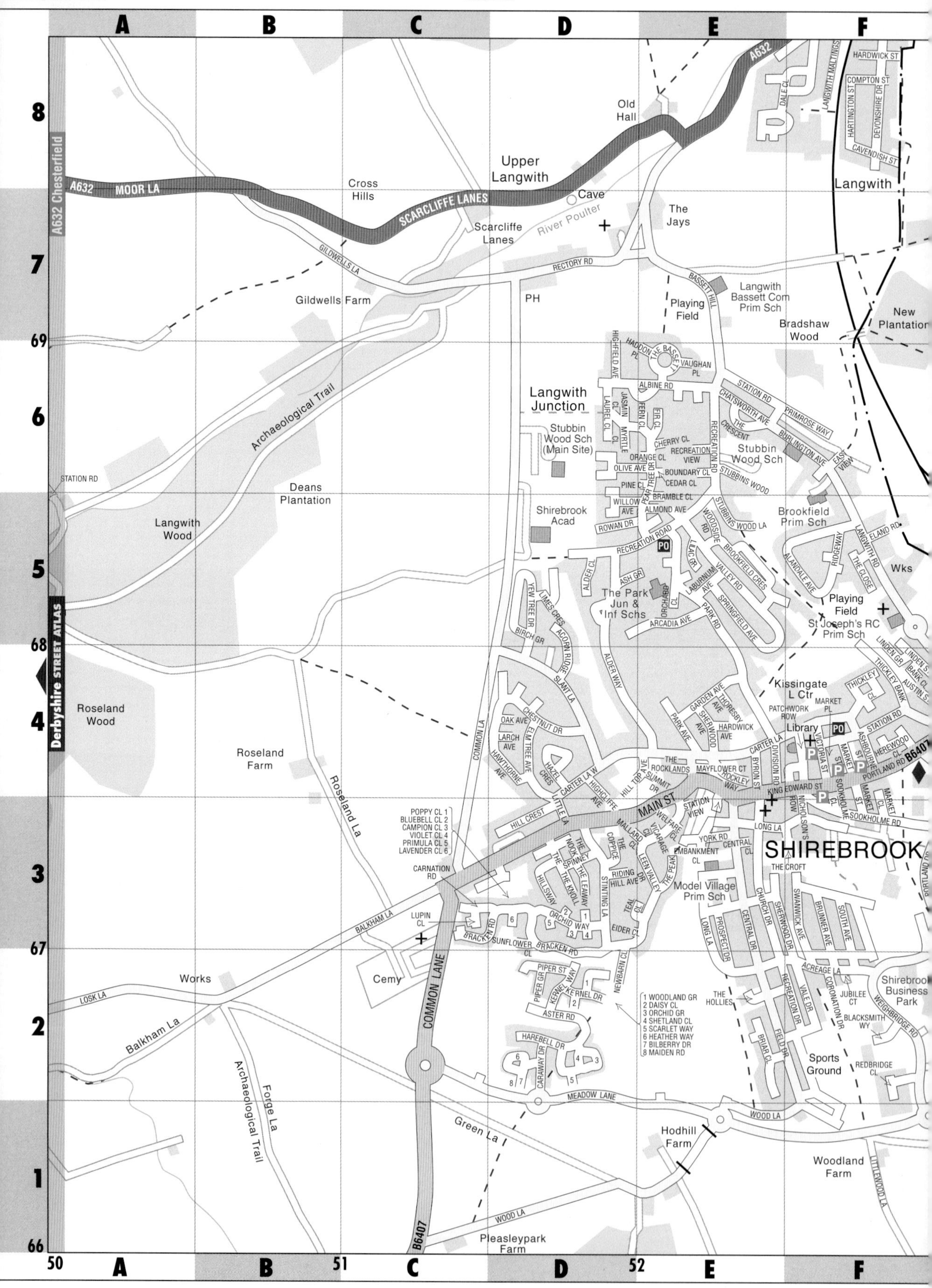

A
B
C
D
E
F
8
7
69
6
5
68
4
3
67
2
1
66
50
51
52
A632 Chesterfield
Derbyshire STREET ATLAS
A632
MOOR LA
SCARCLIFFE LANES
Upper Langwith
Old Hall
Cross Hills
Cave
Scarcliffe Lanes
River Poulter
The Jays
Langwith
HARDWICK ST
COMPTON ST
DALE CL
LANGWITH MALTINGS
HARTINGTON ST
DEVONSHIRE DR
CAVENDISH ST
GILDWELLS LA
RECTORY RD
Gildwells Farm
PH
BASSETT HILL
Playing Field
Langwith Bassett Com Prim Sch
Bradshaw Wood
New Plantation
Archaeological Trail
Langwith Junction
Stubbin Wood Sch (Main Site)
HADDON PL
THE BASSETT
VAUGHAN PL
HIGHFIELD AVE
ALBINE RD
STATION RD
CHATSWORTH AVE
THE CRESCENT
PRIMROSE WAY
BURLINGTON AVE
EASY VIEW
JASMIN CL
LAUREL CL
MYRTLE CL
FERN CL
FIR CL
CHERRY CL
RECREATION VIEW
RECREATION RD
ORANGE CL
OLIVE AVE
BOUNDARY CL
CEDAR CL
PINE CL
PEAR TREE DR
BRAMBLE CL
WILLOW AVE
ALMOND AVE
ROWAN DR
Stubbin Wood Sch
STUBBINS WOOD
STUBBINS WOOD LA
WOODSIDE RD
Brookfield Prim Sch
STATION RD
Deans Plantation
Langwith Wood
Shirebrook Acad
RECREATION ROAD
PO
LILAC GR
BROOKFIELD CRES
VALLEY RD
ALANDALE AVE
RIDGEWAY
LANGWITH RD
THE CLOSE
ELAND RD
Wks
ALDER CL
ASH GR
The Park Jun & Inf Schs
ORCHARD CL
LABURNUM AVE
PARK RD
SPRINGFIELD AVE
ARCADIA AVE
Playing Field
St Joseph's RC Prim Sch
YEW TREE DR
LIMES CRES
BIRCH GR
ACORN RIDGE
SLANT LA
ALDER WAY
LINDEN GR
LINDEN S
BANK CL
THICKLEY BANK
AUSTIN S
THICKLEY CL
Roseland Wood
Roseland Farm
Roseland La
CHESTNUT DR
OAK AVE
LARCH AVE
ELM TREE AVE
HAWTHORNE AVE
HAZEL CRES
COMMON LA
GARDEN AVE
THORESBY AVE
SHERWOOD AVE
PARK AVE
HARDWICK AVE
Kissingate L Ctr
PATCHWORK ROW
MARKET PL
Library
PO
STATION RD
CARTER LA
DIVISION RD
VICTORIA ST
MARKET ST
ASHBOURNE ST
HEREWOOD CL
PORTLAND RD
B6407
THE ROCKLANDS
MAYFLOWER CT
ROCKLEY WAY
BYRON ST
HILL TOP AVE
SUMMIT DR
CARTER LA W
HIGHCLIFFE AVE
LITTLE LA
HILL CREST
MAIN ST
STATION VIEW
KING EDWARD ST
NICHOLSON'S ROW
SOOKHOLME RD
MARKET CL
P
POPPY CL 1
BLUEBELL CL 2
CAMPION CL 3
VIOLET CL 4
PRIMULA CL 5
LAVENDER CL 6
LONG LA
WELFARE CL
VICARAGE CL
MALLARD CL
COPPICE
YORK RD
CENTRAL CL
EMBANKMENT CL
SHIREBROOK
THE CROFT
CARNATION RD
THE SPINNEY
THE MOOR
THE LEAWAY
THE KNOLL
HILLSWAY
RIDING HILL AVE
STINTING LA
THE COPPICE
LEEN VALLEY
THE PEAK
Model Village Prim Sch
TEAL CL
EIDER CL
ORCHID WAY
CHURCH DR
CENTRAL DR
SHERWOOD DR
SWANWICK AVE
BRUNNER AVE
SOUTH AVE
LONG LA
PROSPECT DR
BALKHAM LA
LUPIN CL
BRACKEN RD
SUNFLOWER CL
BRACKEN RD
Cemy
COMMON LANE
PIPER ST
PIPER GR
KERNEL WAY
KERNEL DR
ASTER RD
NEWBARN CL
1 WOODLAND GR
2 DAISY CL
3 ORCHID GR
4 SHETLAND CL
5 SCARLET WAY
6 HEATHER WAY
7 BILBERRY DR
8 MAIDEN RD
THE HOLLIES
RECREATION DR
VALE DR
ACREAGE LA
CORONATION DR
JUBILEE CT
BLACKSMITH WY
Shirebrook Business Park
WEIGHBRIDGE RD
Works
LOSK LA
Balkham La
HAREBELL DR
CARAWAY DR
BRIAR CL
FIELD DR
Sports Ground
REDBRIDGE CL
MEADOW LANE
WOOD LA
Archaeological Trail
Forge La
Green La
Hodhill Farm
Woodland Farm
LITTLEWOOD LA
WOOD LA
B6407
Pleasleypark Farm

87

59
74

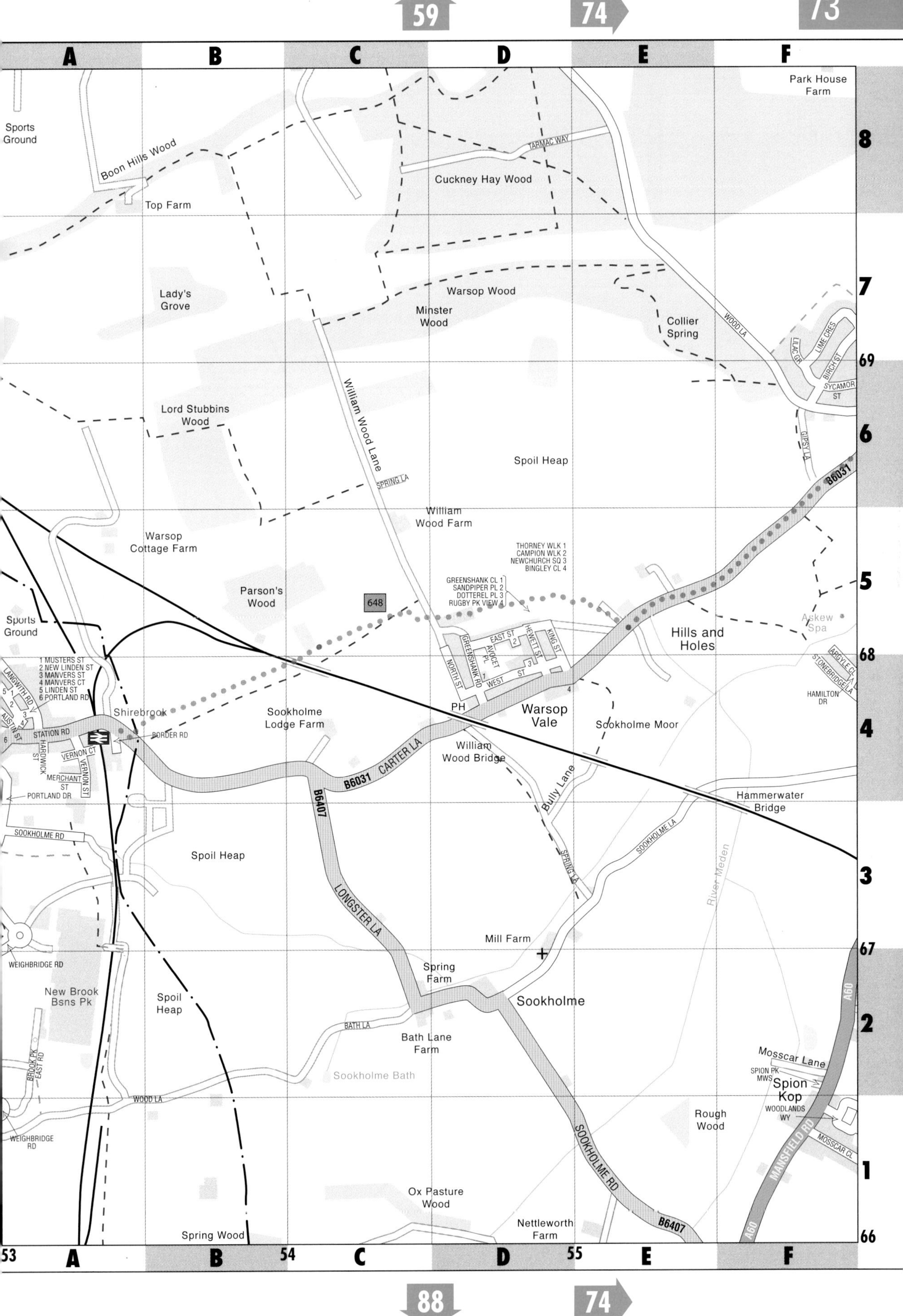

Sports Ground
Boon Hills Wood
Top Farm
Cuckney Hay Wood
TARMAC WAY
Park House Farm
Lady's Grove
Warsop Wood
Minster Wood
Collier Spring
WOOD LA
LILAC GR
LIME CRES
BIRCH ST
SYCAMORE ST
Lord Stubbins Wood
William Wood Lane
SPRING LA
Spoil Heap
GIPSY LA
B6031
William Wood Farm
Warsop Cottage Farm
THORNEY WLK 1
CAMPION WLK 2
NEWCHURCH SQ 3
BINGLEY CL 4
Parson's Wood
648
GREENSHANK CL 1
SANDPIPER PL 2
DOTTEREL PL 3
RUGBY PK VIEW 4
Sports Ground
Askew Spa
Hills and Holes
EAST ST
HEWETT ST
KING ST
GREENSHANK RD
AVOCET PL
NORTH ST
WEST ST
ARGYLE CL
STONEBRIDGE LA
HAMILTON DR
1 MUSTERS ST
2 NEW LINDEN ST
3 MANVERS ST
4 MANVERS CT
5 LINDEN ST
6 PORTLAND RD
LANGWITH RD
AUSTIN ST
Shirebrook
STATION RD
BORDER RD
Sookholme Lodge Farm
PH
Warsop Vale
Sookholme Moor
HARDWICK ST
VERNON CT
VERNON ST
MERCHANT ST
PORTLAND DR
CARTER LA
B6031
William Wood Bridge
Bully Lane
Hammerwater Bridge
B6407
SOOKHOLME RD
Spoil Heap
SOOKHOLME LA
SPRING LA
River Meden
LONGSTER LA
Mill Farm
WEIGHBRIDGE RD
New Brook Bsns Pk
Spoil Heap
Spring Farm
Sookholme
A60
BATH LA
Bath Lane Farm
BROOK PK
EAST RD
Sookholme Bath
Mosscar Lane
SPION PK MWS
Spion Kop
WOODLANDS WY
WOOD LA
Rough Wood
WEIGHBRIDGE RD
SOOKHOLME RD
MOSSCAR CL
MANSFIELD RD
Ox Pasture Wood
Spring Wood
Nettleworth Farm
B6407
A60
A B C D E F
8 7 69 6 5 68 4 3 67 2 1 66
53 54 55

88
74

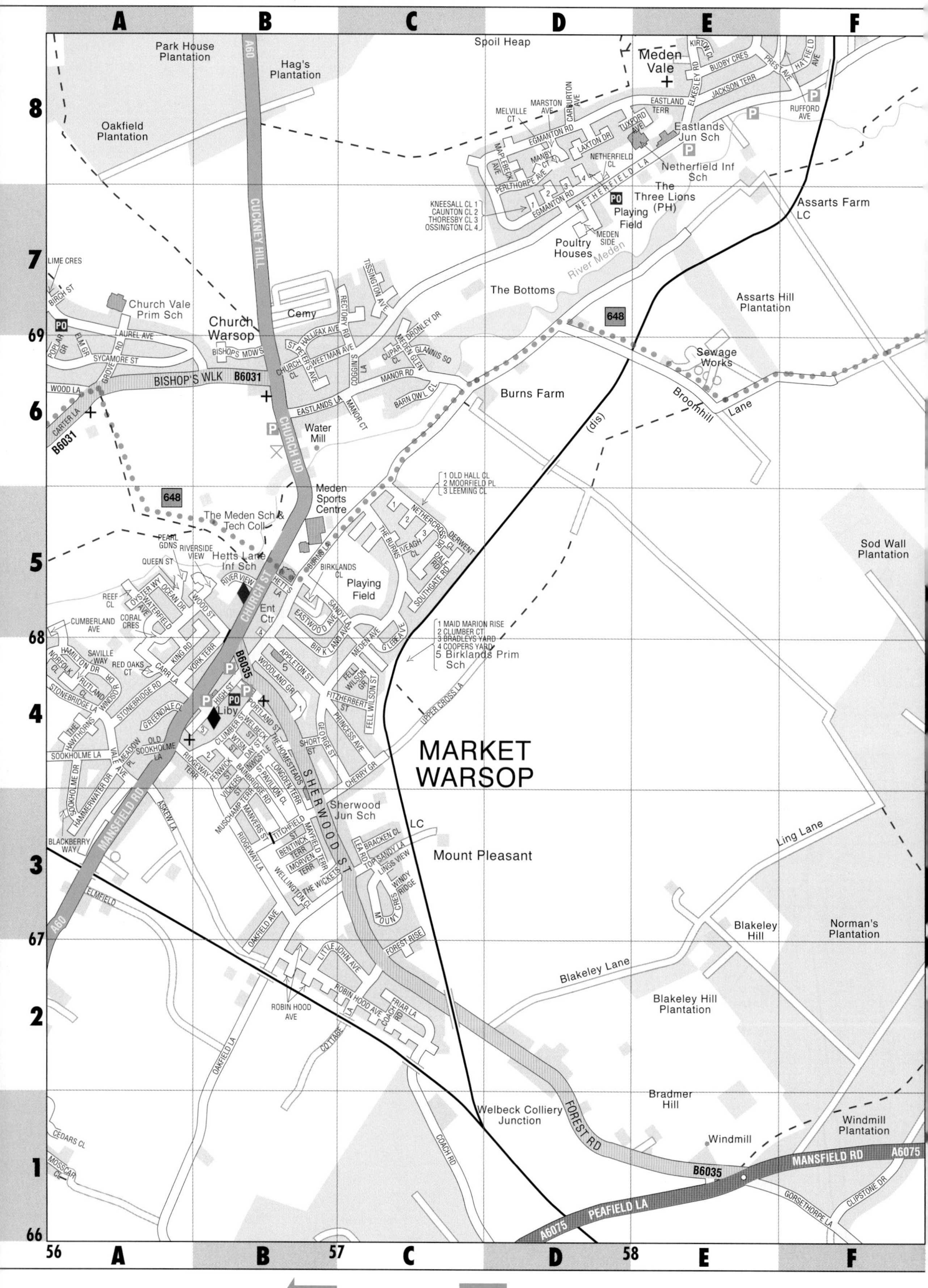

A   B   C   D   E   F

8

7

LIME CRES
BIRCH ST
POPLAR GR
ELM GR
SYCAMORE ST
PO
Church Vale Prim Sch
Church Warsop
LAUREL AVE
GROVE ST
BISHOPS MDWS
BISHOPS WLK   B6031
WOOD LA
CARTER LA
B6031
648

Park House Plantation

Oakfield Plantation

Hag's Plantation

CUCKNEY HILL

A60

Spoil Heap

Meden Vale

ELKESLEY RD
BUDBY CRES
JACKSON TERR
PRIESS AVE
HATFIELD
RUFFORD AVE
P   P   P
KIRKBY RD
MELVILLE CT
MARSTON AVE
CARBURTON AVE
EASTLAND TERR
TUXFORD AVE
Eastlands Jun Sch
P
Netherfield Inf Sch
MAPLEBECK AVE
EGMANTON RD
MANSFIELD CT
NETHERFIELD LA
PERLTHORPE AVE
EGMANTON RD
KNEESALL CL 1
CAUNTON CL 2
THORESBY CL 3
OSSINGTON CL 4
PO   The Three Lions (PH)
Playing Field
MEDEN SIDE
Poultry Houses
River Meden
648
Assarts Farm LC

Assarts Hill Plantation

The Bottoms
Sewage Works

6

69

Cemy
RECTORY RD
TISSINGTON AVE
HALLIFAX AVE
SWEETMANI AVE
ST PETER'S AVE
CHURCH CL
WESTWOOD
EASTLANDS LA
MANOR CT
MANOR RD
BARN OWL CL
CIPAR DR
BRONLEY DR
THE GLEN
S GLANNIS SQ
Burns Farm
(dis)
BROOKHILL LANE
Broomhill

Water Mill
P
CHURCH RD
648
The Meden Sch & Tech Coll
PEARL GDNS
RIVERSIDE VIEW
Hetts Lane Inf Sch
Meden Sports Centre
1 OLD HALL CL
2 MOORFIELD PL
3 LEEMING CL
Sod Wall Plantation

5

68

QUEEN ST
REEF CL
OYSTER WY
WATERFIELD
OCEAN DR
CORAL CRES
CUMBERLAND AVE
SAVILLE WAY
RED OAKS CT
KING RD
YORK TERR
HETTS LA
RIVER VIEW
WOOD ST
CHURCH ST
B6035
Ent Ctr
Birklands Inf Sch
BIRKLANDS CL
EASTWOOD AVE
SANDY LA
APPLETON ST
WOODLAND GR
BIRK LAND AVE
FELL WILSON TER
NETHERDREW
DERWENT
THE BURNS
IVEAGH CL
SOUTHGATE RD
GIBB ST
1 MAID MARION RISE
2 CLUMBER CT
3 BRADLEYS YARD
4 COOPERS YARD
5 Birklands Prim Sch

Playing Field

4

3

67

2

1

66

HAMILTON DR
NORFOLK CL
VAUTLAND
STONEBRIDGE LA
STONEBRIDGE RD
GREENDALE CL
TIME
HAWTHORNS
MEADOW
OLD SOOKHOLME LA
SOOKHOLME LA
SOOKHOLME DR
HAMMERWATER DR
Blackberry Way
ASKEW LA
A60
MANSFIELD RD
ELMFIELD
CEDARS CL
MOSSCAR
Mount Pleasant

P   Liby
PO   P
HIGH ST
PORTLAND ST
AXELBECK ST
CLUMBER ST
FENWICK
DAY ST
BAINES ST
BANBRIDGE RD
THE HOMESTEADS
CHERRY GR
GEORGE ST
SHORT ST
KINGESS AVE
FITZHERBERT ST
FELL ST
WILLOW GR
MEDEN AVE
SHERWOOD ST
OAKFIELD AVE
UPPER CROSS LA
MARKET WARSOP
LC
Sherwood Jun Sch
VICKERS ST
MUSGRAVE ST
STANVERS ST
RIDGEWAY LA
TITTOFIELD ST
BENTINCK TERR
MAYFIELD TERR
MORVEN TERR
WELLINGTON TERR
LEA BRACKEN DL
TOP SANDY LA
LINGS VIEW
MOUNT
WINDY RIDGE
FOREST RISE
ROBIN HOOD AVE
ROBIN HOOD AVE
LITTLE JOHN AVE
FRIAR LA
COTTAGE LA
COACH RD
OAKFIELD LA
WELBECK COLLIERY JUNCTION
FOREST RD
Blakeley Lane
Blakeley Hill
Blakeley Hill Plantation
Bradmer Hill
Windmill
Ling Lane
Norman's Plantation
Windmill Plantation
B6035   MANSFIELD RD   A6075
A6075   PEAFIELD LA
GORSETHORPE LA
GLIPSTONE DR

A   B   C   D   E   F

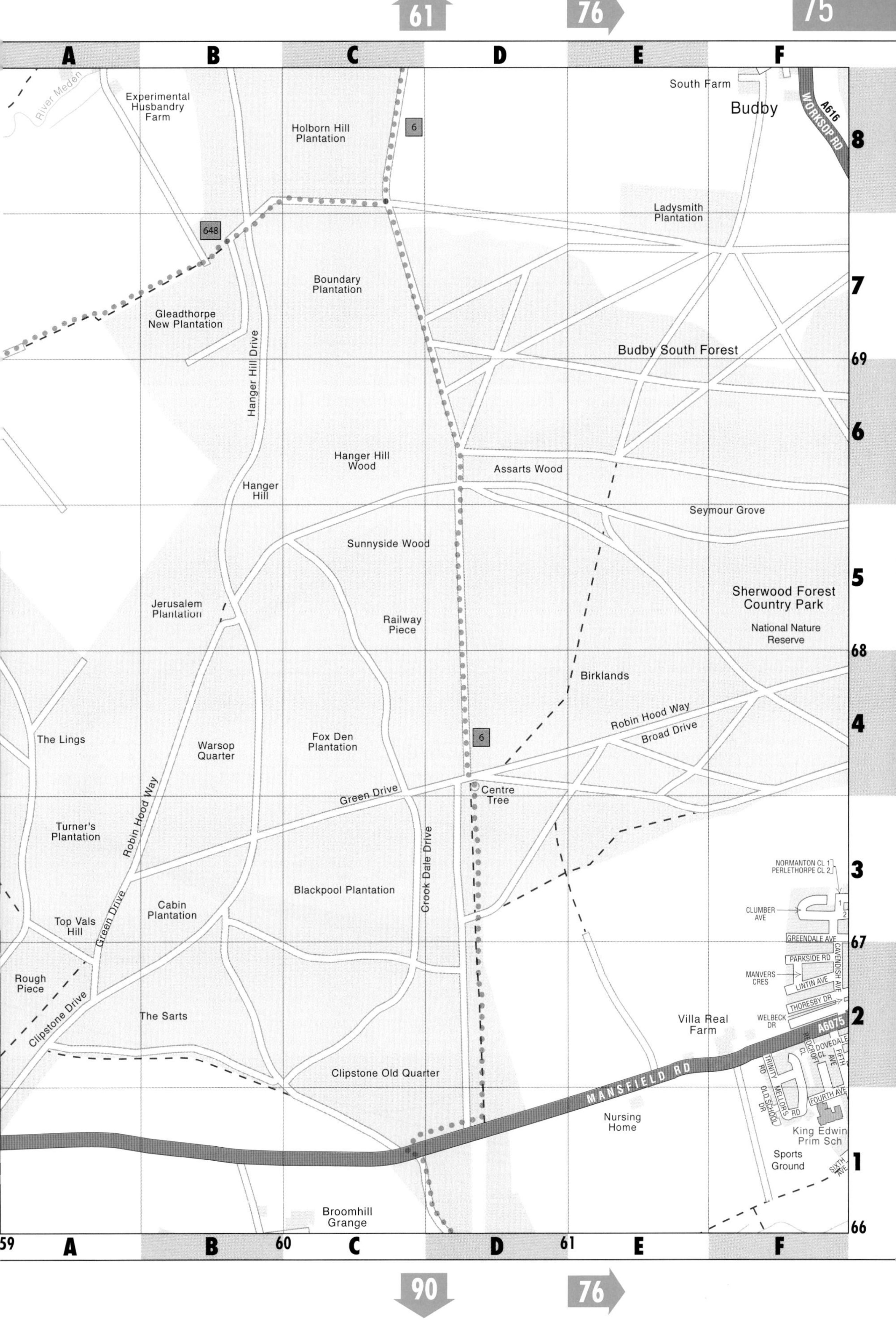

A　B　C　D　E　F

River Meden

Experimental
Husbandry
Farm

Holborn Hill
Plantation

6

South Farm

Budby

A616 WORKSOP RD

8

648

Gleadthorpe
New Plantation

Boundary
Plantation

Ladysmith
Plantation

7

Hanger Hill Drive

Budby South Forest

69

6

Hanger Hill
Wood

Hanger
Hill

Assarts Wood

Seymour Grove

Jerusalem
Plantation

Sunnyside Wood

Railway
Piece

Sherwood Forest
Country Park

National Nature
Reserve

5

68

Birklands

The Lings

Warsop
Quarter

Fox Den
Plantation

Robin Hood Way

Robin Hood Way

Broad Drive

4

Turner's
Plantation

Green Drive

Centre
Tree

6

Crook Dale Drive

NORMANTON CL 1
PERLETHORPE CL 2

3

CLUMBER
AVE

1
2

2
1

GREENDALE AVE

67

Top Vals
Hill

Cabin
Plantation

Blackpool Plantation

PARKSIDE RD

MANVERS
CRES

LINTIN AVE

CAVENDISH AVE

THORESBY DR

2

Rough
Piece

Clipstone Drive

The Sarts

Clipstone Old Quarter

Villa Real
Farm

WELBECK
DR

A6075

DOVEDALE AVE

Fifth

MANSFIELD RD

TRINITY RD

MELLORS RD

OLD SCHOOL DR

FOURTH AVE

Nursing
Home

King Edwin
Prim Sch

Sports
Ground

SIXTH AVE

1

Broomhill
Grange

66

75
62

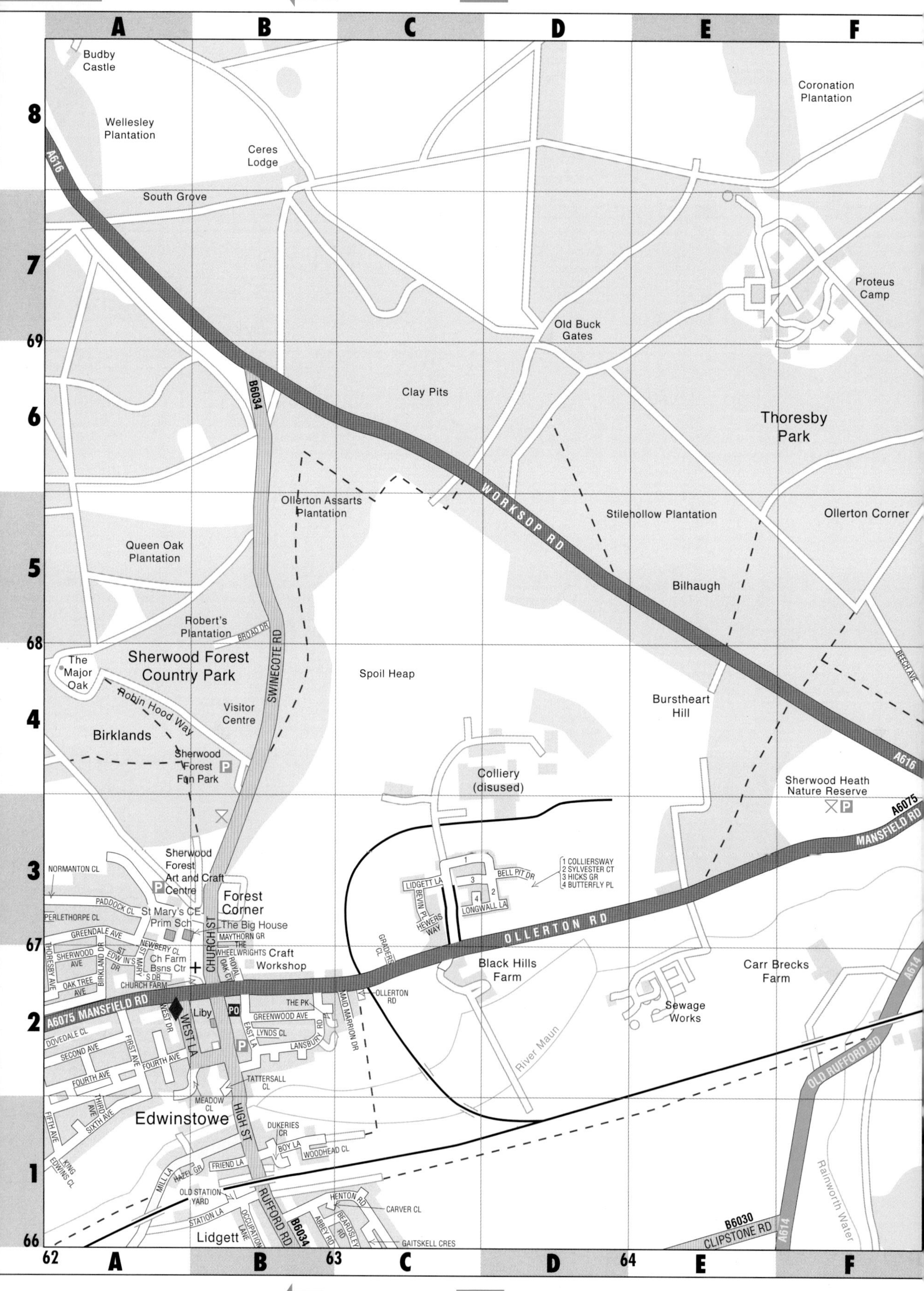
A
B
C
D
E
F
8
7
69
6
5
68
4
3
67
2
1
66
62
63
64
Budby Castle
Wellesley Plantation
Ceres Lodge
South Grove
Coronation Plantation
Proteus Camp
Old Buck Gates
Clay Pits
Thoresby Park
A616
B6034
WORKSOP RD
Ollerton Assarts Plantation
Stilehollow Plantation
Ollerton Corner
Queen Oak Plantation
Bilhaugh
Robert's Plantation
BROAD DR
SWINECOTE RD
Sherwood Forest Country Park
The Major Oak
Robin Hood Way
Visitor Centre
Spoil Heap
Burstheart Hill
BEECH AVE
Birklands
Sherwood Forest Fun Park
Colliery (disused)
Sherwood Heath Nature Reserve
A6075
MANSFIELD RD
Sherwood Forest Art and Craft Centre
NORMANTON CL
1 COLLIERSWAY
2 SYLVESTER CT
3 HICKS GR
4 BUTTERFLY PL
BELL PIT DR
LIDGETT LA
BEVIN PL
HEWERS WAY
LONGWALL LA
Forest Corner
PADDOCK CL
St Mary's CE Prim Sch
PERLETHORPE CL
The Big House
MAYTHORN GR
GREENDALE AVE
NEWBERY CL
THE WHEELWRIGHTS
Craft Workshop
CHURCH ST
OAK CT
ROYAL
SHERWOOD AVE
ST MARY'S DR
EDWIN'S DR
Ch Farm Bsns Ctr
THORESBY AVE
BIRKLAND DR
OAK TREE AVE
CHURCH FARM
GRAFTERS CL
OLLERTON RD
Black Hills Farm
Carr Brecks Farm
A614
A6075 MANSFIELD RD
WEST DR
WEST LA
Liby
PO
THE PK
GREENWOOD AVE
MAID MARRION DR
OLLERTON RD
Sewage Works
DOVEDALE CL
FIRST AVE
EAST LA
LYNDS CL
LANSBURY RD
SECOND AVE
FOURTH AVE
River Maun
OLD RUFFORD RD
FOURTH AVE
TATTERSALL CL
THIRD AVE
MEADOW CL
SIXTH AVE
HIGH ST
Edwinstowe
DUKERIES CR
FIFTH AVE
BOY LA
WOODHEAD CL
KING EDWINS CL
MILL LA
HAZEL GR
FRIEND LA
OLD STATION YARD
RUFFORD RD
HENTON RD
CARVER CL
Rainworth Water
STATION LA
OCCUPATION LANE
ABBEY RD
BEARDSLEY RD
B6030
CLIPSTONE RD
Lidgett
GAITSKELL CRES

75
91

63
78

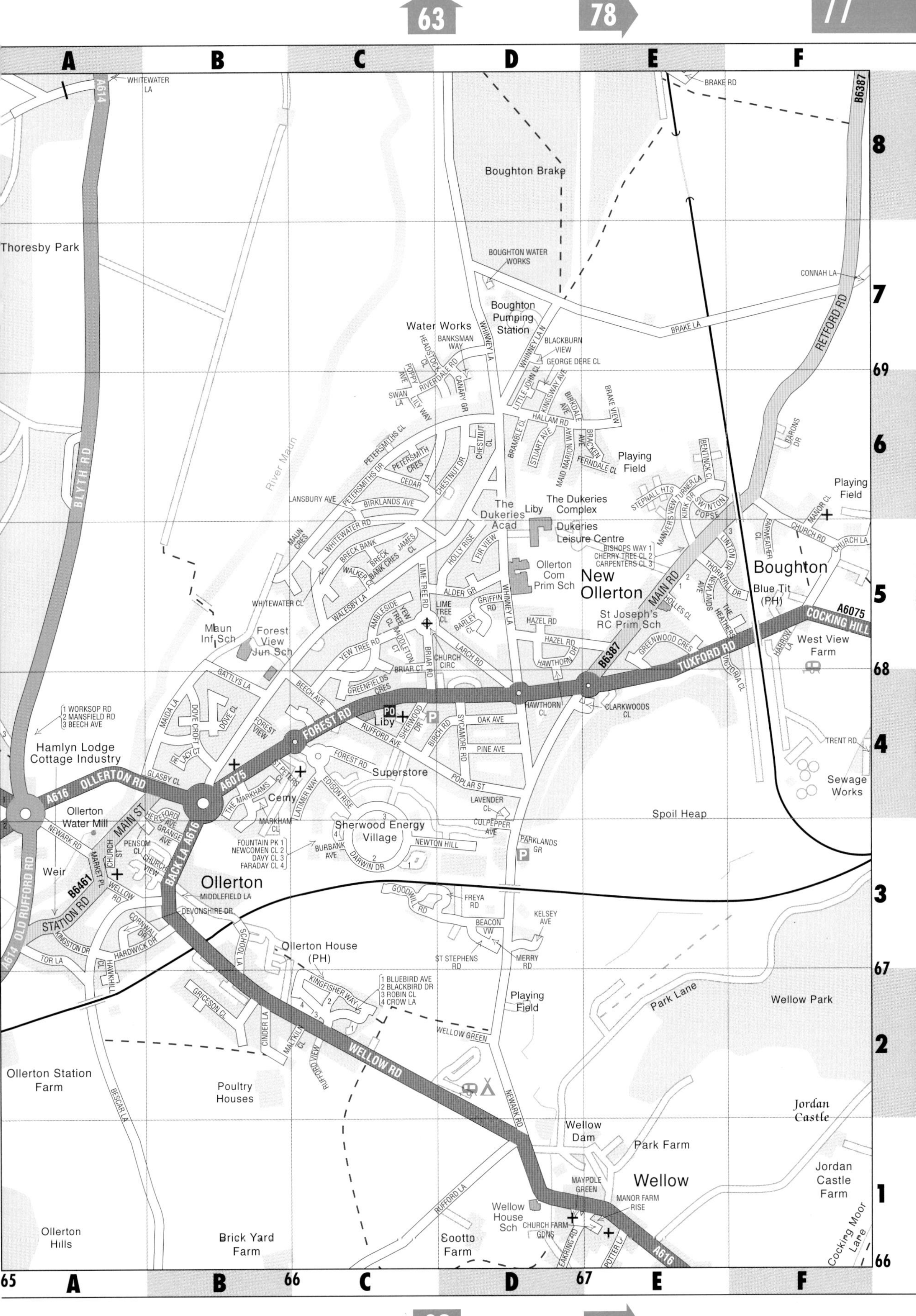
A
B
C
D
E
F
8
7
69
6
5
68
4
3
67
2
1
66
65
66
67
Thoresby Park
WHITEWATER LA
A614
BLYTH RD
BRAKE RD
B6387
Boughton Brake
BOUGHTON WATER WORKS
Boughton Pumping Station
Water Works
CONNAH LA
BRAKE LA
RETFORD RD
BANKSMAN WAY
HEADSTOCK CL
RIVERDALE RD
POPPY AVE
SWAN LA
LILY WAY
CANARY GR
WHINNEY LA
BLACKBURN VIEW
GEORGE DERE CL
LITTLE JOHN CL
KINGSWAY AVE
BIRKDALE AVE
BRAKE VIEW
HALLAM RD
BRAMBLE CL
STUART AVE
MAID MARION WAY
BRACKEN AVE
FERNDALE CL
Playing Field
BARONS DR
PETERSMITHS CL
PETERSMITH CRES
PETERSMITHS DR
CEDAR LA
CHESTNUT CL
CHESTNUT DR
BIRKLANDS AVE
LANSBURY AVE
River Maun
The Dukeries Acad
Liby
The Dukeries Complex
Dukeries Leisure Centre
BISHOPS WAY 1
CHERRY TREE CL 2
CARPENTERS CL 3
STEPNALL HTS
MANVERS VIEW
KIRK DR
TURNER LA
BENTINCK CL
SWINTON COPSE
MANOR CL
CHURCH RD
CHURCH LA
FAIRWEATHER CL
LINTON DR
THORNHILL DR
NEWLANDS AVE
HOLLES CL
THE HEATHERS
Boughton
Blue Tit (PH)
A6075
COCKING HILL
MAUN CRES
WHITEWATER RD
BRECK BANK
BRECK BANK CRES
JAMES CL
WALKER CL
HOLLY RISE
FIR VIEW
Ollerton Com Prim Sch
New Ollerton
MAIN RD
WHITEWATER CL
WALESBY LA
AMBLESIDE
LIME TREE RD
ALDER GR
GRIFFIN RD
LIME TREE CL
BARLEY CL
HAZEL RD
St Joseph's RC Prim Sch
Maun Inf Sch
Forest View Jun Sch
YEW TREE CL
YEW TREE RD
MIDDLETON CT
BRIAR RD
CHURCH CIRC
LARCH RD
HAWTHORN DR
GREENWOOD CRES
TUXFORD RD
VICTORIA CL
HARROW LA
West View Farm
GATTLYS LA
BRIAR CT
GREENFIELDS CRES
BEECH AVE
HAWTHORN CL
CLARKWOODS CL
1 WORKSOP RD
2 MANSFIELD RD
3 BEECH AVE
MAIDA LA
DOVE CROFT
DOVE CL
FOREST VIEW
FOREST RD
PO
Liby
SHERWOOD DR
BIRCH RD
SYCAMORE RD
OAK AVE
PINE AVE
TRENT RD
Hamlyn Lodge Cottage Industry
LACY CT
RUFFORD AVE
FOREST RD
Superstore
POPLAR ST
Sewage Works
A616
OLLERTON RD
GLASBY CL
A6075
ST PETERS
THE MARKHAMS
Cemy
LATIMER WAY
EDISON RISE
LAVENDER CL
Spoil Heap
Ollerton Water Mill
NEWARK RD
HEREFORD AVE
GRANGE AVE
MAIN ST
MARKHAM CL
Sherwood Energy Village
CULPEPPER AVE
PARKLANDS GR
PENSOM CL
CHURCH ST
CHURCH VIEW
FOUNTAIN PK 1
NEWCOMEN CL 2
DAVY CL 3
FARADAY CL 4
BURBANK AVE
NEWTON HILL
DARWIN DR
Weir
MARKET PL
B6461
WELLOW RD
BACK LA
Ollerton
MIDDLEFIELD LA
OLD RUFFORD RD
STATION RD
DEVONSHIRE DR
CORNWALL DR
GOODWILL RD
FREYA RD
BEACON VW
KELSEY AVE
KINGSTON DR
HARDWICK DR
SCHOOL LA
Ollerton House (PH)
ST STEPHENS RD
MERRY RD
TOR LA
HAWKHILL CL
1 BLUEBIRD AVE
2 BLACKBIRD DR
3 ROBIN CL
4 CROW LA
KINGFISHER WAY
GRICESON CL
Playing Field
Park Lane
Wellow Park
CINDER LA
MALTKILN CL
WELLOW GREEN
WELLOW RD
Ollerton Station Farm
RUFFORD VIEW
Poultry Houses
BESCAR LA
NEWARK RD
Jordan Castle
Wellow Dam
Park Farm
Wellow
Jordan Castle Farm
MAYPOLE GREEN
MANOR FARM RISE
RUFFORD LA
Wellow House Sch
CHURCH FARM GDNS
EAKRING RD
POTTER LA
A616
Cocking Moor Lane
Ollerton Hills
Brick Yard Farm
Scotto Farm

92
78

A　　B　　C　　D　　E　　F

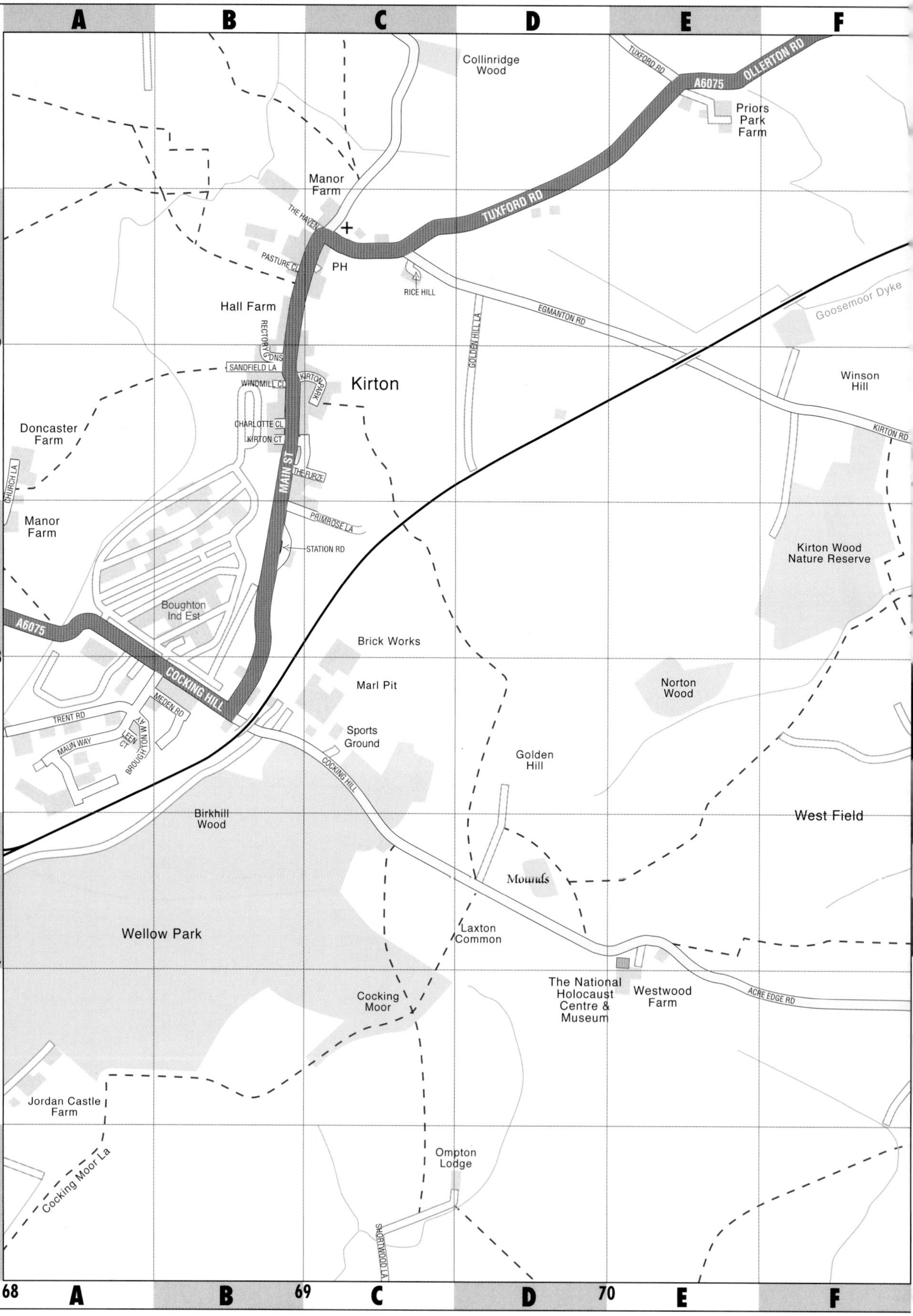

8

Collinridge Wood

TUXFORD RD

A6075 OLLERTON RD

Priors Park Farm

7

Manor Farm

THE HAVEN

PASTURE CL

PH

+

RICE HILL

TUXFORD RD

Goosemoor Dyke

EGMANTON RD

Hall Farm

69

RECTORY GDNS

SANDFIELD LA

WINDMILL CL

KIRTON PARK

GOLDBY HILL LA

Winson Hill

6

Doncaster Farm

Kirton

CHARLOTTE CL

KIRTON CT

MAIN ST

THE FURZE

KIRTON RD

CHURCH LA

PRIMROSE LA

Kirton Wood Nature Reserve

Manor Farm

STATION RD

5

A6075

Boughton Ind Est

68

Brick Works

Norton Wood

COCKING HILL

TRENT RD

MEDEN RD

Marl Pit

4

MAIN WAY

BROUGHTON WAY

KEEN CT

Sports Ground

COCKING HILL

Golden Hill

West Field

Birkhill Wood

Mounds

3

Wellow Park

Laxton Common

67

Cocking Moor

The National Holocaust Centre & Museum

Westwood Farm

ACRE EDGE RD

2

Jordan Castle Farm

Cocking Moor La

Ompton Lodge

1

SHORTWOOD LA

66

68　　A　　B　　69　　C　　D　　70　　E　　F

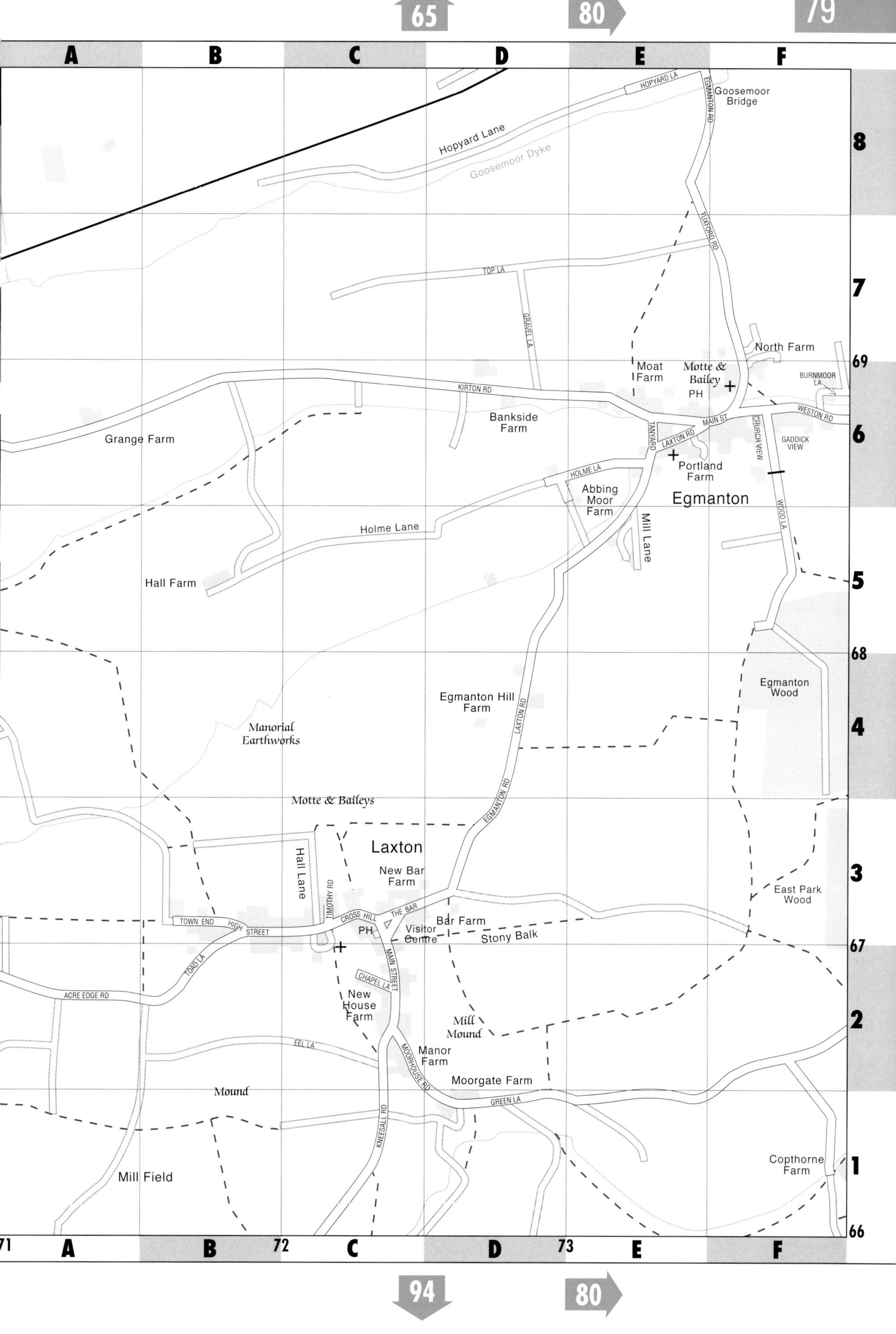
A
B
C
D
E
F
Hopyard Lane
HOPYARD LA
EGMANTON RD
Goosemoor Bridge
Goosemoor Dyke
8
TUXFORD RD
TOP LA
7
GRAVEL LA
North Farm
Moat Farm
Motte & Bailey
PH
69
BURNMOOR LA
KIRTON RD
WESTON RD
Bankside Farm
Grange Farm
TANYARD
MAIN ST
LAXTON RD
CHURCH VIEW
GADDICK VIEW
6
Portland Farm
HOLME LA
Abbing Moor Farm
Egmanton
WOOD LA
Holme Lane
Mill Lane
Hall Farm
5
68
Egmanton Wood
Egmanton Hill Farm
LAXTON RD
4
Manorial Earthworks
EGMANTON RD
Motte & Baileys
Laxton
Hall Lane
New Bar Farm
3
East Park Wood
TIMOTHY RD
THE BAR
CROSS HILL
TOWN END
HIGH STREET
Bar Farm
PH
Visitor Centre
Stony Balk
67
TOAD LA
CHAPEL LA
MAIN STREET
ACRE EDGE RD
New House Farm
Mill Mound
2
EEL LA
MOORHOUSE RD
Manor Farm
Moorgate Farm
Mound
GREEN LA
KNEESALL RD
1
Copthorne Farm
Mill Field
66
71
72
73

A   B   C   D   E   F

8

7

69

6

5

68

4

3

67

2

1

66

B1164

BURNMOOR LA

A1

Stone Road End Farm

Egmanton Crossing
LC
Windmill (dis)

Ruddings Cottage

NORMANTON RD

Goosemoor Dyke

GREAT NORTH RD

Scarthingmoor Mill

WESTON RD

Scarthingmoor House Farm

Gipsy Lodge Farm

Lady Wood

Scarthingmoor Farm

Scarthingmoor Cottage Farm

Bell Farm

B1164

THACK LA

Egmanton Common Farm

LADYWOOD LA

BELL LA

Egmanton Wood

Ladywood Farm

MOORHOUSE RD

East Park Wood

Moorhouse Beck

WADNAL LA

A1

Breck's Farm

Breck Cottage

GREEN LA

Aggrie House Farm

Church Farm
MOORHOUSE RD

Moorhouse

Thorpe Farm

Wadnal Plantation

Cocked Hat Plantation

OSSINGTON RD

Copthorne Farm

Brookdale Farm

MOORHOUSE RD

North Park Farm

Commonside Plantation

74   A   B   75   C   D   76   E   F

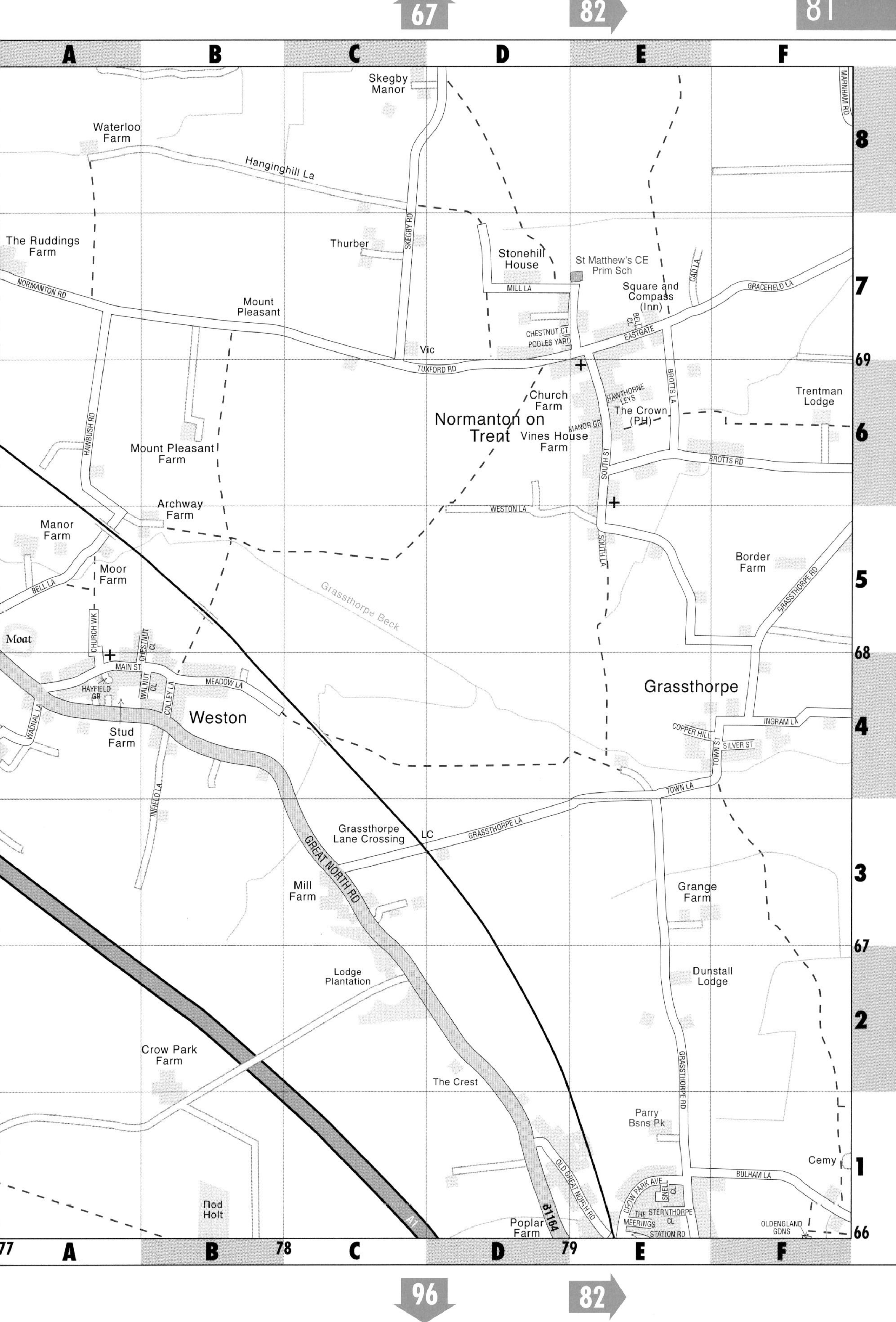
A
B
C
D
E
F
8
7
69
6
5
68
4
3
67
2
1
66
77
78
79
Skegby Manor
Waterloo Farm
Hanginghill La
MARNHAM RD
The Ruddings Farm
Thurber
SKEGBY RD
Stonehill House
St Matthew's CE Prim Sch
CAD LA
Square and Compass (Inn)
GRACEFIELD LA
NORMANTON RD
Mount Pleasant
MILL LA
BELL CL
EASTGATE
CHESTNUT CT
POOLES YARD
Vic
TUXFORD RD
Church Farm
HAWTHORNE LEYS
BROTTS LA
The Crown (PH)
Trentman Lodge
Normanton on Trent
Vines House Farm
MANOR GR
HAWBUSH RD
Mount Pleasant Farm
SOUTH ST
BROTTS RD
Archway Farm
WESTON LA
Manor Farm
SOUTH LA
Moor Farm
Border Farm
BELL LA
GRASSTHORPE RD
Grassthorpe Beck
Moat
CHURCH WK
CHESTNUT CL
MAIN ST
MEADOW LA
HAYFIELD GR
WALNUT CL
COLLEY LA
Grassthorpe
WADNAL LA
Weston
Stud Farm
COPPER HILL
INGRAM LA
SILVER ST
TOWN ST
TOWN LA
INFIELD LA
Grassthorpe Lane Crossing
LC
GRASSTHORPE LA
GREAT NORTH RD
Mill Farm
Grange Farm
Lodge Plantation
Dunstall Lodge
Crow Park Farm
The Crest
GRASSTHORPE RD
Parry Bsns Pk
Cemy
OLD GREAT NORTH RD
CROW PARK AVE
SNELL CL
BULHAM LA
THE STERNTHORPE CL
MEERINGS
STATION RD
OLDENGLAND GDNS
Nod Holt
A1
B1164
Poplar Farm

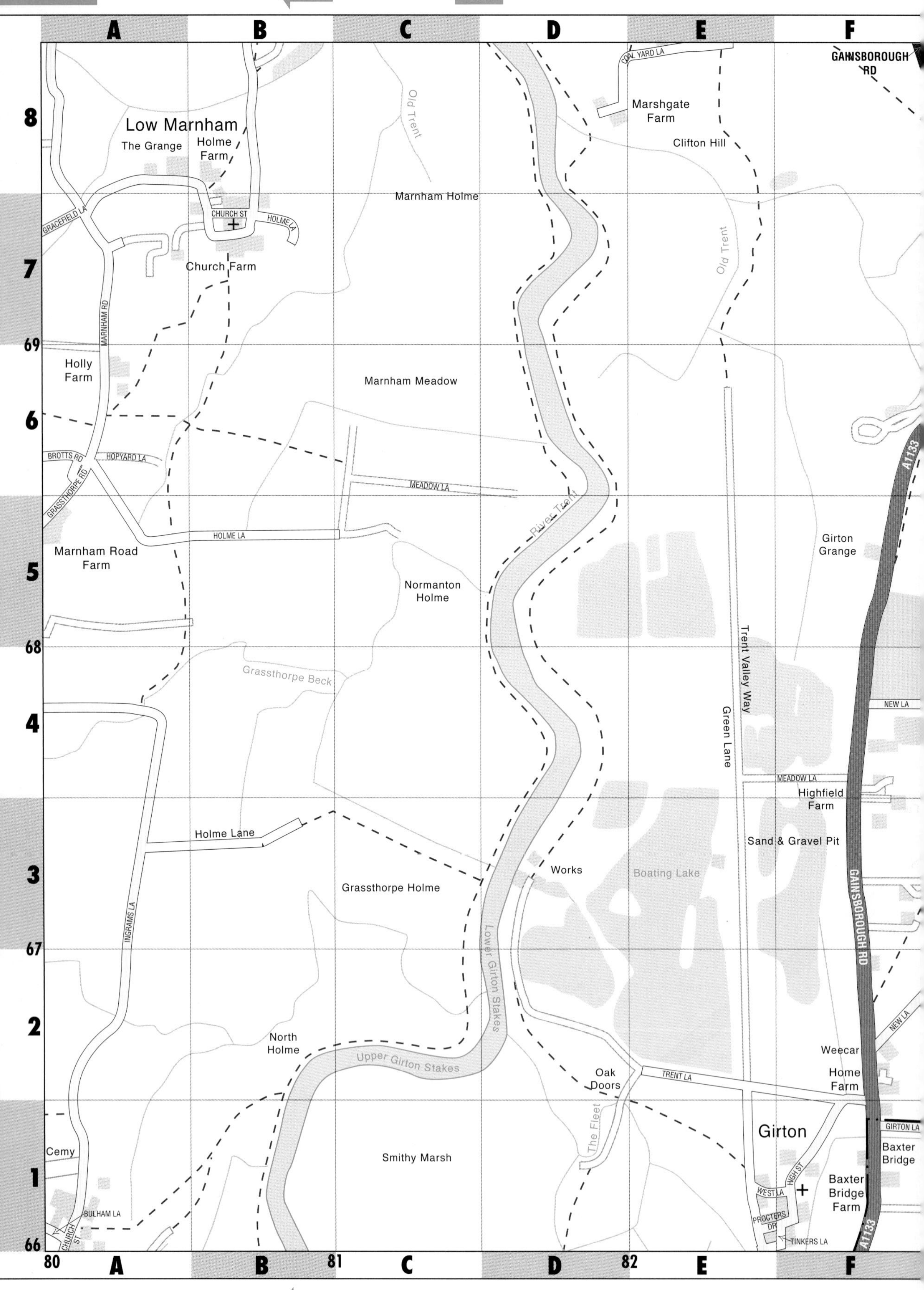

A B C D E F

GAINSBOROUGH RD

8

Low Marnham

The Grange

Holme Farm

Marshgate Farm

Clifton Hill

Old Trent

Marnham Holme

GRACEFIELD LA

CHURCH ST

HOLME LA

7

Church Farm

Old Trent

A1133

69

Holly Farm

Marnham Meadow

MARNHAM RD

6

BROTTS RD

HOPYARD LA

MEADOW LA

Girton Grange

GRASSTHORPE RD

HOLME LA

Marnham Road Farm

River Trent

5

Normanton Holme

Trent Valley Way

68

Grassthorpe Beck

Green Lane

NEW LA

4

MEADOW LA

Highfield Farm

Holme Lane

Sand & Gravel Pit

GAINSBOROUGH RD

3

INGRAMS LA

Grassthorpe Holme

Works

Boating Lake

67

Lower Girton Stakes

2

North Holme

Upper Girton Stakes

Oak Doors

TRENT LA

Weecar

Home Farm

NEW LA

The Fleet

Girton

GIRTON LA

Cemy

HIGH ST

Baxter Bridge

1

Smithy Marsh

WEST LA

PROCTERS DR

Baxter Bridge Farm

CHURCH ST

BULHAM LA

A1133

TINKERS LA

66

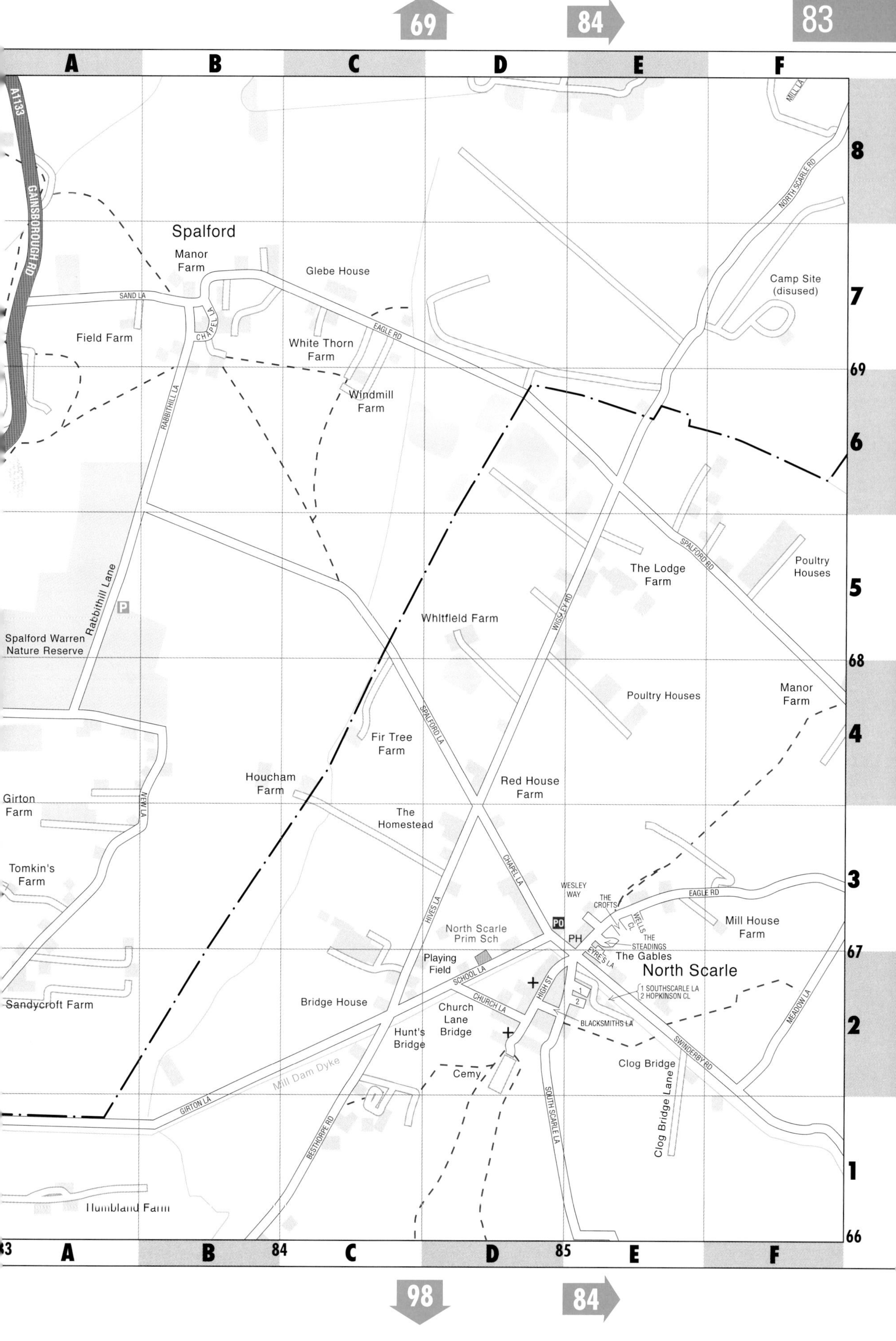

A B C D E F

8

Camp Site
(disused)

7

69

6

5

68

4

3

67

2

1

66

Spalford

Manor
Farm

Glebe House

SAND LA

Field Farm

CHAPEL LA

White Thorn
Farm

Windmill
Farm

RABBITHILL LA

Rabbithill Lane

P

Spalford Warren
Nature Reserve

EAGLE RD

NORTH SCARLE RD

MILL LA

The Lodge
Farm

Poultry
Houses

SPALFORD RD

Whitfield Farm

WIGS EY RD

SPALFORD LA

Fir Tree
Farm

Houcham
Farm

Girton
Farm

NEW LA

Tomkin's
Farm

The
Homestead

Red House
Farm

CHAPEL LA

Poultry Houses

Manor
Farm

Sandycroft Farm

HIVES LA

North Scarle
Prim Sch

Playing
Field

SCHOOL LA

Bridge House

CHURCH LA

Church
Lane
Bridge

Hunt's
Bridge

HIGH ST

WESLEY
WAY

PO

PH

FYRE'S LA

THE
CROFTS

WELLS
CL

THE
STEADINGS

The Gables

North Scarle

1
2

1 SOUTHSCARLE LA
2 HOPKINSON CL

BLACKSMITHS LA

EAGLE RD

Mill House
Farm

MEADOW LA

SWINDERBY RD

Clog Bridge

Clog Bridge Lane

SOUTH SCARLE LA

Cemy

Mill Dam Dyke

GIRTON LA

BESTHORPE RD

Humbland Farm

GAINSBOROUGH RD

A1133

83
70

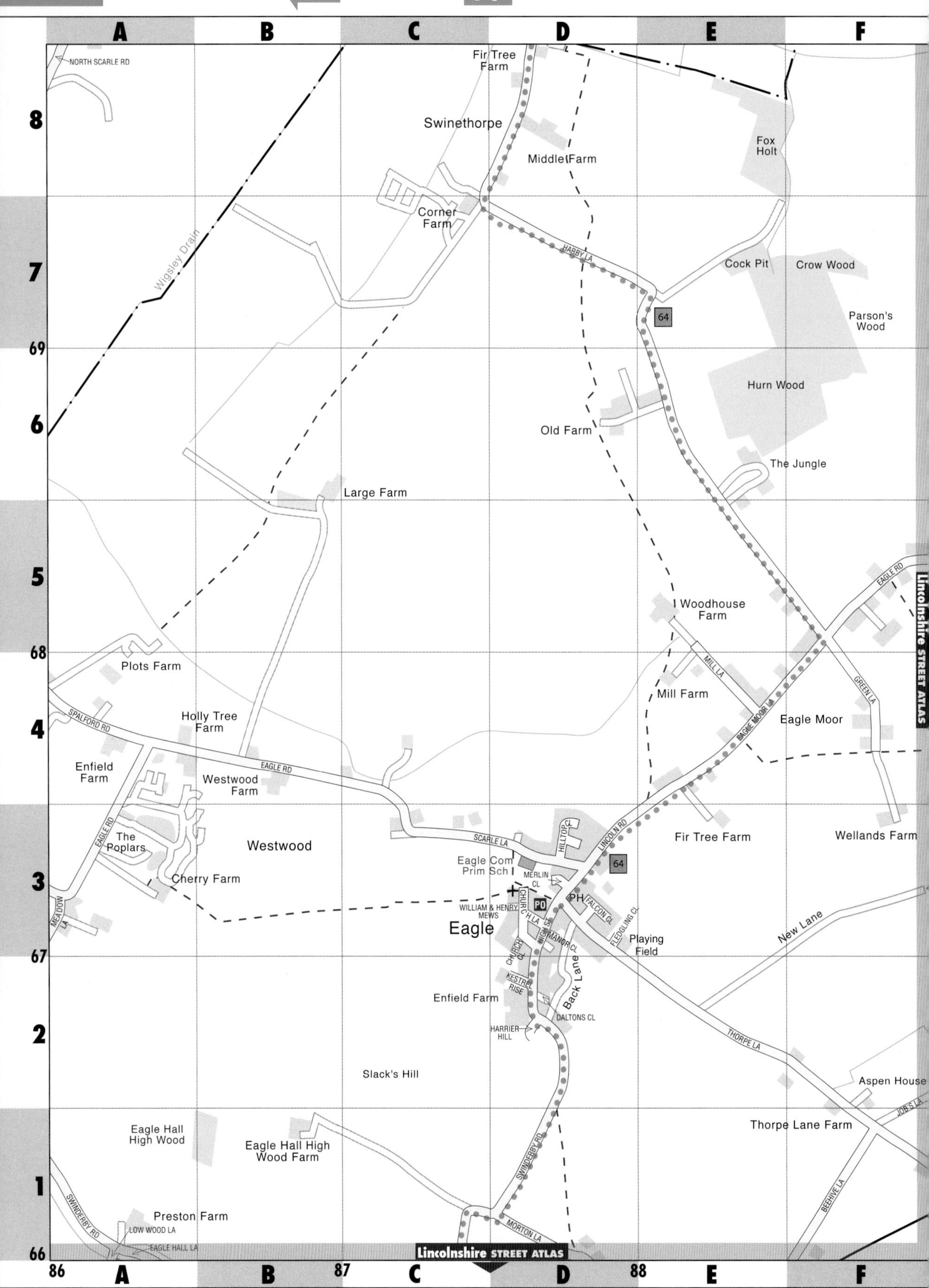

A
B
C
D
E
F
8
7
69
6
5
68
4
3
67
2
1
66
86
87
88
NORTH SCARLE RD
Fir Tree Farm
Swinethorpe
Middle Farm
Fox Holt
Corner Farm
Wigsley Drain
HARBY LA
Cock Pit
Crow Wood
64
Parson's Wood
Hurn Wood
Old Farm
The Jungle
Large Farm
Woodhouse Farm
EAGLE RD
Plots Farm
MILL LA
Mill Farm
GREEN LA
SPALFORD RD
Holly Tree Farm
EAGLE MOOR LA
Eagle Moor
Enfield Farm
Westwood Farm
EAGLE RD
EAGLE RD
The Poplars
Westwood
HILLTOP CL
LINCOLN RD
SCARLE LA
Fir Tree Farm
Wellands Farm
Eagle Com Prim Sch
64
MERLIN CL
Cherry Farm
PH
FALCON CL
FLEDGLING CL
MEADOW LA
WILLIAM & HENRY MEWS
PO
CHURCH LA
Eagle
MANOR CL
Playing Field
New Lane
CHURCH CL
KESTREL RISE
Back Lane
Enfield Farm
DALTONS CL
HARRIER HILL
THORPE LA
Slack's Hill
Aspen House
JOB'S LA
Thorpe Lane Farm
Eagle Hall High Wood
Eagle Hall High Wood Farm
SWINDERBY RD
SWINDERBY RD
BEEHIVE LA
Preston Farm
LOW WOOD LA
EAGLE HALL LA
MORTON LA
Lincolnshire STREET ATLAS

83

86

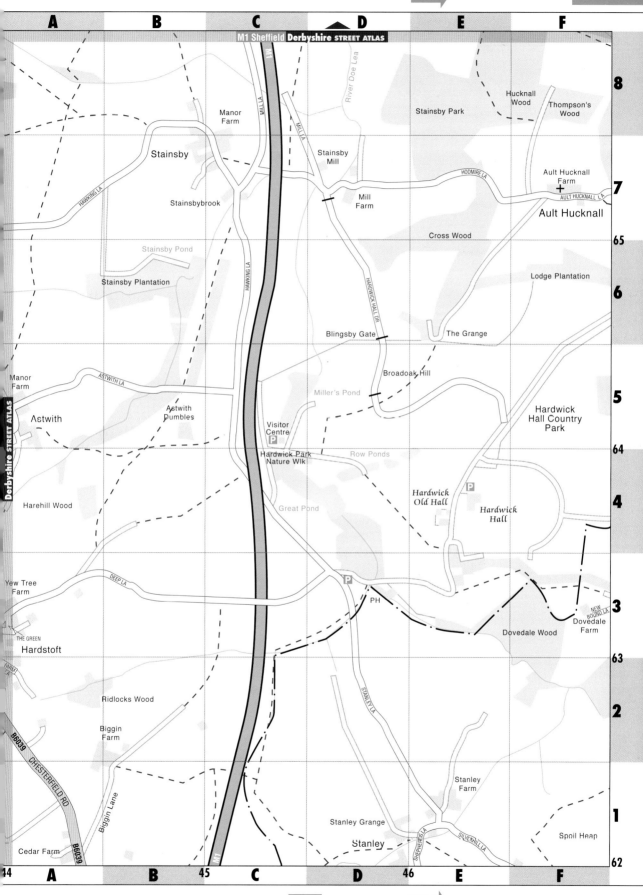

A
B
C
D
E
F
M1 Sheffield Derbyshire STREET ATLAS
M1
MILL LA
River Doe Lea
Manor Farm
Stainsby Park
Hucknall Wood
Thompson's Wood
8
Stainsby
Stainsby Mill
HODMIRE LA
Ault Hucknall Farm
7
HAWKING LA
Stainsbybrook
Mill Farm
AULT HUCKNALL LA
Ault Hucknall
Cross Wood
65
Stainsby Pond
HAWKING LA
Lodge Plantation
Stainsby Plantation
HARDWICK HALL DR
6
Blingsby Gate
The Grange
Manor Farm
ASTWITH LA
Broadoak Hill
Miller's Pond
5
Astwith
Astwith Dumbles
Visitor Centre
Hardwick Hall Country Park
P
Derbyshire STREET ATLAS
Hardwick Park Nature Wlk
Row Ponds
64
P
Hardwick Old Hall
Harehill Wood
Hardwick Hall
4
Great Pond
Yew Tree Farm
DEEP LA
P
PH
3
NEW BOUND LA
Dovedale Farm
Dovedale Wood
THE GREEN
Hardstoft
63
FARM LA
STANLEY LA
Ridlocks Wood
2
Biggin Farm
B6039
CHESTERFIELD RD
Stanley Farm
Biggin Lane
1
Stanley Grange
Spoil Heap
SHEPHERDS LA
SILVERHILL LA
Cedar Farm
B6039
Stanley
M1
62
44
A
B
45
C
D
46
E
F

99

86

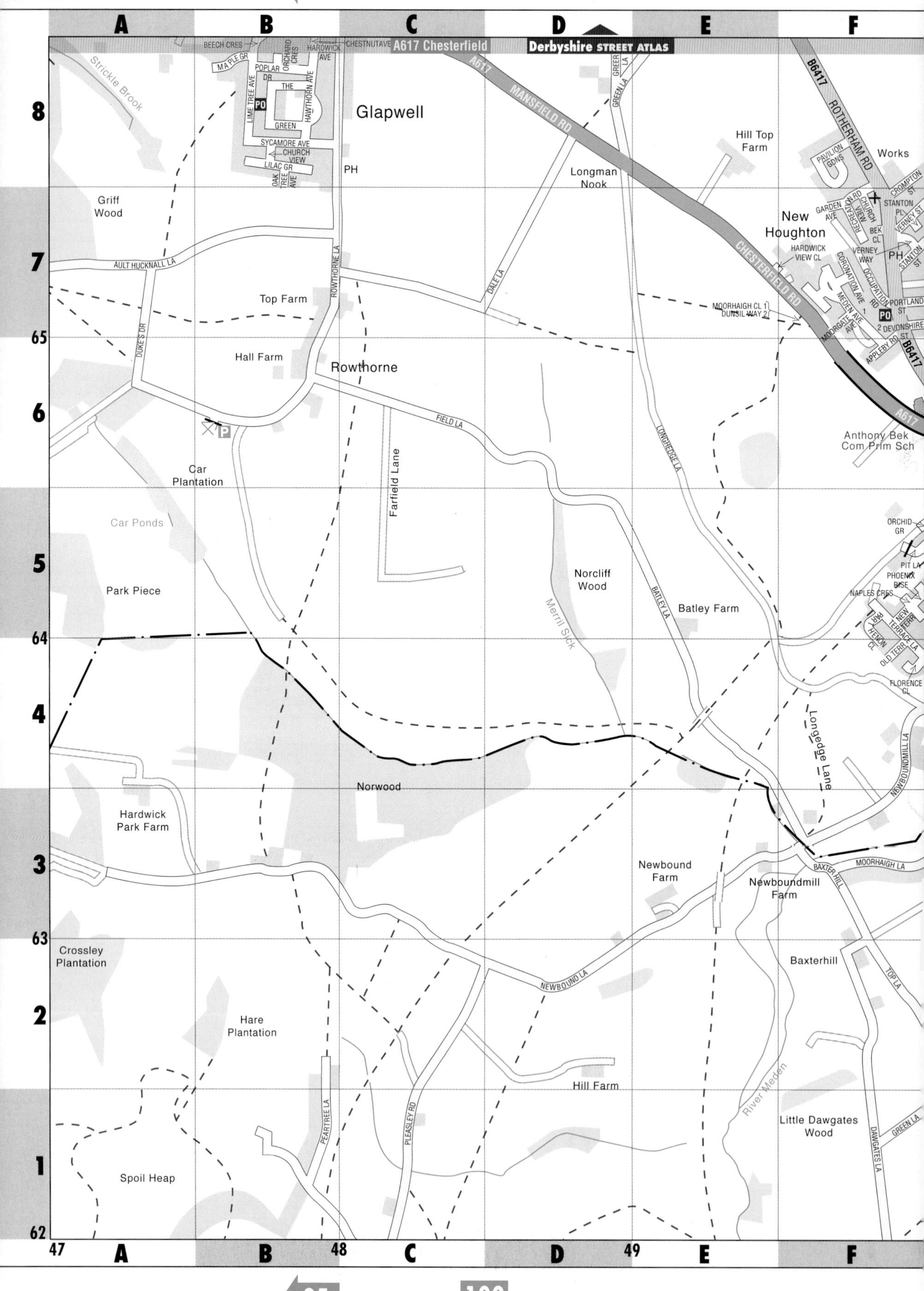

Derbyshire STREET ATLAS

Glapwell

New Houghton

Griff Wood

Top Farm

Hall Farm

Rowthorne

Car Plantation

Car Ponds

Park Piece

Norcliff Wood

Batley Farm

Hill Top Farm

Longman Nook

Anthony Bek Com Prim Sch

Works

Farfield Lane

Merril Sick

Longedge Lane

Norwood

Hardwick Park Farm

Newbound Farm

Newboundmill Farm

Baxterhill

Crossley Plantation

Hare Plantation

Hill Farm

Little Dawgates Wood

Spoil Heap

River Meden

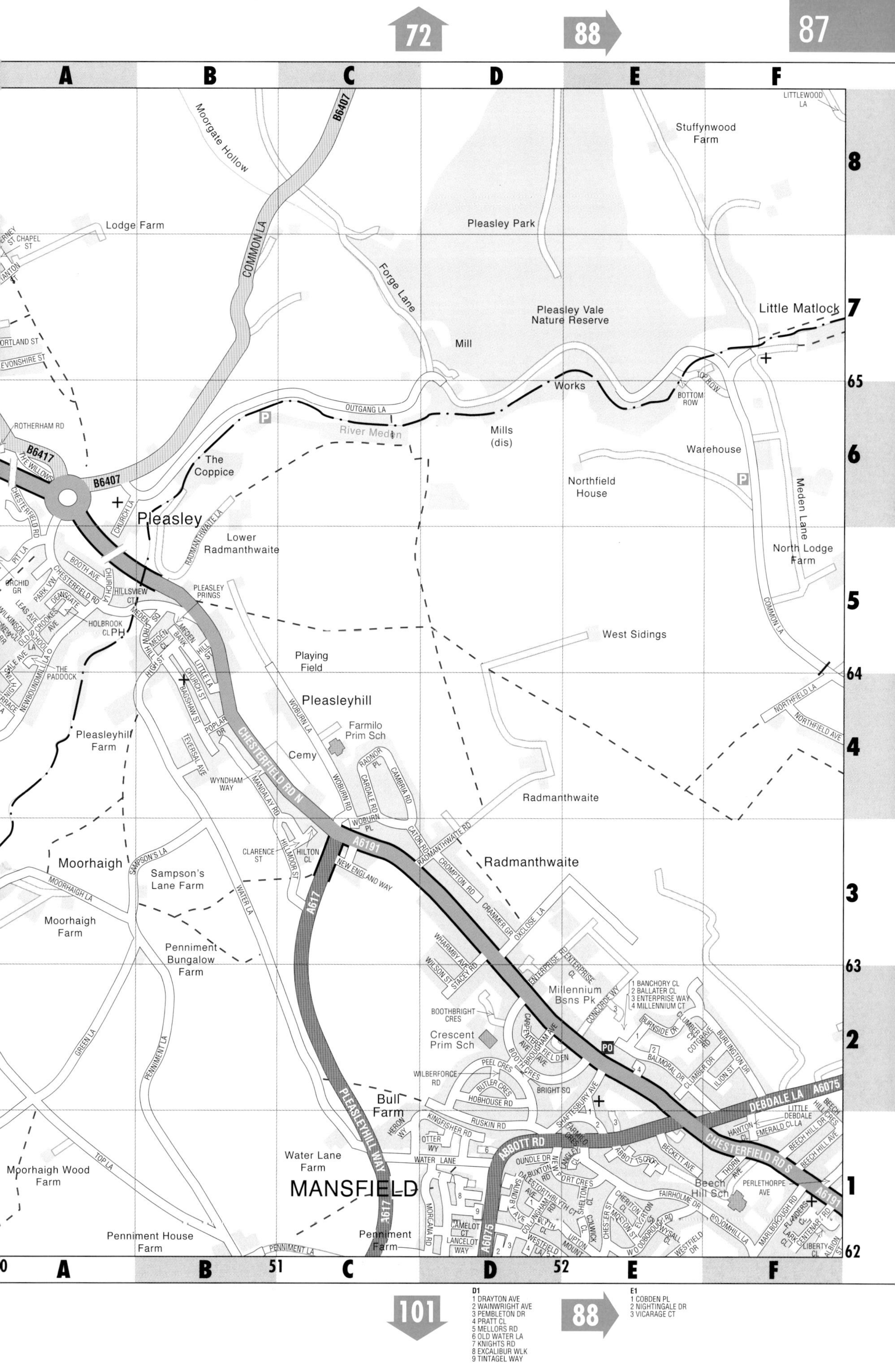

A | B | C | D | E | F

8
7
65
6
5
64
4
3
63
2
1
62

LITTLEWOOD LA

Stuffynwood Farm

Moorgate Hollow

COMMON LA

B6407

Pleasley Park

Lodge Farm

CHAPEL ST

PORTLAND ST

DEVONSHIRE ST

Forge Lane

Pleasley Vale Nature Reserve

Mill

Little Matlock

Works

TOP ROW
BOTTOM ROW

ROTHERHAM RD

Outgang La

River Meden

Mills (dis)

Warehouse

B6417

THE WILLOWS

B6407

CHESTERFIELD RD

The Coppice

Northfield House

Meden Lane

CHURCH LA

Pleasley

RADMANTHWAITE LA

Lower Radmanthwaite

North Lodge Farm

ORCHID GR

PARK VW

CHESTERFIELD RD

BOOTH AVE

Hillsview Ct

Pleasley Prings

COMMON LA

PIT LA

CROOKE AVE
LEAS AVE

GEMSGATE

CHURCH LA

CRESCENT

CRESCENT

WILKINSON
AVE

NEW RD

HOLBROOK CL PH

HIGH ST

MEDEN BANK

LITTLE LA

WOBURN LA

Playing Field

West Sidings

NORTHFIELD LA

THE PADDOCK

BAGSHAW ST

CHURCH ST

POPLAR DR

Pleasleyhill

Farmilo Prim Sch

NORTHFIELD AVE

NEWBOUND LA

TERRACE

Pleasleyhill Farm

EVERSALL AVE

MANDALAY RD

CHESTERFIELD RD N

Cemy

RADNOR PL

CARDALE RD

WOBURN RD

CAMBRIA RD

WYNDHAM WAY

WOBURN PL

Radmanthwaite

Moorhaigh

SAMPSON'S LA

Sampson's Lane Farm

CLARENCE ST

HILLMOOR ST

HILTON CL

A6191

NEW ENGLAND WAY

CATOR CLOSE

RADMANTHWAITE RD

CROMPTON RD

CRAMMER GR

ONCLOSE LA

Radmanthwaite

MOORHAIGH LA

WATER LA

A617

Moorhaigh Farm

GREEN LA

Penniment Bungalow Farm

PENNIMENT LA

WHARMBY AVE
WILSON ST
STACEY RD

BOOTHBRIGHT CRES

ENTERPRISE CL

Millennium Bsns Pk

CONCORDE WY

1 BANCHORY CL
2 BALLATER CL
3 ENTERPRISE WAY
4 MILLENNIUM CT

BURNSIDE DR

BALMORAL DR

CLIMBER DR

COTGRAVE RD

BURLINGTON DR

TILTON DR

63

2

Crescent Prim Sch

CARPENTER GRAM AVE

SHELDEN

PO

Bull Farm

PLEASLEYHILL WAY

WILBERFORCE RD

PEEL CRES

BUTLER CRES

HOBHOUSE RD

BRIGHT SQ

SHAFTESBURY AVE

DEBDALE LA

A6075

LITTLE DEBDALE CL

BEECH

Water Lane Farm

HERON WY

KINGFISHER RD

RUSKIN RD

CHESTERFIELD RD S

HAWTON

BEECH HILL DR

BEECH HILL RD

Moorhaigh Wood Farm

TOP LA

OTTER CL

Water Lane

ABBOTT RD

OUNDLE DR

BUXTON CL

BECKETT AVE

ABBOT'S CROFT

FAIRHOLME RD

Beech Hill Sch

PERLETHORPE AVE

A6191

MANSFIELD

A617

MORGANA RD

CAMELOT WAY
LANCELOT WAY

TINTAGEL WAY

NEWPORT CRES

CHERITON CT

CHIWICK

CHES JR ST

FIXTON

WOODBOROUGH RD
YALL RD

WESTFIELD LA

LIPTON MOUNT

WESTFIELD DR

ROOMHILL RD

MARLBOROUGH RD

CENTENARY RD

ANDERS RD

THORN CL

LASK
CENTENARY

LIBERTY RD

Penniment House Farm

PENNIMENT LA

Penniment Farm

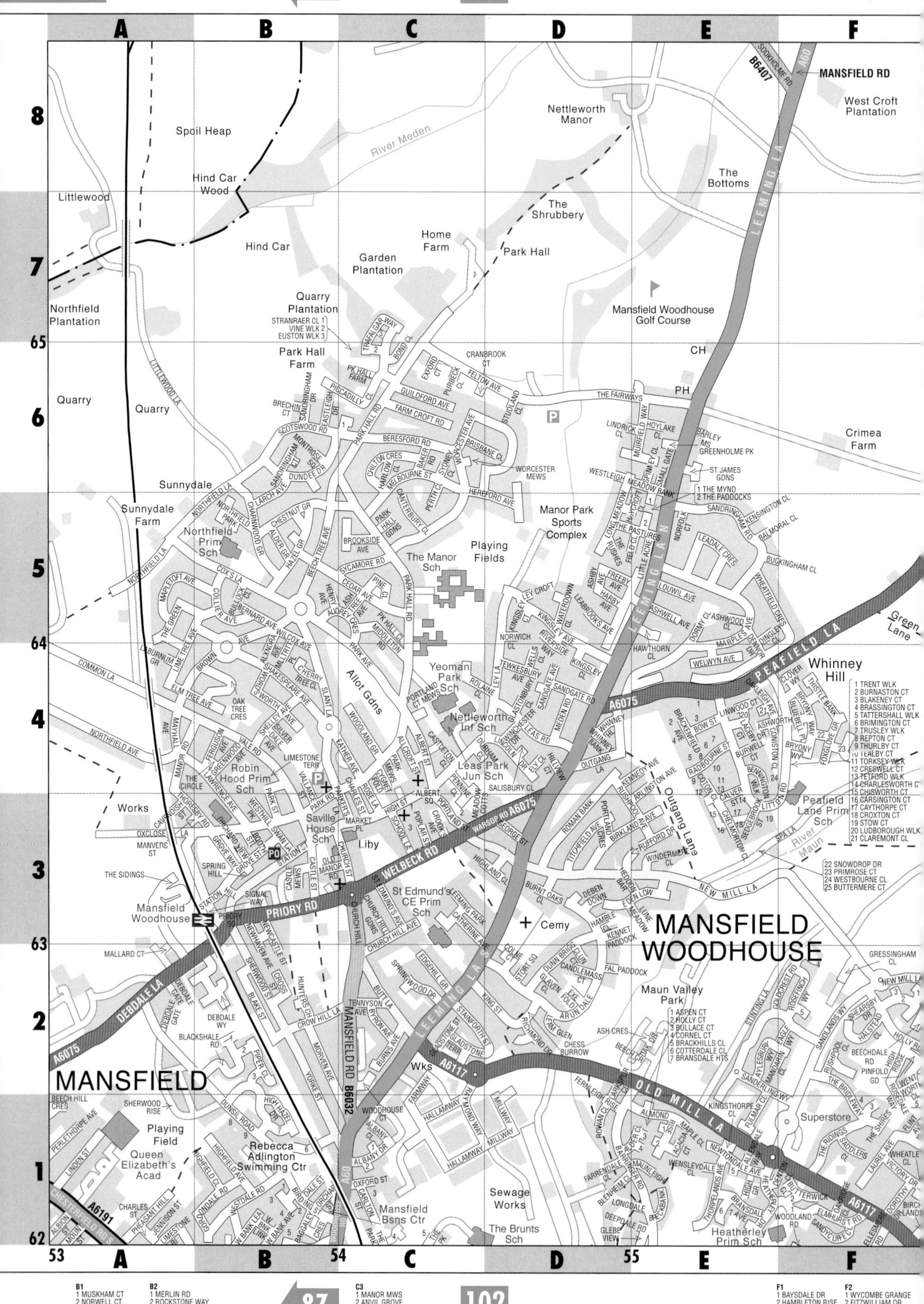

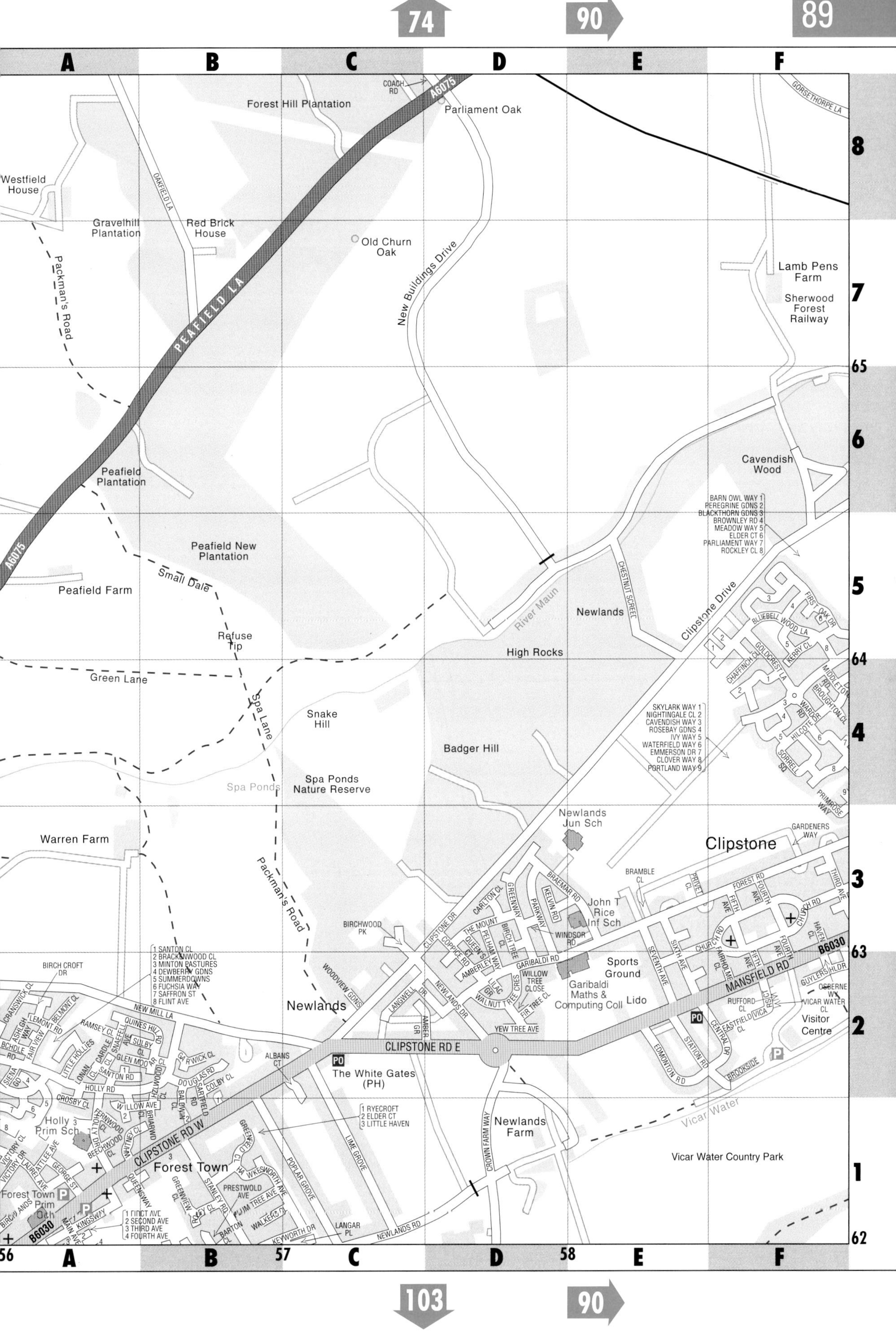
74
90
A
B
C
D
E
F
Forest Hill Plantation
Parliament Oak
Westfield House
Gravelhill Plantation
Red Brick House
Old Churn Oak
New Buildings Drive
Packman's Road
PEAFIELD LA
A6075
Lamb Pens Farm
Sherwood Forest Railway
Cavendish Wood
Peafield Plantation
Peafield New Plantation
Small Dale
Peafield Farm
Refuse Tip
River Maun
Newlands
High Rocks
Clipstone Drive
Green Lane
Spa Lane
Snake Hill
Badger Hill
Spa Ponds
Spa Ponds Nature Reserve
Newlands Jun Sch
Warren Farm
Clipstone
John T Rice Inf Sch
Sports Ground
Garibaldi Maths & Computing Coll
Lido
Newlands
CLIPSTONE RD E
The White Gates (PH)
MANSFIELD RD
B6030
Visitor Centre
Newlands Farm
Vicar Water
Vicar Water Country Park
CLIPSTONE RD W
Holly Prim Sch
Forest Town
Forest Town Prim
56
57
58
62
63
64
65
1
2
3
4
5
6
7
8
103
90

89
75

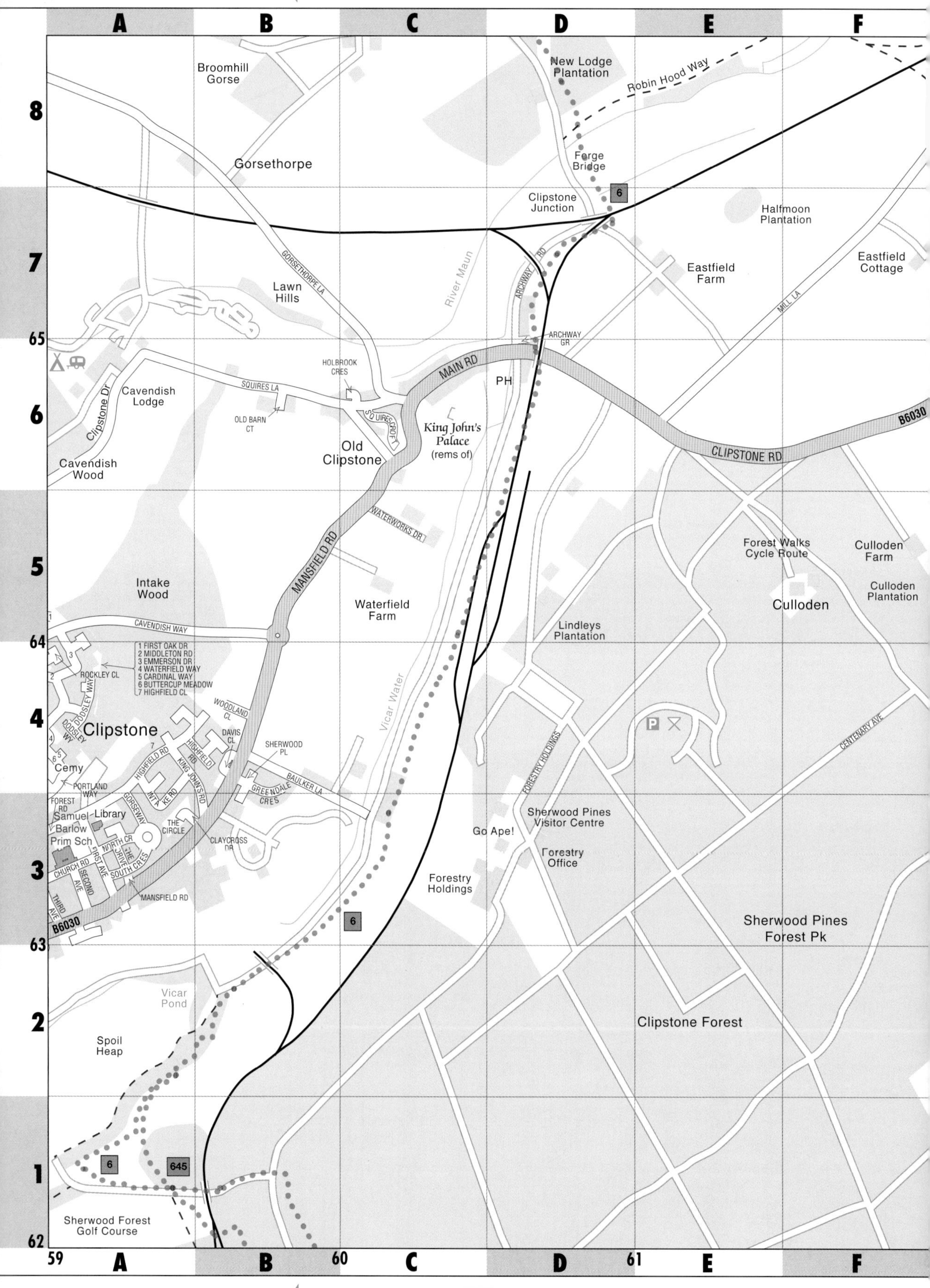
A
B
C
D
E
F
8
7
65
6
5
64
4
3
63
2
1
62
59
60
61
Broomhill
Gorse
New Lodge
Plantation
Robin Hood Way
Gorsethorpe
Forge
Bridge
Clipstone
Junction
6
Halfmoon
Plantation
Eastfield
Farm
Eastfield
Cottage
GORSETHORPE LA
Lawn
Hills
River Maun
ARCHWAY RD
MILL LA
ARCHWAY
GR
HOLBROOK
CRES
MAIN RD
PH
Cavendish
Lodge
SQUIRES LA
OLD BARN
CT
SQUIRES CROFT
King John's
Palace
(rems of)
B6030
Clipstone Dr
Old
Clipstone
CLIPSTONE RD
Cavendish
Wood
WATERWORKS DR
Forest Walks
Cycle Route
Culloden
Farm
MANSFIELD RD
Intake
Wood
Waterfield
Farm
Culloden
Plantation
Culloden
CAVENDISH WAY
Lindleys
Plantation
1 FIRST OAK DR
2 MIDDLETON RD
3 EMMERSON DR
4 WATERFIELD WAY
5 CARDINAL WAY
6 BUTTERCUP MEADOW
7 HIGHFIELD CL
ROCKLEY CL
DODSLEY WAY
WOODLAND
CL
Vicar Water
CENTENARY AVE
Clipstone
DAVIS
CL
HIGHFIELD
RD
SHERWOOD
PL
FORESTRY HOLDINGS
Cemy
HIGHFIELD RD
KING JOHN'S RD
BAULKER LA
PORTLAND
WAY
GREENDALE
CRES
FOREST
RD
Samuel
Barlow
Prim Sch
Library
GORSEWAY
THE
CIRCLE
Sherwood Pines
Visitor Centre
Go Ape!
CLAYCROSS
DR
Forestry
Office
NORTH CR
THE DRIVE
FIRST AVE
CHURCH RD
SECOND
AVE
SOUTH CRES
Forestry
Holdings
THIRD
AVE
MANSFIELD RD
B6030
6
Sherwood Pines
Forest Pk
Vicar
Pond
Spoil
Heap
Clipstone Forest
6
645
Sherwood Forest
Golf Course

89
104

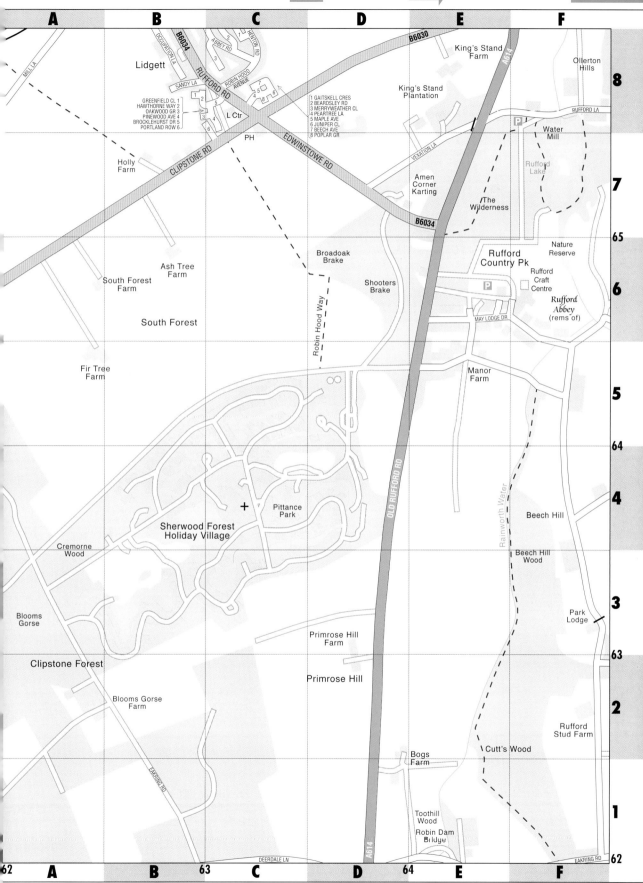

A B C D E F

8

7

65

6

5

64

4

3

63

2

1

62

Lidgett

B6034
ABBEY RD
HEITON RD
B6030
A614
King's Stand Farm
Ollerton Hills

OCCUPATION LA
RUFFORD RD
ROBIN HOOD AVENUE
SANDY LA
King's Stand Plantation
Rufford LA

GREENFIELD CL 1
HAWTHORNE WAY 2
OAKWOOD GR 3
PINEWOOD AVE 4
BROCKLEHURST DR 5
PORTLAND ROW 6

1 GAITSKELL CRES
2 BEARDSLEY RD
3 MERRYWEATHER CL
4 PEARTREE LA
5 MAPLE AVE
6 JUNIPER CL
7 BEECH AVE
8 POPLAR GR

L Ctr

P
Water Mill

PH
EDWINSTOWE RD
VEXATION LA
Rufford Lake

Holly Farm
CLIPSTONE RD
Amen Corner Karting
The Wilderness

B6034

Broadoak Brake
Nature Reserve

Ash Tree Farm
Rufford Country Pk

Shooters Brake
Rufford Craft Centre

South Forest Farm
Rufford Abbey (rems of)

South Forest
ROBIN HOOD WAY
P
MAY LODGE DR

Fir Tree Farm
Manor Farm

Rainworth Water
Beech Hill

Sherwood Forest Holiday Village
+
Pittance Park
OLD RUFFORD RD
Beech Hill Wood

Cremorne Wood

Blooms Gorse
Park Lodge

Primrose Hill Farm

Clipstone Forest
Primrose Hill

EAKRING RD
Blooms Gorse Farm
Rufford Stud Farm

Cutt's Wood
Bogs Farm

Toothill Wood
Robin Dam Bridge
A614
DEERDALE LN
EAKRING RD

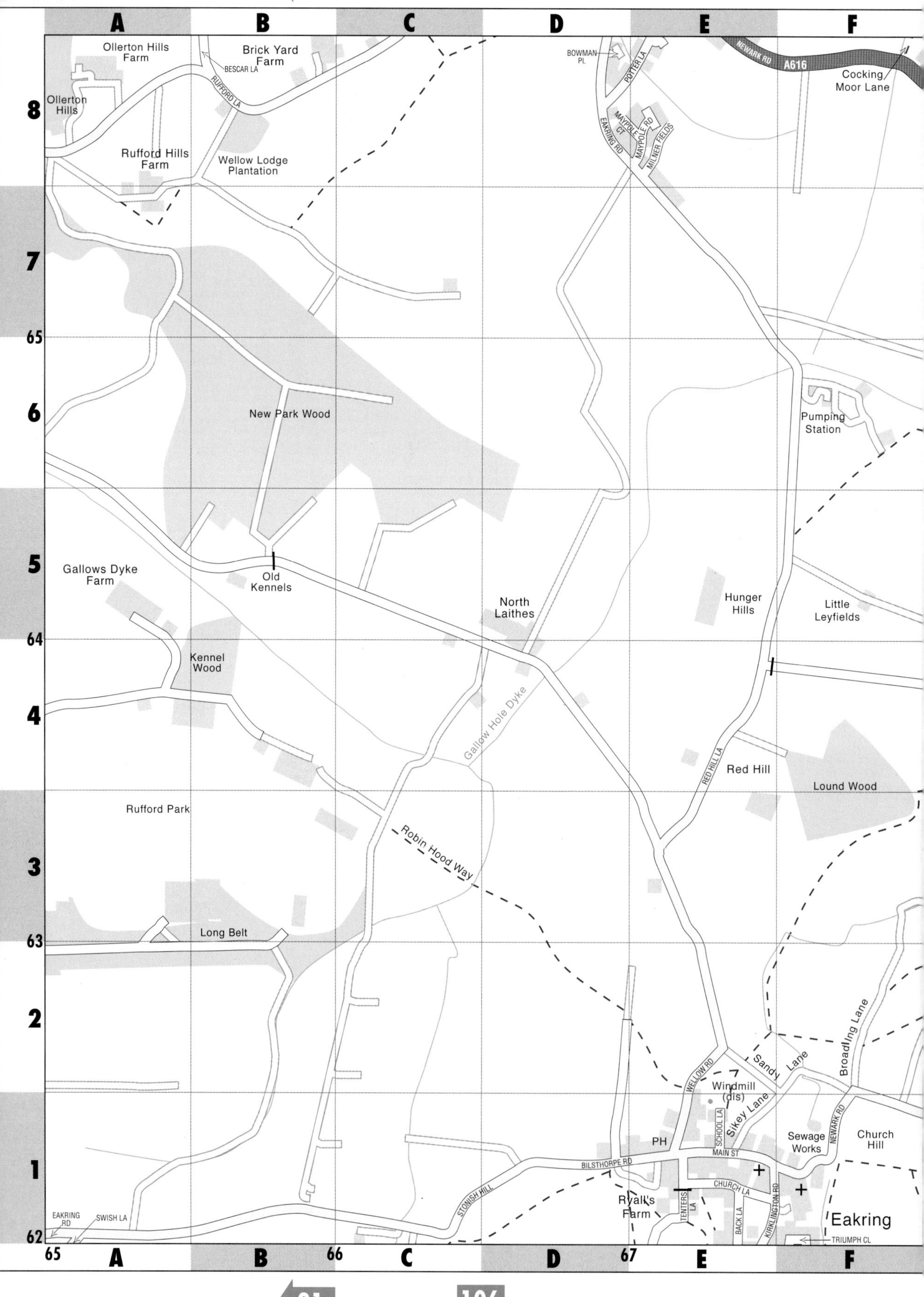

A B C D E F

8

7

65

6

5

64

4

3

63

2

1

62

Ollerton Hills Farm

Brick Yard Farm

BESCAR LA

RUFFORD LA

Ollerton Hills

Rufford Hills Farm

Wellow Lodge Plantation

BOWMAN PL

POTTER LA

NEWARK RD A616

Cocking Moor Lane

MAYPOLE GT

EAKRING RD

MAYPOLE RD

MILNER FIELDS

New Park Wood

Pumping Station

Gallows Dyke Farm

Old Kennels

North Laithes

Hunger Hills

Little Leyfields

Kennel Wood

Gallow Hole Dyke

RED HILL LA

Red Hill

Lound Wood

Rufford Park

Robin Hood Way

Long Belt

Broadling Lane

Sandy Lane

Windmill (dis)

WELLOW RD

SCHOOL LA

Sikey Lane

NEWARK RD

Sewage Works

Church Hill

PH

MAIN ST

BILSTHORPE RD

STONISH HILL

Ryall's Farm

TENTERS LA

CHURCH LA

BACK LA

KIRKLINGTON RD

Eakring

EAKRING RD

SWISH LA

TRIUMPH CL

65 A B 66 C D 67 E F

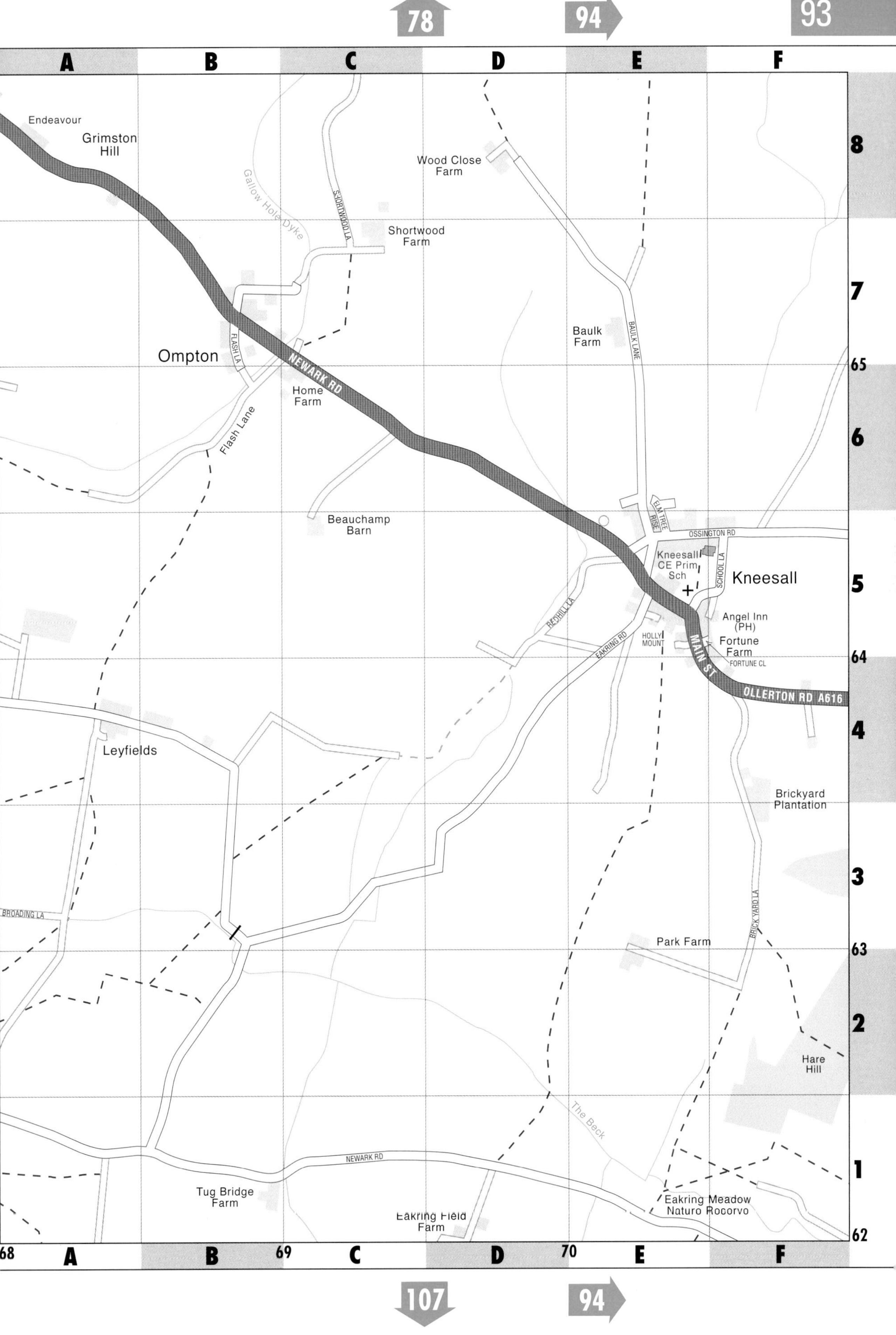
A
B
C
D
E
F
Endeavour
Grimston Hill
Gallow Hole Dyke
SHORTWOOD LA
Wood Close Farm
Shortwood Farm
Baulk Farm
BAULK LANE
FLASH LA
Ompton
NEWARK RD
Home Farm
Flash Lane
Beauchamp Barn
ELM TREE RISE
OSSINGTON RD
Kneesall CE Prim Sch
SCHOOL LA
Kneesall
REDHILL LA
Angel Inn (PH)
HOLLY MOUNT
EAKRING RD
MAIN ST
Fortune Farm
FORTUNE CL
OLLERTON RD A616
Leyfields
Brickyard Plantation
BROADING LA
BRICK YARD LA
Park Farm
Hare Hill
The Beck
NEWARK RD
Tug Bridge Farm
Eakring Field Farm
Eakring Meadow Nature Reserve
8
7
65
6
5
64
4
3
63
2
1
62
68
69
70

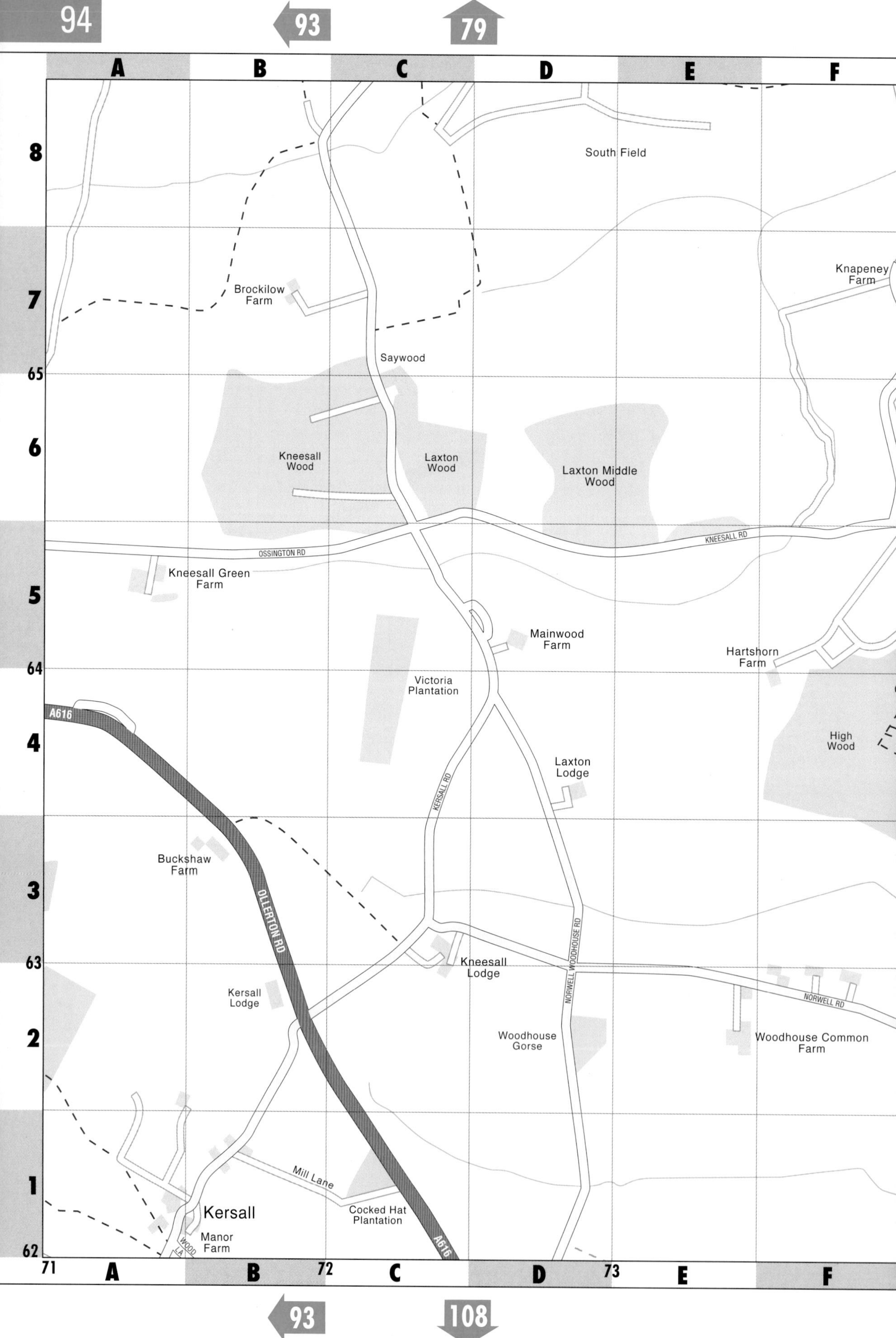

93
79

A **B** **C** **D** **E** **F**

8

South Field

7

Knapeney
Farm

Brockilow
Farm

65

Saywood

6

Kneesall
Wood

Laxton
Wood

Laxton Middle
Wood

KNEESALL RD

OSSINGTON RD

Kneesall Green
Farm

5

Mainwood
Farm

Hartshorn
Farm

64

Victoria
Plantation

4

A616

High
Wood

Laxton
Lodge

KERSALL RD

3

Buckshaw
Farm

OLLERTON RD

NORWELL WOODHOUSE RD

63

Kneesall
Lodge

NORWELL RD

Kersall
Lodge

2

Woodhouse
Gorse

Woodhouse Common
Farm

Mill Lane

1

Kersall

Cocked Hat
Plantation

A616

Manor
Farm

WOOD LA

62

71 **A** **B** **72** **C** **D** **73** **E** **F**

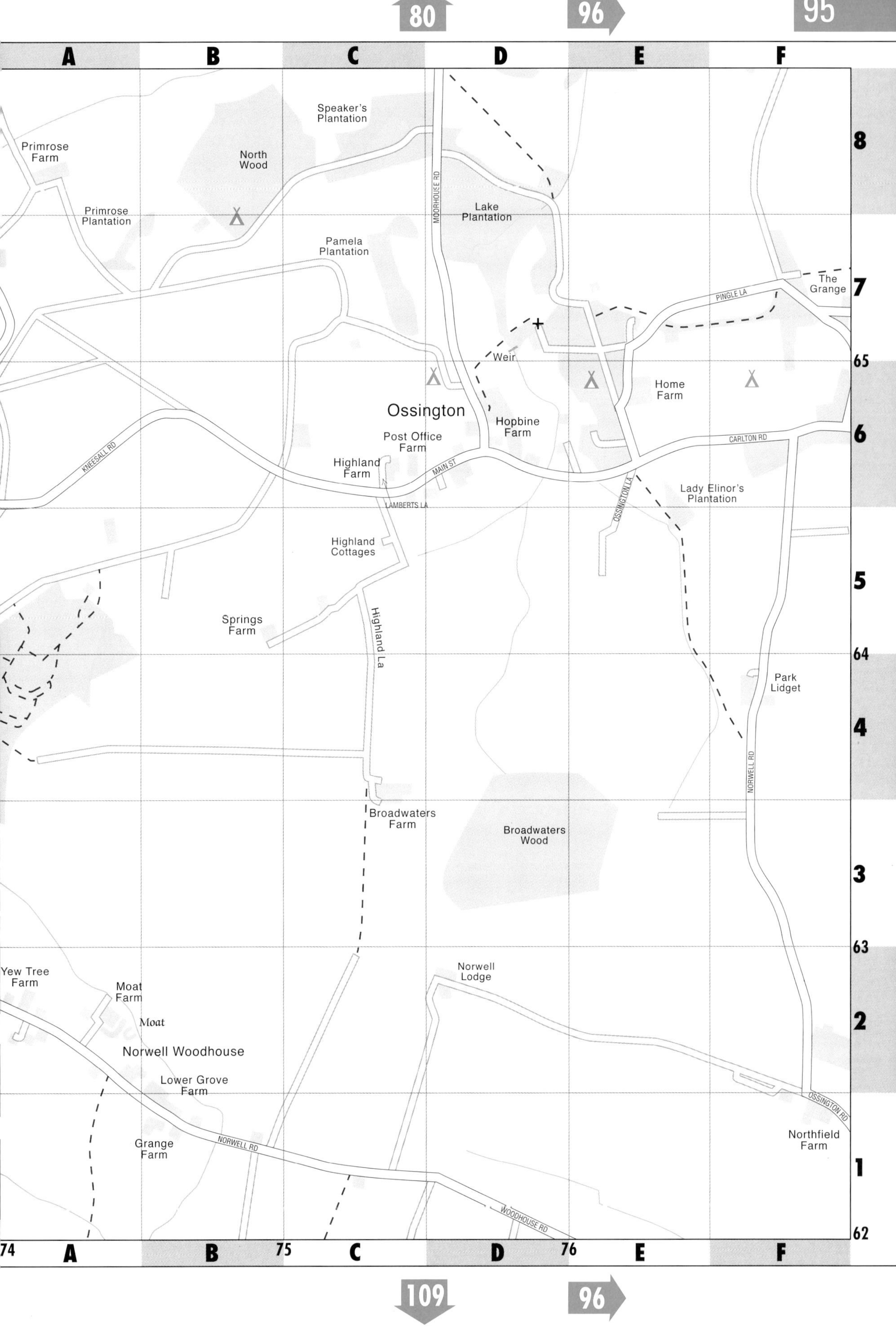
80
96
A
B
C
D
E
F
Speaker's Plantation
Primrose Farm
North Wood
Primrose Plantation
MOORHOUSE RD
Lake Plantation
Pamela Plantation
The Grange
PINGLE LA
Weir
Ossington
Home Farm
Hopbine Farm
Post Office Farm
CARLTON RD
KNEESALL RD
Highland Farm
MAIN ST
LAMBERTS LA
OSSINGTON LA
Lady Elinor's Plantation
Highland Cottages
Springs Farm
Highland La
Park Lidget
NORWELL RD
Broadwaters Farm
Broadwaters Wood
Yew Tree Farm
Norwell Lodge
Moat Farm
Moat
Norwell Woodhouse
Lower Grove Farm
OSSINGTON RD
Northfield Farm
Grange Farm
NORWELL RD
WOODHOUSE RD
8
7
65
6
5
64
4
3
63
2
1
62
74
75
76
109
96

95
81

A B C D E F

8

Common Farm

OSSINGTON RD

Brimblebeck Lane

Lady Charlotte's Plantation

Barrel Hill

B1164

OLD GREAT NORTH RD

Crow Park Bridge

STATION RD

GRASSTHORPE RD

FORGE CL

HIGH ST

PH

HEMPLANDS LA

NURSERY LA

HOUNSFIELD WAY

STRAWBERRY FIELDS

ROSE FARM DR

TWITCH LA

THE CLUCK TOOLS

Liby

FREDERICK CL 1
WILLOW HOLT 2
THE VINES 3
OLD ENGLAND GDNS 4

BARREL HILL RD

POPLAR CL

PALMER

MILL LA

MAIN ST

Windmill

7

The Grange

Sutton on Trent

OSSINGTON LA

EAVES LA

MAIN ST

SHIRES WAY

FLORAL VILLAS

65

PINGLE LA

6

CARLTON RD

Carlton Wood

Stud Farm

Works

Works

GREAT NORTH RD

5

OSSINGTON RD

Castlehill

LC

Great Northern Inn (PH)

B1164

FERRY LANE

CHURCH LANE

64

Whiteley Plantation

THE FARMSTEAD 1
OLD BELL LA 2

B1164

MAIN ST

4

Hill Farm

Carlton-on-Trent

3

Willoughby Farm

63

CARLTON LA

2

Willoughby Farm

The Beck

Sewage Works

OLD NORTH ROAD

1

OSSINGTON RD

The Poplars

Vicarage

GREAT NORTH RD

62

77 A B 78 C D 79 E F

A
B
C
D
E
F
Sutton-on-Trent Prim Sch
FIRST HOLME LA
Holme Farm
MIDDLE HOLME LA
TRAFALGAR SQ
FAR HOLME LA
South Holme
Spring Head
GREEN LA
HIGH ST
A1133
The Holly House Farm
TINKER'S LA
Trent Valley Way
GAINSBOROUGH RD
The Fleet
The Manor
FAR HOLME LA
SAND LA
SANDERS CL
FLEET LA
Meering Lane
Primrose Hill
Works
Besthorpe Nature Reserve
PINGS CL 1
CHURCH LA 2
OLD SCHOOL LA 3
WADDINGTON LA 4
LOW RD
MAIN RD
The Rhymes
CARLTON LA
Besthorpe
Besthorpe Wharf
Trent La
TRENT LA
River Trent
Mill Farm
CHURCH LA
Windmill
Carlton Holme
Hoehill Lane
Carlton Rack
BESTHORPE RD
Ferry Farm
1 CHURCH LA
2 FERRY LA
Besthorpe Nature Reserve
West View Farm
The Beck
The Fleet
Carlton Ferry Lane
COLLINGHAM RD
LUMBERT WAY
A1133
BESTHORPE RD
OLD NORTH RD
Sand and Gravel Pit
Sewage Works
Northcroft Lane
Pitomy Farm
PITOMY DR 1
HICKMAN GR 2
CARLTON FERRY LA
Ferry Lane Farm
Sand and Gravel Pit
CHURCH LA
LOW ST
A1
8
7
65
6
5
64
4
3
63
2
1
62
80
81
82

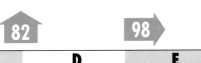

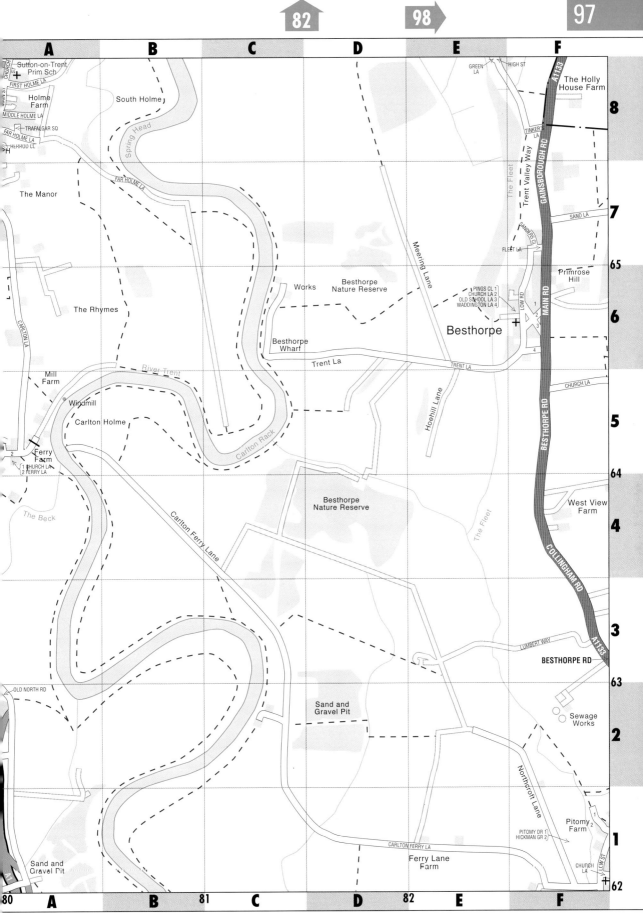

97
83

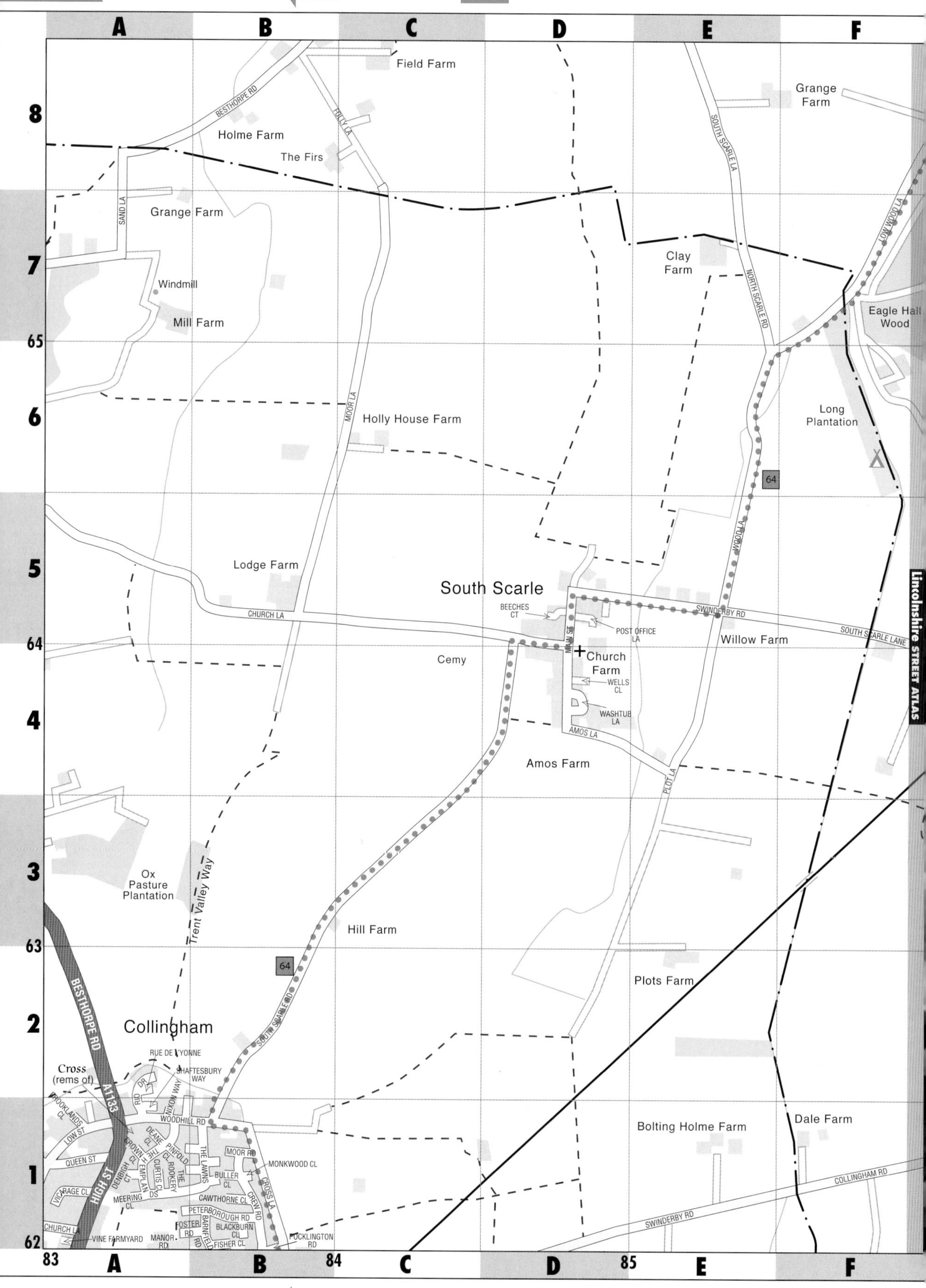
A
B
C
D
E
F
8
7
65
6
5
64
4
3
63
2
1
62
83
84
85
Field Farm
Grange Farm
Holme Farm
The Firs
BESTHORPE RD
FOLLY LA
SOUTH SCARLE LA
Grange Farm
SAND LA
Windmill
Mill Farm
Clay Farm
NORTH SCARLE RD
LOW WOOD LA
Eagle Hall Wood
MOOR LA
Holly House Farm
Long Plantation
64
WOOD LA
Lodge Farm
South Scarle
CHURCH LA
BEECHES CT
MAIN ST
POST OFFICE LA
SWINDERBY RD
SOUTH SCARLE LANE
Willow Farm
Cemy
Church Farm
WELLS CL
WASHTUB LA
AMOS LA
Amos Farm
PLOT LA
Ox Pasture Plantation
Trent Valley Way
Hill Farm
64
SOUTH SCARLE RD
Plots Farm
BESTHORPE RD
Collingham
A1133
RUE DE L'YONNE
SHAFTESBURY WAY
Cross (rems of)
BROOKLANDS CL
LOW ST
QUEEN ST
HIGH ST
VICARAGE CL
CHURCH LA
VINE FARMYARD
MANOR RD
WOODHILL RD
NIXON WAY
DEANE CL
PINFOLD CL
THE LAWNS
MOOR RD
MONKWOOD CL
BULLER CL
CROSS LA
CAWTHORNE CL
CREW RD
PETERBOROUGH RD
BLACKBURN CL
FOSTER RD
BARNFIELD RD
FISHER CL
POCKLINGTON RD
DENBIGH CL
MEERING CL
Bolting Holme Farm
Dale Farm
SWINDERBY RD
COLLINGHAM RD
Lincolnshire STREET ATLAS

97
112

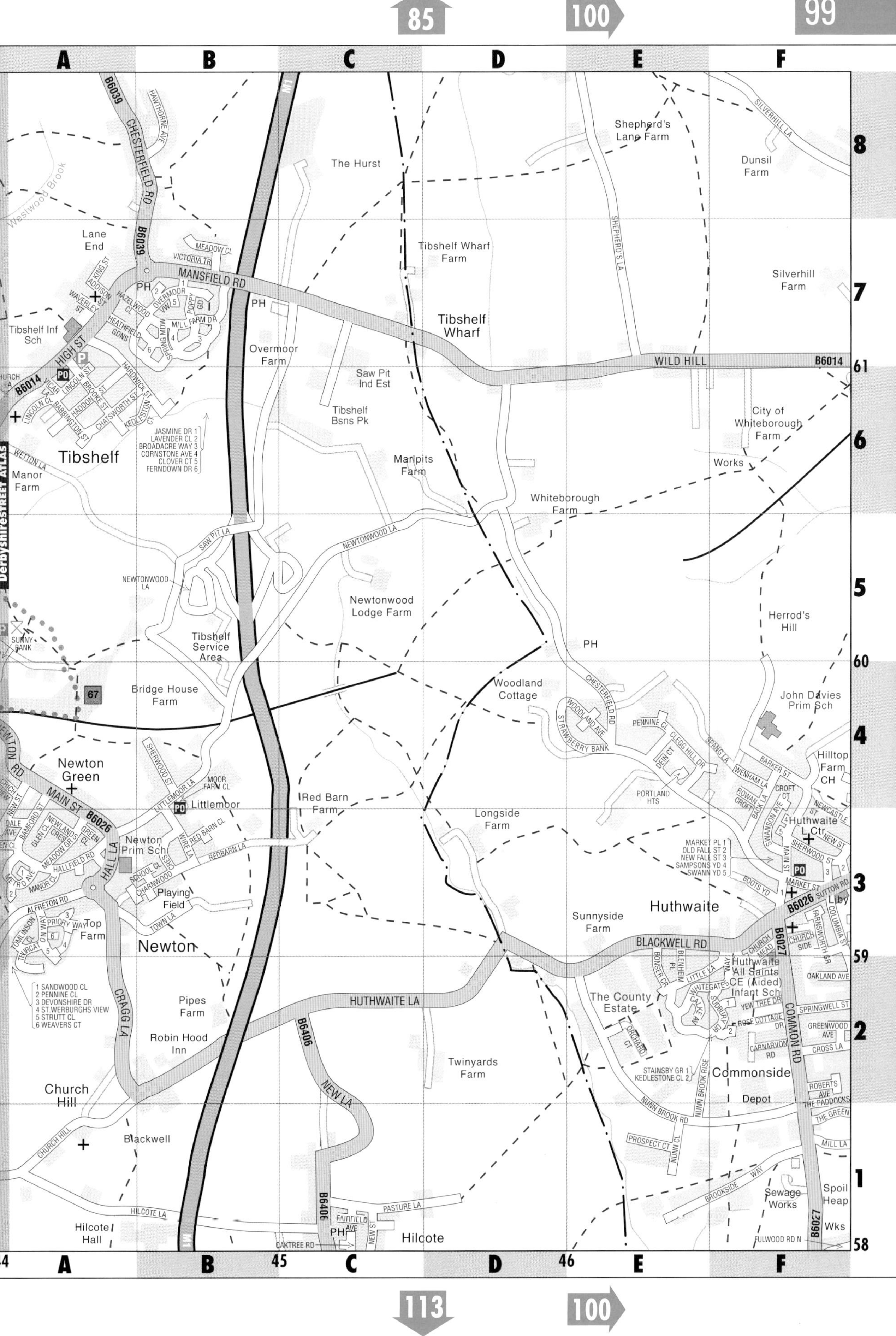
Tibshelf
Lane End
Tibshelf Inf Sch
Manor Farm
The Hurst
Tibshelf Wharf Farm
Tibshelf Wharf
Overmoor Farm
Saw Pit Ind Est
Tibshelf Bsns Pk
Marlpits Farm
Shepherd's Lane Farm
Dunsil Farm
Silverhill Farm
City of Whiteborough Farm
Works
Whiteborough Farm
Newtonwood Lodge Farm
Tibshelf Service Area
Herrod's Hill
Bridge House Farm
Woodland Cottage
John Davies Prim Sch
Newton Green
Littlemoor
Red Barn Farm
Longside Farm
Hilltop Farm
Newton Prim Sch
Playing Field
Top Farm
Newton
Huthwaite
Sunnyside Farm
Huthwaite L Ctr
Huthwaite All Saints CE (Aided) Infant Sch
The County Estate
Pipes Farm
Robin Hood Inn
Twinyards Farm
Commonside
Depot
Church Hill
Blackwell
Sewage Works
Spoil Heap
Wks
Hilcote Hall
Hilcote
MANSFIELD RD
CHESTERFIELD RD
HIGH ST
WILD HILL
B6014
B6039
B6026
B6027
B6406
M1
BLACKWELL RD
HUTHWAITE LA
NEW LA
CRAGG LA
MAIN ST
HALL LA
NEWTON RD
NEWTONWOOD LA
SAW PIT LA
SHEPHERD'S LA
SILVERHILL LA
COMMON RD
NUNN BROOK RD
BROOKSIDE WAY
HILCOTE LA
PASTURE LA
CHURCH HILL
JASMINE DR 1
LAVENDER CL 2
BROADACRE WAY 3
CORNSTONE AVE 4
CLOVER CT 5
FERNDOWN DR 6
1 SANDWOOD CL
2 PENNINE CL
3 DEVONSHIRE DR
4 ST.WERBURGHS VIEW
5 STRUTT CL
6 WEAVERS CT
MARKET PL 1
OLD FALL ST 2
NEW FALL ST 3
SAMPSONS YD 4
SWANN YD 5
STAINSBY GR 1
KEDLESTONE CL 2
Derbyshire STREET ATLAS
A B C D E F
8 7 61 6 5 60 4 3 59 2 1 58
44 45 46

D1
1 NETHER FIELD GRANGE
2 ROODS CL
E2
1 WINDRUSH CL

F3
1 NORTHERN BRIDGE RD
2 GRESHAM CL
3 CHATSWORTH
F4
1 MANSFIELD RD
2 REDCLIFFE ST

F1
1 KINGS MILL RD E
2 JEPHSON RD
3 ASHWOOD CL
F2
1 MARKET PL
2 ALBERT SQ
3 VICTORIA ST
4 PORTLAND CL

87
102

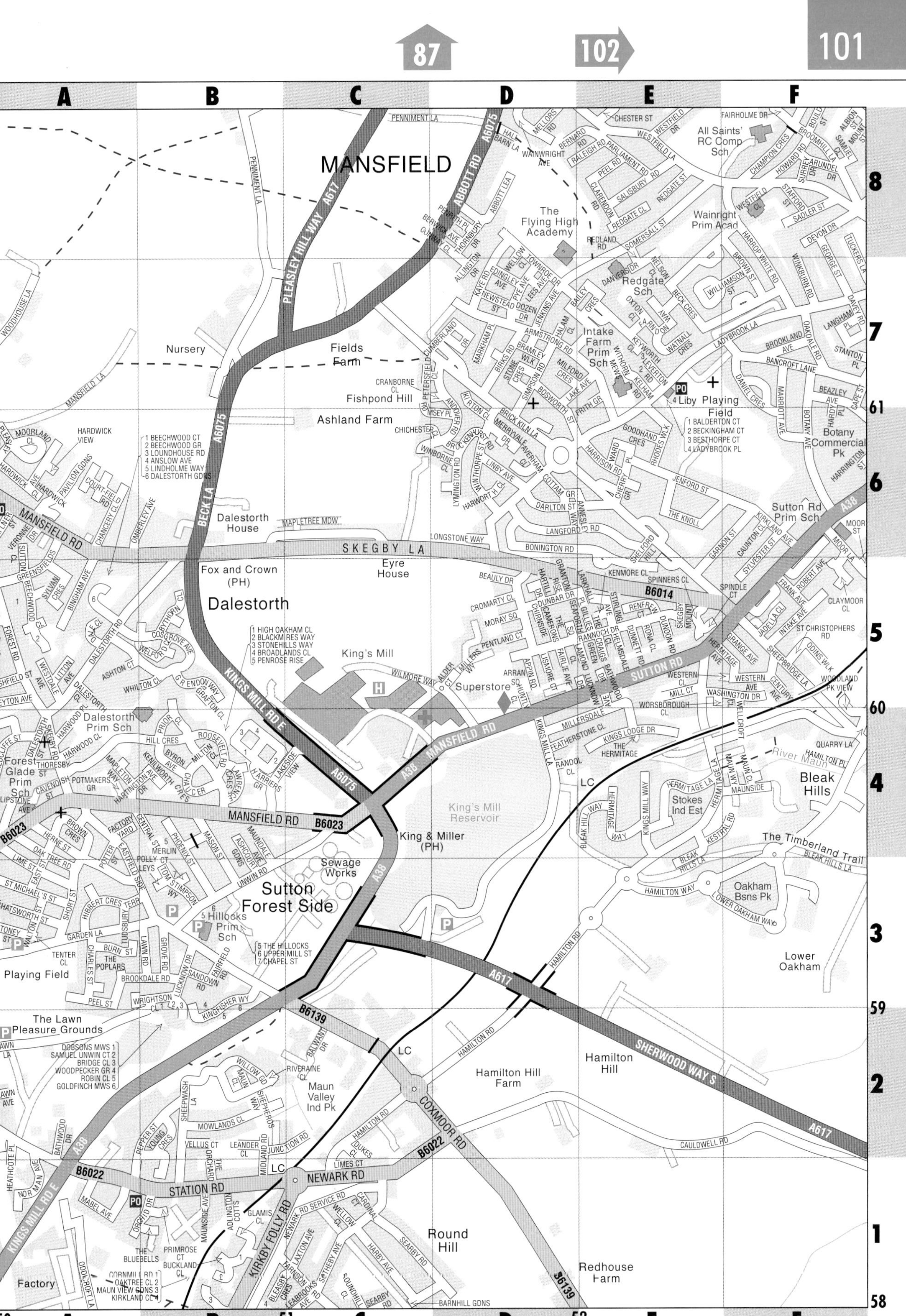
MANSFIELD
Nursery
Fields Farm
Fishpond Hill
Ashland Farm
Dalestorth House
Fox and Crown (PH)
Eyre House
Dalestorth
King's Mill
Superstore
Dalestorth Prim Sch
Forest Glade Prim Sch
King's Mill Reservoir
King & Miller (PH)
Sewage Works
Sutton Forest Side
Hillocks Prim Sch
Playing Field
The Lawn Pleasure Grounds
Maun Valley Ind Pk
Hamilton Hill Farm
Hamilton Hill
Round Hill
Redhouse Farm
Factory
The Flying High Academy
Redgate Sch
Intake Farm Prim Sch
Wainright Prim Acad
All Saints' RC Comp Sch
Liby Playing Field
Botany Commercial Pk
Sutton Rd Prim Sch
Stokes Ind Est
Bleak Hills
The Timberland Trail
Oakham Bsns Pk
Lower Oakham
River Maun
SKEGBY LA
MANSFIELD RD
SUTTON RD
KINGS MILL RD E
SHERWOOD WAY S
PLEASLEY HILL WAY
ABBOTT RD
BECK LA
STATION RD
NEWARK RD
COXMOOR RD
KIRKBY FOLLY RD
A38
A617
A6075
B6014
B6022
B6023
B6139
A
B
C
D
E
F
1
2
3
4
5
6
7
8
50
51
52
58
59
60
61

115
102

102

A7
1 THE ROOKERY
2 MOUNT PLEASANT
3 THORESBY ST
4 NEWCASTLE ST
5 BROWNING ST
6 KIPLING ST
7 BEARDALL ST
8 CORPORATION ST
9 ST JOHN'S PL
10 TENNYSON ST
11 LAYTON BURROUGHS
12 CASTLE ST
13 ST JOHNS VIEW

◀ 101

B5
1 RADFORD ST
2 PEACOCK ST
3 GARDEN RD
4 CLERKSON ST
5 COMMERCIAL ST
6 STATION ST

▲ 88

7 HIGHFIELD TERR
8 WHARF RD
9 GROVE ST
10 SHERWOOD ST
11 ACORN BSNS PK
12 BEECH AVE

13 CONTINUATION
14 COMMERCIAL GATE

B7
1 WEST GATE
2 CLIFTON PL
3 ECLIPSE YD
4 ALFRED CT
5 HANDLEY ARC
6 CLERKSON'S ALLEY

7 TOOTHILL RD
8 STOCKWELL GATE
9 MARKET PL
10 QUEEN ST
11 QUAKER LA
12 MARKET HOUSE PL
13 EXCHANGE ROW

14 QUEENS WLK
15 MARKET ST
16 Mansfield Coll of Art and
   Design/VisionStudio Sch
17 OLD MEETING HOUSE YARD
18 West Nottinghamshire C

MANSFIELD

◀ 101

C5
1 ST MARGARET ST
2 ST CATHERINE ST
3 ST ANDREW ST
4 ASHBERY CL
5 BLACKTHORN DR
6 FERNDALE

▲ 116

E1
1 FARTHING WAY
2 MERCURY WAY
3 SATURN WAY
4 ORION GR

E2
1 JUPITER MWS
2 MOONBEAM WAY
3 STAR WLK
4 CHESTNUT HILL
5 SATURN WAY

F5
1 EARLSWOOD DR
2 BREWERS WAY
3 ESKDALE CL
4 RYEDALE AVE
5 THE DUKERIES

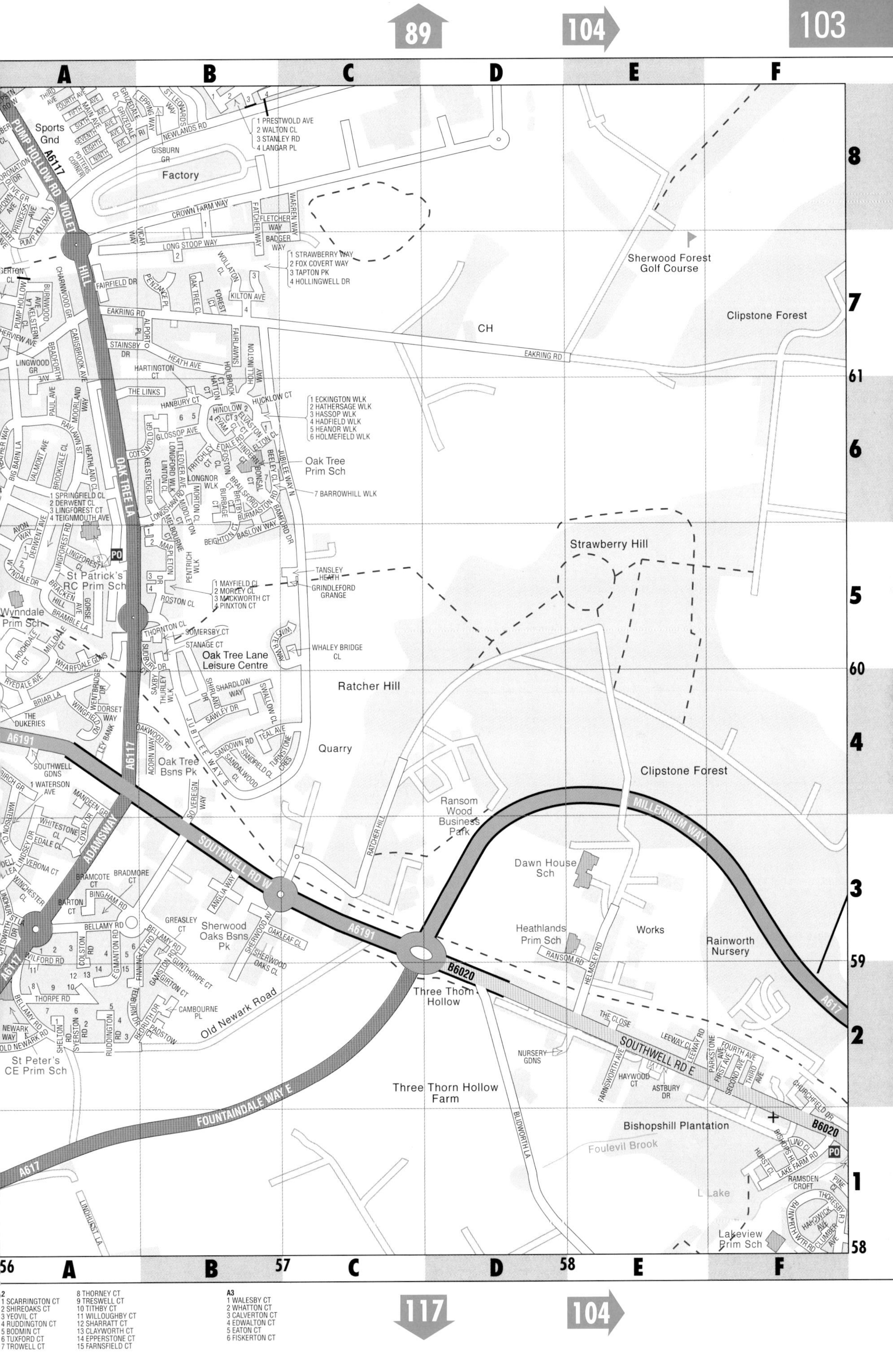

A　B　C　D　E　F

Sports Gnd

Factory

CROWN FARM WAY

LONG STOOP WAY

1 PRESTWOLD AVE
2 WALTON CL
3 STANLEY RD
4 LANGAR PL

1 STRAWBERRY WAY
2 FOX COVERT WAY
3 TAPTON PK
4 HOLLINGWELL DR

Sherwood Forest Golf Course

Clipstone Forest

CH

EAKRING RD

FAIRFIELD DR

EAKRING RD

THE LINKS

HANBURY CT

1 ECKINGTON WLK
2 HATHERSAGE WLK
3 HASSOP WLK
4 HADFIELD WLK
5 HEANOR WLK
6 HOLMEFIELD WLK

Oak Tree Prim Sch

7 BARROWHILL WLK

Strawberry Hill

1 SPRINGFIELD CL
2 DERWENT CL
3 LINGFOREST CL
4 TEIGNMOUTH AVE

St Patrick's RC Prim Sch

PO

1 MAYFIELD CL
2 MORLEY CL
3 MACKWORTH CT
4 PINXTON CT

Tansley Heath

Grindleford Grange

Wynndale Prim Sch

Oak Tree Lane Leisure Centre

WHALEY BRIDGE CL

Ratcher Hill

THE DUKERIES

60

Quarry

Oak Tree Bsns Pk

A6191

Clipstone Forest

SOUTHWELL RD W

A6191

Ransom Wood Business Park

MILLENNIUM WAY

ADAMS WAY

Dawn House Sch

Works

Rainworth Nursery

Southwell GDNS
WATERSON AVE

Sherwood Oaks Bsns Pk

Heathlands Prim Sch

RANSOM RD

A6117

Old Newark Road

B6020

Three Thorn Hollow

SOUTHWELL RD E

St Peter's CE Prim Sch

THE CLOSE

NURSERY GDNS

B6020

PO

FOUNTAINDALE WAY E

Three Thorn Hollow Farm

Bishopshill Plantation

Foulevil Brook

A617

L Lake

Lakeview Prim Sch

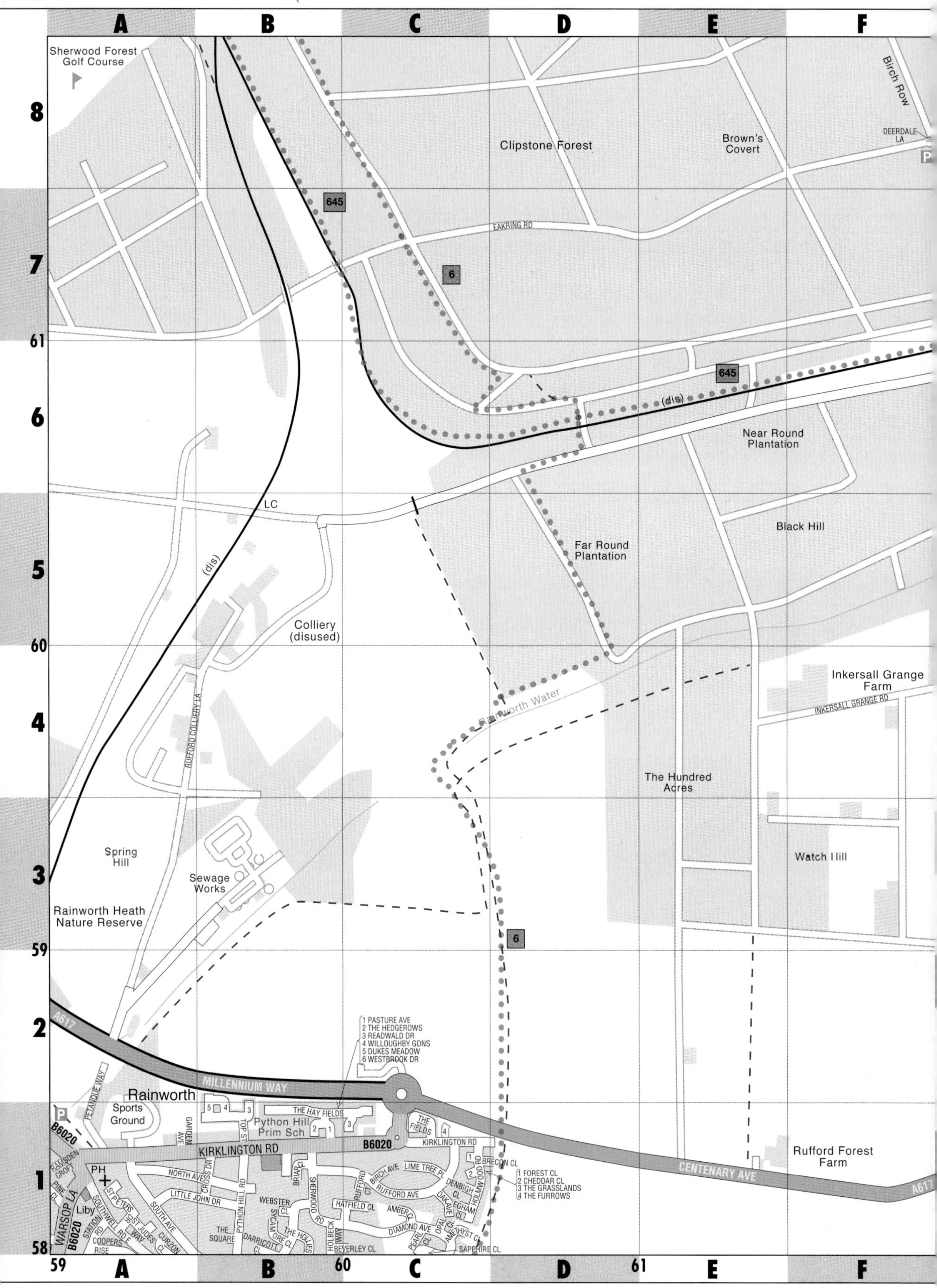

Sherwood Forest
Golf Course

Clipstone Forest

Brown's
Covert

Birch Row

DEERDALE
LA

EAKRING RD

645

6

645

(dis)

Near Round
Plantation

LC

Far Round
Plantation

Black Hill

(dis)

Colliery
(disused)

RUFFORD COLLIERY LA

Rainworth Water

Inkersall Grange
Farm

INKERSALL GRANGE RD

The Hundred
Acres

Watch Hill

Spring
Hill

Sewage
Works

6

Rainworth Heath
Nature Reserve

A617

Rainworth

1 PASTURE AVE
2 THE HEDGEROWS
3 READWALD DR
4 WILLOUGHBY GDNS
5 DUKES MEADOW
6 WESTBROOK DR

MILLENNIUM WAY

Sports
Ground

PETERDALE WAY

P

THE HAY FIELDS

5 4

Python Hill
Prim Sch

GARDEN
AVE

TOP ST

3

2 1

3

THE
FIELDS

4

KIRKLINGTON RD

B6020

Rufford Forest
Farm

CENTENARY AVE

A617

B6020

KIRKLINGTON RD

BRIAR CL

PYTHON HILL RD

BIRCH AVE

SYCAMORE CL

DENBIGH
CL

RUFFORD AVE

LIME TREE PL

BRECON CL

1 FOREST CL
2 CHEDDAR CL
3 THE GRASSLANDS
4 THE FURROWS

WARSOP LA

B6020

PINE AV

RAWSON
CROFT

PH

Liby

ST PETERS CL

SOUTHWELL RD W

STATION
RD

ST JUDES CL

CROSS ST

CURZON CL

NORTH AVE

SOUTH AVE

LITTLE JOHN DR

SHERWOOD RD

WEBSTER CL

HATFIELD CL

HOLBECK
WY

BEVERLEY CL

DIAMOND AVE

PEAR TREE

AMBER

OAK AV

EGHAM
CL

AMETHYST CL

SAPPHIRE CL

4

3

THE
HOLLIES

THE
SQUARE

DARRICOTT
CL

COOPERS
RISE

91
106

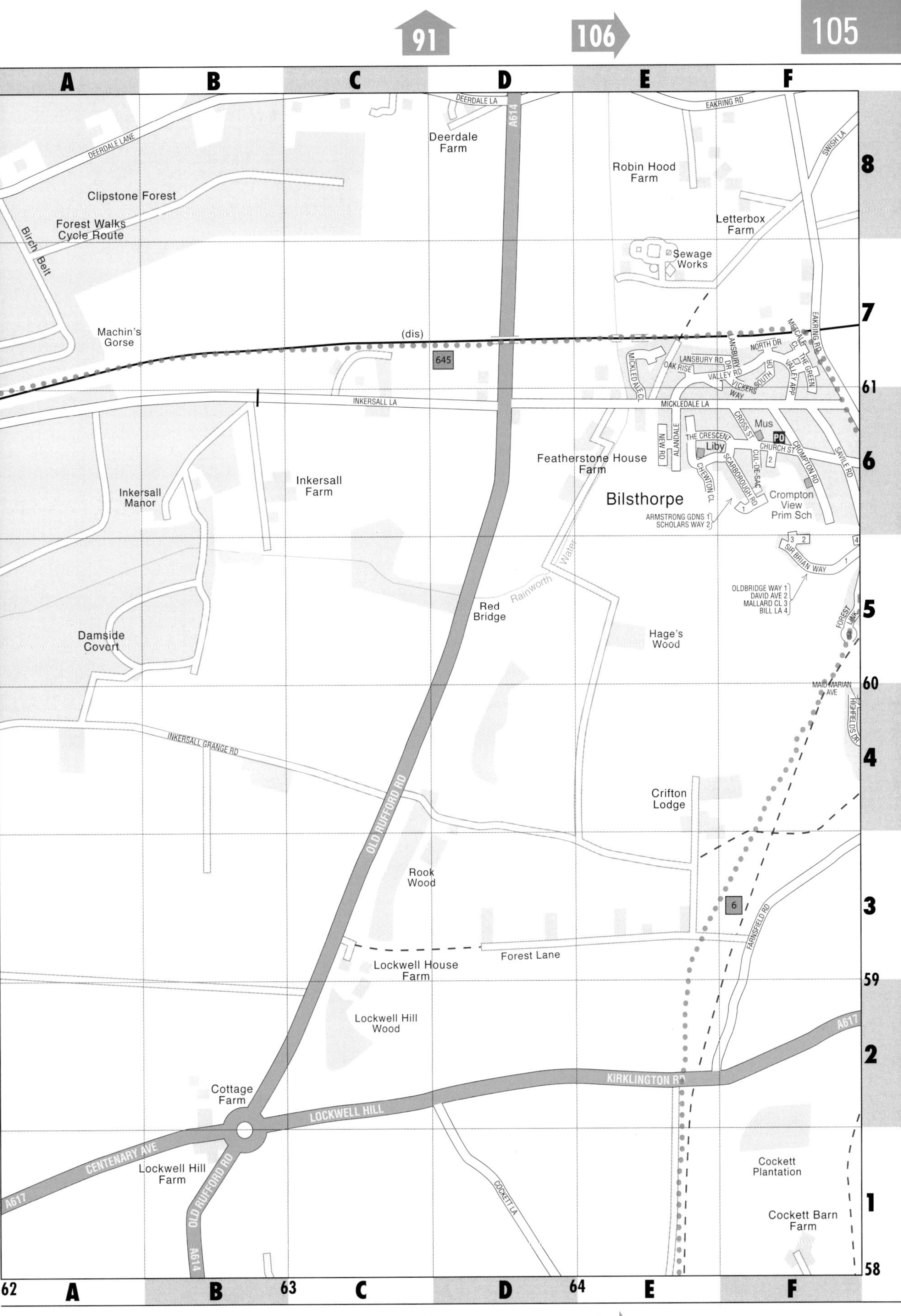
A
B
C
D
E
F
8
7
61
6
5
60
4
3
59
2
1
58
62
63
64
DEERDALE LANE
DEERDALE LA
A614
Deerdale Farm
EAKRING RD
Robin Hood Farm
SWISH LA
Clipstone Forest
Forest Walks Cycle Route
Birch Belt
Letterbox Farm
Sewage Works
Machin's Gorse
(dis)
645
METCALF CL
EAKRING RD
NORTH DR
LANSBURY RD
OAK RISE
LANSBURY DR
VALLEY RD
VICKERS WAY
SOUTH DR
VALLEY APP
THE GREEN
MICKLED ALE CL
INKERSALL LA
MICKLEDALE LA
NEW RD
ALANDALE
THE CRESCENT
Liby
Mus
CROSS ST
PO
CHURCH ST
CROMPTON RD
SAVILE RD
CUL-DE-SAC
SCARBOROUGH RD
CHEWTON CL
Featherstone House Farm
Inkersall Farm
Inkersall Manor
Bilsthorpe
Crompton View Prim Sch
ARMSTRONG GDNS 1
SCHOLARS WAY 2
SIR BRIAN WAY
OLDBRIDGE WAY 1
DAVID AVE 2
MALLARD CL 3
BILL LA 4
Rainworth Water
Red Bridge
FOREST LINK
Damside Covert
Hage's Wood
MAID MARIAN AVE
HIGHFIELDS DR
INKERSALL GRANGE RD
Crifton Lodge
OLD RUFFORD RD
Rook Wood
6
FARNSFIELD RD
Forest Lane
Lockwell House Farm
Lockwell Hill Wood
A617
KIRKLINGTON RD
Cottage Farm
LOCKWELL HILL
CENTENARY AVE
Lockwell Hill Farm
OLD RUFFORD RD
A614
COCKETT LA
Cockett Plantation
Cockett Barn Farm

62 A B 63 C D 64 E F

119
106

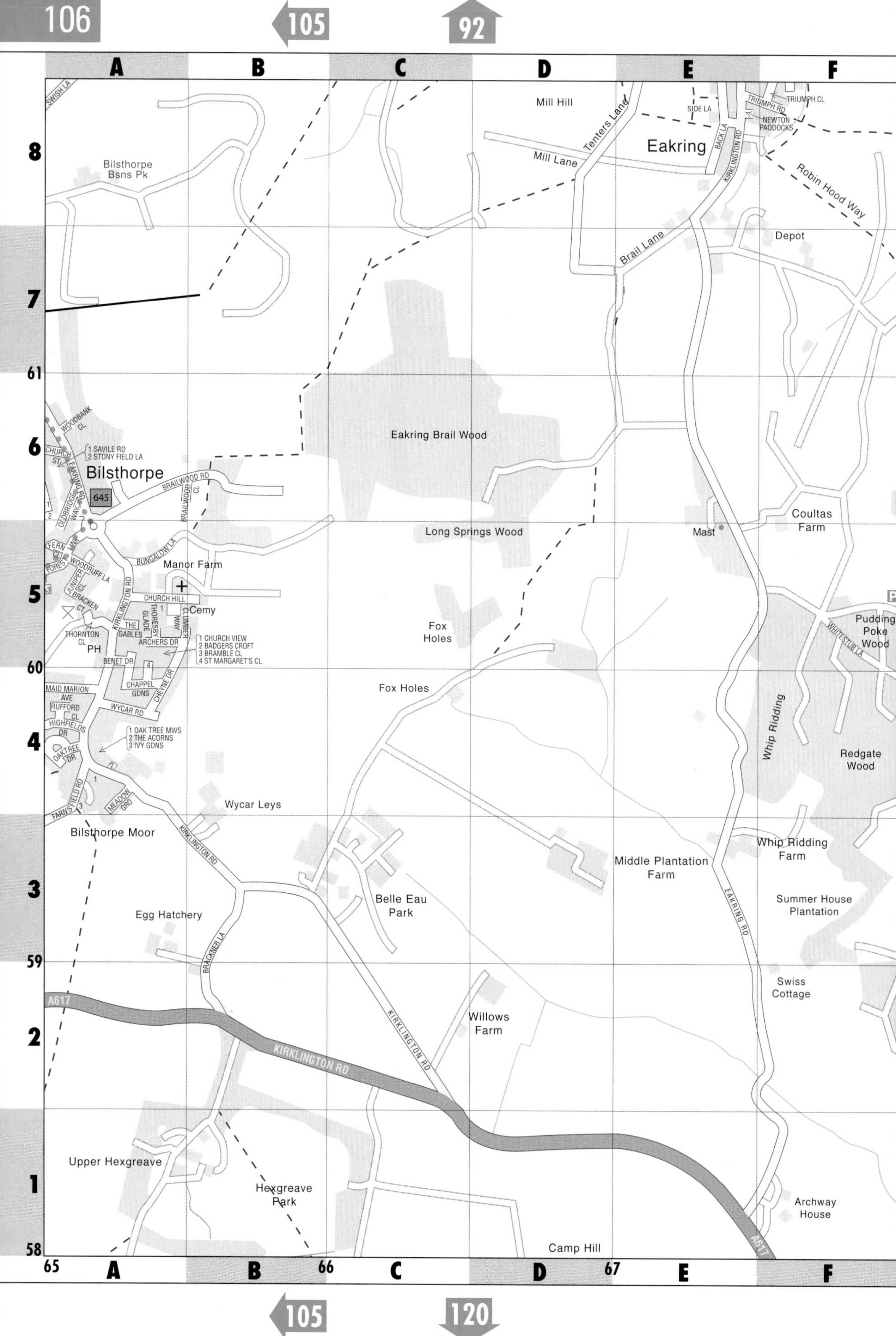

A B C D E F

8

7

61

6

5

60

4

3

59

2

1

58

SWISH LA

Bilsthorpe
Bsns Pk

Mill Hill

Mill Lane

Tenters Land

SIDE LA

Eakring

TRIUMPH RD
TRIUMPH CL
NEWTON
PADDOCKS

BACK LA
KIRKLINGTON RD

Robin Hood Way

Brail Lane

Depot

WOODBANK CL

1 SAVILE RD
2 STONY FIELD LA

CHURCH ST

Bilsthorpe

645

OLDBRIDGE WAY
EAKRING RD

BRAILWOOD RD
BRAILWOOD CL

Eakring Brail Wood

Coultas
Farm

Long Springs Wood

Mast

BUNGALOW LA

Manor Farm

FERN RD
FLORE

WOODRUFF LA

THORESBY GLADE

CLUMBER WAY

Cemy

CHURCH HILL

THORNTON CL

PH

THE GABLES

ARCHERS DR

BENET DR

CHAPPEL GDNS

KIRKLINGTON RD

BRACKEN CT

1 CHURCH VIEW
2 BADGERS CROFT
3 BRAMBLE CL
4 ST MARGARET'S CL

Fox
Holes

P

Pudding
Poke
Wood

WHITESTUB LA

Whip Ridding

Redgate
Wood

MAID MARION AVE

RUFFORD CL

HIGHFIELDS DR

OAKTREE DR

WYCAR RD

CHEYNE DR

Fox Holes

1 OAK TREE MWS
2 THE ACORNS
3 IVY GDNS

Whip Ridding
Farm

FARNSFIELD RD

MEADOW GRO

Wycar Leys

KIRKLINGTON RD

Middle Plantation
Farm

Summer House
Plantation

Bilsthorpe Moor

Egg Hatchery

BRACKNER LA

Belle Eau
Park

EAKRING RD

Swiss
Cottage

59

A617

Willows
Farm

KIRKLINGTON RD

Upper Hexgreave

Hexgreave
Park

Camp Hill

Archway
House

A617

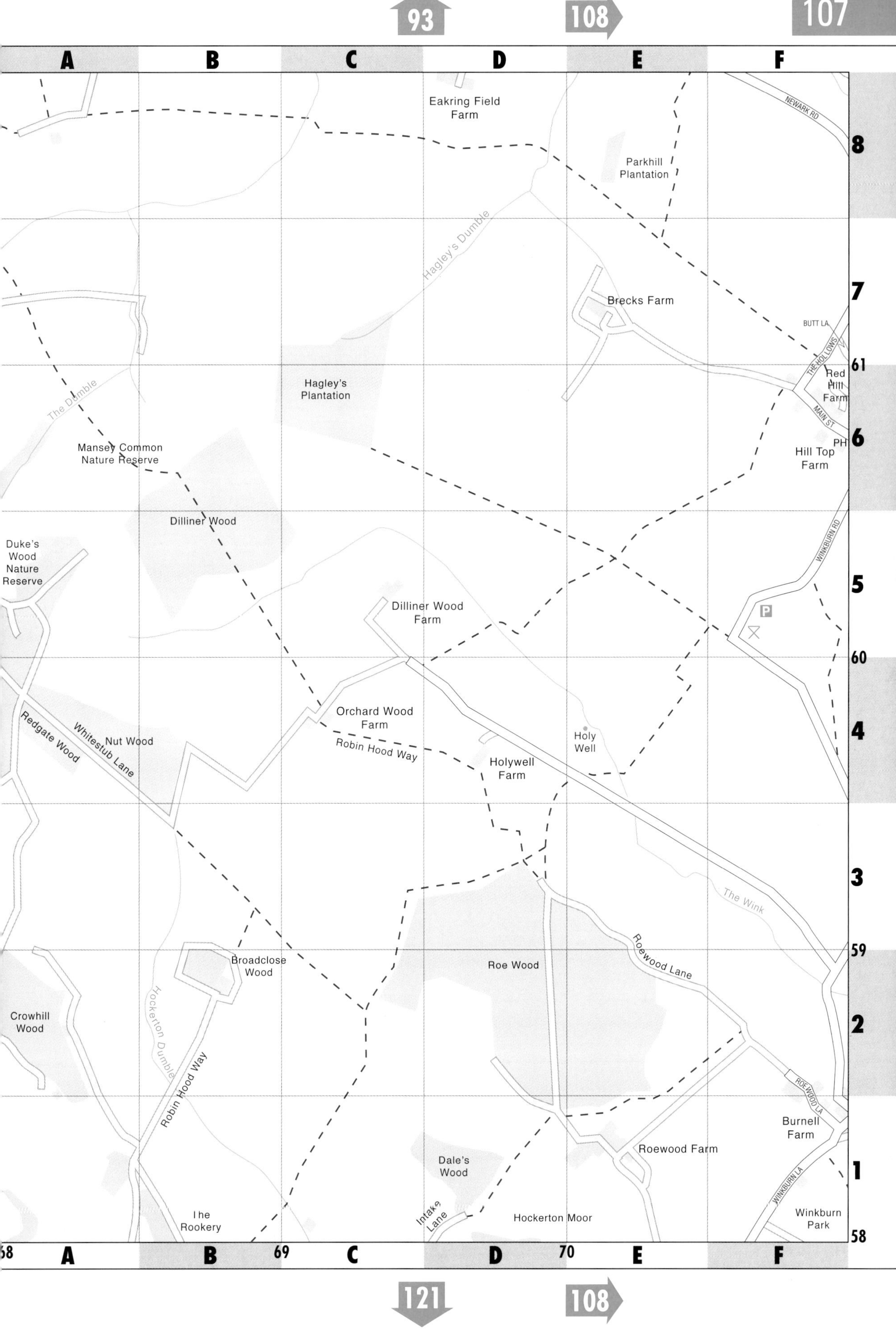
93
108
A
B
C
D
E
F
Eakring Field Farm
Newark Rd
Parkhill Plantation
Hagley's Dumble
Brecks Farm
Butt La
The Hollows
Red Hill Farm
Main St
PH
Hill Top Farm
The Dumble
Hagley's Plantation
Mansey Common Nature Reserve
Dilliner Wood
Duke's Wood Nature Reserve
Winkburn Rd
Dilliner Wood Farm
Orchard Wood Farm
Robin Hood Way
Holy Well
Holywell Farm
Redgate Wood
Whitestub Lane
Nut Wood
The Wink
Roewood Lane
Broadclose Wood
Roe Wood
Crowhill Wood
Hockerton Dumble
Robin Hood Way
Roewood La
Burnell Farm
Roewood Farm
Dale's Wood
Winkburn La
Intake Lane
The Rookery
Hockerton Moor
Winkburn Park
8
7
61
6
5
60
4
3
59
2
1
58
68
69
70
121
108

107
94

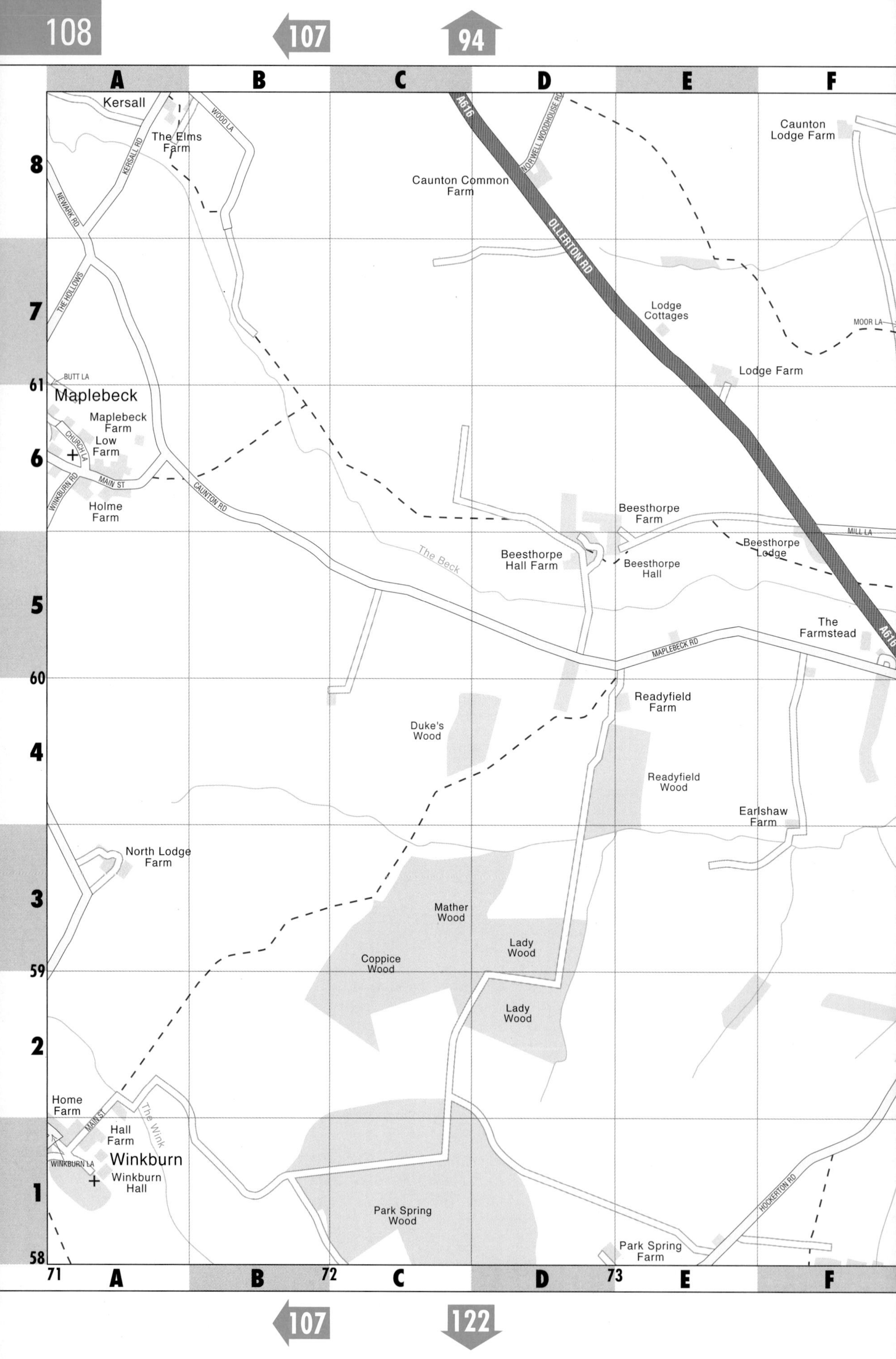
Kersall
The Elms Farm
WOOD LA
KERSALL RD
NEWARK RD
A616
NORWELL WOODHOUSE RD
Caunton Common Farm
OLLERTON RD
Caunton Lodge Farm
THE HOLLOWS
Lodge Cottages
MOOR LA
BUTT LA
Maplebeck
Maplebeck Farm
Lodge Farm
CHURCH LA
Low Farm
MAIN ST
WINKBURN RD
Holme Farm
CAUNTON RD
Beesthorpe Farm
MILL LA
Beesthorpe Hall Farm
The Beck
Beesthorpe Hall
Beesthorpe Lodge
The Farmstead
A616
MAPLEBECK RD
Readyfield Farm
Duke's Wood
Readyfield Wood
Earlshaw Farm
North Lodge Farm
Mather Wood
Lady Wood
Coppice Wood
Lady Wood
Home Farm
MAIN ST
The Wink
Hall Farm
Winkburn
WINKBURN LA
Winkburn Hall
HOCKERTON RD
Park Spring Wood
Park Spring Farm
A B C D E F
8 7 61 6 5 60 4 3 59 2 1 58
71 72 73

107
122

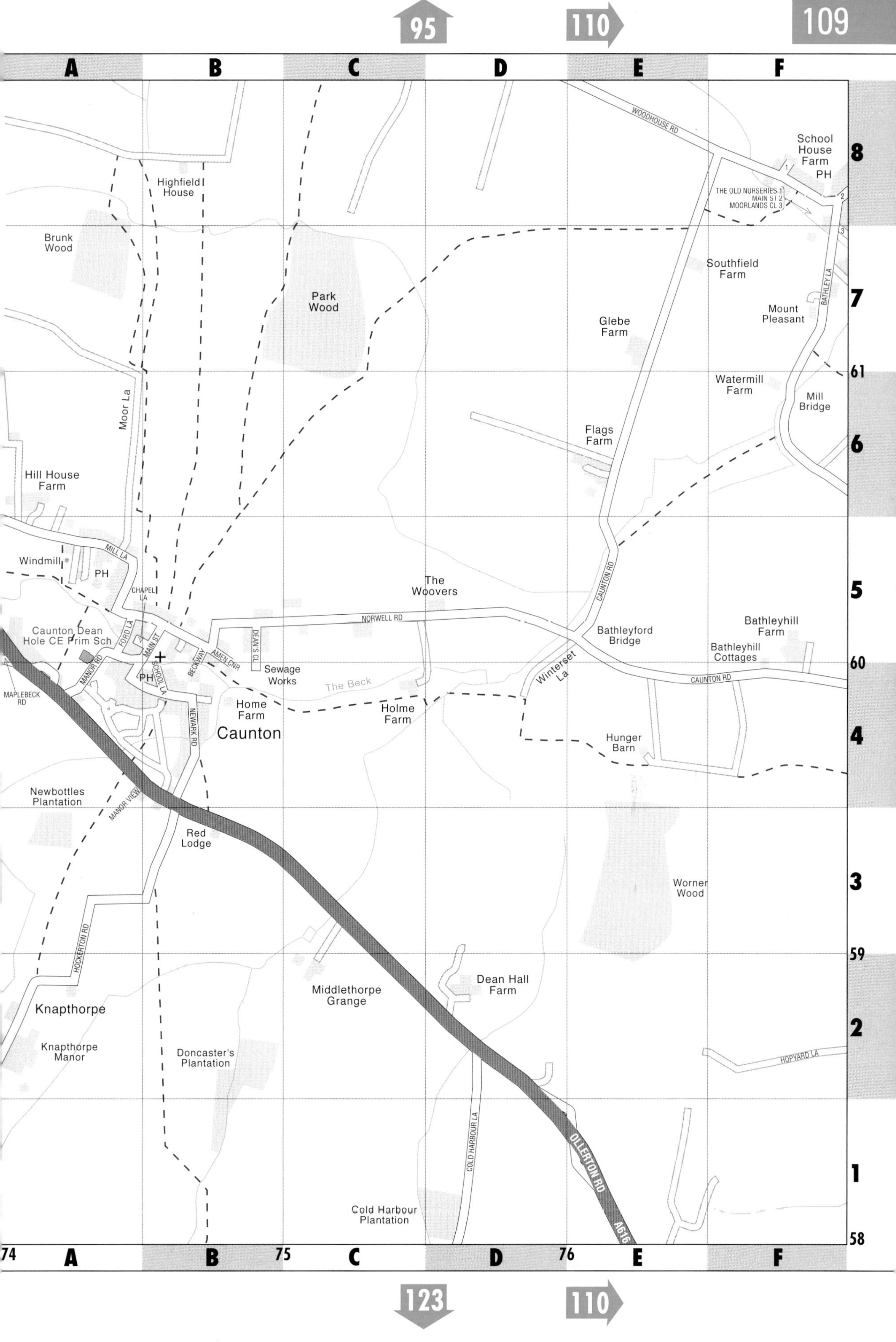

A B C D E F

8
7
61
6
5
60
4
3
59
2
1
58

74 75 76

WOODHOUSE RD

School House Farm PH

THE OLD NURSERIES 1
MAIN ST 2
MOORLANDS CL 3

Highfield House

Brunk Wood

Park Wood

Southfield Farm

Mount Pleasant

BATHLEY LA

Glebe Farm

Watermill Farm

Mill Bridge

Moor La

Flags Farm

Hill House Farm

CAUNTON RD

The Woovers

Windmill
PH

MILL LA

CHAPEL LA

NORWELL RD

Bathleyford Bridge

Bathleyhill Farm

Bathleyhill Cottages

Caunton Dean Hole CE Prim Sch

FORD LA

MAIN ST

BECK LA

AMEN CNR

DEAN'S CL

Sewage Works

The Beck

Winterset La

CAUNTON RD

MAPLEBECK RD

MANOR RD

PH

SCHOOL LA

Home Farm

Holme Farm

Hunger Barn

NEWARK RD

Caunton

Newbottles Plantation

MANOR VIEW

Red Lodge

Worner Wood

HOCKERTON RD

Knapthorpe

Middlethorpe Grange

Dean Hall Farm

Knapthorpe Manor

Doncaster's Plantation

HOPYARD LA

COLD HARBOUR LA

OLLERTON RD A616

Cold Harbour Plantation

109
96

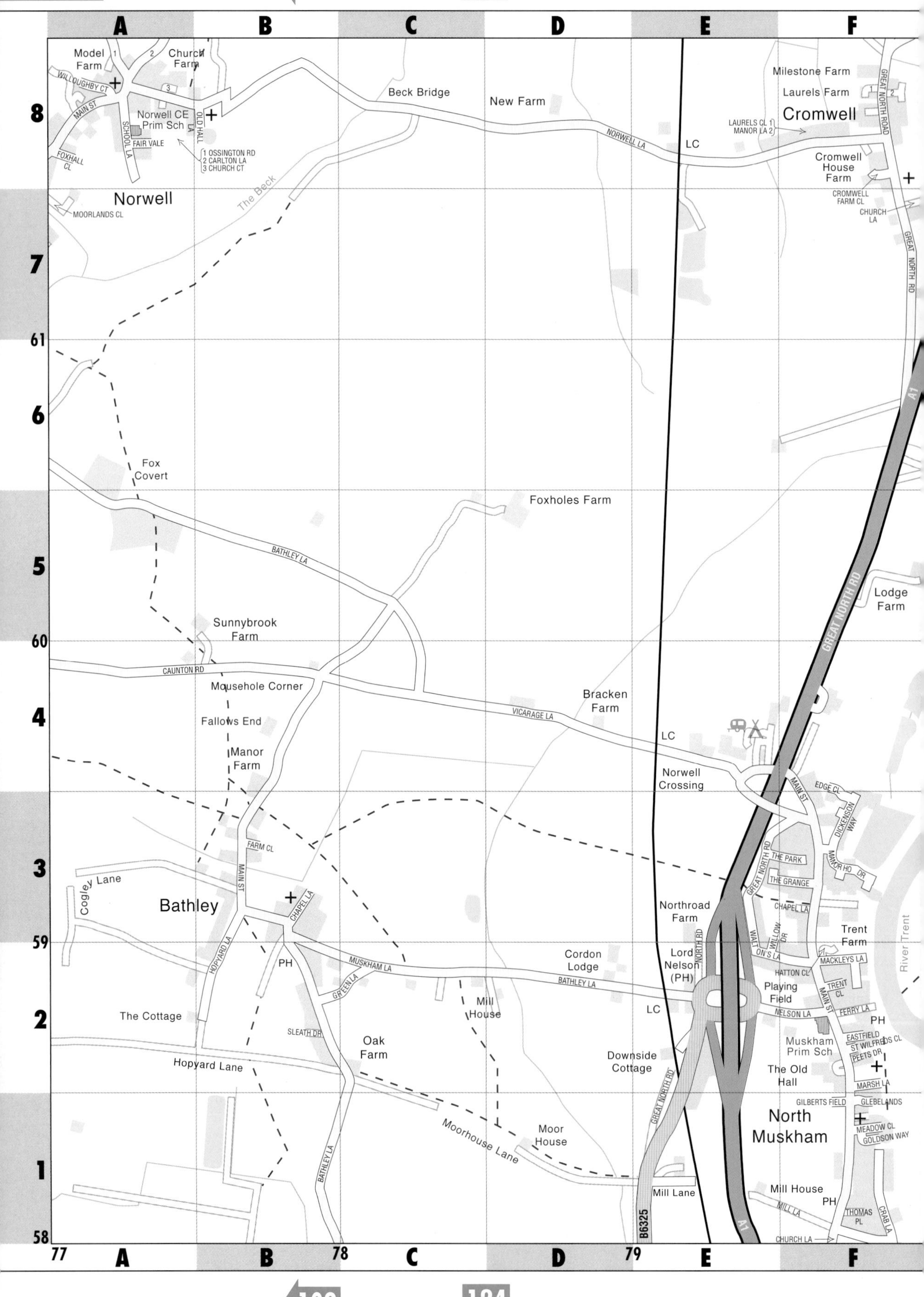

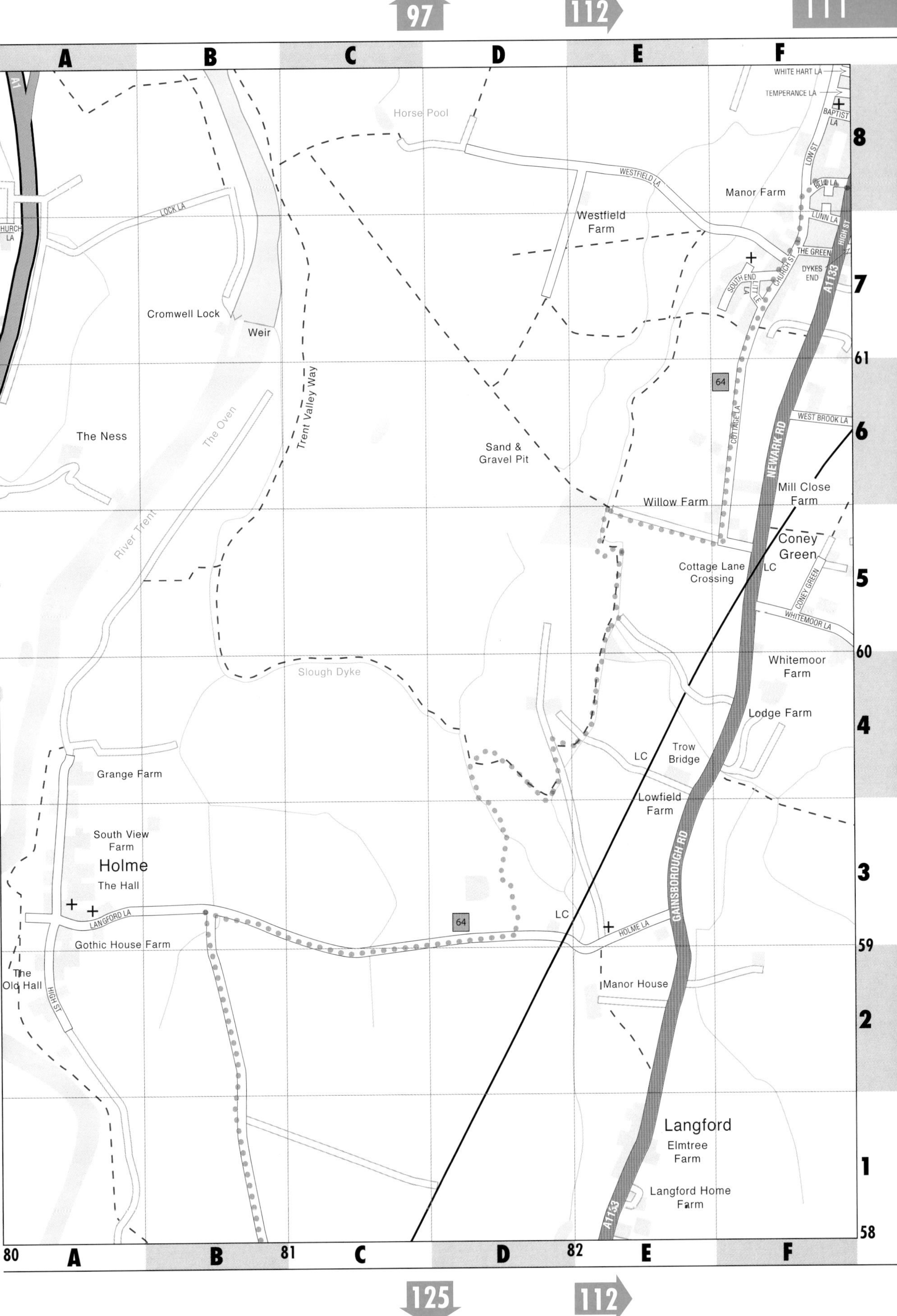

A   B   C   D   E   F

8

WHITE HART LA
TEMPERANCE LA
BAPTIST LA

Horse Pool

WESTFIELD LA

Manor Farm

LOW ST

Westfield
Farm

CHURCH LA

BLUE LA

LUNN LA

THE GREEN

HIGH ST

7

DYKES
END

SOUTH END

LITTLE LA

A1133

61

CHURCH ST

Cromwell Lock

LOCK LA

Weir

64

WEST BROOK LA

NEWARK RD

6

Trent Valley Way

The Oven

The Ness

Sand &
Gravel Pit

COTTAGE LA

Mill Close
Farm

Willow Farm

Coney
Green

River Trent

Cottage Lane
Crossing

LC

5

CONEY GREEN

WHITEMOOR LA

60

Whitemoor
Farm

Slough Dyke

Lodge Farm

4

LC

Trow
Bridge

Lowfield
Farm

GAINSBOROUGH RD

3

Grange Farm

LC

South View
Farm

Holme

The Hall

59

LANGFORD LA

Gothic House Farm

Holme La

HOLME LA

64

LC

Manor House

The
Old Hall

HIGH ST

2

Langford

Elmtree
Farm

1

A1133

Langford Home
Farm

58

80   A   B   81   C   D   82   E   F

111
98

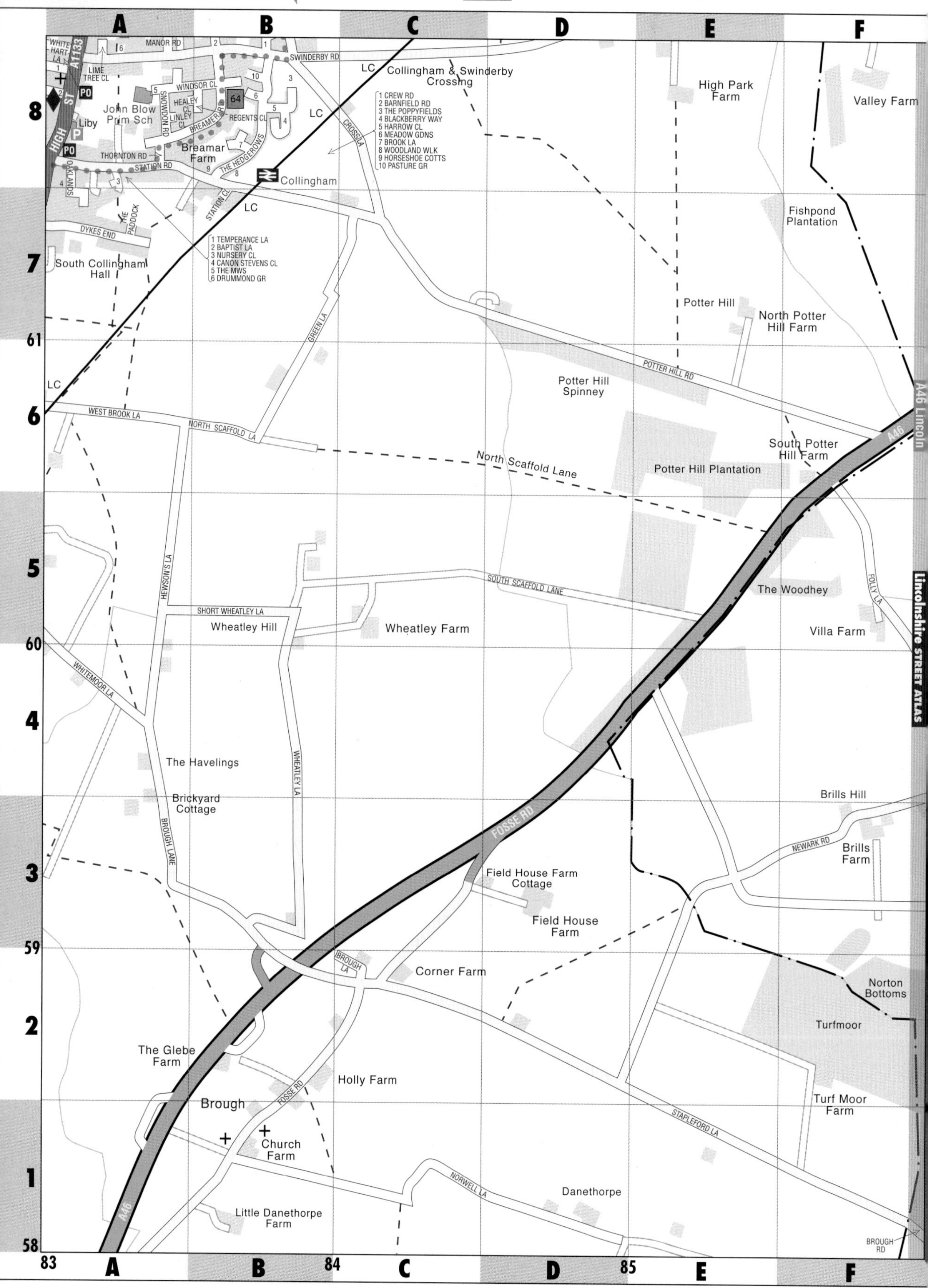
A
B
C
D
E
F
8
7
61
6
5
60
4
3
59
2
1
58
83
84
85
WHITE HART LA
A1133
HIGH ST
LIME TREE CL
MANOR RD
SWINDERBY RD
LC
Collingham & Swinderby Crossing
High Park Farm
Valley Farm
John Blow Prim Sch
Liby
PO
WINDSOR CL
SNOWDON RD
HEALEY CL
LINLEY CL
BREAMER RD
REGENTS CL
64
Breamar Farm
THORNTON RD
STATION RD
THE HEDGEROWS
OAKLANDS
Collingham
CROSS LA
1 CREW RD
2 BARNFIELD RD
3 THE POPPYFIELDS
4 BLACKBERRY WAY
5 HARROW CL
6 MEADOW GDNS
7 BROOK LA
8 WOODLAND WLK
9 HORSESHOE COTTS
10 PASTURE GR
STATION CL
THE PADDOCK
DYKES END
1 TEMPERANCE LA
2 BAPTIST LA
3 NURSERY CL
4 CANON STEVENS CL
5 THE MWS
6 DRUMMOND GR
South Collingham Hall
Fishpond Plantation
GREEN LA
Potter Hill
North Potter Hill Farm
POTTER HILL RD
Potter Hill Spinney
WEST BROOK LA
NORTH SCAFFOLD LA
North Scaffold Lane
South Potter Hill Farm
Potter Hill Plantation
A46
A46 Lincoln
SOUTH SCAFFOLD LANE
The Woodhey
FOLLY LA
HEWSON'S LA
SHORT WHEATLEY LA
Wheatley Hill
Wheatley Farm
Villa Farm
WHITEMOOR LA
The Havelings
WHEATLEY LA
Brickyard Cottage
BROUGH LANE
FOSSE RD
Brills Hill
NEWARK RD
Brills Farm
Field House Farm Cottage
Field House Farm
BROUGH LA
Corner Farm
Norton Bottoms
Turfmoor
The Glebe Farm
Holly Farm
Brough
Turf Moor Farm
STAPLEFORD LA
Church Farm
NORWELL LA
Danethorpe
Little Danethorpe Farm
BROUGH RD

111
126

99
114

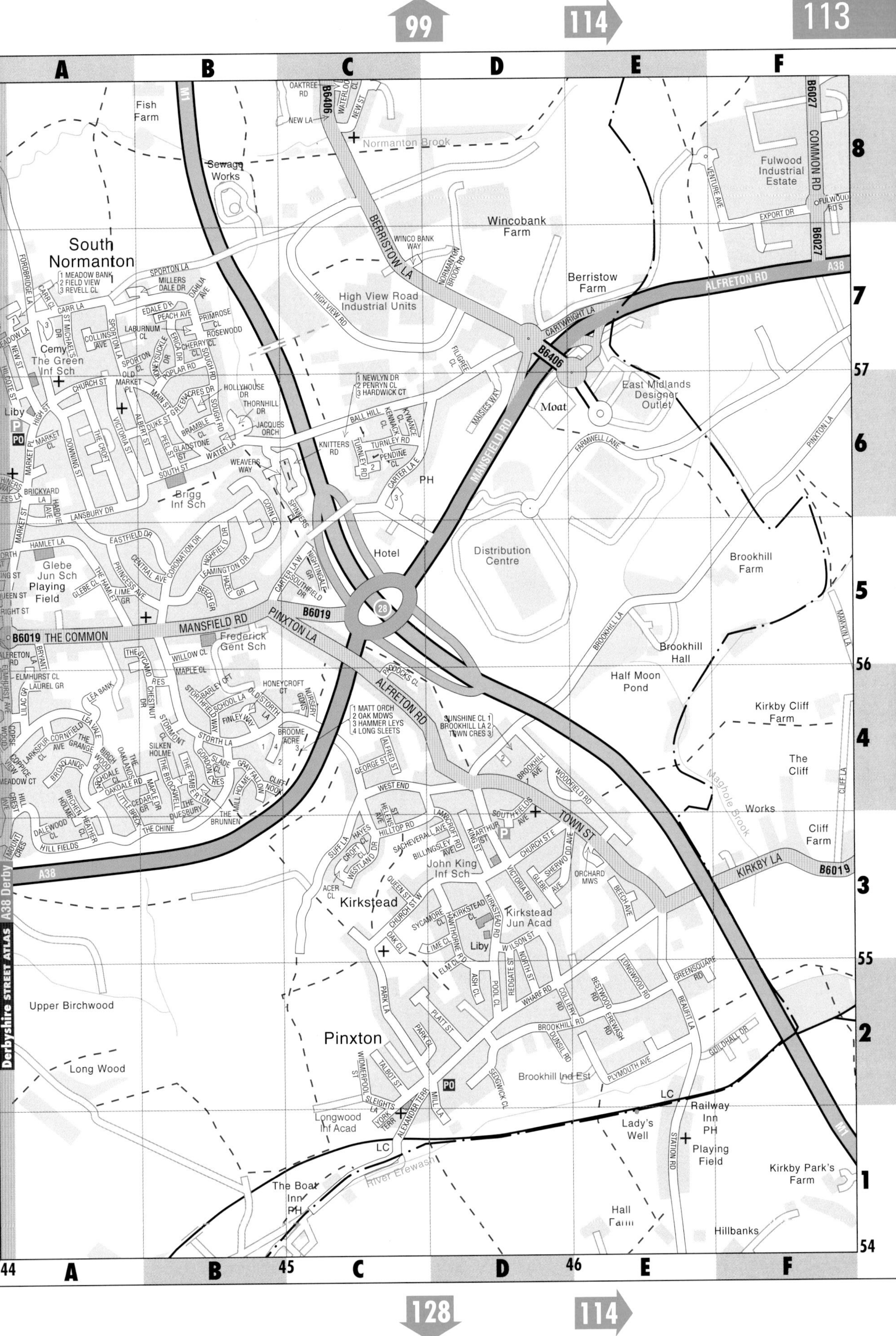
A
B
C
D
E
F
8
7
57
6
5
56
4
3
55
2
1
54
44
45
46
Fish Farm
Sewage Works
Normanton Brook
South Normanton
1 MEADOW BANK
2 FIELD VIEW
3 REVELL CL
Wincobank Farm
Berristow Farm
High View Road Industrial Units
Fulwood Industrial Estate
COMMON RD
EXPORT DR
VENTURE AVE
B6027
A38
ALFRETON RD
CARTWRIGHT LA
B6406
BERRISTOW LA
WINCO BANK WAY
HIGH VIEW RD
NORMANTON BROOK RD
SPORTON LA
MILLERS DALE DR
CARR LA
Cemy
The Green Inf Sch
CHURCH ST
MARKET PL
Liby
PO
East Midlands Designer Outlet
Moat
1 NEWLYN DR
2 PENRYN CL
3 HARDWICK CT
BALL HILL
KNITTERS RD
TURNLEY RD
PENDINE CL
CARTER LA E
PH
FARMWELL LANE
MANSFIELD RD
MAISIES WAY
PINXTON LA
Brigg Inf Sch
WATER LA
SOUTH ST
WEAVERS WAY
SPINNERS
Hotel
Distribution Centre
Brookhill Farm
Glebe Jun Sch
Playing Field
EASTFIELD DR
LANSBURY DR
HAMLET LA
B6019 THE COMMON
MANSFIELD RD
B6019
PINXTON LA
28
Frederick Gent Sch
M1
Brookhill Hall
Half Moon Pond
BROOKHILL LA
Kirkby Cliff Farm
The Cliff
Works
Magnole Brook
Cliff Farm
KIRKBY LA
B6019
1 MATT ORCH
2 OAK MDWS
3 HAMMER LEYS
4 LONG SLEETS
SUNSHINE CL 1
BROOKHILL LA 2
TOWN CRES 3
ALFRETON RD
TOWN ST
WEST END
GEORGE ST
ALFRED ST
John King Inf Sch
Kirkstead
Kirkstead Jun Acad
ORCHARD MWS
STORTH LA
HONEYCROFT CT
BROOME ACRE
THE BRUNNEN
THE CHINE
HILL FIELDS
DALEWOOD CL
A38
Upper Birchwood
Long Wood
Pinxton
PARK LA
PLATT ST
WHARF RD
BROOKHILL RD
LONGWOOD RD
GREENSQUARE RD
BEAUFIT LA
GUILDHALL DR
PLYMOUTH AVE
Brookhill Ind Est
PO
LC
Railway Inn PH
Lady's Well
Playing Field
STATION RD
Longwood Inf Acad
SLEIGHTS LA
ALEXANDER TERR
MILL LA
LC
River Erewash
The Boat Inn PH
Hall Farm
Hillbanks
Kirkby Park's Farm
Derbyshire STREET ATLAS
A38 Derby

128
114

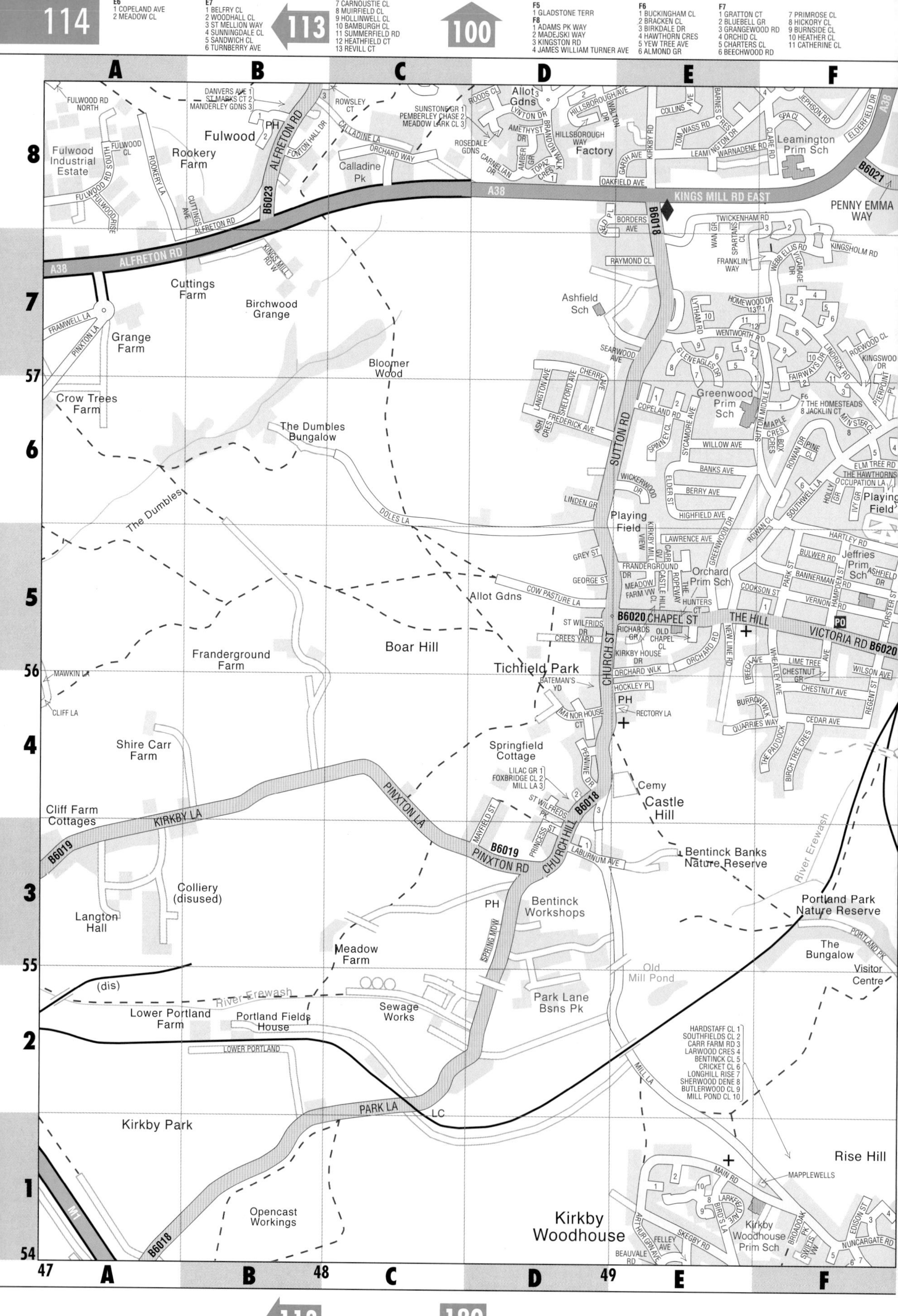

E6
1 COPELAND AVE
2 MEADOW CL

E7
1 BELFRY CL
2 WOODHALL CL
3 ST MELLION WAY
4 SUNNINGDALE CL
5 SANDWICH CL
6 TURNBERRY AVE

7 CARNOUSTIE CL
8 MUIRFIELD CL
9 HOLLINWELL CL
10 BAMBURGH CL
11 SUMMERFIELD RD
12 HEATHFIELD CT
13 REVILL CT

F5
1 GLADSTONE TERR
F8
1 ADAMS PK WAY
2 MADEJSKI WAY
3 KINGSTON RD
4 JAMES WILLIAM TURNER AVE

F6
1 BUCKINGHAM CL
2 BRACKEN CL
3 BIRKDALE DR
4 HAWTHORN CRES
5 YEW TREE AVE
6 ALMOND GR

F7
1 GRATTON CT
2 BLUEBELL GR
3 GRANGEWOOD RD
4 ORCHID CL
5 CHARTERS CL
6 BEECHWOOD RD

7 PRIMROSE CL
8 HICKORY CL
9 BURNSIDE CL
10 HEATHER CL
11 CATHERINE CL

113
100
113
129

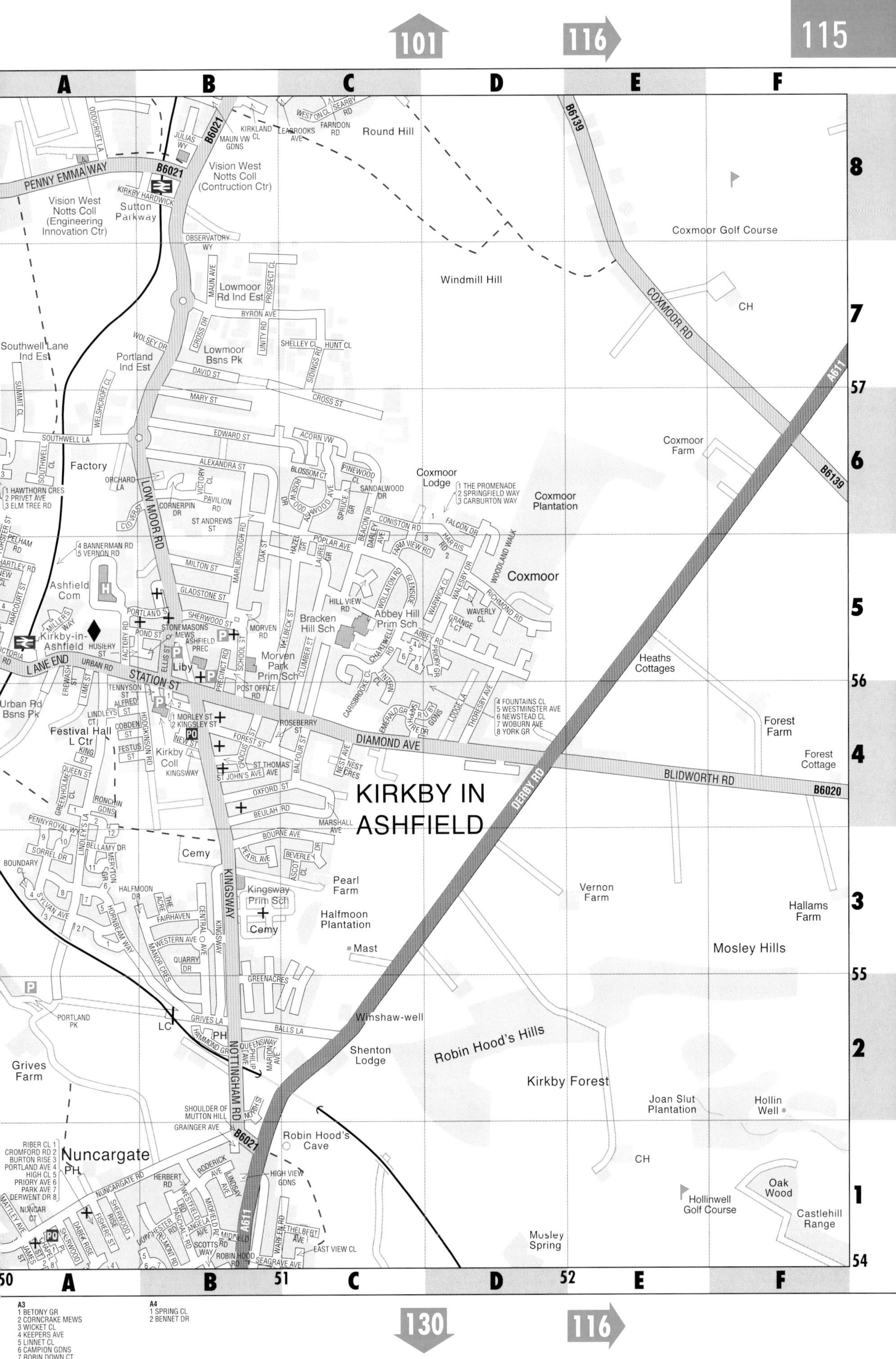

KIRKBY IN ASHFIELD

A3
1 BETONY GR
2 CORNCRAKE MEWS
3 WICKET CL
4 KEEPERS AVE
5 LINNET CL
6 CAMPION GDNS
7 ROBIN DOWN CT
8 HAREBELL CL
9 AMARELLA LA

A4
1 SPRING CL
2 BENNET DR

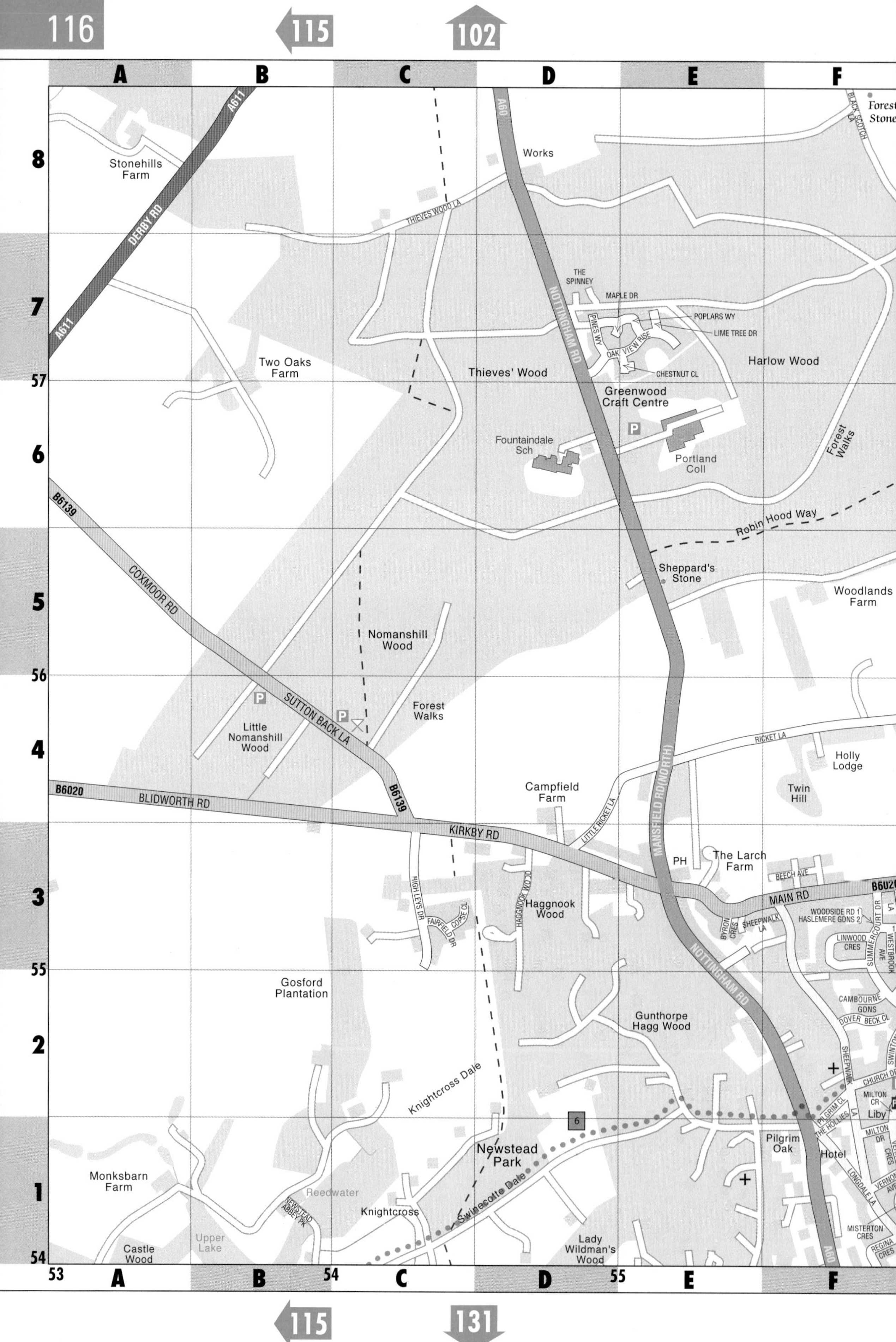

A B C D E F

8

7

57

6

5

56

4

3

55

2

1

54

Stonehills Farm

DERBY RD

A611

B6139

COXMOOR RD

B6020

BLIDWORTH RD

B6139

SUTTON BACK LA

Two Oaks Farm

THIEVES WOOD LA

A60

NOTTINGHAM RD

Works

Forest Stone

BLACK SCOTCH

THE SPINNEY

PINES WY

MAPLE DR

OAK VIEW RISE

POPLARS WY

LIME TREE DR

CHESTNUT CL

Harlow Wood

Thieves' Wood

Greenwood Craft Centre

P

Fountaindale Sch

Portland Coll

Forest Walks

Robin Hood Way

Sheppard's Stone

Woodlands Farm

Nomanshill Wood

P

Forest Walks

P

Little Nomanshill Wood

RICKET LA

MANSFIELD RD (WORTH)

Holly Lodge

Twin Hill

KIRKBY RD

LITTLE RICKET LA

Campfield Farm

PH

The Larch Farm

BEECH AVE

MAIN RD

B6020

WOODSIDE RD 1
HASLEMERE GDNS 2

LINWOOD CRES

CAMBOURNE GDNS

DOVER BECK CL

HAGGNOOK WOOD DR

HIGHLEYS DR

FAIRFIELD DR

COPSE CL

Haggnook Wood

SHEEPWALK LA

BYRON CRES

SUMMERCOURT DR

LA

WESTBROOK

2

Gosford Plantation

Gunthorpe Hagg Wood

NOTTINGHAM RD

SWINTON CT

SHEEPWALK

+

CHURCH DR

MILTON CR

Liby

PO

Knightcross Dale

6

Newstead Park

PILGRIM CL

THE HOLLIES

Pilgrim Oak

Hotel

MILTON DR

VERNON

CRES

Monksbarn Farm

Reedwater

Upper Lake

NEWSTEAD ABBEY PK

Knightcross

Swinecote Dale

Lady Wildman's Wood

+

LONGDALE LA

VERNON AVE

MISTERTON CRES

REGINA CRES

A60

Castle Wood

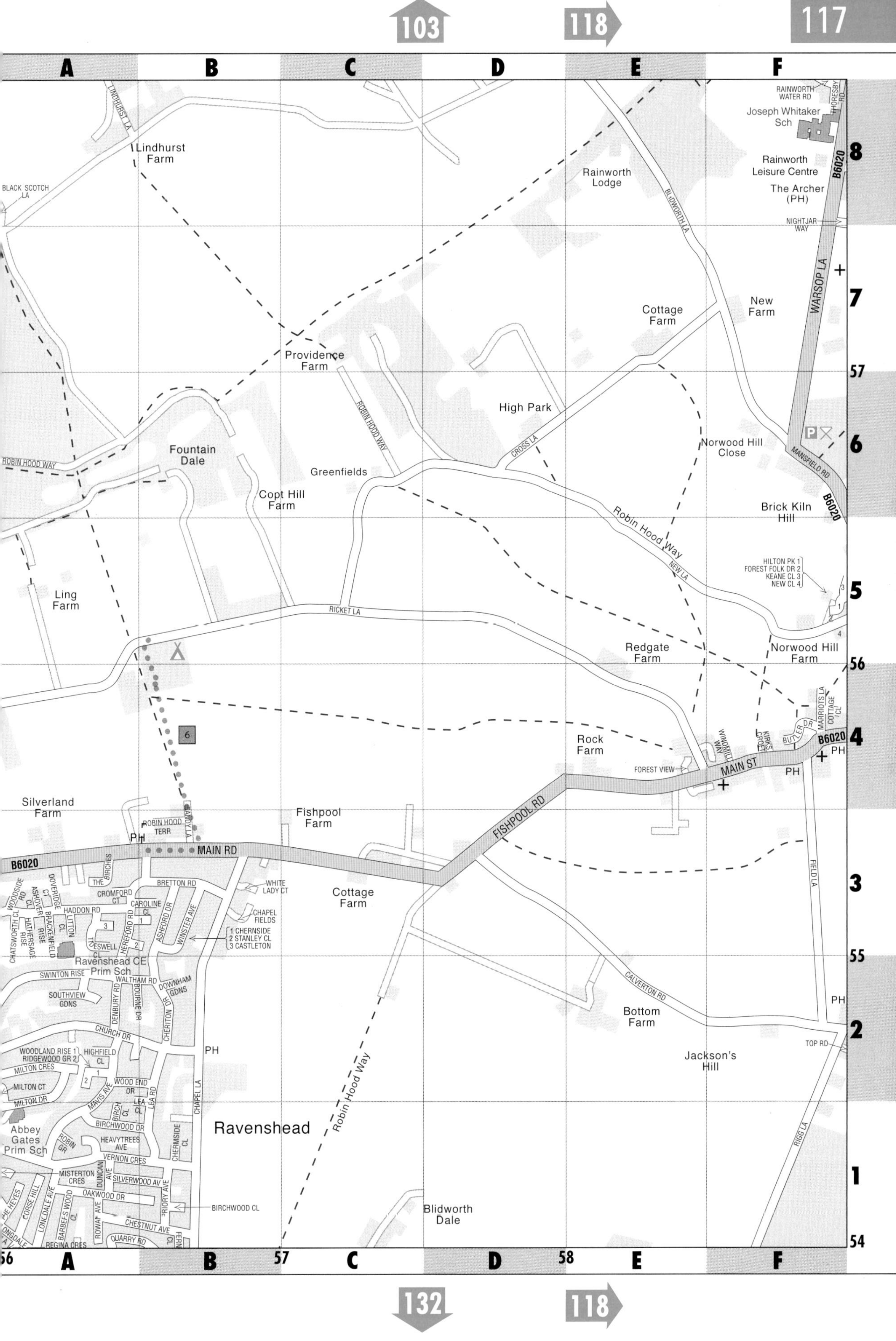
103
118
A
B
C
D
E
F
Lindhurst Farm
Rainworth Water Rd
Joseph Whitaker Sch
Rainworth Leisure Centre
The Archer (PH)
Rainworth Lodge
Black Scotch La
Nightjar Way
Warsop La
B6020
New Farm
Cottage Farm
Providence Farm
High Park
Norwood Hill Close
Mansfield Rd
Robin Hood Way
Fountain Dale
Greenfields
Copt Hill Farm
Brick Kiln Hill
Cross La
Robin Hood Way
New La
Ling Farm
Ricket La
Redgate Farm
Norwood Hill Farm
Rock Farm
Forest View
Windmill Way
Kirks Croft
Butler Dr
Marriots La
Cottage Cl
Main St
Fishpool Rd
Silverland Farm
Fishpool Farm
Robin Hood Terr
Sandy La
Main Rd
Cottage Farm
White Lady Ct
Chapel Fields
Field La
Calverton Rd
Bottom Farm
Jackson's Hill
Top Rd
Ravenshead CE Prim Sch
Ravenshead
Abbey Gates Prim Sch
Robin Hood Way
Rigg La
Blidworth Dale
Chapel La
56
57
58
54
55
132
118

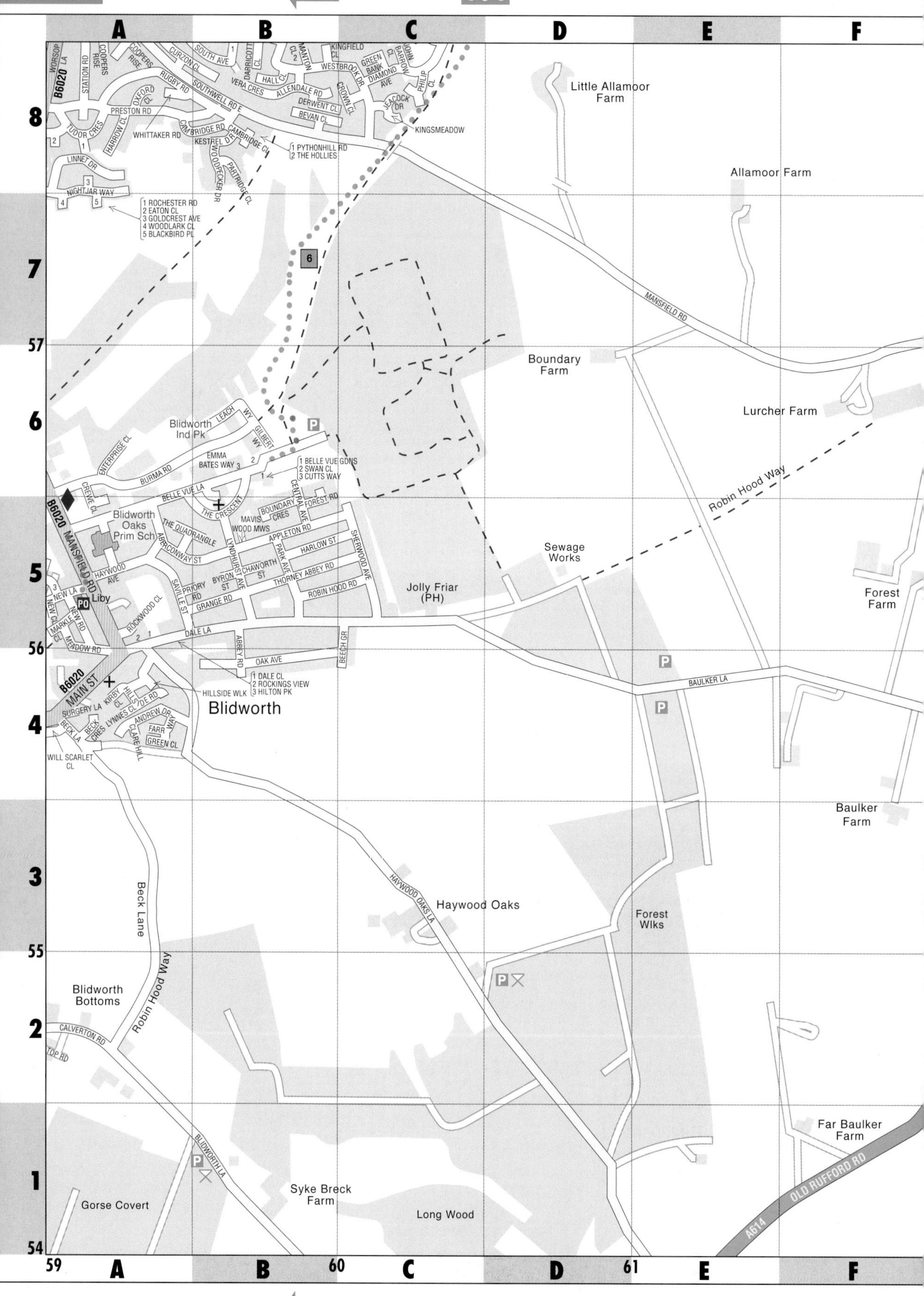

8

1 PYTHONHILL RD
2 THE HOLLIES

KINGSMEADOW

Little Allamoor
Farm

Allamoor Farm

1 ROCHESTER RD
2 EATON CL
3 GOLDCREST AVE
4 WOODLARK CL
5 BLACKBIRD PL

7

6

57

Mansfield Rd

Boundary
Farm

Lurcher Farm

Blidworth
Ind Pk

1 BELLE VUE GDNS
2 SWAN CL
3 CUTTS WAY

Robin Hood Way

Blidworth
Oaks
Prim Sch

Sewage
Works

Forest
Farm

5

Jolly Friar
(PH)

56

1 DALE CL
2 ROCKINGS VIEW
3 HILTON PK

Baulker La

Blidworth

4

Baulker
Farm

WILL SCARLET
CL

3

Beck Lane

Haywood Oaks

Forest
Wlks

55

Robin Hood Way

Blidworth
Bottoms

2

CALVERTON RD

TOP RD

Far Baulker
Farm

1

Gorse Covert

Syke Breck
Farm

Long Wood

Old Rufford Rd

A614

54

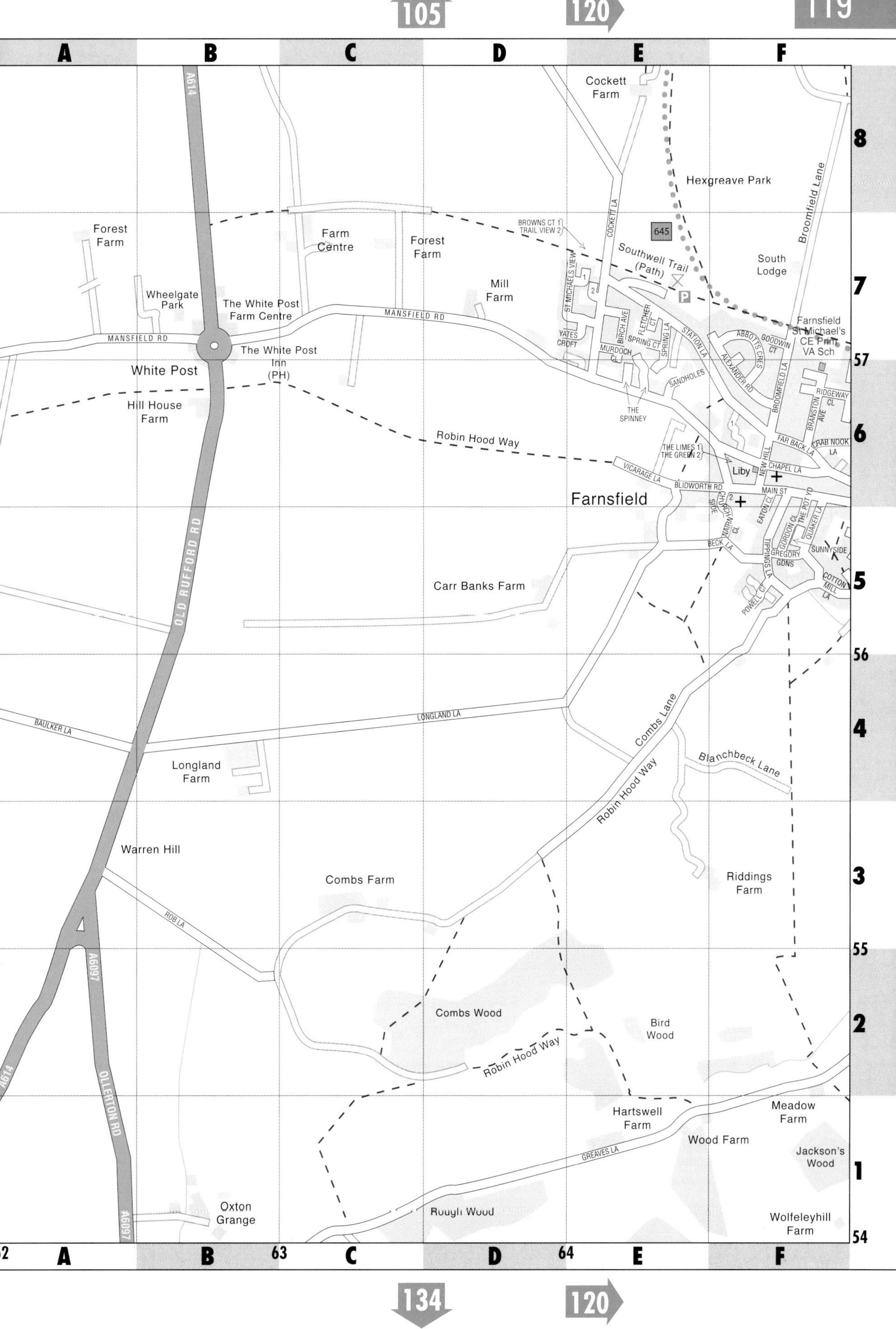
105
120
A
B
C
D
E
F
8
7
57
6
5
56
4
3
55
2
1
54
Cockett Farm
Hexgreave Park
Broomfield Lane
BROWNS CT 1
TRAIL VIEW 2
COCKETT LA
645
Southwell Trail (Path)
South Lodge
Forest Farm
Farm Centre
Forest Farm
Mill Farm
Wheelgate Park
The White Post Farm Centre
A614
MANSFIELD RD
MANSFIELD RD
The White Post Inn (PH)
White Post
Hill House Farm
ST MICHAELS VIEW
YATES CROFT
BIRCH AVE
FLETCHER CT
SPRING CT
SPRING LA
MURDOCH CL
STATION LA
ABBOTTS CRES
GOODWIN CT
ALEXANDER RD
Farnsfield St Michael's CE Prim VA Sch
SANDHOLES
THE SPINNEY
BROOMFIELD LA
RIDGEWAY CL
BRANSTON AVE
FAR BACK LA
CRAB NOOK LA
Robin Hood Way
THE LIMES 1
THE GREEN 2
Liby
NEW HILL
CHAPEL LA
VICARAGE LA
BLIDWORTH RD
MAIN ST
Farnsfield
CHURCH SIDE
NAIRN CL
EATON CL
THE POT YD
GORDON CL
QUAKER LA
BECK LA
TIPPINGS LA
GREGORY GDNS
SUNNYSIDE
COTTON MILL LA
POWELL CT
OLD RUFFORD RD
Carr Banks Farm
BAULKER LA
LONGLAND LA
Longland Farm
Combs Lane
Robin Hood Way
Blanchbeck Lane
Warren Hill
Combs Farm
Riddings Farm
ROB LA
A6097
Combs Wood
Bird Wood
Robin Hood Way
A614
OLLERTON RD
Hartswell Farm
Meadow Farm
Wood Farm
Jackson's Wood
GREAVES LA
Oxton Grange
Rough Wood
Wolfeleyhill Farm
A6097
62
63
64
134
120

119
106

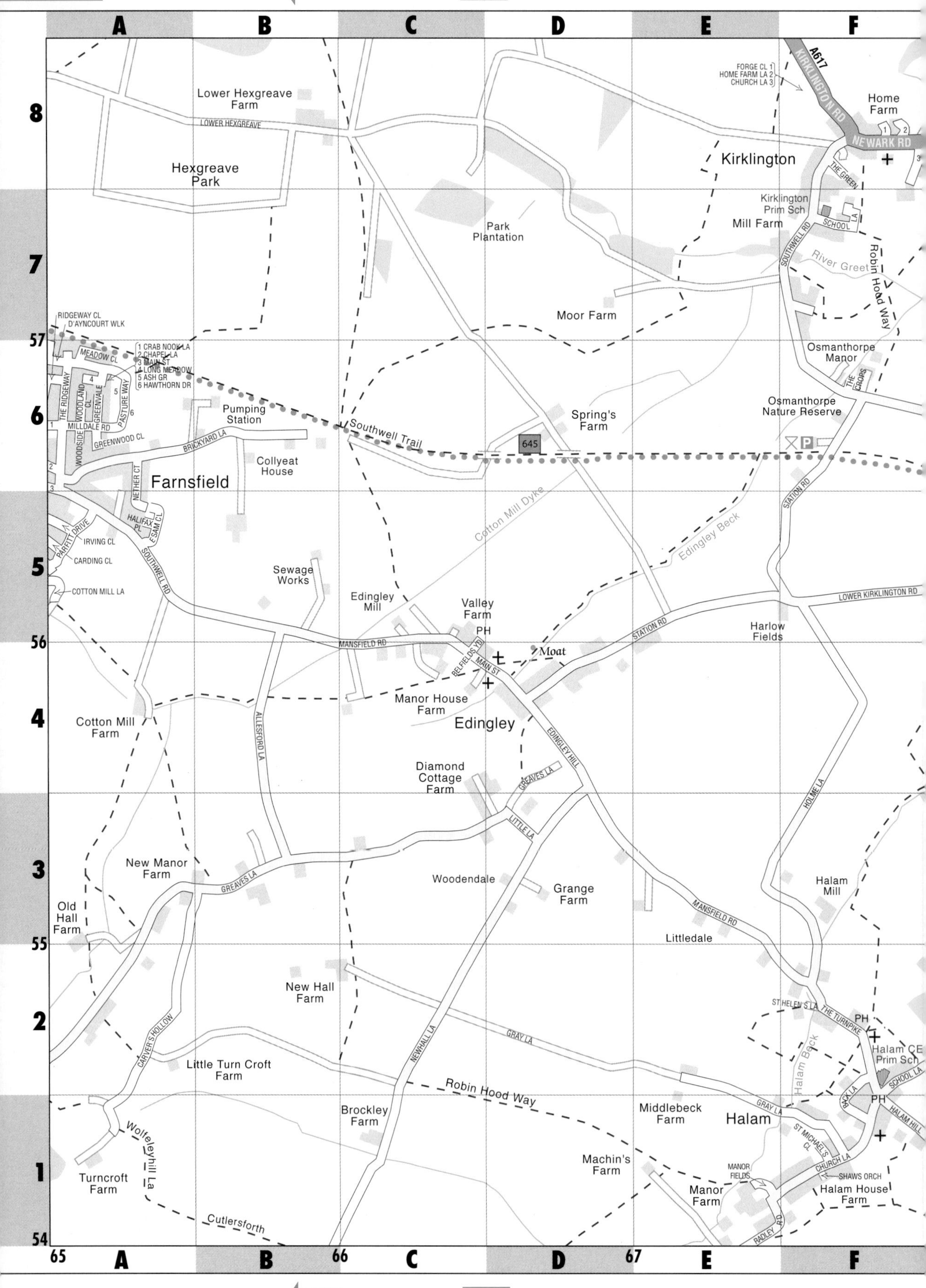
A
B
C
D
E
F
8
7
6
5
4
3
2
1
57
56
55
54
65
66
67
Lower Hexgreave Farm
LOWER HEXGREAVE
Hexgreave Park
Park Plantation
Kirklington
A617
KIRKLINGTON RD
NEWARK RD
FORGE CL 1
HOME FARM LA 2
CHURCH LA 3
Home Farm
THE GREEN
Kirklington Prim Sch
SCHOOL LA
Mill Farm
SOUTHWELL RD
River Greet
Robin Hood Way
Moor Farm
Osmanthorpe Manor
THE CROPS
Osmanthorpe Nature Reserve
Spring's Farm
645
RIDGEWAY CL
D'AYNCOURT WLK
MEADOW CL
1 CRAB NOOK LA
2 CHAPEL LA
3 MAIN ST
4 LONG MEADOW
5 ASH GR
6 HAWTHORN DR
THE RIDGEWAY
WOODLAND CL
GREENVALE
PASTURE WAY
MILLDALE RD
WOODSIDE
GREENWOOD CL
BRICKYARD LA
Pumping Station
Southwell Trail
Collyeat House
Farnsfield
NETHER CT
HALIFAX PL
ESAM CL
PARFITT DRIVE
IRVING CL
CARDING CL
COTTON MILL LA
SOUTHWELL RD
Cotton Mill Dyke
Edingley Beck
STATION RD
Sewage Works
Edingley Mill
Valley Farm
PH
MANSFIELD RD
BELFIELDS YD
MAIN ST
Moat
STATION RD
LOWER KIRKLINGTON RD
Harlow Fields
Manor House Farm
Edingley
Cotton Mill Farm
ALLESFORD LA
EDINGLEY HILL
Diamond Cottage Farm
GREAVES LA
LITTLE LA
HOLME LA
New Manor Farm
GREAVES LA
Woodendale
Grange Farm
Halam Mill
Old Hall Farm
MANSFIELD RD
Littledale
New Hall Farm
ST HELEN'S LA
THE TURNPIKE
PH
Halam CE Prim Sch
Halam Beck
SCHOOL LA
CARVER'S HOLLOW
GRAY LA
NEWHALL LA
Little Turn Croft Farm
Robin Hood Way
Brockley Farm
Middlebeck Farm
Halam
GRAY LA
BACK LA
PH
HALAM HILL
Wolfeleyhill La
Turncroft Farm
Machin's Farm
ST MICHAELS CL
CHURCH LA
SHAWS ORCH
MANOR FIELDS
Manor Farm
Halam House Farm
RADLEY RD
Cutlersforth

119
135

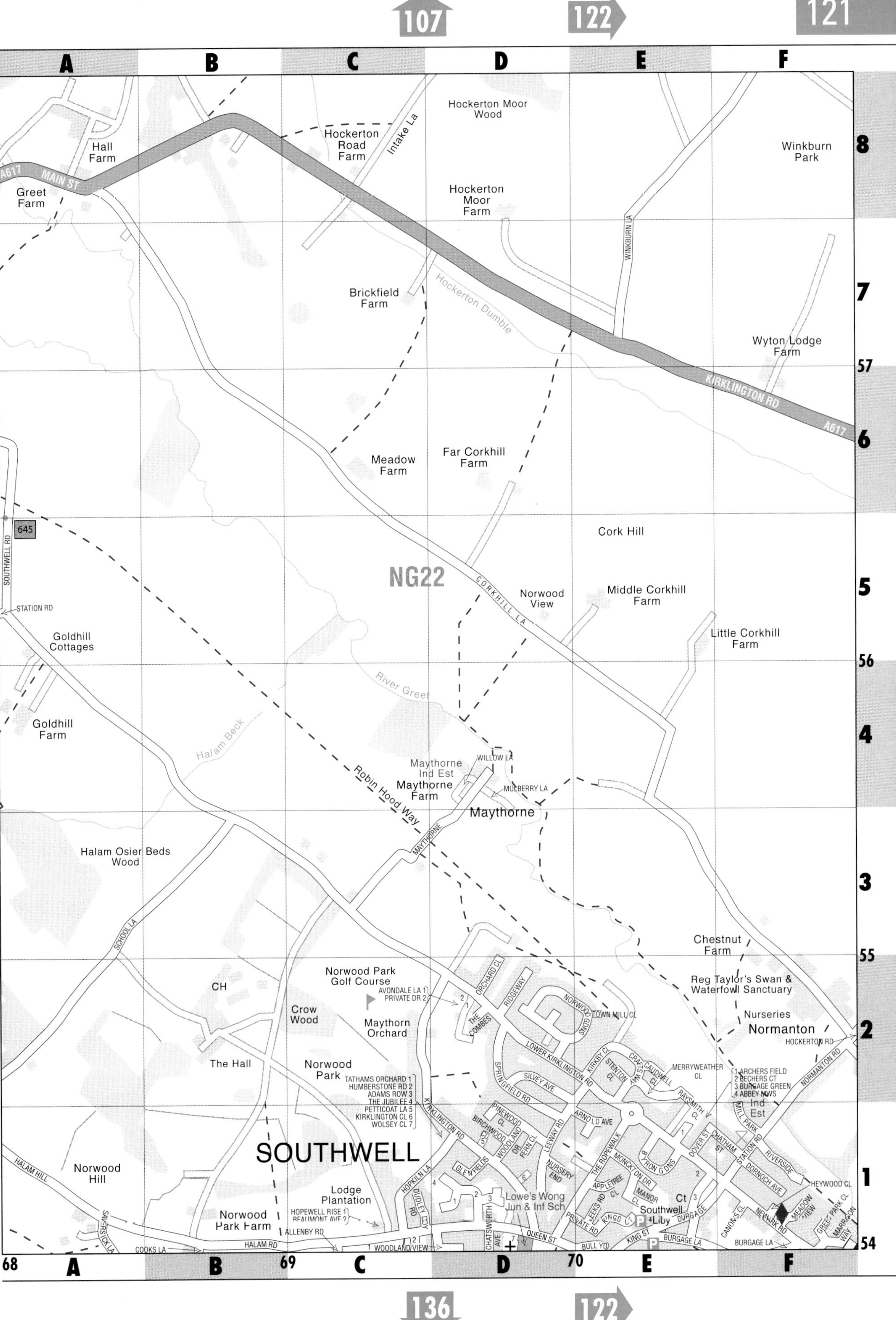

8

Hall Farm

A617 MAIN ST

Greet Farm

Hockerton Road Farm

Intake La

Hockerton Moor Wood

Winkburn Park

Hockerton Moor Farm

WINKBURN LA

7

Brickfield Farm

Hockerton Dumble

Wyton Lodge Farm

57

KIRKLINGTON RD

A617

6

Meadow Farm

Far Corkhill Farm

Cork Hill

645

SOUTHWELL RD

NG22

CORKHILL LA

Norwood View

Middle Corkhill Farm

5

STATION RD

Goldhill Cottages

Little Corkhill Farm

56

River Greet

Goldhill Farm

Halam Beck

4

Robin Hood Way

Maythorne Ind Est

WILLOW LA

Maythorne Farm

MULBERRY LA

Maythorne

MAYTHORNE

Halam Osier Beds Wood

3

SCHOOL LA

Chestnut Farm

55

Norwood Park Golf Course

Reg Taylor's Swan & Waterfowl Sanctuary

CH

AVONDALE LA 1
PRIVATE DR 2

ORCHARD CL

RIDGEWAY

TOWN MILL CL

Nurseries

Normanton

2

Crow Wood

Maythorn Orchard

THE COMBERS

NORWOOD GDNS

KIRKBY CL

STENTON CL

CRAFTS WAY

CAUDHILL CL

MERRYWEATHER CL

HOCKERTON RD

NORMANTON RD

The Hall

Norwood Park

TATHAMS ORCHARD 1
HUMBERSTONE RD 2
ADAMS ROW 3
THE JUBILEE 4
PETTICOAT LA 5
KIRKLINGTON CL 6
WOLSEY CL 7

LOWER KIRKLINGTON RD

SILVEY AVE

ARNOLD AVE

RANSAITH

1 ARCHERS FIELD
2 BECHERS CT
3 BURGAGE GREEN
4 ABBEY NEWS

Ind Est

MILL PARK

RIVERSIDE

SOUTHWELL

KIRKLINGTON RD

HOPKILN LA

DUDLEY CL

GLEWFIELDS

PINEWOOD CL

BIRCHWOOD

WOODLAND DR

FERN CL

LEYWAY RD

NURSERY END

SPRINGFIELD RD

THE ROPEWALK

MONCKTON RD

APPLETREE

MANOR

DOVER CL

CHATHAM ST

STATION

DORNOCH AVE

HEYWOOD CL

Norwood Hill

SALFERS CL LA

Lodge Plantation

HOPEWELL RISE 1
BEAUMONT AVE 2

ALLENBY RD

CHATSWORTH AVE

Lowe's Wong Jun & Inf Sch

LEEKS RD

PRIVATE RD

KING ST

KING CL

Ct

Southwell Liby

P

BURGAGE

CANON CL

NEWARK RD

MEADOW VIEW

GRES PARK CL

MARRIGAN WAY

1

Norwood Park Farm

COOKS LA

HALAM RD

WOODLAND VIEW

QUEEN ST

BULL YD

P

BURGAGE LA

BURGAGE LA

54

A **B** **C** **D** **E** **F**

8

Winkburn Park

Park Spring Wood

Newlands Farm

Newfields Farm

Park Leys

BROADGATE LA

7

HOCKERTON RD

57

Sunnybank Farm

6 A617 KIRKLINGTON RD

THE PADDOCKS

HOCKERTON HTS

PH

Hockerton

Woodside Farm

CAUNTON RD

CHURCH LA

Cheveral Wood

Hockerton Grange

Manor Farm

GABLES DR

Hockerton Dumble

NEWARK RD

Cheverals

The Wink

5

Gorse Hill

56

WHEATGRASS HILL

Upton Lodge

Lodge Farm

4

Spring Wood Farm

MICKLEBARROW HILL A617

3

Hockerwood

Hopyard Farm

Car Dyke

The Mill

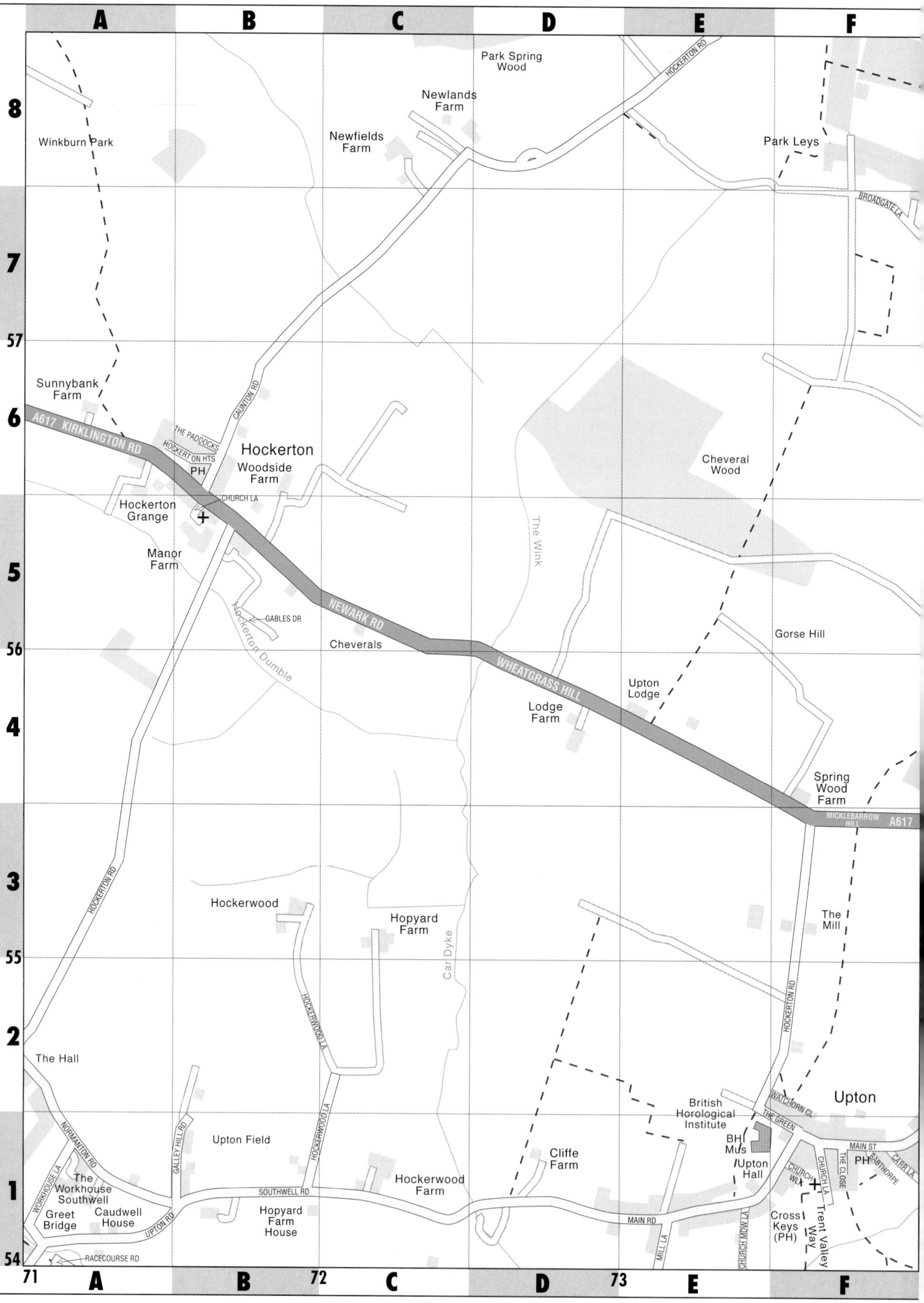

HOCKERTON RD

55

The Hall

HOCKERTON RD

HOCKERWOOD LA

2

Upton Field

British Horological Institute

WATCHORN CL

Upton

THE GREEN

NORMANTON RD

GALLEY HILL RD

UPTON RD

Cliffe Farm

BHI Mus

Upton Hall

MAIN ST

SPARTHORPE

CARR LA

CHURCH WLK

CHURCH LA

THE CLOSE

1

WORKHOUSE LA

The Workhouse Southwell

Caudwell House

SOUTHWELL RD

Hopyard Farm House

Hockerwood Farm

MAIN RD

MILL LA

CHURCH MOW LA

Cross Keys (PH)

Trent Valley Way

Greet Bridge

RACECOURSE RD

54

71 **A** **B** 72 **C** **D** 73 **E** **F**

A   B   C   D   E   F

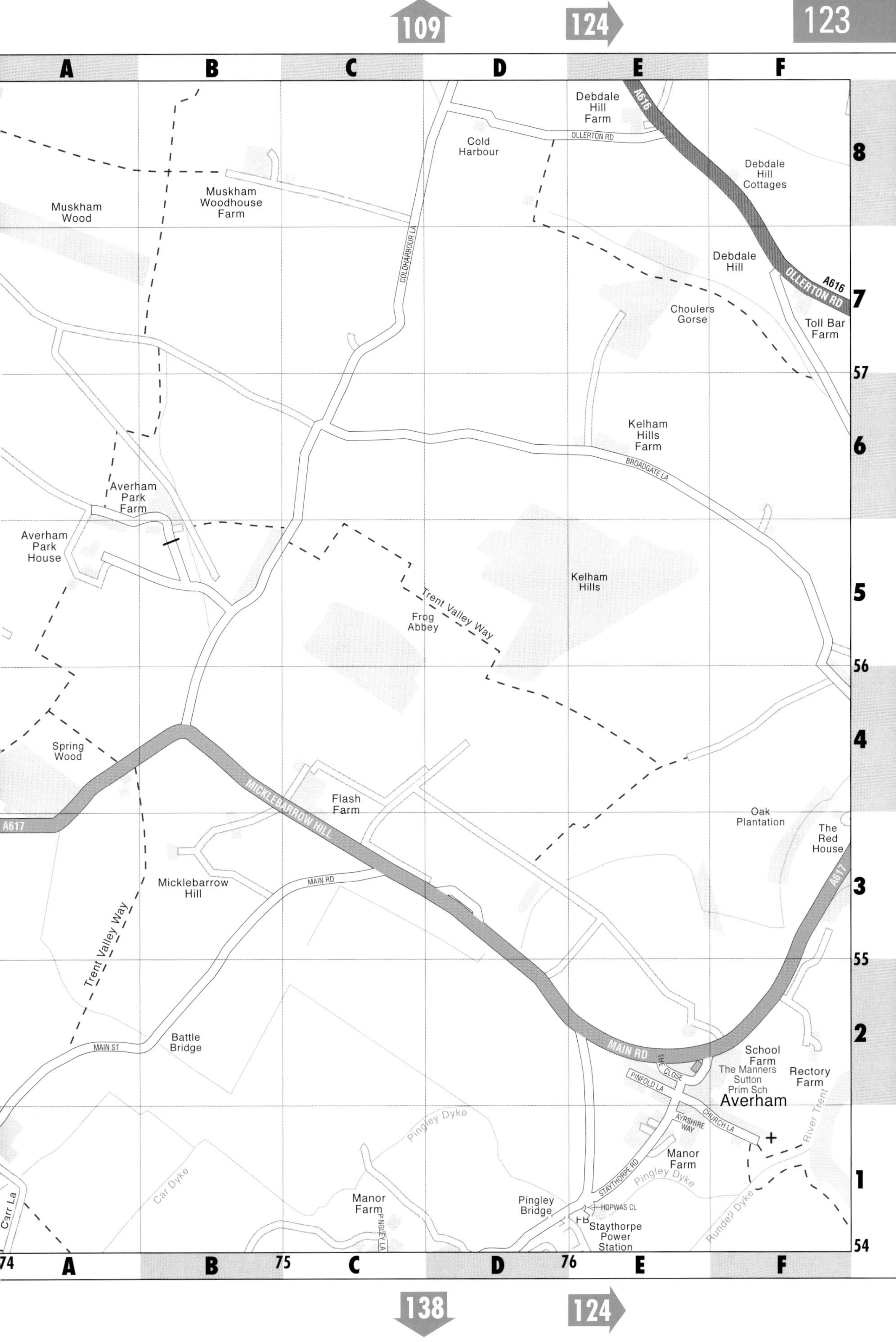

Debdale Hill Farm

OLLERTON RD

Cold Harbour

Debdale Hill Cottages

A616

8

Muskham Wood

Muskham Woodhouse Farm

Debdale Hill

OLLERTON RD

A616

7

Choulers Gorse

Toll Bar Farm

57

Kelham Hills Farm

BROADGATE LA

6

Averham Park Farm

Averham Park House

Kelham Hills

5

Trent Valley Way

Frog Abbey

56

Spring Wood

4

A617

Flash Farm

MICKLEBARROW HILL

Oak Plantation

The Red House

A617

Trent Valley Way

Micklebarrow Hill

MAIN RD

3

55

MAIN ST

Battle Bridge

MAIN RD

THE CLOSE

School Farm
The Manners Sutton Prim Sch

Rectory Farm

2

PINFOLD LA

Averham

CHURCH LA

AYRSHIRE WAY

River Trent

Pingley Dyke

STAYTHORPE RD

Manor Farm

Pingley Dyke

1

Carr La

Manor Farm

PINGLEY LA

Car Dyke

Pingley Bridge

HOPWAS CL

Staythorpe Power Station

Rundel Dyke

54

74   A   B   75   C   D   76   E   F

123
110

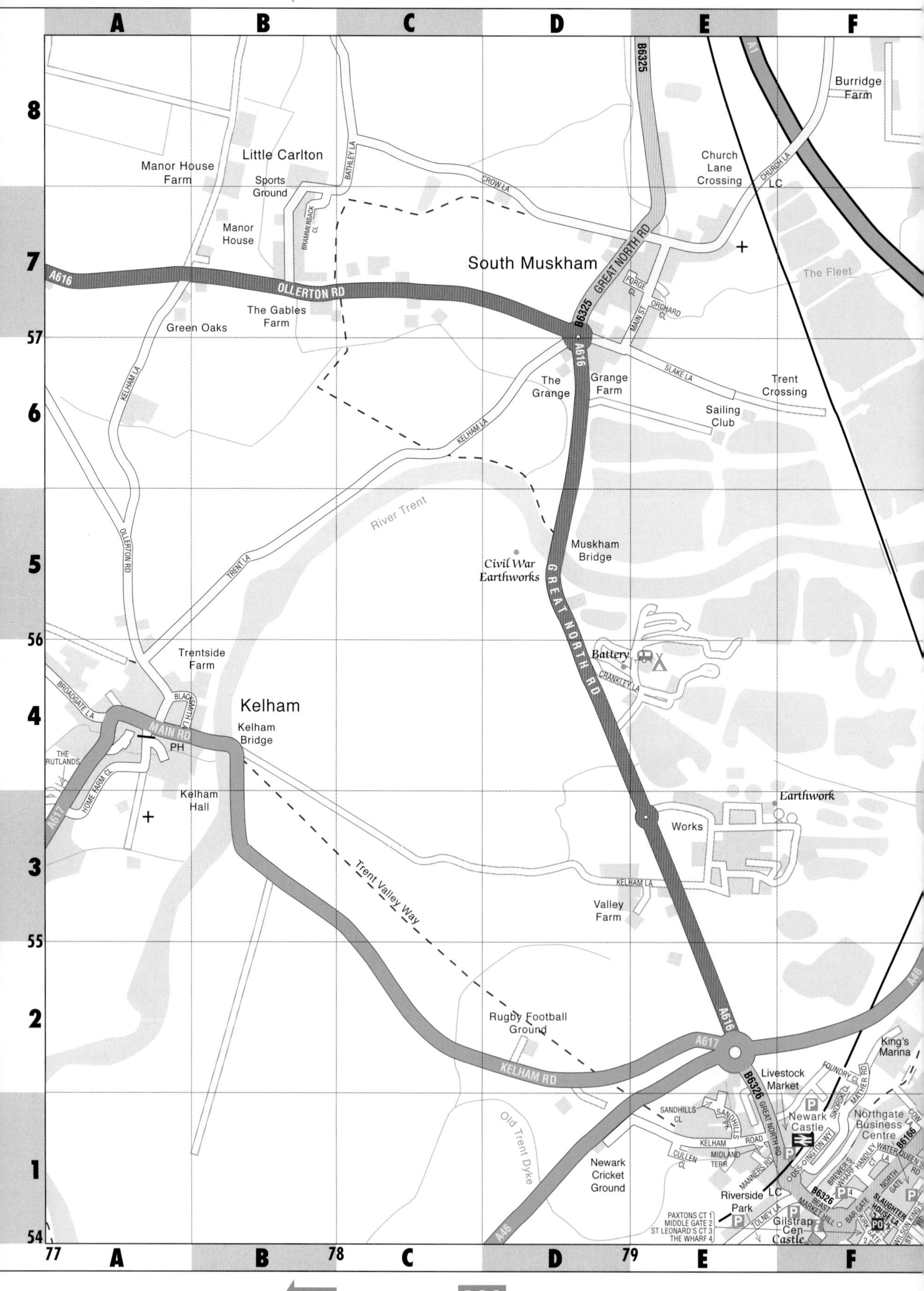
Little Carlton
Manor House Farm
Sports Ground
Manor House
South Muskham
Church Lane Crossing
Burridge Farm
The Fleet
Green Oaks
The Gables Farm
The Grange
Grange Farm
Trent Crossing
Sailing Club
River Trent
Muskham Bridge
Civil War Earthworks
Battery
Trentside Farm
Kelham
Kelham Bridge
PH
Kelham Hall
Earthwork
Works
Valley Farm
Trent Valley Way
Rugby Football Ground
Old Trent Dyke
Newark Cricket Ground
Riverside Park
Livestock Market
Newark Castle
Northgate Business Centre
King's Marina
Gilstrap Cen
Castle
A616
OLLERTON RD
B6325
GREAT NORTH RD
A617
KELHAM RD
A46
B6326
A1
MAIN RD
OLLERTON RD
KELHAM LA
TRENT LA
CROW LA
BATHLEY LA
BRAMMERSACK CL
SLAKE LA
CHURCH LA
FORGE CL
MAIN ST
ORCHARD CL
CRANKLEY LA
BROADGATE LA
BLACKSMITH LA
THE RUTLANDS
HOME FARM CL
SANDHILLS CL
KELHAM ROAD
CULLEN CL
MIDLAND TERR
MANNERS RD
TOLNEY LA
PAXTONS CT 1
MIDDLE GATE 2
ST LEONARD'S CT 3
THE WHARF 4
LC
A B C D E F
8 7 57 6 5 56 4 3 55 2 1 54
77 78 79

123
139

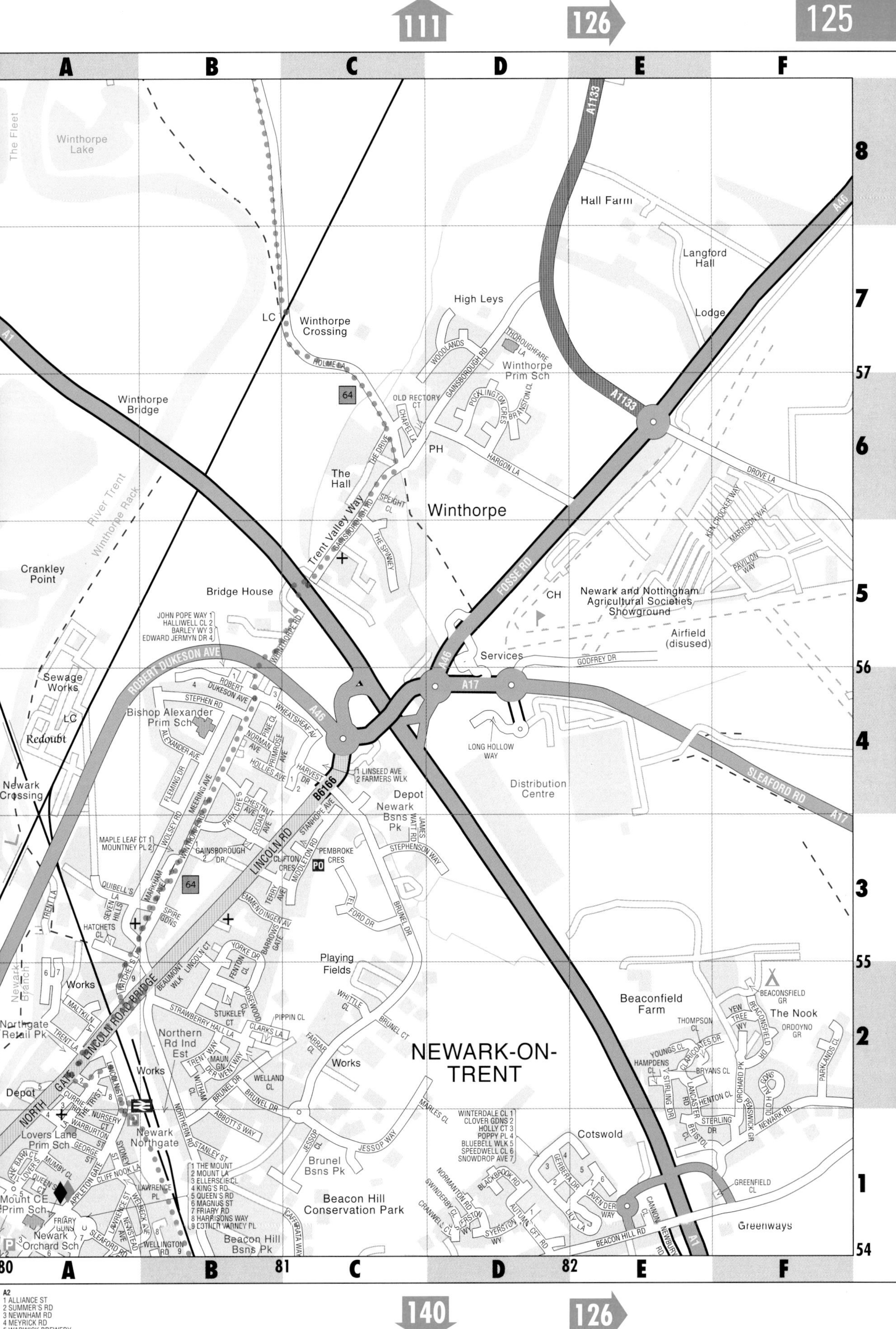

A2
1 ALLIANCE ST
2 SUMMER'S RD
3 NEWNHAM RD
4 MEYRICK RD
5 WARWICK BREWERY
6 WATERS EDGE
7 KINGS SCONCE AVE
8 HIGGINS CL
9 APPLE TREE CL

A B C D E F

8

Thorpe Field
Farm

Danethorpe Hill

7

High
Wood

Danethorpe Hill
Farm

Little Danethorpe
Farm

57

6

Lingspot
Farm

Langford Moor
Farm

Langford Moor

5

Newark Air
Museum

Stapleford Wood

56

HIGHFIELD DR

PAILINGS RIDE

CODDINGTON LA

4

Northlea

Drove Cottage
Farm

DROVE LA

STAPLEFORD LA

3

The Bungalow

A17

Moor
Brats

The
Cottage

Moor
Plantation

Flawford
Farm

55

THE
GREEN

MORGANS CL

THORPE CL

PARKES CL

ROSS CL

Sports
Ground

Coddington
Moor

The
Tinderbox

2

Coddington

Hall
Farm

BECKINGHAM RD

SLEAFORD RD

A17

NEWARK RD

VALLEY VIEW

BROWNLOW'S HILL

CHAPEL LA

MAIN ST

PH

OLD MANOR CT

Kelwick
Wood

1

Coddington
CE Prim Sch

HOUGHS
YARD

Manor
Farm

Vale Farm

CH

Newark Golf Course

BALDERTON LA

LONG LA

54

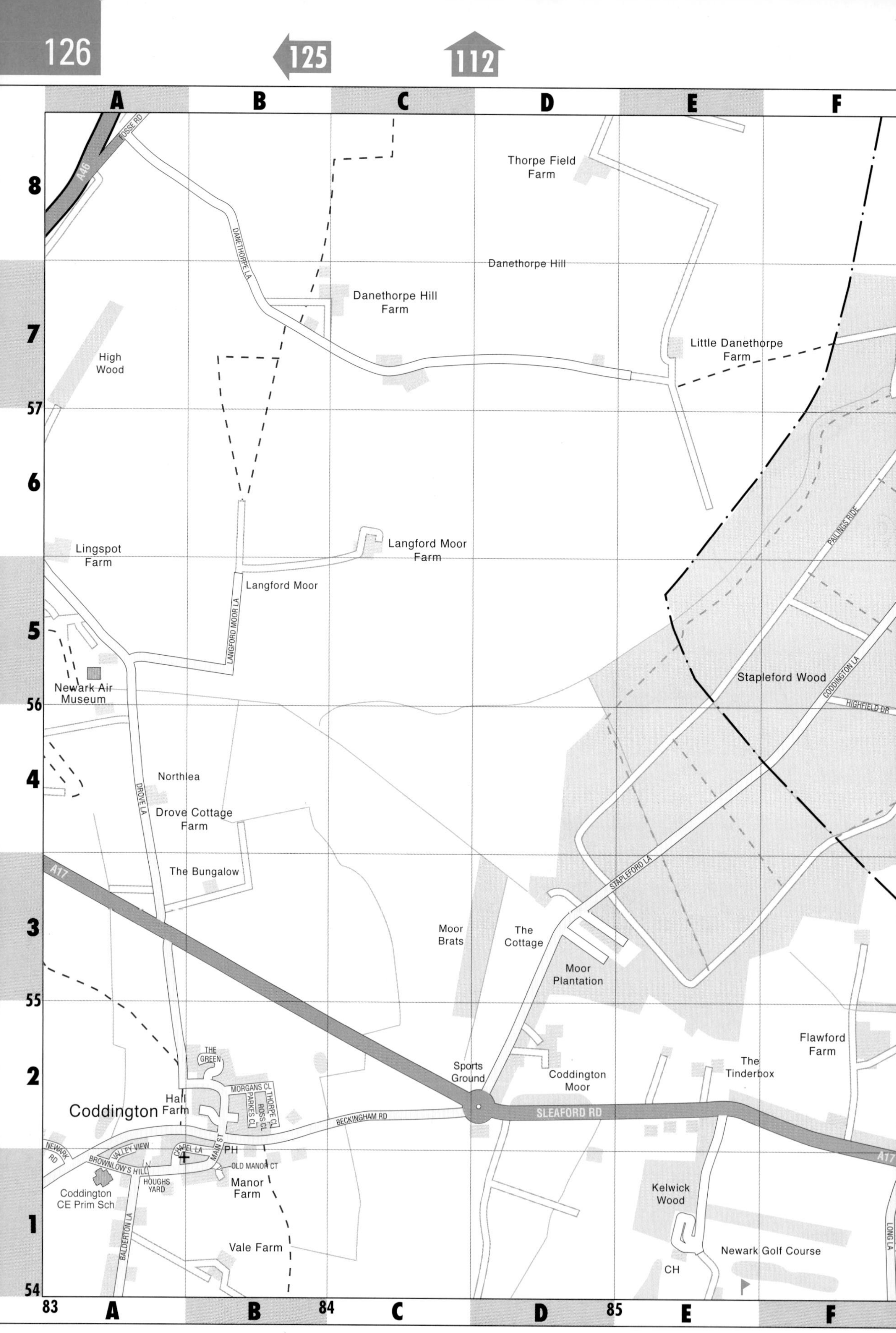

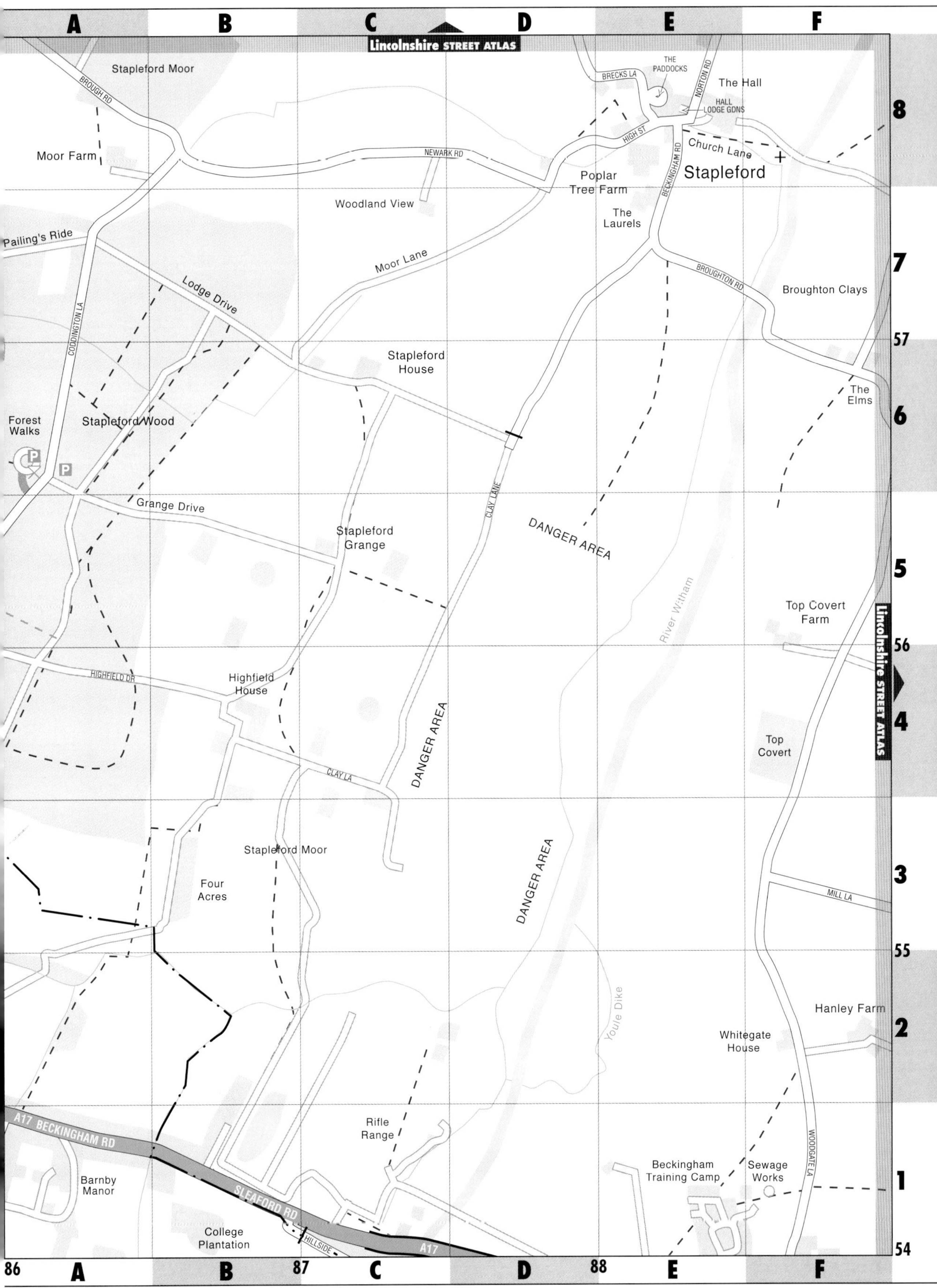

Stapleford Moor

Moor Farm

BROUGH RD

Pailing's Ride

CODDINGTON LA

Forest Walks

Stapleford Wood

Lodge Drive

Newark Rd

Woodland View

Moor Lane

Stapleford House

Grange Drive

HIGHFIELD DR

Highfield House

Stapleford Grange

CLAY LA

Stapleford Moor

Four Acres

CLAY LANE

DANGER AREA

DANGER AREA

DANGER AREA

River Witham

Youle Dike

BRECKS LA

THE PADDOCKS

HIGH ST

NORTON RD

The Hall

HALL LODGE GDNS

BECKINGHAM RD

Church Lane

Stapleford

Poplar Tree Farm

The Laurels

BROUGHTON RD

Broughton Clays

The Elms

Top Covert Farm

Top Covert

MILL LA

Hanley Farm

Whitegate House

WOODGATE LA

Rifle Range

Beckingham Training Camp

Sewage Works

A17 BECKINGHAM RD

Barnby Manor

SLEAFORD RD

College Plantation

HILLSIDE

A17

113

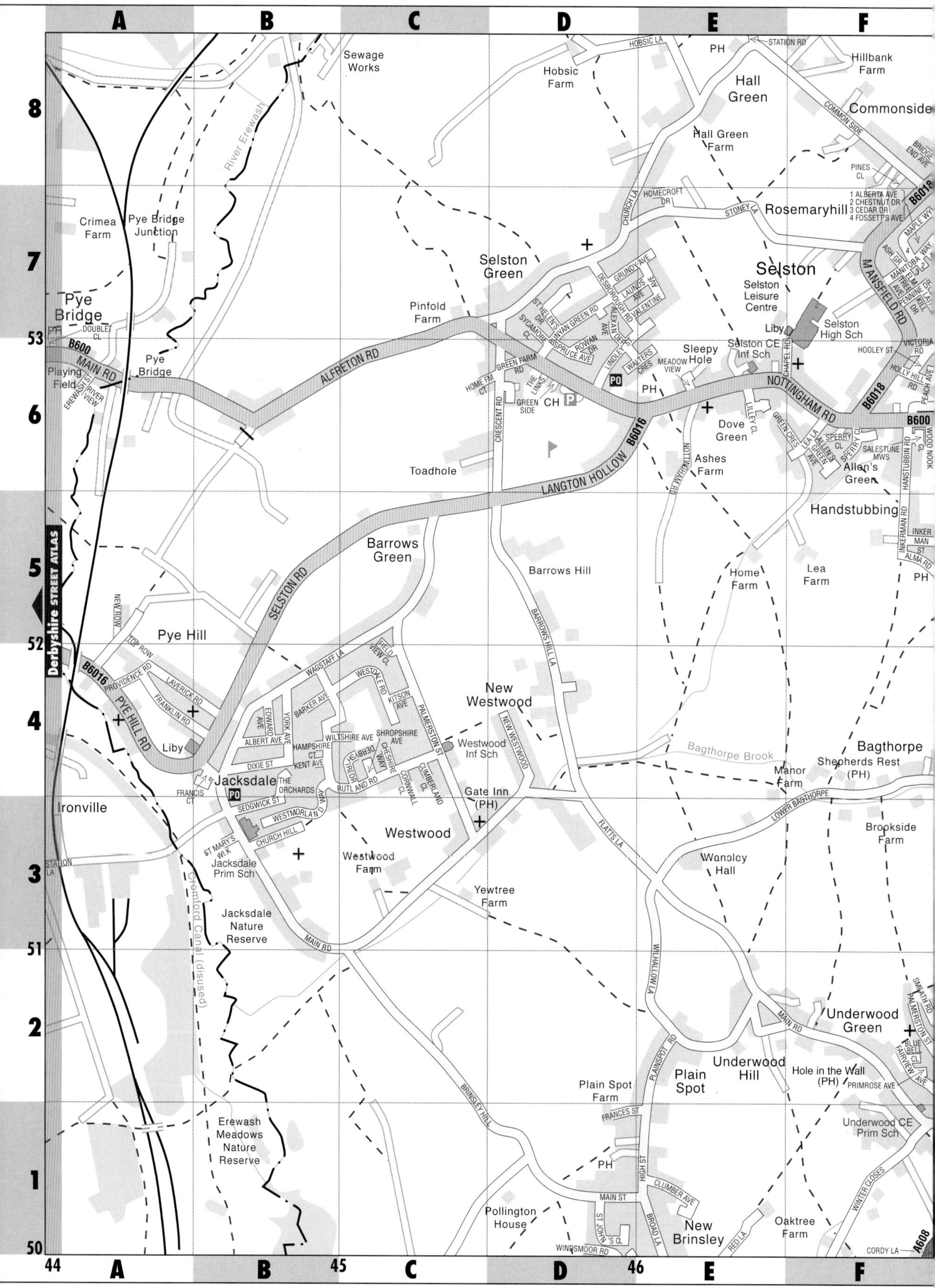
A
B
C
D
E
F
8
7
6
5
4
3
2
1
53
52
51
50
44
45
46
Sewage Works
Hobsic Farm
HOBSIC LA
PH
STATION RD
Hillbank Farm
Hall Green
Commonside
COMMON SIDE
Hall Green Farm
PINES CL
HOMECROFT DR
STONEY LA
Rosemaryhill
1 ALBERTA AVE
2 CHESTNUT DR
3 CEDAR DR
4 FOSSETT'S AVE
B6018
MAPLE WY
Crimea Farm
Pye Bridge Junction
River Erewash
Selston Green
Selston
Selston Leisure Centre
MANSFIELD RD
Pye Bridge
DOUBLET CL
B600
MAIN RD
Pinfold Farm
ALFRETON RD
Liby
Selston High Sch
Selston CE Inf Sch
Sleepy Hole
MEADOW VIEW
HOOLEY ST
VICTORIA RD
Pye Bridge
Playing Field
EREWASH ST
RIVER VIEW
GREEN FARM RD
HOME FM CT
THE LINKS
GREEN SIDE
CH
PO
PH
NOTTINGHAM RD
CHAPEL RD
Dove Green
LILLEY CL
B6016
CRESCENT RD
Toadhole
Ashes Farm
SPERRY CL
SALESTUNE MWS
Allen's Green
HANSTUBBIN RD
WOOD NOOK
LANGTON HOLLOW
Handstubbing
INKERMAN RD
INKER MAN ST
ALMA RD
Barrows Green
Barrows Hill
Home Farm
Lea Farm
PH
SELSTON RD
NEW ROW
Pye Hill
TOP ROW
BARROWS HILL LA
PROVIDENCE RD
LAVERICK RD
FRANKLIN RD
WAGSTAFF LA
FIELD VIEW CL
WESTDALE RD
KITSON AVE
New Westwood
PALMERSTON ST
BARKER AVE
EDWARD AVE
YORK AVE
ALBERT AVE
WILTSHIRE AVE
SHROPSHIRE AVE
HAMPSHIRE CT
NEW WESTWOOD
PYE HILL RD
Liby
Westwood Inf Sch
Bagthorpe Brook
Bagthorpe
Shepherds Rest (PH)
DIXIE ST
KENT AVE
DERBY TER
CHESHIRE WAY
CUMBERLAND CL
CORNWALL CL
Manor Farm
Jacksdale
THE ORCHARDS
RUTLAND RD
Gate Inn (PH)
FRANCIS CT
PO
SEDGWICK ST
WESTMORLAND WAY
Ironville
LOWER BAGTHORPE
Brookside Farm
ST MARY'S WLK
CHURCH HILL
Westwood
FLATTS LA
STATION LA
Jacksdale Prim Sch
Westwood Farm
Wansley Hall
Cromford Canal (disused)
Yewtree Farm
Jacksdale Nature Reserve
MAIN RD
WILHALLOW LA
SMITH RD
PALMERSTON ST
Underwood Green
MAIN RD
BLUE BELL CL
FAIRVIEW AVE
PLAINSPOT RD
Underwood Hill
Plain Spot
Hole in the Wall (PH)
PRIMROSE AVE
Plain Spot Farm
BRINSLEY HILL
Erewash Meadows Nature Reserve
FRANCES ST
Underwood CE Prim Sch
PH
HIGH ST
CLUMBER AVE
WINTER CLOSES
MAIN ST
Pollington House
ST JOHN'S CL
BROAD LA
New Brinsley
RED LA
Oaktree Farm
A608
WINDSMOOR RD
CORDY LA
Derbyshire STREET ATLAS

143

114
130

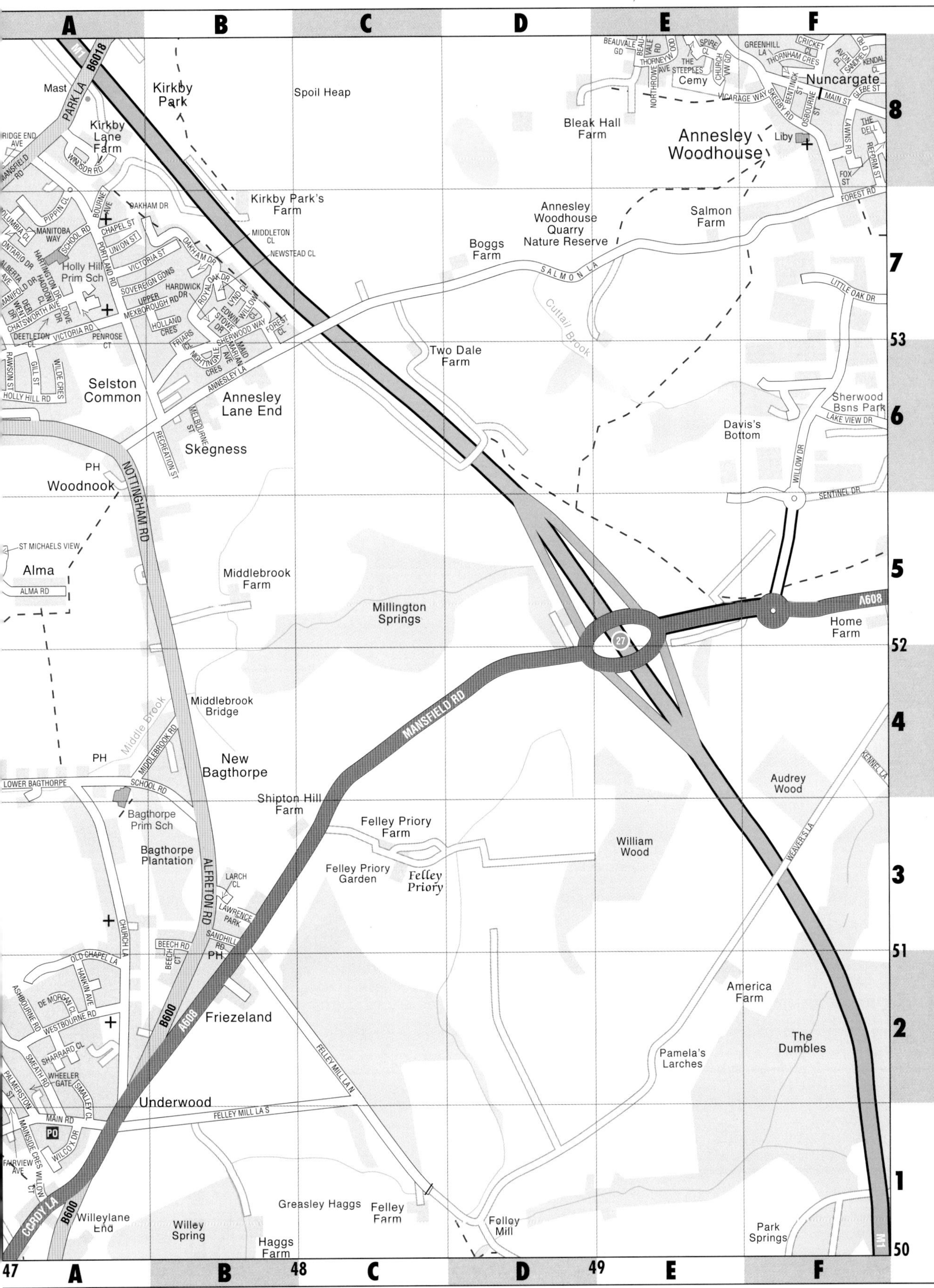
A
B
C
D
E
F
Mast
Kirkby Park
Spoil Heap
Kirkby Lane Farm
Bleak Hall Farm
Annesley Woodhouse
Nuncargate
Liby
Kirkby Park's Farm
Annesley Woodhouse Quarry Nature Reserve
Salmon Farm
Boggs Farm
Holly Hill Prim Sch
Salmon La
Cuttail Brook
Two Dale Farm
Selston Common
Annesley Lane End
Skegness
Sherwood Bsns Park
Davis's Bottom
PH
Woodnook
Nottingham Rd
Alma
Middlebrook Farm
Millington Springs
A608
Home Farm
Middlebrook Bridge
Mansfield Rd
New Bagthorpe
Lower Bagthorpe
Audrey Wood
Bagthorpe Prim Sch
Shipton Hill Farm
Felley Priory Farm
Bagthorpe Plantation
William Wood
Felley Priory Garden
Felley Priory
Alfreton Rd
Friezeland
America Farm
The Dumbles
Pamela's Larches
Underwood
Felley Mill La N
Felley Mill La S
Greasley Haggs
Felley Farm
Felley Mill
Willeylane End
Willey Spring
Haggs Farm
Park Springs
M1
B600
B6018
47
48
49
50
51
52
53
1
2
3
4
5
6
7
8

144
130

129
115

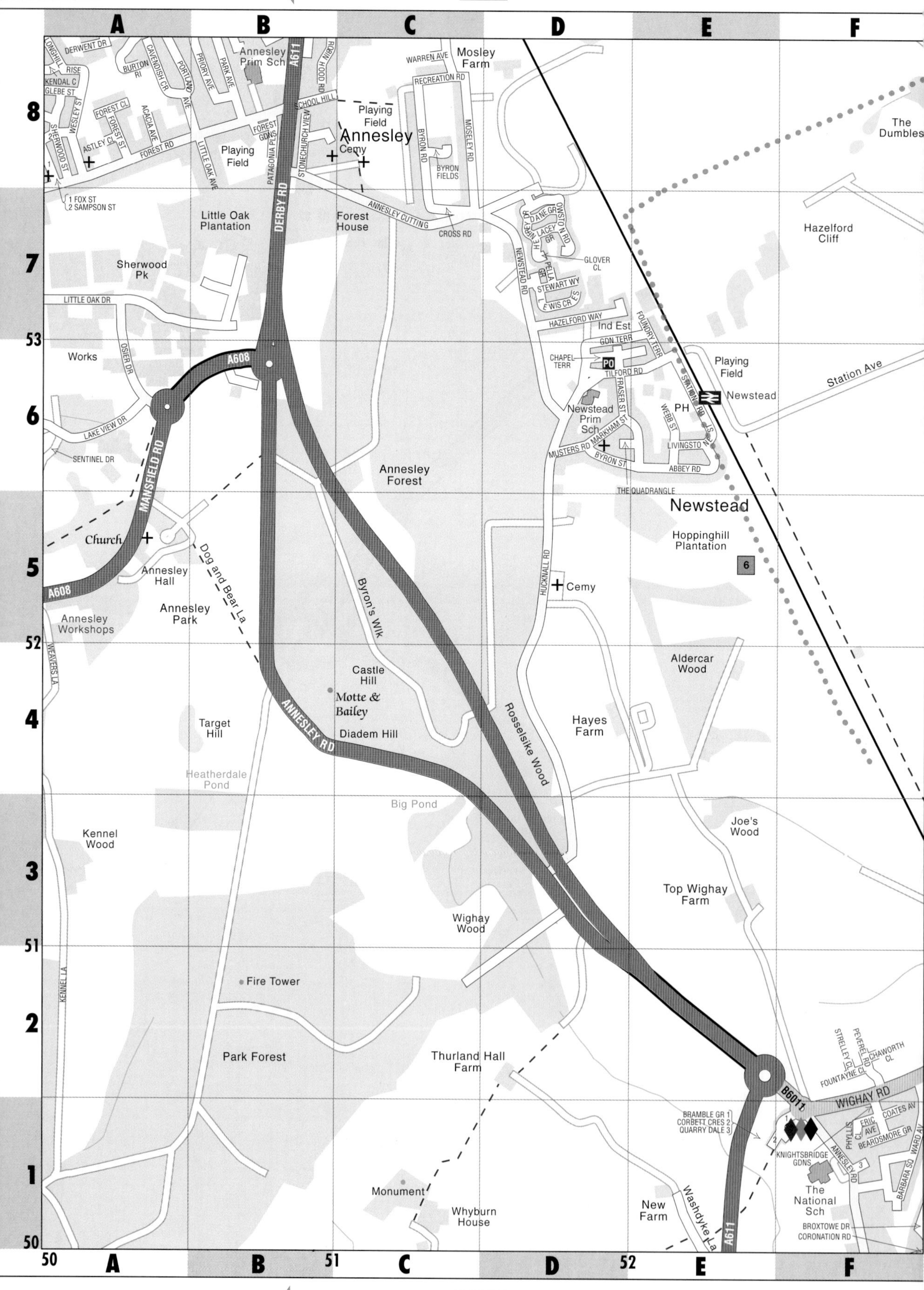
Annesley
Newstead
Annesley Forest
Annesley Park
Annesley Hall
Little Oak Plantation
Sherwood Pk
Forest House
Playing Field
Mosley Farm
The Dumbles
Hazelford Cliff
Playing Field
Station Ave
Hoppinghill Plantation
Aldercar Wood
Hayes Farm
Rosselsike Wood
Byron's Wlk
Dog and Bear La
Castle Hill
Motte & Bailey
Diadem Hill
Target Hill
Heatherdale Pond
Big Pond
Kennel Wood
Joe's Wood
Top Wighay Farm
Wighay Wood
Fire Tower
Park Forest
Thurland Hall Farm
Monument
Whyburn House
New Farm
Washdyke La
The National Sch
Annesley Workshops
Works
Church
Cemy
A611
A608
B6011
DERBY RD
ANNESLEY RD
MANSFIELD RD
HUCKNALL RD
NEWSTEAD RD
WIGHAY RD
LITTLE OAK DR
LAKE VIEW DR
SENTINEL DR
OSIER DR
WEAVERS LA
KENNEL LA
Annesley Prim Sch
Newstead Prim Sch
Ind Est
PO
PH
THE QUADRANGLE
ABBEY RD
BYRON ST
MUSTERS RD
MARKHAM ST
FRASER ST
WEBB ST
LIVINGSTON
TILFORD RD
GDN TERR
CHAPEL TERR
HAZELFORD WAY
STEWART WY
LEWIS CR
GLOVER CL
ANNESLEY CUTTING
CROSS RD
BYRON FIELDS
BYRON RD
MOSELEY RD
RECREATION RD
WARREN AVE
SCHOOL HILL
STONECHURCH VIEW
PATAGONIA PL
LITTLE OAK AVE
FOREST RD
FOREST GDNS
ACACIA AVE
FOREST CL
ASTLEY CL
SHERWOOD ST
WESLEY ST
GLEBE ST
KENDAL C
RISE
LONGHILL
DERWENT DR
BURTON RI
CAVENDISH CR
PORTLAND AVE
PRIORY AVE
PARK AVE
ROBIN HOOD RD
1 FOX ST
2 SAMPSON ST
BRAMBLE GR 1
CORBETT CRES 2
QUARRY DALE 3
KNIGHTSBRIDGE GDNS
FOUNTAYNE CL
STRELLEY CL
PEVEREL RD
CHAWORTH CL
COATES AV
ERIC AVE
PHYLLIS CL
BEARDSMORE GR
WARD AV
BARBARA SQ
ANNESLEY RD
BROXTOWE DR
CORONATION RD
A B C D E F
8 7 6 5 4 3 2 1
53 52 51 50
50 51 52

129
145

116
132

A
B
C
D
E
F
8
7
53
6
5
52
4
3
51
2
1
50
54
55
Castle Wood
Upper Lake
Newstead Abbey & Gardens
Priory (remains of)
Abbey Wood
Black Hills
Newstead Park
Poet's Corner Wood
Garden Lake
Poet's Corner
Hawk Lawn
Robin Hood Way
River Leen
Ravenshead Wood
Station Avenue
Limekiln Wood
Gibbetdale Wood
BLIDWORTH WAYE
Lower Lake
Johnny Sherwood
Quarry Banks Farm
Quarry Holes
Jack o'Sherwood
The Firs
MAIN ST
DANNERS HILL
Quarry Banks
Weir Mills Farm
HALL LA
Playing Field
Top Farm
BREAK LA
Mons
Papplewick Hall and Gardens
King Edward's Plantation
QUARRY LA
Church Plantation
Linby Cum Papplewick CE Prim Sch
Linby
Cross
Papplewick
PH
BLACKSMITHS CT
LINBY LA
FOREST LA
B6011
Castle Mill Farm
LC
WIGHAY RD
MOOR RD
NUNN CL 1
VINCENT CL 2
BAXTER CL 3
CRANSWICK CL 4
BASS CL 5
ASKEW RD 6
GRANGEMOOR 7
PAPPLEWICK FARM CL 8
Warp Mill
Papplewick Moor
CHADBURN RD
Robin Hood Way
PAPPLEWICK LA
Grange Farm
Holy Cross RC Prim Sch
PARK GATE 1
ST MICHAEL'S VIEW 2
LINBY RD 3
BROXTOWE DR
CORONATION RD
VICTORIA GR
WATERLOO RD
SHERWOOD WLK
HAZEL WAY
CHURCH LA
HAYDEN LA
DOROTHY AVE
DELIA AVE
ALISON AVE
MARION AVE
DEVITT DR
CHRISTINE CL
BERNARD AVE
SUSAN CL
ALEXANDER CL
FRANCES GR
DAWN CL
ETHEL AVE
VAUGHAN AVE
ROSSLYN DR
RYKNIELD RD
CORINTHIAN CL
KELBROOK RD
OSPREY GR
PEREGRINE RD
FALCON WY
PAPPLEWICK GRANGE
HOLBECK RD
AVOCET
B683
A60
NOTTINGHAM RD
MANSFIELD RD
REGINA CR
NEWSTEAD ABBEY PK
PO
P

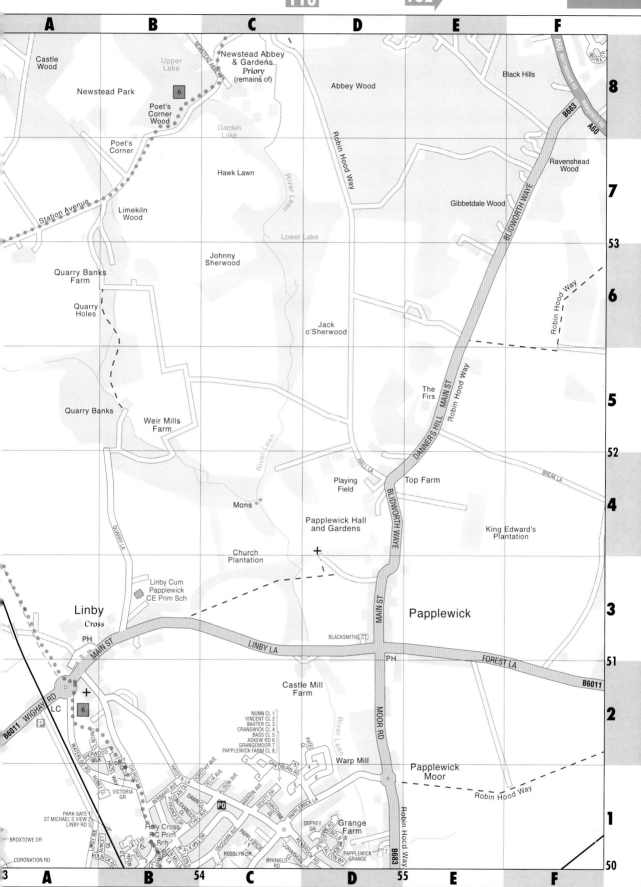

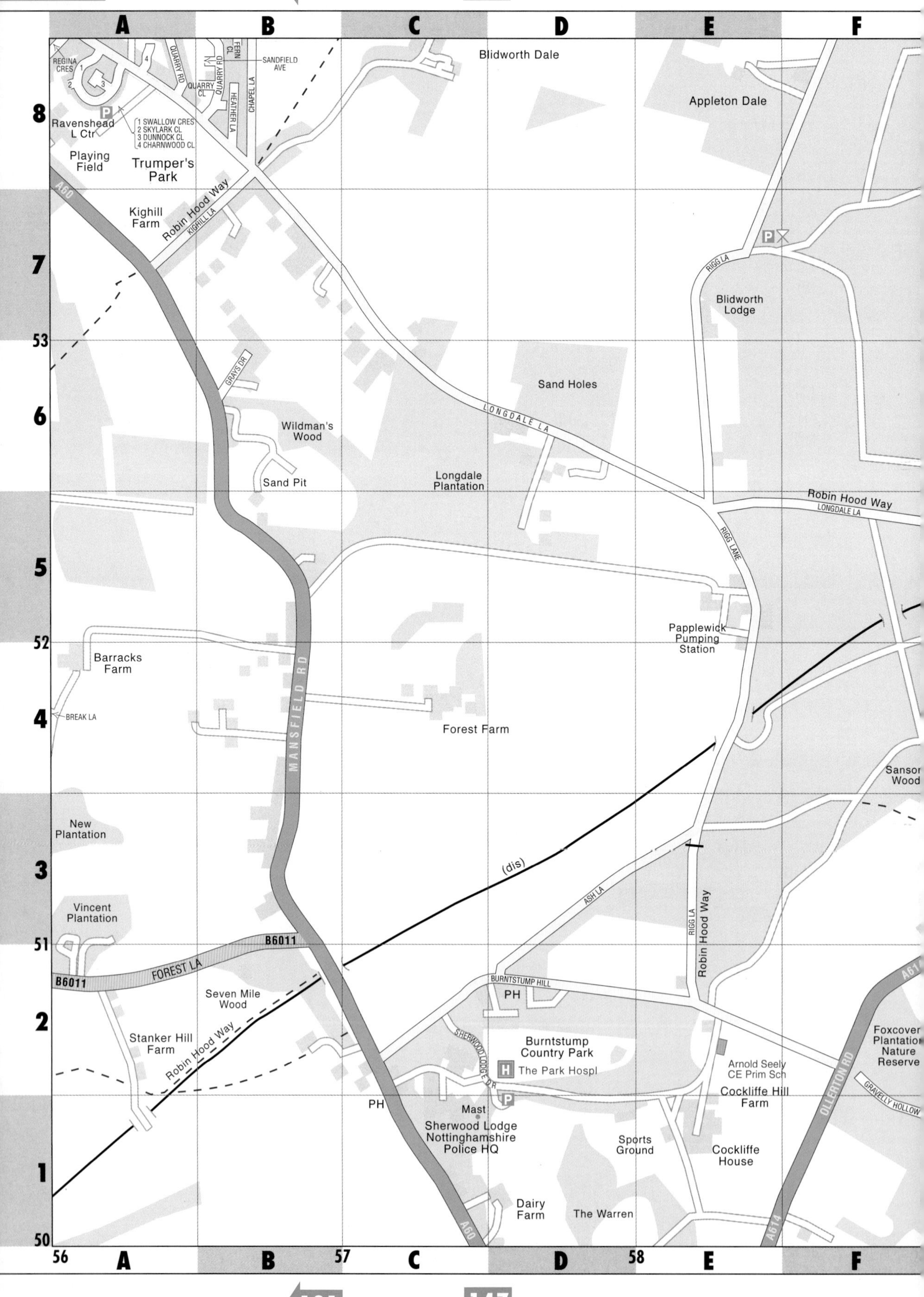
A
B
C
D
E
F
8
7
53
6
5
52
4
3
51
2
1
50
56
57
58
Blidworth Dale
Appleton Dale
REGINA CRES
SANDFIELD AVE
QUARRY RD
QUARRY CL
FERN CL
HEATHER LA
CHAPEL LA
Ravenshead L Ctr
1 SWALLOW CRES
2 SKYLARK CL
3 DUNNOCK CL
4 CHARNWOOD CL
Playing Field
Trumper's Park
A60
Kighill Farm
Robin Hood Way
KIGHILL LA
RIGG LA
Blidworth Lodge
GRAYS DR
Sand Holes
LONGDALE LA
Wildman's Wood
Sand Pit
Longdale Plantation
Robin Hood Way
LONGDALE LA
RIGG LANE
Papplewick Pumping Station
Barracks Farm
MANSFIELD RD
BREAK LA
Forest Farm
Sansom Wood
New Plantation
(dis)
ASH LA
RIGG LA
Robin Hood Way
Vincent Plantation
B6011
FOREST LA
B6011
BURNTSTUMP HILL
PH
Seven Mile Wood
Stanker Hill Farm
Robin Hood Way
SHERWOOD LODGE DR
Burntstump Country Park
The Park Hospl
Arnold Seely CE Prim Sch
Foxcover Plantation Nature Reserve
OLLERTON RD
GRAVELLY HOLLOW
Cockliffe Hill Farm
PH
Mast
Sherwood Lodge Nottinghamshire Police HQ
Sports Ground
Cockliffe House
Dairy Farm
The Warren
A60
A614
A614

118
134

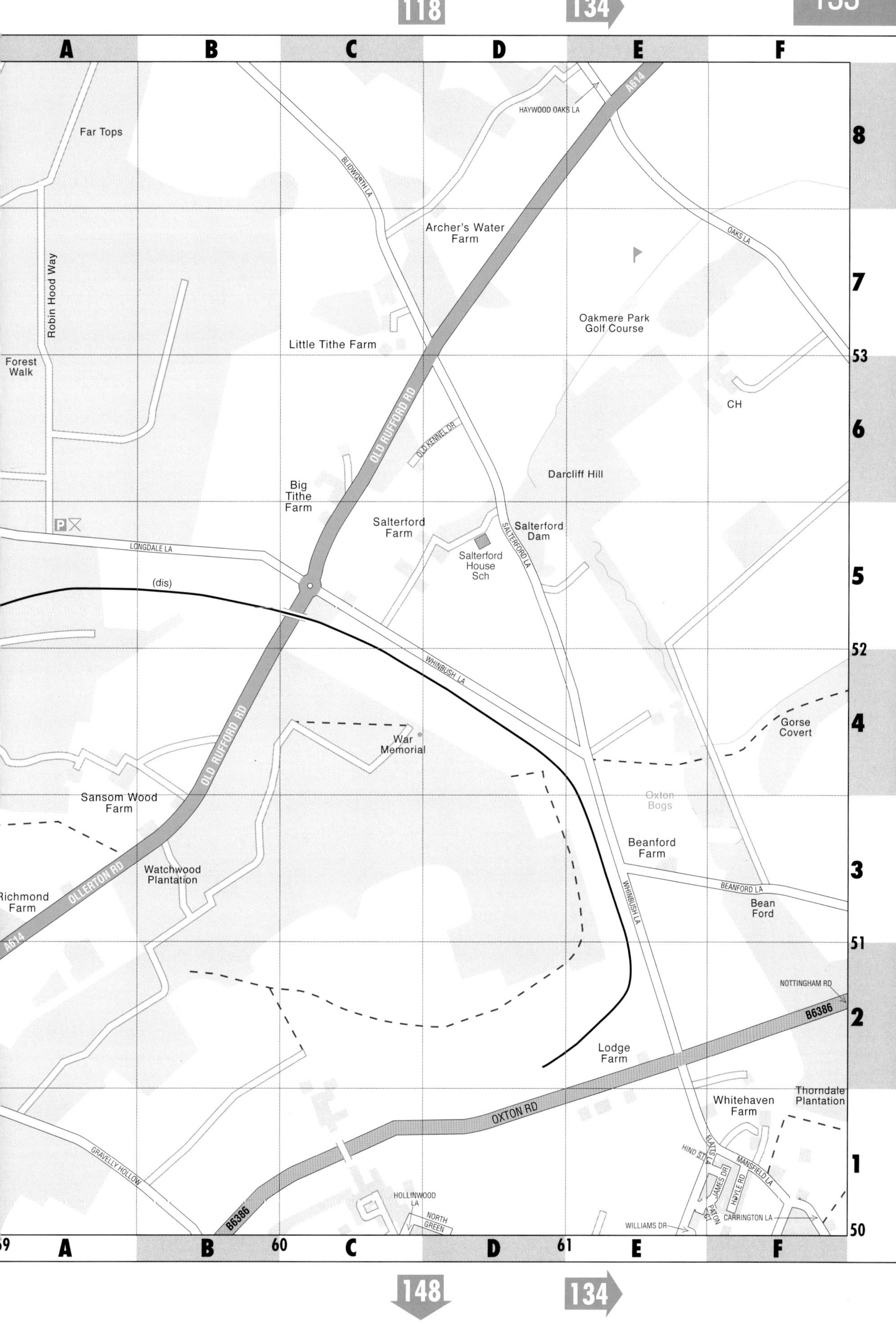
A
B
C
D
E
F
8
7
6
5
4
3
2
1
53
52
51
50
59
60
61
Far Tops
HAYWOOD OAKS LA
A614
BLIDWORTH LA
Robin Hood Way
Archer's Water Farm
OAKS LA
Oakmere Park Golf Course
Little Tithe Farm
Forest Walk
CH
OLD RUFFORD RD
OLD KENNEL DR
Darcliff Hill
Big Tithe Farm
Salterford Farm
Salterford Dam
LONGDALE LA
Salterford House Sch
SALTERFORD LA
(dis)
WHINBUSH LA
Gorse Covert
War Memorial
Oxton Bogs
Sansom Wood Farm
Beanford Farm
Watchwood Plantation
WHINBUSH LA
BEANFORD LA
Bean Ford
Richmond Farm
OLLERTON RD
NOTTINGHAM RD
B6386
Lodge Farm
OXTON RD
Thorndale Plantation
Whitehaven Farm
FLATTS LA
HIND ST
MANSFIELD LA
JAMES DR
HOYLE RD
GRAVELLY HOLLOW
HOLLINWOOD LA
NORTH GREEN
PATON CT
CARRINGTON LA
WILLIAMS DR
B6386

148
134

133
119

A B C D E F

8

7

53

6

5

52

4

3

51

2

1

50

Margaret's Spring

Horsepasture Wood

Robin Hood Way

Loath Hill

Robin Hood Hill

Fallows Farm

Far Leys Holt

Dairy Farm

A6097

OLLERTON RD

Moorfields Farm

OXTON BYPASS

OAKS LA

Godson Plantation

Cockglode Plantation

FOREST RD

WINDMILL HILL

Windmill Hill

HONEYKNAB LA

Oxton Dumble

Far Leys

Oxton Hill Farm

OXTON HILL

OXTON BYEPASS

P

Hatfield Lane

CHAPEL LA

THE ORCHARDS

PO

Oxton

BLIND LA

Deer Leap

SOUTHWELL RD

Middlehey Sch

Birkhouse Wood

MANOR CL

Salterford House Sch

ELMCROFT

MAIN ST

NEW RD

SANDY LA

Holly Lodge

Nether Field

Rossellewood Farm

SCHOOL GDNS

WATER LA

PH

BEANFORD LA

SOUTHWELL RD

B6386   NOTTINGHAM RD

Thorndale Plantation

OXTON BYPASS

Mill Farm

Dover Beck

EPPERSTONE RD

A6097

Epperstone Park

Park Farm

62   A   B   63   C   D   64   E   F

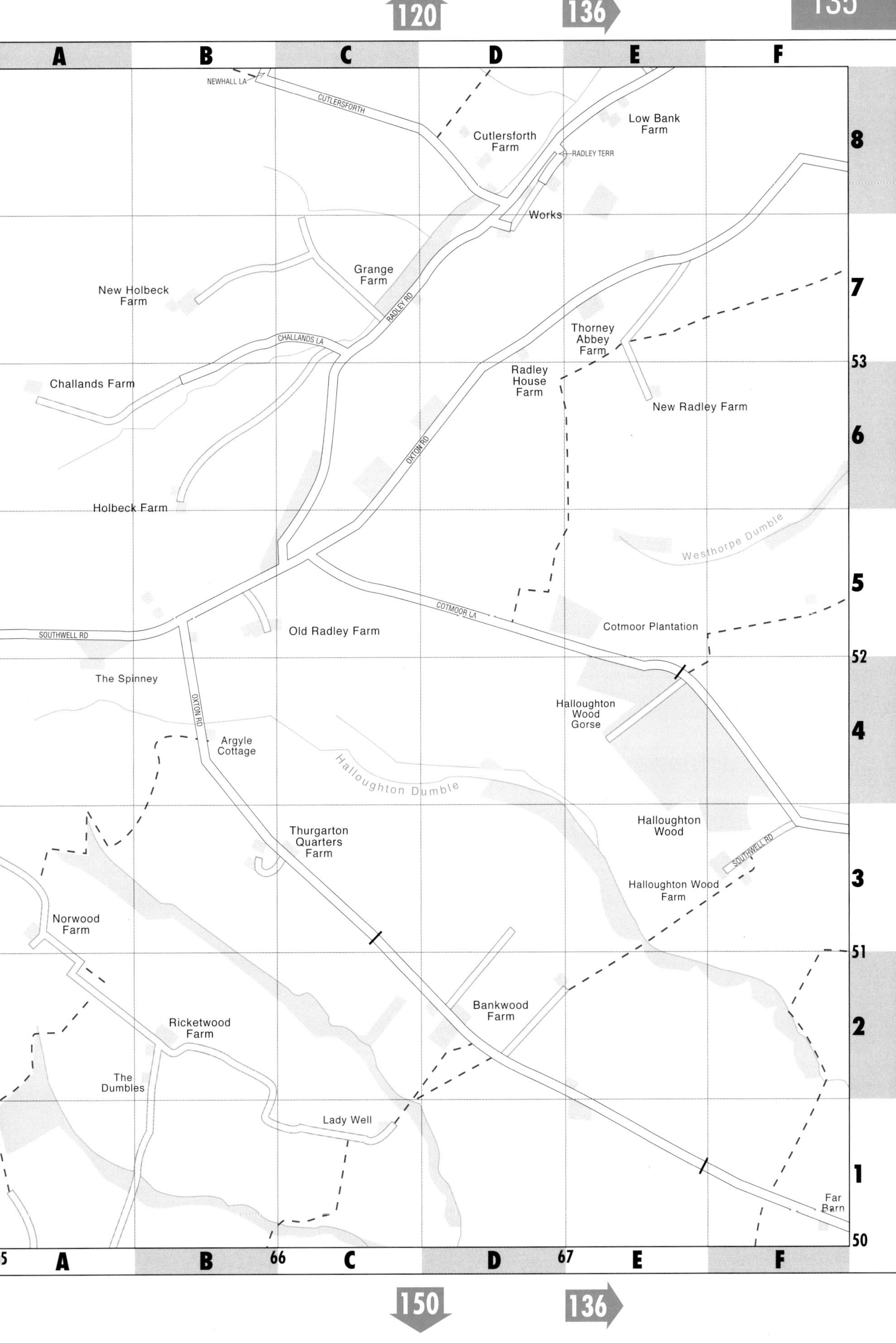

120
136

A   B   C   D   E   F

8
7
53
6
5
52
4
3
51
2
1
50

NEWHALL LA
CUTLERSFORTH
Cutlersforth Farm
Low Bank Farm
RADLEY TERR
Works
Grange Farm
New Holbeck Farm
RADLEY RD
CHALLANDS LA
Thorney Abbey Farm
Radley House Farm
Challands Farm
New Radley Farm
OXTON RD
Holbeck Farm
Westhorpe Dumble
SOUTHWELL RD
Old Radley Farm
COTMOOR LA
Cotmoor Plantation
The Spinney
OXTON RD
Halloughton Wood Gorse
Argyle Cottage
Halloughton Dumble
Thurgarton Quarters Farm
Halloughton Wood
Halloughton Wood Farm
SOUTHWELL RD
Norwood Farm
Ricketwood Farm
Bankwood Farm
The Dumbles
Lady Well
Far Barn

5   A   B   66   C   D   67   E   F

150
136

135
121

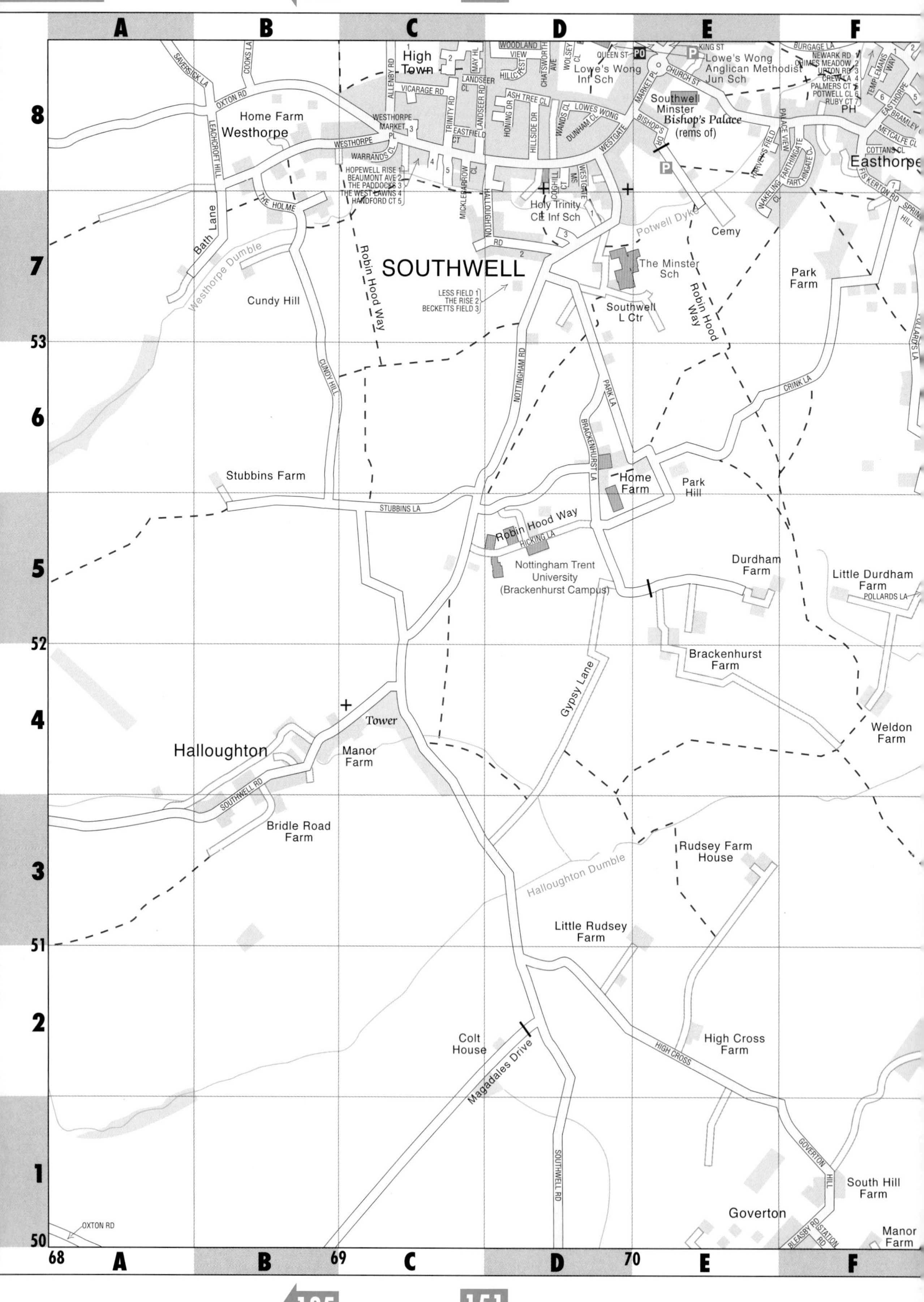

SOUTHWELL

High Town

Home Farm
Westhorpe

Cundy Hill

LESS FIELD 1
THE RISE 2
BECKETTS FIELD 3

Southwell
Minster
Bishop's Palace
(rems of)

Southwell
L Ctr

The Minster
Sch

Lowe's Wong
Inf Sch

Lowe's Wong
Anglican Methodist

Lowe's Wong
Anglican Methodist
Jun Sch

Holy Trinity
CE Inf Sch

Easthorpe

Park
Farm

Cemy

Robin Hood Way

Stubbins Farm

STUBBINS LA

Robin Hood Way

HICKING LA

Home
Farm

Park
Hill

Nottingham Trent
University
(Brackenhurst Campus)

Durdham
Farm

Little Durdham
Farm

POLLARDS LA

Brackenhurst
Farm

Weldon
Farm

Halloughton

Tower

Manor
Farm

Gypsy Lane

Bridle Road
Farm

Halloughton Dumble

Rudsey Farm
House

Little Rudsey
Farm

Colt
House

Magdales Drive

High Cross
Farm

High Cross

South Hill
Farm

Goverton

Manor
Farm

OXTON RD

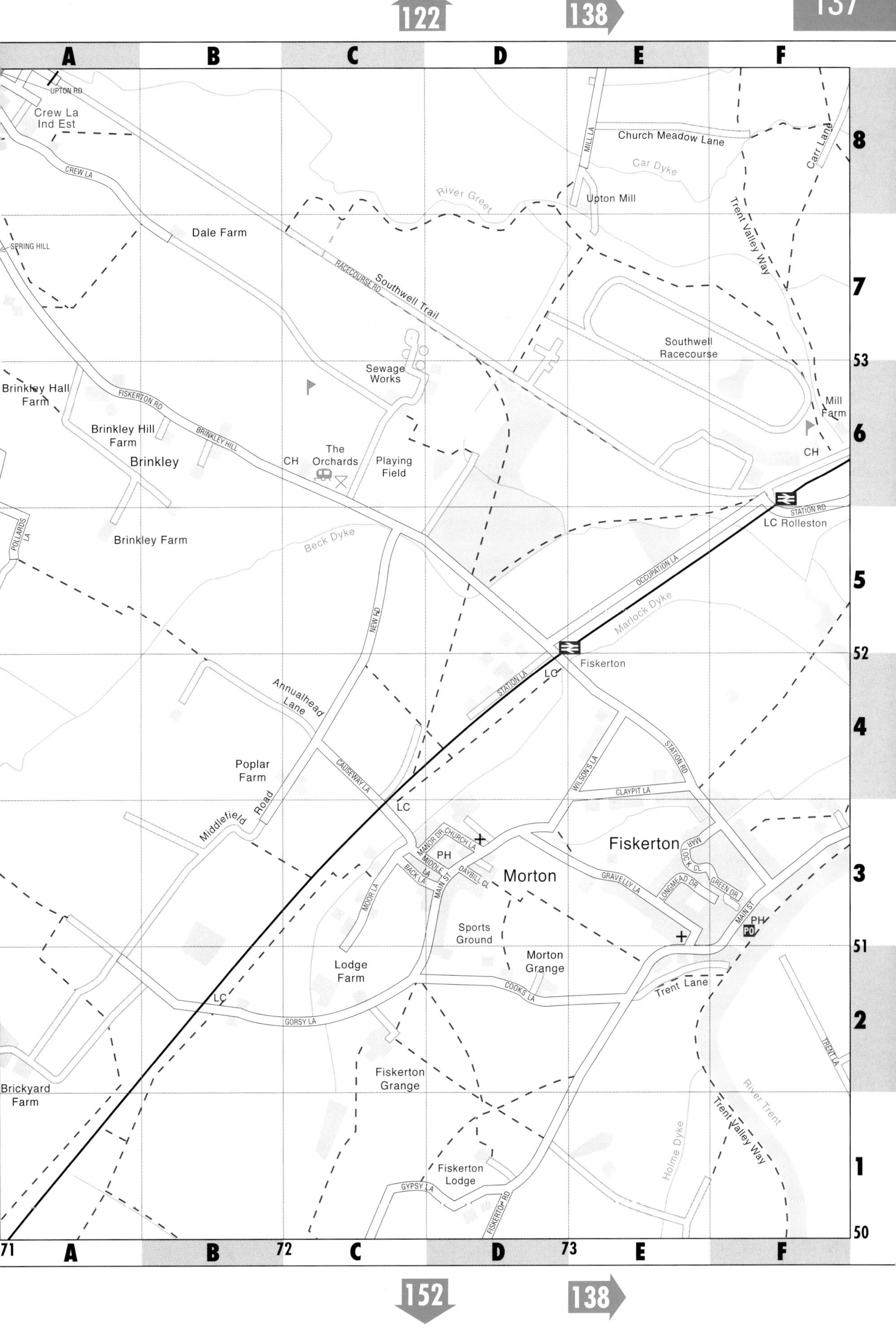

122

138

A B C D E F

UPTON RD.
Crew La
Ind Est

8

Church Meadow Lane

Car Dyke

Carr Lane

CREW LA

SPRING HILL

Dale Farm

River Greet

MILL LA

Upton Mill

Trent Valley Way

7

RACECOURSE RD

Southwell Trail

53

Brinkley Hall
Farm

FISKERTON RD

Brinkley Hill
Farm

BRINKLEY HILL

Brinkley

Sewage
Works

Southwell
Racecourse

Mill
Farm

6

CH

The
Orchards

Playing
Field

CH

POLLARDS LA

Brinkley Farm

Beck Dyke

STATION RD

LC Rolleston

5

NEW RD

OCCUPATION LA

Marlock Dyke

Annualhead
Lane

STATION LA

LC

Fiskerton

52

CAUSEWAY LA

4

Poplar
Farm

WILSON'S LA

CLAYPIT LA

STATION RD

Middlefield Road

LC

MOOR LA

MANOR DR

CHURCH LA

BACK LA

MIDDLE LA

MAIN ST

DAYBILL CL

Morton

Fiskerton

GRAVELLY LA

LONGMEAD DR

GREEN DR

MAR

CL

3

PH

Sports
Ground

Morton
Grange

COOKS LA

PH
PO

51

Lodge
Farm

Trent Lane

LC

GORSY LA

River Trent

2

Brickyard
Farm

Fiskerton
Grange

TRENT LA

Holme Dyke

Trent Valley Way

1

GYPSY LA

Fiskerton
Lodge

FISKERTON RD

50

71

A

72

B

C

73

D

E

F

152

138

← 137
123

A B C D E F

CARR LA

8

PINGLEY CL
PINGLEY LA

Staythorpe

Staythorpe
Power Station

BERAY GDNS

7

LC

HUGHS CL

LC

STAYTHORPE RD

LC

53

Baagarley Rack

LONG LA

CROFT FARM CL

GOODWINS CT

6

MANOR LA

CROFT CL

Greenaway

Rolleston
Gorse

Farndon Ponds
Nature
Reserve

Moats

LC

GREENAWAY

The Crown Inn
(PH)

Rundell Dyke

Farndon
Willow
Holt Nat Reserve

LC

STATION RD

CORNER FARM CL

5

Ferry
(P)

Rolleston

HOLLY CT

Rolleston Field

The Brittania
(PH)

P

NORTH END
TEL
CROFT

WYKE LA

52

Norwood
Farm

FISKERTON RD

MARRISON CT 1
CALFORNIA RD 2
NURSERY AVE 3

CHAPEL LA

MARSH LA

PO

River Green

Trent Valley Way

Swillow Lane

CHURCH ST

MAIN ST

4

Fiskerton
Mill

WYKE LA
WEST
END

PREBENDS CL
CROSS LA

ST SCHOOL LA

ST PETERS CL

P

Main St

OLD HALL CL

River Trent

3

Gawburn Nip

51

FOSSE RD

2

A1133

TRENT LA

Gawburn Holt

AD PONTEM
ROMAN FORT
& SETTLEMENT

MAIN ST

1

P

Wharf
Farm

Thorpe

TRENT LA

CHURCH LA

Stoke
Hall

The Park

50

74 A B 75 C D 76 E F

← 137
153

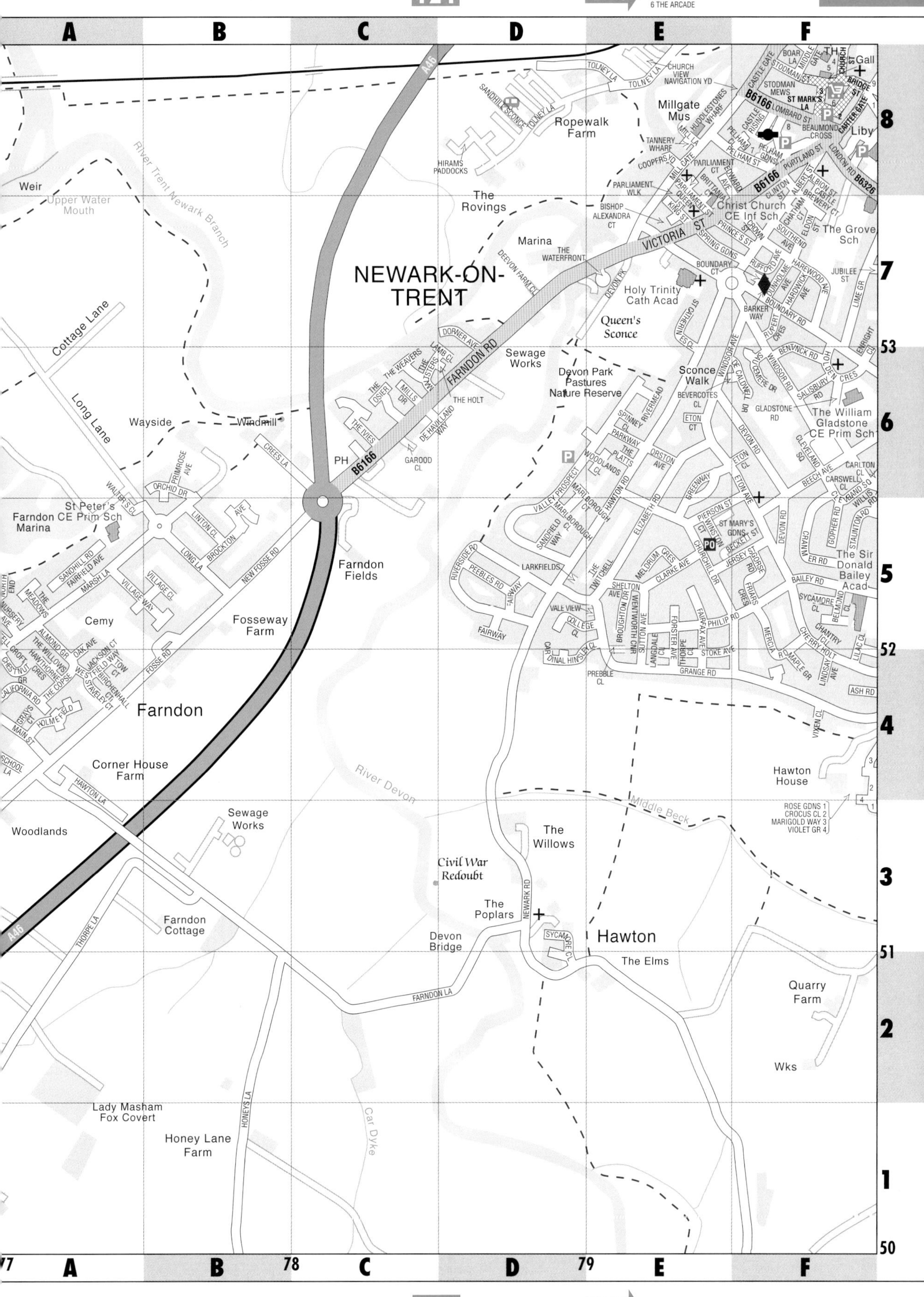

124

140

F8
1 BALDERTON GATE
2 SARACEN'S HEAD YD
3 ST MARK'S PL
4 QUEEN'S HEAD CT
5 CHAIN LA
6 THE ARCADE

7 BAINBRIDGE CT
8 MARTINDALE LA
9 APPLETON GATE

NEWARK-ON-TRENT

Farndon

Hawton

A8
1 WELLINGTON RD
2 FRIARY RD
3 LINDUM ST
4 PULFORD CL

B8
1 HARRISONS WAY
2 ESTHER VARNEY PL
3 THE CROSSINGS
4 MASSEY CT
5 THE SIDINGS
6 SAM DERRY CL

A7
1 POLLARD CL
2 SYDNEY GDNS
3 SYDNEY TERR

◁ **139**   △ **125**

NEWARK-ON-TRENT

Theatre
Newark Coll
Newark Mus
Magnus St
Sleaford Rd
Beacon Hill Rd
Beacon Hill

1 OAK VIEW
2 CAFFERATA WAY

Whomsley Cl
Hounsfield Cl
Ransome Cl
Gresham Cl
Hutchinson Rd

1 LILBURNE CL
2 LEVELLERS WAY
3 NASEBY RD
4 CLUDD AV
5 ROBINSON CL
6 IRETON AVE
7 ADWALTON CL
8 THE HEIGHTS
9 THE WOODLANDS
10 SEACROFT

The Close
Barnby Gate
Clay La
South Lodge
Clay Lane
The Firs

Barnby Crossing
Highfields Sch
LC
Barnby Rd
The Hollies
Green Hill Farm

Newark Magnus CE Sch
Magnums Com Sports Ctr
Newcastle Ave
Cemy
The Barnby Road Acad
64
Newstead Lodge

Newark Orch Sch
Allot Gdns
Sports Ground
Grove Sports Ctr
Playing Field

1 LORD HAWKE WAY
2 PAVILLION MWS
3 HALL DR
4 STADIUM AVE

Oliver Quibell Inf Sch
Allot Gdns
New Balderton
Blackthorne Cl

Newark Academy

Groveview Rd
Playing Field
LC
Field House Farm

1 ALEXANDER MWS
2 JASMINE CT

Christ Church CE Prim Sch
Kingfisher Cl
John Hunt Prim Sch
Chuter Ede Prim Sch (Balderton Site)
Knott's Ct
Hillary Way Kennedy Wk
Manthorpe House

Sports Ground
64
1 LACE MEAD
2 WEAVER AVE
3 THE ALNEEDLE WAY
4 SWIFT DR
5 FURROW CL
6 CARDINGTON WAY
7 CHARTERS DR
8 SPINNERS WAY
9 CLOVERFIELD PL
10 MARIGOLD WAY
11 BOWBRIDGE L

Liby
Byron Ct
Marshall Cl
Main St
Gamage Cl

1 QUEEN ST
2 VICARAGE GDNS
3 HALL GDNS
4 BRIDGE CT

1 BAKEWELL CT
2 SHEPPARDS CT
Cemy

Buckminster Rd 1
Avro Rd 2
Wickenby Av 3
Halifax Rd 4

Chuter Ede Prim Sch (Fernwood Annex)

Balderton

Sewage Works

1 QUEENS FARM GDNS
2 NURSERY GDNS
Blackberry Wy
Ainsdale Cl
Dale Cres

Bow Bridge
Middle Beck
Works

Cottage Cl 1
Inglewood Cl 2
Kirton Cl 3

Works

Goldstraw La 1
Read Cl 2
The Newlands 3

Fernwood Bsns Pk
PH
The Suthers Sch
Goodwin La
B6326

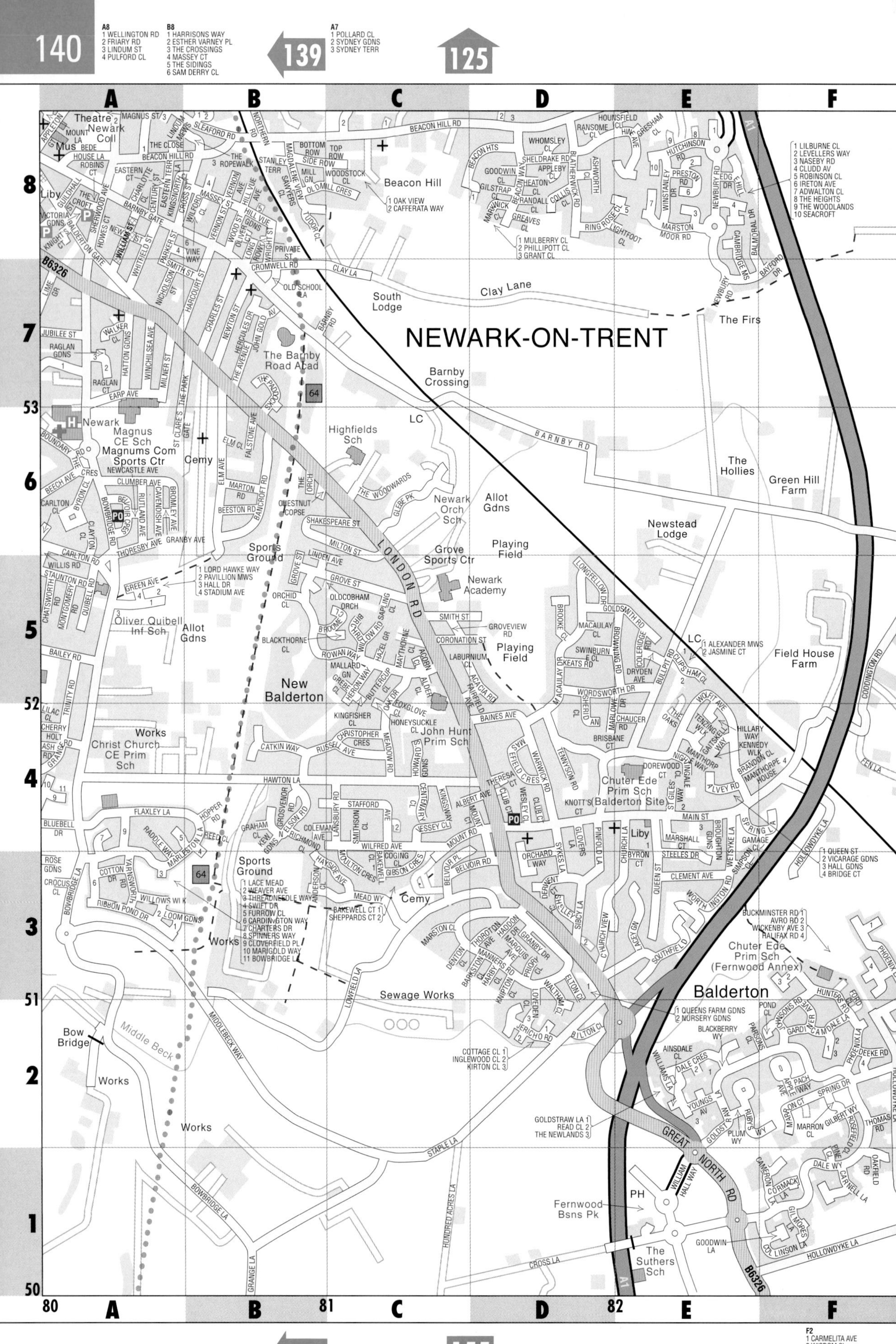

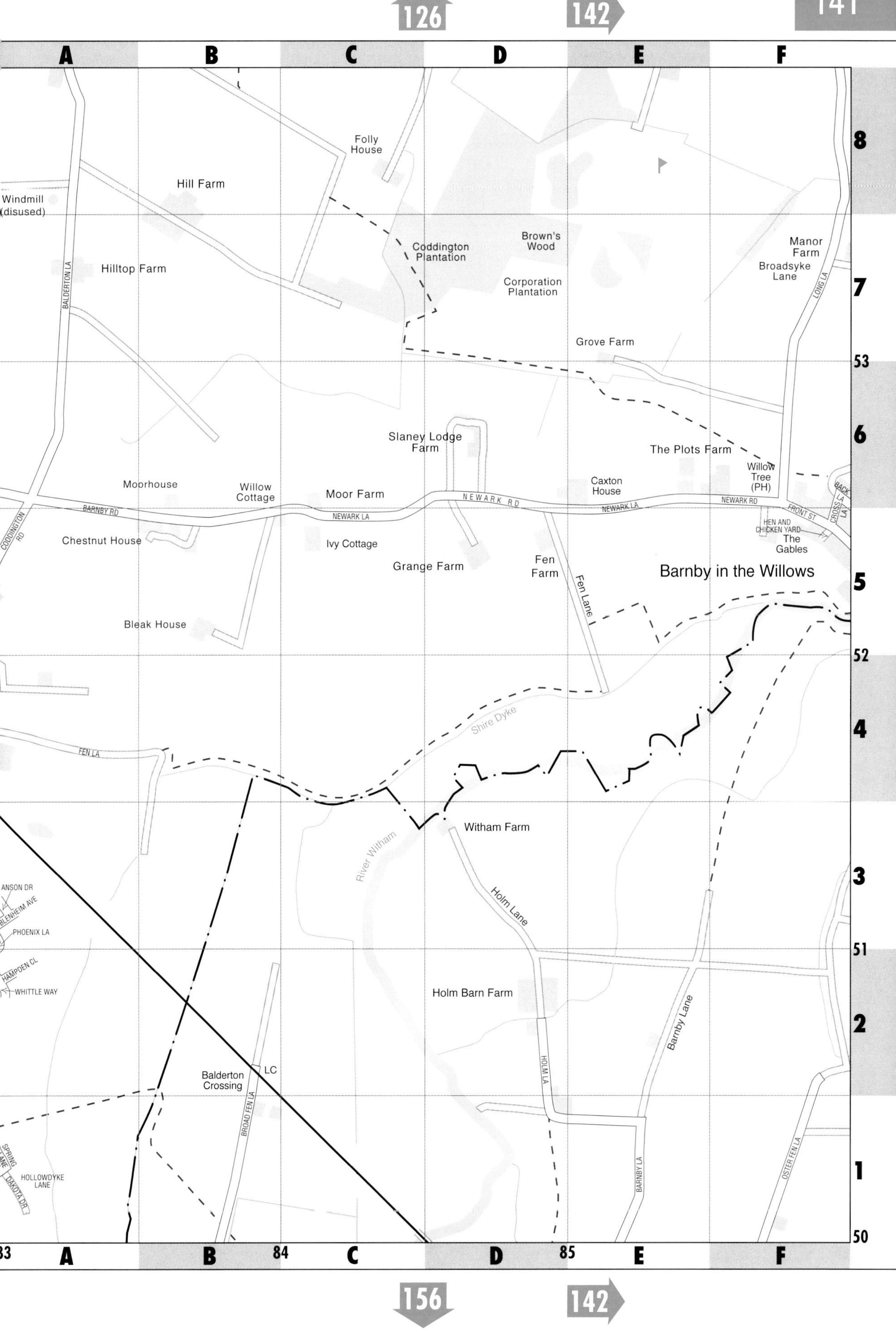
A
B
C
D
E
F
Folly House
Hill Farm
Windmill (disused)
Coddington Plantation
Brown's Wood
Manor Farm
Broadsyke Lane
Hilltop Farm
BALDERTON LA
Corporation Plantation
LONG LA
Grove Farm
Slaney Lodge Farm
The Plots Farm
Willow Tree (PH)
Moorhouse
Willow Cottage
Moor Farm
Caxton House
BARNBY RD
NEWARK LA
NEWARK RD
NEWARK LA
NEWARK RD
FRONT ST
BACK LA
CROSS LA
CODDINGTON RD
Chestnut House
Ivy Cottage
HEN AND CHICKEN YARD
The Gables
Grange Farm
Fen Farm
Fen Lane
Barnby in the Willows
Bleak House
Shire Dyke
FEN LA
Witham Farm
River Witham
ANSON DR
BLENHEIM AVE
PHOENIX LA
Holm Lane
HAMPDEN CL
WHITTLE WAY
Holm Barn Farm
Barnby Lane
HOLM LA
LC
Balderton Crossing
BROAD FEN LA
SPRING LANE
DAKOTA DR
HOLLOWDYKE LANE
BARNBY LA
OSTER FEN LA
8
7
53
6
5
52
4
3
51
2
1
50
83
84
85

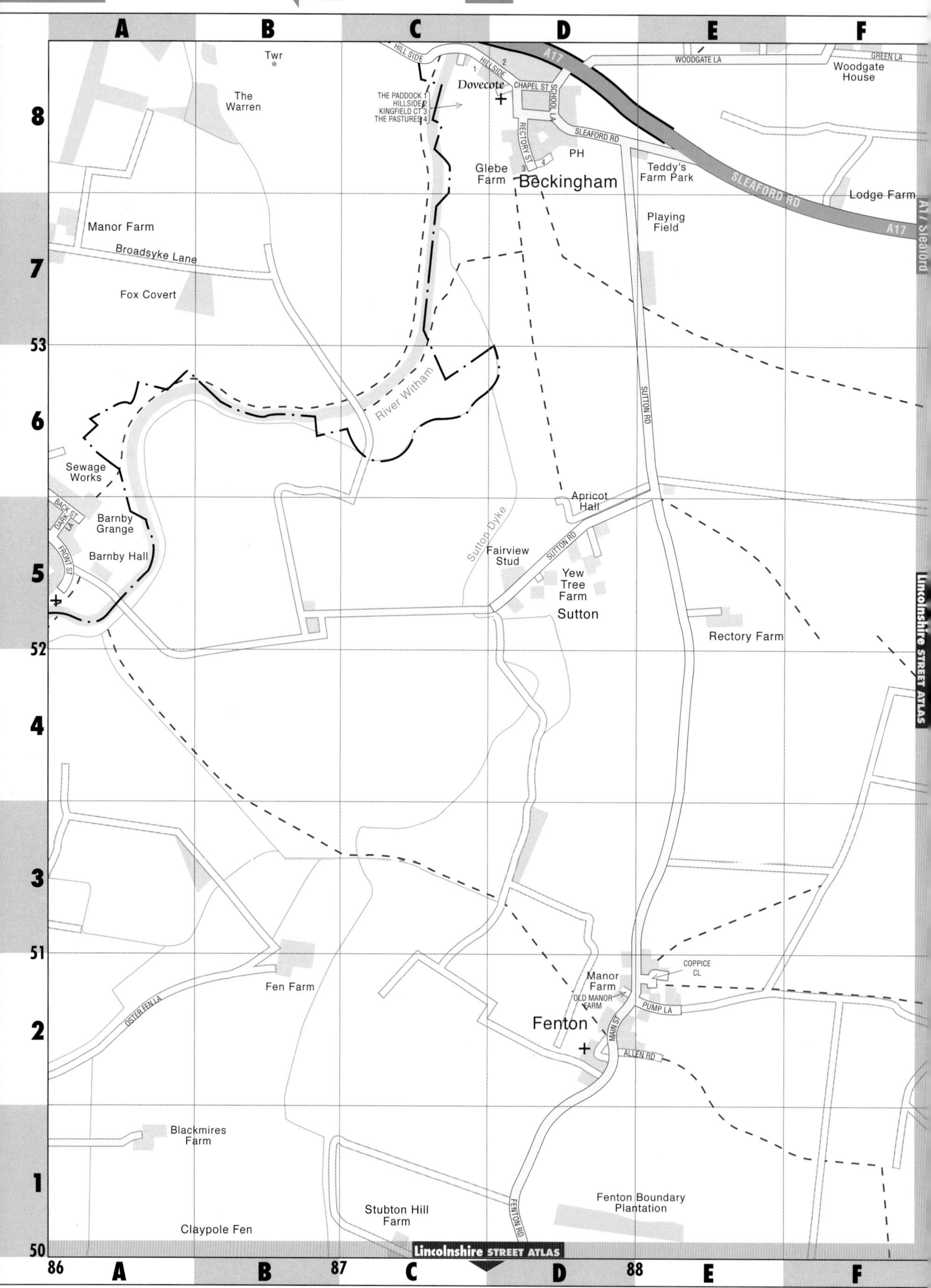

Twr

The Warren

HILL SIDE

HILL SIDE

A17

WOODGATE LA

GREEN LA

Woodgate House

Dovecote

THE PADDOCK 1
HILLSIDE 2
KINGFIELD CT 3
THE PASTURES 4

Chapel St

SCHOOL LA

RECTORY ST

Sleaford Rd

SLEAFORD RD

A17 Sleaford

Glebe Farm

PH

Beckingham

Teddy's Farm Park

Lodge Farm

A17

Manor Farm

Broadsyke Lane

Playing Field

Fox Covert

River Witham

BACK ST

DARK LA

Sewage Works

FRONT ST

Barnby Grange

Sutton Dyke

Apricot Hall

SUTTON RD

Barnby Hall

Fairview Stud

Yew Tree Farm

Sutton

Rectory Farm

OSTER FEN LA

Fen Farm

Manor Farm

OLD MANOR FARM

COPPICE CL

PUMP LA

Fenton

MAIN ST

ALLEN RD

Blackmires Farm

FENTON RD

Fenton Boundary Plantation

Stubton Hill Farm

Claypole Fen

Lincolnshire STREET ATLAS

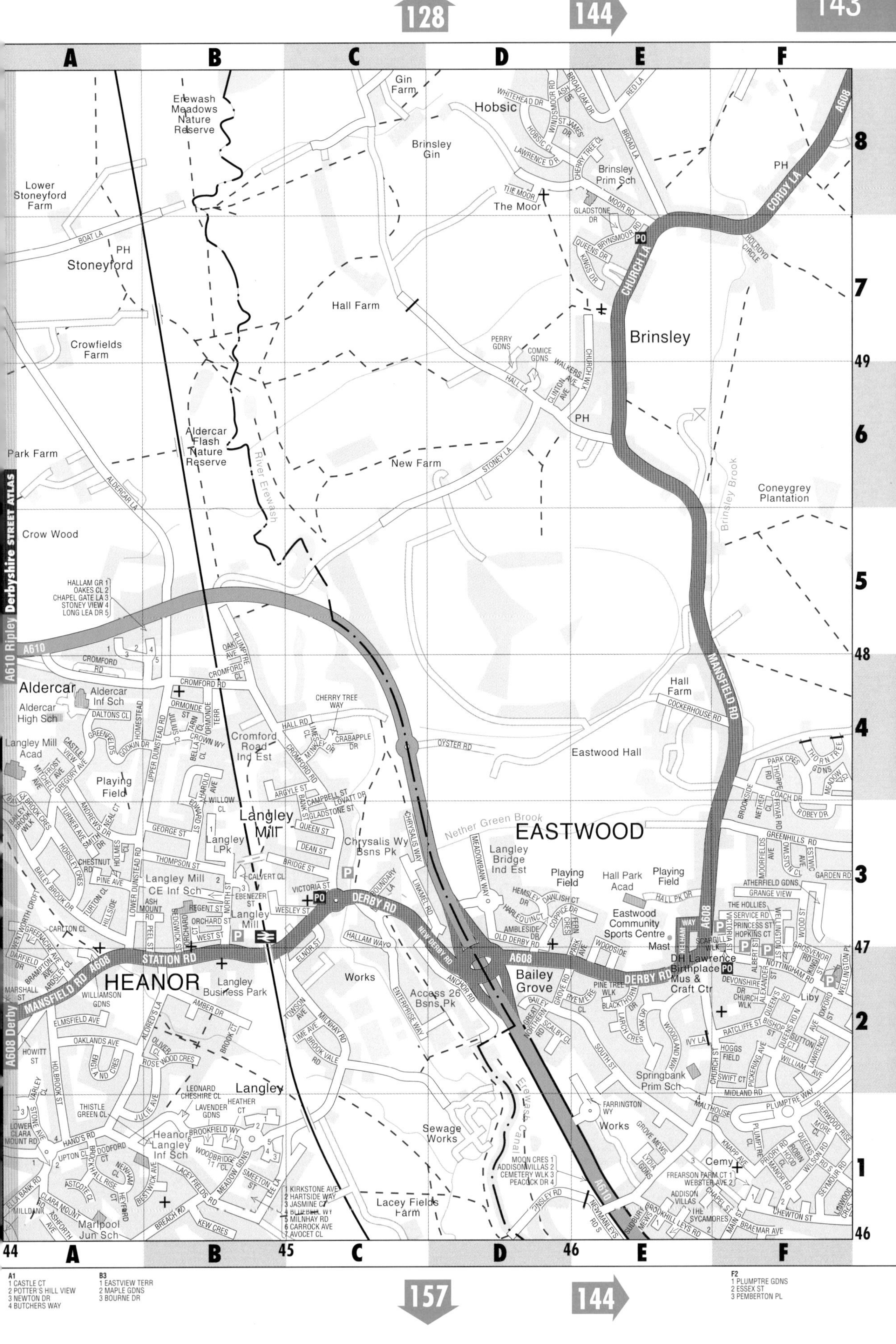
128
144
A
B
C
D
E
F
8
7
49
6
5
48
4
3
47
2
1
46
44
45
46
Derbyshire STREET ATLAS
A610 Ripley
A608 Derby
Gin Farm
Erewash Meadows Nature Reserve
Hobsic
Brinsley Gin
Lower Stoneyford Farm
BOAT LA
PH
Stoneyford
Hall Farm
The Moor
Brinsley Prim Sch
Crowfields Farm
Brinsley
Park Farm
Aldercar Flash Nature Reserve
River Erewash
New Farm
STONEY LA
ALDERCAR LA
Crow Wood
Coneygrey Plantation
Brinsley Brook
CHURCH LA
CORDY LA
HOLROYD CIRCLE
A608
MANSFIELD RD
HALLAM GR 1
OAKES CL 2
CHAPEL GATE LA 3
STONEY VIEW 4
LONG LEA DR 5
A610
CROMFORD RD
Aldercar
Aldercar Inf Sch
Aldercar High Sch
Langley Mill Acad
Playing Field
Cromford Road Ind Est
Hall Farm
COCKERHOUSE RD
OYSTER RD
Eastwood Hall
Langley Mill
Langley Pk
Chrysalis Wy Bsns Pk
Nether Green Brook
EASTWOOD
Langley Bridge Ind Est
Playing Field
Hall Park Acad
Playing Field
Langley Mill CE Inf Sch
Eastwood Community Sports Centre
Mast
DH Lawrence Birthplace Mus & Craft Ctr
DERBY RD
STATION RD
HEANOR
Langley Business Park
Works
Access 26 Bsns Pk
Bailey Grove
Liby
Langley
Heanor Langley Inf Sch
Sewage Works
Erewash Canal
Springbank Prim Sch
Works
Cemy
Lacey Fields Farm
Marlpool Jun Sch
MOON CRES 1
ADDISON VILLAS 2
CEMETERY WLK 3
PEACOCK DR 4
1 KIRKSTONE AVE
2 HARTSIDE WAY
3 JASMINE CT
4 BLUEBELL WY
5 MILNHAY RD
6 CARROCK AVE
7 AVOCET CL
FREARSON FARM CT 1
WEBSTER AVE 2
A1
1 CASTLE CT
2 POTTER'S HILL VIEW
3 NEWTON DR
4 BUTCHERS WAY
B3
1 EASTVIEW TERR
2 MAPLE GDNS
3 BOURNE DR
F2
1 PLUMPTRE GDNS
2 ESSEX ST
3 PEMBERTON PL
157
144

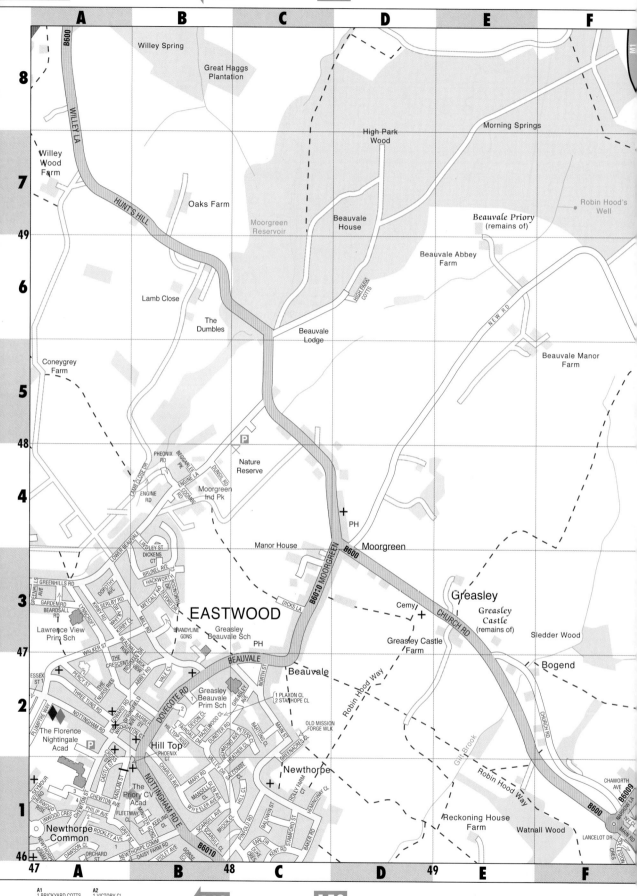
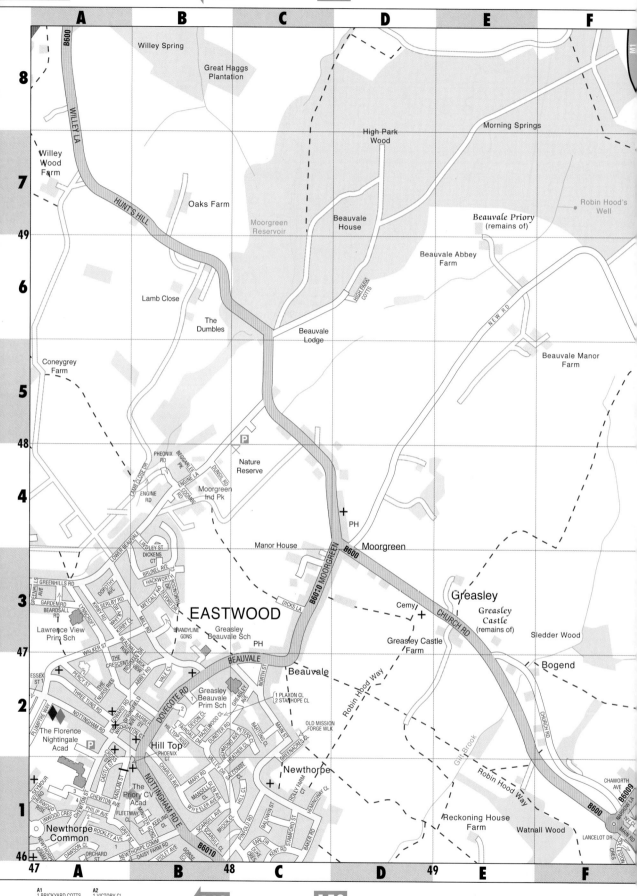

Willey Spring

Great Haggs Plantation

High Park Wood

Morning Springs

Robin Hood's Well

Willey Wood Farm

B600

WILLEY LA

HUNT'S HILL

Oaks Farm

Moorgreen Reservoir

Beauvale House

Beauvale Priory (remains of)

Beauvale Abbey Farm

Lamb Close

The Dumbles

Beauvale Lodge

HIGH PARK COTTS

NEW RD

Beauvale Manor Farm

Coneygrey Farm

P

Nature Reserve

PHEONIX RD

BEGGARLEE PK

LAMB CLOSE DR

DUNSIL RD

Moorgreen Ind Pk

ENGINE LA

COOMBE

ENGINE RD

Manor House

PH

B6010 MOORGREEN

B600

Moorgreen

Greasley

Greasley Castle (remains of)

Sledder Wood

LOWER BEAUVALE

FOLEY ST

DICKENS CT

BRUNEL AVE

HACKWORTH

BOSWORTH

METCALF

TELFORD

DICKS LA

EASTWOOD

CHURCH RD

Cemy

GREENHILLS RD

GARDEN RD

BEARDSALL RD

LYNNCROFT

KIRBY RD

MILL RD

WHIT

KIRBY RD

SERLBY RD

DOROTHY AVE

GREENHILLS AVE

Lawrence View Prim Sch

BRANDLINE GDNS

Greasley Beauvale Sch

PH

Greasley Castle Farm

Bogend

WALKER ST

PERCY ST

THE NURSERIES

THE CRESCENT

INGHAM MSK

ABBEY RD

VALE CL

BEAUVALE

WORTH ST

Robin Hood Way

CHURCH RD

ESSEX ST

THREE TUNS RD

BARBER

WALFORD CT

SPRINGFIELD

LEONARD AVE

DOVECOTE RD

Greasley Beauvale Prim Sch

DEVON CL

GREASLEY AVE

Beauvale

1 PLAXON CL 2 STANHOPE CL

OLD MISSION FORGE WLK

Robin Hood Way

PLUMPTRE WAY

The Florence Nightingale Acad

P

NOTTINGHAM RD

WAUGHTON CL

HILL TOP RISE

FAIRDALE DR

DUNSTER RD

RAYMOND DR

HAZELWOOD DR

MARY RD

PETERS CT

BARTONS CL

GREENACRES CL

MAIN ST

HOLLY FARM CT

Gilt Brook

CHAWORTH AVE

B6009

SEYMOUR

CASTLE CRES

CHEWTON ST

The Priory CV Acad

PHOENIX CT

CHARLES AVE

GLEN AVE

HEATHER CL

SALCOMBE

Newthorpe

Reckoning House Farm

Watnall Wood

LANCELOT DR

MAIN RD

ILKESTON

CRES

NARROW LA

B600

SEYMOUR RISE

LINWOOD CRES

CHEWTON

PHILIP AVE

FLEETWAY CL

MANSELL

WHEELER AVE

HOLLY CL

BALDWIN CT

STAMFORD ST

BAKER RD

KENT RD

EARL DR

BECK

Hill Top

Newthorpe Common

ROCKLEY AVE

GREY ST

KEELING CL

SCARGILL AVE

SCARGILL CL

VIOLET CL

GORSE

B6010

PINFOLD LA

NOTTINGHAM RD E

LINWOOD

DAWSON CL

ORCHARD ST

NEWTHORPE COMM

DAISY FARM CL

130
146

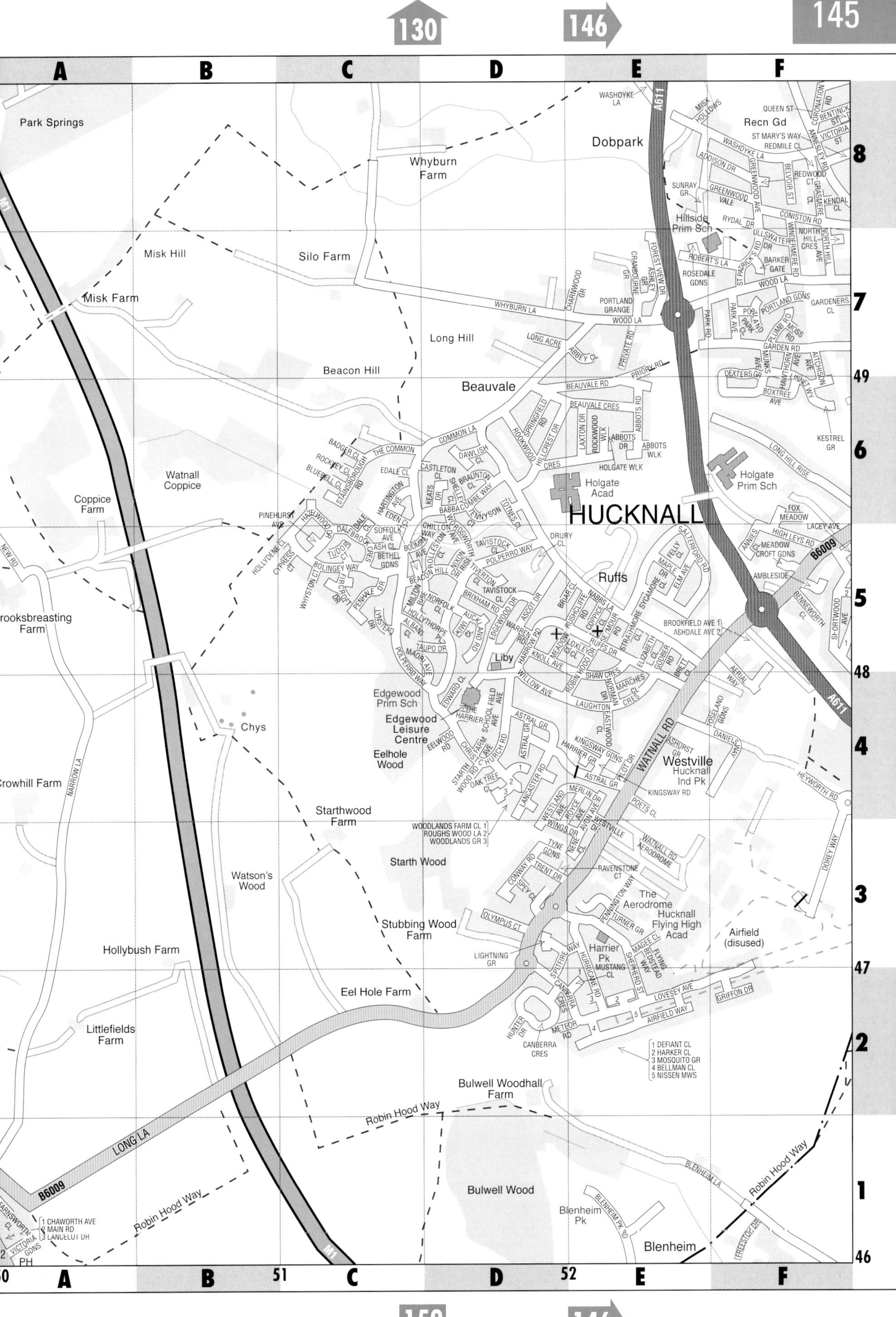
A
B
C
D
E
F
8
7
49
6
5
48
4
3
47
2
1
46
50
51
52
Park Springs
Whyburn Farm
Dobpark
Recn Gd
Misk Hill
Silo Farm
Misk Farm
Hillside Prim Sch
Long Hill
Beacon Hill
Beauvale
Watnall Coppice
Coppice Farm
Holgate Acad
Holgate Prim Sch
HUCKNALL
Ruffs
Brooksbreasting Farm
Liby
Edgewood Prim Sch
Edgewood Leisure Centre
Eelhole Wood
Chys
Crowhill Farm
Westville
Hucknall Ind Pk
Starthwood Farm
Starth Wood
Watson's Wood
The Aerodrome
Hucknall Flying High Acad
Stubbing Wood Farm
Airfield (disused)
Hollybush Farm
Harrier Pk
Eel Hole Farm
Littlefields Farm
Bulwell Woodhall Farm
Robin Hood Way
Bulwell Wood
Blenheim Pk
Blenheim
M1
A611
B6009
LONG LA
WATNALL RD
WHYBURN LA
WOOD LA
COMMON LA
THE COMMON
BEAUVALE RD
BEAUVALE CRES
HOLGATE WLK
LONG HILL RISE
NARROW LA
NEW RD
BLENHEIM LA
LOVESEY AVE
AIRFIELD WAY
GRIFFON DR
KINGSWAY RD
HEYWORTH RD
DOREY WAY
WOODLANDS FARM CL 1
ROUGHS WOOD LA 2
WOODLANDS GR 3
1 DEFIANT CL
2 HARKER CL
3 MOSQUITO GR
4 BELLMAN CL
5 NISSEN MWS
1 CHAWORTH AVE
2 MAIN RD
3 LANCELOT DR
BROOKFIELD AVE 1
ASHDALE AVE 2

159
146

146

B7
3 Byron Bsns Ctr

B8
1 BOATSWAIN DR
2 LOVELACE WLK
3 BLATHERWICK CL

◀ 145

▲ 131

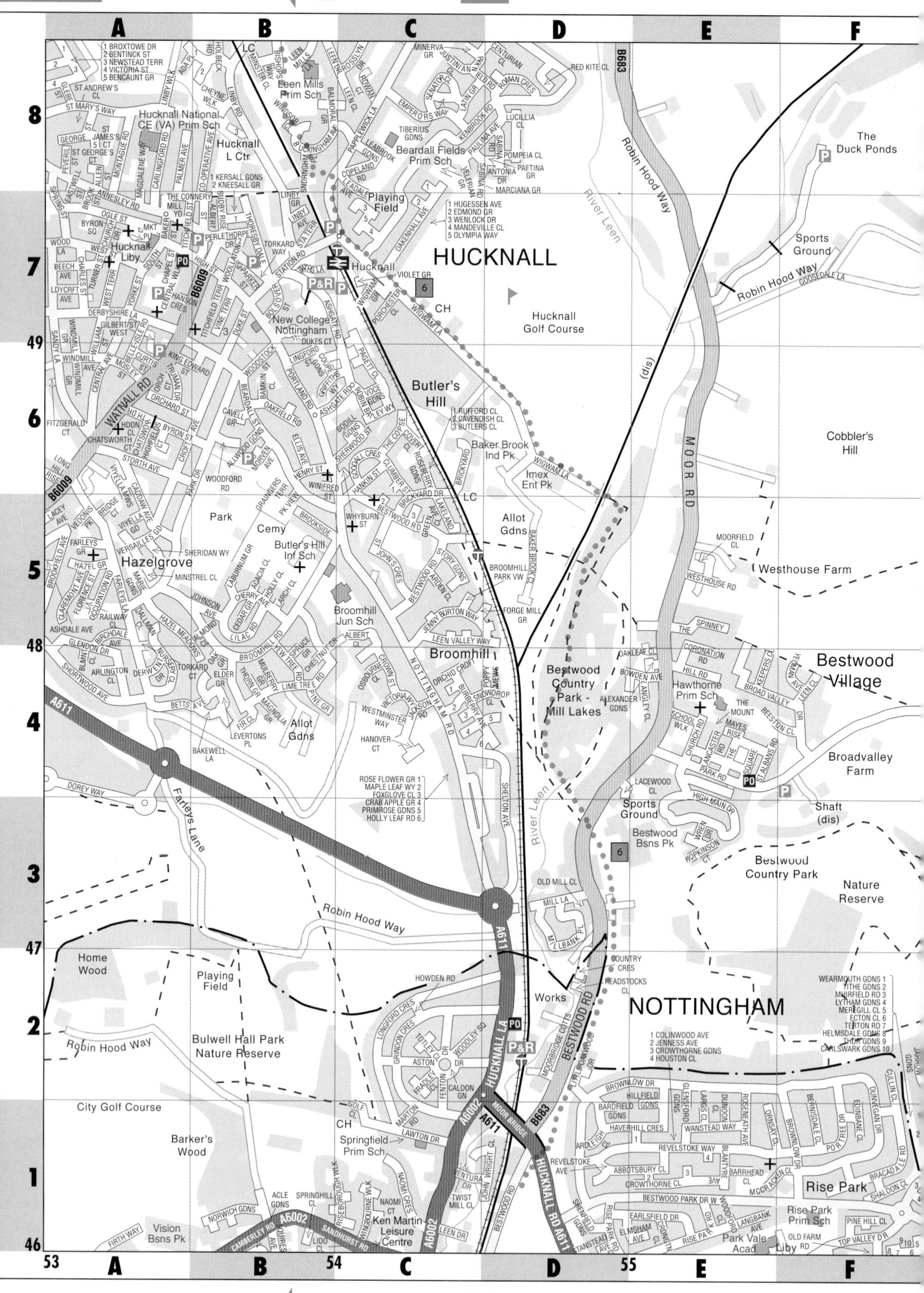

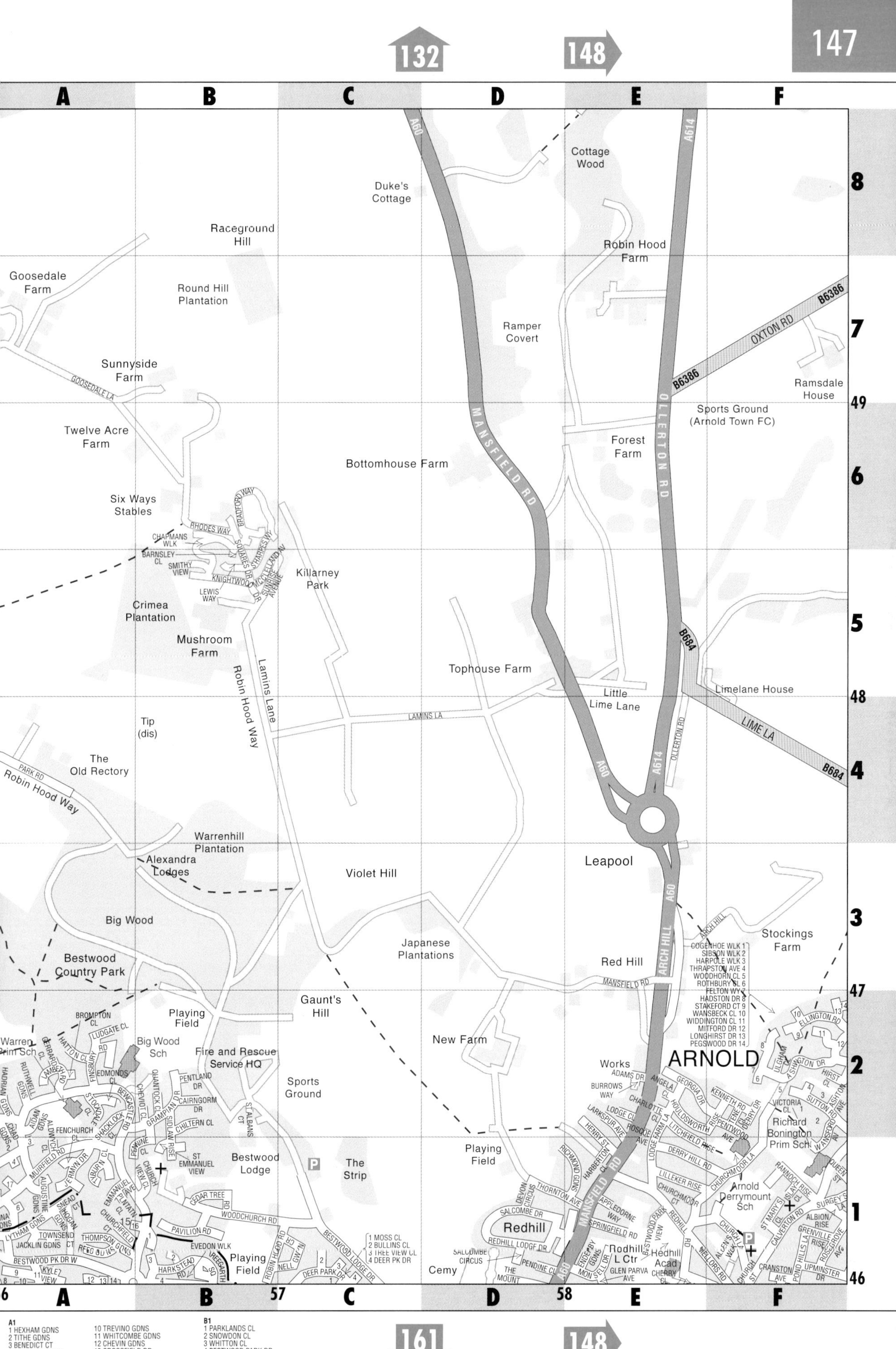

A B C D E F

8
7
49
6
5
48
4
3
47
2
1
46

Cottage Wood

Duke's Cottage

Raceground Hill

Robin Hood Farm

Goosedale Farm

Round Hill Plantation

Ramper Covert

OXTON RD
B6386

Sunnyside Farm

B6386

Ramsdale House

GOOSEDALE LA

Sports Ground (Arnold Town FC)

Twelve Acre Farm

MANSFIELD RD

Bottomhouse Farm

Forest Farm

Six Ways Stables

BRADFORD WAY
RHODES WAY

CHAPMANS WLK
BARNSLEY CL
SMITHY VIEW
KNIGHTWOOD
LEWIS WAY
SQUIRES DR
STRIKES W
MICKLEDON
SUNDALE AVENUE

Killarney Park

OLLERTON RD

Crimea Plantation

Mushroom Farm

Lamins Lane

Tophouse Farm

B684

Little Lime Lane

Limelane House

LAMINS LA

OLLERTON RD

LIME LA
B684

Robin Hood Way

Tip (dis)

The Old Rectory

PARK RD

A614

Robin Hood Way

A60

Warrenhill Plantation

Leapool

Stockings Farm

Alexandra Lodges

Violet Hill

Red Hill

ARCH HILL

Arch Hill

COGENHOE WLK 1
SIBSON WLK 2
HARPOLE WLK 3
THRAPSTON AVE 4
WOODHORN CL 5
ROTHBURY CL 6
FELTON WY 7
HADSTON DR 8
STAKEFORD CT 9
WANSBECK CL 10
WIDDINGTON CL 11
MITFORD DR 12
LONGHIRST DR 13
PEGSWOOD DR 14

Big Wood

Japanese Plantations

MANSFIELD RD

47

ELLINGTON RD

Bestwood Country Park

Gaunt's Hill

New Farm

ARNOLD

Warren Prim Sch

BROMPTON CL
LUDGATE CL
HATTON CL

Playing Field

Big Wood Sch

Fire and Rescue Service HQ

Works

ADAMS DR
BURROWS WAY
ANGELA
CHARLOTTE
GEORGIAN
KENNETH RD
SERPENTINE
VICTORIA CL
ULGHAM
KINGSTON DR
HIRST
SUTTON LA

Richard Bonington Prim Sch

Sports Ground

New Farm

HADRIAN GDNS
STOCKDALE CL
RUTHWELL
JARRATT CL
SHACKLOCK
BEWCASTLE RD
CHEVIOT CL
QUANTOCK
GRAMPIAN
SIDLAW RISE
PENTLAND DR
CAIRNGORM DR
CHILTERN CL
ST ALBANS CT

St Emmanuel View

Bestwood Lodge

The Strip

Playing Field

LARKSPUR AVE
HENRY ST
LODGE CL
ROSOE
CHARTFIELD
LITCHFIELD RISE
DERRY HILL RD
LILLEKER RISE
CHURCHMOOR LA

Arnold Derrymount Sch

WANSBOROUGH

FENCHURCH
MURFIELD
EMLYN DR
BURN
AUGUSTINE GDNS
LYTHAM
TOWNSEND
JACKLIN GDNS
BESTWOOD PK DR W
KYLE2 VIEW

EMMANUEL
CT WATH
NEW
CHURCHFIELD
CEDAR TREE RD
WOODCHURCH RD
ST

HARKSTEAD
EVEDON WLK
PAVILION RD
ROBIN HOOD DR
BESTWOOD LODGE DR
DEER PARK DR
NELL

1 MOSS CL
2 BULLINS CL
3 TREE VIEW CL
4 DEER PK DR

THORNTON AVE
RICHMOND GDNS
DEVON
CIRCUS
SALCOMBE DR

Redhill

Redhill Lodge Dr
SALCOMBE CIRCUS
PENDINE CL
THE MOUNT
GLEN PARVA AVE

Cemy

APPLEDORNE
SPRINGFIELD RD
CHURCHMOOR
REDHILL
CHERRY

Redhill L Ctr

Redhill Acad

Redhill Acad
CHERRY

MELLORS RD
ST MARY'S
PEMBREY
CALVERTON RD
RANNOCH RISE
CHIRN
CRANSTON
AVE
POND HILLS LA
CHERRY
ALBION RISE
GRENVILLE
RISE
UPMINSTER
DR
QUEEN
SURGEY
SWANSEA

Bestwood Lodge

Playing Field

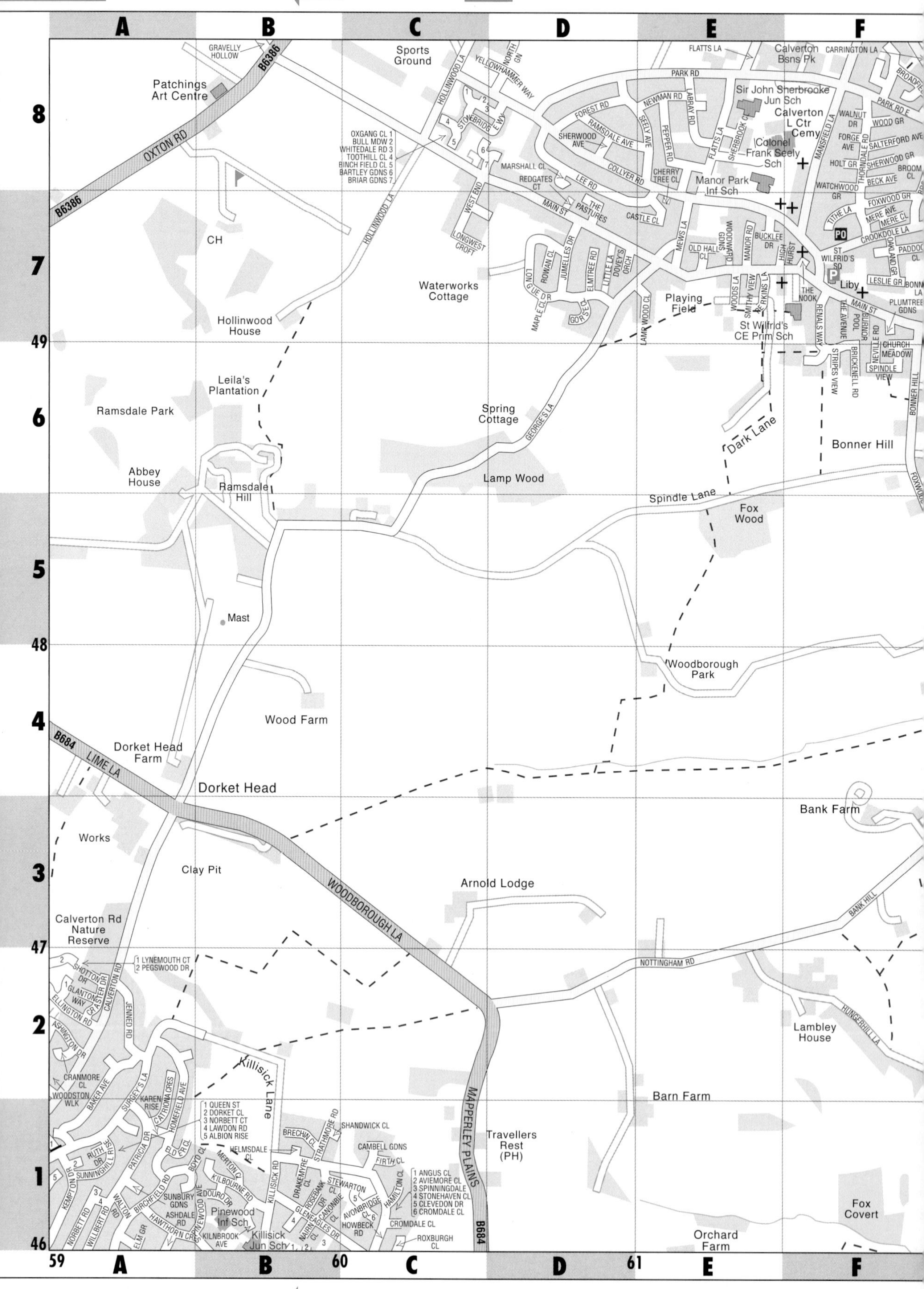

Gravelly Hollow

B6386

Patchings Art Centre

Sports Ground

OXTON RD

B6386

CH

Hollinwood House

Leila's Plantation

Ramsdale Park

Abbey House

Ramsdale Hill

Mast

Wood Farm

B684   LIME LA

Dorket Head Farm

Dorket Head

Works

Clay Pit

Calverton Rd Nature Reserve

1 LYNEMOUTH CT
2 PEGSWOOD DR

SHOTTON DR

2
1 GLANTONFELL WAY
ELLINGTON WAY

CALVERTON RD

JENNER RD

Killisick Lane

CRANMORE CL

WOODSTON WLK

BAKER AVE

SURREY'S LA

KAREN RISE

CATRIONA RISE

HOMEFIELD AVE

1 QUEEN ST
2 DORKET CL
3 NORBETT CT
4 LAWDON RD
5 ALBION RISE

BRECHIN CL

STRATHMORE RD

SHANDWICK CL

CAMBELL GDNS

FIRTH CL

1 ANGUS CL
2 AVIEMORE CL
3 SPINNINGDALE
4 STONEHAVEN CL
5 CLEVEDON DR
6 CROMDALE CL

HELMSDALE

MERTON CL

KILBOURNE RD

KILLISICK RD

DRAKEMYRE CL

ROSEBANK

GLENEAGLES DR

STEWARTON CL

AVONBRIDGE CL

HAWKTON CL

CROMDALE CL

ROXBURGH CL

HOWBECK RD

MAPPERLEY PLAINS

B684

WOODBOROUGH LA

Arnold Lodge

Travellers Rest (PH)

Barn Farm

Orchard Farm

Fox Covert

Bank Farm

BANK HILL

HUNGERHILL LA

Lambley House

NOTTINGHAM RD

Woodborough Park

Spindle Lane

Fox Wood

Dark Lane

Bonner Hill

BONNER HILL

FOXWOOD

Lamp Wood

GEORGE'S LA

Spring Cottage

Waterworks Cottage

HOLLINWOOD LA

HOLLINWOOD LA

YELLOWHAMMER WAY

NORTH DR

STONEBRIDGE LA

OXGANG CL 1
BULL MDW 2
WHITEDALE RD 3
TOOTHILL CL 4
BINCH FIELD CL 5
BARTLEY GDNS 6
BRIAR GDNS 7

MARSHALL CL

REDGATES CT

WEST END

LONGWEST CROFT

MAPLE CL

LONGUE DR

ROWAN CL

JUMELLES DR

GORSE CL

ELMTREE RD

LITTLE LA

DOVEY'S ORCH

LANE VW

Playing Field

OLD HALL CL

Manor Park Inf Sch

MEWS LA

CHERRY TREE CL

SEELY AVE

PEPPER RD

ABRAY RD

Sir John Sherbrooke Jun Sch

Calverton L Ctr

Colonel Frank Seely Sch

Calverton Cemy

MAIN ST

THE PASTURES

CASTLE CL

BUCKLEE DR

HIGH HURST

MANOR RD

WOODS LA

IRVINS LA

SMITH VIEW

St Wilfrid's CE Prim Sch

ST WILFRID'S SQ

Liby

PO

Main St

REVALS WAY

THE NOOK

THE AVENUE

MEADOW

CHURCH MEADOW

BRICKENHILL RD

STRIPES VIEW

SPINDLE VIEW

FLATTS LA

Calverton Bsns Pk

CARRINGTON LA

PARK RD

NEWMAN RD

FOREST RD

RAMSDALE AVE

SHERWOOD AVE

LEE RD

COLLYER RD

BROADFIELD

PARK RD E

WALNUT DR

FORGE GR

SALTERFORD AVE

SHERWOOD GR

BROOM CL

HOLT GR

BECK AVE

WATCHWOOD GR

FOXWOOD GR

MERE AVE

MERE CL

CROOKDOLE LA

TITHE LA

PADDOCK CL

LESLIE RD

BONNY LA

PLUMTREE GDNS

WALTON

NORBETT RD

WILLBERT RD

ELM GR

KEMPTON DR

SUNNINGHILL RISE

RUTH DR

WAVERLEY CL

PATRICIA DR

BIRCHFIELD RD

ASHDALE RD

HAWTHORN CRES

KILNBROOK AVE

Killisick Jun Sch

Pinewood Inf Sch

SUNBURY GDNS

NEWDOUR DR

FLOYD CL

GOYDEN CL

MAIN CL

CALCOMBE

ASHWORTH DR

ASHINGTON DR

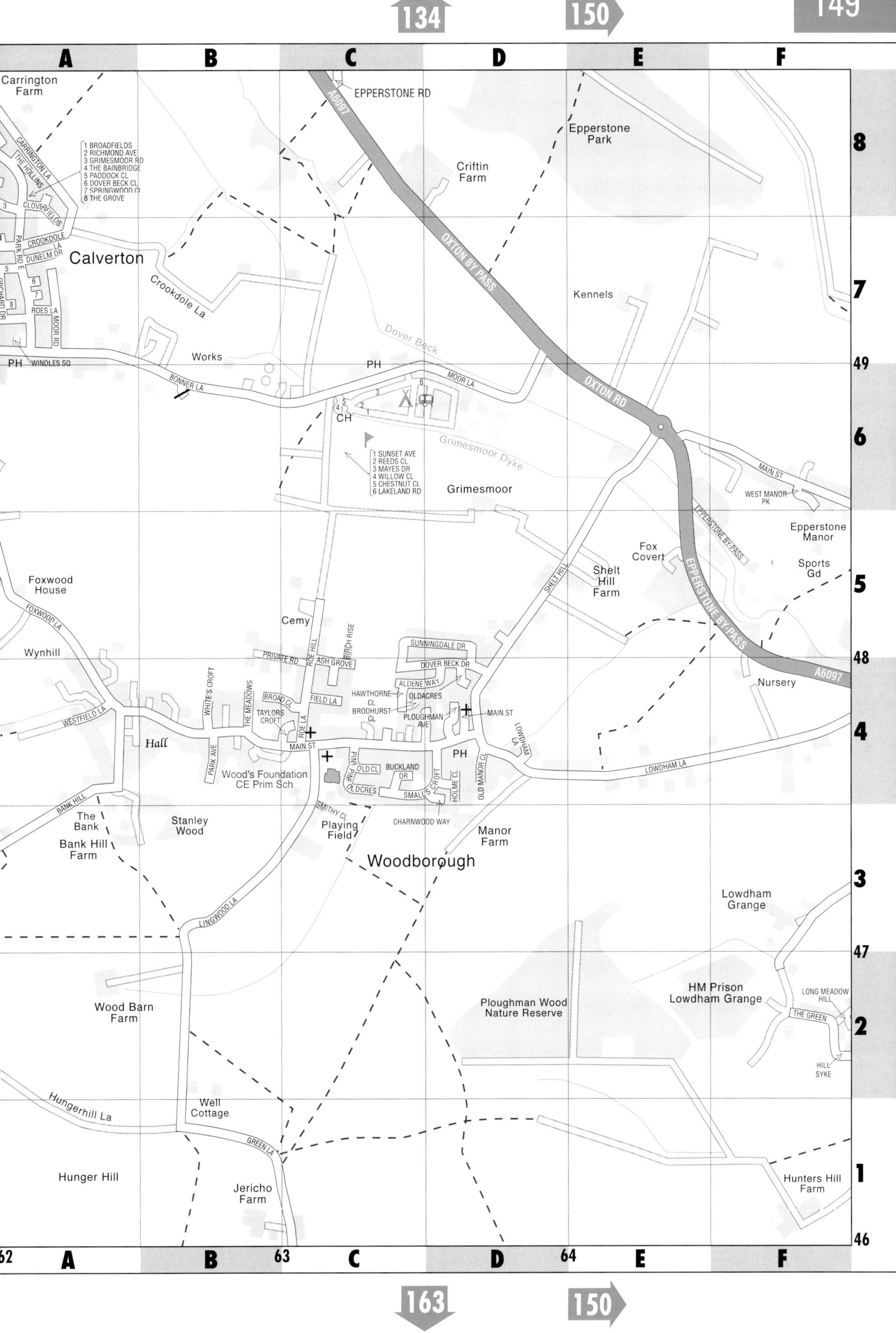
134
150
A
B
C
D
E
F
Carrington Farm
EPPERSTONE RD
A6097
Epperstone Park
8
CARRINGTON LA
THE HOLLINS
1 BROADFIELDS
2 RICHMOND AVE
3 GRIMESMOOR RD
4 THE BAINBRIDGE
5 PADDOCK CL
6 DOVER BECK CL
7 SPRINGWOOD CL
8 THE GROVE
Criftin Farm
CLOVERFIELDS
CROOKDOLE LA
DUNELM DR
PARK RD E
Calverton
OXTON BY PASS
7
Crookdole La
Kennels
ROES LA
MOOR RD
ORCHARD DR
Dover Beck
Works
PH
WINDLES SQ
BONNER LA
PH
MOOR LA
49
OXTON RD
CH
Grimesmoor Dyke
6
1 SUNSET AVE
2 REEDS CL
3 MAYES DR
4 WILLOW CL
5 CHESTNUT CL
6 LAKELAND RD
Grimesmoor
MAIN ST
WEST MANOR PK
EPPERSTONE BY-PASS
Epperstone Manor
Fox Covert
Sports Gd
Foxwood House
Shelt Hill Farm
SHELT HILL
5
FOXWOOD LA
EPPERSTONE BY-PASS
Cemy
BIRCH RISE
Wynhill
SUNNINGDALE DR
PRIVATE RD
ROE HILL
ASH GROVE
DOVER BECK DR
48
A6097
Nursery
WHITE'S CROFT
THE MEADOWS
ALDENE WAY
HAWTHORNE CL
OLDACRES
BROAD CL
FIELD LA
BRODHURST CL
TAYLORS CROFT
PLOUGHMAN AVE
MAIN ST
WESTFIELD LA
ROE LA
LOWDHAM LA
4
Hall
MAIN ST
PH
PARK AVE
PINFOLD CL
BUCKLAND DR
OLDCRES
SMALLS CROFT
HOLME CL
OLD MANOR CL
LOWDHAM LA
Wood's Foundation CE Prim Sch
BANK HILL
The Bank
Stanley Wood
SMITHY CL
Playing Field
CHARNWOOD WAY
Manor Farm
Bank Hill Farm
Woodborough
3
Lowdham Grange
LINGWOOD LA
47
HM Prison Lowdham Grange
LONG MEADOW HILL
Wood Barn Farm
Ploughman Wood Nature Reserve
THE GREEN
2
HILL SYKE
Hungerhill La
Well Cottage
GREEN LA
1
Hunger Hill
Jericho Farm
Hunters Hill Farm
46
62
63
64
163
150

A B C D E F

8

Hill Farm

Brockwood Farm

Thurgarton Beck

Starling Hall

Foxhole Wood

Cottage Farm

Thistly Coppice

7

Green Acres

Souther Wood

Southerwood Barn

Eastwood Farm

Hagg Farm

49

Hagg Cottage

Chapel La
NEEPS CROFT
Order Beck
Hagg Lane

6

CHURCH LA

Epperstone

Bentley Wood

PH

HAGG LA

MAIN ST
BLAND LA
TOAD LA
Dovecote

1 PADDOCK FARM COTTS
2 MANOR WLK

Netherfield Farm

PARR LA

5

Order Beck
LOWDHAM RD

Netherfield Farm House

Playing Field

48

Wash Bridge

Leland's Dumble

A6097 OXTON RD

4

LOWDHAM LA

Gonalston

Nursery

EPPERSTONE BY-PASS
OLD EPPERSTONE RD

Car Holt Farm

GONALSTON LA

Dover Beck

MAIN ST

Lowdham Mill

3

Nurseries

Eliment Hill Farm

Vicarage

Carr Beck Barn

The Hut

The Hermitage

Cliff Mill

47

Cemy

EPPERSTONE RD

1 PASTURE VIEW
2 DOVER BECK CL
3 THE OLD DAIRY

Cliff Mill Farm

Grove Farm

Lowdham CE Sch
The Old Hall

THE LEYS
MOUNT PLEASANT
NURSERY GDNS

RECTORY HILL

2

LONG MEADOW HILL

CHURCH LA

Liby

RIVERS LANE RD
BARKER HILL

Barker Hill

Norrisdene

HILL SYKE

Motte

STONEY BANK
TON LA
PLOUGH LA

THE PRIORS

ST MARY'S CL

BLACKTHORNE DR

SOUTHWELL RD

THE GREEN

ROCKLEYS VIEW

Cooker Beck

LAMBLEY RD

PH
RED LA

MANOR HOUSE CL
MAIN ST
PO

PH
CRANLEIGH DR

CHARTA MWS

1 NOTTINGHAM RD
2 VICTORIA AVE
3 WORCESTER CL

BROOKSIDE
THE CORNER
MORLEY'S
MAGNA CL

WILLOW HOLT

OLD TANNERY DRIVE

1

PH

SOMERVALE DRIVE
STATION RD
BECKS CL
NEWTON CL
LIME TREE GDNS
LAMBOURNE CRES
BLENHEIM AVE

PH

46

Lowdham

A6097

RUSSEY CL

CAYTHORPE RD

65 A 66 B C 67 D E F

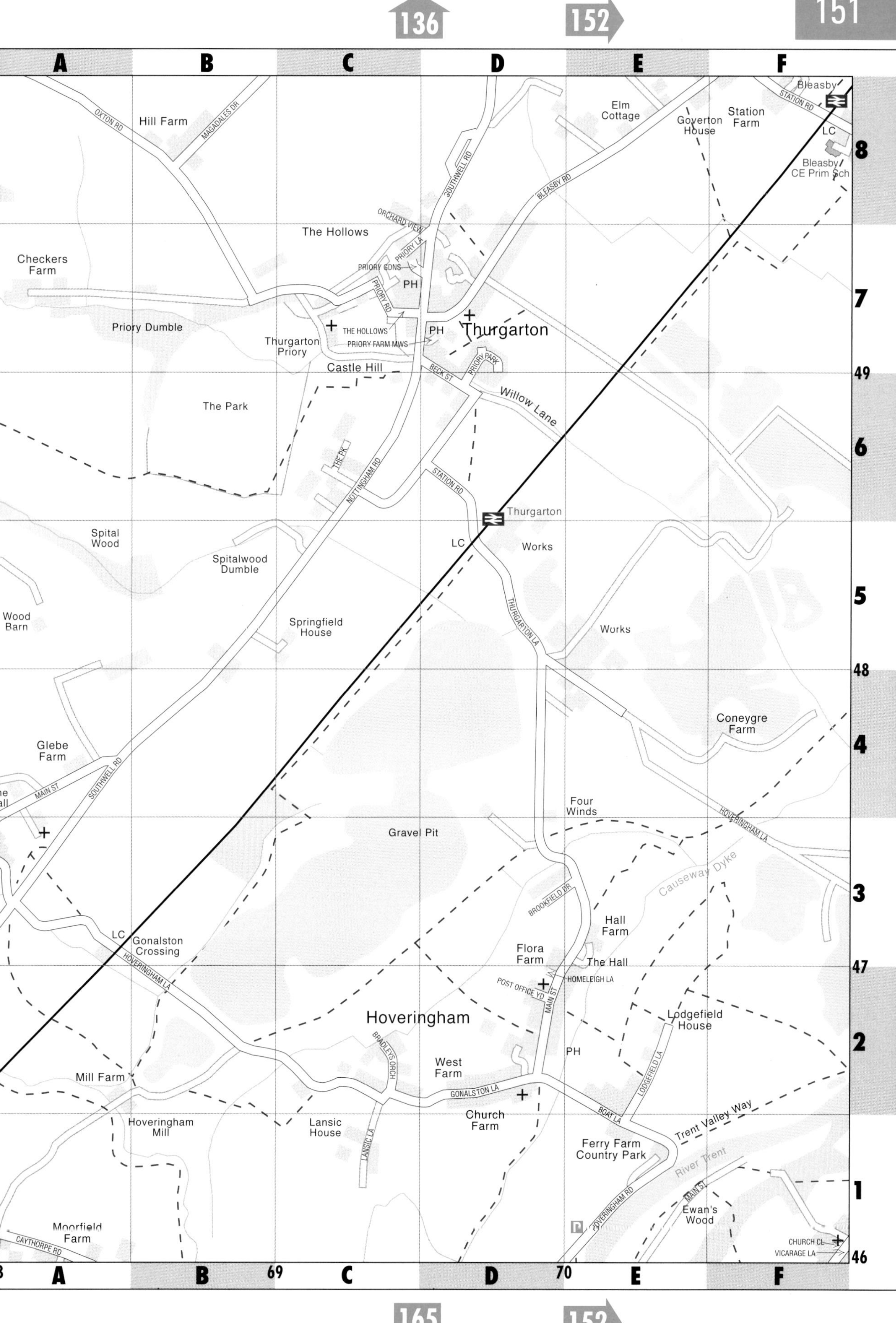
A
B
C
D
E
F
Hill Farm
OXTON RD
MAGADALES DR
SOUTHWELL RD
Elm Cottage
Goverton House
Station Farm
Bleasby
STATION RD
LC
Bleasby CE Prim Sch
BLEASBY RD
8
ORCHARD VIEW
The Hollows
PRIORY LA
PRIORY GDNS
PH
PRIORY RD
Checkers Farm
7
Priory Dumble
THE HOLLOWS
PRIORY FARM MWS
PH
Thurgarton
Thurgarton Priory
Castle Hill
BECK ST
PRIORY PARK
49
The Park
Willow Lane
THE PK
NOTTINGHAM RD
STATION RD
6
Thurgarton
Spital Wood
LC
Works
Spitalwood Dumble
5
Wood Barn
Springfield House
THURGARTON LA
Works
48
Coneygre Farm
Glebe Farm
SOUTHWELL RD
MAIN ST
4
Four Winds
HOVERINGHAM LA
Gravel Pit
Causeway Dyke
3
BROOKFIELD DR
Hall Farm
LC
Gonalston Crossing
Flora Farm
The Hall
HOVERINGHAM LA
HOMELEIGH LA
47
POST OFFICE YD
MAIN ST
Lodgefield House
Hoveringham
BRADLEYS ORCH
West Farm
PH
2
LODGEFIELD LA
Mill Farm
GONALSTON LA
BOAT LA
Hoveringham Mill
Lansic House
Church Farm
Trent Valley Way
LANSIC LA
Ferry Farm Country Park
River Trent
1
HOVERINGHAM RD
MAIN ST
Ewan's Wood
Moorfield Farm
CAYTHORPE RD
CHURCH CL
VICARAGE LA
46
8
69
70

151
137

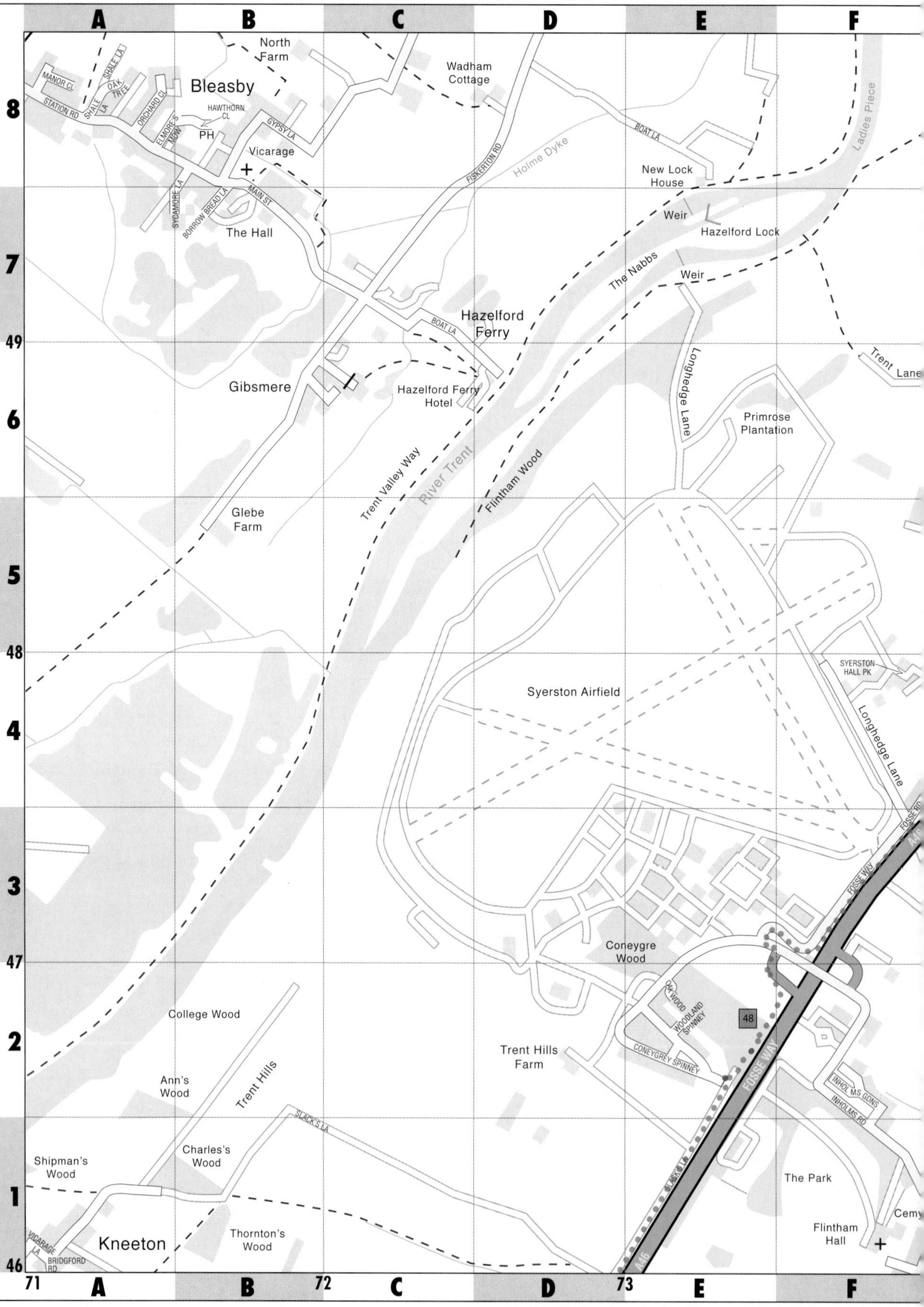

A **B** **C** **D** **E** **F**

North Farm

Wadham Cottage

Bleasby

MANOR CL

STATION RD

SHALE LA

OAK TREE

ELMORE'S MDW

ORCHARD CL

HAWTHORN CL

GYPSY LA

PH

Vicarage

SYCAMORE LA

BORROW BREAD LA

MAIN ST

The Hall

FISKERTON RD

Holme Dyke

BOAT LA

New Lock House

Weir

Hazelford Lock

The Nabbs

Weir

8

7

49

Hazelford Ferry

BOAT LA

Gibsmere

Hazelford Ferry Hotel

Longhedge Lane

Primrose Plantation

6

Trent Valley Way

River Trent

Flintham Wood

Glebe Farm

Ladies Piece

Trent Lane

5

48

Syerston Airfield

SYERSTON HALL PK

Longhedge Lane

4

FOSSE WAY

FOSSE RD

3

47

Coneygre Wood

OAK WOOD

WOODLAND SPINNEY

48

FOSSE WAY

College Wood

CONEYGREY SPINNEY

Trent Hills Farm

INHOLMS GDNS

INHOLMS RD

2

Ann's Wood

Trent Hills

SLACK'S LA

Shipman's Wood

Charles's Wood

CONEYGREY SPINNEY

The Park

Cem

1

VICARAGE LA

BRIDGFORD RD

Kneeton

Thornton's Wood

A46

Flintham Hall

46

71 **A** **72** **B** **C** **73** **D** **E** **F**

138
154

A B C D E F

8
7
49
6
5
48
4
3
47
2
1
46

Manor Farm
Grange Fram
TRENT LA
CHURCH LA
SCHOOL LA
Hall Farm
Stoke Wood
PH
East Stoke
A46
MAIN ST
HUMBER LA
BROWNLOW CL
MOOR LA
FOSSE RD
The Old Vicarage
ELSTON LA
Cedar Cottage
Trent Lane
Mill Hill House
ELSTON LA
Elston Lodge Farm
WILLOW RUNDLE DR
Stoke Fields Farm
CHAPEL FARM CL
Elston Towers
All Saints Anglican Methodist Prim Sch
Elston Chapel
Lady Pit Farm
LOW ST
OLD CHAPEL LA
Codders Dyke
FOSSE RD
LODGE LA
PINFOLD LA
THE SPINNEY
TUDOR OAKS
Elston
CHURCH LA
CARRGATE LA
ELSTON HALL
TOP ST
THE GREEN
TOAD LA
CENTRAL DR
WINSTON DR
DARWIN CL
SYERSTON HALL PK
PADDOCKS CL 1
THE PADDOCKS 2
PH
MILL RD
THE ORCHARD
Sewage Works
Carrgate Lane
The Windmill
Syerston
A46
GREENGATE
MAIN ST
The Rookery
Low Farm
Gundykes Plantation
BRECKS LA
Croft House
HAWKSWORTH RD
MOOR LA
DOGHILL LA
Hawksworth Road
Lineham Plantation
LINEHAM LA
Longhedge Lane
Ash Holt
CROSS LA
Sewage Works
Brecks Plantation
Hill Farm
DEADWONG LA
Flintham
INHOLMS RD
Flintham Prim Sch
Flintham Mus
WOOD'S LA

74 A B 75 C D 76 E F

167
154

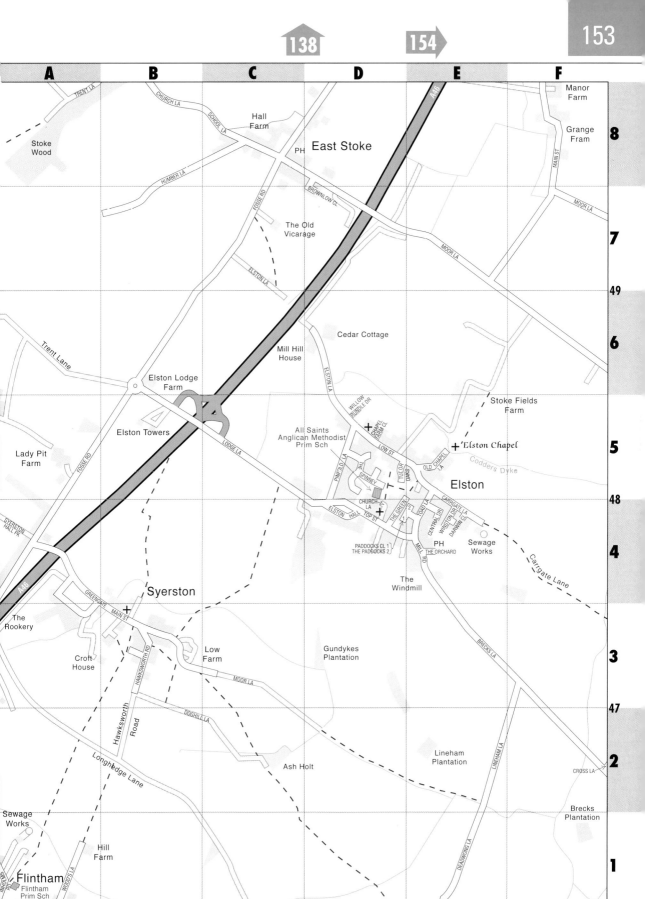

153
139

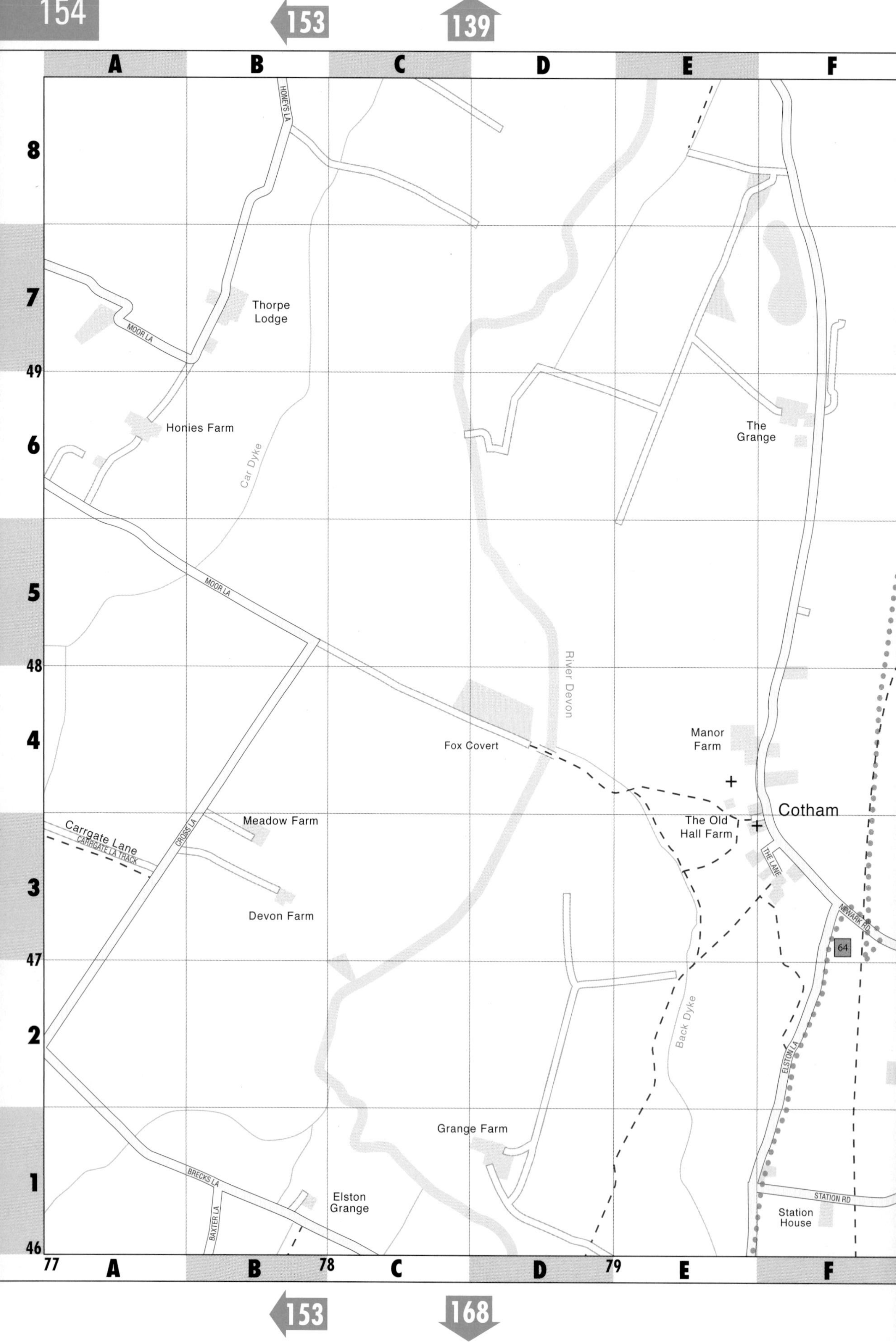

153
168

A B C D E F

8

7

49

6

5

48

4

3

47

2

1

46

77 A B 78 C D 79 E F

HONEY'S LA

MOOR LA

Thorpe
Lodge

Honies Farm

Car Dyke

MOOR LA

The
Grange

River Devon

Manor
Farm

Fox Covert

The Old
Hall Farm

Cotham

THE LANE

NEWARK RD

64

Carrgate Lane
CARRGATE LA TRACK

CROSS LA

Meadow Farm

Devon Farm

Back Dyke

ELSTON LA

Grange Farm

BRECKS LA

BAXTER LA

Elston
Grange

STATION RD

Station
House

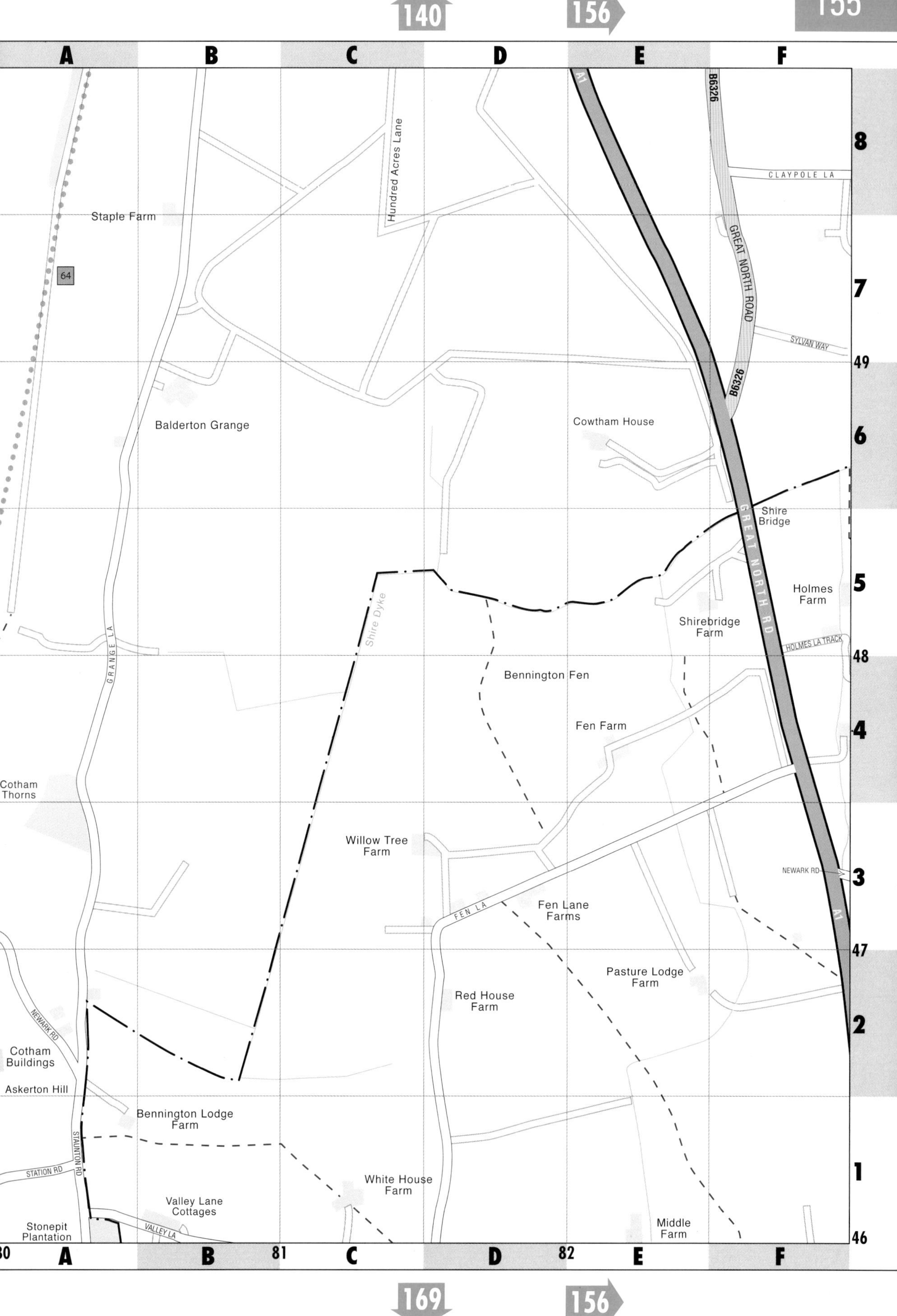

8
7
49
6
5
48
4
3
47
2
1
46

Staple Farm

64

Hundred Acres Lane

Balderton Grange

A1

B6326

GREAT NORTH ROAD

CLAYPOLE LA

SYLVAN WAY

B6326

Cowtham House

Shire Bridge

GREAT NORTH RD

Holmes Farm

Shirebridge Farm

HOLMES LA TRACK

Shire Dyke

Bennington Fen

Fen Farm

GRANGE LA

Cotham Thorns

Willow Tree Farm

FEN LA

Fen Lane Farms

NEWARK RD

A1

NEWARK RD

Red House Farm

Pasture Lodge Farm

Cotham Buildings

Askerton Hill

Bennington Lodge Farm

STAUNTON RD

STATION RD

White House Farm

Valley Lane Cottages

Middle Farm

Stonepit Plantation

VALLEY LA

155
141

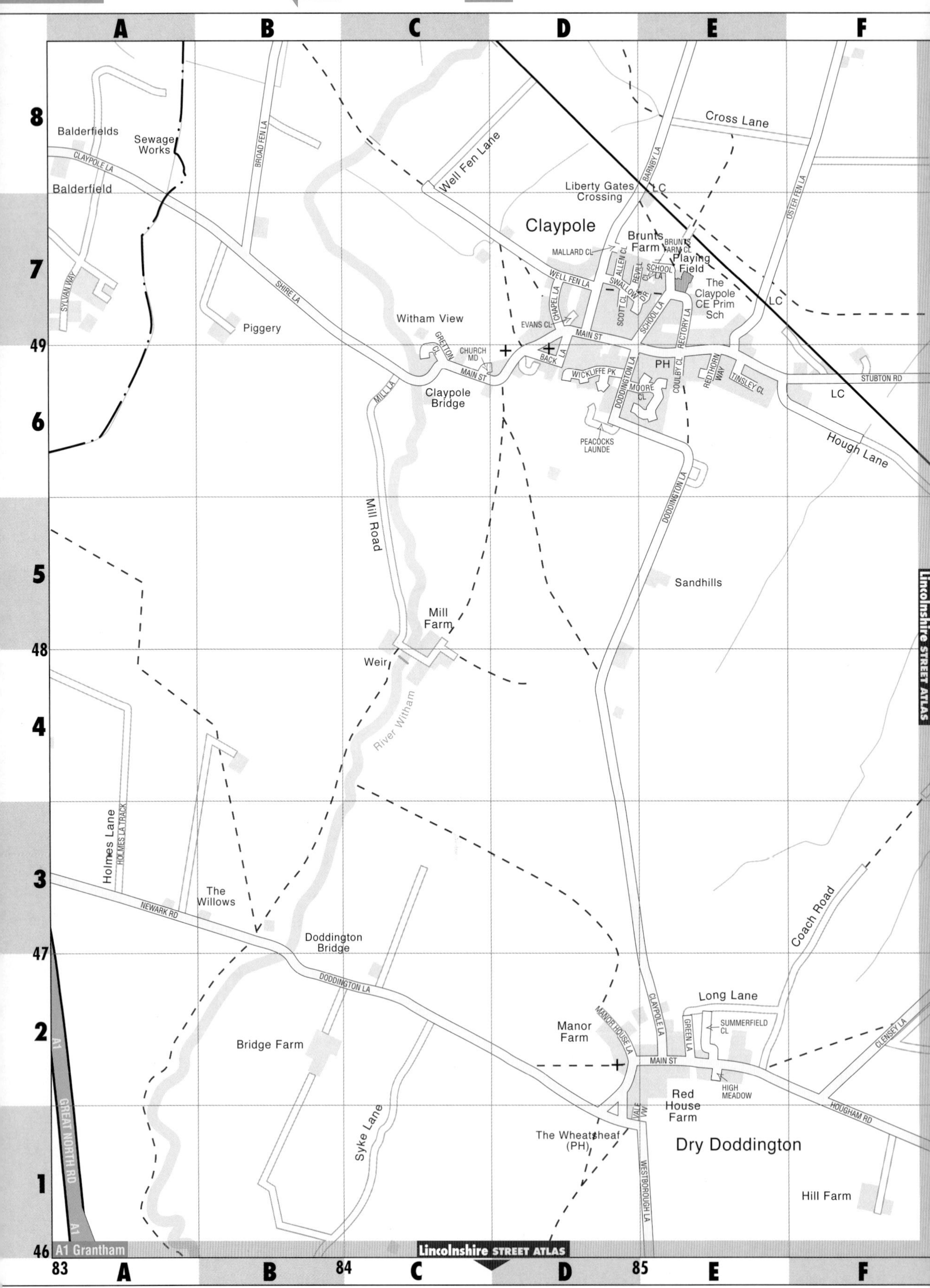
A
B
C
D
E
F
8
7
49
6
5
48
4
3
47
2
1
46
83
84
85
Balderfields
Sewage Works
CLAYPOLE LA
Balderfield
BROAD FEN LA
Well Fen Lane
Cross Lane
BARNBY LA
Liberty Gates Crossing
LC
OSTER FEN LA
Claypole
Brunts Farm
BRUNTS FARM CL
MALLARD CL
ALLEN CL
REVILL CL
SCHOOL LA
Playing Field
The Claypole CE Prim Sch
WELL FEN LA
SWALLOW DR
SHIRE LA
SYLVAN WAY
Piggery
Witham View
CHAPEL LA
SCOTT CL
SCHOOL LA
RECTORY LA
EVANS CL
MAIN ST
GRETTON CL
CHURCH MD
BACK LA
WICKLIFFE PK
DODDINGTON LA
PH
COULBY CL
REDTHORN WAY
TINSLEY CL
STUBTON RD
MAIN ST
MILL LA
Claypole Bridge
MOORE CL
PEACOCKS LAUNDE
Hough Lane
Mill Road
DODDINGTON LA
Sandhills
Mill Farm
Weir
River Witham
Holmes Lane
HOLMES LA TRACK
The Willows
NEWARK RD
Doddington Bridge
DODDINGTON LA
Coach Road
Long Lane
Manor Farm
MANOR HOUSE LA
CLAYPOLE LA
GREEN LA
SUMMERFIELD CL
CLENSEY LA
Bridge Farm
MAIN ST
HIGH MEADOW
Red House Farm
HOUGHAM RD
A1
GREAT NORTH RD
Syke Lane
The Wheatsheaf (PH)
VALE VW
WESTBOROUGH LA
Dry Doddington
Hill Farm
A1 Grantham
Lincolnshire STREET ATLAS

155

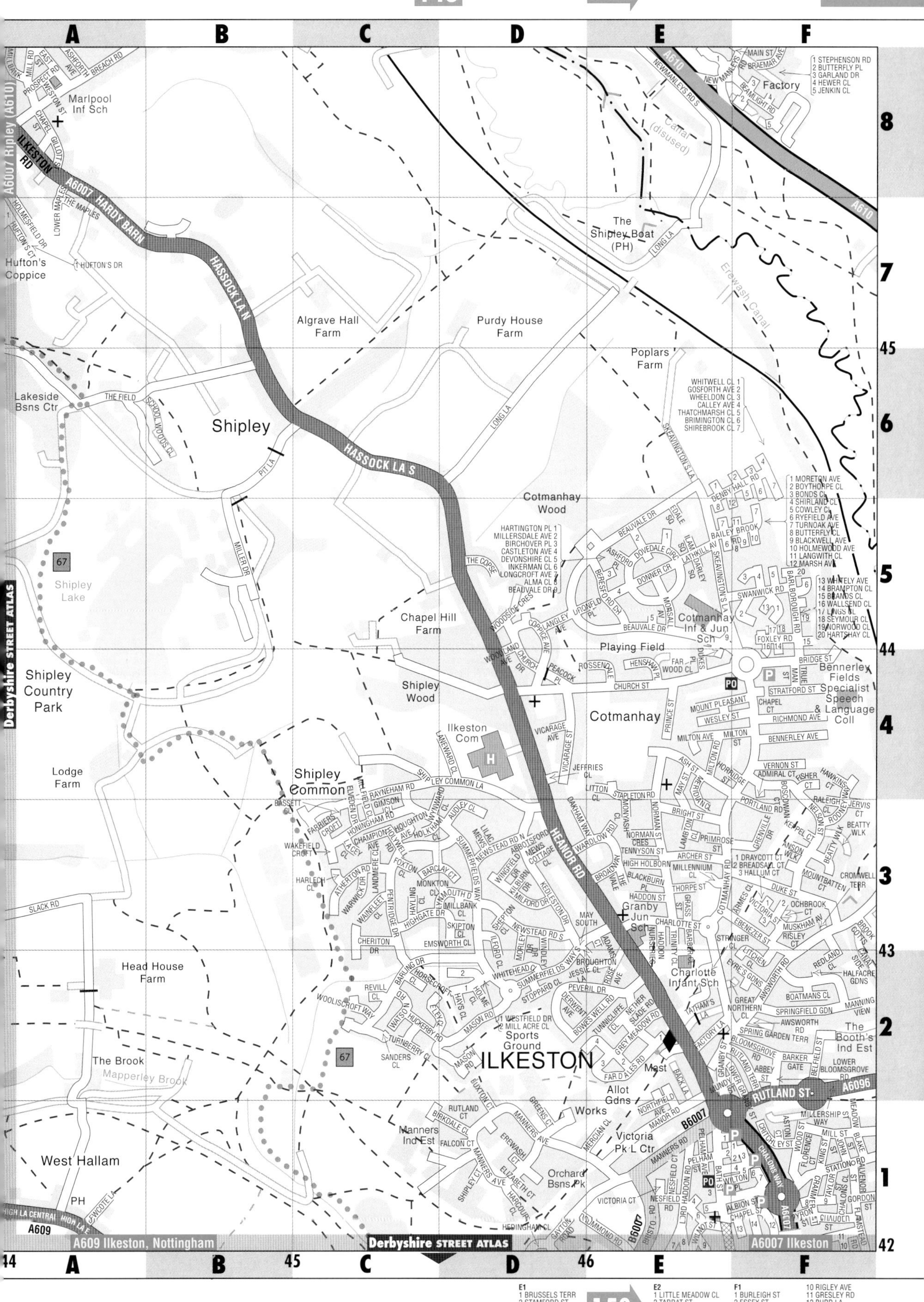

157
144

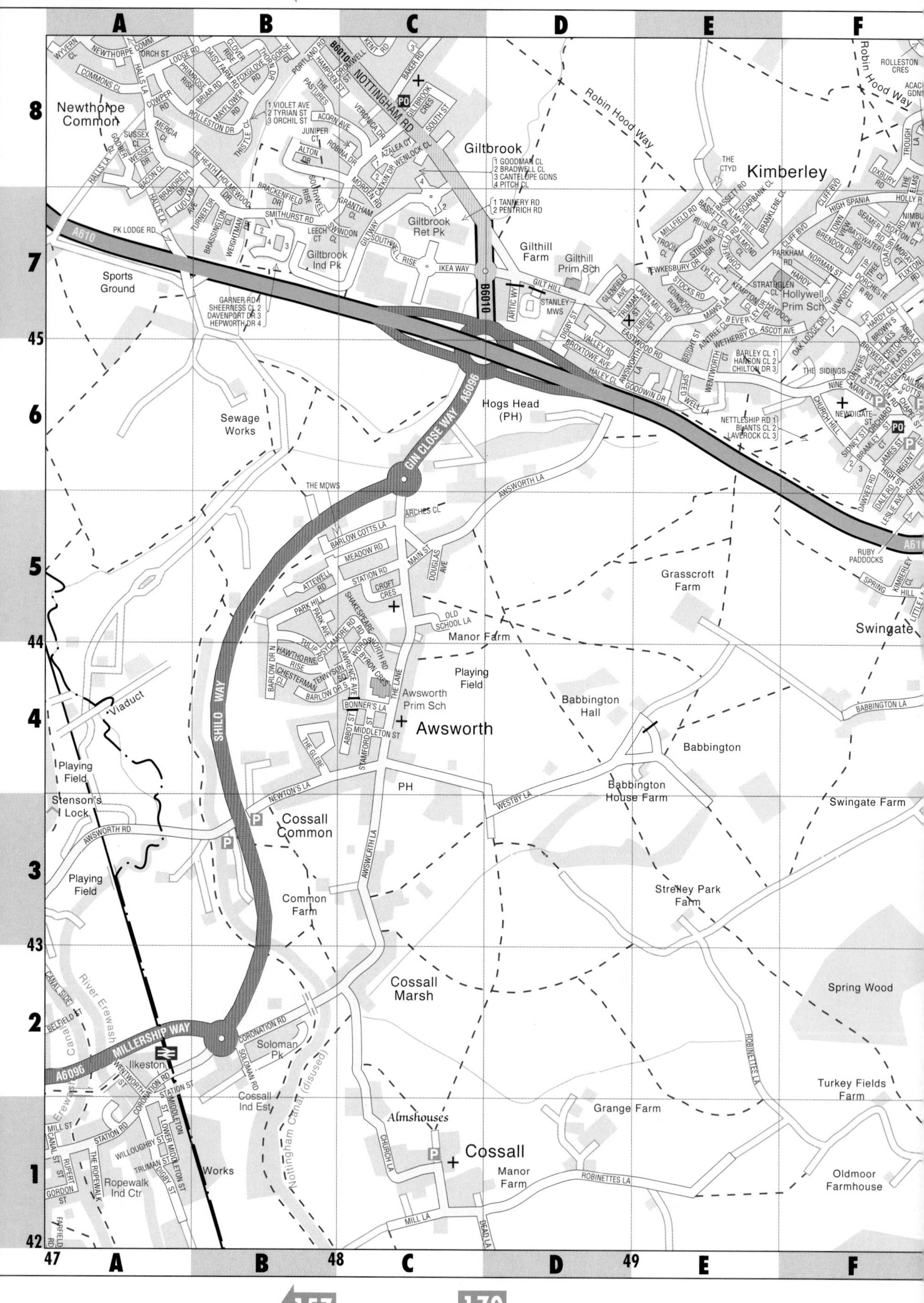
A
B
C
D
E
F
8
7
45
6
5
44
4
3
43
2
1
42
47
48
49
Newthorpe Common
Giltbrook
Kimberley
Robin Hood Way
Giltbrook Ret Pk
Giltbrook Ind Pk
Gilthill Farm
Gilthill Prim Sch
Hollywell Prim Sch
Sports Ground
Sewage Works
Hogs Head (PH)
NOTTINGHAM RD
GIN CLOSE WAY
SHILO WAY
A610
A6096
B6010
Grasscroft Farm
Swingate
Manor Farm
Playing Field
Babbington Hall
Babbington
Babbington House Farm
Awsworth Prim Sch
Awsworth
Viaduct
Playing Field
Stenson's Lock
Cossall Common
Swingate Farm
Strelley Park Farm
Common Farm
Cossall Marsh
Spring Wood
River Erewash
Erewash Canal
MILLERSHIP WAY
Ilkeston
Soloman Pk
Cossall Ind Est
Nottingham Canal (disused)
Turkey Fields Farm
Grange Farm
Almshouses
Cossall
Manor Farm
Oldmoor Farmhouse
Works
Ropewalk Ind Ctr
ROBINETTES LA
MILL LA
DEAD LA
CHURCH LA
AWSWORTH LA
AWSWORTH RD
NEWTON'S LA
WESTBY LA
CORONATION RD
SOLOMAN RD
STATION RD
BABBINGTON LA
Tha Sidings
PK LODGE RD
IKEA WAY
GILT HILL
STANLEY MWS
1 VIOLET AVE
2 TYRIAN ST
3 ORCHIL ST
1 GOODMAN CL
2 BRADWELL CL
3 CANTELUPE GDNS
4 PITCH CL
1 TANNERY RD
2 PENTRICH RD
GARNER RD 1
SHEERNESS CL 2
DAVENPORT DR 3
HEPWORTH DR 4
BARLEY CL 1
HANSON CL 2
CHILTON DR 3
NETTLESHIP RD 1
BLANTS CL 2
LAVEROCK CL 3
RUBY PADDOCKS

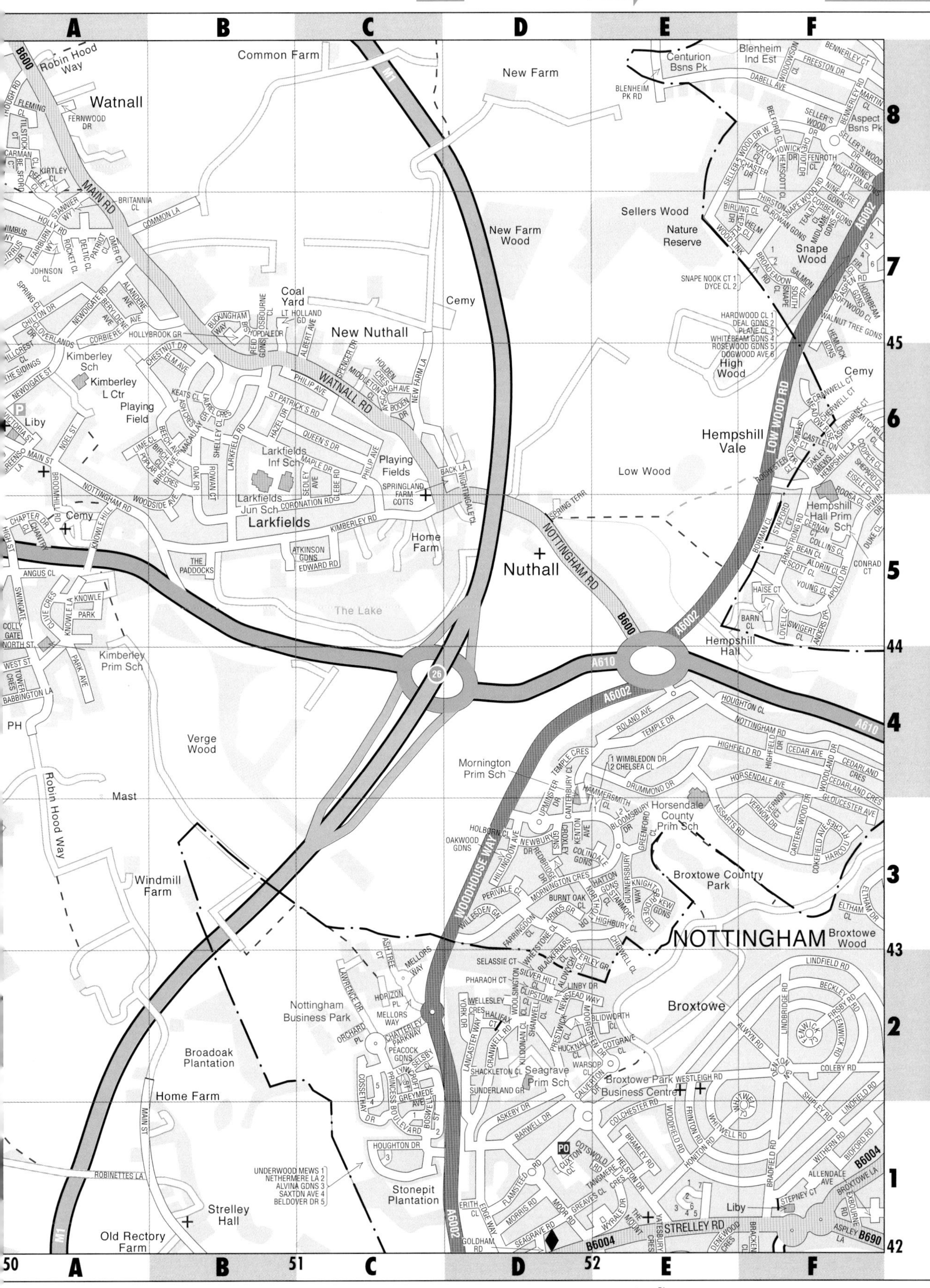

E1
1 ROSEMARY CL
2 LAVENDER CL
3 MAGNOLIA CL
4 HONEYSUCKLE CL
5 JASMINE CL
6 BRIDGE GREEN WALK
7 LILAC CL

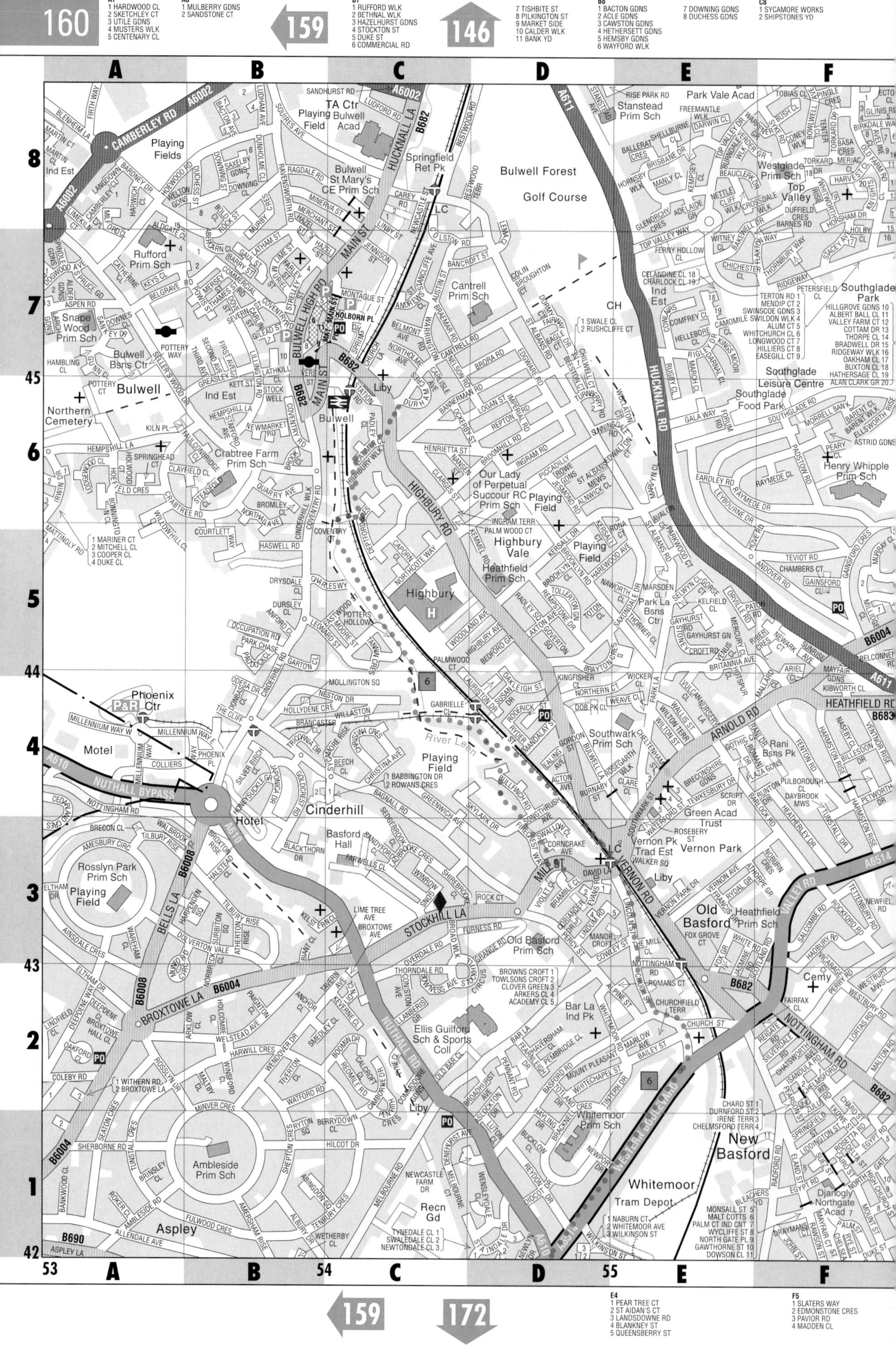

160
A7
1 HARDWOOD CL
2 SKETCHLEY CT
3 UTILE GDNS
4 MUSTERS WLK
5 CENTENARY CL
A8
1 MULBERRY GDNS
2 SANDSTONE CT
159
B7
1 RUFFORD WLK
2 BETHNAL WLK
3 HAZELHURST GDNS
4 STOCKTON ST
5 DUKE ST
6 COMMERCIAL RD
146
7 TISHBITE ST
8 PILKINGTON ST
9 MARKET SIDE
10 CALDER WLK
11 BANK YD
B8
1 BACTON GDNS
2 ACLE GDNS
3 CAWSTON GDNS
4 HETHERSETT GDNS
5 HEMSBY GDNS
6 WAYFORD WLK
7 DOWNING GDNS
8 DUCHESS GDNS
C8
1 SYCAMORE WORKS
2 SHIPSTONES YD
A B C D E F
8 7 6 5 4 3 2 1
45 44 43 42
53 54 55
Bulwell
Bulwell Forest Golf Course
Top Valley
Highbury Vale
Cinderhill
Old Basford
New Basford
Whitemoor
Aspley
Vernon Park
Southglade Park
159
172
E4
1 PEAR TREE CT
2 ST AIDAN'S CT
3 LANDSDOWNE RD
4 BLANKNEY ST
5 QUEENSBERRY ST
F5
1 SLATERS WAY
2 EDMONSTONE CRES
3 PAVIOR RD
4 MADDEN CL

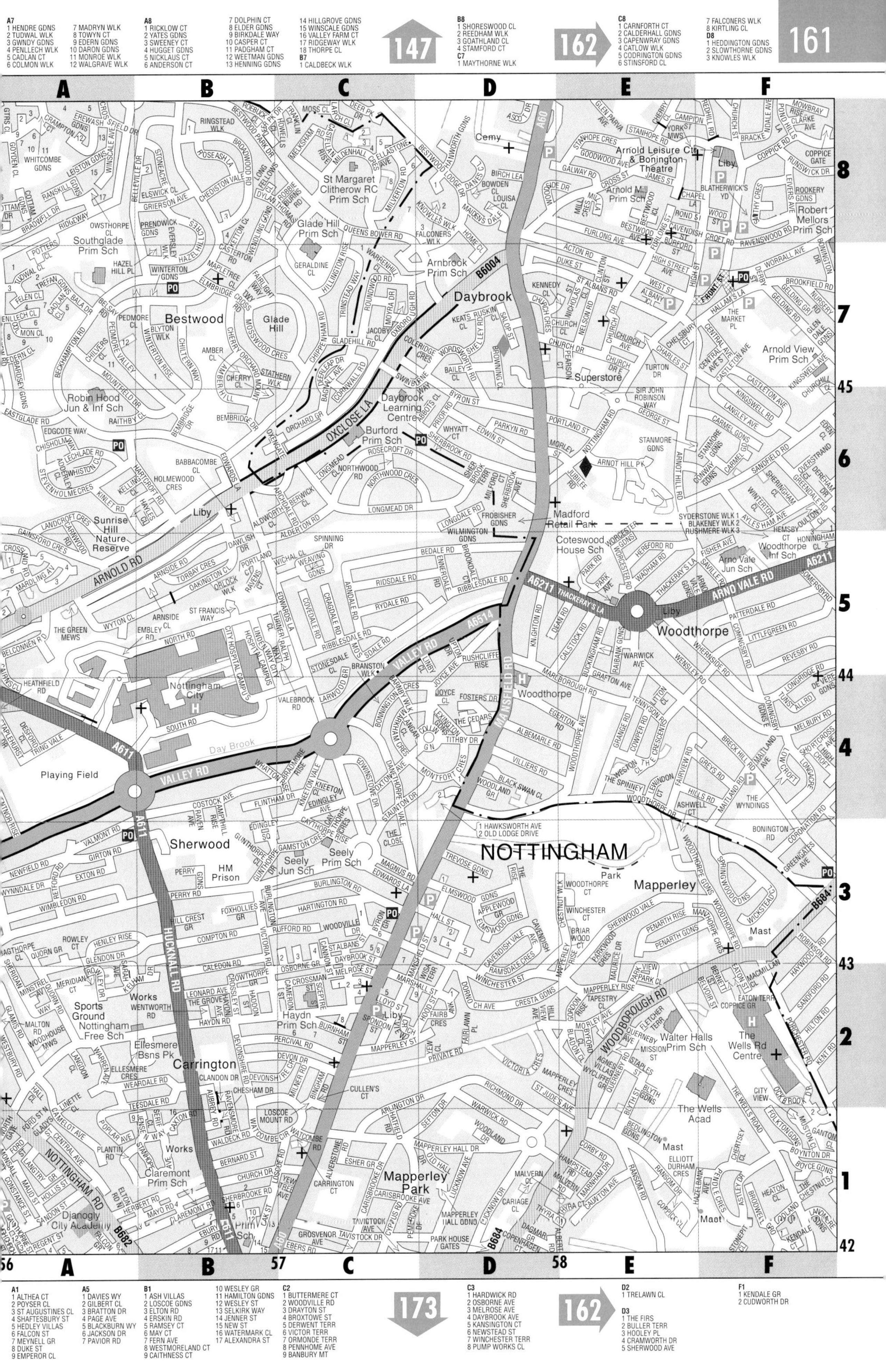

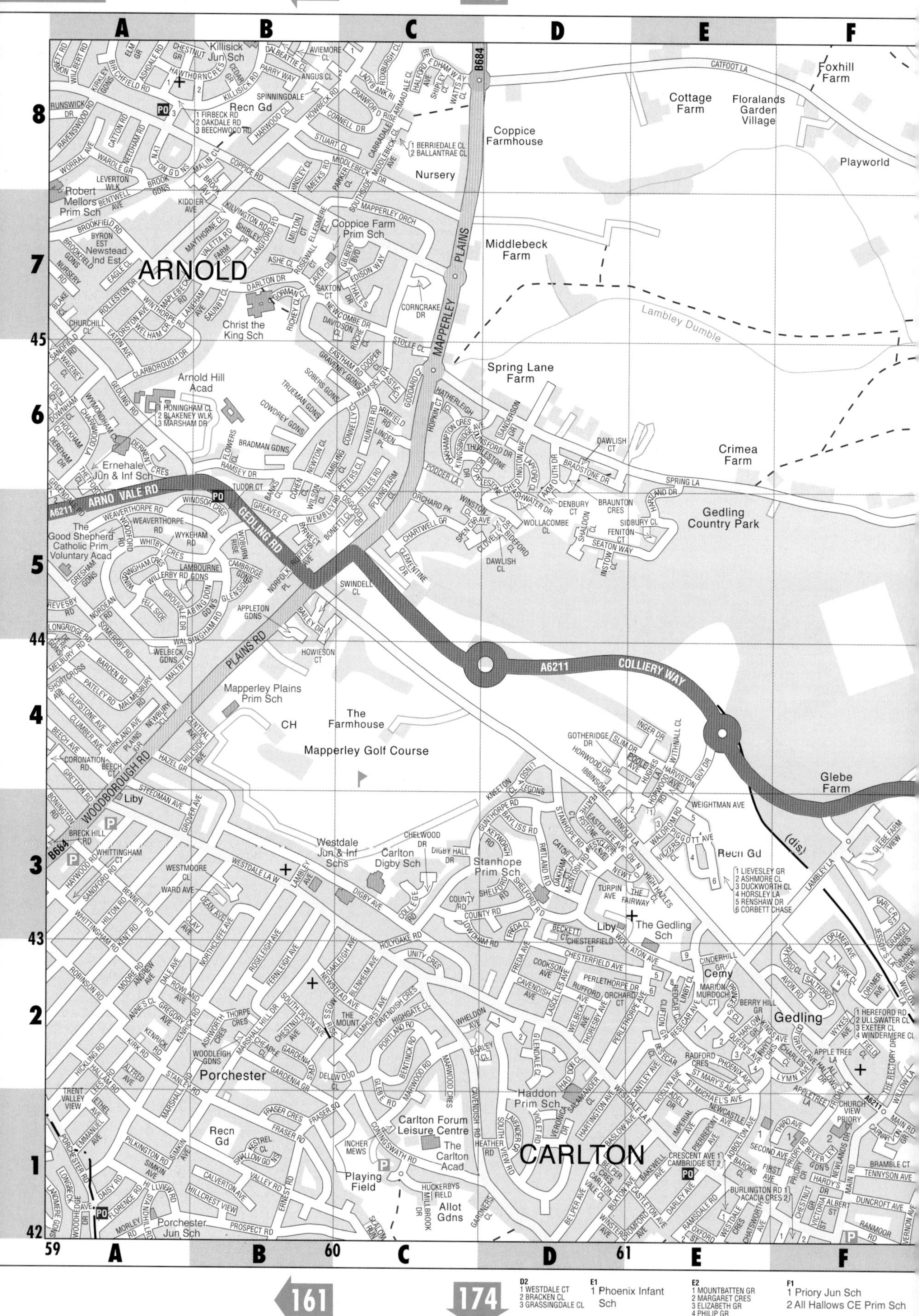

D2
1 WESTDALE CT
2 BRACKEN CL
3 GRASSINGDALE CL

E1
1 Phoenix Infant
Sch

E2
1 MOUNTBATTEN GR
2 MARGARET CRES
3 ELIZABETH GR
4 PHILIP GR
5 PERLETHORPE CL
6 PERLETHORPE CRES
7 STOREY AV
8 HUCKNALL CRES
9 BABBINGTON CRES

F1
1 Priory Jun Sch
2 All Hallows CE Prim Sch

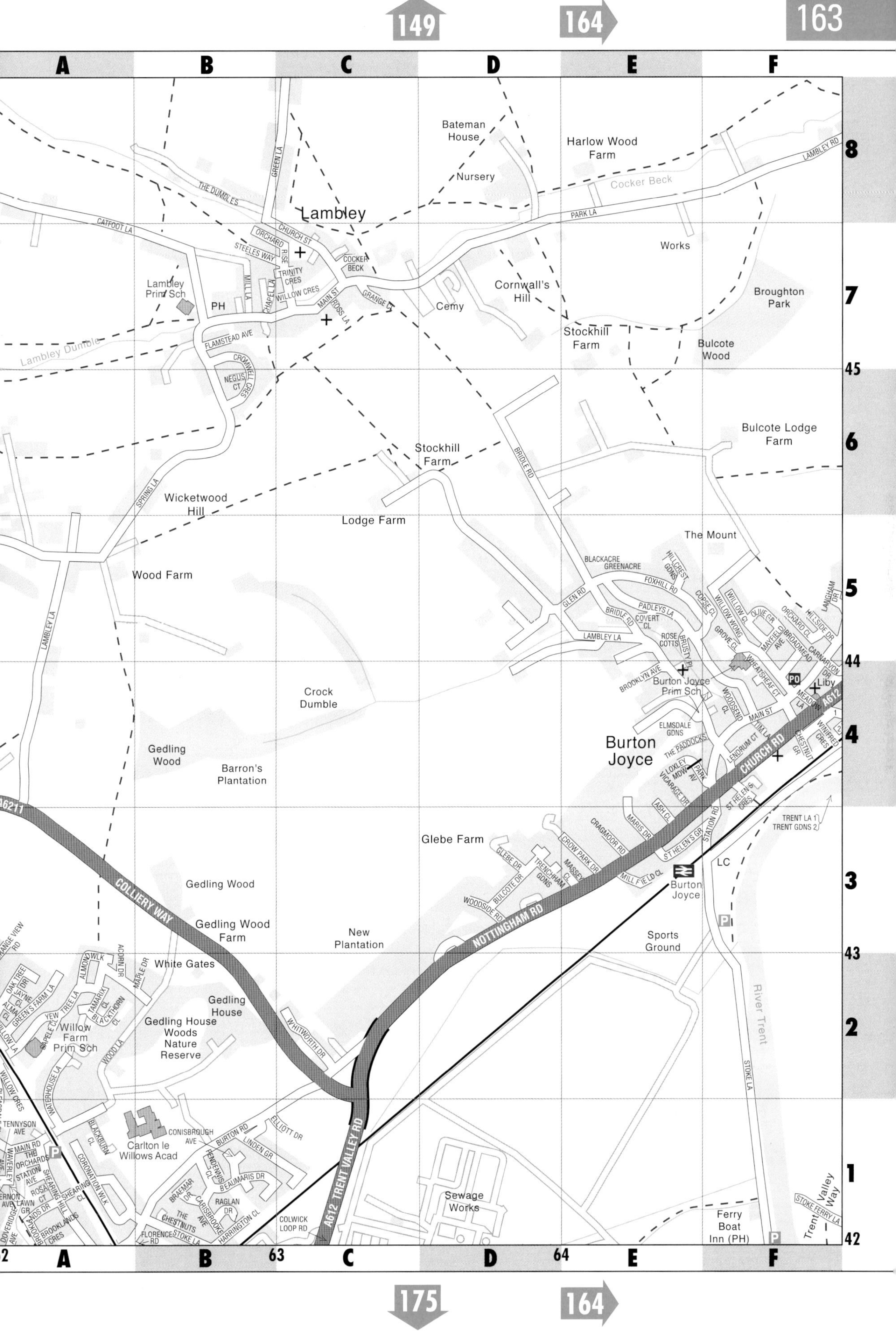

A B C D E F

8
45
7
6
5
44
4
43
3
2
1
42

THE DUMBLES
CATFOOT LA
Lambley
Lambley Prim Sch
PH
FLAMSTEAD AVE
CROMWELL CRES
NEGUS CT
ORCHARD RISE
STEELES WAY
CHURCH ST
TRINITY CRES
WILLOW CRES
PAPER LA
MILL LA
MAIN ST
CROSS LA
GRANGE CT
GREEN LA
Bateman House
Nursery
Cocker Beck
Harlow Wood Farm
Cornwall's Hill
Cemy
Stockhill Farm
PARK LA
Works
Cocker Beck
Broughton Park
Bulcote Wood
LAMBLEY CY RD

Lambley Dumble
SPRING LA
Wicketwood Hill
Stockhill Farm
BRIDLE RD
Bulcote Lodge Farm

Wood Farm
LAMBLEY LA
Lodge Farm
The Mount
BLACKACRE GREENACRE
HILLCREST GDNS
FOXHILL RD
GLEN RD
BRIDLE RD
PADLEYS LA
COVERT CL
LAMBLEY LA
Rose Cotts
COPSE CL
WILLOW MONG
WILLOW CL
OLIVE GR
GROVE CL
BRISTOL RD
MANVERS AVE
ORCHARD CL
CARNARVON
HILLSIDE DR
LANGHAM DR
BROADMEAD

Crock Dumble
BROOKLYN AVE
Burton Joyce Prim Sch
WHEATSHEAF CT
WOODSEND
Burton Joyce
PO
Liby
MAIN ST
CHURCH RD
A612
MEADOW
WINIFRED CRES
CHESTNUT
ELMSDALE GDNS
The Paddocks
LENDRUM CT
PARK AVE
LOXLEY MDW
A6211
Gedling Wood
Barron's Plantation
COLLIERY WAY
VICARAGE DR
ASH CL
MARIS DR
CRAGMOOR RD
St HELEN'S GR
St HELEN'S CRES
STATION RD
Trent La 1
TRENT GDNS 2
Glebe Farm
CROW PARK DR
GLEBE DR
TRENCHAM GDNS
MASSON CT
MILL FIELD CL
Burton Joyce
LC
New Plantation
Gedling Wood Farm
Gedling House
White Gates
WOODSIDE RD
BULCOTE DR
NOTTINGHAM RD
Sports Ground
River Trent

Gedling House Woods Nature Reserve
Willow Farm Prim Sch
WHITWORTH DR
A612 TRENT VALLEY RD
STOKE LA

OAK TREE AVE
JAYNE CL
ALMON WLK
ACORN DR
APPLE TREE LA
GREEN'S FARM LA
TAMARIX CL
MAPLE DR
YEW TREE LA
ALDER CL
WOOD LA
BLACKTHORN CL
MARBLE VIEW
ABLE DR
WATERHOUSE LA
WILLOW CRES
TENNYSON AVE
MAIN RD
STATION AVE
WAVERLEY
SHEARING HILL CL
CORONATION WLK
BLACKBURN
The Orchard
P
Carlton le Willows Acad
CONISBROUGH AVE
BRAEMAR DR
CARISBROOKE DR
PENDENNIS CL
BURTON RD
LINDEN GR
ELLIOTT DR
RAGLAN DR
BEAUMARIS DR
The Chestnuts
FLORENCE
STOKE LA
COLWICK LOOP RD
HARRINGTON CL
Sewage Works
Ferry Boat Inn (PH)
P
STOKE FERRY LA
Trent Valley Way
TRENT VALLEY WAY

2 63 64

163
150
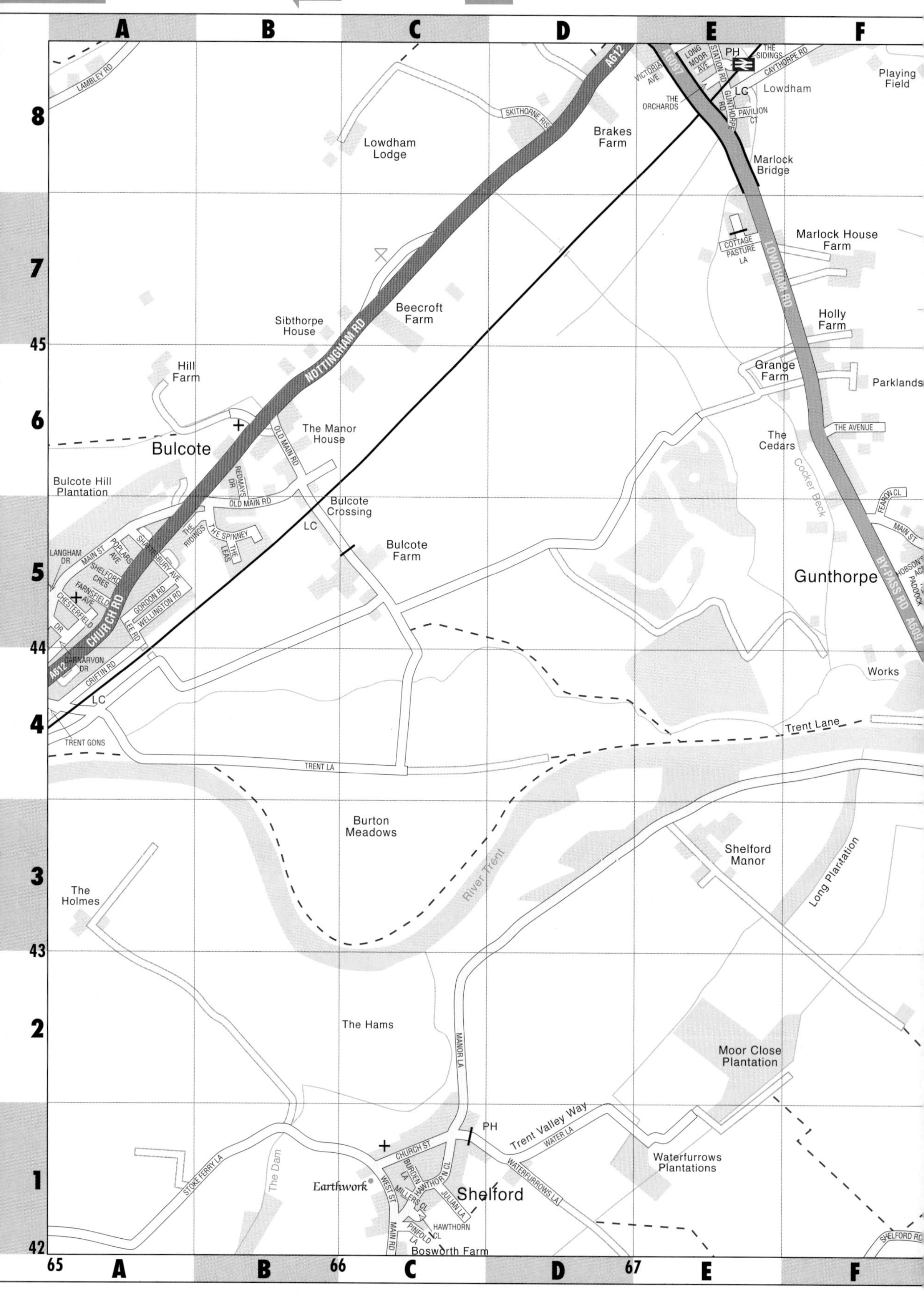
A
B
C
D
E
F
8
7
45
6
5
44
4
3
43
2
1
42
65
66
67
LAMBLEY RD
Lowdham Lodge
SKITHORNE RISE
A612
Brakes Farm
VICTORIA AVE
A6097
LONG MOOR AVE
STATION RD
PH
THE SIDINGS
CAYTHORPE RD
THE ORCHARDS
LC
Lowdham
GUNTHORPE RD
PAVILION CT
Playing Field
Marlock Bridge
COTTAGE PASTURE LA
LOWDHAM RD
Marlock House Farm
Beecroft Farm
Sibthorpe House
NOTTINGHAM RD
Holly Farm
Hill Farm
Grange Farm
Parklands
THE AVENUE
The Manor House
OLD MAIN RD
Bulcote
The Cedars
Cocker Beck
Bulcote Hill Plantation
REDMAYS DR
OLD MAIN RD
Bulcote Crossing
FEARON CL
LC
THE RIDINGS
THE SPINNEY
THE LEAS
MAIN ST
LANGHAM DR
MAIN ST
POPLARS AVE
SHAFTESBURY AVE
Bulcote Farm
SHELFORD CRES
FARNSFIELD AVE
CHESTERFIELD DR
GORDON RD
WELLINGTON RD
CHURCH RD
LEE RD
Gunthorpe
HOBSON'S ACRE
PADDOCK
BY-PASS RD
A6097
CARNARVON DR
CRIFTIN RD
A612
Works
LC
Trent Lane
TRENT GDNS
TRENT LA
Burton Meadows
Shelford Manor
River Trent
Long Plantation
The Holmes
The Hams
MANOR LA
Moor Close Plantation
PH
Trent Valley Way
WATER LA
CHURCH ST
Waterfurrows Plantations
WATERFURROWS LA
BURDEN LA
HAWTHORN CL
JULIAN LA
STOKE FERRY LA
The Dam
Earthwork
WEST ST
MILLERS CL
Shelford
PINFOLD LA
HAWTHORN CL
MAIN RD
Bosworth Farm
SHELFORD RD
163
176

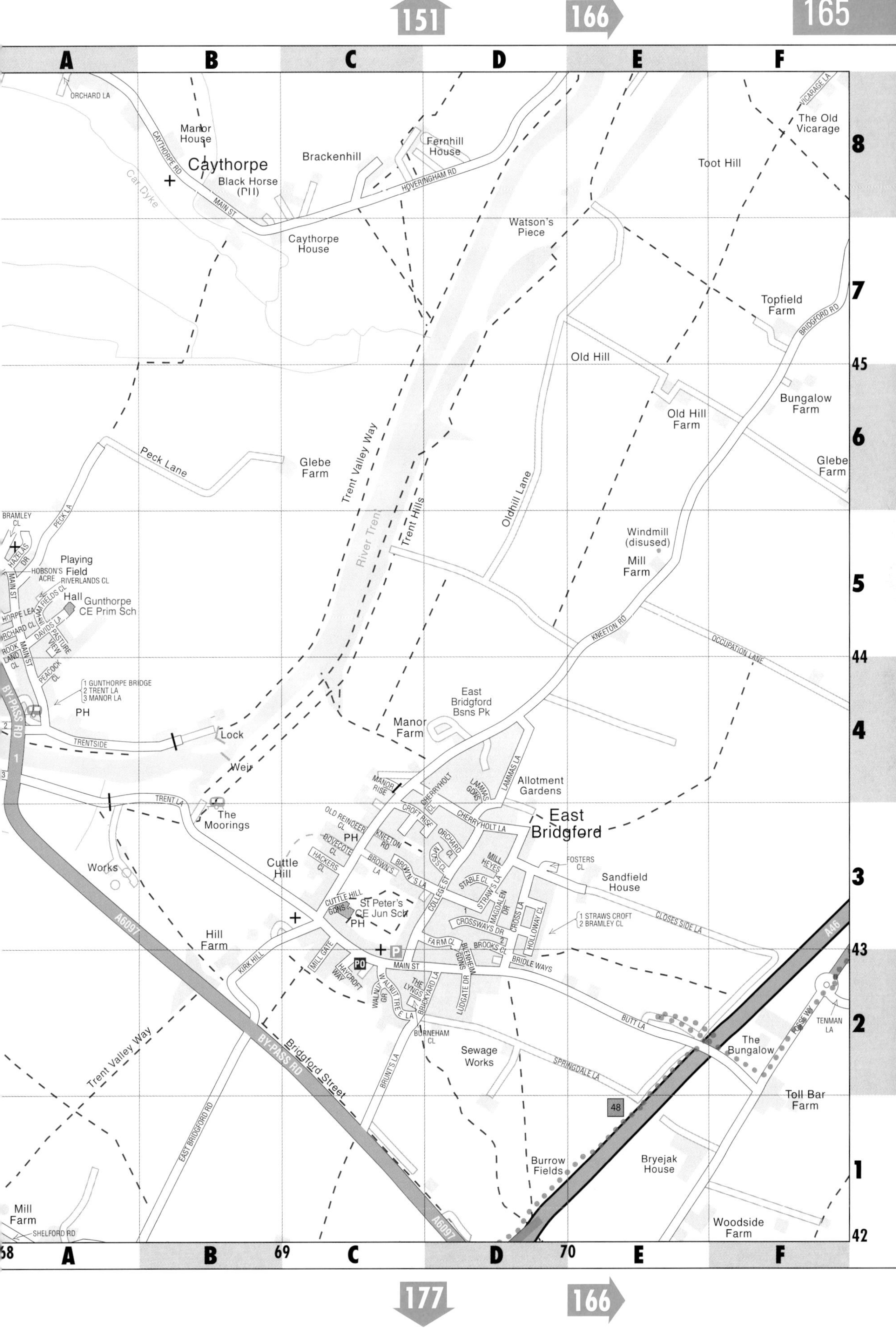
151
166
A
B
C
D
E
F
8
7
6
5
4
3
2
1
45
44
43
42
ORCHARD LA
Manor House
Caythorpe
CAYTHORPE RD
Car Dyke
Black Horse (PH)
MAIN ST
Brackenhill
Fernhill House
HOVERINGHAM RD
Caythorpe House
VICARAGE LA
The Old Vicarage
Toot Hill
Watson's Piece
Topfield Farm
BRIDGFORD RD
Old Hill
Old Hill Farm
Bungalow Farm
Peck Lane
Glebe Farm
Trent Valley Way
Trent Hills
River Trent
Oldhill Lane
Glebe Farm
BRAMLEY CL
PECK LA
HAZELAS DR
Playing Field
HOBSON'S ACRE
RIVERLANDS CL
MAIN ST
Hall
Gunthorpe CE Prim Sch
DAVIDS LA
PASTURE VIEW
PEACOCK CL
1 GUNTHORPE BRIDGE
2 TRENT LA
3 MANOR LA
PH
BY-PASS RD
TRENTSIDE
Lock
Weir
Windmill (disused)
Mill Farm
KNEETON RD
OCCUPATION LANE
East Bridgford Bsns Pk
Manor Farm
LAMMAS GDNS
LAMMAS LA
Allotment Gardens
MANOR RISE
CHERRYHOLT
CROFT RISE
CHERRYHOLT LA
East Bridgford
TRENT LA
The Moorings
OLD REINDEER CL
PH
KNEETON RD
ORCHARD CL
DOVECOTE CL
HACKERS CL
BROWN'S LA
MILL HEYES
FOSTERS CL
Sandfield House
Works
Cuttle Hill
STABLE CL
STRAW'S LA
COLLEGE ST
CUTTLE HILL GDNS
St Peter's CE Jun Sch
PH
CROSSWAYS DR
MAGDALEN DR
CROSS LA
HOLLOWAY CL
1 STRAWS CROFT
2 BRAMLEY CL
CLOSES SIDE LA
A6097
Hill Farm
KIRK HILL
MILL GATE
HAYCROFT WAY
PO
P
MAIN ST
FARM CL
BROOKS CL
BLENHEIM GDNS
BRIDLE WAYS
A46
WALNUT GR
WALNUT TREE LA
THE LYNGS
BRICKYARD LA
LUDGATE DR
BUTT LA
FOSSE WY
TENMAN LA
Trent Valley Way
BY-PASS RD
Bridgford Street
BURNEHAM CL
Sewage Works
The Bungalow
BRUNT'S LA
SPRINGDALE LA
Toll Bar Farm
EAST BRIDGFORD RD
48
Burrow Fields
Bryejak House
Mill Farm
SHELFORD RD
Woodside Farm
68
69
70
177
166

165
152

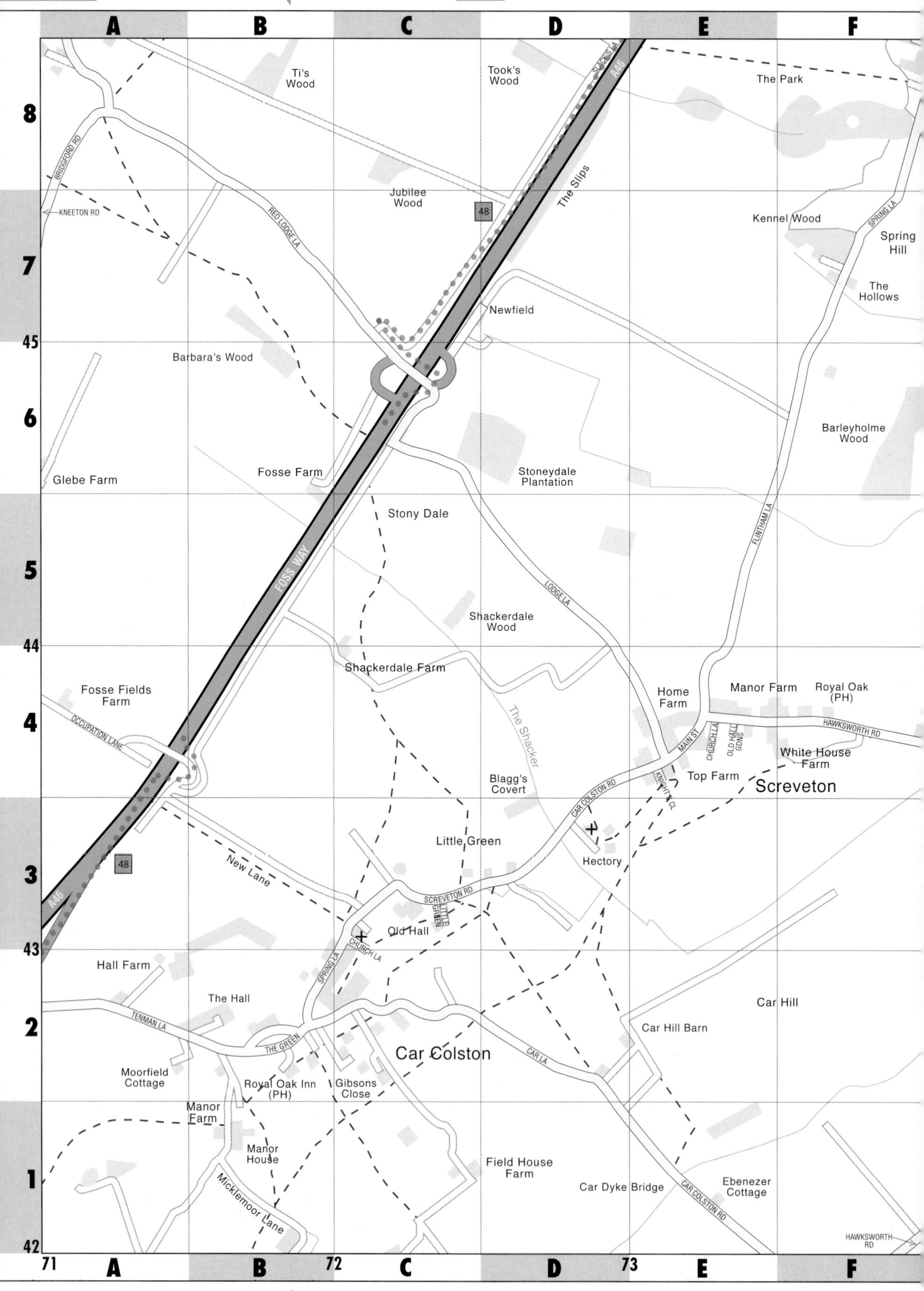
Ti's Wood
Took's Wood
The Park
BRIDGFORD RD
KNEETON RD
RED LODGE LA
Jubilee Wood
48
The Slips
A46
SLACK'S LA
Kennel Wood
SPRING LA
Spring Hill
The Hollows
Newfield
Barbara's Wood
Barleyholme Wood
Glebe Farm
Fosse Farm
Stoneydale Plantation
Stony Dale
FLINTHAM LA
FOSS WAY
LODGE LA
Shackerdale Wood
Shackerdale Farm
Fosse Fields Farm
Home Farm
Manor Farm
Royal Oak (PH)
OCCUPATION LANE
The Shacker
HAWKSWORTH RD
MAIN ST
CHURCH LA
OLD HALL GDNS
White House Farm
Blagg's Covert
Top Farm
Screveton
CAR COLSTON RD
KNIGHT'S CL
Little Green
Hectory
New Lane
SCREVETON RD
LITTLE GREEN
Old Hall
CHURCH LA
Hall Farm
SPRING LA
The Hall
TENMAN LA
Car Hill
Car Hill Barn
THE GREEN
Car Colston
CAR LA
Moorfield Cottage
Royal Oak Inn (PH)
Gibsons Close
Manor Farm
Manor House
Field House Farm
Car Dyke Bridge
CAR COLSTON RD
Ebenezer Cottage
Micklemoor Lane
HAWKSWORTH RD
A B C D E F
8 7 6 5 4 3 2 1
45 44 43 42
71 72 73

165
178

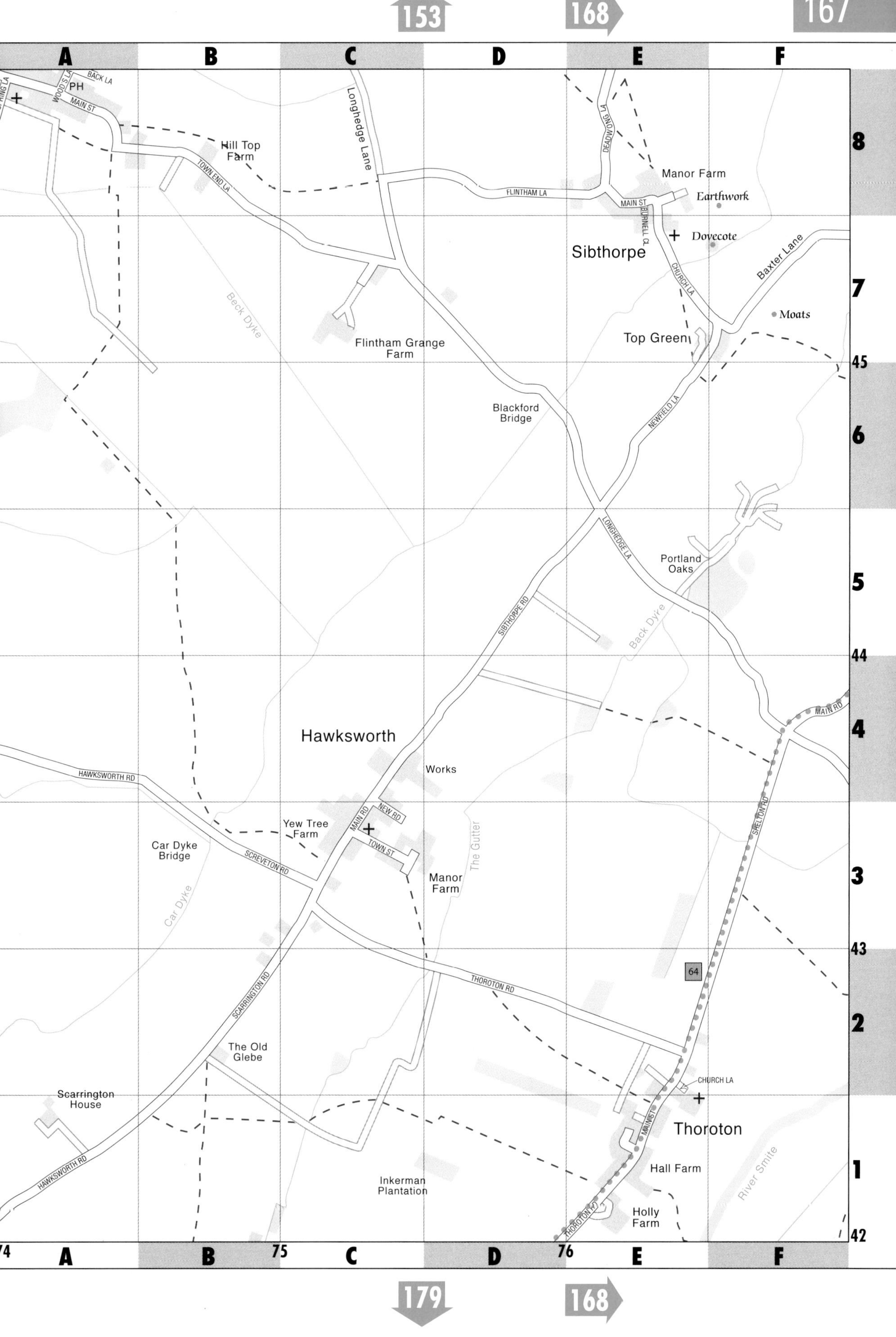

A B C D E F

RING LA
WOOD'S LA
BACK LA
PH
MAIN ST
Hill Top Farm
TOWN END LA
Longhedge Lane
DEADMAN LA
BURNELL CL
Manor Farm
Earthwork
MAIN ST
Dovecote
Sibthorpe
Baxter Lane
CHURCH LA
FLINTHAM LA
Beck Dyke
Top Green
Moats
Flintham Grange Farm
Blackford Bridge
NEWFIELD LA
LONGHEDGE LA
Portland Oaks
Back Dyke
SIBTHORPE RD
MAIN RD
Hawksworth
Works
HAWKSWORTH RD
SHELTON RD
Yew Tree Farm
NEW RD
MAIN RD
Car Dyke Bridge
SCREVETON RD
TOWN ST
The Gutter
Manor Farm
Car Dyke
64
SCARRINGTON RD
THOROTON RD
The Old Glebe
Scarrington House
CHURCH LA
MAIN ST
Thoroton
HAWKSWORTH RD
Inkerman Plantation
River Smite
Hall Farm
THOROTON RD
Holly Farm

167
154

A **B** **C** **D** **E** **F**

8

Firs Farm

BAXTER LA

Back Dyke

BRECKS LA

Wensor
Bridge

ELSTON LA

Booth's
Farm

7

Fox
Covert

Limekiln
Covert

ELSTON RD

Staunton Grange

45

64

Shelton

Hall Farm

Shelton House
Farm

Fourteen Acre
Covert

6

The Hall

ST ANN'S WAY

Staunton
Works

Manor Farm

Little
Orchard

Fishpond
Plantation

River Smite

5

Top Farm

MAIN RD

Fairfields

44

River Devon

4

Brickyard
Plantation

SHELTON LA

Works

Greenacres

3

Shelton Lodge
Farm

Lane Side

Flawborough

43

LONGHEDGE LA

Flawborough
Hall

Manor Farm

Manor Farm

MANOR FARM CL

2

Oscar
Bridge

Stonehouse
Farm

MAIN ST

Sunnymede

NEWARK RD

ORSTON LA

FLAWBOROUGH RD

1

Chestnut Farm

Grange Farm

Alverton

MILL LA

42

77 **A** **B** 78 **C** **D** 79 **E** **F**

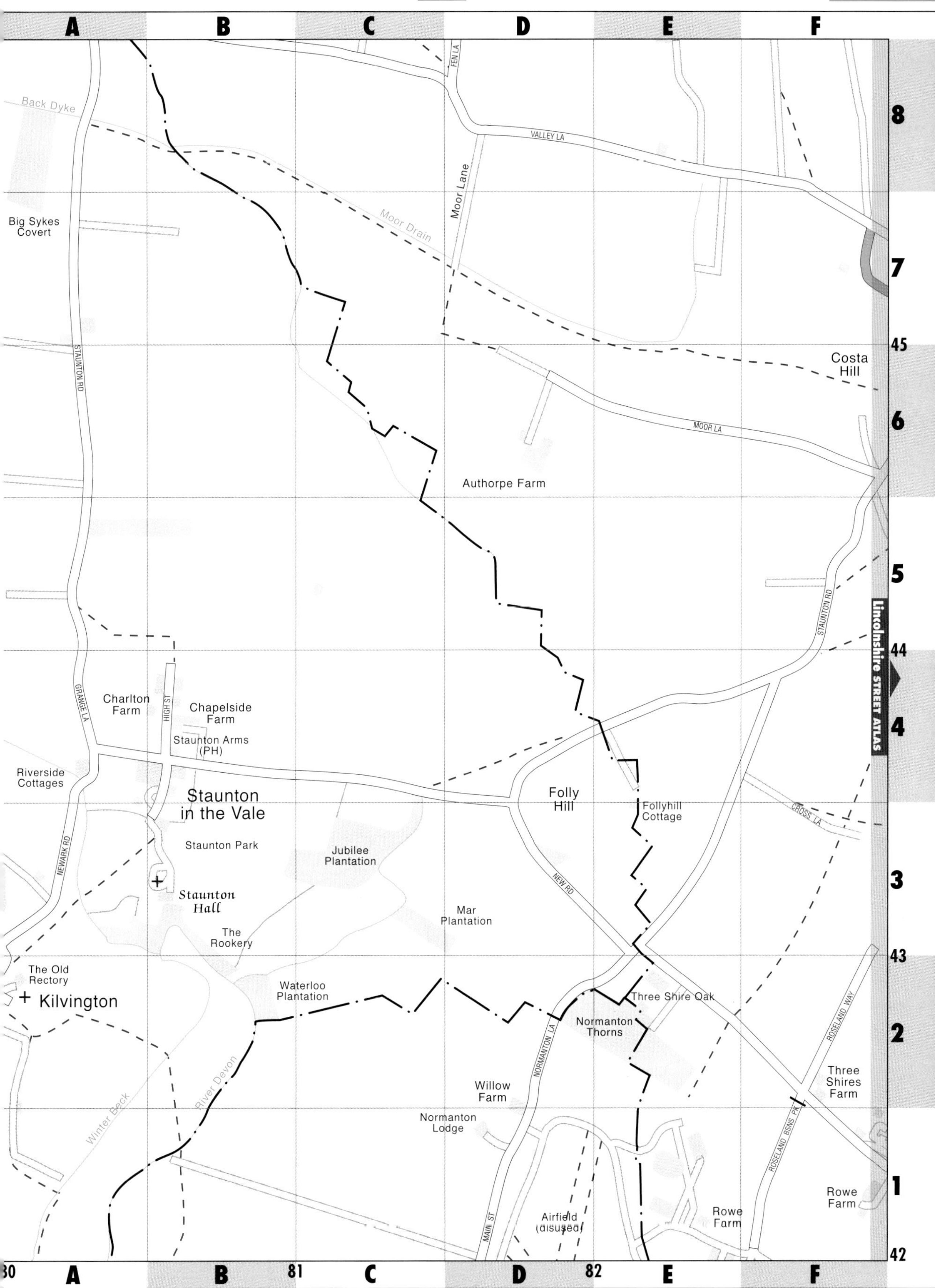

8

Back Dyke

Big Sykes
Covert

7

45

STAUNTON RD

Moor Drain

Moor Lane

FEN LA

VALLEY LA

Costa
Hill

MOOR LA

6

Authorpe Farm

STAUNTON RD

5

44

4

GRANGE LA

Charlton
Farm

HIGH ST

Chapelside
Farm

Staunton Arms
(PH)

Riverside
Cottages

NEWARK RD

**Staunton
in the Vale**

Staunton Park

Jubilee
Plantation

*Staunton
Hall*

The
Rookery

Folly
Hill

Follyhill
Cottage

CROSS LA

3

Mar
Plantation

NEW RD

The Old
Rectory

Kilvington

Waterloo
Plantation

Three Shire Oak

43

Normanton
Thorns

NORMANTON LA

ROSELAND WAY

2

Winter Beck

River Devon

Willow
Farm

Three
Shires
Farm

Normanton
Lodge

ROSELAND BSNS PK

1

MAIN ST

Airfield
(disused)

Rowe
Farm

Rowe
Farm

42

158

A7
1 BROMLEY CT
2 REDBRIDGE CL
3 KENSINGTON GDNS
4 ST JOHNS RD
5 CONCORDE CL
6 Kensington Jun Acad

A   B   C   D   E   F

Oldmoor Wood

MILL LA

DIGBY ST

Robbinetts Arm (dis)

DEAD LA

Cemy

Larklands

Larklands Inf Sch

River Erewash

ILKESTON

Shortwood Farm

Mast

Nottingham Canal Nature Reserve

Field House

Shortwood Farm

Gallows Inn

Meadow Farm

Robin Hood Way

Trowell Service Area

Trowell Moor

Moor Cottages

Grange Wood

Shortwood House

NOTTINGHAM RD

Trowell

ILKESTON RD

Uplands Farm

NOTTINGHAM RD   A609

Trowell Hall

Playing Field

Trpwell Junction

Hill Rise

Trowell CE Prim Sch

Potter's Plantation

Factories

Hallam Fields Lock

Festival Cres

Hallam Fields

Sewage Works

Crompton Rd Ind Est

Swancar Farm

Nottingham Canal (disused)

Works

67

Junction Lock

STAPLEFORD RD

Stapleford Rd

Northern Dr

Field Farm

STAPLEFORD

Stapleford Hill

LC

1 WAGTAIL CL
2 FIELD FARM WAY
3 GOLDFINCH CL
4 SKYLARK RI
5 DUNNOCK DR

LOW'S LA

PH

TROWELL RD

ILKESTON RD

1 SHERICAN CT
2 ADELAIDE CL
3 CANBERRA CT
4 DRYDEN CT

Stanton-by-Dale

Faraday Ct

The Crescent

HICKINGS LA

Moorbridge La

Playing Field

Jubilee House Christian Sch

M1

Ilkeston Gate

Stanton Gate

Stanton Gate

CH

PEATFIELD CT

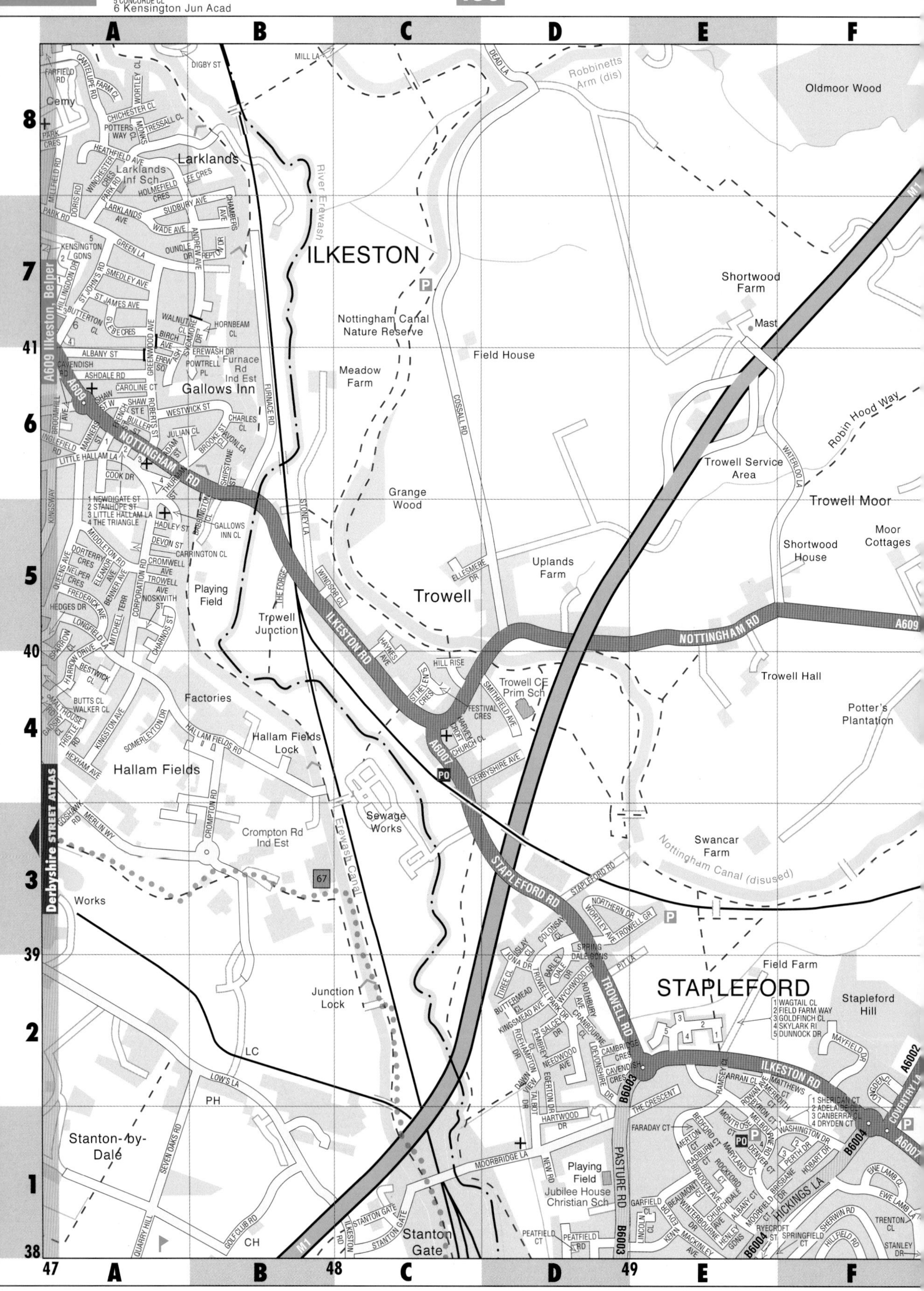

182

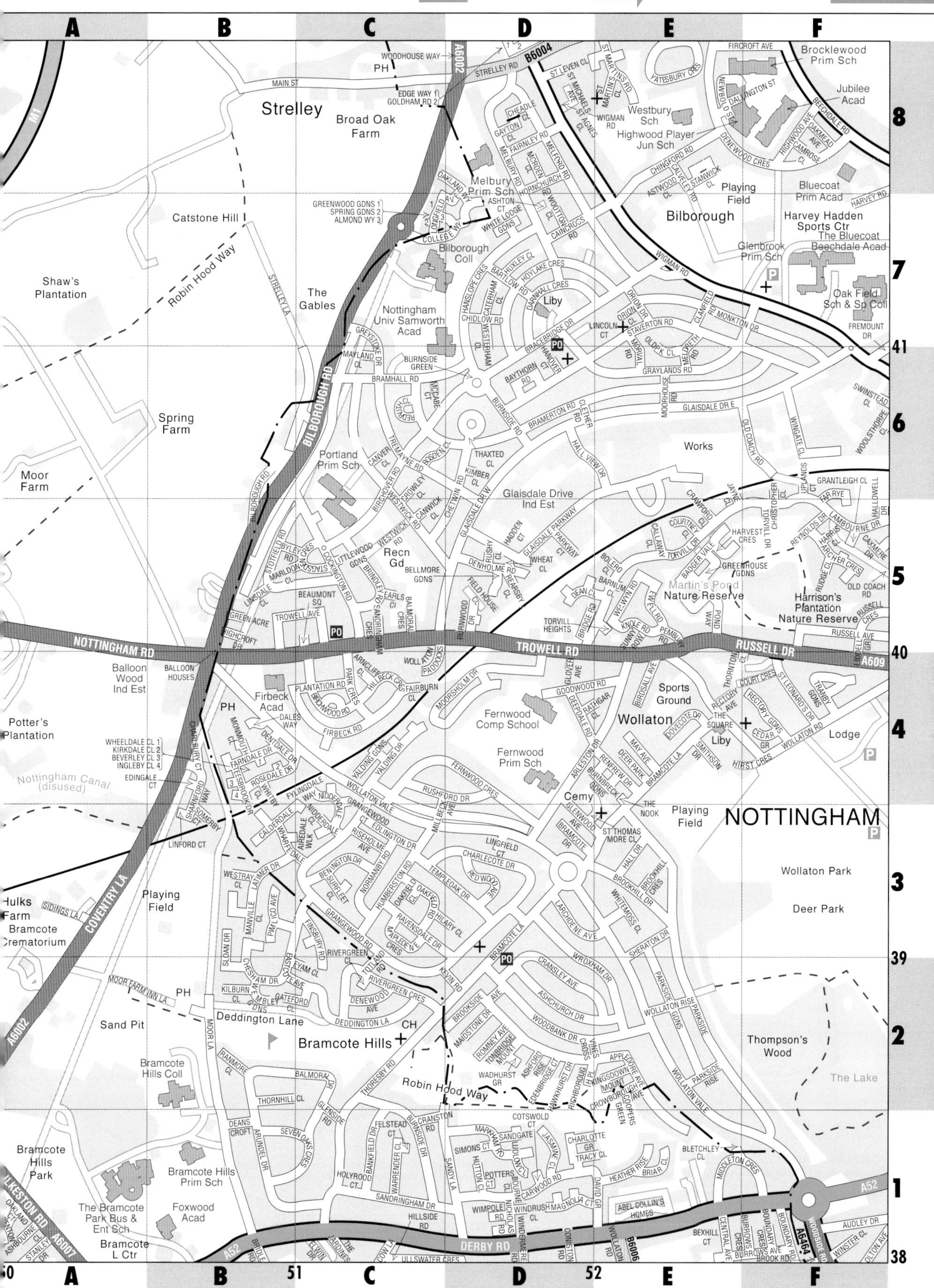
A
B
C
D
E
F
8
7
41
6
5
40
4
3
39
2
1
38
50
51
52
M1
A6002
B6004
Strelley
Broad Oak Farm
MAIN ST
WOODHOUSE WAY
EDGE WAY 1
GOLDHAM RD 2
STRELLEY RD
PH
Catstone Hill
Robin Hood Way
Shaw's Plantation
STRELLEY LA
The Gables
BILBOROUGH RD
Spring Farm
Moor Farm
Melbury Prim Sch
Bilborough Coll
Nottingham Univ Samworth Acad
GREENWOOD GDNS 1
SPRING GDNS 2
ALMOND WY 3
COLLEGE WY
OAKLAND AV
ASHTON CT
WHITE LODGE GDNS
GAYTON CL
CHEADLE CL
FAIRNLEY RD
MELBURY RD
MCRDEN CL
MELFORD RD
HORNCHURCH RD
WOOTTON CL
CAINCROSS RD
ST LEVEN CL
ST MICHAELS AVE
ST AGNES CL
ST MARTIN'S RD
WIGMAN RD
YATESBURY CRES
FIRCROFT AVE
Brocklewood Prim Sch
NEWBOLD ST
DALLINGTON ST
Jubilee Acad
BEECHDALE RD
Westbury Sch
Highwood Player Jun Sch
DENEWOOD CRES
HIGHWOOD AVE
OAKMEAD AVE
CAMROSE CL
CHINGFORD RD
ASTWOOD CL
CALVELEY RD
STANWICK CL
Playing Field
Bilborough
Bluecoat Prim Acad
HARVEY RD
Harvey Hadden Sports Ctr
The Bluecoat Beechdale Acad
Glenbrook Prim Sch
Oak Field Sch & Sp Coll
FREMOUNT DR
HUXLEY CL
HOYLAKE CRES
HANSLOPE CRES
BARTLOW RD
CATERHAM CL
DARNHALL CRES
Liby
CHIDLOW RD
WESTERHAM CL
BRACEBRIDGE DR
LINCOLN CT
ORION DR
ORION CL
STAVERTON RD
CLANFIELD RD
MONKTON DR
OLDPARK CL
MORVAL RD
MELDRETH RD
GRAYLANDS RD
PO
HANOVER CT
BAYTHORN RD
GREYSTONE DR
MAYLAND CL
BURNSIDE GREEN
BRAMHALL RD
MCCABE CT
BURNSIDE RD
BRAMERTON RD
CLETHER RD
MOORHOUSE RD
GLAISDALE DR E
OLD COACH RD
WINGATE CL
SWINSTEAD CL
WOOLSTHORPE CL
Works
HALL VIEW DR
THAXTED CL
KIMBER CL
Portland Prim Sch
CANVER CL
TREMAYNE RD
BOSDEN CL
BIRCHOVER RD
CROWLEY CL
CANWICK CL
WESTWICK RD
CHETWIN RD
GLAISDALE DR W
Glaisdale Drive Ind Est
HADDEN CT
GLAISDALE PARKWAY
CRAWFORD CL
JAYNE CL
CHRISTOPHER CL
UPLANDS CT
GRANTLEIGH CL
FAR RYE
HALLOWELL DR
COURTNEY CL
CALLAWAY CL
TORVILL DR
HARVEST CRES
REYNOLDS DR
LAMBOURNE DR
HARRIS CL
CAXMERE DR
ARCHER CRES
BADGER VALE
GREENHOUSE GDNS
RUDGE CL
OLD COACH RD
Martin's Pond Nature Reserve
Harrison's Plantation Nature Reserve
RUSSELL CRES
RUSSELL AVE
BILBOROUGH RD
STOTFIELD RD
BYLEY RD
MARLDON CL
STAGSDEN CRES
COCKINGTON RD
LITTLEWOOD GDNS
WESTWICK RD
Recn Gd
BELLMORE GDNS
RUSHY CL
DENHOLME RD
WHEAT CL
BOLERO CL
BARNUM CL
DEAN CL
WELWYN RD
EWELL RD
KNOLE RD
SUNNY ROW
PEMBURY RD
POND WAY
LINSDALE CL
BEAUMONT SQ
TROWELL AVE
EARLS CL
BALMORAL CRES
SANDRINGHAM CRES
BURNWOOD DR
FIELD HOUSE CL
KEARSBY CL
TORVILL HEIGHTS
BRIDGE RD
GREEN ACRE
HIGHCROFT
NOTTINGHAM RD
TROWELL RD
RUSSELL DR
A609
LIDDELL CL
Balloon Wood Ind Est
BALLOON HOUSES
Potter's Plantation
Firbeck Acad
ARNCLIFFE CL
PARK CRES
HILLBECK CRES
WOLLATON PADDOCKS
FAIRBURN CL
PLANTATION RD
BROADWOOD RD
DALES WAY
FIRBECK RD
MOORSHOLM DR
Fernwood Comp School
GLOVER AVE
GOODWOOD RD
DEEPDALE RD
RATHGAR CL
BIRDSALL AVE
Sports Ground
Wollaton
THORNTON CL
RECTORY AVE
COURT CRES
ST LEONARD'S DR
TRAMBY GDNS
RECTORY GDNS
CEDAR GR
DOVECOTE DR
THE SQUARE
HIRST CRES
WOLLATON RD
Lodge
WHEELDALE CL 1
KIRKDALE CL 2
BEVERLEY CL 3
INGLEBY CL 4
EDINGALE CT
CHARLBURY CT
MONMOUTH CL
DENTDALE DR
FARNDALE DR
ROSEDALE DR
TEESBROOK DR
WHITBY CL
Nottingham Canal (disused)
YALDING GDNS
YALDING DR
Fernwood Prim Sch
FERNWOOD CRES
RUSHFORD DR
MILLBECK AVE
MAY AVE
DEER PARK
BRAMCOTE LA
SMITHSON DR
ARLESTON DR
RENFREW DR
BURNBRECK GDNS
Cemy
THE NOOK
Playing Field
NOTTINGHAM
SHARNFORD WAY
SOMERBY CT
LINFORD CT
FYLINGDALE WAY
NIDDERDALE
CALDERDALE
AIREDALE WLK
WHARFEDALE
GRANGEWOOD RD
WOLLATON VALE
EDLINGTON DR
RISEHOLME AVE
LINGFIELD CT
CHARLECOTE DR
GLENWOOD AVE
BRAMCOTE DR
ST THOMAS MORE CL
HALL DR
BROOKHILL CRES
BROOKHILL DR
Wollaton Park
Deer Park
WESTRAY CL
LATIMER DR
MANVILLE CL
PIMLICO AVE
BENINGTON DR
SURFLEET CL
NORMANBY RD
HUMBERSTON RD
OAKFIELD CL
OAKFIELD RD
TEMPLEOAK DR
RED OAK AVE
HILARY CL
RAVENSDALE DR
MAPLEDENE CRES
WHITEMOSS CL
LARCHDENE AVE
WROXHAM DR
SHERATON DR
Playing Field
Hulks Farm
Bramcote Crematorium
SIDINGS LA
COVENTRY LA
SLOAN DR
FINSBURY RD
EASTCOTE AVE
EYAM CL
RIVERGREEN CL
TOTLAND RD
RIVERGREEN CRES
KEVIN RD
CRANSLEY AVE
ASHCHURCH DR
PARKSIDE GDNS
WOLLATON RISE
PARKSIDE
MOOR FARM INN LA
PH
CHESHAM DR
KILBURN CL
WEMBLEY GDNS
GATEFORD CL
DENEWOOD CRES
DEDDINGTON LA
Deddington Lane
CH
BROOKSIDE AVE
MAIDSTONE DR
ROMNEY AVE
TONBRIDGE MOUNT
WOODBANK DR
VINES CROSS
APPLEDORE AVE
Sand Pit
MOOR LA
Bramcote Hills
Thompson's Wood
The Lake
Bramcote Hills Coll
RANMORE CL
BALMORAL DR
THORNHILL CL
GLENSIDE RD
THORESBY RD
Robin Hood Way
WADHURST GR
ASHFORD RISE
EDENBRIDGE CT
HAWKHURST DR
RIGHBOROUG
KINGSDOWN MOUNT
CROWBOROUGH AVE
GREEN
COOPERS
WOLLATON VALE
PARKSIDE RISE
DEANS CROFT
ARUNDEL DR
SEVEN OAKS CRES
FELSTEAD CT
CRANSTON RD
BANKFIELD DR
BURNSIDE DR
COTSWOLD CT
MARKHAM RD
SANDGATE
SIMONS CT
HUTTON CL
LUDLOW CL
JASMINE CL
CHARLOTTE GR
TRACY CL
BLETCHLEY CT
MIDDLETON CRES
HEATHER RISE
BRIAR CL
A52
Bramcote Hills Park
Bramcote Hills Prim Sch
HOLYROOD CT
WARRENDER CL
SANDY LA
POTTERS CT
BOURNE CL
CARWOOD RD
DAVID GR
SANDRINGHAM DR
WIMPOLE RD
NICHOLAS RD
WINDRUSH CL
MAGNOLIA CT
ABEL COLLIN'S HOMES
ILKESTON RD
A6007
OAKLAND CT
ASHBOURNE CL
STANLEY DR
The Bramcote Park Bus & Ent Sch
Foxwood Acad
Bramcote L Ctr
BRIDLE RD
ELVIN DR
THE JARDINES
COW LA
HILLSIDE RD
ULLSWATER CRES
DERBY RD
WINDERMERE RD
CONISTON RD
WOLLATON RD
B6006
BEXHILL CT
CENTRAL AVE
BURROWS CRES
BOUNDARY CRES
BURROWS AVE
BROOK RD
BOUNDARY RD
A6464
WOODSIDE RD
AUDLEY DR
WINSTER CL
OLTON AVE

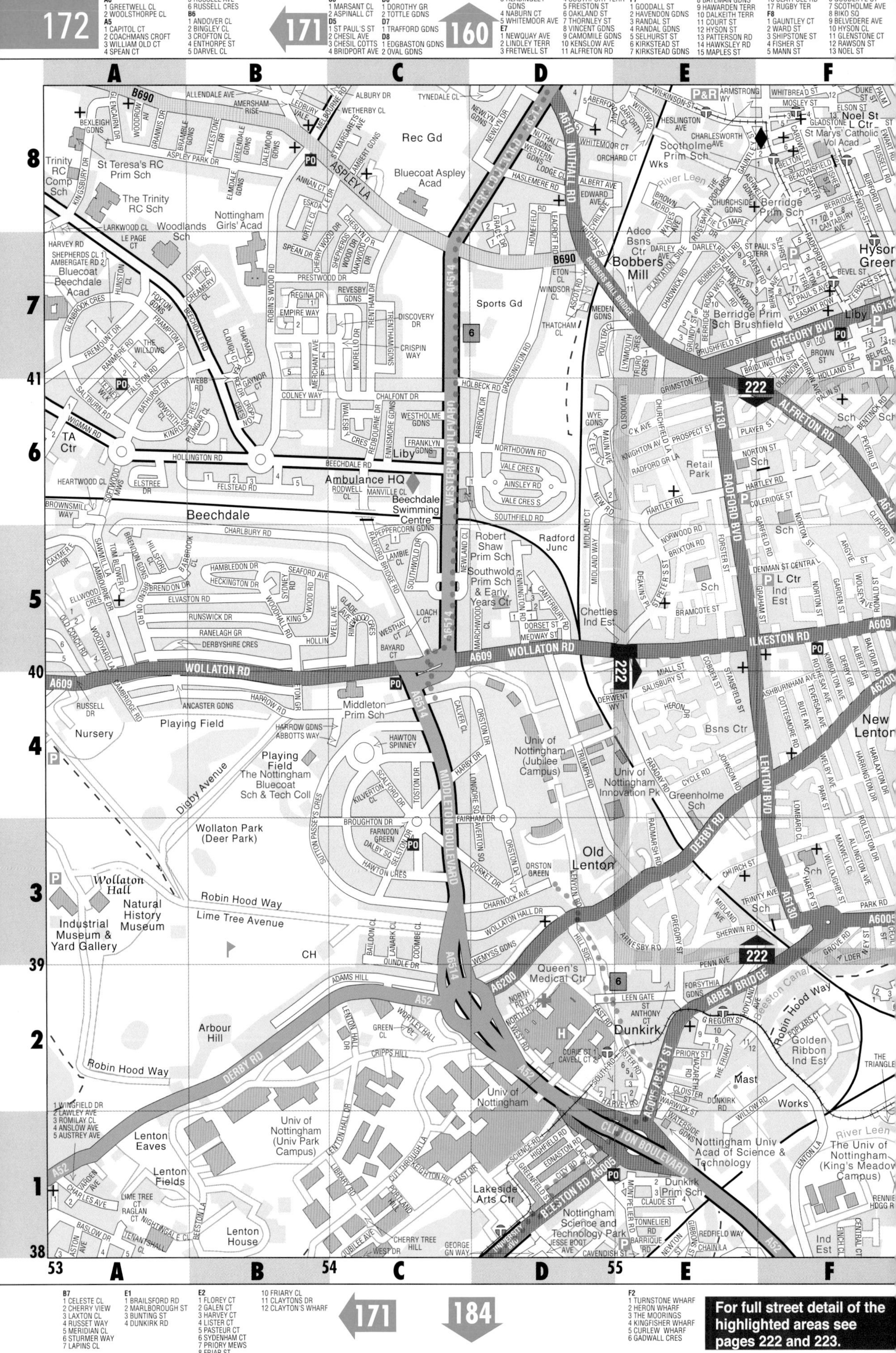
172
A6
1 GREETWELL CL
2 WOOLSTHORPE CL
A5
1 CAPITOL CT
2 COACHMANS CROFT
3 WILLIAM OLD CT
4 SPEAN CT
5 RUSSELL AVE
6 RUSSELL CRES
B6
1 ANDOVER CL
2 BINGLEY CL
3 CROFTON CL
4 ENTHORPE ST
5 DARVEL CL
171
C5
1 MARSANT CL
2 ASPINALL CT
D5
1 ST PAUL'S ST
2 CHESIL AVE
3 CHESIL COTTS
4 BRIDPORT AVE
D6
1 DOROTHY GR
2 TOTTLE GDNS
D7
1 TRAFFORD GDNS
D8
1 EDGBASTON GDNS
2 OVAL GDNS
160
3 HEADINGLEY GDNS
4 NABURN CT
5 WHITEMOOR AVE
E7
1 NEWQUAY AVE
2 LINDLEY TERR
3 FRETWELL ST
4 SOUTHPORT TERR
5 FREISTON ST
6 OAKLAND ST
7 THORNLEY ST
8 VINCENT GDNS
9 CAMOMILE GDNS
10 KENSLOW AVE
11 ALFRETON RD
F7
1 GOODALL ST
2 HAVENDON GDNS
3 RANDAL ST
4 RANDAL GDNS
5 SELHURST ST
6 KIRKSTEAD ST
7 KIRKSTEAD GDNS
8 BATEMAN GDNS
9 HAWARDEN TERR
10 DALKEITH TERR
11 COURT ST
12 HYSON ST
13 PATTERSON RD
14 HAWKSLEY RD
15 MAPLES ST
16 CLAYPOLE RD
17 RUGBY TER
F8
1 GAUNTLEY CT
2 WARD ST
3 SHIPSTONE ST
4 FISHER ST
5 MANN ST
6 GOODLIFFE ST
7 SCOTHOLME AVE
8 BIKO SQ
9 BELVEDERE AVE
10 HYSON CL
11 GLENSTONE CT
12 RAWSON ST
13 NOEL ST
A
B
C
D
E
F
8
7
41
6
5
40
4
3
39
2
1
38
53
54
55
St Teresa's RC Prim Sch
Trinity RC Comp Sch
The Trinity RC Sch
Nottingham Girls' Acad
Woodlands Sch
Bluecoat Beechdale Acad
Rec Gd
Bluecoat Aspley Acad
Sports Gd
Scotholme Prim Sch
Berridge Prim Sch
Bobbers Mill
Berridge Prim Sch Brushfield
St Marys' Catholic Vol Acad
Noel St L Ctr
Hyson Green
Beechdale
Ambulance HQ
Beechdale Swimming Centre
Robert Shaw Prim Sch
Southwold Prim Sch & Early Years Ctr
Radford Junc
Chettles Ind Est
Retail Park
222
WOLLATON RD
ILKESTON RD
Middleton Prim Sch
Playing Field
Nursery
Playing Field
The Nottingham Bluecoat Sch & Tech Coll
Univ of Nottingham (Jubilee Campus)
Univ of Nottingham Innovation Pk
Greenholme Sch
Bsns Ctr
New Lenton
Wollaton Park (Deer Park)
Wollaton Hall
Natural History Museum
Industrial Museum & Yard Gallery
Robin Hood Way
Lime Tree Avenue
Old Lenton
Queen's Medical Ctr
Dunkirk
Arbour Hill
Golden Ribbon Ind Est
Univ of Nottingham
Univ of Nottingham (Univ Park Campus)
Lenton Eaves
Lenton Fields
Lenton House
Lakeside Arts Ctr
Nottingham Science and Technology Park
Nottingham Univ Acad of Science & Technology
Dunkirk Prim Sch
The Univ of Nottingham (King's Meadow Campus)
Ind Est
1 WINGFIELD DR
2 LAWLEY AVE
3 ROMILAY CL
4 ONSLOW AVE
5 AUSTREY AVE
B7
1 CELESTE CL
2 CHERRY VIEW
3 LAXTON CL
4 RUSSET WAY
5 MERIDIAN CL
6 STURMER WAY
7 LAPINS CL
E1
1 BRAILSFORD RD
2 MARLBOROUGH ST
3 BUNTING ST
4 DUNKIRK RD
E2
1 FLOREY CT
2 GALEN CT
3 HARVEY CT
4 LISTER CT
5 PASTEUR CT
6 SYDENHAM CT
7 PRIORY MEWS
8 FRIAR ST
9 OLD CHURCH ST
10 FRIARY CL
11 CLAYTONS DR
12 CLAYTON'S WHARF
171
184
F2
1 TURNSTONE WHARF
2 HERON WHARF
3 THE MOORINGS
4 KINGFISHER WHARF
5 CURLEW WHARF
6 GADWALL CRES
For full street detail of the highlighted areas see pages 222 and 223.

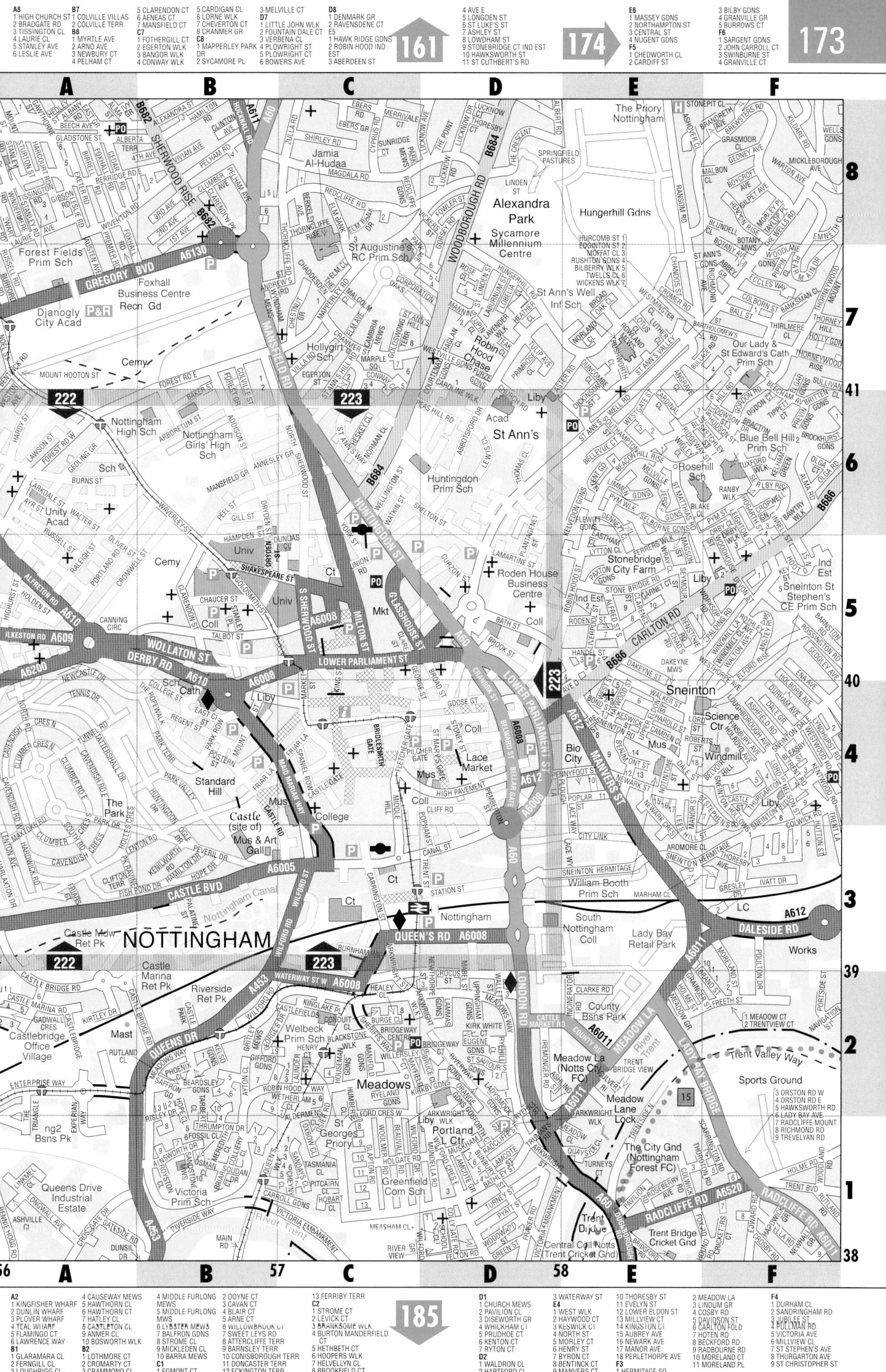
173
A8
1 HIGH CHURCH ST
2 BRADGATE RD
3 TISSINGTON CL
4 LAURIE CL
5 STANLEY AVE
6 LESLIE AVE
B7
1 COLVILLE VILLAS
2 COLVILLE TERR
B8
1 MYRTLE AVE
2 ARNO AVE
3 NEWBURY CT
4 PELHAM CT
5 CLARENDON CT
6 AENEAS CT
7 MANSFIELD CT
C7
1 FOTHERGILL CT
2 EGERTON WLK
3 BANGOR WLK
4 CONWAY WLK
5 CARDIGAN CL
6 LORNE WLK
7 CHEVERTON CT
8 CRANMER GR
C8
1 MAPPERLEY PARK DR
2 SYCAMORE PL
3 MELVILLE CT
D7
1 LITTLE JOHN WLK
2 FOUNTAIN DALE CT
3 VERBENA CL
4 PLOWRIGHT ST
5 PLOWRIGHT CT
6 BOWERS AVE
D8
1 DENMARK GR
2 RAVENSDENE CT
E5
1 HAWK RIDGE GDNS
2 ROBIN HOOD IND EST
3 ABERDEEN ST
161
4 AVE E
5 LONGDEN ST
6 ST LUKE'S ST
7 ASHLEY ST
8 LOWDHAM ST
9 STONEBRIDGE CT IND EST
10 HAWKSWORTH ST
11 ST CUTHBERT'S RD
174
E6
1 MASSEY GDNS
2 NORTHAMPTON ST
3 CENTRAL ST
4 NUGENT GDNS
F5
1 CHEDWORTH CL
2 CARDIFF ST
3 BILBY GDNS
4 GRANVILLE GR
5 BURROWS CT
F6
1 SARGENT GDNS
2 JOHN CARROLL CT
3 SWINBURNE ST
4 GRANVILLE CT
A
B
C
D
E
F
8
7
41
6
5
40
4
3
39
2
1
38
56
57
58
222
223
The Priory Nottingham
Jamia Al-Hudaa
Alexandra Park
Sycamore Millennium Centre
Hungerhill Gdns
Forest Fields Prim Sch
Foxhall Business Centre
Recn Gd
Djanogly City Acad
St Augustine's RC Prim Sch
St Ann's Well Inf Sch
Hollygirt Sch
Robin Hood Chase
Our Lady & St Edward's Cath Prim Sch
Nottingham High Sch
Nottingham Girls' High Sch
St Ann's
Huntingdon Prim Sch
Blue Bell Hill Prim Sch
Rosehill Sch
Unity Acad
Stonebridge City Farm
Roden House Business Centre
Sneinton St Stephen's CE Prim Sch
Univ
Mkt
Sneinton
Science Ctr
Windmill
Standard Hill
The Park
Castle (site of)
Mus & Art Gall
College
Lace Market
Bio City
William Booth Prim Sch
South Nottingham Coll
Lady Bay Retail Park
Nottingham
NOTTINGHAM
Castle Mdw Ret Pk
Castle Marina Ret Pk
Riverside Ret Pk
Castlebridge Office Village
Welbeck Prim Sch
Meadows
County Bsns Park
Meadow La (Notts Cty FC)
Meadow Lane Lock
Trent Valley Way
Sports Ground
St Georges Priory
Portland L Ctr
Greenfield Com Sch
ng2 Bsns Pk
Victoria Prim Sch
Queens Drive Industrial Estate
The City Gnd (Nottingham Forest FC)
Trent Bridge
Trent Bridge Cricket Gnd
Central Coll Notts (Trent Cricket Gnd)
River Trent
Nottingham Canal
Works
A2
1 KINGFISHER WHARF
2 DUNLIN WHARF
3 PLOVER WHARF
4 TEAL WHARF
5 FLAMINGO CT
6 LAWRENCE WAY
B1
1 GLARAMARA CL
2 FERNGILL CL
3 LOUGHRIGG CL
4 CAUSEWAY MEWS
5 HAWTHORN CL
6 HAWTHORN CT
7 HATLEY CL
8 CASTLETON CL
9 ANMER CL
10 BOSWORTH WLK
B2
1 LOTHMORE CT
2 CROMARTY CT
3 CRAMMOND CL
4 MIDDLE FURLONG MEWS
5 MIDDLE FURLONG MWS
6 LYBSTER MEWS
7 BALFRON GDNS
8 STROME CL
9 MICKLEDEN CL
10 BARRA MEWS
C1
1 EGMONT CT
2 DOYNE CT
3 CAVAN CT
4 BLAIR CT
5 ARNE CT
6 WILLOWBROOK CT
7 SWEET LEYS RD
8 ATTERCLIFFE TERR
9 BARNSLEY TERR
10 CONISBOROUGH TERR
11 DONCASTER TERR
12 ECKINGTON TERR
13 FERRIBY TERR
C2
1 STROME CT
2 LEVICK CT
3 BRANKSOME WLK
4 BURTON MANDERFIELD CT
5 HETHBETH CT
6 HOOPERS WLK
7 HELVELLYN CL
8 BROOKFIELD CT
185
D1
1 CHURCH MEWS
2 PAVILION CL
3 DISEWORTH GR
4 WHICKHAM CT
5 PRUDHOE CT
6 KENTON CT
7 RYTON CT
D2
1 WALDRON CL
2 HARTFORD CL
3 WATERWAY ST
E4
1 WEST WLK
2 HAYWOOD CT
3 KESWICK CT
4 NORTH ST
5 MORLEY CT
6 HENRY ST
7 BYRON CT
8 BENTINCK CT
9 MANVERS CT
10 THORESBY ST
11 EVELYN ST
12 LOWER ELDON ST
13 MILLVIEW CT
14 KINGSTON CT
15 AUBREY AVE
16 NEWARK AVE
17 MANOR AVE
18 PERLETHORPE AVE
F3
1 HERMITAGE SQ
2 MEADOW LA
3 LINDUM GR
4 COSBY RD
5 DAVIDSON ST
6 CARLTON FOLD
7 HOTEN RD
8 BECKFORD RD
9 RADBOURNE RD
10 MORELAND CT
11 MORELAND PL
F4
1 DURHAM CL
2 SANDRINGHAM RD
3 JUBILEE ST
4 PULLMAN RD
5 VICTORIA AVE
6 MILLVIEW CL
7 ST STEPHEN'S AVE
8 THURGARTON AVE
9 ST CHRISTOPHER ST

173
162

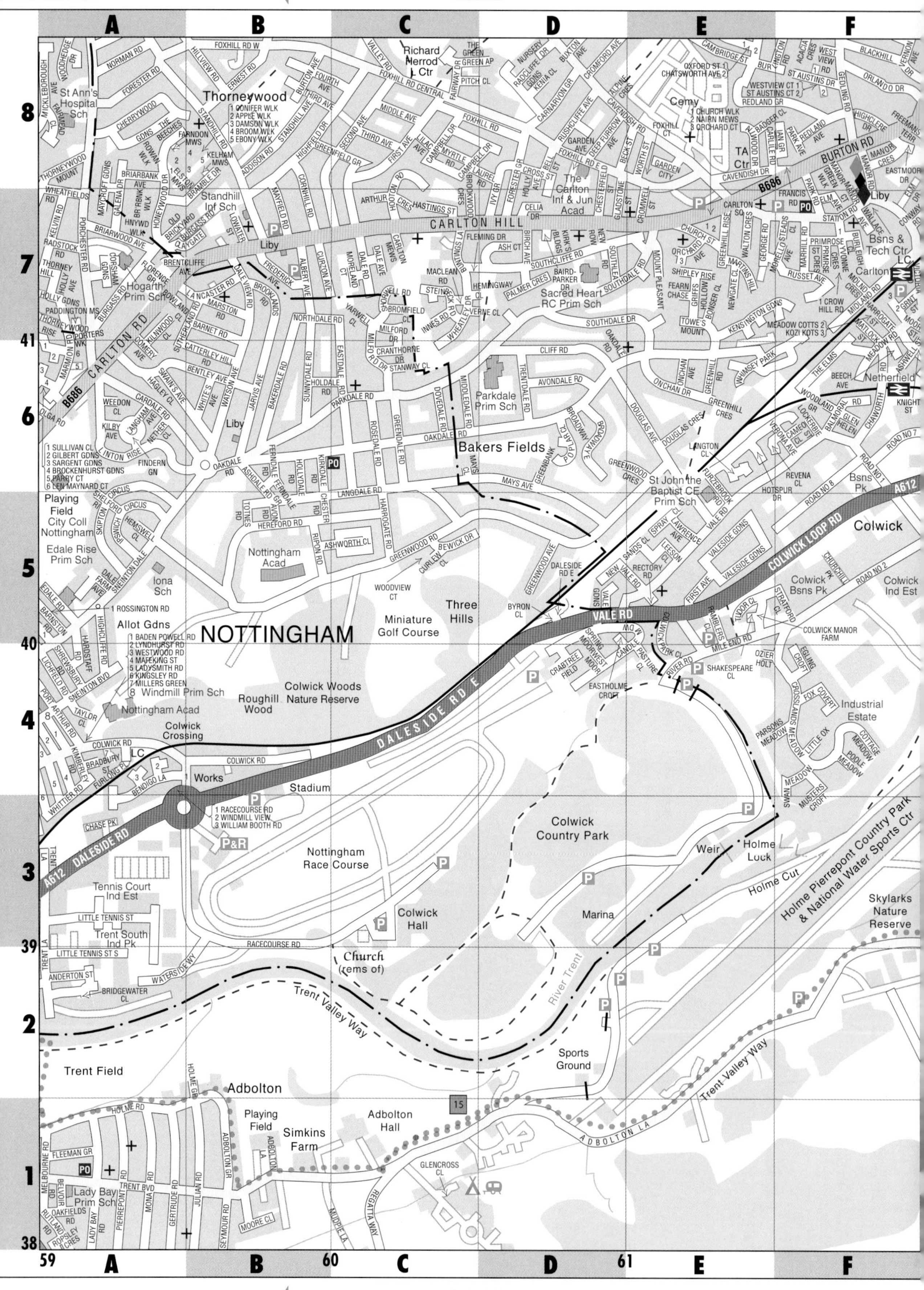
A
B
C
D
E
F
8
7
41
6
5
40
4
3
39
2
1
38
59
60
61
Thorneywood
St Ann's Hospital Sch
Richard Herrod L Ctr
Cemy
TA Ctr
Liby
Standhill Inf Sch
Hogarth Prim Sch
CARLTON HILL
CARLTON RD
BURTON RD
B686
The Carlton Inf & Jun Acad
Sacred Heart RC Prim Sch
Bsns & Tech Ctr
Carlton
Netherfield
Parkdale Prim Sch
Bakers Fields
St John the Baptist CE Prim Sch
Colwick
Playing Field
City Coll Nottingham
Edale Rise Prim Sch
Iona Sch
Nottingham Acad
Miniature Golf Course
Three Hills
Allot Gdns
NOTTINGHAM
Windmill Prim Sch
Nottingham Acad
Colwick Woods Nature Reserve
Roughill Wood
Colwick Crossing
Works
Stadium
DALESIDE RD E
DALESIDE RD
A612
COLWICK LOOP RD
VALE RD
Colwick Bsns Pk
Colwick Ind Est
Industrial Estate
Colwick Country Park
Nottingham Race Course
Tennis Court Ind Est
Trent South Ind Pk
Colwick Hall
Church (rems of)
Marina
Weir
Holme Lock
Holme Cut
Holme Pierrepont Country Park & National Water Sports Ctr
Skylarks Nature Reserve
River Trent
Trent Valley Way
Trent Field
Sports Ground
Adbolton
Playing Field
Simkins Farm
Adbolton Hall
ADBOLTON LA
Lady Bay Prim Sch
15

173
186

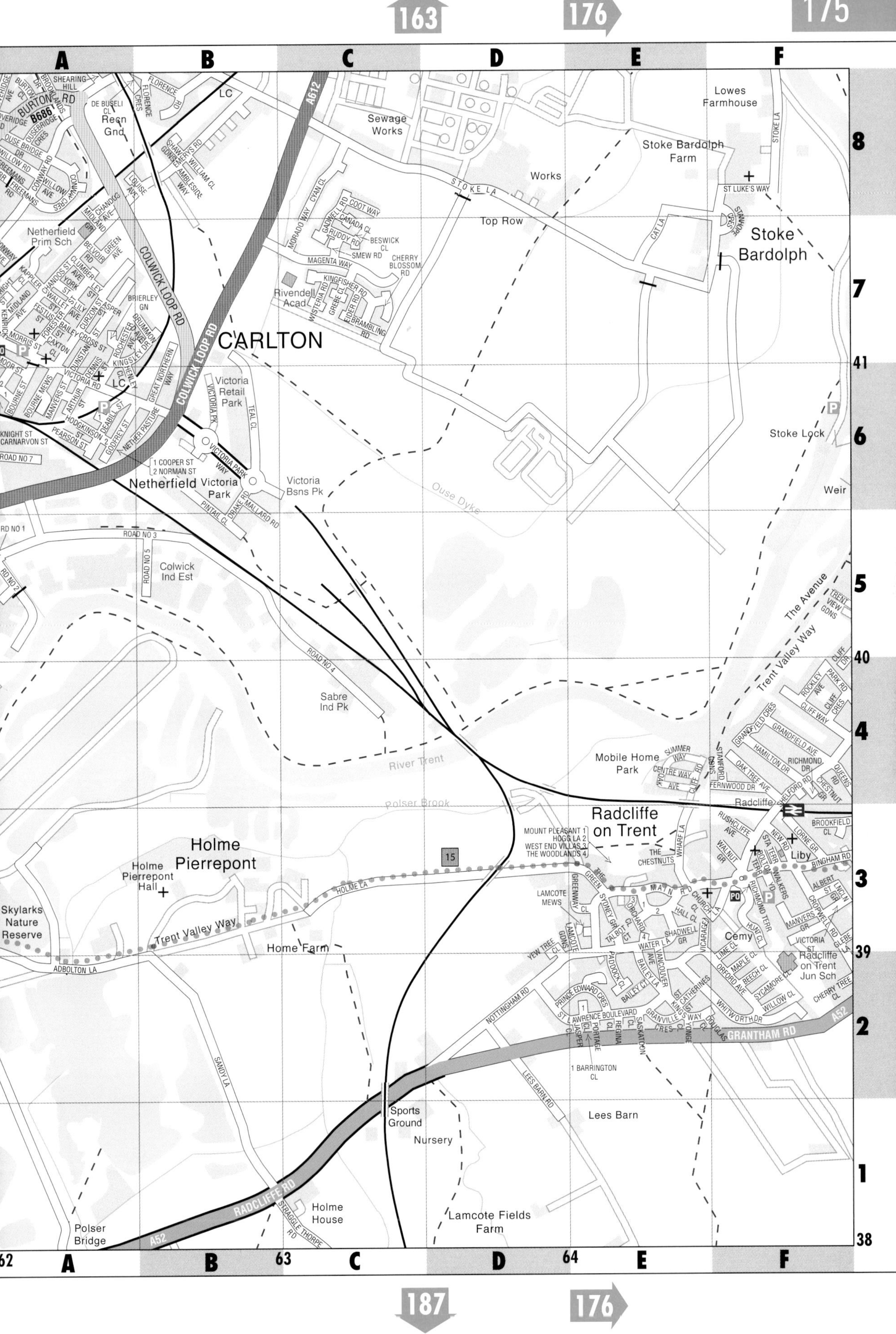
A
B
C
D
E
F
8
7
41
6
5
40
4
3
39
2
1
38
62
63
64
CARLTON
Netherfield
Victoria Park
Victoria Retail Park
Victoria Bsns Pk
Colwick Ind Est
Sabre Ind Pk
Sewage Works
Works
Top Row
Lowes Farmhouse
Stoke Bardolph Farm
Stoke Bardolph
Stoke Lock
Weir
Ouse Dyke
River Trent
Polser Brook
Mobile Home Park
Radcliffe on Trent
Radcliffe
Holme Pierrepont
Holme Pierrepont Hall
Skylarks Nature Reserve
Home Farm
Trent Valley Way
The Avenue
Sports Ground
Nursery
Lees Barn
Lamcote Fields Farm
Holme House
Polser Bridge
Netherfield Prim Sch
Rivendell Acad
Recn Gnd
Cemy
Liby
Radcliffe on Trent Jun Sch
COLWICK LOOP RD
A612
B686
BURTON RD
STOKE LA
HOLME LA
ADBOLTON LA
SANDY LA
RADCLIFFE RD
A52
GRANTHAM RD
NOTTINGHAM RD
LEES BARN RD
MAIN RD
ROAD NO 1
ROAD NO 2
ROAD NO 3
ROAD NO 4
ROAD NO 5
ROAD NO 7
KNIGHT ST
CARNARVON ST
1 COOPER ST
2 NORMAN ST
MOUNT PLEASANT 1
HOGG LA 2
WEST END VILLAS 3
THE WOODLANDS 4
1 BARRINGTON CL
LAWRENCE BOULEVARD
PRINCE EDWARD CRES
WHARF LA
THE CHESTNUTS
LAMCOTE MEWS
15
LC

175
164

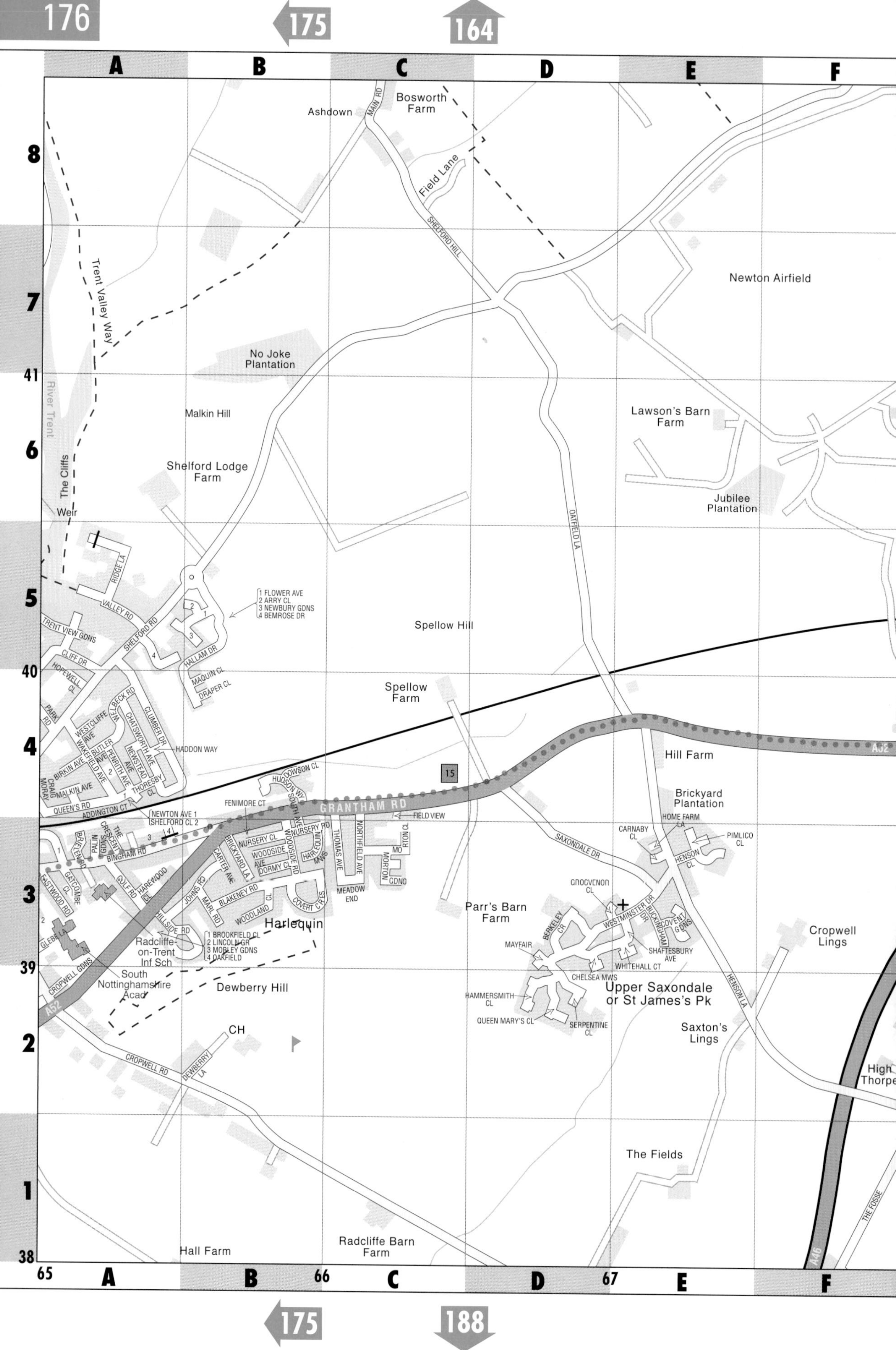
A
B
C
D
E
F
8
7
41
6
5
40
4
3
39
2
1
38
65
66
67
Ashdown
MAIN RD
Bosworth
Farm
Field Lane
SHELFORD HILL
Newton Airfield
Trent Valley Way
River Trent
No Joke
Plantation
Malkin Hill
Lawson's Barn
Farm
Shelford Lodge
Farm
The Cliffs
Weir
Jubilee
Plantation
OATFIELD LA
RIDGE LA
VALLEY RD
1 FLOWER AVE
2 ARRY CL
3 NEWBURY GDNS
4 BEMROSE DR
Spellow Hill
TRENT VIEW GDNS
SHELFORD RD
HALLAM DR
CLIFF DR
HOPEWELL CL
MAQUIN CL
DRAPER CL
Spellow
Farm
PARK RD
WESTCLIFFE AVE
CHATSWORTH AVE
CLUMBER DR
HADDON WAY
BUTLER AVE
PENRITH AVE
NEWSTEAD AVE
WAKEFIELD AVE
BIRKIN AVE
MALKIN AVE
CRAIG MORAY
THORESBY CL
QUEEN'S RD
ADDINGTON CT
NEWTON AVE 1
SHELFORD CL 2
FENIMORE CT
DOWSON CL
HUDSON WY
SOUTH AVE
GRANTHAM RD
FIELD VIEW
15
Hill Farm
A52
Brickyard
Plantation
HOME FARM LA
CARNABY CL
PIMLICO CL
HENSON CL
SAXONDALE DR
PALIN GDNS
THE CRESCENT
BINGHAM RD
NURSERY CL
NURSERY RD
WOODSIDE AVE
WOODSIDE RD
DORMY CL
BRICKYARD LA
CARTER AVE
HARLEQUIN MWS
THOMAS AVE
NORTHFIELD AVE
MORTON GDNS
MEADOW END
GATCOMBE CL
EASTWOOD RD
GULF RD
HAREWOOD CL
JOHNS RD
MARL RD
BLAKENEY RD
WOODLAND
COVERT CRES
Parr's Barn
Farm
GROSVENOR CL
WESTMINSTER DR
BUCKINGHAM DR
COVENT GDNS
BERKELEY CR
MAYFAIR
SHAFTESBURY AVE
WHITEHALL CT
CHELSEA MWS
Upper Saxondale
or St James's Pk
HAMMERSMITH CL
QUEEN MARY'S CL
SERPENTINE CL
Harlequin
HILLSIDE RD
1 BROOKFIELD CL
2 LINCOLN GR
3 MOBLEY GDNS
4 OAKFIELD
GLEBE LA
Radcliffe-
on-Trent
Inf Sch
South
Nottinghamshire
Acad
CROPWELL GDNS
Dewberry Hill
Cropwell
Lings
HENSON LA
Saxton's
Lings
CH
CROPWELL RD
DEWBERRY LA
High
Thorpe
The Fields
THE FOSSE
A46
Hall Farm
Radcliffe Barn
Farm

175
188

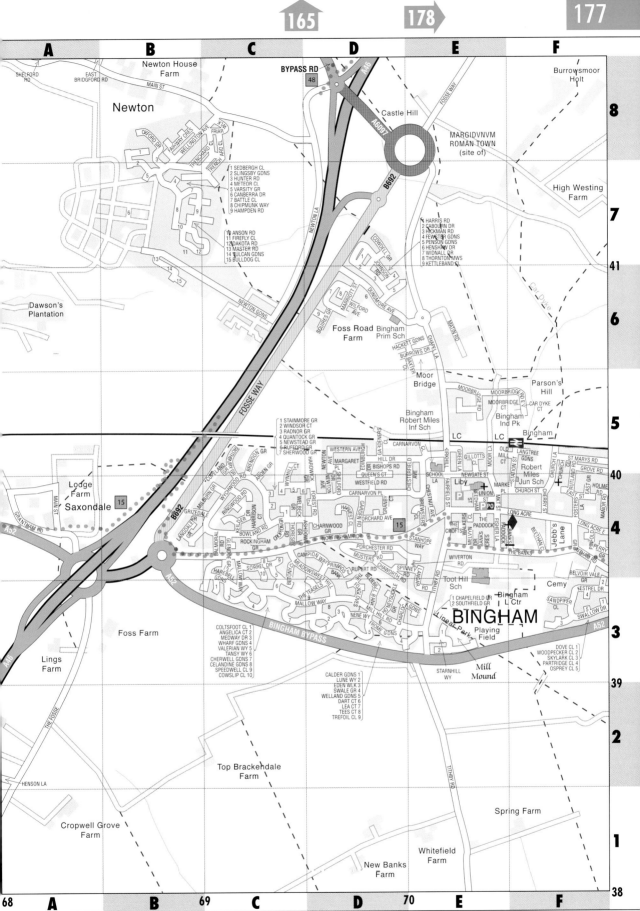

165
178

A B C D E F

Newton House Farm

Burrowsmoor Holt

Newton

Castle Hill

MARGIDVNVM ROMAN TOWN (site of)

High Westing Farm

1 SEDBERGH CL
2 SLINGSBY GDNS
3 HUNTER RD
4 METEOR CL
5 VARSITY GR
6 CANBERRA DR
7 BATTLE CL
8 CHIPMUNK WAY
9 HAMPDEN RD
10 ANSON RD
11 FIREFLY CL
12 DAKOTA RD
13 MASTER RD
14 VULCAN GDNS
15 BULLDOG CL

1 HARRIS RD
2 CABOURN DR
3 HICKMAN RD
4 FEWSTER GDNS
5 PENSON GDNS
6 HENSHAW DR
7 WIDNALL DR
8 THORNTON MWS
9 KETTLEBAND CL

Dawson's Plantation

Foss Road Farm

Bingham Prim Sch

Moor Bridge

Parson's Hill

Bingham Robert Miles Inf Sch

Bingham Ind Pk

1 STAINMORE GR
2 WINDSOR CT
3 RADNOR GR
4 QUANTOCK GR
5 NEWSTEAD GR
6 RUFFORD GR
7 SHERWOOD GR

Lodge Farm

Saxondale

Liby

Robert Miles Jun Sch

Toot Hill Sch

Cemy

1 CHAPELFIELD GR
2 SOUTHFIELD GR

Bingham L Ctr

BINGHAM

Playing Field

Foss Farm

Lings Farm

COLTSFOOT CL 1
ANGELICA CL 2
MEDWAY DR 3
WHARF GDNS 4
VALERIAN WY 5
TANSY WY 6
CHERWELL GDNS 7
CELANDINE GDNS 8
SPEEDWELL CL 9
COWSLIP CL 10

CALDER GDNS 1
LUNE WY 2
EDEN WLK 3
SWALE GR 4
WELLAND GDNS 5
DART CT 6
LEA CT 7
TEES CT 8
TREFOIL CL 9

DOVE CL 1
WOODPECKER CL 2
SKYLARK CL 3
PARTRIDGE CL 4
OSPREY CL 5

Mill Mound

Top Brackendale Farm

Spring Farm

Cropwell Grove Farm

Whitefield Farm

New Banks Farm

68 A B 69 C D 70 E F

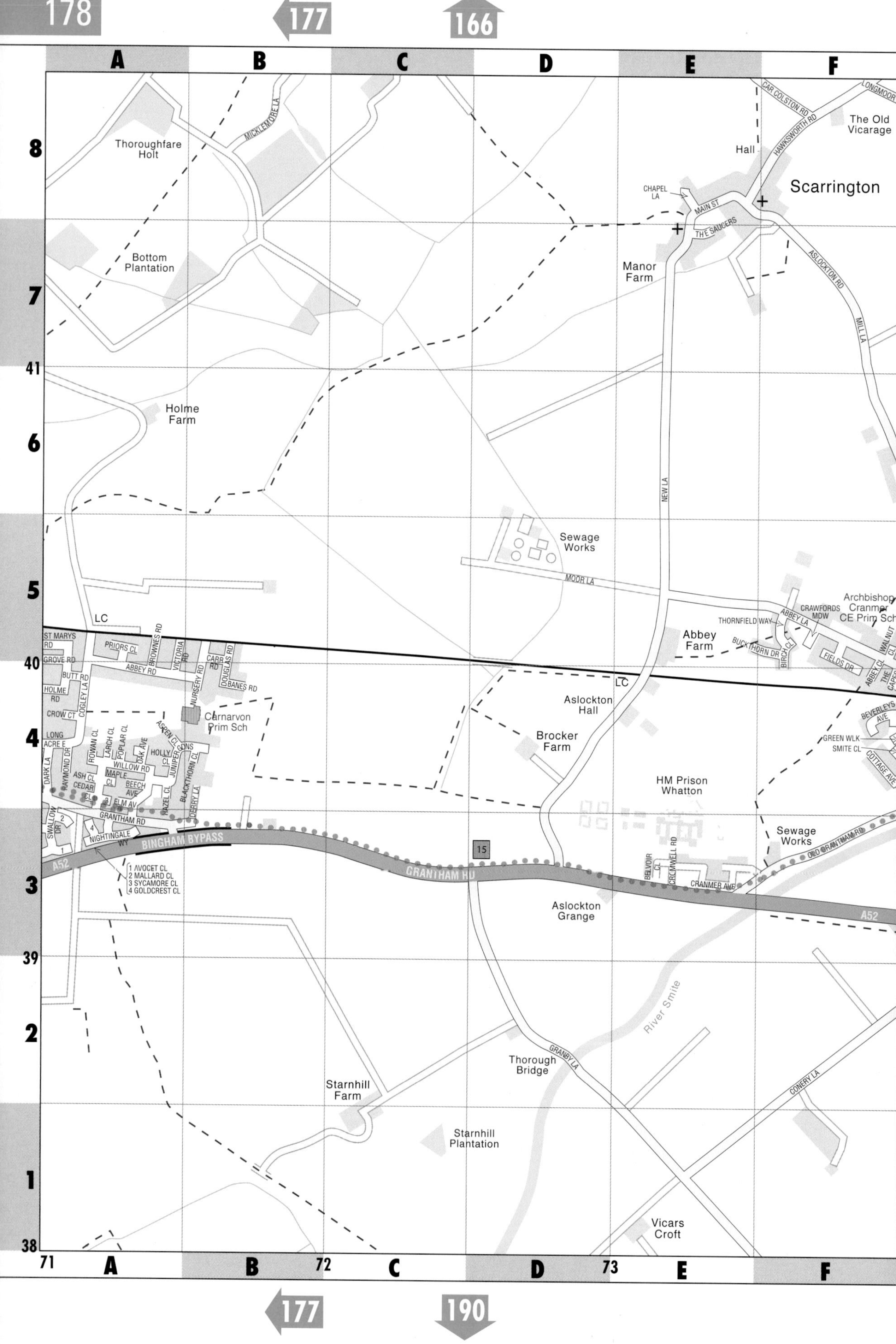

A B C D E F

8 Thoroughfare Holt

Hall

CAR COLSTON RD LONGMOOR L

The Old Vicarage

HAWKSWORTH RD

Scarrington

Bottom Plantation

CHAPEL LA

MAIN ST

THE SAUCERS

7 Manor Farm

ASLOCKTON RD

MILL LA

41

6 Holme Farm

NEW LA

5 Sewage Works

MOOR LA

Archbishop Cranmer CE Prim Sch

CRAWFORDS MDW

LC

ABBEY LA

THORNFIELD WAY

40 ST MARYS RD GROVE RD PRIORS CL BROWNES RD VICTORIA RD CARR RD DOUGLAS RD

BUTT RD ABBEY RD BANES RD

HOLME RD COGLEY LA NURSERY RD

CROW CT

Carnarvon Prim Sch

Abbey Farm

BUCKTHORN DR BIRCH CL

FIELDS DR ABBEY CL THE CAPES WALNUT

LC

BEVERLEYS AVE

4 LONG ACRE E RAYMOND DR ROWAN CL LARCH CL POPLAR CL ASPEN CL OAK AVE HOLLY CL JUNIPER CL BLACKTHORN CL

DARK LA ASH CL CEDAR CL WILLOW RD MAPLE CL BEECH AVE HAZEL CL DERRY LA

Aslockton Hall

Brocker Farm

HM Prison Whatton

GREEN WLK SMITE CL COTTAGE AVE

Sewage Works

SWALLOW DR ELM AV NIGHTINGALE WY GRANTHAM RD

1 AVOCET CL
2 MALLARD CL
3 SYCAMORE CL
4 GOLDCREST CL

BINGHAM BYPASS

15

GRANTHAM RD

BELVOIR CROMWELL RD CRANMER AVE OLD GRANTHAM RD

3 A52 A52

Aslockton Grange

39

River Smite

2 GRANBY LA

Thorough Bridge

Starnhill Farm

CONERY LA

Starnhill Plantation

1 Vicars Croft

38

167
180

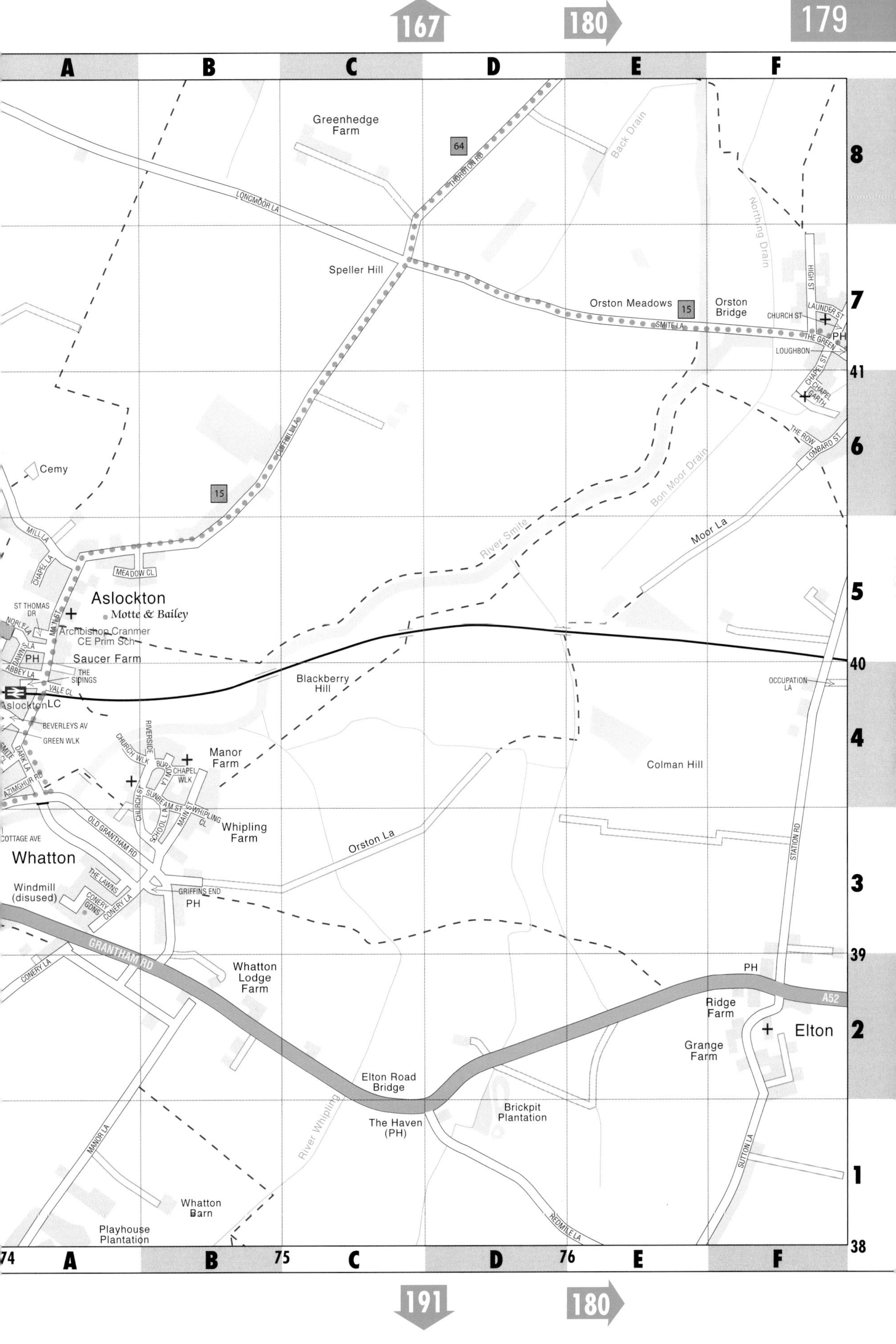
A
B
C
D
E
F
Greenhedge Farm
64
THOROTON RD
Back Drain
LONGMOOR LA
Northing Drain
Speller Hill
HIGH ST
Orston Meadows
15
Orston Bridge
LAUNDER ST
CHURCH ST
SMITE LA
THE GREEN
PH
LOUGHBON
CHAPEL ST
CHAPEL GARTH
THE ROW
LOMBARD ST
CLIFF HILL LA
Bon Moor Drain
Cemy
15
River Smite
MILL LA
Moor La
CHAPEL LA
MEADOW CL
Aslockton
ST THOMAS DR
Motte & Bailey
NORLEA LA
MAIN ST
Archbishop Cranmer CE Prim Sch
DAWN'S LA
PH
Saucer Farm
ABBEY LA
THE SIDINGS
VALE CL
Blackberry Hill
OCCUPATION LA
Aslockton
LC
BEVERLEYS AV
GREEN WLK
RIVERSIDE
CHURCH WLK
Manor Farm
DARK LA
SMITE
BURGH LA
CHAPEL WLK
Colman Hill
AZIMGHUR RD
SUNBEAM ST
CHURCH ST
SCHOOL LA
MAIN ST
WHIPLING CL
Whipling Farm
OLD GRANTHAM RD
COTTAGE AVE
Whatton
Orston La
STATION RD
THE LAWNS
Windmill (disused)
CONERY GDNS
CONERY LA
GRIFFINS END
PH
GRANTHAM RD
CONERY LA
Whatton Lodge Farm
PH
Ridge Farm
A52
Elton
Grange Farm
Elton Road Bridge
The Haven (PH)
Brickpit Plantation
River Whipling
MANOR LA
SUTTON LA
Whatton Barn
Playhouse Plantation
HEDMILE LA
8
7
41
6
5
40
4
3
39
2
1
38
74
75
76

191
180

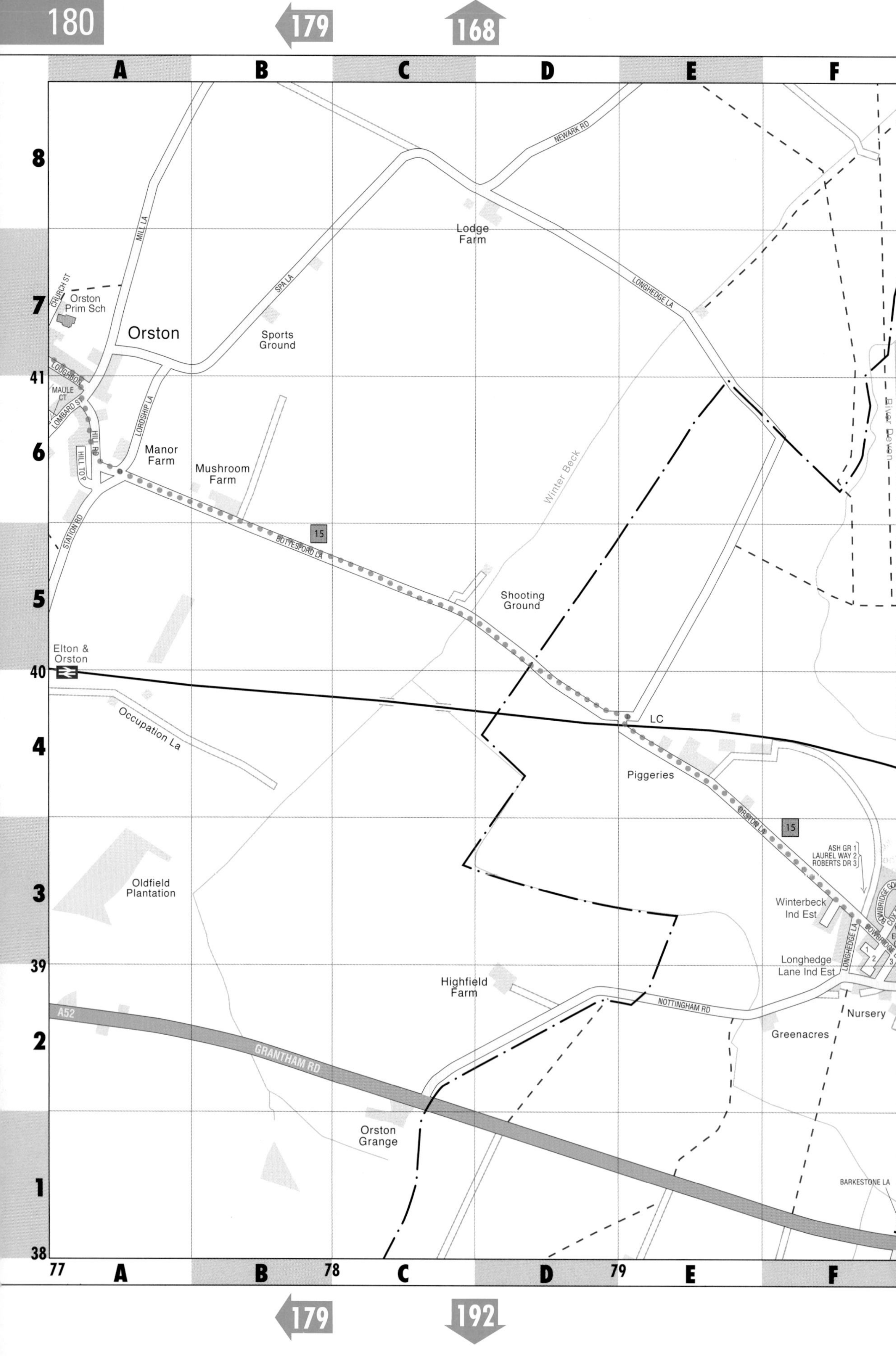

A B C D E F

8

NEWARK RD

Lodge
Farm

LONGHEDGE LA

7

CHURCH ST

Orston
Prim Sch

Orston

MILL LA

SPA LA

Sports
Ground

41

LONGHO

MAULE
CT

LOMBARD ST

LORDSHIP LA

HILL RD

6

HILL TOP

Manor
Farm

Mushroom
Farm

STATION RD

Winter Beck

BOTTESFORD LA

15

5

Shooting
Ground

Elton &
Orston

40

Occupation La

LC

Piggeries

ORSTON LA

15

ASH GR 1
LAUREL WAY 2
ROBERTS DR 3

4

Winterbeck
Ind Est

SCRIMSHIRE

3

Oldfield
Plantation

Longhedge
Lane Ind Est

LONGHEDGE LA

Nursery

39

Highfield
Farm

NOTTINGHAM RD

Greenacres

A52

2

GRANTHAM RD

Orston
Grange

BARKESTONE LA

1

38

77

A

B

78

C

D

79

E

F

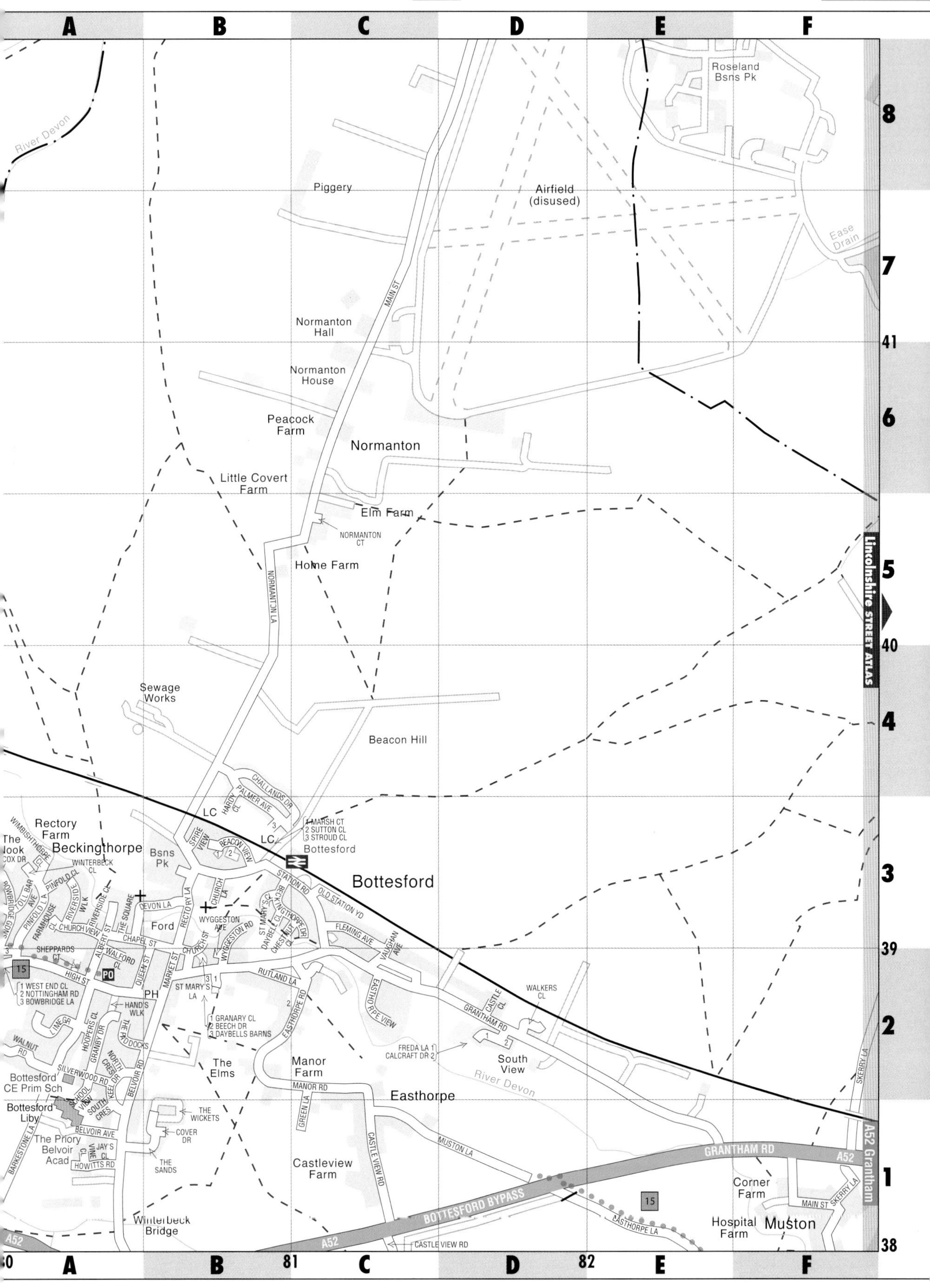

Roseland Bsns Pk

Ease Drain

Piggery

Airfield (disused)

Normanton Hall

Normanton House

Peacock Farm

Normanton

Little Covert Farm

Elm Farm

NORMANTON CT

Home Farm

Lincolnshire STREET ATLAS

Sewage Works

Beacon Hill

CHALLANDS DR

PALMER AVE

HARDYS CL

LC

SPIRE VIEW

BEACON VIEW

LC

1 MARSH CT
2 SUTTON CL
3 STROUD CL
Bottesford

Rectory Farm

Beckingthorpe

Bsns Pk

WINTERBECK CL

WIMBISHTHORPE

The Nook

COX DR

RIVERSIDE CL

PINFOLD CL

PINFOLD AVE

CHURCH VIEW

FARMHOUSE CL

ALBERT ST

THE SQUARE

DEVON LA

CHURCH ST

WYGGESTON AVE

Ford

CHURCH LA

RECTORY LA

STATION RD

KINGTHORPE ST

DAYBELL CL

CHESTNUT CL

ST MARY'S

OLD STATION YD

Bottesford

FLEMING AVE

WALTHAM AVE

WALKERS CL

SHEPPARDS

WALFORD CL

HIGH ST

PO

PH

MARKET ST

QUEEN ST

ST MARY'S LA

CHAPEL ST

RUTLAND LA

EASTHORPE RD

GREEN LA

RODE VIEW

GRANTHAM RD

CASTLE CL

1 WEST END CL
2 NOTTINGHAM RD
3 BOWBRIDGE LA

15

WALNUT RD

LIME GR

GRANBYS CL

NORMAN CRES

BELVOIR RD

HAND'S WLK

THE DOCKS

1 GRANARY CL
2 BEECH DR
3 DAYBELLS BARNS

The Elms

Manor Farm

1 FREDA LA
CALCRAFT DR 2

South View

Bottesford CE Prim Sch

Bottesford Liby

The Priory Belvoir Acad

BARKESTONE LA

HOWITTS RD

SCHOOL LA

SOUTH CRES

SILVERWOOD CL

BELVOIR AVE

JAY'S VINE CL

THE WICKETS

COVER DR

THE SANDS

MANOR RD

Easthorpe

River Devon

Castleview Farm

Winterbeck Bridge

BOTTESFORD BYPASS

A52

CASTLE VIEW RD

MUSTON LA

CASTLE VIEW RD

EASTHORPE LA

15

GRANTHAM RD

A52 Grantham

SKERRY LA

Corner Farm

MAIN ST

Hospital Farm

Muston

A52

A5
1 FRIESLAND DR
2 PAIGE GDNS
C6
1 BROOKFIELD MWS
2 BRAMBLE CT

E8
1 MACKINLEY AVE
2 SHERWIN RD
F8
1 PLACKETT CL
2 PARKER GDNS

170

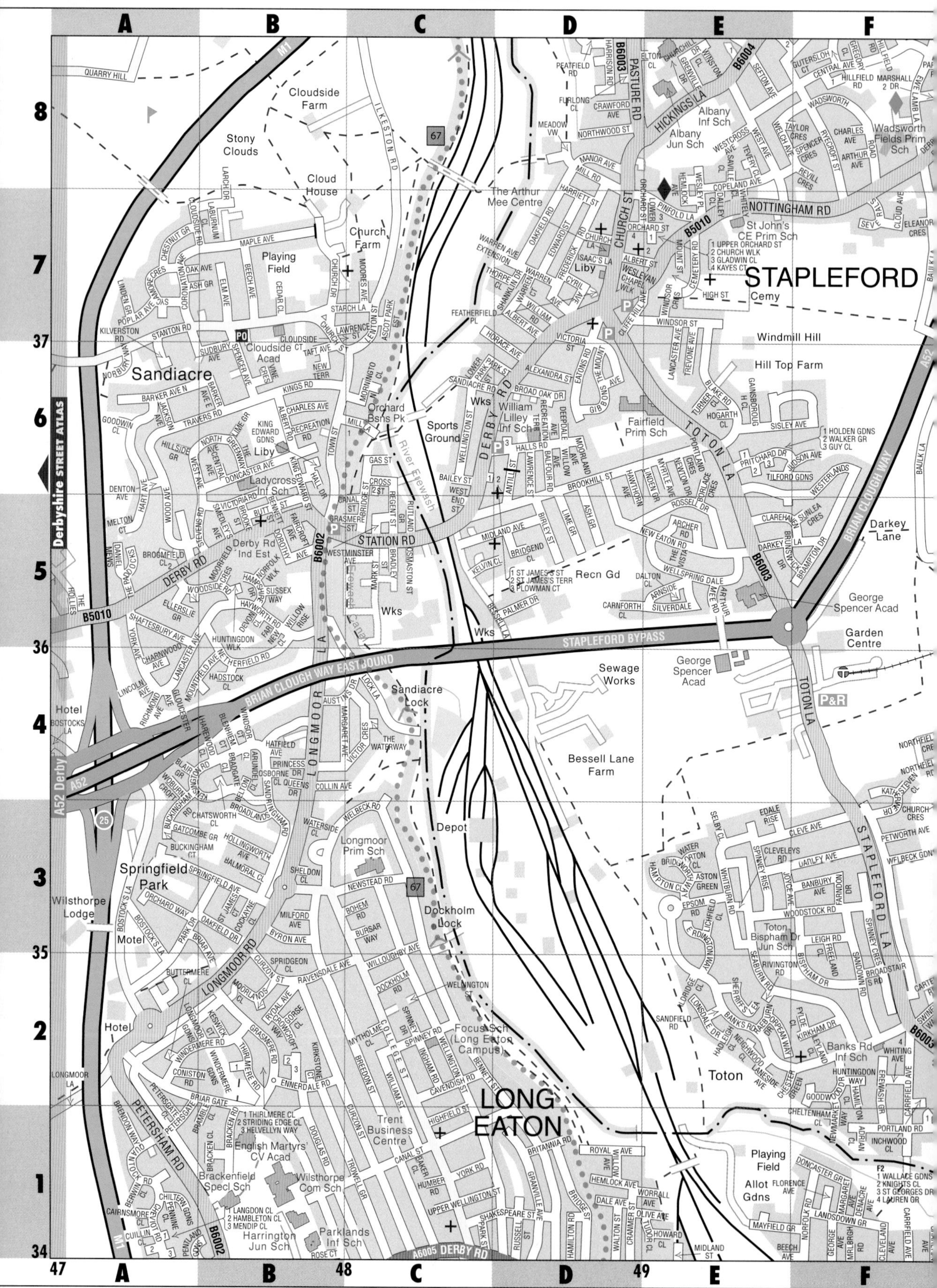

193

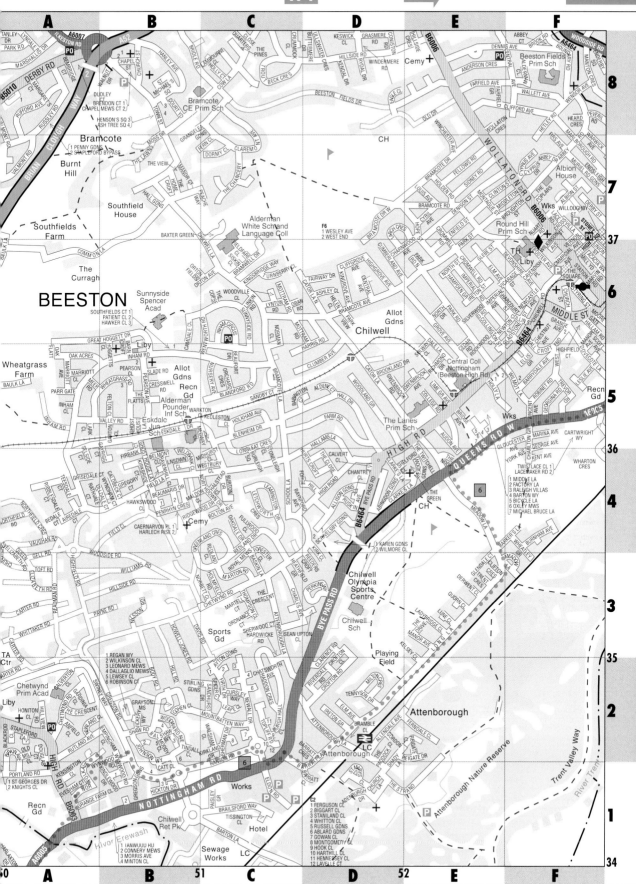

171
184

A B C D E F

8 7 37 6 5 36 4 3 35 2 1 34

BEESTON

Bramcote
Burnt Hill
Southfield House
Southfields Farm
The Curragh
Wheatgrass Farm
Bramcote CE Prim Sch
Alderman White Sch and Language Coll
Sunnyside Spencer Acad
Alderman Pounder Inf Sch
Eskdale Jun Sch
Allot Gdns
Recn Gd
Chilwell
Central Coll Nottingham (Beeston High Rd)
The Lanes Prim Sch
Beeston Fields Prim Sch
Albion House
Round Hill Prim Sch
TH
Liby
Wks
The Square
Chilwell Olympia Sports Centre
Chilwell Sch
Playing Field
Sports Gd
Chetwynd Prim Acad
Attenborough
Attenborough Nature Reserve
Trent Valley Way
River Trent
Works
Chilwell Ret Pk
Hotel
Sewage Works
Hivor Erewash
Cemy
CH
LC

HIGH RD
QUEENS RD W
NOTTINGHAM RD
BYE PASS RD
WOLLATON RD
MIDDLE ST
BRIAN CLOUGH WAY
DERBY RD

1 DUDLEY CT
BRENDON CT 1
CHAPEL MEWS CT 2
HENSON'S SQ 3
ASH TREE SQ 4
1 PENNY GDNS
2 STAPLEFORD BYPASS

F6
1 WESLEY AVE
2 WEST END

SOUTHFIELDS CT 1
PATIENT CL 2
HAWKER CL 3

CAERNARVON PL 1
HARLECH RISE 2

1 KAREN GDNS
2 WILMORE CL

TWISTLACE CL 1
LACEMAKER RD 2

1 MIDDLE LA
2 FACTORY LA
3 RALEIGH VILLAS
4 BARTON WY
5 BICYCLE LA
6 OXLEY MWS
7 MICHAEL BRUCE LA

1 REGAN WY
2 WILKINSON CL
3 LEONARD MEWS
4 DALLAGLIO MEWS
5 LEWSEY CL
6 ROBINSON CT

1 ST GEORGES DR
2 KNIGHTS CL

1 IANWOOD RD
2 CONNERY MEWS
3 MORRIS AVE
4 MINTON CL

C2
1 FERGUSON CL
2 BIGGART CL
3 STANILAND CL
4 WHITTON CL
5 RUSSELL GDNS
6 ABLARD GDNS
7 GOWAN CL
8 MONTGOMERY CL
9 HOOK CL
10 HARTHILL CL
11 HENNESSEY CL
12 LAVELLE CT

50 A B 51 C D 52 E F

194
184

183
172

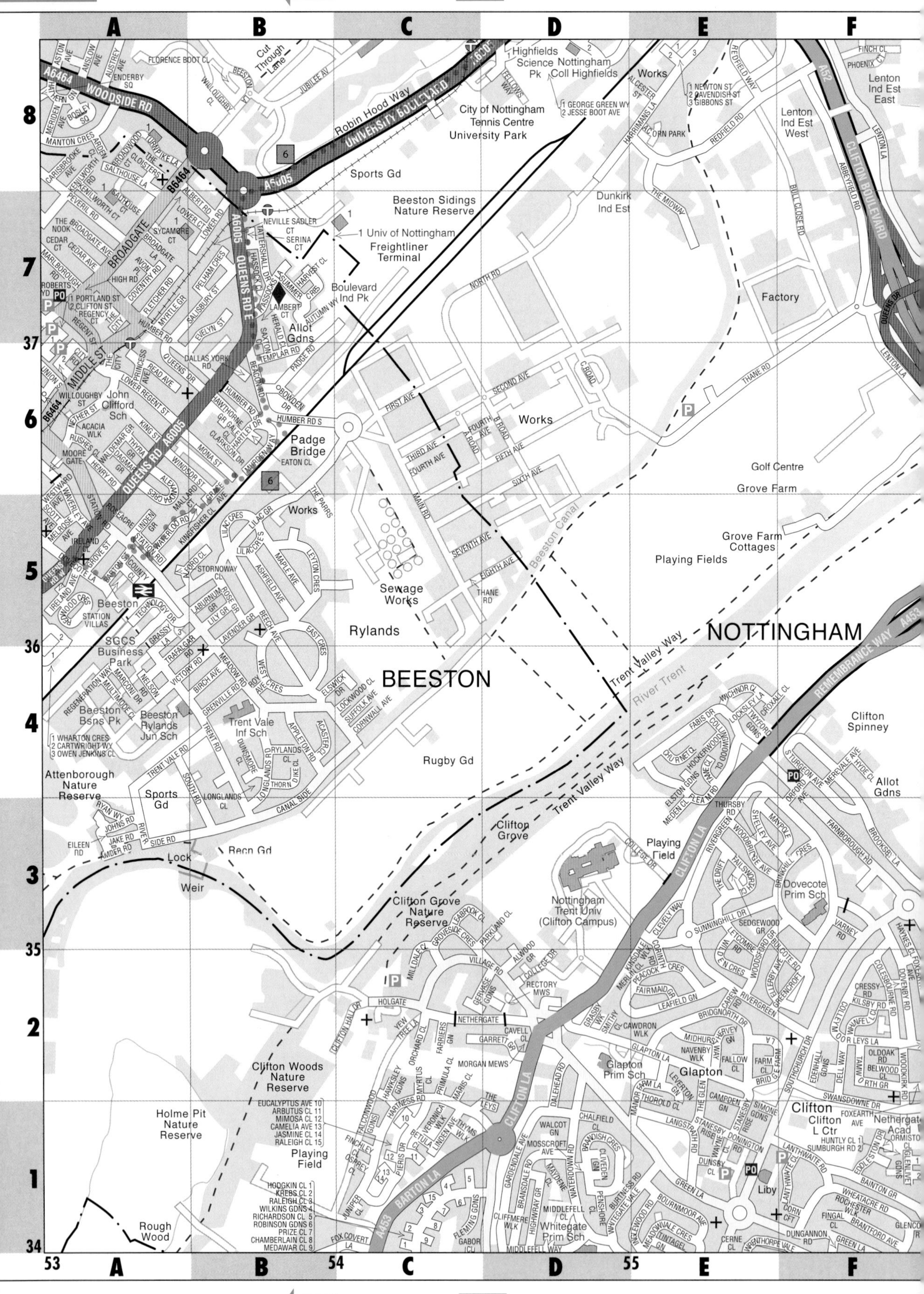
A B C D E F
BEESTON
NOTTINGHAM
WOODSIDE RD
UNIVERSITY BOULEVARD
Robin Hood Way
QUEENS RD E
QUEENS RD
BROADGATE
MIDDLE ST
CLIFTON BOULEVARD
REMEMBRANCE WAY
CLIFTON LA
BARTON LA
Highfields Science Pk
Nottingham Coll Highfields
City of Nottingham Tennis Centre
University Park
Sports Gd
Beeston Sidings Nature Reserve
Univ of Nottingham
Freightliner Terminal
Boulevard Ind Pk
Allot Gdns
Dunkirk Ind Est
Lenton Ind Est East
Lenton Ind Est West
Factory
Works
John Clifford Sch
Padge Bridge
Sewage Works
Rylands
Beeston
SGCS Business Park
Beeston Bsns Pk
Beeston Rylands Jun Sch
Trent Vale Inf Sch
Rugby Gd
Golf Centre
Grove Farm
Grove Farm Cottages
Playing Fields
Beeston Canal
Trent Valley Way
River Trent
Clifton Spinney
Allot Gdns
Attenborough Nature Reserve
Sports Gd
Lock
Weir
Recn Gd
Clifton Grove
Playing Field
Nottingham Trent Univ (Clifton Campus)
Clifton Grove Nature Reserve
Dovecote Prim Sch
Clifton Woods Nature Reserve
Holme Pit Nature Reserve
Playing Field
Glapton Prim Sch
Glapton
Clifton
Clifton L Ctr
Liby
Whitegate Prim Sch
Rough Wood
8 7 6 5 4 3 2 1
37 36 35 34
53 54 55

173

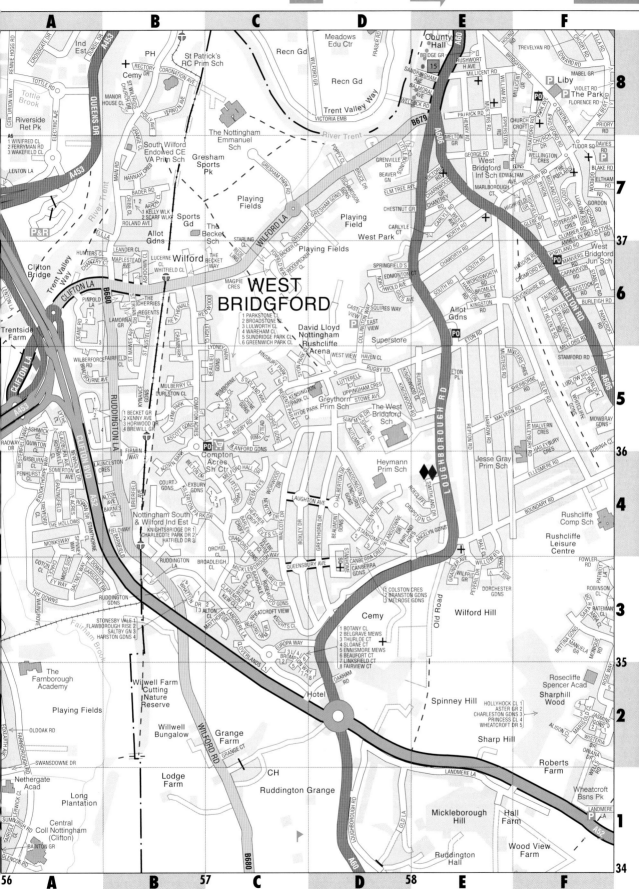

A B C D E F

8 7 6 5 4 3 2 1

37 36 35 34

WEST BRIDGFORD

Meadows Edu Ctr
County Hall
Recn Gd
Trent Valley Way
Victoria Emb
River Trent
Ind Est
Queens Dr
A453
PH
Cemy
St Patrick's RC Prim Sch
Tottle Brook
Riverside Ret Pk
Lenton La
Manor House Cl
The Nottingham Emmanuel Sch
South Wilford Endowed CE VA Prim Sch
Gresham Sports Pk
Playing Fields
Sports Gd
The Becket Sch
Allot Gdns
Wilford
Wilford La
Clifton Bridge
Clifton La
Trentside Farm
P&R
Playing Field
West Park
Playing Fields
Liby
The Park
West Bridgford Inf Sch
West Bridgford Jun Sch
Melton Rd
A606
A60
B679
Loughborough Rd
David Lloyd Nottingham Rushcliffe Arena
Superstore
Allot Gdns
Greythorn Prim Sch
The West Bridgford Sch
Heymann Prim Sch
Jesse Gray Prim Sch
Compton Acres Sh Ctr
Ruddington La
Clifton Bvd
A52
B680
Nottingham South & Wilford Ind Est
Rushcliffe Comp Sch
Rushcliffe Leisure Centre
Wilford Hill
Cemy
Old Road
Rosecliffe Spencer Acad
Sharphill Wood
Spinney Hill
Sharp Hill
Roberts Farm
Wheatcroft Bsns Pk
The Farnborough Academy
Playing Fields
Wilwell Farm Cutting Nature Reserve
Willwell Bungalow
Grange Farm
Wilford Rd
Hotel
Fairham Brook
Nethergate Acad
Long Plantation
Central Coll Nottingham (Clifton)
Lodge Farm
CH
Ruddington Grange
Landmere La
Mickleborough Hill
Hall Farm
Wood View Farm
Ruddington Hall

56 A B 57 C D 58 E F

196

186

185
174

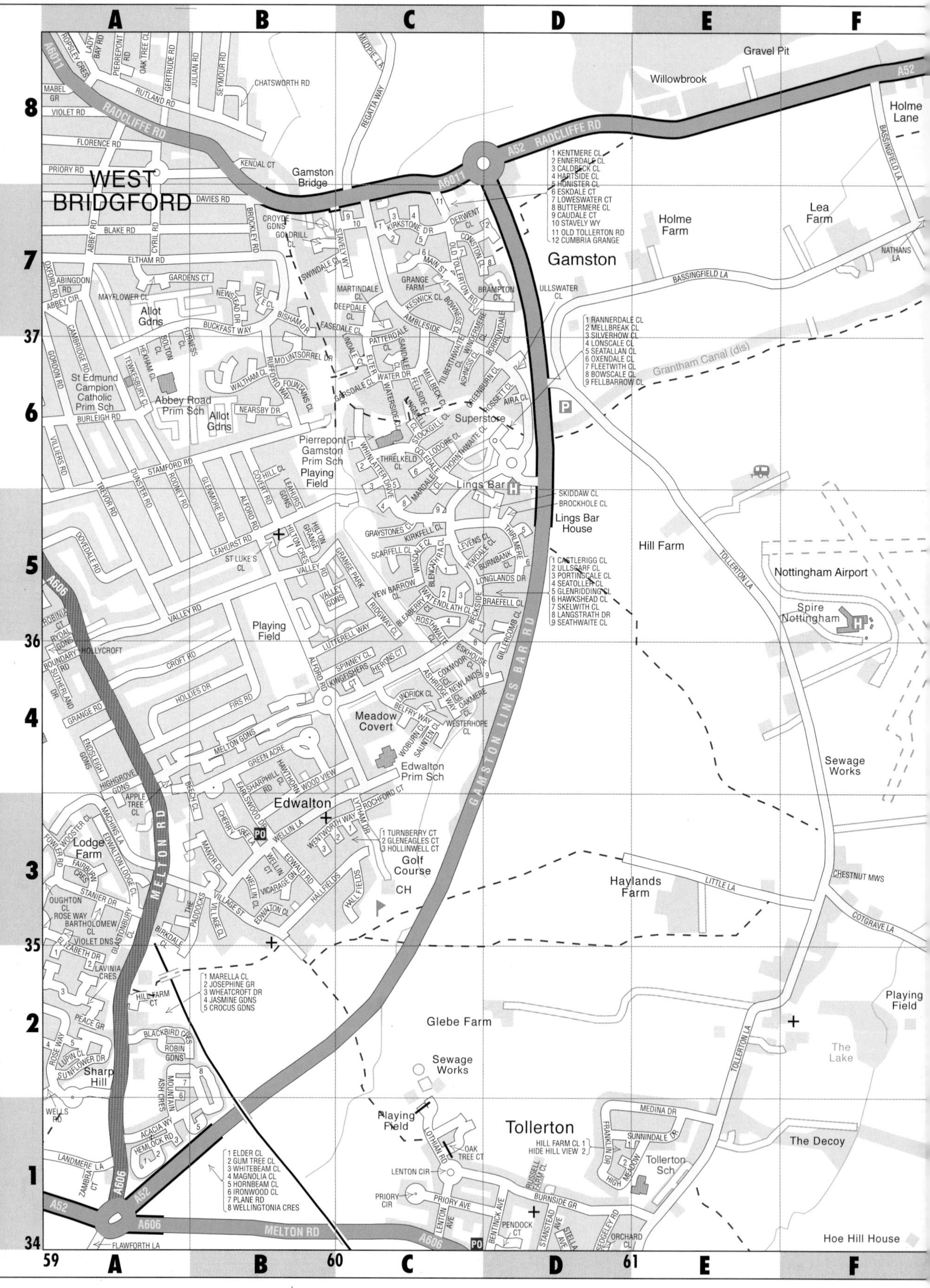
A
B
C
D
E
F
8
7
37
6
5
36
4
3
35
2
1
34
59
60
61
WEST BRIDGFORD
Gamston
Edwalton
Tollerton
Gamston Bridge
Willowbrook
Gravel Pit
Holme Lane
Holme Farm
Lea Farm
NATHANS LA
BASSINGFIELD LA
Grantham Canal (dis)
A52
RADCLIFFE RD
A6011
A606
MELTON RD
GAMSTON LINGS BAR RD
TOLLERTON LA
LITTLE LA
COTGRAVE LA
CHESTNUT MWS
1 KENTMERE CL
2 ENNERDALE CL
3 CALDBECK CL
4 HARTSIDE CL
5 HONISTER CL
6 ESKDALE CT
7 LOWESWATER CT
8 BUTTERMERE CL
9 CAUDALE CT
10 STAVELY WY
11 OLD TOLLERTON RD
12 CUMBRIA GRANGE
ULLSWATER CL
1 RANNERDALE CL
2 MELLBREAK CL
3 SILVERHOW CL
4 LONSCALE CL
5 OXENDALE CL
6 FLEETWITH CL
7 FLEETWITH CL
8 BOWSCALE CL
9 FELLBARROW CL
SKIDDAW CL
BROCKHOLE CL
Lings Bar House
Lings Bar
Superstore
1 CASTLERIGG CL
2 ULLSCARF CL
3 PORTINSCALE CL
4 SEATOLLER CL
5 GLENRIDDING CL
6 HAWKSHEAD CL
7 SKELWITH CL
8 LANGSTRATH DR
9 SEATHWAITE CL
Hill Farm
Nottingham Airport
Spire Nottingham
Sewage Works
Haylands Farm
Playing Field
The Lake
Glebe Farm
The Decoy
Hoe Hill House
Tollerton Sch
MEDINA DR
SUNNINDALE DR
FRANKLIN DR
HIGH MEADOW
HILL FARM CL 1
HIDE HILL VIEW 2
BURNSIDE GR
RUSSELL FARM CL
STANSTEAD AVE
STELLA AVE
SEDGELEY RD
ORCHARD CL
PENDOCK CT
BENTINCK AVE
LENTON AVE
PRIORY AVE
PRIORY CIR
LENTON CIR
LOTHIAN RD
OAK TREE CT
Golf Course
CH
1 TURNBERRY CT
2 GLENEAGLES CT
3 HOLLINWELL CT
Edwalton Prim Sch
Meadow Covert
WESTERHOPE CL
Pierrepont Gamston Prim Sch
Playing Field
Abbey Road Prim Sch
St Edmund Campion Catholic Prim Sch
Allot Gdns
Lodge Farm
Sharp Hill
1 MARELLA CL
2 JOSEPHINE GR
3 WHEATCROFT DR
4 JASMINE GDNS
5 CROCUS GDNS
1 ELDER CL
2 GUM TREE CL
3 WHITEBEAM CL
4 MAGNOLIA CL
5 HORNBEAM CL
6 IRONWOOD CL
7 PLANE RD
8 WELLINGTONIA CRES
FLAWFORTH LA
LANDMERE LA
ZAMBRA CT
HEMLOCK RD
ACACIA WY
ASH CRES
MOUNTAIN ROBIN
BLACKBIRD CRES
HILL FARM CT
PEACE GR
SUNFLOWER DR
LUPIN CL
ROSE WAY
WELLS RD
VIOLET DNS
ELIZABETH DR
LAVINIA CRES
BARTHOLOMEW CL
ROSE WAY
OUGHTON CL
STANIER DR
FAIRBURN CRES
EDWALTON LODGE CL
GLASTONBURY CL
BIRKDALE CL
THE PADDOCKS
VILLAGE ST
VILLAGE CL
EDWALTON CL
VICARAGE GN
WELLIN CT
WELLIN CL
WELLIN LA
MANOR CL
CHERRY TREE LA
EARLSWOOD DR
BEECH CL
APPLE TREE CL
HIGHGROVE GDNS
MACHINS LA
WOOSTER CL
FOWLER RD
ENDSLEIGH GDNS
GRANGE RD
SUTHERLAND DR
BOUNDARY RD
HOLLYCROFT
RYDAL GDNS
ROBINIA CT
DOVEDALE RD
TREVOR RD
DUNSTER RD
ROMNEY RD
GLENMORE RD
ALFORD RD
COVERT RD
HILL CL
LEAHURST GDNS
LEAHURST RD
ST LUKE'S CL
HILTON CRES
HILTON GRANGE
VALLEY RD
VALLEY GDNS
GRANGE PARK
CROFT RD
HOLLIES DR
FIRS RD
MELTON GDNS
GREEN ACRE
SHARPHILL RD
HAWTHORN CL
WOOD VIEW
WENTWORTH WAY
LYTHAM DR
ROCHFORD CT
EDWALD RD
HALLFIELDS
HALL FIELDS
SPINNEY CL
KINGFISHERS CT
HERONS CT
LUTTERELL WAY
RIDGWAY CL
YEW BARROW CL
BLEABERRY CL
ROSTHWAITE CL
WATENDLATH CL
BECKSIDE
BRAEFELL CL
GILLERCOMB CL
ESKHOUSE CL
COXMOOR CL
NEWLANDS CL
OAKMERE CL
ASHRIDGE WAY
LINDRICK CL
BELFRY WAY
WOBURN CL
SAUNTEN CL
GRAYSTONES CL
KIRKFELL CL
SCARFELL CL
WASDALE CL
BLENCATHRA CL
LEVENS CL
YEWDALE CL
BURNBANK CL
LONGLANDS DR
THIRLMERE
THRELKELD CL
WHINLATTER DRIVE
MARDALE CL
COLEDALE
LODORE CL
THORNTHWAITE CL
STOCKGILL CL
LINGMELL CL
WATERSIDE CL
GARSDALE CL
FELLSIDE CL
MILLBECK CL
TILBERTHWAITE CL
ASHNESS CL
GREENBURN CL
ROSSETT CL
AIRA CL
WINDERMERE
BORROWDALE
AMBLESIDE
KESWICK CL
BOWNESS CL
BRAMPTON CT
CONISTON CL
DERWENT CL
KIRKSTONE DR
MAIN ST
GRANGE FARM
OLD TOLLERTON RD
MARTINDALE CL
DEEPDALE CL
EASEDALE CL
LINDALE CL
PATTERDALE CL
SANDALE CL
ELTERWATER DR
WATER DR
SWINDALE CL
STAVELY WY
GOLDRILL CL
CROYDE GDNS
BISHAM DR
MOUNTSORREL DR
RUFFORD WAY
FOUNTAINS CL
WALTHAM CL
NEARSBY DR
NEWSTEAD DR
DALE CL
BUCKFAST WAY
FURNESS CL
BOLTON CL
HEXHAM CL
TEWKESBURY CL
CAMBRIDGE RD
GORDON RD
VILLIERS RD
BURLEIGH RD
STAMFORD RD
MAYFLOWER CL
GARDENS CT
ELTHAM RD
ABINGDON RD
ABBEY CIR
OXFORD RD
ABBEY RD
CYRIL RD
BLAKE RD
DAVIES RD
BROCKLEY RD
KENDAL CT
PRIORY RD
FLORENCE RD
VIOLET RD
MABEL GR
RUTLAND RD
CHATSWORTH RD
ROPSLEY CRES
LADY BAY RD
PIERREPONT RD
OAK TREE CL
GERTRUDE RD
JULIAN RD
SEYMOUR RD
MUDPIE LA
REGATTA WAY
BASSINGFIELD LA
PO

185
197

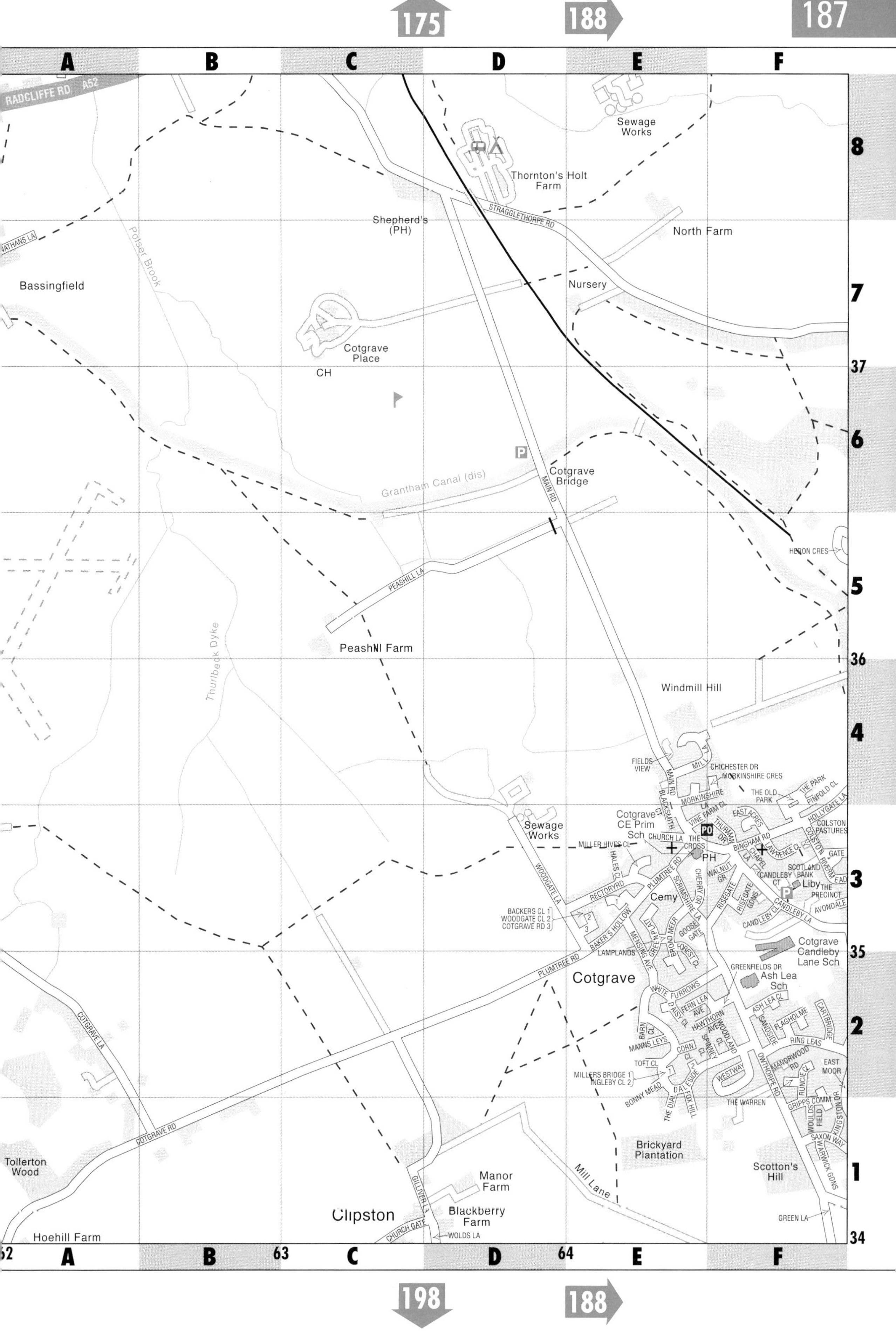

RADCLIFFE RD A52

| A | B | C | D | E | F |

8

Sewage Works

Thornton's Holt Farm

STRAGGLETHORPE RD

North Farm

Shepherd's (PH)

Bassingfield

Nursery

7

37

Cotgrave Place

CH

6

Grantham Canal (dis)

Cotgrave Bridge

MAIN RD

HERON CRES

PEASHILL LA

5

Thurlbeck Dyke

36

Peashill Farm

Windmill Hill

4

FIELDS VIEW

CHICHESTER DR
MORKINSHIRE CRES

THE PARK
PINFOLD LA

THE OLD PARK

HOLLYGATE LA
COLSTON PASTURES

MORKINSHIRE LA
VINE FARM CL
EAST ACRES

Cotgrave CE Prim Sch

CHURCH LA
THE CROSS
PH

BINGHAM RD

SCOTLAND BANK
THE PRECINCT
AVONDALE

Sewage Works

MILLER HIVES CL

WOODGATE LA

HALES CL

RECTORY RD

BAKER'S HOLLOW

Cemy

CANDLEBY CT
Liby

P

BACKERS CL 1
WOODGATE CL 2
COTGRAVE RD 3

CANDLEBY LA

Cotgrave Candleby Lane Sch

35

PLUMTREE RD

LAMPLANDS

GREENFIELDS DR

Ash Lea Sch

ASH LEA CL

Cotgrave

WHITE FURROWS

HAWTHORN AVE

WOODLAND

PLAGHOLME
CARTBRIDGE
RING LEAS

2

MANNS LEYS

CORN CL

WESTWAY

MANORWOOD RD

EAST MOOR

MILLERS BRIDGE 1
INGLEBY CL 2

BONNY MEAD

THE WARREN

GRIPPS COMM FIELD

Tollerton Wood

COTGRAVE LA

COTGRAVE RD

Brickyard Plantation

Scotton's Hill

1

Hoehill Farm

Clipston

Manor Farm

Blackberry Farm

Mill Lane

GREEN LA

WOLDS LA

34

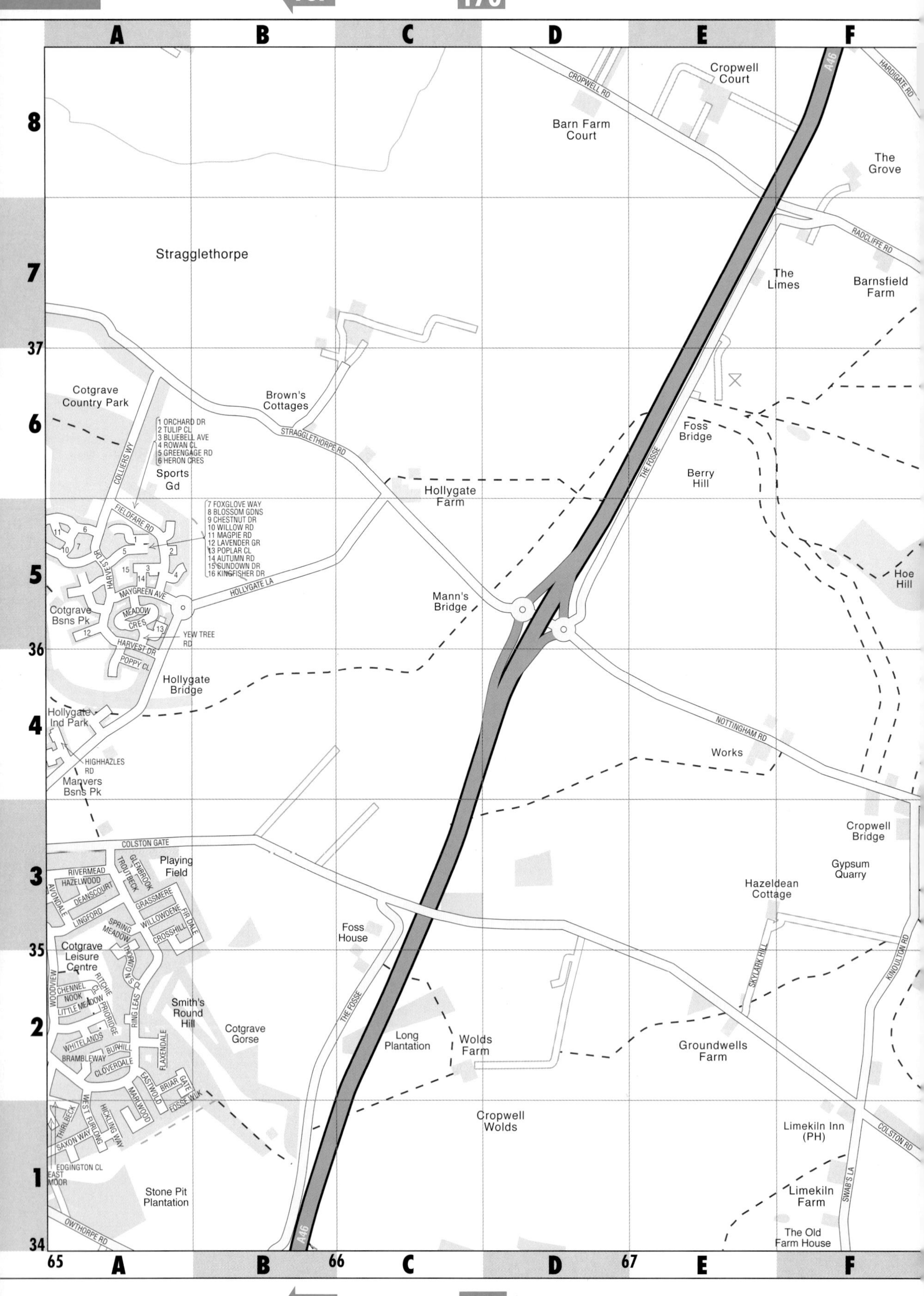

A   B   C   D   E   F

8

Cropwell
Court

Barn Farm
Court

Cropwell Rd

The
Grove

Hardgate Rd

Stragglethorpe

7

Radcliffe Rd

The
Limes

Barnsfield
Farm

37

Cotgrave
Country Park

Brown's
Cottages

Stragglethorpe Rd

Colliers Wy

Foss
Bridge

6

1 ORCHARD DR
2 TULIP CL
3 BLUEBELL AVE
4 ROWAN CL
5 GREENGAGE RD
6 HERON CRES

Sports
Gd

Fieldfare Rd

Hollygate
Farm

Berry
Hill

The Fosse

7 FOXGLOVE WAY
8 BLOSSOM GDNS
9 CHESTNUT DR
10 WILLOW RD
11 MAGPIE RD
12 LAVENDER GR
13 POPLAR CL
14 AUTUMN RD
15 SUNDOWN DR
16 KINGFISHER DR

Hoe
Hill

5

11 6
10 7   1
5   2
15 3
14 4

Harvest Rd

Maygreen Ave

Hollygate La

Mann's
Bridge

Cotgrave
Bsns Pk

Meadow
Cres

13

Yew Tree
Rd

36

12

Harvest Dr

Poppy Cl

Hollygate
Bridge

Nottingham Rd

Hollygate
Ind Park

Highhazles
Rd

Works

4

Manvers
Bsns Pk

Cropwell
Bridge

Colston Gate

Playing
Field

Gypsum
Quarry

3

Rivermead
Hazelwood
Deanscourt

Glenbrook
Troutbeck

Grassmere
Willowdene
Fir Dale
Crosshill

Hazeldean
Cottage

Avondale
Lingford
Spring
Meadow
Thornton's

Skylark Hill

Kinoulton Rd

35

Cotgrave
Leisure
Centre

Foss
House

Woodview
Chennel
Nook
Little Meadow

Ritchie
Ringrose

Ring Leas

Smith's
Round
Hill

The Fosse

Long
Plantation

Wolds
Farm

Groundwells
Farm

2

Whitelands
Brambleway
Burhill
Cloverdale

Malwood

Eastham
Briar Gate
Flaxendale

Cotgrave
Gorse

Colston Rd

Thin Beck
Saxon Way

West Furlong
Huckling Van
Old
Fosse Wlk

Cropwell
Wolds

Limekiln Inn
(PH)

1

Edgington Cl
East
Moor

Swab's La

Limekiln
Farm

Stone Pit
Plantation

Owthorpe Rd

A46

The Old
Farm House

34

65   A   B   66   C   D   67   E   F

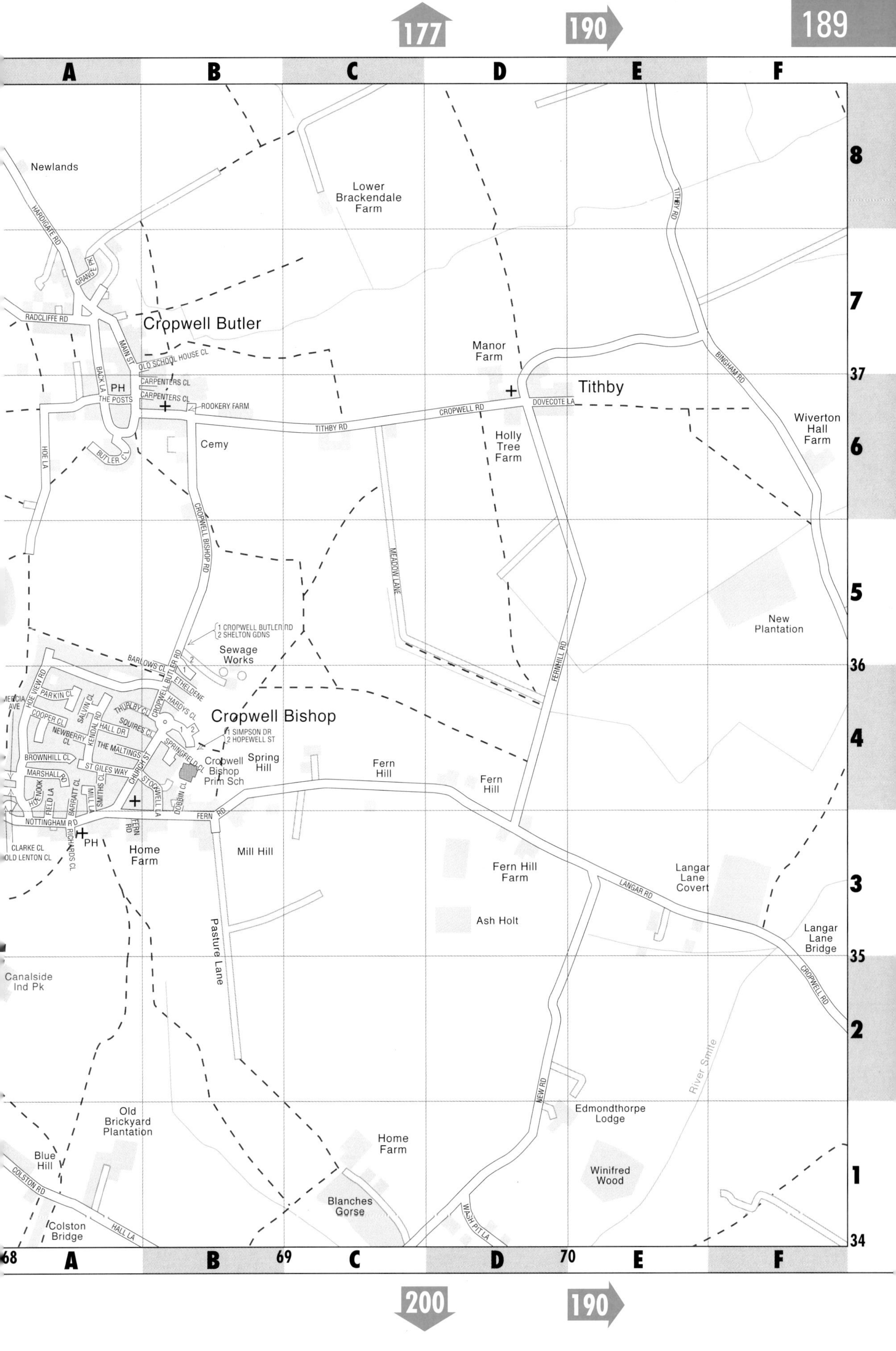

A **B** **C** **D** **E** **F**

8

Newlands

Lower
Brackendale
Farm

HARDIGATE RD

GRANGE LA

7

RADCLIFFE RD

Cropwell Butler

Manor
Farm

Tithby

MAIN ST

BACK LA

PH

OLD SCHOOL HOUSE CL

CARPENTERS CL

CARPENTERS CL

37

THE POSTS

ROOKERY FARM

Cropwell Rd

DOVECOTE LA

Wiverton
Hall
Farm

TITHBY RD

BINGHAM RD

HOE LA

BUTLER CL

TITHBY RD

Cemy

Holly
Tree
Farm

6

CROPWELL BISHOP RD

MEADOW LANE

5

1 CROPWELL BUTLER RD
2 SHELTON GDNS

Sewage
Works

FERNHILL RD

New
Plantation

36

BARLOWS CL

BP ETHELDENE

HARDYS CL

Cropwell Bishop

MERCIA
AVE

HOE VIEW RD

PARKIN CL

SALVIN CL

THURLBY CL

HALL DR

SQUIRES CL

KENDAL CL

1

4

NEWBERRY
CL

COOPER CL

THE MALTINGS

CROPWELL BUTLER RD

1 SIMPSON DR
2 HOPEWELL ST

Spring
Hill

Fern
Hill

Fern
Hill

BROWNHILL CL

ST GILES WAY

SPRINGFIELD CL

STOCKWELL LA

Cropwell
Bishop
Prim Sch

MARSHALL
CL

SMITHS CL

MILL LA

DOBBIN CL

FERN
RD

Mill Hill

Fern Hill
Farm

Langar
Lane
Covert

3

BARRATT CL

FIELD LA

CHURCH ST

Fern
RD

LANGAR RD

Langar
Lane
Bridge

OXBOW CL

RICHARDS CL

CLARKE CL

OLD LENTON CL

PH

Home
Farm

Ash Holt

35

CROPWELL RD

Canalside
Ind Pk

Pasture Lane

2

COLSTON RD

Old
Brickyard
Plantation

Home
Farm

NEW RD

Edmondthorpe
Lodge

River Smite

190

Blue
Hill

Blanches
Gorse

Winifred
Wood

1

HALL LA

Colston
Bridge

WASH PIT LA

34

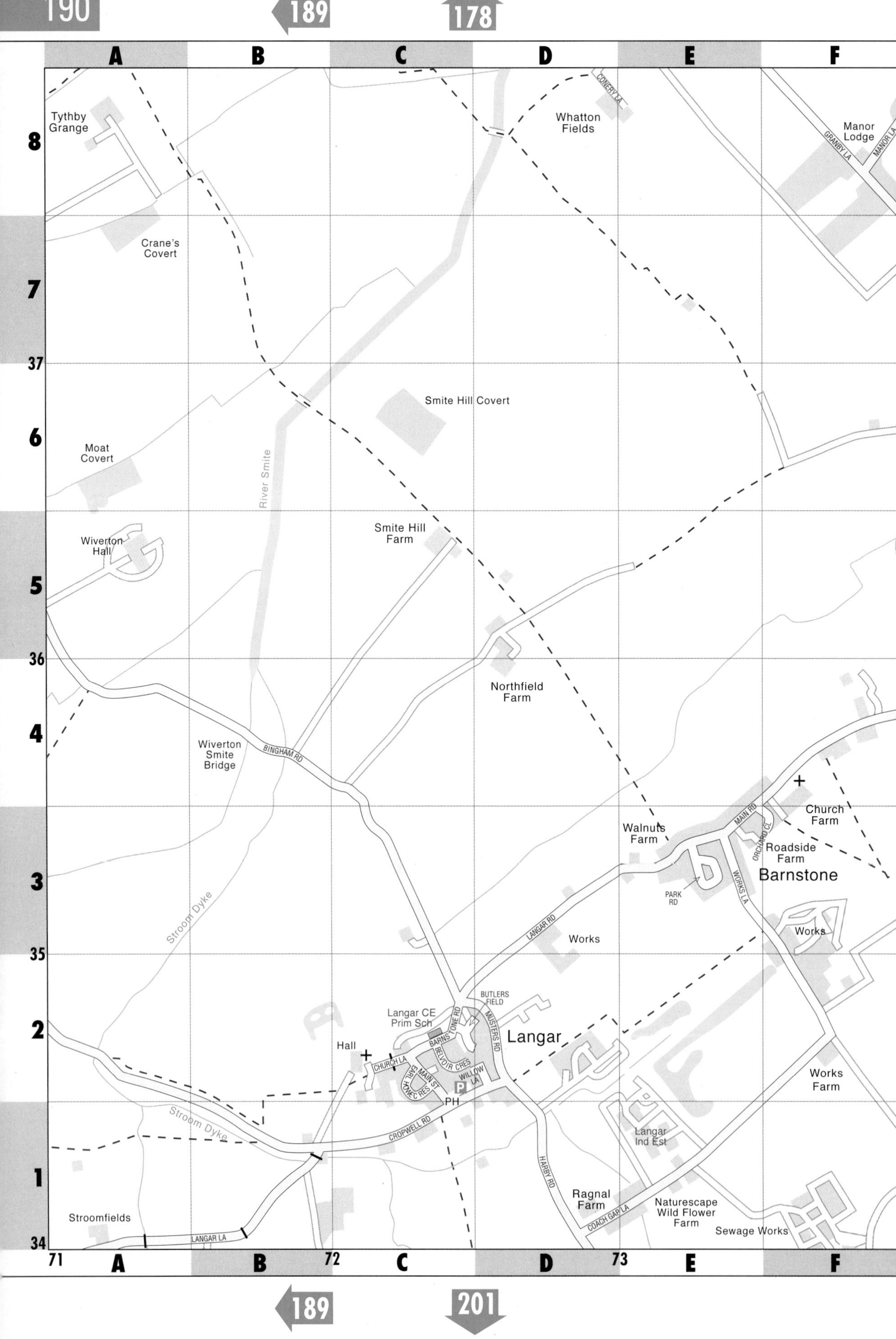

189
178
189
201

A   **B**   **C**   **D**   **E**   **F**

Tythby
Grange

Whatton
Fields

CONERY LA

Manor
Lodge

GRANBY LA

MANOR LA

8

Crane's
Covert

7

37

Smite Hill Covert

River Smite

6

Moat
Covert

Smite Hill
Farm

Wiverton
Hall

5

36

Northfield
Farm

Church
Farm

4

Wiverton
Smite
Bridge

BINGHAM RD

Walnuts
Farm

MAIN RD

ORCHARD CL

Roadside
Farm

Barnstone

WORKS LA

3

Stroom Dyke

PARK
RD

Works

Works

35

Langar RD

Works

BUTLERS
FIELD

2

Langar CE
Prim Sch

BARNSTONE RD

MUSTERS RD

Langar

Works
Farm

Hall

CHURCH LA

BELVOIR CRES

MAIN ST

MMFC RES

WILLOW
LA

Stroom Dyke

PH

CROPWELL RD

HARBY RD

Langar
Ind Est

1

Ragnal
Farm

COACH GAP LA

Naturescape
Wild Flower
Farm

Stroomfields

LANGAR LA

Sewage Works

34

71   **A**   **B**   **72**   **C**   **D**   **73**   **E**   **F**

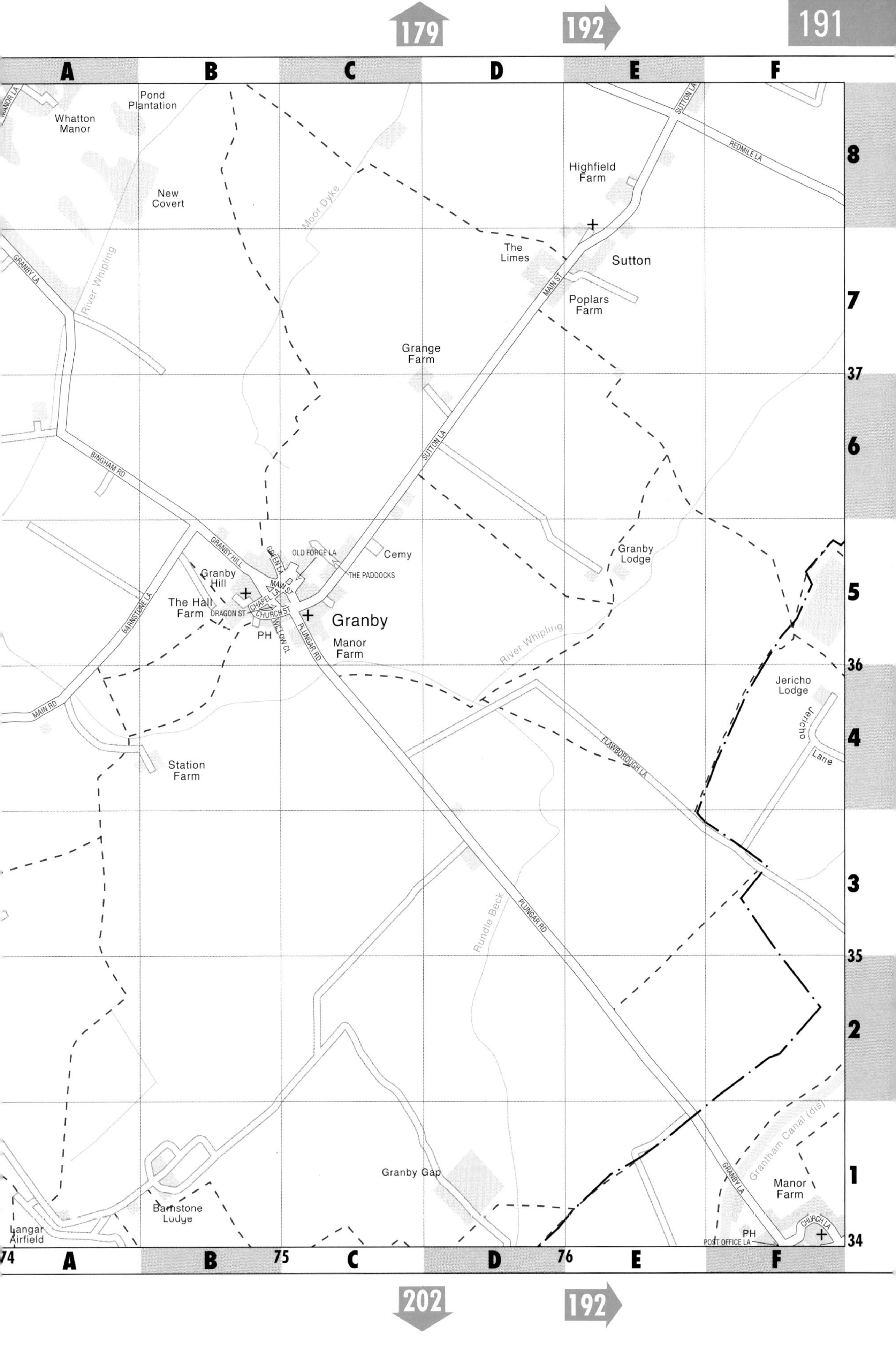

A B C D E F

8
7
37
6
5
36
4
3
35
2
1
34

74 A B 75 C D 76 E F

MANOR LA
Whatton Manor
Pond Plantation
New Covert
GRANBY LA
River Whipling
Moor Dyke
Highfield Farm
SUTTON LA
REDMILE LA
The Limes
Sutton
MAIN ST
Poplars Farm
Grange Farm
BINGHAM RD
SUTTON LA
Granby Hill
GREEN LA
Old Forge La
THE PADDOCKS
Cemy
Granby Lodge
Granby Hill
MAIN ST
CHAPEL LA
DRAGON ST
CHURCH ST
WICLOW CL
The Hall Farm
PH
Granby
Manor Farm
PLUNGAR RD
River Whipling
BARNSTONE LA
MAIN RD
Station Farm
FLAWBOROUGH LA
Jericho Lodge
Jericho Lane
36
Rundle Beck
PLUNGAR RD
35
Grantham Canal (dis)
Granby Gap
Barnstone Lodge
Langar Airfield
GRANBY LA
Manor Farm
PH
POST OFFICE LA
CHURCH LA

A B C D E F

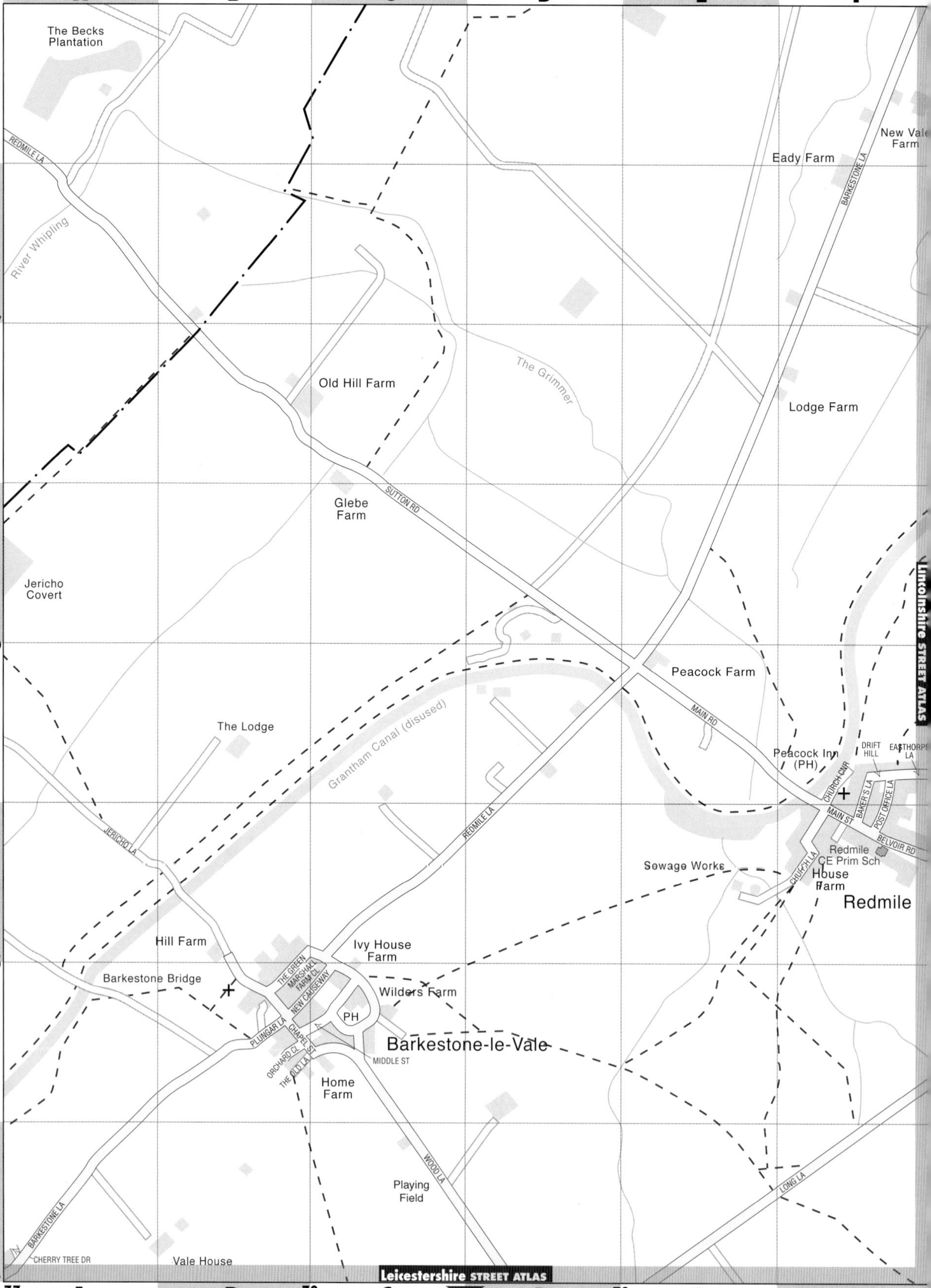

8

The Becks Plantation

REDMILE LA

7

River Whipling

37

6

Old Hill Farm

The Grimmer

Eady Farm

New Vale Farm

BARKESTONE LA

Lodge Farm

Glebe Farm

SUTTON RD

5

Jericho Covert

36

Peacock Farm

Lincolnshire STREET ATLAS

The Lodge

4

Grantham Canal (disused)

MAIN RD

Peacock Inn (PH)

DRIFT HILL

EASTHORPE LA

REDMILE LA

CHURCH CNR

BAKER'S LA

POST OFFICE LA

JERICHO LA

MAIN ST

Sewage Works

Redmile CE Prim Sch

BELVOIR RD

House Farm

3

Hill Farm

CHURCH LA

Redmile

Barkestone Bridge

Ivy House Farm

35

THE GREEN
MARSHALL FARM CL

NEW CAUSEWAY

Wilders Farm

PLUNGAR LA

PH

2

ORCHARD CL
THE OLD LA
CHAPEL LA

Barkestone-le-Vale

MIDDLE ST

Home Farm

WOOD LA

LONG LA

Playing Field

1

BARKESTONE LA

34

CHERRY TREE DR

Vale House

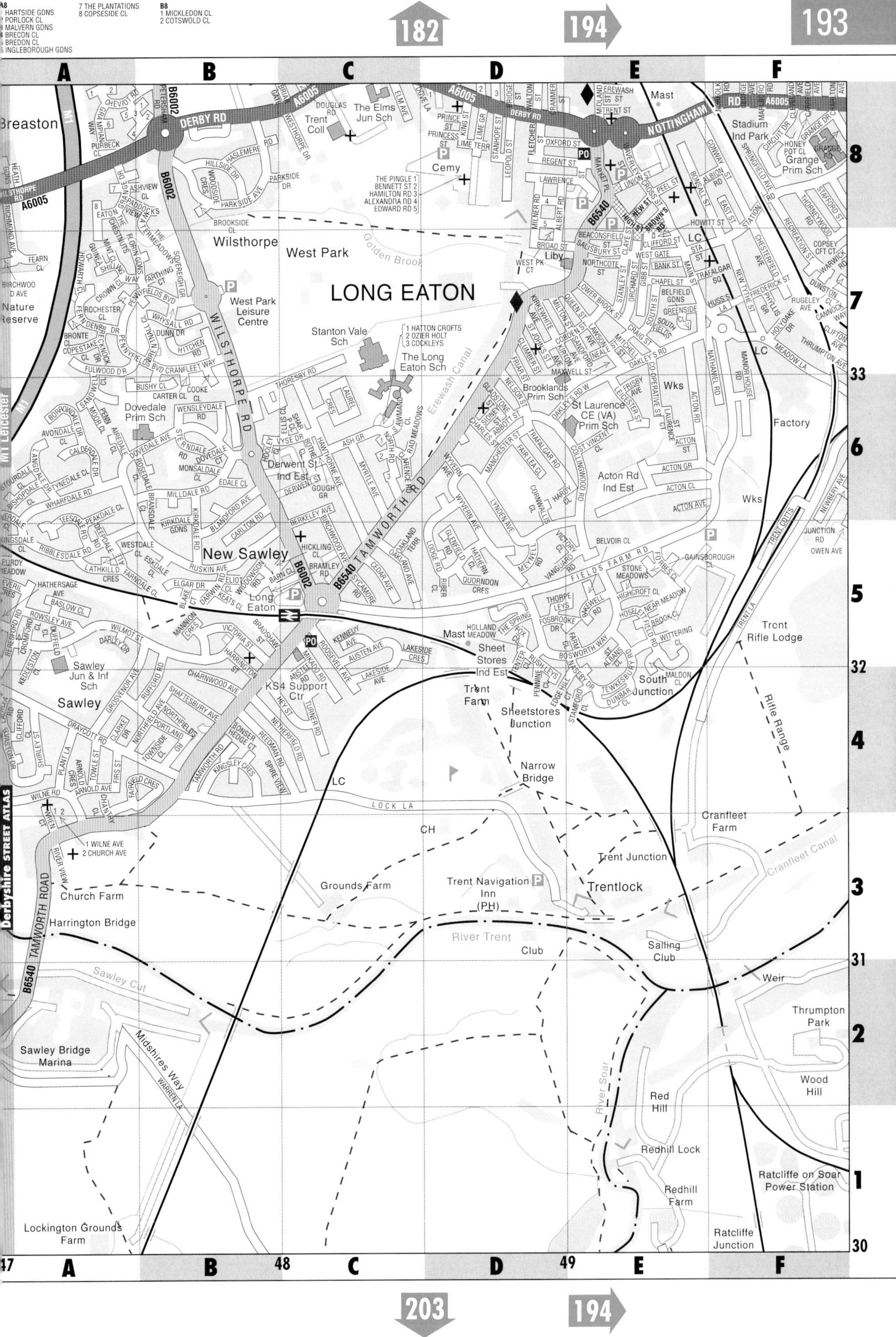
A8
1 HARTSIDE GDNS
2 PORLOCK CL
3 MALVERN GDNS
4 BRECON CL
5 BREDON CL
6 INGLEBOROUGH GDNS
7 THE PLANTATIONS
8 COPSESIDE CL
B8
1 MICKLEDON CL
2 COTSWOLD CL
182
194
A
B
C
D
E
F
Breaston
M1
DERBY RD
A6005
B6002
Trent Coll
The Elms Jun Sch
Cemy
Mast
NOTTINGHAM RD
Stadium Ind Park
Grange Prim Sch
Wilsthorpe
West Park
Golden Brook
LONG EATON
West Park Leisure Centre
WILSTHORPE RD
Stanton Vale Sch
1 HATTON CROFTS
2 OZIER HOLT
3 COCKLEYS
The Long Eaton Sch
Erewash Canal
THE PINGLE 1
BENNETT ST 2
HAMILTON RD 3
ALEXANDRA RD 4
EDWARD RD 5
Liby
MARKET PL
HIGH ST
Nature Reserve
Dovedale Prim Sch
Brooklands Prim Sch
St Laurence CE (VA) Prim Sch
Wks
Factory
Derwent St Ind Est
Acton Rd Ind Est
TAMWORTH RD
B6540
New Sawley
Long Eaton
FIELDS FARM RD
Sawley Jun & Inf Sch
Sawley
Mast
Sheet Stores Ind Est
KS4 Support Ctr
Trent Farm
Sheetstores Junction
South Junction
Trent Rifle Lodge
Rifle Range
Narrow Bridge
LC
LOCK LA
CH
Cranfleet Farm
Trent Junction
Trentlock
Cranfleet Canal
1 WILNE AVE
2 CHURCH AVE
Church Farm
Harrington Bridge
TAMWORTH ROAD
Grounds Farm
Trent Navigation Inn (PH)
River Trent
Club
Sailing Club
Weir
Sawley Cut
Thrumpton Park
Sawley Bridge Marina
Midshires Way
WARREN LA
Wood Hill
Red Hill
River Soar
Redhill Lock
Redhill Farm
Ratcliffe on Soar Power Station
Lockington Grounds Farm
Ratcliffe Junction
8
7
33
6
5
32
4
3
31
2
1
30
47
48
49
Derbyshire STREET ATLAS
M1 Leicester

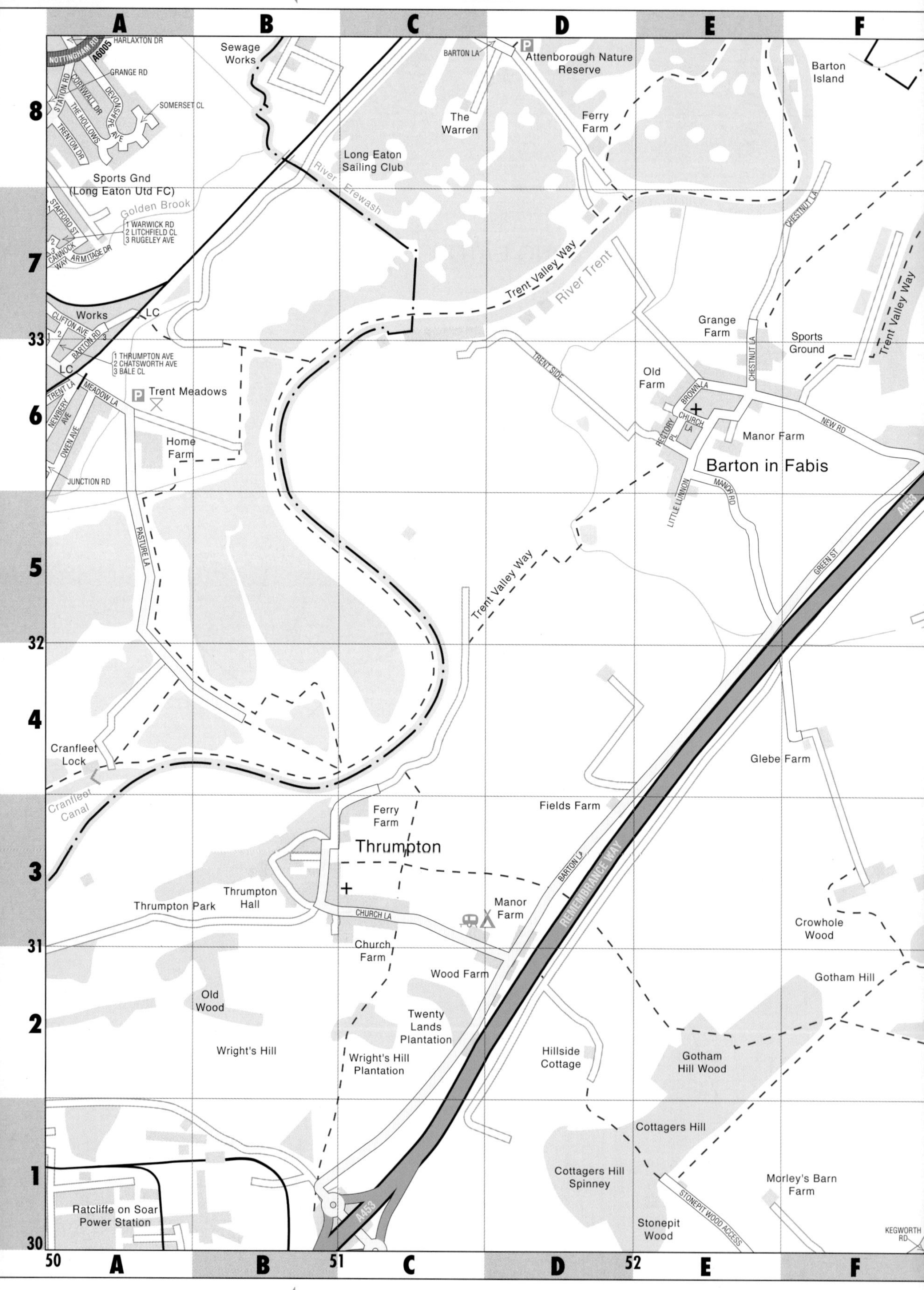

Sewage Works

BARTON LA

Attenborough Nature Reserve

The Warren

Ferry Farm

Barton Island

Long Eaton Sailing Club

River Erewash

Golden Brook

Sports Gnd (Long Eaton Utd FC)

1 WARWICK RD
2 LITCHFIELD CL
3 RUGELEY AVE

Trent Valley Way

River Trent

Grange Farm

Sports Ground

Old Farm

Works   LC

1 THRUMPTON AVE
2 CHATSWORTH AVE
3 BALE CL

LC

Trent Meadows

Home Farm

JUNCTION RD

PASTURE LA

TRENT SIDE

CHURCH LA

RECTORY PL

Manor Farm

Barton in Fabis

LITTLE LUNNON

MANOR RD

NEW RD

GREEN ST

A453

Trent Valley Way

Cranfleet Lock

Cranfleet Canal

Glebe Farm

Fields Farm

Ferry Farm

Thrumpton

Thrumpton Park

Thrumpton Hall

CHURCH LA

Manor Farm

Church Farm

Wood Farm

Old Wood

Wright's Hill

Twenty Lands Plantation

Wright's Hill Plantation

Hillside Cottage

REMEMBRANCE WAY

BARTON LA

Crowhole Wood

Gotham Hill

Cottagers Hill

Gotham Hill Wood

Cottagers Hill Spinney

Ratcliffe on Soar Power Station

A453

Stonepit Wood

STONEPIT WOOD ACCESS

Morley's Barn Farm

KEGWORTH RD

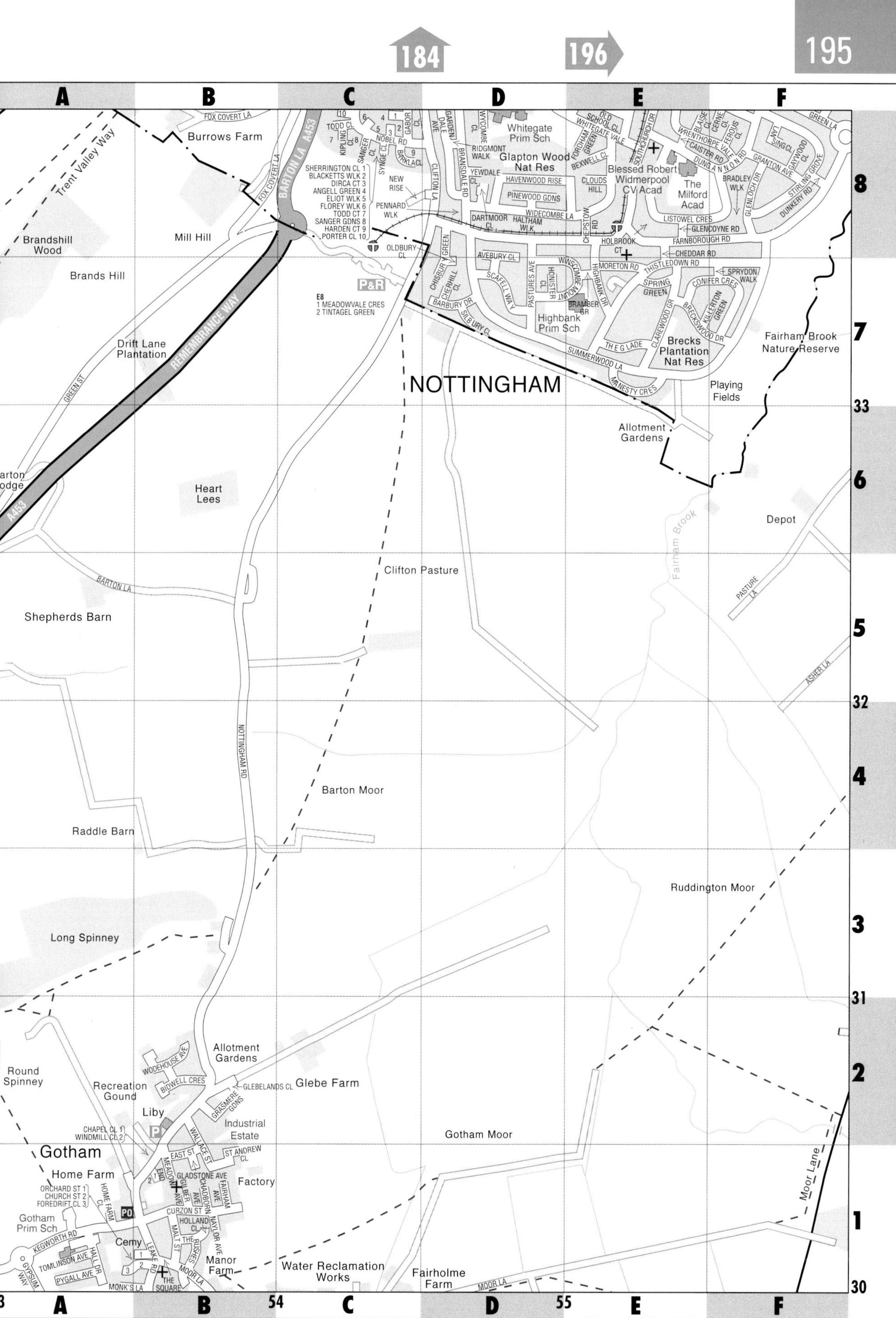

A B C D E F

8
7
33
6
5
32
4
3
31
2
1
30

Trent Valley Way

Fox Covert La

Burrows Farm

BARTON LA A453

Brandshill Wood

Mill Hill

Brands Hill

GREEN ST

REMEMBRANCE WAY

FOX COVERT LA

Drift Lane Plantation

A453

arton odge

Heart Lees

BARTON LA

Shepherds Barn

NOTTINGHAM RD

Clifton Pasture

Barton Moor

Raddle Barn

Long Spinney

Round Spinney

Recreation Gound

WODEHOUSE AVE

BIDWELL CRES

Allotment Gardens

GLEBELANDS CL

Glebe Farm

Liby

GRASMERE GDNS

Industrial Estate

CHAPEL CL 1
WINDMILL CL 2

Gotham

Home Farm

ORCHARD ST 1
CHURCH ST 2
FOREDRIFT CL 3

Gotham Prim Sch

Cemy

KEGWORTH RD

TOMLINSON AVE

PYGALL AVE

HALL DR

HOME FARM

GYPSUM WAY

MONK'S LA

LEAKE RD

THE SQUARE

MOOR LA

Manor Farm

Water Reclamation Works

Fairholme Farm

Gotham Moor

MEADOW END

EAST ST

WALLIS ST

ST ANDREW CL

GLADSTONE AVE

Factory

CURZON ST

HOLLAND CL

NAYLOR AVE

MALT ST

THE RUSHES

FAIRHAM AVE

MACBORN AVE

BELPER AVE

ST END

Ruddington Moor

Fairham Brook

Fairham Brook Nature Reserve

Depot

PASTURE LA

ASHER LA

Moor Lane

MOOR LA

30

TODD CL
KIPLING CL
SHERRINGTON CL 1
BLACKETTS WLK 2
DIRCA CT 3
ANGELL GREEN 4
ELIOT WLK 5
FLOREY WLK 6
TODD CT 7
SANGER GDNS 8
HARDEN CT 9
PORTER CL 10

SYNGE CL

NOBEL RD

GABOR

SANGER CL

BARKLA CL

NEW RISE

PENNARD WLK

CLIFTON AVE

BRANSDALE RD

CLIFTON LA

WYCOMBE CL

GARDENIA DALE AVE

RIDGMONT WALK

YEWDALE CL

Whitegate Prim Sch

Glapton Wood Nat Res

HAVENWOOD GDNS

PINEWOOD GDNS

WIDECOMBE LA

DARTMOOR CL

HALTHAM WLK

OLDBURY CL

CHISBURY GREEN

CHERNILL CL

BARBURY DR

SILBURY CL

AVEBURY CL

PASTURES AVE

SCAFELL WAY

HONISTER CL

WINSCOMBE CL

HIGHBANK DR

BRAMBER GR

Highbank Prim Sch

THE GLADE

SUMMERWOOD LA

AMESTY CRES

OLD SCHOOL CL

WHITEGATE VALE

FORTHAM GREEN RD

BEXWELL CL

SOUTHCHURCH DR

CHEPSTOW RD

HOLBROOK CT

MORETON RD

THISTLEDOWN RD

CLAREWOOD GR

BRECKSWOOD DR

KILVERTON GREEN

CONIFER CRES

SPRING GREEN

Brecks Plantation Nat Res

WRENTHORPE VALE

CAISTOR RD

DUNGANNON RD

Blessed Robert Widmerpool CV Acad

The Milford Acad

LISTOWEL CRES

GLENCOYNE RD

FARNBOROUGH RD

CHEDDAR RD

SPRYDON WALK

GLENLOCH DR

STIRLING GR

GRANTON AVE

BRADLEY WLK

GREEN LA

SISING CL

HAYWOOD GROVE

DUNKERY RD

Playing Fields

Allotment Gardens

P&R

P&R

PO

E8
1 MEADOWVALE CRES
2 TINTAGEL GREEN

195
185

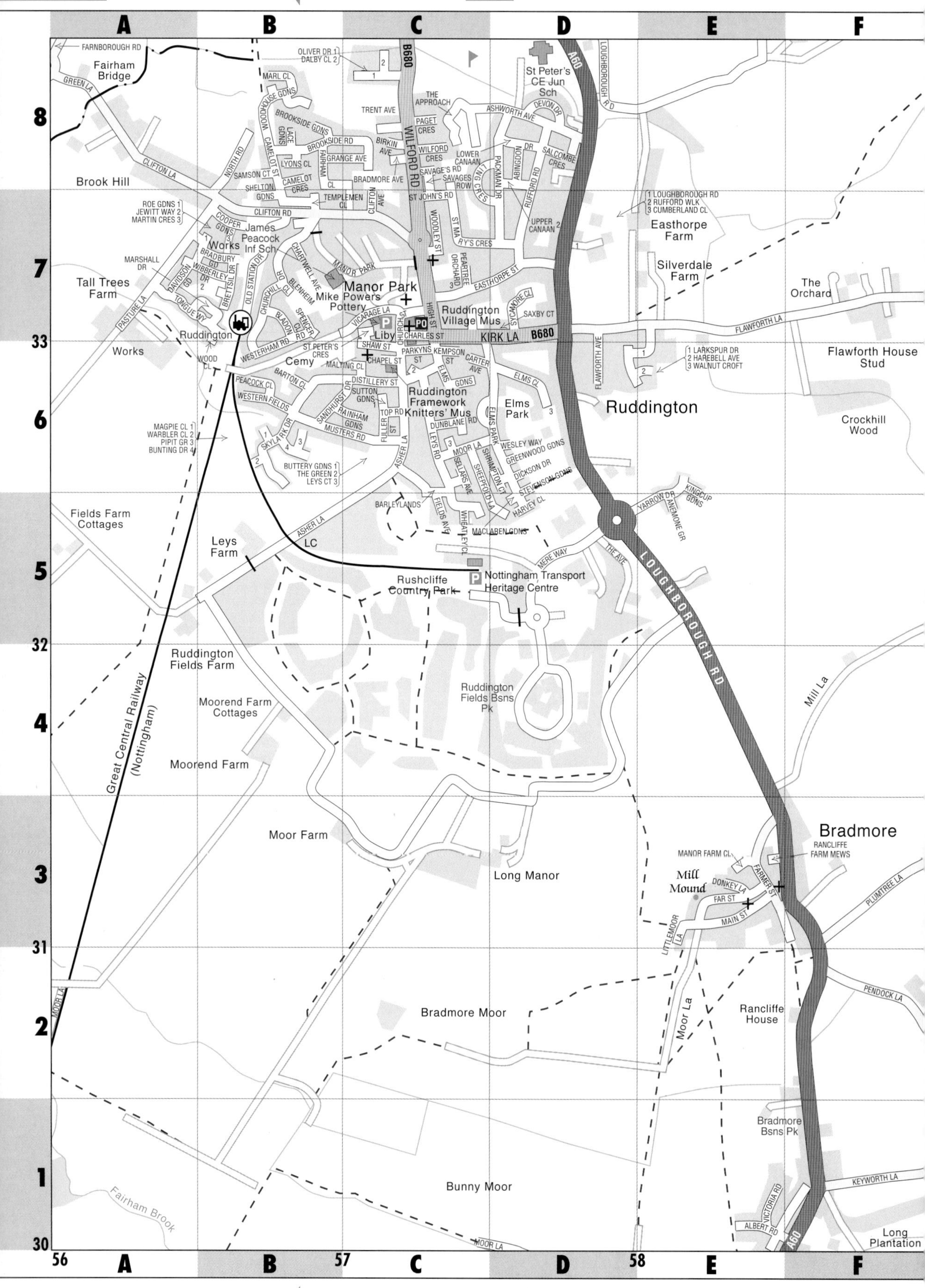
Fairham Bridge
Brook Hill
Tall Trees Farm
Works
Ruddington
James Peacock Inf Sch
Manor Park
Mike Powers Pottery
Liby
Cemy
Ruddington Village Mus
Ruddington Framework Knitters' Mus
Elms Park
St Peter's CE Jun Sch
Easthorpe Farm
Silverdale Farm
The Orchard
Flawforth House Stud
Crockhill Wood
Ruddington
Fields Farm Cottages
Leys Farm
Rushcliffe Country Park
Nottingham Transport Heritage Centre
Ruddington Fields Farm
Moorend Farm Cottages
Moorend Farm
Ruddington Fields Bsns Pk
Great Central Railway (Nottingham)
Moor Farm
Long Manor
Mill Mound
Bradmore
Bradmore Moor
Rancliffe House
Bradmore Bsns Pk
Bunny Moor
Fairham Brook
Long Plantation
WILFORD RD
LOUGHBOROUGH RD
KIRK LA
FLAWFORTH LA
ASHER LA
CLIFTON RD
Mill La
Moor La
PLUMTREE LA
PENDOCK LA
KEYWORTH LA
MOOR LA
A60
B680

195
206

186
198

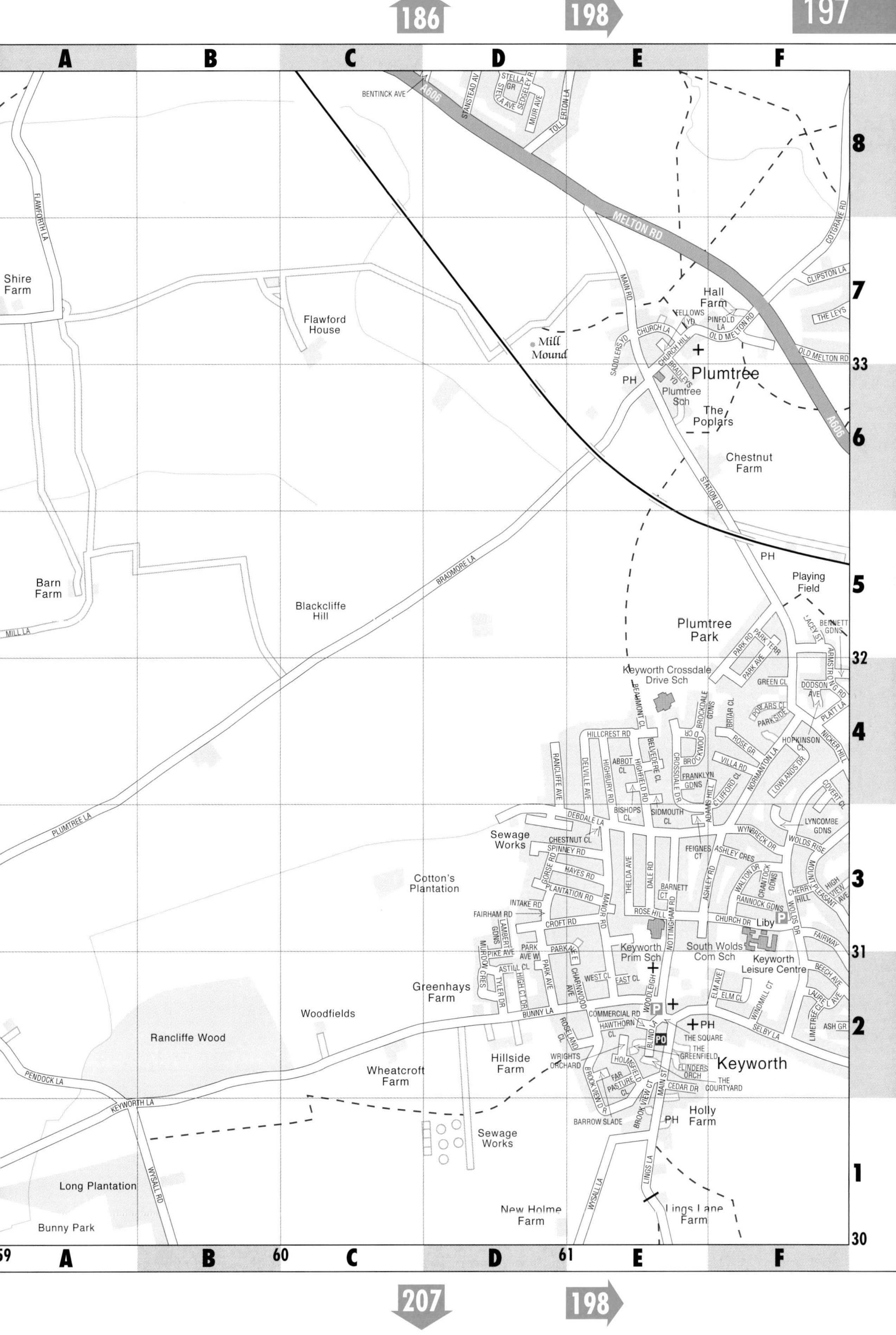
A
B
C
D
E
F
8
7
33
6
5
32
4
3
31
2
1
30
59
60
61
Shire Farm
Flawford House
Mill Mound
Barn Farm
Blackcliffe Hill
Cotton's Plantation
Sewage Works
Greenhays Farm
Woodfields
Rancliffe Wood
Hillside Farm
Wheatcroft Farm
Long Plantation
Bunny Park
New Holme Farm
Lings Lane Farm
Holly Farm
Keyworth
Plumtree
Plumtree Sch
Hall Farm
The Poplars
Chestnut Farm
Playing Field
Plumtree Park
Keyworth Crossdale Drive Sch
Keyworth Prim Sch
South Wolds Com Sch
Keyworth Leisure Centre
Liby
PH
PO
MELTON RD
A606
BENTINCK AVE
STANSTEAD AV
STELLA GR
STELLA AVE
SEDGLEY R
MUIR AVE
TOLLERTON LA
FLAWFORTH LA
MAIN RD
CHURCH LA
CHURCH HILL
FELLOWS YD
PINFOLD LA
OLD MELTON RD
SADDLERS YD
BRADLEYS YD
COTGRAVE RD
CLIPSTON LA
THE LEYS
STATION RD
BRADMORE LA
MILL LA
PLUMTREE LA
PARK RD
PARK TERR
PARK AVE
LACEY ST
BENNETT GDNS
ARMSTRONG RD
GREEN CL
DODSON AVE
PLATT LA
NICKER HILL
HOPKINSON CL
LOWLANDS DR
COVERT CL
LYNCOMBE GDNS
WOLDS RISE
MOUNT PLEASANT
HIGH VIEW AVE
CHERRY HILL
WOLDS DR
FAIRWAY
BEECH AVE
LAUREL AVE
LIMETREE CL
ASH GR
SELBY LA
WINDMILL CT
ELM AVE
ELM CL
BEAUMONT CL
BROCKDALE GDNS
BRIAR CL
POPLARS CL
PARKSIDE
ROSE GR
VILLA RD
NORMANTON LA
HILLCREST RD
RANCLIFFE AVE
DELVILLE AVE
HIGHBURY RD
ABBOT CL
HIGHFIELD RD
BELVEDERE CL
CROSSDALE DR
BROCKWOOD CR
FRANKLYN GDNS
ADAMS HILL
CLIFFORD CL
BISHOPS CL
SIDMOUTH CL
DEBDALE LA
CHESTNUT CL
SPINNEY RD
HAYES RD
GORSE RD
PLANTATION RD
INTAKE RD
FAIRHAM RD
CROFT RD
MANOR RD
THELDA AVE
DALE RD
BARNETT CT
ROSE HILL
NOTTINGHAM RD
FEIGNES CT
ASHLEY CRES
ASHLEY RD
WYNBRECK DR
WALTON DR
CRANTOCK GDNS
RANNOCK GDNS
CHURCH DR
LAMBERT GDNS
MURDEN CRES
PIKE AVE
PARK AVE W
PARK AVE E
ASTILL CL
TYLER DR
HIGH CL DR
CHARNWOOD AVE
WEST CL
EAST CL
WOODLEIGH
BUNNY LA
COMMERCIAL RD
HAWTHORN CL
ROSELAND CL
BLIND LA
THE SQUARE
THE GREENFIELD
FLINDERS ORCH
THE COURTYARD
WRIGHTS ORCHARD
HOLMSFIELD
FAR PASTURE CL
BROOK VIEW DR
BROOK VIEW CT
MAIN ST
CEDAR DR
BARROW SLADE
LINGS LA
WYSALL LA
WYSALL RD
PENDOCK LA
KEYWORTH LA

207
198

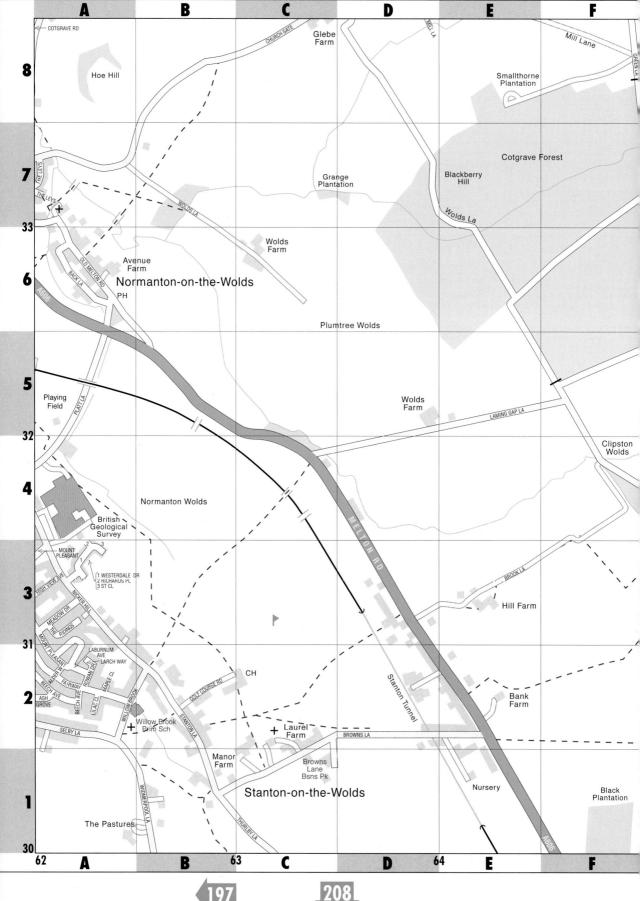

← COTGRAVE RD

Hoe Hill

CHURCH GATE

Glebe Farm

MILL LA

Mill Lane

GREEN LA

Smallthorne Plantation

Cotgrave Forest

THE LEYS

Grange Plantation

Blackberry Hill

Wolds La

WOLDS LA

THE LEYS

Avenue Farm

Wolds Farm

Normanton-on-the-Wolds

PH

OLD MELTON RD

BACK LA

A606

Plumtree Wolds

Wolds Farm

LAMING GAP LA

Playing Field

PLATTS LA

Clipston Wolds

British Geological Survey

Normanton Wolds

MOUNT PLEASANT

1 WESTERDALE DR
2 RICHARDS PL
3 ST CL

MELTON RD

BROOK LA

Hill Farm

HIGH VIEW AVE

NICKER HILL

MEADOW DR

THE RIDINGS

MOUNT PLEASANT

LABURNUM AVE

LARCH WAY

Stanton Tunnel

Bank Farm

BEECH AVE

ALDER W

FAIRWAY

ROWAN DR

LILAC CL

MAPLE CL

WILLOW BROOK

STANTON LA

GOLF COURSE RD

CH

ASH GROVE

SELBY LA

Willow Brook Prim Sch

Laurel Farm

BROWNS LA

Browns Lane Bsns Pk

Nursery

Black Plantation

Manor Farm

WIDMERPOOL LA

Stanton-on-the-Wolds

THURLBY LA

The Pastures

A606

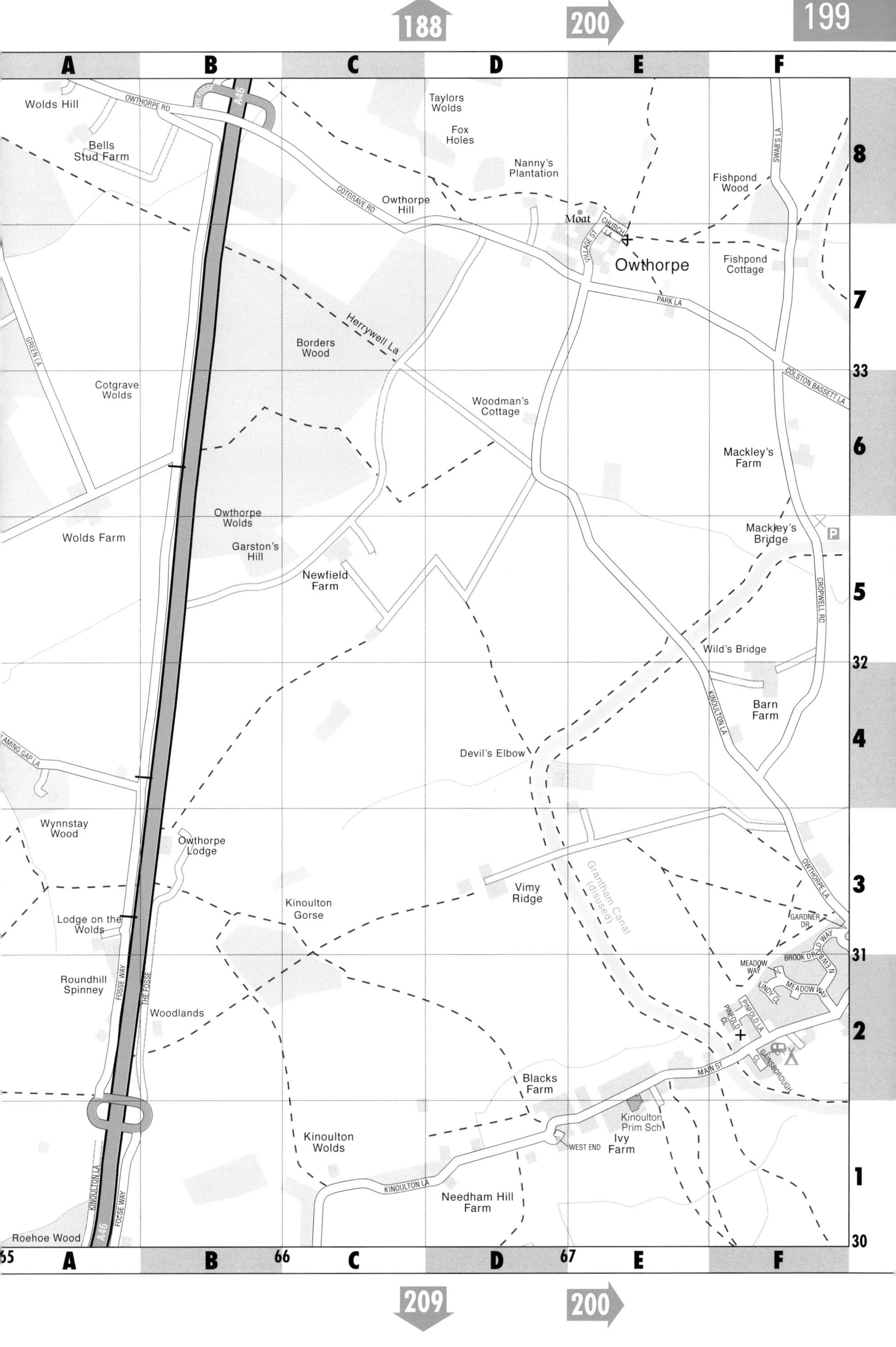
188
200
A
B
C
D
E
F
Wolds Hill
OWTHORPE RD
THE FOSSE
A46
Taylors Wolds
Fox Holes
Bells Stud Farm
Nanny's Plantation
Fishpond Wood
SWAB'S LA
COTGRAVE RD
Owthorpe Hill
Moat
CHURCH LA
VILLAGE ST
Owthorpe
Fishpond Cottage
PARK LA
Herrywell La
Borders Wood
GREEN LA
Cotgrave Wolds
Woodman's Cottage
COLSTON BASSETT LA
Mackley's Farm
Owthorpe Wolds
Wolds Farm
Garston's Hill
Mackley's Bridge
Newfield Farm
CROPWELL RD
Wild's Bridge
KINOULTON LA
Barn Farm
AMING GAP LA
Devil's Elbow
Wynnstay Wood
Owthorpe Lodge
Grantham Canal (disused)
Vimy Ridge
OWTHORPE LA
Kinoulton Gorse
Lodge on the Wolds
GARDNER DR
MEADOW WAY
BROOK DR
NEWBOLD WAY
LINDY CL
MEADOW WAY
Roundhill Spinney
FOSSE WAY
THE FOSSE
Woodlands
PINFOLD CL
PINFOLD LA
GAINSBOROUGH CL
Blacks Farm
MAIN ST
Kinoulton Prim Sch
Kinoulton Wolds
WEST END
Ivy Farm
KINOULTON LA
Needham Hill Farm
KINOULTON LA
A46
FOSSE WAY
Roehoe Wood
8
7
33
6
5
32
4
3
31
2
1
30
65
66
67
209
200

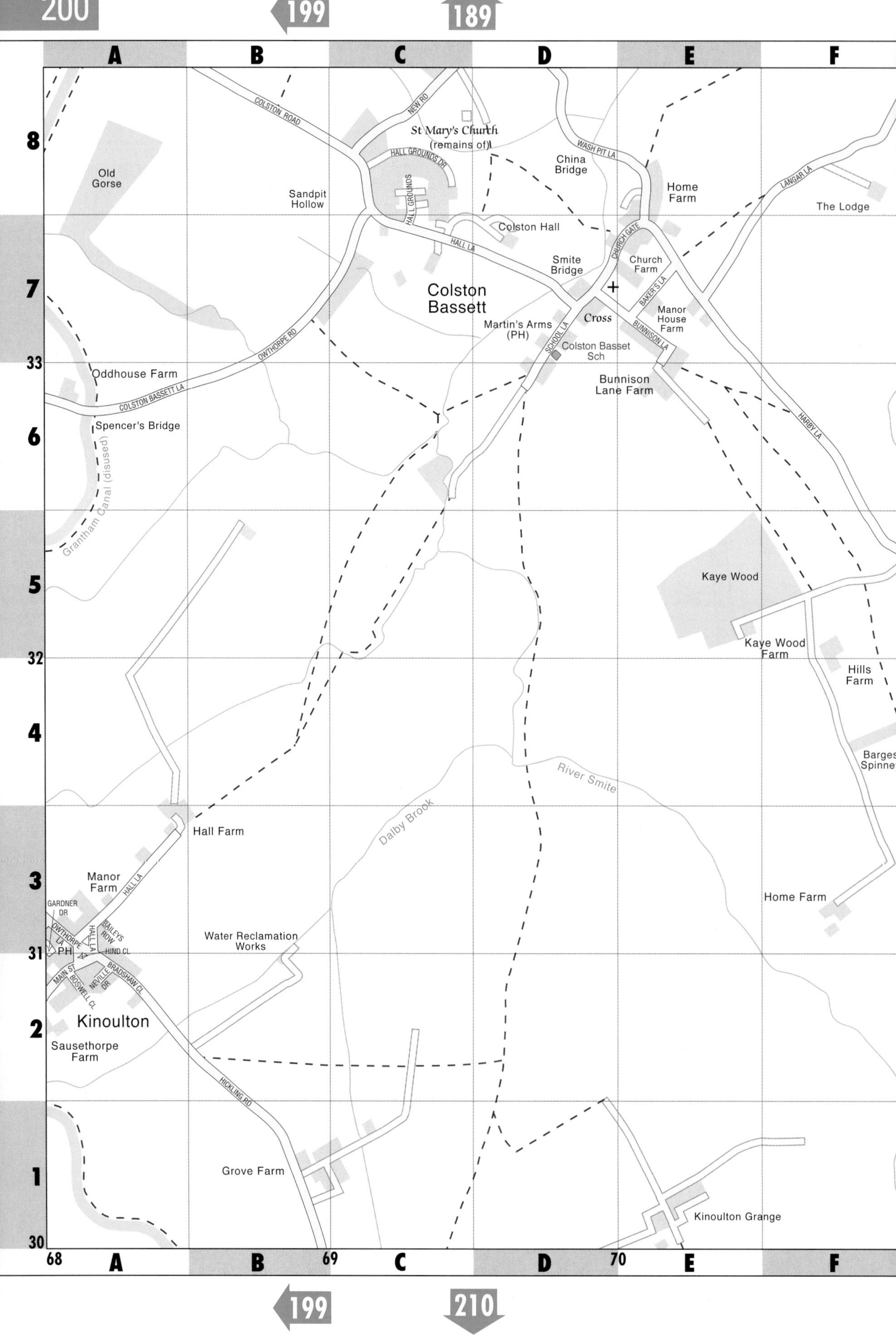

A   B   C   D   E   F

8

St Mary's Church
(remains of)

COLSTON ROAD

NEW RD

HALL GROUNDS DR

WASH PIT LA

China
Bridge

Home
Farm

LANGAR LA

The Lodge

Old
Gorse

Sandpit
Hollow

HALL GROUNDS

Colston Hall

Colston Hall

CHURCH GATE

Church
Farm

BAKER'S LA

HALL LA

Smite
Bridge

Manor
House
Farm

7

Colston
Bassett

+

Cross

OWTHORPE RD

Martin's Arms
(PH)

SCHOOL LA

BUNNISON LA

33

Oddhouse Farm

Colston Basset
Sch

Bunnison
Lane Farm

COLSTON BASSETT LA

6

Spencer's Bridge

HARBY LA

Grantham Canal (disused)

Kaye Wood

5

Kaye Wood
Farm

Hills
Farm

32

4

River Smite

Barges
Spinney

Dalby Brook

Hall Farm

3

Manor
Farm

HALL LA

Home Farm

GARDNER
DR

OWTHORPE

BAILEY'S
ROW

Water Reclamation
Works

HIND CL

31

PH

MAIN ST

HALL LA

BOSWELL CL

NEVILLE DR

BRADSHAW CL

2

Kinoulton

Sausethorpe
Farm

HICKLING RD

1

Grove Farm

Kinoulton Grange

30

68   A   B   69   C   D   70   E   F

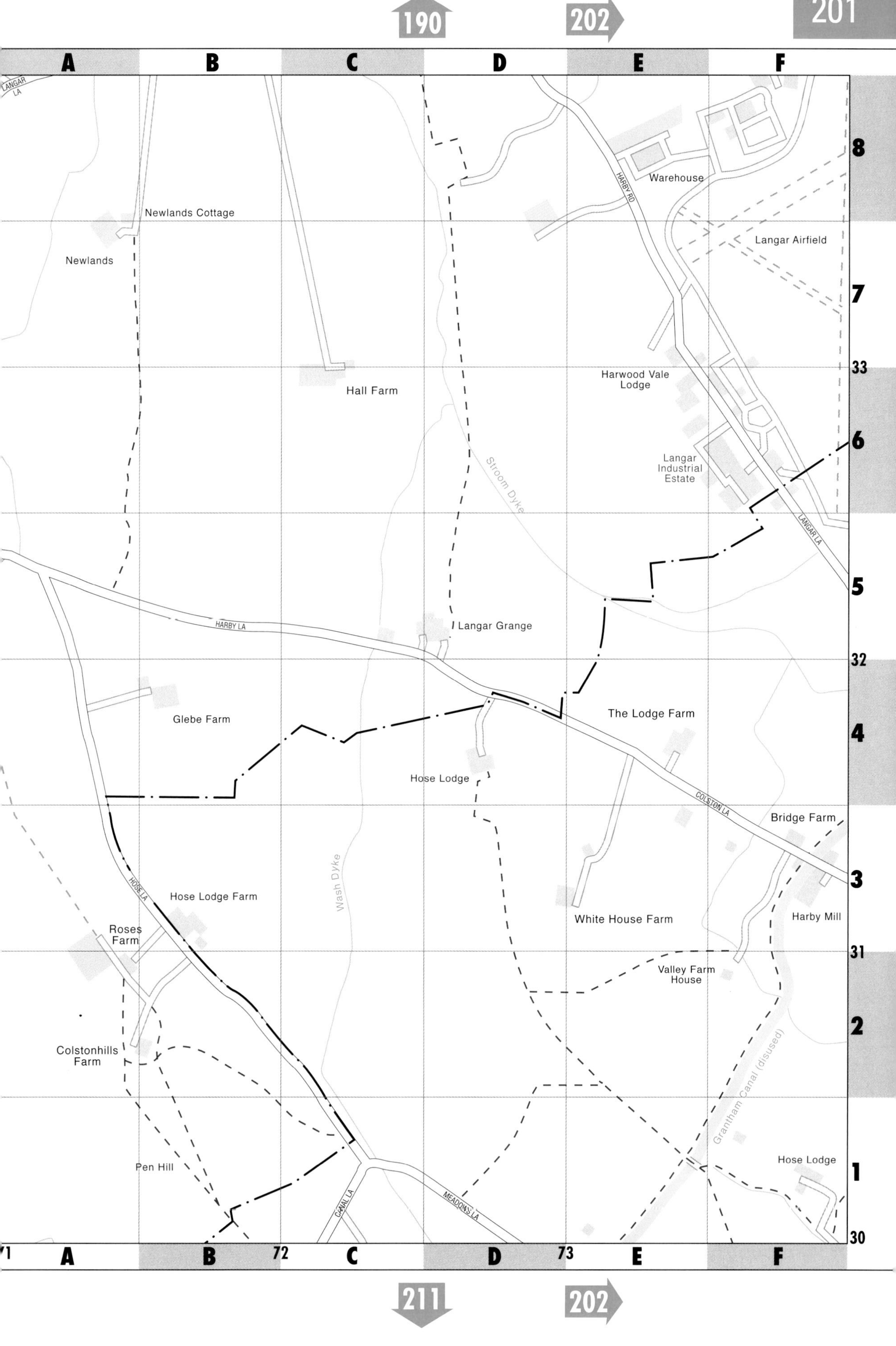
190
202
A
B
C
D
E
F
LANGAR LA
Newlands Cottage
Newlands
Warehouse
HARBY RD
Langar Airfield
Hall Farm
Harwood Vale Lodge
Langar Industrial Estate
Stroom Dyke
LANGAR LA
Langar Grange
HARBY LA
Glebe Farm
The Lodge Farm
Hose Lodge
COLSTON LA
Bridge Farm
Wash Dyke
HOSE LA
Hose Lodge Farm
Roses Farm
White House Farm
Harby Mill
Valley Farm House
Colstonhills Farm
Grantham Canal (disused)
Pen Hill
Hose Lodge
CANAL LA
MEADOWS LA
8
7
33
6
5
32
4
3
31
2
1
30
71
72
73
211
202

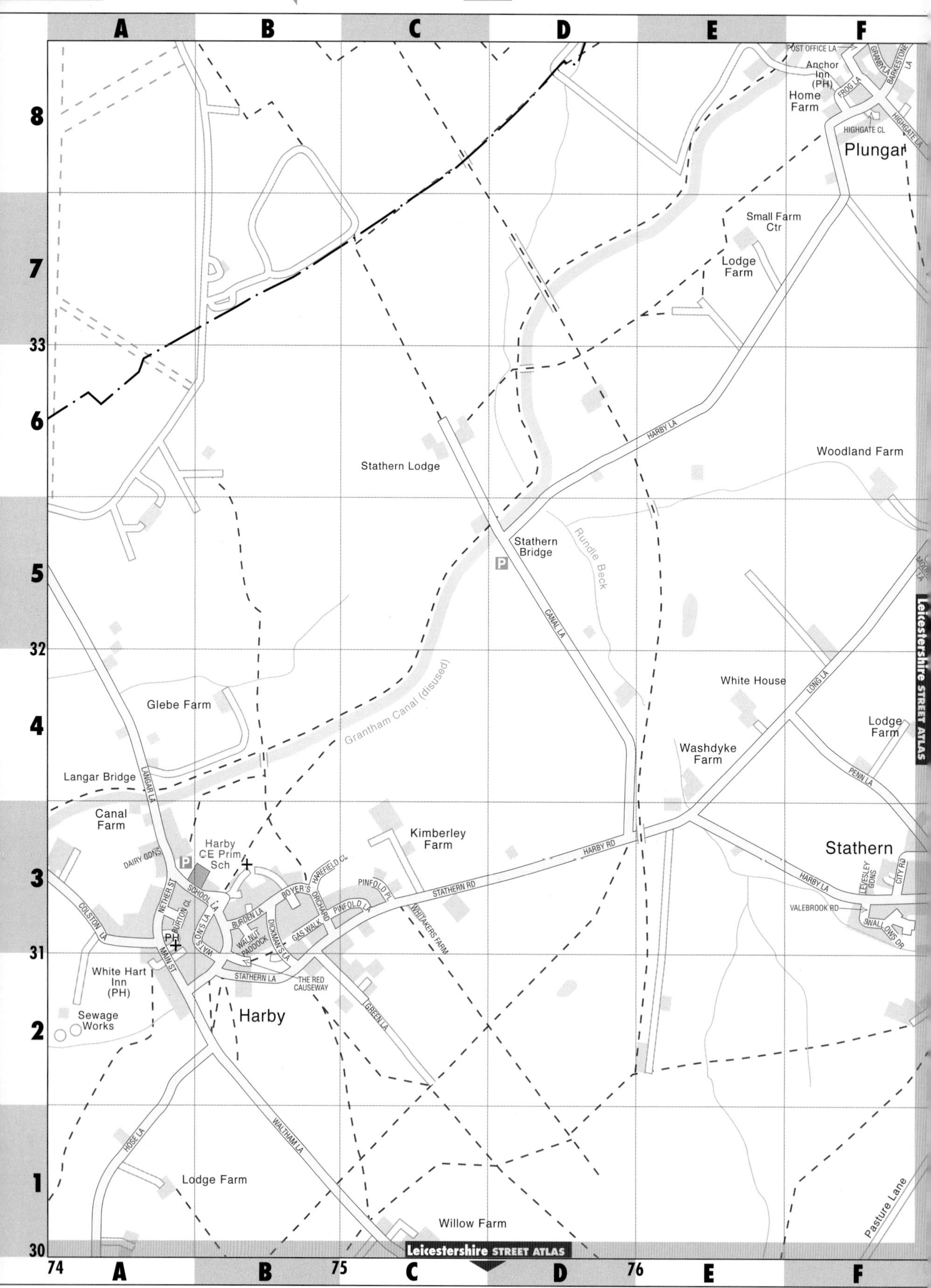

A B C D E F

8

7

33

6

Stathern Lodge

Stathern Bridge

Woodland Farm

HARBY LA

Rundle Beck

POST OFFICE LA

Anchor Inn (PH)

Home Farm

FROG LA

GRANTLEY LA

BARKESTONE

HIGHGATE LA

HIGHGATE CL

Plungar

Small Farm Ctr

Lodge Farm

White House

LONG LA

Lodge Farm

PENN LA

Stathern

EVESLEY GDNS

CITY RD

HARBY LA

VALEBROOK RD

SWALLOWS DR

Washdyke Farm

5

32

4

P

CANAL LA

Grantham Canal (disused)

Glebe Farm

Langar Bridge

LANGAR LA

Canal Farm

DAIRY GDNS

Harby CE Prim Sch

P

Kimberley Farm

HAREFIELD CL

PINFOLD ST

PINFOLD LA

Stathern Rd

HARBY RD

3

31

COLSTON LA

NETHER ST

WAT SON'S LA

SCHOOL LA

BURTON CL

BURGEN LA

WALNUT PADDOCK

DICKMAN'S LA

BOYER'S ORCHARD

GAS WALK

WHITAKERS FARM

PH

PH

White Hart Inn (PH)

MAIN ST

STATHERN LA

THE RED CAUSEWAY

GREEN LA

Harby

Sewage Works

2

HOSE LA

WALTHAM LA

Lodge Farm

Willow Farm

Pasture Lane

1

30

74 A B 75 C D 76 E F

Leicestershire STREET ATLAS

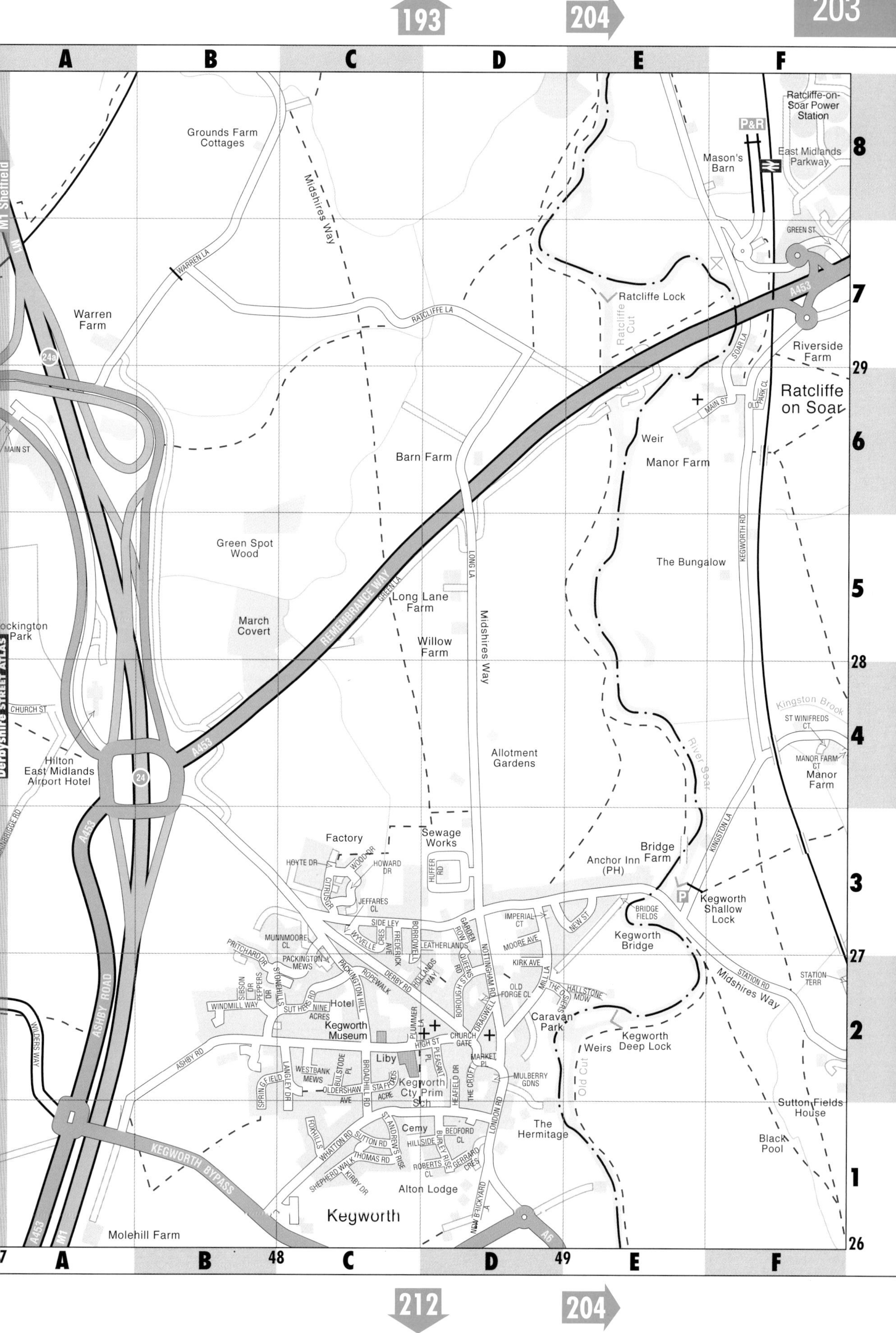
193
204
A
B
C
D
E
F
8
7
29
6
5
28
4
3
27
2
1
26
48
49
212
204
Grounds Farm Cottages
Midshires Way
Ratcliffe-on-Soar Power Station
P&R
Mason's Barn
East Midlands Parkway
M1 Sheffield
GREEN ST
WARREN LA
Warren Farm
RATCLIFFE LA
Ratcliffe Lock
Ratcliffe Cut
A453
Riverside Farm
24a
SOAR LA
Ratcliffe on Soar
MAIN ST
OLD PARK CL
MAIN ST
Weir
Manor Farm
Barn Farm
Green Spot Wood
KEGWORTH RD
The Bungalow
LONG LA
REMEMBRANCE WAY
GREEN LA
Long Lane Farm
Midshires Way
Lockington Park
March Covert
Willow Farm
Derbyshire STREET ATLAS
Kingston Brook
ST WINIFREDS CT
CHURCH ST
River Soar
Hilton East Midlands Airport Hotel
24
Allotment Gardens
MANOR FARM CT
Manor Farm
A453
Factory
Sewage Works
KINGSTON LA
Bridge Farm
HOYTE DR
WOOD DR
HOWARD DR
Anchor Inn (PH)
HUFFER RD
CITRUS GR
JEFFARES CL
P
Kegworth Shallow Lock
BRIDGE FIELDS
SIDE LEY
IMPERIAL CT
NEW ST
MUNNMOORE CL
WYVELLE CRES
FREDERICK AVE
BORROWELL
GARDEN ROW
LEATHERLANDS
MOORE AVE
Kegworth Bridge
PRITCHARD DR
PACKINGTON MEWS
DERBY RD
HOLLANDS WAY
QUEENS RD
NOTTINGHAM RD
KIRK AVE
STATION RD
STATION TERR
Midshires Way
ROPEWALK
PACKINGTON HILL
BOROUGH ST
OLD FORGE CL
MILL LA
THE DRIVE
HALLSTONE MDW
SIBSON DR
PEPPERS DR
STONEHILLS
WINDMILL WAY
SUTHERS RD
NINE ACRES
Hotel
DRAGWELL
Caravan Park
Kegworth Museum
PLUMMER LA
HIGH ST
CHURCH GATE
Kegworth Deep Lock
WILDERS WAY
ASHBY RD
ASHBY ROAD
Weirs
Liby
PLEASANT PL
MARKET PL
WESTBANK MEWS
BULSTODE PL
MULBERRY GDNS
SPRINGFIELD
LANGLEY DR
OLDERSHAW AVE
BROADHILL RD
STAFFORD ACRE
Kegworth Cty Prim Sch
HEAFIELD DR
THE CROFT
LONDON RD
Old Cut
Sutton Fields House
FOXHILLS
WHATTON RD
SUTTON RD
ST ANDREW'S RISE
Cemy
HILLSIDE
BURLEY RISE
BEDFORD CL
The Hermitage
KEGWORTH BYPASS
THOMAS RD
GERRARD CRES
ROBERTS CL
Black Pool
SHEPHERD WALK
KIRBY DR
Alton Lodge
NEW BRICKYARD LA
A6
Kegworth
A453
M1
Molehill Farm

203
194

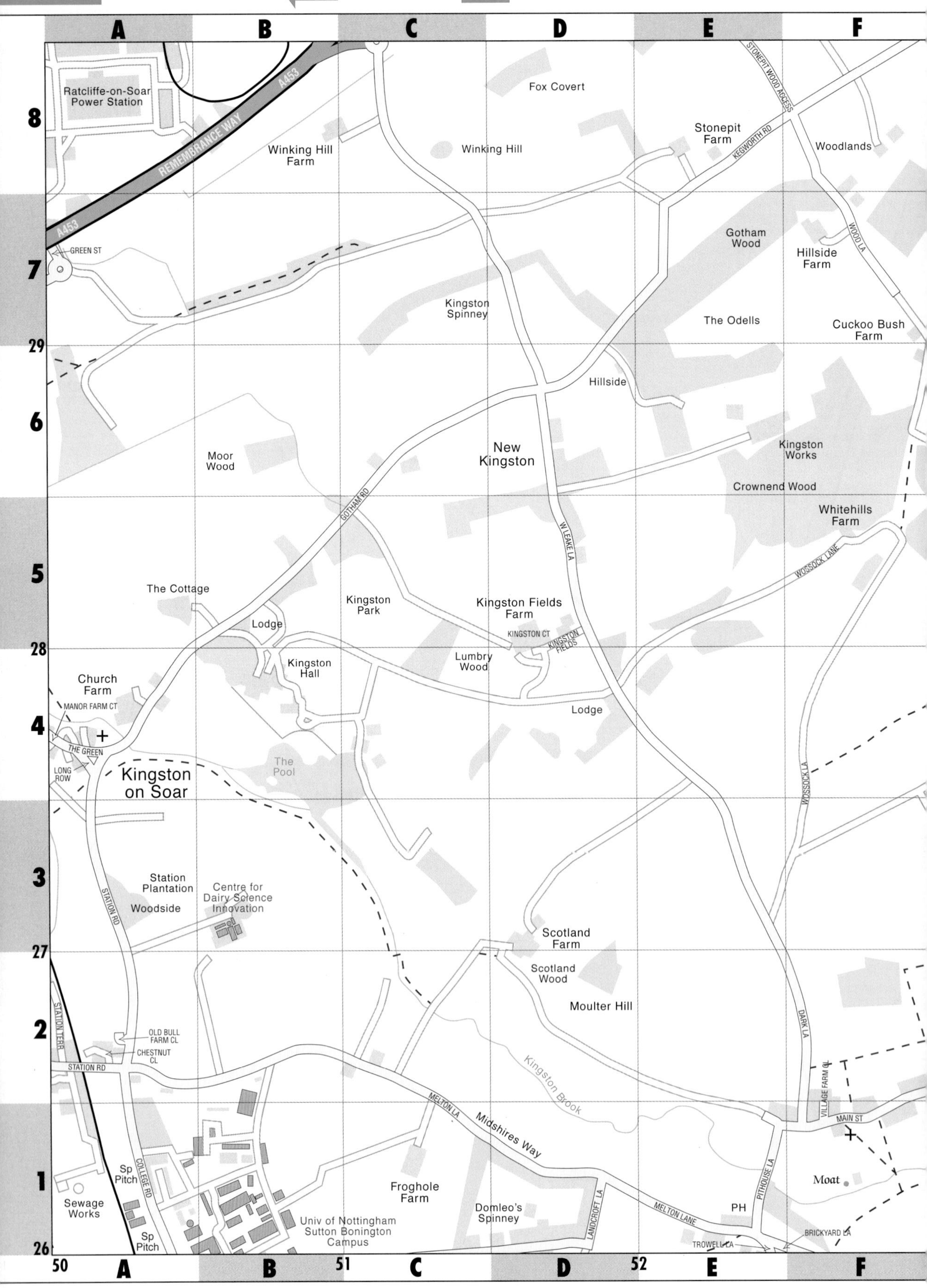
A
B
C
D
E
F
8
7
29
6
5
28
4
3
27
2
1
26
50
51
52
Ratcliffe-on-Soar Power Station
A453
REMEMBRANCE WAY
Winking Hill Farm
Winking Hill
Fox Covert
Stonepit Farm
STONEPIT WOOD ACCESS
KEGWORTH RD
Woodlands
GREEN ST
Gotham Wood
Hillside Farm
WOOD LA
Kingston Spinney
The Odells
Cuckoo Bush Farm
Hillside
Moor Wood
New Kingston
Kingston Works
Crownend Wood
Whitehills Farm
GOTHAM RD
W LEAKE LA
WOSSOCK LANE
The Cottage
Kingston Park
Kingston Fields Farm
Lodge
KINGSTON CT
KINGSTON FIELDS
Church Farm
Kingston Hall
Lumbry Wood
MANOR FARM CT
Lodge
THE GREEN
LONG ROW
Kingston on Soar
The Pool
WOSSOCK LA
Station Plantation
Centre for Dairy Science Innovation
Woodside
STATION RD
Scotland Farm
Scotland Wood
Moulter Hill
STATION TERR
OLD BULL FARM CL
CHESTNUT CL
STATION RD
DARK LA
Kingston Brook
MELTON LA
Midshires Way
VILLAGE FARM CL
MAIN ST
Sp Pitch
COLLEGE RD
Froghole Farm
PITHOUSE LA
Moat
Sewage Works
Domleo's Spinney
LANDCROFT LA
MELTON LANE
PH
Univ of Nottingham Sutton Bonington Campus
Sp Pitch
TROWELL LA
BRICKYARD LA

203
213

195
206

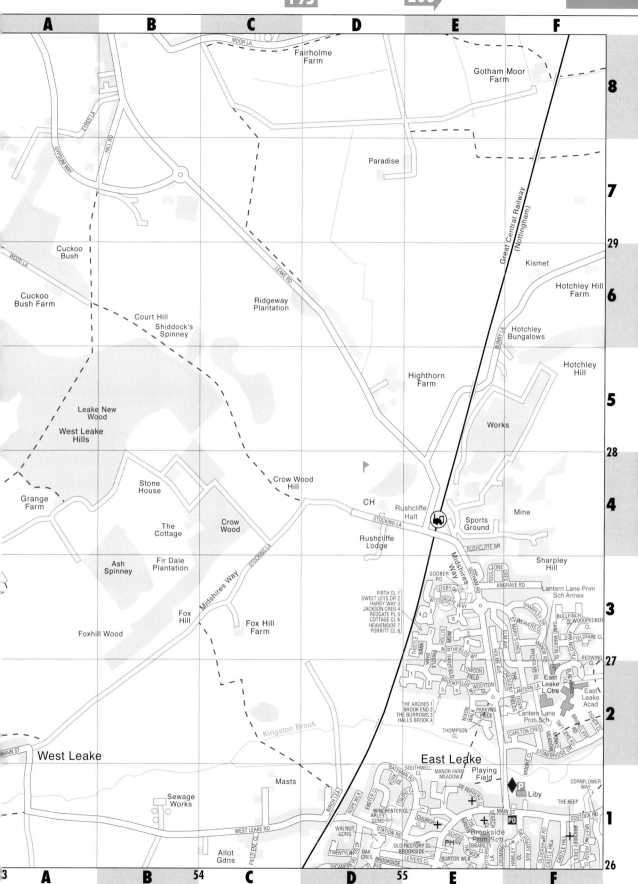
Fairholme Farm
Gotham Moor Farm
Paradise
Cuckoo Bush
Cuckoo Bush Farm
Court Hill
Shiddock's Spinney
Ridgeway Plantation
Great Central Railway (Nottingham)
Kismet
Hotchley Hill Farm
Hotchley Bungalows
Hotchley Hill
Highthorn Farm
Works
Leake New Wood
West Leake Hills
Stone House
Crow Wood Hill
Grange Farm
CH
Rushcliffe Halt
Sports Ground
Mine
The Cottage
Crow Wood
Rushcliffe Lodge
Ash Spinney
Fir Dale Plantation
Sharpley Hill
Midshires Way
Fox Hill
Fox Hill Farm
Foxhill Wood
Kingston Brook
West Leake
East Leake
Masts
Sewage Works
Allot Gdns
Playing Field
Liby
Brookside Prim Sch
East Leake L Ctre
East Leake Acad
Lantern Lane Prim Sch
Lantern Lane Prim Sch Annex
MOOR LA
EYRES LA
HILL RD
GYPSUM WAY
WOOD LA
LEAKE RD
BUNNY LA
STOCKING LA
RUSHCLIFFE GR
GOTHAM RD
WEST LEAKE RD
MAIN ST
BIRCH LEA
FIELD END CL
COSTOCK RD
FIRTH CL 1
SWEET LEYS DR 2
HARDY WAY 3
JACKSON CRES 4
REDGATE PL 5
COTTAGE CL 6
HEAVENSIDE 7
PORRITT CL 8
THE ARCHES 1
BROOK END 2
THE BURROWS 3
HALLS BROOK 4

205
196

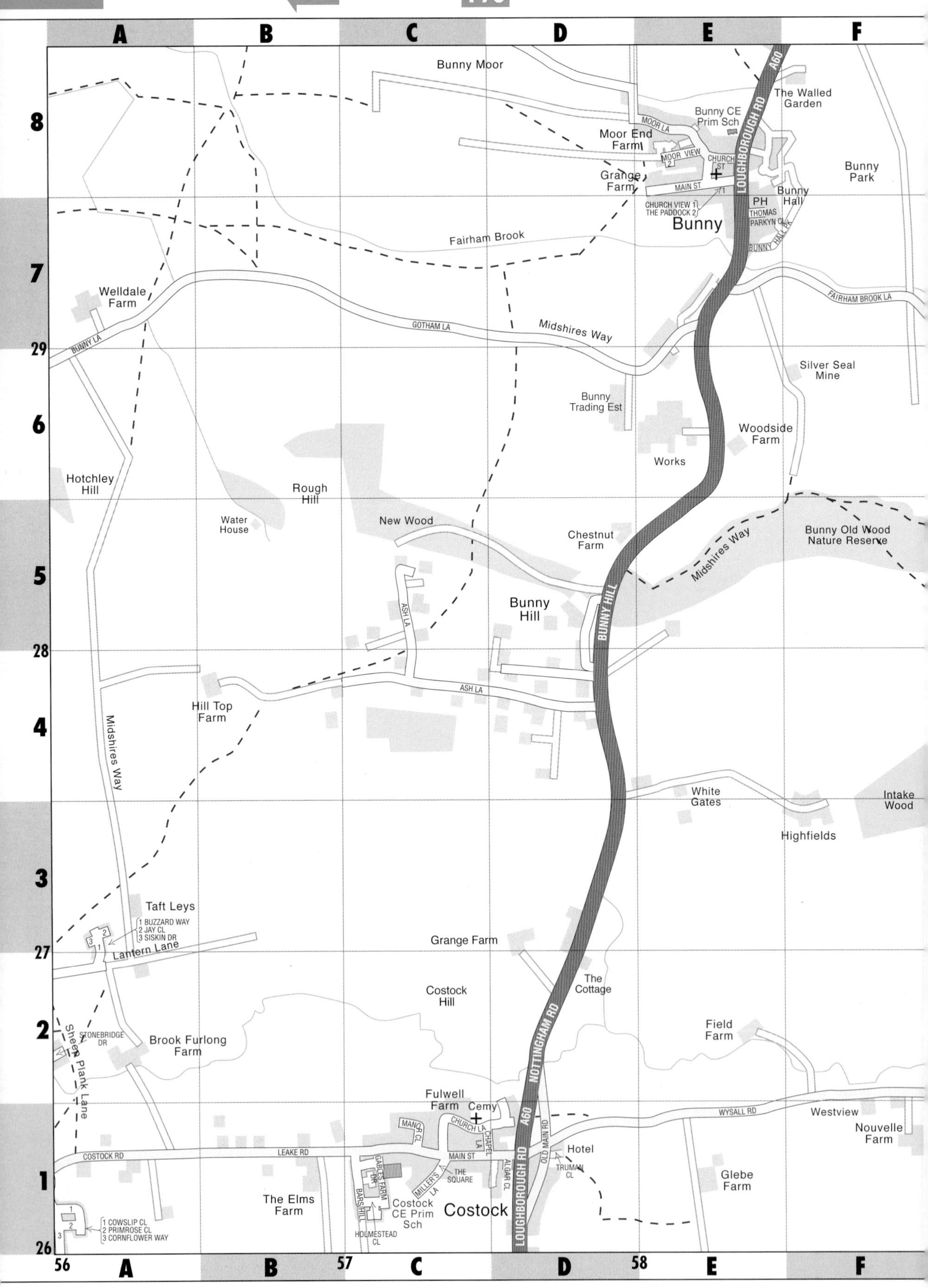
A
B
C
D
E
F
Bunny Moor
The Walled Garden
Bunny CE Prim Sch
MOOR LA
Moor End Farm
MOOR VIEW
CHURCH ST
Grange Farm
MAIN ST
CHURCH VIEW 1
THE PADDOCK 2
Bunny
PH
THOMAS PARKYN CL
BUNNY HALL PK
Bunny Hall
Bunny Park
LOUGHBOROUGH RD
A60
Fairham Brook
Welldale Farm
BUNNY LA
GOTHAM LA
Midshires Way
FAIRHAM BROOK LA
Silver Seal Mine
Bunny Trading Est
Woodside Farm
Works
Hotchley Hill
Rough Hill
Water House
New Wood
Chestnut Farm
Midshires Way
Bunny Old Wood Nature Reserve
ASH LA
Bunny Hill
BUNNY HILL
ASH LA
Hill Top Farm
Midshires Way
White Gates
Highfields
Intake Wood
Taft Leys
1 BUZZARD WAY
2 JAY CL
3 SISKIN DR
Lantern Lane
Grange Farm
The Cottage
Costock Hill
NOTTINGHAM RD
Sheep Plank Lane
STONEBRIDGE DR
Brook Furlong Farm
Field Farm
Fulwell Farm
Cemy
MANOR CL
CHURCH LA
CHAPEL LA
WYSALL RD
Westview
Nouvelle Farm
COSTOCK RD
LEAKE RD
MAIN ST
GABLES FARM DR
MILLER'S LA
THE SQUARE
ALGAR CL
OLD MAIN RD
Hotel
TRUMAN CL
Glebe Farm
The Elms Farm
BARS HILL
Costock CE Prim Sch
Costock
HOLMESTEAD CL
1 COWSLIP CL
2 PRIMROSE CL
3 CORNFLOWER WAY
8
7
29
6
5
28
4
3
27
2
1
26
56
57
58

205
215

197
208

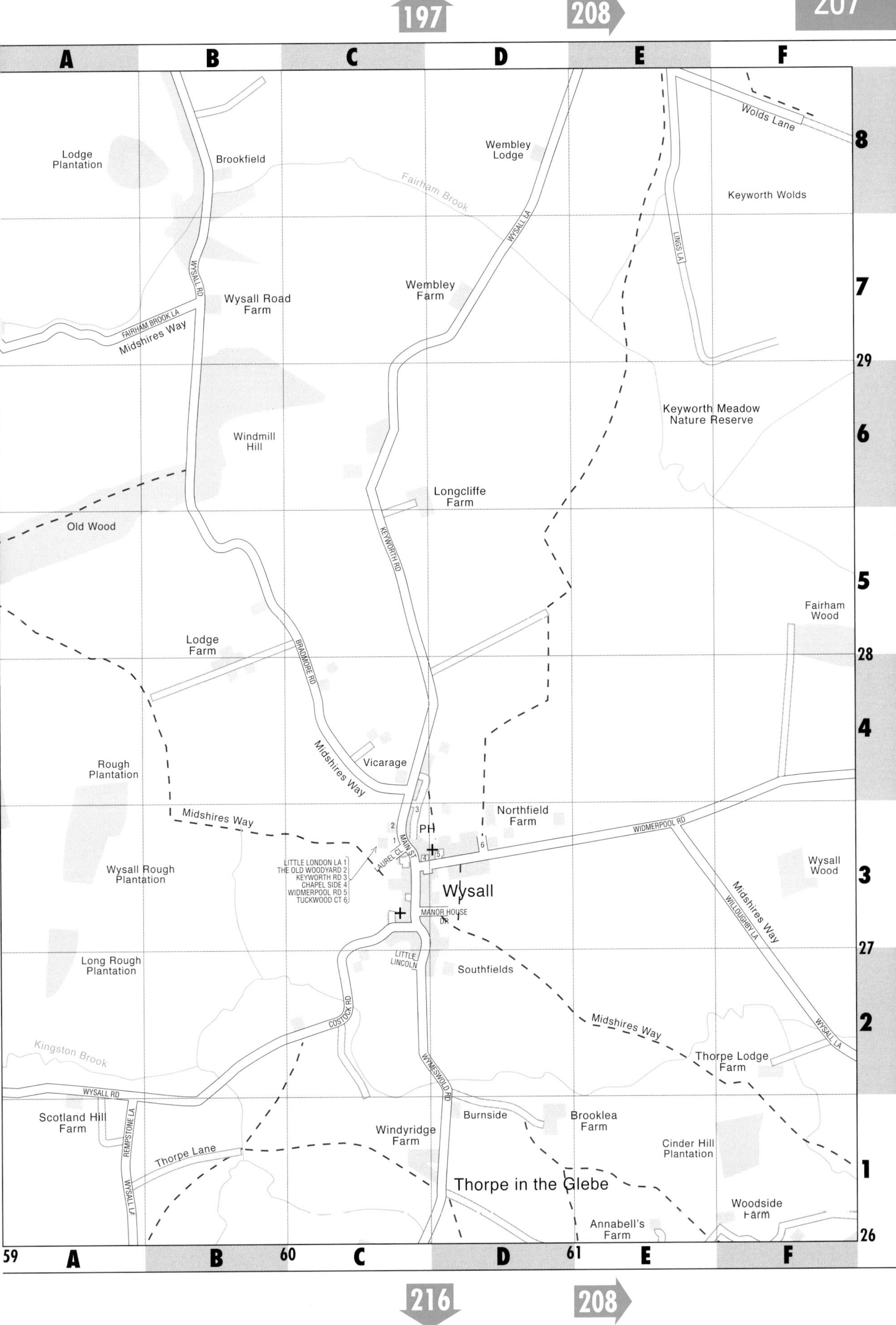
Lodge Plantation
Brookfield
Wembley Lodge
Fairham Brook
Wolds Lane
Keyworth Wolds
WYSALL LA
LINGS LA
WYSALL RD
Wembley Farm
Wysall Road Farm
FAIRHAM BROOK LA
Midshires Way
Keyworth Meadow Nature Reserve
Windmill Hill
Longcliffe Farm
Old Wood
KEYWORTH RD
Fairham Wood
Lodge Farm
BRADMORE RD
Rough Plantation
Midshires Way
Vicarage
Northfield Farm
PH
WIDMERPOOL RD
Midshires Way
LITTLE LONDON LA 1
THE OLD WOODYARD 2
KEYWORTH RD 3
CHAPEL SIDE 4
WIDMERPOOL RD 5
TUCKWOOD CT 6
LAUREL CL
MAIN ST
Wysall Rough Plantation
Wysall
MANOR HOUSE DR
Wysall Wood
Midshires Way
WILLOUGHBY LA
Long Rough Plantation
LITTLE LINCOLN
Southfields
COSTOCK RD
Midshires Way
Kingston Brook
WYSALL LA
Thorpe Lodge Farm
WYSALL RD
WYMESWOLD RD
Scotland Hill Farm
REMPSTONE LA
Burnside
Brooklea Farm
Windyridge Farm
Thorpe Lane
Cinder Hill Plantation
WYSALL LA
Thorpe in the Glebe
Woodside Farm
Annabell's Farm
A B C D E F
8 7 29 6 5 28 4 3 27 2 1 26
59 60 61

216
208

207
198

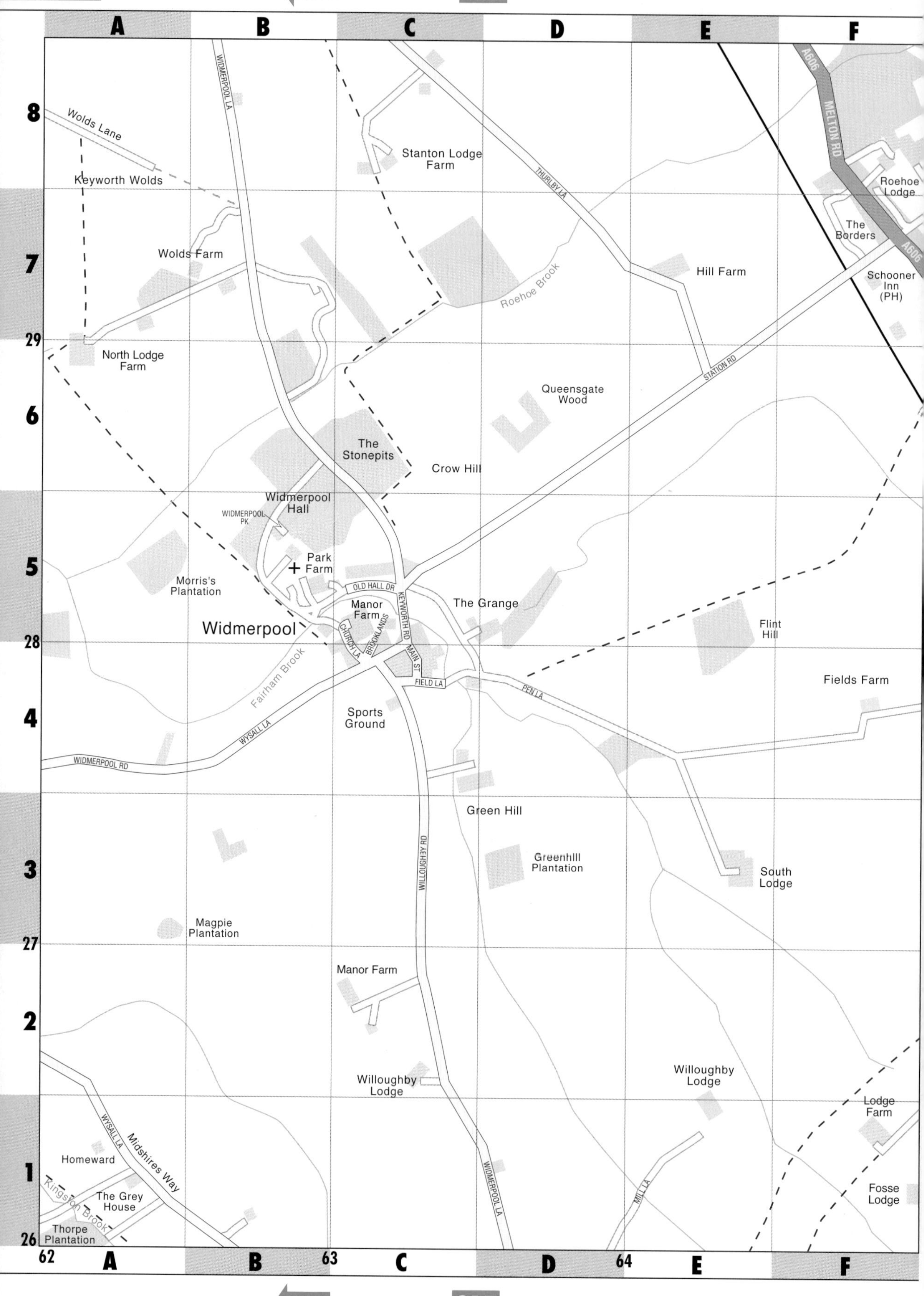
A
B
C
D
E
F
8
7
29
6
5
28
4
3
27
2
1
26
62
63
64
Wolds Lane
Keyworth Wolds
Wolds Farm
North Lodge Farm
WIDMERPOOL LA
Stanton Lodge Farm
THURLBY LA
Roehoe Brook
Hill Farm
A606
MELTON RD
Roehoe Lodge
The Borders
Schooner Inn (PH)
STATION RD
Queensgate Wood
The Stonepits
Crow Hill
Widmerpool Hall
WIDMERPOOL PK
Park Farm
Morris's Plantation
OLD HALL DR
Manor Farm
KEYWORTH RD
The Grange
Widmerpool
CHURCH LA
BROOKLANDS
MAIN ST
FIELD LA
PEN LA
Flint Hill
Fields Farm
Fairham Brook
WYSALL LA
Sports Ground
WIDMERPOOL RD
Green Hill
Greenhill Plantation
South Lodge
WILLOUGHBY RD
Magpie Plantation
Manor Farm
Willoughby Lodge
Willoughby Lodge
Lodge Farm
Homeward
Midshires Way
The Grey House
Kingston Brook
Thorpe Plantation
WIDMERPOOL LA
MILL LA
Fosse Lodge

207
217

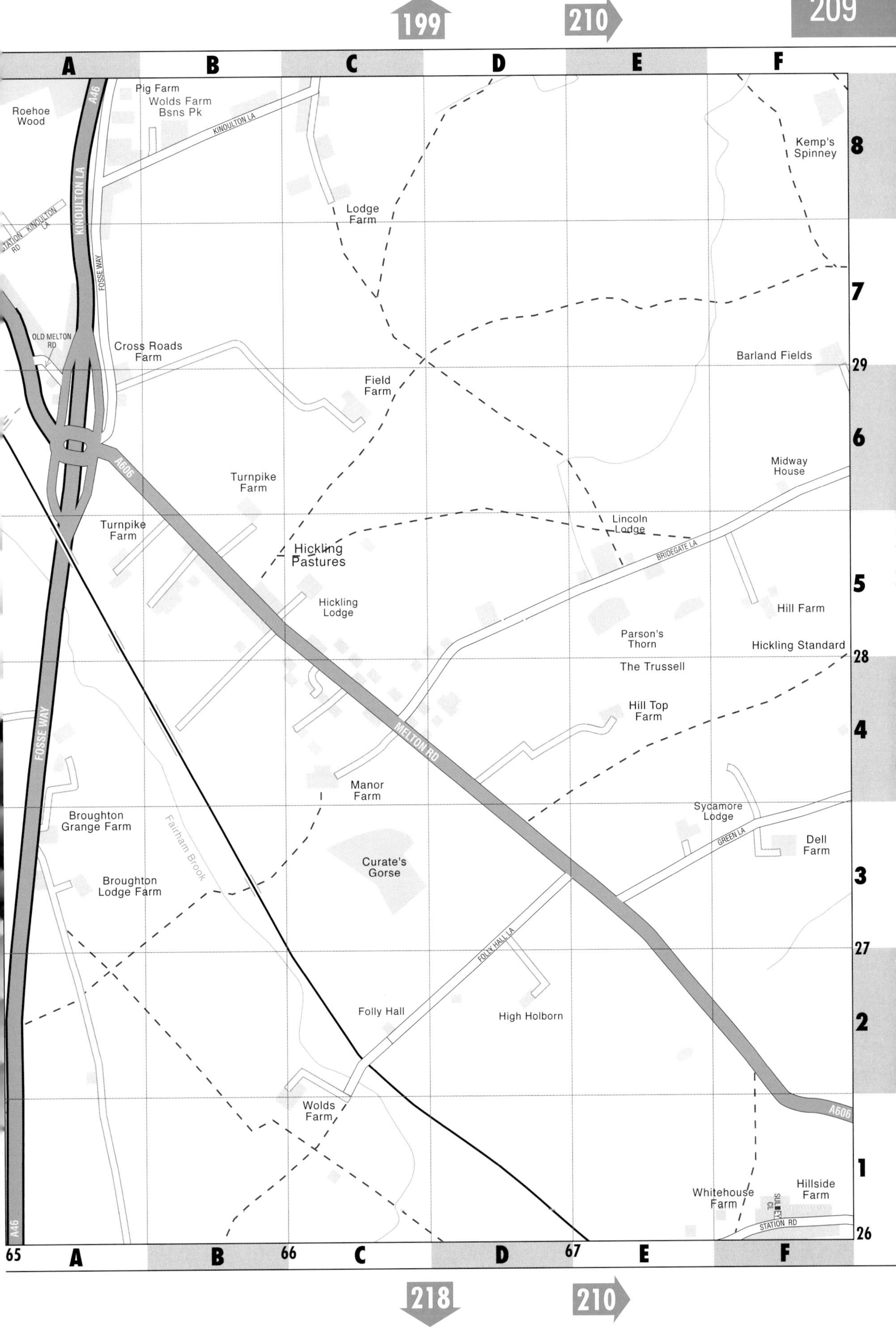

A B C D E F

8

Roehoe Wood

Pig Farm
Wolds Farm
Bsns Pk

KINOULTON LA

Kemp's Spinney

KINOULTON LA

FOSSE WAY

Lodge Farm

7

STATION KINOULTON LA
RD

OLD MELTON RD

Cross Roads Farm

Barland Fields

29

A606

Field Farm

6

Turnpike Farm

Midway House

Turnpike Farm

Lincoln Lodge

Hickling Pastures

BRIDEGATE LA

5

Hickling Lodge

Hill Farm

Parson's Thorn

Hickling Standard

28

The Trussell

FOSSE WAY

Hill Top Farm

4

MELTON RD

Manor Farm

Sycamore Lodge

Broughton Grange Farm

Fairham Brook

GREEN LA

Dell Farm

Curate's Gorse

3

Broughton Lodge Farm

27

FOLLY HALL LA

2

Folly Hall

High Holborn

A606

Wolds Farm

1

Whitehouse Farm

Hillside Farm

STATION RD

26

65 A B 66 C D 67 E F

209
200

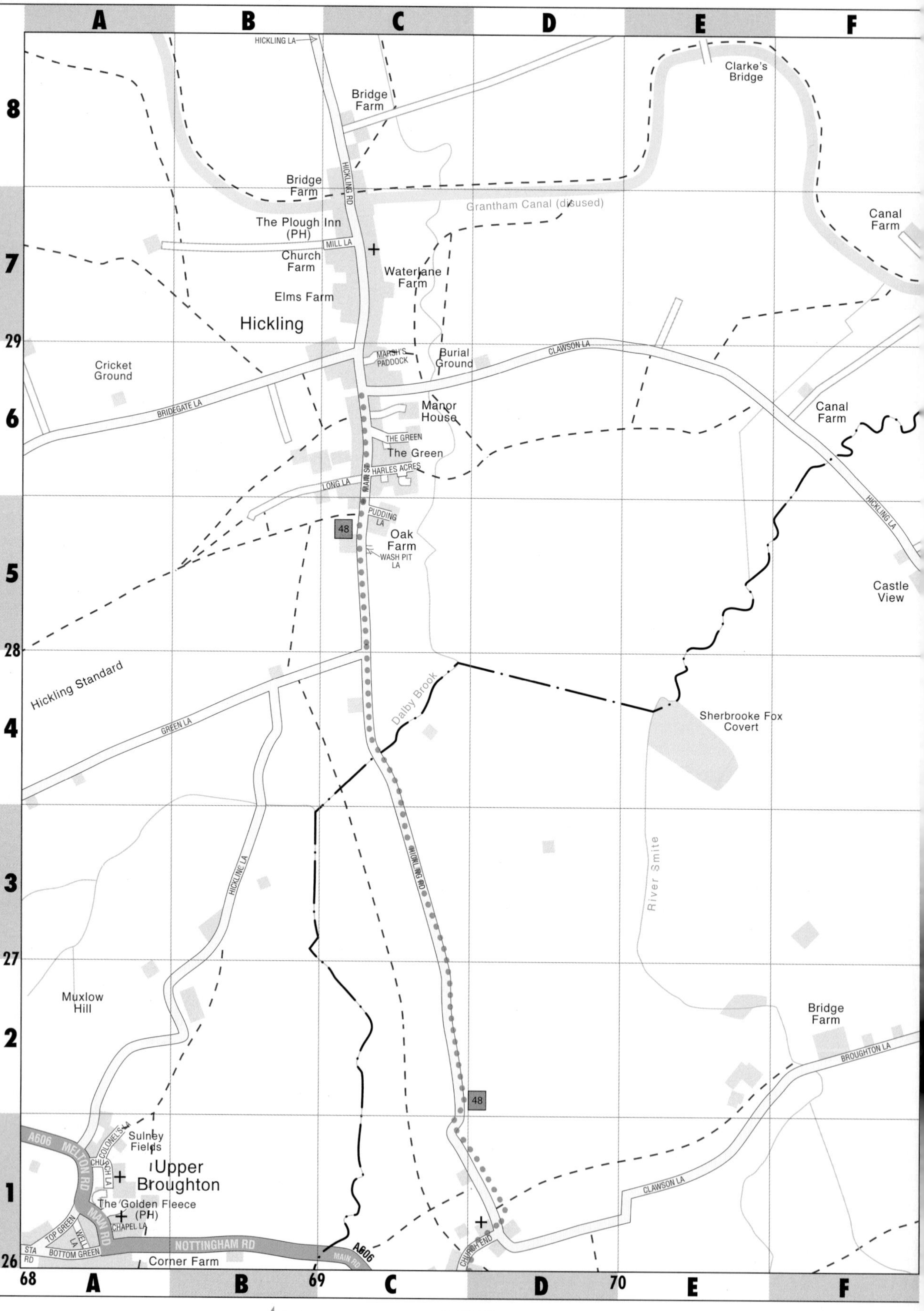

A   B   C   D   E   F

8

HICKLING LA

Bridge
Farm

Clarke's
Bridge

Bridge
Farm

HICKLING RD

MILL LA

Grantham Canal (disused)

Canal
Farm

The Plough Inn
(PH)

Church
Farm

7

Waterlane
Farm

Elms Farm

Hickling

29

Cricket
Ground

Marsh's
Paddock

Burial
Ground

CLAWSON LA

BRIDEGATE LA

Manor
House

Canal
Farm

6

THE GREEN

The Green

HICKLING LA

LONG LA

WAIN SD

HARLES ACRES

PUDDING LA

48

Oak
Farm

WASH PIT
LA

Castle
View

5

28

Hickling Standard

Dalby Brook

Sherbrooke Fox
Covert

GREEN LA

4

River Smite

HICKLING LA

WAIN RD

3

27

Muxlow
Hill

Bridge
Farm

2

BROUGHTON LA

48

A606

MELTON RD

COLONELS LA

Sulney
Fields

Upper
Broughton

CLAWSON LA

1

MAIN RD

CHU...LA

The Golden Fleece
(PH)

CHAPEL LA

TOP GREEN

WELL LA

STA
RD

BOTTOM GREEN

NOTTINGHAM RD

MAIN RD

A606

Corner Farm

CHURCH END

26

68   A   B   69   C   D   70   E   F

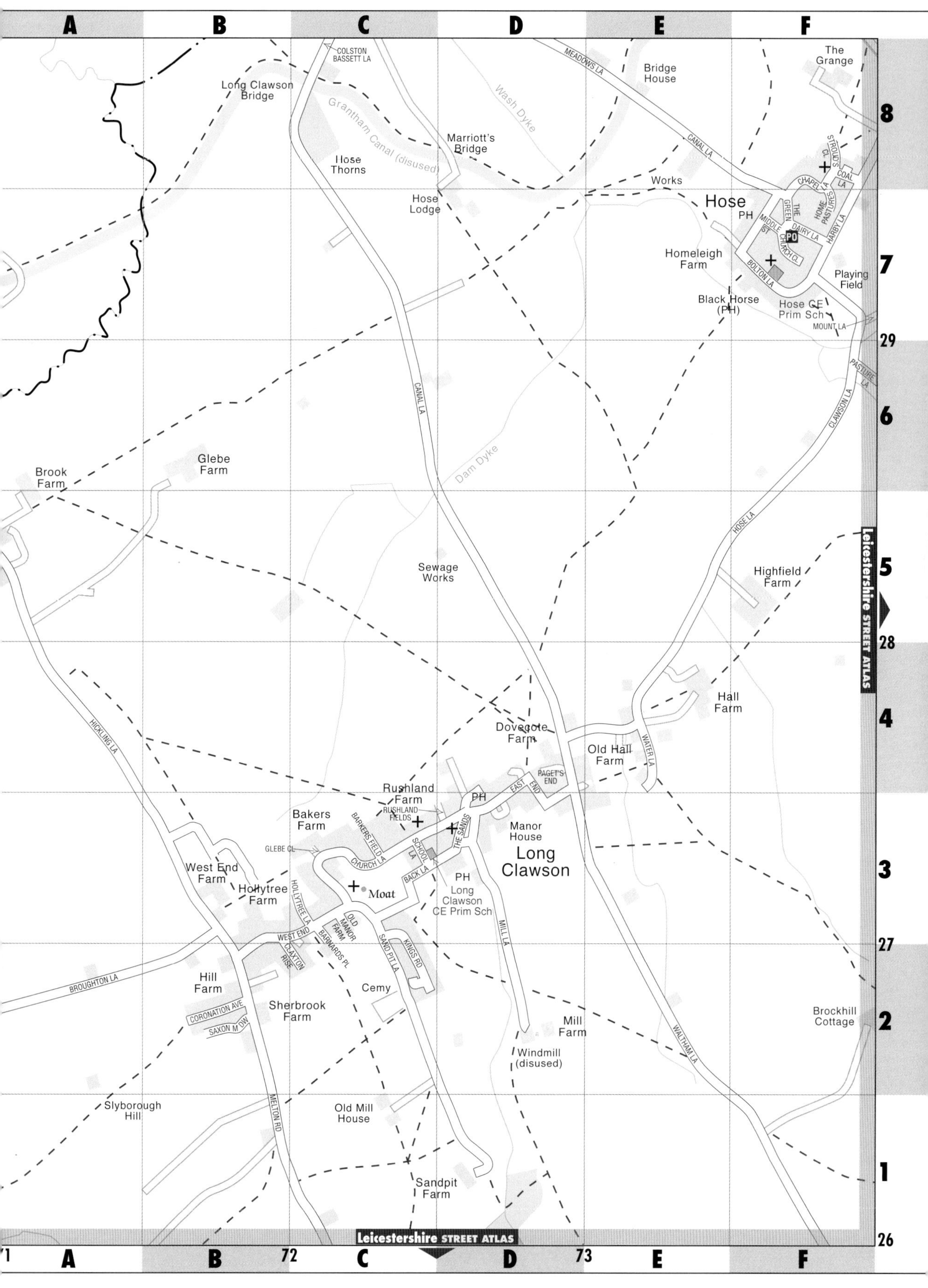
A
B
C
D
E
F
COLSTON BASSETT LA
Long Clawson Bridge
Grantham Canal (disused)
Hose Thorns
Marriott's Bridge
Wash Dyke
MEADOWS LA
Bridge House
The Grange
CANAL LA
Works
Hose Lodge
Hose
PH
Homeleigh Farm
Black Horse (PH)
Hose CE Prim Sch
Playing Field
MOUNT LA
PASTURE LA
CLAWSON LA
CHAPEL LA
COAL LA
HARBY LA
HOME PASTURES
THE GREEN
MIDDLE ST
DAIRY LA
CHURCH CL
BOLTON LA
STROUDS CL
PO
CANAL LA
Dam Dyke
Brook Farm
Glebe Farm
Sewage Works
HOSE LA
Highfield Farm
Hall Farm
HICKLING LA
Dovecote Farm
Old Hall Farm
WATER LA
PAGET'S END
EAST END
Rushland Farm
RUSHLAND FIELDS
PH
Bakers Farm
BARKERS FIELD
CHURCH LA
THE SANDS
SCHOOL LA
BACK LA
Manor House
Long Clawson
GLEBE CL
West End Farm
Hollytree Farm
Moat
PH
Long Clawson CE Prim Sch
HOLLYTREE LA
OLD MANOR FARM
BARNARDS PL
WEST END
CLAXTON RISE
SAND PIT LA
KINGS RD
MILL LA
BROUGHTON LA
Hill Farm
CORONATION AVE
SAXON M DW
Sherbrook Farm
Cemy
Mill Farm
Windmill (disused)
WALTHAM LA
Brockhill Cottage
Slyborough Hill
MELTON RD
Old Mill House
Sandpit Farm
8
7
29
6
5
28
4
3
27
2
1
26
71
72
73
Leicestershire STREET ATLAS

203

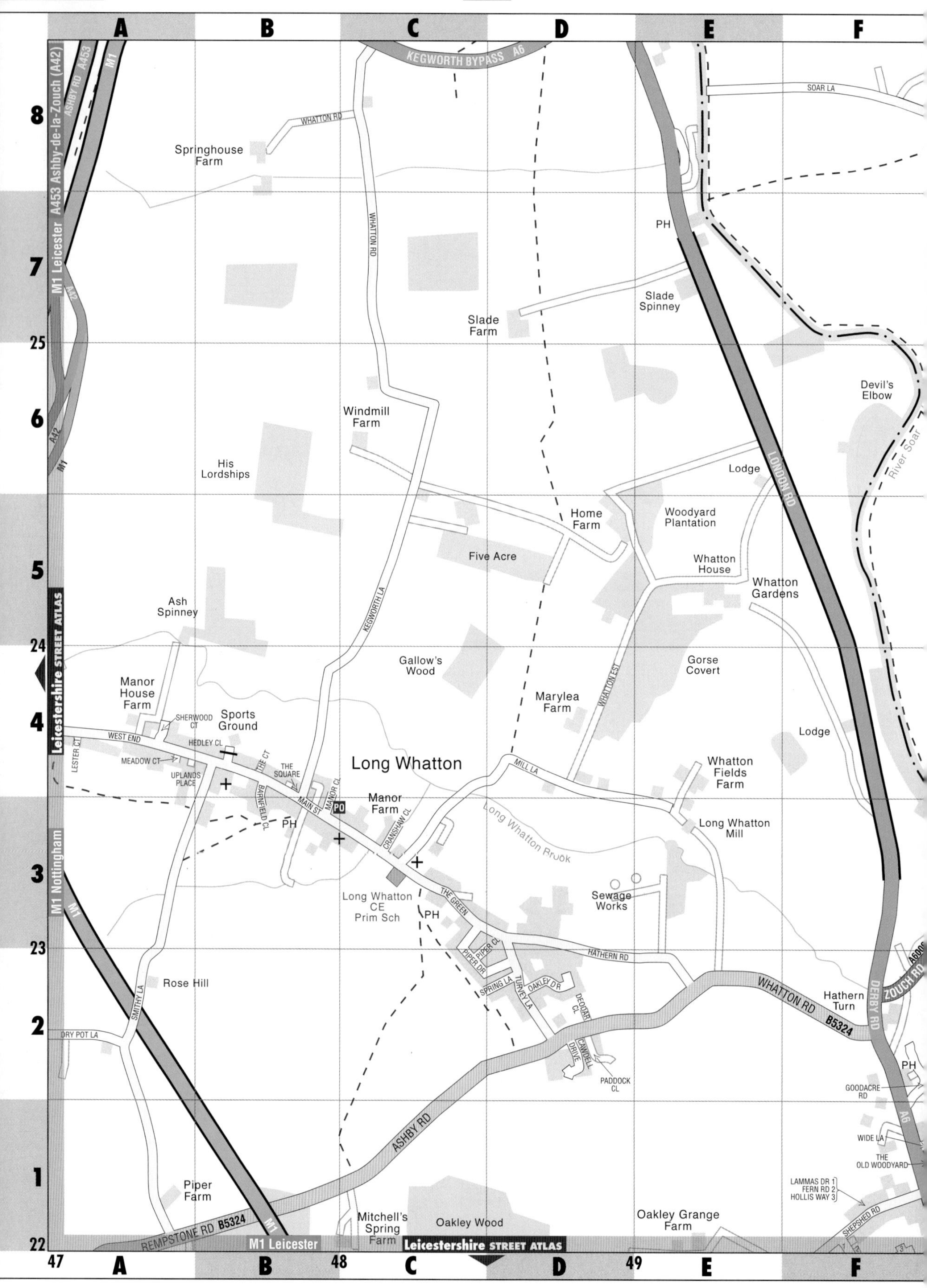

8

KEGWORTH BYPASS A6

ASHBY RD   A453

WHATTON RD

Springhouse
Farm

SOAR LA

7

M1 Leicester A453 Ashby-de-la-Zouch (A42)

WHATTON RD

PH

25

Slade
Spinney

Slade
Farm

6

A42

M1

Windmill
Farm

His
Lordships

LONDON RD

River Soar

Devil's
Elbow

Lodge

5

KEGWORTH LA

Five Acre

Home
Farm

Woodyard
Plantation

Whatton
House

Whatton
Gardens

Ash
Spinney

24

Gallow's
Wood

WHATTON LA

Gorse
Covert

Leicestershire STREET ATLAS

Manor
House
Farm

SHERWOOD
CT

Sports
Ground

Marylea
Farm

Lodge

4

WEST END

LESTER CT

MEADOW CT

HEDLEY CL

THE CT

THE
SQUARE

UPLANDS
PLACE

BARNFIELD CL

MAIN ST

MANOR CL

Long Whatton

MILL LA

Whatton
Fields
Farm

Long Whatton
Mill

Manor
Farm

PO

PH

CRANSHAW CL

Long Whatton Brook

Long Whatton
Mill

3

M1 Nottingham

M1

THE GREEN

PH

Long Whatton
CE
Prim Sch

Sewage
Works

23

Rose Hill

SMITH LA

PIPER CL

PIPER DR

SPRING LA

TURLEY LA

OAKLEY DR

DECOBBE CL

HATHERN RD

WHATTON RD
B5324

DERBY RD

ZOUCH RD

A6

Hathern
Turn

PH

2

DRY POT LA

CANDELL
DRIVE

PADDOCK
CL

GOODACRE
RD

WIDE LA

THE
OLD WOODYARD

1

Piper
Farm

Mitchell's
Spring
Farm

Oakley Wood

Oakley Grange
Farm

LAMMAS DR 1
FERN RD 2
HOLLIS WAY 3

SHEPSHED RD

22

REMPSTONE RD B5324

M1 Leicester

Leicestershire STREET ATLAS

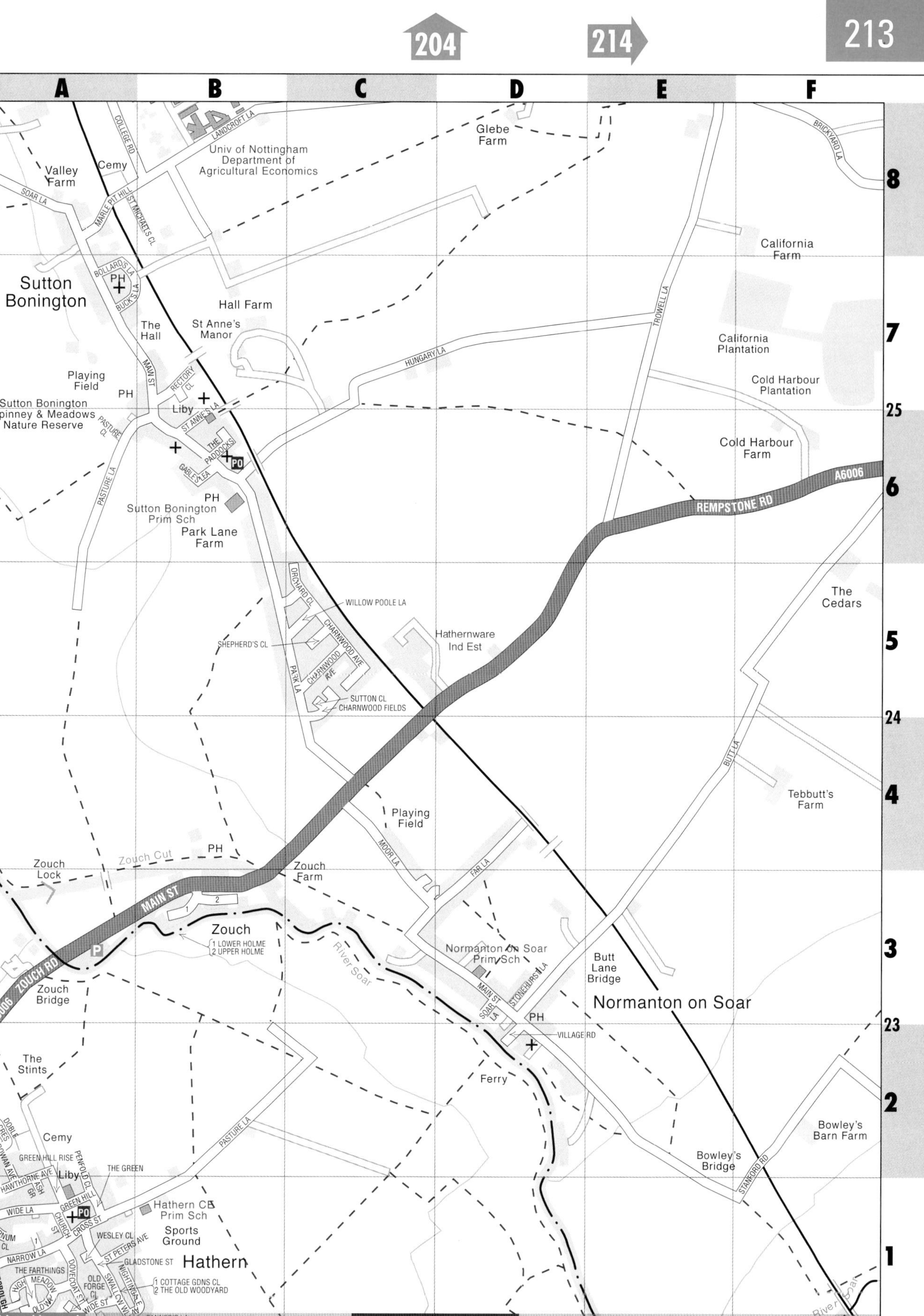

Sutton Bonington

Valley Farm

Cemy

Univ of Nottingham Department of Agricultural Economics

Glebe Farm

California Farm

8

California Plantation

Hall Farm

St Anne's Manor

The Hall

Cold Harbour Plantation

Hungary La

7

25

The Paddocks

Liby

PO

Cold Harbour Farm

PH

Sutton Bonington Prim Sch

Park Lane Farm

REMPSTONE RD   A6006

6

Playing Field

PH

Sutton Bonington Spinney & Meadows Nature Reserve

Pasture Cl

Pasture La

Orchard Cl

Willow Poole La

The Cedars

Shepherd's Cl

Charnwood Ave

Hathernware Ind Est

5

Sutton Cl
Charnwood Fields

Butt La

24

Tebbutt's Farm

4

Playing Field

Moor La

Zouch Cut

PH

Zouch Lock

Zouch Farm

Far La

Butt Lane Bridge

3

Zouch

1 LOWER HOLME
2 UPPER HOLME

Normanton on Soar Prim Sch

Stonehurst La

Normanton on Soar

MAIN ST

ZOUCH RD

A6006

Zouch Bridge

River Soar

Soar La

PH

VILLAGE RD

23

The Stints

Ferry

2

Bowley's Barn Farm

Cemy

Liby

The Green

Green Hill Rise

Hawthorne Ave

Pasture La

Bowley's Bridge

Stanford Rd

PO

Hathern CE Prim Sch

Sports Ground

Hathern

Wide La

Wesley Cl

St Peters Ave

Gladstone St

1 COTTAGE GDNS CL
2 THE OLD WOODYARD

Narrow La

The Farthings

Old Forge

Swan La

River Soar

1

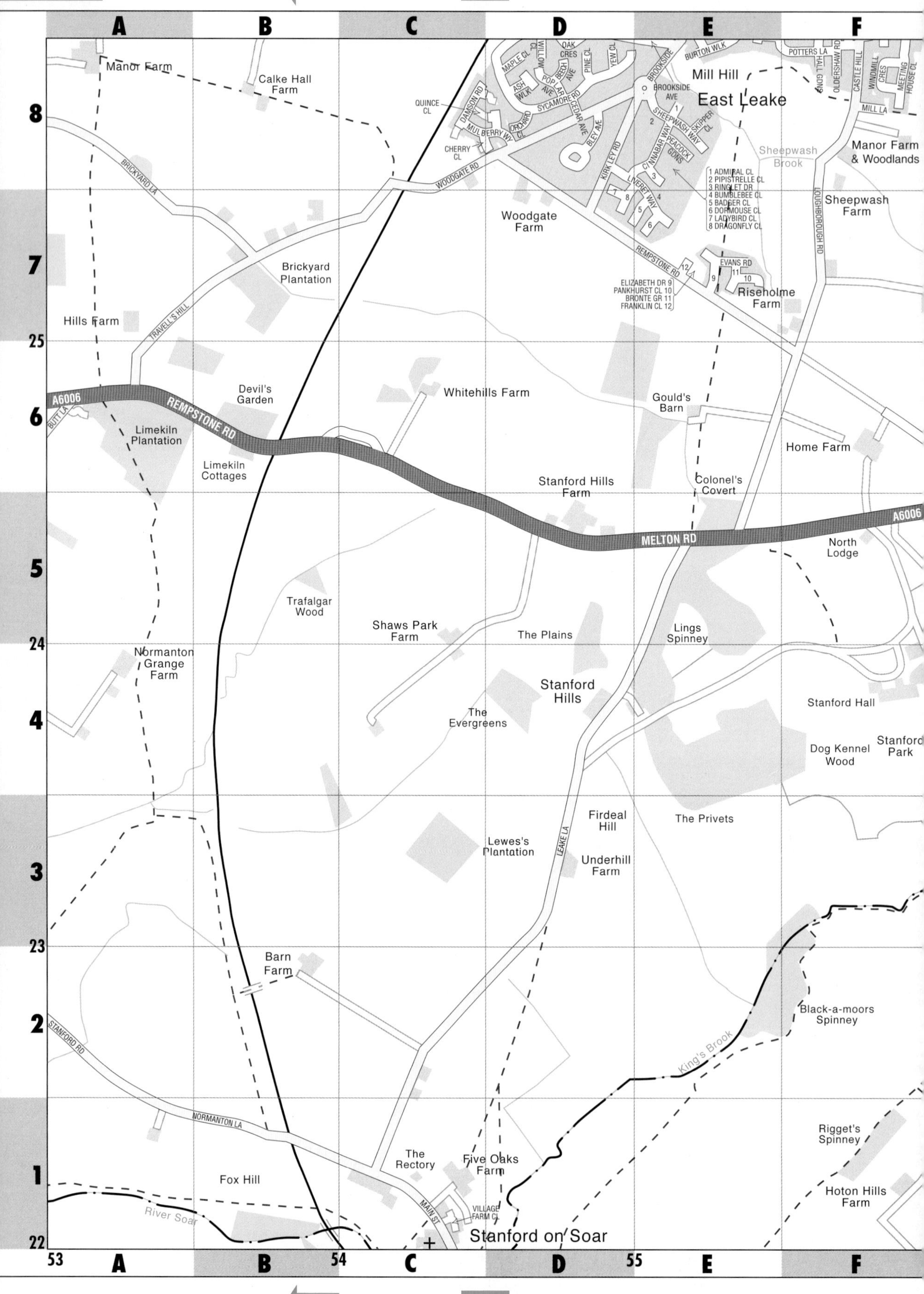

A B C D E F

8
7
25
6
5
24
4
3
23
2
1
22

Manor Farm

Calke Hall Farm

Brickyard LA

Brickyard Plantation

Hills Farm

Travell's Hill

A6006
BUTT LA

REMPSTONE RD

Devil's Garden

Limekiln Plantation

Limekiln Cottages

Normanton Grange Farm

Stanford RD

NORMANTON LA

Fox Hill

River Soar

Barn Farm

Woodgate RD

Woodgate Farm

Whitehills Farm

Stanford Hills Farm

Trafalgar Wood

Shaws Park Farm

The Plains

Stanford Hills

The Evergreens

Lewes's Plantation

LEAKE LA

Firdeal Hill

Underhill Farm

The Privets

King's Brook

The Rectory

Five Oaks Farm

MAIN ST

VILLIAGE FARM CL

Stanford on Soar

QUINCE CL

MAPLE CL
MOTTIM
ASH WLK
POP
BIRCH
PINE CL
YEW CL

OAK CRES

DANSON RD
MULBERRY WAY
ORCHARD CL
SYCAMORE RD
CEDAR AVE

CHERRY CL

KIRK LEY RD

REY AVE

BROOKSIDE

BURTON WLK

Mill Hill

BROOKSIDE AVE

East Leake

POTTERS LA
HALL GDNS
OLDERSHAW RD
CASTLE HILL
WINDMILL CRES
MILL LA
MEETING HOUSE CL

SHEEPWASH
SKIPPER CL
CINNABAR WAY
PEACOCK GDNS

NEREY WAY

1 ADMIRAL CL
2 PIPISTRELLE CL
3 RINGLET DR
4 BUMBLEBEE CL
5 BADGER CL
6 DORMOUSE CL
7 LADYBIRD CL
8 DRAGONFLY CL

REMPSTONE RD

EVANS RD

ELIZABETH DR 9
PANKHURST CL 10
BRONTE GR 11
FRANKLIN CL 12

Sheepwash Brook

Manor Farm & Woodlands

Sheepwash Farm

LOUGHBOROUGH RD

Riseholme Farm

Gould's Barn

Colonel's Covert

Home Farm

MELTON RD
A6006

North Lodge

Lings Spinney

Stanford Hall

Dog Kennel Wood

Stanford Park

Black-a-moors Spinney

Rigget's Spinney

Hoton Hills Farm

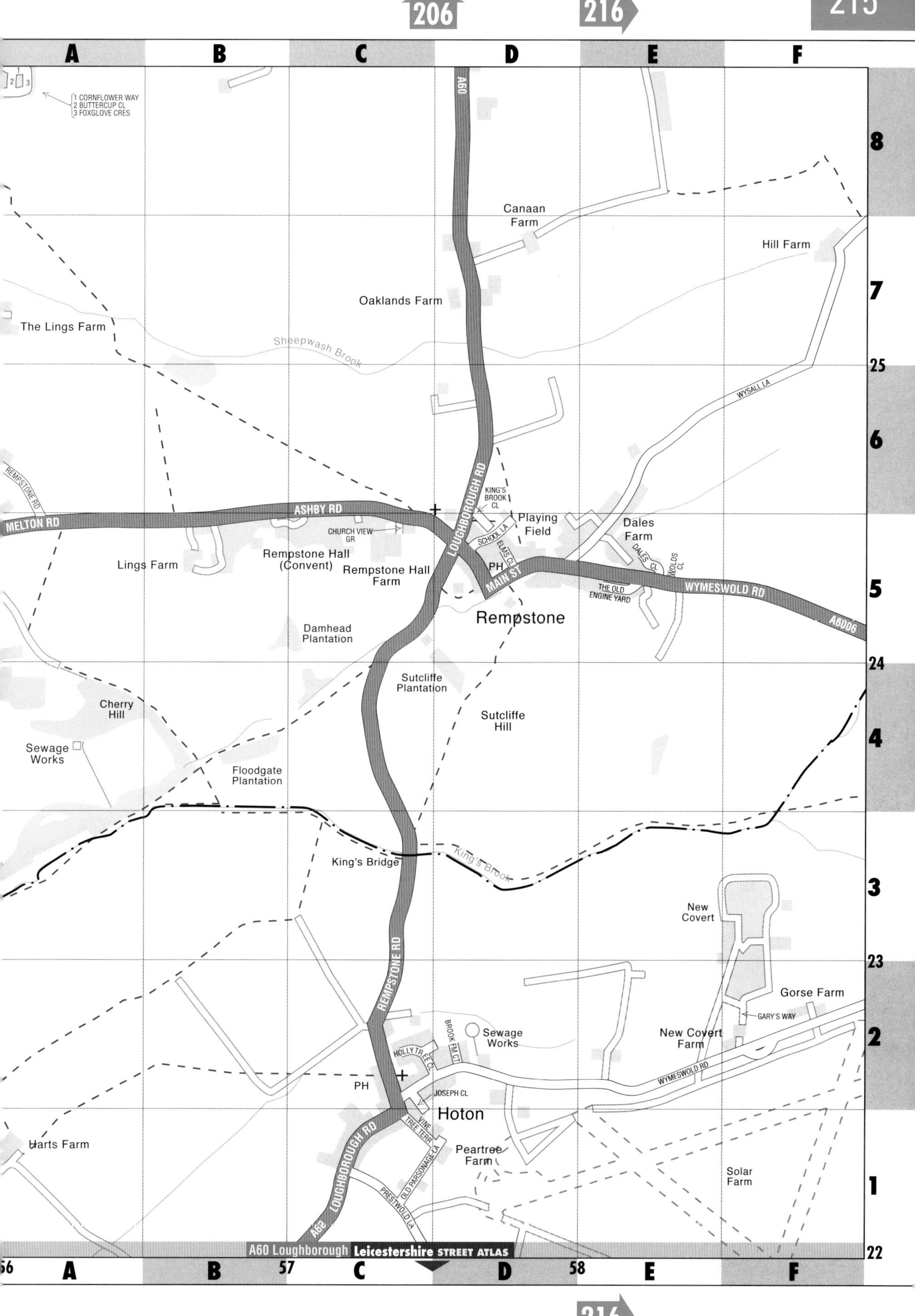
A
B
C
D
E
F
8
7
6
5
4
3
2
1
25
24
23
22
56
57
58
1 CORNFLOWER WAY
2 BUTTERCUP CL
3 FOXGLOVE CRES
A60
Canaan Farm
Hill Farm
Oaklands Farm
The Lings Farm
Sheepwash Brook
WYSALL LA
REMPSTONE RD
MELTON RD
ASHBY RD
LOUGHBOROUGH RD
KING'S BROOK CL
Playing Field
SCHOOL LA
ELMS CL
Dales Farm
DALES CL
WOLDS CL
CHURCH VIEW GR
Lings Farm
Rempstone Hall (Convent)
Rempstone Hall Farm
PH
MAIN ST
THE OLD ENGINE YARD
WYMESWOLD RD
A6006
Rempstone
Damhead Plantation
Sutcliffe Plantation
Sutcliffe Hill
Cherry Hill
Sewage Works
Floodgate Plantation
King's Bridge
King's Brook
New Covert
Gorse Farm
GARY'S WAY
New Covert Farm
REMPSTONE RD
BROOK FM CT
Sewage Works
HOLLY TREE CL
PH
JOSEPH CL
Hoton
VINE TREE TERR
Harts Farm
Peartree Farm
OLD PARSONAGE LA
PRESTWOLD LA
Solar Farm
A60 Loughborough
A6

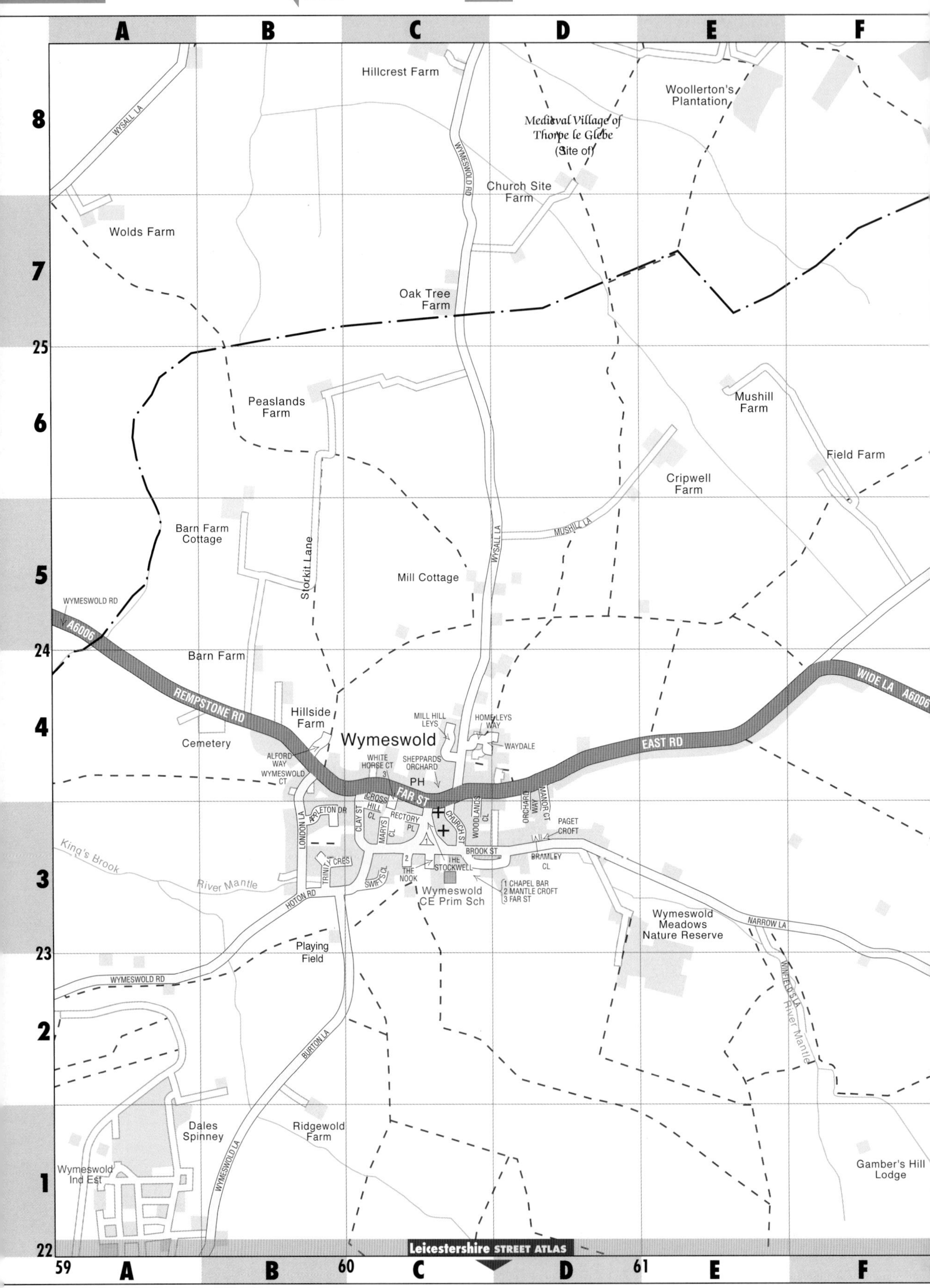

	A	B	C	D	E	F

Hillcrest Farm

Medieval Village of
Thorpe le Glebe
(Site of)

Woollerton's
Plantation

WYSALL LA

Wolds Farm

Church Site
Farm

WYMESWOLD RD

8

7

Oak Tree
Farm

25

Peaslands
Farm

Mushill
Farm

6

Field Farm

Cripwell
Farm

Barn Farm
Cottage

Storkit Lane

WYSALL LA

MUSHILL LA

5

Mill Cottage

WYMESWOLD RD

A6006

Barn Farm

24

REMPSTONE RD

WIDE LA A6006

Hillside
Farm

MILL HILL
LEYS

HOMELEYS
WAY

Wymeswold

4

Cemetery

ALFORD
WAY
WYMESWOLD
CT

WAYDALE

EAST RD

WHITE
HORSE CT
3

SHEPPARDS
ORCHARD

PH

FAR ST

APPLETON DR

CROSS
HILL
CL

CLAY ST

RECTORY
PL

WOODLANCS
CL

ORCHARD
WAY

PAGET
CROFT

LONDON LA

MARYS
CL

CHURCH ST

BROOK ST

King's Brook

TRINITY CRES

SWIFTS CL

2
THE
NOOK

1
THE
STOCKWELL

BRAMLEY
CL

NARROW LA

WINFIELD LA

River Mantle

HOTON RD

3

Wymeswold
CE Prim Sch

1 CHAPEL BAR
2 MANTLE CROFT
3 FAR ST

Wymeswold
Meadows
Nature Reserve

River Mantle

23

WYMESWOLD RD

Playing
Field

BURTON LA

2

Dales
Spinney

Ridgewold
Farm

WYMESWOLD LA

Gamber's Hill
Lodge

1

Wymeswold
Ind Est

22

59	A	B	60	C	D	61	E	F

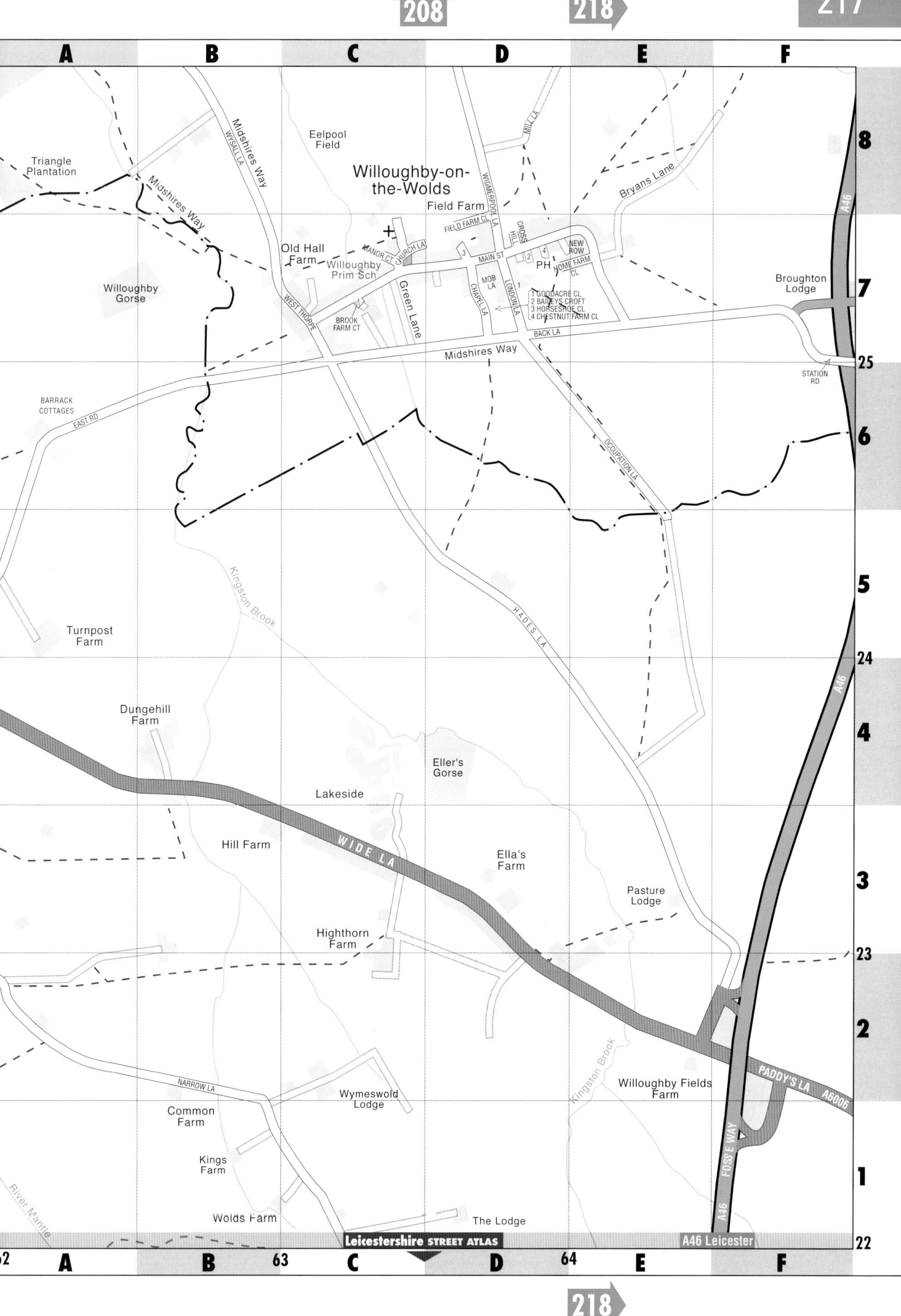
A
B
C
D
E
F
Triangle Plantation
Eelpool Field
Willoughby-on-the-Wolds
Midshires Way
WYSALL LA
Midshires Way
MILL LA
Bryans Lane
Field Farm
WIDMERPOOL LA
FIELD FARM CL
CROSS HILL
Old Hall Farm
MANOR CT
CHURCH LA
Willoughby Prim Sch
MAIN ST
NEW ROW
PH
HOME FARM CL
Willoughby Gorse
MOB LA
CHAPEL LA
LONDON LA
1 GOODACRE CL
2 BAILEYS CROFT
3 HORSESHOE CL
4 CHESTNUT FARM CL
Broughton Lodge
Green Lane
WEST THORPE
BROOK FARM CT
BACK LA
Midshires Way
STATION RD
A46
BARRACK COTTAGES
EAST RD
OCCUPATION LA
Kingston Brook
HADES LA
Turnpost Farm
Dungehill Farm
Eller's Gorse
Lakeside
Hill Farm
WIDE LA
Ella's Farm
Pasture Lodge
Highthorn Farm
Kingston Brook
Willoughby Fields Farm
PADDY'S LA
A6006
NARROW LA
Wymeswold Lodge
Common Farm
Kings Farm
FOSSE WAY
River Mantle
Wolds Farm
The Lodge
8
7
25
6
5
24
4
3
23
2
1
22
62
63
64
A46 Leicester

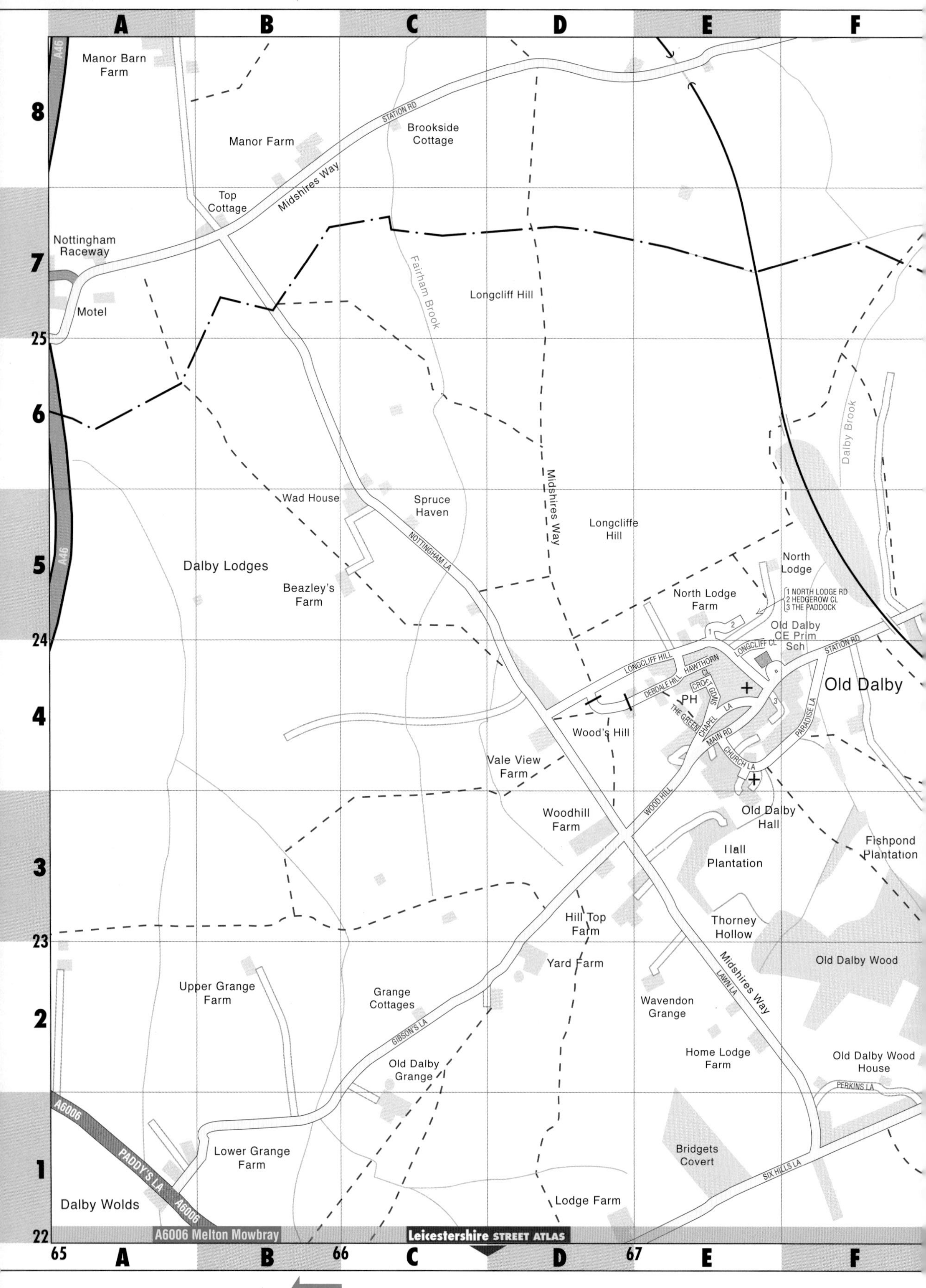

Manor Barn Farm

Manor Farm

Brookside Cottage

STATION RD

Midshires Way

Top Cottage

Nottingham Raceway

Motel

Fairham Brook

Longcliff Hill

Wad House

Spruce Haven

Dalby Lodges

Beazley's Farm

NOTTINGHAM LA

Midshires Way

Longcliffe Hill

North Lodge

1 NORTH LODGE RD
2 HEDGEROW CL
3 THE PADDOCK

North Lodge Farm

Old Dalby CE Prim Sch

LONGCLIFF CL

STATION RD

LONGCLIFF HILL

DEBDALE HILL

HAWTHORN CL

CROFT GDNS

CHAPEL LA

Old Dalby

PH

THE GREEN

MAIN RD

PARADISE LA

Wood's Hill

Vale View Farm

CHURCH LA

Old Dalby Hall

Fishpond Plantation

Woodhill Farm

WOOD HILL

Hall Plantation

Thorney Hollow

Hill Top Farm

Yard Farm

Old Dalby Wood

Upper Grange Farm

Grange Cottages

GIBSON'S LA

Wavendon Grange

Midshires Way

LAWN LA

Old Dalby Grange

Home Lodge Farm

Old Dalby Wood House

PERKINS LA

A6006

PADDY'S LA

A6006

Lower Grange Farm

Bridgets Covert

SIX HILLS LA

Dalby Wolds

Lodge Farm

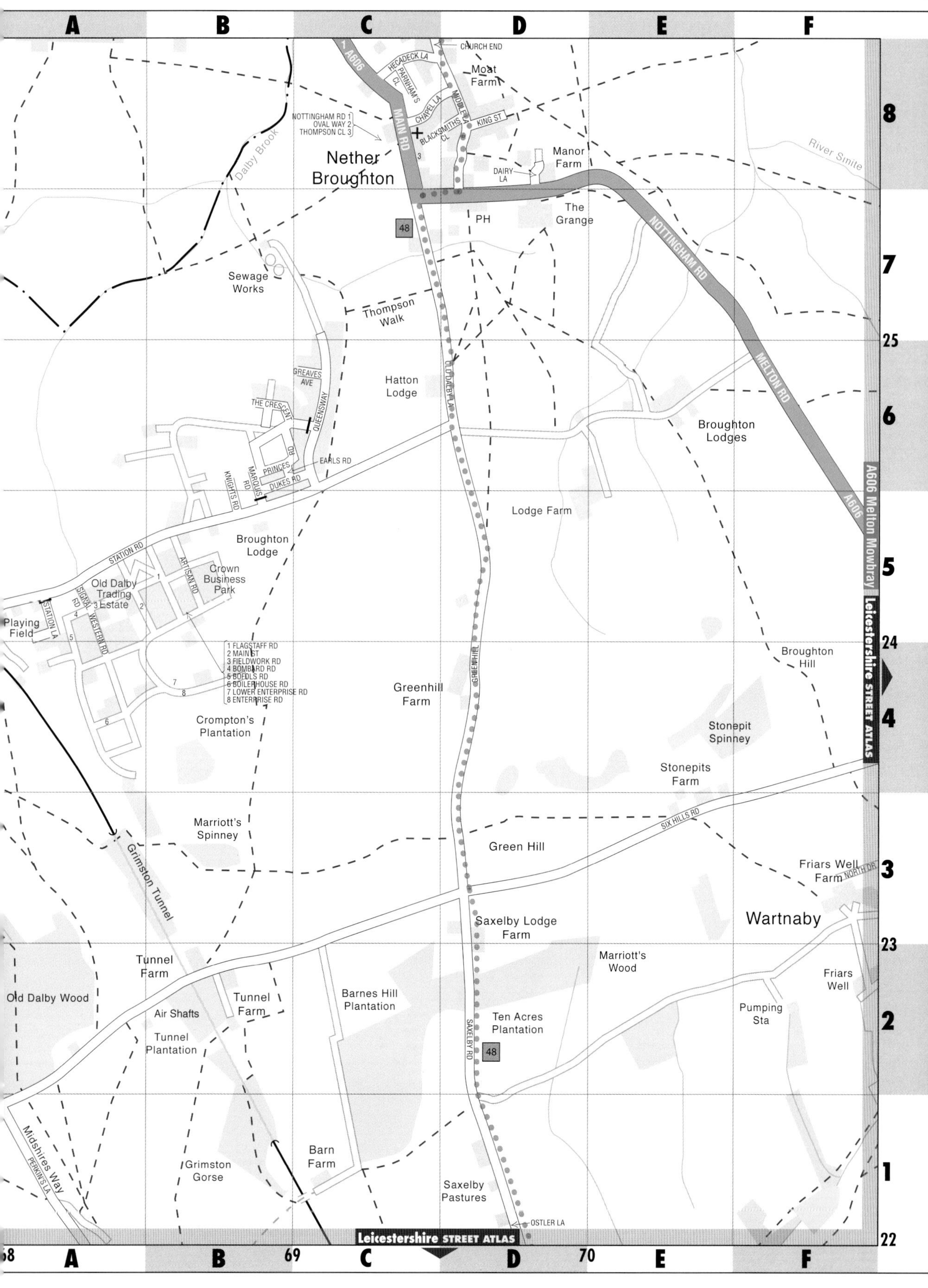

A B C D E F

8
7
25
6
5
24
4
3
23
2
1
22

CHURCH END
Moat Farm
HECADECK LA
PARRHAM'S CL
A606
MAIN RD
CHAPEL LA
MUM LA
KING ST
NOTTINGHAM RD 1
OVAL WAY 2
THOMPSON CL 3
BLACKSMITHS CL
Manor Farm
DAIRY LA
Nether Broughton
48
PH
The Grange
NOTTINGHAM RD
MELTON RD
River Smite

Sewage Works
Thompson Walk
GREAVES AVE
THE CRESCENT
QUEENSWAY
Hatton Lodge
Broughton Lodges

MARQUIS DR
PRINCES DR
EARLS RD
DUKES RD
KNIGHTS RD
STATION RD
Broughton Lodge
ARTISAN RD
Crown Business Park
Lodge Farm

A606 Melton Mowbray
Leicestershire STREET ATLAS

Old Dalby Trading Estate
SIGNAL RD
WESTERN RD
STATION LA
Playing Field

1 FLAGSTAFF RD
2 MAIN ST
3 FIELDWORK RD
4 BOMBARD RD
5 BOELS RD
6 BOILERHOUSE RD
7 LOWER ENTERPRISE RD
8 ENTERPRISE RD

Greenhill Farm
Broughton Hill
Crompton's Plantation
Stonepit Spinney
Stonepits Farm

SIX HILLS RD
Marriott's Spinney
Green Hill
Friars Well Farm
NORTH DR
Wartnaby

Grimston Tunnel
Saxelby Lodge Farm
Marriott's Wood
Friars Well

Tunnel Farm
Barnes Hill Plantation
SAXELBY RD
Ten Acres Plantation
Pumping Sta
Old Dalby Wood
Air Shafts
Tunnel Farm
Tunnel Plantation
48

Midshires Way
PERKINS LA
Grimston Gorse
Barn Farm
Saxelby Pastures
OSTLER LA

68 A B 69 C D 70 E F

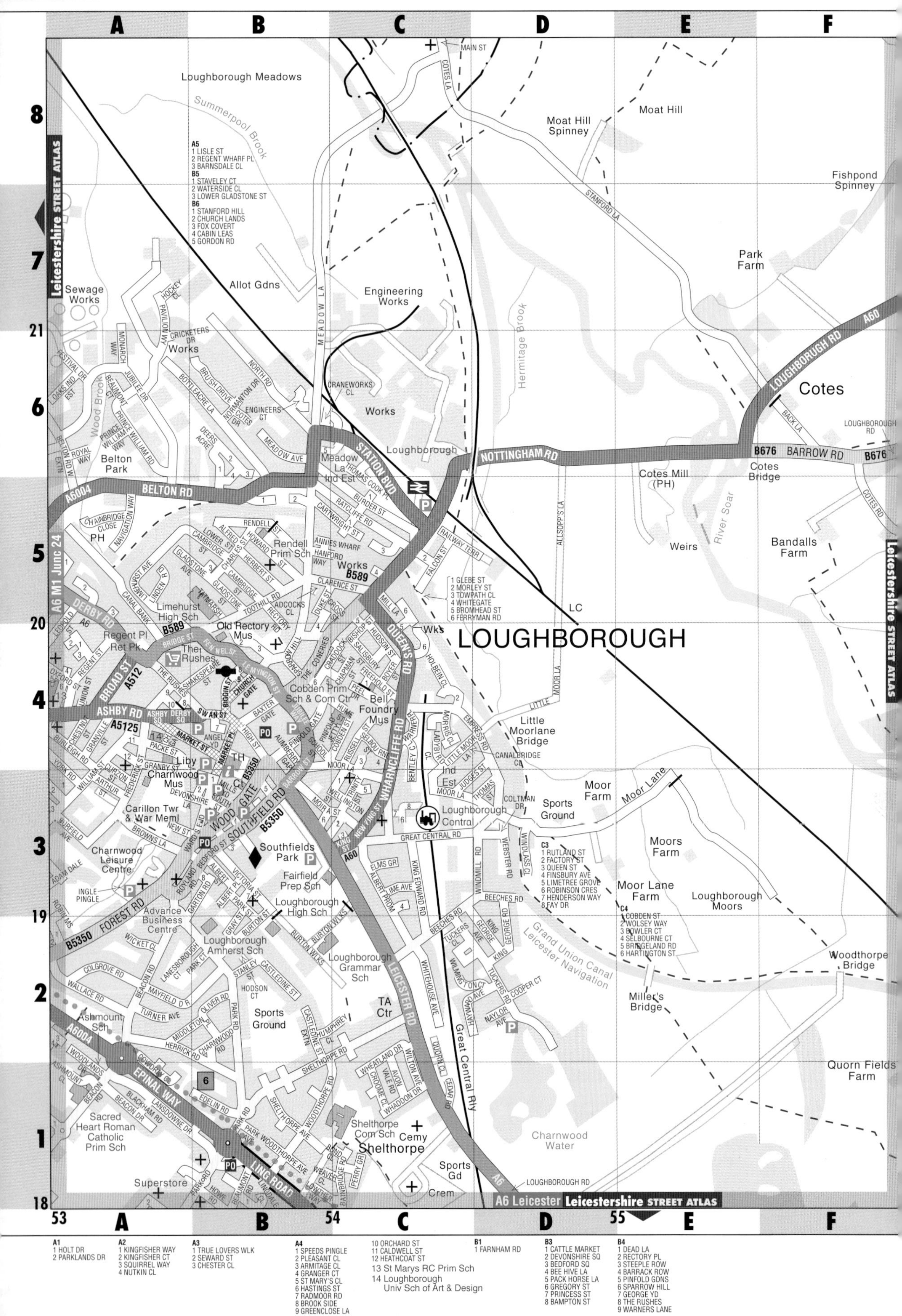

A1
1 HOLT DR
2 PARKLANDS DR

A2
1 KINGFISHER WAY
2 KINGFISHER CT
3 SQUIRREL WAY
4 NUTKIN CL

A3
1 TRUE LOVERS WLK
2 SEWARD ST
3 CHESTER CL

A4
1 SPEEDS PINGLE
2 PLEASANT CL
3 ARMITAGE CL
4 GRANGER CT
5 ST MARY'S CL
6 HASTINGS ST
7 RADMOOR RD
8 BROOK SIDE
9 GREENCLOSE LA

10 ORCHARD ST
11 CALDWELL ST
12 HEATHCOAT ST
13 St Marys RC Prim Sch
14 Loughborough
    Univ Sch of Art & Design

B1
1 FARNHAM RD

B3
1 CATTLE MARKET
2 DEVONSHIRE SQ
3 BEDFORD SQ
4 BEE HIVE LA
5 PACK HORSE LA
6 GREGORY ST
7 PRINCESS ST
8 BAMPTON ST

B4
1 DEAD LA
2 RECTORY PL
3 STEEPLE ROW
4 BARRACK ROW
5 PINFOLD GDNS
6 SPARROW HILL
7 GEORGE YD
8 THE RUSHES
9 WARNERS LANE

Nottingham approaches

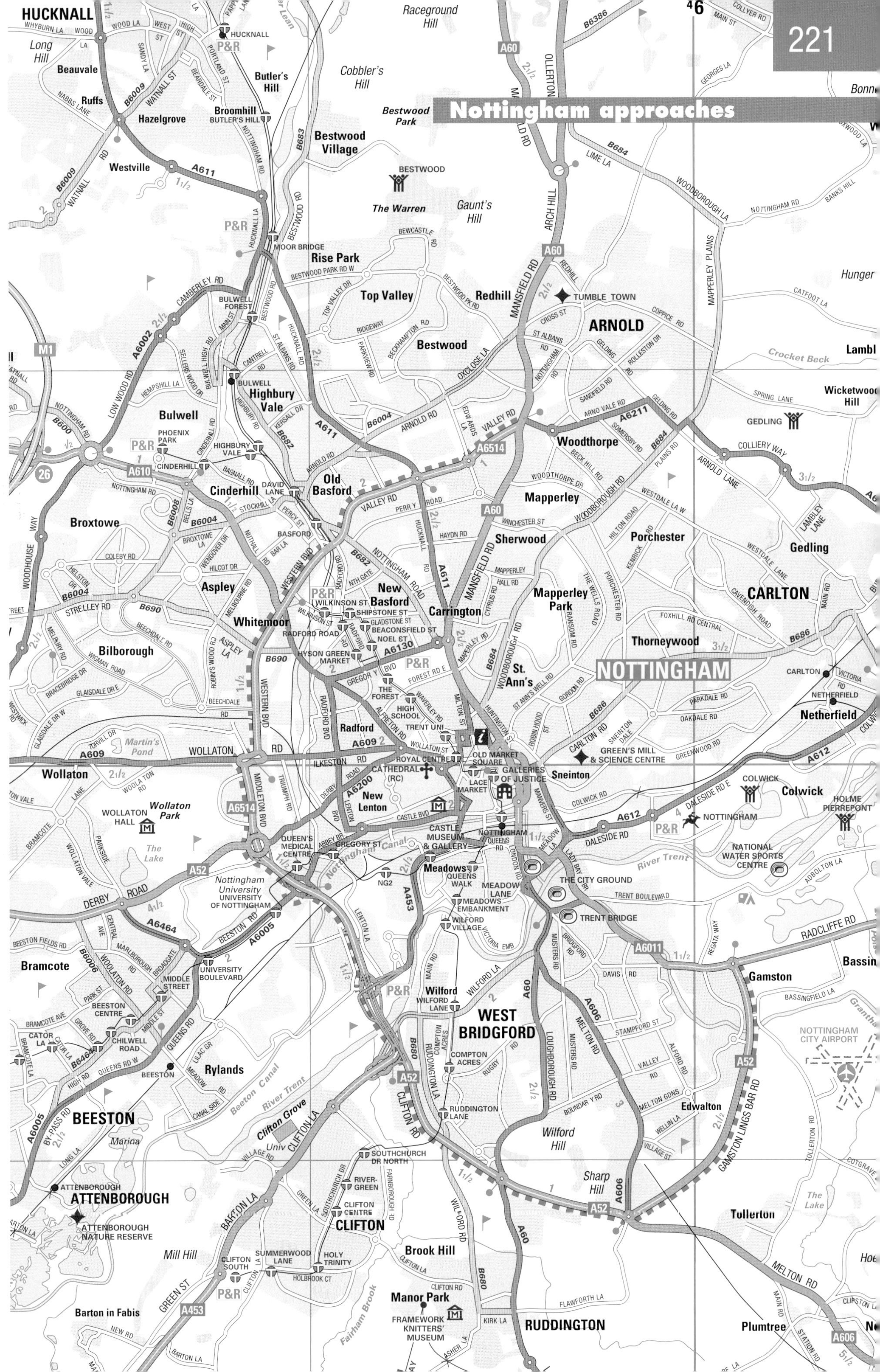
HUCKNALL
WHYBURN LA
WOOD LA
Long Hill
Beauvale
Ruffs
NABBS LANE
Hazelgrove
Westville
B6009
WATNALL RD
WATNALL ST
SANDY LA
PORTLAND ST
BEARDALL ST
HUCKNALL
P&R
Butler's Hill
Broomhill
BUTLER'S HILL
NOTTINGHAM RD
A611
Raceground Hill
Cobbler's Hill
Bestwood Park
B683
Bestwood Village
BESTWOOD
The Warren
Gaunt's Hill
BESTWOOD RD
HUCKNALL LA
MOOR BRIDGE
Rise Park
BESTWOOD PARK RD W
BEWCASTLE RD
Top Valley
Redhill
TOP VALLEY DR
RIDGEWAY
BECKHAMPTON RD
Bestwood
CAMBERLEY RD
BULWELL FOREST
A6002
M1
BULWELL
Highbury Vale
Bulwell
HEMPSHILL LA
LOW WOOD RD
NOTTINGHAM RD
B600
26
PHOENIX PARK
HIGHBURY VALE
CINDERHILL
A610
Cinderhill
DAVID LANE
STOCKHILL LA
Old Basford
Broxtowe
B6008
B6004
BROXTOWE LA
BASFORD
WOODHOUSE WAY
COLEBY RD
HILCOT DR
Aspley
B6004
STRELLEY RD
B690
Whitemoor
WESTERN BVD
New Basford
WILKINSON ST
SHIPSTONE ST
GLADSTONE ST
BEACONSFIELD ST
NOEL ST
RADFORD ROAD
HYSON GREEN MARKET
A6130
Carrington
Bilborough
WIGMAN ROAD
BRACEBRIDGE DR
GLAISDALE DR E
BEECHDALE RD
ASPLEY LA
B690
THE FOREST
HIGH SCHOOL
TRENT UNI
Radford
A609
WOLLATON ST
ROYAL CENTRE
OLD MARKET SQUARE
CATHEDRAL (RC)
LACE MARKET
GALLERIES OF JUSTICE
Sneinton
Martin's Pond
A609
WOLLATON RD
Wollaton
ILKESTON RD
A6200
New Lenton
Wollaton Park
WOLLATON HALL
The Lake
A6514
MIDDLETON BVD
CASTLE BVD
CASTLE MUSEUM & GALLERY
NOTTINGHAM
QUEEN'S MEDICAL CENTRE
GREGORY ST
Nottingham Canal
Meadows
QUEENS WALK
NG2
A453
MEADOW LANE
MEADOWS EMBANKMENT
WILFORD VILLAGE
A52
DERBY ROAD
A6464
Nottingham University
UNIVERSITY OF NOTTINGHAM
BEESTON RD
A6005
UNIVERSITY BOULEVARD
MIDDLE STREET
Bramcote
B6006
BEESTON CENTRE
CHILWELL ROAD
CATOR LA
B6464
QUEENS RD
Rylands
BEESTON
Beeston Canal
River Trent
BEESTON
A6005
Marina
Clifton Grove
Univ
CLIFTON LA
ATTENBOROUGH
ATTENBOROUGH NATURE RESERVE
Mill Hill
CLIFTON SOUTH
SUMMERWOOD LANE
HOLY TRINITY
CLIFTON
CLIFTON CENTRE
RIVERGREEN
SOUTHCHURCH DR NORTH
BARTON LA
Barton in Fabis
GREEN ST
A453
P&R
Fairham Brook
Brook Hill
Manor Park
FRAMEWORK KNITTERS' MUSEUM
RUDDINGTON
B680
A52
CLIFTON RD
RUDDINGTON LANE
COMPTON ACRES
Wilford
WILFORD LANE
WILFORD LA
WEST BRIDGFORD
LOUGHBOROUGH RD
A60
A606
MELTON RD
Wilford Hill
Sharp Hill
A52
Edwalton
GAMSTON LINGS BAR RD
Gamston
NOTTINGHAM CITY AIRPORT
Tollerton
The Lake
Plumtree
MELTON RD
A606
THE CITY GROUND
TRENT BOULEVARD
TRENT BRIDGE
A6011
RADCLIFFE RD
Bassingfield
NATIONAL WATER SPORTS CENTRE
River Trent
DALESIDE RD
A612
NOTTINGHAM
Colwick
COLWICK
HOLME PIERREPONT
GREEN'S MILL & SCIENCE CENTRE
CARLTON RD
B686
NOTTINGHAM
St. Ann's
Thorneywood
CARLTON
Netherfield
NETHERFIELD
CARLTON
A612
Gedling
Porchester
Mapperley Park
Sherwood
MANSFIELD RD
A60
Mapperley
Woodthorpe
A6211
B684
WOODBOROUGH RD
A6514
VALLEY RD
ARNOLD RD
B6004
ARNOLD
TUMBLE TOWN
MANSFIELD RD
A60
ARCH HILL
OLLERTON RD
A60
B6386
B684
WOODBOROUGH LA
MAPPERLEY PLAINS
Hunger Hill
Crocket Beck
Lambley
Wicketwood Hill
GEDLING
COLLIERY WAY
ARNOLD LANE
WESTDALE LANE
CARLTON

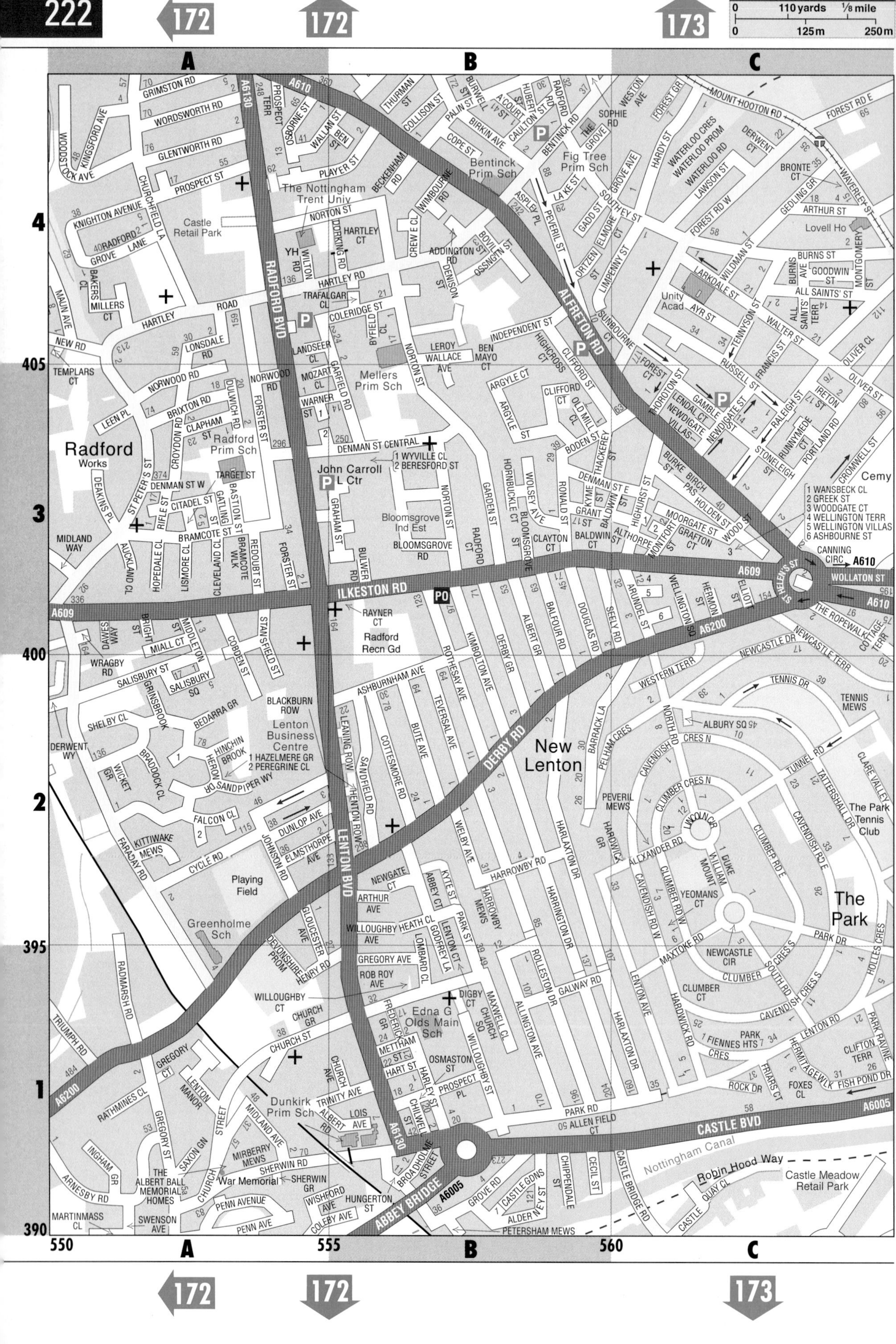

172
172
173
Scale: 7 inches to 1 mile
0 110 yards 1/8 mile
0 125m 250m
A
B
C
4
405
3
400
2
395
1
390
550
555
560
GRIMSTON RD
WORDSWORTH RD
GLENTWORTH RD
KINGSFORD AVE
WOODSTOCK AVE
PROSPECT ST
KNIGHTON AVENUE
CHURCHFIELD LA
RADFORD GROVE LANE
Castle Retail Park
BAKERS CL
MAUN AVE
MILLERS CT
HARTLEY ROAD
NEW RD
TEMPLARS CT
LONSDALE RD
NORWOOD RD
BRIXTON RD
CLAPHAM ST
DULWICH RD
CROYDON RD
LEEN PL
Radford
Works
Radford Prim Sch
TARGET ST
DENMAN ST W
DEAKINS PL
ST PETER'S ST
RIFLE ST
CITADEL ST
GATLING ST
BASTION ST
BRAMCOTE ST
BRAMCOTE WLK
MIDLAND WAY
AUCKLAND CL
HOPEDALE CL
LISMORE CL
CLEVELAND CL
REDOUBT ST
FORSTER ST
A609
A610
A6130
RADFORD BVD
PROSPECT TERR
OSBORNE ST
WALLAN ST
BEN ST
PLAYER ST
The Nottingham Trent Univ
BECKENHAM RD
NORTON ST
HARTLEY CT
YH
WILTON RD
DORKING RD
HARTLEY RD
TRAFALGAR CL
COLERIDGE ST
BYFIELD CL
LANDSEER CL
MOZART CL
WARNER ST
GARFIELD RD
Mellers Prim Sch
LEROY WALLACE AVE
BEN MAYO CT
DENMAN ST CENTRAL
1 WYVILLE CL
2 BERESFORD ST
John Carroll L Ctr
GRAHAM ST
Bloomsgrove Ind Est
BLOOMSGROVE RD
BULWER RD
THURMAN ST
COLLISON ST
PALIN ST
BURWELL ST
BIRKIN AVE
COPE ST
WIMBOURNE RD
CREW E CL
ADDINGTON RD
DENISON ST
BOVILL ST
OSSINGTON ST
Bentinck Prim Sch
CAULTON ST
HUBERT ST
RADFORD RD
BENTINCK RD
THE GROVE
SOPHIE RD
Fig Tree Prim Sch
WESTON AVE
ASPLEY PL
PEVERIL ST
LAKE ST
GADD ST
ELMORE CT
SOUTHEY ST
GROVE AVE
ORTZEN ST
LIMPENNY ST
ALFRETON RD
INDEPENDENT ST
HIGHCROSS CT
CLIFFORD ST
ARGYLE CT
ARGYLE ST
CLIFFORD CT
OLD MILL CL
BODEN ST
THACKEREY ST
GARDEN ST
RADFORD CT
HORNBUCKLE CT
WOLSEY AVE
BLOOMSGROVE ST
RONALD ST
CLAYTON CT
DENMAN ST E
GRANT ST
BALDWIN ST
BALDWIN CT
HIGHURST ST
ALTHORPE ST
MONTFORT ST
MOORGATE ST
GRAFTON CT
ILKESTON RD
PO
RAYNER CT
Radford Recn Gd
HARDY ST
FOREST GR
MOUNT HOOTON RD
FOREST RD E
WATERLOO CRES
WATERLOO PROM
WATERLOO RD
DERWENT CT
LAWSON ST
FOREST RD W
BRONTE CT
GEDLING GR
ARTHUR ST
WAVERLEY ST
Lovell Ho
WILDMAN ST
LARKDALE ST
BURNS ST
BURNS AVE
GOODWIN ST
MONTGOMERY ST
ALL SAINTS' ST
ALL SAINTS' TERR
Unity Acad
AYR ST
TENNYSON ST
WALTER ST
SUNBOURNE CT
FOREST CT
FRANCIS ST
OLIVER CL
OLIVER ST
RUSSELL ST
THOROTON ST
LENDAL CT
NEWDIGATE VILLAS
GAMBLE ST
NEWDIGATE ST
RALEIGH ST
IRETON ST
RUNNYMEDE CT
PORTLAND RD
STONELEIGH ST
CROMWELL ST
Cemy
BURKE ST
BIRCH PAS
HOLDEN ST
WOOD ST
1 WANSBECK CL
2 GREEK ST
3 WOODGATE CT
4 WELLINGTON TERR
5 WELLINGTON VILLAS
6 ASHBOURNE ST
CANNING CIRC
WOLLATON ST
ST HELEN'S ST
THE ROPEWALK
COTTAGE TERR
NEWCASTLE DR
NEWCASTLE TERR
A6200
ELLIOTT ST
HERMON ST
WELLINGTON SQ
ARUNDEL ST
SEELY RD
DOUGLAS RD
BALFOUR RD
ALBERT GR
DERBY GR
KIMBOLTON AVE
ROTHESAY AVE
TEVERSAL AVE
BUTE AVE
COTTESMORE RD
ASHBURNHAM AVE
DERBY RD
BRIGHT ST
DAWES WAY
MIALL CT
MIDDLETON ST
COBDEN ST
STANSFIELD ST
WRAGBY RD
SALISBURY ST
SALISBURY SQ
GRINSBROOK
SHELBY CL
BEDARRA GR
DERWENT WY
WICKET GR
BRADDOCK CL
HINCHIN BROOK
HERON DR
SANDPIPER WY
1 HAZELMERE GR
2 PEREGRINE CL
FALCON CL
KITTIWAKE MEWS
FARADAY RD
CYCLE RD
Playing Field
Greenholme Sch
JOHNSON RD
DUNLOP AVE
ELMSTHORPE AVE
BLACKBURN ROW
Lenton Business Centre
LEANING ROW
SANDFIELD RD
HENTON ROW
LENTON BVD
New Lenton
BARRACK LA
PELHAM CRES
WESTERN TERR
TENNIS DR
TENNIS MEWS
NORTH RD
ALBURY SQ
CAVENDISH CRES N
CLUMBER CRES N
TUNNEL RD
TATTERSHALL DR
CLARE VALLEY
PEVERIL MEWS
LINCOLN CIR
HARDWICK GR
ALEXANDER RD
CLUMBER RD E
CAVENDISH RD E
DUKE WILLIAM MOUNT
The Park Tennis Club
YEOMANS CT
CLUMBER RD W
CAVENDISH RD W
The Park
PARK DR
MAXTOKE RD
NEWCASTLE CIR
CLUMBER CRES S
SOUTH RD
CAVENDISH CRES S
HOLLES CRES
CLUMBER CT
HARDWICK RD
PARK RAVINE
LENTON RD
1 FIENNES HTS
PARK CRES
HERMITAGE WLK
CLIFTON TERR
FISH POND DR
ROCK DR
FRIARS CT
FOXES CL
HARLAXTON DR
HARRINGTON DR
HARROWBY RD
HARROWBY MEWS
WELBY AVE
ROLLESTON DR
GALWAY RD
ALLINGTON AVE
LENTON AVE
NEWGATE CT
ARTHUR AVE
ABBEY CT
KYTE ST
PARK ST
LENTON CT
HEATH CL
GODFREY LA
LOMBARD CL
WILLOUGHBY AVE
GREGORY AVE
ROB ROY AVE
WILLOUGHBY CT
DIGBY CT
MAXWELL CL
CHURCH SQ
WILLOUGHBY ST
Edna G Olds Main Sch
FREDERICK GR
METTHAM ST
HART ST
OSMASTON ST
PROSPECT PL
HARLEY ST
CHILWELL ST
DEVONSHIRE PROM
GLOUCESTER AVE
HENRY RD
CHURCH GR
CHURCH ST
CHURCH AVE
TRINITY AVE
Dunkirk Prim Sch
ALBERT RD
LOIS AVE
RADMARSH RD
TRIUMPH RD
A6200
GREGORY CT
LENTON MANOR
RATHMINES CL
GREGORY ST
STREET
MIDLAND AVE
MIRBERRY MEWS
SHERWIN RD
SHERWIN GR
War Memorial
INGHAM GR
SAXON GN
THE ALBERT BALL MEMORIAL HOMES
ARNESBY RD
CHURCH
PENN AVENUE
WISHFORD AVE
HUNGERTON ST
COLEBY AVE
MARTINMASS CL
SWENSON AVE
PENN AVE
ABBEY BRIDGE
A6005
BROADHOLME STREET
A6130
GROVE RD
CASTLE GDNS
ALDER CT
NEY ST
CHIPPENDALE ST
CECIL ST
PARK RD
ALLEN FIELD CT
CASTLE BRIDGE RD
CASTLE BVD
Nottingham Canal
Robin Hood Way
CASTLE QUAY CL
Castle Meadow Retail Park
PETERSHAM MEWS

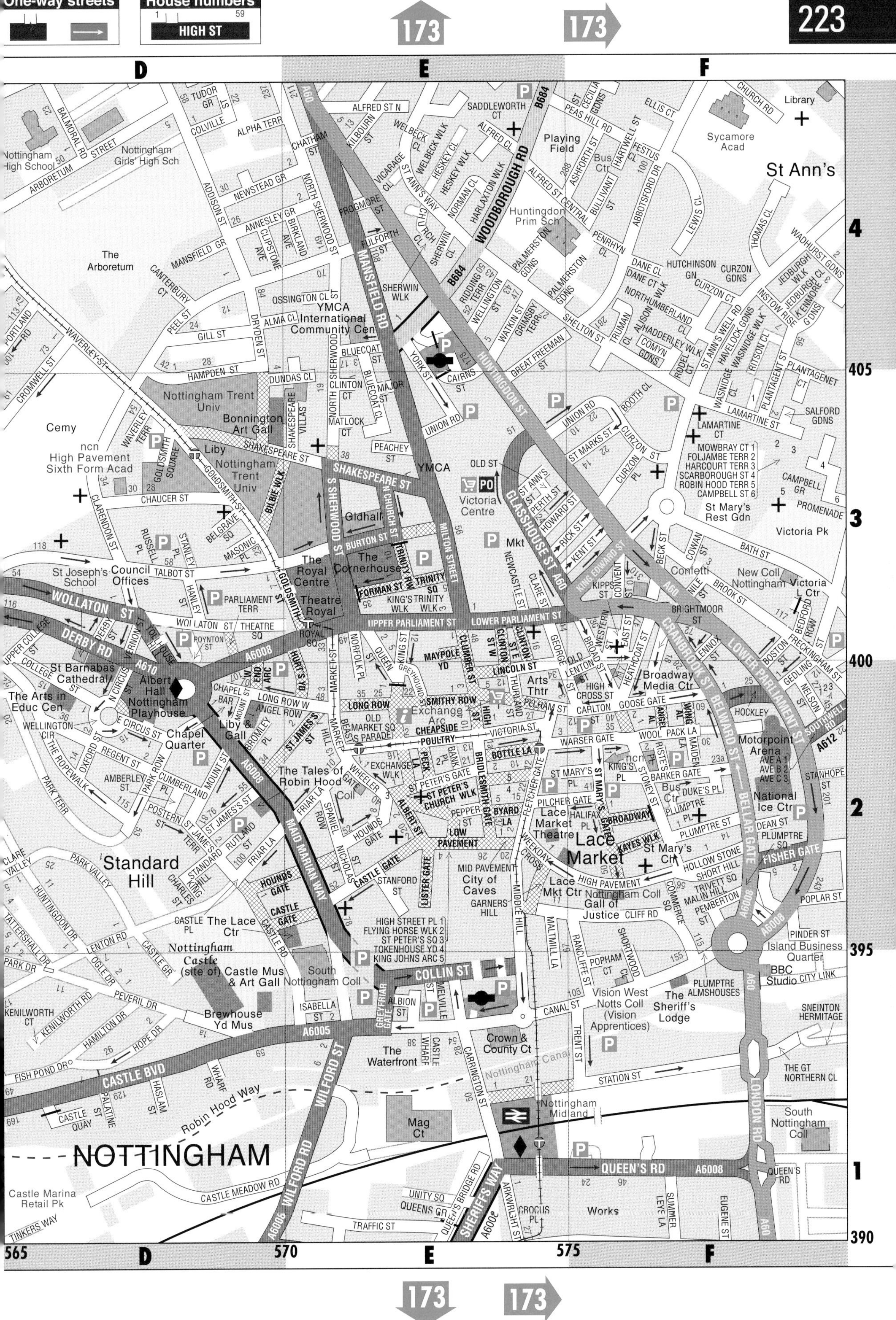

One-way streets
House numbers
1
59
HIGH ST
173
173
D
E
F
4
405
3
400
2
395
1
390
565
570
575
NOTTINGHAM
St Ann's
Lace Market
Standard Hill
The Arboretum
Nottingham High School
Nottingham Girls' High Sch
Sycamore Acad
Library
Playing Field
Huntingdon Prim Sch
YMCA International Community Cen
Nottingham Trent Univ
Bonnington Art Gall
Cemy
ncn High Pavement Sixth Form Acad
Victoria Centre
Mkt
The Royal Centre
Theatre Royal
The Cornerhouse
Gldhall
Council Offices
St Joseph's School
St Barnabas Cathedral
The Arts in Educ Cen
Albert Hall
Nottingham Playhouse
Chapel Quarter
Liby & Gall
The Tales of Robin Hood
Exchange Arc
Broadway Media Ctr
Arts Thtr
Motorpoint Arena
National Ice Ctr
Confetti
New Coll Nottingham
Victoria L Ctr
St Mary's Rest Gdn
Victoria Pk
Lace Market Theatre
Lace Mkt Ctr
Nottingham Coll
Gall of Justice
City of Caves
Island Business Quarter
BBC Studio
The Lace Ctr
Nottingham Castle (site of)
Castle Mus & Art Gall
South Nottingham Coll
Brewhouse Yd Mus
Crown & County Ct
Vision West Notts Coll (Vision Apprentices)
The Sheriff's Lodge
Plumptre Almshouses
Sneinton Hermitage
The Waterfront
Nottingham Midland
Mag Ct
South Nottingham Coll
Castle Marina Retail Pk
Works
Robin Hood Way
Nottingham Canal
MANSFIELD RD
WOODBOROUGH RD
HUNTINGDON ST
GLASSHOUSE ST
SHAKESPEARE ST
UPPER PARLIAMENT ST
LOWER PARLIAMENT ST
WOLLATON ST
DERBY RD
MAID MARIAN WAY
CASTLE BVD
WILFORD ST
WILFORD RD
QUEEN'S RD
LONDON RD
CRANBROOK ST
BELWARD ST
BELLAR GATE
FISHER GATE
COLLIN ST
CARRINGTON ST
STATION ST
CANAL ST
SHERIFFS WAY
LONG ROW
CHEAPSIDE
POULTRY
SMITHY ROW
VICTORIA ST
HIGH PAVEMENT
LOW PAVEMENT
MIDDLE HILL
HOLLOW STONE
WAVERLEY ST
ALFRED ST CENTRAL
HIGH STREET PL 1
FLYING HORSE WLK 2
ST PETER'S SQ 3
TOKENHOUSE YD 4
KING JOHNS ARC 5
MOWBRAY CT 1
FOLJAMBE TERR 2
HARCOURT TERR 3
SCARBOROUGH ST 4
ROBIN HOOD TERR 5
CAMPBELL ST 6
AVE A 1
AVE B 2
AVE C 3
A60
A6008
A610
A6005
A612
B684

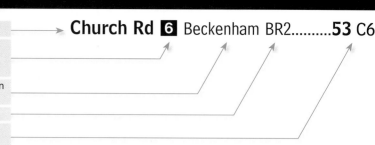

Index

Place name May be abbreviated on the map

Location number Present when a number indicates the place's position in a crowded area of mapping

Locality, town or village Shown when more than one place has the same name

Postcode district District for the indexed place

Page and grid square Page number and grid reference for the standard mapping

Cities, towns and villages are listed in CAPITAL LETTERS

Public and commercial buildings are highlighted in **magenta** **Places of interest** are highlighted in blue with a star★

Abbreviations used in the index

Acad	**Academy**	Comm	**Common**	Gd	**Ground**	L	**Leisure**	Prom	**Promenade**
App	**Approach**	Cott	**Cottage**	Gdn	**Garden**	La	**Lane**	Rd	**Road**
Arc	**Arcade**	Cres	**Crescent**	Gn	**Green**	Liby	**Library**	Recn	**Recreation**
Ave	**Avenue**	Cswy	**Causeway**	Gr	**Grove**	Mdw	**Meadow**	Ret	**Retail**
Bglw	**Bungalow**	Ct	**Court**	H	**Hall**	Meml	**Memorial**	Sh	**Shopping**
Bldg	**Building**	Ctr	**Centre**	Ho	**House**	Mkt	**Market**	Sq	**Square**
Bsns, Bus	**Business**	Ctry	**Country**	Hospl	**Hospital**	Mus	**Museum**	St	**Street**
Bvd	**Boulevard**	Cty	**County**	HQ	**Headquarters**	Orch	**Orchard**	Sta	**Station**
Cath	**Cathedral**	Dr	**Drive**	Hts	**Heights**	Pal	**Palace**	Terr	**Terrace**
Cir	**Circus**	Dro	**Drove**	Ind	**Industrial**	Par	**Parade**	TH	**Town Hall**
Cl	**Close**	Ed	**Education**	Inst	**Institute**	Pas	**Passage**	Univ	**University**
Cnr	**Corner**	Emb	**Embankment**	Int	**International**	Pk	**Park**	Wk, Wlk	**Walk**
Coll	**College**	Est	**Estate**	Intc	**Interchange**	Pl	**Place**	Wr	**Water**
Com	**Community**	Ex	**Exhibition**	Junc	**Junction**	Prec	**Precinct**	Yd	**Yard**

Index of towns, villages, streets, hospitals, industrial estates, railway stations, schools, shopping centres, universities and places of interest

1st–Ald

1st Ave NG7 . . . 173 B8
2nd Ave NG7 . . . 173 B8
3rd Ave NG7 . . . 173 B8
4th Ave NG7 . . . 173 B8

A

Aaron Cl NG11 . . . 185 B7
Abba Cl NG16 . . . 158 F7
Abbey Bridge NG7 . . . 172 E2
Abbey Cir NG2 . . . 186 A7
Abbey Cl
Aslockton NG13 . . . 178 F5
Hucknall NG15 . . . 145 E7
Abbey Ct
Beeston NG9 . . . 183 F8
Mansfield NG18 . . . 102 F7
Nottingham NG7 . . . 222 B2
Abbeydale Dr NG18 . . . 102 D3
Abbey Dr NG9 . . . 183 F7
Abbeyfield Rd NG7 . . . 184 F8
Abbey Gates Prim Sch NG15 . . . 117 A1
Abbey Gr NG3 . . . 173 F7
Abbey Hill Prim Sch NG17 . . . 115 C5
Abbey La NG13 . . . 178 F5
Abbey Mws NG25 . . . 121 E1
Abbey Pk LN1 . . . 44 B2
Abbey Prim Sch NG19 . . . 102 F8
Abbey Rd
Beeston NG9 . . . 183 F7
Bingham NG13 . . . 178 A4
Blidworth NG21 . . . 118 B5
Eastwood NG16 . . . 144 B2
Edwinstowe NG21 . . . 91 C8
Kirkby-in-Ashfield NG17 . . . 115 D5
Mansfield NG18 . . . 102 E7
Mattersey DN10 . . . 20 C7
Newstead NG15 . . . 130 E6
West Bridgford NG2 . . . 186 A7
Abbey Road Prim Sch NG2 . . . 186 A6
Abbey St
Ilkeston DE7 . . . 157 F2
Nottingham NG7 . . . 172 E2
Worksop S80 . . . 35 F2
Abbot Cl NG12 . . . 197 E4
Abbotsbury Cl NG5 . . . 146 E1
Abbots Cl NG5 . . . 161 D6
Abbots Dr NG15 . . . 145 E6
Abbotsford Dr NG3 . . . 223 F4
Abbotsford Mews DE7 . . . 157 D3
Abbots Rd NG15 . . . 145 E6
Abbot St NG16 . . . 158 C4
Abbots Wlk NG15 . . . 145 E6
Abbott Lea NG19 . . . 101 D8
Abbotts Cres NG22 . . . 119 F7
Abbotts Croft NG19 . . . 87 E1
Abbott St NG10 . . . 193 D6
Abbotts Way NG8 . . . 172 C4
Abbott's Way NG24 . . . 125 B1
Abel Collin's Homes NG8 . . . 171 E1
Abercarn Cl NG6 . . . 160 B7
Aberconway St NG21 . . . 118 A5
Aberdeen St 3 NG3 . . . 173 E5
Aberford Ave NG8 . . . 172 D8
Abingdon Dr NG11 . . . 196 D8
Abingdon Gdns
Arnold NG5 . . . 162 B5
Beeston NG9 . . . 183 D4
Abingdon Rd NG2 . . . 186 A7
Abingdon Sq NG8 . . . 160 B1
Abingdon View S81 . . . 35 C8
Abington Ave NG17 . . . 100 F5
Ablard Gdns 6 NG9 . . . 183 C2
Acacia Ave
Annesley Woodhouse NG17 . . . 130 A8
Gainsborough DN21 . . . 15 D1
Torksey Lock LN1 . . . 44 C1
Acacia Cl
Hucknall NG15 . . . 146 B5
Worksop S80 . . . 35 C2
Acacia Cres NG4 . . . 162 F1
Acacia Ct NG19 . . . 88 E1
Acacia Gdns NG16 . . . 158 F8
Acacia Rd NG24 . . . 140 D5
Acacia Wlk NG9 . . . 183 F6
Acacia Wy NG12 . . . 186 A1
Academy Cl NG6 . . . 160 D2
Acaster Cl NG9 . . . 184 B4
Access 26 Bsns Pk NG16 . . . 143 D2
Acer Cl NG16 . . . 113 C3
Ackford Dr S80 . . . 35 D3
Acland St DN21 . . . 15 C1
Acle Gdns NG6 . . . 146 B1
Acorn Ave NG16 . . . 158 B8
Acorn Bank NG2 . . . 185 B4
Acorn Bsns Pk 11 NG18 . . . 102 B6
Acorn Cl NG24 . . . 140 C5
Acorn Dr NG4 . . . 163 A2
Acorn Pk NG7 . . . 184 E8
Acorn Ridge NG20 . . . 72 D5
Acorns The NG22 . . . 106 A4
Acorn Vw NG17 . . . 115 C6
Acorn Way NG18 . . . 103 B4
Acourt St NG7 . . . 222 B4
Acreage La NG20 . . . 72 F2
Acre Edge Rd NG22 . . . 78 F2
Acre The NG17 . . . 115 B3
Acton Ave
Long Eaton NG10 . . . 193 E6
Nottingham NG6 . . . 160 D4
Acton Cl NG10 . . . 193 E6
Acton Gr NG10 . . . 193 E6
Acton Rd
Arnold NG5 . . . 161 E7
Long Eaton NG10 . . . 193 E6
Acton Rd Ind Est NG10 . . . 193 E6
Acton St NG10 . . . 193 E5
Adalia Wlk S81 . . . 25 D1
Adam Dale LE11 . . . 220 A3
Adams Ct DE7 . . . 157 E3
Adams Dr NG5 . . . 147 E2
Adams Hill
Keyworth NG12 . . . 197 F3
Nottingham NG7 . . . 172 C2
Adams Pk Way 1 NG17 . . . 114 F8
Adams Row NG25 . . . 121 D1
Adam St DE7 . . . 170 A6
Adamsway
Mansfield NG18 . . . 102 F2
Mansfield NG18 . . . 103 A3
Adams Way DN21 . . . 44 C8
Ada Pl NG15 . . . 146 B8
ADBOLTON . . . 174 B2
Adbolton Ave NG4 . . . 162 E1
Adbolton Gr NG2 . . . 174 B1
Adbolton La
West Bridgford NG12 . . . 174 D1
West Bridgford NG4 . . . 174 B1
Adco Bsns Ctr NG7 . . . 172 E7
Adcocks Cl LE11 . . . 220 B5
Adderley Cl NG5 . . . 161 A6
Addington Ct NG12 . . . 176 A4
Addington Rd NG7 . . . 222 B4
Addison Dr NG15 . . . 145 F8
Addison Pl LN1 . . . 55 D6
Addison Rd NG4 . . . 174 B8
Addison St
Nottingham NG1 . . . 223 D4
Tibshelf DE55 . . . 99 A7
Addison Villas NG16 . . . 143 E1
Adelaide Cl
Gainsborough DN21 . . . 24 F6
Stapleford NG9 . . . 170 F1
Adelaide Gr NG5 . . . 160 E8
Adel Dr NG4 . . . 162 E1
Adenburgh Dr NG9 . . . 183 D1
Adlington Cotts NG17 . . . 101 B1
Adlington Mws DN21 . . . 24 F6
Admiral Cl LE12 . . . 214 E8
Admiral Ct DE7 . . . 157 F4
Admirals Ct NG18 . . . 102 D5
Adrian Cl NG9 . . . 182 F1
Adrians Cl NG18 . . . 102 E5
Adrian's Wlk DN22 . . . 39 F4
Advance Bsns Ctr LE12 . . . 220 A2
Adwalton Cl 7 NG24 . . . 140 E8
Aegir Cl DN21 . . . 24 F6
Aegir Specl Acad DN21 . . . 15 F2
Aeneas Ct 6 NG5 . . . 173 B8
Aerial Way NG15 . . . 145 F5
Aerodrome The NG15 . . . 145 E3
Agnes Villas NG3 . . . 161 E2
Aidan Gdns NG5 . . . 147 A2
Ainsdale Cl NG24 . . . 140 E2
Ainsdale Cres NG8 . . . 160 A3
Ainsdale Gn DN22 . . . 39 D3
Ainsley Rd NG8 . . . 172 D6
Ainsworth Dr NG2 . . . 173 B1
Aintree Cl NG16 . . . 158 E7
Aira Cl NG2 . . . 186 D6
Airedale S81 . . . 36 A7
Airedale Ave DN11 . . . 8 A8
Airedale Cl NG10 . . . 193 A6
Airedale Ct NG9 . . . 183 A4
Airedale Wlk NG8 . . . 171 C3
Airfield Way NG6 . . . 145 E2
Aisby Wlk DN21 . . . 24 F7
Aitchison Ave NG15 . . . 145 F7
Alan Clark Gr 20 NG5 . . . 160 F8
Alandale NG22 . . . 105 E6
Alandale Ave NG20 . . . 72 F5
Alandene Ave NG16 . . . 159 A7
Albans Ct NG21 . . . 89 C2
Albany Cl
Arnold NG5 . . . 161 E7
Hucknall NG15 . . . 145 C5
Mansfield Woodhouse NG19 . . . 88 C1
Albany Ct NG9 . . . 170 E1
Albany Dr NG19 . . . 88 C1
Albany Inf Sch NG9 . . . 182 E8
Albany Jun Sch NG9 . . . 182 E8
Albany Pl NG19 . . . 88 C1
Albany Rd NG7 . . . 173 A8
Albany St
Gainsborough DN21 . . . 15 C2
Ilkeston DE7 . . . 170 A6
Albemarle Rd NG5 . . . 161 D4
Alberta Ave NG16 . . . 129 A7
Alberta Terr NG7 . . . 173 A8
Albert Ave
Balderton NG24 . . . 140 C4
Carlton NG4 . . . 174 B7
Nottingham NG8 . . . 172 D8
Nuthall NG16 . . . 159 C6
Stapleford NG9 . . . 182 D7
Westwood NG16 . . . 128 B4
Albert Ball Cl NG5 . . . 160 F8
Albert Cl NG15 . . . 146 C5
Albert Dr NG7 . . . 222 B3
Albert Hall★ NG1 . . . 223 D2
Albert Pl LE11 . . . 220 B3
Albert Prom LE11 . . . 220 C3
Albert Rd
Beeston NG9 . . . 184 B7
Bunny NG11 . . . 196 E1
Long Eaton NG10 . . . 193 D8
Nottingham NG7 . . . 222 A1
Nottingham, Alexander Park NG3 . . . 173 D8
Retford DN22 . . . 39 E6
Sandiacre NG10 . . . 182 B6
West Bridgford NG2 . . . 185 F8
Albert Sq NG17 . . . 100 E2
Albert St
Bottesford NG13 . . . 181 A3
Carlton NG4 . . . 162 F1
Eastwood NG16 . . . 143 F3
Hucknall NG15 . . . 146 B7
Loughborough LE11 . . . 220 B3
Mansfield NG18 . . . 102 B6
Mansfield Woodhouse NG19 . . . 88 C4
Newark-on-Trent NG24 . . . 139 F8
Nottingham NG1 . . . 223 E2
Radcliffe on Trent NG12 . . . 175 F3
South Normanton DE55 . . . 113 B6
Stanton Hill NG17 . . . 100 C6
Stapleford NG9 . . . 182 D7
Worksop S80 . . . 35 F3
Albert Terr DN21 . . . 24 D8
Albine Rd NG20 . . . 72 E6
Albion Cl S80 . . . 35 F3
Albion House NG9 . . . 183 F7
Albion Rd
Long Eaton NG10 . . . 193 F8
Sutton in Ashfield NG17 . . . 100 F2
Albion Rise NG5 . . . 147 F1
Albion St
Beeston NG9 . . . 183 F7
Ilkeston DE7 . . . 157 F1
Mansfield NG19 . . . 87 F1
Mansfield NG19 . . . 101 F8
Newark-on-Trent NG24 . . . 139 F8
Nottingham NG1 . . . 223 E1
Albion Terr DN10 . . . 7 B1
Albury Dr NG8 . . . 160 B1
Albury Sq NG7 . . . 222 C2
Alcester St NG7 . . . 184 E8
Alcock Ave NG18 . . . 102 E7
Alconbury Way S81 . . . 35 C8
Aldene Ct NG9 . . . 183 D5
Aldene Way NG14 . . . 149 C4
ALDERCAR . . . 143 A4
Aldercar Flash Nature Reserve★ NG16 . . . 143 B6
Aldercar High Sch NG16 . . . 143 A4
Aldercar Inf Sch NG16 . . . 143 A4
Aldercar La NG16 . . . 143 A6
Alder Cl
Mansfield NG19 . . . 88 D1
New Balderton NG24 . . . 140 C5
Shirebrook NG20 . . . 72 D5
Worksop S80 . . . 35 E1
Alder Ct NG19 . . . 101 D5
Alder Gdns NG6 . . . 160 A7
Alder Gr
Mansfield Woodhouse NG19 . . . 88 B5
New Ollerton NG22 . . . 77 D5
Alderman Cl NG9 . . . 183 F8
Alderman Pounder Inf Sch NG9 . . . 183 B5
Alderman White Sch and Language Coll NG9 . . . 183 C7
Aldermens Cl NG2 . . . 173 C2
Alderney St NG7 . . . 222 B1
Alderson Cl DN11 . . . 8 B8
Alderson Dr DN11 . . . 8 B8
Alderson Rd S80 . . . 35 E1
Alders The 5 DN21 . . . 15 F1
Alderton Chase DN21 . . . 15 C3
Alderton Rd NG5 . . . 161 C6
Alder Way
Keyworth NG12 . . . 198 A2
Shirebrook NG20 . . . 72 D4
Sutton in Ashfield NG17 . . . 100 D3
Aldgate Cl NG6 . . . 160 A8
Aldred's La DE75 . . . 143 B2
Aldridge Cl NG9 . . . 182 E2
Aldrin Cl NG6 . . . 159 F5

Aldworth Cl NG5 161 C6
Aldwych Cl
Nottingham NG5 147 A1
Nuthall NG16 159 D2
Alec Rose Gr DN21 24 F7
Alexander Ave
Newark-on-Trent NG24 125 B4
Selston NG16 128 D7
Alexander Cl NG15 131 B1
Alexander Gdns NG15 146 E4
Alexander Mws NG24 140 E5
Alexander Rd
Farnsfield NG22 119 F6
Nottingham NG7 222 C2
Alexander St NG16 143 F2
Alexander Terr NG16 113 C1
Alexandra Ave
Mansfield NG18 102 B4
Mansfield Woodhouse NG19 88 B5
Sutton in Ashfield NG17 100 F4
Alexandra Cres NG9 184 A6
Alexandra Rd
Bircotes DN11 9 B4
Long Eaton NG10 193 D8
Alexandra St
Kirkby-in-Ashfield NG17 115 B6
Nottingham NG5 161 B1
Nottingham NG5 173 B8
Stapleford NG9 182 D6
Alexandra Terr NG17 100 C6
Alford Cl NG9 184 B5
Alford Rd NG2 186 B5
Alford Way LE12 216 B4
Alfred Ave NG3 162 A2
Alfred Cl NG3 223 E4
Alfred Ct 4 NG18 102 B7
Alfred St Central NG3 223 E4
Alfred St N NG3 223 E4
Alfred St S NG3 173 E5
Alfred St
Gainsborough DN21 15 C1
Kirkby-in-Ashfield NG17 115 A4
Loughborough LE11 220 B5
Pinxton NG16 113 C4
Sutton in Ashfield NG17 100 F4
Alfreton Rd
Huthwaite NG17 113 F7
Newton DE55 99 A3
Nottingham NG7 222 B4
11 Nottingham NG8 172 E7
Pinxton NG16 113 C4
Selston, Selston Green DE55, NG16 128 C6
Selston, Underwood NG16 129 B3
South Normanton DE55 113 A5
South Normanton DE55 113 D6
Sutton in Ashfield NG17 100 D4
Algar Cl LE12 206 D1
Alison Ave NG15 131 C1
Alison Cl NG12 185 F2
Alison Wlk NG3 223 F4
Allcroft St NG19 88 C4
Allenby Rd NG25 136 C8
Allen Cl NG23 156 D7
Allendale Ave
Beeston NG9 183 D2
Nottingham NG16 159 F1
Nottingham NG8 160 A1
Allendale Rd NG21 118 B8
Allendale Way NG19 88 E1
Allen Dr NG18 102 F5
Allen Field Ct NG7 222 B1
Allen Rd NG23 142 D2
Allen's Gn Ave NG16 128 F6
Allen St
Hucknall NG15 146 A8
Worksop S80 35 E3
Allen's Wlk NG5 147 F1
Allesford La NG22 120 B4
All Hallows CE Prim Sch 2 NG4 162 F1
All Hallows Cl DN22 39 E4
All Hallows Dr NG4 162 F2
All Hallows St DN22 39 E4
All Hallows View DN22 39 E4
Alliance St NG24 125 A2
Allington Ave NG7 222 B1
Allington Dr NG19 101 D7
Allison Ave DN22 40 B3
Allison Gdns NG9 183 D4
All Saints Anglican Methodist Prim Sch NG23 153 D5
All Saints' CE Inf Sch NG17 99 F2
All Saints Ct NG17 100 A2
All Saints Harworth CE (Aided) Prim Sch
Harworth DN11 8 F3
Harworth DN11 9 A4
All Saints' RC Comp Sch NG19 101 F8
All Saints' St NG7 222 C4
All Saints' Terr NG7 222 C4
Allsopp Dr S81 35 F6
Allsopp's La LE11 220 D5
Allwood Cl NG18 102 E8
Allwood Dr NG4 174 E8
Allwood Gdns NG15 146 B6
Alma Cl
Carlton NG4 163 A2
Ilkeston DE7 157 E5
Nottingham NG1 223 E4
Alma Hill NG16 158 E7
Alma Rd
Nottingham NG3 173 F6
Retford DN22 40 A7
Selston NG16 129 A5
Alma St NG7 173 A8
Almond Ave NG20 72 E5
Almond Cl
Hucknall NG15 146 B5
Kimberley NG16 158 E7
Saxilby LN1 57 B4
Almond Gr
Farndon NG24 139 A5
6 Kirkby-in-Ashfield NG17 114 F6
Worksop S80 35 E1
Almond Rise NG19 88 E1
Almond Way NG8 171 C7
Almond Wlk NG4 163 A2
Alnwick Cl NG6 160 D6
Alpha Terr NG1 223 D4
Alpine Cres
Carlton NG4 174 D8
Torksey Lock LN1 44 C1
Alpine Ct S80 35 C2
Alpine St NG6 160 E2
Alport Pl NG18 103 B7
Althea Ct 1 NG7 161 A1
Althorpe St NG7 222 C3
Alton Ave NG11 185 B4
Alton Cl NG11 185 C3
Alton Dr NG16 158 B8
Alum Ct NG5 160 F8
Alvenor St DE7 157 F1
Alverstone Rd NG3 161 C1
Alvey Rd NG24 140 E4
Alvina Gdns NG8 159 C1
Alway Cres DN22 39 C8
Alwood Gr NG11 184 D2
Alwyn Rd NG8 159 F2
Amanda Ave S81 25 E6
Amanda Rd DN11 8 F4
Amarella La 9 NG17 115 A3
Amber Cl
Nottingham NG5 161 B7
Rainworth NG21 104 C1
Amber Dr NG16 143 B2
Ambergate Rd NG8 172 A7
Amber Gr
Kirkby-in-Ashfield NG17 114 D8
Newlands NG19 89 D2
Amber Hill NG5 161 B7
Amberley NG19 89 D2
Amberley St NG1 223 D2
Amber Rd NG9 184 A3
Amber St NG18 102 C5
Ambleside
Hucknall NG15 145 F5
New Ollerton NG22 77 C5
West Bridgford NG2 186 C7
Ambleside Dr NG16 143 D3
Ambleside Grange S81 35 F8
Ambleside Prim Sch NG8 160 B1
Ambleside Rd NG8 160 A1
Ambleside Way NG4 175 B8
Amcott Ave
Misterton DN10 14 A8
Walkeringham DN10 13 F8
Amcott Way DN22 39 E7
Amelia Ct DN22 29 C2
Amen Cnr NG23 109 B5
Amen Cnr Karting★ NG22 91 E7
America Gdns NG22 65 F3
Amersham Rise NG8 160 B1
Amesbury Circ NG8 160 A3
Amethy St Gdns NG18 102 D4
Amethyst Cl NG21 104 C1
Amherst Rise 4 S81 35 D8
Amos La NG23 98 D4
Ampthill Rise NG5 161 B4
Amrthyst Dr NG17 114 D8
Anastasia Cl DN21 15 C3
Ancaster Gdns NG8 172 A4
Anchor Cl NG8 160 B2
Anchor Rd NG16 143 D2
Anders Dr NG6 159 F5
Anderson Cl NG24 140 B3
Anderson Cres NG9 183 E8
Anderson Ct 6 NG5 161 A8
Anderson Rd DN21 24 F2
Anderson Way NG21 75 F1
Anderton St NG4 174 A2
Andover Cl 1 NG8 172 B6
Andover Rd
Mansfield NG19 101 D7
Nottingham NG5 160 E5
Andrew Ave
Ilkeston DE7 170 B7
Nottingham NG3 162 A2
Andrew Dr NG21 118 A4
Andrews Dr NG16 143 A3
Anemone Gr NG11 196 E5
Anfield Cl NG9 183 A2
Anford Cl NG6 160 B5
Angela Ave NG17 115 B1
Angela Cl NG5 147 E2
Angel Alley NG1 223 F2
Angelica Ct NG13 177 C3
Angell Gn NG11 195 C8
Angel Row NG1 223 E2
Angel Row Gall★ NG1 223 D2
Angel Yd LE11 220 B4
Anglia Way NG18 103 B3
Angrave Cl NG3 173 E7
Angus Cl
Arnold NG5 148 B1
Arnold NG5 162 B8
Kimberley NG16 159 A5
Anmer Cl 9 NG2 173 B1
Anna Cl NG12 185 F3
Annan Ct NG8 172 B8
Anne's Cl NG3 162 A2
ANNESLEY 130 C8
Annesley Cutting NG15 130 C7
Annesley Gr
Nottingham NG1 223 D4
Nottingham NG14 173 B6
Annesley La NG16 129 B6
Annesley Prim Sch NG17 130 B8
Annesley Rd
Hucknall NG15 145 F8
West Bridgford NG2 185 F7
Annesley Way NG19 101 D6
ANNESLEY WOODHOUSE 129 E8
Annesley Woodhouse Quarry Nature Reserve★ NG17 129 D7
Annesley Workshops NG15 130 A5
Annies Cl NG15 145 F5
Annies Wharf LE11 220 B5
Anslow Ave
Beeston NG9 184 A8
Dalestorth NG17 101 A5
Sutton in Ashfield NG17 100 F5
Anson Dr NG24 141 A3
Anson Rd NG13 177 B7
Anson Wlk DE7 157 F3
Anstee Rd NG10 193 C4
Anstey Rise NG3 173 F5
Anston Ave S81 35 E5
Anthony Bek Com Prim Sch NG19 86 F6
Antill St NG9 182 D6
Antonia Dr NG15 146 D8
Anvil Ct NG18 102 B4
Anvil Grove 2 NG19 88 C3
Apley Cl DN21 24 F7
Apollo Dr NG6 159 F5
Appin Rd NG19 101 D5
Apple Ave NG24 140 F2
Appleby Cl NG24 140 D8
Appleby Ct S81 35 F8
Appleby Rd NG19 86 F6
Appledore Ave NG8 171 E2
Appledorne Way NG5 147 E1
Appleton Dr LE12 216 B3
Appleton Gate
Newark-on-Trent NG24 125 A1
9 Newark-on-Trent NG24 139 F8
Appleton Gdns NG3 162 B5
Appleton Rd
Beeston NG9 184 B4
Blidworth NG21 118 B5
Appleton St NG20 74 B4
Appletree Cl NG25 121 E1
Apple Tree Cl
9 Newark-on-Trent NG24 125 A2
West Bridgford NG12 186 A4
Appletree La NG4 162 F1
Apple Tree La NG4 162 F2
Apple Wlk NG4 174 A8
Applewood Cl S81 35 D8
Applewood Gr NG5 161 D3
Approach The NG11 196 C8
Arboretum St NG1 223 D4
Arbrook Dr NG8 172 D8
Arbutus Cl NG11 184 C1
Arcade The NG24 139 F8
Arcadia Ave NG20 72 E5
Archbishop Cranmer CE Prim Sch
NG13 179 A5
Aslockton NG13 178 F5
Archdale Rd NG5 161 C6
Archer Cres NG8 171 F5
Archer Rd NG9 182 E5
Archers Dr NG22 106 A5
Archers Field NG25 121 E1
Archer St DE7 157 E3
Arches Cl NG16 158 C5
Arches Rd NG19 102 D5
Arches The LE12 205 E2
Arch Hill
Arnold NG5 147 E3
Arnold NG5 147 F3
Archway Gr NG21 90 D6
Archway Rd NG21 90 D7
Arden Cl
Beeston NG9 184 A8
Hucknall NG15 146 C5
Arden Gr NG13 177 C5
Ardleigh Cl NG5 146 D1
Ardmore Cl NG2 173 F3
Ardsley Cl DE75 143 A2
Argosy Cl DN10 9 F8
Argyle Cl NG20 73 F4
Argyle Ct NG7 222 B3
Argyle St
Langley Mill NG16 143 C4
Mansfield NG18 102 E6
Nottingham NG7 222 B3
Ariel Cl NG6 160 F5
Arkers Cl NG6 160 D3
Arklow Cl NG8 160 B2
Arkwright St
Gainsborough DN21 15 C1
Nottingham NG2 173 C3
Arkwright Wlk
Nottingham NG14 173 D2
Nottingham NG2 173 C2
Arleston Dr NG8 171 D4
Arley Gdns LE12 205 D1
Arlington Ave NG19 88 E4
Arlington Cl NG15 146 A4
Arlington Dr NG3 161 C2
Arlington Way DN22 39 F7
Armadale Cl NG5 162 C8
Armes Cl DE7 157 F3
Armfield Rd NG5 162 C6
Armitage Cl 8 LE11 220 A4
Armitage Dr NG10 194 A7
Armstrong Gdns NG22 105 F6
Armstrong Rd
Keyworth NG12 197 F4
Mansfield NG19 101 D7
Nottingham NG6 159 F5
Retford DN22 39 F7
Arnbrook Prim Sch NG5 161 D7
Arncliff Cl NG8 171 C4
Arndale Rd NG5 161 C5
Arne Ct 5 NG2 173 C1
Arnesby Rd NG7 222 A1
Arno Ave 2 NG7 173 B8
ARNOLD 162 A7
Arnold Ave
Long Eaton NG10 193 A4
Retford DN22 40 B3
Southwell NG25 121 E1
Arnold Cres NG10 193 A4
Arnold Derrymount Sch NG5 147 F1
Arnold Hill Acad NG5 162 A6
Arnold La NG3 162 D4
Arnold L Ctr NG5 161 E8
Arnold Mill Prim Sch NG5 161 E8
Arnold Rd NG5 161 A5
Arnold Seely CE Prim Sch NG5 132 E2
Arnold View Prim Sch NG5 161 F7
Arnos Gr NG8 159 D3
Arnot Hill Pk NG5 161 E6
Arnot Hill Rd NG5 161 E6
Arno Vale Gdns NG5 161 E5
Arno Vale Jun Sch NG5 161 F5
Arno Vale Rd NG5 161 F5
Arnside NG9 182 E5
Arnside Cl NG5 161 B5
Arnside Rd NG5 161 B5
Arran Cl NG9 170 E2
Arran Sq NG19 101 D5
Arry Cl NG12 176 B5
Arthur Ave
Nottingham NG7 222 B2
Stapleford NG9 182 F8
Arthur Cres NG4 174 C7
Arthur Gn Ave NG17 114 E1
Arthur Lee Centre The NG9 182 D7
Arthur Mee Rd NG9 182 E5
Arthur Rd DN21 15 D2
Arthur Short Cl S80 45 A6
Arthur St
Carlton NG4 175 A6
Mansfield NG18 102 C6
Nottingham NG7 222 C4
Pinxton NG16 113 D3
Artic Way NG16 158 D7
Artisan Rd LE14 219 B5
Arum Croft DN22 39 D4
Arun Dale NG19 88 D2
Arundel Cl
Gainsborough DN21 15 E2
Sandiacre NG10 182 B4
Arundel Dr
Beeston NG9 171 B1
Carlton in Lindrick S81 25 F6
Carlton in Lindrick S81 26 A6
Mansfield NG19 101 F8
Ranskill DN22 19 B5
Arundel St NG7 222 C3
Arundel Way DN22 39 C8
Arundel Wlk DN11 9 B5
Ascot Ave NG16 158 E7
Ascot Cl NG17 115 C3
Ascot Dr
Arnold NG5 161 D8
Hucknall NG15 145 D5
Mansfield NG18 102 F7
Ascot Pk Est NG10 182 B4
Ascot Rd NG8 172 D7
Ascott Gdns NG2 185 A5
Ashbourne Cl NG9 171 A1
Ashbourne Ct NG6 159 F6
Ashbourne Rd NG16 129 A2
Ashbourne St
Nottingham NG7 222 C3
Shirebrook NG20 72 F4
Ashburnham Ave
Nottingham NG7 222 B2
Nottingham NG8 172 F4
Ashby Ave NG19 88 D5
Ashby Rd
Kegworth DE74 203 A2
Kegworth DE74 203 B2
Long Whatton LE12 212 C1
Loughborough LE11 220 A4
Rempstone LE12 215 C6
Ashby Sq LE11 220 A4
Ashchurch Dr NG8 171 D2
Ash Cl
Bingham NG13 178 A4
Burton Joyce NG14 163 E4
Dunham-on-Trent NG22 54 C2
Hucknall NG15 145 C5
Pinxton NG16 113 D2
Worksop S80 35 C1
Ashcourt Gdns NG17 101 B4
Ash Cres
Kirkby-in-Ashfield NG17 114 D6
Mansfield Woodhouse NG19 88 E2
Nuthall NG16 159 B6
Ashcroft DN22 39 D4
Ashcroft Rd DN21 24 D6
Ash Ct NG4 174 D7
Ashdale Ave
Hucknall NG15 145 F5
Hucknall NG15 146 A5
Ashdale Rd
Arnold NG5 162 A8
Ilkeston DE7 170 A6
Nottingham NG3 174 B6
Ashdown Cl NG11 185 B6
Ashdown Gr NG13 177 D4
Ashdown Way DN10 6 E1
Ashe Cl NG5 162 B7
Asher La
Ruddington NG11 195 F5
Ruddington NG11 196 B5
Ruddington NG11 196 C6
Ashes Pk Ave
Worksop S81 25 D1
Worksop S81 35 D8
Ashfield Ave
Beeston NG9 184 B5
Mansfield NG18 102 B7
Ashfield Coll NG17 100 D2
Ashfield Com Hospl NG17 115 A5
Ashfield Ct DN10 11 C4
Ashfield Dr NG17 114 F5
Ashfield Grange LN1 56 F4
Ashfield Prec NG17 115 B5
Ashfield Rd
Huthwaite NG17 100 B3
Nottingham NG2 173 F4
Ashfield Sch NG17 114 D7
Ashfield St NG17 101 A5
Ashford Ct DN22 39 D4
Ashford Dr NG15 117 B3
Ashford Pl DE7 157 E5
Ashford Rise
Nottingham NG8 171 D2
Sutton in Ashfield NG17 100 E4
Ashforth Ave DE75 143 A1
Ashforth St NG3 223 F4
Ashgate NG17 100 D3
Ashgate Rd
Hucknall NG15 146 B6
HUCKNALL NG15 146 B7
Ash Gr
Brinsley NG16 143 D8
Farnsfield NG22 120 A6
Gainsborough DN21 15 D2
Hathern LE12 213 A1
Keyworth NG12 198 A2
Long Eaton NG10 193 C6
Sandiacre NG10 182 A7
Selston NG16 128 F7
Shirebrook NG20 72 D5
Stapleford NG9 182 D5
Sutton in Ashfield NG17 100 D7
Woodborough NG14 149 C4
Ash Holt Dr S81 35 F8
Ash Holt Ind Pk DN9 1 A5
Ashington Dr
Arnold NG5 147 F2
Arnold NG5 148 A2
Ash La
Costock LE12 206 C4
Papplewick NG15 132 D3
Ranskill DN22 19 A3
Ashland Rd NG17 100 C3
Ashland Rd W NG17 100 B3
Ashlands Cl NG17 100 B3
Ashlea DN10 6 E2
Ash Lea Cl NG12 187 F2
Ash Lea Sch NG12 187 F2
Ashleigh Dr NG17 100 D2
Ashleigh Way NG19 89 A2
Ashley Cl NG9 183 D6
Ashley Cres NG12 197 F3
Ashley Ct S81 35 F5
Ashley Gr NG15 145 E7
Ashley La DN22 41 F2
Ashley Rd
Keyworth NG12 197 E3
Worksop S81 35 E6
Ashley St 7 NG3 173 E5
Ashley Terr S80 35 F3
Ashling St NG2 173 D2
Ashmore Ave NG17 100 C2
Ashmore Cl
2 Carlton NG4 162 E3
Carlton NG5 162 E3
Ashmount Cl LE11 220 A1
Ash Mount Rd NG16 143 B3
Ashmount Sch LE11 220 A1
Ashness Cl NG2 186 C6
Ashover Cl
Nottingham NG3 173 E8
Ravenshead NG15 117 B3
Ash Rd NG24 139 F4
Ashridge Way NG2 186 C4
Ash St DE7 157 E4
Ashton Ave NG5 147 F2
Ashton Ct
Nottingham NG8 171 D7
Sutton in Ashfield NG17 101 A5
Ash Tree Ave
Bawtry DN10 9 F7
Mansfield Woodhouse NG19 88 C5
Ash Tree Cl
2 Shireoaks S81 35 A7
Southwell NG25 136 D8
Ash Tree Ct NG8 159 C2
Ash Tree Sq NG9 183 B8
Ashurst Gr NG15 145 E4
Ashvale Ind Est NG22 66 A2
Ashvale Rd NG22 66 A2
Ash Vale Rd NG22 64 A2
Ashview Cl NG10 193 A8
Ash Villas 1 NG7 161 B1
Ashville Cl NG2 173 A1
Ashwater Dr NG3 162 D5
Ashwell Ave NG19 88 E5
Ashwell Ct NG5 161 E3
Ashwell Gdns NG7 172 E8
Ashwell St NG4 174 F6
Ashwick Cl NG11 185 A5
Ash Wlk LE12 214 D8
Ashwood Ave NG17 115 C6
Ashwood Cl
Mansfield Woodhouse NG19 88 E5
3 Sutton in Ashfield NG17 100 F1
Ashwood Rd S80 35 B2
Ashworth Ave NG11 196 C8
Ashworth Bsns Ctr NG1 223 F4
Ashworth Cl
Newark-on-Trent NG24 140 D8
Nottingham NG3 174 C5
Ashworth Cres
North Leverton with Habblesthorpe DN22 32 C1
Nottingham NG3 162 B2
Ashworth Dr NG19 88 E4
Askeby Dr NG8 159 D1
Askew La NG20 74 A3
Askew Rd NG15 131 D1
ASKHAM 51 F2
Askham La DN22 52 B5
Askham Rd NG22 51 F1
ASLOCKTON 179 A5
Aslockton Dr NG8 160 D2
Aslockton Rd NG13 178 F7
Aslockton Sta NG13 179 A4
Aspect Bsns Pk NG6 159 F8
Aspen Cl
Bingham NG13 178 A4
Laughterton LN1 55 B4
Tuxford NG22 66 A2
Walesby NG22 64 A2
Aspen Ct
Gainsborough DN21 15 F2
Mansfield NG19 88 E1
Tuxford NG22 66 A2
Aspen Rd NG6 159 F7
Asper St NG4 175 A7
Aspinall Ct 2 NG8 172 C5
Aspley La NG8 172 C8
Aspley Pk Dr NG8 172 B8
Aspley Pl NG7 222 B4
Aspley Rd NG17 100 D3
Asquith Mews NG18 102 E6
Asquith Prim Sch NG18 102 E6
Asquith St
Gainsborough DN21 15 B2
Mansfield NG18 102 E6
Assarts Rd NG16 159 E3
Astbury Dr NG21 103 E2
Astcote Cl DE75 143 A1
Aster Gr 2 NG12 185 F2
Aster Rd
Nottingham NG3 173 E7
Shirebrook NG20 72 D2
Astill Cl NG12 197 D2
Astle Ct NG5 162 C6
Astley Cl NG17 130 A8
Astley Dr NG3 161 F1
Aston Ave NG9 172 A1
Aston Ct DE7 157 F1
Aston Dr NG6 146 C2
Aston Gn NG9 182 E3
Astral Gr NG15 145 E4
Astrid Gdns NG5 160 F6
ASTWITH 85 A5
Astwith La S44, S45 85 B5
Astwood Cl NG8 171 E8
Athelstan Rd S80 35 F1
Atherfield Gdns NG16 143 F3
Atherton Rd DE7 157 C3
Atherton Rise NG8 160 B3
Athorpe Gr NG6 160 E3
Atkin La NG18 102 B3
Atkinson Gdns NG16 159 C5
ATTENBOROUGH 183 E2
Attenborough La NG9 183 C3
Attenborough Nature Reserve★ NG9 183 E1
Attenborough Sta NG9 183 D2
Attercliffe Terr 8 NG2 173 C1
Attewell Rd NG16 158 B5
Attlee Ave NG19 89 A1
Aubrey Ave 15 NG2 173 E4
Aubrey Rd NG5 161 B2
Auckland Cl NG7 222 A3
Auckland Rd
Hucknall NG15 145 D5
Retford DN22 39 C8
Audley Cl DE7 157 D3
Audley Dr NG9 171 F1
Audon Ave NG9 183 E5
Audrey Cres NG19 88 C5
Augustine Gdns NG5 147 A1
AULT HUCKNALL 85 F7
Ault Hucknall La
Ault Hucknall S44 85 F7
Ault Hucknall S44 86 A7
Aumberry Gap LE11 220 B4
Aurillac Way DN22 29 D2
Austen Ave
Long Eaton NG10 193 C5
Nottingham NG7 173 A7
AUSTERFIELD 3 C2
Austin Cl NG18 102 E8
Austin Dr DN21 24 E6
Austin Gr 12 NG17 115 A3

Austins Dr NG10 182 B4
Austin St
  Nottingham NG6 160 C7
  Shirebrook NG20 73 A4
Austrey Ave NG9 184 A8
Autumn Cft Rd NG24 125 D1
Autumn Cl NG12 185 D5
Autumn Rd NG12 188 A5
Autumn Way NG9 184 B7
Avalon Cl NG6 160 E6
Avalon Gdns DN11 9 A5
Avebury Cl NG11 195 D8
Aveling Way
  Shireoaks S81 34 F8
  Shireoaks S81 35 A8
Avenue A NG1 223 F2
Avenue B NG1 223 F2
Avenue C NG1 223 F2
Avenue Cl NG5 160 F8
Avenue D NG1 173 E4
Avenue E 4 NG1 173 E5
Avenue Rd DN22 39 F5
Avenue The
  Calverton NG14 148 F7
  Gainsborough DN21 15 E2
  Gunthorpe NG14 164 F6
  Mansfield NG18 102 E3
  Newark-on-Trent NG24 140 B7
  Sutton in Ashfield NG17 100 E1
AVERHAM 123 F2
Averham Cl NG19 101 D6
Averton Sq NG8 172 D3
Ave The
  Milton NG22 65 A7
  Ruddington NG11 196 D5
Aviary Way S81 36 B8
Aviemore Cl NG5 162 B8
Avocet Cl
  Bingham NG13 178 A3
  Heanor DE75 143 B1
  Hucknall NG15 131 B1
Avocet Gr S81 35 C6
Avocet Pl NG20 73 E4
Avon Ave NG15 145 E4
Avonbridge Cl NG5 148 C1
Avon Cl NG17 129 F8
Avondale
  Cotgrave NG12 188 A3
  Mansfield NG18 102 E7
Avondale Cl NG10 193 A6
Avondale La NG25 121 D2
Avondale Rd NG4 174 D6
Avon Gdns NG2 185 F7
Avonlea Cl DE7 170 B6
Avon Pl NG9 184 A7
Avon Rd
  Carlton NG4 162 F2
  Nottingham NG3 174 B5
Avon Rise DN22 40 A7
Avon Vale Rd LE11 220 C1
Avon Way
  Mansfield NG18 103 A5
  Worksop S81 35 E7
Avro Rd NG24 140 F3
AWSWORTH 158 C4
Awsworth La NG16 158 D6
Awsworth Prim Sch
  NG16 158 C4
Awsworth Rd DE7 157 F2
Axford Cl NG4 162 F2
Axmouth Dr NG5 162 D6
Aylesbury Wy NG19 88 E2
Aylesham Ave NG5 161 F6
Aylestone Dr NG8 172 B8
Ayrshire Way NG23 123 E1
Ayr St NG7 222 C4
Ayscough Ave NG16 159 C6
Ayton Cl NG2 173 D2
Ayton Gdns NG9 183 C2
Azalea Ct NG16 158 C8
Azimghur Rd NG13 179 A4
Azure Pl S81 25 D1

B

Babbacombe Cl NG5 161 B6
Babbacombe Way
  NG15 145 D6
Babbage Way S80 35 E4
Babbington Cl DE7 170 B5
Babbington Cres NG4 162 E2
Babbington Dr NG6 160 C4
Babbington La NG16 158 F4
Babbington St DE55 99 A6
Babington Ct NG9 183 C5
Babthorpe NG23 122 F1
BABWORTH 39 A6
Babworth Cres DN22 39 C6
Babworth Ct NG18 102 D7
Babworth Mws DN22 39 D6
Babworth Rd DN22 39 B6
Backers Cl NG12 187 E3
Back La
  Claypole NG23 156 D6
  Cotes LE12 220 F6
  Cropwell Butler NG12 189 A6
  Eakring NG22 106 E8
  East Markham NG22 66 A7
  Flintham NG23 167 A8
  Halam NG22 120 F2
  Huthwaite NG17 99 F3
  Ilkeston DE7 157 E2
  Keyworth NG12 198 A6
  Long Clawson LE14 211 C3
  Misson DN10 4 B2
  Morton NG25 137 C3
  North Clifton NG23 68 E5
Back La *continued*
  Nuthall NG16 159 D6
  Ollerton NG22 77 B3
  Ranskill DN22 19 A4
  Sutton in Ashfield NG17 100 F6
  Thorpe Salvin S80 34 A6
  Willoughby-on-t-W LE12 217 D7
Back St
  Barnby in the Willows
  NG24 142 A5
  East Stockwith DN21 7 D1
  South Clifton NG23 68 E1
Back Terr DN22 39 F8
Bacon Cl NG16 158 A8
Bacon La NG22 65 C5
Bacon St DN21 24 D6
Bacopa Dr DN22 40 A4
Bacton Ave NG6 160 B8
Bacton Gdns 1 NG6 160 B8
Baden Powell Rd NG2 174 A4
Bader NG11 185 B7
Bader Rise DN10 20 A8
Bader View DN10 20 A8
Badger Cl
  East Leake LE12 214 E7
  Hucknall NG15 145 C6
  Nottingham NG4 174 E8
  West Bridgford NG12 185 C6
Badgers Chase DN22 29 F1
Badgers Croft NG22 106 A5
Badger Vale NG9 171 E5
Badger Way NG19 103 B7
Baggaley Cres NG19 88 B1
Bagnall Ave NG5 161 C7
Bagnall Rd NG6 160 C4
Bagshaw St NG19 87 B4
Bagthorpe Cl NG5 161 A3
Bagthorpe Prim Sch
  NG16 129 A4
Baildon Cl NG8 172 C3
Bailey Brook Cres
  NG16 143 A4
Bailey Brook Dr NG16 143 A3
Bailey Brook Rd DE7 157 F5
Bailey Brook Wlk
  NG16 143 A3
Bailey Cl NG5 161 D7
Bailey Cres NG19 101 E7
Bailey Ct NG12 175 E2
Bailey Dr NG3 162 B5
Bailey Gr Rd NG16 143 D2
Bailey La NG12 175 E2
Bailey Rd NG24 139 F5
Baileys Croft LE12 217 D7
Baileys Row NG12 200 A2
Bailey St
  Carlton NG4 175 A7
  Nottingham NG6 160 E2
  Stapleford NG9 182 C6
Bainbridge Ct 7 NG24 139 F8
Bainbridge Rd
  Loughborough LE11 220 C1
  Market Warsop NG20 74 B4
Bainbridge Terr NG17 100 D6
Bainbridge The NG14 149 A7
Bainbrigge Rd DE74 203 A3
Baines Ave NG24 140 D4
Baines Rd DN21 24 F8
Bainton Gr NG7 184 F1
Baird-Parker Dr NG4 174 D7
Baker Ave
  Arnold NG5 148 A2
  Gringley on the Hill DN10 12 E2
Baker Brook Cl NG15 146 D5
Baker Brook Ind Pk
  NG15 146 C6
Baker Cl
  Long Eaton NG10 182 C1
  Worksop S81 35 D5
Bakerdale Rd NG3 174 B6
Baker La NG20 60 A2
Baker Rd
  Eastwood NG16 144 C1
  Mansfield Woodhouse
  NG19 88 C6
Bakers Cl NG7 222 A4
BAKERS FIELDS 174 C6
Baker's Hollow NG12 187 E3
Baker's La
  Colston Bassett NG12 200 E7
  Redmile NG13 192 F3
Baker St
  Hucknall NG15 146 A7
  13 Ilkeston DE7 157 F1
  Nottingham NG1 173 B7
Bakewell Ave NG4 162 E1
Bakewell Cl NG24 140 C4
Bakewell Dr NG5 160 E7
Bakewell La NG15 146 B4
Bakewell Rd NG10 193 E5
Bala Dr NG5 161 A7
BALDERTON 140 E3
Balderton Ct NG19 101 E7
Balderton Gate NG24 140 A8
Balderton La NG24 141 A7
Baldwin Cl NG19 89 B2
Baldwin Ct NG7 222 B3
Baldwin St
  Eastwood NG16 144 C1
  Nottingham NG7 222 C3
Balfour Rd
  Nottingham NG7 222 B3
  Stapleford NG9 182 D6
Balfour St
  Gainsborough DN21 15 C1
  Kirkby-in-Ashfield NG17 115 C4
Balfron Gdns 7 NG2 173 B2
Balkham La NG20 72 C3
Ballantrae Cl NG5 162 B8
Ballater Cl NG19 87 E2
Ballerat Cres NG5 160 E8
Ballerini Way LN1 57 C3
Ball Hill DE55 113 C6
Balloon Houses NG9 171 B4
Balloon Wood Ind Est
  NG8 171 A4
Balls La NG17 115 C2
Ball St NG3 173 F7
Balmoral Ave NG2 185 E8
Balmoral Cl
  Carlton in Lindrick S81 25 F6
  Mansfield Woodhouse
  NG19 88 E5
  Sandiacre NG10 182 B3
Balmoral Cres NG8 171 C5
Balmoral Ct DN11 9 B5
Balmoral Dr
  Beeston NG9 171 C2
  Mansfield NG19 87 E2
  Newark-on-Trent NG24 140 E8
Balmoral Gr NG15 146 B8
Balmoral Rd
  Bingham NG13 177 C4
  Carlton NG4 174 F6
  Nottingham NG1 223 D4
Balshaw Way NG9 183 B2
Balwant Dr NG17 101 C2
Bamburgh Cl 10 NG17 114 E7
Bamford Dr NG18 103 B6
Bamford St DE55 99 A3
Bamkin Cl NG15 146 B6
Bampton St 8 LE11 220 B3
Banbury Ave NG9 182 F3
Banbury Mount 9
  NG5 161 C2
Banchory Cl NG19 87 E2
Bancroft La NG18 101 F7
Bancroft Rd NG24 140 B6
Bancroft St NG6 160 C7
Banes Rd NG13 178 B4
Bangor Wlk 3 NG3 173 C7
Bank Ave NG17 100 E1
Bank Cl
  Creswell S80 58 D8
  Shirebrook NG20 72 F4
Bank End Cl NG18 102 D4
Bank End Rd DN10 1 C4
Bankfield Dr NG9 171 C1
Bank Hill NG14 149 A4
Bank Pl NG1 223 E2
Banks Ave NG17 114 E6
Banks Cl NG5 162 B6
Banks Cres NG13 177 E4
Bank Side DN22 39 F3
Banksman Cl NG14 173 F7
Banksman Way NG22 77 D7
Banks Paddock
  NG13 177 F4
Banks Rd NG9 182 E2
Banks Road Inf Sch
  NG9 182 F2
Bank St
  Langley Mill NG16 143 C3
  Long Eaton NG10 193 E7
Banks The NG13 177 F4
Bankwood Cl NG8 160 A1
Bank Yd 11 NG6 160 B7
Bannerman Rd
  Kirkby-in-Ashfield NG17 114 F5
  Nottingham NG6 160 C6
Baptist La
  Collingham NG23 111 F8
  Collingham NG23 112 A7
Barbara Sq NG15 130 F1
Barber Cl DE7 157 F3
Barber St NG16 144 B2
Barbers Wood Cl
  NG15 117 A1
Barbrook Cl NG8 172 A5
Barbury Dr NG11 195 D7
Barclay Ct DE7 157 C3
Barden Rd NG3 162 A4
Bardfield Gdns NG5 146 D1
Bardney Dr NG6 160 A8
Bardsey Gdns NG5 161 A7
Barent Cl NG5 160 F6
Barent Wlk NG5 160 F6
Barford Cl
  Shireoaks S81 34 F8
  Shireoaks S81 35 A8
Bar Gate NG24 124 F1
Barker Ave
  Sutton in Ashfield
  NG17 100 D7
  Westwood NG16 128 B4
Barker Ave E NG10 182 A6
Barker Ave N NG10 182 A6
Barker Gate
  Hucknall NG15 145 F7
  Ilkeston DE7 157 F2
  Nottingham NG1 223 F2
Barker Hades Rd S81 16 B3
Barker Hill NG14 150 E2
Barkers Field LE14 211 C3
Barker's La NG9 183 E4
Barker St NG17 99 F4
Barker Way NG24 139 F7
Barkestone La
  Bottesford NG13 181 A1
  Plungar NG13 192 A1
  Plungar NG13 202 F8
BARKESTONE-LE-
  VALE 192 C2
Barkla Cl NG11 195 C8
Barkston Cl NG24 140 D3
Bar La NG6 160 D2
Bar La Ind Pk NG6 160 D2
Barlborough Rd DE7 157 F5
Barley Cl
  Carlton NG5 162 D2
  Kimberley NG16 158 F7
  New Ollerton NG22 77 D5
Barley Croft
  South Normanton DE55 113 B4
  West Bridgford NG2 185 C4
Barley Dale Dr NG9 170 D2
Barleylands NG11 196 C6
Barley Ms NG19 88 E6
Barley Wy 4 NG24 125 B4
Barling Dr DE7 157 C2
Barlock Rd NG6 160 E4
Barlow Cotts La NG16 158 B5
Barlow Dr N NG16 158 B4
Barlow Dr S NG16 158 B4
Barlows Cl NG12 189 B4
Barnards Pl LE14 211 C3
Barnby Gate NG24 140 A8
BARNBY IN THE
  WILLOWS 141 F5
Barnby La NG23 156 E8
BARNBY MOOR 28 C5
Barnby Rd
  Newark-on-Trent NG24 140 B7
  Newark-on-Trent NG24 140 D6
Barnby Road Acad The
  NG24 140 B7
Barnby Wlk NG5 161 C4
Barn Cl
  Cotgrave NG12 187 E2
  Mansfield NG18 102 F5
  Nottingham NG16 159 F5
  Worksop S81 36 A7
Barn Croft
  Beeston NG9 183 B5
  Mansfield NG18 102 F6
Barndale Cl NG2 185 C3
Barnes Cl NG11 185 B4
Barnes Cres NG17 114 E8
Barnes Ct DN22 29 D2
Barnes Rd NG5 160 E8
Barnet Rd NG3 174 B7
Barnett Ct NG12 197 E3
Barnfield NG11 185 B4
Barnfield Cl LE12 212 B4
Barnfield Rd
  Collingham NG23 98 B1
  Collingham NG23 112 B8
Barnhill Gdns NG17 101 C1
Barn La DN22 32 D1
Barn Owl Cl NG20 74 C6
Barn Owl Way NG21 89 F5
Barnsdale Cl LE11 220 A5
Barnsley Cl NG6 147 B5
Barnsley Terr 9 NG2 173 C1
BARNSTONE 190 F3
Barnstone La NG13 191 A5
Barnstone Rd NG13 190 C2
Barnston Rd NG2 174 A5
Barnum Cl NG8 171 E5
Barn Vw DN10 20 A8
Barons Cl NG4 162 E1
Barons Dr NG22 77 F6
Barrack Cotts LE12 217 A6
Barrack La NG7 222 B2
Barrack Row 4 LE11 220 B4
Barra Mews 10 NG2 173 B2
Barratt Cl
  Beeston NG9 183 D1
  Cropwell Bishop NG12 189 A4
Barratt Cres NG9 183 D2
Barratt La NG9 183 D1
Bar Rd DN10 23 C7
Bar Rd N DN10 23 C8
Bar Rd S DN10 23 C8
Barrel Hill Rd NG23 96 E7
Barrhead Cl NG5 146 E1
Barringer Rd NG19 88 D1
Barrington Cl NG12 175 E2
Barrique Rd NG7 172 E1
Barrowby Ct S81 36 A5
Barrowhill Wlk NG18 103 B6
Barrow Rd LE12 220 F6
Barrows Gate NG24 125 B3
Barrows Hill La NG16 128 D5
Barrow Slade NG12 197 E2
Barrow St LE11 220 B3
Barrydale Ave NG9 183 F5
Barry St NG6 160 B7
Bars Hill LE12 206 C1
Bar The NG22 79 C3
Bartholomew Cl NG12 186 A3
Bartley Gdns NG14 148 C8
Bartlow Rd NG8 171 D7
Barton Cl
  Mansfield Woodhouse
  NG19 89 B1
  Ruddington NG11 196 B6
BARTON IN FABIS 194 E6
Barton La
  Barton in Fabis NG11 195 A5
  Beeston NG9 183 C1
  Beeston NG9 194 D8
  Long Eaton NG11 194 D3
  Nottingham NG11 184 C1
Barton Rd NG10 194 A6
Bartons Cl NG16 144 C2
Barton St NG9 184 A5
Barton Wy NG9 183 E5
Barwell Dr NG8 159 D1
Basa Cres NG5 160 F8
Basford Hall NG6 160 C3
Basford Rd NG6 160 D2
Baskin La NG9 183 C3
Baslow Ave NG4 162 D1
Baslow Cl NG10 193 A5
Baslow Dr NG9 172 A1
Baslow Way NG18 103 B5
Bass Cl NG15 131 C1
Bassetlaw District General
  Hospl S81 36 A5
Bassetlaw Leisure
  Centre S80 35 F3
Bassetlaw Mus* DN22 39 F7
Bassett Cl
  Ilkeston DE7 157 C3
  Kimberley NG16 158 E7
Bassett Hill NG20 72 E7
Bassett Rd NG16 158 E7
Bassett The NG20 72 E6
Bassingfield La NG12 186 F8
Bastion St NG7 222 A3
Bateman Cl NG12 185 F3
Bateman Gdns 8 NG7 172 F7
Bateman Rd LE12 205 E1
Bateman's Yd NG17 114 D4
Bath La
  Mansfield NG18 102 C8
  Market Warsop NG19 73 C2
BATHLEY 110 A3
Bathley La
  Bathley NG23 110 B5
  Little Carlton NG23 124 C7
  Norwell NG23 109 F7
  South Muskham NG23 110 B1
Bathley St NG2 173 D1
Baths La NG15 146 B7
Bath St
  Ilkeston DE7 157 E1
  Mansfield NG18 102 B6
  Nottingham NG1 223 F3
  Nottingham NG14 173 D5
  Sutton in Ashfield NG17 100 F4
Bathurst Dr NG8 172 A6
Bathurst Terr
  Creswell NG20 58 F2
  Whaley Thorns NG20 58 F2
  Whaley Thorns NG20 59 A2
Bathwood Dr
  Mansfield NG17, NG18 101 E5
  Sutton in Ashfield NG17,
  NG18 101 A2
Batley La NG19 86 E4
Battle Cl NG13 177 B7
Baulker La
  Blidworth NG21 118 E4
  Clipstone NG21 90 B4
  Farnsfield NG22 119 A4
Baulk La
  Beeston NG9 183 A6
  Harworth DN11 8 F5
  Kneesall NG22 93 E7
  Stapleford NG9 183 A5
  Torworth DN22 19 A2
  Worksop S81 35 E5
Baulk The
  Clarborough DN22 40 E8
  Worksop S81 35 F5
Baum's La NG18 102 C5
BAWTRY 10 B7
Bawtry Cl DN11 8 F4
Bawtry Mayflower
  Prim Sch DN10 10 A8
Bawtry Rd
  Bawtry DN10 10 C8
  Bircotes DN10 9 C1
  Blyth S81 18 A6
  Everton DN10 11 A3
  Finningley DN10 3 E8
  Harworth DN11 9 A5
  Misson DN10 4 A3
  Tickhill DN11 8 E7
Bawtry Wlk NG3 173 F6
Baxter Cl
  Bingham NG13 177 E6
  Hucknall NG15 131 C1
Baxter Green NG9 183 B7
Baxter Hill NG19 86 F3
Baxter La
  Sibthorpe NG23 154 B1
  Sibthorpe NG23 168 A8
Baxter St LE11 220 B4
Bayard Ct NG8 172 C5
Bayard St DN21 15 C1
Bayford Dr NG24 140 F7
Bayliss Rd NG4 162 D3
Baysdale Dr 1 NG19 88 F1
Bayswater Rd NG16 158 F7
Baythorn Rd NG8 171 D6
Beacon Dr
  Kirkby-in-Ashfield
  NG17 115 C6
  Loughborough LE11 220 A1
Beacon Hill Bsns Pk
  NG24 125 B1
Beacon Hill Conservation
  Park* NG24 125 C1
Beacon Hill Dr NG15 145 D5
Beacon Hill Rd
  Gringley on the Hill
  DN10 13 A2
  Newark-on-Trent NG24 140 C8
Beacon Hill Rise NG3 173 E6
Beacon Hts NG24 140 D8
Beacon Rd
  Beeston NG9 184 B6
  Loughborough LE11 220 A2
Beaconsfield Dr NG24 125 F2
Beaconsfield Green
  NG24 125 F2
Beaconsfield St
  Long Eaton NG10 193 E7
  Nottingham NG7 172 F8
Beacon View NG13 181 B3
Beacon Vw NG22 77 D3
Beacon Way NG24 140 D8
Beacon Wlk DN10 13 A2
Beamlight Rd DE7 157 F8
Bean Ave S80 36 B3
Bean Cl NG6 159 F5
Beanford La
  Calverton NG14 133 F3
  Oxton NG25 134 A3
Beardall Fields
  Prim Sch NG15 146 C8
Beardall St
  Hucknall NG15 146 B6
  7 Mansfield NG18 102 A7
Beardsall Rd NG16 144 A3
Beardsall's Row DN22 39 F7
Beardsley Gdns NG2 173 B2
Beardsley Rd NG21 76 C1
Beardsmore Gr NG15 130 F1
Beast Mkt Hill
  Newark-on-Trent NG24 124 F1
  Nottingham NG1 223 E2
Beatty Wlk DE7 157 F3
Beauclerk Dr NG5 160 E8
Beaufit La NG16 113 E2
Beaufort Ct NG11 185 C3
Beaufort Dr NG9 183 C5
Beaufort Gdns DN10 9 F7
Beaufort St DN21 15 C3
Beaufort Way S81 35 E8
Beaulieu Gdns NG2 185 C5
Beauly Dr NG19 101 D5
Beaumaris Dr
  Beeston NG9 183 B4
  Carlton NG4 163 B1
Beaumond Cross NG24 139 F8
Beaumont Ave
  Mansfield NG18 102 F5
  Southwell NG25 121 C1
  Southwell NG25 136 C8
Beaumont Cl
  Keyworth NG12 197 E4
  Stapleford NG9 170 E1
Beaumont Ct LE11 220 A6
Beaumont Gdns NG2 185 D4
Beaumont Rd LE11 220 B1
Beaumont Rise S80 35 D3
Beaumont Sq NG9 171 C5
Beaumont St
  Gainsborough DN21 24 D8
  Nottingham NG2 173 E4
Beaumont Wlk NG24 125 B2
Beauvale NG16 144 C2
Beauvale Cres NG15 145 E6
Beauvale Dr DE7 157 E5
Beauvale Rd
  Annesley Woodhouse
  NG17 129 E8
  Hucknall NG15 145 E6
  Nottingham NG2 173 C1
Beauvale Rise NG16 144 A3
Beaver Gn 5 NG12 185 D7
Beaver Pl S80 35 F3
Beazley Ave NG18 101 F7
Bechers Ct NG25 121 E1
Beck Ave NG14 148 F8
Beck Cres
  Blidworth NG21 118 A4
  Mansfield NG19 101 E7
Beck Dr DN21 14 A5
Beckenham Rd NG7 222 B4
Becket Gr NG11 185 A5
Becket Sch The NG2 185 B7
Beckett Ave
  Carlton in Lindrick S81 25 F7
  Gainsborough DN21 15 E2
  Mansfield NG19 87 E1
Beckett Ct NG4 162 D3
Becketts Field NG25 136 D7
Beckett St NG24 139 F5
Becket Way The NG12 185 B6
Beckford Rd 8 NG2 173 F3
Beckhampton Rd NG5 161 A7
BECKINGHAM
  Lincs 142 D8
  Notts 14 B1
Beckingham Ct NG19 101 E7
Beckingham Prim Sch
  DN10 14 B1
Beckingham Rd
  Beckingham NG24 127 A1
  Coddington NG24 126 C2
  Stapleford LN6 127 E8
  Walkeringham DN10 14 A4
Beckingthorpe Dr
  NG13 181 B3
Beck La
  Blidworth NG21 118 A4
  Clayworth DN22 21 E4
  Farnsfield NG22 119 F5
  Sutton in Ashfield NG17,
  NG19 101 B6
  West Markham NG22 65 B3
Beckland Hill NG22 65 F6
Beckley Rd NG8 159 F2
Beckon Mdw DN10 23 C8
Beckside
  Lowdham NG14 150 E1
  West Bridgford NG2 186 C5
Beck St
  Carlton NG4 174 E8
  Nottingham NG1 223 F3
  Thurgarton NG14 151 D7
Beckway NG23 109 B5
Bedale S81 36 A8
Bedale Ct NG9 183 A4
Bedale Rd NG5 161 D5
Bedarra Gr NG7 222 A2
Bede Cl NG5 147 A1
Bede House La NG24 140 A8
Bede Ling NG2 185 C6
Bedford Ave NG18 102 E7
Bedford Cl DE74 203 D1
Bedford Ct
  Bawtry DN10 9 F7
  Stapleford NG9 170 E1
Bedford Gr NG6 160 D5
Bedford Row NG1 223 F3
Bedford Sq 3 LE11 220 B3
Bedford St LE11 220 B3
Bedlam Row LN1 57 A3
Bedlington Gdns NG3 161 E1

Beecham Ave NG3 173 F7
Beech Ave
Beeston NG9 184 B5
Bingham NG13 178 A4
Carlton NG4 174 F6
East Leake LE12 214 D8
Edwinstowe NG22 76 F4
Gainsborough DN21 15 D2
Hucknall NG15 146 A7
Huthwaite NG17 100 A3
Keyworth NG12 198 A2
Kirkby-in-Ashfield NG17 114 F5
Lidgett NG21 91 C8
Long Eaton NG10 182 F1
12 Mansfield NG18 102 B6
New Ollerton NG22 77 C4
Nottingham, Hyson Green NG7 173 A8
Nottingham, Mapperley NG3 162 A4
Nuthall NG16 159 B6
Ollerton NG22 77 A4
Pinxton NG16 113 E3
Ravenshead NG15 116 F3
Sandiacre NG10 182 B7
Tickhill DN11 8 B7
Worksop S81 35 F6
Beech Cl
Gringley on the Hill DN10 12 F2
Nottingham NG6 160 C4
Radcliffe on Trent NG12 175 F2
West Bridgford NG12 186 A4
Beech Cres
Glapwell S44 86 B8
Mansfield Woodhouse NG19 88 D2
Beechcroft S81 36 A6
Beech Ct
Nottingham NG3 162 A4
Selston NG16 129 B3
BEECHDALE 172 B6
Beechdale Ave NG17 100 F4
Beechdale Cres NG17 100 F4
Beechdale Rd
Mansfield Woodhouse NG19 89 A2
Nottingham NG8 172 B7
Beechdale Swimming Ctr NG8 172 C6
Beech Dr NG13 181 B2
Beecher La DN10 14 B1
Beeches Ct NG23 98 D5
Beeches Rd LE11 220 C2
Beeches The
Carlton NG3 174 A8
Sutton in Ashfield NG17 100 D7
Tuxford NG22 65 F2
Beech Gr
Blidworth NG21 118 C5
Carlton in Lindrick S81 25 E7
South Normanton DE55 113 B5
Beech Hill Ave NG19 87 F1
Beech Hill Cres NG19 87 F1
Beech Hill Dr NG19 87 F1
Beech Hill Sch NG19 87 F1
Beech Rd
Harworth DN11 9 A5
Selston NG16 129 B3
Beech St NG17 100 D7
Beech Tree Ave NG19 88 B5
Beechways DN22 39 D4
Beech Wlk DN22 50 B4
Beechwood Cl
Mansfield Woodhouse NG19 89 A1
Sutton in Ashfield NG17 101 A5
Beechwood Cres DN22 37 F6
Beechwood Ct NG17 101 A5
Beechwood Dr DN22 38 D6
Beechwood Gr NG17 101 A5
Beechwood Rd
Arnold NG5 162 A8
6 Kirkby-in-Ashfield NG17 114 F7
Beedham Way NG5 162 C8
Beehive La LN6 84 F1
Bee Hive La 4 LE11 220 B3
Beehive St DN22 39 F6
Beeley Ave NG17 100 E1
Beeley Cl NG18 103 B6
BEESTON 183 A6
Beeston Bsns Pk NG9 184 A4
Beeston Cl NG6 146 F4
Beeston Ct NG6 160 D6
Beeston Fields Dr NG9 183 D8
Beeston Fields Prim Sch NG9 183 F8
Beeston La NG9 184 B8
Beeston Rd
Newark-on-Trent NG24 140 B5
Nottingham NG7 172 D1
Beeston Rylands Jun Sch NG9 184 A4
Beeston Sidings Nature Reserve* NG11 184 C7
Beeston Sta NG9 184 A5
Beethan Cl NG13 177 F4
Beggarlee Pk NG16 144 B4
Behay Gdns NG23 138 C8
Beighton Ct NG18 103 B5
Beighton St NG17 100 F3
Bek Cl NG19 86 F7
Belconnen Rd NG5 161 A5
Beldover Dr 5 NG16 159 C2
Belfield Gdns NG10 193 E7
Belfields Yd NG22 120 C4
Belfmoor Cl S80 45 A5
Belford Cl NG6 159 F8
Belfry Cl 1 NG17 114 E7
Belfry Rise S81 36 B8
Belfry Way NG2 186 C4
Belgrave Ct DN10 9 F7
Belgrave Mews NG11 185 C3
Belgrave Rd NG6 160 A7
Belgrave Sq NG1 223 D3
Belgravia Ct 2 S81 35 E7
Bella Cl NG16 143 B4
Bellamy Dr NG17 115 A3
Bellamy Rd NG18 103 A2
Bellar Gate NG1 223 F2
Bell Cl NG23 81 E7
Belle-Isle Rd NG15 146 A7
Belleville Dr NG5 161 B8
Bellevue Ct NG3 173 E6
Belle Vue Gdns NG21 118 B6
Belle Vue La NG21 118 A6
Bell Foundry Mus* LE11 220 C4
Bell La
Collingham NG23 111 F8
Nottingham NG11 185 A7
Weston NG23 80 F5
Weston NG23 81 A5
Bellmore Gdns NG8 171 D5
Bell Pit Dr NG21 76 D3
Bellsfield Cl S80 45 A5
Bells La NG8 160 A3
Bell St NG4 174 D8
Bell View NG18 102 C7
Belmond Cl NG24 139 F5
Belmont Ave NG6 160 C7
Belmont Cl
Beeston NG9 183 B4
Hucknall NG15 146 A4
Mansfield Woodhouse NG19 89 A2
Belmont Rd NG17 115 B1
Belper Ave NG4 162 D1
Belper Cres NG4 162 D1
Belper Rd NG7 172 F7
Belper St NG18 102 D7
Belper Way NG18 102 D7
Belsay Rd NG5 161 A7
Belsford Ct NG16 159 A8
Belton Cl NG10 182 B4
Belton Dr NG2 185 B4
Belton Rd LE11 220 A5
Belton Rd W Extension LE11 220 A6
Belton St NG7 172 F8
Belt Rd The DN21 15 E3
Belvedere Ave 9 NG7 172 F8
Belvedere St NG18 102 B6
Belvoir Ave NG13 181 A1
Belvoir Cl
Aslockton NG13 178 E3
Long Eaton NG10 193 E5
Belvoir Cres
Langar NG13 190 C2
Newark-on-Trent NG24 140 A6
Belvoir Hill NG2 173 F4
Belvoir Pl NG24 140 D4
Belvoir Rd
Balderton NG24 140 D3
Bottesford NG13 181 A2
Carlton NG4 175 A7
Redmile NG13 192 F3
West Bridgford NG2 174 A1
Belvoir St
Hucknall NG15 145 F8
Nottingham NG3 161 F2
Belvoir Terr DN21 15 B4
Belvoir Vale Gr NG13 177 F4
Belward St NG1 223 F2
Belwood Cl NG7 184 F2
Bembridge S81 36 B6
Bembridge Ct NG9 183 A8
Bembridge Dr NG5 161 B6
Bemrose Dr NG12 176 A5
Bencaunt Grove NG15 146 A8
Bendigo La NG2 174 A4
Benedict Ct 3 NG5 147 A1
Benet Dr NG22 106 A5
Benington Dr NG8 171 C3
Ben Mayo Ct NG7 222 B4
Benner Ave DE7 170 A5
Bennerley Ave DE7 157 F4
Bennerley Ct NG6 159 F8
Bennerley Fields Specialist Speech & Language Coll DE7 157 F4
Bennerley Rd NG6 159 F8
Bennet Dr 2 NG17 115 A4
Bennett Ave NG18 102 F6
Bennett Gdns NG12 197 F4
Bennett Rd NG3 162 A3
Bennett St
Long Eaton NG10 182 C2
Nottingham NG3 161 F2
Sandiacre NG10 182 B5
Benneworth Cl NG15 145 F5
Bennington Wlk NG19 88 E4
Ben St NG7 222 B4
Benick St NG18 102 D7
Bentinck Ave NG12 186 D1
Bentinck Banks Nature Reserve* NG17 114 E3
Bentinck Cl
Annesley Woodhouse NG17 114 F1
Boughton NG22 77 E6
Bentinck Ct 8 NG2 173 E4
Bentinck Prim Sch NG7 222 B1
Bentinck Rd
Carlton NG4 162 C2
Newark-on-Trent NG24 139 F6
Nottingham NG7 222 B4
Bentinck St
Annesley Woodhouse NG17 129 F8
Hodthorpe S80 45 C6
Bentinck St *continued*
Hucknall NG15 145 F8
Sutton in Ashfield NG17 100 F3
Bentinck Terr NG20 74 B3
Bentinck Workshops NG17 114 D3
Bentinick Ct S80 46 F8
Bentley Ave NG3 174 B6
Bentley Cl LE11 220 C4
Bentwell Ave NG5 162 A7
Beresford Dr DE7 157 E5
Beresford Rd
Long Eaton NG10 193 A5
Mansfield Woodhouse NG19 88 C6
Beresford St
Mansfield NG18 102 D6
Nottingham NG7 222 A3
Berkeley Ave
Long Eaton NG10 193 C6
Nottingham NG3 173 C8
Berkeley Cres NG12 176 D3
Berkeley Rd NG18 102 C5
Bernard Ave
Hucknall NG15 131 B1
Mansfield Woodhouse NG19 88 B5
Bernard Rd NG19 101 E8
Bernard St NG5 161 B1
Bernisdale Cl NG5 146 F1
Berridge Adult Ctr The NG7 173 A8
Berridge Jun Sch NG7 172 E7
Berridge Prim Sch NG7 172 F8
Berridge Prim Sch Brushfield NG7 172 E7
Berridge Rd E NG7 173 A8
Berridge Rd W NG7 172 E7
Berriedale Cl NG5 162 C8
Berristow Grange NG17 100 D1
Berristow La DE55 113 C7
Berry Ave NG17 114 E6
Berrydown Cl NG8 160 C1
Berry Hill Cl NG18 102 C4
Berry Hill Gdns NG18 102 F4
Berry Hill Gr NG4 162 E2
Berry Hill La
Mansfield NG18 102 C4
Mansfield NG18 102 D4
Berry Hill Mews NG18 102 D4
Berry Hill Prim Sch NG18 102 F4
Berry Hill Rd NG18 102 C4
Berry Pk Lea NG18 102 D3
Berwick Ave NG19 101 D8
Berwick Cl NG5 161 C6
Berwin Cl NG10 182 A1
Beryldene Ave NG16 159 A7
Bescar La
Ollerton NG22 77 A2
Rufford NG22 92 B8
Bescoby St DN22 39 F6
Besecar Ave NG4 162 E2
Besecar Cl NG4 162 E2
Bessell La NG9 182 D5
Bessemer Dr NG18 102 B4
Bessingham Dr NG11 185 C3
BESTHORPE 97 E6
Besthorpe Ct NG19 101 E7
Besthorpe Nature Reserve (North)* NG23 97 D6
Besthorpe Nature Reserve (South)* NG23 97 D4
Besthorpe Rd
Besthorpe NG23 97 F3
Collingham NG23 98 A2
North Scarle LN6 83 C1
Bestwick Ave DE75 143 B1
Bestwick Cl DE7 170 A4
BESTWOOD 161 B7
Bestwood Ave NG5 161 E8
Bestwood Bsns Pk NG6 146 E3
Bestwood Cl NG5 161 E8
Bestwood Country Park - Mill Lakes* NG6 146 B2
Bestwood Ctry Pk* NG6 146 F3
Bestwood Lodge Dr NG5 161 D8
Bestwood Park Drive 4 NG5 147 B1
Bestwood Pk Dr NG5 161 B8
Bestwood Pk Dr W NG5 146 E1
Bestwood Pk View NG5 147 E1
Bestwood Rd
Hucknall NG15 146 C5
Nottingham NG6 146 D2
Pinxton NG16 113 E2
Bestwood Terr NG6 160 C8
BESTWOOD VILLAGE 146 F4
Beswick Cl NG4 175 C7
Betford Gate DN22 41 D8
Bethel Gdns NG15 145 C5
Bethel Terr S80 34 E7
Bethnal Wlk 2 NG6 160 B7
Betony Cl NG13 177 C4
Betony Gr 1 NG17 115 A3
Bettina Gdns NG12 185 F3
Betts Ave NG15 146 A4
Bettys La DN21 24 E4
Betula Cl NG11 184 C1
Beulah Rd NG17 115 B4
Bevan Cl NG21 118 B8
Bevel St NG7 172 F7
Bevercotes Cl NG24 139 F6
Bevercotes La NG22 65 D3
Bevercotes Rd NG22 64 C3
Beverley Cl
Nottingham NG8 171 B4
Rainworth NG21 104 B1
Beverley Dr
Kimberley NG16 158 E7
Kirkby-in-Ashfield NG17 115 C3
Mansfield NG18 102 D2
Beverley Gdns NG4 162 F1
Beverley Rd DN11 9 A4
Beverleys Ave NG13 178 F4
Beverley Wlk S81 25 E7
Bevin Pl NG21 76 C3
Bewcastle Rd NG5 147 A2
Bewick Dr NG3 174 C5
Bexhill Ct NG8 171 E1
Bexwell Cl NG11 195 E8
BHI Mus* NG25 122 E1
Biant Cl NG8 160 B3
Bicycle La NG9 183 E5
Biddleston Ct NG17 100 D5
Bideford Cl NG3 162 D5
Bidford Rd NG8 159 F1
Bidwell Cres NG11 195 B2
Big Barn La NG18 102 F5
Biggart Cl 2 NG9 183 C2
Biggin St LE11 220 B4
Big House The NG21 76 B3
Big La DN22 30 D3
Bigsby Rd
Retford DN22 30 A1
Retford DN22 39 F8
Big Wood Sch NG5 147 B2
Biko Sq 8 NG7 172 F8
Bilberry Dr NG20 72 D2
Bilberry Wlk NG3 173 E7
Bilbie Wlk NG1 223 D3
BILBOROUGH 171 E7
Bilborough Coll NG8 171 C7
Bilborough Rd NG8 171 C6
Bilby Gdns 3 NG3 173 F5
Billesdon Dr NG5 160 F4
Billingsley Ave NG16 113 D3
Bill La NG22 105 F5
Billy Button La
Torworth DN22 19 A1
Torworth S81 27 F8
BILSTHORPE 105 E6
Bilsthorpe Bsns Pk NG22 106 A8
Bilsthorpe Heritage Museum* NG22 105 F6
Bilsthorpe Rd NG22 92 D1
Bilton Cl NG24 140 D2
Binbrook Ct DN10 9 F6
Binch Field Cl NG14 148 C8
BINGHAM 177 E3
Bingham Ave NG17 101 A5
Bingham Bypass
Bingham NG13 177 C3
Bingham NG13 178 A3
Bingham Ind Pk NG13 177 E5
Bingham L Ctr NG13 177 F3
Bingham Prim Sch NG13 177 D6
Bingham Rd
Cotgrave NG12 187 F3
Granby NG13 191 A6
Langar NG13 190 B4
Mansfield NG18 103 A3
Nottingham NG5 161 C2
Radcliffe on Trent NG12 176 A3
Bingham Robert Miles Inf Sch NG13 177 E5
Bingham Sta NG13 177 F5
Bingley Cl 2 NG8 172 B6
Bingley Cres 11 NG17 115 A3
BioCity NG8 173 E4
Birch Ave
Beeston NG9 184 B4
Carlton NG4 174 D7
Farnsfield NG22 119 E7
Ilkeston DE7 170 A7
Nuthall NG16 159 B6
Rainworth NG21 104 C1
Birch Cl
Aslockton NG13 178 F5
Nuthall NG16 159 B6
Rampton DN22 42 F2
Ranskill DN22 19 C4
Ravenshead NG15 117 A1
Birch Croft Dr NG19 89 A2
Birchcroft Rd DN22 39 E8
Birch Ct NG22 65 F2
Birchdale Ave NG15 145 A5
Birchenhall Ct NG24 139 A4
Birchen Holme DE55 113 A4
Birches The NG15 117 A3
Birchfield Dr S80 35 B2
Birchfield Rd NG5 148 A1
Birch Gr
Gainsborough DN21 15 D2
Mansfield NG18 103 A4
Shirebrook NG20 72 D5
Birchlands NG19 88 F1
Birch Lea
Arnold NG5 161 D8
East Leake LE12 205 D1
Birchover Pl DE7 157 E5
Birchover Rd NG8 171 C6
Birch Pas NG7 222 C3
Birch Rd
Hodthorpe S80 45 C6
New Balderton NG24 140 C5
New Ollerton NG22 77 D4
Birch Rise NG14 149 C5
Birch St NG20 73 F6
Birch Tree Cl NG19 89 D3
Birch Tree Cres NG17 114 F4
Birchwood Ave
Breaston NG10 193 A7
Birchwood Ave *continued*
Long Eaton NG10 193 C5
Birchwood Cl
Ravenshead NG15 117 B1
South Normanton DE55 113 A4
Southwell NG25 121 D1
Sutton in Ashfield NG17 100 E6
Birchwood Dr
Ravenshead NG15 117 A1
Sutton in Ashfield NG17 100 D7
Birchwood Pk NG19 89 C3
Birchwood Rd NG8 171 C4
Birchwood View DN21 15 F1
BIRCOTES 9 D4
Bircotes L Ctr DN11 9 C4
Bird Cl NG18 102 C3
Birdcroft La DN10 14 A5
Birding St NG19 88 B1
Birdsall Ave NG8 171 E4
Bird's La NG17 114 E1
Birkdale S81 36 B6
Birkdale Ave NG22 77 D6
Birkdale Cl
Ilkeston DE7 157 D1
West Bridgford NG12 186 A3
Birkdale Dr 3 NG17 114 F6
Birkdale Gr DN22 39 D2
Birkdale Sq DN21 15 E3
Birkdale Way
Nottingham NG5 160 F8
9 Nottingham NG5 161 A8
Birkin Ave
Beeston NG9 183 A2
Nottingham NG7 172 F7
Radcliffe on Trent NG12 176 A4
Ruddington NG11 196 C8
Birkland Ave
Mansfield Woodhouse NG19 88 D3
Market Warsop NG20 74 B4
Nottingham, Mapperley NG3 162 A4
Nottingham, St Ann's NG1 223 E4
Birkland Dr NG21 76 A2
Birkland La NG23 68 F1
Birklands Ave
New Ollerton NG22 77 C6
Worksop S80 36 C1
Birklands Cl NG20 74 B5
Birklands Prim Sch NG20 74 B5
Birkland St NG18 102 D7
Birks Cl S80 45 C6
Birks Rd NG19 101 D7
Birley St NG9 182 D5
Birling Cl NG6 159 F7
Birrell Rd NG7 173 A8
Birrel St DN21 15 B2
Bisham Dr NG2 186 B7
Bishop Alexander Prim Sch NG24 125 A4
Bishop Alexandra Ct NG24 139 E7
Bishopdale S81 36 A7
Bishopdale Cl NG10 193 A6
Bishopdale Dr NG16 159 B7
Bishopfield La DN22 19 A5
Bishops Cl NG12 197 E4
Bishop's Dr NG25 136 E8
Bishops Hill NG21 103 F1
Bishops Mdws NG20 74 B6
Bishops Rd NG13 177 D5
Bishop St
Eastwood NG16 143 F2
Loughborough LE11 220 C4
Mansfield NG18 102 B5
Sutton in Ashfield NG17 100 E3
Bishops Way
Boughton NG22 77 E5
Hucknall NG15 146 B8
Bishop's Wlk NG20 74 A6
Bispham Dr NG9 182 F2
Blackacre NG14 163 E5
Black Beny DN10 4 D1
Blackberry Way
Collingham NG23 112 B8
Market Warsop NG20 74 A3
Newark-on-Trent NG24 140 E2
Blackbird Av 8 S81 35 C7
Blackbird Cl LE12 205 F2
Blackbird Cres NG12 186 A2
Blackbird Dr NG22 77 C2
Blackbird Pl NG21 118 A8
Blackbrook Rd NG24 125 D1
Blackburn Cl
Carlton NG4 163 A1
Collingham NG23 98 B1
Blackburn Pl DE7 157 E3
Blackburn Row NG7 222 B2
Blackburn View NG22 77 D7
Blackburn Wy 5 NG5 161 A5
Blackcliff Field Cl S80 45 A5
Blacketts Wlk NG11 195 C8
Blackfriars Cl NG8 159 D3
Blackham Rd LE11 220 A1
Black Hereford Way DN22 39 C4
Blackhill Dr NG4 174 F8
Black La LN6 71 F1
Blackmires Way NG17 101 B4
Black Rock Wy NG19 102 D5
Blackrod Cl NG9 183 A2
Black Scotch Cl
Mansfield NG18 102 E3
Mansfield NG18 102 E4
Black Scotch La
Harlow Wood NG18 117 A8
Ravenshead NG18 116 F8
Blackshale Rd NG19 88 B2
Blacksmith Ct NG12 187 E4
Blacksmith La
Kelham NG23 124 A4
Torworth DN22 19 B2
Blacksmiths Cl LE14 219 D8
Blacksmiths Ct NG15 131 D3
Blacksmiths La LN6 83 D2
Blacksmiths Mws S81 35 C8
Blacksmith Wy NG20 72 F2
Blackstone Dr S81 34 F8
Blackstone Wlk NG2 173 C2
Blackstope La
4 Retford DN22 39 F7
Retford DN22 40 A7
Blackstope La East DN22 40 B6
Black Swan Cl NG5 161 D4
Blackthorn Cl
Bingham NG13 178 B4
Carlton NG4 163 A2
1 Gainsborough DN21 15 F1
Blackthorn Dr
5 Mansfield NG18 102 C5
Nottingham NG6 160 B3
Blackthorne Cl NG24 140 B5
Blackthorne Dr NG14 150 D2
Blackthorn Gdns NG21 89 F5
Blackthorn Way NG17 100 C1
Blackwell Rd NG17 99 E3
Blackwith Ave DE7 157 F5
Blades Dr LN1 57 A5
Bladon Cl NG3 161 E2
Bladon Rd NG11 196 B7
Blair Ct 4 NG2 173 C1
Blair Gr NG10 182 A4
Blaise Cl NG11 195 E8
Blake Cl
Arnold NG5 162 A7
Nottingham NG14 173 E5
Blake Cres NG18 102 E7
Blake Ct NG10 193 B5
Blakeney Ct NG19 88 E4
Blakeney Dr NG18 102 C4
Blakeney Rd NG12 176 B3
Blakeney Wlk NG5 161 F5
Blake Rd
Stapleford NG9 182 E6
West Bridgford NG2 186 A7
Blake St
Ilkeston DE7 157 F1
Mansfield Woodhouse NG19 88 B2
Blandford Ave NG10 193 B5
Blandford Dr DN22 39 D4
Blandford Gdns NG2 185 C5
Blandford Rd NG9 183 C5
Bland La NG14 150 A5
Blankney Cl LN1 57 A4
Blankney St 4 NG5 160 E4
Blants Cl NG16 158 F6
Blantyre Ave NG5 146 E1
Blatherwick Cl 3 NG15 146 B8
Blatherwick Rd NG24 140 D8
Blatherwick's Yd NG5 161 F8
Bleaberry Cl NG2 186 C5
Bleachers Yd NG7 160 F1
Bleak Hills La NG18 101 E4
Bleak Hills Lane NG18 102 A4
Bleak Hill Way NG18 101 E4
BLEASBY 152 B8
Bleasby CE Prim Sch NG14 151 F8
Bleasby Cres NG17 101 B1
Bleasby Rd NG14 151 D8
Bleasby St NG2 173 F4
Bleasby Sta NG14 151 F8
Bleasdale Cl NG4 163 A2
Bleinham Pk NG6 145 E1
Blencathra Cl NG2 186 C5
Blenheim Ave
Fernwood NG24 141 A3
Lowdham NG14 150 E1
Nottingham NG3 162 C2
Blenheim Cl
Mansfield NG19 88 D1
Ruddington NG11 196 B7
Skellingthorpe LN6 71 F4
Blenheim Dr NG9 183 C5
Blenheim Gdns NG13 165 D2
Blenheim Ind Est NG6 159 F8
Blenheim La NG6, NG15 145 E1
Blenheim Pk Rd
Nottingham NG16 159 E8
Nottingham NG6 145 E1
Blenheim Pl NG17 99 E3
Blenheim Rise
Bawtry DN10 9 F6
Worksop S81 35 E8
Blenheim Ct NG10 182 B4
Blessed Robert Widmerpool CV Acad NG11 195 E8
Bletchley Cl NG9 171 E1
Bley Ave LE12 214 D8
BLIDWORTH 118 B4
Blidworth Cl NG8 159 E2
Blidworth Ind Pk NG21 118 B6
Blidworth La
Blidworth NG21 133 C8
Mansfield NG21 103 D1
Rainworth NG21 117 E8
Blidworth Oaks Primary Sch NG21 118 A5
Blidworth Rd
Farnsfield NG22 119 E6
Kirkby-in-Ashfield NG15 115 E4
Blidworth Waye NG15 131 F7

Blind La
Keyworth NG12 . . . 197 E2
Oxton NG25 . . . 134 C4
Bloomgrove Rd DE7 . . . 157 F2
Bloomsbury Dr NG16 . . 159 E3
Bloomsbury Gdns
NG18 . . . 102 E4
Bloomsgrove Ind Est
NG7 . . . 222 B3
Bloomsgrove Rd NG7 . . 222 B3
Bloomsgrove St NG7 . . . 222 B3
Blossom Ct NG17 . . . 115 C6
Blossom Gdns NG12 . . . 188 A5
Blossom Gr DN22 . . . 40 A3
Blue Albion St DN22 . . . 39 D4
Blue Barn La NG20 . . . 59 C3
Bluebell Ave NG12 . . . 188 A5
Bluebell Bank NG13 . . . 177 D3
Bluebell Cl
Carlton in Lindrick S81 . . . 26 A7
Hucknall NG15 . . . 145 C6
Selston NG16 . . . 128 F2
Shirebrook NG20 . . . 72 D3
Stanton Hill NG17 . . . 100 B6
Blue Bell Ct DN22 . . . 19 B4
Bluebell Dr NG24 . . . 140 A4
Bluebell Gr 2 NG17 . . . 114 F7
Blue Bell Hill Prim Sch
NG3 . . . 173 F6
Blue Bell Hill Rd NG3 . . 173 E6
Bluebell Pl NG19 . . . 88 F4
Bluebells The NG17 . . . 101 B1
Bluebell Wlk NG24 . . . 125 E1
Bluebell Wood La
Clipstone NG21 . . . 89 F4
Mansfield NG21 . . . 89 F5
Bluebell Wood Way
NG17 . . . 100 C1
Bluebell Wy NG16 . . . 143 B1
Blue Bell Yd NG22 . . . 65 F3
Bluebird Ave NG22 . . . 77 C2
Bluecoat Aspley Acad
NG8 . . . 172 C8
Bluecoat Beechdale Acad
NG8 . . . 172 A7
Bluecoat Beechdale Acad
The NG9 . . . 171 F7
Bluecoat Cl NG1 . . . 223 E3
Bluecoat Prim Acad
NG9 . . . 171 F8
Bluecoat St NG1 . . . 223 E4
Blundell Cl NG3 . . . 173 F8
BLYTH . . . 18 A3
Blyth Cl NG19 . . . 87 D1
Blyth Ct NG19 . . . 87 D1
Blyth Gdns
Blyth S81 . . . 18 B2
Nottingham NG3 . . . 161 E2
Blyth Gr
Worksop S81 . . . 35 F5
Worksop S81 . . . 36 A5
Blyth Hall S81 . . . 18 A3
Blyth Rd
Blyth, Bilby S81, DN22 . . . 27 E5
Blyth, Nornay S81 . . . 18 A7
Carlton in Lindrick DN22 . . 26 E3
Elkesley S80 . . . 48 F4
Firbeck S81 . . . 16 C7
Harworth DN11 . . . 8 F3
Hodsock S81 . . . 27 A7
New Ollerton NG22 . . . 77 A6
Oldcotes S81 . . . 16 F6
Ranskill DN22 . . . 19 A4
Walesby NG22 . . . 63 A3
Worksop, Kilton S81 . . . 36 B6
Blyth St NG3 . . . 161 E2
Blyton Rd DN21 . . . 15 C4
Blyton Wlk NG5 . . . 161 B7
Boar La NG24 . . . 139 F8
Boat La
Aldercar NG16 . . . 143 A7
Bleasby NG14 . . . 152 C7
Bleasby NG14 . . . 152 E8
Hoveringham NG14 . . . 151 E2
Boatmans Cl DE7 . . . 157 F2
Boatswain Dr 1 NG15 . 146 B8
BOBBERS MILL . . . 172 E7
Bobbers Mill Bridge
NG7 . . . 172 D7
Bobbers Mill Rd NG7 . . . 172 E7
Bobrainsforth Way 7
DN21 . . . 15 F2
Boden Dr NG16 . . . 159 C6
Boden St NG7 . . . 222 B3
Bodill Gdns NG15 . . . 146 C6
Bodmin Ave NG15 . . . 145 C5
Bodmin Ct 5 NG18 . . . 103 A2
Bodmin Dr NG8 . . . 160 C2
Body Rd NG9 . . . 183 B2
Bofols Rd LE14 . . . 219 A5
Bogg La NG22 . . . 64 A1
Bohem Rd NG10 . . . 182 C3
Boilerhouse Rd LE14 . . . 219 A4
Bold Cl NG6 . . . 160 B8
BOLE . . . 23 E3
Bole La DN22 . . . 23 D3
Bolero Cl NG8 . . . 171 E5
Bolham La DN22 . . . 29 F1
Bolham Way DN22 . . . 29 F2
Bolingey Way NG15 . . . 145 C5
Bollard's La LE12 . . . 213 A7
Bolsover St
Hucknall NG15 . . . 146 B7
Mansfield NG18 . . . 102 D6
Bolton Ave NG9 . . . 183 C4
Bolton Cl NG2 . . . 186 A7
Bolton La LE14 . . . 211 F7
Bolton Terr NG12 . . . 175 F3
Bombard Rd LE14 . . . 219 A5
Bond Cl
Loughborough LE11 . . . 220 C1
Mansfield Woodhouse
NG19 . . . 88 C6
Bond St
Arnold NG5 . . . 161 E8
Nottingham NG2 . . . 173 E4
Bonemill La
Clarborough DN22 . . . 30 D2
Worksop S81 . . . 35 D5
Bonetti Cl NG5 . . . 162 C5
Boniface Gdns 4 NG5 . 147 A1
Bonington Art Gall★
NG1 . . . 223 D3
Bonington Dr NG5 . . . 161 F7
Bonington Rd
Arnold NG5 . . . 161 F4
Mansfield NG19 . . . 101 E6
Nottingham NG3 . . . 162 A3
Bonington Theatre★
NG5 . . . 161 E8
Bonner Hill NG14 . . . 148 F6
Bonner La NG14 . . . 149 B6
Bonner'S La NG16 . . . 158 C4
Bonnington Cl NG6 . . . 160 A6
Bonnington Cres NG5 . . 161 C4
Bonny Mead NG12 . . . 187 E2
Bonsal Ct NG18 . . . 103 B6
Bonsall St NG10 . . . 193 E8
Bonser Cl NG4 . . . 174 E7
Bonser Cres NG17 . . . 99 E2
Bonser Gdns NG17 . . . 100 D2
Bonser Hedge Ct NG10 193 B4
Booth Ave NG19 . . . 87 A5
Booth Cl NG3 . . . 223 F3
Booth Cres NG19 . . . 87 D2
Booth's Ind Est The
DE7 . . . 157 F2
Booth St NG19 . . . 88 B3
Boots Yd NG17 . . . 99 F3
Border Rd NG20 . . . 73 A4
Borders Ave NG17 . . . 114 E8
Borlace Cres NG9 . . . 182 E6
Borman Cl NG6 . . . 159 F5
Borough St DE74 . . . 203 D2
Borrow Bread La NG14 152 B7
Borrowdale Cl NG2 . . . 186 D6
Borrowdale Dr NG10 . . . 193 A6
Borrowell DE74 . . . 203 C3
Boscombe Rd S81 . . . 35 C8
Boscowan Ct DE7 . . . 157 F4
Bosden Cl NG8 . . . 171 C6
Bosley Sq NG9 . . . 184 A8
Bostocks La NG10 . . . 182 A4
Bostock's La NG10 . . . 182 A3
Boston St NG1 . . . 223 F3
Boswell Cl
Kinoulton NG12 . . . 200 A2
Mansfield NG18 . . . 102 C3
Boswell St NG8 . . . 159 C1
Bosworth Dr NG16 . . . 144 B3
Bosworth St NG19 . . . 101 D7
Bosworth Way NG10 . . . 193 E5
Bosworth Wlk 10 NG2 . . 173 B1
Botany Ave
Mansfield NG18 . . . 101 F6
Nottingham NG3 . . . 173 F7
Botany Cl NG11 . . . 185 C2
Botany Mws NG14 . . . 173 F7
BOTHAMSALL . . . 63 E7
Bothe Cl NG10 . . . 193 C6
BOTTESFORD . . . 181 C3
Bottesford Bypass
NG13 . . . 181 D1
Bottesford CE Prim Sch
NG13 . . . 181 A2
Bottesford La NG13 . . . 180 B5
Bottesford Sta NG13 . . . 181 C3
Bottleacre La LE11 . . . 220 B6
Bottle La NG1 . . . 223 E2
Bottom Gn LE14 . . . 210 A1
Bottom Row
Mansfield NG19 . . . 87 E6
Newark-on-Trent NG24 . . 140 B8
BOUGHTON . . . 77 F5
Boughton Cl NG17 . . . 100 F5
Boughton Ind Est NG22 . 78 B5
Boughton Ppg Sta★
NG22 . . . 77 D7
Boughton Rd S80 . . . 35 A5
Boughton Water Works
NG22 . . . 77 D7
Boulevard Ind Pk NG7 . . 184 C7
Boundary Cl
Kirkby-in-Ashfield
NG17 . . . 115 A3
Shirebrook NG20 . . . 72 E6
Boundary Cres
Beeston NG9 . . . 171 F1
Blidworth NG21 . . . 118 B5
Boundary Ct NG24 . . . 139 F7
Boundary La NG16 . . . 143 C3
Boundary Rd
Beeston NG9 . . . 183 F8
Newark-on-Trent NG24 . . 139 F7
West Bridgford NG2 . . . 185 F4
Boundary Row S80 . . . 35 F2
Boundary Wlk NG20 . . . 58 F1
Bourne Ave
Kirkby-in-Ashfield
NG17 . . . 115 B3
Selston NG16 . . . 129 A7
Bourne Cl NG9 . . . 171 D1
Bourne Dr NG15 . . . 117 A2
Bourne Mews NG4 . . . 175 A6
Bourne St NG4 . . . 175 A6
Bournmoor Ave NG7 . . . 184 E1
Bovill St NG7 . . . 222 B4
Bovington Ct DN22 . . . 29 E1
Bowbridge Gdns NG13 181 A3
Bowbridge La
Balderton NG24 . . . 140 B1
Bottesford NG13 . . . 180 F3
Newark-on-Trent NG24 . . 140 A4
New Balderton NG24 . . . 140 A3
Bowbridge Rd NG24 . . . 140 A6
Bowden Ave NG6 . . . 146 E4
Bowden Cl NG5 . . . 161 D8
Bowden Dr NG9 . . . 184 B6
Bowers Ave 6 NG3 . . . 173 D7
Bowes Well Rd DE7 . . . 157 E2
Bowland Cl NG3 . . . 174 A7
Bowland Rd NG13 . . . 177 C4
Bowler Ct 3 LE11 . . . 220 C4
Bowling Gn Rd DN21 . . . 15 B1
Bowling St NG18 . . . 102 D6
Bowlwell Ave NG5 . . . 160 F8
Bowman Pl NG22 . . . 92 D1
Bowness Ave NG6 . . . 160 C2
Bowness Cl NG2 . . . 186 C7
Bowne St NG17 . . . 100 F3
Bowscale Cl NG2 . . . 186 C5
Bow St NG19 . . . 88 E4
Box Cres NG17 . . . 114 F6
Boxley Dr NG2 . . . 185 C4
Boxtree Ave NG15 . . . 145 F6
Boyce Gdns NG3 . . . 161 F1
Boycroft Ave NG3 . . . 173 F8
Boyd Cl NG5 . . . 148 A1
Boyer's Orch LE14 . . . 202 B3
Boyer St LE11 . . . 220 C4
Boy La NG21 . . . 76 B1
Boynton Dr NG3 . . . 161 F1
Boythorpe Cl DE7 . . . 157 F5
Bracadale Rd NG5 . . . 146 F1
BRACEBRIDGE . . . 36 A3
Bracebridge S80 . . . 36 B3
Bracebridge Ave S80 . . . 36 B3
Bracebridge Ct S80 . . . 36 A2
Bracebridge Dr NG8 . . . 171 D7
Bracey Rise NG2 . . . 185 E3
Bracken Ave NG22 . . . 77 E6
Brackenbury Rd LN1 . . . 57 A5
Bracken Cl
2 Carlton NG4 . . . 162 D2
Gainsborough DN21 . . . 15 B3
2 Kirkby-in-Ashfield
NG17 . . . 114 F6
Long Eaton NG10 . . . 182 B1
Market Warsop NG20 . . . 74 C3
Nottingham NG8 . . . 159 F1
Bracken Ct
Bilsthorpe NG22 . . . 106 A5
Harworth DN11 . . . 8 E4
Brackendale Ave NG5 . . 161 F8
Brackendale Dr NG22 . . . 64 A2
Brackenfield Ave NG19 . 88 E4
Brackenfield Dr NG16 . . 158 B7
Brackenfield Rise
NG15 . . . 117 A3
Brackenfield Specl Sch
NG10 . . . 182 B1
Bracken Hill NG18 . . . 103 A5
Bracken Hill La
Austerfield DN10 . . . 3 F7
Misson DN10 . . . 4 A5
Misson DN10 . . . 4 A7
Bracken Hill Sch NG17 . 115 C5
Bracken La
Retford DN22 . . . 40 B5
Retford DN22 . . . 40 C7
Bracken Lane Prim Sch
DN22 . . . 40 A5
Bracken Rd
Long Eaton NG10 . . . 182 B1
Shirebrook NG20 . . . 72 D3
Bracken Way
Harworth DN11 . . . 8 D4
Harworth DN11 . . . 8 E4
Brackenwood Cl NG19 . . 89 A1
Brackhills Cl NG19 . . . 88 E1
Bracknell Cres NG8 . . . 160 D1
Brackner La NG22 . . . 106 B3
Bracton Dr NG3 . . . 173 F6
Bradbourne Ave NG11 . 185 A5
Bradbury Gd NG11 . . . 196 B7
Bradbury St NG2 . . . 174 A4
Bradden Ave NG9 . . . 170 E1
Bradder Way NG18 . . . 102 A5
Braddock Cl NG7 . . . 222 A2
Bradfield Rd NG8 . . . 159 F1
Bradford Way NG6 . . . 147 B6
Bradforth Ave NG18 . . . 103 A7
Bradgate Cl NG10 . . . 182 B4
Bradgate Rd 2 NG7 . . . 173 A8
Bradleys Orch NG14 . . . 151 C2
Bradley St NG10 . . . 182 C5
Bradleys Yard 3
NG20 . . . 74 B4
Bradman Gdns NG5 . . . 162 B6
BRADMORE . . . 196 F3
Bradmore Ave NG11 . . . 196 C8
Bradmore Bsns Pk
NG11 . . . 196 F1
Bradmore Ct NG18 . . . 103 A3
Bradmore La NG12 . . . 197 D5
Bradmore Rd NG12 . . . 207 C4
Bradmore Rise NG5 . . . 161 C4
Bradshaw Cl NG12 . . . 200 A2
Bradshaw St NG10 . . . 193 B5
Bradshaw Way DN21 . . . 24 E7
Bradstone Dr NG5 . . . 162 D6
Bradwell Cl NG16 . . . 158 C8
Bradwell Dr NG5 . . . 161 A8
Braeburn Mws DN10 . . . 10 A7
Braefell Cl NG2 . . . 186 D5
Braemar Ave NG16 . . . 143 F1
Braemar Dr NG4 . . . 163 B1
Braemar Rd
Clipstone NG19 . . . 89 E3
Nottingham NG6 . . . 160 C7
Brailsford Ct
Harworth DN11 . . . 8 E4
Mansfield NG18 . . . 103 B6
Brailsford Rd 1 NG7 . . 172 E1
Brailsford Way NG9 . . . 183 C1
Brailwood Cl NG22 . . . 106 A6
Brailwood Rd NG22 . . . 106 A6
Brake La NG22 . . . 77 E7
Brake Rd
Boughton NG22 . . . 77 E8
Walesby NG22 . . . 63 D1
Brake View NG22 . . . 77 E6
Bramber Gr NG11 . . . 195 E7
Bramble Cl
Beeston NG9 . . . 183 D2
Bilsthorpe NG22 . . . 106 A5
Clipstone NG21 . . . 89 E3
Long Eaton NG10 . . . 182 B1
New Ollerton NG22 . . . 77 D6
North Leverton with
Habblesthorpe DN22 . . . 42 D8
Nottingham NG6 . . . 160 D3
Shirebrook NG20 . . . 72 E6
South Normanton DE55 . . 113 B6
Bramble Croft NG17 . . . 100 C1
Bramble Ct
Carlton NG4 . . . 162 F1
2 Sandiacre NG10 . . . 182 C6
Stapleford NG10 . . . 182 C6
Bramble Dr NG3 . . . 174 B8
Bramble Gdns NG8 . . . 172 A8
Bramble Gr NG15 . . . 130 F1
Bramble La NG18 . . . 103 A5
Bramble Rd DN22 . . . 40 B4
Brambles The
Newton on Trent LN1 . . . 55 A1
Retford DN22 . . . 39 F7
Walesby NG22 . . . 64 A2
Brambleway NG12 . . . 188 A2
Bramble Way DN11 . . . 8 E4
Brambling Cl NG18 . . . 102 E7
Brambling Rd NG4 . . . 175 C7
Bramblings The S81 . . . 35 C7
BRAMCOTE . . . 183 A7
Bramcote Ave NG9 . . . 183 D6
Bramcote CE Prim Sch
NG9 . . . 183 B8
Bramcote Ct NG18 . . . 103 A3
Bramcote Dr
Beeston NG9 . . . 183 E7
Nottingham NG8 . . . 171 D3
Retford DN22 . . . 39 D5
Bramcote Dr W NG9 . . . 183 D7
BRAMCOTE HILLS . . . 171 C2
Bramcote Hills Coll
NG9 . . . 171 B2
Bramcote Hills Prim Sch
NG9 . . . 171 B1
Bramcote La
Beeston NG9 . . . 183 C5
Nottingham NG8 . . . 171 D3
Bramcote L Ctr NG9 . . . 171 A1
Bramcote Park Bus & Ent
Sch The NG9 . . . 171 A1
Bramcote Rd NG9 . . . 183 E7
Bramcote St NG7 . . . 222 A3
Bramcote Wlk NG7 . . . 222 A3
Bramerton Rd NG8 . . . 171 D6
Bramhall Rd NG8 . . . 171 C6
Bramley Cl
East Bridgford NG13 . . . 165 D3
East Leake LE12 . . . 205 E1
Gunthorpe NG14 . . . 165 A5
Southwell NG25 . . . 136 F8
Wymeswold LE12 . . . 216 D3
Bramley Ct
Gainsborough DN21 . . . 15 E1
Kimberley NG16 . . . 158 F6
Sutton in Ashfield NG17 . 100 F3
Bramley Rd
Long Eaton NG10 . . . 193 B5
Nottingham NG8 . . . 159 E1
Bramley Way DN10 . . . 14 B8
Bramley Wlk NG19 . . . 101 D7
Bramling Cross Mws
S81 . . . 25 C1
Brammersack Cl NG23 124 B7
Brampton Ave DE75 . . . 143 A2
Brampton Cl 14 DE7 . . . 157 F5
Brampton Ct NG2 . . . 186 C7
Brampton Dr NG9 . . . 182 F5
Brampton La LN1 . . . 44 C4
Bramwell Dr NG9 . . . 183 C6
Brancaster Cl NG6 . . . 160 B4
Brancliffe La S81 . . . 34 F7
Brandish Cres NG11 . . . 184 D1
Brand La NG17 . . . 100 C5
Brandon Cl NG24 . . . 140 E4
Brandon Walk NG17 . . . 114 D8
Brandreth Ave
Nottingham NG3 . . . 173 F8
Sutton in Ashfield NG17 . 100 D4
Brandreth Dr NG16 . . . 158 A8
Brands Cl 15 DE7 . . . 157 F5
Brand St NG2 . . . 173 F2
Brandyline Gdns NG16 . 144 B3
Branklene Cl NG16 . . . 158 E7
Branksome Wlk 3
NG2 . . . 173 C2
Bransdale S81 . . . 36 A8
Bransdale Ave NG19 . . . 88 E1
Bransdale Cl NG10 . . . 193 B6
Bransdale Hts NG19 . . . 88 E1
Bransdale Rd NG11 . . . 184 D1
Branston Ave NG22 . . . 119 F6
Branston Cl NG24 . . . 125 D6
Branston Gdns NG2 . . . 185 D4
Branston Wlk NG5 . . . 161 C4
Brantford Ave NG7 . . . 184 F1
Brantingham Gdns DN10 . 3 A1
Brassington Cl NG16 . . . 158 B7
Brassington Ct NG19 . . . 88 E4
Bratton Dr 3 NG5 . . . 161 A5
Braunton Cl NG15 . . . 145 D6
Braunton Cres NG5 . . . 162 D6
Bray Ct S81 . . . 34 F8
Brayton Cres NG6 . . . 160 D5
B Rd NG9 . . . 184 D6
Breach Rd DE75 . . . 157 A8
Breadsall Ct DE7 . . . 157 F3
Break La
Papplewick NG15 . . . 131 F4
Papplewick NG15 . . . 132 A4
Breamer Rd NG23 . . . 112 B8
BREASTON . . . 193 A8
Brechin S81 . . . 36 B5
Brechin Cl NG5 . . . 148 B1
Brechin Ct NG19 . . . 88 B6
Breckbank NG19 . . . 88 E1
Breck Bank NG22 . . . 77 C5
Breck Bank Cres NG22 . . 77 C5
Breck Hill Rd NG3 . . . 161 F4
Breck La DN10 . . . 20 A8
Brecknock Dr NG10 . . . 193 A7
Brecks La
Elston NG23 . . . 154 B1
Shelton NG23 . . . 168 C8
Stapleford LN6 . . . 127 E8
Brecks Plantation Nature
Reserve★ NG11 . . . 195 D8
Brecks Rd DN22 . . . 39 D3
Breckswood Dr NG11 . . 195 E7
Brecon Cl
4 Long Eaton NG10 . . . 193 A8
Nottingham NG8 . . . 160 A3
Rainworth NG21 . . . 104 C1
Breconshire Gdns NG6 160 E3
Bredon Cl 5 NG10 . . . 193 A8
Breedon St NG10 . . . 182 C2
Brendon Ct NG9 . . . 183 B8
Brendon Dr
Kimberley NG16 . . . 158 F7
Nottingham NG8 . . . 172 A5
Brendon Gdns NG8 . . . 172 A5
Brendon Gr NG13 . . . 177 C5
Brendon Rd NG8 . . . 172 A5
Brendon Way NG10 . . . 182 A1
Brentcliffe Ave NG3 . . . 174 A7
Brentnall Cl NG10 . . . 193 B7
Bretby Ct NG18 . . . 103 B6
Brett Cl NG15 . . . 145 E5
Bretton Rd NG15 . . . 117 B3
Brettsil Dr NG11 . . . 196 B7
Brewers Way NG18 . . . 102 F5
Brewer's Wharf NG24 . . 124 F1
Brewery La
Everton DN10 . . . 11 C3
Retford DN22 . . . 39 F6
Brewery St NG16 . . . 158 F6
Brewhouse Yd Mus-The
Mus of Nottingham Life★
NG7 . . . 223 D1
Brewill Gr NG11 . . . 185 A5
Brewster Rd DN21 . . . 24 F6
Brewsters Cl NG13 . . . 177 E4
Brewsters Rd NG3 . . . 173 F8
Brewsters Way DN22 . . . 29 C1
Brewsters Wlk DN10 . . . 10 A8
Brian Clough Way
Stapleford NG9 . . . 182 D5
Stapleford NG9 . . . 182 F5
Brian Clough Way
Eastbound NG10 . . . 182 B4
Briar Ave NG10 . . . 182 B3
Briarbank Ave NG3 . . . 174 A8
Briarbank Wlk NG3 . . . 174 A7
Briar Cl
Beeston NG9 . . . 171 E1
Elkesley DN22 . . . 50 B4
Hucknall NG15 . . . 145 E5
Keyworth NG12 . . . 197 F4
Rainworth NG21 . . . 104 B1
Stanton Hill NG17 . . . 100 C6
Worksop S80 . . . 35 C2
Briar Ct
Harworth DN11 . . . 8 E4
New Ollerton NG22 . . . 77 C5
Nottingham NG2 . . . 173 B1
Briar Gate
Cotgrave NG12 . . . 188 A2
Long Eaton NG10 . . . 182 B2
Briar Gdns NG14 . . . 148 C8
Briar Gn DN11 . . . 8 E4
Briar La NG18 . . . 103 A4
Briar Lea
Retford DN22 . . . 39 D4
Worksop S80 . . . 35 C2
Briar Rd
Eastwood NG16 . . . 158 B8
New Ollerton NG22 . . . 77 C5
Briars The DN10 . . . 4 B3
Briarwood Ave NG3 . . . 174 A7
Briarwood Cl NG19 . . . 89 B1
Briarwood Ct NG3 . . . 161 E3
Briber Hill
Blyth S81 . . . 18 A1
Blyth S81 . . . 27 A8
Briber Rd S81 . . . 18 A2
Brich Gr LN1 . . . 44 C1
Brickcliffe Rd LE12 . . . 205 F2
Brickenell Rd NG14 . . . 148 F6
Brickenhole La DN10 . . . 13 F5
Brickings Way DN22 . . . 32 D5
Brick Kiln La NG18 . . . 101 D7
Brickley Cres LE12 . . . 205 F1
Brickyard NG15 . . . 146 C6
Brickyard Cotts 1
NG16 . . . 144 A1
Brickyard Dr NG15 . . . 146 C5
Brickyard La
East Bridgford NG13 . . . 165 C2
East Leake LE12 . . . 214 A8
Brickyard La *continued*
Farnsfield NG22 . . . 120 B6
Misson DN10 . . . 4 D4
Norton and Cuckney NG20 59 F5
Radcliffe on Trent NG12 . 176 B3
South Normanton DE55 . 113 A6
Sutton Bonington LE12 . . 213 F8
Walkeringham DN10 . . . 13 C6
Brick Yard La NG22 . . . 93 F3
Brickyard Way DN11 . . . 9 A2
Brick Yd Rd DN22 . . . 50 C6
Bride Church La DN11 . . . 8 A7
Bridegate La LE14 . . . 209 E5
Bridge Ave NG9 . . . 183 E5
Bridge Cl
Sutton Forest Side
NG17 . . . 101 B3
Whitwell S80 . . . 45 A5
Bridge Ct
Balderton NG24 . . . 140 E4
Hucknall NG15 . . . 146 A5
Bridge End Ave NG16 . . 128 F8
Bridge Farm La NG7 . . . 184 E2
Bridge Fields DE74 . . . 203 E3
Bridgegate DN22 . . . 39 E7
Bridge Gn Wlk 6 NG8 . 159 E1
Bridge Gr NG2 . . . 185 E8
Bridge House Ct S81 . . . 26 A5
Bridge La Ct DN10 . . . 10 A6
Bridgeland Rd 10 LE11 220 B4
Bridgend Cl NG9 . . . 182 D5
Bridge Pl
Saxilby LN1 . . . 57 B3
Worksop S80 . . . 35 E3
Bridge Rd
Gainsborough DN21 . . . 24 D7
Nottingham NG8 . . . 171 D5
Bridge St
Gainsborough DN21 . . . 24 C7
Ilkeston DE7 . . . 157 F4
Langley Mill NG16 . . . 143 C3
Long Eaton NG10 . . . 182 D1
Loughborough LE11 . . . 220 A4
Mansfield NG18 . . . 102 C7
Newark-on-Trent NG24 . . 139 F8
Sandiacre NG10 . . . 182 C6
Saxilby LN1 . . . 57 B3
Worksop S80 . . . 35 E2
Bridgeway Ct NG2 . . . 173 D2
Bridgeway Ctr NG2 . . . 173 C2
Bridgford Rd
Kneeton NG13 . . . 165 F7
Kneeton NG13 . . . 166 A8
West Bridgford NG2 . . . 185 F8
Bridgford St NG18 . . . 102 F5
Bridgnorth Dr NG7 . . . 184 E2
Bridgnorth Way NG9 . . . 182 E3
Bridle Cl NG17 . . . 100 B6
Bridle Rd
Beeston NG9 . . . 183 B8
Burton Joyce NG14 . . . 163 D6
Burton Joyce NG14 . . . 163 E5
Bridlesmith Gate
Nottingham NG1 . . . 223 E2
Nottingham NG14 . . . 173 C4
Bridle Ways NG13 . . . 165 D2
Bridleway The NG19 . . . 88 F1
Bridlington St NG7 . . . 172 F7
Bridon Cl DN22 . . . 39 E4
Bridport Ave 4 NG8 . . . 172 D5
Brielen Rd NG12 . . . 176 A3
Brierfield Ave NG11 . . . 185 B4
Brierley Forest Pk★
NG17 . . . 100 A2
Brierley Forest Prim Sch
NG17 . . . 100 D3
Brierley Gn NG4 . . . 175 A7
Brierley Ind Est NG17 . . 100 D5
Brierley Pk Ck NG17 . . . 100 C5
Brierly Cotts NG17 . . . 100 E3
Brierly Rd NG17 . . . 100 D4
Brigg Inf Sch DE55 . . . 113 B6
Brightmoor St NG1 . . . 223 F3
Bright Sq NG19 . . . 87 D2
Bright St
Gainsborough DN21 . . . 24 C8
Ilkeston DE7 . . . 157 E3
Kimberley NG16 . . . 158 E6
Nottingham NG7 . . . 222 A3
South Normanton DE55 . 113 A5
Brimington Cl DE7 . . . 157 F6
Brimington Ct NG19 . . . 88 E4
Brimstone Way S81 . . . 25 D1
Brindley Gr DN22 . . . 29 A6
Brindley Rd NG8 . . . 171 C5
Brinkhill Cres NG11 . . . 184 F3
Brinkley Hill NG25 . . . 137 B6
BRINSLEY . . . 143 E7
Brinsley Cl NG8 . . . 160 A1
Brinsley Hill NG16 . . . 128 C2
Brinsley Prim Sch
NG16 . . . 143 E8
Brinsley Way DN11 . . . 9 B3
Brisbane Cl NG19 . . . 88 C6
Brisbane Ct NG24 . . . 140 D4
Brisbane Dr
Nottingham NG5 . . . 160 E8
Stapleford NG9 . . . 170 E1
Bristol Cl NG24 . . . 125 E1
Bristol Rd DE7 . . . 157 E1
Britannia Ave NG6 . . . 160 E5
Britannia Cl NG16 . . . 159 A7
Britannia Rd NG10 . . . 182 D1
Britannia Terr DN21 . . . 24 D7
British Fields NG22 . . . 65 D3
British Horological Inst★
NG23 . . . 122 E2
Brittania Ct NG24 . . . 139 E8
Britten Gdns NG3 . . . 173 F6
Brixham Rd NG15 . . . 145 D5
Brixton Rd NG7 . . . 222 A3

Brixworth Way DN22 40 B8
Broadacre Way 3 DE55 99 B7
Broad Cl NG14 149 C4
Broad Dr NG21 76 B5
Broad Eadow Rd NG6 159 F7
Broad Fen La NG23 156 B8
Broadfields NG14 148 F8
Broadgate NG9 184 A7
Broad Gate NG22 66 E7
Broadgate Ave NG9 184 A7
Broadgate La
Beeston NG9 184 A7
Kelham NG23 123 E6
Kelham NG25 122 F7
Broad Gores DN22 30 D3
Broadhill Rd DE74 203 C2
BROADHOLME 57 B1
Broadholme Rd LN1 57 A2
Broadholme St NG7 222 B1
Broadhurst Ave NG6 160 D2
Broading La NG22 93 A3
Broadings La DN22 54 A6
Broad La
Brinsley NG16 143 E8
Hodthorpe S80 45 D6
South Leverton DN22 43 B6
Broadlands
Sandiacre NG10 182 B3
South Normanton DE55 113 A4
Broadlands Cl NG17 101 B4
Broadleaf Cl NG17 100 D2
Broadleigh Cl NG11 185 C3
Broadleigh Ct DN22 39 D4
Broad Marsh Sh Ctr
NG1 223 E2
Broadmead NG14 163 F5
Broad Meer NG12 187 E3
Broad Oak Cl NG3 173 E7
Broad Oak Dr
Brinsley NG16 143 E8
Stapleford NG9 182 D6
Broadoak Pk NG17 114 F1
Broad Pl S80 45 C6
Broad St
Long Eaton NG10 193 D7
Loughborough LE11 220 A4
Nottingham NG1 223 F3
Broadstairs Rd NG9 182 F2
Broadstone Cl NG2 185 C5
Broad Valley Dr NG6 146 E4
Broadway
Carlton NG3 174 D6
Ilkeston DE7 157 E3
Nottingham NG1 223 F2
Broadway E NG4 174 D6
Broadway Ind Est
NG18 102 C6
Broadway Media Ctr*
NG1 223 F2
Broadway The NG18 102 C6
Broad Wlk NG6 160 C3
Broadwood Ct NG9 184 A8
Broadwood Rd NG5 161 B8
Brockdale Gdns NG12 197 E4
Brockenhurst Gdns
NG3 174 A6
Brockenhurst Rd
NG19 101 D6
Brockhall Rise DE75 143 A1
Brockhole Cl NG2 186 D5
Brockhurst Gdns NG3 173 F6
Brocklehurst Dr NG21 91 C8
Brocklesby Cl DN21 24 F7
Brocklewood Prim
NG8 171 F8
Brockley Rd NG2 186 B7
Brockton Ave NG24 139 B5
Brockwell The DE55 113 B4
Brockwood Cres NG12 197 E4
Brodhurst Cl NG14 149 C4
Brodwell Grove NG3 161 F1
Bromfield Ct NG3 174 C7
Bromhead St LE11 220 C5
Bromley Ave NG24 140 A6
Bromley Cl NG6 160 B6
Bromley Ct 1 DE7 170 A7
Bromley Pl NG1 223 D2
Bromley Rd NG2 185 E6
Brompton Cl NG5 147 A2
Brompton Way NG11 185 C3
Bronte Cl NG10 193 A7
Bronte Ct NG7 222 C4
Bronte Gr LE12 214 E7
Brook Ave NG5 162 B8
Brook Cl
Eastwood NG16 144 B1
Long Eaton NG10 193 E5
Nottingham NG6 160 B6
Brook Cotts DE7 157 F3
Brook Ct NG16 143 B2
Brookdale Ct NG5 161 D5
Brookdale Rd NG17 101 B3
Brook Dr NG12 199 F2
Brooke Cl
Balderton NG24 140 D5
Worksop S81 36 C4
Brook End LE12 205 E2
Brooke St
Ilkeston DE7 170 B6
Sandiacre NG10 182 B5
Brook Farm Ct LE12 217 C7
Brookfield Ave
Hucknall NG15 145 F5
Hucknall NG15 146 A5
Sutton in Ashfield NG17 100 D4
Brookfield Cl
Radcliffe on Trent
NG12 175 F3
Radcliffe on Trent NG12 176 A3
Brookfield Cres NG20 72 E5
Brookfield Ct 8 NG2 173 C2
Brookfield Dr NG14 151 D3
Brookfield Gdns NG5 162 A7
Brookfield Mws 1
NG10 182 C6
Brookfield Rd NG5 162 A7
Brookfields Way LE12 205 E2
Brookfield Way DE75 143 B1
Brook Gdns NG5 162 A8
Brookhill Ave NG16 113 D4
Brookhill Cres NG8 171 E3
Brookhill Dr NG8 171 E3
Brookhill Ind Est NG16 113 D2
Brookhill La
Pinxton NG16 113 D4
Pinxton NG16 113 E5
Brookhill Leys Prim Sch
NG16 144 A2
Brookhill Leys Rd
NG16 143 E1
Brookhill Rd NG16 113 D2
Brookhill St NG9 182 D6
Brook La
Collingham NG23 112 B8
3 Gainsborough DN21 15 F2
Stanton-on-the-Wolds
NG12 198 E3
Brookland Ave NG18 101 F7
Brookland Cl NG14 165 A5
Brookland Dr NG9 183 D5
Brooklands NG12 208 C4
Brooklands Cl NG23 98 A1
Brooklands Cres NG4 163 A1
Brooklands Dr NG4 163 A1
Brooklands Prim Sch
NG10 193 D7
Brooklands Rd NG3 174 B7
Brooklyn Ave NG14 163 E5
Brooklyn Cl NG6 160 D5
Brooklyn Rd NG6 160 D5
Brook Pk East Rd NG20 73 A2
Brook Rd NG9 183 F8
Brooksby La NG11 184 F3
Brooks Cl NG13 165 D3
Brookside
Clipstone NG21 89 F2
East Leake LE12 214 E8
Eastwood NG16 143 F4
Hucknall NG15 146 B5
Lowdham NG14 150 D1
Brook Side 8 LE11 220 A4
Brookside Ave
East Leake LE12 205 D1
Mansfield Woodhouse
NG19 88 C5
Nottingham NG8 171 D2
Brookside Cl NG10 193 B8
Brookside Gdns NG11 196 B8
Brookside Rd NG11 196 B8
Brookside Way NG17 99 F1
Brookside Wlk DN11 9 B4
Brook St
Hucknall NG15 146 A7
Nottingham NG1 223 F3
Sutton in Ashfield NG17 100 E2
Tibshelf DE55 99 A6
Wymeswold LE12 216 C3
Brook Terr S80 35 E1
Brookthorpe Way
NG11 185 A4
Brookvale Cl NG18 103 A6
Brook Vale Rd NG16 143 C2
Brook View Ct NG12 197 E1
Brook View Dr NG12 197 E2
Brookview Lound Hall Est
DN22 64 E7
Brookwood Cres NG4 174 C7
Broom Cl
Calverton NG14 148 F8
Carlton in Lindrick S81 25 D1
Tickhill DN11 8 B7
Worksop S81 25 D1
Broome Acre DE55 113 C4
Broome Cl NG24 140 B5
Broomfield Cl NG10 182 A5
Broomfield La
Farnsfield NG22 119 F6
Mattersey DN10 19 E7
Mattersey Thorpe DN10 20 A8
Broomhill Ave
Ilkeston DE7 170 A6
Worksop S81 35 F8
Broomhill Jun Sch
NG15 146 B5
Broomhill La
Mansfield NG19 87 F1
Mansfield NG19 101 F8
Broomhill Pk View
NG15 146 C5
Broomhill Rd
Hucknall NG15 146 B4
Kimberley NG16 159 A6
Nottingham NG6 160 D6
Broom Hills LN1 55 C5
Broom Rd NG14 148 F8
Broomston La DN9 2 E2
Broom Wlk NG4 174 B8
Brora Rd NG6 160 D7
Brotts La NG23 81 E6
Brotts Rd NG23 81 F6
BROUGH 112 B1
Brougham Ave NG19 87 D2
Brough La
Brough NG23 112 D3
Brough NG23 112 C2
Elkesley DN22 50 B3
Brough Rd LN6 127 A8
Broughton Cl
Clipstone NG21 89 F4
Ilkeston DE7 157 D2
Broughton Dr
Newark-on-Trent NG24 139 E5
Broughton Dr *continued*
Nottingham NG8 172 C3
Broughton Gdns NG24 140 E4
Broughton La LE14 211 A2
Broughton Rd LN6 127 E7
Broughton St NG9 183 F7
Broughton Way NG22 78 A4
Brown Ave NG19 88 B4
Brown Cres NG17 101 A4
Brownes Rd NG13 178 A5
Brownhill Cl NG12 189 A4
Browning Cl
Arnold NG5 161 D7
Worksop S81 36 B5
Browning Rd NG24 140 E5
Browning St 5 NG18 102 A7
Brown La
Barton in Fabis NG11 194 E6
Thorney NG23 70 D5
Brownley Rd NG21 89 F5
Brownlow Cl NG23 153 D7
Brownlow Dr NG5 146 F1
Brownlow's Hill NG24 126 A1
Brown Md Rd NG8 172 E8
Browns Croft NG6 160 D3
Brown's Flats NG16 158 F7
Browns La
Loughborough LE11 220 A3
Stanton-on-the-Wolds
NG12 198 D2
Brown's La NG13 165 C3
Browns Lane Bsns Pk
NG12 198 C1
Brownsmill Way NG8 172 A6
Brown's Rd NG10 193 E8
Brown St
Mansfield NG19 101 F7
Nottingham NG7 172 F7
Brown Wood La NG23 70 B6
BROXHOLME 57 E8
Broxholme La LN1 57 C6
Broxton Rise NG8 160 B3
Broxtowe Ave
Kimberley NG16 158 D6
Nottingham NG8 160 C2
Broxtowe Ctry Pk*
NG8 159 E3
Broxtowe Dr
Hucknall NG15 131 A1
Mansfield NG18 102 C6
Broxtowe Hall Cl NG8 160 A2
Broxtowe La NG8 160 A2
Broxtowe Pk Bsns Ctr
NG8 159 E2
Broxtowe St 4 NG5 161 C2
Bruce Cl NG2 173 D2
Bruce Dr NG2 185 D7
Brunel Ave NG16 144 B3
Brunel Bsns Pk NG24 125 C1
Brunel Cl DN11 8 F2
Brunel Dr NG24 125 C2
Brunel Gate DN11 8 F2
Brunnen The DE55 113 B4
Brunner Ave NG20 72 F3
Brunswick Dr NG9 182 E5
Bruntings The NG18 102 F7
Brunts Bsns Ctr NG18 102 C8
Brunts Farm Cl NG23 156 E7
Brunt's La NG13 165 C2
Brunts Sch The NG18 88 D1
Brunts St NG18 102 C6
Brush Dr LE11 220 B6
Brushfield St NG7 172 E7
Brussels Terr 1 DE7 157 E1
Brusty Pl NG14 163 E5
Bryans Cl
Coddington NG24 125 E2
Styrrup DN11 9 A2
Bryans Cl La DN10 3 F3
Bryant La DE55 113 A5
Bryndale Cl DN11 9 C4
Brynsmoor Rd NG16 143 E7
Bryony Way NG19 88 F4
Buckfast Way NG2 186 B7
Buckingham Ave NG15 146 B8
Buckingham Cl
1 Kirkby-in-Ashfield
NG17 114 F6
Mansfield Woodhouse
NG19 88 E5
Buckingham Ct
Harworth DN11 9 A5
Sandiacre NG10 182 A3
Buckingham Dr NG12 176 E3
Buckingham Rd
Arnold NG5 161 E5
Sandiacre NG10 182 A3
Buckingham Rise S81 35 E7
Buckingham Way
NG16 159 B7
Buckland Cl NG17 101 B1
Buckland Dr NG14 149 C4
Bucklee Dr NG14 148 E8
Bucklow Cl NG8 160 D1
Buckminster Rd NG24 140 F3
Buck's La LE12 213 A7
Buckthorn Dr NG13 178 F5
BUDBY 75 F8
Budby Ave NG18 102 F6
Budby Cres NG20 74 E8
Budby Rd
Cuckney NG20 60 B3
Norton and Cuckney NG20 61 A3
Budby Rise NG15 146 B7
BULCOTE 164 A6
Bulcote Dr NG14 163 D3
Bulcote Rd NG11 184 E3
Bulgrave Mews NG2 185 C3
Bulham La
Sutton on Trent NG23 81 F1
Sutton-on-Trent NG23 82 A1
Bullace Ct NG19 88 E1
Bullace Rd NG3 173 E7
Bull Cl Rd NG7 184 F7
Bulldog Cl NG13 177 B6
Buller Cl NG23 98 B1
Buller St DE7 170 A6
Buller Terr 2 NG5 161 D3
Bullfinch Cl LE12 205 F3
Bullfinch Rd NG6 160 D4
Bullins Cl NG5 147 C1
Bullivant Ave S80 58 C8
Bullivant St NG3 223 F4
Bull Meadow NG14 148 C8
Bullock Cl NG19 88 B5
Bullpit Rd NG24 140 E5
Bull Yd
Southwell NG25 121 E1
Worksop S80 35 E2
Bulstode Pl DE74 203 C2
BULWELL 160 A6
Bulwell Acad NG6 160 C8
Bulwell Bsns Ctr NG6 160 A7
Bulwell Hall Pk Nature
Reserve* NG6 146 B2
Bulwell High Rd NG6 160 B7
Bulwell La NG6 160 D4
Bulwell St Mary's CE Prim
Sch NG6 160 C8
Bulwell Sta NG6 160 C6
Bulwer Rd
Kirkby-in-Ashfield NG17 114 F5
Nottingham NG7 222 B3
Bumblebee Cl LE12 214 E7
Bumblebee La S81 27 A6
Bunbury St NG2 173 D1
Bungalow La NG22 106 A5
Bunnison La NG12 200 E7
BUNNY 206 E7
Bunny CE Prim Sch
NG11 206 E8
Bunny Hall Pk NG11 206 E7
Bunny Hill LE12, NG11 206 D5
Bunny La
East Leake NG11 205 E6
Keyworth NG12 197 D2
Bunny Trad Est NG11 206 D6
Bunny Wood Nature
Reserve* NG11 206 F5
Bunting Dr NG11 196 B6
Buntings La NG4 174 C7
Bunting St 3 NG7 172 E1
Bunyan Gn Rd NG16 128 D7
Burbage Ct NG18 103 B6
Burbank Ave NG22 77 C3
Burberry Ave NG15 146 C4
Burden Cres DN22 53 B8
Burden La
Harby LE14 202 B3
Shelford NG12 164 C1
Burder St LE11 220 C5
Burfield Ave LE11 220 A3
Burford Prim Sch
NG5 161 C6
Burford Rd NG7 172 F8
Burford St NG5 161 E8
Burgage NG25 121 E1
Burgage Green NG25 121 E1
Burgage La NG25 121 E1
Burgass Rd
Carlton NG4 174 B7
Nottingham NG3 174 A7
Burge Cl NG2 173 C2
Burgh Cl DN21 24 E7
Burgh Hall Cl NG9 183 C2
Burhill NG12 188 A2
Burke St NG7 222 C3
Burleigh Cl NG4 174 F7
Burleigh Ct NG22 65 F3
Burleigh Rd
Loughborough LE11 220 A4
West Bridgford NG2 186 A6
Burleigh Rise NG22 65 F3
Burleigh Sq NG9 183 C4
Burleigh St 1 DE7 157 F1
Burley DN10 13 E6
Burley Rise DE74 203 D1
Burlington Ave
Nottingham NG5 161 B3
Shirebrook NG20 72 F6
Burlington Dr NG19 87 F2
Burlington Rd
Carlton NG4 174 F8
Nottingham NG5 161 C3
Burma Rd NG21 118 A6
Burmaston Rd NG18 103 B6
Burnaby St NG6 160 D4
Burnaston Ct NG19 88 E4
Burnbank Cl NG2 186 D5
Burnbreck Gdns NG8 171 E4
Burndale Wlk NG5 160 E8
Burneham Cl NG13 165 C2
Burnell Cl NG23 167 E7
Burnham Ave NG9 183 F4
Burnham Ct NG18 102 C4
Burnham St NG5 161 C2
Burnham Way NG1 173 C3
Burnmoor La
Egmanton NG22 79 F6
Egmanton NG22 80 A7
Egmanton NG22 80 B8
Burnor Pool NG14 148 F7
Burns Ave
Mansfield Woodhouse
NG19 88 C2
Nottingham NG7 222 C4
Burnside Cl 9 NG17 114 F7
Burnside Dr
Beeston NG9 171 C1
Mansfield NG19 87 E2
Burnside Green NG8 171 D6
Burnside Grove NG12 186 D1
Burnside Rd
Nottingham NG8 171 D6
West Bridgford NG2 185 E5
Burns La NG20 74 B5
Burns Rd S81 36 B4
Burns St
Gainsborough DN21 15 B2
Mansfield NG18 102 A7
Nottingham NG7 222 C4
Burn St NG17 101 A3
Burns The NG20 74 C5
Burntleys Rd DN22 30 D7
Burnt Oak Cl NG16 159 D3
Burnt Oaks Cl NG19 88 D3
Burntstump Ctry Pk*
NG5 132 D1
Burntstump Hill NG5 132 D2
Burnwood Ave NG18 103 A7
Burnwood Dr NG8 171 D5
Burr La 12 DE7 157 F1
Burrows Ave NG9 171 F1
Burrows Cres NG9 171 F1
Burrows Ct NG3 173 F5
Burrows Dr NG13 177 E6
Burrows The LE12 205 E2
Burrows Way NG5 147 E2
Burrow Wlk NG17 114 E4
Bursar Way NG10 182 C3
Burtness Rd NG7 184 D1
Burton Ave NG4 174 A7
Burton Cl
Carlton NG4 175 A8
Harby LE14 202 A3
Burton Dr
Beeston NG9 183 C4
3 Retford DN22 39 F6
BURTON JOYCE 163 E4
Burton Joyce Prim Sch
NG14 163 F4
Burton Joyce Sta
NG14 163 E3
Burton La
Whatton NG13 179 B4
Wymeswold LE12 216 B2
Burton Manderfield Ct 4
NG2 173 C2
Burton Rd
Carlton NG4 175 A8
Sutton in Ashfield NG17 100 C3
Burton Rise
Annesley NG17 130 A8
Annesley Woodhouse
NG17 115 A1
Walesby NG22 64 A1
Burton St
Gainsborough DN21 24 D7
Loughborough LE11 220 B2
Nottingham NG1 223 E3
Burton Wlk LE12 214 E8
Burton Wlks LE11 220 B2
Burwell Ct NG19 88 E4
Burwell St NG7 222 B4
Bush Cl NG5 160 F8
Bushmead Mews 4 S80 35 F2
Bushy Cl NG10 193 A6
Buskeyfield La NG20 59 F4
Butchers Mws DN22 54 B5
Butchers Way 4 DE75 143 A1
Bute Ave NG7 222 B2
Butler Ave NG12 176 A4
Butler Cl NG12 189 A6
Butler Cres NG19 87 D2
Butler Dr NG21 117 F4
Butlers Cl NG15 146 C5
Butlers Field NG13 190 C2
Butler's Hill Infant Sch
NG15 146 B5
Butlerwood Cl 9
NG17 114 E1
Butten Mdw DN10 3 C2
Buttercup Cl
East Leake LE12 215 A8
New Balderton NG24 140 C5
Buttercup Meadow
NG21 90 A4
Butterfly Cl DE7 157 F5
Butterfly Pl
2 Eastwood DE7 157 F8
Edwinstowe NG21 76 C3
Butterhall Cl S80 45 A5
Buttermarket Sh Ctr
NG24 139 F8
Buttermead Cl NG9 170 D2
Buttermere Cl
Long Eaton NG10 182 A2
West Bridgford NG2 186 D7
Buttermere Ct
Mansfield Woodhouse
NG19 88 E3
1 Nottingham NG5 161 C2
Buttermere Dr NG9 183 D8
Butterton Cl DE7 170 A7
Butterwick Cl NG19 88 F1
Buttery Gdns NG11 196 C6
Buttery La NG17 100 E7
Butt Hill S80 45 A6
Butt La
East Bridgford NG13 165 E2
Mansfield Woodhouse
NG19 88 C2
Maplebeck NG22 107 F7
Maplebeck NG22 108 A7
Normanton on S LE12 213 C4
Butt Rd NG13 178 A4
Butts Cl DE7 170 A4
Butt St NG10 182 B5
Buxton Ave NG4 162 D1
Buxton Cl NG5 160 F8
Buxton Ct DE7 157 D1
Buxton Rd NG19 87 D1
Buzzard Way LE12 206 A3
Byard La NG1 223 E2
Bycroft Rd DN21 15 C4
Bye Pass Rd
Beeston NG9 183 D3
Gunthorpe NG14 164 F5
Bye Path Rd DN22 39 F8
Byfield Cl NG7 222 B4
Byford Cl NG3 161 E2
Byley Rd NG8 171 B5
Bypass Rd NG13 177 D8
Byrne Ct NG5 162 B5
Byron Ave
Kirkby-in-Ashfield
NG17 115 B7
Long Eaton NG10 182 B3
Mansfield Woodhouse
NG19 88 C2
Sutton in Ashfield NG17 101 B4
Byron Bsns Ctr 3
NG15 146 B7
Byron Cl
Darlton NG22 67 A8
Newark-on-Trent NG24 140 A6
Nottingham NG4 174 D5
Byron Cres
Awsworth NG16 158 C4
Ravenshead NG15 116 E3
Byron Ct
Balderton NG24 140 E3
7 Nottingham NG2 173 E4
Stapleford NG9 170 E2
Byron Est NG5 162 A7
Byron Fields NG15 130 E6
Byron Gdns NG25 121 E1
Byron Gr NG5 161 C3
Byron Rd
Annesley NG15 130 C8
West Bridgford NG2 185 F7
Byron Square
NG15 146 B7
Byron St
Arnold NG5 161 D6
Blidworth NG21 118 B5
Hucknall NG15 146 A6
Ilkeston DE7 157 F1
Mansfield NG18 102 A7
Newstead NG15 130 D6
Shirebrook NG20 72 E4
Byron Way S81 36 B4
Bythorn Cl NG17 101 B5

C

Cabin Leas 4 LE11 220 B5
Cabourn Dr NG13 177 D6
Caddaw Ave NG15 146 A5
Caddow La
Clarborough and Welham
DN22 41 C8
Retford DN22 31 C1
Caddow View DN22 32 D5
Cad La NG23 81 E7
Cadlan Cl NG5 161 A7
Cadlan Ct 5 NG5 161 A7
Caenby Cl DN21 24 F7
Caernarvon Pl NG9 183 B4
Cafferata Way
Newark-on-Trent NG24 125 C1
Newark-on-Trent NG24 140 C8
Caincross Rd NG8 171 D7
Cairngorm Dr
Mansfield NG19 102 D5
Nottingham NG5 147 B2
Cairns Cl NG5 161 A5
Cairnsmore Cl NG10 182 A1
Cairns St NG1 223 E3
Cairo St NG7 160 F1
Caister Rd NG11 195 E8
Caithness Ct 9 NG5 161 B1
Calcraft Dr NG13 181 D2
Calcroft Cl NG8 160 C2
Caldbeck Cl NG2 186 C7
Caldbeck Ct NG9 183 B4
Caldbeck Wlk 1 NG5 161 B7
Calder Ave DN21 15 F2
Calderdale NG8 171 B3
Calderdale Dr NG10 193 A6
Calder Gdns NG13 177 D3
Calderhall Gdns 2
NG5 161 C8
Calder Wlk 10 NG6 160 B7
Caldon Gn NG6 146 C2
Caldwell St 11 LE11 220 A4
Caledonian Rd
Retford DN22 39 F5
Retford DN22 40 A5
Caledon Rd NG5 161 B3
Calf Croft S80 45 A5
Calfornia Rd NG24 138 F4
California Rd NG24 139 A4
Calke Ave NG17 99 E2
Calladine Cl NG17 100 D1
Calladine Gr NG17 100 D1
Calladine La NG17 114 C8
Calladine Pk NG17 114 C8
Callaway Cl NG8 171 E5
Callerdale Gr NG22 66 A2
Calley Ave DE7 157 F6
Calstock Rd NG5 161 C5
Calveley Rd NG8 171 E8
Calver Cl NG8 172 C4
Calver St NG19 88 E4
Calvert Cl
Beeston NG9 183 D4
Heanor NG16 143 B3
CALVERTON 149 A7
Calverton Ave NG4 162 B1

Calverton Bsns Park NG14 148 F8
Calverton Cl NG9 183 A2
Calverton Ct 3 NG18 103 A3
Calverton Dr NG8 159 D2
Calverton Forum Leisure Ctr NG4 162 C1
Calverton Rd
Arnold NG5 148 A2
Blidworth NG21 117 E2
Blidworth NG21 118 A2
Calverton Road Nature Reserve* NG5 148 A3
Cambell Gdns NG5 148 C1
Camberley Ct NG6 160 A8
Camberley Rd NG6 160 A8
Camborne Cl DN22 29 E1
Camborne Cres DN22 29 E1
Camborne Dr NG8 160 C2
Camborne Ms DN22 29 E1
Cambourne Gdns NG15 116 F2
Cambourne Pl NG18 103 B2
Cambrai Terr S80 35 E4
Cambria Mews NG3 173 C7
Cambria Rd NG19 87 C4
Cambridge Cl NG21 118 B8
Cambridge Cres NG9 170 D2
Cambridge Gdns NG5 162 B5
Cambridge Ms NG24 140 E8
Cambridge Rd
Harworth DN11 8 F4
Nottingham NG8 172 A4
Rainworth NG21 118 A8
West Bridgford NG2 186 A6
Cambridge St
Carlton NG4 174 E8
Loughborough LE11 220 B5
Mansfield NG18 102 A5
Camb's La DN22 31 D8
Camdale Cl NG9 183 B6
Camdale La NG24 140 F2
Camden Cl NG2 173 E4
Camelia Ave NG11 184 C1
Camelot Ave NG5 161 A1
Camelot Cres NG11 196 B8
Camelot St NG19 87 D1
Camelot St NG11 196 B8
Cameo Cl NG4 174 F6
Cameron La NG24 140 E1
Cameron St NG5 161 C2
Camerons The NG19 101 D5
Camomile Cl NG5 160 E7
Camomile Gdns 9 NG7 172 E7
Campbell Cl
Nottingham NG6 160 A1
Worksop S81 35 F8
Campbell Dr NG4 174 C8
Campbell Gr NG3 223 F3
Campbell St
Gainsborough DN21 15 B1
Langley Mill NG16 143 C4
Nottingham NG3 223 F3
Campden Gn NG7 184 E2
Campion Cl NG20 72 D3
Campion Gdns 6 NG17 115 A3
Campion St NG5 161 E8
Campion Way NG13 177 D4
Camrose Cl NG8 171 F8
Canada Cl NG4 175 C8
Canalbridge Cl LE11 220 C4
Canal Ct LN1 57 A3
Canal La
Harby NG13 202 D5
Hose LE14 211 C6
West Stockwith DN10 7 D2
Canal Rd S80 35 F3
Canal Side
Beeston NG9 184 B3
Ilkeston DE7 157 F1
Ilkeston DE7 158 A2
Canalside Industrial Park NG12 189 A2
Canal St
Ilkeston DE7 158 A1
Long Eaton NG10 182 C1
Nottingham NG1 223 E1
Retford DN22 39 F6
Sandiacre NG10 182 C5
Canal Terr S80 36 A3
Canary Gr NG22 77 D6
Canberra Cl NG9 170 F1
Canberra Cres
Hucknall NG15 145 F5
Hucknall NG6 145 D2
West Bridgford NG2 185 D3
Canberra Dr NG13 177 B7
Canberra Gdns NG2 185 D3
Candleby Cl NG12 187 F3
Candleby Ct NG12 187 F3
Candleby La NG12 187 F3
Candlemass Ct NG19 88 D2
Candle Mdw NG2 174 D5
Canning Circ NG7 222 C3
Cannock Way NG10 194 A7
Cannon Cl NG24 125 E1
Cannon Sq DN22 39 F8
Cannon St NG5 161 C3
Canonbie Cl NG5 148 B1
Canon Cook Cl LN1 57 A5
Canon's Cl NG25 121 F1
Canon Stevens Cl NG23 112 A7
Cantabury Ave NG7 172 F8
Cantelupe Gdns NG16 158 C8
Cantelupe Rd DE7 170 A8
Canterbury Cl
Mansfield Woodhouse NG19 88 C5
Nuthall NG16 159 D3
Retford DN22 39 E5
Worksop S81 36 A7
Canterbury Ct NG1 223 D4
Canterbury Rd NG8 172 D5
Canterbury Wlk S81 25 E7
Cantley Ave NG4 162 E2
Cantrell Prim Sch NG6 160 C7
Cantrell Rd NG6 160 C7
Canver Cl NG8 171 C6
Canwick Cl NG8 171 C5
Canwick Way DN21 15 E3
Cape Honey Way S81 25 D1
Capenwray Gdns 3 NG5 161 C8
Cape St NG18 101 F7
Capes The NG13 178 F4
Capitol Ct 1 NG8 172 A5
Caporn Cl NG6 160 C5
Capps Pl NG22 66 A2
Capt Ball Meml Homes NG7 222 A1
Caraway Dr NG20 72 D2
Carburton Ave NG20 74 D8
Carburton Border* S80 61 F6
Carburton La NG20 60 D5
Carburton Way NG17 115 D6
CAR COLSTON 166 C6
Car Colston Rd
Car Colston NG13 166 E1
Scarrington NG13 178 F8
Screveton NG13 166 D4
Cardale Rd
Nottingham NG3 174 A6
Radmanthwaite NG19 87 C4
Cardiff St 2 NG3 173 F5
Cardigan Cl 5 NG3 173 C7
Cardinal Cl NG3 173 E6
Cardinal Hinsley Cl NG24 139 D4
Cardinal Way NG21 90 A4
Carding Cl NG22 120 A5
Cardington Cl NG5 146 E1
Cardington Way NG24 140 A4
Cardle Cl NG19 89 A2
Cardwell St NG7 172 F8
Car Dyke Ct NG13 177 F5
Carew Rd NG7 184 E2
Carey Rd NG6 160 C8
Cariage Cl NG5 161 D1
Carisbrook Ave NG18 103 A7
Carisbrooke Ave
Beeston NG9 184 A8
Carlton NG4 163 B1
Nottingham NG3 161 C1
Carisbrooke Cl NG17 115 C5
Carisbrooke Dr NG3 161 C1
Car La NG13 166 D2
Carlile Rd NG4 174 E8
Carling Ave S80 35 D3
Carlingford Rd NG15 146 A8
Carlin St NG6 160 B7
Carlisle Ave NG6 160 C7
Carlisle Mws 6 DN21 15 D1
Carlisle St DN21 15 D1
Carlswark Gdns NG5 146 F1
CARLTON 162 D1
Carlton Acad The NG4 162 C1
Carlton Ave S81 35 E6
Carlton Bsns & Tech Ctr NG4 174 F7
Carlton Central Jun Sch NG4 174 D8
Carlton Cl
Clipstone NG19 89 D3
Heanor DE75 143 A3
Newark-on-Trent NG24 139 F6
Worksop S81 35 E7
Carlton Cres LE12 205 F2
Carlton Digby Sch NG3 162 C3
Carlton Dr DN10 9 F6
Carlton Ferry La NG23 97 D1
Carlton Fold 6 NG2 173 F3
Carlton Forum L Ctr NG4 162 C1
Carlton Hall La S81 25 F5
Carlton Hill NG4 174 C7
Carlton Inf & Jun Acad The NG4 174 D8
CARLTON IN LINDRICK 25 F5
Carlton La
Broxholme LN1 57 F7
Norwell NG23 96 C2
Norwell NG23 110 A8
Sutton on Trent NG23 97 A6
Carlton le Willows Acad NG4 163 A1
Carlton Mews NG4 174 C7
CARLTON-ON-TRENT 96 E4
Carlton Phoenix Ind Est S80 36 A4
Carlton Rd
Long Eaton NG10 193 B5
Newark-on-Trent NG24 140 A5
Nottingham NG3 173 E5
Ossington NG23 95 F6
Ossington NG23 96 A6
South Carlton S81 25 F4
Worksop S80, S81 35 F5
Carlton Sq NG4 174 E7
Carlton St
Mansfield Woodhouse NG19 88 C1
Nottingham NG1 223 F2
Carlton Sta NG4 174 F7
Carlton Vale Cl NG4 162 D1
Carlyle Ct NG12 185 E7
Carlyle Rd NG2 185 E7
Carman Cl NG16 159 A8
Carmel Gdns NG5 161 F6
Carmelita Ave 1 NG24 140 F2
Carnaby Cl NG12 176 E3
Carnarvon Cl NG13 177 E5
Carnarvon Dr NG14 164 A5
Carnarvon Gr
Carlton, Gedling NG4 162 F1
Carlton, Thorneywood NG4 174 D8
Sutton in Ashfield NG17 100 B3
Carnarvon Pl NG13 177 D4
Carnarvon Prim Sch NG13 178 B4
Carnarvon Rd
Huthwaite NG17 99 F2
West Bridgford NG2 185 F6
Carnarvon St
Carlton NG4 175 A6
Teversal NG17 100 B7
Carnation Rd NG20 72 C3
Carnelian Dr NG17 114 D8
Carnell La NG24 140 F1
Carnforth Cl NG9 182 D5
Carnforth Ct 1 NG5 161 C8
Carnoustie S81 36 B5
Carnoustie Cl 7 NG17 114 E7
Carnwood Rd NG5 161 A5
Carolgate DN22 39 F6
Carolgate Ct 4 DN22 39 F6
Caroline Cl NG15 117 B3
Caroline Ct DE7 170 A6
Caroline Wlk NG3 173 D6
Carpenter Ave NG19 87 D2
Carpenters Cl
Cropwell Butler NG12 189 B6
Kirton NG22 77 F5
Carradale Cl NG5 162 C8
Carr Cl DE55 113 A7
Carr Farm Rd NG17 114 F1
Carrfield Ave NG10 182 F1
Carrfield Cl NG17 100 D3
Carrgate La NG23 153 E5
Carrgate La Track NG23 154 A3
Carr Gr NG17 114 E5
CARR HILL 11 A4
Carr Hill Prim Sch DN22 29 F1
Carr Hill Way DN22 29 F1
CARRINGTON 161 B2
Carrington Cl NG9 170 A5
Carrington Ct NG5 161 C1
Carrington La NG14 149 A8
Carrington Prim Sch NG5 161 B1
Carrington St NG1 223 E1
Carrion Pl NG18 102 F2
Carrion Vw 5 S81 35 D6
Carr La
Blyton DN21 15 C8
Doddington LN6 71 B3
East Stockwith DN21 7 E1
Gainsborough DN21 24 C6
Market Warsop NG20 74 A4
Misterton DN10 6 E2
South Normanton DE55 113 A7
Styrrup DN11 8 D1
Styrrup DN11 17 D8
Upton NG23 122 F1
Upton NG23 138 A8
Carrock Ave DE75 143 B1
Carroll Gdns NG2 173 C1
Carr Rd
Bingham NG13 178 B5
Gringley on the Hill DN10 12 C6
Retford DN22 39 E6
Carr View DN10 11 C3
Carsic La NG17 100 E3
Carsic Rd NG17 100 D4
Carsington Ct NG19 88 E3
Carson Rd DN21 15 C2
Carswell Cl NG24 139 F6
Cartbridge NG12 187 F2
Carter Ave
Radcliffe on Trent NG12 176 B3
Ruddington NG11 196 C6
Carter Gate NG24 139 F8
Carter La
Mansfield NG18 102 E6
Shirebrook NG20 72 E4
Warsop Vale NG19 73 C4
Carter La E DE55 113 C6
Carter La W
Shirebrook NG20 72 D4
South Normanton DE55 113 C5
Carter Rd NG9 183 A3
Carters Wood Dr NG16 159 F3
Carton Rd S81 26 A5
Cartwright Cl NG22 54 A2
Cartwright La DE55 113 D7
Cartwright St
Loughborough LE11 220 C5
Shireoaks S81 34 F7
Cartwright Way
Beeston NG9 183 F5
Beeston NG9 184 A5
Carver Cl NG21 76 B1
Carver's Hollow NG22 120 A2
Carver St NG7 172 F8
Carwood Rd NG9 171 D1
Caskgate St DN21 24 C8
Casper Ct 10 NG5 161 A8
Caspian Cl 4 NG19 88 F2
Castellan Rise NG5 161 C8
Casterton Rd NG5 161 B7
Castle Brewery Ct NG24 139 F7
Castlebridge NG2 173 A2
Castlebridge Office Village NG2 173 A2
Castle Bridge Rd NG2 173 A2
Castle Bvd NG7 222 C1
Castle Cl
Bottesford NG13 181 D2
Calverton NG14 148 E7
Castle Ct 1 DE75 143 A1
Castledine St Extension LE11 220 B2
Castledine St LE11 220 B2
Castle Farm La S80 46 D7
Castlefields NG2 173 C2
Castle Gate
Newark-on-Trent NG24 139 F8
Nottingham NG1 223 E2
Tickhill DN11 8 A7
Castle Gdns NG7 222 B1
Castle Gr NG7 223 D1
Castle Hill LE12 205 F1
Castle Hill Cl NG17 114 E5
Castle Marina Pk NG2 173 A2
Castle Marina Rd NG2 173 A2
Castle Mdw Rd NG2 223 D1
Castle Mdw Ret Pk NG7 222 C1
Castle Mews NG19 88 B3
Castle Mus & Art Gall* NG7 223 D1
Castle Pk NG2 173 B2
Castle Pl NG1 223 D2
Castle Quay NG7 223 D1
Castle Quay Cl NG7 222 C1
Castle Rd NG1 223 D2
Castlerigg Cl NG2 186 C5
Castle Rising NG24 139 F8
Castle St
Eastwood NG16 144 A1
12 Mansfield NG18 102 A7
Mansfield Woodhouse NG19 88 B3
Nottingham NG2 173 F4
Worksop S80 35 E2
Castleton Ave
Arnold NG5 161 F6
Carlton NG4 162 E1
Ilkeston DE7 157 E5
Castleton Cl
Hucknall NG15 145 D6
Mansfield Woodhouse NG19 88 C4
8 Nottingham NG2 173 B1
Ravenshead NG15 117 A3
Castleton Ct NG6 159 F6
Castle View
Aldercar NG16 143 A4
West Bridgford NG2 185 D6
Castle View Rd NG13 181 C1
Castle Wood Acad DN10 10 A8
Caterham Cl NG8 171 D7
Catfoot La NG4 162 E8
Catherine Ave NG19 88 C3
Catherine Cl
11 Kirkby-in-Ashfield NG17 114 F7
Morton DN21 15 C3
Nottingham NG6 160 A7
Catkin Dr NG16 158 C8
Catkin Way NG24 140 B4
Cat La NG14 175 D8
Catlow Wlk 4 NG5 161 C8
Caton Cl NG17 100 D3
Cator Cl NG4 162 D3
Cator La NG9 183 D5
Cator La N NG9 183 D6
Cator Rd NG19 87 C3
Catriona Cres NG5 148 A1
Catt Cl NG9 183 B1
Catterley Hill Rd NG3 174 B6
Cattle Mkt 1 LE11 220 B3
Cattle Mkt Rd NG2 173 D2
Cattle Rd DN10 6 C1
Catton Rd NG5 162 A8
Caudale Ct NG2 186 C7
Caudwell Cl NG25 121 E2
Caudwell Dr NG18 102 C3
Cauldwell Rd
Mansfield NG18 102 A1
Mansfield NG18 102 B1
Sutton in Ashfield NG17 101 E2
Caulton St NG7 222 B4
CAUNTON 109 B4
Caunton Ave NG3 161 E1
Caunton Cl
Mansfield NG18 101 F6
Meden Vale NG20 74 D7
Caunton Dean CE Hole Prim Sch NG23 109 A5
Caunton Rd
Bathley NG23 109 E4
Caunton NG23 109 E5
Hockerton NG25 122 B6
Maplebeck NG22 108 B6
Caunt's Cres NG17 100 D3
Causeway DN21 24 E3
Causeway La
Gamston DN22 51 B7
Gamston DN22 51 C7
Morton NG25 137 C4
Causeway Mews 4 NG2 173 B1
Cavan Ct 3 NG2 173 C1
Cavell Cl
Nottingham NG11 184 D2
Woodbeck DN22 53 B8
Cavell Ct NG7 172 D2
Cavell Gr NG15 146 B6
Cavendish Ave
Carlton NG4 162 D2
Edwinstowe NG21 75 F2
Cavendish Ave *continued*
Newark-on-Trent NG24 140 A6
Nottingham NG5 161 D3
Sutton in Ashfield NG17 100 E3
Cavendish Cl
Bawtry DN10 9 F6
Hucknall NG15 146 C5
Cavendish Cres
Annesley Woodhouse NG17 130 A8
Carlton NG4 162 C2
Kirkby-in-Ashfield NG17 115 A4
Stapleford NG9 170 D2
Cavendish Cres N NG7 222 C2
Cavendish Cres S NG7 222 C1
Cavendish Dr
Carlton NG4 174 E8
Lea DN21 24 F2
Cavendish Pl NG9 183 F6
Cavendish Rd
Carlton NG4 162 C1
Ilkeston DE7 170 A6
Long Eaton NG10 182 C2
Retford DN22 40 B4
Worksop S80 47 A8
Cavendish Rd E NG7 222 C2
Cavendish Rd W
Nottingham NG14 173 A4
Nottingham NG7 222 C2
Cavendish St
Arnold NG5 161 E8
Langwith NG20 72 F8
Mansfield NG18 102 C5
Mansfield Woodhouse NG19 88 A3
Nottingham NG7 184 E8
Sutton in Ashfield NG17 101 A4
Cavendish Vale NG5 161 D3
Cavendish Way
Clipstone NG21 89 F4
Clipstone NG21 90 A5
Cave's La DN10 13 D6
Cawdell Dr LE12 212 D2
Cawdron Wlk NG7 184 E2
Cawston Gdns 3 NG6 160 B8
Cawthorne Cl NG23 98 B1
Cawthorne Way NG18 102 F7
Caxmere Dr NG8 171 F5
Caxton Cl NG4 175 A7
Caxton Rd NG5 161 B1
CAYTHORPE 165 B8
Caythorpe Cres NG5 161 C3
Caythorpe Ct NG19 88 E3
Caythorpe Rd NG14 150 F1
Caythorpe Rise NG5 161 C3
Cecil Cl S80 35 A4
Cecil St
Gainsborough DN21 15 C1
Nottingham NG7 222 B1
Cedar Ave
Beeston NG9 184 A7
East Leake LE12 214 D8
Kirkby-in-Ashfield NG17 114 F4
Long Eaton NG10 193 C5
Mansfield Woodhouse NG19 88 C5
Newark-on-Trent NG24 125 B3
Nuthall NG16 159 F4
Cedar Cl
Carlton in Lindrick S81 25 E7
Gainsborough DN21 15 B3
Sandiacre NG10 182 B7
Shirebrook NG20 72 E6
Sutton in Ashfield NG17 100 D7
Torksey Lock LN1 44 C1
Cedar Ct NG9 184 A7
Cedar Dr
Keyworth NG12 197 E2
Selston NG16 128 F7
5 Shireoaks S81 35 A7
Cedar Gr
Arnold NG5 162 B8
Hucknall NG15 146 B5
Nottingham NG8 171 F4
South Normanton DE55 113 B4
Cedar La NG22 77 C6
Cedarland Cres NG16 159 F4
Cedar Rd
Beeston NG9 183 E5
Loughborough LE11 220 C1
Nottingham NG7 173 A8
Cedars Cl NG20 74 A1
Cedar St NG18 102 C5
Cedars The NG5 161 D4
Cedar Tree Rd
Elkesley DN22 50 A3
Nottingham NG5 147 B1
Cedar Tree View DN22 50 B3
Celandine Cl NG5 160 E7
Celandine Gdns NG13 177 C4
Celery Mdws DN22 30 D4
Celeste Cl 1 NG8 172 B7
Celia Dr NG4 174 D7
Celtic Fields S81 35 D7
Celtic Point S81 35 D7
Cemetery Rd
Langold S81 16 F3
Stapleford NG9 182 E7
Worksop S80 36 A2
Cemetery Wlk NG16 143 E1
Centenary Ave
Bilsthorpe NG22 105 A1
Kings Clipstone NG21 90 F4
Rainworth NG22 104 E1
Centenary Cl
New Balderton NG24 140 C4
5 Nottingham NG6 160 A8
Centenary Rd NG19 87 F1
Central Ave
Arnold NG5 161 F7
Beeston NG9 183 F8
Central Ave *continued*
Beeston, Chilwell NG9 183 D6
Blidworth NG21 118 B5
Creswell S80 58 D8
Hucknall NG15 146 A6
Kirkby-in-Ashfield NG17 115 B3
Mansfield NG18 102 C5
Nottingham, Mapperley NG3 162 A4
Nottingham, New Basford NG7, NG5 161 A1
Sandiacre NG10 182 B6
South Normanton DE55 113 B5
Stapleford NG9 182 F8
Walesby NG22 64 A1
West Bridgford NG2 185 F8
Worksop S80 35 E3
Central Ave S NG5 161 F7
Central Cl NG20 72 E3
Central Coll Nottingham (Beeston High Rd) NG9 183 E5
Central Coll Nottingham (Clifton) NG11 185 A1
Central Coll Notts (Wheeler Gate) NG1 223 E2
Central Ct NG7 172 F1
Central Dr
Bawtry DN10 10 A8
Clipstone NG21 89 F2
Elston NG23 153 E4
Shirebrook NG20 72 E3
Central St
3 Nottingham NG3 173 E6
Sutton in Ashfield NG17 101 B4
Central Wlk NG15 146 A7
Centre Way NG12 175 E4
Centurian Cl NG15 146 D8
Centurion Bsns Pk NG6 159 E8
Centurion Way NG11 185 A8
Century Ave NG18 101 F5
Century La LN1 57 A5
Century Rd DN22 39 E5
Century St NG24 140 A8
Cernan Ct NG6 159 F5
Cerne Cl NG7 184 E1
Chaceley Way NG11 185 A3
Chadborn Ave NG11 195 B1
Chadburn Rd
Hucknall NG15 131 C2
Mansfield NG18 102 E8
Chaddesden The NG3 173 C7
Chad Gdns NG5 147 A2
Chadwick Rd NG7 172 E7
Chadwick Way DN22 53 B8
Chaffinch Cl
Clipstone NG21 89 F4
Mansfield NG18 102 F7
Chaffinch Mews S81 35 C7
Chainbridge Cl LE11 220 A5
Chainbridge La DN22 29 D8
Chainbridge Nature Reserve* DN22 30 A8
Chainbridge Rd DN22 30 B8
Chain Bridge Rd DN22 29 C8
Chain La
5 Newark-on-Trent NG24 139 F8
Nottingham NG7 172 E1
Chalfield Cl NG11 184 D1
Chalfont Dr NG8 172 C6
Challands Dr NG13 181 B4
Challands La NG22 135 C7
Chalons Cl DE7 157 F1
Chamberlain Cl NG11 184 C1
Chambers Ave DE7 170 B7
Chambers Ct NG5 160 F5
Champion Ave DE7 157 C3
Champion Cres NG19 101 F8
Chancery Cl NG17 101 A6
Chancery Ct NG11 185 A6
Chancery La DN22 39 E6
Chancery The NG9 183 C7
Chandos Ave NG4 175 A8
Chandos Ct NG22 65 F3
Chandos St
Carlton NG4 175 A7
Nottingham NG3 173 E7
Chantrey Cl NG9 183 D4
Chantrey Rd NG2 185 E7
Chantry Cl
Kimberley NG16 159 A5
Long Eaton NG10 193 A4
Newark-on-Trent NG24 139 F5
Chantry The NG18 102 F5
Chantry Wlk NG22 65 F3
Chapel Bank DN10 1 F2
Chapel Bar
Nottingham NG1 223 D2
Wymeswold LE12 216 C3
Chapel Baulk DN9 2 B1
Chapel Cl
Gotham NG11 195 B1
Misterton DN10 6 F2
Walesby NG22 64 A2
Chapel Ct DE7 157 F4
Chapel Dr
Gamston DN22 51 A5
Worksop S80 35 B5
Chapel Farm Cl NG23 153 D5
Chapelfield Gr NG13 177 E3
Chapel Fields NG15 117 B3
Chapel Garth NG13 179 F6
Chapelgate DN22 39 F7
Chapel Gate S81 26 A5
Chapelgate Ct 3 DN22 39 F7
Chapel Gate La NG16 143 A5
Chapel La
Arnold NG5 161 E8
Aslockton NG13 179 A5

Chapel La *continued*
Bathley NG23 . . . . . 110 B3
Bingham NG13 . . . . . 177 E6
Bingham NG13 . . . . . 178 E8
Caunton NG23 . . . . . 109 A5
Claypole NG23 . . . . . 156 D7
Coddington NG24 . . . . . 126 B1
Costock LE12 . . . . . 206 C1
Cotgrave NG12 . . . . . 187 F3
Epperstone NG14 . . . . . 150 A6
Everton DN10 . . . . . 11 C3
Farndon NG24 . . . . . 138 F4
Farnsfield NG22 . . . . . 119 F5
Granby NG13 . . . . . 191 B5
Hose LE14 . . . . . 211 F8
Lambley NG4 . . . . . 163 B7
Laxton NG22 . . . . . 79 C2
Misterton DN10 . . . . . 6 F2
Morton DN21 . . . . . 15 B4
Nether Broughton LE14 . . 219 C8
North Scarle LN6 . . . . . 83 D3
Old Dalby LE14 . . . . . 218 E4
Oxton NG25 . . . . . 134 C4
Ravenshead NG15 . . . . . 117 B2
Scrooby DN10 . . . . . 10 A2
Spalford NG23 . . . . . 83 B7
Upper Broughton LE14 . . 210 A1
Walesby NG22 . . . . . 64 A2
Willoughby-on-t-W LE12 . 217 D7
Winthorpe NG24 . . . . . 125 C6
Chapel Mews Ct NG9 . . 183 B8
Chapel Pl NG16 . . . . . 158 F6
Chapel Quarter Bsns Development NG1 . . . 223 D2
Chapel Rd NG16 . . . . . 128 E6
Chapel Side NG12 . . . . . 207 C3
Chapel St
Annesley Woodhouse NG17 . . . . . 115 A1
Barkestone-le-Vale NG13 . . . . . 192 B2
Beckingham LN5 . . . . . 142 D8
Beeston NG9 . . . . . 183 B8
Bottesford NG13 . . . . . 181 A3
Eastwood NG16 . . . . . 143 F1
Heanor DE75 . . . . . 157 A8
Hucknall NG15 . . . . . 146 A7
8 Ilkeston DE7 . . . . . 157 F1
Kimberley NG16 . . . . . 158 F6
Kirkby-in-Ashfield NG17 . 114 E5
Long Eaton NG10 . . . . . 193 E7
New Houghton NG19 . . . . . 87 A7
Orston NG13 . . . . . 179 F7
Ruddington NG11 . . . . . 196 C6
Selston NG16 . . . . . 129 A7
Sutton Forest Side NG17 101 B3
Whaley Thorns NG20 . . . . . 59 A3
Chapel Stalth DN21 . . . . . 24 C8
Chapel Terr NG15 . . . . . 130 D6
Chapel Wlk
Whatton-in-the-Vale NG13 . . . . . 179 B4
Worksop S80 . . . . . 35 E2
Chapel Yard LN1 . . . . . 57 A3
Chapman Ct NG8 . . . . . 172 B7
Chapman St LE11 . . . . . 220 C4
Chapmans Wlk NG6 . . . . . 147 B6
Chappel Gdns NG22 . . . . . 106 A4
Chapter Dr NG16 . . . . . 159 A5
Chard St NG7 . . . . . 160 F2
Charlbury Ct NG9 . . . . . 171 B4
Charlbury Rd NG8 . . . . . 172 B5
Charlecote Dr NG8 . . . . . 171 D3
Charlecote Pk Dr NG2 . 185 C4
Charles Ave
Beeston NG9 . . . . . 172 A1
Beeston, Chilwell NG9 . . . 183 C3
Eastwood NG16 . . . . . 144 B1
Sandiacre NG10 . . . . . 182 B6
Stapleford NG9 . . . . . 182 F8
Charles Baines Com Prim Sch DN21 . . . . . 24 F8
Charles Cl
Carlton NG4 . . . . . 162 F2
Ilkeston DE7 . . . . . 170 B6
Charles St
Arnold NG5 . . . . . 161 E7
Gainsborough DN21 . . . . . 15 D1
Hucknall NG15 . . . . . 146 A7
Long Eaton NG10 . . . . . 193 D6
Loughborough LE11 . . . . . 220 B5
Mansfield NG19 . . . . . 88 A1
Mansfield Woodhouse NG19 . . . . . 88 C3
Newark-on-Trent NG24 . . 140 B7
Ruddington NG11 . . . . . 196 C7
Sutton in Ashfield NG17 . 101 A3
Charleston Gdns 3 NG12 . . . . . 185 F2
Charles Way NG6 . . . . . 160 B5
Charlesworth Ave NG7 172 E8
Charlesworth Ct NG19 . . 88 E3
Charlock Cl NG5 . . . . . 160 E7
Charlock Gdns NG13 . . . 177 D3
Charlotte Cl
Arnold NG5 . . . . . 147 E2
Kirton NG22 . . . . . 78 B6
Newark-on-Trent NG24 . . 140 A8
Charlotte Gr NG9 . . . . . 171 D1
Charlton Ave NG10 . . . . . 182 F1
Charlton Gr NG9 . . . . . 183 F5
Charlton Rd S81 . . . . . 26 A2
Charnock Ave NG8 . . . . . 172 D3
Charnos St DE7 . . . . . 170 A5
Charnwood Ave
Beeston NG9 . . . . . 183 E6
Keyworth NG12 . . . . . 197 E2
Long Eaton NG10 . . . . . 193 B4
Sandiacre NG10 . . . . . 182 A4
Sutton Bonington LE12 . . 213 C5
Charnwood Cl NG15 . . . 132 A8
Charnwood Cres DE55 . . 99 B3
Charnwood Fields LE12 . . . . . 213 C5
Charnwood Gr
Bingham NG13 . . . . . 177 D4
Hucknall NG15 . . . . . 145 E7
Mansfield NG18 . . . . . 103 A7
Mansfield Woodhouse NG19 . . . . . 88 B5
West Bridgford NG2 . . . . . 185 E7
Charnwood La NG5 . . . . . 162 A6
Charnwood L Ctr LE11 . 220 A3
Charnwood Mus* LE11 . . . . . 220 A3
Charnwood Rd LE11 . . . 220 B2
Charnwood St NG17 . . . 100 C1
Charnwood Way NG14 . 149 D4
Charta Mws NG14 . . . . . 150 E1
Charter Ct DN22 . . . . . 39 D8
Charter Pl NG22 . . . . . 66 A2
Charters Cl 5 NG17 . . . 114 F7
Charters Dr NG24 . . . . . 140 A4
Chartwell Ave NG11 . . . . . 196 B7
Chartwell Gr NG3 . . . . . 162 C5
Chartwell Rd NG17 . . . . . 115 C5
Chase Pk NG2 . . . . . 174 A3
Chatham Ct NG24 . . . . . 139 F7
Chatham St
Nottingham NG1 . . . . . 223 E4
Southwell NG25 . . . . . 121 F1
Chatsworth NG17 . . . . . 100 F3
Chatsworth Ave
Beeston NG9 . . . . . 183 C2
Carlton NG4 . . . . . 162 E1
Long Eaton NG10 . . . . . 194 A6
Nottingham NG7 . . . . . 160 F2
Radcliffe on Trent NG12 . 176 A4
Selston NG16 . . . . . 129 A7
Shirebrook NG20 . . . . . 72 E6
Southwell NG25 . . . . . 121 D1
Chatsworth Cl
Mansfield NG18 . . . . . 102 E2
Ravenshead NG15 . . . . . 117 A3
Sandiacre NG10 . . . . . 182 B4
Sutton in Ashfield NG17 . 100 F5
Chatsworth Ct
Harworth DN11 . . . . . 9 B5
Hucknall NG15 . . . . . 146 A6
Chatsworth Dr
Hucknall NG15 . . . . . 146 A6
Mansfield NG18 . . . . . 102 E2
Chatsworth Rd
Creswell S80 . . . . . 58 C8
Newark-on-Trent NG24 . . 140 A5
West Bridgford NG2 . . . . . 186 B8
Worksop S81 . . . . . 35 F7
Chatsworth St
Sutton in Ashfield NG17 . . . . . 101 A3
Tibshelf DE55 . . . . . 99 A6
Chatterley Parkway NG16 . . . . . 159 C2
Chaucer Cres NG17 . . . . . 101 B4
Chaucer Rd NG24 . . . . . 140 E4
Chaucer St
Ilkeston DE7 . . . . . 157 F1
Mansfield NG18 . . . . . 102 A7
Nottingham NG1 . . . . . 223 D3
Chaworth Ave NG16 . . . 145 A1
Chaworth Cl NG15 . . . . . 130 F2
Chaworth Rd
Bingham NG13 . . . . . 177 D4
Carlton NG4 . . . . . 174 F6
West Bridgford NG2 . . . . . 185 E6
Chaworth St NG21 . . . . . 118 B5
Cheadle Cl
Nottingham, Bilborough NG8 . . . . . 171 D8
Nottingham, Portchester NG3 . . . . . 162 B2
Cheapside
Nottingham NG1 . . . . . 223 E2
Worksop S80 . . . . . 36 A2
Cheddar Cl NG21 . . . . . 104 C1
Cheddar Rd NG11 . . . . . 195 E8
Chedington Ave NG3 . . . 162 D6
Chediston Vale NG5 . . . 161 B8
Chedworth Cl 1 NG3 . . 173 F5
Chelmesford Mews Rd DN22 . . . . . 39 E4
Chelmorton Cl NG19 . . . . . 88 E3
Chelmsford Rd NG7 . . . . . 160 F2
Chelmsford Terr NG7 . . 160 F2
Chelsea Cl NG16 . . . . . 159 E3
Chelsea St NG7 . . . . . 160 F1
Cheltenham Cl NG9 . . . . . 182 F1
Cheltenham Ct NG18 . . 102 F7
Cheltenham St NG6 . . . . . 160 E4
Chelwood Dr NG5 . . . . . 162 C3
Chennel Nook NG12 . . . 188 A2
Chepstow Rd NG11 . . . . . 195 E8
Chepstow Wlk NG18 . . . 102 F7
Chequers Cl DN22 . . . . . 38 A6
Chequers La NG22 . . . . . 54 B2
Cherhill Cl NG11 . . . . . 195 D7
Cheriton Cl NG19 . . . . . 87 E1
Cheriton Dr
Ravenshead NG15 . . . . . 117 B2
Shipley DE7 . . . . . 157 C3
Chermside Cl NG15 . . . . . 117 B1
Chernside NG15 . . . . . 117 A3
Cherries The NG12 . . . . . 185 B6
Cherry Ave
Hucknall NG15 . . . . . 146 B5
Kirkby-in-Ashfield NG17 . 114 D7
Cherry Cl
Arnold NG5 . . . . . 161 E8
East Leake LE12 . . . . . 214 C8
Nottingham NG5 . . . . . 161 B7
Shirebrook NG20 . . . . . 72 E6
South Normanton DE55 . . 113 B7
Cherry Gr
Mansfield NG18 . . . . . 101 E6
Market Warsop NG20 . . . 74 C4
Cherry Hill NG12 . . . . . 197 F3
Cherry Holt
Newark-on-Trent NG24 . . 139 F5
Retford DN22 . . . . . 29 D1
Cherryholt Cl NG13 . . . 165 D3
Cherryholt La NG13 . . . 165 D3
Cherry La NG18 . . . . . 102 B3
Cherry Orch NG12 . . . . . 187 E3
Cherry Orch Mount NG5 . . . . . 161 B7
Cherry St NG13 . . . . . 177 F4
Cherry Tree Ave S81 . . . . 34 F7
Cherry Tree Cl
Boughton NG22 . . . . . 77 E5
Brinsley NG16 . . . . . 143 E8
Calverton NG5 . . . . . 148 E8
Mansfield Woodhouse NG19 . . . . . 88 B4
Radcliffe on Trent NG12 . 175 F2
Ranskill DN22 . . . . . 19 C4
Cherry Tree Dr NG13 . . . 192 A1
Cherry Tree Hill NG7 . . . 172 C1
Cherry Tree La NG12 . . . 186 B3
Cherry Tree Rd DN21 . . . 15 E1
Cherry Tree Way NG16 143 C4
Cherry Tree Wlk DN22 . . 19 C5
Cherry View 2 NG8 . . . 172 B7
Cherry Wood Dr NG8 . . . 172 B7
Cherrywood Gdns NG3 174 A8
Chertsey Cl NG3 . . . . . 161 F1
Cherwell Ct NG6 . . . . . 159 F6
Cherwell Gdns NG13 . . . 177 C3
Chesham Dr
Beeston NG9 . . . . . 171 B2
Nottingham NG5 . . . . . 161 B1
Cheshire Way NG16 . . . . . 128 C4
Chesil Ave 2 NG8 . . . . . 172 D5
Chesil Cotts 3 NG8 . . . . . 172 D5
Cheslyn Dr NG8 . . . . . 172 C8
Chesnut Cl NG23 . . . . . 81 A4
Chesnut Gdn NG17 . . . . . 100 D1
Chess Burrow NG19 . . . . . 88 D2
Chester Cl 3 LE11 . . . . . 220 A3
Chesterfield Ave
Bingham NG13 . . . . . 177 E5
Carlton NG4 . . . . . 162 D2
Long Eaton NG10 . . . . . 193 F7
Chesterfield Ct NG4 . . . 162 D3
Chesterfield Dr
Burton Joyce NG14 . . . . . 164 A5
Retford DN22 . . . . . 40 A7
Chesterfield Rd
Darfoulds S80 . . . . . 34 F1
Darfoulds S80 . . . . . 35 A1
Hardstoft DE55 . . . . . 85 A1
Huthwaite NG17 . . . . . 99 E4
New Houghton NG19 . . . . . 86 E7
Pleasley NG19 . . . . . 87 A5
Chesterfield Rd N NG19 . 87 C4
Chesterfield Rd S
Mansfield NG18 . . . . . 102 A8
Mansfield NG18 . . . . . 102 B8
Chesterfield St NG4 . . . 174 D7
Chester Gn NG9 . . . . . 182 E2
Chesterman Cl NG16 . . . 158 B4
Chester Rd NG3 . . . . . 174 B5
Chester St
Mansfield NG19 . . . . . 87 E1
Mansfield NG19 . . . . . 101 E8
Chesterton Dr S81 . . . . . 36 B5
Chestnut Ave
Beeston NG9 . . . . . 183 F6
Bingham NG13 . . . . . 177 E4
Gainsborough DN21 . . . . . 15 D2
Glapwell S44 . . . . . 86 B8
Kirkby-in-Ashfield NG17 . 114 F4
Newark-on-Trent NG24 . . 125 B4
Nottingham NG3 . . . . . 162 B2
Ravenshead NG15 . . . . . 117 B1
Retford DN22 . . . . . 39 D4
Chestnut Cl
Bottesford NG13 . . . . . 181 C3
Calverton NG14 . . . . . 149 C6
Church End DN21 . . . . . 14 A5
Keyworth NG12 . . . . . 197 E3
New Ollerton NG22 . . . . . 77 D6
Ravenshead NG18 . . . . . 116 E7
Sutton Bonington LE12 . . 204 A2
Worksop S80 . . . . . 35 E1
Chestnut Copse NG24 . . 140 B6
Chestnut Cres LN1 . . . . . 44 C1
Chestnut Ct NG23 . . . . . 81 E7
Chestnut Dr
Bawtry DN10 . . . . . 9 F7
Cotgrave NG12 . . . . . 188 A5
Mansfield NG18 . . . . . 102 E8
New Ollerton NG22 . . . . . 77 D6
Nuthall NG16 . . . . . 159 B6
Selston NG16 . . . . . 128 F7
Shirebrook NG20 . . . . . 72 D4
South Normanton DE55 . . 113 B4
Chestnut Farm Cl LE12 . . . . . 217 D7
Chestnut Gdns NG17 . . . 100 D1
Chestnut Gr
Arnold NG5 . . . . . 162 A8
Burton Joyce NG14 . . . . . 163 F4
Carlton NG4 . . . . . 162 F1
Farndon NG24 . . . . . 139 A4
Hucknall NG15 . . . . . 146 B4
Kirkby-in-Ashfield NG17 . 114 F5
Mansfield Woodhouse NG19 . . . . . 88 B5
Nottingham NG3 . . . . . 173 C7
Radcliffe on Trent NG12 . 175 F4
Sandiacre NG10 . . . . . 182 A7
West Bridgford NG2 . . . . . 185 D7
Chestnut Hill NG18 . . . . . 102 E2
Chestnut La NG11 . . . . . 194 E6
Chestnut Mews NG18 . . 102 E2
Chestnut Mws NG12 . . . 186 F3
Chestnut Rd
Langley Mill NG16 . . . . . 143 A3
Langold S81 . . . . . 16 F4
Chestnut Screed NG21 . . 89 E5
Chestnut St LE11 . . . . . 220 A4
Chestnuts The
Carlton NG4 . . . . . 163 B1
Long Eaton NG10 . . . . . 193 A8
Nottingham NG3 . . . . . 161 F1
Radcliffe on Trent NG12 . 175 E3
Chestnut Walk NG5 . . . . . 161 E3
Chestnut Way NG22 . . . . . 66 A2
Chettles Ind Est NG8 . . . 172 D5
Chetwin Rd NG8 . . . . . 171 D5
Chetwynd Prim Acad NG9 . . . . . 183 A2
Chetwynd Rd
Beeston, Chilwell NG9 . . 183 C3
Beeston, Toton NG9 . . . . . 183 A2
Cheverton Ct 7 NG3 . . . 173 C7
Chevin Gdns 12 NG5 . . . 147 A1
Cheviot Cl NG5 . . . . . 147 B2
Cheviot Ct S81 . . . . . 25 E7
Cheviot Dr NG6 . . . . . 159 F8
Cheviot Rd NG10 . . . . . 182 A1
Chewton Ave NG16 . . . . . 144 A1
Chewton Cl NG22 . . . . . 105 E6
Chewton St NG16 . . . . . 144 A1
Cheyne Dr NG22 . . . . . 106 A4
Cheyne Wlk
Bawtry DN10 . . . . . 9 F7
HUCKNALL NG15 . . . . . 146 B8
Retford DN22 . . . . . 39 D4
Cheyny Cl NG2 . . . . . 173 C1
Chichester Cl
Ilkeston DE7 . . . . . 170 A8
Mansfield NG19 . . . . . 101 D6
Nottingham NG5 . . . . . 160 E7
Chichester Dr NG12 . . . 187 E4
Chichester Wlk S81 . . . . . 25 E7
Chidlow Rd NG8 . . . . . 171 D7
Chigwell Cl NG8 . . . . . 159 E3
Chillon Way NG15 . . . . . 145 D6
Chiltern Cl NG5 . . . . . 147 B2
Chiltern Gdns NG10 . . . 182 A1
Chiltern Way
Carlton in Lindrick S81 . . . 25 E7
Nottingham NG5 . . . . . 161 B7
Chilton Cres NG19 . . . . . 88 C6
Chilton Dr
Kimberley NG16 . . . . . 158 F7
Watnall NG16 . . . . . 159 A7
Chilvers Cl NG5 . . . . . 161 A7
CHILWELL 183 D6
Chilwell Ct NG6 . . . . . 160 D7
Chilwell La NG9 . . . . . 183 C6
Chilwell Olympia NG9 . . 183 D3
Chilwell Rd NG9 . . . . . 183 F6
Chilwell Ret Pk NG9 . . . 183 A2
Chilwell Sch NG9 . . . . . 183 D3
Chilwell St NG7 . . . . . 222 B1
Chimes Mdw NG25 . . . . . 136 F8
Chine Gdns NG2 . . . . . 185 C5
Chine The DE55 . . . . . 113 B3
Chingford Rd NG8 . . . . . 171 E8
Chiomere DN22 . . . . . 39 D4
Chipmunk Way NG13 . . 177 B7
Chippendale St NG7 . . . 222 B1
Chippenham Rd NG5 . . . 161 C7
Chirnside NG19 . . . . . 101 D5
Chisbury Gn NG11 . . . . . 195 D7
Chisholm Way NG5 . . . . . 161 A6
Chisworth Ct NG19 . . . . . 88 E3
Christ Church CE Inf Sch NG24 . . . . . 139 E7
Christ Church CE Prim Sch NG24 . . . . . 140 A4
Christchurch Rd NG15 . 145 D4
Christina Ave NG6 . . . . . 160 C4
Christina Cres NG6 . . . . . 160 C4
Christine Cl NG15 . . . . . 131 C1
Christopher Cl NG8 . . . . . 171 F6
Christopher Cres NG24 . . . . . 140 C4
Christ the King Sch NG5 . . . . . 162 B7
Chrysalis Way NG16 . . . . . 143 C3
Chrysalis Way Bsns Pk DE75 . . . . . 143 C3
Church Ave
Arnold NG5 . . . . . 161 E7
Long Eaton NG10 . . . . . 193 A4
Nottingham NG7 . . . . . 222 B1
Sutton in Ashfield NG17 . 100 D2
Church Circ NG22 . . . . . 77 C5
Church Cl
Arnold NG5 . . . . . 161 E7
Bingham NG13 . . . . . 177 F5
Church Warsop NG20 . . . 74 B6
Eagle LN6 . . . . . 84 D3
East Leake LE12 . . . . . 205 E1
Hose LE14 . . . . . 211 F7
Kneeton NG13 . . . . . 151 F1
North Wheatley DN22 . . . . . 31 E8
Nottingham NG3 . . . . . 223 E4
Radcliffe on Trent NG12 . 175 E3
Trowell NG9 . . . . . 170 C4
Church Cnr NG13 . . . . . 192 F4
Church Cres
Arnold NG5 . . . . . 161 D7
Beeston NG10 . . . . . 182 F3
Beeston NG9 . . . . . 183 A3
Church Croft NG2 . . . . . 185 F8
Church Ct NG23 . . . . . 110 A8
Churchdale Ave NG9 . . . 170 E1
Church Dr
Arnold NG5 . . . . . 161 E7
Hucknall NG15 . . . . . 146 A7
Church Dr *continued*
Ilkeston DE7 . . . . . 157 D4
Keyworth NG12 . . . . . 197 F3
Misterton DN10 . . . . . 6 E2
Nottingham NG5 . . . . . 161 B1
Ravenshead NG15 . . . . . 117 A2
Sandiacre NG10 . . . . . 182 B7
Shirebrook NG20 . . . . . 72 E3
West Bridgford NG2 . . . . . 185 F7
Church Dr E NG5 . . . . . 161 E7
Church End LE14 . . . . . 210 C1
Church Farm NG21 . . . . . 76 A2
Church Farm Bsns Ctr NG21 . . . . . 76 A2
Church Farm Gdns NG22 . . . . . 77 E1
Church Field Cl S81 . . . . . 26 A5
Churchfield Ct NG5 . . . . . 147 A1
Churchfield Dr NG21 . . . 103 F2
Churchfield La NG7 . . . . . 222 A4
Churchfield Terr NG7 . . 160 E2
Churchgate DN22 . . . . . 39 F7
Church Gate
Colston Bassett NG12 . . . 200 E7
Cotgrave NG12 . . . . . 198 C8
Kegworth DE74 . . . . . 203 D2
Loughborough LE11 . . . . . 220 A4
Loughborough LE11 . . . . . 220 B4
Church Gr NG7 . . . . . 222 A1
Church Hill
Bilsthorpe NG22 . . . . . 106 A5
Jacksdale NG16 . . . . . 128 B3
Keyworth NG12 . . . . . 197 E7
Kimberley NG16 . . . . . 158 F6
Kirkby-in-Ashfield NG17 . 114 D3
Mansfield Woodhouse NG19 . . . . . 88 C3
Newton DE55 . . . . . 99 A1
North Wheatley DN22 . . . . . 31 E8
Sutton in Ashfield NG17 . 100 E2
Church Hill Ave NG19 . . . 88 C3
Church Hill Gdns NG19 . . 88 C3
Churchill Cl NG5 . . . . . 161 F6
Churchill Dr
Newark-on-Trent NG24 . . 139 E5
Ruddington NG11 . . . . . 196 B7
Stapleford NG9 . . . . . 182 E8
Churchill Pk NG4 . . . . . 174 C3
Churchill Way
Lea DN21 . . . . . 24 F3
Worksop S81 . . . . . 25 D1
Worksop S81 . . . . . 35 D8
Church La
Arnold NG5 . . . . . 147 F1
Askham NG22 . . . . . 52 A3
Austerfield DN10 . . . . . 3 C2
Averham NG23 . . . . . 123 F1
Babworth DN22 . . . . . 39 A6
Balderton NG24 . . . . . 140 E4
Barton in Fabis NG11 . . . 194 E6
Beeston NG9 . . . . . 183 D1
Besthorpe NG23 . . . . . 97 E6
Besthorpe NG23 . . . . . 98 B5
Bingham NG13 . . . . . 177 F5
Bothamsall DN22 . . . . . 63 F7
Bottesford NG13 . . . . . 181 B3
Boughton NG22 . . . . . 77 F5
Brinsley NG16 . . . . . 143 E7
Car Colston NG13 . . . . . 166 C3
Carlton in Lindrick S81 . . . 25 F4
Carlton-on-Trent NG23 . . . 96 F4
Carlton-on-Trent NG23 . . . 97 A5
Clarborough DN22 . . . . . 30 E3
Clayworth DN22 . . . . . 21 D5
Collingham NG23 . . . . . 98 A1
Cossall NG16 . . . . . 158 C1
Costock LE12 . . . . . 206 C1
Cotgrave NG12 . . . . . 187 E3
Cromwell NG23 . . . . . 110 F7
Eagle LN6 . . . . . 84 D3
Eakring NG22 . . . . . 92 E1
East Drayton DN22 . . . . . 53 A3
East Stoke NG23 . . . . . 138 B1
East Stoke NG23 . . . . . 153 B8
Elston NG23 . . . . . 153 D4
Epperstone NG14 . . . . . 150 A6
Gamston DN22 . . . . . 50 F4
Halam NG22 . . . . . 120 F1
Harworth DN11 . . . . . 8 F4
Hayton DN22 . . . . . 30 C5
Hockerton NG25 . . . . . 122 B5
Hucknall NG15 . . . . . 131 B1
Kirklington NG22 . . . . . 120 E8
Langar NG13 . . . . . 190 C2
Letwell S81 . . . . . 16 A2
Long Clawson LE14 . . . . . 211 C3
Lowdham NG14 . . . . . 150 C2
Mansfield NG18 . . . . . 102 C6
Maplebeck NG22 . . . . . 108 A6
Misterton DN10 . . . . . 6 E2
Morton NG25 . . . . . 137 D3
North Clifton NG23 . . . . . 68 D3
North Scarle LN6 . . . . . 83 D2
Nottingham NG6 . . . . . 160 C7
Old Dalby LE14 . . . . . 218 E4
Owthorpe NG12 . . . . . 199 E8
Pleasley NG19 . . . . . 87 A6
Plumtree NG12 . . . . . 197 E7
Plungar NG13 . . . . . 191 F1
Redmile NG13 . . . . . 192 F3
Retford DN22 . . . . . 39 E4
Saxilby LN1 . . . . . 56 F5
Screveton NG13 . . . . . 166 E4
Scrooby DN10 . . . . . 10 A2
Selston, Selston Green NG16 . . . . . 128 D7
Selston, Underwood NG16 . . . . . 129 A3
Sibthorpe NG23 . . . . . 167 E7
South Muskham NG23 . . . 124 E7
Stapleford NG9 . . . . . 182 D7
Church La *continued*
Sutton in Ashfield NG17 . 100 E2
Thoroton NG23 . . . . . 167 E2
Thrumpton NG11 . . . . . 194 C3
Tibshelf DE55 . . . . . 99 A6
Tickhill DN11 . . . . . 8 A7
Torksey LN1 . . . . . 44 B2
Upper Broughton LE14 . . 210 A1
Upton NG23 . . . . . 122 F1
West Drayton DN22 . . . . . 50 F2
Widmerpool NG12 . . . . . 208 C5
Willoughby-on-t-W LE12 . 217 C7
Church Lands 2 LE11 . . 220 B6
Church Mdw
Calverton NG14 . . . . . 148 F7
Claypole NG23 . . . . . 156 C6
Church Mdw La NG23 . . 122 E1
Church Mead NG17 . . . . . 99 F3
Church Mews
1 Nottingham NG2 . . . . . 173 D1
Sutton in Ashfield NG17 . 100 E2
Churchmoor Ct NG5 . . . 147 E1
Churchmoor La NG5 . . . 147 F1
Church Rd
Bestwood Village NG6 . . . 146 E4
Bircotes DN11 . . . . . 9 C4
Burton Joyce NG14 . . . . . 163 F4
Church Warsop NG20 . . . 74 B6
Clipstone NG21 . . . . . 89 F3
Eastwood NG16 . . . . . 144 F2
Greasley NG16 . . . . . 144 E3
Harby NG23 . . . . . 70 D1
Nottingham NG3 . . . . . 223 F4
Saxilby LN1 . . . . . 57 A4
Church St E NG16 . . . . . 113 D4
Church St W NG16 . . . . . 113 D4
Church Side
Farnsfield NG22 . . . . . 119 F6
Huthwaite NG17 . . . . . 99 F3
Mansfield NG18 . . . . . 102 C6
Churchside Gdns NG7 . 172 E8
Church Sq NG7 . . . . . 222 B1
Church St
Arnold NG5 . . . . . 161 F8
Bawtry DN10 . . . . . 10 A6
Beckingham DN10 . . . . . 14 B1
Beeston NG9 . . . . . 183 F6
Beeston, Bramcote NG9 . 183 B8
Bilsthorpe NG22 . . . . . 105 F6
Bingham NG13 . . . . . 177 F4
Bottesford NG13 . . . . . 181 B2
Bunny NG11 . . . . . 206 E8
Carlton NG4 . . . . . 174 E7
Collingham NG23 . . . . . 111 F7
Cropwell Bishop NG12 . . 189 A4
East Markham NG22 . . . . . 66 A6
Eastwood NG16 . . . . . 143 F2
Edwinstowe NG21 . . . . . 76 B2
Everton DN10 . . . . . 11 C3
Farndon NG24 . . . . . 138 F4
Gainsborough DN21 . . . . . 15 C1
Gotham NG11 . . . . . 195 B1
Granby NG13 . . . . . 191 B5
Hathern LE12 . . . . . 213 A1
Headon DN22 . . . . . 52 B7
Ilkeston DE7 . . . . . 157 E4
Kegworth DE74 . . . . . 203 A4
Kirkby-in-Ashfield NG17 . 114 D4
Lambley NG4 . . . . . 163 C7
Langold S81 . . . . . 16 E2
Low Marnham NG23 . . . . . 82 B7
Mansfield NG18 . . . . . 102 B7
Mansfield Woodhouse NG19 . . . . . 88 C3
Market Warsop NG20 . . . 74 B5
Misson DN10 . . . . . 4 C2
Misterton DN10 . . . . . 6 E2
Newark-on-Trent NG24 . . 139 F8
North Wheatley DN22 . . . 31 E8
Nottingham NG7 . . . . . 222 A1
Nottingham, Old Basford NG6 . . . . . 160 E2
Ollerton NG22 . . . . . 77 A3
Orston NG13 . . . . . 179 F7
Orston NG13 . . . . . 180 A7
Pleasleyhill NG19 . . . . . 87 B4
Ruddington NG11 . . . . . 196 C7
Sandiacre NG10 . . . . . 182 B7
Shelford NG12 . . . . . 164 C1
South Leverton DN22 . . . 42 C7
South Normanton DE55 . . 113 A6
Southwell NG25 . . . . . 136 E8
Stapleford NG9 . . . . . 182 D7
Sturton le Steeple DN22 . . 32 D4
Sutton in Ashfield NG17 . 100 E2
Sutton on Trent NG23 . . . 97 A8
Whaley Thorns NG20 . . . . . 59 A2
Whatton NG13 . . . . . 179 A3
Wymeswold LE12 . . . . . 216 C3
Church Vale Prim Sch NG20 . . . . . 74 A7
Church View
Balderton NG24 . . . . . 140 D3
Beckingham DN10 . . . . . 14 B1
Bilsthorpe NG22 . . . . . 106 A5
Bottesford NG13 . . . . . 181 A3
Bunny NG11 . . . . . 206 E8
Carlton NG4 . . . . . 162 F1
Egmanton NG22 . . . . . 79 F6
Glapwell S44 . . . . . 86 B8
Newark-on-Trent NG24 . . 139 E8
New Houghton NG19 . . . . . 86 F7
Ollerton NG22 . . . . . 77 B3
Saxilby LN1 . . . . . 57 A5
Scrooby DN10 . . . . . 10 A2
Stanton Hill NG17 . . . . . 100 D6
Church View Cl NG5 . . . 147 B1
Church View Gd NG17 . 129 E8

Church View Gr LE12 .. **215** F6
Church Walk
Bawtry DN10 ..... **10** A7
Brinsley NG16 ..... **143** E7
Carlton NG4 ..... **174** E7
Eastwood NG16 ..... **143** F2
Harworth DN11 ..... **8** E4
Stapleford NG9 ..... **182** E7
Upton NG23 ..... **122** F1
Weston NG23 ..... **81** A5
Whatton NG13 ..... **179** B4
Worksop S80 ..... **35** F3
CHURCH WARSOP **74** A7
Church Way
Sutton DN22 ..... **29** A6
Sutton cum Lound DN22 .. **29** A6
Church Yard LN1 ..... **55** A1
Churnet Cl NG11 ..... **184** E4
Chuter Ede Prim Sch
NG24 ..... **140** E4
Chuter Ede Prim Sch (Fernwood Annex) ... **140** F3
CINDERHILL **160** B4
Cinderhill Gr NG4 ..... **162** E2
Cinderhill Rd NG6 ..... **160** B5
Cinderhill Wlk NG6 ..... **160** B6
Cinder La NG22 ..... **77** B2
Cinnabar Way LE12 ..... **214** E8
Circle The NG19 ..... **88** B4
Circuit Dr NG10 ..... **193** F8
Cirrus Dr NG16 ..... **159** A7
Citadel St NG7 ..... **222** A3
Citrus Gr DE74 ..... **203** C3
City Coll Nottingham
NG4 ..... **174** A6
City Gd (Nottingham Forest FC) The NG2 ..... **173** E1
City Gnd (Nottingham Forest FC) The NG2 ... **173** E1
City Hospital Campus NG5
161 ..... **B5**
City Link NG1, NG2 ..... **173** F3
City of Caves NG1 ..... **223** E2
City of Nottingham Tennis Ctr NG7 ..... **184** C8
City Rd
Beeston NG9 ..... **184** A6
Nottingham NG7 ..... **172** D1
Stathern LE14 ..... **202** F3
City The NG9 ..... **184** A6
City View NG5 ..... **161** F1
Clandon Dr NG5 ..... **161** B2
Clanfield Rd NG8 ..... **171** E7
Clapham St NG7 ..... **222** A3
Clara Mount Rd DE75 .. **143** A1
CLARBOROUGH **30** E4
Clarborough Dr NG5 ... **162** A6
Clarborough Hill DN22 .. **30** E4
Clarborough Prim Sch
DN22 ..... **30** E3
Clarborough Tunnel Nature Reserve DN22 ..... **31** C2
Clare Cl NG6 ..... **160** E4
Clarehaven NG9 ..... **182** E5
Clare Hill NG21 ..... **118** A4
Claremont Ave
Beeston NG9 ..... **183** C7
Hucknall NG15 ..... **146** A5
Claremont Dr NG11 ..... **185** C3
Claremont Prim Sch
NG5 ..... **161** B1
Claremont Rd
Gainsborough DN21 ..... **24** F6
Nottingham NG5 ..... **161** B1
Claremount Cl NG19 .... **88** E4
Clarence Rd
Beeston NG9 ..... **183** D3
Long Eaton NG10 ..... **193** C6
Worksop S80 ..... **35** E4
Clarence St
Loughborough LE11 ..... **220** C5
Mansfield NG18 ..... **102** A6
Nottingham NG3 ..... **173** E5
Pleasleyhill NG19 ..... **87** C3
Clarendon Ct 5 NG5 ... **173** B8
Clarendon Dr S81 ..... **35** D6
Clarendon Pk NG5 ..... **173** B8
Clarendon Rd NG19 .... **101** E8
Clarendon St NG1 ..... **223** D3
Clare Rd NG17 ..... **114** F8
Clare St
Nottingham NG1 ..... **223** E3
Nottingham NG14 ..... **173** C5
Clare Valley
Nottingham NG7 ..... **222** C2
Nottingham NG7 ..... **223** D2
Clarewood Gr NG11 .... **195** E7
Clarges St NG6 ..... **160** C6
Claricoates Dr NG24 ... **125** E2
Clarke Ave
Arnold NG5 ..... **161** F8
Newark-on-Trent NG24 .. **139** E5
Clarke Cl NG12 ..... **189** A4
Clarke Dr NG10 ..... **193** A4
Clarke Rd NG2 ..... **173** E2
Clarke's La NG9 ..... **183** D4
Clark La NG22 ..... **65** F2
Clarks La NG24 ..... **125** B2
Clarkson Dr NG9 ..... **184** B6
Clarkwoods Cl NG22 .... **77** E4
Clater's Cl DN22 ..... **40** A8
Claude St NG7 ..... **172** E1
Clawson La
Hickling LE14 ..... **210** D6
Hose LE14 ..... **211** F6
Nether Broughton LE14 .. **210** E1
Claxton Rise LE14 ..... **211** C2
Clay Ave NG3 ..... **162** A3
Claycross Dr NG21 ..... **90** A3
Claye St NG10 ..... **193** E7
Clayfield Cl NG6 ..... **160** A6
Claygate NG3 ..... **174** A7
Clay La
Fenton LN1 ..... **55** D7
Newark-on-Trent NG24 .. **140** C7
Stapleford NG24 ..... **127** C4
Claylands Ave
Worksop S81 ..... **35** C6
Worksop S81 ..... **35** D6
Claylands Cl S81 ..... **35** D5
Claylands La S81 ..... **35** D6
Claymoor Cl NG19 ..... **101** F5
Claypit La NG25 ..... **137** E3
CLAYPOLE **156** D7
Claypole CE Prim Sch The
NG23 ..... **156** E7
Claypole La
Dry Doddington NG23 ... **156** E2
Fernwood NG23 ..... **156** A8
Fernwood NG24 ..... **155** F8
Claypole Rd 16 NG7 .... **172** F7
Clay St LE12 ..... **216** C3
Claythorne Dr DN21 ..... **24** E8
Clayton Cl NG24 ..... **140** A6
Clayton Ct NG7 ..... **222** B3
Claytons Dr 11 NG7 .... **172** E2
Clayton's Wharf 12
NG7 ..... **172** E2
CLAYWORTH **21** D6
Clayworth Comm DN22 . **21** E3
Clayworth Ct 13 NG18 .. **103** A2
Clayworth Rd DN10 ..... **12** F1
Clegg Hill Dr NG17 ..... **99** E4
Clement Ave NG24 ..... **140** E3
Clementine Dr NG3 ..... **162** C5
Clensey La NG23 ..... **156** F2
Clerkson's Alley 6
NG18 ..... **102** B7
Clerkson St 4 NG18 ... **102** B6
Clether Rd NG8 ..... **171** D6
Cleve Ave NG9 ..... **182** E3
Clevedon Dr 5 NG5 ... **148** C1
Cleveland Ave NG10 ... **182** F1
Cleveland Cl
Carlton in Lindrick S81 ... **25** E7
Nottingham NG7 ..... **222** A3
Cleveland Sq NG24 ..... **139** F6
Cleveland St DN21 ..... **24** D7
Cleveleys Rd NG9 ..... **182** E3
Clevely Way NG11 ..... **184** E3
Cliff Bvd NG16 ..... **158** F7
Cliff Cres NG12 ..... **175** F4
Cliff Dr NG12 ..... **176** A5
Cliffe Hill Ave NG9 ..... **182** D7
Cliff Gate NG22 ..... **65** C8
Cliffgrove Ave NG9 ..... **183** D6
Cliffhill La NG13 ..... **179** C6
Cliff La NG16 ..... **113** F4
Cliffmere Wlk NG11 ..... **184** D1
Cliff Nook DE55 ..... **113** B4
Cliff Nook La NG24 ..... **125** A1
Clifford Ave NG9 ..... **183** F8
Clifford Cl
Keyworth NG12 ..... **197** F4
Long Eaton NG10 ..... **193** A4
Clifford Ct NG7 ..... **222** B3
Clifford St
Long Eaton NG10 ..... **193** E7
Mansfield NG18 ..... **102** B4
Nottingham NG7 ..... **222** B3
Cliff Rd
Carlton NG4 ..... **174** D6
Nottingham NG1 ..... **223** F2
Radcliffe on Trent NG12 . **175** E4
Cliff St NG18 ..... **102** C7
Cliff The NG6 ..... **160** B4
Cliff Way NG12 ..... **175** F4
CLIFTON **184** F1
Clifton Ave
Long Eaton NG10 ..... **194** A7
Ruddington NG11 ..... **196** C7
Clifton Bvd NG7 ..... **184** F8
Clifton Cres
Beeston NG9 ..... **183** E3
Newark-on-Trent NG24 .. **125** B3
Clifton Gdns NG18 ..... **102** F4
Clifton Gr
Carlton NG4 ..... **162** E2
Mansfield NG18 ..... **102** F4
Clifton Grove Nature Reserve NG11 ..... **184** C3
Clifton La
Nottingham NG11 ..... **184** E3
Ruddington NG11 ..... **196** A8
Thorney NG23 ..... **69** E4
Clifton L Ctr NG11 ..... **184** F1
Clifton Pl 2 NG18 ..... **102** B7
Clifton Rd NG11 ..... **196** B7
Clifton St NG9 ..... **184** A6
Clifton Terr
Nottingham NG14 ..... **173** A3
Nottingham NG7 ..... **222** C1
Clifton Way DN22 ..... **39** C8
Clifton Woods Nature Reserve NG11 ..... **184** C3
Clinthill La S80 ..... **45** A7
Clinton Ave
Brinsley NG16 ..... **143** D6
Nottingham NG5 ..... **173** B8
Clinton Ct NG1 ..... **223** E3
Clinton Gdn La NG22 ..... **65** F2
Clinton Gdns NG22 ..... **66** A2
Clinton St E NG1 ..... **223** E3
Clinton St W NG1 ..... **223** E3
Clinton St
Arnold NG5 ..... **161** E7
Beeston NG9 ..... **183** E7
Newark-on-Trent NG24 .. **139** F8
Worksop S80 ..... **36** A1
Clinton Terr DN21 ..... **24** D7
Clipsham Cl NG24 ..... **140** E5
CLIPSTON **187** C1
CLIPSTONE **89** F3
Clipstone Ave
Mansfield NG18 ..... **102** C8
Nottingham NG1 ..... **223** D4
Nottingham, Mapperley
NG3 ..... **162** A4
Sutton in Ashfield NG17 . **101** A4
Clipstone Cl NG8 ..... **159** D2
Clipstone Dr
Clipstone NG19 ..... **89** D3
Kings Clipstone NG20 .... **74** F1
Clipstone Rd
Edwinstowe NG22 ..... **76** E1
Kings Clipstone NG21 .... **90** E6
Lidgett NG21 ..... **91** B7
Clipstone Rd E NG19 .... **89** C2
Clipstone Rd W NG19 ... **89** B1
Clipston La NG12 ..... **197** F7
Clive Cres NG16 ..... **159** A5
Cliveden Gn NG11 ..... **184** D1
Cloister St NG7 ..... **172** E2
Cloisters The NG9 ..... **184** A8
Close Quarters NG9 .... **183** C8
Closes Side La NG13 ... **165** E3
Close The
Averham NG23 ..... **123** E2
Beeston NG9 ..... **183** D4
Mansfield NG21 ..... **103** F2
Newark-on-Trent NG24 .. **140** A8
Nottingham NG5 ..... **161** C3
Shirebrook NG20 ..... **72** F5
Upton NG23 ..... **122** F1
Cloud Ave NG9 ..... **182** F7
Clouds Hill NG11 ..... **195** E8
Cloudside Acad NG10 .. **182** B6
Cloudside Ct NG10 ..... **182** C7
Cloudside Rd NG10 ..... **182** A7
Clough Ct NG8 ..... **172** B7
Clovelly Dr NG3 ..... **162** D5
Clover Cl S81 ..... **36** B7
Clover Ct 5 DE55 ..... **99** B7
Cloverdale NG12 ..... **188** A2
Cloverfield Pl NG24 ..... **140** A4
Cloverfields NG14 ..... **149** A8
Clover Gdns NG24 ..... **125** D1
Clover Gn NG6 ..... **160** D3
Cloverlands NG11 ..... **185** C3
Cloverlands Dr NG16 .... **159** A7
Clover Rise NG16 ..... **158** B8
Clover St NG17 ..... **115** A6
Clover Way
Clipstone NG21 ..... **89** F4
Mansfield Woodhouse
NG19 ..... **88** F4
Club Ct NG24 ..... **140** D4
Cludd Ave NG24 ..... **140** E8
Clumber Ave
Beeston NG9 ..... **183** D5
Brinsley NG16 ..... **128** E1
Carlton NG4 ..... **175** A7
Edwinstowe NG21 ..... **75** F3
Mansfield NG21 ..... **103** F1
Newark-on-Trent NG24 .. **140** A6
Nottingham, Hyson Green
NG5 ..... **173** B8
Nottingham, Mapperley
NG3 ..... **162** A4
Clumber Cres NG17 .... **100** C6
Clumber Cres N NG7 ... **222** C2
Clumber Cres S NG7 ... **222** C1
Clumber Ct
Mansfield NG19 ..... **87** E2
Market Warsop NG20 .... **74** B4
Nottingham NG7 ..... **222** C1
Clumber Dr
Mansfield NG19 ..... **87** E2
Radcliffe on Trent NG12 . **176** A4
Clumber La S80 ..... **47** F3
Clumber Pk Ctry Pk
S80 ..... **48** B3
Clumber Pl S80 ..... **35** E3
Clumber Rd
Clumber and Hardwick
S80 ..... **47** F6
Clumber and Hardwick
S80 ..... **48** A6
West Bridgford NG2 .... **185** F7
Worksop S80 ..... **47** B5
Clumber Rd E NG7 ..... **222** C2
Clumber Rd W NG7 .... **222** C2
Clumber St
Hucknall NG15 ..... **146** C6
Kirkby-in-Ashfield NG17 . **115** C5
Long Eaton NG10 ..... **193** D7
Mansfield NG18 ..... **102** B7
Market Warsop NG20 .... **74** B4
Nottingham NG1 ..... **223** E3
Retford DN22 ..... **39** E6
Sutton in Ashfield NG17 . **100** D2
Clumber Way NG22 ..... **106** A5
Clun Ct NG19 ..... **88** D2
Clyro Pl
Sutton DN22 ..... **28** F6
Sutton cum Lound DN22 .. **28** F6
Coach Cl S81 ..... **35** A7
Coach Cres S81 ..... **35** A7
Coach Dr NG16 ..... **143** F4
Coach Gap La NG13 .... **190** D1
Coachmans Croft 2
NG8 ..... **172** A5
Coach Rd
Market Warsop NG20 .... **74** C1
Shireoaks S81 ..... **34** F6
Worksop S81 ..... **35** A7
Coalfields Cl NG17 ..... **100** C1
Coal La LE14 ..... **211** F8
Coalpit La
Elkesley DN22 ..... **49** F4
Coalpit La *continued*
Elkesley DN22 ..... **50** A4
Coal Rd S81 ..... **36** E5
Coal Yd La NG23 ..... **82** E8
COATES **43** E7
Coates Ave NG15 ..... **130** F1
Coates Rd DN22 ..... **43** D8
Coatsby Rd NG16 ..... **158** F7
Cobblestone Dr NG18 .. **102** D5
Cobden Pl
1 Mansfield NG19 ..... **87** E1
Mansfield NG19 ..... **87** E2
Cobden Prim Sch & Com Ctr LE11 ..... **220** B4
Cobden St
Gainsborough DN21 ..... **24** C8
Kirkby-in-Ashfield NG17 . **115** A4
Long Eaton NG10 ..... **193** E7
1 Loughborough LE11 .. **220** C4
Nottingham NG7 ..... **222** A3
Nottingham NG8 ..... **172** E4
Coburn St NG17 ..... **100** F1
Cobwell Rd DN22 ..... **39** E6
Cochrane Terr NG17 ... **100** D6
Cockayne Cl NG10 ..... **182** B3
Cocker Beck NG4 ..... **163** C7
Cockerels Roost LN1 .... **55** A1
Cockerhouse Rd NG16 . **143** E4
Cockett La NG22 ..... **119** E7
Cocketts Hill NG22 ..... **54** B2
Cockhill Cl DN10 ..... **10** A6
Cock Hill La DN10 ..... **10** A6
Cocking Hill
Boughton NG22 ..... **77** F5
Kirton NG22 ..... **78** B4
Kirton NG22 ..... **78** C4
Cocking La DN22 ..... **42** C2
Cockington Rd NG8 ..... **171** C5
Cockle Cl NG18 ..... **102** E5
Cockleys NG10 ..... **193** C6
Cockshut La NG20 ..... **59** A4
CODDINGTON **126** A2
Coddington CE Prim Sch
NG24 ..... **126** A1
Coddington La LN6 ..... **127** A6
Coddington Rd NG24 ... **140** F5
Codrington Gdns 5
NG5 ..... **161** C8
Cogenhoe Wlk NG5 ..... **147** F2
Coggin's La NG20 ..... **74** C6
Coghill Ct NG25 ..... **136** D8
Coging Cl NG24 ..... **140** C3
Cogley La NG13 ..... **178** A4
Cohen Cl
Arnold NG5 ..... **162** B6
Beeston NG9 ..... **183** B2
Cokefield Ave NG16 .... **159** F3
Colbeck St S80 ..... **35** E3
Colborn St NG3 ..... **173** F7
Colby Cl NG19 ..... **89** B2
Coldharbour La NG23 .. **123** C7
Cold Harbour La NG23 . **109** D1
Coleby Ave NG7 ..... **222** A1
Coleby Rd NG8 ..... **159** F2
Coledale NG2 ..... **186** C6
Coleman Ave NG24 ..... **140** B4
Coleridge Cres NG5 .... **161** D7
Coleridge Rd
Balderton NG24 ..... **140** E5
Worksop S81 ..... **36** B5
Coleridge St NG7 ..... **222** B4
Colesbourne Rd NG7 ... **184** F2
Colgrove Rd LE11 ..... **220** A2
Colin Broughton Ct
NG6 ..... **160** D7
Colindale Gdns NG16 .. **159** E3
Colinwood Ave NG5 .... **146** E1
College Cl NG24 ..... **139** D5
College Dr
Nottingham NG11 ..... **184** D2
Nottingham NG11 ..... **184** E3
College La
East Markham NG22 ..... **66** A7
Worksop S80 ..... **36** B1
College Rd
Beeston NG9 ..... **183** E5
Carlton NG3 ..... **162** C3
Sutton Bonington LE12 . **204** A1
College Side 5 NG18 ... **88** C1
College St
East Bridgford NG13 .... **165** D3
Long Eaton NG10 ..... **182** C2
Nottingham NG1 ..... **223** D2
College Way NG8 ..... **171** C7
Colley La NG23 ..... **81** B4
Colleymoor Leys La
NG7 ..... **184** F2
Collier Ave NG19 ..... **88** B5
Collier Gdns S81 ..... **16** E1
Colliersway NG21 ..... **76** C3
Colliers Way NG6 ..... **160** A4
Colliers Wy NG12 ..... **188** A5
Colliery Cl NG2 ..... **173** B1
Colliery Rd
Bircotes DN11 ..... **9** B3
Creswell S80 ..... **58** E8
Pinxton NG16 ..... **113** D2
Colliery Way
Carlton NG4 ..... **163** B3
Carlton NG5 ..... **162** E4
Collin Ave NG10 ..... **182** B4
COLLINGHAM **98** A2
Collingham Rd
Besthorpe NG23 ..... **97** F4
Collingham LN6 ..... **98** F1
Mansfield NG19 ..... **87** D1
Newton on Trent LN1 .... **69** A8
North Clifton NG23 ..... **68** F5
Collingham Sta NG23 .. **112** B8
Collin Gn NG5 ..... **161** D4
Collington St NG9 ..... **183** E6
Collington Way NG2 ... **185** D6
Collingwood Cl NG11 .. **184** E4
Collingwood Rd NG10 .. **193** E6
Collinridge View NG22 .. **64** A2
Collins Ave
South Normanton DE55 .. **113** A7
Sutton in Ashfield NG17 . **114** E7
Collins Cl NG6 ..... **159** F5
Collinson La NG24 ..... **140** F1
Collin St
Beeston NG9 ..... **183** F6
Nottingham NG1 ..... **223** E1
Collins Wlk DN22 ..... **39** F7
Collis Cl NG24 ..... **140** D8
Collison St NG7 ..... **222** B4
Collyer Rd NG14 ..... **148** D8
Colly Gate NG16 ..... **159** A5
Collygate Rd NG2 ..... **173** D1
Colmon Cl NG5 ..... **161** A7
Colmon Wlk 6 NG5 ... **161** A7
Colne Ct NG19 ..... **88** D2
Colney Way NG8 ..... **172** B6
Colonel Frank Seely Sch
NG14 ..... **148** E8
Colonel's La LE14 ..... **210** A1
Colonsay Cl NG9 ..... **170** D3
Colsterdale S81 ..... **36** B8
COLSTON BASSETT **200** C7
Colston Bassett La
Hose LE14 ..... **211** C8
Owthorpe NG12 ..... **199** F6
Owthorpe NG12 ..... **200** A6
Colston Bassett Sch
NG12 ..... **200** D7
Colston Cres NG2 ..... **185** D4
Colston Gate NG12 ..... **188** A3
Colston La LE14 ..... **201** E4
Colston Pastures NG12 **187** E3
Colston Rd
Colston Bassett NG12 ... **200** B8
Cropwell Bishop NG12 ... **189** A1
Mansfield NG18 ..... **103** A3
Nottingham NG6 ..... **160** C7
Coltman Dr LE11 ..... **220** D3
Colton St DN10 ..... **6** E2
Coltsfoot Cl NG13 ..... **177** C3
Columbia Ave
Mansfield NG18 ..... **102** F5
Sutton in Ashfield NG17 . **100** C2
Columbia Cl NG16 ..... **129** A7
Columbia St NG17 ..... **100** A2
Columbus Ct S80 ..... **35** C2
Colville St NG1 ..... **173** B7
Colville Terr
Gainsborough DN21 ..... **24** D8
2 Nottingham NG1 ..... **173** B7
Colville Villas 1 NG1 .. **173** B7
COLWICK **174** F5
Colwick Bsns Pk NG4 .. **174** F5
Colwick Cl NG19 ..... **87** E1
Colwick Ctry Pk NG2 **174** D3
Colwick Hall NG2 ..... **174** C3
Colwick Ind Est NG4 ... **174** F5
Colwick Loop Rd
Carlton NG4 ..... **163** C1
Carlton NG4 ..... **175** A6
Carlton NG4 ..... **175** B6
Colwick Manor Farm
NG4 ..... **174** E5
Colwick Pk Cl NG4 ..... **174** E5
Colwick Rd
Nottingham NG2 ..... **174** B4
West Bridgford NG2 .... **173** E1
Colwick Woods Nature Reserve NG2 ..... **174** B4
Combes The NG25 ..... **121** D2
Comery Ave NG3 ..... **174** A6
Comet Dr 2 NG16 ..... **144** A2
Comfrey Cl NG5 ..... **160** E7
Comice Gdns NG16 ..... **143** D6
Commerce Sq NG1 ..... **223** F2
Commercial Ave NG9 ... **183** F6
Commercial Gate
NG18 ..... **102** B6
Commercial Rd
Keyworth NG12 ..... **197** E2
6 Nottingham NG6 ..... **160** B7
Commercial St 5
NG18 ..... **102** B6
Commodore Gdns
NG8 ..... **160** C2
Common La
Beeston NG9 ..... **183** A6
Blyth S81 ..... **18** B4
Harworth DN11 ..... **8** D4
Hucknall NG15 ..... **145** D6
Mansfield Woodhouse
NG19 ..... **88** A4
Ranskill DN22 ..... **19** C4
Shirebrook NG20 ..... **72** C2
Sturton le Steeple DN22 .. **32** E6
Watnall NG16 ..... **159** B7
Common Rd
Huthwaite NG17 ..... **99** F2
Retford DN22 ..... **39** F7
Thorpe Salvin S80 ..... **34** A5
Commons Cl NG16 ..... **158** A8
Common Side NG16 .... **128** F8
Common The
Hucknall NG15 ..... **145** C6
South Normanton DE55 .. **113** B6
Community Way S80 .... **36** B1
Compton Acres NG2 .... **185** B5
Compton Acres Sh Ctr
NG2 ..... **185** C5
Compton Rd NG5 ..... **161** B3
Compton St NG20 ..... **72** F8
Comyn Gdns NG3 ..... **223** F4
Concorde Cl 5 DE7 .... **170** A7
Concorde Wy NG19 ..... **87** E2
Conduit Cl NG2 ..... **173** C2
Coneries The LE11 ..... **220** B4
Conery Gdns NG13 ..... **179** A3
Conery La
Whatton NG13 ..... **178** F2
Whatton-in-the-Vale
NG13 ..... **190** D8
Coney Green NG23 ..... **111** F5
Coneygrey Spinney
NG23 ..... **152** E2
Confetti NG7 ..... **222** F3
Conifer Cres NG11 ..... **195** E7
Conifer Wlk NG3 ..... **174** A8
Coningsby Ave S81 ..... **35** C8
Coningsby Cl DN21 ..... **24** F8
Coningsby Gdns East
NG5 ..... **161** F4
Coningsby Rd NG5 ..... **161** F5
Coningswath Rd NG4 .. **162** C1
Conisborough Terr 10
NG2 ..... **173** C1
Conisbrough Ave NG4 . **163** B1
Coniston Ave NG6 ..... **160** C2
Coniston Cl
Mansfield Woodhouse
NG19 ..... **88** E4
West Bridgford NG2 .... **186** C7
Coniston Rd
Beeston NG9 ..... **183** D8
Hucknall NG15 ..... **145** F8
Kirkby-in-Ashfield NG17 . **115** C6
Long Eaton NG10 ..... **182** A2
Worksop S81 ..... **35** E8
Connah La NG22 ..... **77** F7
Connaught Rd DN21 .... **15** D2
Connelly Cl NG5 ..... **162** C6
Connery Mews NG9 ..... **183** B1
Connery The NG15 ..... **146** A7
Conrad Cl S80 ..... **36** B3
Conrad Ct NG16 ..... **159** F5
Constance St NG7 ..... **161** A1
Continuation NG18 ..... **102** B6
Convent St NG1 ..... **223** F3
Conway Ave NG4 ..... **175** A7
Conway Cl
Mansfield NG19 ..... **101** D8
Nottingham NG3 ..... **173** C7
Conway Cres NG4 ..... **175** A8
Conway Dr S81 ..... **25** F6
Conway Gdns
Arnold NG5 ..... **161** F6
Retford DN22 ..... **39** B8
Conway Rd
Carlton NG4 ..... **175** A8
Hucknall NG15 ..... **145** D3
Conway St NG10 ..... **193** F8
Conway Wlk 4 NG3 .... **173** C7
Cook Dr DE7 ..... **170** A6
Cooke Cl NG10 ..... **193** B7
Cooks La
Fiskerton NG25 ..... **137** D2
Southwell NG25 ..... **136** B8
Cookson Ave NG4 ..... **162** D2
Cookson St NG17 ..... **114** E5
Coombe Cl NG8 ..... **172** C3
Coombe Rd NG16 ..... **144** B4
Co-Operative Ave
NG15 ..... **146** B8
Co-Operative St
Long Eaton NG10 ..... **193** E6
Stanton Hill NG17 ..... **100** C6
Cooper Cl
Arnold NG5 ..... **162** C6
Cropwell Bishop NG12 ... **189** A4
Nottingham NG6 ..... **159** F6
Cooper Ct LE11 ..... **220** D2
Cooper Gdns NG11 ..... **196** B7
Coopers Gn NG8 ..... **171** E2
Coopers Rise NG21 ..... **104** A1
Cooper St NG4 ..... **175** A6
Coopers Yard 4 NG20 .. **74** B4
Coopers Yd NG24 ..... **139** E8
Coot Way NG4 ..... **175** C8
Copeland Ave
1 Kirkby-in-Ashfield
NG17 ..... **114** E6
Stapleford NG9 ..... **182** E8
Copeland Gr NG13 ..... **177** C5
Copeland Rd
Hucknall NG15 ..... **146** C8
Kirkby-in-Ashfield NG17 . **114** E6
Copenhagen Ct NG3 .... **161** D1
Cope St NG7 ..... **222** B4
Copestake Cl NG10 ..... **193** A7
Copper Beech Cl DN21 .. **24** E4
Copper Hill NG23 ..... **81** E4
Coppice Ave DE7 ..... **157** D5
Coppice Cl
Fenton NG23 ..... **142** E2
Hucknall NG15 ..... **145** E5
Nottingham NG5 ..... **161** E1
Coppice Croft NG17 .... **100** C1
Coppice Dr NG16 ..... **143** D3
Coppice Form Prim Sch
NG5 ..... **162** B7
Coppicegate NG5 ..... **161** F8
Coppice Gr NG3 ..... **161** E1
Coppice Rd
Arnold NG5 ..... **162** B8
Clipstone NG19 ..... **89** D3
Worksop S81 ..... **35** F7
Coppice The
Barnby Moor DN22 ..... **28** D5
Shirebrook NG20 ..... **72** D3
Coppice View DE55 ..... **113** A4
Coppice Way DN11 ..... **9** A3
Copplestone Dr NG3 ... **162** C6
Coppywood Cl NG17 ... **100** B7
Copse Cl
Burton Joyce NG14 ..... **163** F5
Ravenshead NG15 ..... **116** C3
Copseside Cl 8 NG10 .. **193** A8

Copse The
Beeston NG9 183 C6
Farndon NG24 139 A4
Hucknall NG15 146 C6
Ilkeston DE7 157 D5
Mansfield NG18 102 C2
Stanton Hill NG17 100 C5
Copsewood DE55 113 A4
Coral Cres NG20 74 A5
Corben Gdns NG6 159 F7
Corbett Chase 6 NG4 162 E3
Corbett Cres NG15 130 F1
Corbiere Ave NG16 159 A7
Corby Rd NG3 161 E1
Cordy La
Brinsley NG16 143 F8
Underwood NG16 128 F1
Corene Ave NG17 100 E1
Coriander Dr NG6 160 D3
Corinthian Cl NG15 131 C1
Corinth Rd NG7 184 E2
Corkhill La NG22 121 D5
Cormack La NG24 140 F1
Corn Cft NG11 184 F1
Corn Cl
Cotgrave NG12 187 E2
South Normanton DE55 113 A5
Corncrake Ave NG6 160 D3
Corncrake Dr NG5 162 C7
Corncrake Mews 2
NG17 115 A3
Cornelia Mws DN22 40 A4
Cornell Dr NG5 162 C8
Corner Croft NG17 100 A3
Corner Farm Cl
Rolleston NG23 138 A6
Sutton cum Lound DN22 29 A6
Corner Farm Dr DN10 11 C3
Cornerhouse The*
NG1 223 E3
Cornerpin Dr NG17 115 B6
Corner The NG14 150 D1
Cornfield Ave DE55 113 A4
Cornfield Cl S81 26 A7
Cornfield Rd NG16 158 E7
Cornflower Way
East Leake LE12 205 F1
East Leake LE12 215 A8
Cornhill Rd NG4 174 B7
Cornley Rd DN10 6 C3
Corn Mill La S81 25 C3
Cornmill Rd
Sutton Forest Side
NG17 101 B1
Sutton in Ashfield NG17 101 B1
Cornstone Ave 4 DE55 99 B7
Cornwall Ave
Beeston NG9 184 C4
Mansfield NG18 102 F6
Cornwall Cl NG16 128 C4
Cornwall Dr
Barton in Fabis NG10 194 A8
Ollerton NG22 77 A3
Cornwallis Cl NG10 193 D6
Cornwall Rd
Arnold NG5 161 C7
Retford DN22 30 A1
Shireoaks S81 34 F7
Coronation Ave
Long Clawson LE14 211 B2
Misson DN10 4 B3
New Houghton NG19 86 F7
Nottingham NG11 185 B8
Sandiacre NG10 182 A7
Coronation Dr
Mansfield NG19 103 A8
Shirebrook NG20 72 F2
South Normanton DE55 113 B6
Coronation Rd
Arnold NG3 161 F3
Awsworth DE7 158 A1
Bestwood Village NG6 146 E4
Cossall NG16 158 B2
Hucknall NG15 145 F8
Nuthall NG16 159 C5
Coronation St
Mansfield NG18 102 D6
New Balderton NG24 140 C5
Retford DN22 39 E6
Sutton in Ashfield NG17 100 E1
Whitwell S80 45 A6
Coronation Wlk NG4 163 A1
Corporation Oaks
NG3 173 C7
Corporation Rd DE7 170 A5
Corporation St 8
NG18 102 A7
Corringham Rd DN21 15 F1
Corsham Gdns NG3 174 A7
Cosby Dr LE12 205 E3
Cosby Rd 4 NG2 173 F3
Cosgrove Ave NG17 101 B5
COSSALL 158 C1
Cossall Ind Est NG16 158 B2
Cossall Rd NG9 170 D5
Cossethay Dr NG8 159 C2
Costhorpe Ind Est S81 16 E1
Costhorpe Villas S81 16 E1
COSTOCK 206 C1
Costock Ave NG5 161 B4
Costock Rd
East Leake LE12 206 A1
Wysall NG12 207 C2
COTES 220 F6
Cotes Dr LE11 220 B6
Cotes La LE11 220 C8
Cotes Rd LE12 220 F5
Coteswood House Sch
NG5 161 E5
COTGRAVE 187 E2
Cotgrave Ave NG4 162 F2
Cotgrave Bsns Pk
NG12 188 A4
Cotgrave Candleby Lane
School NG12 187 F3
Cotgrave CE Prim Sch
NG12 187 E3
Cotgrave Cl NG8 159 E2
Cotgrave Ctry Pk*
NG12 188 A6
Cotgrave La NG12 187 A2
Cotgrave L Ctr NG12 188 A3
Cotgrave Rd
Cotgrave NG12 187 A1
Cotgrave NG12 187 E3
Mansfield NG19 87 F2
Owthorpe NG12 199 C8
COTHAM 154 F4
COTMANHAY 157 E4
Cotmanhay Rd DE7 157 E3
Cotmoor La NG25 135 D5
Coton Cl
Mansfield Woodhouse
NG19 88 E4
Nottingham NG11 185 A3
Cotswold Cl 2 NG10 193 B8
Cotswold Ct
Beeston NG9 171 D1
Carlton in Lindrick S81 25 E7
Cotswold Gr NG18 103 B6
Cotswold Rd NG8 159 E1
Cottage Ave NG13 178 F4
Cottage Cl
Balderton NG24 140 D2
Blidworth NG21 117 F4
East Leake LE12 205 E3
Ilkeston DE7 157 D3
Stanton Hill NG17 100 C6
Cottage Gdns Cl LE12 213 A1
Cottage La
Collingham NG23 111 F6
Market Warsop NG20 74 C2
North Clifton NG23 69 B4
Cottage Mdw NG4 174 F4
Cottage Pasture La
NG14 164 E7
Cottage Terr NG1 222 C3
COTTAM 43 D4
Cottam Dr NG5 161 A8
Cottam Gdns NG5 161 A8
Cottam Gr NG19 101 D6
Cottam La DN22 42 D6
Cottam Rd
Cottam DN22 43 C4
South Leverton DN22 42 E7
Cottans Cl NG25 136 F8
Cotterdale Cl NG19 88 E1
Cotterhill Cl S81 25 D1
Cottesmore Rd NG7 222 D2
Cotton Dr NG24 140 A4
Cotton Mill La NG22 120 A5
Cottonwood Rd NG17 100 C5
Coulby Cl NG23 156 E6
Coulton's Ave NG17 100 C3
Coulton's Cl NG17 100 C3
Country Cres NG15 146 D2
County Bsns Pk NG2 173 E2
County Cl NG9 184 A5
County Estate The NG17 99 E2
County Rd
Carlton NG4 162 C3
Nottingham NG2 173 E2
Coupe Gdns NG15 146 B6
Coupland Cl 6 DN21 15 F1
Court Cres NG8 171 F4
Courtenay Gdns NG3 173 D7
Court-Field Rd NG17 101 A6
Court Gdns NG11 185 B4
Courtlett Way NG6 160 B5
Courtney Cl NG8 171 E5
Court St 11 NG7 172 F7
Court The LE12 212 B4
Courtyard The NG12 197 E2
Court Yd NG9 183 B8
Covedale Rd NG5 161 C5
Covent Gdns NG12 176 E3
Coventry Ct NG6 160 C5
Coventry Dr S81 36 A6
Coventry La NG9 171 A3
Coventry Rd
Beeston NG9 184 A7
Nottingham NG6 160 B6
Cove Rd DN9 2 E6
Coverdale S81 36 B7
Cover Dr NG13 181 B1
Covert Cl
Burton Joyce NG14 163 E5
Hucknall NG15 146 C6
Keyworth NG12 197 F4
Covert Rd NG2 186 B6
Cowan St NG1 223 F3
Cowdell Gr NG13 177 D7
Cowdray Cl LE11 220 A1
Cowdrey Gdns NG5 162 B6
Cow La
Beeston NG9 183 C8
Newark-on-Trent NG24 124 F1
Cowlairs NG5 160 E7
Cowley Cl DE7 157 F5
Cowley St NG6 160 D3
Cowpasture La
Sturton le Steeple DN21 33 C6
Sutton in Ashfield NG17 100 E1
Cow Pasture La
Kirkby-in-Ashfield
NG17 114 D5
Misson DN10 4 F5
Cow Pature La DN9 5 A5
Cowper Cl S81 36 B5
Cowper Rd
Arnold NG5 161 E4
Eastwood NG16 158 A8
Cowper Rise S81 36 B5
Cowpes Cl NG17 100 E4
Cowslip Cl
Bingham NG13 177 C3
East Leake LE12 206 A1
Cowslip Dr S81 25 F7
Cox Dr NG13 180 F3
Coxmoor Cl NG2 186 C4
Coxmoor Ct 14 NG5 147 A1
Coxmoor Rd NG17,
NG15 115 E7
Cox's Hill DN21 15 D1
Cox's La NG19 88 B5
Crabapple Dr NG16 143 C4
Crab Apple Gr NG15 146 C4
Crab La NG23 110 F1
Crab Nook La NG22 119 F6
Crabtree Farm Prim Sch
NG6 160 B6
Crabtree Field NG2 174 D4
Crabtree La
Beckingham DN10 22 F7
Beckingham DN10 23 A8
High Marnham NG23 67 D2
Crabtree Rd NG6 160 A6
Craddock St LE11 220 B4
Crafts Way NG25 121 E1
Cragdale Rd NG5 161 C5
Cragg La DE55 99 A2
Cragmoor Rd NG14 163 E3
Crags Bsns Pk S80 58 E8
Crags Rd
Belph S80 45 B3
Creswell S80 45 A1
Craig Moray NG12 176 A4
Craigs Gn NG19 101 E5
Craig St NG10 193 E7
Craigston Rd S81 25 E6
Crammond Cl 3 NG2 173 B2
Crampton Cl NG17 100 B3
Crampton Ct NG5 161 A8
Crampton Rd NG18 102 E8
Cramworth Gr 4 NG5 161 D3
Cranberry Cl NG2 185 B5
Cranborne Cl NG19 101 D7
Cranbourne Cl NG9 170 D2
Cranbourne Gr NG15 145 F7
Cranbrook Ct NG19 88 C6
Cranbrook St NG1 223 F3
Craneworks Cl LE11 220 B6
Cranfleet Way NG10 193 B7
Cranford Gdns NG2 185 C4
Crankley La NG23 124 D4
Cranleigh Dr NG14 150 D1
Cranmer Ave NG13 178 E3
Cranmer Gr
8 Nottingham NG3 173 C7
Radmanthwaite NG19 87 D3
Cranmer Rd NG24 139 F5
Cranmer St
Ilkeston DE7 157 F1
Long Eaton NG10 182 D1
Nottingham NG3 173 C7
Cranmore Cl NG5 148 A2
Cranshaw Cl LE12 212 C3
Cransley Ave NG8 171 D2
Cranston Ave NG5 147 F1
Cranston Rd NG9 171 C1
Cranswick Cl
Hucknall NG15 131 D1
Mansfield Woodhouse
NG19 89 A2
Cranthorne Dr NG3 174 C6
Crantock Gdns NG12 197 E3
Cranwell Cl NG24 125 D1
Cranwell Ct NG6 159 F6
Cranwell Rd NG8 159 D2
Craster Dr
Arnold NG5 148 A2
Nottingham NG6 159 F8
Craster St NG17 100 E1
Crathie Rd S81 25 E6
Craven Rd NG7 172 E7
Crawford Ave NG9 182 D8
Crawford Cl NG8 171 E5
Crawford Rise NG5 162 C8
Crawfords Mdw NG13 178 F5
C Rd NG9 184 D6
Creamery Cl NG8 172 B7
Crees La NG24 139 B6
Crees Yard NG17 114 A4
Crescent Ave NG4 162 E1
Crescent Prim Sch
NG19 87 D2
Crescent Rd NG16 128 D6
Crescent The
Arnold NG5 161 E4
Beckingham DN10 14 B1
Beeston, Chilwell NG9 183 C3
Beeston, Toton NG9 183 A2
Bilsthorpe NG22 105 E6
Bircotes DN11 9 C4
Blidworth NG21 118 B5
East Leake LE12 205 F2
Eastwood NG16 144 A2
Lea DN21 24 F2
Mansfield NG18 102 C3
Newark-on-Trent NG24 140 A6
Nottingham NG3 173 D8
Old Dalby LE14 219 B6
Radcliffe on Trent NG12 176 A3
Retford DN22 39 D6
Shirebrook NG20 72 E6
Stapleford NG9 170 E2
Sutton in Ashfield NG17 100 D7
Cresswell Rd
Beeston NG9 183 B5
Worksop S80 35 E4
Cresswell St S80 35 E3
Cressy Rd NG7 184 F2
Cresta Gdns NG3 161 D2
CRESWELL 58 D8
Creswell Crags Mus & Ed
Ctr* S80 45 B1
Creswell Ct NG19 88 E4
Creswell Rd
Cuckney NG20 59 E3
Cuckney NG20 60 A3
Crewe Cl
Blidworth NG21 118 A6
Nottingham NG7 222 B4
Crewe Rd DN11 9 B4
Crew La NG25 137 A8
Crew La Ind Est NG25 137 A8
Crew Rd
Collingham NG23 98 B1
Collingham NG23 112 B8
Crew Yard The DN10 11 C3
Cribb Cl NG11 185 B7
Crich View
Newton DE55 99 A4
Nottingham NG5 161 C2
Cricket Cl NG17 129 F8
Cricketers Ct NG2 173 F1
Cricketers Dr LE11 220 A6
Cricket Field La DN22 39 E8
Cricket Green LN1 57 A5
Criftin Rd NG14 164 A4
Crink La NG25 136 F6
Cripps Hill NG7 172 C2
Crispin Way NG8 172 C7
Critchley St DE7 157 F1
Critch's Flats NG16 158 F6
Crocus Close
Newark-on-Trent NG24 139 F4
Newark-on-Trent NG24 140 A4
Crocus Gardens 5
NG12 186 A2
Crocus St
Kirkby-in-Ashfield
NG17 115 B4
Nottingham NG2 173 D2
Croft Ave
Hucknall NG15 146 A6
Mansfield NG18 102 C2
Croft Cl
Pinxton NG16 113 C3
Rolleston NG23 138 A6
Croft Cres NG16 158 C5
Croft Ct NG17 99 F4
Croft Dr DN11 8 A8
Crofters View DN22 39 E8
Croft Farm Cl
Everton DN10 11 C3
Rolleston NG23 138 B6
Croft Gdns LE14 218 E4
Crofton Cl
Beeston NG9 183 D3
3 Nottingham NG8 172 D6
Crofton Rd NG9 183 D2
Croft Prim Sch NG17 100 F2
Croft Rd
Arnold NG5 161 F8
Finningley DN10 1 A1
Keyworth NG12 197 D3
West Bridgford NG12 186 A4
Croft Rise NG13 165 C3
Crofts The
Bingham NG13 177 E4
North Scarle LN6 83 E3
Croft The
Beckingham DN10 23 C8
Kegworth DE74 203 D2
Newark-on-Trent NG24 140 A8
Retford DN22 39 F8
Shirebrook NG20 72 E3
South Normanton DE55 113 A6
Stanton Hill NG17 100 C5
Croft Way DN10 11 C3
Croft Wlk S80 45 A6
Cromarty Cl NG19 101 D5
Cromarty Ct 2 NG2 173 B2
Cromdale Cl NG5 148 C1
Cromer Cl NG18 102 C4
Cromer Rd NG3 173 E7
Cromford Ave
Carlton NG4 174 D8
Mansfield NG18 102 A4
Cromford Cl
Aldercar NG16 143 B4
Long Eaton NG10 193 A5
Cromford Rd
Annesley Woodhouse
NG17 115 A1
Langley Mill NG16 143 B4
West Bridgford NG2 185 F6
Cromford Road Ind Est
DE75 143 B4
Cromford St
Gainsborough DN21 15 C1
2 Gainsborough DN21 15 D1
Crompton Rd
Bilsthorpe NG22 105 F6
Ilkeston DE7 170 B3
Radmanthwaite NG19 87 D3
Crompton St
New Houghton NG19 86 F8
Teversal NG17 100 B7
Crompton View Prim Sch
NG22 105 F6
CROMWELL 110 E7
Cromwell Ave
Ilkeston DE7 170 A5
Lea DN21 24 F3
Cromwell Cres NG4 163 B7
Cromwell Dr LE12 205 E1
Cromwell Farm Cl
NG23 110 F8
Cromwell Rd
Aslockton NG13 178 E3
Beeston NG9 183 E6
Newark-on-Trent NG24 140 B7
Cromwell St
Carlton NG4 174 E7
Eastwood NG16 158 C8
Gainsborough DN21 24 D6
Mansfield NG18 102 C6
Nottingham NG7 222 C3
Cromwell Terr DE7 157 F3
Crookdole La NG14 148 F7
Crooked Billet St DN21 15 B4
Crookes Ave NG19 87 A5
Crookford Hill
Clumber and Hardwick
DN22 48 E3
Elkesley DN22 49 E3
Crook's Ave NG19 88 C3
Croome Cl LE11 220 C1
Crops The NG22 120 F6
Cropston Cl NG2 185 E4
Cropton Cres NG8 172 B6
Cropton Gr NG13 177 C4
CROPWELL BISHOP 189 B4
Cropwell Bishop Prim Sch
NG12 189 B4
Cropwell Bishop Rd
NG12 189 B6
CROPWELL BUTLER 189 B7
Cropwell Butler Rd
Cropwell Bishop NG12 189 B4
Cropwell Bishop NG12 189 B5
Cropwell Ct NG18 102 D7
Cropwell Gdns NG12 176 A2
Cropwell Gn NG3 173 F6
Cropwell Rd
Colston Bassett NG12 189 F2
Cropwell Butler NG12 188 D8
Langar NG13 190 C1
Owthorpe NG12 199 F5
Radcliffe on Trent NG12 176 A2
Tithby NG13 189 D6
Crosby Cl NG19 89 A1
Crosby Rd NG2 185 F8
Cross Comm La DN22 33 A5
Crossdale Dr NG12 197 E4
Crossdale Wlk NG5 160 E8
Cross Dr
Kirkby-in-Ashfield
NG17 115 B7
Rainworth NG21 104 B1
Crossfield Dr
13 Nottingham NG5 147 A1
Nottingham NG5 161 A8
Crossgate Dr NG2 173 A1
Crosshill NG12 188 A3
Cross Hill
Gringley on the Hill DN10 12 F2
Laxton NG22 79 C3
Cross Hill Cl LE12 216 C3
Crossings The 3
NG24 140 B8
Cross La
Austerfield DN10 3 C5
Balderton NG24 140 D1
Blidworth NG21 117 D6
Collingham NG23 112 C8
East Bridgford NG13 165 D3
Elkesley DN22 49 F4
Elston NG23 153 F2
Elston NG23 154 A3
Farndon NG24 138 F4
Gringley on the Hill DN10 5 A1
Harby NG23 70 D2
Long Bennington NG13 169 F3
Staunton in the Vale
NG23 169 F2
Crossland Rd NG5 161 A5
Crosslands Mdw NG4 174 F4
Crossley Ave NG17 100 A3
Crossley Hill La S81 26 C4
Crossley St NG5 161 B2
Crossman St NG5 161 C2
Cross Rd NG15 130 C7
Cross Row
Huthwaite NG17 100 A2
Stanton Hill NG17 100 C5
Cross St
Arnold NG5 161 E8
Barnby in the Willows
NG24 141 F5
Beeston NG9 183 F7
Bilsthorpe NG22 105 F6
Carlton, Netherfield NG4 175 A7
Carlton, Thorneywood
NG4 174 D8
Eastwood NG16 144 A2
4 Gainsborough DN21 15 D1
Gainsborough DN21 24 D8
Hathern LE12 213 A1
Kirkby-in-Ashfield NG17 115 C6
Langold S81 16 E3
Long Eaton NG10 193 E8
Loughborough LE11 220 C5
Mansfield Woodhouse
NG19 88 B2
Morton DN21 15 B4
Newark-on-Trent NG24 140 B8
Retford DN22 40 A6
Sandiacre NG10 182 C6
Sturton le Steeple DN22 32 D5
Cross The
Carlton in Lindrick S81 26 A6
Cotgrave NG12 187 E3
Crossways
East Markham NG22 66 A7
Retford DN22 39 F8
Crossways Dr NG13 165 D3
Crowborough Ave NG8 171 E2
Crowcroft Way NG10 182 B2
Crow Ct NG13 178 A4
Crow Hill NG19 87 B5
Crow Hill Ct NG18 102 B8
Crow Hill Dr NG18 102 B8
Crow Hill La NG19 88 B2
Crow Hill Rd NG4 174 F7
Crow Hl Ri NG18 102 B8
Crow La
Ollerton NG22 77 C2
South Muskham
NG23, NG24 124 D7
Crowley Cl NG8 171 C6
Crown Ave NG19 103 A8
Crown Cl
Collingham NG23 98 A1
Long Eaton NG10 193 A7
Rainworth NG21 118 C8
Crown Ct DN22 32 D5
Crown Farm Way
Forest Town NG19 89 D1
Mansfield NG19 103 B8
Crown St
Mansfield NG18 102 F6
Newark-on-Trent NG24 139 F7
Nottingham NG15 146 C4
Worksop S80 35 E4
Crown Wy NG16 143 B4
Crow Pk Ave NG23 81 E1
Crow Pk Dr NG14 163 E3
Crowthorne Cl NG5 146 E1
Crowthorne Gardens
NG5 146 E1
Crowtrees Dr NG17 100 D1
Croxall Cl NG11 184 E4
Croxley Gdns NG16 159 D3
Croxton Ct NG19 88 E3
Croyde Gdns NG12 186 B7
Croydon Rd NG7 222 A3
Crummock Cl NG9 183 C8
Crystal Ct S81 25 D1
CUCKNEY 60 A4
Cuckney CE Prim Sch
NG20 60 A2
Cuckney Hill
Church Warsop NG20 74 B7
Cuckney NG20 60 B1
Cuckney Rd NG20 61 D3
Cuckoo Holt S81 35 C7
Cuckstool The NG23 96 F8
Cudworth Dr NG3 161 F2
Cuillin Cl NG10 182 A1
Cul-de-sac NG22 105 F6
Cullen Cl NG24 124 E1
Cullen's Ct NG5 161 C2
Cullin Cl NG5 146 F2
Culpepper Ave NG22 77 D3
Cultivation Rd 4
NG16 144 A1
Culvert Rise NG14 173 E2
Cumberland Ave
Beeston NG9 183 D6
Market Warsop NG20 74 A5
Cumberland Cl
Bircotes DN11 9 D4
Carlton in Lindrick S81 25 F7
Ruddington NG11 196 D7
Westwood NG16 128 C4
Cumberland
Drive NG19 101 D7
Cumberland
Place NG1 223 D2
Cumbria Grange 12
NG12 186 C7
Cumbria Rd S81 36 A6
Cundy Hill NG25 136 B6
Cunningham Close
DN10 19 F8
Cupar Cl NG20 74 C6
Curbar Cl NG19 102 D5
Curie Ct NG7 172 D2
Curlew Cl NG3 174 C5
Curlew Wharf 5 NG7 172 F2
Currie Rd NG24 125 A2
Cursley Way NG9 183 C2
Curtis Cl NG23 98 A1
Curtis St NG15 146 A6
Curzon Ave NG4 174 B7
Curzon Cl NG21 118 A8
Curzon Ct NG3 223 F4
Curzon Dr S81 35 F7
Curzon Gdns NG3 223 F4
Curzon Pl NG3 223 F3
Curzon St
Carlton NG4 175 A7
Gainsborough DN21 15 C2
Gotham NG11 195 B1
Long Eaton NG10 182 B2
Loughborough LE11 220 A3
Nottingham NG3 223 F3
Cusworth Way S80 35 D3
Cuthbert Pl DN22 29 F1
Cuthberts Ave
Worksop S80 47 A7
Worksop S80 47 B7
Cutlersforth NG22 135 C8
Cut Throat La DN22 41 B8
Cut Through La NG8 172 C1
Cuttings Ave NG17 114 B8
Cutts Way NG21 118 B6
Cuxton Cl NG8 159 D1
Cyan Close NG4 175 C8
Cycle Rd NG7 222 A2
Cygnet Fold NG19 88 C4
Cypress Ct NG15 145 C5
Cyprus Ave NG9 183 F7
Cyprus Dr NG9 183 F7
Cyprus Rd NG3 161 C1
Cyril Ave
Beeston NG9 183 E7
Nottingham NG8 172 D8
Stapleford NG9 182 D7
Cyril Rd NG2 186 A7

D

Dabek Rise NG17 115 A1
Dabell Ave NG6 159 F8
Dadley Rd S81 25 F7
Dadsley Rd DN11 8 A8
Dagmar Gr
Beeston NG9 184 A6
Nottingham NG3 161 D1
Dahlia Ave DE55 113 B7
Dairy Farm Ct DN21 7 E2
Dairyfield Dr S80 59 E8
Dairy Gdns LE14 202 A3
Dairy La
Hose LE14 211 F7
Nether Broughton LE14 219 D8
Dairy Square NG8 172 B7
Daisy Cl
Cotgrave NG12 187 E2
Shirebrook NG20 72 D2
Daisy Farm Rd NG16 158 B8
Daisy Rd NG3 162 A1
Dakeyne Mws NG14 173 E4
Dakeyne St NG3 173 E5
Dakota Dr NG24 141 A1
Dakota Rd NG13 177 B7
Dalbeattie Cl NG5 162 B8
Dalby Cl NG11 196 B8
Dalby Sq NG8 172 C3
Dale Ave
Carlton NG4 174 C7
Long Eaton NG10 182 D1
Newton DE55 99 A3
Nottingham NG3 162 A2
Dalebrook Cres NG15 145 C5
Dale Cl
Blidworth NG21 118 A5
Hucknall NG15 145 C5
Langwith NG20 72 E8
Retford DN22 39 E3
Sutton in Ashfield NG17 101 A5
West Bridgford NG2 186 B7
Whaley Thorns NG20 58 F1
Dale Cres NG24 140 E2
Dale Farm Ave NG3 174 A5
Dale Gr NG2 173 F4
Dalehead Rd NG11 184 D2
Dale La
Ault Hucknall S44 86 D7
Beeston NG9 183 E5
Blidworth NG21 118 B5
Dalemoor Gdns NG8 172 B8
Dale Rd
Carlton NG4 174 C7
Keyworth NG12 197 E3
Kimberley NG16 158 F5
Market Warsop NG20 74 C5
Dales Ave NG17 100 F5
Dales Cl LE12 215 E5
Daleside NG12 187 E2
Daleside Rd NG2 174 A3
Daleside Rd E
Nottingham NG2, NG3 174 C4
Nottingham NG4 174 D5
Dales La DN10 4 F4
Dale St
Mansfield NG19 88 B1
Nottingham NG2 173 E4
Dalestorth Ave NG19 87 D1
Dalestorth Cl NG17 101 A5
Dalestorth Gdns NG17 101 A5
Dalestorth Prim Sch
NG17 101 A4
Dalestorth Rd NG17 101 A5
Dalestorth St NG17 101 A4
Dales Way NG9 171 B4
DALESWORTH 101 B5
Dale View Rd NG3 174 B7
Dalewood Cl DE55 113 A3
Dale Wy NG24 140 F1
Dalkeith Terr 10 NG7 172 F7
Dallaglio Mews NG9 183 B2
Dallas St NG18 102 A6
Dallas York Rd NG9 184 B6
Dalley Cl NG9 182 F7
Dallington St NG9 171 F8
Dallman Cl NG15 146 A5
Dalton Cl NG9 182 E5
Dalton Gr DN10 10 A8
Daltons Cl
Aldercar NG16 143 A4
Eagle LN6 84 D2
Dame Flogan St NG18 102 B6
Dame La DN10 4 B2
Dam Rd DN11 8 A6
Damson Rd LE12 214 C8
Damson Wlk NG3 174 B8
Dane Cl NG3 223 F4
Dane Ct NG3 223 F4
Dane Gr NG15 130 D7
Danes Cl NG5 161 D8
Danesfield Rd S80 35 F1
Daneshill Gravel Pits Nature Reserve★
DN22 19 D1
Daneshill Rd
Lound DN22 20 A1
Lound DN22 29 C8
Danes Rd DN21 15 F1
Danethorpe La NG24 126 B8
Danethorpe Vale NG5 161 C4
Daniel Cres NG18 101 F7
Daniel Mews NG10 182 A5
Daniels Way NG15 145 F4
Danners Hill NG15 131 E5
Danvers Ave NG17 114 B8
Danvers Dr NG19 101 E7
Darbyshire Cl NG23 70 D2
Darfield Ct DN11 8 A7
Darfield Dr DE75 143 A2
Darkey La NG9 182 E5
Dark La
Aslockton NG13 179 A4
Barnby in the Willows
NG24 142 A5
Bingham NG13 178 A4
West Leake LE12 204 F2
Darley Ave
Beeston NG9 182 F3
Carlton NG4 162 E1
Kirkby-in-Ashfield NG17 115 C5
Nottingham NG7 172 E7
Darleydale Cl NG18 102 D3
Darley Dr NG10 193 A5
Darley Rd NG7 172 E7
Darley Sq DE7 157 E5
DARLTON 67 B7
Darlton Dr NG5 162 B7
Darlton Rd
Darlton NG22 67 A8
Darlton NG22 67 D8
Dunham-on-Trent NG22 54 B1
East Drayton DN22 53 A1
Ragnall NG22 53 F1
Tuxford NG22 66 C4
Darlton St NG19 101 D6
Darnal Cl NG5 160 E7
Darnhall Cres NG8 171 D7
Daron Gdns 10 NG5 161 A7
Darrel Rd DN22 39 E5
Darricott Cl NG21 118 B8
Dart Ct NG13 177 D3
Dartmoor Cl NG11 195 D8
Darvel Cl 5 NG8 172 B6
Darwin Cl
Elston NG23 153 E4
Mansfield NG18 102 C3
Nottingham NG5 160 E8
Darwin Dr
New Ollerton NG22 77 C3
Woodbeck DN22 42 B1
Darwin Rd NG10 193 B5
Darwin St DN21 24 D6
Daubeney Ave LN1 57 B3
Davenport Dr NG16 158 B7
Davey Rd NG18 102 A7
David Ave NG22 105 F5
David Gr NG9 171 E1
David La NG6 160 D3
Davids La NG14 165 A5
Davidson Cl NG5 162 C7
Davidson Gd NG11 196 A7
Davidson St 5 NG2 173 F3
David St NG17 115 B7
Davies Ave NG17 100 E3
Davies Cl NG17 100 E3
Davies Rd NG2 186 A7
Davies Way 1 NG5 161 A5
Davis Cl NG21 90 B4
Davis Rd NG9 183 B3
Davy Cl
Hucknall NG15 131 B2
New Ollerton NG22 77 C3
Dawber St S81 35 D7
Dawes Way NG7 222 A3
Dawgates La NG19 86 F1
Dawlish Cl
Carlton NG3 162 D5
Hucknall NG15 145 D6
Dawlish Ct
Arnold NG5 162 D6
Eastwood NG16 143 D3
Dawlish Dr NG5 161 B5
Dawn Cl NG15 131 C1
Dawn House School
NG21 103 F3
Dawn's La NG13 179 A5
Dawn View NG9 170 D2
Dawson Cl NG16 144 A1
Dawver Rd NG16 158 F6
Daybell Cl NG13 181 B3
Daybells Barns NG13 181 B2
Daybill Cl NG25 137 D3
DAYBROOK 161 D7
Daybrook Ave 4 NG5 161 C3
Daybrook Learning Centre
NG5 161 C8
Daybrook Mws NG5 160 F4
Daybrook St NG5 161 C3
D'Ayncourt Wlk NG22 120 A6
Day St NG20 74 B4
Deabill St NG4 175 A6
Dead La
Cossall NG16 158 D1
1 Loughborough LE11 220 B4
Deadwong La NG23 153 E1
Deakins Ct NG18 102 C6
Deakins Pl NG7 222 A3
Deal Gdns NG6 159 F7
Dean Ave NG3 162 A3
Dean Cl
Mansfield NG18 102 C4
Nottingham NG8 171 D5
Deane Cl NG23 98 A1
Deane Rd NG2 185 A6
Dean Rd NG5 161 E5
Deans Cl DN10 6 E2
Dean's Cl NG23 109 B5
Deanscourt NG12 188 A3
Deans Croft NG9 171 B1
Deansgate NG19 87 A5
Dean St
Langley Mill NG16 143 C3
Nottingham NG1 223 F2
Death La DN22 21 D6
Debdale Gate NG19 88 A2
Debdale Hill LE14 218 E4
Debdale La
Keyworth NG12 197 E3
Mansfield NG19 88 A2
Debdale Wy NG19 88 B2
Debdhill Rd DN10 6 E2
Deben Down NG19 88 D3
De Brouwer Cl DN22 39 F5
De Buseli Cl NG4 175 A8
De Caldwell Dr NG24 139 F6
Deddington La NG9 171 C2
Deeley Cl NG16 159 A7
Deepdale Ave NG9 182 D6
Deepdale Cl NG2 186 C7
Deepdale Gdns NG17 100 F4
Deepdale Pk NG17 100 F4
Deepdale Rd
Long Eaton NG10 193 A5
Mansfield NG19 88 E1
Nottingham NG8 171 D4
Deepdale St NG17 100 F4
Deepdene Cl NG8 160 A2
Deepdene Way NG8 160 A2
Deep Furrow Ave NG4 174 D8
Deep La S45 85 B3
Deeps La DN10 4 B7
Deerdale La
Bilsthorpe NG22 105 A8
Edwinstowe NG21 91 C1
Rainworth NG21 104 F8
Deerlands Way DN10 23 C8
Deerleap Dr NG5 161 C7
Deer Pk NG8 171 E4
Deer Pk Dr
Arnold NG5 147 C1
4 Nottingham NG5 147 C1
Nottingham NG5 161 B8
Nottingham NG5 161 C8
Deers Acre LE11 220 B6
Dees La DN10 4 B7
Deetleton Cl NG16 129 A7
Deevon Farm Cl NG24 139 D7
De Ferrers Cl LE12 205 E1
De Havilland Way
NG24 139 C6
Dein Ct DE55 99 E4
De Lacy Ct NG22 77 B4
Delamere Cl NG18 102 C4
Delamere Dr NG18 102 C4
Delia Ave NG15 131 C1
Dell Lea NG18 103 A3
Dell The NG17 129 F8
Dell Way NG7 184 F2
Dellwood Cl NG4 162 C2
Delta St NG7 160 F1
Deltic Cl NG16 159 A7
Delville Ave NG12 197 E4
De Morgan Cl NG16 129 A2
Denacre Ave NG10 182 F1
Denbigh Ave 3 S81 35 E7
Denbigh Cl NG21 104 C1
Denbigh Ct NG23 98 A1
Denbury Ct NG5 162 D6
Denbury Rd NG15 117 A2
Denby Dr NG18 102 D2
Denby Hall Rd DE7 157 F6
Dendy Dr DN22 53 B8
Dene Cl DN10 20 B7
Denehurst Ave NG8 160 C1
Dene The S80 35 C2
Denewood Ave NG9 171 C2
Denewood Cres NG8 171 E8
Denholme Rd NG8 171 D5
Denison Ave DN22 40 A4
Denison St
Beeston NG9 183 E7
Nottingham NG7 222 B4
Denman Cl DN22 39 D8
Denman St Central
NG7 222 B3
Denman St E NG7 222 B3
Denman St W NG7 222 A3
Denmark Grove 1
NG3 173 D8
Dennett Cl NG3 173 E6
Dennis Ave NG9 183 E8
Dennis Brown Ct LN1 57 B3
Dennis St
Carlton NG4 175 A7
Worksop S80 35 F2
Dennor Dr NG19 88 E5
Denstone Rd NG3 173 E5
Dentdale Dr NG8 171 B4
Denton Ave NG10 182 A6
Denton Cl
Balderton NG24 140 C3
Mansfield NG19 88 E1
Denton Dr NG2 185 D4
Denton Gn NG8 159 F2
Denver Ct NG9 170 E1
Deodar Cl LE12 212 D2
Deptford Cres NG6 160 C5
Derby Gr NG7 222 B3
Derby Rd
Annesley Woodhouse NG15,
NG17 130 B7
Beeston NG9 171 D1
Eastwood NG16 143 E2
Hathern LE12 212 F2
Kegworth DE74 203 C2
Kirkby-in-Ashfield NG17 115 D4
Langley Mill NG16 143 C3
Long Eaton NG10 193 B8
Loughborough LE11 220 A5
Mansfield NG17, NG18 116 B8
Nottingham NG7 222 B2
Sandiacre NG10 182 A5
Derbyshire Ave NG9 170 D4
Derbyshire Cres NG8 172 A5
Derbyshire Dr NG16 128 C4
Derbyshire La NG15 146 A7
Derby Sq LE11 220 A4
Derby St
Arnold NG5 161 F7
Beeston NG9 183 F7
Mansfield NG18 102 C6
Nottingham NG1 223 D3
Dereham Dr NG5 162 A6
Derry Dr NG5 147 F2
Derry Hill Rd NG5 147 E1
Derry La NG13 178 B3
Derwent Ave
Ilkeston DE7 157 D2
Mansfield NG18 103 A5
Derwent Cl
Beeston NG9 183 E3
Mansfield NG18 103 A5
Market Warsop NG20 74 C5
Rainworth NG21 118 B8
West Bridgford NG2 186 C7
Worksop S81 35 F6
Derwent Cres NG5 162 A6
Derwent Ct
Balderton NG24 140 D3
Nottingham NG7 222 C4
Derwent Dr
Annesley Woodhouse
NG17 130 A8
Hucknall NG15 146 A4
Nuncargate NG17 115 A1
Selston NG16 129 A7
Derwent St Ind Est
NG10 193 D6
Derwent St NG10 193 C6
Derwent Terr 5 NG5 161 C2
Derwent Way
Newark-on-Trent NG24 125 B2
Nottingham NG7 172 D4
Nottingham NG7 222 A2
Desborough Rd NG16 128 D7
Desford Cl NG5 161 A4
De Vere Gdns NG5 162 A4
Devitt Dr NG15 131 C1
Devon Cir NG5 147 D1
Devon Cl
Eastwood NG16 144 B2
Sandiacre NG10 182 B5
Devon Dr
Mansfield NG19 101 F8
Nottingham NG5 161 C2
Ruddington NG11 196 D8
Devon La NG13 181 B3
Devon Pk NG24 139 E7
Devon Pk Pastures Nature Reserve★ NG24 139 D6
Devon Rd NG24 139 F6
Devonshire Ave
Beeston NG9 183 F6
Long Eaton NG10 194 A8
Devonshire Cl
Ilkeston DE7 157 E5
1 Sutton in Ashfield
NG17 100 A2
Devonshire Cres NG5 161 B2
Devonshire Dr
Eastwood NG16 143 F2
Langwith NG20 72 F8
3 Newton DE55 99 A3
Ollerton NG22 77 A3
Stapleford NG9 170 D2
Devonshire La LE11 220 B3
Devonshire Promenade
NG7 222 A1
Devonshire Rd
Harworth DN11 8 F4
Nottingham NG5 161 B2
Retford DN22 39 D6
West Bridgford NG2 185 F6
Devonshire Sq 2 LE11 220 B3
Devonshire St
New Houghton NG19 87 A7
Worksop S80 35 F2
Devon St
Ilkeston DE7 170 A5
Nottingham NG3 173 F5
Dewberry Gdns NG19 89 A2
Dewberry La NG12 176 B2
Dexters Gr NG15 145 F7
DH Lawrence Birthplace Mus★ NG16 143 F3
Dial The NG12 187 E1
Diamond Ave
Kirkby-in-Ashfield
NG17 115 C4
Rainworth NG21 104 C1
Dianthus Gr DN22 40 B4
Dickens Ct NG16 144 B3
Dickenson Terr DN21 24 D7
Dickenson Way NG23 110 F3
Dickens Rd S81 36 B3
Dickinson St NG3 173 E7
Dickman's La LE14 202 B3
Dicks La NG16 144 C3
Dickson Dr NG11 196 D6
Didcot Dr NG8 160 D1
Digby Ave NG3 162 C3
Digby Ct NG7 222 B1
Digby Hall Dr NG4 162 C3
Digby St
Cossall DE7 158 A1
Ilkeston DE7 170 A8
Kimberley NG16 158 D7
Diggles Lodge La
Barnby Moor DN22 28 B4
Barnby Moor S81 27 F3
Dingle Ct DN22 19 B5
Dingley Cl NG19 88 E5
Dirca Ct NG11 195 C8
Discovery Dr NG8 172 C7
Diseworth Gr 3 NG2 173 D1
Distillery St NG11 196 C6
Division Rd NG20 72 E4
Dixie St NG16 128 B4
Djanogly City Acad
Nottingham NG7 161 A1
Nottingham NG7 173 A7
Djanogly Northgate Acad
NG7 160 F1
Dobbin Cl NG12 189 B4
Doble Cres LE12 213 A2
Dob Pk Cl NG6 160 D4
Dobsons Mws NG17 101 B3
Dockholm Rd NG10 182 C2
Dock Rd S80 35 E3
DODDINGTON 71 C1
Doddington Hall★ LN6 71 B1
Doddington La
Claypole NG23 156 B2
Dry Doddington NG23 156 E5
Dodford Ct DE75 143 A1
Dodsley Way NG21 90 A4
Dodson Ave NG12 197 F4
Dog & Duck La DN21 15 B4
Doghill La NG23 153 B2
Dog La DN10 10 A2
Dogwood Ave
Nottingham NG16 159 F7
Nottingham NG6 160 A7
Dolegate Rd DN22 53 A4
Doles La
Kirkby-in-Ashfield
NG17 114 C6
Whitwell S80 45 B7
Dolphin Ct 7 NG5 161 A8
Dominie Cross Rd
DN22 39 F6
Donbas Cl NG6 160 B4
Doncaster Ave NG10 182 B6
Doncaster By Pass
Blyth DN11 17 F7
Blyth S81 18 A6
Doncaster Gr NG10 182 F1
Doncaster Rd
Austerfield DN10 3 A1
Bawtry DN10 10 A8
Carlton in Lindrick S81 25 F7
Carlton in Lindrick S81 26 A6
Langold S81 16 F3
Tickhill DN11 8 A8
Westwoodside DN9 2 E3
Doncaster Sheffield Airport
DN10 3 B7
Doncaster Terr 11
NG2 173 C1
Donington Rd NG7 184 E1
Donkey La NG11 196 E3
Donner Cres DE7 157 E5
Dooland Dr NG3 161 F1
Dorchester Cl NG18 102 D2
Dorchester Dr NG18 102 D2
Dorchester Gdns NG2 185 E3
Dorchester Rd
Annesley Woodhouse
NG17 115 B1
Harworth DN11 9 B5
Kimberley NG16 158 F7
Doreen Dr NG17 100 D2
Dorewood Ct NG24 140 E4
Dorey Way NG15 146 A4
Doris Rd DE7 170 A7
Dorket Cl NG5 148 A1
Dorket Dr NG8 172 D3
Dorking Rd NG7 222 B4
Dormer Dr S80 35 B5
Dormouse Cl LE12 214 E7
Dormy Cl
Beeston NG9 183 C7
Mansfield Woodhouse
NG19 88 E5
Radcliffe on Trent NG12 176 B3
Dormy Ct NG6 160 D7
Dorner Ave NG24 139 D7
Dornoch Ave
Nottingham NG5 161 D2
Southwell NG25 121 F1
Dorothy Ave
Eastwood NG16 144 A3
Hucknall NG15 131 B1
Mansfield Woodhouse
NG19 88 C1
Sandiacre NG10 182 B5
Dorothy Dr NG19 88 F1
Dorothy Gr 1 NG8 172 D6
Dorset Dr DN11 8 F4
Dorset Gdns NG2 185 C5
Dorset St NG8 172 D5
Dorset Way NG18 103 A4
Dorterry Cres DE7 170 A5
Dorton Ave DN21 24 F8
Dotterel Pl NG20 73 E4
Doublet Cl NG16 128 A6
Douglas Ave
Awsworth NG16 158 C5
Carlton NG4 174 E6
Douglas Cl NG12 175 E2
Douglas Cres NG4 174 E6
Douglas Ct NG9 183 A2
Douglas Rd
Bingham NG13 178 B4
Long Eaton NG10 182 B1
Long Eaton NG10 193 C8
Mansfield Woodhouse
NG19 89 B2
Nottingham NG7 222 B3
Sutton in Ashfield NG17 100 D2
Douro Dr NG5 148 B1
Dove Cl
Bingham NG13 177 F3
11 Gainsborough DN21 15 F1
Ollerton NG22 77 B4
Worksop S81 35 E7
Dovecoat St LE12 213 A1
Dovecote Cl NG13 165 C3
Dovecote Dr NG8 171 E4
Dovecote La
Beeston NG9 184 A5
Tithby NG13 189 D6
Dovecote Prim Sch
NG11 184 F3
Dovecote Rd NG16 144 B2
Dove Croft NG22 77 B4
Dovedale Ave
Long Eaton NG10 193 A6
Sutton in Ashfield NG17 100 D1
Dovedale Cir DE7 157 E5
Dovedale Cl
Edwinstowe NG21 76 A2
Mansfield NG18 102 D3
Dovedale Ct NG10 193 B6
Dovedale Prim Sch
NG10 193 A6
Dovedale Rd
Nottingham NG3 174 C6
West Bridgford NG2 186 A5
Dove Dr NG16 129 A7
Dove La NG10 193 C8
Dovenby Rd NG7 184 F2
Dover Beck Cl
Calverton NG14 149 A7
Lowdham NG14 150 D2
Ravenshead NG15 116 F2
Dover Beck Dr NG14 149 D4
Dover Bottom DN22 50 D3
Doveridge Ave NG4 175 A8
Doveridge Ct NG15 117 A3
Doveridge Rd NG4 175 A8
Dover St NG25 121 E1
Dove St NG6 160 B7
Dovey's Orch NG14 148 D7
Downes Cl NG6 160 A7
Downham Cl NG5 162 A6
Downham Gdns NG15 117 B2
Downing Cl NG6 160 B8
Downing Gdns 7
NG6 160 B8
Downing St
Nottingham NG6 160 B8
South Normanton DE55 113 A6
Sutton in Ashfield NG17 100 F3
Downs The
4 Mansfield Woodhouse
NG19 88 F1
Nottingham NG11 185 A3
Dowson Cl
11 Nottingham NG7 160 F1
Radcliffe on Trent NG12 176 B4
Dowson St NG3 173 F6
Doyne Ct 2 NG2 173 C1
Dozen Dr NG19 101 D7
Dragonfly Cl LE12 214 D7
Dragon St NG13 191 B5
Dragwell DE74 203 D2
DRAKEHOLES 11 F1
Drakemyre Cl NG5 148 B1
Drake Rd NG4 175 B6
Drake St DN21 24 D6
Draper Cl NG12 176 B4
Draycott Ct DE7 157 F3
Draycott Rd NG10 193 A4
Draymans Ct NG7 160 F1
Drayton Ave NG19 87 D1
Drayton Rd
Stokeham DN22 53 C5
Upton DN22 52 C4
Drayton St 3 NG5 161 C2
Drift Hill NG13 192 F4
Drift The
Hucknall NG15 131 B1
Nottingham NG11 184 E3
Drinking Pit La
Welbeck S80 46 D3
Welbeck S80 47 C4
Whitwell S80 46 B3
Drinsey Nook La NG23 70 C7
Drive The
Beeston NG9 183 E3
Clipstone NG21 90 A3
Gainsborough DN21 24 F7
Winthorpe NG24 125 C6
Drive The Pk La DN22 30 A1
Drmonde Terr 7 NG3 161 C2
Dronfield Pl DE7 157 D5
Dronley Dr NG20 74 C7
Drove La NG24 126 A4
Drovers Ct DN21 24 E5
Droversdale Rd DN11 9 C4
Drummond Ave NG4 175 B7
Drummond Dr NG16 159 E4
Drummond Gr NG23 112 A7
Drummond Rd DE7 157 E1
Drury Cl NG15 145 D5
Drury La DN11 8 A7
Dryden Ave NG24 140 E5
Dryden Ct NG9 170 E1
Dryden Dale S81 36 B3
Dryden St
Nottingham NG1 223 D4
Nottingham NG14 173 B5
DRY DODDINGTON 156 E1
Dry Pot La LE12 212 A2
Drysdale Cl NG6 160 B5
Duchess Gdns 8 NG6 160 B8
Duchess St
Nottingham NG6 160 B8
Whitwell S80 45 A6
Ducie La DN22 23 E3
Duckworth Cl 3 NG4 162 E3
Dudley Ct NG9 183 A8
Dudley Doy Rd NG25 121 C1
Duesbury The DE55 113 B4
Duffield Cl NG10 193 A5
Duffield Cres NG5 160 F8
Duke Cl NG6 160 A5
Duke Cres NG16 144 C1
Duke Pl S80 35 E3

Dukeries Acad The NG22 77 D5
Dukeries Bsns Ctr S80 36 B2
Dukeries Cl S81 35 C6
Dukeries Complex The★ NG22 77 D5
Dukeries Cres
 Edwinstowe NG21 76 B1
 Worksop S80 36 C1
Dukeries Industrial Estate The S81 35 C6
Dukeries L Ctr NG22 77 D6
Dukeries The
 Mansfield NG18 102 F5
 Mansfield NG18 103 A4
Dukeries Way S81 35 C6
Dukes Cl NG17 101 C2
Dukes Ct NG15 146 B7
Duke's Dr S44 86 A7
Dukes Meadow NG21 104 B1
Dukes Pl DE7 157 E4
Duke's Pl NG1 223 F2
Dukes Rd LE14 219 B6
Duke St
 Arnold NG5 161 E7
 Hucknall NG15 146 B7
 Huthwaite NG17 100 A3
 Ilkeston DE7 157 F3
 Loughborough LE11 220 B5
 8 Nottingham NG5 161 A1
 5 Nottingham NG7 160 B7
 Retford DN22 39 E6
 South Normanton DE55 113 B6
 Sutton in Ashfield NG17 100 E2
 Whitwell S80 45 A6
Duke's Terr DN10 10 A7
Duke's Wood Nature Reserve★ NG22 107 A5
Duke William Mount NG7 222 C2
Dulverton Vale NG8 160 B3
Dulwich Rd NG7 222 A3
Dumb Hall La S80 34 B4
Dumbles The
 Lambley NG4 163 B8
 Sutton in Ashfield NG17 100 C1
Dunbar Cl
 Gainsborough DN21 15 E2
 Long Eaton NG10 193 E4
Dunbar Dr NG19 101 D5
Dunblane Rd NG11 196 C6
Duncan Ave NG15 117 A1
Duncombe Cl NG3 173 E7
Duncroft Ave NG4 162 F1
Dundas Cl
 Nottingham NG1 223 E3
 Nottingham NG14 173 C5
Dundee Dr NG19 88 B6
Dunelm Cl NG17 100 C3
Dunelm Dr NG14 149 A7
Dungannon Rd NG11 195 E8
Dunham Cl
 Newton on Trent LN1 55 A1
 Southwell NG25 136 D8
DUNHAM-ON-TRENT 54 C2
Dunham-on-Trent CE Prim Sch NG22 54 A1
Dunham Rd
 Laneham DN22 54 A4
 Laneham DN22 54 A5
 Newton on Trent DN22, LN1 54 E1
 Newton on Trent LN1 55 A1
Dunholme Ave NG24 139 F7
Dunholme Cl
 Gainsborough DN21 24 E8
 Nottingham NG6 160 B8
Dunholme Rd DN21 24 E7
Dunkery Rd NG11 195 F8
DUNKIRK 172 E2
Dunkirk Ind Est NG7 184 D7
Dunkirk Prim School (Abbey Campus) NG7 222 B1
Dunkirk Prim Sch (Highfield Campus) NG7 172 E1
Dunkirk Rd 4 NG7 172 E1
Dunlin Wharf 2 NG2 173 A2
Dunlop Ave NG7 222 A2
Dunn Brigg NG19 88 D2
Dunn Dr NG10 193 B7
Dunnett Rd NG19 101 E5
Dunnock Cl NG15 132 A8
Dunnock Dr NG9 170 E2
Dunoon Cl NG5 146 E1
Dunoon Rd NG19 101 E5
Dunsby Cl NG7 184 E1
Dunsford Dr NG3 162 C6
Dunsil Cl NG19 88 B1
Dunsil Ct NG19 88 B1
Dunsil Dr NG11 185 A8
Dunsil Rd
 Eastwood NG16 144 B4
 Mansfield NG19 88 B1
 Pinxton NG16 113 D2
Dunsil Way NG19 86 F7
Dunsmore Avenue NG13 177 D6
Dunsmore Cl NG9 184 B4
Dunstall Wlk DN21 24 F7
Dunstan Cres S80 35 F1
Dunstan St NG4 175 A7
Dunster Rd
 Eastwood NG16 144 B1
 Gainsborough DN21 15 E2
 West Bridgford NG2 186 A6
Dunston Cl NG10 193 F7
Dunstone Rd DN22 41 E8
Dunvegan Dr NG5 146 F2
Dunwoody Cl NG18 102 F7
Durham Ave NG2 173 F4
Durham Cl
 Mansfield Woodhouse NG19 88 C4
 1 Nottingham NG2 173 F4
 Worksop S81 36 A7
Durham Cres NG6 160 C6
Durham Gr DN22 30 A1
Durham St 3 DE7 157 F1
Durlston Cl NG2 185 B5
Durnford St NG7 160 F2
Dursley Cl NG6 160 B5
Dyce Cl NG6 159 F7
Dykes End NG23 112 A8
Dylan Thomas Rd NG5 161 C8
Dyscarr Cl S81 16 F3
Dyscarr Wood Nature Reserve★ S81 16 E3

E

EAGLE 84 C3
Eagle Cl
 Arnold NG5 162 A7
 Beeston NG9 183 D8
Eagle Com Prim Sch LN6 84 D3
Eagle Ct NG6 160 D7
Eagle Moor La LN6 84 F4
Eagle Pl DN22 39 F7
Eagle Rd
 Eagle LN6 84 B4
 Eagle Moor LN6 84 F5
 North Scarle LN6 83 E3
 Spalford NG23 83 C7
Eagle Wy NG19 88 F2
EAKRING 92 F1
Eakring Cl NG18 102 F7
Eakring Meadow Nature Reserve★ NG22 93 E1
Eakring Rd
 Bilsthorpe NG22 105 E8
 Kirklington NG22 106 E3
 Kneesall NG22 93 E5
 Mansfield NG18, NG21, NG22 103 D7
 Rufford NG22 91 B1
 Rufford NG22 91 F1
 Rufford NG22 92 A8
 Wellow NG22 92 D8
Ealing Ave NG6 160 D4
Eardley Rd NG5 160 E6
Earl Cres NG4 162 F3
Earl Dr NG16 144 C1
Earles Ct DN22 29 C1
Earl Howe Cres NG13 190 C2
Earls Cl NG8 171 C5
Earlsfield Dr NG5 146 E1
Earls Rd LE14 219 B6
Earlswood Dr
 Mansfield NG18 102 F5
 West Bridgford NG12 186 B4
Earp Ave NG24 140 A7
Easedale Cl NG2 186 C7
Easegill Ct NG5 160 F8
East Acres NG12 187 F3
EAST BRIDGFORD 165 D3
East Bridgford Bsns Pk NG13 165 D4
East Bridgford Rd
 East Bridgford NG13 165 B1
 Newton NG13 177 A8
East Cir St NG1 223 D2
East Cl NG12 197 E2
Eastcliffe Ave NG4 162 D3
Eastcote Ave NG9 171 B2
East Cres NG9 184 B5
Eastcroft LN1 57 A5
Eastcroft La NG22 52 A2
Eastdale Rd NG3 174 C6
East Dr NG7 172 C1
EAST DRAYTON 53 A3
East End LE14 211 D4
Eastern Ave DN21 15 F1
Eastern Ct NG24 140 A8
Eastern Terr La NG24 140 A8
Eastfield
 North Muskham NG23 110 F2
 North Wheatley DN22 31 E8
Eastfield Cl NG21 89 F2
Eastfield Ct NG25 136 C8
Eastfield Dr DE55 113 A5
Eastfield Meadow DN22 31 E8
Eastfield Pk NG22 66 B4
Eastfield Side NG17 101 A4
Eastgate
 Normanton on Trent NG23 81 E7
 Worksop S80 35 F3
East Gate S81 36 A3
Eastglade Rd NG5 161 A6
East Gr
 Bingham NG13 177 F4
 Nottingham NG7 173 A8
Eastham Cl NG3 173 E6
Eastham Rd NG5 162 C6
Eastholme Croft NG2 174 D5
Easthorpe NG25 136 F8
Easthorpe La NG13 192 F4
Easthorpe Rd NG13 181 C2
Easthorpe St NG11 196 C7
Easthorpe View NG13 181 C2
East La NG21 76 B2
Eastlands Jun Sch NG20 74 E8
Eastlands La NG20 74 B6
Eastland Terr NG20 74 E8
EAST LEAKE 205 E2
East Leake Acad LE12 205 F2
East Leake L Ctr LE12 205 F2
Eastleigh Dr NG19 88 B6
EAST MARKHAM 65 F7
East Markham Prim Sch
 East Markham NG22 65 F8
 East Markham NG22 66 A7
East Meadow Rd NG22 52 B1
East Midlands Designer Outlet NG17 113 E6
East Midlands Parkway NG11 203 F8
East Moor
 Cotgrave NG12 187 F2
 Cotgrave NG12 188 A1
Eastmoor Dr NG4 174 F8
East Rd
 Nottingham NG8 172 D2
 Willoughby-on-the-Wolds LE12 217 A6
 Wymeswold LE12 216 E4
East St
 Bingham NG13 177 F4
 Bole DN22 23 E3
 Gotham NG11 195 B1
 Harworth DN11 9 A5
 Heanor DE75 157 A8
 Long Eaton NG10 193 F8
 Market Warsop NG20 73 D5
 Nottingham NG1 223 F3
 Retford DN22 39 F6
 Sutton in Ashfield NG17 101 A3
EAST STOCKWITH 7 E1
EAST STOKE 153 D8
East View
 Bawtry DN10 10 A8
 East Markham NG22 65 F6
 Shirebrook NG20 72 F6
 West Bridgford NG2 185 D6
 Whaley Thornes NG20 59 A3
East View Cl NG17 115 C1
Eastwell St NG15 146 A8
East Wlk DN22 39 C8
Eastwold NG12 188 A2
EASTWOOD 143 E3
Eastwood Ave NG20 74 B5
Eastwood Cl NG15 145 E4
Eastwood Com Sports Ctr NG16 143 E3
Eastwood Ct
 Worksop S81 25 F1
 Worksop S81 35 F8
Eastwood La DN10 4 D3
Eastwood Rd
 Kimberley NG16 158 E6
 Radcliffe on Trent NG12 176 A3
Eastwood St NG6 160 C5
Easy Par S80 45 A5
Eather Ave NG19 88 C4
EATON 40 A1
Eaton Ave NG5 162 A7
Eaton Cl
 Beeston NG9 184 B6
 Farnsfield NG22 119 F6
 Rainworth NG21 118 A8
Eaton Ct 5 NG18 103 A3
Eaton Grange Dr NG10 193 A8
Eaton Hall DN22 40 A1
Eatons Rd NG9 182 D6
Eaton St NG3 161 F2
Eaton Terr NG3 161 F2
Eaton Wood Nature Reserve★ DN22 51 D8
Eaves La NG23 96 E8
Ebenezer St
 Ilkeston DE7 157 F3
 Langley Mill NG16 143 B3
Ebers Gr NG3 173 C8
Ebers Rd NG3 173 C8
Ebony Wlk NG3 174 B8
Ebury Rd NG5 161 B1
Eckington Terr 12 NG2 173 C1
Eckington Wlk NG18 103 B6
Eclipse Yd 3 NG18 102 B7
Ecton Cl NG5 146 F1
Edale Cl
 Hucknall NG15 145 C6
 Long Eaton NG10 193 B6
 Mansfield NG18 103 A3
Edale Ct NG17 100 E4
Edale Dr DE55 113 B7
Edale Rd
 Mansfield NG18 103 B6
 Nottingham NG2 174 A5
Edale Rise NG9 182 E3
Edale Rise Prim Sch NG2 174 A5
Edale Sq DE7 157 E5
Eddery View NG18 102 F7
Eddison Cl S81 36 A7
Eddison Pk Ave S81 35 E8
Eddleston Dr NG7 184 F1
Edelin Rd LE11 220 B1
Edenbridge Ct NG8 171 D2
Eden Cl
 Arnold NG5 162 A6
 Hucknall NG15 145 C6
Eden Ct DN22 39 E3
Edenhall Cl NG22 66 A2
Edenhall Gdns NG7 184 F2
Eden Low NG19 88 E3
Eden Wlk NG13 177 D3
Edern Cl NG5 161 A7
Edern Gdns 9 NG5 161 A7
Edgar Ave NG18 102 C8
Edgbaston Dr DN22 39 E5
Edgbaston Gdns 1 NG8 172 D8
Edgcote Way NG5 161 A6
Edge Cl NG23 110 F4
Edge Hill Ct NG10 193 D4
Edgehill Dr NG24 140 E8
Edgehill Gr NG19 88 C2
Edge Way NG8 159 D1
Edgewood Dr NG15 145 D5
Edgewood Leisure Centre NG15 145 D4
Edgewood Prim Sch NG15 145 C4
Edgewood Rd NG16 158 F6
Edgington Cl NG12 188 A1
Edginton St NG3 173 F7
Edgware Rd NG6 160 D7
Edinbane Cl NG5 146 F1
Edinboro Row NG16 158 E7
Edinburgh Dr NG13 177 D5
Edinburgh Rd
 Worksop S80 36 B1
 Worksop S80 47 B8
Edinburgh Wlk S80 47 A8
Edingale Ct NG9 171 B4
EDINGLEY 120 C4
Edingley Ave
 Mansfield NG19 101 D7
 Nottingham NG5 161 C4
Edingley Hill NG22 120 D4
Edingley Sq NG5 161 B3
Edison Rise NG22 77 C4
Edison St NG17 114 F1
Edison Way NG5 162 C7
Edlington Dr NG8 171 C3
Edmond Gr NG15 146 C7
Edmonds Cl NG5 147 A2
Edmonstone Cres 2 NG5 160 F5
Edmonton Ct NG2 185 D6
Edmonton Rd NG21 89 E2
Edna G Olds Main Sch NG7 222 B1
Ednaston Rd NG7 172 D1
Edwald Rd NG12 186 B3
Edwaltam Ave NG2 185 E7
EDWALTON 186 B3
Edwalton Cl NG12 186 B3
Edwalton Ct
 4 Mansfield NG18 103 A3
 Nottingham NG6 160 E6
Edwalton Lodge Cl NG12 186 A3
Edwalton Prim Sch NG12 186 C4
Edward Ave
 Newark-on-Trent NG24 139 E8
 Nottingham NG8 172 D8
 Sutton in Ashfield NG17 100 E4
 Westwood NG16 128 B4
Edward Cl NG15 145 D4
Edward Jermyn Dr NG24 125 B4
Edward Rd
 Eastwood NG16 144 A2
 Gainsborough DN21 15 D1
 Long Eaton NG10 193 D8
 Nuthall NG16 159 C5
 West Bridgford NG2 185 F8
Edwards Ct S80 35 D3
Edwards La NG5 161 C5
Edward St
 Aldercar NG16 143 B3
 Kirkby-in-Ashfield NG17 115 B6
 Stapleford NG9 182 D7
 Worksop S80 35 F4
Edwin St
 Arnold NG5 161 D6
 Sutton in Ashfield NG17 100 E3
EDWINSTOWE 76 A1
Edwinstowe Dr
 Nottingham NG5 161 C4
 Selston NG16 129 B7
Edwinstowe Rd NG21 91 C7
Eel La NG22 79 C2
Eel Pool Rd DN10 11 E1
Eelwood Rd NG15 145 D4
Egerton Cl NG18 103 A7
Egerton Dr NG9 170 D2
Egerton Rd NG5 161 E4
Egerton St NG3 173 C7
Egerton Wlk 2 NG3 173 C7
Egham Cl NG21 104 C1
Egling Croft NG4 174 F4
EGMANTON 79 E6
Egmanton Rd
 Egmanton NG22 79 E8
 Kirton NG22 78 D7
 Laxton NG22 79 D3
 Mansfield NG18 103 A3
 Meden Vale NG20 74 D7
 Tuxford NG22 65 E1
Egmont Ct 1 NG2 173 C1
Egypt Rd NG7 160 F1
Eider Cl NG20 72 D3
Eider Rd NG4 175 C7
Eighth Ave
 Beeston NG9 184 C5
 Mansfield NG19 103 A8
Eileen Rd NG9 184 A3
Eisele Cl NG6 159 F6
Ekowe St NG7 160 F2
Eland Rd NG20 72 F5
Eland St NG7 160 F1
Elder Cl
 Arnold NG5 148 A1
 1 Edwalton NG12 186 A1
Elder Ct
 Clipstone NG21 89 F5
 Forest Town NG19 89 B1
Elderfield Dr NG17 114 F8
Elder Gdns 8 NG5 161 A8
Elder Gr NG15 146 B4
Elder Pl 3 S81 35 A7
Elder St
 Kirkby-in-Ashfield NG17 114 E6
 Sutton in Ashfield NG17 100 E7
Eldon Gn NG22 65 F3
Eldon Rd NG9 183 C1
Eldon St
 Newark-on-Trent NG24 139 F7
 Tuxford NG22 65 F3
Eleanor Ave DE7 170 A5
Eleanor Cres NG9 182 F7
Electric Ave NG11 185 A8
Eley Cl DE7 157 C2
Elford Rise NG3 173 F5
Elgar Dr NG10 193 B5
Elgar Gdns NG3 173 F7
Eliot Cl
 Gainsborough DN21 24 F7
 Long Eaton NG10 193 B5
Eliot Wlk NG11 195 C8
Elizabethan Academy The DN22 29 D1
Elizabethan Gdns DN22 39 D6
Elizabeth Cl
 Gainsborough DN21 15 C3
 Hucknall NG15 145 E5
Elizabeth Ct DE7 157 D1
Elizabeth Dr
 East Leake LE12 214 E7
 Edwalton NG12 186 A2
Elizabeth Gr NG4 162 E2
Elizabeth Rd
 Beeston NG9 183 A3
 Newark-on-Trent NG24 139 E5
ELKESLEY 50 B3
Elkesley Bridge DN22 48 F4
Elkesley Bridge Rd DN22 50 A4
Elkesley Ind Est DN22 50 C4
Elkesley Prim Sch DN22 50 A3
Elkesley Rd NG20 74 E8
Ella Bank Rd DE75 143 A1
Ella Rd NG2 173 F1
Ellastone Ave NG5 161 C8
Ellerby Ave NG7 184 E2
Ellerslie Cl NG24 125 A1
Ellerslie Gr NG10 182 A5
Ellesmere Bsns Pk NG5 161 B2
Ellesmere Cl NG5 162 B7
Ellesmere Dr NG9 170 C5
Ellesmere Rd
 Mansfield NG18 102 F8
 West Bridgford NG2 185 F4
Ellington Rd
 Arnold NG5 147 F2
 Arnold NG5 148 A2
Elliott Cl DN22 39 F5
Elliott Dr NG4 163 C1
Elliott Durhamcres NG5 161 E1
Elliott St NG7 222 C3
Ellis Ave NG15 146 B6
Ellis Cl NG10 193 C6
Ellis Ct NG3 223 F4
Ellis Gr NG9 183 F5
Ellis Guilford Sch & Sports Coll NG6 160 C2
Ellis St NG17 115 B5
Ellsworth Rise NG5 160 F6
Ellwood Cres NG8 172 A5
Elma La NG20 59 D6
Elm Ave
 Beeston, Attenborough NG9 183 D2
 Beeston, Chilwell NG9 183 E6
 Bingham NG13 178 A4
 Carlton NG4 174 F7
 East Leake LE12 205 F3
 Hucknall NG15 145 E5
 Keyworth NG12 197 F2
 Long Eaton NG10 193 C8
 Newark-on-Trent NG24 140 B6
 Nottingham NG3 173 C7
 Nuthall NG16 159 B6
 Sandiacre NG10 182 B7
Elm Bank NG3 173 C8
Elm Bank Dr NG3 173 C8
Elmbridge NG5 161 B7
Elm Cl
 Keyworth NG12 197 F2
 Newark-on-Trent NG24 140 B6
 Nottingham NG3 173 C7
 Pinxton NG16 113 D2
 Saxilby LN1 57 B4
Elmcroft NG25 134 B3
Elm Croft DN11 8 A8
Elmdale Gdns NG8 172 B8
Elm Dr NG4 174 F7
Elmfield NG20 74 A3
Elm Gr
 Arnold NG5 148 A1
 Church Warsop NG20 74 A6
Elmhurst Ave
 Nottingham NG3 162 C2
 South Normanton DE55 113 A4
Elmhurst Cl DE55 113 A4
Elmhurst Dr NG17 100 A3
Elmhurst Rd NG19 88 F1
Elmore Ct NG7 222 B4
Elmore's Mdw NG14 152 A8
Elms Cl
 Rempstone LE12 215 D5
 Ruddington NG11 196 D6
Elmsdale Gdns NG14 163 F4
Elmsfield Ave DE75 143 A2
Elms Gdns NG11 196 C6
Elms Gr LE11 220 C3
Elmsham Ave NG5 146 E1
Elms Jun Sch The NG10 193 C8
Elmsmere Dr
 Oldcotes S81 16 F6
 Oldcotes S81 17 A6
Elms Pk NG11 196 D6
Elms Rd S80 35 F4
Elms The
 Carlton NG4 174 F6
 Watnall NG16 158 F8
Elmsthorpe Ave NG7 222 A2
Elmswood Gdns NG5 161 D3
ELMTON 58 A7
Elmton Cl S80 58 D8
Elmton Rd S80 58 D8
Elmtree Ave NG16 128 F7
Elm Tree Ave
 Mansfield Woodhouse NG19 88 A4
 Shirebrook NG20 72 D4
 West Bridgford NG2 185 D7
Elmtree Cl S81 34 F7
Elm Tree Ct S80 35 F2
Elm Tree Dr DN10 9 F7
Elm Tree Pl DN22 50 B4
Elmtree Rd NG14 148 D7
Elm Tree Rd NG17 114 F6
Elm Tree Rise NG22 93 E5
Elm Tree St NG18 102 C7
Elm Wlk DN22 40 A5
Elmwood Cl DN22 30 A1
Elmwood Ct S80 35 B2
Elnor St NG16 143 C3
Elsham Wlk DN21 24 F8
Elson St NG7 172 F8
ELSTON 153 E5
Elston Gdns NG11 184 E4
Elston Hall NG23 153 D4
Elston La
 Cotham NG23 154 F2
 Cotham NG23 168 E8
 East Stoke NG23 153 C7
 Elston NG23 153 D6
Elston Mws NG4 174 A8
Elston Rd NG23 168 D7
Elswick Cl NG5 161 B8
Elswick Dr NG9 184 C4
Elterwater Dr NG2 186 C6
Eltham Cl NG8 159 F3
Eltham Dr NG8 160 A2
Eltham Rd NG2 186 A7
Elton Cl
 Balderton NG24 140 D3
 Mansfield NG18 103 B6
 Stapleford NG9 182 D8
Elton & Orston Sta NG13 180 A5
Elton Rd
 Mansfield NG18 102 F6
 3 Nottingham NG5 161 B1
Elton Rd N NG5 161 A1
Elton Terr NG7 172 F7
Elvaston Ct NG18 103 B6
Elvaston Dr NG10 193 A4
Elvaston Rd NG8 172 B5
Elveden Dr DE7 157 C3
Elwin Dr NG8 171 C1
Ely Cl
 Mansfield Woodhouse NG19 88 D4
 Worksop S80 36 A2
Embankment Cl NG20 72 E3
Embley Rd NG5 161 A5
Emerald Cl NG19 87 F1
Emerald Gr NG17 115 C4
Emerys Rd NG4 175 B8
Emma Bates Way NG21 118 B6
Emmanuel Ave
 Nottingham, Portchester NG3 162 A1
 Nottingham, Rise Park NG5 147 A1
Emmendingen Av NG24 125 B3
Emmerson Dr
 Clipstone NG21 89 F4
 Clipstone NG21 90 A4
 Clipstone NG21 90 A5
Emneth Cl NG3 173 F8
Emperor Cl 9 NG5 161 A1
Empingham Cl NG9 183 B2
Empire St NG18 102 D6
Empire Way NG8 172 B7
Empress Rd LE11 220 D4
Emsworth Ave DN22 29 E1
Emsworth Cl DE7 157 D3
Ena Ave NG2 173 F5
Enderby Cres
 Gainsborough DN21 24 E7
 Mansfield NG18 102 F6
Enderby Gdns NG5 147 E1
Enderby Sq NG9 183 F8
Endor Rd NG18 102 F1
Endsleigh Gdns
 Beeston NG9 183 F7
 West Bridgford NG12 186 A4
Enfield Ct NG23 70 D2
Enfield St NG9 183 E7
Engineers Ct LE11 220 B6
Engine La NG16 144 B4
Engine Rd NG16 144 B4
England Cres DE75 143 A2
English Martyrs' CV Acad NG10 182 B1
Ennerdale Cl NG2 186 C7
Ennerdale Rd
 Long Eaton NG10 182 B2
 Nottingham NG5 161 D5
Ennismore Mews NG11 185 C2
Enright Cl NG24 139 F6
Enterprise Bsns Ctr S81 35 F8
Enterprise Cl NG21 118 A6

Enterprise Rd
Old Dalby LE14 219 B4
Pleasley NG19 87 D2
Enterprise Way
Heanor NG16 143 C2
3 Mansfield NG19 87 E2
Nottingham NG2 173 A2
Retford DN22 39 F5
Enterprise Wy NG21 118 A6
Enthorpe St 4 NG8 172 B6
Epinal Way LE11 220 A1
EPPERSTONE 150 A6
Epperstone By-pass
Epperstone NG14 150 B4
Woodborough NG14 149 E5
Epperstone Ct 14
NG18 103 A2
Epperstone Rd
Lowdham NG14 150 D2
Oxton NG25 134 C1
West Bridgford NG2 185 E8
Epping Way NG19 103 B8
Epsom Rd NG9 182 E3
Epsom St NG18 102 F6
Erdington Way NG9 182 E3
Erewash Ct DE7 157 D1
Erewash Dr DE7 170 B6
Erewash Gdns NG5 161 A8
Erewash Gr NG9 182 F2
Erewash Meadows Nature Reserve★
Aldercar NG16 143 B8
Jacksdale NG16 128 B1
Erewash Rd NG16 113 E2
Erewash Sq DE7 170 A6
Erewash St
Kirkby-in-Ashfield NG17 115 A5
Long Eaton NG10 193 E8
Pye Bridge DE55 128 A6
Erica Dr DE55 113 B7
Eric Ave NG15 130 F1
Erith Cl NG8 159 D1
Ernehale Jun & Inf Sch
NG5 162 A6
Ernest Rd NG4 162 B1
Ernie White Cl LN1 56 F5
Erskine Rd 4 NG5 161 B1
Esam Cl NG22 120 A5
Esher Gr NG3 161 C1
Eshton Rise
Austerfield DN10 3 A1
Bawtry DN10 10 A8
Eskdale Cl
Long Eaton NG10 193 B5
Mansfield NG18 102 F5
Eskdale Ct NG2 186 C7
Eskdale Dr
Beeston NG9 183 B5
Nottingham NG8 172 B8
Worksop S81 35 E8
Eskdale Jun Sch NG9 183 B5
Eskhouse Cl NG2 186 C4
Eskil Way DN22 50 A4
Essex Dr DN11 9 D4
Essex Rd DN11 9 D4
Essex St
2 Eastwood NG16 143 F2
2 Ilkeston DE7 157 F1
Estfeld Cl DN11 8 A8
Esther Varney Pl
Newark-on-Trent NG24 125 B1
2 Newark-on-Trent NG24 140 B8
Estwic Ave NG16 143 F3
Ethel Ave
Hucknall NG15 131 C1
Nottingham NG3 162 A1
Ethelbert Ave NG17 115 C1
Etheldene NG12 189 B4
Ethel Rd NG2 185 F7
Etherington St DN21 24 D8
Eton Cl
Newark-on-Trent NG24 139 F6
Nottingham NG8 172 D7
Eton Ct NG24 139 E6
Eton Gr NG8 172 B4
Eton Pl NG12 185 E5
Eton Rd NG2 185 E6
Eucalyptus Ave NG11 184 C1
Eugene Gdns NG2 173 D2
Eugene St NG2 223 F1
Europa Way NG2 185 C3
Euston Wlk NG19 88 C6
Evans Ave NG17 100 C3
Evans Cl NG23 156 D7
Evans Rd
East Leake LE12 214 E7
Nottingham NG6 160 D3
Evedon Wlk NG5 147 B1
Evelyn St
Beeston NG9 184 B7
11 Nottingham NG2 173 E4
Eversley Wlk NG5 161 B8
EVERTON 11 C3
Everton Prim Sch DN10 11 B3
Everton Sluice La DN10 11 C4
Everton St NG19 87 E1
Evesham Ct NG9 183 A1
Evesham Mews 7 S80 35 F2
Ewart Rd NG7 173 A8
Ewe Lamb Cl NG9 170 F1
Ewe Lamb La NG9 170 F1
Ewell Rd NG8 171 E5
Exbourne Rd NG8 159 F1
Exbury Gdns NG2 185 B4
Excalibur Wlk 8 NG19 87 D1
Exchange Arc NG1 223 E2
Exchange Rd NG2 185 F7
Exchange Row 13
NG18 102 B7
Exchange St DN22 39 E7
Exchange Wlk NG1 223 E2
Exe Fold NG19 88 D2
Exeter Cl
Carlton NG4 162 F2
East Leake LE12 205 D1
Exeter Rd
Nottingham NG7 173 A8
West Bridgford NG2 185 F6
Exford Ct NG19 88 C6
Experian Wy NG2 173 A1
Explore Way S80 34 D1
Export Dr NG17 113 F8
Exton Rd NG5 161 A3
Eyam Cl
Beeston NG9 171 C2
Mansfield NG18 103 B6
Eyres Cl NG17 100 F6
Eyre's Gdns DE7 157 F2
Eyres La NG11 205 A8
Eyre's La LN6 83 E3
Eyre St NG2 173 E4

F

Fabis Dr NG11 184 E4
Fackley Rd NG17 100 C6
Fackley Way NG17 100 C6
Factory La
Beeston NG9 183 E5
Ilkeston DE7 157 E2
Factory Rd NG17 115 A5
Factory St 2 LE11 220 C3
Factory Yd NG17 101 A4
Failsworth Cl NG11 184 E3
Fairbank Cres NG5 161 D2
Fairburn Cl NG8 171 C4
Fairburn Cres NG12 186 A3
Fairburn Wy NG16 159 A7
Faircroft Ave NG10 182 B5
Fairdale Dr NG16 144 B2
Fairfax Cl
Gainsborough DN21 24 F6
Nottingham NG7 160 F2
Fairfield DN22 39 E3
Fairfield Ave
Farndon NG24 139 A5
Hilcote DE55 99 C1
New Balderton NG24 140 C5
Fairfield Cl
Nether Langwith NG20 59 A2
Nottingham NG11 185 B5
Fairfield Cres NG10 193 A4
Fairfield Dr
Mansfield NG18 103 A7
Ravenshead NG15 116 C3
Fairfield Prep Sch
LE11 220 B3
Fairfield Prim Sch
NG9 182 D6
Fairfield Rd NG17 101 B3
Fairfield St NG13 177 E4
Fairham Ave NG11 195 B1
Fairham Brook La
Bunny NG11 206 F7
Bunny NG11 207 A7
Fairham Cl NG11 196 B8
Fairham Dr NG8 172 D4
Fairham Rd NG12 197 D3
Fairhaven NG17 115 B3
Fairholme Cl NG21 89 F2
Fairholme Dr
Mansfield NG19 87 E1
Mansfield NG19 101 F8
Fairisle Cl NG11 185 A1
Fairland Cres NG2 185 D4
Fairlawn Pl NG5 161 D2
Fairlawns NG18 103 B7
Fair Lea Cl NG10 193 D6
Fairlie Ave NG19 101 D5
Fairlight Way NG5 161 B7
Fairmaid Gr NG7 184 E2
Fairmead Cl NG3 174 A8
Fairnley Rd NG8 171 D8
Fair Vale NG23 110 A8
Fair View NG19 89 A2
Fairview Ave
Selston NG16 128 F2
Underwood NG16 129 A1
Fairview Ct NG11 185 D2
Fairview Rd NG5 161 E4
Fairway
Keyworth NG12 198 A2
Newark-on-Trent NG24 139 D5
Retford DN22 39 D4
Fairway Cres NG13 177 B8
Fairway Dr
Beeston NG9 183 D6
Nottingham NG4 174 C8
Nottingham NG6 160 D7
Fairways Dr NG17 114 F7
Fairways The
Mansfield Woodhouse NG19 88 D6
Torksey LN1 44 C2
Fairway The NG4 162 E3
Fairweather Cl NG22 77 F5
Falcon Cl
Eagle LN6 84 D3
Nottingham NG7 222 A2
Falcon Ct DE7 157 D1
Falcon Dr NG17 115 D6
Falconers Wlk
7 Arnold NG5 161 C8
Nottingham NG5 161 D8
Falcon Gr
7 Gainsborough DN21 15 F1
Falcon Gr *continued*
Nottingham NG7 161 A1
Falcon St
Loughborough LE11 220 C5
6 Nottingham NG7 161 A1
Falcon Way
East Leake LE12 205 F3
Papplewick NG15 131 D1
Falconwood Gdns
NG11 184 C1
Fallow Cl
Nottingham NG7 184 E2
Retford DN22 29 E1
Fallow Croft LN1 57 A5
Fallow Ct S81 36 B7
Fallow Way NG18 102 E1
Fal Paddock NG19 88 D2
Falstone Ave NG24 140 B6
Falston Rd NG8 172 A7
Faraday Ave NG22 66 A3
Faraday Cl
Harworth DN11 8 F3
New Ollerton NG22 77 C3
Faraday Ct NG9 170 E1
Faraday Rd
Mansfield NG18 102 E5
Nottingham NG7 222 A2
Far Back La NG22 119 F6
Far Clay Gr S81 34 F7
Far Croft Ave NG17 100 C3
Far Dales Rd DE7 157 E2
Farfield Ave NG9 183 E8
Farfield Gr NG9 183 E8
Farfield Rd DE7 170 A8
Farhill La NG22 68 A7
Far Holme La
Sutton on Trent NG23 97 A8
Sutton-on-Trent NG23 97 B7
Far La LE12 213 D3
Farleigh Dr
1 Harworth DN11 8 F5
Harworth DN11 9 A5
Farleys Gr NG15 146 A5
Farleys La NG15 146 A5
Farley St NG6 160 B7
Farm Ave NG15 145 D4
Farm Cl
Bathley NG23 110 B3
East Bridgford NG13 165 D3
Ilkeston DE7 170 A8
Long Eaton NG10 193 E5
North Leverton with Habblesthorpe DN22 32 C1
Nottingham NG7 184 E2
Farm Croft Rd NG19 88 C6
Farm Ct NG20 59 A1
Farmers Branch S81 36 A7
Farmers Cl NG17 100 A1
Farmer St NG11 196 E3
Farmers Wlk NG24 125 C4
Farm Gr S81 36 B7
Farmhouse Cl NG13 181 A3
Farmilo Cres NG19 87 E1
Farmilo Prim Sch NG19 87 C4
Farm La
East Markham NG22 65 F7
Hardstoft S45 85 A2
Farm Rd
Arnold NG5 162 B7
Beeston NG9 183 D5
Farmstead The NG23 96 F4
Farm View DN22 39 E3
Farm View Rd NG17 115 C5
Farmway NG19 88 C2
Farnborough Acad The
NG11 185 A2
Farnborough Rd NG11 185 A2
Farndale S81 36 B7
Farndale Cl
Long Eaton NG10 193 A5
Sutton in Ashfield NG17 100 F5
Farndale Dr NG8 171 B4
Farndale Rd NG17 100 F5
FARNDON 139 B4
Farndon Dr NG9 182 F3
Farndon Gn NG8 172 C3
Farndon Gr S81 35 D7
Farndon La NG24 139 C2
Farndon Mws NG4 174 B8
Farndon Ponds Nature Reserve★ NG24 138 F6
Farndon Rd
Newark-on-Trent NG24, NG23 139 D6
Sutton in Ashfield NG17 101 D1
Farndon Way NG19 101 E7
Farndon Willow Holt Nature Reserve★
NG24 138 F5
Farnes Ct S81 36 B5
Far New Cl NG10 182 B5
Farnham Rd 1 LE11 220 B1
FARNSFIELD 119 E6
Farnsfield Ave NG14 164 A5
Farnsfield Ct 15 NG18 103 A2
Farnsfield Rd
Bilsthorpe NG22 105 F3
Bilsthorpe NG22 106 A4
Farnsfield St Michael's CE Prim VA Sch NG22 119 F7
Farnsworth Ave NG21 103 E2
Farnsworth Cl NG16 145 A1
Farnsworth Gr NG17 99 F3
Far Pasture Cl NG12 197 E2
Farrar Cl NG24 125 C2
Far Rd NG22 67 D4
Farrendale Cl NG19 88 D1
Farriers Croft DE7 157 C3
Farriers Gn NG11 184 C2
Farringdon Cl NG8 159 D3
Farrington Wy NG16 143 E1
Farr Way NG21 118 A4
Far Rye NG8 171 F6
Far St
Bradmore NG11 196 E3
Wymeswold LE12 216 C4
Farthingate NG25 136 F8
Farthingate Cl NG25 136 F8
Farthing Ct NG10 193 B7
Farthings The LE12 213 A1
Farthing Way 1 NG18 102 E1
Farwells Cl NG6 160 C3
Far Wood Cl DE7 157 E4
Faulconbridge Cl NG6 160 B6
Fawcett St DN21 15 C1
Fay Dr 8 LE11 220 C3
Fearn Chase NG4 174 E7
Fearn Cl DE72 193 A7
Fearnleigh Dr NG6 160 D2
Fearon Cl NG14 164 F5
Featherbed La S80 34 F1
Featherfield Pl NG9 182 D7
Featherston Ave S80 36 B2
Featherstone Cl
Carlton NG4 162 D3
Mansfield NG18 101 D4
Feignes Ct NG12 197 E3
Feilding Way DN21 15 E1
Felen Cl NG5 161 A7
Fellbarrow Cl NG2 186 C5
Fell Croft NG24 139 A5
Felley Ave NG17 114 E1
Felley Mill La N NG16 129 C2
Felley Mill La S NG16 129 B1
Felley Priory Gdn★
NG16 129 C3
Fellows Rd NG9 183 E7
Fellows Way NG9 184 D8
Fellows Yd NG12 197 E7
Fell Side NG5 162 A5
Fellside Cl NG2 186 C6
Fell Wilson St NG20 74 C4
Felly Cl NG15 145 E5
Felly Mill La S NG16 129 B1
Felstead Ct NG9 171 C1
Felton Ave NG19 88 C6
Felton Cl NG9 183 B5
Felton Rd NG2 173 D1
Felton Way NG5 147 F2
Fenchurch Cl NG5 147 A1
Fen Cl DE55 99 A3
Fenimore Ct NG12 176 B3
Fenton Ct NG5 162 E5
Fen La
Balderton NG23 155 D3
Balderton NG24 141 A4
Fennec Dr S81 35 B7
Fennel St LE11 220 B4
Fenroth Cl NG6 159 F8
FENTON
Balderton 142 D2
Saxilby 55 D6
Fenton Cl NG24 125 B2
Fenton Dr NG6 146 C2
Fenton Fields LN1 55 D6
Fenton Rd
Fenton NG23 142 D1
Nottingham NG5 160 F4
Fenwick Cl NG8 159 F2
Fenwick Rd NG8 159 F2
Fenwick St NG20 74 B4
Ferguson Ave NG19 88 B4
Ferguson Cl 1 NG9 183 C2
Fern Ave 7 NG5 161 B1
Fern Bank Ave NG22 64 A1
Fern Cl
Beeston NG9 183 C7
Bilsthorpe NG22 106 A5
Ravenshead NG15 117 B1
Ravenshead NG15 132 B8
Shirebrook NG20 72 E6
Southwell NG25 121 D1
Fern Cres NG16 143 D3
Ferndale 6 NG18 102 C5
Ferndale Cl
Beeston NG9 183 E2
New Ollerton NG22 77 E6
Ferndale Gr NG3 174 B6
Ferndale Rd NG3 174 B6
Ferndene Dr NG10 193 A7
Ferndown Dr 6 DE55 99 B7
Ferngill Cl 2 NG2 173 B1
Fernhill Rd NG12 189 D4
Fern Lea Ave NG12 187 E2
Fernleigh Ave NG3 162 B2
Fernleigh Rise NG19 88 D1
Fern Rd
Cropwell Bishop NG12 189 A3
Cropwell Bishop NG12 189 B3
Hathern LE12 212 F1
Ferns Meadows DN22 42 C8
Fern St NG17 100 E4
Fernwood Bsns Pk
NG24 140 E1
Fernwood Cl NG19 89 A1
Fernwood Comp Sch
NG8 171 D4
Fernwood Cres NG8 171 D4
Fernwood Dr NG12 175 F4
Fernwood Prim Sch
NG8 171 D4
Ferny Hollow Cl NG5 160 E8
Ferous Cl NG11 195 F8
Ferrers Wlk NG3 173 E5
Ferriby Terr 13 NG2 173 C1
Ferry Farm Ctry Pk★
NG14 151 E1
Ferryla LN1 56 B2
Ferry La
Carlton-on-Trent NG23 96 F5
Carlton-on-Trent NG23 97 A5
Everton DN10 11 C3
Ferry La *continued*
Kettlethorpe LN1 55 F4
North Muskham NG23 110 F2
Ferryman Rd
Loughborough LE11 220 C5
2 West Bridgford NG2 185 A6
Festival Ave DN11 9 A4
Festival Cres NG9 170 C4
Festival Dr LE11 220 A6
Festival Hall L Ctr
NG17 115 A4
Festus Cl NG3 223 F4
Festus St
Carlton NG4 175 A7
Kirkby-in-Ashfield NG17 115 A4
Fewster Gdns NG13 177 D6
Field Ave
Hucknall NG15 145 D4
Saxilby LN1 57 A5
Field Cl
Beeston NG9 183 B4
Carlton NG4 162 F2
Mansfield Woodhouse NG19 88 D5
Worksop S81 36 A7
Field Dr NG20 72 E2
Fielden Ave NG19 87 D2
Field End Cl LE12 205 C1
Fieldfare Cl
Beeston NG9 183 C6
East Leake LE12 205 F3
Fieldfare Dr S81 35 C7
Field Farm Way NG9 170 E2
Field House Cl NG8 171 D5
Fieldings The NG17 100 B2
Field La
Ault Hucknall NG19, S44 86 C6
Beeston NG9 183 B4
Blidworth NG21 117 F3
Cropwell Bishop NG12 189 A4
Morton DN21 15 A4
Widmerpool NG11 208 C4
Woodborough NG14 149 C4
Wroot DN9 2 B8
Field Maple Dr NG7 172 E8
Field Pl NG17 114 D8
Fields Ave NG11 196 C5
Fields Dr NG13 178 F5
Fields End DN10 6 E1
Fields Farm Rd NG10 193 E5
Fields The NG21 104 C1
Fields View NG12 187 E4
Field The DE75 157 A6
Field View
Radcliffe on Trent NG12 176 C4
Saxilby LN1 57 A5
South Normanton DE55 113 A7
Sutton in Ashfield NG17 100 C1
Field View Cl NG16 128 C4
Fieldway NG11 185 B4
Fieldwork Rd LE14 219 A5
Fiennes Cres NG7 222 C1
Fifth Ave
Beeston NG9 184 D6
Clipstone NG21 89 F3
Edwinstowe NG21 75 F2
Mansfield NG19 103 A8
Fiftyeights Rd DN10 1 D3
Fig Tree Prim Sch
NG7 222 B4
Filigree Cl DE55 113 D7
Finch Cl NG7 184 F8
Finchley Cl NG11 184 C1
Findern Ct NG18 103 B6
Findern Gn NG3 174 A6
Fingal Cl NG7 184 E2
Fingle St DN22 32 D1
Fingleton S81 36 B6
Finkell St DN10 12 F3
Finley Way DE55 113 B4
Finney La DN22 51 E1
Finningley Rd NG18 103 A3
Finsbury Ave
4 Loughborough LE11 220 C3
Nottingham NG2 173 F4
Finsbury Pk Cl NG2 185 C5
Finsbury Rd
Beeston NG9 171 C3
Nottingham NG5 147 A2
Firbank Ct NG9 183 B4
FIRBECK 16 A6
Firbeck Acad NG8 171 B4
Firbeck Ave NG18 102 F5
Firbeck Cres S81 16 F3
Firbeck Rd
Arnold NG5 162 A8
Nottingham NG8 171 C4
Fir Cl
HUCKNALL NG15 146 B4
Nottingham NG6 159 F7
Shirebrook NG20 72 E6
Fircroft Ave NG8 171 F8
Fircroft Dr NG15 145 C5
Fir Dale NG12 188 A3
Firecrest Way NG6 160 D3
Firefly Cl NG13 177 B7
Firemen's Row NG17 100 E2
Firmin Way NG12 185 B4
Firs Ave NG9 183 F7
Firsby Rd NG8 159 F2
Firs La S81 27 E3
Firs Rd NG12 186 B4
Firs St NG10 193 A4
First Ave
Beeston NG9 184 C6
Carlton, Colwick NG4 174 E5
Carlton, Gedling NG4 162 F1
Carlton, Thorneywood NG4 174 C8
Clipstone NG21 90 A3
First Ave *continued*
Edwinstowe NG21 76 A2
Mansfield NG21 103 F2
Mansfield Woodhouse NG19 89 A1
Nottingham NG6 160 B7
Firs The 1 NG5 161 D3
First Holme La NG23 97 A8
First Oak Dr
Clipstone NG21 90 A4
Mansfield NG21 89 F5
Firth Cl
Arnold NG5 148 C1
East Leake LE12 205 E3
Firth Dr NG9 183 C2
Firth Rd DN22 39 C8
Firth Way NG6 146 A1
Fir Tree Cl NG19 89 D2
Fir View NG22 77 D5
Fisher Ave NG5 161 F5
Fisher Cl
Collingham NG23 98 B1
East Leake LE12 205 F2
Sutton in Ashfield NG17 100 D5
Fisher Ct DE7 157 F4
Fisher Gate NG1 223 F2
Fisher La
Bingham NG13 177 E4
Mansfield NG18 102 C5
Fishers St NG17 115 A1
Fisher St 4 NG7 172 F8
Fish Pond Dr NG7 223 D1
Fishpool Rd NG21 117 D3
FISKERTON 137 E3
Fiskerton Ct 6 NG18 103 A3
Fiskerton Rd
Bleasby NG25 152 D8
Fiskerton NG25 137 D1
Rolleston NG23 138 B5
Southwell NG25 137 A6
Fiskerton Sta NG25 137 E4
Fitzgerald Ct NG15 146 A6
Fitzherbert St NG20 74 C4
Fitzwilliam Dr 2 NG19 88 F2
Five Acres NG11 185 A4
Five Fields Cl DN22 40 A4
Five Fields La DN22 40 A4
Flagholme NG12 187 F2
Flagstaff Rd LE14 219 A5
Flamingo Ct 5 NG2 173 A2
Flamstead Ave NG4 163 B7
Flamstead Rd DE7 157 F1
Flamsteed Rd NG8 159 D1
Flanders Cl NG19 87 F1
Flash La NG22 93 B7
Flat La S81 16 A6
Flatts La
Calverton NG14 133 E1
Westwood NG16 128 D3
Flatts The NG9 183 B5
FLAWBOROUGH 168 C2
Flawborough La NG13 191 E4
Flawborough Rd NG13 168 E1
Flawborough Rise
NG2 185 B3
Flawforth Ave NG11 196 D6
Flawforth La NG11 196 E7
Flaxendale NG12 188 A2
Flaxley La NG24 140 A4
Flaxton Way NG5 160 F7
Fleam Rd NG11 184 E4
FLEDBOROUGH 68 C5
Fledgling Cl LN6 84 D3
Fleeman Gr NG2 174 A1
Fleet Cl NG7 172 D6
Fleet La NG23 97 F7
Fleetway S81 35 E7
Fleetway Cl NG16 144 B1
Fleetwith Cl NG2 186 C5
Fleming Ave
Bottesford NG13 181 C3
Tuxford NG22 66 A3
Fleming Cl NG16 159 A8
Fleming Dr
Carlton NG4 174 C7
Newark-on-Trent NG24 125 B4
Woodbeck DN22 53 B8
Fleming Gdns NG11 184 C1
Fletcher Ct NG22 119 F7
Fletcher Gate NG1 223 E2
Fletcher Rd NG9 184 A7
Fletcher St NG10 193 D8
Fletcher Terr NG3 161 E2
Fletcher Way NG19 103 B8
Flewitt Gdns NG3 173 E6
Flinders Orch NG12 197 E2
Flint Ave
Forest Town NG19 89 A1
Mansfield Woodhouse NG19 88 F1
FLINTHAM 153 A1
Flintham Dr NG5 161 C4
Flintham La
Screveton NG13 166 E5
Sibthorpe NG23 167 D8
Flintham Mus★ NG23 153 A1
Flintham Prim Sch
NG23 153 A1
Flixton Rd NG16 158 F7
Flood Rd Old Section The
DN10 23 E7
Flood Rd The
Gainsborough DN21 24 B7
Saundby DN10 23 E7
Floralands Gdn Village★
NG4 162 E8
Floral Villas NG23 96 F7
Florence Ave NG10 182 F1
Florence Boot Cl NG9 184 B8
Florence Cl NG19 86 F4
Florence Cres NG4 175 B8

Florence Ct DE7 157 F1
Florence Gr NG3 174 A7
Florence Rd
Carlton NG4 175 B8
Nottingham NG3 162 A1
West Bridgford NG2 186 A8
Florence St NG15 146 A5
Florence Terr DN21 24 F2
Florey Ct 1 NG7 172 E2
Florey Wlk NG11 195 C8
Florin Gdns NG10 193 A7
Florin Way NG18 102 E1
Floss La DN22 43 D4
Floss Mill La DN21 15 B3
Flower Ave NG12 176 B5
Flowers Cl NG5 162 B6
Flying Bedstead Way NG6 145 E2
Flying High Acad The NG19 101 D8
Flying Horse Wlk NG1 223 E2
Focus Sch (Long Eaton Campus) NG10 182 C2
Foley Pl 11 S80 35 F1
Foljambe Terr NG3 223 F3
Folkton Gdns NG3 161 F1
Folly Hall La LE12 209 D3
Folly La
Besthorpe NG23 98 B8
Stapleford LN6 112 F5
Folly Nook La DN22 19 A6
Folly Nook Pk DN22 19 B5
Fonton Hall Dr NG17 114 B8
Forbes Cl NG10 193 E5
Fordbridge La DE55 113 A7
Ford Cl NG24 140 F3
Fordham Gn NG11 195 E8
Ford La NG23 109 A5
Ford St N NG7 161 A1
Ford St NG7 161 A1
Foredrift Cl NG11 195 A1
Forest Ave NG18 102 C5
Forest Cl
Annesley Woodhouse NG17 130 A8
Cotgrave NG12 187 E3
Rainworth NG21 104 C1
Selston NG16 129 B7
Forest Ct
Mansfield NG18 103 B7
Nottingham NG7 222 C3
Forester Cl NG9 183 C4
Forester Gr NG4 174 D8
Forester Rd NG3 174 A8
Forester St NG4 175 A7
Forest Fields Prim Sch NG7 173 A8
Forest Folk Dr NG21 117 F5
Forest Gdns NG15 130 B8
Forest Glade Prim Sch NG17 101 A4
Forest Gr NG7 222 C4
Forest Hill NG18 102 C2
Forest Hill Pk S81 36 B7
Forest Hill Rd S81 36 A7
Forest La
Papplewick NG15 131 E3
Walesby NG22 63 E3
Worksop S80 36 C2
Worksop S80 47 C8
Forest Link NG22 105 F5
Forest Rd
Annesley Woodhouse NG17 130 A8
Bingham NG13 177 D4
Blidworth NG21 118 B5
Calverton NG14 148 D8
Clipstone NG21 89 F3
Clipstone NG21 90 A3
Clumber and Hardwick DN22 48 C5
Elkesley DN22 49 C5
Loughborough LE11 220 A3
Mansfield NG18 102 C5
Market Warsop NG20 74 D1
New Ollerton NG22 77 C4
Oxton NG25 134 B5
Sutton in Ashfield NG17 101 A5
Forest Rd E NG1 173 B7
Forest Rd W NG7 222 C4
Forest Rise
Market Warsop NG20 74 C2
Worksop S80 36 C2
Forestry Holdings NG21 90 D4
Forest St
Annesley Woodhouse NG17 130 A8
Kirkby-in-Ashfield NG17 115 B4
Sutton in Ashfield NG17 100 F2
FOREST TOWN 89 B1
Forest Town Prim Sch NG19 89 A1
Forest View
Blidworth NG21 117 E4
New Ollerton NG22 77 B4
Retford DN22 39 D3
Forest View Dr NG15 145 E7
Forest View Jun Sch
Boughton/Ollerton NG22 77 D5
New Ollerton NG22 77 B5
Forest Wlk S80 36 C1
Forewood La
Treswell DN22 41 F4
Treswell DN22 42 A4
Forge Ave NG14 148 F8
Forge Cl
Kirklington NG22 120 E8
South Muskham NG23 124 E7
Sutton on Trent NG23 96 F8
Forge Hill NG9 183 D4
Forge Mill Gr NG15 146 C5
Forge The NG9 170 B5
Forman St NG1 223 E3
Forrests Yd S80 35 E2
Forrington Pl LN1 57 C3
Forster Ave NG24 139 E5
Forster St
Gainsborough DN21 15 C1
Kirkby-in-Ashfield NG17 114 F5
Nottingham NG7 222 A3
Forsythia Gdns NG7 172 E2
Fortune Cl NG22 93 F5
Forum Rd NG5 160 E6
Fosbrooke Dr NG10 193 D5
Foss Dyke Ct LN1 57 A3
Fossdyke Gdns LN1 57 B3
Fossdyke Paddock LN1 57 A3
Fossdyke Wlk LN1 44 C1
Fosse Gr LN1 57 B3
Fosse Rd
Brough NG23 112 B2
Brough NG23 112 D3
Brough NG23 126 A8
East Stoke NG23 153 C7
Elston NG23 153 A5
Farndon NG24, NG23 139 A4
Syerston NG23 152 F3
Winthorpe NG24 125 D5
Fosse The
Bingham NG13 177 A2
Cotgrave NG12 188 C2
Cotgrave NG12 199 B8
Cropwell Butler NG12 176 F1
Cropwell Butler NG12 188 E6
Fossett's Ave NG16 128 F7
Fosseway 3 DN21 15 F1
Fosse Way
Bingham NG13 177 C5
East Bridgford NG13 165 F2
Flintham NG23 152 E2
Flintham NG23 153 A1
Kinoulton NG12 199 A1
Newton NG13 177 E8
Stanton-on-the-Wolds NG12 199 A2
Widmerpool LE14 209 A7
Widmerpool NG12 209 A4
Willoughby-on-the-Wolds LE12 217 F1
Fosse Wlk NG12 188 A1
Fossil Cl NG14 173 B1
Foss Way NG13 166 B5
Foster Ave NG9 183 F6
Foster Rd NG23 98 A1
Fosters Cl NG13 165 A5
Fosters Dr NG5 161 D4
Fosters La NG13 177 F4
Foster St NG18 102 C6
Foston Cl NG18 103 B6
Fothergill Ct 1 NG3 173 C7
Foundry Cl NG24 124 F2
Foundry Terr NG15 130 D6
Fountain Dale Ct 2 NG3 173 D7
Fountaindale Sch NG18 116 D6
Fountaindale Way E
Mansfield NG18 102 F1
Mansfield NG18 103 B1
Fountaindale Way West NG18 102 F1
Fountain Hill DN10 13 D7
Fountain Hill Rd DN10 13 D7
Fountain Pk NG22 77 C3
Fountains Cl
Kirkby-in-Ashfield NG17 115 C5
West Bridgford NG2 186 B6
Fountayne Cl NG15 130 F2
Four Seasons Sh Ctr NG18 102 B7
Fourth Ave
Beeston NG9 184 C6
Beeston NG9 184 D6
Carlton NG4 174 B8
Clipstone NG21 89 F3
Edwinstowe NG21 76 A2
Mansfield NG19 103 A8
Rainworth NG21 103 F2
Fowler Rd
Edwalton NG12 185 F3
Edwalton NG12 186 A3
Fowler St NG3 173 D8
Foxbridge Cl NG17 114 D4
Foxby Hill DN21 24 E6
Foxby La DN21 24 F6
Foxby Mws DN21 24 E5
Foxby Warren DN21 24 E6
Fox Cl NG10 193 D5
Fox Covert
Carlton NG4 174 F4
3 Loughborough LE11 220 B6
Fox Covert Cl NG17 100 C1
Fox Covert La
Misterton DN10 14 A8
Nottingham NG11 184 C1
Nottingham NG11 195 C8
Walkeringham DN10 13 F8
Foxcovert Plantation Nature Reserve* NG14 132 F2
Fox Covert Way NG19 103 B7
Foxearth Ave NG11 185 A2
Foxes Cl NG7 222 C1
Foxfield Way NG12 185 C6
Foxglove Cl
New Balderton NG24 140 C5
Nottingham NG15 146 C4
Worksop S80 36 B2
Foxglove Cres LE12 215 A8
Foxglove Gr NG19 88 F4
Foxglove Rd NG16 158 B8
Foxgloves The NG13 177 D3
Foxglove Way NG12 188 A5
Fox Gr NG5 160 E3
Fox Gr Ct NG6 160 E3
Foxhall Bsns Ctr NG7 173 B7
Foxhall Cl NG23 110 A8
Foxhall Rd NG7 173 A8
Fox Hill NG12 187 E2
Foxhill Cl NG17 100 B3
Foxhill Ct NG4 174 E8
Foxhill Rd
Burton Joyce NG14 163 E5
Carlton NG4 174 C8
Foxhill Rd Central NG4 174 C8
Foxhill Rd E NG4 174 D8
Foxhill Rd W NG4 174 B8
Foxhills DE74 203 C1
Foxhollies Gr NG5 161 B3
Fox La S80 58 E8
Foxley Rd DE7 157 F5
Fox Mdw NG15 145 F6
Fox Rd
Nottingham NG2 173 E1
Whitwell S80 45 A6
Fox St
Annesley Woodhouse NG16 129 F8
Annesley Woodhouse NG17 130 A8
Creswell S80 58 E8
Sutton in Ashfield NG17 100 F3
Foxton Cl NG6 159 F8
Foxwood Acad NG9 171 B1
Foxwood Cl
Carlton in Lindrick S81 25 D1
Worksop S81 25 D1
Foxwood Gr NG14 148 F7
Foxwood La NG14 149 A5
Fradley Cl NG6 146 C2
Frampton Rd NG8 172 A7
Frances Gr NG15 131 B1
Frances St NG16 128 D1
Francis Chichester Wlk DN21 24 F7
Francis Ct NG16 128 B4
Francis Gr NG6 160 E3
Francis Rd NG4 174 F8
Francis St
Mansfield NG18 102 E7
Nottingham NG7 222 C4
Francis Way DN22 29 F1
Francklin Rd NG14 150 D2
Franderground Dr NG17 114 E5
Frank Ave NG18 101 F5
Frank Ford Cl LN1 56 F5
Franklin Cl
East Leake LE12 214 E7
Nottingham NG5 161 C8
Franklin Dr NG12 186 D1
Franklin Rd NG16 128 A4
Franklin Way NG17 114 E7
Franklyn Gdns
Keyworth NG12 197 E4
Nottingham NG8 172 C6
Fraser Cres NG4 162 B1
Fraser Rd
Carlton NG4 162 B1
Nottingham NG2 173 D1
Fraser Sq NG4 162 B1
Fraser St NG15 130 D6
Frearson Farm Ct NG16 143 F1
Freckingham St NG1 223 F2
Freda Ave NG4 162 D2
Freda Cl NG4 162 D3
Freda La NG13 181 D2
Frederick Ave
Carlton NG4 174 B7
Ilkeston DE7 170 A5
Kegworth DE74 203 C3
Kirkby-in-Ashfield NG17 114 D6
Frederick Cl NG23 96 F8
Frederick Gent Sch DE55 113 B5
Frederick Rd NG9 182 D7
Frederick St
Long Eaton NG10 193 F7
Loughborough LE11 220 A3
Mansfield NG18 102 C6
Retford DN22 39 F6
Sutton in Ashfield NG17 100 C1
Worksop S80 35 E3
Freeby Ave NG19 88 D5
Freehold St LE11 220 C4
Freeland Cl NG9 182 F3
Freeman's La DN22 32 C5
Freemans Rd NG4 175 A8
Freemans Terr NG4 175 A8
Freemantle Wlk NG5 160 E8
Freeston Dr
Nottingham NG6 145 F1
Nottingham NG6 159 F8
Freeth St NG2 173 F2
Freeth Terr NG23 68 E5
Freiston St 5 NG7 172 E7
Fremount Dr NG8 172 A7
French St DE7 170 A6
French Terr NG20 59 A2
Fretwell St 3 NG7 172 E7
Freya Rd NG22 77 D3
Friar La
Market Warsop NG20 74 C2
Nottingham NG1 223 D2
Friars Cl NG16 129 B7
Friars Cres NG24 139 F5
Friars Ct
Nottingham NG14 173 A3
Nottingham NG7 222 C1
Friar St
Long Eaton NG10 193 D7
8 Nottingham NG7 172 E2
Friar Wlk NG13 177 C8
Friary Cl 10 NG7 172 E2
Friary Gdns NG24 125 A1
Friary Rd 2 NG24 140 A8
Friary The NG7 172 E2
Friday La NG4 162 F1
Friend La NG21 76 B1
Frienship Cl LN1 55 B4
Friesland Dr 1 NG10 182 A6
Frinton Rd NG8 159 E1
Frisby Ave NG10 193 E6
Fritchley Ct NG18 103 B6
Frith Gr NG19 101 E7
Frithwood La
Creswell S80 58 D7
Creswell S80 59 A8
Frobisher Gdns NG5 161 D6
Frog La NG13 202 F8
Frogmore St NG1 223 E4
Frome Gdns NG13 177 D3
Front St
Arnold NG5 161 F7
Barnby in the Willows NG24 141 F5
East Stockwith DN21 7 D2
South Clifton NG23 68 E1
Frost Ave NG16 143 A4
Fryar Rd NG16 143 F3
Fuchsia Way NG19 89 A1
Fuggle Dr S81 25 D1
Fulford Ave DN22 39 C8
Fulforth St NG1 223 E4
Fuller Cl NG18 102 B4
Fuller St NG11 196 C6
Fullwood Ave 4 DE7 157 E1
Fullwood Cl NG9 183 C4
Fullwood St 6 DE7 157 E1
Fulmar Cl NG19 88 E1
Fulmar Way S81 35 C7
Fulwood Cl NG17 114 A8
Fulwood Cres NG8 160 B1
Fulwood Dr NG10 193 A7
Fulwood Ind Est DE55 113 F8
Fulwood Rd N
Huthwaite NG17 99 F1
Huthwaite NG17 100 A1
Sutton in Ashfield NG17 114 A8
Fulwood Rd S NG17 114 A8
Fulwood Rise NG17 114 A8
Furlong Ave NG5 161 E8
Furlong Cl NG9 182 D8
Furlong Pl NG4 174 A4
Furlong St NG5 161 E8
Furnace Rd DE7 170 B6
Furnace Road Ind Est DE7 170 B6
Furness Cl NG2 186 A7
Furness Rd NG6 160 C3
Furnival St S80 36 A1
Furrow Cl NG24 140 A4
Furrows The NG21 104 C1
Furzebrook Rd NG4 174 E6
Furze Gdns NG3 173 D7
Furze The NG22 78 C6
Fylde Cl NG9 182 F2
Fylingdale Way NG8 171 C4

G

Gables Dr NG25 122 B5
Gables Farm Dr LE12 206 C1
Gable's Lea LE12 213 B6
Gables The NG22 106 A5
Gabor Ct NG11 195 C8
Gabrielle Cl NG6 160 D4
Gaddick View NG22 79 F6
Gadd St NG7 222 B4
Gadsby Cl DE7 170 A4
Gadwall Cres
Nottingham NG14 173 A2
6 Nottingham NG7 172 F2
Gadwell Mws S80 35 B5
Gadwell Rd NG4 175 C8
Gainas Ave DN21 15 C2
GAINSBOROUGH 24 E5
Gainsborough Acad The DN21 15 F2
Gainsborough Benjamin Adlard Com Sch DN21 24 E6
Gainsborough Central Sta DN21 24 D8
Gainsborough Cl
Kinoulton NG12 199 F2
Long Eaton NG10 193 E5
Stapleford NG9 182 E6
Gainsborough Coll DN21 15 C1
Gainsborough Dr NG24 125 B3
Gainsborough Lea Rd Sta DN21 24 D5
Gainsborough Parish Church CE Prim Sch The DN21 15 C1
Gainsborough Rd
Bawtry DN10 10 A6
Beckingham DN10 13 D1
Besthorpe NG23 97 F7
Bole DN22 23 A3
Everton DN10 11 D2
Girton NG23 82 F1
Gringley on the Hill DN10 12 B1
Langford NG23 111 E3
Lea DN21 24 F2
North Wheatley DN22 22 F1
North Wheatley DN22 31 C8
Saundby DN22 23 C5
Gainsborough Rd *continued*
Saxilby LN1 56 E2
South Clifton NG23 68 F3
South Clifton NG23 82 F8
Spalford NG23 83 A8
Sturton le Steeple DN22 32 C6
Winthorpe NG24 125 C6
Gainsborough Waterfront Enterprise Ctr DN21 24 C6
Gainsborough W Lindsey L Ctr DN21 15 D2
Gainsford Cl NG5 160 F5
Gainsford Cres NG5 160 F5
Gaitskell Cres NG21 76 C1
Gaitskell Way NG24 140 E4
Gala Way
Nottingham NG5 160 E6
Retford DN22 39 F5
Gale Cl NG9 184 B6
Galena Dr NG3 174 A7
Galen Ave DN22 42 A1
Galen Ct 2 NG7 172 E2
Galleries of Justice* NG1 223 F2
Galley Hill Rd NG25 122 B1
Gallows Inn Cl DE7 170 A5
Gally Knight Way S81 16 F3
Galway Ave DN11 9 D5
Galway Cres DN22 39 C8
Galway Dr DN11 9 D5
Galway Mews DN11 9 A3
Galway Rd
Arnold NG5 161 E8
Bircotes DN11 9 D5
Nottingham NG7 222 B1
Gamage Cl NG24 140 F4
Gamble St NG7 222 C3
GAMSTON
Retford 51 A5
West Bridgford 186 D7
Gamston CE Prim Sch DN22 50 F5
Gamston Cres NG5 161 C3
Gamston Lings Bar Rd NG12 186 C3
Gamston Rd NG18 103 B3
Gamston Wood Nature Reserve* DN22 51 D6
Gant Ct DN11 8 A8
Ganton Cl NG3 161 F1
Garbsen Ct 4 S80 35 E2
Garden Ave
Carlton NG4 174 D8
New Houghton NG19 86 F7
Rainworth NG21 104 A1
Shirebrook NG20 72 E4
Garden City NG4 174 E8
Gardendale Ave NG11 184 D1
Gardeners Cl
Hucknall NG15 145 F7
Newton NG13 177 D5
Gardeners Way
Clipstone NG21 89 F3
Worksop S81 35 D6
Gardenia Cres NG3 162 B2
Gardenia Gr NG3 162 B2
Garden La NG17 101 A3
Garden Rd
Bingham NG13 177 D4
Eastwood NG16 144 A3
Hucknall NG15 145 F7
3 Mansfield NG18 102 B6
Garden Row DE74 203 D3
Gardens Ct NG2 186 A7
Garden St NG7 222 B3
Gardiner Ave NG24 140 F2
Gardiner Terr NG17 100 D6
Gardinia Cl NG9 183 A2
Gardner Dr NG12 199 F3
Gardners Cl NG5 162 D1
Garfield Cl NG9 170 E1
Garfield Rd NG7 222 B3
Garfield St DN21 15 C1
Garforth Cl NG8 172 E8
Garibaldi Maths and Computing Coll NG19 89 E2
Garibaldi Rd NG19 89 D2
Garland Dr 3 DE7 157 F8
Garland Rd S81 16 E1
Garner Rd NG16 158 B7
Garners Hill NG1 223 E2
Garnet Cl NG18 102 C5
Garnet Ct NG3 173 E5
Garnet St NG4 174 F7
Garnon St NG18 101 E6
Garood Cl NG24 139 C6
Garratt Ave NG18 102 C7
Garrett Gr NG11 184 D2
Garsdale Cl NG2 186 C6
Garsdale Dr NG11 185 A3
Garside Ave NG17 100 D1
Garside St S80 36 A3
Garth Ave NG17 114 E8
Garth Rd NG18 102 A4
Garton Cl
Beeston NG9 183 B5
Nottingham NG6 160 B5
Garton Rd LE11 220 A3
Garwick Cl NG19 89 B2
Gary's Way LE12 215 F2
Gas St NG10 182 C6
Gas Wlk LE14 202 B3
Gatcombe Cl NG12 176 A3
Gatcombe Gr NG10 182 A3
Gateford Ave S81 35 D6
Gateford Cl
Beeston NG9 171 C2
Worksop S81 35 D7
Gateford Dr S81 35 D6
Gateford Gdns S81 35 D6
Gateford Glade S81 35 D6
Gateford Hill S81 25 C1
Gateford Park Prim Sch S81 35 D8
Gateford Rd
Worksop S81 35 E4
Worksop S81, S80 35 D6
Gateford Rise S81 35 D7
Gateford Toll Bar S81 35 A8
Gatekeeper Way S81 25 D1
Gateside Rd NG2 173 A1
Gatling St NG7 222 A3
Gattlys La NG22 77 B4
Gaul St NG6 160 B7
Gauntley Ct 1 NG7 172 F8
Gauntley St NG7 172 E8
Gautries Cl NG5 161 A8
Gawthorne St NG7 161 A1
Gayhurst Gn NG6 160 E5
Gayhurst Rd NG6 160 E5
Gaynor Ct NG8 172 B6
Gayrigg Ct NG9 183 B4
Gayton Cl NG8 171 D8
Gayton Rd DE7 157 D1
Gaywood Cl NG11 195 F8
Gdn Terr NG15 130 D6
GEDLING 162 F2
Gedling Country Pk* NG4 162 E5
Gedling Gr NG7 222 C4
Gedling Rd
Arnold NG5 162 B5
Carlton NG4 174 F8
Gedling Sch The NG4 162 E3
Gedling St
Mansfield NG18 102 B5
Nottingham NG1 223 F2
Gedney Ave NG3 173 F8
Gelding Gr NG5 161 F7
Gelding House Woods Nature Reserve* NG4 163 B2
Gell Rd NG9 183 A3
Geoff La DN21 24 E5
George Ave
Beeston NG9 183 F5
Long Eaton NG10 182 F1
George Dere Cl NG22 77 D6
George Gn Way NG8 172 D1
George Green Way NG7 184 D8
George Rd
Carlton NG4 174 E7
West Bridgford NG2 185 E7
George's La NG14 148 D6
George Spencer Acad
Stapleford NG9 182 E4
Stapleford NG9 182 E5
George St
Arnold NG5 161 E6
Gainsborough DN21 15 B2
Hucknall NG15 146 A8
Langley Mill NG16 143 B3
Mansfield NG19 101 F8
Mansfield Woodhouse NG19 88 D3
Mansfield Woodhouse, Forest Town NG19 89 A1
Market Warsop NG20 74 B4
Newark-on-Trent NG24 125 A1
Nottingham NG1 223 E3
Pinxton NG16 113 C4
Retford DN22 39 F5
Sutton in Ashfield NG17 100 B3
Whaley Thorns NG20 59 A2
Worksop S80 35 F3
George Yd 7 LE11 220 B4
Georgia Dr NG5 147 E2
Georgina Rd NG9 183 F5
Geraldine Cl NG5 161 C8
Gerard Gr DN22 29 F2
Gerbera Dr NG24 125 D1
Gerrard Cl NG5 147 A2
Gerrard Cres DE74 203 D1
Gertrude Rd NG2 174 A1
Gervase Gdns NG11 184 D2
Ghest Villas S81 16 F1
Ghost House La NG9 183 B4
Gibbet Hill La DN10 9 F4
Gibbons Ave NG9 182 D6
Gibbons St NG7 172 E1
Gibb St NG10 193 E7
Gibdyke DN10 4 C3
Gibson Cres NG24 140 C3
Gibson Ct S81 25 E1
Gibson Rd NG7 173 A8
Gibson's La LE14 218 C2
Gifford Gdns NG2 173 B2
Gilbert Ave
Gotham NG11 195 B1
Tuxford NG22 66 A3
Gilbert Bvd NG5 162 C7
Gilbert Cl 2 NG5 161 A5
Gilbert Gdns NG3 174 A6
Gilbert Rd DN11 9 B4
Gilbert St West NG15 146 A7
Gilberts Field NG23 110 F1
Gilbert Way NG24 140 F2
Gilbert Wy NG21 118 B6
Gilcroft St
Mansfield NG18 102 C6
Sutton in Ashfield NG17 100 E6
Gildingwells Rd S81 16 A2
Gildwells La NG20 72 B7
Gilead St NG6 160 B7
Giles Ave NG2 185 D6
Gillercomb Cl NG2 186 D5
Gill Gn Wlk DN22 30 D4
Gillies The NG19 101 E5

Gilliver La NG12 187 C1
Gillot St DE75 157 A8
Gillotts Cl NG13 177 E5
Gill St
Nottingham NG1 223 D4
Selston NG16 129 A6
Sutton in Ashfield NG17 100 C2
Gilmores La NG24 140 F1
Gilpet Ave NG3 173 F8
Gilstrap Cl NG24 140 D8
Gilstrap Ctr★ NG24 124 E1
GILTBROOK 158 C8
Giltbrook Cres NG16 158 C8
Giltbrook Ind Pk NG16 158 B7
Giltbrook Ret Pk NG16 158 C7
Gilt Hill NG16 158 D7
Gilthill Prim Sch NG16 158 D7
Giltway NG16 158 C7
Gimson Cl DE7 157 C3
Gin Cl Way NG16 158 C6
Gipsy La
Gunthorpe DN9 7 E7
Warsop Vale NG20 73 F6
GIRTON 82 E1
Girton Ct NG18 103 B2
Girton La
Girton NG23 82 F1
North Scarle LN6 83 B1
Girton Rd NG5 161 A3
Gisburn Cl NG11 185 A4
Gisburn Gr NG19 103 B8
Glade Ave NG8 172 C5
Glade Hill Prim Sch
NG5 161 C8
Gladehill Rd NG5 161 C7
Glade The NG11 195 E7
Gladstone Ave
Gotham NG11 195 B1
Loughborough LE11 220 B5
Gladstone Dr NG16 143 E7
Gladstone Pl S80 35 E3
Gladstone Rd NG24 139 F6
Gladstone St
Beeston NG9 183 F6
Carlton NG4 174 D7
Gainsborough DN21 15 C1
Hathern LE12 213 A1
Kirkby-in-Ashfield NG17 115 B5
Langley Mill NG16 143 C4
Long Eaton NG10 193 D6
Loughborough LE11 220 B5
Mansfield NG18 102 D7
Mansfield Woodhouse
NG19 88 C2
Nottingham NG7 173 A8
South Normanton DE55 113 B6
Worksop S80 35 E3
Gladstone Terr
1 Kirkby-in-Ashfield
NG17 114 F5
Mansfield Woodhouse
NG19 88 C2
Gladwin Cl NG9 182 E7
Gladys St NG7 161 A1
Glaisdale S81 36 B7
Glaisdale Dr E NG8 171 E6
Glaisdale Drive Ind Est
NG8 171 D6
Glaisdale Dr W NG8 171 D5
Glaisdale Parkway
NG8 171 D5
Glamis Cl NG17 101 B1
Glamis Rd
Carlton in Lindrick S81 25 E6
Nottingham NG5 161 A2
Glannis Sq NG20 74 C6
Glanton Way NG5 148 A2
Glapton La NG7 184 E2
Glapton Prim Sch
NG11 184 D2
Glapton Rd NG2 173 C1
Glapton Wood Nature Reserve★ NG11 195 D8
GLAPWELL 86 C8
Glaramara Cl 1 NG2 173 B1
Glasby Cl NG22 77 B4
Glasshouse St NG1 223 E3
Glastonbury Cl
Edwalton NG12 186 A3
Mansfield Woodhouse
NG19 88 D4
Glaven Cl NG19 88 D2
Glebe Ave
Market Warsop NG20 74 C4
Pinxton NG16 113 D3
Glebe Cl
Long Clawson LE14 211 C3
North Wheatley DN22 31 E8
South Normanton DE55 113 A5
Worksop S80 35 C3
Glebe Cres DE7 170 A7
Glebe Dr NG14 163 D3
Glebe Farm Cl NG2 185 C4
Glebe Farm View NG4 162 F3
Glebe Jun Sch DE55 113 A5
Glebelands NG23 110 F1
Glebelands Cl NG11 195 B2
Glebe Pk NG24 140 C6
Glebe Rd
Carlton NG4 162 C2
Nuthall NG16 159 C6
West Bridgford NG2 185 F7
Glebe St
Annesley Woodhouse
NG17 129 F8
Beeston NG9 183 E6
Hucknall NG15 146 A8
Loughborough LE11 220 C5
Glebe The
Awsworth NG16 158 B4
Retford DN22 39 D8
Glebe View NG18 102 E8
Gledhill Dr S81 35 B7
Glen Ave NG16 144 B1
Glenbrook NG12 188 A3
Glenbrook Cres NG8 172 A7
Glenbrook Prim Sch
NG8 171 F7
Glencairn Dr NG8 172 A8
Glen Cl DE55 99 A3
Glencoe Rd NG11 185 A1
Glencoyne Rd NG11 195 E8
Glencross Cl NG4 174 C1
Glendale Cl NG4 162 D2
Glendale Ct NG9 183 E3
Glendale Gdns NG5 161 F7
Glendoe Gr NG13 177 C4
Glendon Dr
Hucknall NG15 146 A5
Nottingham NG5 161 A3
Gleneagles Ct NG12 186 C3
Gleneagles Dr
Arnold NG5 148 B1
Kirkby-in-Ashfield NG17 114 E7
Glen Eagles Way DN22 39 D3
Glenfield Ave NG16 158 D7
Glenfield Rd NG10 193 D5
Glen Helen NG4 174 F6
Glenlivet Gdns NG7 184 F1
Glenloch Dr NG11 195 F8
Glen Mooar Cl NG19 89 A2
Glenmore Rd NG2 186 B6
Glenorchy Cres NG5 160 E8
Glen Parva Ave NG5 147 E1
Glen Rd NG14 163 E5
Glenridding Cl NG2 186 D5
Glensford Gdns NG5 146 E2
Glenside
Arnold NG5 162 B5
Kirkby-in-Ashfield NG17 115 C5
Glenside Rd NG9 171 C1
Glen St NG17 100 E4
Glenstone Ct 11 NG7 172 F8
Glen The NG7 184 F2
Glenthorn Cl S81 34 F7
Glentworth Rd NG7 222 A4
Glenwood Ave NG8 171 D3
Glinis Rd NG5 160 F8
Glossop Ave NG18 103 B6
Gloucester Ave
Beeston NG9 183 F5
Nottingham NG7 222 A2
Nuthall NG16 159 F4
Sandiacre NG10 182 A4
Gloucester Rd S81 36 A7
Glover Ave NG8 171 D4
Glover Cl
Newstead NG15 130 D7
South Leverton DN22 42 C6
Glovers Cl NG20 60 A3
Glovers La NG24 140 D4
Goacher's La DN22 31 D8
Go Ape!★ NG21 90 D4
Goatchurch Ct 8 NG5 147 A1
Goathland Cl 3 NG5 161 B8
Godber Cl NG16 158 A8
Godber Rd
East Leake LE12 205 E3
Hucknall NG15 145 E5
Goddard Ct NG5 162 C6
Godfrey Dr NG24 125 E5
Godfrey La NG7 222 B2
Godfrey's Ct S80 35 E3
Godfrey St NG4 175 A6
Godkin Dr NG16 143 A4
Goit La DN33 31 A6
Goldcrest Ave NG21 118 A8
Goldcrest Cl NG13 178 A3
Goldcrest La NG21 89 F4
Goldcrest Rd
Mansfield NG19 88 F2
Nottingham NG6 160 B4
Goldcrest Rise S81 35 C7
Golden Hill La NG22 78 D7
Goldenholme La DN22 43 A1
Golden Ribbon Ind Est
NG2 172 F2
Goldfinch Cl
Mansfield NG18 102 E7
Stapleford NG9 170 E2
Goldfinch Mws NG17 101 B2
Goldham Rd NG8 171 D8
Goldrick Cl DN10 7 B1
Goldrill Cl NG2 186 B7
Goldsmith Rd
Balderton NG24 140 D5
Worksop S81 36 B5
Goldsmith Sq NG1 223 D3
Goldsmith St
Mansfield NG18 102 A7
Nottingham NG1 223 D3
Goldson Way NG23 110 F1
Goldstraw La
Balderton NG24 140 E2
Newark-on-Trent NG24 140 E2
Goldswong Terr NG3 173 C7
Goldthorpe Ave S81 16 F3
Goldthorpe Cl S81 16 F3
Golf Cl NG15 146 C1
Golf Club Rd DE7 170 B1
Golf Course Rd NG12 198 B2
Golf Rd NG12 176 A3
Gomersall Cl DN22 40 A6
Gonalston La
Epperstone NG14 150 D4
Hoveringham NG14 151 D2
Goodacre Cl LE12 217 D7
Goodacre Rd LE12 212 F2
Goodacre St NG18 102 C7
Goodall Cres NG15 146 C5
Goodall St 1 NG7 172 F7
Goodhand Cres NG18 101 E6
Goodliffe St 6 NG7 172 F8
Goodman Cl NG16 158 C8
Good Shepherd Catholic Prim Voluntary Acad
The NG5 62 A5
Goodwill Rd NG22 77 C3
Goodwin Cl
Newark-on-Trent NG24 140 D8
Sandiacre NG10 182 A6
Goodwin Ct NG22 119 F7
Goodwin Dr NG16 158 E6
Goodwin La NG24 140 F1
Goodwins Ct NG23 138 B6
Goodwin St NG7 222 C4
Goodwood Ave NG5 161 E8
Goodwood Dr NG9 182 F2
Goodwood Rd NG8 171 D4
Goodwood Way NG18 102 F7
Goosedale La NG6 147 A7
Goose Gate
Cotgrave NG12 187 E3
Nottingham NG1 223 F2
Goosemoor La
Retford DN22 39 F4
Retford DN22 40 A4
Goosemoor La E DN22 40 A4
Gopher Rd NG24 139 F5
Goransson Walk
S80 35 B5
Gordon Ave NG18 102 E6
Gordonbrae NG18 102 C3
Gordon Cl
Beeston NG9 183 D2
Farnsfield NG22 119 F5
Worksop S80 36 B3
Gordon Cres DE55 113 B4
Gordondale Rd NG19 88 B1
Gordon Rd
Burton Joyce NG14 164 A5
5 Loughborough LE11 220 B6
Nottingham NG3 173 F6
West Bridgford NG2 185 F7
Gordon Rise NG3 161 E2
Gordon Sq NG2 185 F7
Gordon St
Gainsborough DN21 24 D6
Ilkeston DE7 158 A1
Nottingham NG6 160 D4
Gorman Ct NG5 162 B7
Gorse Ave NG18 103 A5
Gorse Cl
Calverton NG14 148 D7
Eastwood NG16 158 B8
Long Eaton NG10 182 B2
Gorse Ct NG6 160 E5
Gorse Hill NG15 117 A1
Gorselands Ave S80 36 C1
Gorse Rd
Keyworth NG12 197 D3
Newark-on-Trent NG24 139 F5
Gorsethorpe La
Kings Clipstone NG20 74 F1
Kings Clipstone NG21 89 F8
Kings Clipstone NG21 90 B7
Gorseway NG21 90 A3
Gorsey Rd NG3 173 D8
Gorsy La NG25 137 C2
Gosforth Ave DE7 157 F6
Gosforth Ct NG2 173 D1
Goshawk Rd DE7 170 A3
GOTHAM 195 A1
Gotham La NG11 206 C7
Gotham Prim Sch
NG11 195 A1
Gotham Rd
East Leake LE12 205 E3
Kingston on Soar NG11 204 C5
Gotheridge Dr NG4 162 D4
Gothic Cl NG6 160 E4
Gough Gr NG10 193 C6
Goverton Hill NG14 136 F1
Goverton Sq NG6 160 D5
Gowan Cl 7 NG9 183 C2
Goyden Cl NG5 161 A8
Grace Ave NG9 184 B6
Grace Dr NG8 172 D8
Gracefield La NG23 81 F7
Grace Rd DN22 39 E4
Graders Cl NG21 76 C2
Grafton Ave NG5 161 E5
Grafton Cl NG17 101 B5
Grafton Ct NG7 222 C3
Grafton St S80 35 E4
Graham Cl NG24 140 B4
Graham St NG7 222 B3
Grainger Ave
Annesley Woodhouse
NG17 115 B1
West Bridgford NG2 185 E3
Grainger St NG2 173 E2
Graingers Terr NG15 146 B6
Grampian Dr NG5 147 B2
Grampian Way NG10 193 A8
Granary Cl
Bottesford NG13 181 B2
Morton DN21 15 B5
Granary Ct
Brampton LN1 44 C4
Carlton in Lindrick S81 26 A6
GRANBY 191 C5
Granby Ave
Mansfield NG18 102 B8
Newark-on-Trent NG24 140 B6
Granby Ct NG13 177 D4
Granby Dr
Balderton NG24 140 D3
Bottesford NG13 181 A2
Granby Hill NG13 191 B5
Granby La
Plungar NG13 191 F1
Whatton NG13 178 D2
Granby St
Ilkeston DE7 157 E2
Loughborough LE11 220 A4
Grandfield Ave NG12 175 F4
Grandfield Cres NG12 175 F4
Grange Ave
Bawtry DN10 9 F8
Beeston NG9 183 F6
Mansfield NG18 101 F5
Misterton DN10 14 A8
Newark-on-Trent NG24 139 E4
Ollerton NG22 77 B3
Ruddington NG11 196 C8
Grange Cl
Carlton in Lindrick S81 26 A6
Lambley NG4 163 C7
Misterton DN10 14 A8
Nottingham NG11 185 B8
Teversal NG17 100 C8
Grange Cres NG4 162 F3
Grange Ct
Kirkby-in-Ashfield
NG17 115 D5
West Bridgford NG2 185 C2
Grange Dr
Harworth DN11 9 A5
Long Eaton NG10 193 F8
Misterton DN10 14 A8
Grange Farm NG12 186 C7
Grange Farm Cl
Beeston NG9 183 A1
Sutton in Ashfield NG17 100 C1
Grange La
Balderton NG24 155 A4
Staunton in the Vale
NG13 169 A4
Worksop S81 37 C3
Grangelea Gdns NG9 183 B8
Grangemoor NG15 131 D1
Grange Pk
Cropwell Butler NG12 189 A7
Gainsborough DN21 15 B5
West Bridgford NG2 186 C5
Grange Prim Sch NG10 193 F8
Granger Ct 4 LE11 220 A4
Grange Rd
Arnold NG5 161 E4
Barton in Fabis NG10 194 A8
Blidworth NG21 118 B5
Long Eaton NG10 193 F8
Nottingham NG6 160 D3
Retford DN22 39 E3
West Bridgford NG2 186 A4
Grange The
North Muskham NG23 110 F3
Retford DN22 39 E3
South Normanton DE55 113 A4
Grange View
Eastwood NG16 143 F3
2 Harworth DN11 8 F5
Harworth DN11 9 A5
Grange View Rd NG4 163 A2
Grange Wlk DN10 7 A1
Grangewood Ct NG8 171 C3
Grangewood Rd
3 Kirkby-in-Ashfield
NG17 114 F7
Nottingham NG8 171 C3
Grannis Dr NG8 172 A8
Grant Cl NG24 140 D8
Grantham Cl NG16 158 C7
Grantham Rd
Bingham NG13 178 C3
Bottesford NG13 181 D2
Muston NG13 181 E1
Orston NG13 180 B2
Radcliffe on Trent NG4 175 F2
Saxondale NG13 177 A4
Whatton-in-the-Vale
NG13 179 A3
Grantleigh Cl NG8 171 F5
Granton Ave NG11 195 F8
Granton Rise NG19 101 D5
Grant St NG7 222 B3
Granville Ave NG10 182 D1
Granville Cres NG12 175 E2
Granville Ct 4 NG3 173 F6
Granville Gr 4 NG3 173 F5
Granville St LE11 220 A4
Grasby Walk NG9 184 D2
Grasmere Cl
Gainsborough DN21 15 E2
Hucknall NG15 145 F8
Grasmere Rd
Beeston NG9 183 D8
Long Eaton NG10 182 B2
Worksop S81 35 F7
Grasmere St NG10 182 C5
Grasmoor Cl NG14 173 F8
Grassingdale Cl
Carlton NG4 162 D2
3 Carlton NG5 162 D2
Grassington Rd NG8 172 D7
Grasslands The
Rainworth NG21 104 B1
Rainworth NG21 104 C1
Grassmere NG12 188 A3
Grass St DE7 157 E3
GRASSTHORPE 81 E4
Grassthorpe La NG23 81 D3
Grassthorpe Rd
Grassthorpe NG23 81 F5
Low Marnham NG23 82 A5
Sutton on Trent NG23 81 E2
Sutton on Trent NG23 96 E8
Grassy La NG9 184 A5
Gratton Ct 1 NG17 114 F7
Gravelholes La DN10 6 E1
Gravel La NG22 79 D7
Gravelly Hollow NG14 133 A1
Gravelly La NG25 137 E3
Gravel Pit La
Bevercotes DN22 64 E7
West Drayton DN22 50 F1
Graveney Gdns NG5 162 C6
Graves Moor La S81 18 E2
Graves Wlk DN22 19 B2
Gray Fallow DE55 113 B4
Gray La
Halam NG22 120 D2
Halam NG22 120 E1
Graylands Rd NG8 171 E6
Grays Dr NG15 132 B6
Grayson Ms NG9 183 B2
Gray St LE11 220 B2
Graystones Cl NG2 186 C5
Grazingfield NG11 185 A4
GREASLEY 144 E3
Greasley Ave NG16 144 C2
Greasley Beauvale Prim
Sch NG16 144 B2
Greasley Beauvale Sch
NG16 144 B3
Greasley Ct NG18 103 B3
Greasley St NG6 160 B7
Greasley Street Ind Est
NG6 160 B6
Great Black La DN11 8 C6
Great Central Rd
Loughborough LE11 220 C3
Mansfield NG18 102 C6
Great Central Rly★
LE11 220 C2
Great Central Sta LE11 220 C3
Great Freeman St NG3 223 E4
Great Hoggett Dr NG9 183 B6
Great La NG22 65 F7
Great Northern Cl DE7 157 F2
Great Northern Cl The
NG2 223 F1
Great Northern Rd
NG16 143 D2
Great Northern Way
NG4 175 B6
Great North Rd
Balderton NG23, NG24 155 F5
Barnby Moor DN22 28 C5
Bathley NG23 110 B3
Bawtry DN10 10 A5
Bircotes DN10 9 F5
Claypole NG24 155 F7
Cromwell NG23 110 F8
Eaton DN22 40 A2
Gamston DN22 51 A4
Gamston DN22 51 A7
Newark-on-Trent NG24 124 E1
North Muskham NG23 110 F2
North Muskham NG23 110 F5
Ranskill DN22 19 B3
Scrooby DN10 10 A2
South Muskham NG23,
NG24 124 D5
West Markham NG22 65 C7
Weston NG23 81 C3
Greaves Ave LE14 219 C6
Greaves Cl
Arnold NG5 162 B5
Newark-on-Trent NG24 140 D8
Nottingham NG8 159 D1
Greaves La NG22 120 B3
Grebe Cl
Carlton NG4 175 C7
New Balderton NG24 140 C5
Greek St NG7 222 C3
Green Acad Trust NG6 160 E4
Greenacre
Burton Joyce NG14 163 E5
Mansfield NG18 102 F5
Stanton Hill NG17 100 C5
Green Acre
Nottingham NG8 171 B5
West Bridgford NG12 186 B4
Greenacre Ave DE75 143 A3
Greenacre Rd
Worksop S81 35 F6
Worksop S81 36 A6
Greenacres NG17 115 B2
Greenacres Cl NG16 144 C2
Greenacres Dr DE55 113 B6
Green Ap NG4 174 C8
Green Ave NG4 175 A7
Greenaway NG23 138 A6
Greenbank NG4 174 D6
Green Bank NG21 118 C8
Greenbank Dr NG17 100 E5
Greenburn Cl NG2 186 D6
Green Cl
Blidworth NG21 118 A4
Hucknall NG15 146 C5
Keyworth NG12 197 F4
Newton DE55 99 A3
Stapleford NG7 172 C2
Greenclose La 9 LE11 220 A4
Green Cres NG16 128 F6
Greencroft NG11 184 F2
Greendale Ave NG21 76 A3
Greendale Cl
Market Warsop NG20 74 A4
Stanton Hill NG17 100 C6
Greendale Cres NG21 90 B4
Greendale Gdns NG8 172 B8
Greendale Rd
Arnold NG5 161 F6
Nottingham NG3 174 C6
Green Dr NG25 137 F3
Green Farm Rd NG16 128 D6
Greenfield Ave S80 45 C6
Greenfield Cl
Coddington NG24 125 F1
Greenfield Cl *continued*
Edwinstowe NG21 91 B8
Mansfield Woodhouse
NG19 89 B1
Greenfield Gr NG4 174 C8
Greenfields NG16 143 A4
Greenfields Com Sch
NG2 173 D1
Greenfields Cres NG22 77 C4
Greenfields Dr NG12 187 F2
Greenfield St NG7 172 D1
Greenfield The NG12 197 E2
Greenfield Way S81 25 F7
Greenfinch Dale S81 35 C7
Greenford Cl NG16 159 E3
Green Fram Ct S81 26 A6
Greengage Rd NG12 188 A5
Greengate NG23 153 A4
Greengate Rd DN22 53 B4
Greengates Ave NG3 161 F3
Greenhalgh Cres 3
DE7 157 E2
Green Hill
Hathern LE12 213 A1
Wartnaby LE14 219 D4
Greenhill Cres NG4 174 E6
Greenhill La NG17 129 F8
Greenhill Rd NG4 174 E6
Greenhill Rise NG4 174 F7
Green Hill Rise LE12 213 A1
Greenhills Ave NG16 144 A3
Greenhills Rd NG16 143 F3
Greenholme Cl NG17 115 A4
Greenholme Pk NG19 88 E6
Greenholme Sch NG7 222 A2
Greenhouse Gdns NG9 171 E5
Green Inf Sch The
DE55 113 A7
Green La
Babworth DN22 38 E5
Bathley NG23 110 B2
Beckingham LN5 142 F8
Bingham NG13 177 E4
Bottesford NG13 181 C1
Clifton NG9 184 D1
Clumber and Hardwick
S80 48 D5
Collingham NG23 112 B7
Cotgrave NG12 187 F1
Cotgrave NG12 198 F8
Cotgrave NG12 199 A7
Darlton NG22 67 C4
Dry Doddington NG23 156 E2
Dunham-on-Trent LN1 68 D8
Eagle LN6 84 F4
Girton NG23 97 E8
Granby NG13 191 B5
Harby LE14 202 C2
Hodthorpe S80 45 C5
Ilkeston DE7 170 A7
Kegworth DE74 203 C5
Lambley NG4 149 B1
Laxton NG22 79 D1
Lea DN21 24 F3
Mansfield NG18 102 C3
Mansfield, Moorhaigh
NG19 87 A2
Nottingham NG7 184 E1
Pleasley S44 86 D8
Ranskill DN10 18 F8
Treswell DN22 42 D4
Upper Broughton LE14 210 A4
Walesby NG22 64 A2
Greenland Cres NG9 183 C4
Greenland Rd NG17 100 E7
Green Leys NG2 185 C4
Green Mews The NG5 161 A5
Green Mile La DN22 38 E8
Green Platt NG12 187 E3
Green Rd DN10 13 A2
Greens Ct DE7 157 D1
Green's Farm La NG4 163 A2
Greensfields NG17 101 A5
Greenshank Cl NG20 73 E4
Greenshank Rd NG20 73 D4
Greenside DN22 42 F2
Green Side NG16 128 D6
Greenside Ave DN22 42 F2
Greenside Cl NG10 193 E7
Greens La NG16 159 A6
Greenspotts La DN22 52 B7
Greensquare Rd NG16 113 E2
Green St
Barton in Fabis NG11 195 A7
Nottingham NG2 173 D1
Ratcliffe on Soar NG11 203 F7
Ratcliffe on Soar NG11 204 A7
Green The
Barkestone-le-Vale
NG13 192 B2
Beckingham DN10 23 C8
Beeston NG9 183 E4
Bilsthorpe NG22 105 F7
Car Colston NG13 166 B2
Carlton in Lindrick S81 26 A6
Coddington NG24 126 B2
Collingham NG23 111 F7
Dunham-on-Trent NG22 54 C1
East Leake LE12 205 E1
Elmton S80 58 B7
Elston NG23 153 D4
Farnsfield NG22 119 F6
Gainsborough DN21 24 F7
Glapwell S44 86 B8
Hardstoft S45 85 A3
Harworth DN11 8 E4
Hathern LE12 213 A1
Hickling LE14 210 C6
Hose LE14 211 F7
Huthwaite NG17 99 F1
Kingston on Soar LE12 204 A4

Green The *continued*
Kirklington NG22 120 F8
Long Whatton LE12 212 C3
Lowdham NG14 149 F2
Lowdham NG14 150 A2
Mansfield Woodhouse NG19 88 A5
Nottingham NG4 174 C8
Orston NG13 179 F7
Perlethorpe NG22 62 F3
Perlethorpe NG22 63 A3
Radcliffe on Trent NG12 175 E3
Ruddington NG11 196 C6
South Clifton NG23 68 E1
Upton NG23 122 F1
Greentrees Ct NG17 100 D1
Greenvale NG22 120 A6
Greenview Cl NG19 89 B1
Greenway
Carlton in Lindrick S81 26 A6
Clipstone NG19 89 D3
Newark-on-Trent NG24 139 E6
Retford DN22 39 D3
Greenway Cl NG12 175 E3
Greenway The NG10 182 B6
Greenwich Ave NG6 160 C4
Greenwich Pk Cl NG2 185 C5
Green Wlk NG13 178 F4
Greenwood Ave
Edwinstowe NG21 76 B2
Harworth DN11 8 F5
Hucknall NG15 145 F8
Huthwaite NG17 99 F2
Huthwaite NG17 100 A2
Ilkeston DE7 170 A7
Mansfield Woodhouse NG19 88 B4
Nottingham NG3 174 D5
Greenwood Cl
Carlton in Lindrick S81 25 D1
Farnsfield NG22 120 A6
Worksop S81 25 D1
Greenwood Cotts NG18 102 F8
Greenwood Craft Ctr* NG18 116 E6
Greenwood Cres
Boughton NG22 77 E5
Carlton NG4 174 E6
Greenwood Dr NG17 114 F5
Greenwood Gdns
Nottingham NG8 171 C7
Ruddington NG11 196 D6
Greenwood Prim Sch NG17 114 E6
Greenwood Rd NG3 174 C5
Greenwood Vale NG15 145 F8
Greer La S44 86 D8
Greet Park Cl NG25 121 F1
Greetwell Cl 1 NG8 172 A6
Gregory Ave
Aldercar NG16 143 A4
Nottingham, New Lenton NG7 222 B1
Nottingham, Portchester NG3 162 A2
Gregory Bvd NG7 173 A7
Gregory Cl NG9 182 F8
Gregory Cres DN11 8 E4
Gregory Ct
Beeston NG9 183 B4
Nottingham NG7 222 A1
Gregory Gdns NG22 119 F5
Gregory St
9 Ilkeston DE7 157 E1
6 Loughborough LE11 220 B3
Nottingham NG7 172 E2
Gregson Gdns NG9 183 B1
Gregson Rd NG9 183 B2
Grendon Way NG17 101 B5
Grenville Dr
Ilkeston DE7 157 F3
Stapleford NG9 182 E8
West Bridgford NG12 185 D7
Grenville Rd NG9 184 B4
Grenville Rise NG5 147 F1
Gresham Cl
Newark-on-Trent NG24 140 E8
Sutton in Ashfield NG17 100 F3
West Bridgford NG2 185 C7
Gresham Gdns
Arnold NG5 162 A5
West Bridgford NG2 185 D7
Gresham Park Rd NG2 185 C7
Gresley Ave DN10 10 A8
Gresley Dr NG2 173 F3
Gresley Rd
11 Ilkeston DE7 157 F1
Retford DN22 39 D5
Gressingham Cl NG19 88 F3
Greta N Rd NG23 96 F3
Gretton Cl NG23 156 C6
Gretton Rd NG3 162 A4
Greyfriar Gate NG1 223 E1
Greyhound St NG1 223 E2
Grey Meadow Rd DE7 157 E2
Greymede Ave NG8 159 C2
Greys Rd NG5 161 F4
Grey St
Eastwood NG16 144 A1
Gainsborough DN21 15 B2
Kirkby-in-Ashfield NG17 114 D5
Greystoke Dr NG8 171 C7
Greystones Rd DN21 15 B3
Greythorn Dr NG2 185 D4
Greythorn Prim Sch NG2 185 D5
Griceson Cl NG22 77 B2
Grierson Ave NG5 161 B8
Grieves Cl DN22 39 F5
Griffin Rd NG22 77 D5
Griffins End NG13 179 B3
Griffiths Way NG15 146 B6
Griffon Dr NG6 145 F2
Griffs Hollow NG4 174 E7
Grimesmoor Rd NG14 149 A8
Grimsby Terr NG3 223 E4
Grimston Rd NG7 222 A4
Grindleford Grange NG18 103 C5
Grindon Cres NG6 146 C2
Gringley Ct DN10 12 F2
GRINGLEY ON THE HILL 12 E1
Gringley Rd
Clayworth DN22 21 D4
Clayworth DN22 21 E6
Misterton DN10 6 E1
Walkeringham DN10 13 E4
Gringley View DN10 11 B4
Grinsbrook NG7 222 A2
Gripps Comm NG12 187 F1
Grisedale Ct NG9 183 A4
Gritley Mews NG2 173 B2
Grives La NG17 115 B2
Grizedale Cl NG19 103 A8
Grizedale Gr NG13 177 B4
Grizedale Ri NG19 103 A8
Grosvenor Ave
Long Eaton NG10 193 A4
Nottingham NG3 161 C1
Sutton in Ashfield NG17 100 D2
Torksey Lock LN1 55 B8
Grosvenor Cl
Radcliffe on Trent NG12 176 D3
Retford DN22 40 A4
Grosvenor Rd
Bircotes DN11 9 B4
Eastwood NG16 143 F2
Langold S81 16 F3
New Balderton NG24 140 B4
Grouville Dr NG5 162 A5
GROVE 40 F4
Grove Ave
Beeston NG9 183 E6
Nottingham NG7 222 C4
Grove Cl NG14 163 F5
Grove Coach Rd DN22 40 B4
Grove Ct 5 S80 35 E2
Grove La DN22 40 B6
Grove Mews NG16 143 E1
Grove Pk DN10 6 F1
Grover Ave NG3 162 A3
Grove Rd
Church Warsop NG20 74 A6
Grove DN22 40 F3
Grove DN22 41 C6
Headon DN22 52 B8
Headon cum Upton DN22 41 A1
Nottingham NG7 222 B1
Retford DN22 40 C3
Sutton in Ashfield NG17 101 B3
Grove Sch The NG24 139 F7
Groveside Cres NG11 184 C3
Grove Sports Ctr NG24 140 C5
Grove St
Beeston NG9 184 A5
6 Mansfield NG18 102 B6
Mansfield Woodhouse NG19 88 B3
New Balderton NG24 140 B5
Retford DN22 39 F7
Grove The
Beckingham DN10 14 B1
Calverton NG14 149 A7
Newton on Trent LN1 55 A1
Nottingham NG7 222 B4
Nottingham, Carrington NG5 161 B2
Groveview Rd NG24 140 C5
Grove Way NG19 88 B3
Grovewood Cl DN10 13 F8
Grove Wood Rd DN10 6 F1
Grove Wood Terr DN10 6 F1
Grundy Ave NG16 128 D7
Grundy Nook S80 45 A5
Grundy St NG7 172 E7
Guildford Ave NG19 88 C6
Guildhall Dr NG16 113 E2
Guildhall St NG24 140 A8
Guinea Cl NG10 193 A7
Gum Tree Cl 2 NG12 186 A1
Gunn Cl NG6 160 A7
Gunnersbury Way NG8 159 E3
GUNTHORPE 164 F5
Gunthorpe Bridge NG13 165 A4
Gunthorpe CE Prim Sch NG14 165 A5
Gunthorpe Cl NG5 161 B3
Gunthorpe Ct NG18 103 B3
Gunthorpe Dr NG5 161 B3
Gunthorpe Rd
Carlton NG4 162 D3
Lowdham NG14 164 E8
West Stockwith DN9 7 E8
Gutersloh Ct NG9 182 F8
Guy Close NG9 182 E6
Guy Drive NG4 162 E4
Guy Gibson Ct DN21 24 F7
Guylers Hill Dr NG21 89 F2
Gwenbrook Ave NG9 183 E5
Gwenbrook Rd NG9 183 D5
Gwndy Gdns 3 NG5 161 A7
Gypsum Way NG11 205 A7
Gypsy La NG14 152 B8

H

Habblesthorpe Cl DN22 32 E1
Habblesthorpe Rd DN22 32 E1
Hackers Cl NG13 165 C3
Hackett Gdns NG13 177 E6
Hackworth Cl NG16 144 B3
Hadbury Rd NG5 160 F3
Hadden Ct NG8 171 D5
Hadderley Wlk NG3 223 F4
Haddon Cl
Carlton NG4 162 D2
Hucknall NG15 146 A6
Selston NG16 129 B7
Haddon Cres NG9 183 C2
Haddon Dr NG24 140 D3
Haddon Nurseries DE7 157 E3
Haddon Pl NG20 72 D7
Haddon Prim Sch NG4 162 D1
Haddon Rd
Mansfield NG18 102 B8
Ravenshead NG15 117 A3
Retford DN22 40 B4
West Bridgford NG2 185 F6
Haddon St
Ilkeston DE7 157 E3
Nottingham NG5 161 B2
Sutton in Ashfield NG17 100 E4
Tibshelf DE55 99 A6
Haddon Way NG12 176 A4
Hades La LE12 217 D5
Hadfield Wlk NG18 103 B6
Hadleigh Cl NG9 182 E2
Hadley St DE7 170 A5
Hadrian Gdns NG5 147 A2
Hadstock Cl NG10 182 B4
Hadston Dr NG5 147 F2
Hagg La
Bawtry DN10 10 E8
Egmanton NG22 80 A5
Epperstone NG14 150 B5
Haggnook Wood NG15 116 D3
Haggonfields Prim Sch S80 35 A4
Hagley Cl NG3 174 A6
Haileybury Cres NG2 185 F5
Haileybury Rd NG2 185 F5
Hainton Cl DN21 24 E7
Haise Ct NG6 159 F5
HALAM 120 E1
Halam CE Prim Sch NG22 120 F2
Halam Cl NG19 101 D7
Halam Hill NG22 121 A1
Halberton Dr NG2 185 D4
Haldane St DN21 15 B1
Haldon Way
Worksop S81 25 D1
Worksop S81 35 C8
Hales Cl NG12 187 E3
Haley Cl NG16 158 D6
Halfacre Gdns DE7 157 F2
Halfmoon Dr NG17 115 B3
Halford Ave NG5 162 C8
Halifax Ct NG8 159 D2
Halifax Dr S81 35 E8
Halifax Pl
Farnsfield NG22 120 A5
Nottingham NG1 223 E2
Halifax Rd NG24 140 F3
Hallam Dr NG12 176 B5
Hallam Fields Rd DE7 170 B4
Hallam Gr NG16 143 A5
Hallam Rd
Beeston NG9 183 F6
New Ollerton NG22 77 D6
Nottingham NG3 162 A2
Hallams La NG9 183 D5
Hallam's La NG5 161 F7
Hallamway NG18 88 C1
Hallam Way NG16 143 C3
Hall Barn La NG19 101 D8
Hall Cl
Nottingham NG5 161 A2
Radcliffe on Trent NG12 175 E3
Rainworth NG21 118 B8
Hall Cl The NG22 66 A7
Hall Croft NG9 183 F5
Hallcroft Ave DN22 39 E8
Hallcroft Ind Est DN22 29 D2
Hallcroft Inf Sch DN22 29 C1
Hallcroft Rd DN22 29 D2
Hall Dr
Beeston NG9 183 D5
Clayworth DN22 21 D5
Cropwell Bishop NG12 189 A4
Gotham NG11 195 A1
Newark-on-Trent NG24 140 A5
Nottingham NG8 171 E3
Sandiacre NG10 182 B6
Worksop S80 35 D2
Worksop S81 37 B4
Hallfield Rd DE55 99 A3
Hallfields NG12 186 B3
Hall Gdns
Balderton NG24 140 E4
Beeston NG9 183 B7
East Leake LE12 214 F8
Hall Grounds NG12 200 D8
Hall Grounds Dr NG12 200 C8
Halliday Cl S80 35 D3
Hallifax Ave NG20 74 B7
Halliwell Cl NG24 125 B4
Hall La
Brinsley NG16 143 D6
Colston Bassett NG12 189 A1
Colston Bassett NG12 200 C7
East Markham NG22 66 A7
Kinoulton NG12 200 A3
Newton DE55 99 A3
Hall La *continued*
Papplewick NG15 131 D4
Hall Lodge Gdns LN6 127 E8
HALLOUGHTON 136 B4
Halloughton Rd NG25 136 D7
Hallowell Dr NG8 171 F5
Hall Park Acad NG16 143 E3
Hall Pk Dr NG16 143 E3
Hall Rd NG16 143 C4
Halls Brook LE12 205 E2
Halls La
Eastwood NG16 158 A7
Newthorpe Common NG16 158 A8
Halls Rd NG9 182 D6
Hall's Rd DN10 13 A3
Hall St
Mansfield NG18 102 E6
Nottingham NG5 161 D3
Sutton in Ashfield NG17 100 E6
Hallstone Mdw DE74 203 D2
Hallum Ct DE7 157 F3
Hall View
Mattersey DN10 20 B7
Worksop S80 35 D2
Hall View Dr NG8 171 D6
Hall Yard LN6 71 C1
Halstead Cl
Beeston NG9 183 C4
Mansfield Woodhouse NG19 88 F2
Nottingham NG8 160 B3
Haltham Gn 2 DN21 24 F8
Haltham Wlk NG11 195 D8
Hamble Cl NG19 88 D3
Hambledon Dr NG8 172 B5
Hambleton Cl NG10 182 A1
Hambleton Ct S81 25 E7
Hambleton Rise 2 NG19 88 F1
Hambling Cl NG6 160 A7
Hamilton Cl
Arnold NG5 148 C1
Beeston NG9 182 F2
Hamilton Dr
Market Warsop NG20 73 F4
Market Warsop NG20 74 A4
Nottingham NG14 173 B3
Nottingham NG7 223 D1
Radcliffe on Trent NG12 175 F4
Hamilton Gdns 11 NG5 161 B1
Hamilton Pl NG18 101 F4
Hamilton Rd
Long Eaton NG10 182 D1
11 Nottingham NG5 161 B1
Nottingham NG5 173 B8
Sutton in Ashfield NG17 101 C2
Hamilton St
Mansfield NG18 102 E6
Worksop S81 35 E6
Hamilton Way NG18 101 E3
Hamlet La DE55 113 A5
Hamlet The DE55 113 A5
Hammer Leys DE55 113 B4
Hammersmith Cl
Nuthall NG16 159 E4
Radcliffe on Trent NG12 176 D2
Hammerwater Dr NG20 74 A3
Hammond Gr NG17 115 B2
Hampden Cl NG24 141 A2
Hampden Gr NG9 183 E6
Hampden Rd NG13 177 B7
Hampdens Cl NG24 125 E2
Hampden St
Eastwood NG16 158 B8
Kirkby-in-Ashfield NG17 114 F5
Nottingham NG1 223 D3
Hampshire Ct NG16 128 B4
Hampshire Dr NG10 182 B5
Hampstead Rd NG3 161 E1
Hampton Cl NG9 182 E3
Hampton Rd NG2 185 E6
Hampton View NG18 102 A4
Hanbury Ct NG18 103 B6
Handel Ct 7 DN21 15 D1
Handel House Sch DN21 15 D1
Handel St NG3 173 E5
Handford Ct NG25 136 C8
Handley Arc 5 NG18 102 B7
Handley Ct NG24 124 F1
Hand's Rd DE75 143 A1
Hand's Wlk NG13 181 A2
Hanford Way LE11 220 B5
Hangar Hill S80 45 A6
Hankin Ave NG16 129 A2
Hankin St NG15 146 C6
Hanley Ave NG9 183 B8
Hanley St NG1 223 D3
Hannah Cres NG11 185 B7
Hannam's Yd DN22 39 D7
Hanover Ct
HUCKNALL NG15 146 C4
Nottingham NG8 171 D6
Hansby Cl DN11 8 B7
Hanslope Cres NG8 171 D7
Hanson Cl NG16 158 F7
Hanson Cres NG15 146 A7
Hanstubbin Rd NG16 128 F6
Hanworth Gdns NG5 161 D8
Harberton Cl NG5 147 E1
HARBY
Leics 202 B2
Notts 70 E2
Harby Ave
Mansfield Woodhouse NG19 88 D5
Sutton in Ashfield NG17 101 C1
Harby Cl NG24 140 D3
Harby Dr NG8 172 C4
Harby La
Colston Bassett NG12 200 F6
Hose LE14 211 F7
Plungar LE14 202 F3
Saxilby NG23 70 F7
Swinethorpe NG23 70 D1
Swinethorpe NG23 84 D7
Harby Queen Eleanor County Prim Sch NG23 70 E3
Harby Rd
Langar NG13 190 D1
Langar NG13 201 E8
Stathern LE14 202 D3
Wigsley NG23 69 F1
Wigsley NG23 70 A1
Harcourt Cl DE7 157 D1
Harcourt Cres NG16 159 F3
Harcourt Pl DN22 40 A4
Harcourt Rd NG7 173 A8
Harcourt St
Beeston NG9 183 E6
Kirkby-in-Ashfield NG17 115 A5
Mansfield NG18 102 D6
Newark-on-Trent NG24 140 B7
Harcourt Terr NG3 223 F3
Harden Ct NG11 195 C8
Hardie Ave DE55 113 A6
Hardigate Rd NG12 189 A8
Hardstaff Cl
Annesley Woodhouse NG17 114 E1
Retford DN22 29 C1
Hardstaff Rd NG2 174 A4
HARDSTOFT 85 A3
Hardwick Ave
Mansfield NG21 103 F1
Newark-on-Trent NG24 139 F7
Shirebrook NG20 72 E4
Sutton in Ashfield NG17 101 A6
Hardwick Cl
Saxilby LN1 56 F4
Sutton in Ashfield NG17 101 A6
Hardwick Cres S80 36 B2
Hardwick Ct
Harworth DN11 9 B5
South Normanton DE55 113 C6
Hardwick Dr
Ollerton NG22 77 A3
Selston NG16 129 B7
Hardwicke Rd NG9 183 C8
Hardwick Gr
Nottingham NG7 222 B2
West Bridgford NG2 173 F1
Hardwick Hall* S44 85 E4
Hardwick Hall Ctry Pk* S44 85 F5
Hardwick Hall Dr S44 85 D6
Hardwick La
Hardwick LN1 56 B4
Sutton in Ashfield NG17 100 F2
Torksey LN1 44 F1
Torksey LN1 55 F8
Torksey LN1 56 A7
Hardwick Old Hall* S44 85 E4
Hardwick Pk Nature Wlk* S44 85 C4
Hardwick Rd
1 Nottingham, Carrington NG5 161 C3
Nottingham, The Park NG7 222 C1
Hardwick Rd E S80 36 B2
Hardwick Rd W S80 36 B2
Hardwick St
Langwith NG20 72 F8
Mansfield NG18 102 D7
Shirebrook NG20 73 A4
Sutton in Ashfield NG17 100 F2
Tibshelf DE55 99 A7
Hardwick Terr S80 48 D4
Hardwick Top Rd S80 48 C5
Hardwick View NG17 101 A6
Hardwick View Cl NG19 86 F7
Hardwood Cl
1 Nottingham NG6 159 F7
1 Nottingham NG6 160 A7
Hardy Barn DE75 157 A7
Hardy Cl
Bottesford NG13 181 B3
Kimberley NG16 158 F7
Long Eaton NG10 193 D6
Hardy Pl NG18 101 F6
Hardys Cl NG12 189 B4
Hardy's Dr NG4 162 F1
Hardy St
Kimberley NG16 158 F7
Nottingham NG7 222 C4
Worksop S80 35 E3
Hardy Way LE12 205 E3
Harebell Cl 8 NG17 115 A3
Harebell Dr NG20 72 D2
Harebell Gdns NG13 177 C3
Harefield LE12 205 E3
Harefield Cl LE14 202 B3
Hareholme St NG18 102 A8
Harewood Ave
Newark-on-Trent NG24 139 F7
Nottingham NG6 160 D5
Retford DN22 39 C5
Harewood Cl
Radcliffe on Trent NG12 176 A3
Sandiacre NG10 182 B4
Harewood Ct DN11 9 B5
Harewood Dr DN10 10 A8
Harewood Rd S81 35 F7
Hargon La NG24 125 D6
Harkstead Rd NG5 147 B1
Harlaxton Dr
Long Eaton NG10 194 A8
Harlaxton Dr *continued*
Nottingham NG14 173 A3
Nottingham NG7 222 B2
Harlaxton Wlk NG3 223 E4
Harlech Cl DE7 157 C3
Harlech Rise NG9 183 B4
Harlequin Cl NG12 176 B3
Harlequin Ct NG16 143 D3
Harlequin Dr S81 25 D1
Harles Acres LE14 210 C6
Harley Cl S80 46 E8
Harley Gall The* S80 45 E1
Harley St NG7 222 B1
Harlow Ave NG18 102 C3
Harlow Cl
Mansfield Woodhouse NG19 88 C6
Sutton in Ashfield NG17 100 F6
Harlow Gr NG4 162 E2
Harlow St NG21 118 B5
Harmston Rise NG5 160 F4
Harold Ave NG16 143 B4
Harold Brace Rd DN21 24 E5
Harold St NG2 173 E4
Harpenden Sq NG8 160 B3
Harper Hill Gdns DN11 9 B3
Harpham Rd DN21 44 B8
Harpole Wlk NG5 147 F2
Harrier Gr NG15 145 E4
Harrier Hill LN6 84 D2
Harrier Pk NG15 145 D2
Harriers Gr NG17 101 B4
Harrier The NG15 145 D4
Harriett St NG9 182 D7
Harrimans La NG7 184 E8
Harrington Cl NG4 163 B1
Harrington Dr NG7 222 B2
Harrington Jun Sch NG10 182 B1
Harrington St
Long Eaton NG10 193 B5
Mansfield NG18 102 A6
Worksop S80 35 D2
Harris Cl NG8 171 F5
Harrison Ct NG13 177 C4
Harrison Dr S81 16 E3
Harrison Rd
Mansfield NG18 101 E6
Stapleford NG9 182 D8
Harrison's Plantation Nature Reserve* NG8 171 F5
Harrisons Way
Newark-on-Trent NG24 125 B1
1 Newark-on-Trent NG24 140 B8
Harris Rd
Beeston NG9 183 D6
Bingham NG13 177 D7
Kirkby-in-Ashfield NG17 115 D6
Harrogate Rd NG3 174 C5
Harrogate St NG4 174 F7
Harrop White Rd NG19 101 F8
Harrowby Mews NG7 222 B2
Harrowby Rd NG7 222 B2
Harrow Cl
Collingham NG23 112 B8
Gainsborough DN21 15 F2
Rainworth NG21 118 A8
Harrow Dr DE7 170 A4
Harrow Gdns NG8 172 C4
Harrow La NG22 77 F5
Harrow Rd
Hucknall NG15 145 D5
Nottingham NG8 172 B4
West Bridgford NG2 185 E5
Harstoft Ave S81 35 F5
Harston Gdns NG2 185 B3
Hart Ave NG10 182 A5
Hartcroft Rd NG5 161 B6
Hartford Cl 2 NG2 173 D2
Harthill Cl 10 NG9 183 C2
Hartill Dr NG19 101 D5
Hartington Ave
Carlton NG4 162 D1
Hucknall NG15 145 C6
Hartington Ct NG18 103 B6
Hartington Dr
Selston NG16 129 A7
Sutton in Ashfield NG17 101 B4
Hartington Pl DE7 157 E5
Hartington Rd NG5 161 C3
Hartington St
Langwith NG20 72 F8
11 Loughborough LE11 220 B4
Hartland Dr NG5 162 E5
Hartland Rd S80 35 E2
Hartley Ct NG7 222 B4
Hartley Dr NG9 184 B6
Hartley Rd
Kirkby-in-Ashfield NG17 114 F5
Nottingham NG7 222 B4
Hartness Rd NG11 184 C1
Harton Cl NG17 100 D6
Hartshay Cl 20 DE7 157 F5
Hartside Cl NG2 186 C7
Hartside Gdns 1 NG10 193 A8
Hartside Wy NG16 143 B1
Hart St NG7 222 B1
Hartwell St NG3 223 F4
Hartwood Dr NG9 170 D1
Harvest Cl
Beeston NG9 184 B7
Bingham NG13 177 D4
Carlton in Lindrick S81 25 F7
Nottingham NG5 160 F8
Worksop S81 36 B7

Harvest Cres NG9 171 E5
Harvest Dr
Cotgrave NG12 188 A5
Newark-on-Trent NG24 125 C4
Harvester Way NG18 102 D1
Harvest La NG17 100 A1
Harvest Rd 3 NG16 144 A1
Harvey Cl NG11 196 D5
Harvey Croft NG9 170 C4
Harvey Ct 3 NG7 172 E2
Harvey Hadden Sports Ctr NG8 171 F7
Harvey Rd
Mansfield NG18 102 E5
Nottingham, Bilborough NG8 171 F7
Nottingham, Dunkirk NG7 172 E2
Harvey's Field NG25 136 E8
Harviston Ave NG4 162 E4
HARWELL 11 A4
Harwell Sluice La DN10 11 D3
Harwich Cl NG6 160 A8
Harwill Cres NG8 160 B2
Harwood Cl
Arnold NG5 162 B8
Sutton in Ashfield NG17 101 A4
Harwood Pl NG17 101 A4
HARWORTH 8 F5
Harworth Ave S81 18 A6
Harworth Cl NG19 101 D6
Haslam St NG7 223 D1
Haslehurst Gdns S80 35 E2
Haslemere Gdns NG15 116 F2
Haslemere Rd
Long Eaton NG10 193 B8
Nottingham NG8 172 D8
Hassock Cl NG9 184 D6
Hassock La N DE75 157 B7
Hassock La S DE75 157 C6
Hassocks La NG9 184 B7
Hassop Wlk NG18 103 B6
Hastings St
Carlton NG4 174 C7
6 Loughborough LE11 220 A4
Haswell Rd NG6 160 B5
Hatchets Cl NG24 125 A3
Hatchet's La NG24 125 A3
Hatfield Ave
Meden Vale NG20 74 F8
Sandiacre NG10 182 B4
Hatfield Cl NG21 104 B1
Hatfield Dr NG2 185 C4
Hatfield Rd NG3 161 C1
Hatfield St DN22 40 A6
Hathaway Dr S81 36 B4
Hather Cl DN22 51 A5
Hatherleigh Cl NG3 162 C6
HATHERN 213 B1
Hathern Cl NG10 193 D5
Hathern Gn NG9 184 A8
Hathern Rd LE12 212 D2
Hathern Turn LE12 212 F2
Hathernware Ind Est LE12 213 D5
Hathersage Ave NG10 193 A5
Hathersage Cl NG5 160 F8
Hathersage Rise NG15 117 A3
Hathersage Way NG17 100 E4
Hathersage Wlk NG18 103 B6
Hatley Cl 7 NG2 173 B1
Hatton Cl
North Muskham NG23 110 F2
Nottingham NG5 147 A2
Hatton Crofts NG10 193 C6
Hatton Ct NG18 103 B6
Hatton Gdns
Newark-on-Trent NG24 140 B8
Nuthall NG8 159 E3
Haughgate Hill DN22 22 B1
HAUGHTON 63 F6
Haughton Mdws
Haughton DN22 63 F5
Haughton DN22 64 A5
Haughton Way
Walesby DN22 63 F2
Walesby NG22 64 A2
Havelock Gdns NG3 223 F4
Haven Cl
Clipstone NG21 89 F3
Sutton in Ashfield NG17 100 D3
West Bridgford NG2 185 D5
Havenden Gdns 2 NG7 172 F7
Haven Hill S81 16 D6
Haven The NG22 78 C7
Havenwood Rise NG11 195 D8
Haverhill Cres NG5 146 D1
Haversham Cl NG6 160 D2
Hawarden Terr 9 NG7 172 F7
Hawbush Rd NG23 81 A6
Hawfinch Mdws DN22 39 E8
Hawker Cl NG9 183 B5
Hawkesworth Ave NG19 89 B1
Hawkhill Cl NG22 77 A3
Hawkhurst Dr NG8 171 D2
Hawking La
Stainsby S44 85 A7
Stainsby S44 85 C6
Hawkins Cl DN11 9 A5
Hawkins Ct DE7 157 F4
Hawk Ridge Gdns 1 NG3 173 E5
Hawkshead Cl NG2 186 D5
Hawksley Gdns NG11 184 C2
Hawksley La DN22 52 B4
Hawksley Rd 14 NG7 172 F7
Hawkswood Cl NG9 183 B4
HAWKSWORTH 167 C4
Hawksworth Ave NG5 161 D4
Hawksworth Rd
Hawksworth NG13 167 B3
Scarrington NG13 166 F1
Scarrington NG13 167 A1
Scarrington NG13 178 F8
Screveton NG13 166 F4
Syerston NG23 153 B3
West Bridgford NG2 173 F1
Hawksworth St
Gainsborough DN21 24 D8
10 Nottingham NG3 173 E5
Hawley Cl LE12 205 F1
Hawson Way S81 35 C7
Hawthorn Ave
Gainsborough DN21 15 D1
Glapwell S44 86 B8
Hucknall NG15 145 F7
Stapleford NG9 182 D6
Torksey Lock LN1 44 C1
Hawthorn Cl
Beckingham DN10 23 B8
Bleasby NG14 152 B8
Keyworth NG12 197 E2
Mansfield Woodhouse NG19 88 E5
New Ollerton NG22 77 D5
5 Nottingham NG2 173 B1
Old Dalby LE14 218 E4
Shelford NG12 164 C1
Shelford NG13 164 C1
West Bridgford NG12 186 B4
Hawthorn Cres
Arnold NG5 148 A1
4 Kirkby-in-Ashfield NG17 114 F6
Kirkby-in-Ashfield NG17 115 A6
Hawthorn Ct 6 NG2 173 B1
Hawthorn Dr
Farnsfield NG22 120 A6
New Ollerton NG22 77 D5
Hawthorne Ave
Hathern LE12 213 A1
Long Eaton NG10 193 C6
Shirebrook NG20 72 D4
Tibshelf DE55 99 B8
Hawthorne Cl
North Leverton with Habblesthorpe DN22 42 D8
Saxilby LN1 57 A5
Stanton Hill NG17 100 B6
Woodborough NG14 149 C4
Hawthorne Cres NG24 139 A4
Hawthorne Gr NG9 184 B6
Hawthorne Leys NG23 81 E6
Hawthorne Prim Sch NG6 146 E4
Hawthorne Rd NG16 113 D3
Hawthorne Rise NG16 158 B4
Hawthornes The NG22 54 C2
Hawthorne Way NG21 91 B8
Hawthorne Wood DN22 39 D6
Hawthorn Gr DN21 15 D1
Hawthorns The
Kirkby-in-Ashfield NG17 114 F6
Market Warsop NG20 74 A4
Walesby NG22 64 A2
Hawthorn Way S81 25 E7
HAWTON 139 E3
Hawton Cl
Gainsborough DN21 15 E2
Mansfield NG19 87 F1
Hawton Cres NG8 172 C3
Hawton La
Farndon NG24 139 A4
New Balderton NG24 140 B4
Hawton Rd NG24 139 E5
Hawton Spinney NG8 172 C4
Haxey Gate Rd DN10 6 F5
Haxey Rd DN10 6 F4
Haycroft Cl NG19 88 E5
Haycroft Way NG13 165 C2
Hayden La NG15 131 B1
Haydn Ave NG5 161 B2
Haydn Prim Sch NG5 161 C2
Haydn Rd NG5 161 B2
Haydock Cl NG16 158 E7
Hayes Cl NG16 113 C3
Hayes Ct DN22 19 B4
Hayes Rd NG12 197 E3
Hayfield Gr NG23 81 A4
Hay Fields The NG21 104 B1
Hayles Cl NG5 161 B6
Hayling Cl DE7 157 C3
Hayling Dr NG8 160 D1
Haymans Corner 3 NG19 88 C3
Haynes Ave NG9 170 C5
Haynes Cl
Nottingham NG11 184 F3
Tuxford NG22 66 A3
Hays Cl DE7 157 D2
Hayside Ave NG24 140 B3
HAYTON 30 D6
Hayton Rd
Hayton DN22 21 D1
Hayton DN22 30 C8
Hayward Ave LE11 220 C2
Haywood Ave NG21 118 A5
Haywood Ct
Mansfield NG21 103 E2
2 Nottingham NG2 173 E4
Haywood Oaks La NG21 118 C3
Haywood Rd NG3 162 A3
Haywood St NG2 173 E4
Hazelas Dr NG14 165 A5
Hazel Bank NG18 102 E8
Hazelbank Ave NG3 161 F1
Hazelby Rd S80 58 E8
Hazel Cl NG13 178 A4
Hazel Cres NG20 72 D4
Hazel Dr NG16 159 B6
Hazelford Way NG15 130 D7
Hazel Gr
Edwinstowe NG21 76 B1
Hucknall NG15 146 A5
Kirkby-in-Ashfield NG17 115 C5
Mansfield Woodhouse NG19 88 B5
New Balderton NG24 140 C5
Nottingham NG3 162 A4
South Normanton DE55 113 B5
Hazel Hill Cres NG5 161 B8
Hazel Hill Pl NG5 161 B7
Hazelhurst Gdns 3 NG6 160 B7
Hazel Mdws NG15 146 A5
Hazelmere Gr NG7 222 A2
Hazelmere Rd S80 58 B8
Hazel Rd NG22 77 D5
Hazel St
Nottingham NG6 160 B8
Sutton in Ashfield NG17 100 D7
Hazel Way NG15 131 B2
Hazelwood NG12 188 A3
Hazelwood Cl
Eastwood NG16 144 B2
Mansfield Woodhouse NG19 89 B2
Tibshelf DE55 99 B7
Hazelwood Dr NG15 145 C6
Hazelwood Gr S80 35 C2
Hazelwood La DN22 41 E1
Hazelwood Rd NG7 172 E7
Headingley Gdns 3 NG8 172 D8
Headingley Rd DN22 39 E4
Headland Ave DN22 50 A3
HEADON 52 B7
Headstead Bank DN22 43 D6
Headstock Cl NG22 77 C7
Headstocks Cl NG15 146 D2
Head Stocks The NG17 100 A1
Heafield Dr DE74 203 D2
Healdswood Inf Sch NG17 100 D6
Healdswood St NG17 100 D7
Healey Cl
Collingham NG23 112 A8
Nottingham NG2 173 C2
HEANOR 143 B2
Heanor Langley Inf Sch DE75 143 B1
Heanor Rd DE7 157 D3
Heanor Wlk NG18 103 B6
Heapham Cres DN21 24 F8
Heapham Rd
Gainsborough DN21 15 E1
3 Gainsborough DN21 24 F8
Heard Cres NG9 183 F8
Heartwood Cl NG8 172 A6
Heath Ave NG18 103 B7
Heath Cl NG7 222 B2
Heathcoat St
12 Loughborough LE11 220 A4
Nottingham NG1 223 F3
Heathcote Pl NG17 101 A1
Heather Cl
Eastwood NG16 144 C2
9 Gainsborough DN21 15 F1
10 Kirkby-in-Ashfield NG17 114 F7
Mansfield NG18 102 A6
Nottingham NG3 173 D7
South Normanton DE55 113 A3
Tickhill DN11 8 B8
Heather Croft NG2 185 C4
Heather Ct DE75 143 B1
Heather La NG15 132 B8
Heatherley Dr
Mansfield NG19 88 E1
Nottingham NG6 160 F4
Heatherley Prim Sch NG19 88 E1
Heather Rd NG4 162 D1
Heather Rise NG9 171 E1
Heathers The NG22 77 F5
Heathervale NG2 185 B6
Heather Way
Mansfield NG18 103 A6
Shirebrook NG20 72 D2
Heathfield Ave DE7 170 A8
Heathfield Ct 12 NG17 114 E7
Heathfield Gdns
Retford DN22 39 E8
Tibshelf DE55 99 A7
Heathfield Gr NG9 183 C3
Heathfield Prim Sch NG6 160 D5
Heathfield Prim Sch (Kersall Rd) NG5 160 D5
Heathfield Prim Sch (Scotland Rd) NG5 160 F3
Heathfield Rd
Nottingham NG5 160 F4
Nottingham NG5 161 A4
Heathfield Wy NG18 102 D5
Heath Gdns DE72 193 A8
Heath Gr S81 25 D1
Heathland Cl NG18 103 A6
Heathlands Prim Sch NG21 103 D3
Heathrington Gdns 9 NG5 147 A1
Heath The NG16 158 B8
Heaton Cl
Newark-on-Trent NG24 140 D8
Nottingham NG3 161 F1
Heaton St DN21 24 D8
Heavenside LE12 205 E3
Heavytrees Ave NG15 117 A1
Hecadeck La LE14 219 C8
HECKDYKE DN10 7 F4
Heckdyke DN10 7 F4
Heckdyke La DN10 7 E5
Heckington Dr NG8 172 B5
Heddington Gdns 1 NG5 161 D8
Heddon Bar NG19 88 E3
Hedgerow Cl
Old Dalby LE14 218 E5
Sutton in Ashfield NG17 100 C1
Hedgerows The
Collingham NG23 112 B8
Rainworth NG21 104 B1
Hedges Dr DE7 170 A5
Hedingham Cl DE7 157 D1
Hedley Cl LE12 212 A4
Hedley St NG7 173 A8
Hedley Villas 5 NG7 161 A1
Heights The NG24 140 E8
Helen Cl NG9 183 D6
Helenship La DN22 54 B7
Hellebore Cl NG5 160 E7
Helm Cl NG6 159 F7
Helmsdale Cl
Arnold NG5 148 B1
Mansfield NG19 101 E5
Helmsdale Gdns NG5 146 F1
Helmsley Rd NG21 103 E3
Helston Dr NG8 159 E1
Helvellyn Cl 7 NG2 173 C2
Helvellyn Way NG10 182 B2
Hemingway Cl
Carlton NG4 174 C7
Eastwood NG16 144 C1
Hemlock Ave
Long Eaton NG10 182 D1
Stapleford NG9 182 E8
Hemlock Gdns NG6 159 F6
Hemlock Rd NG12 186 A1
Hemmingfield Cl S81 35 F8
Hemmingfield Cres
Worksop S81 35 F7
Worksop S81 36 A8
Hemmingfield Rd S81 36 A7
Hemmingfield Rise S81 36 A8
Hemmingfield Way S81 36 A8
Hemplands La NG23 96 E8
Hemplands The NG23 98 A1
Hempshill Hall Prim Sch NG6 159 F5
Hempshill La NG6 160 A6
HEMPSHILL VALE 159 E6
Hemsby Ct NG5 161 F6
Hemsby Gdns 5 NG6 160 B8
Hemscott Cl NG6 159 F8
Hemsley Dr NG16 143 D3
Hemswell Cl NG3 174 A5
Hen And Chicken Yard NG24 141 F5
Henderson Way 7 LE11 220 C3
Hendon Rise NG3 173 F8
Hendre Gdns 1 NG5 161 A7
Henfrey Dr NG15 130 D7
Henley Cl NG4 175 A6
Henley Ct DN21 15 C2
Henley Gdns NG9 170 E1
Henley Rise NG5 161 A3
Hennessey Cl 11 NG9 183 C2
Henning Gdns 13 NG5 161 A8
Henning La NG17 100 B1
Hennymoor Cl S80 45 A5
Hennymoor La S80 45 C2
Henrietta St NG6 160 C6
Henry Ave NG19 88 B5
Henry Cl S80 46 F8
Henry Ct NG2 173 C2
Henry Mws DN22 29 F1
Henry Rd
Beeston NG9 184 A6
Nottingham NG7 222 A1
West Bridgford NG2 185 E8
Henry St
Arnold NG5 147 E2
Hucknall NG15 146 B6
6 Nottingham NG2 173 E4
Sutton in Ashfield NG17 100 F1
Henry Whipple Prim Sch NG5 160 F6
Henshaw Dr NG13 177 D6
Henshaw Pl DE7 157 E4
Henson Cl NG12 176 E3
Henson La
Bingham NG13 177 A2
Cropwell Butler NG12 176 E2
Henson's Sq NG9 183 B8
Henton Cl NG24 125 E2
Henton Rd NG21 76 C1
Henton Row NG7 222 B2
Hepple Dr NG6 159 F7
Hepworth Dr NG16 158 B7
Herald Cl NG9 184 B7
Herbert Rd
Annesley Woodhouse NG17 115 B1
Nottingham NG5 161 B1
Herbert St
Loughborough LE11 220 B5
Mansfield NG18 102 A6
Hercules Dr NG24 140 B7
Hereford Ave
Mansfield Woodhouse NG19 88 C6
Ollerton NG22 77 B4
Hereford Cl S81 36 A6
Hereford Rd
Arnold NG5 161 E5
Carlton NG4 162 F2
Nottingham NG3 174 B5
Hereford Rd *continued*
Ravenshead NG15 117 A3
Herewood Cl NG20 72 F4
Hermes Cl DN10 9 F8
Hermitage Ave NG18 101 F5
Hermitage La NG18 101 E4
Hermitage Sq 1 NG2 173 F3
Hermitage The NG18 101 E4
Hermitage Way NG18 101 E4
Hermitage Wlk NG7 222 C1
Hermon St NG7 222 C3
Herne St NG17 101 A4
Heron Cres
Cotgrave NG12 187 F5
Cotgrave NG12 188 A5
Heron Dr
Gainsborough DN21 15 F1
Nottingham NG7 222 A2
Heron Glade S81 35 C7
Herons Ct NG2 186 C4
Heron Way
Mansfield NG19 87 C1
New Balderton NG24 140 C5
Heron Wharf 2 NG7 172 F2
Herrick Rd LE11 220 A2
Herril Ings DN11 8 B8
Herriot Gr DN11 9 A4
Herrod Cl NG23 97 A8
Herrods View NG17 100 C6
Hersbrucker Cl S81 25 D1
Hervey Gn NG7 184 E2
Heskey Cl NG3 223 E4
Heskey Wlk NG3 223 E4
Hesley Rd
Harworth DN11 8 F3
Harworth DN11 9 A3
Heslington Ave NG8 172 E8
Heslop Ct S80 35 D3
Hethbeth Ct 5 NG2 173 C2
Hethersett Gdns 4 NG6 160 B8
Hetley Rd NG9 183 F8
Hett's La NG20 74 B5
Hetts Lane Inf Sch NG20 74 B5
Hewer Cl 4 DE7 157 F8
Hewers Way NG21 76 C3
Hewett St NG20 73 D5
Hewson's La NG23 112 A5
Hexham Ave DE7 170 A4
Hexham Cl
Mansfield NG18 102 F5
West Bridgford NG2 186 A6
Heyes The NG15 117 A1
Heyford Ct DE75 143 A1
Heymann Prim Sch NG2 185 D4
Hey St NG10 193 C4
Heyward St NG18 102 D7
Heywood Cl NG25 121 F1
Heywood St NG18 102 D7
Heyworth Rd NG15 145 F4
Hibbert Cres NG17 101 A3
Hibbert Rd NG18 102 D7
Hicking La
Southwell NG25 136 D5
Southwell NG25 136 D6
Hickings La NG9 182 E8
HICKLING 210 B7
Hickling Cl NG10 193 B5
Hickling Ct NG18 102 D7
Hickling La
Hickling NG12 210 B8
Long Clawson LE14 211 A4
Upper Broughton LE14 210 B3
Hickling Rd
Hickling LE14 210 C3
Kinoulton NG12 200 B2
Nottingham NG3 162 A2
Hickling Way NG12 188 A1
Hickman Cres DN21 15 C4
Hickman Ct DN21 24 E8
Hickman Gr NG23 97 F1
Hickman Rd NG13 177 D6
Hickman St DN21 24 D8
Hickory Cl 8 NG17 114 F7
Hicks Gr NG21 76 C3
Hickton Dr NG9 183 B1
Hide Hill View NG12 186 D1
Higgins Cl 8 NG24 125 A2
Highbank Dr NG11 195 E7
Highbank Prim Sch NG11 195 D7
Highbury Ave NG6 160 D5
Highbury Cl NG8 159 E3
Highbury Hospl NG6 160 C5
Highbury Rd
Keyworth NG12 197 E4
Nottingham NG6 160 C6
Highbury Wlk NG6 160 C6
High Church St NG7 161 A1
High Church Street 1 NG7 173 A8
High Cl NG17 115 B1
Highclere Dr NG4 174 F8
Highcliffe Ave NG20 72 D4
Highcliffe Rd NG3 174 A5
High Common La
Austerfield DN10 3 A6
Tickhill DN11 9 A8
Highcroft NG3 161 F4
Highcroft Cl NG10 193 E5
Highcroft Dr NG8 171 B5
High Cross NG14 136 E2
Highcross Ct NG7 222 B4
Highcross Hill NG25, NG14 136 D3
High Cross St NG1 223 F3
High Ct Dr NG12 197 D2
Highfield DN22 29 C1
Highfield Ave
Kirkby-in-Ashfield NG17 114 E6
Mansfield NG19 88 B1
Shirebrook NG20 72 D6
Highfield Cl
Clipstone NG21 90 A4
Gainsborough DN21 15 E1
Mansfield NG19 88 B1
Ravenshead NG15 117 A2
Highfield Ct NG9 183 F6
Highfield Dr
Bilsthorpe NG22 105 F4
Carlton NG4 174 B8
Nuthall NG16 159 F4
South Normanton DE55 113 B5
Stapleford LN6 127 A4
Highfield Gr
Carlton in Lindrick S81 26 B5
West Bridgford NG2 185 F7
Highfield La S80 36 C1
High Field La DN10 3 B3
Highfield Rd
Bawtry DN10 10 B8
Beeston NG9 183 A3
Clipstone NG21 90 A4
Keyworth NG12 197 E4
Nottingham NG7 172 D1
Nuthall NG16 159 E4
Saxilby LN1 57 A4
Sutton in Ashfield NG17 100 C3
West Bridgford NG2 185 F7
Highfields Ct NG15 146 A6
Highfields Dr NG22 106 A4
Highfields Sch NG24 140 C6
Highfield St NG10 182 C1
Highfield Terr 8 NG18 102 B6
Highfield Villas S81 25 F8
Highfield Way NG18 102 A5
High Gables DN22 19 B5
Highgate Cl
Carlton NG4 162 C2
Plungar NG13 202 F8
Highgate Dr DE7 157 C3
Highgate La NG13 202 F8
High Gr NG19 88 E1
High Grounds Ct S80 35 B4
High Grounds Rd S80 35 C4
High Grounds Way S80 35 B4
Highgrove Ave NG9 183 D6
Highgrove Gdns NG12 186 A4
High Hazel Dr NG19 88 B1
Highhazels Rd NG12 188 A4
High Hazles Cl NG4 162 E3
High Hazles Dr NG17 100 A2
High Hoe Ct S80 36 A3
High Hoe Dr S80 36 A3
High Hoe Rd S80 36 B3
High Holborn DE7 157 E3
High House Rd DN22 31 F4
High Hurst NG14 148 E7
High La Central DE7 157 A1
High La E DE7 157 A1
Highland Cl NG19 88 D3
Highland Dr NG17 100 D1
Highlanders Hill NG18 102 F5
Highland Gr S81 36 A5
Highland Rd NG18 102 E2
High Leys Dr NG15 116 C3
High Leys Rd NG15 145 F5
High Main Dr NG6 146 E3
HIGH MARNHAM 68 B1
High Mdw
Bawtry DN10 9 F7
Hathern LE12 213 A1
Tollerton NG12 186 D1
High Meadow NG23 156 E2
High Oakham Cl NG17 101 B4
High Oakham Dr NG18 102 B3
High Oakham Grange NG18 102 A3
High Oakham Hill NG18 102 A4
High Oakham Pk NG18 102 B3
High Oakham Prim Sch NG18 102 B3
High Oakham Rd NG18 102 B4
High Pavement
Nottingham NG1 223 F2
Sutton in Ashfield NG17 100 E2
High Pk Cotts NG16 144 D6
High Rd
Beeston NG9 184 A7
Beeston, Chilwell NG9 183 D4
Beeston, Toton NG9 183 A1
Carlton in Lindrick S81 26 A5
South Carlton S81 25 F4
High Ridge NG19 88 F2
High St Ave NG5 161 E7
High St Pl NG1 223 E2
High Spania NG16 158 F7
High St
Arnold NG5 161 E7
Austerfield DN10 3 C2
Bawtry DN10 10 A7
Beckingham DN10 23 B8
Blyth S81 18 B2
Bottesford NG13 181 A2
Brinsley NG16 128 E1
Collingham NG23 112 A8
Eagle LN6 84 D3
East Markham NG22 65 F7
Edwinstowe NG21 76 B1
Elkesley DN22 50 B4
Everton DN10 11 C3
Gainsborough DN21 24 D7
Girton NG23 82 F1
Girton NG23 97 E8
Gringley on the Hill DN10 12 F2
Harby NG23 70 E2
Holme NG23 111 A2

High St *continued*
Hucknall NG15 146 B7
Huthwaite NG17 100 A3
Kegworth DE74 203 C2
Kimberley NG16 158 F6
Laxton NG22 79 B3
Long Eaton NG10 193 E8
Loughborough LE11 220 B4
Mansfield Woodhouse NG19 88 C3
Market Warsop NG20 74 B4
Marton DN21 44 C7
Misson DN10 4 B2
Misterton DN10 6 F2
Newton on Trent LN1 55 A1
Newton on Trent LN1 69 A8
North Scarle LN6 83 D2
Nottingham NG1 223 E2
Orston NG13 179 F7
Pleasleyhill NG19 87 B5
Retford DN22 39 E3
Ruddington NG11 196 C7
Saxilby LN1 57 A3
South Clifton NG23 68 E1
South Leverton DN22 42 C6
South Normanton DE55 113 A6
Stanton Hill NG17 100 C6
Stapleford LN6 127 E8
Stapleford NG9 182 E7
Staunton in the Vale NG13 169 B4
Sutton in Ashfield NG17 100 E2
Sutton on Trent NG23 96 F8
Tibshelf DE55 99 A7
Walkeringham DN10 13 F6
High Tor
Mansfield NG18 102 C2
Sutton in Ashfield NG17 100 E7
Highurst St NG7 222 C3
High View Ave NG12 198 A3
High View Gdns NG17 115 B1
High View Rd DE55 113 C7
High View Rd Ind Units DE55 113 C7
Highwood Ave NG8 171 F8
Highwood Player Jun Sch NG8 171 E8
Highwray Gr NG11 184 D1
Hilary Cl NG8 171 D3
Hilcot Dr NG8 160 C1
HILCOTE 99 C1
Hilcote Dr NG19 89 F4
Hilcote La DE55 99 A1
Hilcote St DE55 113 A6
Hillary Way NG24 140 E4
Hillbeck Cres NG8 171 C4
Hill Cl
Eastwood NG16 144 C1
West Bridgford NG2 186 B6
Hill Cres
Gainsborough DN21 15 F1
Sutton in Ashfield NG17 101 B4
Hillcrest NG25 136 D8
Hill Crest NG20 72 D3
Hillcrest Ave DE55 113 A4
Hillcrest Cl NG16 159 A6
Hillcrest Dr NG15 145 D6
Hillcrest Gdns NG14 163 E5
Hill Crest Gr NG5 161 B3
Hillcrest Mews DN22 40 A7
Hillcrest Rd NG12 197 E4
Hillcrest View NG4 162 B1
Hill Dr NG13 177 D5
Hill Farm Cl NG12 186 D1
Hill Farm Ct NG12 186 A2
Hillfield Gdns NG5 146 E1
Hillfield Rd NG9 170 F1
Hill Fields DE55 113 A3
Hill Gdns DN11 9 A4
Hillgrove Gdns 14 NG5 161 A8
Hilliers Ct NG5 160 F8
Hillingdon Ave NG16 159 D3
Hillingdon Dr DE7 170 A7
Hillington Rise NG5 161 C7
Hillmoor St NG19 87 C3
Hillocks Prim Sch NG17 101 B3
Hillocks The NG17 101 B3
Hill Rd
Beeston NG9 183 B2
Bestwood Village NG6 146 E4
Gotham NG11 205 B7
Harworth DN11 9 A4
Orston NG13 180 A6
Hill Rise NG9 170 C4
Hillsborough Ave NG17 114 D8
Hillsborough Way NG17 114 D8
Hillsford Cl NG8 172 A5
Hillside
Beckingham LN5 142 C8
Beckingham LN5 142 D8
Beckingham NG24 127 C1
Kegworth DE74 203 D1
Langley Mill NG16 143 A3
Marton DN21 44 C8
Tuxford NG22 66 B3
Hill Side
Beckingham LN5 142 D8
Nottingham NG7 172 D3
Hillside Ave
Misterton DN10 7 A2
Nottingham NG3 162 A4
Hillside Cres
Beeston NG9 183 E8
Worksop S81 35 F5
Hillside Dr
Burton Joyce NG14 163 F5
Long Eaton NG10 193 B8
Southwell NG25 136 D8
Hillside Gr NG10 182 A6
Hillside Prim Sch NG15 145 E8
Hillside Rd
Beeston, Bramcote NG9 183 D8
Beeston, Chilwell NG9 183 B3
Blidworth NG21 118 A4
Radcliffe on Trent NG12 176 A3
Hillside Wlk NG21 118 A4
Hills Rd NG5 161 F4
Hill St
Pleasleyhill NG19 87 B5
Retford DN22 39 E4
Worksop S80 35 E2
Hillsview Ct NG19 87 A5
Hillsway NG20 72 D3
Hillsway Cres NG18 102 A4
Hill Syke
Lowdham NG14 150 A2
Woodborough NG14 149 F2
Hill The NG17 114 E5
Hill Top NG13 180 A6
Hill Top Ave NG20 72 E4
Hilltop Cl LN6 84 D3
Hill Top Ct DN11 9 A4
Hilltop Rd NG16 113 C3
Hilltop Rise NG16 144 B2
Hill Top View NG17 100 C1
Hillview Ave NG3 161 D2
Hillview Cres DN22 30 E4
Hillview Ct NG19 88 D4
Hillview Rd
Carlton NG4 162 A1
Retford DN22 39 E3
Hill View Rd
Beeston NG9 183 A2
Kirkby-in-Ashfield NG17 115 C5
Hill Vue Ave NG24 140 B8
Hill Vue Gdns NG24 140 B8
Hillwood Cl S80 35 B2
Hilton Cl NG19 87 C3
Hilton Cres NG2 186 B5
Hilton Ct LN1 57 B3
Hilton Grange NG2 186 B5
Hilton Pk
Blidworth NG21 117 F5
Blidworth NG21 118 A5
Hilton Rd NG3 162 A3
Hinchin Brook NG7 222 A2
Hind Cl NG12 200 A2
Hindlow Ct NG18 103 B6
Hind St
Calverton NG14 133 E1
Retford DN22 40 A6
Hine Ave NG24 140 E8
Hine Cl DN22 39 E4
Hinsley Cl NG5 162 B8
Hirams Paddocks NG24 139 D8
Hirst Cl NG5 147 F2
Hirst Cres NG8 171 E4
Hirst Rd DN22 40 A8
Hitchen Rd NG10 193 B7
Hives La LN6 83 D3
Hobart Cl NG2 173 C1
Hobart Dr NG9 170 F1
Hobben Cres NG15 131 D1
Hobhouse Rd NG19 87 D2
Hobsic Cl NG16 143 D8
Hobsic La NG16 128 E8
Hobson's Acre NG14 165 A5
HOCKERTON 122 B6
Hockerton Hts NG23 122 B6
Hockerton Rd
Caunton NG23 108 F1
Knapthorpe NG23 109 A2
Knapthorpe NG23 122 E8
Southwell NG25 121 F2
Southwell NG25, NG23 122 F2
Hockerwood NG11 184 E4
Hockerwood La
Southwell NG23 122 C2
Southwell NG25 122 B2
Hockey Cl LE11 220 A7
Hockley
Nottingham NG1 223 F2
Nottingham NG7 222 F2
Hockley Pl NG17 114 E4
Hodding Rd S80 45 C6
Hodgkin Cl NG11 184 C1
Hodgkinson Rd NG17 115 B4
Hodgkinson St NG4 175 A6
Hodmire La S44 85 E7
HODSOCK 26 E7
Hodsock La
Blyth S81 27 A8
Carlton in Lindrick S81 26 B7
Hodsock Priory Gdns* S81 26 E7
Hodson Ct LE11 220 B2
HODTHORPE 45 C6
Hodthorpe Prim Sch S80 45 C5
Hoefield Cres NG6 160 A6
Hoe La NG12 189 A6
Hoe Nook NG12 189 A4
Hoe View Rd NG12 189 A4
Hoewood Rd NG6 160 A8
Hogan Gdns NG5 147 A1
Hogarth Cl NG9 182 E6
Hogarth Prim Sch NG3 174 A7
Hogarth St NG3 173 F6
Hoggetts Cl NG9 183 B5
Hogg La NG12 175 E3
Hoggs Field NG16 143 F2
HOLBECK 59 C7
Holbeck La S80 59 D8
Holbeck Rd
Hucknall NG15 131 B1
Holbeck Rd *continued*
Nottingham NG8 172 D6
Holbeck Way NG21 104 B1
Holbein Cl LE11 220 C4
Holborn Ave NG2 173 F4
Holborn Cl NG16 159 D3
Holborn Pl NG6 160 C7
Holbrook Cl NG19 87 A5
Holbrook Cres NG21 90 C6
Holbrook Ct
Mansfield NG18 103 B6
Nottingham NG11 195 E8
Holbrook St DE75 143 A2
Holby Cl NG5 160 F8
Holcombe Cl NG8 160 B2
Holdale Rd NG3 174 B6
Holdenby Cl DN22 40 A8
Holden Cres
Newark-on-Trent NG24 139 F6
Nuthall NG16 159 C6
Holden Gdns NG9 182 E6
Holden Rd NG9 183 E7
Holden St
Mansfield NG18 102 A6
Nottingham NG7 222 C3
Holderness Cl DN11 9 A4
Holding S81 36 B5
Holds La DN22 19 B2
Holgate NG11 184 C2
Holgate Acad NG15 145 E6
Holgate Prim Sch NG15 145 F6
Holgate Rd NG2 173 C1
Holgate Wlk NG15 145 E6
Holkham Ave NG9 183 C5
Holkham Cl
Arnold NG5 162 A6
Shipley DE7 157 C3
Holland Cl NG11 195 B1
Holland Cres NG16 129 B7
Holland Mdw NG10 193 D5
Holland St NG7 172 F7
Hollands Way DE74 203 D2
Holles Cl NG22 77 E5
Holles Cres NG7 222 C1
Holles St S80 35 F2
Hollies Ave NG24 125 B4
Hollies Dr NG12 186 A4
Hollies The
Blyth S81 18 B2
Eastwood NG16 143 F2
Rainworth NG21 104 B1
Rainworth NG21 118 B8
Ravenshead NG15 116 F1
Sandiacre NG10 182 A5
Shirebrook NG20 72 E2
Hollington Rd NG8 172 B6
Hollington Way NG18 103 B7
Hollingwell Dr 4 NG18 103 B7
Hollingworth Ave NG10 182 B3
Hollins The NG14 149 A8
Hollinwell Ave NG8 172 C5
Hollinwell Cl 9 NG17 114 E7
Hollinwell Ct NG12 186 B3
Hollinwood La NG14 133 C1
Hollinwood Lane NG14 148 C8
Hollis Mdw LE12 205 E3
Hollis St NG7 161 A1
Hollis Way LE12 212 F1
Holloway Cl NG13 165 D3
Hollowdyke La
Balderton NG24 140 F2
Balderton NG24 140 F3
Hollowgate La
High Marnham NG23 67 F1
South Clifton NG23 68 B1
Hollows The
Long Eaton NG10 194 A8
Maplebeck NG22 108 A7
Nottingham NG11 185 A4
Thurgarton NG14 151 C7
Hollow Stone NG1 223 F2
Holly Ave
Carlton NG4 174 D8
Nottingham, Wilford NG11 185 B8
Hollyberry Croft NG17 100 D1
Holly Blue Way S81 25 D1
Hollybrook Gr NG16 159 B7
Holly Bush Cl DN22 50 B4
Holly Cl
Bingham NG13 178 A4
Hucknall NG15 146 B5
Hollycroft NG2 186 A4
Holly Croft Gr DN11 8 B7
Holly Ct
Beeston NG9 183 C8
Harworth DN11 8 E4
Mansfield NG19 88 E1
Newark-on-Trent NG24 125 D1
Retford DN22 39 F6
Rolleston NG23 138 A5
Hollydale Rd NG3 174 B6
Hollydene Cl NG15 145 C5
Hollydene Cres NG6 160 B4
Holly Dr NG19 89 A1
Holly Farm Ct NG16 144 C1
Hollygate Ind Pk NG12 188 A4
Hollygate La NG12 188 B5
Holly Gdns NG3 173 F7
Hollygirt Sch NG3 173 C7
Holly Gr NG17 114 F6
Holly Hill Prim Sch NG16 129 A7
Holly Hill Rd NG16 129 A6
Hollyhock Cl 1 NG12 185 F2
Hollyhouse Dr DE55 113 B6
Holly La NG9 183 E5
Holly Leaf Rd NG15 146 C4
Hollymount
5 Retford DN22 39 F6
1 Retford DN22 40 A6
Holly Mount NG22 93 E5
Holly Prim Sch NG19 89 A1
Holly Rd
Mansfield Woodhouse NG19 89 A2
Retford DN22 39 F6
Watnall NG16 159 A7
Holly Rise NG22 77 D5
Hollythorpe Pl NG15 145 C5
Hollytree Cl LE12 215 C2
Hollytree La LE14 211 C3
Hollywell Prim Sch NG16 158 F7
HOLME 111 A3
Holme Ave LE12 205 E3
Holme Bsns Pk S81 25 D3
Holme Cl
Ilkeston DE7 157 D2
Woodborough NG14 149 D4
Holmecroft Ave NG17 100 F5
Holmefield NG24 139 A4
Holmefield Cres DE7 170 A8
Holmefield Rd S80 45 A6
Holmefield Wlk NG18 103 B6
Holme Gr NG2 174 B2
Holme La
Egmanton NG22 79 E6
Halam NG22 120 F3
Langford NG23 111 E3
Normanton on T NG23 82 B5
Radcliffe on Trent NG12 175 C3
Rockley DN22 51 C2
Winthorpe NG24 125 D7
HOLME PIERREPONT 175 B3
Holme Pierrepont Ctry Pk* NG12 174 F3
Holme Pierrepont Hall* NG12 175 B3
Holme Pit Nature Reserve* NG11 184 C3
Holme Rd
Bingham NG13 178 A4
West Bridgford NG2 174 A1
Holmes Cl NG16 143 A3
Holmesfield Dr DE75 157 A7
Holmes La Track
Dry Doddington NG23 156 A3
Long Bennington NG23 155 F5
Holmes Rd DN22 39 F7
Holme St NG2 173 E2
Holmestead Cl LE12 206 C1
Holme The NG25 136 B7
Holme Way S81 25 D1
Holme Wlk DN21 15 F1
Holmewood Ave DE7 157 F5
Holmewood Cres NG5 161 B6
Holmewood Dr NG16 158 B8
Holmfield Cl S81 36 A5
Holmfield Rd NG9 183 C3
Holmhurst Cl S81 35 E5
Holmsfield NG12 197 E2
Holmwood Rd NG21 104 C1
Holroyd Ave NG2 173 F4
Holroyd Circle NG16 143 F7
Holt Dr 1 LE11 220 A1
Holt Gr NG14 148 F7
Holt The
Gainsborough DN21 15 F1
Newark-on-Trent NG24 139 D6
Holwood Ct NG6 160 A6
Holy Cross RC Prim Sch NG15 131 B1
Holy Family RC Prim Sch S80 47 A8
Holyoake Rd NG3 162 C3
Holyrood Ct NG9 171 C1
Holy Trinity Cath Acad NG24 139 E7
Holy Trinity CE Inf Sch NG25 136 D7
Holywell Rd DE7 157 C3
Home Cl NG5 161 D8
Homecroft Dr NG16 128 E7
Home Croft The NG9 183 B7
Home Farm Cl
Gotham NG11 195 A1
Kelham NG24 124 A3
Laughterton LN1 55 B4
Newark-on-Trent NG24 124 A4
Willoughby-on-the-Wolds LE12 217 E7
Homefarm La NG23 70 A6
Home Farm La
Kirklington NG22 120 E8
Upper Saxondale NG12 176 E3
Homefield Ave NG5 148 A1
Homefield Cl NG22 53 B3
Homefield Croft DN10 10 A2
Homefield Rd NG8 172 D7
Home Fm Ct NG16 128 D6
Homelands The NG17 100 F1
Homeleigh La NG14 151 E2
Home Leys Way LE12 216 C4
Home Mdws DN11 8 A6
Home Pastures LE14 211 F7
Home Rise DN22 32 C1
Homestead NG16 143 A4
Homesteads The
Kirkby-in-Ashfield NG17 114 F6
Market Warsop NG20 74 B4
Homewood Dr NG17 114 E7
Honey Bee Gdns NG17 100 C5
Honeycroft Ct DE55 113 B4
Honeyknab La NG25 134 D5
Honey Pot Cl NG10 193 F8
Honeys La NG23 139 B1
Honeysuckle Cl
New Balderton NG24 140 C4
Honeysuckle Cl *continued*
4 Nottingham NG8 159 E1
Honeysuckle Dr DE55 113 B7
Honeysuckle Gr
Bingham NG13 177 D3
Nottingham NG6 160 B4
Honeywood Dr NG3 174 A7
Honeywood Wlk NG3 174 A7
Honing Dr NG25 136 D8
Honingham Cl NG5 162 A6
Honingham Rd DE7 157 C3
Honister Cl
Mansfield NG18 102 C4
Nottingham NG11 195 D7
West Bridgford NG2 186 C7
Honister Ct NG18 102 C4
Honiton Cl NG9 183 A2
Honiton Rd NG8 159 E1
Hood St NG5 161 D2
Hook Cl 9 NG9 183 C2
Hooley Cl NG10 193 B6
Hooley Pl 3 NG5 161 D3
Hooley St NG16 128 F6
Hoopers Cl NG13 181 A2
Hoopers Wlk 6 NG2 173 C2
Hooton Rd NG4 174 C7
Hooton St NG3 173 F5
Hope Cl NG2 173 D2
Hopedale Cl NG7 222 A3
Hope Dr NG7 223 D1
Hope St
Beeston NG9 183 E7
Mansfield NG18 102 D6
Hopewell Cl NG12 176 A4
Hopewell Rise
Southwell NG25 121 C1
Southwell NG25 136 C8
Hopewell St NG12 189 B4
Hopkiln La NG25 121 C1
Hopkin Ct NG5 162 C6
Hopkins Ct NG16 143 F3
Hopkinson Cl
Keyworth NG12 197 F4
North Scarle LN6 83 E2
Hopkinson Ct NG6 146 E3
Hopper Rd NG24 140 A4
Hopwas Cl NG23 123 E1
Hopwood Rd NG5 162 E3
Hopyard La
Bathley NG23 109 F2
Cromwell NG23 110 B2
Egmanton NG22 79 E8
Normanton on T NG23 82 A6
Tuxford NG22 65 E1
Horace Ave NG9 182 D6
Horizon Pl NG8 159 C2
Hornbeam Cl
6 Edwalton NG12 186 B1
Ilkeston DE7 170 B7
Hornbeam Gdns NG6 159 F7
Hornbeam Way NG17 115 A3
Hornbuckle Ct NG7 222 B3
Hornchurch Rd NG8 171 D8
Horne La NG22 54 C1
Hornsby Wlk NG5 160 E8
Horridge St DE7 157 F4
Horsecroft Cl DE7 157 C2
Horsendale Ave NG16 159 F4
Horsendale County Prim Sch NG16 159 E3
Horseshoe Cl LE12 217 D7
Horseshoe Cotts NG23 112 B8
Horseshoe Rise DN10 13 F5
Horsewells St DN10 12 F2
Horsham Dr NG5 160 F8
Horsley Cres NG16 143 A3
Horsley La 4 NG4 162 E3
Horsley Rd DN21 15 B3
Horwood Dr
Carlton NG4 162 D4
West Bridgford NG11 185 A5
HOSE 211 F7
Hose CE Prim Sch LE14 211 F7
Hose La
Colston Bassett LE14 201 A3
Harby LE14 202 A1
Hose LE14 211 F5
Hoselett Field Rd NG10 193 E5
Hosiery St NG17 115 A5
Hospital Rd DN22 39 E7
Hotchkin Ave LN1 57 C3
Hoten Rd 7 NG2 173 F3
HOTON 215 D1
Hoton Rd LE12 216 B3
Hotspur Cl NG6 160 E5
Hotspur Rd DN21 15 C2
Houfton Rd NG18 102 E8
Hougham Rd NG23 156 F1
Houghs Yard NG24 126 A1
Houghton Ave DE7 157 C3
Houghton Cl NG16 159 E4
Houldsworth Rise NG5 147 E2
Hound Rd NG2 185 E8
Hounds Gate NG1 223 D2
Hounsfield Cl NG24 140 E8
Hounsfield Way NG23 96 F8
Houseman Gdns NG2 173 C2
Houston Cl NG5 146 E1
Hove Chase DN22 39 E4
Hove Rd NG5 160 E5
HOVERINGHAM 151 D2
Hoveringham La
Hoveringham NG14 151 B2
Kneeton NG14 151 F3
Hoveringham Rd NG14 165 C8
Howard Cl NG10 182 E1
Howard Dr DE74 203 C3
Howard Rd
Bircotes DN11 9 C4
Howard Rd *continued*
Mansfield NG19 101 F8
Howard's Gdns NG24 140 C4
Howard St
Loughborough LE11 220 B5
Nottingham NG1 223 E3
Sutton in Ashfield NG17 100 F4
Worksop S80 36 B2
Howarth Cl NG10 193 A7
Howbeck La
Clarborough DN22 30 E4
Clarborough DN22 31 A4
Howbeck Rd NG5 162 B8
Howden Rd NG6 146 C1
Howell-Jones Rd NG9 183 B3
Howells Cl NG5 161 C8
Howe Rd LE11 220 B1
Howes Ct NG24 140 A8
Howick Dr NG6 159 F8
Howieson Ct NG3 162 B5
Howitts Rd NG13 181 A1
Howitt St
Heanor DE75 143 A2
Long Eaton NG10 193 E7
Hoylake Cl
Gainsborough DN21 15 E3
Mansfield Woodhouse NG19 88 E6
Hoylake Cres NG8 171 D7
Hoyland Ave NG7 172 E2
Hoyle Rd NG14 133 F1
Hoyte Dr DE74 203 C3
Hubert St NG7 222 B4
Huckerby Rd DE7 157 C2
Huckerbys Field NG4 162 C1
Hucklow Ct NG18 103 B6
HUCKNALL 145 E6
Hucknall Cl NG8 159 D2
Hucknall Cres NG4 162 E2
Hucknall Flying High Acad NG15 145 E3
Hucknall Ind Pk NG15 145 E4
Hucknall La NG6 146 D2
Hucknall L Ctr NG15 146 B8
Hucknall National CE (VA) Prim Sch NG15 146 A8
Hucknall Rd
Newstead NG15 130 D5
Nottingham NG6 160 E6
Hucknall Sta NG15 146 C7
Huddlestones Wharf NG24 139 E8
Hudson St
Loughborough LE11 220 C4
Nottingham NG3 173 F6
Hudson Wy NG12 176 B4
Huffer Rd DE74 203 D3
Hufton's Ct DE75 157 A7
Hufton's Dr DE75 157 A7
Hugessen Ave NG15 146 C8
Hugget Gdns 4 NG5 161 A8
Hughes Ford Way LN1 57 B3
Hughes La NG4 162 E4
Hughs Cl NG23 138 C7
Humber Cl NG2 173 C2
Humber La NG23 153 B8
Humber Rd
Beeston NG9 184 A7
Long Eaton NG10 182 C1
Humber Rd S NG9 184 B6
Humber St
Retford DN22 40 A6
Worksop S80 35 E4
Humberstone Rd NG25 121 D1
Humberston Rd NG8 171 C3
Hume St LE11 220 C4
Humphrey Cl LE11 220 B2
Humphries Gdns S80 35 E1
Hundred Acre La S81 26 C3
Hundred Acres La NG24 140 D1
Hundreds La DN10 5 B2
Hungary La LE12 213 C7
Hungerhill La NG5 148 F2
Hungerhill Rd NG3 173 D7
Hungerton St NG7 222 B1
Hunston Cl NG8 172 A7
Hunt Cl
Kirkby-in-Ashfield NG17 115 C7
Radcliffe on Trent NG12 175 F3
Hunter Dr NG6 145 D2
Hunter Rd
Arnold NG5 162 C6
Newton NG13 177 B8
Hunters Chase NG19 88 B2
Hunters Cl NG11 185 A6
Hunters Ct NG17 114 E5
Hunter's Dr DN10 12 E2
Hunters Rd NG24 140 F3
Huntingdon Dr NG7 223 D2
Huntingdon Prim Sch NG3 223 E4
Huntingdon St NG1 223 E3
Huntingdon Way NG9 182 F2
Huntingdon Wlk NG10 182 B5
Huntly Cl
Mansfield NG19 101 D5
Nottingham NG7 184 F1
Hunt's Hill NG16 144 A7
Huntsman Pl DN22 19 B2
Hurcomb St NG3 173 F7
Hurrican Rd NG15 145 E2
Hurst Cl NG21 103 F1
Hurts Croft NG9 183 D4
Hurt's Yd NG1 223 E2
Huss's La NG10 193 F7

Hutchinson Gn NG3 223 F4
Hutchinson Rd NG24 140 E8
HUTHWAITE 99 E3
Huthwaite All Saints CE (Aided) Infant Sch NG17 99 F4
Huthwaite La DE55 99 C2
Huthwaite L Ctr NG17 99 F3
Huthwaite Rd NG17 100 C2
Hutton Cl NG9 171 D1
Hutton St NG2 173 F3
Huxley Cl NG8 171 D7
Hyde Cl NG11 184 F4
Hyde Pk Cl NG2 185 C5
Hyson Cl 10 NG7 172 F8
HYSON GREEN 172 F7
Hyson St 12 NG7 172 F7

I

Ian Gr NG4 174 F8
Ibbinson Ct NG4 162 D4
IBTE Mus of Telecommunications★ S81 35 F2
Idle Bank DN9 2 D5
Idle Ct DN10 10 A7
Idle Valley Nature Reserve★ DN22 29 B3
Idlevalley Rd DN22 39 E8
Idle View DN22 29 F1
Idlewells Sh Ctr NG17 100 E2
Ikea Way NG16 158 C7
Ilam Sq DE7 157 E5
Ilford Cl DE7 157 D3
Ilion St NG19 87 F2
ILKESTON 157 D2, 170 B7
Ilkeston Com Hospl DE7 157 D4
Ilkeston Rd
Sandiacre NG10 182 C8
Stapleford NG9 170 F2
Trowell NG9 170 C5
Ilkeston Sta DE7 158 A2
Imex Ent Pk NG15 146 D6
Imperial Ave
Beeston NG9 183 E6
Carlton NG4 162 E1
Imperial Ct DE74 203 D3
Imperial Rd
Beeston NG9 183 E6
Nottingham NG6 160 D6
Incher Mews NG5 162 C1
Inchwood Cl NG9 182 F2
Incinerator Rd NG2 173 E2
Independent St NG7 222 B4
Industrial Mus & Yd Gall★ NG8 172 A3
Infield La
Cuckney NG20 60 B5
North Leverton with Habblesthorpe DN22 32 E1
Weston NG23 81 B3
Ingamells Dr LN1 57 C3
Inger Dr NG4 162 E4
Ingham Gr NG7 222 A1
Ingham Rd
Bawtry DN10 9 F8
Long Eaton NG10 182 C2
Ingleborough Gdns 6 NG10 193 A8
Ingleby Cl
Cotgrave NG12 187 E2
Nottingham NG8 171 B4
Ingleby Medieval Village of★ LN1 57 A8
Inglefield Rd DE7 170 A6
Inglemere Cl S81 36 A5
Ingle Pingle LE11 220 A3
Inglewood Cl NG24 140 D2
Inglewood Rd NG7 184 E1
Ingram Rd NG6 160 D6
Ingrams La NG23 82 A3
Ingram Terr NG6 160 C6
Ings Rd DN10 12 E6
Inham Cir NG9 183 C6
Inham Cl NG9 183 A5
Inham Fields Cl NG14 165 A5
Inham Rd
Beeston NG9 183 A5
Beeston NG9 183 B5
Inholms Gdns NG23 152 F2
Inholms Rd NG23 152 F2
Inkerman Cl DE7 157 E5
Inkerman Rd NG16 128 F5
Inkerman St NG16 128 F5
Inkersall Grange Rd
Bilsthorpe NG22 105 B4
Rainworth NG21 104 F4
Inkersall La NG22 105 C6
Innes Rd NG4 174 C7
Institute St NG17 100 C6
Instow Cl NG5 162 D5
Instow Rise NG3 223 F4
Intake Ave NG18 101 F5
Intake Farm Prim Sch NG19 101 E7
Intake Rd
Clipstone NG21 90 A3
Keyworth NG12 197 D3
intu Victoria Ctr NG1 223 E3
Iona Cl DN21 15 E2
Iona Dr NG9 170 D2
Iona Gdns NG5 147 A1
Iona Sch NG3 174 A5
Ipswich Cir NG3 174 A5
Ireland Ave NG9 184 A5
Ireland Cl NG9 184 A5
Iremonger Rd NG2 173 D2
Irene Terr NG7 160 F2
Ireton Ave 6 NG24 140 E8
Ireton Gr NG9 183 D2
Ireton St
Beeston NG9 183 E6
Nottingham NG7 222 C3
Ironwood Cl 6 NG12 186 A2
Irving Cl NG22 120 A5
Irwin Dr NG6 160 A6
Isaac's La NG9 182 D7
Isabella St NG7 223 E1
Isandula Rd NG7 160 F2
Island Bsns Quarter NG1 223 F1
Islay Cl
Arnold NG5 147 F1
Stapleford NG9 170 D3
Ivatt Cl DN10 10 A8
Ivatt Dr NG2 173 F3
Iveagh Cl NG20 74 C5
Ivel Cres S81 34 F8
Ives Cl NG2 185 C4
Ivies The NG24 139 C6
Ivy Cl NG16 144 F1
Ivy Cottage La LN1 56 E4
Ivy Gdns NG22 106 A4
Ivy Gr
Carlton NG4 174 D7
Kirkby-in-Ashfield NG17 114 F6
Nottingham NG7 173 A8
Ivy La NG16 143 E2
Ivy Lodge La S81 16 B3
Ivy Way NG21 89 F4

J

Jacklin Ct NG17 114 F6
Jacklin Gdns NG5 147 A1
Jacksdale Nature Reserve★ NG16 128 B3
Jacksdale Prim Sch NG16 128 B3
Jackson Ave
8 Ilkeston DE7 157 E1
Sandiacre NG10 182 A6
Jackson Cres LE12 205 E3
Jackson Dr 6 NG5 161 A5
Jackson Rd NG15 146 C4
Jacksons Hill
Perlethorpe NG22 62 F3
Perlethorpe NG22 63 A2
Jackson Terr NG20 74 E8
Jacoby Cl NG5 161 C7
Jacques Orch DE55 113 B6
Jade Ct NG18 102 D4
Jadella Cl NG19 101 F5
Jake Rd NG9 184 A3
James Cl NG22 77 C5
James Dr NG14 133 F1
James' Murray Mews NG18 102 C7
James Peacock Inf Sch NG11 196 B7
James St
Annesley Woodhouse NG17 115 A1
Arnold NG5 161 E8
Kimberley NG16 158 F6
Worksop S80 35 E5
James Watt Rd NG24 125 C3
James William Turner Ave
Sutton in Ashfield NG17 100 E1
4 Sutton in Ashfield NG17 114 F8
Jamia Al-Hudaa Ind NG3 173 C8
Japan Rd DN21 15 B1
Japonica Dr NG6 160 B4
Jardine S81 36 B6
Jardines The NG9 171 C1
Jarrow Ct DN21 15 F2
Jarrow Gdns NG5 146 F2
Jarvis Ave NG3 174 B6
Jasmin Cl NG20 72 D6
Jasmine Cl
Beeston NG9 171 D1
5 Nottingham, Broxtowe NG8 159 E1
Nottingham, Glapton NG11 184 C1
Jasmine Ct
Balderton NG24 140 E5
Nottingham NG16 143 B1
Jasmine Dr DE55 99 B7
Jasmine Gdns
Edwalton NG12 185 F2
4 Edwalton NG12 186 A2
Jasmine Rd NG5 160 E3
Jasper Cl NG12 175 E2
Jay Cl LE12 206 A3
Jayne Cl
Carlton NG4 163 A2
Nottingham NG8 171 E5
Jay's Cl NG13 181 A1
Jeacock Dr NG21 118 C8
Jean Revill Cl LN1 56 F5
Jedburgh Cl NG3 223 F4
Jedburgh Wlk NG3 223 F4
Jeffares Cl DE74 203 C3
Jeffries Cl DE7 157 D4
Jeffries Prim Sch NG17 114 F5
Jellicoe St NG20 59 A2
Jenford St NG18 101 E6
Jenkin Close 5 DE7 157 F8
Jenkins Ave
Mansfield NG19 101 D7
Retford DN22 39 F5
Jenned Rd NG5 148 A2
Jenner St 14 NG5 161 B1
Jenness Ave NG5 146 E1
Jennison St
Mansfield NG19 88 A1
Nottingham NG6 160 C7
Jenny Beckett's La NG18 102 F4
Jenny Burton Way NG15 146 C5
Jensen Way NG5 161 B1
Jephson Rd
2 Sutton in Ashfield NG17 100 F1
Sutton in Ashfield NG17 114 F8
Jericho La NG13 192 A3
Jericho Rd NG24 140 D2
Jermyn Dr NG5 147 A1
Jersey Gdns NG3 173 E6
Jersey St NG24 139 F5
Jerusalem LN6 71 F2
Jerusalem Rd LN6 71 F3
Jervis Ct DE7 157 F3
Jesmond Rd NG6 160 D6
Jesse Boot Ave
Nottingham NG7 184 D8
Nottingham NG8 172 D1
Jesse Gray Prim Sch NG2 185 E4
Jessie La DE7 157 D2
Jessop Cl NG24 125 C1
Jessop's La NG4 162 F2
Jessop Way NG24 125 C1
Jewitt Way NG11 196 B7
Job La DN10 20 B7
Job's La LN6 84 F2
Jockey La DN22 50 A5
John Barrow Cl NG21 118 C8
John Blow Prim Sch NG23 112 A8
John Carroll Ct 2 NG3 173 F6
John Carroll L Ctr NG7 222 B3
John Clifford Sch NG9 184 A6
John Coupland Hospl DN21 15 B3
John Gold Av NG24 140 B7
John Hunt Prim Sch NG24 140 C4
John Jenkinson Cl DN21 24 F7
John King Inf Sch NG16 113 D3
John King Workshop Mus★ NG16 113 D3
John Pope Way NG24 125 B4
Johnson Ave NG15 146 B5
Johnson Cl NG16 159 A7
Johnson Dr NG18 102 C3
Johnson Rd NG7 222 A2
Johnsons Rd NG24 140 F2
Johnson Way NG9 183 B2
Johns Rd
Beeston NG9 184 A3
Radcliffe on Trent NG12 176 B3
John St
Ilkeston DE7 157 F1
Nottingham NG7 160 F1
Sutton in Ashfield NG17 100 F4
Worksop S80 35 E3
John T Rice Inf Sch NG19 89 E3
John Wright Cl NG5 146 D1
Josephine Gr 2 NG12 186 A2
Joseph Whitaker Sch NG21 117 F8
Joyce Ave
Beeston NG9 182 E3
Nottingham NG5 161 D5
Joyce Cl NG5 161 D4
Jubilee Acad NG8 171 F8
Jubilee Ave
Beeston NG9 184 B8
Nottingham NG8 172 C1
Jubilee Cl DN10 4 B3
Jubilee Cres 1 DN21 15 D1
Jubilee Ct NG20 72 F2
Jubilee Dr LE11 220 A6
Jubilee House Christian Sch NG9 170 D1
Jubilee Rd
Arnold NG5 161 E6
Retford DN22 39 D5
Sutton in Ashfield NG17 100 D3
Jubilee St
Kimberley NG16 158 E7
Newark-on-Trent NG24 140 A7
3 Nottingham NG2 173 F4
Jubilee The NG25 121 D1
Jubilee Way LE11 220 B4
Jubilee Way N NG18 103 C6
Jubilee Way S NG18 103 B4
Judes Pk NG22 65 F7
Judges St LE11 220 C3
Judson Ave NG9 182 F6
Julian Cl DE7 170 A6
Julian La NG12 164 C1
Julian Rd NG2 174 B1
Julias Wy NG17 115 B8
Julie Ave DE75 143 A1
Julius Cl NG16 143 A4
Jumelles Dr NG14 148 D7
Junction Rd
Long Eaton NG10 194 A6
Sutton in Ashfield NG17 101 B2
Juniper Cl
Bilsthorpe NG22 106 A5
Lidgett NG21 91 C8
Juniper Cl *continued*
Nottingham NG11 184 C1
Juniper Ct NG16 158 C8
Juniper Gdns NG13 178 A4
Juniper Way DN21 15 D1
Jupiter Mws 1 NG18 102 E2
Justinian Cl NG15 146 C8

K

Kansington Ct 5 NG5 161 C3
Kappler Cl NG4 175 A7
Karen Gdns NG9 183 D4
Karen Rise NG5 148 A1
Karsten Ave DN21 15 E3
Katherine Dr NG9 182 F4
Kaye Rd NG19 101 D7
Kayes Ct NG9 182 E7
Kayes Wlk NG1 223 F2
Keane Cl NG21 117 F5
Keats Ave NG17 100 B3
Keats Cl
Arnold NG5 161 D7
Long Eaton NG10 193 B5
Nuthall NG16 159 B6
Keats Cres S81 36 B4
Keats Dr NG15 145 D6
Keats Rd NG24 140 D5
Kedleston Cl
Beeston NG9 183 C5
Long Eaton NG10 193 A5
Kedleston Ct DE55 99 B6
Kedleston Dr DE7 157 D3
Kedlestone Cl NG17 99 F2
Kedleston Rd S81 35 F6
Keel Dr NG13 181 A2
Keeling Cl NG16 144 B1
Keepers Ave 4 NG17 115 A3
Keepers Cl NG6 146 E4
Keep The LE12 205 F1
KEGWORTH 203 C1
Kegworth Bypass
Kegworth DE74 203 B1
Kegworth DE74 212 C8
Kegworth La DE74 212 C5
Kegworth Mus★ DE74 203 C2
Kegworth Rd
Gotham NG11 194 F1
Gotham NG11 195 A1
Ratcliffe on Soar NG11 203 F5
Keighton Hill NG7 172 C1
Keilder Dr NG13 177 C4
Kelfield Cl NG6 160 E5
KELHAM 124 B4
Kelham Dr NG5 161 A2
Kelham Gn NG3 173 F6
Kelham La
Kelham NG23 124 A6
Newark-on-Trent NG24 124 D3
Kelham Mws NG4 174 B8
Kelham Rd
Mansfield NG19 101 E7
Newark-on-Trent NG24 124 E1
Kelham Way NG16 143 E3
Keller Ct DN22 53 B8
Kelling Cl NG5 161 A6
Kelly Wlk NG2 185 B7
Kelsey Ave NG22 77 D3
Kelsey Cl NG9 183 E3
Kelso Gdns NG2 173 B2
Kelstedge Dr NG18 103 B6
Kelstern Cl
Mansfield NG18 103 A7
Nottingham NG8 160 C3
Kelvedon Gdns NG3 173 E6
Kelvin Cl NG9 182 C5
Kelvin Rd
Clipstone NG19 89 D3
Nottingham NG3 174 A7
Kemmel Rd NG6 160 D5
Kempsey Cl NG5 160 E8
Kempson St NG11 196 C6
Kempton Cl NG16 158 F7
Kempton Dr NG5 148 A1
Kempton Rd NG18 102 F7
Kenbrook Rd
Hucknall NG15 146 C8
Papplewick NG15 131 D1
Ken Crocker Way NG24 125 E5
Kendal Cl
Annesley Woodhouse NG16 129 F8
Annesley Woodhouse NG17 130 A8
Hucknall NG15 145 F8
Worksop S81 35 E8
Kendal Ct NG2 186 B8
Kendal Dr NG9 183 D8
Kendale Ct NG3 161 F1
Kendale Gr 1 NG5 161 F1
Kendal Rd NG12 189 A4
Kenia Cl NG4 174 D8
Kenilworth Ave NG17 101 B4
Kenilworth Cl
Saxilby LN1 57 A4
Worksop S80 36 A1
Kenilworth Ct
Beeston NG9 184 A7
Nottingham NG7 223 D1
Kenilworth Dr S81 25 F6
Kenilworth Rd
Beeston NG9 184 A8
Nottingham NG14 173 B3
Nottingham NG7 223 D1
Kenley Cl S81 35 D8
Kenmare Cres DN21 24 F6
Ken Martin Leisure Ctr NG6 146 C1
Kenmore Cl NG19 101 E5
Kenmore Gdns NG3 223 F4
Kennack Cl DE55 113 C6
Kennedy Ave
Long Eaton NG10 193 C5
Mansfield Woodhouse NG19 88 D4
Kennedy Cl NG5 161 E7
Kennedy Ct
Walesby NG22 64 A2
Worksop S81 36 A4
Kennedy Dr NG9 170 E1
Kennedy Rise NG22 64 A2
Kennedy Wlk NG24 140 E4
Kennel Dr DN22 28 C5
Kennel La LN6 71 C1
Kenneth Rd NG5 147 F2
Kennet Paddock NG19 88 D3
Kennington Rd NG8 172 D5
Kenny Ave NG11 185 A5
Kenrick Rd NG3 162 A2
Kenrick St NG4 175 A7
Kensington Cl
Beeston NG9 183 A1
Mansfield Woodhouse NG19 88 E5
Sutton in Ashfield NG17 100 E2
Kensington Gdns
Carlton NG4 174 E7
Ilkeston DE7 170 A7
Kensington Gr LN1 55 B8
Kensington Jun Acad (6) DE7 170 A7
Kensington Pk Cl NG2 185 C5
Kensington Rd NG10 182 A4
Kensington Way 1 S81 35 E7
Kenslow Ave 10 NG7 172 E7
Kent Ave
Beeston NG9 183 F4
Westwood NG16 128 B4
Kent Cl S81 36 A6
Kentmere Cl NG2 186 C7
Kenton Ave NG16 159 D3
Kenton Ct 6 NG2 173 D1
Kent Rd
Eastwood NG16 158 C8
Nottingham NG3 162 A3
Kent St NG1 223 F3
Kentwood Rd NG2 173 F4
Kenyon Rd
Nottingham NG7 172 D3
Nottingham NG8 172 D3
Keppel Ct DE7 157 F3
Kernel Dr NG20 72 D2
Kernel Way NG20 72 D2
Kerry Cl NG21 89 F5
KERSALL 94 B1
Kersall Ct NG6 160 D5
Kersall Dr NG6 160 D5
Kersall Gdns NG15 146 B7
Kersall Rd
Kersall NG22 94 C3
Kersall NG22 108 A8
Kestral Dr NG13 177 F3
Kestral Rd NG18 101 E4
Kestrel Av 13 DN21 15 F1
Kestrel Cl NG4 162 B1
Kestrel Dr NG21 118 B8
Kestrel Gr NG15 145 F7
Kestrel Mews S81 35 C7
Kestrel Rise LN6 84 D2
Keswick Cl
Beeston NG9 183 D8
West Bridgford NG2 186 C7
Keswick Ct
Long Eaton NG10 182 B2
3 Nottingham NG2 173 E4
Keswick Rd S81 35 E7
Keswick St NG2 173 E4
Ketlock Hill La DN22 32 C1
Kettleband Cl NG13 177 D6
KETTLETHORPE 55 C4
Kettlethorpe La LN1 55 E4
Kettlethorpe Rd
Fenton LN1 55 D5
Laughterton LN1 55 B5
Ketton Cl NG5 161 B8
Kett St NG6 160 B6
Keverne Cl NG8 160 C2
Kevin Rd NG8 171 D2
Kew Cl NG11 185 C3
Kew Cres DE75 143 B1
Kew Gdns
New Balderton NG24 140 B4
Nuthall NG8 159 E3
Kexby Wlk DN21 24 F7
Keyes Cl DN10 19 F8
Keyes Ct DN10 19 F8
Keyes Gn DN22 19 F8
Keyes Rise DN10 19 F8
Keys Cl NG6 160 A7
Key St NG3 173 F5
KEYWORTH 197 F2
Keyworth Cl NG19 101 E7
Keyworth Crossdale Drive Sch NG12 197 E4
Keyworth Dr NG19 89 C1
Keyworth L Ctr NG12 197 F2
Keyworth Mdw Nature Reserve★ NG12 207 E6
Keyworth Prim Sch NG12 197 E3
Keyworth Rd
Carlton NG4 162 D3
Widmerpool NG12 208 C5
Wysall NG12 207 C3
Wysall NG12 207 C5
Kibworth Cl NG5 160 F4
Kiddier Ave NG5 162 B7
Kid La S81 16 A5
Kighill La NG15 132 B7
Kilbourne Rd NG5 148 B1
Kilbourn St NG3 223 E4
Kilburn Cl NG9 171 B2
Kilby Ave NG3 174 A6
Kildare Rd NG3 173 F8
Kildonan Cl NG8 159 D2
Killerton Gn NG11 195 E7
Killerton Pk Dr NG11 185 B4
Killisick Jun Sch NG5 162 B8
Killisick Rd NG5 162 B8
Kilnbrook Ave NG5 148 B1
Kiln Pl NG6 160 A6
Kilnwood Cl NG3 174 A7
Kilsby Rd NG7 184 F2
Kilton Ave NG18 103 B7
Kilton Cl S81 36 A4
Kilton Cres S81 36 B4
Kilton Glade S81 36 B4
Kilton Hill S81 36 A5
Kilton Rd S80 36 A3
Kilton Terr S80 36 A3
Kilverston Rd NG10 182 A6
Kilverton Cl NG8 172 C4
Kilvington Rd NG5 162 B7
Kimber Cl NG8 171 D6
KIMBERLEY 158 E8
Kimberley Cl NG16 158 F5
Kimberley L Ctr NG16 159 A6
Kimberley Mws DN11 9 B3
Kimberley Prim Sch
Kimberley NG16 158 F6
Kimberley NG16 159 A6
Kimberley Rd
Nottingham NG2 174 A4
Nuthall NG16 159 C5
Kimberley Sch NG16 159 A6
Kimbolton Ave NG7 222 B2
Kindlewood Dr NG9 183 B1
King Charles St NG1 223 D2
Kingcup Gdns NG11 196 E5
King Edward Ave NG18 102 B4
King Edward Gdns NG10 182 B6
King Edward Prim Sch NG18 102 C6
King Edward Rd LE11 220 C3
King Edward St
Hucknall NG15 146 A6
Nottingham NG1 223 F3
Sandiacre NG10 182 B6
Shirebrook NG20 72 F4
King Edward's Terr DN22 39 F6
King Edwin Prim Sch NG21 75 F1
King Edwins Cl NG21 76 A1
Kingerby Cl DN21 24 E7
Kingfield Cl NG21 118 B8
Kingfield Ct LN5 142 D8
Kingfisher Cl
New Balderton NG24 140 C5
Nottingham NG6 160 D4
Kingfisher Ct
Beeston NG9 184 B5
2 Loughborough LE11 220 A2
Kingfisher Dr NG12 188 A4
Kingfisher Rd
Carlton NG4 175 C7
Mansfield NG19 87 D1
Kingfishers Ct NG2 186 C4
Kingfisher Way
1 Loughborough LE11 220 A2
Sutton in Ashfield NG17 101 B3
Kingfisher Wharf
4 Nottingham NG7 172 F2
1 Nottingham NG7 173 A2
Kingfisher Wlk S81 35 C7
Kingfisher Wy NG22 77 C4
King George Ave LE11 220 D2
King George Rd LE11 220 D2
King George V Ave NG18 102 E5
King Johns Arc NG1 223 E2
King John's Rd NG21 90 A4
Kinglake Pl NG2 173 C2
King Rd NG20 74 A4
Kingrove Ave NG9 183 D6
King St E DN21 24 D7
Kings Ave NG4 162 E2
Kingsbridge Ave NG3 162 C6
Kingsbridge Way NG9 183 C6
Kingsbury Dr NG8 172 A8
Kings Ct NG25 121 E1
Kingsdale S81 36 B8
Kingsdale Cl NG10 193 A5
Kingsdown Mount NG8 171 E2
Kings Dr NG16 143 E7
Kingsford Ave NG7 222 A4
Kingshaugh Camp (Ancient Mon)★ NG22 66 F8
Kingsholm Rd NG17 114 F7
Kingsley Ave NG19 88 D5
Kingsley Cl NG19 88 D4
Kingsley Cres NG10 193 B4
Kingsley Ct
Mansfield Woodhouse NG19 88 D5
Worksop S81 36 B4
Kingsley Dr NG4 175 A7
Kingsley Rd NG2 174 A3
Kingsley St NG17 115 B4
Kings Lodge Dr NG18 101 E4
King's Marina★ NG24 124 F2
Kingsmead DN22 39 D3
Kingsmead Ave NG9 170 D2
Kingsmeadow NG21 118 C8
King's Mill★ NG17 101 C5
King's Mill Ctr Hospl NG17 101 C5
Kings Mill La NG18 101 D4

Kings Mill Rd E
1 Sutton in Ashfield NG17 100 F1
Sutton in Ashfield NG17, NG19 114 E8
Kings Mill Rd W NG17 114 B7
Kings Mill Way NG18 101 E4
Kings Moor NG5 160 E7
Kingsnorth Cl NG24 140 A8
King's Pl NG1 223 F2
Kings Rd
Long Clawson LE14 211 C2
Sandiacre NG10 182 B6
King's Rd NG24 124 F1
Kings Sconce Ave 7 NG24 125 A2
Kings Stand NG18 102 E4
King St
Beeston NG9 184 A6
Eastwood NG16 143 E2
Gainsborough DN21 24 D7
Hodthorpe S80 45 C6
Huthwaite NG17 100 B3
Ilkeston DE7 157 F1
Kirkby-in-Ashfield NG17 115 A4
Long Eaton NG10 193 D8
Loughborough LE11 220 C3
Mansfield NG18 102 D7
Mansfield Woodhouse NG19 88 D2
Nether Broughton LE14 219 D8
Newark-on-Trent NG24 139 E7
Nottingham NG1 223 E3
Pinxton NG16 113 D4
South Normanton DE55 113 A5
Southwell NG25 121 E1
Southwell NG25 136 E8
Sutton in Ashfield NG17 100 E2
Tibshelf DE55 99 A7
Warsop Vale NG20 73 D5
Worksop S80 35 E2
Kingsthorpe Cl NG19 88 E1
Kingston Ave DE7 170 A4
Kingston Cl S80 47 C8
Kingston Ct
Kingston on Soar NG11 204 D5
14 Nottingham NG2 173 E4
Kingston Dr
Cotgrave NG12 187 F1
Ollerton NG22 77 A3
Kingston Fields NG11 204 D5
Kingston La DE74 203 F3
KINGSTON ON SOAR 204 A4
Kingston Park Acad S81 25 F6
Kingston Rd
Carlton in Lindrick S81 25 E6
3 Kirkby-in-Ashfield NG17 114 F8
Mansfield NG18 102 D7
West Bridgford NG2 185 E6
Worksop S80 36 B1
Worksop S80 47 B8
Kings Walk NG19 102 D4
Kingsway
Ilkeston DE7 170 A6
Kirkby-in-Ashfield NG17 115 B3
Kirkby-in-Ashfield NG17 115 B4
Mansfield Woodhouse NG19 89 A1
New Balderton NG24 140 C3
Radcliffe on Trent NG12 175 E2
Worksop S81 36 A4
Kings Way S80 45 C6
Kingsway Ave NG22 77 D6
Kingsway Gdns NG15 145 E4
Kingsway Prim Sch NG17 115 B3
Kingsway Rd NG15 145 E4
Kingswell Ave NG5 161 F7
Kingswell Rd NG5 161 F6
Kings Wlk NG18 102 E4
King's Wlk NG1 223 E3
Kingswood Cl S81 16 A5
Kings Wood Cl DN10 10 A8
Kingswood Dr NG17 114 F6
Kingswood Rd
Nottingham NG8 172 B5
West Bridgford NG2 185 D5
Kinlet Rd NG5 161 A6
KINOULTON 200 A2
Kinoulton La
Kinoulton NG12 209 B8
Kinoulton, Owthorpe NG12 199 F4
Stanton-on-the-Wolds NG12 199 A1
Widmerpool NG12 209 A8
Kinoulton Prim Sch NG12 199 E1
Kinoulton Rd NG12 188 F2
Kinsdale Wlk NG11 184 E3
Kipling Cl
Nottingham NG11 195 C8
Worksop S81 35 F5
Kipling St 6 NG18 102 A7
Kipps St NG1 223 F3
Kirby Cl
Blidworth NG21 118 A4
Eastwood NG16 144 A3
Kirby Dr DE74 203 C1
Kirby Rd NG16 144 A3
Kirk Ave DE74 203 D2
Kirkbride Ct NG9 183 B4
Kirkby Cl NG25 121 E2
Kirkby Coll NG17 115 B4
Kirkby Folly Rd NG17 101 B1
Kirkby Gdns NG2 173 D2
Kirkby Hardwick NG17 115 B8
Kirkby House Dr NG17 114 E5
KIRKBY-IN-ASHFIELD 115 C4
Kirkby-in-Ashfield Sta NG17 115 A5
Kirkby La
Pinxton NG16 113 F3
Pinxton NG16 114 B4
Kirkby Mill View NG17 114 E5
Kirkby Rd
Ravenshead NG15 116 C3
Sutton in Ashfield NG17 100 E1
KIRKBY WOODHOUSE 114 D1
Kirkby Woodhouse Prim Sch NG17 114 E1
Kirk Cl NG9 183 D4
Kirkdale Cl NG8 171 B4
Kirkdale Gdns NG10 193 B6
Kirkdale Rd
Long Eaton NG10 193 B6
Nottingham NG3 174 B6
Kirk Dr NG22 77 E6
Kirke Cl NG22 66 B7
Kirke St DN22 39 F7
Kirkewhite Ave NG10 193 D7
Kirkfell Cl NG2 186 C5
Kirk Gate NG24 124 F1
Kirkham Dr NG9 182 F2
Kirkhill NG13 177 E5
Kirk Hill NG13 165 B2
Kirk La NG11 196 C7
Kirkland Ave NG18 101 F6
Kirkland Cl
Sutton Forest Side NG17 101 B1
Sutton in Ashfield NG17 115 B8
Kirkland Dr NG9 183 C2
Kirkley Gdns NG5 162 A8
Kirk Ley Rd LE12 214 D8
KIRKLINGTON 120 E8
Kirklington Cl NG25 121 D1
Kirklington Prim Sch NG22 120 E7
Kirklington Rd
Bilsthorpe NG22 105 D2
Bilsthorpe NG22 106 A3
Bilsthorpe NG22 106 B2
Eakring NG22 106 E8
Hockerton NG25 121 F6
Hockerton NG25 122 A6
Rainworth NG21, NG22 104 C1
Southwell NG25 121 D1
Kirkpatrick Dr S81 35 C7
Kirk Rd NG3 162 A2
Kirk's Bldgs NG4 174 D7
Kirks Croft NG21 117 F4
KIRKSTEAD 113 D3
Kirkstead Cl NG16 113 D3
Kirkstead Gdns 7 NG7 172 F7
Kirkstead Jun Acad NG16 113 D3
Kirkstead Rd NG16 113 D3
Kirkstead St 6 NG7 172 F7
Kirkstone Ave NG16 143 B1
Kirkstone Ct NG10 182 B2
Kirkstone Dr NG2 186 C7
Kirk White Ct NG2 173 D2
Kirtle Cl NG8 172 B8
Kirtley Cl NG16 159 A8
Kirtley Dr NG2 173 A2
Kirtling Cl NG5 161 C8
KIRTON 78 C6
Kirton Ave NG10 193 D7
Kirton Cl
Balderton NG24 140 D2
Mansfield NG19 101 D7
Meden Vale NG20 74 E8
Kirton Ct NG22 78 B6
Kirton Pk NG22 78 C6
Kirton Rd
Egmanton NG22 79 D6
Kirton NG22 78 F6
Kirton Wood Nature Reserve* NG22 78 F5
Kitchener Dr NG18 102 C6
Kitchener Gdns S81 35 E8
Kitchener Terr NG20 59 A2
Kitson Ave NG16 128 C4
Kittiwake Mews NG7 222 A2
Kiwi Cl NG15 145 D5
Knapp Ave NG16 143 F1
Knaton Rd S81 25 E7
KNEESALL 93 F5
Kneesall Cl NG20 74 D7
Kneesall Gr NG15 146 B7
Kneesall Rd
Laxton NG22 79 C1
Ossington NG22 94 E5
Ossington NG23 95 A6
KNEETON 152 A1
Kneeton Cl
Carlton NG4 162 D4
Nottingham NG5 161 C4
Kneeton Rd
East Bridgford NG13 165 C3
East Bridgford NG13 165 E5
Kneeton NG13 166 A7
Kneeton Vale NG5 161 C4
Knighton Av NG7 172 E6
Knighton Ave NG7 222 A4
Knighton Rd NG5 161 D5
Knightsbridge Dr
Nuthall NG8 159 E3
West Bridgford NG2 185 C4
Knightsbridge Gdns NG15 130 F1
Knights Cl
Beeston NG9 182 F2
Beeston NG9 183 A2
Nottingham NG5 160 F8
West Bridgford NG2 185 C3
Knight's Cl NG13 166 E4
Knight's Ct NG24 140 A8
Knights Rd
7 Mansfield NG19 87 D1
Old Dalby LE14 219 B5
Knight St NG4 175 A6
Knights Wlk DN22 29 A6
Knipton Cl NG24 140 D3
Knitters Rd DE55 113 C6
Knole Rd NG8 171 E5
Knoll Ave NG15 145 D5
Knoll The
Mansfield NG18 101 E6
Shirebrook NG20 72 D3
Knott End S81 16 E3
Knott's Ct NG24 140 D4
Knowle Hill NG16 159 A5
Knowle La NG16 159 A5
Knowle Pk NG16 159 A5
Knowles Wlk NG5 161 D8
Kozi Kots NG4 174 F7
Krebs Cl NG11 184 C1
KS4 Support Centre NG10 193 B4
Kyle View NG5 147 A1
Kyme St NG7 222 B3
Kynance Cl DE55 113 C6
Kynance Gdns NG11 185 B5
Kyte St NG7 222 B2

L

Labray Rd NG14 148 E8
Laburnium Cl NG24 140 C5
Laburnum Ave
Gainsborough DN21 15 D2
Keyworth NG12 198 A2
Kirkby-in-Ashfield NG17 114 D3
Shirebrook NG20 72 E5
Laburnum Cl
Hathern LE12 213 A1
Sandiacre NG10 182 B7
South Normanton DE55 113 B7
Worksop S80 35 D1
Laburnum Gr
Beeston NG9 184 B5
Hucknall NG15 146 B5
Mansfield Woodhouse NG19 88 A4
Laburnum Rd S81 16 F4
Laburnum St NG3 173 D7
Laceby Ct NG19 88 E4
Lace Ctr The* NG1 223 D2
Lace Gdns NG11 196 B8
Lacemaker Rd NG9 183 F4
Lace Market Theatre The* NG1 223 E2
Lace Mead NG24 140 A4
Lace Mkt Ctr The* NG1 223 E2
Lace Rd NG9 183 F7
Lace St NG7 172 D1
Lace Way NG14 173 E4
Lacewood Cl NG15 146 E4
Lace Wy NG1 173 E3
Lacey Ave NG15 146 A5
Lacey Cl DE7 157 C3
Lacey Fields Rd DE75 143 B1
Lacey Gn NG24 140 E3
Lacey Gr NG15 130 D7
Lacey St NG12 197 F5
Ladbrooke Cres NG6 160 C3
Ladybank Rise NG5 162 C8
Lady Bay Ave NG2 173 F1
Lady Bay Bridge NG2 173 E2
Lady Bay Prim Sch NG2 174 A1
Lady Bay Rd NG2 174 A1
Lady Bay Ret Pk NG2 173 E3
Ladybird Cl
East Leake LE12 214 D7
Loughborough LE11 220 C4
Ladybridge Cl NG9 183 E3
Ladybrook La NG18 101 F7
Ladybrook Pl NG19 101 E7
Ladybrook Primary Sch NG19 101 D8
Ladycroft Ave NG15 146 A7
Ladycross Inf Sch NG10 182 B6
Ladylea Cl S80 35 B2
Ladylea Rd NG10 193 A4
Lady Lee Quarry Nature Reserve* S80 35 A4
Lady Margaret Cres NG20 60 C5
Ladysmith Rd NG2 174 A4
Ladysmock Gdns NG2 173 D2
Lady Well La DN22 52 B8
Lady Wlk S81 35 C7
Ladywood La NG23 80 E5
Lake Ave NG19 101 E7
Lake Farm Rd NG21 103 F1
Lakeland Ave NG15 146 C5
Lakeland Rd NG14 149 C6
Lakeside Arts Ctr* NG7 172 D1
Lakeside Ave NG10 193 C4
Lakeside Bsns Ctr DE75 157 A6
Lakeside Cres NG10 193 C5
Lakeside View NG17 101 B4
Lake St NG7 222 B4
Lake View S80 61 C6
Lake View Dr NG17 129 F6
Lakeview Prim Sch NG21 103 F1
Lamartine Ct NG3 223 F3
Lamartine St NG3 223 F3
Lamb Cl NG24 139 C7
Lamb Cl Dr NG16 144 B4
Lambcroft Rd NG16 113 D4
Lambert Ct NG9 184 B7
Lambert Gdns
Keyworth NG12 197 D3
Nottingham NG8 172 C8
Lambert Pl LN1 57 A5
Lamberts La NG23 95 C6
Lambert St NG7 172 E7
Lambeth Rd NG5 147 A2
Lambie Cl NG8 172 C5
Lamb La S81 16 C5
LAMBLEY 163 C8
Lambley Ave
Mansfield NG18 102 F5
Nottingham NG3 162 B3
Lambley La
Burton Joyce NG14 163 E5
Carlton NG4 162 F3
Lambley Prim Sch NG4 163 B7
Lambley Rd NG14 150 B1
Lambourne Cl NG9 183 C8
Lambourne Cres NG14 150 F1
Lambourne Dr NG8 172 A5
Lambourne Gdns NG5 162 A5
Lambton Cl DE7 157 E3
Lamcote Gdns NG12 175 E3
Lamcote Gr NG2 173 D1
Lamcote Mews NG4 175 E3
Lamcote St NG2 173 D1
Laming Gap La NG12 198 E5
Lamins La NG5 147 D4
Lammas Cl NG17 100 E2
Lammas Dr LE12 212 F1
Lammas Gdns
East Bridgford NG13 165 D4
Nottingham NG2 173 D2
Lammas La NG13 165 D4
Lammas Rd NG17 100 E2
Lammas Sch The NG17 100 E3
Lamond Cl NG19 101 E5
Lamorna Gr NG11 185 B6
Lamplands NG12 187 E3
Lampman Way S81 16 E1
Lamp Wood Cl NG14 148 E7
Lanark Cl NG8 172 C3
Lancaster Ave
Sandiacre NG10 182 A4
Stapleford NG9 182 E7
Lancaster Cl DN11 8 B7
Lancaster Dr DN10 9 F8
Lancaster Rd
Bestwood Village NG6 146 E4
Gringley on the Hill DN10 22 A8
Hucknall NG15 145 D4
Newark-on-Trent NG24 125 E2
Nottingham NG3 174 B7
Lancaster Way
Nottingham NG8 159 D2
Skellingthorpe LN6 71 F4
Lancaster Wlk S81 35 E8
Lancastrian Way S81 36 A6
Lancelot Dr NG16 145 A1
Lancelot Way NG19 87 D1
Lancelyn Gdns NG2 185 E4
Lancster Cres DN11 8 B7
Landa Gr NG22 66 A3
Landa Gr Pk NG22 66 A3
Landcroft Cres NG5 161 A6
Landcroft La LE12 204 D1
Landmere Cl DE7 157 C3
Landmere Gdns NG3 161 F1
Landmere La
West Bridgford NG11 185 C3
West Bridgford NG11, NG12 185 E1
Landsdowne Ct DN22 39 D4
Landsdowne Rd 3 NG5 160 E4
Landsdown Gr NG10 182 F1
Landseer Cl
Nottingham NG7 222 A4
Southwell NG25 136 C8
Landseer Rd NG25 136 C8
Lane End NG17 115 A5
LANEHAM 54 B6
Laneham Ave NG5 162 A7
Laneham Rd
Dunham-on-Trent NG22 54 A2
Stokeham DN22 53 D6
Laneham St DN22 43 A1
Lanercost Mews 3 S80 35 F2
Lanesborough Ct LE11 220 B2
Laneside Ave NG9 182 E2
Lanes Prim Sch The NG9 183 D5
Lane The
Awsworth NG16 158 C4
Cotham NG23 154 F3
Laneward Cl DE7 157 D4
LANGAR 190 D2
Langar CE Prim Sch NG13 190 C2
Langar Cl NG5 161 C4
Langar Industrial Estate NG13 201 E6
Langar La
Colston Bassett NG12 200 F8
Harby LE14 202 A4
Langar Pl NG19 103 B8
Langar Rd
Bingham NG13 177 E4
Langar NG13 190 D3
Tithby NG12 189 E3
Langdale Cl NG24 139 E4
Langdale Dr
Long Eaton NG10 193 A6
Tickhill DN11 8 B8
Langdale Gr NG13 177 B4
Langdale Rd
Nottingham NG3 174 C5
Worksop S81 35 F7
Langdon Cl
Long Eaton NG10 182 A1
Nottingham NG5 161 A2
Langdown Cl NG6 160 A8
Langer Ind Est NG13 190 E1
LANGFORD 111 E1
Langford La NG23 111 A3
Langford Moor La NG24 126 B5
Langford Rd
Arnold NG5 162 B7
Mansfield NG19 101 D6
Langford St NG17 100 E3
Langham Ave NG3 174 A6
Langham Dr
Burton Joyce NG14 163 F5
Burton Joyce NG14 164 A5
Langham Pl NG18 101 F7
Langholme La DN9 6 C8
Langley Ave
Arnold NG5 161 F6
Ilkeston DE7 157 D5
Langley Bridge Ind Est DE75 143 D3
Langley Cl
Mansfield NG19 87 E1
Nottingham NG6 146 E4
Langley Dr DE74 203 C2
LANGLEY MILL 143 B3
Langley Mill Business Park NG16 143 B2
Langley Mill CE Inf Sch NG16 143 B3
Langley Mill Jun Sch NG16 143 A4
Langley Mill Sta NG16 143 B2
Langley Pk DE75 143 B3
Langley St 1 S80 35 F2
LANGOLD 16 E4
Langold Ctry Pk* S81 16 E2
Langold Dyscarr Com Sch S81 16 D3
Langstrath Dr NG2 186 C4
Langstrath Rd NG7 184 E1
Langton Ave NG17 114 D6
Langton Cl NG4 174 E6
Langton Hollow NG16 128 D6
Langton Rd
Bircotes DN11 9 B3
Sutton in Ashfield NG17 100 E2
Langtree Gdns NG13 177 F5
Langtry Gr NG7 161 A1
Langwell Dr NG19 89 C2
LANGWITH 72 F8
Langwith Bassett Com Prim Sch NG20 72 E7
Langwith Cl DE7 157 F5
Langwith Dr NG20 58 F1
Langwith Lodge Dr NG20 59 B1
Langwith Maltings NG20 72 F8
Langwith Rd
Cuckney NG20 60 A2
Nether Langwith NG20 59 E1
Shirebrook NG20 72 F5
Langwith-Whaley Thorns Sta NG20 58 F2
Lansbury Ave NG22 77 C6
Lansbury Dr
Bilsthorpe NG22 105 F7
South Normanton DE55 113 A6
Lansbury Gdns NG18 102 E8
Lansbury Rd
Bilsthorpe NG22 105 E7
Edwinstowe NG21 76 B2
New Balderton NG24 140 C4
Sutton in Ashfield NG17 100 F1
Lansdall Ave DN21 24 E3
Lansdown Cl NG9 183 B4
Lansdowne Ave NG18 102 D2
Lansdowne Dr
Loughborough LE11 220 A1
West Bridgford NG2 185 D4
Lansic La NG14 151 C1
Lansing Cl NG11 195 F8
Lantern La LE12 205 F2
Lantern La Prim Sch Annex LE12 205 F2
Lanthwaite Cl NG7 184 F1
Lanthwaite Rd NG7 184 F1
Lapford Cl NG3 162 D6
Lapwing Cl DN21 14 B2
Larch Ave
Mansfield Woodhouse NG19 88 B5
Shirebrook NG20 72 D4
Larch Cl
Bingham NG13 178 A4
Friezeland NG16 129 B3
Hucknall NG15 146 B5
Nottingham NG5 161 C8
Larch Cres
Beeston NG9 183 D7
Eastwood NG16 143 E2
Larch Ct DN21 15 E2
Larchdale Cl DE55 113 A4
Larchdene Ave NG8 171 D3
Larch Dr NG10 182 B7
Larch Gdns NG6 160 A7
Larch Rd NG22 77 D5
Larch Way NG12 198 A2
Largs Cl NG5 146 E1
Lark Cl
Beeston NG9 183 A5
Mansfield NG19 87 F1
Larkdale St NG7 222 C4
Larkfield Ave NG17 114 E1
Larkfield Rd NG16 159 B6
Larkfields NG24 139 D5
Larkfields Inf Sch NG16 159 B6
Larkfields Jun Sch NG16 159 B5
Larkhall Pl NG19 101 E5
Larklands Ave DE7 170 A7
Lark Spinney S81 35 C6
Larkspur Ave NG5 147 E2
Larkspur Cl
Mansfield NG19 88 D2
South Normanton DE55 113 A4
Larkwood Cl NG8 172 A8
Larpit Gn S80 45 A5
Larwood Ave S81 36 B5
Larwood Cres NG17 114 F1
Larwood Gr NG5 161 C4
Lascelles Ave NG4 162 D2
Latham St NG6 160 B7
Lathkill Ave DE7 157 E5
Lathkill Cl NG6 160 B7
Lathkilldale Cres NG10 193 A5
Lathkill Dr NG16 128 F7
Latimer Cl NG6 160 C6
Latimer Dr NG9 171 B3
Latimer Way NG22 77 C4
Latin Gr NG15 146 C8
LAUGHTERTON 55 A4
Laughton Ave NG2 185 C4
Laughton Cres NG15 145 E4
Laughton La DN21 15 A5
Laughton Rd DN21 15 C7
Launceston Cres NG11 185 A4
Launder St
Nottingham NG2 173 C2
Orston NG13 179 F7
Launds Ave NG16 128 D7
Laurel Ave
Church Warsop NG20 74 A7
Keyworth NG12 197 F2
Mansfield NG18 102 C5
Mansfield Woodhouse NG19 89 A1
Misterton DN10 6 E3
Laurel Cl
Gainsborough DN21 15 E2
Shirebrook NG20 72 D6
Wysall NG12 207 C3
Laurel Cres
Long Eaton NG10 193 C6
Nuthall NG16 159 B6
Laurel Gr
Kirkby-in-Ashfield NG17 115 C5
South Normanton DE55 113 A4
Laurel Rd NG4 174 C8
Laurels Cl NG23 110 F8
Laurels The DN22 39 E4
Laurence View Prim Sch NG16 144 A3
Lauren Gr NG9 182 F2
Laurie Ave NG7 173 A8
Laurie Cl 4 NG7 173 A8
Lauriston Dr NG6 160 D4
Lavelle Ct NG9 183 D1
Lavender Cl
New Ollerton NG22 77 D4
2 Nottingham NG8 159 E1
Shirebrook NG20 72 D3
Tibshelf DE55 99 B7
Lavender Cres NG4 162 D1
Lavender Gdns DE75 143 B1
Lavender Gr
Beeston NG9 184 B5
Cotgrave NG12 188 A5
Lavender Way NG24 125 E1
Lavender Wlk NG3 173 D7
Lavenham Mews 8 S80 35 F2
Laver Cl NG5 162 B7
Laverick Rd NG16 128 A4
Laverock Cl NG16 158 F6
Lavinia Cres NG12 186 A2
Lawdon Rd NG5 148 A1
Lawley Ave NG9 172 A1
Lawn Ave NG17 100 F2
Lawn Gr NG4 163 A1
Lawn La
Old Dalby LE14 218 E2
Sutton in Ashfield NG17 100 F2
Lawn Mill Rd NG16 158 E7
Lawn Rd
Carlton in Lindrick S81 25 E8
Sutton in Ashfield NG17 101 B3
Lawns Rd NG17 129 F8
Lawns The
Beeston NG9 183 B7
Collingham NG23 98 B1
Whatton NG13 179 A3
Lawnwood Ave DN22 50 A3
Lawnwood La DN22 50 A3
Lawrence Ave
Awsworth NG16 158 C4
Carlton NG4 174 E5
Eastwood NG16 143 F2
Kirkby-in-Ashfield NG17 114 E5
Mansfield Woodhouse NG19 88 B4
Lawrence Cl NG12 187 F3
Lawrence Cres NG17 101 B4
Lawrence Dr
Brinsley NG16 143 D8
Nottingham NG8 159 C2
Lawrence Pk NG16 129 B3
Lawrence Pl NG24 125 A1
Lawrence St
Long Eaton NG10 193 D8
Newark-on-Trent NG24 125 A1
Sandiacre NG10 182 B7
Stapleford NG9 182 D6

Lawrence Way [6] NG2 173 A2
Lawson Ave NG10 193 E7
Lawson Cl DN22 50 F2
Lawson Sq S81 18 B2
Lawson St NG7 222 C4
Lawton Dr NG6 146 C1
LAXTON 79 C3
Laxton Ave
Nottingham NG6 160 D5
Sutton in Ashfield NG17 101 C1
Laxton Cl [3] NG8 172 B7
Laxton Dr
Hucknall NG15 145 E6
Meden Vale NG20 74 D8
Laxton Rd NG22 79 D4
Laxton Visitors Ctr*
NG22 79 C3
Laycock Ave DN10 12 E2
Layton Ave NG18 102 A7
Layton Burroughs [11]
NG18 102 A7
LEA 24 F2
Lea Bank DE55 113 A4
Leabrook Cl NG11 184 C3
Leabrook Gdns NG15 146 C8
Leabrooks Ave
Mansfield Woodhouse
NG19 88 D5
Sutton in Ashfield NG17 101 C1
Leach Cl NG22 54 C1
Leachcroft Hill NG25 136 B8
Leach Wy NG21 118 B6
Lea Cl NG15 117 B2
Leacroft Rd NG8 172 D8
Lea Ct
Bingham NG13 177 D3
Worksop S80 35 C2
Leadale Ave NG15 146 C8
Leadale Cres NG19 88 E5
Lead Hill S80 35 E2
Leaf Cl NG15 131 B1
Leafe Cl NG9 183 C2
Leafield DN22 39 D8
Leafield Gn NG7 184 E2
Leahurst Gdns NG2 186 B6
Leahurst Rd NG2 186 B5
Leake La LE12 214 D3
Leake Rd
Costock LE12 206 B1
Gotham NG11 205 C6
Lea La NG16 128 F6
Leam Glen NG19 88 D2
Leamington Dr
Beeston NG9 183 C4
South Normanton DE55 113 B5
Sutton in Ashfield NG17 114 E8
Leamington Hall NG17 100 E1
Leamington Prim Sch
NG17 114 F8
Leander Cl
Nottingham NG11 185 B6
Sutton Forest Side NG17 101 B2
Leaning Row NG7 222 B2
Lea Rd
Gainsborough DN21 24 E5
Market Warsop NG20 74 C3
Ravenshead NG15 117 B2
Torksey LN1 44 B4
Lea Rd W DN21 24 D5
Leas Ave NG19 87 A5
Leas Park Jun Sch
NG19 88 C4
Leas Rd NG19 88 D4
Leas The NG14 164 B5
Leatherlands DE74 203 D3
Lea Vale DE55 113 A4
Leaverton Mws S81 16 F3
Leaway The NG20 72 D3
Le Brun Sq S81 25 E7
Lechlade Rd NG5 161 A6
Ledbury Vale NG8 172 B8
Leech Ct NG16 158 B7
Lee Cres DE7 170 A8
Leeds Rd S81 34 F7
Leeks Rd NG25 121 E1
Lee La DE75 143 B1
Leeming Cl NG20 74 C5
Leeming Ct DN11 9 F6
Leeming La NG19, NG20 88 E7
Leeming La N NG19 88 E5
Leeming La S NG19 88 C2
Leeming Pk NG19 88 C3
Leeming St NG18 102 B7
Leen Cl
Bestwood Village NG6 146 F4
Hucknall NG15 146 C8
Leen Ct NG22 78 A4
Leen Dr
Hucknall NG15 131 B1
Nottingham NG6 146 C1
Leen Gate NG7 172 E2
Leen Mills La NG15 131 A1
Leen Mills Prim Sch
NG15 146 B8
Leen Pl NG7 222 A3
Leen Valley Dr NG20 72 E3
Leen Valley Way
NG15 146 C5
Lee Rd
Burton Joyce NG14 164 A5
Calverton NG14 148 D8
Lees Ave NG19 101 D7
Lees Barn Rd NG12 175 D2
Lees Hill St NG2 173 E4
Lees La DE55 113 A6
Leeson Cl NG4 174 E5
Lees Rd NG3 162 A2
Leeway Cl NG21 103 E2
Leeway Rd
Mansfield NG21 103 E2
Southwell NG25 121 D1
Legion Dr NG17 100 D6
Leicester Cres S81 35 E7
Leicester Rd LE11 220 C4
Leicester St NG10 193 E6
Leigh Cl NG2 185 C6
Leigh Rd NG9 182 F3
Leighton St NG3 173 F6
Leiston Gdns NG5 161 A8
Leivers Ave NG5 161 F8
Leivers Cl LE12 205 E1
Lema Cl NG6 160 D7
Lemont Rd NG19 89 A2
Lemynton St LE11 220 B4
Lendrum Ct NG14 163 F4
Len Maynard Ct NG4 174 A6
Lennox St NG1 223 F3
Lenton Ave
Nottingham NG7 222 C1
Tollerton NG12 186 C1
Lenton Bvd NG7 222 B2
Lenton Cir NG12 186 C1
Lenton Ct NG7 222 B2
Lenton Hall Dr NG7 172 C1
Lenton Ind Est E NG7 184 F8
Lenton Ind Est W NG7 184 E8
Lenton La NG7 184 F8
Lenton Manor NG7 222 A1
Lenton Prim Sch NG7 222 B1
Lenton Rd NG7 223 D2
Lenton St NG10 182 C7
Leonard Ave NG5 161 B2
Leonard Cheshire Cl
DE75 143 B1
Leonard Mews NG9 183 B2
Leonard St NG6 160 B5
Leopold St
Long Eaton NG10 193 D8
Loughborough LE11 220 A5
Sutton in Ashfield NG17 100 E1
Le Page Ct NG8 172 A7
Leroy Wallace Ave
NG7 222 B4
Lerwick Cl
Nottingham NG11 185 A1
Worksop S81 35 E8
Leslie Ave
Beeston NG9 183 F5
Kimberley NG16 158 F5
[6] Nottingham NG7 173 A8
Leslie Gr NG14 148 F7
Leslie Rd NG7 173 A8
Less Field NG25 136 D7
Letchworth Cres NG9 183 C4
Letcombe Rd NG11 184 E3
LETWELL 16 A3
Levellers Way NG24 140 E8
Levels La
Blaxton DN9 1 A8
Misson DN10 4 B6
Levens Cl NG2 186 C5
Leverton Gn NG7 184 E2
Leverton Rd
Mansfield NG19 101 E7
Retford DN22 40 A8
Retford DN22 40 C7
Sturton le Steeple DN22 32 D4
Levertons Pl NG15 146 B4
Leverton Wlk NG5 162 A8
Levesley Gdns LE14 202 F3
Levick Ct [2] NG2 173 C2
Lewcote La DE7 157 A1
Lewindon Ct NG5 161 E4
Lewis Cl NG3 223 F4
Lewis Cres NG15 130 D7
Lewis St DN21 24 D8
Lewis Way NG6 147 B5
Lewsey Cl NG9 183 B2
Lexington Ct NG22 65 F2
Lexington Gdns
Nottingham NG5 161 D4
Tuxford NG22 65 F2
Ley Bank NG18 103 A4
Leybourne Dr NG5 160 E6
Ley Croft NG19 88 D5
Ley La
East Drayton DN22 53 D3
Mansfield Woodhouse
NG19 88 D4
Leyland Cl NG9 182 F2
Leys Ct NG11 196 C6
Leys La
Gringley on the Hill DN10 12 E2
Tuxford NG22 65 A3
Leys Rd NG11 196 C6
Ley St NG4 175 A7
Leys The
Lowdham NG14 150 D2
Normanton-on-the-Wolds
NG12 197 F7
Nottingham NG11 184 D1
Leyton Ave NG17 101 A5
Leyton Cres NG9 184 B5
Liber Cl NG18 102 F8
Liberty Cl NG19 87 F1
Library Rd NG7 172 C1
Lichfield Ave NG18 102 C2
Lichfield Cl
Beeston NG9 182 E3
Mansfield NG18 102 C2
Worksop S81 36 A7
Lichfield La NG18 102 D3
Lichfield Rd NG2 174 A4
Lichfield Wlk S81 25 E7
Liddell Gr NG8 171 F4
Liddington St NG7 160 F1
Lidget La DN22 40 A8
LIDGETT 91 B8
Lidgett La NG21 76 C3
Lido Cl NG6 145 C1
Lievesley Gr [1] NG4 162 E3
Lifton Ave DN22 29 E1
Lightfoot Cl NG24 140 E8
Lightning Gr NG15 145 D3
Lilac Ave NG4 174 C8
Lilac Cl
Keyworth NG12 198 A2
Newark-on-Trent NG24 139 F4
[7] Nottingham NG8 159 E1
Sutton cum Lound DN22 29 A7
Lilac Cres NG9 184 B5
Lilac Gr
Bawtry DN10 9 F7
Beeston NG9 184 B5
Clipstone NG19 89 D2
Glapwell S44 86 B8
Kirkby-in-Ashfield NG17 114 D4
Market Warsop NG20 73 F7
Shirebrook NG20 72 E5
South Normanton DE55 113 A4
Lilac Mews DE7 157 D3
Lilac Rd NG15 146 B5
Lilac Tree Gr S81 25 E7
Lilburne Cl NG24 140 E8
Lillee Ct S81 36 B5
Lilleker Rise NG5 147 E1
Lilley Cl NG16 128 E6
Lillington Rd NG6 160 B7
Lily Ave NG4 175 A7
Lily Gr NG9 184 B5
Lily La NG24 125 D1
Lily Way NG22 77 C6
Limb Cres NG17 100 F1
Lime Ave
Firbeck S81 16 A6
Huthwaite NG17 100 A3
Langley Mill NG16 143 C2
Loughborough LE11 220 C3
Sutton in Ashfield NG17 100 F4
Lime Cl
Nuthall NG16 159 A6
Pinxton NG16 113 D3
Radcliffe on Trent NG12 175 F3
Torksey Lock LN1 44 B1
Lime Cres NG20 73 F7
Lime Gr
Bottesford NG13 181 A2
Long Eaton NG10 193 D8
Mansfield Woodhouse
NG19 89 C1
Newark-on-Trent NG24 139 F7
Retford DN22 39 D7
Sandiacre NG10 182 B6
South Normanton DE55 113 A5
Stapleford NG9 182 D5
Lime Gr Ave NG9 183 E5
Limehurst Ave LE11 220 A5
Limehurst High Sch
LE11 220 A5
Limekiln Ct NG6 160 A8
Lime Kiln Pl NG18 102 B6
Limekiln Way S81 34 E7
Lime La NG5 147 F4
Limes Ave NG20 59 A2
Limes Cl NG16 143 C4
Limes Cres NG20 72 D5
Limes Ct NG17 101 C1
Lime St
Kirkby-in-Ashfield
NG17 115 A5
Nottingham NG6 160 B7
Sutton in Ashfield NG17 101 A3
Limes The
Beckingham DN10 14 B1
Farnsfield NG22 119 F6
Limestone Ri NG19 102 A8
Limestone Rise NG19 88 A1
Limestone Terr NG19 88 B4
Lime Terr NG10 193 D8
Limetree Ave
Carburton NG22 61 C6
Worksop S80 48 C6
Lime Tree Ave
Carlton in Lindrick S81 25 E7
Gainsborough DN21 15 D1
Glapwell S44 86 B8
Kirkby-in-Ashfield NG17 114 F5
Mansfield Woodhouse
NG19 88 A5
Nottingham NG8 160 C3
Retford DN22 39 D7
Sutton in Ashfield NG17 100 D6
Limetree Cl NG12 197 F2
Lime Tree Cl
Collingham NG23 112 A8
New Ollerton NG22 77 D5
Lime Tree Cres DN10 9 F7
Lime Tree Ct NG9 172 A1
Lime Tree Dr NG18 116 E7
Lime Tree Gdns NG14 150 E1
Limetree Gr [5] LE11 220 C3
Lime Tree Mws S81 36 B5
Lime Tree Pl
Mansfield NG18 102 C6
Rainworth NG21 104 C1
Lime Tree Rd
Elkesley DN22 50 B3
Hucknall NG15 146 B4
New Ollerton NG22 77 C5
Limmen Gdns NG3 173 E6
Limpenny St NG7 222 C4
LINBY 131 A3
Linby Ave
Hucknall NG15 146 B7
Mansfield NG19 101 D6
Linby Cl
Carlton NG4 162 E2
Nottingham NG5 161 D5
Linby Cum Papplewick CE
Prim Sch NG15 131 B3
Linby Dr
Bircotes DN11 9 B3
Nottingham NG8 159 D2
Linby Gr NG15 146 B7
Linby La NG15 131 C3
Linby Rd
Hucknall NG15 131 B1
Hucknall NG15 146 B8
Linby St NG6 160 C8
Linby Wk NG15 131 A1
Linby Wlk NG15 146 A8
Lincoln Ave NG10 182 A4
Lincoln Cir NG7 222 C2
Lincoln Cl
Stapleford NG9 170 E1
Tibshelf DE55 99 A6
Lincoln Ct
Newark-on-Trent NG24 125 B2
Nottingham NG8 171 E7
Lincoln Dr NG19 88 D4
Lincoln Gr
Radcliffe on Trent
NG12 175 F3
Radcliffe on Trent NG12 176 A3
Lincoln La LN1 55 E5
Lincoln Rd
Eagle LN6 84 D3
East Markham NG22 66 A7
East Markham NG22 66 C7
Fenton LN1 55 D6
Newark-on-Trent NG24 125 B3
Saxilby LN1 57 D3
Torksey LN1 44 B1
Tuxford NG22 66 A3
Lincoln Rd Bridge
NG24 125 A2
Lincoln Red Cl DN22 39 C4
Lincoln St
Gainsborough DN21 15 C1
Newark-on-Trent NG24 125 A2
Nottingham NG1 223 E2
Nottingham, Old Basford
NG6 160 E3
Tibshelf DE55 99 A6
Worksop S80 36 A1
Lincoln View S80 36 A2
Lindale Cl NG2 186 C6
Lindbergh Cl S80 35 C2
Lindbridge Rd NG8 159 F2
Lind Cl NG21 103 F1
Linden Ave
New Balderton NG24 140 B5
Nottingham NG11 184 C1
Tuxford NG22 66 A2
Linden Gr
Beeston NG9 184 A5
Carlton NG4 163 B1
Kirkby-in-Ashfield NG17 114 D6
Sandiacre NG10 182 A7
Shirebrook NG20 72 F4
Stapleford NG9 182 E6
Linden Pl NG5 162 C6
Linden Rd
Loughborough LE11 220 A5
Mansfield NG18 102 F8
Linden St
Mansfield NG19 88 A1
Nottingham NG3 173 D7
Shirebrook NG20 72 F4
Shirebrook NG20 73 A4
Linden Terr DN21 24 D7
Linden Way City Hospital
Campus NG5 161 B5
Lindfield Cl NG8 160 A2
Lindfield Rd NG8 159 F2
Lindholme Way
Dalestorth NG17 101 A5
Sutton in Ashfield NG17 100 F5
Lindhurst La NG18 102 F4
Lindhurst Way W
NG18 102 E1
Lindisfarne Gdns [6]
NG5 147 A1
Lindley Ave NG17 100 D2
Lindley's La NG17 115 A3
Lindley St
Eastwood NG16 144 B4
Mansfield NG18 102 A7
Selston NG16 128 D6
Lindley Terr [2] NG7 172 E7
Lindrick DN11 8 A6
Lindrick Cl
Carlton in Lindrick S81 25 F7
Mansfield Woodhouse
NG19 88 D6
West Bridgford NG2 186 C4
Worksop S81 35 F5
Lindrick Ct DN22 39 D2
Lindrick Dr DN21 15 E3
Lindrick La DN11 8 A6
Lindrick Nook S81 35 F6
Lindrick Rd NG17 114 F7
Lindsay Ave
Annesley Woodhouse
NG17 115 B1
Newark-on-Trent NG24 139 F4
Lindsay Cl NG18 102 A6
Lindsey Cl DN21 24 F6
Lindsey Dr
Gainsborough DN21 15 F2
Mansfield NG18 103 A3
Lindsey Rd DN11 9 A5
Lindum Gr [3] NG2 173 F3
Lindum Mews NG24 140 A8
Lindum Rd NG6 160 D3
Lindum St [3] NG24 140 A8
Lindum Wy LN1 44 C1
Lindwall Ct S81 36 B5
Lindy Cl NG12 199 F2
Linecroft La DN10 14 C7
Linette Cl NG5 161 A2
Linford Ct NG9 171 B3
Ling Beeches DN22 39 D4
Ling Cres NG11 196 C8
Lingdale Cl LE11 220 B1
Ling Dr [8] DN21 15 F1
Lingfield Cl
Mansfield NG18 102 F5
Saxilby LN1 57 A4
Lingfield Ct NG8 171 D3
Lingford NG12 188 A3
Lingford St NG15 146 B6
Lingforest Cl NG18 103 A5
Lingforest Ct [3] NG18 103 A5
Lingforest Rd NG18 103 A5
Lingmell Cl NG2 186 C6
Ling Rd LE11 220 B1
Lings Bar Hospl NG2 186 D6
Lings Cl [17] DE7 157 F5
Lings La NG12 207 E7
Lings View NG20 74 C3
Lings Wood La DN10 10 D3
Lingwood Gr
Mansfield NG18 102 F7
Mansfield NG18 103 A7
Lingwood La NG14 149 B3
Linkin Rd NG9 183 C6
Linkmel Cl NG2 173 A1
Linkmel Rd NG16 143 C3
Linksfield Ct NG11 185 C2
Links The
Mansfield NG18 103 B6
Selston NG16 128 D6
Linley Cl NG23 112 A8
Linnell St NG3 173 F6
Linnet Cl [5] NG17 115 A3
Linnet Dr NG21 118 A8
Linnets Dr NG18 102 E7
Linnets The S81 35 D7
Linnet Wy NG15 145 F6
Linsdale Cl NG8 171 B5
Linsdale Gdns NG4 162 D4
Linseed Ave NG24 125 C4
Linseed Gr NG18 102 D1
Lintin Ave NG21 75 F2
Linton Cl
Bawtry DN11 9 F6
Farndon NG24 139 B5
Mansfield NG18 103 B6
Linton Dr NG22 77 F5
Linton Rise NG3 174 A6
Linwood Cl DN21 24 F7
Linwood Cres
Eastwood NG16 144 A1
Ravenshead NG15 116 F3
Linwood Ct NG19 88 E4
Lion Cl NG8 160 C2
Liquorice La S81 26 B4
Lisle St [1] LE11 220 A5
Lismore Cl NG7 222 A3
Lismore Ct NG19 101 D5
Lissington Rd DN21 24 E7
Lister Ct [4] NG7 172 E2
Lister Gate NG1 223 E2
Lister Rd NG7 172 E2
Listowel Cres NG11 195 E8
Litchen Cl DE7 157 F2
Litchfield Cl NG10 194 A7
Litchfield Rise NG5 147 E2
Little Acre NG19 88 E5
Little Barn Ct NG18 102 F6
Little Barn Gdns NG18 102 F5
Little Barn La NG18 102 F6
Little Belt The DN21 15 D3
Littleborough Rd
Littleborough DN22 33 E1
Sturton le Steeple DN22 33 B3
Little Bounds NG11 185 D7
Little Breck DE55 113 A4
LITTLE CARLTON 124 B8
Little Carter La NG18 102 E7
Little Debdale La NG19 87 F1
Little Green NG13 166 C3
Littlegreen Rd NG5 161 F5
LITTLE GRINGLEY DN22 40 E7
Little Gringley La DN22 40 D7
Little Hallam La DE7 170 A6
Little Haven NG19 89 B1
Little Hayes NG2 185 C4
Little Holland Gd NG16 159 B7
Little Hollies NG19 89 A2
Little John Ave NG20 74 C2
Little John Cl NG22 77 D6
Little John Dr NG21 104 A1
Little John Wlk [1]
NG3 173 D7
Little La
Blyth S81 18 B3
Calverton NG14 148 D7
Collingham NG23 111 F7
Edingley NG22 120 D3
Gringley on the Hill DN10 12 F2
Huthwaite NG17 99 E2
Kimberley NG16 158 F5
Pleasleyhill NG19 87 B5
Shirebrook NG20 72 D3
Thorpe Salvin S80 34 B6
Tollerton NG12 186 E3
Little Lincoln NG12 207 C2
Little London La NG12 207 C3
Little Lunnon NG11 194 E6
Little Mdw NG12 188 A2
Little Meadow Cl [1]
DE7 157 E2
Littlemoor La NG11 196 E3
Little Moor La LE11 220 C4
Little Oak Ave NG17 130 A7
Little Oak Dr NG17 129 F7
Little Oakwood Dr
NG5 146 D2
Littleover Ave NG18 103 B6
Little Ox NG4 174 F4
Little Ricket La NG15 116 D3
Little Tennis St S NG2 174 A2
Little Tennis St NG2 174 A3
Little Top La
Lound DN22 20 C1
Lound DN22 29 C8
Little Wlk DN21 7 D1
Littlewood Gdns NG8 171 C5
Littlewood La
Mansfield Woodhouse
NG19 88 A6
Shirebrook NG19 87 F8
Shirebrook NG20 72 F1
Littleworth NG18 102 C5
Litton Ave NG17 101 A5
Litton Cl
Arnold NG5 161 E4
Ilkeston DE7 157 E4
Ravenshead NG15 117 A3
Littondale S81 36 A7
Litton Rd NG19 88 E3
Liveret Way LE12 214 E8
Liverpool St NG3 173 E5
Livingstone St NG15 130 E6
Llanberis Gr NG8 160 C2
Lloyd St NG5 161 C2
Loach Ct NG8 172 C5
Lobelia Cl NG3 173 D7
Lockerbie St NG4 174 F6
Lock La
Collingham NG23 111 B8
Long Eaton NG10 193 C4
Sandiacre NG10 182 C4
Locksley La NG11 184 E4
Lockwell Hill NG22 105 C2
Lockwood Cl
Beeston NG9 184 C4
[16] Nottingham NG5 147 A1
Lockwood Dr DN22 39 D3
Lodge Cl
Arnold NG5 147 E2
Nottingham NG8 172 D8
Lodge Farm La NG5 147 E1
Lodgefield La NG14 151 E2
Lodge La
Elston NG23 153 C5
Kirkby-in-Ashfield NG17 115 D4
Screveton NG13 166 D5
Tuxford NG22 66 A1
Lodge Lane Ind Est
NG22 66 B1
Lodge Rd
Eastwood NG16 158 A8
Long Eaton NG10 193 D5
Lodgewood Cl NG6 160 A6
Lodore Cl NG2 186 C6
Lodore Rd S81 35 F7
Logan St NG6 160 D6
Lois Ave NG7 222 B1
Lombard Cl NG7 222 B2
Lombard St
Newark-on-Trent NG24 139 F8
Orston NG13 180 A6
Lonan Cl NG19 89 A2
London La
Willoughby-on-t-W
LE12 217 D7
Wymeswold LE12 216 B3
London Rd
Kegworth DE74 203 D1
Newark-on-Trent NG24 140 C5
Nottingham NG2 173 D2
Retford DN22 40 A3
Longacre NG5 161 F4
Long Acre NG15 145 D7
Longbeck Ave NG3 162 A1
Longbourne Ct [3] NG19 88 F2
Long Brecks La S81 18 C1
LONG CLAWSON 211 D3
Long Clawson CE Prim Sch
LE14 211 D3
Longcliff Cl LE14 218 E4
Longcliff Hill LE14 218 E4
Longcroft Ave DE7 157 E5
Longcroft View S80 45 A6
Longdale NG19 88 E1
Longdale Ave NG15 117 A1
Longdale La
Arnold NG15 132 F5
Calverton NG21 133 B5
Ravenshead NG15 132 C6
Longdale Rd NG5 161 D6
Longden Cl NG9 170 F2
Longden St [5] NG3 173 E5
Longden Terr
Market Warsop NG20 74 B4
Stanton Hill NG17 100 D6
LONG EATON 193 C7
Long Eaton Sch The
NG10 193 C6
Long Eaton Sta NG10 193 C5
Longfellow Dr
Balderton NG24 140 D5
Worksop S81 36 B4
Longfellows Cl NG5 161 B8
Longfield Ave NG8 171 C7
Longfield La DE7 170 A5
Longford Cres NG6 146 C2
Longford Wlk NG18 103 B6
Longhedge La
Bottesford NG13 180 F3
Flawborough NG13,
NG23 168 A2
Orston NG13 180 E7
Pleasley NG19 86 E6
Sibthorpe NG13 167 E5
Longhill Rise NG17 114 F1
Long Hill Rise NG15 145 F6
Longhirst Dr NG5 147 F2
Long Hollow Way
NG24 125 D4

Longholme Rd DN22 40 B8
Longhurst S81 36 B5
Longhurst View S80 45 A5
Long La
Barkestone-le-Vale NG13 192 F1
Barnby in the Willows NG24 141 F7
Beeston NG9 183 E3
Carlton in Lindrick S81 25 F6
East Drayton DN22 53 C3
Farndon NG24 138 F7
Farndon NG24 139 B5
Hickling LE14 210 C6
Kegworth DE74 203 D5
Shipley DE75 157 D6
Shirebrook NG20 72 E3
Stathern LE14 202 F4
Watnall NG16 145 A1
Longland La NG22 119 D4
Longlands Cl NG9 184 B4
Longlands Dr NG2 186 D5
Longlands Rd NG9 184 B4
Long Lea Dr NG16 143 A5
Longleat Cres NG9 183 C5
Long Mdw
Farnsfield NG22 120 A6
Mansfield Woodhouse NG19 88 D5
Long Mdw Hill NG14 150 A2
Long Mdws DN10 11 B3
Longmead Cl NG5 161 C6
Longmead Dr
Fiskerton NG25 137 E3
Nottingham NG5 161 C6
Long Meadow NG22 120 A6
Longmoor Ave NG14 164 E8
Longmoor Gdns NG10 182 B2
Longmoor La
Long Eaton NG10 182 A2
Scarrington NG13 179 B8
Longmoor Prim Sch NG10 182 C3
Longmoor Rd NG10 182 B2
Longnor Wlk NG18 103 B6
Longore Sq NG8 172 D4
Longridge Rd NG5 161 F4
Long Row
Kingston on Soar LE12 204 A4
Newark-on-Trent NG24 140 B8
Nottingham NG1 223 E2
Long Row W NG1 223 E2
Longshaw Rd NG18 103 B6
Long Sleets DE55 113 C4
Longster La NG20 73 C3
Longstone Way NG19 101 D6
Long Stoop Way NG19 103 B7
Longue Dr NG14 148 D7
Longwall Ave NG2 173 A1
Longwall La NG21 76 D3
Longwest Croft NG14 148 C7
LONG WHATTON 212 C4
Long Whatton CE Prim Sch LE12 212 C3
Longwood Ct NG5 160 F8
Longwood Dr NG17 100 E1
Longwood Inf Acad NG16 113 C2
Longwood Rd NG16 113 E2
Lonscale Cl NG2 186 C5
Lonsdale Dr NG9 182 E1
Lonsdale Rd NG7 222 A4
Loom Gdns NG24 140 A4
Lord Haddon Rd DE7 157 E1
Lord Hawke Way NG24 140 A5
Lord Nelson St NG2 173 F4
Lords Ct DN22 39 E4
Lordship La NG13 180 A6
Lord St
Gainsborough DN21 24 C8
Mansfield NG18 102 B5
Nottingham NG2 173 E4
Lords Wood Rd DN11 8 F2
Lorimer Ave NG4 162 F2
Lorne Gr NG12 175 F3
Lorne Wlk 6 NG3 173 C7
Lortas Rd NG5 160 F2
Loscoe Gdns 2 NG5 161 B2
Loscoe Mount Rd NG5 161 C2
Loscoe Rd NG5 161 C1
Losk La NG20 72 A2
Lothian Rd NG12 186 C1
Lothmore Ct 1 NG2 173 B2
Lotus Cl NG3 173 E7
Loughbon NG13 180 A7
LOUGHBOROUGH 220 C4
Loughborough Amherst Sch LE11 220 B2
Loughborough Ave NG2 173 F4
Loughborough Carillon Tower & War Memorial* LE11 220 B3
Loughborough Gram Sch LE11 220 B2
Loughborough High Sch LE11 220 B3
Loughborough Rd
Bradmore NG11 196 E5
Bunny NG11 206 E8
East Leake LE12 214 F7
Hathern LE12 213 A1
Hoton LE12 215 C1
Loughborough LE11 220 D1
Rempstone LE12 215 D5
Ruddington NG11 196 D7
Ruddington NG11 196 D8
West Bridgford NG12 185 E5
Loughborough Sta LE11 220 C5
Loughborough Univ Sch of Art & Design (14) LE11 220 A4
Loughborough Rd LE12 220 F6
Loughrigg Cl 3 NG2 173 B1
Louis Ave NG9 183 E7
Louise Ave NG4 175 A8
LOUND 29 C8
Lound House Cl NG17 100 F5
Loundhouse Rd NG17 101 A5
Lound House Rd NG17 100 F5
Lound Low Rd DN22 29 D7
Louwil Ave NG19 88 E5
Lovatt Dr NG16 143 C3
Loveden Cl NG24 140 D3
Love La DN21 15 C1
Lovelace Wk 2 NG15 146 B8
Lovell Cl NG6 159 F5
Lovell House Inf Sch NG7 222 C4
Lover's La NG24 125 A1
Lovers Lane Prim Sch NG24 125 A1
Lovesey Ave NG6 145 E2
Lowater St NG4 174 B7
Low Common DN11 8 D4
Lowcroft NG5 161 F4
Lowdam Rd NG14 150 A5
Low Deeps La DN10 1 E1
LOWDHAM 150 D1
Lowdham CE Prim Sch NG14 150 D2
Lowdham La
Woodborough NG14 149 D4
Woodborough NG14 149 E4
Lowdham Rd
Carlton NG4 162 C3
Gunthorpe NG14 164 E7
Lowdham St 8 NG3 173 E5
Lowdham Sta NG14 164 E8
Lower Bagthorpe
Bagthorpe NG16 129 A4
Selston NG16 128 F3
Lower Beauvale NG16 144 A3
Lower Bloomsgrove Rd DE7 157 F2
Lower Brook St NG10 193 E7
Lower Cambridge St LE11 220 B5
Lower Canaan NG11 196 D8
Lower Chapel St 9 DE7 157 F1
Lower Clara Mount Rd DE75 143 A1
Lower Ct NG9 184 B7
Lower Dunstead Rd NG16 143 A3
Lower Eldon St 12 NG2 173 E4
Lower Enterprise Rd LE14 219 B4
Lower Gladstone St 3 LE11 220 B5
Lower Granby St DE7 157 F2
Lower Hexgreave NG22 120 B8
Lower Kirklington Rd
Edingley NG22 120 F5
Southwell NG25 121 D2
Lower Maples DE75 157 A7
Lower Meadow La NG17 100 A2
Lower Middleton St DE7 158 A1
Lower Oakham Way NG18 101 F3
Lower Orch St NG9 182 D7
Lower Parliament St
Nottingham NG1 223 F2
Nottingham NG14 173 C5
Lower Pasture La DN22 31 E8
Lower Pk St NG9 182 C5
Lower Portland NG17 114 B2
Lower Rd NG9 184 B7
Lower Regent St NG9 184 A6
Loweswater Ct NG2 186 C7
Lowes Wong NG25 136 D8
Lowe's Wong Anglican Methodist Jun Sch NG25 136 D8
Lowe's Wong Inf Sch NG25 136 D8
Lowe's Wong Jun & Inf Sch NG25 121 D1
Lowfield DN22 29 D1
Lowfield Cl DN22 19 C4
Lowfield La NG24 140 C2
Low Field La DN10 3 C1
Low Holland La DN22 32 E4
Lowlands Dr NG12 197 F4
LOW MARNHAM 82 A8
Low Mdw Row S81 34 E7
Lowmoor Bsns Pk NG17 115 B7
Low Moor Rd NG17 115 B6
Lowmoor Rd Ind Est NG17 115 B7
Low Pavement NG1 223 E2
Low Rd
Besthorpe NG23 97 F6
Clarborough DN22 30 F5
Hayton DN22 31 A6
North Wheatley DN22 31 C8
Scrooby DN10 10 A2
Sutton in Ashfield NG17 100 F7
Low's La DE7 170 B2
Low St
Beckingham DN10 14 C1
Beckingham DN10 23 C8
Carlton in Lindrick S81 26 A5
Collingham NG23 98 A1
Low St *continued*
Collingham NG23 111 F8
Dunham-on-Trent NG22 54 C2
East Drayton DN22 53 B3
East Markham NG22 66 A6
Elkesley DN22 50 B3
Elston NG23 153 D5
Gringley on the Hill DN10 12 F2
Harby NG23 70 D2
North Wheatley DN22 31 D8
Sutton in Ashfield NG17 100 E2
Torworth DN22 19 B2
Lowther Sq S81 25 E7
Lowther Way LE11 220 B1
Lowtown Cl S80 36 A2
Lowtown St S80 36 A2
Lowtown View S80 36 A2
Low Wood La
Eagle LN6 84 A1
South Scarle LN6 98 F7
Low Wood Rd NG6 159 F6
Loxley Cl NG15 145 E5
Loxley Dr NG18 103 A3
Loxley La S80 45 A5
Loxley Mdw NG14 163 E4
LRONVILLE 128 A3
Lucerne Cl NG11 185 B6
Lucillia Cl NG15 146 D8
Lucknow Ave NG3 161 D1
Lucknow Ct NG3 173 D8
Lucknow Dr
Mansfield NG17, NG18 101 E5
Nottingham NG3 161 D1
Sutton in Ashfield NG17, NG18 101 B3
Lucknow Rd NG3 173 D8
Ludborough Wlk NG19 88 E4
Ludford Cres DN21 24 E7
Ludford Rd NG6 160 C8
Ludgate Cl NG5 147 A2
Ludgate Dr NG13 165 D2
Ludham Ave NG6 160 B8
Ludlam Ave NG16 158 A7
Ludlow Ave NG12 185 F7
Ludlow Cl NG9 171 D1
Ludlow Hill Rd NG2 185 F5
Lulworth Cl NG2 185 C5
Lulworth Ct NG16 158 F7
Lulworth Gr S81 25 D1
Lumbert Way NG23 97 F3
Lumley Dr DN11 8 B7
Lune Cl NG9 183 E3
Lune Mdw NG19 88 E3
Lune Wy NG13 177 D3
Lunness Ct NG18 102 D6
Lunn La NG23 111 F7
Lupin Cl
Edwalton NG12 186 A2
Nottingham NG3 173 D7
Shirebrook NG20 72 C3
Luther Ave NG17 100 E2
Luther Cl NG3 173 E7
Luton Cl NG8 160 D1
Lutterell Ct NG2 185 D5
Lutterell Way NG2 186 C5
Lybster Mews 6 NG2 173 B2
Lydia Gdns NG16 143 E1
Lydney Pk NG2 185 C5
Lyle Cl NG16 158 E7
Lyme Pk NG2 185 B5
Lymington Rd NG19 101 D6
Lymn Ave NG4 162 F2
Lynchet La S81 35 D7
Lyncombe Ct DN22 39 D4
Lyncombe Gdns NG12 197 F8
Lyndale Rd NG9 183 A8
Lynd Cl NG16 129 B7
Lynden Ave NG10 193 D6
Lyndhurst Ave NG21 118 B5
Lyndhurst Gdns NG2 185 D4
Lyndhurst Rd NG2 173 F4
Lynds Cl NG21 76 B2
Lynemouth Ct NG5 148 A2
Lyngs The NG13 165 D2
Lynmouth Cres NG7 172 E7
Lynmouth Dr DE7 157 D3
Lynncroft NG16 144 A3
Lynncroft St NG8 159 C2
Lynnes Cl NG21 118 A4
Lynstead Dr NG15 145 C5
Lynton Gdns NG5 162 A8
Lynton Rd NG9 183 C6
Lyons Cl NG11 196 B8
Lysander Way S81 35 E8
Lytham Dr NG12 186 C3
Lytham Gdns NG5 147 A1
Lytham Rd NG17 114 E7
Lythe Cl NG11 185 A5
Lytton Cl NG3 173 E5

M

Mabel Ave NG17 101 A1
Mabel Gr NG2 186 A8
Mabel St NG2 173 D2
Mable St S80 35 A4
Macaulay Cl
Balderton NG24 140 D5
Worksop S81 36 C4
Macaulay Dr NG24 140 D5
Macaulay Gr NG16 159 B6
Machin Cl NG22 66 B3
Machin Gr S81 35 C7
Machins La NG12 186 A3
Mackinley Ave
Stapleford NG9 170 E1
Stapleford NG9 182 E8
Mackleys La NG23 110 F2
Mackworth Ct NG18 103 B5
Maclaren Gdns NG11 196 D5
Maclean Rd NG4 174 C7
Macmillan Cl NG3 161 F2
Macphail Cres LN1 57 C3
Madden Cl 4 NG5 160 F5
Madejski Way 7 NG17 114 F8
Madford Ret Pk NG5 161 D6
Madison Dr DN10 9 F6
Madryn Wlk 7 NG5 161 A7
Mafeking St NG2 174 A4
Magadales Dr NG14 151 B8
Magdala Rd NG3 173 C8
Magdalen Dr NG13 165 D3
Magdalene View NG24 140 B8
Magdalene Way NG15 146 A7
Magee Cl NG6 145 E2
Magellan Dr S80 35 B2
Magenta Way NG4 175 C7
Mag La NG20 58 D5
Magna Cl NG14 150 E1
Magnolia Cl
4 Edwalton NG12 186 A1
3 Nottingham NG8 159 E1
Magnolia Ct NG9 171 D1
Magnolia Gr NG15 146 B4
Magnums Com Sports Ctr NG24 140 A6
Magnus CE Sch NG24 140 A6
Magnus Rd NG5 161 C3
Magnus St NG24 140 A8
Magpie Cl
Ruddington NG11 196 B6
Worksop S81 35 C7
Magpie Cres NG12 185 C6
Magpie La DN22 32 E1
Magpie Rd NG12 188 A5
Magson St NG3 173 E5
Maida La NG22 77 B4
Maiden Ct LN1 57 B3
Maiden La NG1 223 F2
Maiden Rd NG20 72 D2
Maidens Dale NG5 161 D8
Maid Marian Ave
Bilsthorpe NG22 105 F4
Selston NG16 129 B6
Maid Marian Way NG1 223 E2
Maid Marion Ave NG22 106 A4
Maid Marion Rise 1 NG20 74 B4
Maid Marion Way NG22 77 D6
Maid Marrion Dr NG21 76 C2
Maidstone Dr NG8 171 D2
Main Ave NG19 103 A8
Main Bright Rd 7 NG19 88 B1
Main Bright Walk 6 NG19 88 B1
Main Gate Dr DN11 9 B3
Main La NG12 164 C1
Main Rd
Annesley Woodhouse NG17 114 E1
Averham NG23 123 C3
Averham NG23 123 E2
Barnstone NG13 190 E3
Barnstone NG13 191 A4
Beeston NG9 184 C5
Besthorpe NG23 97 F6
Bevercotes NG22 64 D5
Boughton NG22 77 E5
Carlton NG4 163 A1
Cotgrave NG12 187 E4
Elmton S80 58 A7
Hawksworth NG13 167 C3
Kelham NG23 124 A4
Kings Clipstone NG21 90 C6
Nether Langwith NG20 59 A1
Nottingham NG11 185 B7
Old Dalby LE14 218 E4
Plumtree NG12 197 E7
Pye Bridge DE55 128 A6
Radcliffe on Trent NG12 175 E3
Radcliffe on T, Shelford NG12 176 C8
Ravenshead NG15 117 B3
Redmile NG13 192 E4
Selston NG16 128 F2
Shelford NG13 164 C1
Shelton NG23 167 F4
Shelton NG23 168 A5
Upton NG23 122 E2
Watnall NG16 159 A7
Westwood NG16 128 B3
Wiseton DN10 21 A8
Mainside Cres NG16 129 A1
Main St
Annesley Woodhouse NG17 129 F8
Aslockton NG13 179 A5
Awsworth NG16 158 C5
Balderton NG24 140 E4
Bevercotes NG22 64 F5
Bleasby NG14 152 B7
Blidworth NG21 117 F4
Bothamsall DN22 63 E7
Bothamsall DN22 64 A7
Bottesford NG23 169 D1
Bradmore NG11 196 E3
Brampton LN1 44 C3
Brinsley NG16 128 D1
Broxholme LN1 57 E8
Bunny NG11 206 E8
Burton Joyce NG14 163 F4
Calverton NG14 148 F7
Carlton-on-Trent NG23 96 F4
Caunton NG23 109 B5
Caythorpe NG14 165 B8
Clarborough DN22 30 D6
Clarborough DN22 30 E4
Claypole NG23 156 C6
Claypole NG23 156 D7
Coddington NG24 126 B2
Main St *continued*
Collingham NG23 98 D5
Costock LE12 206 C1
Cropwell Butler NG12 189 A7
Doddington LN6 71 C1
Dry Doddington NG23 156 E2
Dunham-on-Trent NG22 54 C2
Eakring NG22 92 E1
East Bridgford NG13 165 C2
East Leake LE12 205 E1
Eastwood NG16 143 F1
Eastwood, Beauvale NG16 144 C2
Eaton DN22 40 A1
Eaton DN22 50 F8
Eaton DN22 51 A8
Edingley NG22 120 C4
Egmanton NG22 79 F6
Farndon NG24 139 A4
Farnsfield NG22 119 F6
Fenton NG23 142 D2
Fiskerton NG25 137 F3
Flawborough NG13 168 D2
Flintham NG13 167 A8
Flintham NG23 153 A1
Gonalston NG14 150 F3
Gonalston NG14 151 A4
Granby NG13 191 B5
Grove DN22 40 A4
Gunthorpe NG14 165 A5
Harby LE14 202 A3
Harworth DN11 8 E4
Hickling LE14 210 C6
Hoveringham NG14 151 D2
Huthwaite NG17 99 F3
Keyworth NG12 197 E2
Kimberley NG16 158 F6
Kinoulton NG12 199 E2
Kirklington NG25 121 A8
Kirton NG22 78 B6
Kneesall NG22 93 E5
Kneeton NG14 151 E1
Lambley NG4 163 C7
Laneham DN22 54 A5
Langar NG13 190 C2
Laughterton LN1 55 B5
Laxton NG22 79 C2
Linby NG15 131 B3
Lockington DE74 203 A6
Long Eaton NG10 193 E7
Long Whatton LE12 212 B3
Lowdham NG14 150 D2
Maplebeck NG22 107 F6
Maplebeck NG22 108 A6
Mattersey DN10 20 B7
Morton NG25 137 D3
Muston NG13 181 F1
Newton DE55 99 A4
Newton NG13 177 B8
Normanton NG13 181 C7
Normanton on S LE12 213 D3
North Leverton with Habblesthorpe DN22 32 D1
North Muskham NG23 110 F4
Norton NG20 60 C5
Norwell NG23 109 F8
Norwell NG23 110 A8
Nottingham NG6 160 C7
Oldcotes S81 16 F5
Old Dalby LE14 219 A5
Ollerton NG22 77 A3
Ossington NG23 95 D6
Oxton NG25 134 B3
Papplewick NG15 131 E5
Ragnall NG22 68 A8
Rampton DN22 42 F2
Ratcliffe on Soar NG11 203 F6
Redmile NG13 192 F3
Saxondale NG13 177 A4
Scaftworth DN10 10 C4
Scarrington NG13 178 E8
Screveton NG13 166 E4
Sibthorpe NG23 167 E8
South Muskham NG23 124 D7
South Normanton DE55 113 B6
Stanford on Soar LE12 214 C1
Stokeham DN22 53 C7
Strelley NG16 159 A1
Sutton NG13 191 E8
Sutton Bonington LE12 213 B7
Sutton on Trent NG23 96 F7
Syerston NG23 153 B4
Thorney NG23 69 F7
Thoroton NG23 167 E1
Thorpe NG23 153 F8
Thorpe NG24 138 F1
Torksey LN1 44 B2
Upton DN22 52 B5
Upton NG23 122 F1
Walesby NG22 64 A2
West Bridgford NG2 186 C7
West Leake LE12 204 F1
West Markham NG22 65 A7
West Markham NG22 65 C6
Weston NG23 81 A4
West Stockwith DN10 7 E2
Whaley Thorns NG20 58 F2
Whaley Thorns S44 59 A2
Whatton NG13 179 B3
Widmerpool NG11 208 C4
Willoughby-on-t-W LE12 217 D7
Winkburn NG22 108 A1
Wiseton DN10 12 B1
Woodborough NG14 149 C4
Woodborough NG14 149 D4
Wysall NG12 207 C3
Zouch LE12 213 B3
Maisies Way DE55 113 D6
Maitland Ave NG5 161 F4
Maitland Rd NG5 161 F4
Maize Gr NG18 102 E1
Majestic Theatre* DN22 39 E7
Major St NG1 223 E3
Making It!* NG18 102 C6
Malbon Cl NG3 173 F8
Malcolm Cl NG3 173 C7
Maldon Cl
Beeston NG9 183 B4
Long Eaton NG10 193 E5
Malham Cl DN10 9 F8
Malin Cl NG5 162 B8
Malin Hill NG1 223 F2
Malkin Ave NG12 176 A4
Mallard Cl
Bilsthorpe NG22 105 F5
Bingham NG13 178 A3
Claypole NG23 156 D7
Nottingham NG6 160 F4
Shirebrook NG20 72 D3
Mallard Ct
Beeston NG9 184 A5
Mansfield NG19 88 A2
Mallard Gn NG24 140 C5
Mallard Rd NG4 175 B6
Mallards The S81 35 C7
Mallatratt Pl NG19 88 B4
Mallory Dr S80 35 B2
Mallow Way NG13 177 C4
Malmesbury Rd NG3 162 A4
Malpas Ave DN21 15 D1
Maltby Cl NG8 160 B2
Maltby Rd
Mansfield NG18 102 E6
Nottingham NG3 162 A4
Oldcotes S81 16 E6
Malt Cotts NG7 160 F1
Malthouse Cl NG16 143 F1
Malthouse Rd
Ilkeston DE7 170 A4
Whitwell S80 45 A6
Malting Cl NG11 196 C6
Maltings The
Blyth S81 18 B3
Cropwell Bishop NG12 189 A4
Maltkiln Cl NG22 77 C2
Maltkiln La NG24 125 A2
Maltkiln Rd LN1 55 D6
Maltkins The DN22 42 C8
Maltmill La NG1 223 E2
Malton Rd
Nottingham NG5 160 F2
Nottingham NG5 161 A2
Malt St NG11 195 B1
Maltsters The NG24 139 C6
Malvern Cl NG3 161 E1
Malvern Cres NG2 185 F5
Malvern Gdns 3 NG10 193 A8
Malvern Rd
Nottingham NG3 161 E1
West Bridgford NG2 185 E5
Manby Ct NG20 74 D8
Manchester St NG10 193 D6
Mandalay Rd NG19 87 B4
Mandalay St NG6 160 D4
Mandarin Cl NG19 88 E2
Mandeen Gr NG18 103 A4
Manderley Gdns NG17 114 B8
Mandeville Cl NG15 146 C8
Manesty Cres NG11 195 E7
Mangham La DN11 8 A8
Manifold Dr NG16 129 A7
Manifold Gdns NG2 173 C2
Manitoba Way NG16 128 F7
Manly Cl NG5 160 E8
Manners Ave DE7 157 D1
Manners Ind Est DE7 157 F2
Manners Rd
Balderton NG24 140 D3
Ilkeston DE7 157 E1
Newark-on-Trent NG24 124 E1
Manners St DE7 170 A6
Manners Sutton Prim Sch The NG23 123 F2
Manning St NG3 173 D7
Manning View DE7 157 F2
Mannion Cres NG10 193 B5
Manns Leys NG12 187 E2
Mann St 5 NG7 172 F8
Manor Arms Pl NG13 179 F2
Manor Ave
Beeston NG9 183 F5
17 Nottingham NG2 173 E4
Stapleford NG9 182 D8
Manor Bsns Pk DN22 53 A2
Manor Cl
Bleasby NG14 152 A8
Boughton NG22 77 F6
Costock LE12 206 C1
Eagle LN6 84 D3
Gamston DN22 50 F5
Long Whatton LE12 212 B3
Misson DN10 4 C3
Newton DE55 99 A3
Oxton NG25 134 B3
Southwell NG25 121 E1
Teversal NG17 100 C8
Walesby NG22 64 A2
West Bridgford NG12 186 B3
Worksop S80 35 C2
Manor Cres
Carlton NG4 174 F8
Kirkby-in-Ashfield NG17 115 B3
Manor Croft NG6 160 E3
Manor Ct
Beeston NG9 183 B7
Carlton NG4 174 F7
Church Warsop NG20 74 C6
Wymeswold LE12 216 D4

Manor Dr NG25 137 D3
Manor Farm Cl
Bradmore NG11 196 E3
Kilvington NG13 168 F2
Rolleston NG23 138 A6
Manor Farm Ct
Kingston on Soar NG11 203 F4
Kingston on Soar NG11 204 E8
Manor Farm Dr DN22 54 C5
Manor Farm La NG7 184 E2
Manor Farm Mdw
LE12 205 E1
Manor Farm Rise
North Leverton with Habblesthorpe DN22 32 C1
North Leverton with Habblesthorpe DN22 42 C8
Wellow NG22 77 E1
Manor Farm & Woodlands★ LE12 214 F8
Manor Fields NG22 120 E1
Manor Gn Wlk NG4 174 F8
Manor Gr
Austerfield DN10 3 C3
Normanton on Trent NG23 81 E6
North Leverton with Habblesthorpe DN22 32 C1
Worksop S80 35 C2
Manor House Cl
Lowdham NG14 150 D2
West Bridgford NG2 185 B8
Manor House Ct NG17 114 D4
Manor House Dr
North Muskham NG23 110 F3
Wysall NG12 207 C3
Manor House La NG23 156 D2
Manor House Rd NG10 193 F6
Manor La
Broadholme LN6 71 A8
Cromwell NG23 110 F8
Gunthorpe NG13 165 A4
Shelford NG12 164 C2
Whatton NG13 179 A1
Manor Mws 1 NG19 88 C3
Manor Pk NG11 196 C7
Manor Pk Inf Sch NG14 148 E8
Manor Rd
Barton in Fabis NG11 194 E6
Bingham NG13 177 F4
Bottesford NG13 181 C2
Calverton NG14 148 E7
Carlton NG4 174 F8
Caunton NG23 109 A4
Church Warsop NG20 74 C6
Collingham NG23 112 A8
East Leake LE12 205 F3
Eastwood NG16 143 F1
Ilkeston DE7 157 E1
Keyworth NG12 197 E3
Mansfield Woodhouse NG19 88 A4
Morton DN21 15 B4
Saxilby LN1 57 A4
Scrooby DN10 10 A2
Sutton in Ashfield NG17 100 E7
Manor Rise NG13 165 C4
Manor Sch The NG19 88 C5
Manor St
Nottingham NG2 173 E4
Sutton in Ashfield NG17 100 E2
Manor View NG23 109 A4
Manor Wlk NG14 150 A5
Manorwood Rd NG12 187 F2
Manse Ave S80 58 D8
Manse Cl S80 58 D8
Mansell Cl NG16 144 B1
Mansey Common Nature Reserve★ NG22 107 A6
MANSFIELD 102 C8
Mansfield Bsns Ctr NG19 88 B1
Mansfield Coll of Art and Design / VisionStudio Sch 16 NG18 102 B7
Mansfield Com Hospl NG18 102 A6
Mansfield Ct 7 NG5 173 B8
Mansfield Gr
Nottingham NG1 223 D4
Nottingham NG14 173 B6
Mansfield La
Calverton NG14 148 F7
Sutton in Ashfield NG17 101 A7
Mansfield L Ctr NG19 102 A8
Mansfield L Pk★ NG18 102 B5
Mansfield Mus★ NG18 102 C7
Mansfield Rd
Annesley NG15 130 A6
Arnold NG5 147 E3
Arnold NG5, NG15 147 D6
Babworth DN22 38 D3
Blidworth NG21 118 A5
Brinsley NG16 143 F4
Clipstone NG21 90 A3
Clipstone NG21 90 B5
Creswell S80 58 F8
Creswell S80 59 A8
Cuckney NG20 60 B3
Dalesnorth NG17 101 D4
Edingley NG22 120 C5
Edwinstowe NG21 75 E2
Farnsfield NG22 119 B7
Farnsfield NG22 119 C7
Glapwell S44 86 D8
Halam NG22 120 E3
Heanor DE75 143 A2
Mansfield Rd *continued*
Kings Clipstone NG20 74 F1
Mansfield Woodhouse NG19 88 C2
Mansfield Woodhouse NG19 88 F1
Market Warsop NG20 73 F1
1 New Cross NG17 100 F4
Nottingham NG5 161 D4
Ollerton NG22 76 F3
Ollerton NG22 77 A4
Ravenshead NG15 131 F8
Selston NG16 128 F7
Selston, Friezeland NG16 129 C4
South Normanton DE55 113 D6
Sutton in A, Skegby NG17 100 E6
Sutton in A, Sutton Forest Side NG17 101 B4
Tibshelf DE55 99 B7
Worksop DN22 48 A8
Worksop S80 46 A8
Mansfield Rd (North) NG15 116 E3
Mansfield St NG5 161 C2
Mansfield Town Sta NG18 102 B6
MANSFIELD WOODHOUSE 88 E3
Mansfield Woodhouse Sta NG19 88 B3
Manston Way S81 35 C8
Manthorpe Cres NG5 161 F3
Manthorpe House NG24 140 E4
Manthorpe Way NG24 140 E4
Mantle Croft LE12 216 C3
MANTON 36 B1
Manton Cl NG21 118 B8
Manton Cres
Beeston NG9 184 A8
Worksop S80 36 B1
Manton Dale S80 36 B1
Manton Villas S80 36 C1
Manton Wood Enterprise Zone S81 36 F1
Manuela Gr NG12 185 F3
Manvers Bsns Pk NG12 188 A4
Manvers Cres NG21 75 F2
Manvers Ct
Market Warsop NG20 73 A4
9 Nottingham NG2 173 E4
Manvers Gr NG12 175 F3
Manvers Rd
Retford DN22 39 D5
West Bridgford NG2 185 F6
Manvers St
Carlton NG4 175 A6
Mansfield NG18 102 A7
Mansfield Woodhouse NG19 88 A3
Market Warsop NG20 74 B3
Nottingham NG2 173 E4
Shirebrook NG20 73 A4
Worksop S80 35 E3
Manvers View NG22 77 E6
Manville Cl
Beeston NG9 171 B3
Nottingham NG8 172 C6
Maori Ave NG15 145 D5
Maple Ave
Beeston NG9 184 B5
Lidgett NG21 91 C8
Sandiacre NG10 182 B7
Torksey Lock LN1 44 B1
MAPLEBECK 108 A6
Maplebeck Ave NG20 74 D8
Maplebeck Rd
Arnold NG5 162 A7
Caunton NG23 108 E6
Caunton NG23 109 A4
Maple Cl
Calverton NG5 148 D7
East Leake LE12 214 D8
Gainsborough DN21 15 B3
Keyworth NG12 198 A2
Mansfield NG19 88 E1
Radcliffe on Trent NG12 175 F2
South Normanton DE55 113 B4
Tuxford NG22 66 A2
Maple Cres NG17 114 F6
Maple Croft NG18 102 F5
Maple Ct 4 DN21 15 F1
Mapledene Cres NG8 171 C3
Maple Dr
Carlton NG4 163 B2
Elkesley DN22 50 B3
Hucknall NG15 145 E5
Nuthall NG16 159 C6
Ravenshead NG18 116 D7
South Normanton DE55 113 B4
Worksop S81 36 A7
Maple Gr
Bawtry DN10 9 F7
Glapwell S44 86 B8
Newark-on-Trent NG24 139 F4
Maple Leaf Ct NG24 125 A3
Maple Leaf Gdns S80 36 A2
Maple Leaf Way NG15 146 C4
Maples St 15 NG7 172 F7
Maplestead Ave NG11 185 B6
Maples The DE7 157 A7
Mapletoft Ave NG19 88 A5
Mapletoft Ct
Retford DN22 29 B1
RETFORD DN22 39 C8
Mapleton Way NG17 101 A4
Mapletree Cl NG5 161 B7
Mapletree Mdw NG17 101 C6
Maple Wy NG16 128 F7
MAPPERLEY 161 E3
Mapperley Cres NG3 161 E2
Mapperley Hall Dr NG3 161 D2
Mapperley Hall Gdns NG5 161 D1
Mapperley Orch NG5 162 C7
MAPPERLEY PARK 161 E3
Mapperley Pk Dr 1 NG3 173 C8
Mapperley Plains NG3 162 C6
Mapperley Plains Prim Sch NG3 162 B4
Mapperley Rd NG3 173 C7
Mapperley Rise NG3 161 E2
Mapperley St NG5 161 C2
Mappleton Dr NG18 103 B5
Mapplewells NG17 114 F1
Mapplewells Cres NG17 100 B1
Mapplewells Prim Sch NG17 100 B1
Mapplewells Rd NG17 100 C1
Maquin Cl NG12 176 B4
Marbled White Pl S81 25 D1
March Cl NG5 160 E7
Marches Cl NG15 145 E4
Marchwood Cl NG8 172 D5
Marciana Gr NG15 146 C8
Marconi Dr NG9 184 A4
Mardale Cl NG2 186 C6
Mardling Av NG5 161 A5
Marella Cl 1 NG12 186 A2
Margaret Ave
Long Eaton NG10 182 F1
Sandiacre NG10 182 B4
Margaret Cl DN21 15 C3
Margaret Cres 2 NG4 162 E2
Margaret Pl NG13 177 D5
Margaret's Ct NG9 183 A8
Marham Cl NG2 173 E3
Marhill Rd NG4 174 F7
Marie Gdns NG15 146 A5
Marigold Cl NG12 185 F2
Marigold Way
Newark-on-Trent NG24 139 F4
Newark-on-Trent NG24 140 A4
Marina Ave NG9 183 F5
Marina Dr S81 34 F6
Mariner Ct NG6 160 A6
Marion Ave
Hucknall NG15 131 C1
Kirkby-in-Ashfield NG17 115 B2
Marion Murdoch Ct NG4 162 E2
Maris Cl NG11 184 C2
Maris Dr NG14 163 E3
Marjorie St S80 35 A4
Market Cl
Shirebrook NG20 72 F3
South Normanton DE55 113 A6
Market House Pl 12 NG18 102 B7
Market Pl
Bingham NG13 177 E4
Gainsborough DN21 24 C8
Hucknall NG15 146 A7
Huthwaite NG17 99 F3
Kegworth DE74 203 D2
Long Eaton NG10 193 E8
Loughborough LE11 220 B4
9 Mansfield NG18 102 B7
Mansfield Woodhouse NG19 88 C3
Nottingham NG6 160 B7
Ollerton NG22 77 A3
Retford DN22 39 F7
Shirebrook NG20 72 F4
South Normanton DE55 113 A6
Southwell NG25 136 E8
Stanton Hill NG17 100 E2
Tickhill DN11 8 A7
Tuxford NG22 65 F3
Worksop S80 35 F2
Market Pl The NG5 161 F7
Market Side 9 NG6 160 B7
Market St
Bingham NG13 177 E4
Bottesford NG13 181 B2
Gainsborough DN21 24 D8
Huthwaite NG17 99 F3
Loughborough LE11 220 A4
15 Mansfield NG18 102 B7
Nottingham NG1 223 E2
Shirebrook NG20 72 F4
South Normanton DE55 113 A5
Sutton in Ashfield NG17 100 E2
Worksop S80 35 F3
MARKET WARSOP 74 C4
Markham Ave NG24 125 B3
Markham Cl NG22 77 B4
Markham Cres NG5 161 C4
Markham Moor Bridge DN22 65 B8
Markham Pl NG19 101 D7
Markham Rd
Beeston NG9 171 D1
Langold S81 16 E3
Tuxford NG22 65 F4
Markham St NG15 130 D6
Markhams The NG22 77 B4
Mark La NG22 65 F6
Markland La NG20 58 A8
Marklew Cl NG21 118 A5
Mark St NG10 182 C5
Markwick Cl NG24 140 D8
Marlborough Cl
Newark-on-Trent NG24 139 D5
3 Worksop S81 35 D8
Marlborough Ct
Newark-on-Trent NG24 139 D6
West Bridgford NG12 185 F7
Marlborough Rd
Arnold NG5 161 E4
Beeston NG9 183 F7
Kirkby-in-Ashfield NG17 115 B5
Long Eaton NG10 182 F1
Mansfield NG19 87 F1
Marlborough St
Gainsborough DN21 24 D7
2 Nottingham NG7 172 E1
Marl Cl NG11 196 B8
Marldon Cl NG8 171 C5
Marle Pit Hill LE12 213 A8
Marles Cl NG24 125 C2
Marleston La NG24 140 A4
Marlock Cl NG25 137 E3
Marlow Ave NG6 160 E2
Marlowe Dr NG24 140 D4
Marlowe Gdns S81 36 B4
Marlow Rd DN21 15 E2
Marl Rd NG12 176 B3
Marlwood NG12 188 A2
Marly Bank NG18 102 E5
Marmion Rd NG3 174 A6
Marnham Dr NG3 161 E1
Marnham Rd
Low Marnham NG23 82 A7
Marnham NG23 81 F8
Skegby NG23 67 B2
Tuxford NG22 66 D2
Marples Ave NG19 88 E5
Marple Sq NG3 173 C7
Marquis Ave NG24 140 D3
Marquis Gdns
Retford DN22 39 F4
Retford DN22 40 A4
Marquis Rd LE14 219 B6
Marriots La NG21 117 F4
Marriott Ave
Beeston NG9 183 A5
Mansfield NG18 101 F7
Marriott Cl NG9 183 A5
Marriott St NG13 177 D6
Marrison Ct NG24 138 F5
Marrison Way
Southwell NG25 121 F1
Winthorpe NG24 125 F5
Marron Cl NG24 140 F2
Marron Ct NG24 140 F2
Marsant Cl 1 NG8 172 C5
Marsden Cl NG6 160 E5
Marshall Ave NG17 115 C4
Marshall Cl NG5 148 D8
Marshall Ct NG24 140 E4
Marshall Dr
Beeston NG9 183 A8
Ruddington NG11 196 B7
Marshall Farm Cl NG13 192 B2
Marshall Hill Dr NG3 162 B2
Marshall Rd
Cropwell Bishop NG12 189 A4
Nottingham NG3 162 A1
Marshalls Rise
2 Gainsborough DN21 15 D1
Gainsborough DN21 24 D8
Marshall St
Heanor DE75 143 A2
Nottingham NG5 161 C2
Marshall Terr NG17 100 D6
Marsham Dr NG5 162 A6
Marsh Ave DE7 157 F5
Marsh Ct NG13 181 B3
Marsh La
Cottam DN22 43 F4
Farndon NG24 139 A5
Laughterton LN1 55 A4
Misterton DN10 7 B1
Misterton DN21 14 B8
North Leverton with Habblesthorpe DN22 33 D1
North Muskham NG23 110 F2
Saundby DN22 23 D5
Marsh Rd DN10 14 C5
Marsh's Paddock LE14 210 C6
Marston Ave NG20 74 D8
Marston Cl NG24 140 C3
Marston Moor Rd NG24 140 E8
Marston Rd NG3 174 B7
Martin Cl NG6 160 A8
Martin Cres NG11 196 B7
Martin Ct NG6 160 A8
Martindale 8 NG24 139 F8
Martindale Cl NG2 186 C7
Marting Grance Farm La DN10 3 A1
Martin La DN10 9 F8
Martinmass Cl NG7 222 A1
Martins Hill NG4 174 E7
Martin's Pond Nature Reserve★ NG8 171 E5
Martlet Way
Worksop S80 36 A1
Worksop S80 47 A8
MARTON 44 B8
Marton Prim Sch DN21 44 C8
Marton Rd
Beeston NG9 183 C3
Newark-on-Trent NG24 140 B6
Nottingham NG6 146 C1
Martyn Ave NG17 100 F1
Marvin Rd NG9 183 F6
Marvyn Cl NG6 160 E6
Marwood Cres NG4 162 C2
Marwood Rd NG4 162 C2
Maryfield Cl DN22 29 E1
Maryland Ct NG9 170 E1
Mary Rd NG16 144 B1
Marys Cl LE12 216 C3
Marys Gate S80 35 F1
Mary St
Kirkby-in-Ashfield NG17 115 B6
Rhodesia S80 35 B4
Whaley Thorns NG20 59 A2
Masefield Cres NG24 140 D4
Masefield Pl S81 36 B4
Masonic Pl NG1 223 D3
Mason Rd DE7 157 D2
Mason St NG17 101 B4
Massey Cl NG14 163 E3
Massey Ct 4 NG24 140 B8
Massey Gdns 1 NG3 173 E6
Massey St NG24 140 B8
Masson Ct 7 NG5 147 A1
Master Rd NG13 177 B7
Mather Rd NG24 124 F1
Matilda Dr DN22 29 F1
Matin Rd NG13 177 E6
Matlock Ave NG18 102 A5
Matlock Ct NG1 223 E3
Matlock St NG4 174 F7
MATTERSEY 20 C7
Mattersey Ct 4 NG19 88 B1
Mattersey Prim Sch DN10 20 B7
Mattersey Rd
Everton DN10 11 C1
Lound DN22 20 B2
Ranskill DN22 19 D6
Matthews Ct NG9 170 F2
Mattingly Rd NG6 160 A5
Mattley Ave NG17 115 A1
Matt Orch DE55 113 B4
Maud St NG7 161 A1
Maule Ct NG13 180 A6
Maun Ave
Kirkby-in-Ashfield NG17 115 B7
Nottingham NG7 172 D6
Maun Cl
Mansfield NG18 101 F4
Retford DN22 39 F5
Maun Cres NG22 77 C5
Maundale Ave NG17 101 B4
Maun Gn NG24 125 B2
Maun Inf Sch NG22 77 B5
Maunleigh NG19 88 E1
Maunside NG18 101 F4
Maunside Ave NG17 101 B1
Maun Valley Ind Pk NG17 101 C2
Maun View NG18 102 C7
Maun View Gdns
Kirkby-in-Ashfield NG17 115 B8
Sutton Forest Side NG17 101 B1
Maun Way
Mansfield NG18 101 F4
Wellow NG22 78 A4
Maurice Dr NG3 161 E2
Mavis Ave NG15 117 A2
Mavis Wood Mws NG21 118 B5
Mawkin La
Kirkby-in-Ashfield NG17 114 A4
Pinxton NG16 113 F5
Maws La NG16 158 E7
Maxtoke Rd NG7 222 C1
Maxwell Cl NG7 222 B1
May Ave NG8 171 E4
Maycroft Gdns
Carlton NG3 174 A7
Sutton In Ashfield NG17 100 B2
May Ct 6 NG5 161 B1
Maydene Cl NG11 184 D1
Mayes Dr NG14 149 C6
Mayes Rise NG6 146 E4
Mayfair NG12 176 D3
Mayfair Ave NG18 102 D5
Mayfair Cl DN11 8 F4
Mayfair Ct NG7 160 F1
Mayfair Gdns NG5 160 F5
May Fair Pl NG22 66 A2
Mayfair Row 6 S80 35 E2
Mayfield Ave
Burton Joyce NG14 163 F5
Gainsborough DN21 15 B3
Mayfield Cl NG18 103 B5
Mayfield Ct NG2 173 C2
Mayfield Dr
Loughborough LE11 220 A2
Stapleford NG9 170 F2
Mayfield Gr NG10 182 E1
Mayfield Pl NG17 100 D2
Mayfield Rd NG4 174 B7
Mayfield St NG17 114 D3
Mayfield Terr NG20 74 B3
Mayflower Ave DN10 10 A2
Mayflower Cl
Bawtry DN10 10 A8
Gainsborough DN21 24 E4
West Bridgford NG2 186 A7
Mayflower Ct
Austerfield DN10 3 C1
Mansfield NG18 102 B3
Shirebrook NG20 72 E4
Mayflower Jun & Inf Sch DN10 10 B8
Mayflower Rd NG16 158 B8
Mayhall Ave NG19 88 A4
May Hill NG25 136 C8
Mayland Cl NG8 171 C6
May Lodge Dr NG22 91 E6
Mayo Rd NG5 161 B1
Maypole NG11 184 E3
Maypole Ct NG22 92 E8
Maypole Green NG22 77 E1
Maypole Rd NG22 92 E8
Maypole Yd NG1 223 E3
May S DE7 157 D3
Mays Ave NG4 174 D6
Mays Cl NG4 174 C6
Mays La LN1 57 C3
May St DE7 157 E4
Maythorn Cl NG11 185 C3
Maythorne NG25 121 C3
Maythorne Cl
Arnold NG5 162 B7
New Balderton NG24 140 C5
Maythorne Ind Est NG25 121 D4
Maythorne Wlk 1 NG5 161 C7
Maythorn Gr NG21 76 B3
Mccabe Ct NG8 171 C6
Mcclelland Av NG6 147 B5
McCracken Cl NG15 146 E1
Mcintosh Rd NG4 162 D3
Meade Dr S81 36 A7
Meadow Ave
Loughborough LE11 220 B6
Mansfield NG18 102 C5
Meadow Bank
Mansfield Woodhouse NG19 88 E6
South Normanton DE55 113 A7
Meadowbank Day Hospl NG2 173 B1
Meadowbank Way NG16 143 D3
Meadow Cl
Aslockton NG13 179 A5
Eastwood NG16 143 F4
Edwinstowe NG22 76 A2
Farnsfield NG22 120 A6
Hucknall NG15 145 D5
2 Kirkby-in-Ashfield NG17 114 E6
North Muskham NG23 110 F1
Nottingham NG2 173 E1
Retford DN22 29 E1
Tibshelf DE55 99 B7
Meadow Cotts
Carlton NG4 174 F7
Mansfield Woodhouse NG19 88 C3
Meadow Cres NG12 188 A5
Meadow Croft Gdns NG15 145 F5
Meadow Ct
Blyth S81 18 A6
Long Whatton LE12 212 A4
Nottingham NG2 173 F2
South Normanton DE55 113 A4
Meadow Dr
Keyworth NG12 198 A3
Misterton DN10 6 F2
Sutton in Ashfield NG17 100 C3
Tickhill DN11 8 C7
Worksop S80 35 C2
Meadow End
Gotham NG11 195 B1
Radcliffe on Trent NG12 176 C3
Meadow Farm View NG17 114 E5
Meadow Gdns
Beeston NG9 183 E4
Collingham NG23 112 B8
Heanor DE75 143 B1
Meadow Gr
Bilsthorpe NG22 106 A4
Newton DE55 99 A3
Nottingham NG2 173 E2
Meadow La
Beeston NG9 183 E4
Bothamsall DN22 63 E7
Burton Joyco NG14 163 F4
Girton NG23 82 F4
Hodsock S81 17 E4
Long Eaton NG10 193 F7
Loughborough LE11 220 B7
Low Marnham NG23 82 C6
North Scarle LN6 83 F2
2 Nottingham NG2 173 F3
Shirebrook NG20 72 D2
South Normanton DE55 113 A7
Weston NG23 81 B4
Meadow La Ind Est LE11 220 B6
Meadow Lands DN21 15 B5
Meadow Lane Inf Sch NG9 183 E4
Meadow La (Notts County FC) NG2 173 E2
Meadow Lark Cl NG17 114 D8
Meadow Pl NG20 74 A4
Meadow Rd
Awsworth NG16 158 C5
Beeston NG9 184 B4
Blidworth NG21 118 A5
Carlton NG4 174 F7
New Balderton NG24 140 C4
Worksop S80 35 C2
Meadow Rise
Nottingham NG6 159 F6
Saxilby LN1 57 B4
MEADOWS 173 C2
Meadows La LE14 201 D1
Meadow St DE7 157 F1
Meadows The
Awsworth NG16 158 B5
Beckingham DN10 23 B8
Farndon NG24 139 A5
South Wheatley DN22 31 E8
Woodborough NG14 149 B4
Meadows Way NG2 173 C2
Meadowsweet Hill NG13 177 C4

Meadow The
Retford DN22 39 F8
Retford DN22 40 A8
Meadowvale Cres
Nottingham NG11 195 E8
Nottingham NG7 184 E1
Meadow View
Selston NG16 128 E6
Southwell NG25 121 F1
Stapleford NG9 182 D8
Meadow Vw DN10 20 A8
Meadow Way
Clipstone NG21 89 F5
Harworth DN11 8 F5
Kinoulton NG12 199 F2
Meadow Wlk LN1 57 A5
Mead Way NG24 140 C3
Measham Cl NG14 173 D1
Medawar Cl NG11 184 C1
Meden Ave
Market Warsop NG20 74 C5
New Houghton NG19 86 F7
Meden Bank
Bothamsall DN22 63 F7
Pleasleyhill NG19 87 B5
Stanton Hill NG17 100 C6
Meden Cl
Nottingham NG11 184 E3
Pleasleyhill NG19 87 B5
Meden Cres NG17 100 C4
Meden Gdns NG7 172 D7
Meden Glen NG20 74 C6
Meden Rd
Mansfield Woodhouse NG19 88 D4
Wellow NG22 78 B4
Meden Sch & Tech Coll The NG20 74 B5
Meden Side NG20 74 D7
Meden Sports Ctr NG20 74 B5
Meden Sq NG19 87 B5
MEDEN VALE 74 E8
Meden Way DN22 39 F5
Medina Dr NG12 186 E1
Medway DN22 29 D1
Medway Cl NG9 183 C5
Medway Dr NG13 177 C3
Meeks Rd NG5 162 B8
Meering Ave NG24 125 B4
Meering Cl NG23 98 A1
Meerings The NG23 81 E1
Meer Rd NG9 183 A5
Meeting House Cl
East Leake LE12 205 F1
East Leake LE12 214 F8
Meetinghouse La
South Leverton DN22 42 A6
South Leverton DN22 42 B6
Melbourne Ct
Mansfield NG18 103 B6
Nottingham NG8 160 C1
Melbourne Gr DN11 8 F4
Melbourne Rd
Nottingham NG8 160 C1
Stapleford NG9 170 E1
West Bridgford NG2 174 A1
Melbourne St
Mansfield Woodhouse NG19 88 C6
Selston NG16 129 B6
Melbury Prim Sch NG8 171 D8
Melbury Rd
Nottingham, Bilborough NG8 171 D8
Nottingham, Woodthorpe NG3 162 A4
Meldreth Rd NG8 171 E6
Meldrum Cres NG24 139 E5
Meldrum Dr DN21 24 E5
Melford Hall Dr NG2 185 C4
Melford Rd NG8 171 D8
Melksham Rd NG5 161 C8
Mellbreak Cl NG2 186 C6
Mellers Prim Sch NG7 222 B3
Mellish Rd S81 16 E2
Mellors Rd
Arnold NG5 147 F1
Edwinstowe NG22 75 F1
5 Mansfield NG19 87 D1
Mansfield NG19 101 D8
West Bridgford NG2 185 F6
Mellors Way
Nottingham NG16 159 C2
Nottingham NG8 159 C2
Melrose Ave
Beeston NG9 184 A5
Mansfield NG18 102 D5
3 Nottingham NG5 161 C3
Melrose Gdns NG2 185 C4
Melrose Rd DN21 15 C2
Melrose St NG5 161 C2
Melrose Wlk 2 S80 35 F2
Melton Ct NG10 182 A5
Melton Gdns NG12 186 B4
Melton Gr NG2 185 E7
Melton La LE12 204 C2
Melton Rd
East Leake LE12 214 E5
Long Clawson LE14 211 B1
Nether Broughton LE14 219 F6
Plumtree NG12 197 E8
Rempstone LE12 215 A6
Rempstone LE12 215 C6
Stanton-on-the-Wolds NG12 198 D4
Upper Broughton LE14 210 A1
West Bridgford NG12 186 A3
Widmerpool NG12, LE12 209 C4
Melville Ct
Meden Vale NG20 74 D8
Melville Ct *continued*
3 Nottingham NG3 173 C8
Melville Gdns NG3 173 E6
Melville St NG1 223 E1
Melvyn Dr NG13 177 E4
Memorial Ave S80 35 F2
Mendip Cl
Long Eaton NG10 182 A1
Mansfield NG18 102 E4
Mendip Ct
Carlton in Lindrick S81 25 E7
Nottingham NG5 160 F8
Mensing Ave NG12 187 E3
Mercer Rd DN21 15 B2
Merchant Ave NG8 172 B7
Merchants Fold DN22 29 D1
Merchant St
Nottingham NG6 160 B8
Shirebrook NG20 73 A4
Mercia Ave NG12 189 A4
Mercia Cl
Giltbrook NG16 158 A8
Worksop S81 36 A7
Mercia Ct NG17 100 A2
Mercian Cl DE7 157 E1
Mercia Rd NG24 139 F5
Mercury Cl NG6 160 E5
Mercury Way 2 NG18 102 E1
Mere Ave NG14 148 F7
Mere Cl NG14 148 F7
Meredith Cl NG2 173 B1
Meredith Ct NG9 170 E2
Meregill Cl NG5 146 F1
Merevale Ave NG11 184 F4
Merevale Cl NG14 150 E1
Mere Way NG11 196 D5
Meriac Cl NG5 160 F8
Meriden Ave NG9 184 A8
Meridian Cl
Ilkeston DE7 157 E4
5 Nottingham NG8 172 B7
Meridian Ct NG5 161 A2
Merlin Cl
Eagle LN6 84 D3
Nottingham NG7 184 E2
Merlin Ct NG17 101 B3
Merlin Dr NG15 145 E4
Merlin Rd 1 NG19 88 B2
Merlin Way DE7 170 A3
Merrick Dr S81 36 C3
Merrivale Ct NG3 173 C8
Merry Rd NG22 77 D3
Merryvale Dr NG19 101 D6
Merryweather Cl
Edwinstowe NG21 91 C8
Southwell NG25 121 E2
Mersey St NG6 160 B7
Merton Ave DN22 29 E1
Merton Cl NG5 148 B1
Merton Ct NG9 170 E1
Meryton Gr NG17 115 A3
Metcalf Cl NG22 105 F7
Metcalfe Cl NG25 136 F8
Metcalfe Ct DN10 11 C3
Metcalf Rd NG16 144 B3
Meteor Cl NG13 177 B7
Meteor Rd NG6 145 E2
Methuen Ave NG18 102 E6
Metro Ave DE55 99 A3
Mettham St NG7 222 B1
Mews La NG14 148 E8
Mews The
Blyth S81 18 A3
Collingham NG23 112 A7
Meynell Gr 7 NG7 161 A1
Meynell Rd NG10 193 D5
Meynell St DN10 7 F4
Meyrick Rd NG24 125 A1
Miall Ct NG7 222 A3
Miall St NG8 172 E5
Michael Bruce La NG9 183 E5
Micklebarrow Cl NG25 136 C8
Micklebarrow Hill
Averham NG23 123 B4
Upton NG23 122 F3
Mickleborough Ave NG3 174 A8
Mickleborough Way NG2 185 C3
Mickledale Cl NG22 105 E7
Mickledale La NG22 105 E6
Mickleden Cl 9 NG2 173 B2
Mickledon Cl 1 NG10 193 B8
Micklemoor La NG13 178 B8
Middle Ave NG4 174 C8
Middlebeck Ave NG5 162 C8
Middlebeck Dr NG5 162 C8
Middlebeck Way NG24 140 B2
Middlebridge Rd DN10 12 E4
Middlebrook Rd NG16 129 B4
Middledale Rd NG4 174 C6
Middlefell Cl NG9 184 D1
Middlefell Way NG11 184 D1
Middlefield La
Gainsborough DN21 24 E7
Ollerton NG22 77 B3
Middlefield Rd DN22 31 E8
Middle Furlong Gdns 5 NG2 173 B2
Middle Furlong Mews 4 NG2 173 B2
Middle Furlong Mws 5 NG11 173 B2
Middle Gate NG24 139 F8
Middlegate Field Dr S80 45 A5
Middlehey Sch NG25 134 E4
Middle Hill NG1 223 E2
Middle Holme La NG23 97 A8
Middle La
Beeston NG9 183 E5
Middle La *continued*
Morton NG25 137 D3
Nether Broughton LE14 219 D8
Middle Meadow S81 34 E7
Middle Pavement NG1 223 E2
Middle St
Barkestone-le-Vale NG13 192 C2
Beeston NG9 184 A6
Hose LE14 211 F7
Misson DN10 4 C2
Middleton Bvd NG8 172 C3
Middleton Cl
Nuthall NG16 159 C6
Selston NG16 129 B7
Middleton Cres NG9 171 E1
Middleton Ct
Mansfield NG18 103 B6
New Ollerton NG22 77 C5
Middleton Pl LE11 220 A2
Middleton Prim Sch NG8 172 C4
Middleton Rd
Clipstone NG21 89 F4
Clipstone NG21 90 A4
Ilkeston DE7 170 A5
Mansfield Woodhouse NG19 88 C5
Newark-on-Trent NG24 125 C3
Middleton St
Awsworth NG16 158 C4
Beeston NG9 183 F7
Cossall DE7 158 A1
Nottingham NG7 222 A3
Middle Wood La DN10 4 C6
Midfield Rd NG17 115 B1
Midhurst Cl NG9 183 C4
Midhurst Way NG7 184 E2
Midlame Gdns NG6 159 F7
Midland Ave
Carlton NG4 175 A7
Nottingham NG7 222 A1
Stapleford NG9 182 C5
Midland Cotts NG12 185 F7
Midland Cres NG4 174 F7
Midland Ct NG7 172 D5
Midland Gr NG4 175 A8
Midland Rd
Carlton NG4 174 F7
Eastwood NG16 143 F2
Sutton in Ashfield NG17 101 B2
Midland St NG10 193 E8
Midland Terr NG24 124 E1
Midland Way NG7 222 A3
Midland Wy
Mansfield NG18 102 B5
Nottingham NG7 172 D5
Midway The NG7 184 E7
Midworth St NG18 102 B6
Mikado Rd NG10 193 C5
Mike Powers Pottery★ NG11 196 C7
Milburn Gr NG13 177 C4
Mildenhall Cres NG5 161 C8
Mile End Rd NG4 175 A8
Milestone Ct DN22 28 C6
Miles Yd LE11 220 B3
Milfield Cl DN21 15 E3
Milford Acad The NG11 195 E8
Milford Ave NG10 182 B3
Milford Cl NG6 160 A8
Milford Cres NG19 101 D7
Milford Ct NG5 161 D6
Milford Dr
Ilkeston DE7 157 D3
Nottingham NG3 174 C7
Mill Acre Cl DE7 157 D2
Millash La S80 45 B4
Millbank DE75 157 A8
Millbank Cl DE7 157 D3
Millbank Pl NG6 146 D3
Mill Baulk Rd DN10 14 A6
Millbeck Ave NG8 171 C3
Millbeck Cl NG2 186 C6
Mill Bridge Cl DN22 39 E6
Millbrook Dr NG4 162 C1
Mill Bsns Ctr The DN10 12 E2
Mill Cl
Huthwaite NG17 100 A3
Misterton DN10 6 F1
North Leverton with Habblesthorpe DN22 32 C1
Sutton on Trent NG23 96 F8
Mill Cl The NG8 160 E3
Mill Cres
Arnold NG5 161 E8
Whitwell S80 45 A6
Mill Croft NG17 100 E1
Mill Ct NG18 101 E5
Milldale Cl NG11 184 C2
Milldale Ct NG18 103 A5
Milldale Rd
Farnsfield NG22 120 A6
Long Eaton NG10 193 B6
Milldale Wlk NG17 100 E4
Millennium Bsns Pk NG19 87 E2
Millennium Cl DE7 157 E3
Millennium Ct 4 NG19 87 E2
Millennium Way
Mansfield NG18 103 E3
Rainworth NG21 104 B1
Millennium Way E NG6 160 A4
Millennium Way W
Nottingham NG6 160 A4
Nuthall NG6 160 A4
Miller Dr DE7 157 B5
Miller Hives Cl NG12 187 E3
Millers Bridge NG12 187 E2
Millers Cl NG12 164 C1
Millers Ct
Clarborough DN22 30 E4
Nottingham NG7 222 A4
Millersdale Ave
Ilkeston DE7 157 E5
Mansfield NG18 101 E4
Millers Dale Dr DE55 113 B7
Millers Gn 7 NG2 174 A4
Millership Way
Cossall DE7 158 A2
Ilkeston DE7 157 F2
Miller's La LE12 206 C1
Millers Way
Kirkby-in-Ashfield NG17 115 A5
Retford DN22 39 C8
Millers Wy NG17 101 D5
Miller Wy DN21 24 E5
Mill Farm Dr NG17 99 B7
Millfield Ave LN1 57 B4
Millfield Cl
Ilkeston DE7 157 C3
Retford DN22 39 E3
Mill Field Cl
Burton Joyce NG14 163 E3
Harby NG23 70 D2
Millfield Rd
Ilkeston DE7 170 A8
Kimberley NG16 158 E7
Millfield View S80 35 C2
Mill Gate
East Bridgford NG13 165 C3
Newark-on-Trent NG24 139 E8
Millgate Mus★ NG24 139 E8
Mill Gdns S80 35 D2
Mill Gn NG24 140 B8
Mill Heyes NG13 165 D3
Mill Hill
Gringley on the Hill DN10 12 D2
Gringley on the Hill DN10 12 E2
Mill Hill Leys LE12 216 C4
Mill Hill Rd NG13 177 D3
Mill Holme DE55 113 B4
Millicent Gr NG2 185 F8
Millicent Rd NG2 185 E8
Millidge Cl NG5 160 F5
Mill La
Annesley Woodhouse NG17 114 E2
Arnold NG5 161 E8
Aslockton NG13 179 A5
Beckingham NG24 127 F3
Bradmore NG12 197 A5
Caunton NG23 109 A5
Claypole NG23 156 C6
Clayworth DN22 21 F4
Clayworth DN22 22 B4
Clipston NG12 198 D8
Cossall DE7 170 B8
Cossall NG16 158 C1
Cotgrave NG12 187 E4
Eagle LN6 84 E4
East Leake LE12 214 F8
Edwinstowe NG21 76 A1
Hickling LE14 210 C7
Huthwaite NG17 100 A1
Huthwaite NG17 100 A2
Kegworth DE74 203 D2
Kings Clipstone NG21 90 E6
Lambley NG4 163 B7
Lidgett NG21 91 A8
Long Clawson LE14 211 D3
Long Whatton LE12 212 D4
Loughborough LE11 220 C5
Morton DN21 15 C5
Newark-on-Trent NG24 139 E8
Normanton on T NG23 81 D7
North Clifton NG23 68 F5
North Leverton with Habblesthorpe DN22 42 B8
North Muskham NG23 110 F1
Nottingham NG6 146 D3
Orston NG13 180 A7
Pinxton NG16 113 D2
Rockley DN22 51 A2
Sandiacre NG10 182 C6
Saxilby LN1 57 B4
Scarrington NG13 178 F7
Scrooby DN10 10 A3
South Leverton DN22 42 D7
Stainsby S44 85 C8
Tichfield Park NG17 114 D4
Upton NG23 137 E8
Walesby NG22 63 F2
Walkeringham DN10 13 F4
Whitwell S80 45 A6
Wigsley NG23 83 F8
Willoughby-on-t-W LE12 217 D8
Worksop S81 37 D5
Millman Way DN22 29 C1
Mill Mdw View S81 18 B3
Mill Pk NG25 121 F1
Mill Pond Cl NG17 114 E1
Mill Rd
Eastwood NG16 144 B3
Elston NG23 153 E4
Gringley on the Hill DN10 12 E2
Heanor DE75 157 A8
Stapleford NG9 182 D8
Millrise Rd NG19 102 D5
Mills Dr NG24 139 C6
Mill St
Ilkeston DE7 157 E2
Mansfield NG18 102 D6
Nottingham NG6 160 D3
Retford DN22 39 F6
Sutton in Ashfield NG17 100 E2
Worksop S80 35 E4
Millstone Cl NG18 102 E4
Mills Way S80 36 B2
Millview Cl 6 NG2 173 F4
Millview Ct 13 NG2 173 E4
Millway NG19 88 D1
Mill Wlk S80 45 A6
Mill Wood La S80 45 D4
Mill Yd
Beeston NG9 183 F6
Hucknall NG15 146 A7
Milne Ave DN11 9 C4
Milne Dr DN11 9 D4
Milne Gr DN11 9 C4
Milnercroft DN22 29 D1
Milnercroft Gn DN22 29 D1
Milne Rd DN11 9 D4
Milner Fields NG22 92 E8
Milner Rd
Long Eaton NG10 193 D8
Nottingham NG5 161 C2
Milner St
Newark-on-Trent NG24 140 A7
Sutton in Ashfield NG17 101 A6
Milnhay Rd
Heanor NG16 143 C2
Nottingham NG16 143 B1
Milton Ave DE7 157 E4
Milton Cl NG17 101 B4
Milton Cres
Beeston NG9 183 C2
Ravenshead NG15 117 A2
Milton Ct
Arnold NG5 162 B7
Ravenshead NG15 117 A2
Milton Dr
Ravenshead NG15 117 A2
Worksop S81 36 B4
Milton Rd
Gainsborough DN21 15 E2
Ilkeston DE7 157 F4
West Markham NG22 65 B6
Milton Rise NG15 145 C5
Milton St
Ilkeston DE7 157 F4
Kirkby-in-Ashfield NG17 115 B5
Long Eaton NG10 193 D7
Mansfield NG18 102 A7
New Balderton NG24 140 C6
Nottingham NG1 223 E3
Milton Wlk S81 36 B4
Milverton Rd NG5 161 C8
Mimosa Cl NG11 184 C1
Minerva Gr NG15 146 C8
Minerva St NG6 160 B8
Minkley Dr NG16 143 C4
Minster Cl
Hucknall NG15 146 B8
Kirkby-in-Ashfield NG17 114 F6
Minster Gdns NG16 144 B1
Minster Rd DN10 6 E2
Minster Sch The NG25 136 E7
Minstrel Av NG5 161 A2
Minstrel Cl NG15 146 A5
Mint Cl NG10 193 A7
Minton Cl NG9 183 B2
Minton Pastures 3 NG19 89 A1
Minver Cres NG8 160 B2
Mirabelle Way DN11 9 A6
Mirberry Mews NG7 222 A1
Mire La DN22 28 F6
Misk Hollows NG15 145 E8
Misk View NG16 144 B2
Mission Bank DN9 2 A8
Mission Carr Nature Reserve★ DN9 5 A7
Mission St NG5 161 E2
MISSON 4 B2
Misson Bank
Blaxton DN9 1 F4
Misson DN9 1 F5
Misson Prim Sch DN10 4 B3
MISTERTON 6 F1
Misterton Cres
Ravenshead NG15 116 F1
Ravenshead NG15 117 A1
Misterton Ct 3 NG19 88 B1
Misterton Prim Sch DN10 13 F8
Mitchell Ave NG16 143 A4
Mitchell Cl
Nottingham NG6 160 A6
Worksop S81 35 E8
Mitchell St NG10 193 E7
Mitchell Terr DE7 170 A5
Mitford Dr NG5 147 F2
M Lark Cl NG17 100 D1
Moat La DN22 19 B2
Mob La LE12 217 D7
Model La S80 58 E8
Model View S80 58 E8
Model Village S80 58 E8
Model Village Prim Sch NG20 72 E3
Moffat Cl NG3 173 F7
Moira St LE11 220 B3
Mollington Sq NG6 160 B3
Monarch Way LE11 220 A6
Mona Rd NG2 174 A1
Mona St NG9 184 B6
Monckton Dr NG25 121 E1
Monckton Rd
Bircotes DN11 9 C4
Retford DN22 39 C8
Monique Rd NG12 185 F3
Monks Cl DE7 170 A8
Monk's La NG11 195 A1
Monks Mdw LE12 205 F2
Monksway NG11 185 A4
Monks Way S81 34 F7
Monkton Cl DE7 157 C3
Monkton Dr NG8 171 E7
Monkwood Cl NG23 98 B1
Monmouth Cl NG8 171 B4
Monmouth Rd S81 36 A6
Monroe Wlk 11 NG5 161 A7
Monsaldale Cl NG10 193 B6
Monsall Ave DE7 157 E5
Monsall St NG7 160 F1
Monsella Gr DN22 40 A3
Monsell Dr NG5 147 E1
Montague Rd NG15 146 A8
Montague St
Beeston NG9 183 E7
Mansfield NG18 102 E6
Nottingham NG6 160 C7
Montford Rd S81 35 C8
Montfort Cres NG5 161 D4
Montfort St NG7 222 C3
Montgomery Cl 8 NG9 183 C2
Montgomery Rd NG24 140 A5
Montgomery St NG7 222 C4
Montpelier Rd NG7 172 E1
Montrose S81 36 B5
Montrose Ct NG9 170 E1
Montrose Sq NG19 88 B6
Montys Mdw S81 35 D8
Monyash Cl DE7 157 E3
Moody Cl NG9 183 B2
Moonbeam Way 2 NG18 102 E2
Moor Bridge NG6 146 D1
Moorbridge Cotts NG6 146 D2
Moorbridge Ct NG13 177 E5
Moorbridge La NG9 170 D1
Moorbridge Rd NG13 177 E5
Moorbridge Rd E NG13 177 E5
Moore Ave DE74 203 D3
Moore Cl
Claypole NG23 156 D6
East Leake LE12 205 F2
West Bridgford NG2 174 B1
Moore Gate NG9 184 A6
Moore Rd NG3 162 A2
Moores Ave NG10 182 C7
Moore St NG6 160 C5
Moor Farm Cl DE55 99 B4
Moor Farm Inn La NG9 171 A2
Moorfield Cl NG15 146 E5
Moorfield Cres NG10 182 B5
Moorfield Ct NG9 170 E1
Moorfield La
Creswell NG20 58 F4
Whaley Thorns NG20 59 A4
Moorfield Pl NG20 74 C5
Moorfields Ave NG16 143 F3
Moorgate Ave NG19 86 F7
Moorgate Pk DN22 39 F8
Moorgate St NG7 222 C3
Moorgreen NG16 144 C3
Moorgreen Dr NG8 159 D2
Moorgreen Ind Pk NG16 144 B4
Moorgreen Way DN11 9 A3
Moorhades La NG22 53 F8
Moorhaigh Cl NG19 86 F7
Moorhaigh La NG19 87 A3
MOORHOUSE 80 C2
Moorhouse Rd
Egmanton NG22 80 C4
Laxton NG22 79 C2
Moorhouse NG23 80 C2
Moorhouse NG23 80 D1
Nottingham NG8 171 E6
Ossington NG23 95 D8
Moorings The 3 NG7 172 F2
Moor La
Aslockton NG13 178 D5
Beeston NG9 171 B2
Besthorpe NG23 98 C6
Bingham NG13 177 E5
Blyth S81 18 D2
Bradmore NG11 196 E2
Bunny NG11 206 E8
Calverton NG14 149 D6
Caunton NG23 108 F7
Dry Doddington NG23 169 E6
East Stoke NG23 153 E7
Elston NG23 154 B5
Gotham NG11 205 C8
Loughborough LE11 220 C3
Mansfield NG18 101 F6
Morton NG25 137 C3
Normanton on S LE12 213 C4
North Clifton NG23 69 B4
Ruddington NG11 196 C6
South Clifton NG23 69 D3
Stathern NG13 202 F5
Syerston NG23 153 C3
Thorney NG23 69 F4
Thorpe NG23 153 F7
Thorpe NG23 154 A7
Upper Langwith S44 72 A8
Moorland Ave
Stapleford NG9 182 D6
Walkeringham DN10 13 F6
Moorland Cl
Sutton in Ashfield NG17 101 A6
Walkeringham DN10 13 F6
Moorlands Cl
Long Eaton NG10 182 B2
Norwell NG23 109 F8
Norwell NG23 110 A7
Moorland Way NG18 103 A6
Moorland Wlk DN10 13 F6

Moor Rd
Bestwood Village NG6 146 E6
Brinsley NG16 143 E8
Calverton NG14 149 A7
Collingham NG23 98 B1
Nottingham NG8 159 D1
Moorsholm Dr NG8 171 D4
Moor St
Carlton NG4 175 A7
Mansfield NG18 101 F5
Mansfield NG18 102 A6
Moor The NG16 143 D8
Moor Top Rd DN11 8 F5
Moor View NG11 206 E8
Morado Way NG4 175 C7
Moray Ct NG16 158 F7
Moray Sq NG19 101 D5
Morden Cl NG8 171 D8
Morden Rd NG16 158 C8
Moreland Ct
Carlton NG4 174 C7
10 Nottingham NG2 173 F3
Moreland Pl 11 NG2 173 F3
Moreland St NG2 173 F3
Morel Cl NG16 143 F1
Morello Ave NG4 174 F7
Morello Dr NG8 172 C7
Moreton Ave DE7 157 F5
Moreton Rd NG11 195 E7
Morgana Rd NG19 87 D1
Morgan Mews NG7 184 D2
Morgans Cl NG24 126 B2
Morkinshire Cres
NG12 187 F4
Morkinshire La NG12 187 E4
Morley Ave
Nottingham NG3 161 E2
Retford DN22 29 C1
Morley Cl NG18 103 B5
Morley Ct 5 NG2 173 E4
Morley Dr DE7 157 D3
Morley Gdns NG12 176 A3
Morley Pl NG14 173 F8
Morley Rd NG3 162 A1
Morley's Cl NG14 150 E1
Morley St
Arnold NG5 161 D6
Gainsborough DN21 24 C8
Kirkby-in-Ashfield NG17 115 B4
Loughborough LE11 220 C5
Stanton Hill NG17 100 C6
Sutton in Ashfield NG17 100 F3
Mornington Cl NG10 182 C6
Mornington Cres NG8 159 D3
Mornington Prim Sch
NG16 159 D4
Morrell Bank NG5 160 F6
Morris Ave NG9 183 B1
Morris Cl LE11 220 C4
Morris Rd NG8 159 D1
Morris St NG4 175 A7
MORTON
Lincs 15 C4
Notts 137 D3
Morton Carr DN21 14 F7
Morton Cl
Mansfield NG18 103 B6
Morton DN21 15 B4
Radcliffe on Trent NG12 176 C3
Morton Gdns NG12 176 C3
Morton Gr S81 35 E8
Morton Hall Gdns★
DN22 38 A5
Morton La LN6 84 D1
Morton Rd DN21 15 C3
Morton St NG19 87 D2
Morton Terr DN21 15 C2
Morton Trentside Prim Sch
DN21 15 A4
Morval Rd NG8 171 E6
Morven Ave
Hucknall NG15 146 B6
Mansfield Woodhouse
NG19 88 B2
Sutton in Ashfield NG17 100 E2
Morven Park Prim Sch
NG17 115 B5
Morven Rd NG17 115 B5
Morven St S80 58 F8
Morven Terr NG20 74 B3
Mosborough Rd NG17 100 A1
Moseley Rd NG15 130 C8
Moses View S81 35 F4
Mosgrove Cl S81 35 C7
Mosley St
Hucknall NG15 146 A6
Nottingham NG7 172 F8
Mosscar Cl NG20 73 F1
Moss Cl
Arnold NG5 147 C1
East Bridgford NG13 165 D3
Mosscroft Ave NG11 184 D1
Mossdale S81 36 A8
Mossdale Rd
Mansfield NG18 102 E8
Nottingham NG5 161 C5
Moss Dr NG9 183 B7
Moss La LN6 71 F3
Moss Rd NG15 145 F7
Moss Rise NG3 162 B2
Moss Side NG11 185 A3
Mosswood Cres NG5 161 B7
Motorpoint Arena★
NG1 223 F2
Mottram Rd NG9 183 C6
Moulton Cres NG24 140 C3
Mountain Ash Cres
NG12 186 A2
Mount Ave S81 35 E5
Mountbatten Ct DE7 157 F3
Mountbatten Gr NG4 162 E2
Mountbatten Way NG9 183 C2
Mount CE Prim Sch
NG24 125 A1
Mount Cl DN11 8 F5
Mount Cres
Market Warsop NG20 74 C3
South Normanton DE55 113 A3
Mount Ct NG24 140 D4
Mountfield Ave NG10 182 B4
Mountfield Dr NG5 161 A7
Mount Hooton Rd NG7 222 C4
Mount Hooton St NG7 173 A7
Mount La
Hose LE14 211 F7
Newark-on-Trent NG24 140 A8
Mount Milner NG18 102 D6
Mountney Pl NG24 125 A3
Mount Pleasant
Carlton NG4 174 E7
Ilkeston DE7 157 E4
Keyworth NG12 198 A2
Lowdham NG14 150 D2
2 Mansfield NG18 102 A7
Nottingham NG6 160 E2
Radcliffe on Trent NG12 175 E3
Retford DN22 39 F7
Sutton in Ashfield NG17 100 F4
Mount Rd NG24 140 C4
Mountsorrel Dr NG2 186 B6
Mount St
Mansfield NG19 101 F8
Nottingham NG1 223 D2
Nottingham, New Basford
NG7 160 F1
Stapleford NG9 182 E7
Mount The
Arnold NG5 147 D1
Bestwood Village NG6 146 E4
Clipstone NG19 89 D3
Nottingham, Broxtowe
NG8 159 E1
Nottingham, Portchester
NG3 162 C2
Stapleford NG9 182 D6
Mount Vernon Pk DN22 40 A4
Mount View Cl NG18 102 D6
Mowbray Ct NG3 223 F3
Mowbray Gdns NG2 185 F5
Mowbray Rise NG5 161 F8
Mowbray Str DN21 15 C2
Mowcrofts La NG22 68 B7
Mowlands Cl NG17 101 B2
Moyra Dr NG5 161 C7
Mozart Cl NG7 222 A3
Mr Straw's House★ S80 36 A5
Muir Ave NG12 197 D8
Muirfield S81 36 B6
Muirfield Cl 8 NG17 114 E7
Muirfield Rd NG5 147 A1
Muirfield Way NG19 88 E6
Mulberry Cl
4 Mansfield NG18 102 C5
Newark-on-Trent NG24 140 D8
West Bridgford NG2 185 B5
Mulberry Cres S81 25 F7
Mulberry Ct DN10 4 B3
Mulberry Gdns
Kegworth DE74 203 D2
1 Nottingham NG6 160 A8
Mulberry Gr NG15 146 B4
Mulberry La NG25 121 D4
Mulberry Way
East Leake LE12 214 C8
1 Harworth DN11 8 F4
Saxilby LN1 57 A5
Torksey Lock LN1 44 C1
Multimode Cl NG9 184 A4
Mumby Cl NG24 125 A1
Mundella Rd NG2 173 D1
Mundy St DE7 157 E2
Munford Circ NG6 160 B3
Munks Ave NG15 145 F7
Munnmoore Cl DE74 203 C3
Murby Cres NG6 160 B8
Murden Way NG9 184 B6
Murdoch Cl NG22 119 E7
Murdon Cres NG12 197 D2
Muriel Rd NG9 183 F7
Muriel St NG6 160 B7
Murray Cl NG5 160 F5
Murray St NG18 102 B5
Muschamp Terr NG20 74 B3
Mushill La LE12 216 D5
Muskham Ave DE7 157 F3
Muskham Ct 1 NG19 88 B1
Muskham La NG23 110 C2
Muskham Prim Sch
NG23 110 F2
Muskham St NG2 173 D1
Mustang Cl NG15 145 E2
Musters Cres NG2 185 F5
Musters Croft NG4 174 F4
Musters Rd
Bingham NG13 177 D4
Langar NG13 190 D2
Newstead NG15 130 D6
Ruddington NG11 196 C6
West Bridgford NG2 185 E5
Musters St NG20 73 A4
Musters Wlk 4 NG6 160 A7
MUSTON 181 F1
Muston Cl NG3 161 F1
Muston La NG13 181 D1
Mutton La DN10 23 A8
Muttonshire Hill DN22 50 F5
Mynd The NG19 88 E5
Myrtle Ave
Long Eaton NG10 193 C6
Myrtle Ave *continued*
1 Nottingham NG7 173 B8
Stapleford NG9 182 E6
Myrtle Cl NG20 72 D6
Myrtle Gr NG9 184 A7
Myrtle Rd NG4 174 C8
Myrtle St DN22 39 D6
Myrtus Cl NG11 184 C2
Mytholme Cl NG10 182 C2

N

Nabbs La NG15 145 E5
Naburn Ct 4 NG8 172 D8
Nairn Cl
Arnold NG5 148 B1
Farnsfield NG22 119 F5
Nairn Mews NG4 174 E7
Nan Sampson Bank DN9 1 D8
Nansen St NG6 160 C6
Naomi Cres NG6 146 C1
Naomi Ct NG6 146 C1
Naples Cres NG19 86 F5
Narrow La
Austerfield DN10 3 B1
Bawtry DN10 10 B8
Greasley NG16 145 A4
Hathern LE12 213 A1
Wymeswold LE12 217 B2
Naseby Cl NG5 160 F4
Naseby Dr NG10 193 E4
Naseby Rd NG24 140 E8
Nash Cl S81 36 C4
Nathaniel Rd NG10 193 F7
Nathans La
Bassingfield NG12 186 F7
Radcliffe on Trent NG12 187 A7
National Holocaust Ctr &
Mus The★ NG22 78 E3
National Ice Centre★
NG1 223 F2
National Sch The
NG15 130 F1
National Water Sports Ctr
NG12 174 F3
Naturescape Wild Flower
Farm★ NG13 190 E1
Navenby Wlk NG7 184 E2
Navigation Ct LN1 57 B3
Navigation St NG2 173 F2
Navigation Way LE11 220 A5
Navigation Yd NG24 139 F8
Naworth Cl NG6 160 E5
Naylor Ave
Gotham NG11 195 B1
Loughborough LE11 220 D2
Nazareth Rd NG7 172 E2
ncn City (Adams) NG1 223 F2
ncn High Pavement Sixth
Form Acad NG1 223 D3
Neal Ct NG16 143 A3
Neale St NG10 193 E7
Near Mdw NG10 193 E5
Nearsby Dr NG2 186 B6
Nebula Way NG18 102 F1
Needham Rd NG5 162 A8
Needham St NG13 177 E4
Needwood Ave NG9 170 D2
Neeps Croft NG14 150 A6
Negus Ct NG4 163 B6
Neighwood Cl NG9 182 E2
Nell Gwyn Cres NG5 147 C1
Nelper Cres DE7 170 A5
Nelson Cl NG19 101 E7
Nelson La NG23 110 F2
Nelson Rd
Arnold NG5 161 E7
Beeston NG9 184 A4
New Balderton NG24 140 B4
Nottingham NG6 160 C7
Nelson St
Gainsborough DN21 15 C2
Ilkeston DE7 157 F3
Long Eaton NG10 193 D6
Nottingham NG1 223 F2
Retford DN22 39 F6
Nene Cl NG15 145 E3
Nene Wlk S81 35 E7
Nene Wy NG13 177 D3
Neptune Way NG18 102 E2
Nesbitt St NG17 100 F1
Nesfield Ct DE7 157 E1
Nesfield Rd DE7 157 E1
Nest Ave NG17 115 C4
Nest Cres NG17 115 C4
Neston Dr NG6 160 C4
NETHER
BROUGHTON 219 C8
Nether Cl
Eastwood NG16 143 F4
Nottingham NG3 174 A6
Nethercross Dr NG20 74 C5
Nether Ct NG22 120 A6
NETHERFIELD 175 B6
Netherfield Cl NG20 74 D8
Netherfield Inf Sch
NG20 74 D8
Netherfield La
Budby NG22 61 F2
Church Warsop NG20 74 D7
Market Warsop NG20 61 C1
Perlethorpe NG22 62 C3
Perlethorpe NG22 62 F5
Perlethorpe NG22 63 A5
Netherfield Prim Sch
NG4 175 A7
Netherfield Rd
Long Eaton NG10 193 C4
Sandiacre NG10 182 B4
Netherfield Sta NG4 174 F6
Nethergate NG11 184 C2
Nethergate Acad
Clifton NG11 185 A1
Nottingham NG11 184 F1
NETHER LANGWITH 59 B1
Nethermere La NG8 159 C1
Nether Pasture NG4 175 B6
Nether Slade Rd DE7 157 E2
Nether St
Beeston NG9 184 A6
Harby LE14 202 A3
Nether Thorpe Rd S80 34 A5
Netherton Pl S80 36 A1
Netherton Rd S80 47 A7
Nettlecliff Wlk NG5 160 E8
Nettle Croft DN11 8 C7
Nettleship Rd NG16 158 F6
Nettleworth Inf Sch
NG19 88 C4
Neville Dr NG12 200 A2
Neville Rd NG14 148 F6
Neville Sadler Ct NG9 184 B7
Newall Dr
Beeston NG9 183 C2
Everton DN10 11 A1
Newark Air Mus★
NG24 126 A5
Newark Ave 16 NG2 173 E4
Newark Bsns Pk NG24 125 C3
Newark Castle★ NG24 139 F8
Newark Castle Sta
NG24 124 F1
Newark Cl NG18 102 F2
Newark Coll NG24 140 A8
Newark Cres NG2 173 E4
Newark Ct NG5 160 F5
Newark Dr NG18 102 F2
Newark High Acad
NG24 139 F7
Newark Hospl NG24 140 A6
Newark La
Barnby in the Willows
NG24 141 C5
Barnby in the Willows
NG24 141 E5
Newark Mus & Tudor Hall★
NG24 140 A8
Newark North Gate Sta
NG24 125 B1
NEWARK-ON-TRENT 140 C7
Newark Orchard Sch
NG24 140 C6
Newark Rd
Alverton NG13 180 D8
Barnby in the Willows
NG24 141 D6
Barnby in the Willows
NG24 141 F6
Caunton NG23 109 B4
Coddington NG24 125 F1
Collingham LN6 112 F3
Collingham NG23 111 F6
Cotham NG23 154 F3
Cotham NG23 155 A2
Dry Doddington NG23 156 A3
Eakring NG22 92 F1
Eakring NG22 93 C1
Hawton NG24 139 D3
Hockerton NG25 122 C5
Kersall NG22 108 A8
Kilvington NG13 168 F2
Kilvington NG13 169 A3
Kirklington NG22 120 F8
Laughterton LN1 55 B7
Long Bennington NG23 155 F3
Maplebeck NG22 107 F8
Ollerton NG22 77 A3
Ompton NG22 93 C6
Southwell NG25 121 F1
Stapleford LN6 127 C8
Sutton in Ashfield NG17 101 C1
Tuxford NG22 65 F2
Tuxford NG22 66 A2
Wellow NG22 77 D2
Newark Rd Service Rd
NG17 101 B1
Newark St NG2 173 E4
Newark Way NG18 103 A2
NEW BALDERTON 140 B5
Newbarn Cl NG20 72 D2
Newberry Cl NG12 189 A4
Newbery Ave NG10 193 F6
Newbery Cl NG21 76 A3
Newbold St NG9 171 E8
Newbold Way NG12 199 F2
Newbound La NG17 86 C2
New Bound La NG17 85 F3
Newboundmill La NG19 87 A4
New Brickyard La
DE74 203 D1
New Brook Bsns Pk
NG20 73 A2
Newbury Cl NG3 162 A4
Newbury Ct 3 NG5 173 B8
Newbury Dr NG16 159 D3
Newbury Gdns NG12 176 B5
Newbury Mews 5 S80 35 F2
Newbury Rd
Balderton NG24 140 E8
Newark-on-Trent NG24 125 E1
Newcastle Ave
Beeston NG9 183 F6
Carlton NG4 162 E1
Newark-on-Trent NG24 140 A6
Worksop S80 35 E1
Newcastle Cir NG7 222 C2
Newcastle Dr NG7 222 C3
Newcastle Farm Dr
NG8 160 C1
Newcastle St
Huthwaite NG17 100 A3
Newcastle St *continued*
4 Mansfield NG18 102 A7
Mansfield Woodhouse
NG19 88 B3
Market Warsop NG20 74 B4
Nottingham NG1 223 E3
Nottingham, Bulwell NG6 160 C8
Tuxford NG22 65 F2
Worksop S80 35 F2
Newcastle Terr NG7 222 C3
New Cl
Blidworth NG21 117 F5
Blidworth NG21 118 A5
Kirkby-in-Ashfield NG17 115 A5
New Coll Nottingham
Hucknall NG15 146 B7
Nottingham NG3 223 F3
Newcombe Dr NG5 162 C7
Newcomen Cl NG22 77 C3
New Cotts NG20 59 F3
NEW CROSS 100 E4
New Cross St NG17 100 F4
New Cswy NG13 192 C2
New Ct Gdns DN22 40 A5
New Derby Rd NG16 143 C3
Newdigate Rd NG16 159 A7
Newdigate St
Ilkeston DE7 170 A6
Kimberley NG16 159 A6
Nottingham NG7 222 C3
Newdigate Villas NG7 222 C3
New Eaton Rd NG9 182 E5
New England Way NG19 87 C3
New Fall St NG17 99 F3
New Farm La NG16 159 C6
Newfield La NG23 167 E6
Newfield Rd NG5 161 A3
New Fosse Rd NG24 139 B5
Newgate Cl NG4 174 E7
Newgate Ct NG7 222 B2
Newgate La NG18 102 D7
Newgate Lane Prim Sch
NG18 102 C7
Newgate St
Bingham NG13 177 E5
Worksop S80 35 F2
Newhall Gr NG2 173 F1
Newhall La
Edingley NG22 120 C2
Edingley NG22 135 B8
Newham Cl DE75 143 A1
Newhaven Ave NG19 88 B3
New Hill
Farnsfield NG22 119 F6
Walesby NG22 64 A2
New Holles Ct S80 35 F5
Newholm Dr NG11 185 A4
NEW HOUGHTON 86 F7
New Hucknall Way 2
NG17 100 A1
Newings La DN22 42 F8
New Ings La DN21 33 C6
NEWINGTON 10 E8
Newington Rd
Austerfield DN10 3 D1
Austerfield DN10 10 C8
New Inn Wlk DN22 39 F5
New King St LE11 220 C3
New La
Aslockton NG13 178 E6
Blidworth NG21 117 E5
Girton NG23 83 B4
Hilcote DE55 99 C2
Hilcote DE55 113 C8
Stanton Hill NG17 100 D6
Newland Cl
Beeston NG9 183 A2
Nottingham NG8 172 C5
Newlands
Gainsborough DN21 15 E1
Retford DN22 39 D4
Newlands Ave NG22 77 E5
Newlands Cl NG2 186 C4
Newlands Cres DE55 99 A3
Newlands Dr
Carlton NG4 162 F1
Clipstone NG19 89 D2
Newlands Jun Sch
NG19 89 E3
Newlands Rd
Clipstone NG19 89 C1
Mansfield NG19 103 B8
Newlands The NG24 140 E2
NEW LENTON 172 F4
New Linden St NG20 73 A4
New Line Rd NG17 114 E5
Newlyn Dr
Nottingham NG8 172 D8
South Normanton DE55 113 C6
Newlyn Gdns NG8 172 D8
Newmanleys Rd NG16 157 E8
Newmanleys Rd S
NG16 157 E8
Newman Rd NG14 148 E8
Newmarket Rd NG6 160 B6
Newmarket St NG18 102 E6
Newmarket Way NG9 182 F1
New Mill La
Mansfield Woodhouse
NG19 88 E3
Mansfield Woodhouse
NG19 88 F2
Newnham Rd NG24 125 A2
NEW OLLERTON 77 E5
New Pk La 4 NG18 88 C1
New Pl DN22 40 A7
Newport Cres NG19 87 E1
Newport Dr NG8 160 D1
Newquay Ave 1 NG7 172 E7
New Rd
Barton in Fabis NG11 194 F6
New Rd *continued*
Bilsthorpe NG22 105 E6
Blidworth NG21 118 A5
Colston Bassett NG12 189 D2
Firbeck S81 16 A5
Firbeck S81 16 A6
Greasley NG16 144 E6
Hawksworth NG13 167 C3
Morton NG25 137 C5
Nottingham NG7 172 D6
Oxton NG25 134 B3
Radcliffe on Trent NG12 175 F3
Stapleford NG9 170 D1
Staunton in the Vale
NG13 169 D3
Tickhill DN11 8 A7
Treswell DN22 42 C3
New Rise NG11 195 C8
New Row
Carlton NG4 174 D7
Westwood NG16 128 A5
New Scott St NG20 59 A2
New St
Gainsborough DN21 15 C1
Hilcote DE55 113 C8
Huthwaite NG17 99 F3
Huthwaite NG17 100 A3
Kegworth DE74 203 E3
Kirkby-in-Ashfield NG17 115 B4
Long Eaton NG10 193 E8
Loughborough LE11 220 A3
Newark-on-Trent NG24 140 A8
Newton DE55 99 A4
15 Nottingham NG5 161 B1
Retford DN22 39 F6
South Normanton DE55 113 A7
Sutton in Ashfield NG17 100 E2
NEWSTEAD 130 E5
Newstead Abbey & Gdns★
NG15 131 C8
Newstead Abbey Pk
Newstead NG15 116 B1
Newstead NG15 131 B8
Newstead Ave
Newark-on-Trent NG24 125 A1
Nottingham NG3 162 C2
Radcliffe on Trent NG12 176 A4
Newstead Cl
Kirkby-in-Ashfield
NG17 115 C5
Selston NG16 129 B7
Newstead Dr NG2 186 B7
Newstead Gr
Bingham NG13 177 C4
Nottingham NG1 223 D4
Newstead Ind Est NG5 162 A7
Newstead Prim Sch
NG15 130 D6
Newstead Rd
Long Eaton NG10 182 C3
Newstead NG15 130 D7
Newstead Rd S DE7 157 D3
Newstead St
Mansfield NG19 101 D7
6 Nottingham NG5 161 C3
Newstead Sta NG15 130 E6
Newstead Terr NG15 146 A8
Newstead Way NG8 159 D2
New Terr
Pleasley NG19 86 F5
Sandiacre NG10 182 B6
Newthorpe Comm
Eastwood NG16 144 A1
Newthorpe Common
NG16 158 A8
Newthorpe St NG2 173 D2
NEWTON 99 B3
Newton Ave
Bingham NG13 177 D4
Radcliffe on Trent NG12 176 A4
Newton Cl
Arnold NG5 162 B6
1 Gainsborough DN21 24 F8
Lowdham NG14 150 E1
Worksop S81 35 C7
Newtondale Ave NG19 88 E1
Newtondale Cl NG8 160 C1
Newton Dr
3 Heanor DE75 143 A1
Stapleford NG9 182 E6
West Bridgford NG2 185 C4
Newton Gdns NG13 177 C6
Newton Hill NG22 77 C3
Newton La NG13 177 D7
NEWTON ON TRENT 55 A1
Newton Paddocks
NG22 106 E8
Newton Prim Sch DE55 99 A3
Newton Rd
Carlton NG4 162 E3
Kettlethorpe LN1 55 E1
Newton DE55 99 A4
Newton's La NG16 158 B4
Newton St
Beeston NG9 183 E6
Mansfield NG18 102 C6
Newark-on-Trent NG24 140 A7
Nottingham NG7 172 E1
Retford DN22 39 F4
Newtonwood La
Tibshelf DE55 99 B5
Tibshelf DE55 99 C5
New Tythe St NG10 193 F7
New Vale Rd NG4 174 E5
New Westwood NG16 128 D4
ng2 Bsns Pk NG2 173 A1
Nicholas Pl NG22 66 A3
Nicholas Rd NG9 171 D1
Nicholson's Row NG20 72 F3
Nicholson St NG24 140 A7
Nicker Hill NG12 198 A3

Nicklaus Ct **5** NG5 . . . . . **161** A8
Nidderdale NG8 . . . . . . **171** C4
Nidderdale Cl NG8. . . . . **171** C3
Nightingale DN22. . . . . **42** B1
Nightingale Ave
Hathern LE12. . . . . **213** A1
Pleasley NG19 . . . . **87** A4
Nightingale Cl
Balderton NG24. . . . . . . **140** E4
Clipstone NG21 . . . . **89** F4
Mansfield NG21 . . . . **89** F4
Nottingham NG8 . . . . . . **172** A1
Nuthall NG16 . . . . **159** D6
Nightingale Cres NG16 **129** B6
Nightingale Dr NG19. . . **87** E1
Nightingale Gr
South Normanton DE55. . **113** C5
Worksop S81 . . . . **35** D7
Nightingale Way
Bingham NG13. . . . . **178** A3
Woodbeck DN22 . . . . **53** B8
Nightjar Way
Rainworth NG21 . . . . . . **117** F8
Rainworth NG21 . . . . . . **118** A8
Nile St NG1. . . . . **223** F3
Nilsson Rd NG9. . . . . . . **183** B3
Nimbus Wy NG16 . . . . . **159** A7
Nine Acre Gdns NG6. . . **159** F8
Nine Acres DE74. . . . . . **203** C2
Nine Corners NG16 . . . . **158** F6
Nine Scores La DN9. . . . . **1** E7
Ninth Ave NG19. . . . . . . **103** A8
Nixon Rise NG15. . . . . . **145** D5
Nixon Walk LE12. . . . . . **205** E2
Nixon Way NG23. . . . . . . **98** A1
Noble La NG13. . . . . **179** A5
Noburn Cres NG6. . . . . . **160** F3
Noel St
Gainsborough DN21 . . . . . **15** C2
Kimberley NG16. . . . . . . **159** A6
Mansfield NG18. . . . . . . **102** A7
Nottingham NG7 . . . . . . **172** F8
Nook Flatt Rd DN10. . . . **18** A8
Nookin The NG22. . . . . . . **66** B6
Nook The
Beeston NG9 . . . . **184** A7
Beeston, Chilwell NG9. . **183** A4
Calverton NG14 . . . . **148** F7
East Leake LE12 . . . . . . **205** E1
Nottingham NG8 . . . . . . **171** E4
Shirebrook NG20. . . . . . . **72** D3
Norbett Cl NG9 . . . . **183** C3
Norbett Ct NG5. . . . . . . **148** A1
Norbett Rd NG5. . . . . . . **148** A1
Norbreck Cl NG8 . . . . . . **160** B3
Norbridge Acad S81 . . . . **35** E5
Norbury Dr NG18 . . . . . . **102** E4
Norbury Way NG10 . . . . **182** A6
Nordean Rd NG5. . . . . . . **162** A5
Norfolk Ave
Beeston NG9 . . . . **183** A1
Bircotes DN11. . . . . **9** D4
Norfolk Cl
Hucknall NG15. . . . . **145** D5
Market Warsop NG20 . . . . **74** A4
Norfolk Ct NG19 . . . . **88** E5
Norfolk Dr
Bircotes DN11. . . . . **9** C4
Mansfield NG18. . . . . . . **102** B8
Norfolk Gdns NG17 . . . . **100** A2
Norfolk Gr DN11. . . . . **9** C4
Norfolk Pl
Arnold NG5 . . . . **162** B5
Nottingham NG1 . . . . . . **223** E3
Norfolk Rd
Bircotes DN11. . . . . **9** C4
Long Eaton NG10. . . . . . **182** F1
Norfolk St S80. . . . . **35** E2
Norfolk Wlk NG10 . . . . . **182** B5
Norland Cl NG3. . . . . **173** E7
Norman Ave
Newark-on-Trent NG24. . . **125** B4
Sutton in Ashfield NG17 . **101** A1
Normanby Rd NG8. . . . . **171** C3
Norman Cl
Beeston NG9 . . . . **183** C6
Nottingham NG1 . . . . . . **173** C6
Nottingham NG3 . . . . . . **223** E4
Norman Cres DE7. . . . . . **157** E3
Norman Dr
Eastwood NG16. . . . . . . **144** B2
Hucknall NG15. . . . . **145** E4
Norman Rd NG3 . . . . **174** A8
Norman St
Carlton NG4. . . . . **175** A4
Ilkeston DE7 . . . . **157** E3
Kimberley NG16. . . . . . . **158** F7
Normanton Brook Rd
DE55. . . . . **113** D7
Normanton Cl NG21 . . . . **75** F3
Normanton Ct NG13 . . . **181** C5
Normanton Dr
Loughborough LE11. . . . . **220** B6
Mansfield NG18. . . . . . . **102** E7
Normanton La
Bothamsall DN22. . . . . . . **63** C7
Bothamsall S80. . . . . **49** A1
Bottesford NG13. . . . . . . **181** B5
Bottesford NG23. . . . . . . **169** D2
Keyworth NG12. . . . . . . **197** F4
Stanford on Soar LE12. . . **214** B1
**NORMANTON ON
SOAR**. **213** E3
Normanton on Soar Prim
Sch LE12. . . . . **213** D3
**NORMANTON-ON-THE-
WOLDS**. **198** A6
**NORMANTON ON
TRENT**. **81** D6
Normanton Rd
Newark-on-Trent NG24. . . **125** D1

Normanton Rd continued
Southwell NG25. . . . . . . **121** F2
Weston NG23. . . . . **80** F7
Weston NG23. . . . . **81** A7
Nornay Cl S81. . . . . **18** A4
Northall Ave NG6. . . . . . **160** B6
Northampton St 2
NG3. . . . . **173** E6
North Ave
Bawtry DN10. . . . . **10** A8
Rainworth NG21 . . . . . . **104** A1
Sandiacre NG10 . . . . **182** B6
North Carr Rd DN10. . . . . **7** C3
North Church St NG1 . . . **223** E3
North Cir St NG1. . . . . . . **223** D2
Northcliffe Ave NG3 . . . **162** B2
NORTH CLIFTON **68** E6
North Clifton Prim Sch
NG23. . . . . **68** E3
Northcote St NG10. . . . . **193** E7
Northcote Way NG6. . . . **160** C5
North County Prim Sch
DN21. . . . . **15** B2
North Cres
Bottesford NG13 . . . . . . **181** A2
Clipstone NG21 . . . . **90** A3
Northcroft LN1. . . . . **57** A5
Northdale Rd NG3. . . . . . **174** B7
Northdown Dr NG9. . . . . **183** C4
Northdown Rd NG8. . . . . **172** D1
North Dr
Beeston NG9 . . . . **183** E6
Bilsthorpe NG22 . . . . . . **105** F7
Wartnaby LE14 . . . . **219** F3
North End NG24 . . . . **138** F5
Northern Bridge Rd
NG17. . . . . **100** F3
Northern Ct NG6. . . . . . . **160** D4
Northern Dr NG9 . . . . . . **170** D3
Northern Rd NG24 . . . . . **125** B1
Northern Rd Ind Est
NG24. . . . . **125** B1
Northern View NG17. . . **100** F3
North Farm La
Budby NG22. . . . . **61** F1
Carlton in Lindrick S81 . . . **26** A6
Northfield Ave
Ilkeston DE7 . . . . **157** E2
Long Eaton NG10. . . . . . **193** A4
Mansfield Woodhouse
NG19 . . . . **88** A4
Radcliffe on Trent NG12 . **176** C3
Northfield Cl NG18. . . . . **102** E6
Northfield Cres NG9 . . . **183** A4
Northfield Dr NG18 . . . . **102** E6
Northfield La
Mansfield Woodhouse
NG19 . . . . **88** A5
Treswell DN22 . . . . **42** B4
Northfield Pk NG19 . . . . . **88** B5
Northfield Prim Sch
NG19 . . . . **88** B5
Northfield Rd
Beeston NG9 . . . . **183** A4
North Leverton with
Habblesthorpe DN22. . . **33** B1
Northfield Rise LN1. . . . . **56** F4
Northfields NG10 . . . . . . **193** B4
Northfields Cl NG17. . . . **100** E3
Northfields Way LE12. . . **205** D2
Northfield Way DN22 . . . **39** D8
North Gate
Newark-on-Trent NG24. . **125** A2
Nottingham NG5 . . . . . . **161** A2
Nottingham NG7 . . . . . . **160** F1
Tickhill DN11. . . . . **8** A8
Northgate Bsns Ctr
NG24. . . . . **124** F1
North Gate Pl NG7 . . . . . **160** F1
Northgate Ret Pk
NG24. . . . . **125** A2
Northgate St 4 DE7 . . . **157** F1
North Gn
Calverton NG14 . . . . **133** D1
Calverton NG5 . . . . **148** D8
East Drayton DN22 . . . . . . **53** B3
North Hill Ave NG15. . . . **145** F7
North Hill Cres NG15. . . **145** F7
North Leverton CE Prim
Sch DN22 . . . . **32** F1
North Leverton Windmill★
DN22 . . . . **32** B1
**NORTH LEVERTON WITH
HABBLESTHORPE** . . . **42** D8
North Leys Rd DN22. . . . . **43** C8
North Lodge LE14. . . . . . **218** E5
North Marsh Rd DN22. . . **15** C2
North Moor Dr DN10. . . . **13** F6
North Moor Rd DN10. . . . **13** F6
NORTH MUSKHAM. . . . **110** E1
North Nottinghamshire Coll
1 East Retford DN22. . . . **39** F6
Worksop S81 . . . . **35** F5
Northolme DN21. . . . . **15** D1
Northolme Ave NG6. . . . **160** C7
Northolme View 8
DN21. . . . . **15** D1
Northolt Dr NG8 . . . . . . **159** D3
North Par DN21. . . . . **24** F7
North Pk NG18. . . . . **102** E3
North Rd
Long Eaton NG10. . . . . . **193** C6
Loughborough LE11. . . . . **220** B6
North Muskham NG23. . . **110** D2
Nottingham NG5 . . . . . . **161** B5
Nottingham NG7 . . . . . . **222** C2
Nottingham NG9 . . . . . . **184** D7
Retford DN22. . . . . **29** B2
Ruddington NG11. . . . . . **196** B7
West Bridgford NG2 . . . . **185** E7
West Burton DN22. . . . . . **32** D8

North Rd 1 NG8. . . . . . . **172** D2
North Rd 2 NG8. . . . . . . **172** D2
Northrowe NG17. . . . . . . **129** E8
North Scaffold La
NG23. . . . . **112** B2
NORTH SCARLE **83** E2
North Scarle Prim Sch
LN6. . . . . **83** D2
North Scarle Rd
South Scarle NG23 . . . . . . **98** E7
Wigsley NG23 . . . . **70** A1
Wigsley NG23 . . . . **83** F8
Wigsley NG23 . . . . **84** A8
North Sherwood St
NG1. . . . . **223** E4
Northside La DN22. . . . . . **32** F1
Northside Wlk NG5 . . . . **147** F2
North St
Beeston NG9 . . . . **183** E6
Eastwood NG16. . . . . . . **144** C2
Gainsborough DN21 . . . . . **15** C1
Huthwaite NG17 . . . . . . **100** A3
7 Ilkeston DE7. . . . . . . **157** F1
Kimberley NG16. . . . . . . **159** A5
Kirkby-in-Ashfield NG17 . **115** B2
Langley Mill NG16 . . . . . **143** B3
Morton DN21. . . . . **15** A4
4 Nottingham NG2. . . . **173** E4
Pinxton NG16. . . . . **113** D3
South Normanton DE55. . **113** A5
Sturton le Steeple DN22. . . **32** D6
Sutton in Ashfield NG17 . **100** F3
Warsop Vale NG20 . . . . . . **73** D4
Whaley Thorns NG20. . . . . **59** A2
Northumberland Ave
S81 . . . . **25** E8
Northumberland Cl
NG3. . . . . **223** F4
Northumbria Cl S81 . . . . . **36** B6
Northumbria Dr DN22. . . **39** D5
North Warren Rd DN21. . **15** B2
North Way S81 . . . . **25** F7
NORTH WHEATLEY **31** D8
North Wheatley CE Prim
Sch DN22 . . . . **31** E8
North Wlk DN22 . . . . **39** C8
Northwold Ave NG2. . . . **185** D6
Northwood Ave NG17. . . **100** D4
Northwood Cres NG5. . . **161** C6
Northwood Rd NG5 . . . . **161** C6
Northwood St NG9. . . . . **182** D8
Norton La NG20 . . . . **60** B3
Norton Rd LN6 . . . . **127** E8
Norton St NG7. . . . . **222** B3
NORWELL **110** A7
Norwell CE Prim Sch
NG23. . . . . **110** A8
Norwell Ct 2 NG19 . . . . . **88** B1
Norwell La
Brough NG23 . . . . **112** C1
Cromwell NG23 . . . . **110** D8
Norwell Rd
Caunton NG23 . . . . **109** C5
Norwell NG22 . . . . **94** F2
Norwell Woodhouse NG23 **95** B1
Ossington NG23 . . . . **95** F4
Norwell Woodhouse Rd
Caunton NG23 . . . . **108** D8
Norwell NG22 . . . . **94** D2
Norwich Cl NG19 . . . . **88** D5
Norwich Gdns NG6 . . . . **146** B1
Norwith Hill DN10 . . . . . . **3** D1
Norwood Cl
13 Ilkeston DE7 . . . . . . **157** F5
Sutton in Ashfield NG17 . **100** B3
Norwood Gdns NG25. . . **121** E2
Norwood La NG20 . . . . . . **58** E5
Norwood Rd NG7 . . . . . . **222** A3
Noskwith St DE7. . . . . . . **170** A5
Nostell Mews 6 S80. . . . **35** F2
Notintone St NG2. . . . . . **173** E4
NOTTINGHAM **173** B3
Nottingham Acad NG2 . **174** A4
Nottingham Acad The
NG3. . . . . **174** B5
Nottingham Airport
NG12 . . . . **186** F5
Nottingham Arts Theatre★
NG1 . . . . **223** E2
**Nottingham Bluecoat Sch &
Tech Coll The** NG8 . . **172** B4
Nottingham Bsns Pk
NG8 . . . . **159** C2
**Nottingham Canal Nature
Reserve★** NG9 . . . . . . **170** C2
Nottingham Castle (site
of)★ NG7 . . . . **223** D2
Nottingham Cath★
NG1. . . . . **223** D2
Nottingham City Hospl
NG5 . . . . **161** A4
Nottingham Coll NG7 . . **222** F2
Nottingham Coll Highfields
NG7 . . . . **184** D8
**Nottingham Emmanuel Sch
The** NG11 . . . . **185** C8
Nottingham Free Sch
NG5. . . . . **161** A2
Nottingham Girls' Acad
NG8 . . . . **172** B8
Nottingham Girls' High Sch
NG1 . . . . **223** D3
Nottingham High Sch
NG7 . . . . **223** D4
**Nottingham High Sch
(Lovell House Inf Sch)**
NG7 . . . . **222** C4
Nottingham Ice Ctr & Arena
NG1. . . . . **223** F2
Nottingham La LE14 . . . **218** C5

Nottingham Playhouse★
NG1. . . . . **223** D2
Nottingham Racecourse★
NG2 . . . . **174** B3
Nottingham Rd
Arnold NG5 . . . . **161** E6
Beeston NG9 . . . . **183** B1
Bingham NG13. . . . . **177** D4
Bottesford NG13 . . . . . . **180** E2
Burton Joyce NG14 . . . . **163** D3
Costock LE12 . . . . **206** D2
Cropwell Bishop NG12. . **188** E4
Eastwood NG16. . . . . . . **144** A2
Eastwood, Giltbrook
NG16. . . . . **158** C8
Gotham NG11 . . . . **195** B4
Gunthorpe NG14 . . . . . . **164** B6
Hucknall NG15. . . . . **146** C4
Ilkeston DE7 . . . . **170** A4
Kegworth DE74 . . . . **203** D2
Keyworth NG12 . . . . **197** E3
Kimberley NG16. . . . . . . **159** A5
Kirkby-in-Ashfield NG17 . **115** B2
Long Eaton NG10. . . . . . **193** C8
Loughborough LE11. . . . . **220** D6
Mansfield NG18. . . . . . . **102** C3
Nether Broughton LE14. . **219** D8
Nether Broughton LE14. . **219** E7
Nottingham, New Basford
NG7 . . . . **160** F1
Nuthall NG16 . . . . **159** F4
Oxton NG25 . . . . **134** A2
Radcliffe on Trent NG12 . **175** D2
Ravenshead NG15. . . . . . **116** E3
Ravenshead NG15. . . . . . **131** F8
Selston NG16. . . . . **128** E6
Selston NG16. . . . . **129** A6
Southwell NG25. . . . . . . **136** D6
Stapleford NG9 . . . . **182** E7
Thurgarton NG14 . . . . . . **151** C6
Trowell NG9 . . . . **170** E5
Upper Broughton LE14 . . **210** A3
Woodborough NG14 . . . . **149** C5
Nottingham Rd E NG16 **144** B1
Nottingham Science &
Tech Pk NG2 . . . . **172** D1
Nottingham Sta NG2. . . **223** F1
Nottingham South &
Wilford Ind Est NG2. . **185** B4
**Nottingham Transport
Heritage Ctr★** NG11 . . **196** C5
Nottingham Trent Univ
(Brackenhurst Campus)
NG25 . . . . **136** D5
Nottingham Trent Univ
(Clifton Campus)
NG11. . . . . **184** D3
Nottingham Trent Univ The
NG7 . . . . **222** A4
Nottingham NG1 . . . . . . **223** D3
Nottingham Univ Acad of
Science & Technology
NG7 . . . . **172** E1
Nottingham Univ
Samworth Acad NG8 . **171** C7
Nuart Rd NG9. . . . . **183** F6
Nugent Gdn NG3 . . . . . . **173** E6
Nugent Gdns 4 NG3. . . **173** E6
Nuncar Ct NG17. . . . . . . **115** A1
NUNCARGATE **115** A1
Nuncargate Rd NG17. . . **115** A1
Nunn Brook Rd NG17 . . . **99** E2
Nunn Brook Rise NG17. . **99** E2
Nunn Cl
Hucknall NG15. . . . . **131** C1
Huthwaite NG17 . . . . **99** E1
Nurseries The NG16 . . . **144** A2
Nursery Ave
Beeston NG9 . . . . **183** C5
Farndon NG24 . . . . **138** F4
Farndon NG24 . . . . **139** A5
Sutton in Ashfield NG17 . **100** C5
Nursery Cl
Collingham NG23 . . . . . . **112** A4
Hucknall NG15. . . . . **146** A4
Radcliffe on Trent NG12 . **176** B3
Saxilby LN1 . . . . **57** B4
Nursery Ct
Mansfield NG18. . . . . . . **102** C8
Newark-on-Trent NG24. . **125** A1
Nursery Dr NG4. . . . . **174** D8
Nursery End NG25 . . . . . **121** D1
Nursery Gdns
Balderton NG24. . . . . . . **140** E2
Beckingham DN10 . . . . . . **23** C8
Mansfield NG21. . . . . . . **103** D2
South Normanton DE55. . **113** C4
Worksop S80 . . . . **35** B2
Nursery La
Morton DN21. . . . . **15** A5
Nottingham NG6 . . . . . . **160** E4
Sutton on Trent NG23 . . . **96** F8
Nursery Rd
Arnold NG5 . . . . **162** A5
Bingham NG13. . . . . **178** A4
Radcliffe on Trent NG12 . **176** B3
Nursery St NG18. . . . . . . **102** C8
Nursery Vale NG17. . . . . . **15** B5
Nursury Gdns NG14. . . . **150** D2
Nutcroft Way DN10 . . . . . **11** A4
NUTHALL **159** D5
Nuthall Bypass NG6. . . . **160** A4
Nuthall Gardens NG8 . . **172** D8
Nuthall Rd NG8. . . . . **160** C2
Nuthatch Cres S81. . . . . . **25** D1
Nutkin Close 4
LE11 . . . . **220** A2

O

Oak Acres NG9 . . . . **183** A5
Oak Ave
Aldercar NG16 . . . . **143** B5
Bingham NG13. . . . . **178** A4
Blidworth NG21 . . . . **118** B4
Farndon NG24 . . . . **139** A4
Mansfield NG18. . . . . . . **102** C8
New Ollerton NG22 . . . . . **77** D4
Radcliffe on Trent NG12 . **175** E4
Rainworth NG21 . . . . . . **104** C1
Sandiacre NG10 . . . . **182** A7
Shirebrook NG20. . . . . . . **72** D4
Oak Bank Cl NG18 . . . . . **102** B8
Oak Cl
Pinxton NG16. . . . . **113** C3
Worksop S80 . . . . **35** E1
Oak Cres LE12 . . . . **214** D8
Oakdale Dr NG9 . . . . **183** C4
Oakdale Rd
Arnold NG5 . . . . **162** B8
Carlton NG3 . . . . **174** C6
Carlton NG4 . . . . **174** D7
Mansfield NG18. . . . . . . **101** F7
Nottingham NG4 . . . . . . **174** B6
Retford DN22. . . . . **39** E8
South Normanton DE55. . **113** C4
Oak Dr
Eastwood NG16. . . . . . . **143** E2
Mansfield Woodhouse
NG19 . . . . **88** E2
New Balderton NG24. . . . **140** C4
Nuthall NG16 . . . . **159** B6
Torksey Lock LN1. . . . . . . **44** B1
Oakenhall Ave NG15 . . . **146** C2
Oakes Cl NG16. . . . . **143** A5
Oakfield
Radcliffe on Trent
NG12 . . . . **176** A3
Saxilby LN1 . . . . **57** A3
Oakfield Ave
Market Warsop NG20 . . . . **74** B3
Sutton in Ashfield NG17 . **114** E8
Oakfield Cl
Mansfield NG18. . . . . . . **102** F2
Nottingham NG8 . . . . . . **171** C3
Oakfield Dr NG10 . . . . . . **182** B3
Oakfield La NG20 . . . . **74** B2
Oakfield Rd
Hucknall NG15. . . . . **146** B6
Newark-on-Trent NG24. . **140** F1
Nottingham NG8 . . . . . . **171** C3
Stapleford NG9 . . . . **182** D7
Oak Field School and
Sports Coll NG8 . . . . . **171** F7
Oakfields Rd NG2. . . . . . **174** A1
Oak Flatt NG9 . . . . **183** A5
Oakford Cl NG8. . . . . **160** A2
Oak Gr NG15. . . . . **146** A4
Oakham Bsns Pk NG18. . **101** F3
Oakham Cl
Mansfield NG18. . . . . . . **102** B4
Nottingham NG5 . . . . . . **160** F7
Oakham Ct NG5 . . . . **162** D3
Oakham Dr
Carlton in Lindrick S81 . . . **25** E4
Selston NG16. . . . . **129** B7
Oakhampton Cres NG3 **162** E6
Oakham Rd NG11. . . . . . **185** D2
Oakholme Ave S81 . . . . . . **35** F5
Oakholme Rise S81 . . . . . **35** F6
Oakington Cl NG5 . . . . . **161** B5
Oakland Ave
Huthwaite NG17 . . . . **99** F5
Long Eaton NG10. . . . . . **193** C5
Oakland Ct NG9 . . . . **171** A1
Oakland Gr NG14 . . . . . . **148** F7
Oakland Rd NG18 . . . . . . **102** F8
Oaklands NG23 . . . . **112** A8
Oaklands Ave DE75 . . . . **143** A2
Oaklands Dr DN11 . . . . **8** D2
Oakland St 6 NG7. . . . . . **172** E7
Oaklands The DE55 . . . . **113** A4
Oaklands Terr NG10 . . . . **193** C5
Oakland Way NG8 . . . . . **171** D8
Oakleaf Cl
Bestwood Village NG15. . **146** E4
Mansfield NG18. . . . . . . **103** B3
Oakleaf Cres NG17. . . . . **100** C5
Oakleigh Ave
Mansfield Woodhouse
NG19 . . . . **88** A4
Nottingham NG3 . . . . . . **162** C2
Oakleigh St NG6. . . . . . . **160** D4
Oakley Dr LE12 . . . . **212** D2
Oakley Mews NG6 . . . . . **159** F6
Oakley's Rd NG10. . . . . . **193** E7
Oakley's Rd W NG10 . . . **193** D6
Oak Lodge Dr NG16. . . . **158** F7
Oak Mdws DE55 . . . . . . **113** B4
Oakmead Ave NG18 . . . . **171** F8
Oakmere Cl NG2. . . . . . . **186** C4
Oakridge Cl NG19. . . . . . . **88** F1
Oak Rise NG22. . . . . **105** E2
Oaks Ave S80. . . . . **58** C8
Oaks Cl DN22 . . . . **19** B5
Oaksetts Dr S80 . . . . **45** E2
Oaks Ind Est LE11. . . . . . **220** A4
Oaks La
Oxton NG25 . . . . **133** F7
Walkeringham DN10 . . . . **13** C6
Oak St
Kirkby-in-Ashfield
NG17 . . . . **115** B5
Nottingham NG5 . . . . . . **161** B1
Sutton in Ashfield NG17 . **100** D7

Oaks The
Mansfield NG18. . . . . . . **102** C3
Newark-on-Trent NG24. . **140** E4
Oaktree Ave 2 DN21 . . . . **15** F2
Oak Tree Ave
Edwinstowe NG21 . . . . . . **76** A2
Glapwell S44 . . . . **86** B8
Nottingham NG4 . . . . . . **175** F4
Oak Tree Bsns Pk
NG18 . . . . **103** B4
Oaktree Cl NG17. . . . . . . **101** B1
Oak Tree Cl
Hucknall NG15. . . . . **145** D4
Mansfield NG18. . . . . . . **103** B7
West Bridgford NG2 . . . . **186** A8
Oak Tree Cres NG19 . . . . **88** B4
Oak Tree Ct NG12. . . . . . **186** C1
Oaktree Dr NG22 . . . . . . **106** A4
Oak Tree Dr NG4 . . . . . . **163** A2
Oak Tree La NG18 . . . . . . **103** A6
Oak Tree La L Ctr
NG18 . . . . **103** B5
Oak Tree Mws NG22 . . . **106** A4
Oak Tree Prim Sch
NG18 . . . . **103** C6
Oaktree Rd
Hilcote DE55 . . . . **99** C1
Hilcote DE55 . . . . **113** C8
Oak Tree Rd
Bawtry DN10. . . . . **9** F7
Sutton in Ashfield NG17 . **101** A4
Oak Tree Rise S81 . . . . . . **25** E7
Oak View NG24 . . . . **140** C8
Oak View Rise NG18 . . . **116** D7
Oakwood NG23 . . . . **152** E2
Oakwood Dr
Nottingham NG8 . . . . . . **172** C7
Ravenshead NG15. . . . . . **117** A1
Oakwood Gdns NG16 . . **159** D3
Oakwood Gr NG21 . . . . . . **91** B8
Oakwood Mews S80 . . . . **35** C3
Oakwood Rd NG18. . . . . **103** B4
Oatfield La NG12. . . . . . . **176** D6
Oban Rd NG9. . . . . **183** C6
Observatory Way NG17 . **115** B8
Occupation La
Broadholme LN1 . . . . **57** B1
Broadholme LN1 . . . . **71** B8
Edwinstowe NG21 . . . . . . **76** B1
Kirkby-in-Ashfield NG17 . **114** F8
Orston NG13 . . . . **179** F4
Rolleston NG25 . . . . **137** E5
Willoughby-on-t-W LE12 . **217** E6
Occupation Rd
Hucknall NG15. . . . . **146** A5
New Houghton NG19. . . . . **86** F7
Nottingham NG6 . . . . . . **160** B5
Ocean Dr NG20 . . . . **74** A5
Ochbrook Ct DE7 . . . . . . **157** F3
Ockbrook Dr 2 NG3. . . . **161** F1
Ockerby St NG6. . . . . **160** C6
Oddicroft La NG17. . . . . **101** A1
Odesa Dr NG6. . . . . **160** B4
Odins Wlk NG18 . . . . **101** F5
Off The Ave NG17. . . . . . **100** E1
Ogdon Ct NG3 . . . . **173** F6
Ogle Dr
Nottingham NG1 . . . . . . **173** B3
Nottingham NG7 . . . . . . **223** D1
Ogle St NG15. . . . . **146** A2
Oldacres NG14 . . . . **149** D4
Old Bakery Way **3**
NG18. . . . . **88** C1
Old Bar Cl NG6. . . . . **160** C2
Old Barn Cl NG21. . . . . . . **90** B6
Old Basford Prim Sch
NG6. . . . . **160** D3
Old Bawtry Rd DN10 . . . . . **3** C6
Old Bell La NG23. . . . . **96** F4
Old Blyth Rd
Barnby Moor S81. . . . . . . **27** F1
Ranby DN22. . . . . **38** A6
Ranby S81 . . . . **37** F8
Scofton DN22. . . . . **37** F7
Old Bowling Gn The
S81 . . . . **35** B4
Old Brickyard NG3. . . . . **174** A7
Oldbridge Way
Bilsthorpe NG22 . . . . . . **105** F5
Bilsthorpe NG22 . . . . . . **106** A6
Old Bull Farm Cl LE12. . **204** A3
Oldbury Cl NG11. . . . . . . **195** D7
Old Chapel Cl NG17 . . . . **114** E5
Old Chapel La
Elston NG23 . . . . **153** E5
Selston NG16. . . . . **129** A3
Old Church St 9 NG7. . . **172** F2
OLD CLIPSTONE **90** C6
Old Coach Rd
Nottingham NG8 . . . . . . **171** F5
Nottingham NG8 . . . . . . **171** F6
Worksop S80 . . . . **47** E7
Oldcobham Orch
NG24. . . . . **140** C5
OLDCOTES. **17** A6
Old Ctyd The DN21. . . . . . **24** C8
Old Dairy The NG14. . . . **150** D2
OLD DALBY **218** F4
Old Dalby CE Prim Sch
LE14. . . . . **218** E4
Old Dalby CE Sch LE14 . **218** E4
Old Dalby La LE14. . . . . . **219** D6
Old Derby Rd NG16 . . . . **143** D3
Old Dr NG9 . . . . **183** E8
Old Engine Yd The
LE12. . . . . **215** E5
Old England Gdns NG23. . **81** F1

Old England Gdns NG23 96 F8
Old Epperstone Rd
NG14 150 B4
Oldershaw Ave DE74 203 C2
Oldershaw Rd LE12 205 F1
Old Farm Rd NG5 160 F8
Old Forge Cl
Hathern LE12 213 A1
Kegworth DE74 203 C2
Misterton DN10 6 F2
Old Forge La NG13 191 C5
Old Forge Rd DN10 6 E2
Old Gateford Rd S81 35 C8
Old Gdns The DN22 39 E4
Old Grantham Rd
Aslockton NG13 178 F3
Whatton NG13 179 A3
Old Great North Rd
NG23 96 E8
Old Hall Cl
Calverton NG14 148 E7
Farndon NG24 138 F4
Market Warsop NG20 74 C5
Old Hall Dr
Nottingham NG3 161 D2
Retford DN22 39 D6
Widmerpool NG12 208 C5
Old Hall Gdns
Coddington NG24 125 F2
Screveton NG13 166 E4
Old Hall La
East Markham NG22 65 F7
Norwell NG23 110 B8
Old Hall The★ DN21 15 C1
Old Haxey Rd DN10 6 F3
Old Kennel Dr NG14 133 D6
Old Kiln La 2 NG16 144 A1
Oldknow St NG7 172 F7
Old La NG12 185 D1
Old La The NG13 192 B2
OLD LENTON 172 D3
Old Lenton Cl NG12 189 A4
Old Lenton St NG1 223 F2
Old Liby Arts Ctr The★
NG18 102 B7
Old Lodge Dr NG5 161 D4
Old London Rd
Babworth DN22 49 F8
Barnby Moor DN22 28 C3
West Drayton DN22 50 F2
Old Main Rd
Bulcote NG14 164 B5
Costock LE12 206 D1
Old Maltings The DN10 6 F1
Old Manor Cl NG14 149 D4
Old Manor Ct NG24 126 B1
Old Manor Farm NG23 142 D2
Old Manor Rd NG19 88 B3
Old Meeting House Yard
NG18 102 B7
Old Melton Rd
Normanton-on-the-Wolds
NG12 197 F7
Normanton-on-the-Wolds
NG12 198 A6
Plumtree NG12 197 F7
Widmerpool NG12 209 A7
Old Mill Cl
Beeston NG9 183 A2
Bestwood Village NG6 146 D3
Nottingham NG7 222 B3
Old Mill Cres NG24 140 B8
Old Mill Ct NG13 177 F5
Old Mill La
Cuckney NG20 60 B3
Mansfield NG19 88 E1
Old Mission Forge Wlk
NG16 144 C2
Old Mkt Pl
Mansfield NG18 102 B7
South Normanton DE55 113 A6
Old Mkt Sq NG1 223 E2
Old Newark Rd NG18 102 E2
Old North Rd NG23 97 A2
Old North Road NG23 96 F6
Old Nurseries The
NG23 109 F8
Oldoak Rd NG11 185 A2
Old Park Cl NG9 171 E6
Old Parsonage La
LE12 215 C1
Old Pits Cl LN6 71 F3
Old Pk Cl NG11 203 F6
Old Pk The NG12 187 F4
Old Post Office St DN10 11 C3
Old Rd NG17 100 F7
Old Rectory Cl LE12 205 E1
Old Rectory Ct NG24 125 C6
Old Rectory Mus & Wildlife
Gdn★ LE11 220 B4
Old Reindeer Cl NG13 165 C3
Old Rufford Rd
Bilsthorpe NG22 105 C4
Calverton NG14 133 C6
Edwinstowe NG22 91 D4
Farnsfield NG22 119 B5
Ollerton NG22 77 A3
Old Sch Cl NG11 195 E8
Old Sch House Cl
NG12 189 B7
Old Sch La NG19 87 A5
Old School Dr NG21 75 F1
Old School La
Awsworth NG16 158 C5
Besthorpe NG23 97 E6
Newark-on-Trent NG24 140 B7
Old School Pl 10 S80 35 F2
Old Showfields DN21 15 D2
Old Sookholme La
NG20 74 A4
Old St NG1 223 E3
Old Stack Yard The LN1 55 D6
Old Station Dr NG11 196 B7
Old Station Yard NG21 76 B1
Old Sta Yd NG13 181 C3
Old Storth La DE55 113 B4
Old Sykes La LN1 56 D4
Old Tannery Dr NG14 150 E1
Old Terr NG19 86 F4
Old Tollerton Rd
11 Gamston NG12 186 C7
West Bridgford NG2 186 C7
Old Trent Rd DN10 14 F1
Old Walled Gdns DN22 40 F4
Old Water La 6 NG19 87 D1
Old Way LE12 213 A1
Old Wood LN6 71 E6
Old Woodyard The
Hathern LE12 212 F1
Hathern LE12 213 A1
Wysall NG12 207 C3
Olga Ct NG3 173 F6
Olga Rd NG3 173 F6
Olive Ave
Long Eaton NG10 182 E1
Shirebrook NG20 72 D6
Olive Ct NG17 100 F4
Olive Gr
Burton Joyce NG14 163 F5
Mansfield NG19 103 A8
Oliver Cl
Heanor DE75 143 B2
Nottingham NG7 222 C4
Oliver Ct NG24 140 B8
Oliver Dr NG11 196 B8
Oliver Quibell Inf Sch
NG24 140 A5
Oliver Rd LE11 220 B2
Oliver St NG7 222 C3
OLLERTON 77 B3
Ollerton Com Prim Sch
NG22 77 D5
Ollerton Rd
Arnold NG5 147 E6
Averham NG23 123 E8
Calverton NG14 132 F2
Carburton NG22 61 D6
Caunton NG23 108 D8
Eaton DN22 50 E8
Edwinstowe NG21 76 C2
Edwinstowe NG21 76 D3
Farnsfield NG22 119 A1
Gamston DN22 50 E5
Kelham NG23 124 A5
Kersall NG22 94 B3
Kirton NG22 78 F8
Kneesall NG22 93 F4
Ollerton NG22 77 A4
Retford DN22 39 E2
Retford DN22 39 E4
South Muskham NG23 124 B7
Tuxford NG22 65 C2
Worksop S80 47 B4
Ollerton Water Mill★
NG22 77 A3
Olton Ave NG9 171 F1
Olympia Way 5 NG15 146 C7
Olympus Ct NG15 145 D3
Omberley Ave NG17 101 B6
Omer Ct NG16 159 A7
OMPTON 93 B7
Onchan Ave NG4 174 E6
One Call Stadium
(Mansfield Town FC)
NG18 102 B5
Ontario Dr NG16 129 A7
Opal Cl
Mansfield NG18 102 E4
Rainworth NG21 104 C1
Opal Gr DN11 9 B5
Orange Cl NG20 72 E6
Orange Croft
Tickhill DN11 8 B7
Tickhill DN11 8 B8
Orange Gdns NG2 173 D2
Orange Tip Cl S81 25 D1
Orby Cl NG3 173 F6
Orby Wlk NG3 173 F6
Orchard Ave
Bingham NG13 177 D4
Carlton NG4 174 E7
Orchard Bsns Pk
Ilkeston DE7 157 D1
Sandiacre NG10 182 C6
Orchard Cl
Barkestone-le-Vale
NG13 192 B2
Barnstone NG13 190 F3
Bleasby NG14 152 A8
Burton Joyce NG14 163 F5
East Bridgford NG13 165 D3
East Leake LE12 214 D8
Gunthorpe NG14 165 A5
Mansfield NG18 102 C2
Morton DN21 15 B5
Newton on Trent LN1 55 A1
North Leverton with
Habblesthorpe DN22 42 D8
Radcliffe on Trent NG12 175 E3
Shirebrook NG20 72 E5
South Muskham NG23 124 E7
Southwell NG25 121 D2
Sutton Bonington LE12 213 C5
Tollerton NG12 186 D1
Orchard Cres
Beeston NG9 183 C5
Glapwell S44 86 B8
Tuxford NG22 65 F2
Orchard Croft DN10 10 A7
Orchard Ct
Carlton NG4 174 E7
Gedling NG4 162 D2
Hucknall NG15 146 A6
Huthwaite NG17 99 E2
Langley Mill NG16 143 B3
Nottingham NG8 172 E8
Thorney NG23 69 F7
Orchard Dr
Calverton NG14 149 A7
Cotgrave NG12 188 A5
Orchard Gr
Arnold NG5 161 C6
Misterton DN10 14 A8
Walkeringham DN10 13 F8
Orchard La
Caythorpe NG14 165 A8
Kirkby-in-Ashfield NG17 115 B6
Saxilby LN1 57 A4
South Leverton DN22 42 C7
Orchard Leigh DN22 39 D4
Orchard Mws NG16 113 E3
Orchard Pk
Arnold NG5 162 C5
Newark-on-Trent NG24 125 F2
Orchard Pl NG8 159 C2
Orchard Prim Sch
NG17 114 E5
Orchard Rd NG17 114 E5
Orchard Rise
Beckingham DN10 23 C8
Lambley NG4 163 C7
Orchard Sch DN22 42 C7
Orchardside Rd NG22 65 F6
Orchard St
Eastwood NG16 144 A1
Gotham NG11 195 B1
Hucknall NG15 146 A6
Kimberley NG16 158 F6
Langley Mill NG16 143 B3
Long Eaton NG10 193 E7
10 Loughborough LE11 220 A4
Mansfield NG19 88 B1
Stapleford NG9 182 D7
Orchards The
Carlton NG4 163 A1
Lowdham NG14 164 E8
Oxton NG25 134 C4
Westwood NG16 128 B4
Orchard The
Elston NG23 153 E4
Newark-on-Trent NG24 140 B6
Sutton in Ashfield NG17 101 B1
Orchard View
Mansfield Woodhouse
NG19 88 B3
Thurgarton NG14 151 C8
Orchard Way
Balderton NG24 140 D3
Sandiacre NG10 182 A3
Sutton in Ashfield NG17 114 C8
Wymeswold LE12 216 D3
Orchard Wlk NG17 114 E5
Orchid Cl
4 Kirkby-in-Ashfield
NG17 114 F7
New Balderton NG24 140 B5
West Bridgford NG11 185 C4
Orchid Croft NG15 146 C4
Orchid Dr
Farndon NG24 139 B6
Sutton in Ashfield NG17 101 B1
Orchid Gr
Pleasley NG19 86 F5
Pleasley NG19 87 A5
Shirebrook NG20 72 D2
Orchid Way NG20 72 D3
Orchil St NG16 158 B8
Orch St NG16 158 A8
Ordoyno Gr NG24 125 F2
Ordsall Cl NG18 102 E6
Ordsall Pk Cl DN22 39 D6
Ordsall Pk Dr DN22 39 D6
Ordsall Pk Rd DN22 39 D6
Ordsall Prim Sch DN22 39 D4
Ordsall Rd DN22 39 C5
Orford Ave
Nottingham NG11 184 F4
Radcliffe on Trent NG12 175 F2
Oriana Dr NG12 185 F2
Orion Cl NG8 171 E7
Orion Dr NG8 171 E7
Orion Gr 4 NG18 102 E1
Orlando Dr NG4 174 F8
Orlock Wlk NG5 161 B5
Ormiston Cl NG11 184 F1
Ormonde St NG16 143 B4
Ormonde Terr
Aldercar NG16 143 B4
Nottingham NG5 161 C2
Ornsay Cl NG5 146 E1
Orpean Way NG9 182 E2
ORSTON 180 A7
Orston Ave
Arnold NG5 162 A7
Newark-on-Trent NG24 139 E6
Orston Dr NG8 172 D4
Orston Gn NG8 172 D3
Orston La
Bottesford NG13 180 F3
Flawborough NG13 168 B1
Orston Prim Sch NG13 180 A7
Orston Rd E NG2 173 F1
Orston Rd W NG2 173 E1
Orton Ave NG9 183 C6
Orton Fields NG9 183 B6
Ortzen St NG7 222 B4
Orville Rd NG5 160 E5
Osberne Wy NG19 89 F2
Osberton Rd DN22 39 F6
Osberton View S81 36 B5
Osborne Ave 2 NG5 161 C3
Osborne Cl NG10 182 B4
Osborne Gr NG5 161 C3
Osborne St NG7 222 A4
Osbourne Cl
Nottingham NG15 146 C4
Watnall NG16 159 B7
Osbourne St NG17 129 F8
Osgood Rd NG5 162 C5
Osier Dr NG15 130 A6
Osier Fields LE12 205 F2
Osier Rd NG2 173 C2
Osiers The
Kegworth DE74 203 D2
Newark-on-Trent NG24 139 C6
Osman Cl NG2 173 B1
Osmanthorpe Nature
Reserve★ NG22 120 F6
Osmaston St
Nottingham NG7 222 B1
Sandiacre NG10 182 C5
Osprey Cl
Bingham NG13 177 F3
Nottingham NG11 184 C1
Osprey Gr NG15 131 D1
OSSINGTON 95 D6
Ossington Cl
Meden Vale NG20 74 D8
Nottingham NG1 223 E4
Ossington La
Ossington NG23 95 E6
Sutton on Trent NG23 96 E7
Ossington Rd
Carlton-on-Trent NG23 96 C5
Kneesall NG22 93 E5
Kneesall NG22 94 B5
Moorhouse NG23 80 C1
Norwell NG23 95 F1
Norwell NG23 96 A1
Norwell NG23 110 A8
Sutton on Trent NG23 96 C8
Ossington St NG7 222 B4
Ossington Way NG24 124 F1
Oster Fen La
Claypole NG23 142 A2
Claypole NG23 156 F7
Osterley Gr NG8 159 D2
Ostler La LE14 219 D1
Otter Ave LN1 57 A4
Otter Way NG19 87 D1
Oughton Cl NG12 186 A3
Oulton Cl NG5 161 F6
Oundle Dr
Ilkeston DE7 170 A7
Mansfield NG19 87 D1
Nottingham NG8 172 C3
Our Lady of Perpetual
Succour RC Prim Sch
NG6 160 D6
Our Lady & St Edward's
Cath Prim Sch NG3 173 F7
Oursham St NG17 100 F2
Ousebridge Cres NG4 175 A8
Ouse Bridge Dr NG4 175 A8
Outgang La
Mansfield Woodhouse
NG19 88 D4
Pleasley NG19 87 C6
Treswell DN22 42 F4
Out Gang Road
Cottam DN22 43 B4
Cottam DN22 43 C4
Outram St NG17 100 F3
Outwood Acad Portland
S80 35 F1
Worksop S80 46 F8
Outwood Acad Valley
S81 35 E6
Oval Gdns 2 NG8 172 D8
Oval The
Retford DN22 39 D4
Sutton in Ashfield NG17 100 D4
Tickhill DN11 8 B8
Torksey Lock LN1 55 B8
Oval Way LE14 219 C8
Overdale Ave NG17 100 E7
Overdale Cl NG10 193 A6
Overdale Rd NG6 160 C3
Overend Rd S80 35 F4
Overmoor View DE55 99 B7
Overstone Cl NG17 100 F5
Overstrand Cl NG5 161 F6
Owday La S81 25 D3
Owen Ave NG10 194 A6
Owen Jenkins Cl 3
NG9 184 A5
Owlston Cl NG16 143 F3
Owsthorpe Cl NG5 161 A8
Owston Ferry Rd DN9 7 D7
Owston Rd
Newstead NG15 130 D7
West Stockwith DN10 7 C4
OWTHORPE 199 E7
Owthorpe Gr NG5 161 B2
Owthorpe La
Kinoulton NG12 199 F3
Kinoulton NG12 200 A2
Owthorpe Rd
Colston Bassett NG12 200 B7
Cotgrave NG12 187 F2
Oxborough Rd NG5 161 C7
Oxbow Cl NG2 173 C1
Oxbury Rd NG16 158 F8
Oxclose La
Mansfield Woodhouse
NG19 88 A3
Nottingham NG5 161 C6
Radmanthwaite NG19 87 D3
Oxcroft La NG20 58 A8
Oxendale Cl NG2 186 C6
Oxengate NG5 161 C6
Oxford Cl NG21 118 A8
Oxford Dr
Harworth DN11 8 F5
Newton NG13 177 B8
Oxford Rd
Carlton in Lindrick S81 25 F6
West Bridgford NG2 186 A7
Oxford St
Carlton NG4 174 E8
Eastwood NG16 143 F2
Kirkby-in-Ashfield NG17 115 B4
Long Eaton NG10 193 D8
Loughborough LE11 220 A4
Mansfield Woodhouse
NG19 88 C1
Nottingham NG1 223 D2
Sutton in Ashfield NG17 100 D2
Oxgang Cl NG14 148 C8
Oxley Mws NG9 183 E5
Oxpasture La NG20 58 B6
OXTON 134 C4
Oxton Ave NG5 161 C4
Oxton Bypass
Epperstone NG14 149 D7
Oxton NG25 134 A4
Oxton NG25 134 B2
Oxton Cl
Mansfield NG19 101 E7
Retford DN22 39 E3
Oxton Hill NG25 134 F5
Oxton Rd
Calverton NG14 133 D1
Caythorpe NG14 151 A1
Epperstone NG14 149 E6
Epperstone NG14 150 A4
Oxton NG25 135 B4
Southwell NG25 135 C6
Thurgarton NG25 136 A1
Oyster Rd NG16 143 F3
Oyster Way NG20 74 A5
Ozier Holt
Carlton NG4 174 E4
Long Eaton NG10 193 C6

P

Pach Way NG24 140 F2
Packe St LE11 220 A4
Packet Landing The
DN21 7 A2
Pack Horse La 5
LE11 220 B3
Packington Hill DE74 203 C2
Packman Dr NG11 196 D8
Paddington Ms NG3 174 A7
Paddock Cl
Calverton NG14 148 F7
Edwinstowe NG21 76 A3
Long Whatton LE12 212 D2
Mansfield NG18 102 B3
Nottingham NG6 160 B5
Radcliffe on Trent NG12 175 E2
Paddock Farm Cotts
NG14 150 A5
Paddock Gr S81 18 A6
Paddocks Cl
Elston NG23 153 D4
Pinxton NG16 113 C4
Paddocks The
Beckingham DN10 14 B1
Bottesford NG13 181 A2
Burton Joyce NG14 163 E4
Elston NG23 153 E4
Granby NG13 191 C5
Hockerton NG25 122 B6
Huthwaite DE55 99 F1
Lound DN22 20 C2
Mansfield Woodhouse
NG19 88 E5
Marton DN21 44 C8
Newark-on-Trent NG24 140 B7
Newton on Trent LN1 55 A1
Sandiacre NG10 182 A5
Southwell NG25 136 C8
Stapleford LN6 127 E8
Sutton Bonington LE12 213 B6
West Bridgford NG12 186 B3
Worksop S80 35 B5
Worksop S81 36 B7
Paddocks View
NG10 193 A8
Paddock The
Beckingham LN5 142 D8
Beeston NG9 183 D2
Bingham NG13 177 E4
Bunny NG11 206 E8
Collingham NG23 112 A7
Gunthorpe NG13, NG14 164 F5
Kirkby-in-Ashfield NG17 114 F4
Old Dalby LE14 218 E4
Pleasley NG19 87 A5
Retford DN22 40 A4
Stanton Hill NG17 100 C5
Tickhill DN11 8 B8
Paddock View LN1 57 A5
Paddy's La LE14 218 A1
Padge Rd NG9 184 B6
Padgham Ct 11 NG5 161 A8
Padley Cl NG6 160 C6
Padley Hill NG18 102 A6
Padleys La NG14 163 E5
Padstow Cl NG18 103 B2
Padstow Rd NG5 160 F6
Paetina Gr NG15 146 D8
Pagdin Dr DN11 8 E1
Page Ave 4 NG5 161 A5
Paget Cres NG11 196 C8
Paget Croft LE12 216 D3
Paget St 3 LE11 220 A5
Pagett Cl NG15 146 C6
Paige Gdns
2 Sandiacre NG10 182 A6
Stapleford NG10 182 A5
Paignton Cl NG8 160 B2
Pailings Ride NG24 126 F6
Paisley Gr NG9 183 C1
Palace Theatre★
NG24 140 A8
Palace View NG25 136 F8
Palatine St
Nottingham NG1 173 B3
Nottingham NG7 223 D1
Paling Cres NG17 100 E3
Palin Gdns NG12 176 A3
Palin St NG7 222 B4
Palm Ct Ind Ctr NG7 160 F1
Palmer Ave
Bottesford NG13 181 B4
Hucknall NG15 146 A8
Palmer Cres NG4 174 D7
Palmer Dr NG9 182 D5
Palmer Rd
Retford DN22 30 A1
Sutton on Trent NG23 96 F8
Palmers Ct 5 NG25 136 F8
Palmerston Gdns NG3 223 E4
Palmerston St
Selston NG16 128 F2
Underwood NG16 129 A2
Westwood NG16 128 C4
Palm St NG7 160 F1
Palmwood Ct NG6 160 C5
Palm Wood Ct NG6 160 C6
Pankhurst Cl LE12 214 E7
Paper Mill La DN11 8 C8
PAPPLEWICK 131 D3
Papplewick Farm Cl
NG15 131 D1
Papplewick Grange
NG15 131 D1
Papplewick Hall & Gdns★
NG15 131 D4
Papplewick La
Hucknall NG15 131 C2
Hucknall NG15 146 C8
Papplewick Ppg Sta★
NG15 132 E5
Paradise La LE14 218 F4
Parfitt Dr NG22 120 A5
Parish Mws 5 DN21 15 D1
Park Ave
Annesley Woodhouse
NG17 130 B8
Arnold NG5 161 E5
Awsworth NG16 158 B5
Blidworth NG21 118 B5
Burton Joyce NG14 163 E4
Carlton NG4 174 F8
Eastwood NG16 143 E3
Hucknall NG15 145 F7
Keyworth NG12 197 F4
Kimberley NG16 159 A4
Loughborough LE11 220 B1
Mansfield NG18 102 C8
Mansfield Woodhouse
NG19 88 C4
Misterton DN10 6 E3
Nottingham NG3 173 C7
Shirebrook NG20 72 E4
West Bridgford NG2 185 F8
Woodborough NG14 149 B4
Park Ave E NG12 197 D3
Park Ave W NG12 197 D3
Park Chase NG6 160 B5
Park Cl
Lea DN21 24 F1
Nottingham NG3 161 E2
Pinxton NG16 113 C2
Park Cres
Eastwood NG16 143 F4
Ilkeston DE7 170 A8
Newark-on-Trent NG24 125 B4
Nottingham NG8 171 C4
Retford DN22 40 A8
Parkcroft Rd NG2 185 F6
Park Ct
Loughborough LE11 220 B2
Mansfield NG18 102 C8
Parkdale Prim Sch
NG4 174 D6
Parkdale Rd NG3 174 C6
Park Dr
Blyth S81 18 A3
Hucknall NG15 146 B6
Nottingham NG7 222 C2
Sandiacre NG10 182 A3
Park Drain DN10 2 D2
Parker Cl NG5 162 C8
Parker Gdns NG9 182 F8
Parker's La NG19 88 C3
Parker St
Hucknall NG15 146 B7
Newark-on-Trent NG24 140 A8
Parkes Cl NG24 126 B2
Park Farm Cotts LN1 55 F1
Park Gate NG15 131 B1
Park Gdn NG17 100 A3
Park Hall Cl NG19 88 C5
Park Hall Farm NG19 88 C6
Park Hall Gdns NG19 88 C5
Park Hall Rd NG19 88 C5
Parkham Rd NG16 158 F7
Park Hill NG16 158 B5
Park Hill Dr S81 16 A5
Park Hospl The NG5 132 D2
Park House Gates NG3 161 D1
Park Hts NG7 222 C1
Parkin Cl NG12 189 A4
Park La
Elkesley DN22 50 C3
Holbeck NG20 59 C6

Park La *continued*
Kirkby-in-Ashfield NG17 114 C2
Lambley NG4 163 E8
Mansfield NG18 102 B5
Nottingham NG6 160 E4
Owthorpe NG12 199 E7
Pinxton NG16 113 C2
Retford DN22 40 A8
Southwell NG25 136 D6
Sutton Bonington LE12 213 C5
Wigsley NG23 70 A2
Parkland Cl
Mansfield NG18 102 E2
Nottingham NG11 184 D3
Parklands Cl
Coddington NG24 125 F2
[1] Nottingham NG5 147 B1
Parklands Dr [2] LE11 220 A1
Parklands Gr NG22 77 D3
Parklands Inf Sch
NG10 182 B1
Parkland View NG17 100 A2
Park Lane Bsns Ctr
NG6 160 E5
Park Lane Bsns Pk
NG17 114 D2
Park Lodge Rd NG16 158 A7
Park Mews
Mansfield Woodhouse
NG19 88 C4
Nottingham NG3 173 C8
Retford DN22 40 A8
Park Mws NG17 100 F6
Park Pl S80 35 F1
Park Ravine
Nottingham NG14 173 A3
Nottingham NG7 222 C1
Park Rd
Arnold NG5 161 E5
Barnstone NG13 190 E3
Bawtry DN10 9 F7
Beeston, Bramcote
NG9 183 A8
Beeston, Chilwell NG9 183 E6
Bestwood Village NG6 146 E4
Calverton NG14 148 E7
Carlton NG4 174 F7
Hucknall NG15 145 F7
Ilkeston DE7 170 A7
Keyworth NG12 197 F5
Loughborough LE11 220 B2
Mansfield Woodhouse
NG19 88 B3
Nottingham NG7 222 B1
Radcliffe on Trent NG12 175 F4
Shirebrook NG20 72 E5
Park Rd E NG14 149 A7
Park Rd N NG9 183 E6
Park Row NG1 223 D2
Parkside
Huthwaite NG17 100 A3
Keyworth NG12 197 F4
Nottingham NG8 171 E2
Parkside Ave NG10 193 B8
Parkside Dr NG10 193 B8
Parkside Gdns NG8 171 E2
Parkside Rd NG21 75 F2
Parkside Rise NG8 171 E2
Parkside Way DN21 24 F5
Park Springs Rd DN21 24 F6
Park St
Beeston NG9 183 E6
Kirkby-in-Ashfield NG17 114 F5
Long Eaton NG10 182 C1
Loughborough LE11 220 B3
Mansfield Woodhouse
NG19 88 B3
Nottingham NG7 222 B2
Stapleford NG9 182 C5
Sutton in Ashfield NG17 100 F3
Parkstone Ave NG21 103 F2
Parkstone Cl NG2 185 C5
Park Terr
Keyworth NG12 197 F5
Nottingham NG1 223 D2
PARK THE 173 A4
Park The
Cotgrave NG12 187 F4
Edwinstowe NG21 76 B2
Fackley NG17 100 A7
Mansfield NG18 102 C8
Newark-on-Trent NG24 140 A7
North Muskham NG23 110 F3
Thurgarton NG14 151 C6
Park Vale Acad
Nottingham NG15 146 E1
Nottingham NG5 160 E8
Park Valley NG7 223 D2
Park View
Beeston NG9 183 D6
HUCKNALL NG15 146 B5
Nottingham NG3 161 E2
Pleasley NG19 87 A5
Whaley Thorns NG20 58 F2
Whaley Thorns NG20 59 A2
Worksop S81 35 E7
Parkview Rd NG5 161 A7
Park View Way NG18 102 C5
Parkway
Clipstone NG19 89 D3
Newark-on-Trent NG24 139 E6
Sutton in Ashfield NG17 100 B3
Whitwell S80 45 A6
Parkway Ct NG8 171 D5
Parkwood Cres NG5 161 E3
Parkwood Ct NG6 160 E5
Parkyn Rd NG5 161 D6
Parkyns Piece LE12 205 E2
Parkyns St NG11 196 C6
Parliament Ct NG24 139 E8
Parliament Rd NG19 101 E8
Parliament St
Newark-on-Trent NG24 139 E7
Sutton in Ashfield NG17 100 F2
Parliament Terr NG1 223 D3
Parliament Way NG21 89 F5
Parliament Wlk NG24 139 E8
Parman Ct LN1 57 C3
Parnell St DN21 24 C8
Parnham's Cl LE14 219 C8
Parr Gate NG9 183 A5
Parr La NG14 150 A5
Parrs The NG9 184 B6
Parry Bsns Pk NG23 81 E1
Parry Ct [5] NG3 174 A6
Parry Way NG5 162 B8
Parson La NG22 65 C6
Parsons Cl NG24 140 E2
Parsons Mdw NG4 174 F4
Parthenon Cl NG19 86 F5
Partridge Cl
Bingham NG13 177 F3
Blidworth NG21 118 B8
Paschall Rd NG17 115 B1
Pasteur Ct [5] NG7 172 E2
Pasture Ave NG21 104 B1
Pasture Cl
Carlton NG2 174 E4
Kirton NG22 78 B7
Stanton Hill NG17 100 C5
Sutton Bonington LE12 213 A6
Worksop S80 35 C2
Pasture Gr NG23 112 B8
Pasture La
Hathern LE12 213 B2
Hilcote DE55 99 C1
Hose LE14 211 F6
Long Eaton NG10 194 A5
Ruddington NG11 196 A7
Sutton Bonington LE12 213 A6
Pasture Rd
Gainsborough DN21 24 F8
Stapleford NG9 170 D1
Pastures Ave NG11 195 D7
Pastures The
Bawtry DN10 10 A6
Beckingham LN5 142 D8
Calverton NG14 148 D7
Eastwood NG16 158 B8
Mansfield Woodhouse
NG19 88 E5
Rampton DN22 43 A1
Tuxford NG22 65 E2
Pasture View
Gunthorpe NG14 165 A5
Lowdham NG14 150 D2
Pasture Way
Farnsfield NG22 120 A6
Tickhill DN11 8 B8
Patagonia Pl NG15 130 B8
Patchills The NG18 102 F7
Patchings Art Ctr★
NG14 148 A8
Patchwork Row
Shirebrook NG20 72 E3
Shirebrook NG20 72 F4
Pateley Rd NG3 162 A4
Pates Cl NG15 131 D2
Patient Cl NG9 183 B5
Paton Ct NG14 133 F1
Paton Rd NG5 160 E5
Patricia Dr NG5 148 A1
Patrick Rd NG2 185 E8
Patriot Cl NG16 159 A7
Patriot La NG12 185 F3
Patterdale Cl NG2 186 C6
Patterdale Rd NG5 161 F5
Patterson Pl NG18 102 D7
Patterson Rd [13] NG7 172 F7
Paul Ave NG18 103 A6
Paulina Ave NG15 146 C8
Paulson's Dr NG18 102 B7
Pavilion Cl
Market Warsop NG20 74 B4
[2] Nottingham NG2 173 D1
Pavilion Ct NG14 164 E8
Pavilion Gdns
New Houghton NG19 86 F8
Sutton in Ashfield NG17 101 A6
Pavilion Rd
Kirkby-in-Ashfield
NG17 115 B6
Nottingham NG5 147 B1
West Bridgford NG2 173 E1
Pavilion Way NG24 125 F5
Pavillion Mws NG24 140 A5
Pavillion Way LE11 220 A7
Pavior Rd [3] NG5 160 F5
Paviour Rd NG5 160 F5
Paxton Gdns NG3 173 E5
Paxtons Ct NG24 124 F1
Payne Rd NG9 183 B3
Peace Gr NG12 186 A2
Peach Ave
Selston NG16 128 F6
South Normanton DE55 113 B7
Peache Way NG9 183 C7
Peachey St NG1 223 E3
Peacock Cl
Gunthorpe NG14 165 A4
Ruddington NG11 196 B6
Peacock Cres NG7 184 E2
Peacock Dr NG16 143 F2
Peacock Gdns
East Leake LE12 214 E8
Nottingham NG8 159 C2
Peacock Pl
[10] Gainsborough DN21 15 F1
Ilkeston DE7 157 D4
Peacocks Launde
NG23 156 D6
Peacock St [2] NG18 102 B6
Peacock Way S81 25 E1
Peafield La NG19 88 E4
Peafield Lane Prim Sch
NG19 88 F4
Peakdale Cl NG10 193 A6
Peake's Croft DN10 10 A7
Peak Hill Cl
Carlton in Lindrick S81 25 D1
Worksop S81 25 D1
Peak The NG20 72 E3
Pearce Dr NG8 172 B7
Pearl Ave NG17 115 B3
Pearl Cl NG21 104 C1
Pearl Dr S81 25 D1
Pearl Gdns NG20 74 A5
Pearmain Dr NG3 173 F7
Pearson Ave NG9 183 B5
Pearson Cl NG9 183 B5
Pearson Ct NG5 161 E7
Pearson St
Carlton NG4 175 A6
Nottingham NG7 160 F2
Pear Tree Cl DN22 30 D4
Pear Tree Ct [1] NG6 160 E4
Pear Tree Dr NG20 72 E6
Peartree La
Lidgett NG21 91 C8
Teversal NG17 86 B2
Pear Tree La NG17 100 C8
Peartree Orch NG11 196 C7
Peary Cl NG5 160 F6
Peashill La NG12 187 C5
Peas Hill Rd NG3 223 F4
Peat Carr Bank
Finningley DN9 1 D4
Finningley DN9 1 E7
Peatfield Ct NG9 170 A5
Peatfield Rd NG9 170 D1
Peck La
Gunthorpe NG14 165 A5
Nottingham NG1 223 E2
Pecks Hill NG18 102 E7
Pedmore Cl NG5 161 B7
Pedmore Valley NG5 161 A7
Peebles Rd NG24 139 D5
Peel Ave
Retford DN22 40 B3
Tuxford NG22 65 F2
Peel Cres NG19 87 D2
Peel Dr LE11 220 C4
Peel Rd NG19 101 E8
Peel St
Langley Mill NG16 143 B3
Long Eaton NG10 193 E8
Nottingham NG1 223 D4
South Normanton DE55 113 B6
Sutton in Ashfield NG17 101 A3
Peets Dr NG23 110 F2
Pegswood Dr
Arnold NG5 147 F2
Woodborough NG5 148 A2
Pelham Ave
Ilkeston DE7 157 E1
Nottingham NG5 173 B8
Pelham Cl NG24 139 F8
Pelham Cres
Beeston NG9 184 B7
Nottingham NG7 222 B2
Pelham Ct [4] NG5 173 B8
Pelham Gdns NG24 139 F8
Pelham Rd
Kirkby-in-Ashfield
NG17 115 A6
Nottingham NG5 173 B8
Retford DN22 39 D6
Pelham St
Mansfield NG18 102 C7
Newark-on-Trent NG24 139 F8
Nottingham NG1 223 E2
Sutton in Ashfield NG17 100 D2
Worksop S80 36 A1
Pelham Way NG19 89 D3
Pella Crove NG15 130 D7
Pemberley Ch NG17 100 D1
Pemberley Chase
NG17 114 D8
Pemberton Gr
Bawtry DN10 10 A6
Bawtry DN11 9 F6
Pemberton Pl [3] NG16 143 F2
Pemberton St NG1 223 F2
Pemberton The DE55 113 B4
Pembleton Dr [3] NG19 87 D1
Pembrey Cl NG9 170 D2
Pembridge Cl NG6 160 D2
Pembroke Cres NG24 125 C3
Pembroke Dr
Carlton in Lindrick S81 25 E6
Nottingham NG3 161 C1
Pembroke Rd S81 34 F7
Pembury Rd NG8 171 E5
Penarth Gdns NG5 161 E3
Penarth Rise NG5 161 E3
Pendean Way NG17 100 D1
Pendeen Cl DN21 15 E2
Pendennis Cl NG4 163 B1
Pendine Cl
Arnold NG5 147 D1
South Normanton DE55 113 C6
Pendle Cres NG3 161 F1
Pendock Ct NG12 186 D1
Pendock La NG12 197 A2
Penfold Cl LE12 213 A1
Penhale Dr NG15 145 C5
Penhurst Cl NG11 185 A4
Pen La NG12 208 D4
Penllech Cl NG5 161 A7
Penllech Wlk [4] NG5 161 A7
Pennant Rd NG6 160 D2
Pennard Wlk NG11 195 D8
Penn Ave NG7 222 A1
Pennhome Ave [8]
NG5 161 C2
Penniment La NG19 87 B2
Pennine Cl
Huthwaite NG17 99 E4
Long Eaton, Breaston
NG10 182 A1
Long Eaton, New Sawley
NG10 193 D4
Mansfield Woodhouse
NG19 88 C4
Newton DE55 99 A3
Nottingham NG5 147 B1
Pennine Dr
Kirkby-in-Ashfield
NG17 114 D4
Selston NG16 128 F7
Pennington Way NG15 145 E3
Pennington Wlk DN22 40 A6
Penn La LE14 202 F4
Penn Moor Cl NG10 193 A6
Penn St NG17 100 F3
Penny Emma Way
Kirkby-in-Ashfield
NG17 115 A8
Sutton in Ashfield NG17 114 F8
Pennyfields Bvd NG10 193 A7
Pennyfoot St NG1 173 E4
Penny Gdns NG9 183 A8
Penny Gn S80 45 A5
Pennyroyal Way NG17 115 A4
Penny Way NG18 102 D1
Penrhyn Cl NG3 223 F4
Penrhyn Cres NG9 183 B4
Penrith Ave NG12 176 A4
Penrith Cres NG8 160 C2
Penrith Pl NG19 101 D8
Penrose Ct NG16 129 A7
Penrose Rise NG17 101 B4
Penryn Cl DE55 113 C6
Penshore Cl NG11 184 D1
Pensom Cl NG22 77 B3
Penson Gdns NG13 177 D6
Penswick Gr NG24 125 F2
Pentland Ct NG19 101 D5
Pentland Dr
Carlton in Lindrick S81 25 E7
Nottingham NG5 147 B2
Pentland Gdns NG10 182 A1
Pentrich Rd NG16 158 C7
Pentrich Wlk NG18 103 B5
Pentwood Ave NG5 147 F2
Penzance Pl NG18 103 B7
Peppercorn Gdns NG8 172 C5
Pepperly Hill Cl DN22 50 A3
Pepperly Rise DN22 50 A4
Pepper Rd NG14 148 E8
Peppers Dr DE74 203 B2
Pepper St
Nottingham NG1 223 E2
Sutton in Ashfield NG17 101 B2
Percival Cl NG17 100 E3
Percival Cres NG17 100 E3
Percival Rd NG5 161 C2
Percival St S81 35 E5
Percy St
Eastwood NG16 144 A2
Nottingham NG6 160 D3
Sutton in Ashfield NG17 100 D2
Peregrine Cl NG7 222 A2
Peregrine Ct S81 35 C7
Peregrine Gdns NG21 89 F5
Peregrine Rd NG15 131 D1
Perivale Cl NG16 159 D3
Perkins La
Calverton NG5 148 E7
Grimston LE14 218 F2
Perkin's La LE14 219 A1
Perkins Way NG9 183 D3
PERLETHORPE 62 F3
Perlethorpe Ave
Carlton NG4 162 E2
Mansfield NG19 88 A1
[18] Nottingham NG1 173 E4
Perlethorpe Cl
[5] Carlton NG4 162 E2
Edwinstowe NG21 75 F3
Perlethorpe Cres [6]
NG4 162 E2
Perlethorpe Dr
Carlton NG4 162 E2
Hucknall NG15 146 B7
Perlethorpe Rd DN22 63 D7
Perlthorpe Ave NG20 74 D8
Perry Gdns
Brinsley NG16 143 D7
Nottingham NG5 161 B3
Perry Gr
Bingham NG13 177 F4
Loughborough LE11 220 C1
Perry Rd NG5 161 B3
Pershore Dr DN11 9 B5
Perth Cl NG19 88 C5
Perth Dr NG9 170 F1
Perth St NG1 223 E3
Petanque Way NG21 104 A1
Peterborough Rd NG23 98 B1
Peters Cl
Arnold NG5 162 C6
Eastwood NG16 144 C2
Petersfield Cl
Mansfield NG19 101 C8
Nottingham NG5 160 F7
Petersgate NG10 182 A1
Petersgate Cl NG10 182 A1
Petersham Mews NG7 222 B1
Petersham Rd NG10 182 A1
Petersmith Cres NG22 77 C6
Petersmiths Cl NG22 77 C6
Petersmiths Dr NG22 77 C6
Petticoat La NG25 121 D1
Petworth Ave NG9 182 F3
Petworth Dr NG5 160 F4
Peverel Rd NG15 130 F2
Peveril Cres NG10 193 A5
Peveril Dr
Ilkeston DE7 157 D2
Nottingham NG7 223 D1
Sutton in Ashfield NG17 100 C2
West Bridgford NG2 185 E3
Peveril Mews NG7 222 C2
Peveril Rd NG9 184 A7
Peveril St
Hucknall NG15 146 A8
Nottingham NG7 222 B4
Pharaoh Ct NG8 159 D2
Pheasant Hill NG19 88 A1
Pheonix Rd NG16 144 B4
Philip Ave
Eastwood NG16 144 A1
Kirkby-in-Ashfield NG17 115 B2
Nuthall NG16 159 C6
Philip Cl NG21 118 C8
Philip Gr NG4 162 E2
Philip Rd NG24 139 E5
Phillipott Cl NG24 140 D8
Phoenix Ave NG4 162 E2
Phoenix Cl
Mansfield NG18 102 E1
Nottingham NG2 173 B2
Phoenix Ct
Eastwood NG16 144 A1
Gainsborough DN21 24 F7
Nottingham NG7 184 F8
Phoenix Ctr NG6 160 A4
Phoenix Inf Sch [1]
NG4 162 E1
Phoenix La
Fernwood NG24 140 F3
Fernwood NG24 141 A3
Newark-on-Trent NG24 140 F2
Phoenix Pl NG6 160 B4
Phoenix Rise NG19 86 F5
Phoenix St NG17 101 B4
Phyllis Cl NG15 130 F1
Phyllis Gr NG10 193 F7
Piccadilly NG6 160 D6
Piccadilly Cl NG19 88 C6
Pickard St NG18 102 E7
Pickering Ave NG16 143 F2
Pieris Dr NG11 184 C1
Pierpoint Pl NG17 114 F6
Pierrepont Ave NG4 162 E1
Pierrepont Gamston Prim
Sch NG2 186 B6
Pierrepont Rd NG2 174 A1
Pierson St NG24 139 E5
Piggott Ave NG5 162 E3
Pike Ave NG12 197 D2
Pilcher Gate NG1 223 E2
Pilgrim Cl
Ranby DN22 38 E6
Ravenshead NG15 116 F2
Pilgrim Ct S81 34 F7
Pilgrim Rise DN10 3 C1
Pilgrims App DN21 24 F6
Pilgrims Way DN21 24 F6
Pilgrim Way S80 35 F2
Pilkington Rd NG3 162 A1
Pilkington St [8] NG6 160 B7
Pillared House La DN21 24 D7
Pilot Dr NG15 145 E4
Pimlico Ave NG9 171 B3
Pimlico Cl NG12 176 E3
Pinder St NG1 223 F2
Pine Ave
Langley Mill NG16 143 A3
New Ollerton NG22 77 D4
Pine Cl
East Leake LE12 214 D8
Everton DN10 11 C3
Kirkby-in-Ashfield NG17 114 F6
Mansfield NG21 103 F1
Mansfield Woodhouse
NG19 88 C5
Newark-on-Trent NG24 125 B4
Newark-on-Trent NG24 140 F1
Shirebrook NG20 72 E6
Pine Hill Cl NG5 146 F1
Pinehurst Ave NG15 145 C5
Pines Cl NG16 128 F8
Pines The
Beeston NG9 183 C8
Gainsborough DN21 24 F6
Worksop S80 35 F2
Pines Way NG18 116 D7
Pine Tree Cl S80 35 E1
Pine Tree Wlk NG16 143 E2
Pineview Cl NG18 102 F2
Pinewood Ave
Arnold NG5 148 B1
Edwinstowe NG21 91 C8
Pinewood Cl
Kirkby-in-Ashfield
NG17 115 C6
Southwell NG25 121 D1
Pinewood Dr NG18 102 F2
Pinewood Gdns NG11 195 D8
Pinewood Inf Sch NG5 148 B1
Pinfold NG13 177 F4
Pinfold Cl
Bottesford NG13 181 A3
Collingham NG23 98 A1
Cotgrave NG12 187 F4
East Markham NG22 65 F7
Kinoulton NG12 199 F2
Lound DN22 20 C1
Skegby NG17 100 F6
Woodborough NG14 149 C4
Pinfold Cres NG14 149 C4
Pinfold Dr S81 25 F7
Pinfold Gate LE11 220 B4
Pinfold Gdns [5] LE11 220 B4
Pinfold Jetty LE11 220 C4
Pinfold La
Averham NG23 123 E2
Balderton NG24 140 D3
Bottesford NG13 181 A3
Clarborough DN22 40 E8
Elston NG23 153 D5
Harby LE14 202 C3
Harwell DN10 11 B4
Kinoulton NG12 199 F2
Misterton DN10 6 E2
Nottingham NG11 185 B6
Plumtree NG12 197 F7
Shelford NG12 164 C1
Stapleford NG9 182 E7
Styrrup DN11 8 D2
Pinfold Pl LE14 202 C3
Pinfold Rd NG16 144 C1
Pinfold The DN10 4 B2
Pingle Cl
Gainsborough DN21 24 E8
Worksop S81 34 E7
Pingle Cres NG5 160 F8
Pingle La
Ossington NG23 95 F7
Ossington NG23 96 A7
Pingle The NG10 193 D8
Pingley Cl NG23 138 C8
Pingley La NG23 138 C8
Pings Cl NG23 97 E6
Pintail Cl NG4 175 B5
Pintail Meadow S80 35 B5
Pinter La DN21 24 E5
PINXTON 113 C2
Pinxton Ct NG18 103 B5
Pinxton La
Kirkby in A, Fulwood
NG17 114 A7
Kirkby in A, Tichfield Park
NG17 114 C4
South Normanton DE55 113 C5
Pinxton Rd NG17 114 D3
Piper Cl
Hucknall NG15 131 B1
Long Whatton LE12 212 C2
Mansfield NG19 88 B2
Piper Dr LE12 212 C2
Piper Gr NG20 72 D2
Piper La S80 61 D7
Piper St NG20 72 D2
Pipistrelle Cl LE12 214 E8
Pipit Gr NG11 196 B6
Pippin Cl
Newark-on-Trent NG24 125 B2
Nottingham NG3 173 F7
Selston NG16 129 A7
Walkeringham DN10 14 B8
Pippistrelle Cl DN22 42 D8
Pitcairn Cl NG2 173 C1
Pitch Cl
Giltbrook NG16 158 C8
Nottingham NG4 174 C8
Pit Hill NG20 59 A1
Pithouse La LE12 204 E1
Pit La
Mansfield NG19 87 A5
Pleasley NG19 86 F5
Shipley DE75 157 B6
Stapleford NG9 170 D2
Pitomy Dr NG23 97 F1
Pitt Hill NG20 58 F2
Pitt La DN10 12 F3
Plackett Cl NG9 182 F8
Plains Farm Cl NG3 162 C5
Plains Gr NG3 162 A4
Plainspot Rd NG16 128 E2
Plains Rd NG3 162 B4
Plane Cl NG6 159 F7
Plane Rd [7] NG12 186 A2
Plantagenet Ct NG3 223 F3
Plantagenet St
Nottingham NG14 173 D5
Nottingham NG3 223 F3
Plantation Ave NG22 66 A7
Plantation Cl NG5 147 A1
Plantation Dr DN10 11 A1
Plantation Hill S81 36 B4
Plantation La S81 27 B8
Plantation Rd
East Markham NG22 66 A6
Keyworth NG12 197 D3
Nottingham NG8 171 C4
Plantation Side NG7 172 E7
Plantations The [7]
NG10 193 A8
Plantin Rd NG5 161 B1
Plant La NG10 193 A4
Plants Yd S80 35 E2
Platt La NG12 198 A5
Platt St NG16 113 D2
Platts The NG24 139 E5
Plaxton Cl NG16 144 B2
Player St NG7 222 B4
Playworld★ NG4 162 F8
Plaza Gdns NG6 160 E4
Pleasant Cl [2] LE11 220 A4
Pleasant Pl DE74 203 D2
Pleasant Row NG7 172 F7
PLEASLEY 87 D6
PLEASLEYHILL 87 C4
Pleasleyhill Way NG19 87 C1
Pleasley Hill Way
NG19 101 C7
Pleasley Prings NG19 87 B5
Pleasley Rd
Fackley NG17 100 B7
Skegby NG17 100 F6

Pleasley Rd *continued*
Sutton in Ashfield NG17 101 A6
Teversal NG17 86 C1
Pleasley Vale Nature Reserve★ NG19 87 D7
Plot La NG23 98 E4
Plough Dr S81 25 F7
Plough Hill DN22 42 D7
Plough La
Lowdham NG14 150 D1
Nottingham NG2 173 E4
Ploughman Ave NG14 149 D4
Ploughmans Gr NG17 100 A1
Ploughman Wood Nature Reserve★ NG14 149 D2
Plover Dene S81 35 C7
Plover Wharf 3 NG2 173 A2
Plowman Ct NG9 182 D6
Plowright Ct 5 NG3 173 D7
Plowright St 4 NG3 173 D7
Plumb Rd NG15 145 F7
Plummer La DE74 203 C2
Plumptre NG16 143 B5
Plumptre Almshouses NG1 223 F1
Plumptre Cl NG16 143 F1
Plumptre Gdns 1 NG16 143 F2
Plumptre Pl NG1 223 F2
Plumptre Sq NG1 223 F2
Plumptre St NG1 223 F2
Plumptre Way NG16 143 F1
PLUMTREE 197 E6
Plum Tree DN22 32 D1
Plum Tree Ave NG19 89 B1
Plum Tree Cl DN22 30 D4
Plum Tree Ct DN22 32 D1
Plumtree Gdns NG14 148 F7
Plumtree La
Bradmore NG11 196 F3
Bradmore NG12 197 A3
Plumtree Rd
Bircotes DN11 9 C6
Cotgrave NG12 187 E3
Plumtree Sch NG12 197 E6
Plum Way NG24 140 E2
PLUNGAR 202 F8
Plungar Cl NG8 172 B6
Plungar La
Barkestone-le-Vale NG13 192 A1
Barkestone-le-Vale NG13 192 B2
Plungar Rd
Granby NG13 191 C5
Granby NG13 191 D3
Plymouth Ave NG16 113 E2
Plymouth Cl DN21 24 F6
Poachers Ct LN1 57 A3
Pochard Cl 5 NG19 88 F2
Pocklington Cres NG24 125 D6
Pocklington Rd NG23 98 B1
Podder La NG3 162 C6
Poets Cl NG15 145 E4
Point The NG3 173 D8
Pollard Cl 1 NG24 140 A7
Pollard Dr NG18 102 C7
Pollards La
Southwell NG25 136 F5
Southwell NG25 137 A5
Pollard's La NG25 136 F7
Polly Leys NG17 101 B3
Polly Taylor's Rd NG23 67 E1
Polperro Way NG15 145 D5
Pompeia Cl NG15 146 D8
Pond Cl NG24 140 F2
Pond Hills La
Arnold NG5 147 F1
Arnold NG5 161 F8
Pond St NG17 115 B5
Pond Way NG9 171 E5
Pool Cl NG16 113 D2
Poole Ave NG5 162 E4
Poole Mdw NG12 174 F4
Pooles Yard NG23 81 E7
Popham Ct NG1 223 F1
Poplar Ave
East Leake LE12 214 D8
Kirkby-in-Ashfield NG17 115 C5
Nottingham NG5 161 A1
Sandiacre NG10 182 A7
Poplar Cl
Bingham NG13 178 A4
Carlton NG3 174 D6
Cotgrave NG12 188 A4
Sutton on Trent NG23 96 F8
Worksop S80 35 D1
Poplar Cres NG16 159 B6
Poplar Dr
Glapwell S44 86 B8
Pleasleyhill NG19 87 B4
Poplar Gr
Church Warsop NG20 74 A6
Lidgett NG21 91 C8
Mansfield Woodhouse NG19 89 C1
Poplar Rd DE55 113 B7
Poplars Ave NG14 164 A5
Poplars Cl NG12 197 F4
Poplars Ct NG8 172 F2
Poplar St
Mansfield Woodhouse NG19 88 C3
New Ollerton NG22 77 D4
Nottingham NG1 173 E4
Retford DN22 39 F6
Poplars The
Beeston NG9 183 F7
Nottingham NG7 172 E8
Ranskill DN22 19 A4
Sutton in Ashfield NG17 101 A3
West Bridgford NG2 185 F7
Whitwell S80 45 A5
Poplars Way NG18 116 E7
Poppy Cl
Shirebrook NG20 72 D3
West Bridgford NG12 185 D7
Poppyfields The NG23 112 B8
Poppy Field Way
Carlton in Lindrick S81 25 F7
Carlton in Lindrick S81 26 A7
Poppy Gdn DE55 99 B7
Poppy Mews NG15 146 D4
Poppy Pl NG24 125 D1
PORCHESTER 162 B2
Porchester Cl NG15 146 C7
Porchester Jun Sch NG4 162 A1
Porchester Rd
Bingham NG13 177 D4
Nottingham NG3 162 A1
Porlock Cl 2 NG10 193 A8
Porritt Cl 8 LE12 205 E3
Portage Cl NG12 175 E2
Port Arthur Rd NG2 174 A4
Porter Cl NG11 195 C8
Porters Wk NG3 174 A7
Portinscale Cl NG2 186 C5
Portland Coll NG18 116 E6
Portland Cres
Mansfield Woodhouse NG19 88 D3
Meden Vale NG20 60 E1
Stapleford NG9 182 E6
Portland Ct NG5 161 B5
Portland Ct Mews NG19 88 C4
Portland Dr
Shirebrook NG20 72 F3
Shirebrook NG20 73 A4
Portland Gdns NG15 145 F7
Portland Grange NG15 145 E7
Portland Hill NG7 172 C1
Portland Hts DE55 99 E4
Portland Ind Est NG17 115 B7
Portland L Ctr NG2 173 D1
Portland Mdws DN22 29 A6
Portland Pk
Kirkby-in-Ashfield NG17 114 F3
Nuncargate NG17 115 A2
Portland Pk Cl NG15 145 F7
Portland Pk Nature Reserve★ NG17 114 F3
Portland Pl
Sutton DN22 29 A6
Worksop S80 35 F4
Portland Prim Sch NG8 171 C5
Portland Rd
Beeston NG9 182 F1
Carlton NG4 162 C2
Eastwood NG16 158 B8
Hucknall NG15 146 B6
Ilkeston DE7 157 F3
Long Eaton NG10 193 B4
Nottingham NG7 222 C3
Retford DN22 39 D5
Selston NG16 129 A7
Shirebrook NG20 72 F4
Shirebrook NG20 73 A4
West Bridgford NG2 185 F6
Whaley Thorns NG20 59 A2
Portland Ret Pk NG18 102 A5
Portland Row NG21 91 C8
Portland Sq NG17 100 F2
Portland St
Arnold NG5 161 E6
Beeston NG9 184 A7
Mansfield NG18 102 B6
Mansfield Woodhouse NG19 88 C3
Market Warsop NG20 74 B4
Newark-on-Trent NG24 139 F8
New Houghton NG19 87 A7
Sutton in Ashfield NG17 100 F2
Worksop S80 35 E3
Portland Terr
Gainsborough DN21 24 D7
Whaley Thorns NG20 59 A2
Portland Way
Clipstone NG21 89 F4
Clipstone NG21 90 A4
Portman Ct DN10 9 F7
Portree Dr NG5 146 F1
Portside St NG14 173 F2
Postern St NG1 223 D2
Posthill Cl S80 45 A6
Post Office La
Plungar NG13 202 F8
Redmile NG13 192 F3
Post Office Lane NG23 98 D5
Post Office Rd NG17 115 B5
Post Office Yd NG14 151 D2
Posts The NG12 189 A6
Potmakers Gr NG17 101 A4
Potter Hill Rd NG23 112 E6
Potter La NG22 92 D8
Potters Cl NG5 161 A7
Potters Corner NG19 103 A8
Potters Ct NG9 171 D1
Potter's Hill View 2 DE75 143 A1
Potters Hollow NG6 160 C5
Potters La LE12 214 F8
Potters Nook S81 34 F7
Potter St
Sutton in Ashfield NG17 101 A4
Potter St *continued*
Worksop S80 35 F2
Potters Way DE7 170 A8
Pottery Ct NG6 160 A7
Pottery Way NG6 160 A7
Potwell Cl NG25 136 F8
Pot Yd The NG22 119 F6
Poulter Cl NG7 172 D7
Poulter Rise DN22 50 A5
Poulter St
Langwith NG20 59 A1
Whaley Thorns NG20 58 F1
Poulter View DN22 39 F5
Poulton Dr NG2 173 E2
Poultry NG1 223 E2
Powell Ct NG22 119 F5
Powell Gdns 1 S81 35 D8
Powtrell Pl DE7 170 B6
Poynton St NG1 223 D3
Poyser Cl 2 NG7 161 A1
Pratt Cl 4 NG19 87 D1
Prebble Cl NG24 139 E5
Prebends Cl NG24 138 F4
Precinct Rd NG17 115 B5
Precinct The NG12 187 F3
Premier Rd NG7 173 A8
Prendwick Gdns NG5 161 B8
President Pl DN11 9 A6
Prest Ave NG20 74 E8
Preston Rd
Balderton NG24 140 E8
Rainworth NG21 118 A8
Prestwick Cl NG8 159 D2
Prestwold Ave
Mansfield NG19 103 B8
Mansfield Woodhouse NG19 89 B1
Prestwold La LE12 215 C1
Prestwood Dr NG8 172 B7
Previn Gdns NG3 173 F6
Priestgate NG22 65 E6
Priestsic Prim Sch NG17 100 F3
Priestsic Rd NG17 100 E3
Primerose Ct S81 26 A7
Primrose Ave
Farndon NG24 139 B6
Newark-on-Trent NG24 125 B4
Selston NG16 128 F2
Primrose Bank NG13 177 D4
Primrose Cl
East Leake LE12 206 A1
7 Kirkby-in-Ashfield NG17 114 F7
Nottingham NG3 173 D7
South Normanton DE55 113 B7
Primrose Cres NG4 174 F7
Primrose Ct
Mansfield Woodhouse NG19 88 F4
Sutton in Ashfield NG17 101 B1
Primrose Gdns NG15 146 D4
Primrose La NG22 78 C5
Primrose Rise NG16 158 A8
Primrose St
Carlton NG4 174 F7
Gainsborough DN21 24 D7
Ilkeston DE7 157 E3
Primrose Way
Clipstone NG21 89 F4
Shirebrook NG20 72 F6
Sutton in Ashfield NG17 100 C1
Worksop S81 36 A6
Prim Sch of St Mary & St Martin The S81 18 B2
Primula Cl
Nottingham NG11 184 C2
Shirebrook NG20 72 D3
Primula Gr 10 NG17 115 A3
Prince Charles Rd S81 35 D6
Prince Edward Cres NG12 175 E2
Prince of Wales St DN22 39 E6
Princes Rd LE14 219 B6
Princess Anne Rd S81 35 E6
Princess Ave
Beeston NG9 184 A6
Mansfield NG19 103 A8
Market Warsop NG20 74 C4
South Normanton DE55 113 A5
Princess Bvd NG8 159 C2
Princess Cl
Carlton NG4 162 E2
4 Edwalton NG12 185 F2
Princess Diana Ct DN21 15 C3
Princess Dr NG10 182 B4
Princess St
Eastwood NG16 143 F3
Kirkby-in-Ashfield NG17 114 D3
Long Eaton NG10 193 D8
7 Loughborough LE11 220 B3
Princes St NG18 102 A5
Prince's St NG24 139 F7
Princess Wlk DN21 15 F1
Prince St
Ilkeston DE7 157 E4
Long Eaton NG10 193 D8
Prince William Rd LE11 220 A6
Prince William Way LE11 220 A6
Prior Cl NG17 101 B4
Prioridge NG12 188 A2
Prior Rd NG5 161 D6
Priors Cl NG13 178 A5
Priors The NG14 150 D2
Priorswell Rd S80 35 F2
Priory Ave
Annesley Woodhouse NG17 115 B1
Priory Ave *continued*
Annesley Woodhouse NG17 130 B8
Ravenshead NG15 117 B1
Tollerton NG12 186 C1
Priory Belvoir Acad The NG13 181 A1
Priory Cir NG12 186 C1
Priory Cl
Balderton NG24 140 D3
Blyth S81 18 A3
Gainsborough DN21 24 F8
Mattersey DN10 20 A6
Priory Cres NG4 162 F1
Priory Ct NG4 162 F1
Priory Ctr The S80 35 E4
Priory CV Acad The NG16 144 B1
Priory Farm Mws NG14 151 D7
Priory Gdns NG14 151 C7
Priory Gr NG17 115 D5
Priory Jun Sch 1 NG4 162 F1
Priory La NG14 151 C7
Priory Mews 7 NG7 172 E2
Priory Mws S80 35 E2
Priory Nottingham Hospl The (Private) NG3 173 E8
Priory Pk NG14 151 D7
Priory Rd
Blidworth NG21 118 A5
Carlton NG4 162 F1
Eastwood NG16 143 F1
Hucknall NG15 145 E7
Mansfield Woodhouse NG19 88 B3
West Bridgford NG2 186 A8
Priory Sq NG19 88 B3
Priory St NG7 172 E2
Priory Way DE55 99 A3
Pritchard Dr
Kegworth DE74 203 B3
Stapleford NG9 182 E6
Private Dr NG25 121 D2
Private Rd
Hucknall NG15 145 E7
Nottingham NG5, NG3 161 D2
Southwell NG25 121 E1
Woodborough NG14 149 B5
Private St NG24 140 B8
Privet Ave NG17 115 A6
Privet Cl NG21 89 E3
Prize Cl NG11 184 C1
Procters Dr NG23 82 E1
Promenade NG3 223 F3
Promenade The NG17 115 D6
Prospect Cl NG17 115 B7
Prospect Ct NG17 99 E1
Prospect Dr
Shirebrook NG20 72 E3
Worksop S81 35 F6
Prospect Hill Inf Sch S81 36 A6
Prospect Hill Jun Sch S81 36 A7
Prospect Mws DN10 6 F2
Prospect Pl
Nottingham NG7 222 B1
Sutton in Ashfield NG17 100 E1
Prospect Prec S81 36 A6
Prospect Rd
Carlton NG4 162 B1
Heanor DE75 157 A8
Prospect St
Mansfield NG18 102 D6
Nottingham NG7 222 A4
Prospect Terr
Gainsborough DN21 24 D7
Nottingham NG7 222 A4
Providence Pl 5 DE7 157 E1
Providence Rd NG16 128 A4
Prudhoe Ct 5 NG2 173 D1
Pudding La LE14 210 C5
Puggy La S81 36 D6
Pulborough Cl NG5 160 F4
Pulford Cl 4 NG24 140 A8
Pullman Rd 4 NG2 173 F4
Pump Hollow La NG18 103 A7
Pump Hollow Rd NG19 103 A8
Pump La
Fenton NG23 142 E2
Walesby NG22 64 A2
Pump Works Cl 8 NG5 161 C3
Purbeck Cl
Long Eaton NG10 193 A8
Mansfield Woodhouse NG19 88 C6
Purbeck Dr NG2 185 C5
Purdy Mdw NG10 193 A5
Pureland Japanese Gdn and Meditation Ctr★ NG23 68 E5
Pyatt St NG2 173 D1
Pye Ave NG19 101 D7
PYE BRIDGE 128 A7
Pye Hill Rd NG16 128 A4
Pygall Ave NG11 195 A1
Pym St NG3 173 F6
Pym Wlk NG3 173 E6
Pythonhill Rd NG21 118 B8
Python Hill Rd NG21 104 B1

Q

Quadrangle The
Blidworth NG21 118 A5
Newstead NG15 130 D6
Quakefield Rd NG22 66 B6
Quaker La
Farnsfield NG22 119 F5
11 Mansfield NG18 102 B7
Quaker Way NG18 102 B7
Quantock Cl NG5 147 B2
Quantock Gr NG13 177 C4
Quantock Rd NG10 182 A1
Quantum Bsns Pk DN22 42 E8
Quarries Way NG17 114 E4
Quarry Ave NG6 160 B6
Quarry Bank NG18 102 D4
Quarry Cl NG15 132 B8
Quarry Dale NG15 130 F1
Quarrydale Acad NG17 100 E5
Quarrydale Ave NG17 100 F5
Quarrydale Dr NG17 100 E5
Quarrydale Rd NG17 100 F4
Quarry Dale Vw NG18 102 E5
Quarry Dr NG17 115 B3
Quarry Gr S81 35 C7
Quarry Hill NG10 182 A8
Quarry La
Linby NG15 131 B4
Mansfield NG18 101 F4
Mansfield NG18 102 A5
Quarry Rd NG15 132 B8
Quarry Yd NG17 100 E2
Quartz Ave NG18 102 E4
Quayside Cl NG2 173 E1
Queen Elizabeth Acad NG19 88 A1
Queen Elizabeth Cres S80 35 A4
Queen Elizabeth Rd NG9 183 A3
Queen Elizabeth's High Sch DN21 15 C3
Queen Mary's Cl NG12 176 D2
Queens Ave DE7 170 A5
Queen's Ave NG4 162 E2
Queensberry St 5 NG6 160 E4
Queens Bower Rd NG5 161 C8
Queen's Bridge Rd NG2 223 E1
Queensbury Ave NG2 185 C3
Queens Cl
East Markham NG22 66 A7
Hodthorpe S80 45 C5
Queen's Cres DN10 10 A7
Queen's Ct
Bingham NG13 177 D5
Clipstone NG19 89 D3
Newark-on-Trent NG24 125 A1
Queens Dr
Beeston NG9 184 A6
Brinsley NG16 143 E7
Nottingham NG11 185 A8
Nottingham NG7 184 F7
Sandiacre NG10 182 B4
Queen's Dr NG16 159 C6
Queens Dr Ind Est NG2 173 A1
Queens Farm Gdns NG24 140 E2
Queensfield DN21 15 B3
Queens Gr NG2 223 E1
Queen's Head Ct NG24 139 F8
Queen's Medical Ctr (Univ Hospl) NG7 172 D2
Queens Rd
Beeston NG9 184 A6
Carlton in Lindrick S81 25 F7
Hodthorpe S80 45 C6
Kegworth DE74 203 D2
Queen's Rd
Loughborough LE11 220 C4
Newark-on-Trent NG24 125 A1
Nottingham NG2 223 F1
Radcliffe on Trent NG12 176 A4
Queens Rd E NG9 184 B7
Queens Rd N NG16 143 F2
Queens Rd S NG16 143 F1
Queens Rd W NG9 183 E4
Queen's Royal Lancers & Nottinghamshire Yeomanry Mus The★ NG22 62 D3
Queen's Sq NG16 143 F2
Queen St
Arnold NG5 148 A1
Balderton NG24 140 E3
Balderton NG24 140 E4
Bottesford NG13 181 A2
Collingham NG23 98 A1
Gainsborough DN21 24 D7
Hucknall NG15 145 F8
Kirkby-in-Ashfield NG17 115 A4
Langley Mill NG16 143 C3
Long Eaton NG10 193 E7
3 Loughborough LE11 220 C3
10 Mansfield NG18 102 B7
Market Warsop NG20 74 A5
Newark-on-Trent NG24 139 E7
Nottingham NG1 223 E3
Pinxton NG16 113 C3
Retford DN22 39 D6
South Normanton DE55 113 A5
Southwell NG25 121 D1
Southwell NG25 136 E8
Sutton in Ashfield NG17 100 F4
Worksop S80 35 F2
Queensway
Gainsborough DN21 24 F8
Kirkby-in-Ashfield NG17 115 B2
Mansfield Woodhouse NG19 89 A1
Nether Broughton LE14 219 C6
Saxilby LN1 57 B3
Skellingthorpe LN6 71 F3
Worksop S81 35 F4
Queensway Ct LN1 57 B3
Queens Wlk 14 NG18 102 B7
Queen's Wlk
Nether Langwith NG20 59 A1
Nottingham NG2 173 B1
Querneby Ave NG3 161 E2
Querneby Rd NG3 161 E2
Quibell Rd NG24 140 A5
Quibell's La NG24 125 A3
Quince Cl LE12 214 C8
Quines Hill Rd NG19 89 A2
Quinton Cl NG11 185 A5
Quorn Cl
Beeston NG9 183 E3
Loughborough LE11 220 C2
Quorndon Cres NG10 193 D5
Quorn Gr NG5 161 A3
Quorn Rd NG5 161 A2

R

Rabbithill La NG23 83 B6
Racecourse Rd
Brinkley NG25 137 C7
Mansfield NG18 102 E5
Nottingham NG2 174 A4
Nottingham NG4 174 B3
Southwell NG25 122 A1
Rachel Cl DN21 15 C3
Rackhills Cl NG19 88 E1
Radbourne Rd 9 NG2 173 F3
Radbourne St NG19 88 E4
Radburn Ct NG9 170 E1
Radcliffe Gdns NG4 174 D8
Radcliffe Mount NG2 173 F1
RADCLIFFE ON TRENT 175 E3
Radcliffe-on-Trent Inf Sch NG12 176 A3
Radcliffe on Trent Jun Sch NG12 175 F2
Radcliffe Rd
Carlton NG12 175 B1
Cropwell Butler NG12 188 F7
Cropwell Butler NG12 189 A7
West Bridgford NG12 186 A8
West Bridgford NG2 186 D8
Radcliffe St NG2 173 D1
Radcliffe Sta NG12 175 F3
Raddle Way NG24 140 A4
RADFORD 222 A3
Radford Bridge Rd NG8 172 C5
Radford Bvd NG7 222 A4
Radford Cres NG4 162 E2
Radford Ct NG7 222 B4
Radford Gr La NG7 222 A4
Radford Prim Sch NG7 222 A3
Radford Rd
Nottingham NG7 172 F7
Nottingham NG7 222 B4
Radford St
1 Mansfield NG18 102 B6
Worksop S80 36 B1
Radley Rd NG22 135 C7
Radleys La
Perlethorpe NG22 62 F3
Perlwthorpe NG22 63 A3
Radley Sq NG6 160 D5
Radley Terr NG22 135 D8
RADMANTHWAITE 87 D3
Radmanthwaite La NG19 87 B5
Radmanthwaite Rd NG19 87 D3
Radmarsh Rd NG7 222 A1
Rad Mdws NG10 193 C6
Radmoor Rd 7 LE11 220 A4
Radnor Gr NG13 177 C4
Radnor Pl NG19 87 C4
Radstock Rd NG3 174 A7
Radway Dr NG11 185 A5
Raeburn Dr NG9 182 E2
Ragdale Rd NG6 160 B8
Raglan Cl NG3 173 D7
Raglan Ct
Beeston NG9 172 A1
Newark-on-Trent NG24 140 A7
Raglan Dr NG4 163 B1
Raglan Gdns NG24 140 A7
Raglan Rd DN22 40 A7
Raglan St NG16 144 A1
RAGNALL 68 A8
Raibank Gdns NG5 161 E5
Railway Ave S80 58 D8
Railway Cl NG15 146 A5
Railway Cotts NG16 158 F6
Railway Ct LN1 57 A3
Railway Terr LE11 220 C5
Raines Ave S81 35 E6
Raines Pk Rd S81 35 E7
Rainham Gdns NG11 196 C6
RAINWORTH 104 A1
Rainworth Heath Nature Reserve★ NG21 104 A3
Rainworth L Ctr NG21 117 F8
Rainworth Water Rd NG18 117 F8
Rainworth Wr Rd NG21 103 F1
Raithby Cl NG5 161 A6
Raleigh Cl
Ilkeston DE7 157 F3
Nottingham NG11 184 C1
Raleigh Rd NG19 101 E8
Raleigh St NG7 222 C3
Raleigh Villas NG9 183 E5
Ralf Cl NG2 185 E4
Ralph Way NG5 161 C5
Ramblers Cl NG4 174 E5

Ramper La LN1 55 D6
Ramper Rd
Letwell S81 16 A3
Saundby DN22 23 D7
RAMPTON 42 F1
Rampton Gn Rd DN22 42 F1
Rampton Hospl DN22 53 B8
Rampton La DN22 42 D5
Rampton Prim Sch DN22 42 D1
Rampton Rd
Laneham DN22 54 A6
Rampton DN22 42 E3
Ramsdale Ave NG14 148 D8
Ramsdale Cres NG5 161 D2
Ramsdale Rd NG4 162 E1
Ramsden Ave S81 16 F2
Ramsden Cres S81 25 F7
Ramsden Croft
Mansfield NG21 103 F1
Rainworth NG21 104 A1
Ramsden Prim Sch
Carlton in Lindrick S81 25 F5
Carlton in Lindrick S81 26 A5
Ramsey Cl
Mansfield Woodhouse NG19 89 A2
Stapleford NG9 170 E2
Ramsey Ct 5 NG5 161 B1
Ramsey Dr NG5 162 C6
RANBY 38 A6
Ranby CE Prim Sch DN22 38 A7
Ranby Wlk NG3 173 F6
Rancliffe Ave NG12 197 D4
Rancliffe Farm Mews NG11 196 E3
Rancliffe St NG1 223 F1
Randal Gdns 4 NG7 172 F7
Randall Cl NG24 140 D8
Randall Pk Way DN22 29 C2
Randall Way DN22 29 C1
Randal St 3 NG7 172 F7
Randol Cl NG18 101 D4
Ranelagh Gr NG8 172 B5
Rani Bsns Pk NG6 160 F4
Rani Dr NG6 160 F4
Ranmere Rd NG8 172 A7
Ranmoor Rd NG4 162 F1
Ranmore Cl NG9 171 B2
Rannerdale Cl NG2 186 C6
Rannoch Dr NG19 101 E5
Rannoch Rise NG5 147 F1
Rannock Gdns NG12 197 F3
RANSKILL 19 B4
Ranskill Gdns NG5 161 A8
Ranskill Prim Sch DN22 19 B5
Ranskill Rd DN22 19 E6
Ransom Dr NG3 161 E1
Ransome Cl NG24 140 D8
Ransom Rd
Mansfield NG21 103 D3
Nottingham NG3 173 E8
Ransom Wood Bsns Pk NG21 103 D4
Ranson Rd NG9 183 C2
Ratcher Hill NG18 103 C3
Ratcher Way NG19 103 B8
Ratcliffe Gate NG18 102 C6
Ratcliffe La
Darfoulds S80 45 E7
Ratcliffe on Soar DE74 203 C7
RATCLIFFE ON SOAR 203 F6
Ratcliffe Rd LE11 220 C5
Ratcliffe St NG16 143 F2
Rathgar Cl NG8 171 D4
Rathmines Cl NG7 222 A1
Rathvale Ct NG9 183 A4
Raven Ave NG5 161 B4
Ravencroft La DN10 14 B1
Ravendale Rd DN21 24 E7
Ravenhill Cl NG9 183 B4
Ravenscourt S81 36 A6
Ravens Ct NG5 161 B6
Ravensdale Ave
Long Eaton NG10 182 B2
Mansfield NG18 102 D8
Ravensdale Dr NG8 171 C3
Ravensdale Rd NG18 102 E8
Ravensdene Ct 2 NG3 173 D8
Ravensfleet Rd DN21 7 F3
RAVENSHEAD 117 B1
Ravenshead CE Prim Sch NG15 117 A2
Ravenshill Cl DN22 19 B4
Ravensmore Rd NG5 161 B2
Ravenstone Ct NG15 145 D3
Ravenswood Rd NG5 162 A8
Ravensworth Rd NG6 160 B8
Rawson St
Nottingham NG7 160 F1
Selston NG16 129 A6
Raylawn St NG18 103 A6
Raymede Cl NG5 160 F6
Raymede Dr NG5 160 E6
Raymond Cl NG17 114 E7
Raymond Dr NG13 178 A4
Raymond Way NG19 88 C1
Raymoth La S81 35 E7
Rayneham Rd DE7 157 C4
Rayner Ct NG7 222 B3
Raynford Ave NG9 183 C4
Raysmith Cl NG25 121 E2
Rayton Ct DN11 9 A4
Rayton Farm La S80 36 F2
Rayton La
Worksop S81 36 C3
Worksop S81 36 F4
Rayton Spur S81 36 B3
Read Ave NG9 184 A6
Read Cl NG24 140 E2
Readman Rd NG9 183 A3
Read Robinson Ave LN1 57 A5
Readwald Dr NG21 104 B1
Rearsby Cl NG8 171 D5
Rebecca Adlington Swimming Centre NG19 88 B1
Recreation Dr NG20 72 F2
Recreation Rd
Annesley NG15 130 C8
New Houghton NG19 86 F7
Sandiacre NG10 182 B6
Shirebrook NG20 72 E6
Recreation St
Long Eaton NG10 193 F8
Mansfield NG18 102 C7
Selston NG16 129 B6
Recreation Terr NG9 182 D6
Recreation View NG20 72 E6
Rectors Gate DN22 39 E8
Rectory Ave
Gainsborough DN21 15 D1
Nottingham NG8 171 E4
Rectory Cl LE12 213 B7
Rectory Dr NG11 185 B8
Rectory Dr The NG4 162 F2
Rectory Gdns
Beckingham DN10 14 B1
Kirton NG22 78 B6
Nottingham NG8 171 F4
Rectory La
Bottesford NG13 181 B3
Claypole NG23 156 E7
Gamston DN22 50 F5
Gamston DN22 51 A5
Kirkby-in-Ashfield NG17 114 E4
Lea DN21 24 F2
Rectory Mws NG9 184 D2
Rectory Pl
Barton in Fabis NG11 194 E6
2 Loughborough LE11 220 B4
Wymeswold LE12 216 C3
Rectory Rd
Carlton NG4 174 E5
Church Warsop NG20 74 C7
Cotgrave NG12 187 E3
Loughborough LE11 220 B5
Retford DN22 39 E7
Shirebrook NG20 72 D7
Treswell DN22 42 B3
West Bridgford NG2 185 F7
Rectory St LN5 142 D8
Red Admiral Rd S81 25 D1
Red Barn Cl DE55 99 B3
Redbarn La DE55 99 B3
Redbarn Way NG17 100 C1
Redbourne Dr NG8 172 C6
Redbridge Cl
2 Ilkeston DE7 170 A7
Shirebrook NG20 72 F2
Redbridge Dr NG16 159 D3
Redcar Cl
Carlton NG4 162 E2
Mansfield NG18 102 E5
Red Causeway The LE14 202 B2
Redcliffe Gdns NG3 173 C8
Redcliffe Rd
Mansfield NG18 102 D6
Nottingham NG3 173 C8
Redcliffe St
2 New Cross NG17 100 F4
Sutton in Ashfield NG17 101 A4
Redcroft Cl NG21 75 F2
Redfield Rd NG7 184 E8
Redfield Way NG7 184 E8
Red Flats La DN22 30 F4
Redforde Pk Ave DN22 29 C1
Redforde Pk Dr DN22 29 C1
Redforde Pk Rd DN22 29 C1
Red Fox Ave NG17 100 C5
Redgate Cl NG19 101 E8
Redgate Pl LE12 205 E3
Redgate Sch NG19 101 E7
Redgates Ct NG14 148 D7
Redgate St
Mansfield NG19 101 E8
Pinxton NG16 113 D2
Redhill Acad NG5 147 E1
Redhill La
Bothamsall DN22 63 E8
Ompton NG22 93 D5
Sturton le Steeple DN22 32 A6
Red Hill La NG22 92 E4
Redhill L Ctr NG5 147 E1
Redhill Lodge Dr NG5 147 D1
Redhill Rd NG5 147 E1
Redholme Cl S81 25 F7
Red Kite Cl
Hucknall NG15 146 D8
6 Worksop S81 35 C7
Red La
Brinsley NG16 128 E1
Carlton in Lindrick S81 26 A2
Lowdham NG14 150 D1
Redland Ave NG4 174 F8
Redland Cl
Beeston NG9 183 C4
Ilkeston DE7 157 F2
Redland Dr NG9 183 C4
Redland Gr NG4 174 E8
Redland Rd NG19 101 E8
Redlands Prim Sch S80 35 D4
Red Lodge La NG13 166 B7
Redman Cl DN21 15 E2
Redmays Dr NG14 164 B6
REDMILE 192 F3
Redmile CE Prim Sch NG13 192 F3
Redmile Cl NG15 145 F8
Redmile La
Barkestone-le-Vale NG13 192 D3
Elton-on-the-Hill NG13 192 A8
Sutton NG13 179 D1
Sutton NG13 191 F8
Redmile Rd NG8 160 C2
Red Oaks Ct NG20 74 A4
Redoubt St NG7 222 A3
Redruth Cl NG8 171 C6
Redruth Dr NG18 103 B2
Redthorn Way NG23 156 E6
Redwing Cl
East Leake LE12 205 F2
Worksop S81 35 C6
Redwood NG2 185 C6
Redwood Ave NG8 171 D3
Redwood Cres NG9 184 A5
Redwood Ct
Hucknall NG15 145 F8
Mansfield NG18 102 D4
Reed Cl NG24 140 A4
Reeders Croft NG9 183 D3
Reedham Wlk 2 NG5 161 B8
Reedman Rd NG10 193 B4
Reeds Cl NG14 149 C6
Reef Cl NG20 74 A5
Rees Gdns NG5 147 A1
Rees Row DN22 42 B1
Reform St
Annesley Woodhouse NG17 129 F8
Sutton in Ashfield NG17 100 F2
Regal Arts Ctr* S80 35 F4
Regal Dr NG18 102 C3
Regan Way NG9 183 B2
Regatta Way NG2 186 C8
Regency Ct NG9 184 A7
Regeneration Way NG9 184 A4
Regent Circle LN1 55 B8
Regents Cl NG23 112 B8
Regents Pk Cl NG2 185 C5
Regents Pl NG12 185 B6
Regent St
Beeston NG9 184 A7
Kimberley NG16 158 F6
Kirkby-in-Ashfield NG17 114 F4
Langley Mill NG16 143 B3
Long Eaton NG10 193 D8
Loughborough LE11 220 A4
Mansfield NG18 102 B7
Nottingham, New Basford NG7 161 A1
Nottingham, Standard Hill NG1 223 D2
Stapleford NG10 182 C5
Sutton in Ashfield NG17 100 D2
Regent Wharf Pl 2 LE11 220 A5
Regina Cl NG12 175 E2
Regina Cres NG15 116 F1
Reg Taylor's Swan & Waterfowl Sanctuary* NG25 121 F2
Reid Gdns NG16 159 B7
Reigate Cl NG9 183 E2
Reigate Dr NG9 183 E2
Reigate Rd NG7 160 F2
Reindeer St NG18 102 E6
Remembrance Way
Barton in Fabis NG11 195 B7
Kegworth DE74 203 C5
Long Eaton NG11 194 D3
Nottingham NG9 184 F5
Ratcliffe on Soar NG11 204 B8
REMPSTONE 215 D5
Rempstone Dr NG6 160 D5
Rempstone La NG12 207 A1
Rempstone Rd
East Leake LE12 214 E7
East Leake, Stanford Hills LE12 214 A6
Hoton LE12 215 C2
Sutton Bonington LE12 213 E6
Wymeswold LE12 216 A4
Renals Way NG14 148 F7
Rendell Prim Sch LE11 220 B5
Renfrew Ct NG19 101 E5
Renfrew Dr NG8 171 E4
Rennie Hogg Rd
Nottingham NG12 185 A8
Nottingham NG14 173 A1
Nottingham NG8 172 F1
Renshaw Dr 5 NG4 162 E3
Repton Ct NG19 88 E4
Repton Dr DE7 170 B7
Repton Rd
Nottingham NG6 160 D6
West Bridgford NG2 185 E5
RETFORD 39 E8
Retford Education Centre DN22 39 C6
Retford Gate DN22 41 E7
Retford Hospl DN22 39 D8
Retford La DN22 41 F1
Retford L Ctr DN22 39 C6
Retford Little Theatre* DN22 39 E6
Retford Oaks Acad DN22 39 C6
Retford Rd
Askham DN22 52 E3
Barnby Moor DN22 28 B6
Blyth S81 18 B2
Boughton NG22 77 F7
East Drayton NG22 53 A3
Eaton DN22 40 B1
Gamston DN22 51 D7
Headon cum Upton DN22 52 A6
Mattersey DN10 20 C6
Retford Rd *continued*
North Leverton with Habblesthorpe DN22 41 F8
North Wheatley DN22 31 C7
North Wheatley DN22 31 C8
Nottingham NG5 161 A3
Rampton DN22 42 D1
Ranby S81 37 C4
South Leverton DN22 42 A8
Torworth S81 27 F8
Walesby NG22 64 A1
West Markham DN22 65 D5
Woodbeck DN22 52 E7
Woodbeck DN22 53 A7
Worksop S80 36 C2
Retford Sta DN22 39 E5
Revell Cl NG16 113 F3
Revelstoke Ave NG5 146 D1
Revelstoke Way NG5 146 E1
Revesby Gdns NG8 172 C7
Revesby Rd NG5 161 F5
Revill Cl
Claypole NG23 156 D7
Ilkeston DE7 157 C2
Revill Cres NG9 182 F8
Revill Ct 13 NG17 114 E7
Reydon Dr NG8 160 D1
Reynolds Dr NG8 171 F5
RHODESIA 35 A4
Rhodes Way NG6 147 B6
Rhodes Wlk NG18 101 E6
Rhyl Cres NG4 162 E2
Ribblesdale S81 36 A8
Ribblesdale Ct NG9 183 A4
Ribblesdale Rd
Long Eaton NG10 193 A5
Nottingham NG5 161 C5
Ribbon Pond Dr NG24 140 A4
Riber Cl
Annesley Woodhouse NG17 115 A1
Long Eaton NG10 193 D5
Riber Cres NG5 160 F5
Rice Hill NG22 78 C7
Richard Bonington Prim Sch NG5 147 F1
Richard Herrod Ctr NG4 174 D8
Richards Cl NG12 189 A3
Richards Gr NG17 114 E5
Richardson Cl NG11 184 C1
Richardson Gdns NG12 185 D7
Richardson Rise DN21 24 F7
Richards Pl NG12 198 A3
Richard St DN22 40 A5
Richborough Pl NG8 171 D2
Richey Cl NG5 162 B7
Richmond Ave
Breaston DE72 193 A8
Calverton NG14 149 A8
Eastwood NG16 144 B2
Ilkeston DE7 157 F4
Nottingham NG3 173 F7
Sandiacre NG10 182 A4
Richmond Cl NG24 140 B4
Richmond Dr
Beeston NG9 183 E5
Mansfield Woodhouse NG19 88 D2
Nottingham NG3 161 D2
Radcliffe on Trent NG12 175 F4
Richmond Gdns NG5 147 E1
Richmond La DN10 9 F6
Richmond Rd
Carlton in Lindrick S81 25 E6
Gainsborough DN21 24 F8
Kirkby-in-Ashfield NG17 115 D5
Retford DN22 30 A1
West Bridgford NG2 173 F1
Worksop S80 36 A1
Richmond St NG18 102 F5
Richmond Terr NG12 175 F3
Ricket La
Blidworth NG21 117 C5
Ravenshead NG15 116 F4
Ricklow Ct 1 NG5 161 A8
Rick St NG1 223 F3
Riddell Ave S81 16 E3
Ridding La DN10 3 A4
Ridding Terr NG3 223 E4
Ridge Cl NG17 100 D3
Ridge Hill NG14 150 D2
Ridge La NG12 176 A5
Ridgeway
Nottingham NG5 161 A8
Shirebrook NG20 72 F5
Southwell NG25 121 D2
Worksop S81 36 B6
Ridgeway Cl NG22 119 F6
Ridgeway La NG20 74 B3
Ridgeway St NG3 173 E6
Ridgeway Terr NG20 74 B4
Ridgeway The NG22 120 A6
Ridgeway Wlk 17 NG5 161 A8
Ridgewood Dr NG9 183 C4
Ridgewood Gr NG15 117 A2
Ridgmont Wlk NG11 195 D8
Ridgway Cl NG2 186 C5
Riding Hill Av NG20 72 D3
Riding La DN10 3 A4
Ridings The
Bulcote NG14 164 B5
Keyworth NG12 198 A3
Mansfield Woodhouse NG19 88 F1
Ridsdale Rd NG5 161 C5
Rifle St NG7 222 A3
Rigg La
Arnold NG5 132 E3
Blidworth NG21 132 E7
Rigg La *continued*
Hucknall NG15 132 E5
Rigley Ave 10 DE7 157 F1
Rigley Dr NG5 160 E7
Riley Ave NG17 100 C3
Riley Cl NG17 100 C3
Ringer La S80 58 A8
Ring Leas NG12 188 A2
Ringlet Dr LE12 214 E8
Ringrose Cl NG24 140 D8
Ringstead Cl NG2 185 C5
Ringstead Wlk NG5 161 B8
Ringwood S81 36 A6
Ringwood Ave NG18 102 C4
Ringwood Cres NG8 172 C5
Ringwood Rd NG13 177 C4
Rio Dr NG23 98 A2
Ripon Rd NG3 174 B5
Risborough Wlk NG6 146 C1
Risegate NG12 187 F3
Riseholme Ave NG8 171 C3
Riseholme Rd DN21 24 F7
Rise Park Prim Sch NG5 146 F1
Rise Pk Rd NG5 146 E1
Rise The
Nottingham NG5 161 D3
Southwell NG25 136 D7
Risley Ct DE7 157 F3
Risley Dr NG2 173 B2
Rise's Pl NG2 223 F2
Ritchie Cl NG12 188 A2
Ritson Cl NG3 223 F4
Rivendell Acad NG4 175 C7
Riveraine Cl NG17 101 B2
River Cl DN22 29 F1
Riverdale Rd
Beeston NG9 183 C2
New Ollerton NG22 77 C6
Rivergreen NG11 184 E3
Rivergreen Cl NG9 171 C2
Rivergreen Cres NG9 171 C2
River La
Misson DN10 4 C2
Misson DN10 5 A2
Retford DN22 39 E7
Riverlands Cl NG13 165 A5
River Maun Rec Ctr NG18 102 D8
Rivermead
Cotgrave NG12 188 A3
Newark-on-Trent NG24 139 E6
River Rd NG4 174 E4
Riverside
Southwell NG25 121 F1
Whatton NG13 179 B4
Riverside App DN21 15 B1
Riverside Cl
Bottesford NG13 181 A3
Cuckney NG20 60 A3
Riverside Ct LN1 57 C2
Riverside Mws LN1 57 B3
Riverside Rd
Beeston NG9 184 A3
Newark-on-Trent NG24 139 D5
Riverside Ret Pk NG11 185 A8
Riverside View NG20 74 B5
Riverside Way
Mansfield Woodhouse NG19 88 D5
Nottingham NG2 173 B1
Riverside Wlk NG13 181 A3
River View
Laneham DN22 54 C7
Long Eaton NG10 193 A3
Market Warsop NG20 74 B5
Nottingham NG2 173 D1
Pye Bridge DE55 128 A6
Retford DN22 39 E3
Riverview Cotts DN10 4 C2
Riverway Gdns NG2 173 D2
Rivington Rd NG9 182 E2
Road No 1
Carlton NG4 174 F6
Carlton NG4 175 A5
Road No 2
Carlton NG4 174 F5
Carlton NG4 175 A5
Road No 3 NG4 175 A5
Road No 4 NG4 175 C5
Road No 5 NG4 175 B5
Road No 7 NG4 174 F6
Road No 8 NG4 174 F5
Roadwood La NG23 69 F8
Robbie Burns Rd NG5 161 C8
Robert Ave NG18 101 F5
Robert Dukeson Ave NG24 125 B4
Robert Mellors Prim Sch
NG5 162 A8
Arnold NG5 161 F8
Robert Miles Jun Sch NG13 177 F4
Roberts Ave NG17 99 F2
Roberts Cl
Dunham-on-Trent NG22 54 A1
Kegworth DE74 203 D1
Ragnall NG22 68 A8
Robert Shaw Prim Sch NG8 172 D6
Robert's La NG15 145 E7
Robertson Gr S80 35 B5
Roberts St
Ilkeston DE7 170 A6
Nottingham NG2 173 E4
Roberts Yd NG9 184 A7
Robey Cl
Hucknall NG15 131 A1
Mansfield Woodhouse NG19 89 B1
Robey Dr NG16 143 F3
Robey Vale S81 34 F8
Robina Dr NG16 158 C8
Robin Bailey Way NG15 146 C6
Robin Cl
Ollerton NG22 77 C2
Sutton Forest Side NG17 101 B2
Robin Down Cl NG18 102 D2
Robin Down Ct
7 Kirkby-in-Ashfield NG17 115 A3
Mansfield NG18 102 C2
Robin Down La NG18 102 C2
Robinet Rd NG9 183 F5
Robinettes La
Cossall NG16 158 D1
Cossall NG16 158 E2
Strelley NG16 159 A1
Robin Gdns NG12 186 A2
Robin Gr NG15 117 A1
Robin Hood Ave
Edwinstowe NG21 91 C8
Market Warsop NG20 74 C2
Robin Hood Cl NG16 143 F1
Robin Hood Dr NG15 145 E5
Robin Hood Ind Est 2 NG3 173 E5
Robin Hood Jun & Inf Sch NG5 161 A6
Robin Hood Prim Sch NG19 88 B4
Robin Hood Rd
Annesley Woodhouse NG17 130 B8
Arnold NG5 147 B1
Blidworth NG21 118 B5
Robin Hood's Cave* NG22 63 C2
Robin Hood St NG3 173 E5
Robin Hood Terr
Nottingham NG3 223 F3
Ravenshead NG15 117 B3
Robin Hood Way
Blidworth NG21 117 C6
Harlow Wood NG21 117 A6
Nottingham NG2 173 C2
Robinia Ct NG2 186 A5
Robin Mews LE11 220 A3
Robins Ct NG24 140 A8
Robinson Cl
Edwalton NG12 185 F3
Newark-on-Trent NG24 140 E8
Robinson Cres 6 LE11 220 C3
Robinson Ct NG9 183 B2
Robinson Dr S80 35 E1
Robinson Gdns NG11 184 C1
Robinson Rd NG3 162 A2
Robin's Wood Rd NG8 172 B7
Robin Way S81 35 B7
Rob La NG22 119 B3
Rob Roy Ave NG7 222 B1
Rochdale Ct NG18 103 A5
Roche Cl NG5 162 C7
Rochester Ave NG4 175 A7
Rochester Cl
Long Eaton NG10 193 A7
Worksop S81 36 A7
Rochester Ct NG6 159 F6
Rochester Rd NG21 118 A8
Rochester Wlk NG7 184 F1
Rochford Ct NG12 186 C3
Rockcliffe Grange NG18 102 C2
Rock Ct
Mansfield NG18 102 C7
Nottingham NG6 160 D3
Rock Dr NG7 222 C1
Rocket Cl NG16 159 A7
Rockford Ct NG9 170 E1
Rockford Rd NG5 160 F3
Rock Hill NG18 102 D6
Rock Hl Gd NG18 102 D6
Rockingham Gr NG13 177 C4
Rockings View NG21 118 A5
Rocklands The NG20 72 E4
ROCKLEY 51 A2
Rockley Ave
Eastwood NG16 144 A1
Radcliffe on Trent NG12 175 F4
Rockley Cl
Clipstone NG21 89 F5
Clipstone NG21 90 A4
Hucknall NG15 145 C6
Rockleys View
Lowdham NG14 150 A1
Lowdham NG14 150 A2
Rockley Way NG20 72 E4
Rock St
Mansfield NG18 102 D6
Nottingham NG6 160 B8
Rockstone Way 2 NG19 88 B2
Rock Valley NG18 102 C7
Rockwood Cl NG21 118 A5
Rockwood Wlk NG15 145 E6
Rodel Ct NG3 223 F4
Roden House Bsns Ctr NG3 173 D5
Roden St NG3 173 E5
Roderick Ave NG17 115 B1
Roderick St NG6 160 D4
Rodery The NG18 102 E5
Rodney Rd NG2 186 A6
Rodney Way DE7 157 F3
Rodwell Cl NG8 172 C6
Roebuck Cl NG5 161 B8
Roebuck Dr NG18 102 B3
Roebuck Way S80 48 B8
Roecliffe NG2 185 E4

Roe Gdns NG11 196 B7
Roehampton Dr NG9 170 D2
Roe Hill NG14 149 C5
Roe La NG14 149 C4
Roes La NG14 149 A7
Roewood Cl NG17 114 F7
Roewood La NG22 107 F2
Roger Cl NG17 100 F5
Roker Cl NG8 160 A1
Rolaine Cl NG19 88 C4
Roland Ave
Nottingham NG11 185 B7
Nuthall NG16 159 E4
ROLLESTON 138 A5
Rolleston Cl NG15 145 D5
Rolleston Cres NG16 144 F1
Rolleston Dr
Arnold NG5 162 A7
Eastwood NG16 158 B8
Nottingham NG7 222 B1
Rolleston Sta NG25 137 F6
Roman Bank NG19 88 D3
Roman Bank La DN10 18 E6
Roman Cres NG15 146 D8
Roman Dr NG6 160 E4
Roman Rd S81 35 D7
Romans Ct NG6 160 E2
Romilay Cl NG9 172 A1
Romney Ave NG8 171 D2
Romsey Pl NG19 101 D6
Rona Cl NG19 101 E5
Rona Ct NG6 160 E5
Ronald St NG7 222 B3
Ronchin Gdns NG17 115 A4
Roods Cl NG17 114 D8
Rook Cl LN1 56 F4
Rookery Farm NG12 189 B6
Rookery Gdns NG5 161 F8
Rookery La NG17 114 A8
Rookery The
Collingham NG23 98 A1
1 Mansfield NG18 102 A7
Rook's La DN10 6 E2
Rookwood Cl NG9 183 E6
Rookwood Cres NG15 145 D6
Rooley Ave NG17 100 C3
Rooley Dr NG17 100 C3
Roosa Cl NG6 159 F5
Roosevelt Ave NG10 193 C5
Roosevelt Rd NG17 101 B4
Rooth St NG18 102 B6
Ropery Rd DN21 15 B2
Ropewalk DE74 203 C2
Ropewalk Ind Ctr DE7 158 A1
Ropewalk The
Ilkeston DE7 158 A1
Newark-on-Trent NG24 140 B8
Nottingham NG1 223 D2
Southwell NG25 121 E1
Ropeway The NG17 114 E5
Rope Wlk LE12 205 D1
Ropsley Cres NG2 186 A8
Rosa Ct NG4 163 A1
Roscoe Ave NG5 147 E2
Roseacre NG9 184 A5
Rose Ash La NG5 161 B8
Rose Ave
Ilkeston DE7 157 E2
Retford DN22 40 A4
Rosebank Dr NG5 148 B1
Rosebay Av NG7 172 D8
Rosebay Gdns NG21 89 F4
Roseberry Ave NG2 173 E1
Roseberry Gdns NG15 146 C6
Roseberry St NG17 115 C4
Roseberry Cl S80 35 E3
Rosebery Hill NG18 102 C6
Rosebery St NG6 160 E3
Rosebowl Gdns DN22 39 E4
Rose Cl NG3 173 D7
Rosecliffe Spencer Acad
NG12 185 F2
Rose Cottage Dr NG17 99 F2
Rose Cotts NG14 163 E5
Rosecroft Dr NG5 161 C6
Rose Ct NG10 182 B1
Rosedale S81 36 A8
Rosedale Cl NG10 193 B6
Rosedale Dr NG8 171 B4
Rosedale Gdns
Mansfield NG19 102 D5
Sutton in Ashfield NG17 114 D8
Rosedale La NG15 116 F3
Rosedale Rd NG3 174 C6
Rosedale Way NG19 88 F2
Rose Farm Dr NG23 96 F8
Rosefield Cl NG24 140 F2
Rosefields DN21 15 E1
Rosefinch Wy NG19 88 F2
Rose Flower Gr NG15 146 C4
Rosegarth Wlk NG6 160 D4
Rose Gdns
Newark-on-Trent NG24 139 F4
Newark-on-Trent NG24 140 A4
RETFORD DN22 39 D8
Rose Gr
Beeston NG9 184 B5
Keyworth NG12 197 F4
Rosegrove Ave NG5 147 F1
Rose Hill NG12 197 E3
Rosehill Cl LN1 57 A4
Rosehill Sch NG3 173 E6
Rose La NG19 88 C4
Roseland Bsns Ctr
NG23 181 E8
Roseland Bsns Pk
NG23 169 F1
Roseland Way NG23 69 F2
Rose Lea DN22 39 D4
Roseleigh Ave NG3 162 B2
Rosemary Ave NG18 102 A8
Rosemary Cl 1 NG8 159 E1
Rosemary St NG18 102 A7
Rose Mdws DN22 28 D5
Rosemont Cl NG17 100 F6
Roseneath Ave NG5 146 E1
Rose Tree Pl 6 S81 35 A7
Rosetta Rd NG7 160 F1
Rosewall Ct NG5 162 B7
Roseway DN21 15 C1
Rose Way
Edwalton NG12 185 F2
Edwalton NG12 186 A2
Edwalton NG12 186 A3
Rosewood Cl
Carlton in Lindrick S81 25 D1
Newark-on-Trent NG24 125 B2
South Normanton DE55 113 B7
Worksop S81 25 D1
Rosewood Cres DE75 143 B2
Rosewood Ct DN22 39 C5
Rosewood Dr NG17 115 C6
Rosewood Gdns
Nottingham NG6 159 F7
West Bridgford NG2 185 C3
Rosings Ct NG17 100 E1
Roslyn Ave NG4 162 E2
Ross Cl
Coddington NG24 126 B2
Lowdham NG14 150 E1
Rossell Dr NG9 182 E5
Rossendale DE7 157 E4
Rossett Cl NG2 186 D6
Rossetti Gdns S81 36 C3
Rossington Bsns Pk
DN22 39 E5
Rossington Rd NG2 173 F5
Ross La NG4 163 C7
Rosslyn Dr
Hucknall NG15 146 C8
Nottingham NG8 160 A2
Rosslyn Park Primary Sch
NG16 160 A3
Rosthwaite Cl NG2 186 C5
Roston Cl NG18 103 B5
Rothbury Ave NG9 170 D2
Rothbury Cl NG5 147 F2
Rothbury Gr NG13 177 C5
Rotherham Baulk S81 25 C7
Rotherham Rd NG19 86 F8
Rothesay Ave NG7 222 B2
Rothley Ave NG3 173 F5
Rothwell Cl
Gainsborough DN21 24 E8
Nottingham NG11 185 A4
Rotunda The DN10 23 C8
Roughs Wood La
NG15 145 D4
Roulstone Cres LE12 205 E3
Roundhill Cl NG17 101 C1
Round Hill Prim Sch
NG9 183 F7
Roundhouse Cres S81 35 D7
Roundwood Rd NG5 161 C7
Rowan Ave
Hathern LE12 213 A2
Ravenshead NG15 117 A1
Saxilby LN1 57 A5
Stapleford NG9 170 E2
Rowan Cl
Calverton NG14 148 D7
Cotgrave NG12 188 A5
Kirkby-in-Ashfield NG17 114 F6
Mansfield NG19 88 D1
Rowan Cres S80 35 E1
Rowan Croft NG17 99 F4
Rowan Ct
HUCKNALL NG15 146 C8
Nuthall NG16 159 B6
Rowan Dr
Keyworth NG12 198 A2
Kirkby-in-Ashfield NG17 114 F6
Nottingham NG11 185 A4
Selston NG16 128 D6
Shirebrook NG20 72 D5
Rowan Gdns NG6 159 F7
Rowans Cres NG6 160 B4
Rowans The
2 Gainsborough DN21 15 F1
Saxilby LN1 56 F4
Rowan Way NG24 140 B5
Rowan Wlk NG3 174 A8
Rowe Gdns NG6 160 D6
Rowland Ave NG3 162 A2
Rowland Mews NG3 173 E7
Rowley Ct NG5 161 A2
Rowley Dr NG5 161 A2
Rowsley Ave NG10 193 A5
Rowsley Ct NG17 114 C8
Rowston Cl DN21 15 C2
Row The NG13 179 F6
Rowthorne La S44 86 B7
Roxburgh Cl
Arnold NG5 162 C8
Woodborough NG5 148 C1
Roxton Ct NG16 158 F7
Royal Ave NG10 182 D1
Royal Cres S81 35 E6
Royal Ctr (Theatre Royal & Royal Concert Hall)*
NG1 223 E3
Royal Mews NG9 183 C3
Royal Oak Ct NG21 76 B2
Royal Oak Dr NG16 129 B7
Royal Way LE11 220 A6
Roy Ave NG9 184 B4
Royce Ave NG15 145 E4
Royds Cres S80 35 A5
Royland Rd LE11 220 A3
Royston Cl NG2 173 B1
Ruby Ct NG25 136 F8
Ruby Gdns NG17 115 D4
Ruby Paddocks NG16 158 F5
Rubys Way NG24 140 E2
Ruby Wy NG18 102 C5
RUDDINGTON 196 D6
Ruddington Ct 4
NG18 103 A2
Ruddington Fields Bsns Pk
NG11 196 D4
Ruddington Framework Knitters Mus* NG11 196 C6
Ruddington Gdns
NG12 185 B3
Ruddington La
Nottingham NG11 185 B5
West Bridgford NG12 185 B3
Ruddington Rd NG18 103 A2
Ruddington Village Mus*
NG11 196 C7
Ruddy Rd NG4 175 C7
Rudge Cl NG8 171 F5
Rue de L'Yonne NG23 98 A2
Ruffles Ave NG5 162 B5
Rufford Abbey* NG22 91 F6
Rufford Ave
Beeston NG9 183 A8
Carlton NG4 162 D2
Mansfield NG18 102 C7
Meden Vale NG20 74 F8
Newark-on-Trent NG24 139 F7
New Ollerton NG22 77 C4
Rainworth NG21 104 C1
Retford DN22 39 D3
Rufford Cl
Bilsthorpe NG22 106 A4
Clipstone NG21 89 F2
East Markham NG22 65 F7
Hucknall NG15 146 C5
Sutton in Ashfield NG17 100 F5
Rufford Colliery La
NG21 104 A4
Rufford Craft Ctr*
NG22 91 F6
Rufford Ct NG21 104 C1
Rufford Ctry Pk* NG22 91 E6
Rufford Dr NG19 88 E3
Rufford Gr NG13 177 C4
Rufford La
Edwinstowe NG22 91 F8
Wellow NG22 92 B8
Rufford Primary Sch
NG6 160 A7
Rufford Rd
Edwinstowe NG21 91 C8
Long Eaton NG10 193 B4
Nottingham NG5 161 C3
Ruddington NG11 196 D7
Rufford St S80 47 B8
Rufford View NG22 77 C2
Rufford Way NG2 186 B6
Rufford Wlk
1 Nottingham NG6 160 B7
Ruddington NG11 196 D7
Ruffs Dr NG15 145 E5
Rugby Cl NG5 160 E7
Rugby Pk View NG20 73 E4
Rugby Rd
Rainworth NG21 118 A8
West Bridgford NG2 185 C5
Rugby Terr 17 NG7 172 F7
Rugeley Ave NG10 194 A7
Ruislip Cl NG16 158 E7
Runcie Cl NG12 187 F2
Runnymede Ct NG7 222 C3
Runswick Dr
Arnold NG5 161 F8
Nottingham NG8 172 B5
Runton Dr NG6 160 F4
Rupert Cres NG24 139 F7
Rupert Rd NG13 177 D4
Rupert St DE7 158 A1
Rushcliffe Arena*
NG2 185 D6
Rushcliffe Ave
Carlton NG4 174 D8
Radcliffe on Trent NG12 175 F3
Rushcliffe Comp Sch
NG2 185 F4
Rushcliffe Ct NG6 160 D6
Rushcliffe Ctry Pk*
NG11 196 C5
Rushcliffe Gr LE12 205 E4
Rushcliffe L Ctr NG2 185 F4
Rushcliffe Rd NG15 145 E5
Rushcliffe Rise NG5 161 D5
Rushes Cl NG9 184 A6
Rushes Sh Ctr The
LE12 220 A4
Rushes The
Gotham NG11 195 B1
8 Loughborough LE12 220 B4
Mansfield Woodhouse
NG19 88 D5
Rushey Cl S80 36 B2
Rushford Dr NG8 171 D4
Rushland Fields LE14 211 D3
Rushley Manor NG18 102 D1
Rush Leys NG10 193 D5
Rushley View NG17 100 C1
Rushmere Wlk NG5 161 F5
Rushpool Ave NG19 88 D4
Rushpool Cl NG19 88 F2
Rushton Gdns NG3 173 F7
Rushworth Ave NG2 185 E8
Rushworth Cl NG3 173 E7
Rushy Cl NG8 171 D5
Ruskin Ave NG10 193 B5
Ruskin Cl NG5 161 D7
Ruskin Rd NG19 87 D1
Ruskin St DN21 24 D6
Russell Ave
Harworth DN11 8 F4
New Balderton NG24 140 B4
5 Nottingham NG8 172 A5
Russell Cres 6 NG8 172 A5
Russell Dr
Nottingham NG8 171 F5
Nottingham NG8 172 A4
Russell Farm Cl NG12 186 D1
Russell Gdns 5 NG9 183 C2
Russell Pl NG1 223 D3
Russell Rd NG7 172 F8
Russell St
Long Eaton NG10 182 D1
Loughborough LE11 220 C4
Nottingham NG7 222 C3
Sutton in Ashfield NG17 100 F3
Russet Ave NG4 174 F7
Russet Gr DN10 10 A7
Russet Way 4 NG8 172 B7
Russey Cl NG14 150 E1
Russley Rd NG9 183 A8
Ruth Dr NG5 148 A1
Rutherford Ave NG18 102 E4
Rutherglen Pk 9 LN1 57 A5
Ruthwell Gdns NG5 147 A2
Rutland Ave
Beeston NG9 183 A2
Newark-on-Trent NG24 140 A6
Rutland Cl
Market Warsop NG20 74 A4
Nottingham NG14 173 B2
Rutland Cres DN11 8 F5
Rutland Ct DE7 157 D1
Rutland Dr
Harworth DN11 8 F5
Harworth DN11 9 A5
Rutland Gr NG10 182 C5
Rutland La NG13 181 B2
Rutland Rd
Bingham NG13 177 F5
Carlton NG4 162 D3
Retford DN22 40 B4
West Bridgford NG2 186 A8
Westwood NG16 128 C4
Rutland St
Ilkeston DE7 157 F2
1 Loughborough LE11 220 C3
Mansfield NG18 102 C5
Nottingham NG1 223 D2
Rutlands The NG23 124 A4
Rutland Terr DE7 157 F2
Ryan Way NG9 184 A3
Rydal Ave NG10 182 B2
Rydal Dr
Beeston NG9 183 D8
Hucknall NG15 145 F8
Worksop S81 35 E8
Rydale Gdns DN10 3 A1
Rydale Rd NG5 161 C5
Rydal Gdns NG2 186 A5
Rydal Gr NG6 160 E3
Ryder St NG6 160 D4
Ryecroft NG19 89 B1
Rye Croft DN11 8 A8
Ryecroft St NG9 182 F8
Ryedale Ave
Mansfield NG18 102 F5
Mansfield NG18 103 A5
Ryehill Cl NG2 173 D2
Ryehill St NG2 173 D2
Ryeholme Cl LE12 205 F3
Ryeland Gdns NG2 173 C2
Ryemere Cl NG16 143 E2
Rye St NG7 160 F1
Ryknield Rd
Hucknall NG15 146 C8
Papplewick NG15 131 D1
Rylands Cl NG9 184 B4
Ryton Cl S81 18 B2
Ryton Ct 7 NG2 173 D1
Ryton Fields S81 18 B2
Ryton Pl S80 35 F3
Ryton Sq NG8 160 B1
Ryton St S80 35 F3

S

Sabina Rd
HUCKNALL NG15 146 C8
Hucknall NG15 146 D8
Sabre Ind Pk NG4 175 C4
Sacheverall Ave NG16 113 D3
Sacred Heart RC Prim Sch
NG4 174 D7
Sacred Heart Roman Catholic Prim Sch
LE11 220 A1
Saddlers Cl NG19 88 F1
Saddlers Courtyard
DN10 10 A6
Saddlers Yd NG12 197 E7
Saddleworth Ct NG3 223 E4
Sadler St NG19 101 F8
Saffron Gdns NG2 173 B2
Saffron St
Forest Town NG19 89 A1
5 Mansfield Woodhouse
NG19 88 F1
St Agnes Cl NG8 171 D8
St Aidan's Ct 2 NG6 160 E4
St Albans Cl NG10 193 E5
St Albans Ct NG5 147 B2
St Albans Mews NG6 160 D6
St Albans Rd
Arnold NG5 161 E7
Bestwood Village NG6 146 E4
Nottingham NG6 160 D7
St Albans St NG5 161 C3
St Andrew Cl NG11 195 B1
St Andrew's CE Prim Sch
NG17 100 F6
St Andrews Cl NG6 160 C7
St Andrew's Cl NG15 146 A8
St Andrews Cres NG17 100 F6
St Andrews Dr LN1 56 F4
St Andrew's Rd NG3 173 B7
St Andrew's Rise DE74 203 C1
St Andrews St
Kirkby-in-Ashfield
NG17 115 B6
Sutton in Ashfield NG17 100 E6
St Andrew St NG18 102 C5
St Andrews Way DN22 39 E3
St Anne's CE Prim Sch
S80 35 D2
St Annes Cl S80 35 C3
St Annes Dr S80 35 C2
St Anne's La LE12 213 B6
St Annes Mews S80 35 C3
St Annes View S80 35 C3
St Annes Way S80 35 C3
ST ANN'S 173 D6
St Ann's Gdns NG3 173 E7
St Ann's Hill NG3 173 C7
St Ann's Hill Rd NG3 173 C7
St Ann's Hospital Sch
NG4 174 A8
St Ann's St NG1 223 E3
St Ann's Valley NG3 173 E7
St Ann's Way
Nottingham NG3 223 E4
Shelton NG23 168 C6
St Ann's Well Inf Sch
NG3 173 E7
St Ann's Well Rd NG3 173 E6
St Anthony Ct NG7 172 E2
St Augustines Cl 3
NG7 161 A1
St Augustine's RC Prim Sch
NG3 173 C8
St Augustine's Sch S81 36 B4
St Austell Dr NG11 185 B6
St Austins Ct NG4 174 F8
St Austins Dr NG4 174 F8
St Bartholomews Ct
DN22 29 A6
St Bartholomew's Rd
NG3 173 F7
St Botolphs Cl LN1 57 B5
St Botpolphs Gate LN1 57 A5
St Catherines Cl NG24 139 F7
St Catherines St NG12 175 E2
St Catherine St NG18 102 C5
St Cecilia Gdns NG3 223 F4
St Chad's Cl NG18 102 C3
St Chad's Rd NG3 173 E5
St Christophers Rd
NG18 101 F5
St Christopher St 9
NG2 173 F4
St Cl NG12 198 A3
St Clare's Gate NG24 140 A6
St Cuthbert's Rd 11
NG3 173 E5
St Cuthbert St S80 35 F1
St David's Cl S81 36 A6
St Edmund Campion Catholic Prim Sch
NG2 186 A6
St Edmund's Ave NG19 88 C3
St Edmund's CE Prim Sch
NG19 88 C3
St Edwin's Dr NG21 76 A2
St Emmanuel View
NG5 147 B1
St Ervan Rd NG11 185 B6
St Francis Hospl NG5 161 B5
St Francis Way NG5 161 B5
St George's CE Com Prim Sch DN21 24 F6
St Georges Cl DN21 24 E7
St George's Ct NG15 146 A8
St Georges Dr
Beeston NG9 182 F2
Beeston NG9 183 A2
St George's Dr NG2 173 B2
St George's Ms LN1 56 F4
St Georges Priory NG2 173 C2
St Giles Cl DN22 39 C8
St Giles School DN22 39 C7
St Giles Way NG12 189 A4
St Giles' Way NG24 140 E4
St Helens Ave NG16 113 C3
St Helen's Cres
Burton Joyce NG14 163 F4
Trowell NG9 170 C4
St Helen's Dr NG16 128 D7
St Helen's Gr NG14 163 E3
St Helen's La NG22 120 F2
St Helen's Rd
Retford DN22 40 B4
West Bridgford NG2 185 F6
St Helen's St NG7 222 C3
St James Ave DE7 170 A7
St James Ct NG10 182 B3
St James' Dr NG16 143 D8
St James Gdns NG19 88 E6
St James's Ct NG15 146 A8
St James's St
Nottingham NG1 223 D2
Stapleford NG9 182 C6
St James's Terr NG9 182 D6
St Jame's Terr NG1 223 D2
St John's Ave NG17 115 B4
St John's CE Prim Sch
Stapleford NG9 182 E7
Worksop S81 35 E7
St John's Cl NG16 128 D1
St John's Cres NG15 146 C5
St Johns Ct S80 35 E3
St Johns Ctr* NG18 102 A7
St John's Dr DN22 30 D4
St John's Pl 9 NG18 102 A7
St Johns Rd 4 DE7 170 A7
St John's Rd
Ilkeston DE7 170 A7
Ruddington NG11 196 C7
St John's St NG10 193 D7
St John St
Mansfield NG18 102 B7
Retford DN22 39 F7
St John's Terr DN21 24 D7
St Johns View NG18 102 A7
St John the Baptist CE Prim Sch NG4 174 E6
St Joseph's RC Prim Sch
Boughton/Ollerton NG22 77 E5
Retford DN22 39 D7
Shirebrook NG20 72 F5
St Joseph's Sch NG1 223 D3
St Jude's Ave NG3 161 E2
St Judes Way NG21 104 A1
St Laurence CE Prim Sch
NG10 193 E6
St Laurence Ct NG10 193 E6
St Lawrence Bvd NG12 175 E2
St Leonard's DN11 8 A7
St Leonard's Ct NG24 124 F1
St Leonard's Dr NG8 171 F4
St Leonards Way NG19 103 B8
St Leven Cl NG8 171 D8
St Luke's CE Prim Sch
S81 34 F8
St Luke's Cl NG2 186 B5
St Luke's St 6 NG3 173 E5
St Lukes Way DN22 53 A8
St Luke's Way NG14 175 F8
St Margaret Clitherow RC Prim Sch NG5 161 C8
St Margarets Ave NG8 172 C8
St Margaret'S Cl NG22 106 A5
St Margaret St NG18 102 C5
St Mark's Cl S81 35 D8
St Marks Ct NG17 114 B8
St Mark's La NG24 139 F8
St Mark's Pl NG24 139 F8
St Marks St NG3 223 F3
St Marrys Cl DN21 14 A5
St Martin's Ave DN10 9 F7
St Martins Cl
Blyth S81 18 B2
North Leverton with Habblesthorpe DN22 42 C8
St Martin's Cl
Firbeck S81 16 A6
Nottingham NG8 171 E8
St Martins Rd DN22 42 C8
St Martin's Rd NG8 171 E8
St Martin's Wlk S80 45 C6
St Mary Magdalene CE Prim Sch NG17 100 C3
St Mary's Ave NG4 162 E2
St Mary's Catholic Voluntary Acad NG7 172 F8
St Mary's CE Prim Sch
NG21 76 A3
St Mary's Church*
NG1 223 F2
St Marys Cl NG9 183 D1
St Mary's Cl
Arnold NG5 147 F1
Bottesford NG13 181 B3
5 Loughborough LE11 220 A4
Lowdham NG14 150 D2
St Mary's Cres
East Leake LE12 205 F3
Ruddington NG11 196 C7
Tickhill DN11 8 A7
St Mary's Ct NG17 100 D4
St Mary's Dr NG21 76 A2
St Mary's Gate
Nottingham NG1 223 F2
Tickhill DN11 8 A7
St Mary's Gdns NG24 139 F5
St Mary's La NG13 181 B2
St Marys Mews DN11 8 A7
St Mary's Pl NG1 223 F2
St Mary's RC Prim Sch 13
LE11 220 A4
St Marys Rd NG13 177 F5
St Mary's Rd
Sutton in Ashfield
NG17 100 D3
Tickhill DN11 8 A7
St Mary's Way NG15 146 A8
St Mary's Wlk NG16 128 B3
St Matthew's CE Prim Sch
NG23 81 E7
St Matthias Rd NG3 173 E6
St Mawes Ave NG11 185 B6
St Mellion Way 3
NG17 114 E7
St Michaels Ave NG8 171 D8
St Michael's Ave NG4 162 E2
St Michaels Cl LE12 213 A8
St Michael's Cl NG22 120 F1
St Michael's Dr DE55 113 A7
St Michael's Gn DN22 39 D8
St Michael's Sq NG9 183 B8
St Michael's St NG17 101 A3
St Michaels View
Farnsfield NG22 119 E7
Selston NG16 129 A5
St Michael's View
NG15 131 B1
St Nicholas Cl NG5 161 E7
St Nicholas St NG1 223 E2
St Nicholas Way
DN10 10 A6
St Oswalds NG22 54 C2

St Patrick's RC Prim Sch
Clifton NG11 185 B8
Mansfield NG18 103 A5
St Patrick's Rd
Hucknall NG15 145 F7
Nuthall NG16 159 C6
St Paul's Ave NG7 172 F7
St Paul's Rd
Gainsborough DN21 15 B3
Worksop S80 36 A2
St Paul's St 1 NG8 172 D5
St Paul's Terr NG7 172 F7
St Peters Ave LE12 213 A1
St Peter's Ave NG20 74 B6
St Peter's CE Jun Sch
East Bridgford NG13 165 C3
Ruddington NG11 196 D8
St Peters CE Prim Sch
DN10 12 E2
St Peter's CE Prim Sch
Farndon NG24 139 A5
Mansfield NG18 103 A2
St Peter's Church Walk
NG1 223 E2
St Peters Cl
East Stockwith DN21 7 E2
Farndon NG24 138 F4
New Ollerton NG22 77 B4
St Peter's Cres NG11 196 C7
St Peters Ct LN1 55 A1
St Peters Dr NG21 104 A1
St Peter's Gate NG1 223 E2
St Peter's La DN22 21 D5
St Peter's Ret Pk NG18 102 B6
St Peter's Sq NG1 223 E2
St Peter's St NG7 222 A3
St Peter's Way NG18 102 C6
St Philip Neri with St Bede Roman Catholic Voluntary Acad NG19 102 A8
St Saviour's Cl DN22 40 A8
St Saviour's Gdns NG2 173 D2
St Stephen's Ave 7
NG2 173 F4
St Stephens Rd NG22 77 D3
St Stephen's Rd
Nottingham NG2 173 F4
Retford DN22 40 B4
St Swithun's CE Prim Sch
1 DN22 39 F7
St Swithuns Gn 2 DN22 39 F7
St Teresa's RC Prim Sch
NG8 172 A8
St Thomas' Ave NG17 115 B4
St Thomas Dr NG13 179 A5
St Thomas More Cl
NG9 171 D3
St Vincent Cl NG10 193 E6
St Wilfreds Cl NG23 110 F2
St Wilfreds Pk NG17 114 D4
St Wilfrid's CE Prim Sch
NG14 148 E7
St Wilfrids Church Dr
NG2 185 B8
St Wilfrids Dr NG17 114 D5
St Wilfrid's Sq NG14 148 F7
St Winifreds Ct NG11 203 F4
Salamander Cl NG4 162 D2
Salcey Dr NG9 170 D2
Salcombe Cir NG5 147 D1
Salcombe Cl NG16 144 C1
Salcombe Cres NG11 196 D8
Salcombe Dr NG5 147 D1
Salcombe Gr DN10 9 F8
Salcombe Rd NG5 160 F3
Salestune Mws NG16 128 F6
Salford Gdns NG3 223 F3
Salisbury Ave LE12 205 F1
Salisbury Cl
Mansfield Woodhouse NG19 88 D4
Morton DN21 15 B5
Saxilby LN1 57 A4
Worksop S80 35 E4
Salisbury Rd
Mansfield NG19 101 E8
Newark-on-Trent NG24 139 F6
Salisbury Sq NG7 222 A2
Salisbury St
Beeston NG9 184 B7
Gainsborough DN21 15 C2
Long Eaton NG10 193 E7
Loughborough LE11 220 C4
Nottingham NG7 222 A2
Sallie Bank La LN1 55 B4
Salmon Cl NG6 159 F7
Salmon La NG17 129 D7
Salop St NG5 161 D7
Saltburn Rd NG8 172 A6
Saltby Gn NG2 185 B3
Salterford Ave NG14 148 F8
Salterford House Sch
NG25 134 B3
Calverton NG14 133 D5
Salterford La NG14 133 D5
Salterford Rd NG15 145 E5
Saltford Cl NG4 162 F2
Salt Hill S81 16 B5
Salthouse Ct NG9 184 A7
Salthouse La NG9 184 A8
Saltney Way NG11 185 A3
Salvin Cl NG12 189 A4
Sam Derry Cl 6 NG24 140 B8
Samian Cl S81 35 E7
Sampson's La NG19 87 B3
Sampson St NG17 130 A8
Samson Ct NG11 196 B8
Samuel Barlow Prim Sch
NG21 90 A3
Samuel Brunts Way
NG18 102 C8
Samuel Cl NG19 101 F8
Samuel Unwin Ct
NG17 101 B3
Samworth Church Acad
NG18 102 F7
Sandale Cl NG2 186 C6
Sandalwood Cl NG18 103 B4
Sandalwood Dr NG17 115 C6
Sandays Cl NG2 173 C1
Sandbeck Ct DN10 10 A8
Sandby Ct NG9 183 C5
Sanderling Wy NG19 88 E2
Sanders Ave NG18 102 E8
Sanders Cl
Besthorpe NG23 97 F7
Ilkeston DE7 157 C2
Sanderson Dr NG3 162 D6
Sandersons Bank DN9 1 F4
Sanderson's Bank DN9 2 B3
Sandfield Ave NG15 132 B8
Sandfield Cl NG18 103 B4
Sandfield La NG22 78 B6
Sandfield Rd
Annesley Woodhouse NG17 129 F8
Arnold NG5 161 F5
Beeston NG9 182 E2
Nottingham NG7 222 B2
Sandfield Way NG24 139 D5
Sandford Ave NG10 193 E7
Sandford Rd NG3 162 A3
Sandgate NG9 171 D1
Sandgate Ave NG19 88 D4
Sandgate Rd NG19 88 D4
Sandhill La DN22 32 D6
Sandhill Rd
Farndon NG24 139 A5
Selston NG16 129 B3
Sandhills Cl NG24 124 E1
Sandhill Sconce NG24 139 D8
Sandhills Pk NG24 124 E1
Sandhill St S80 35 E3
Sandholes NG22 119 E6
Sandhurst Ave NG18 102 C4
Sandhurst Dr
Beeston NG9 183 C2
Ruddington NG11 196 B6
Sandhurst Rd NG6 146 C1
SANDIACRE 182 A6
Sandiacre Rd NG9 182 C6
Sand La
Besthorpe NG23 97 F7
Broadholme NG23 70 E8
Spalford NG23 83 A7
Torksey LN1 44 C2
Sand Martin Cl LE12 205 F3
Sandmartins S81 35 C7
Sandmartins Cl NG18 102 C5
Sandon St NG7 161 A1
Sandown Rd
Beeston NG9 182 F2
Mansfield NG18 103 B4
Sutton in Ashfield NG17 101 B3
Sandpiper Cl NG13 177 F3
Sandpiper Pl NG20 73 E5
Sandpiper Way NG7 222 A2
Sand Pit La LE14 211 C3
Sandringham Ave NG2 185 E8
Sandringham Cres
Nottingham NG8 171 C5
Worksop S81 35 E6
Sandringham Ct
Harworth DN11 9 A5
Mansfield Woodhouse NG19 88 B6
Sandringham Dr
Beeston NG9 171 C1
Mansfield Woodhouse NG19 88 B6
Sandringham Pl NG15 146 B8
Sandringham Rd
Mansfield Woodhouse NG19 88 E5
2 Nottingham NG2 173 F4
Retford DN22 29 D1
Sandiacre NG10 182 B3
Sandrock Rd DN11 8 F5
Sands Cl NG4 174 E5
Sandsfield La DN21 24 D6
Sandside NG12 187 F2
Sands The
Bottesford NG13 181 B1
Long Clawson LE14 211 D3
Sandstone Ct 2 NG6 160 A8
Sandstone Mws NG14 173 B1
Sandstone Pl NG18 102 E5
Sandwell Cl NG10 193 A6
Sandwich Cl 5 NG17 114 E7
Sandwood Cl DE55 99 A3
Sandycliffe Cl NG19 88 F1
Sandyford Cl NG6 160 C3
Sandy Gr NG18 102 D7
Sandy La
Bawtry DN10 10 A7
Beeston NG9 171 D1
Carlton NG12 175 B2
Edwinstowe NG21 91 B8
Gamston DN22 50 F4
Hucknall NG15 146 A7
Mansfield NG18 102 D7
Market Warsop NG20 74 B5
Oxton NG25 134 C3
Ravenshead NG15 117 B3
Worksop S80 35 D4
Sandy La Ind Est S80 35 D4
Sandymount DN11 9 A5
Sandymount E DN11 9 A4
Sandymount W DN11 9 A4
Sanger Cl NG11 195 C8
Sanger Gdns NG11 195 C8
Sankey Dr NG6 160 A7
Santon Cl NG19 89 A2
Santon Rd NG19 89 A2
Sapele Cl NG4 163 A2
Sapling Cl NG24 140 C5
Sapphire Cl NG21 104 C1
Sapphire Dr NG17 115 C4
Sapphire St NG18 102 C5
Saracen Cl DN21 24 F6
Saracen La DN10 9 F2
Saracen's Head Yd
NG24 139 F8
Saracens La DN10 10 A2
Sarah Ave NG5 161 A2
Sarah Dr NG12 185 F3
Sargent Gdns 1 NG3 173 F6
Sartfield Rd NG19 89 B2
Saskatoon Cl NG12 175 E2
Saturn Rd NG18 102 E2
Saturn Way 3 NG18 102 E1
Saucemere Dr NG24 139 F6
Saucers The NG13 178 E7
Saunby Cl NG5 162 B7
SAUNDBY 23 C6
Saundby Ave NG19 87 D1
Saundby Rd DN22 23 D4
Savage's Rd NG11 196 C8
Savages Row NG11 196 C8
Saversick La NG25 136 A8
Savile Rd
Bilsthorpe NG22 105 F6
Bilsthorpe NG22 106 A6
Savile St DN22 39 E6
Saville Cl NG9 182 E8
Saville House Sch NG19 88 B3
Saville Rd
Arnold NG5 161 F5
Sutton in Ashfield NG17 100 F6
Saville St NG21 118 B5
Saville Way NG20 74 A4
SAWLEY 193 A4
Sawley Dr NG18 103 B4
Sawley Jun & Inf Sch
NG10 193 A5
Sawmill La NG8 172 A5
Saw Pit Ind Est DE55 99 C6
Saw Pit La DE55 99 B5
Sawyers Cl NG24 140 B8
Saxby Ct NG11 196 D7
Saxby Dr NG18 103 B4
Saxelby Gdns NG6 160 B8
Saxelbye Rd LE14 219 D2
SAXILBY 56 F4
Saxilby Ent Pk LN1 57 E2
Saxilby Rd
Broxholme LN1 57 D6
Doddington LN6 71 B3
Saxilby LN1 57 A1
Saxilby LN1 57 F2
Skellingthorpe LN6 71 F8
Saxilby Sta LN1 57 A3
SAXONDALE 177 A4
Saxondale Dr
Nottingham NG6 160 E5
Radcliffe on Trent NG12 176 D3
Saxon Gn NG7 222 A1
Saxon Mdw LE14 211 B2
Saxon Way
Cotgrave NG12 188 A1
Harworth DN11 8 F4
Saxton Ave 4 NG16 159 C1
Saxton Cl
Beeston NG9 184 B6
Worksop S80 35 D2
Saxton Ct NG5 162 B7
Scafell Way NG11 195 D7
Scalby Cl NG16 143 D2
Scalford Dr NG8 172 C4
Scampton Rd S81 35 D8
Scampton Way DN21 24 F7
Scarborough Rd NG22 105 F6
Scarborough St NG3 223 F3
Scarbrough Cl DN11 8 A7
Scarcliffe Ct NG17 100 F3
Scarcliffe La NG20 72 C7
Scarcliffe St NG18 102 D6
Scarcliffe Terr NG20 59 A2
Scarfell Cl NG2 186 C5
Scarf Wlk NG2 185 B7
Scargill Ave NG16 144 B1
Scargill Cl NG16 144 B1
Scargill Wlk NG16 143 F3
Scarle La LN6 84 C3
Scarlet Way NG20 72 D2
SCARRINGTON 178 F8
Scarrington Ct 1
NG18 103 A2
Scarrington Rd
Hawksworth NG13 167 B2
West Bridgford NG2 173 F1
Sceptre St NG5 161 C2
Scholars Place S80 46 F8
Scholars Way NG22 105 F6
School Ave NG15 145 D4
School Cl
Newton DE55 99 B3
Nottingham NG2 173 D1
School Gdns NG25 134 B3
School Gn LE12 205 E1
School Hill NG15 130 B8
School House La DN10 13 F6
School La
Beckingham LN5 142 D8
Beeston NG9 183 C4
Bingham NG13 177 E5
Caunton NG23 109 B4
Claypole NG23 156 E7
Colston Bassett NG12 200 D7
Cuckney NG20 59 F3
Cuckney NG20 60 A3
Eakring NG22 92 E1
East Stoke NG23 153 C8
School La *continued*
Farndon NG24 139 A4
Halam NG22 121 A3
Harby LE14 202 A3
Kirklington NG22 120 F7
Kneesall NG22 93 F5
Long Clawson LE14 211 C3
Mansfield Woodhouse NG19 88 C3
North Scarle LN6 83 D2
Norwell NG23 110 A8
Ollerton NG22 77 B3
Rempstone LE12 215 D5
Saxilby LN1 57 A1
Saxilby LN1 70 F8
South Normanton DE55 113 B4
Whatton NG13 179 B3
School Rd
Langold S81 16 E3
Selston NG16 129 A7
School St
Kirkby-in-Ashfield NG17 115 B5
Loughborough LE11 220 B4
School View NG13 181 A2
School Wlk
Bawtry DN10 10 A7
Bestwood Village NG6 146 E4
School Woods Cl DE75 157 B6
Schrimshire's Rd
North Leverton with Habblesthorpe DN22 32 A1
North Leverton with Habblesthorpe DN22 42 A8
Schrog Hill DN22 41 B8
Science Rd NG7 172 D1
Scofton Cl S81 35 C8
Scolars Way NG19 102 D5
Scollins Ct 4 DE7 157 E2
Scotholme Ave 7 NG7 172 F8
Scotholme Prim Sch
NG7 172 F8
Scot La DN10 10 A7
Scotland Bank NG12 187 F3
Scotland Rd NG5 160 F3
Scotswood Rd NG19 88 B6
Scott Ave NG9 184 A5
Scott Cl
Claypole NG23 156 D7
Nottingham NG6 159 F5
Worksop S81 36 C4
Scotton Sq DN22 29 D1
Scott St DN21 15 C1
Scotts Way NG17 115 B1
Scratta La S80 34 C2
SCREVETON 166 E4
Screveton Rd
Car Colston NG13 166 C3
Hawksworth NG13 167 B3
Scrimshire La NG12 187 E3
Script Dr NG6 160 E4
Scrivelsby Gdns NG9 183 D4
SCROOBY 10 A2
Scrooby Cl DN11 9 A4
Scrooby Rd
Bircotes DN11 9 C4
Harworth DN11 8 F3
Seaburn Rd NG9 182 E2
Seacroft NG24 140 E8
Seaford Ave NG8 172 B5
Seaforth Sq NG19 101 D5
Seagrave Ave NG17 115 B1
Seagrave Prim Sch
NG8 159 D2
Seagrave Rd NG8 159 D1
Seamer Rd NG16 158 F7
Sean Upton Cl NG9 183 D3
Searby Rd NG17 101 C1
Searwood Ave NG17 114 E7
Seatallen Cl NG2 186 C6
Seathwaite Cl NG2 186 D4
Seatoller Cl NG2 186 C5
Seaton Cres NG8 160 A1
Seaton Way NG5 162 D5
Second Ave
Beeston NG9 184 C6
Carlton, Gedling NG4 162 F1
Carlton, Thorneywood NG4 174 C8
Clipstone NG21 90 A3
Edwinstowe NG21 76 A2
Mansfield NG21 103 F2
Mansfield Woodhouse NG19 89 A1
Nottingham NG6 160 B7
Sedbergh Cl NG13 177 B8
Sedgebrook Cl NG6 160 C3
Sedgebrook St NG19 88 E3
Sedgeley Rd NG12 186 D1
Sedgewood Gr NG11 184 E3
Sedgley Ave NG2 173 F5
Sedgmere DN22 39 D4
Sedgwick Cl NG16 113 D2
Sedgwick St
Langley Mill NG16 143 B3
Westwood NG16 128 B3
Sedley Ave NG16 159 C6
Seely Ave NG14 148 E8
Seely Jun Sch NG5 161 C3
Seely Prim Sch NG5 161 C3
Seely Rd NG7 222 C3
Sefton Ave NG9 182 E8
Sefton Dr NG3 161 D2
Selassie Ct NG8 159 D2
Selborne Gdns NG14 173 E6
Selbourne Ct 4 LE11 220 C4
Selbourne St LE11 220 C4
Selby Cl NG9 182 E3
Selby La NG12 197 F2
Selby Rd
Styrrup DN11 8 E2
Selby Rd *continued*
West Bridgford NG2 185 F5
Selhurst Ct NG7 172 F7
Selhurst St 5 NG7 172 F7
Selkirk Way 13 NG5 161 B1
Sellars Ave NG11 196 C6
Seller's Wood Dr NG6 160 A7
Seller's Wood Dr W
NG6 159 F8
Sellers Wood Nature Reserve* NG6 159 E7
Selsby Cl NG16 159 C2
Selsey Ct DN22 29 E1
Selside Ct NG9 183 A4
SELSTON 128 E7
Selston CE Inf Sch
NG16 128 E6
Selston Cl DN11 9 A3
Selston Dr NG8 172 C3
Selston High Sch NG16 128 F7
Selston L Ctr NG16 128 E7
Selston Rd NG16 128 B5
Selwyn Cl NG6 160 E5
Selwyn St NG18 102 E5
Senator Cl NG15 146 C8
Sennen Ct DN22 29 E1
Sentinel Dr
Annesley Woodhouse NG15 130 A6
Annesley Woodhouse NG16 129 F5
Serif Cl NG5 161 B1
Serina Ct NG9 184 B7
Serlby Pk DN10 18 D8
Serlby Pk Acad
Bircotes DN11 8 B4
Bircotes DN11 9 C5
Serlby Pk Dr DN11 9 C4
Serlby Rd
Eastwood NG16 144 A3
Styrrup DN11 9 A2
Serlby Rise NG3 173 F6
Serotine Rd S81 35 B7
Serpentine Cl NG12 176 D2
Service Rd NG16 143 F3
Seven Hills NG24 125 A3
Seven Oaks Cres NG9 171 C1
Seven Oaks Rd DE7 170 A1
Seventh Ave
Beeston NG9 184 C5
Clipstone NG21 89 E2
Mansfield NG19 103 A8
Severals NG9 182 F7
Severn St NG6 160 B7
Seward St 2 LE11 220 A3
Seymour Cl 18 DE7 157 F5
Seymour Rd
Eastwood NG16 143 F1
Hucknall NG15 145 E5
West Bridgford NG2 186 B8
Seymour St NG3 173 E5
SGCS Bsns Pk NG11 184 A5
Shackleton Cl NG8 159 D2
Shacklock Cl NG5 147 A2
Shadwell Gr NG12 175 E3
Shady La NG9 183 D2
Shaftesbury Ave
Burton Joyce NG14 164 A5
Long Eaton NG10 193 B4
Mansfield NG19 87 E2
Radcliffe on Trent NG12 176 E3
Sandiacre NG10 182 A5
Shaftesbury St 4 NG7 161 A1
Shaftesbury Way NG23 98 A1
Shakespeare Ave NG19 88 B4
Shakespeare Cl NG4 174 E5
Shakespeare Rd NG16 158 C5
Shakespeare St
Gainsborough DN21 24 D6
Long Eaton NG10 182 D1
Loughborough LE11 220 B4
New Balderton NG24 140 B6
Nottingham NG1 223 E3
Worksop S81 36 B4
Shakespeare Villas
NG1 223 E3
Shaldon Cl
Arnold NG5 162 D5
Nottingham NG5 146 F1
Shale La NG14 152 A8
Shandwick Cl NG5 148 B1
Shanklin Dr NG9 182 D7
Shanwell Cl NG8 159 D2
Shardlow Way NG18 103 B4
Sharnford Way NG9 171 B3
Sharp Cl NG10 193 C6
Sharpes Wy NG6 147 B5
Sharphill Rd NG12 186 B4
Sharpley Dr LE12 205 F3
Sharrard Cl NG16 129 A2
Sharrat Ct 12 NG18 103 A2
Shaw Cres NG15 145 E4
Shaw Croft NG17 100 F5
Shaw Gdns NG4 175 B8
Shaw Rd
Beeston NG9 183 B2
Gringley on the Hill DN10 12 F3
Gringley on the Hill DN10 12 F4
Shaw St E DE7 170 A6
Shaw St W DE7 170 A6
Shaws Orch NG22 120 F1
Shaw St
Mansfield NG18 102 E7
Ruddington NG11 196 C6
Worksop S80 35 E3
Sheaf Pl S81 35 E7
Shearing Cl NG4 163 A1
Shearing Hill
Carlton NG4 163 A1
Carlton NG4 175 A7
Shearsby Dr NG19 88 F2
Sheepbridge La NG18 101 F5
Sheepfold La NG11 196 C6
Sheepwalk La
Ravenshead NG15 116 F2
Ravenshead NG15 116 F3
Sheepwash La
Sutton in Ashfield NG17 101 B2
Tickhill DN11 8 E8
Sheepwash Way LE12 214 E8
Sheerness Cl NG16 158 B7
Sheet Stores Ind Est
NG10 193 D5
Sheffield Rd
Blyth S81 17 F3
Blyth S81 18 A3
Kettlethorpe LN1 55 F1
Kettlethorpe LN1 56 B1
Shelby Cl NG7 222 A2
Sheldon Cl
Long Eaton NG10 182 B3
New Cross NG17 100 E4
Sheldrake Rd NG24 140 D8
SHELFORD 164 C1
Shelford Ave NG17 114 D6
Shelford Cl
Beeston NG9 183 D4
Radcliffe on Trent NG12 176 A4
Shelford Cres NG14 164 A5
Shelford Dr NG13 177 D4
Shelford Hill
Mansfield NG19 101 E6
Radcliffe on Trent NG12 176 C7
Shelford Rd
Carlton NG4 162 D3
Newton NG13 165 A1
Newton NG13 177 A8
Radcliffe on Trent NG12 176 A5
Shelford NG13 164 F1
Shelford Rise NG3 174 A5
Shellburne Cl NG5 160 E8
Shelley Ave
Mansfield Woodhouse NG19 88 B4
Nottingham NG11 184 E3
Shelley Cl
Balderton NG24 140 D3
Hucknall NG15 145 D6
Kirkby-in-Ashfield NG17 115 C7
Nuthall NG16 159 B6
Shelley Rd NG5 161 D7
Shelley St S80 36 A3
Shelthorpe Ave LE11 220 B1
Shelthorpe Com Sch
LE11 220 C1
Shelthorpe Rd LE11 220 B1
SHELTON 168 C6
Shelton Ave
Hucknall NG15 146 D4
Newark-on-Trent NG24 139 E5
Shelton Cl NG19 87 E1
Shelton Gdns
Cropwell Bishop NG12 189 B5
Ruddington NG11 196 B7
Shelton La NG13 168 C4
Shelton Rd
Mansfield NG18 103 A2
Thoroton NG23 167 F3
Shelton St NG3 223 F4
Shenfield Gdns NG5 146 D1
Shepard Cl NG6 159 F6
Shepherds Ave S81 35 F5
Shepherd's Ave S81 36 A5
Shepherds Cl NG8 172 A7
Shepherd's Cl LE12 213 C5
Shepherds Oak NG17 100 F6
Shepherd St NG6 145 E2
Shepherds Way NG17 101 B2
Shepherds Wood Dr
NG8 172 C7
Shepherd Wlk DE74 203 C1
Sheppards Ct NG13 181 A2
Shepshed Rd LE12 212 F1
Shepton Cl DE7 157 D3
Shepton Cres NG8 160 B1
Sheraton Dr NG8 171 E3
Sherborne Rd
Nottingham NG8 160 A1
West Bridgford NG2 185 F5
Sherbrook Ave NG5 161 D6
Sherbrook Cl NG14 148 E8
Sherbrooke Rd NG5 161 B1
Sherbrook Rd NG5 161 D6
Sherbrook Terr NG5 161 D6
Sheridan Cl NG24 140 D5
Sheridan Ct NG9 170 F1
Sheridan Wy
Hucknall NG15 146 A5
Nottingham NG5 161 A3
Sheriff's Lodge The*
NG1 223 F1
Sheriffs Way NG2 173 C2
Sheringham Cl NG5 161 F6
Sheringham Dr NG18 102 C5
Sherman Dr NG9 183 C2
Sherriff's Lea NG9 182 E2
Sherrington Cl NG11 195 C8
Sherview Ave NG18 103 A7
Sherwin Cl NG3 223 E4
Sherwin Gr NG7 222 A1
Sherwin Rd
Nottingham NG7 222 A1
Stapleford NG9 170 F1
Stapleford NG9 182 E8
Sherwin Wlk NG3 223 E4
SHERWOOD 161 B3
Sherwood Ave
Blidworth NG21 118 C5
Calverton NG14 148 D8

Sherwood Ave *continued*
Edwinstowe NG21 76 A2
Mansfield NG18 103 B3
Newark-on-Trent NG24 140 A8
5 Nottingham NG5 161 D3
Pinxton NG16 113 D3
Shirebrook NG20 72 E4
Sherwood Bsns Pk NG15 129 F6
Sherwood Cl NG18 102 E7
Sherwood Cres S81 18 A2
Sherwood Ct
Beeston NG9 183 C3
Long Whatton LE12 212 A4
Sherwood Dene 8 NG17 114 E1
Sherwood Dr
New Ollerton NG22 77 C4
Shirebrook NG20 72 E3
Worksop S80 47 F8
Worksop S80 48 A8
Sherwood Energy Village★ NG22 77 C3
Sherwood Forest Art & Craft Ctr★ NG21 76 A3
Sherwood Forest Ctry Pk★ NG22 76 A4
Sherwood Forest Farm Pk★ NG20 89 F7
Sherwood Forest Fun Pk★ NG22 76 B4
Sherwood Forest Railway★ NG21 89 F7
Sherwood Gr
Bingham NG13 177 D4
Calverton NG14 148 F8
Sherwood Hall Gdns NG18 102 F8
Sherwood Hall Rd NG18 102 E7
Sherwood Heath Nature Reserve★ NG22 76 F4
Sherwood Jun Sch NG20 74 B3
Sherwood Lodge Dr NG5 132 C2
Sherwood Oaks Bsns Pk NG18 103 B3
Sherwood Oaks Cl NG18 103 B3
Sherwood Pines Forest Pk★ NG21 90 E3
Sherwood Pl
Annesley Woodhouse NG17 115 A1
Clipstone NG21 90 B4
Sherwood Rd
Harworth DN11 8 F5
Rainworth NG21 104 B1
Retford DN22 39 E3
Sutton in Ashfield NG17 100 E1
Worksop S80 35 F4
Sherwood Rise
Annesley Woodhouse NG17 115 A1
Eastwood NG16 143 F1
Mansfield Woodhouse NG19 88 A2
Nottingham NG7 173 B8
Sherwood St
Annesley Woodhouse NG17 130 A8
Hucknall NG15 146 C6
Huthwaite NG17 99 F3
Kirkby-in-Ashfield NG17 115 B5
10 Mansfield NG18 102 B6
Mansfield Woodhouse NG19 88 B2
Market Warsop NG20 74 B3
Newton DE55 99 B4
Sherwood Vale NG5 161 E3
Sherwood Way NG16 129 B7
Sherwood Way S NG17 101 E2
Sherwood Way South NG18 102 B1
Sherwood Wlk NG15 131 A2
Shetland Cl
Mansfield Woodhouse NG19 88 F1
Shirebrook NG20 72 D2
Shet Land Cl 3 NG19 88 F1
Shetlands The
Retford DN22 29 F1
Retford DN22 30 A1
Shilling Rd NG18 102 D1
Shilling Way NG10 193 A7
Shilo Way NG16 158 B4
Shiners Way DE55 113 A6
Shining Cliff Ct DN10 9 F8
SHIPLEY 157 B6
Shipley Cl NG5 162 C8
Shipley Ct DE7 157 D1
Shipley Ctry Pk★ DE75 157 A4
Shipley Rd NG8 159 F2
Shipley Rise NG4 174 E7
Shipstone St
Ilkeston DE7 170 B6
3 Nottingham NG7 172 F8
Shipstones Yard NG6 160 C8
Shipstones Yd NG6 160 C8
Shirburn Ave NG18 102 C8
SHIREBROOK 72 F3
Shirebrook Acad NG20 72 D5
Shirebrook Bsns Pk NG20 72 F2
Shirebrook Cl DE7 157 F6
Shirebrooke Cl NG6 160 C3
Shirebrook Sta NG20 73 A4
Shire Cl S81 26 A7
Shire La NG23, NG24 156 B7
SHIREOAKS 34 E6
Shireoaks Comm
Shireoaks S81 34 F7
Shireoaks S81 35 A7
Shireoaks Ct 2 NG18 103 A2
Shireoaks Rd S80 35 B5
Shireoaks Row S81 34 E7
Shireoaks Sta S81 34 E7
Shireoak Triangle Bsns Pk S81 35 A7
Shires The
Mansfield Woodhouse NG19 88 F1
Sutton in Ashfield NG17 100 D1
Shires Way NG23 96 F7
Shirland Cl DE7 157 F5
Shirland Dr NG18 103 B4
Shirley Dr NG5 162 B7
Shirley Rd NG3 173 C8
Shirley St NG10 193 A4
Shoreswood Cl 1 NG5 161 B8
Shortcross Ave NG3 161 F4
Short Hill NG1 223 F2
Shortleys Rd DN22 54 D8
Short St
Market Warsop NG20 74 B4
Sutton in Ashfield NG17 101 A3
Short Wheatley La NG23 112 B5
Shortwood Ave NG15 145 F5
Shortwood Cl NG1 223 F1
Shortwood La NG22 93 C8
Shorwell Rd NG3 174 C7
Shotton Dr NG5 148 A2
Shoulder of Mutton Hill NG17 115 B1
Shrewsbury Rd
Bircotes DN11 9 B4
Nottingham NG2 174 A4
Worksop S80 36 B2
Shrewsbury View DN22 29 C1
Shrimpton Ct NG11 196 D6
Shropshire Ave NG16 128 C4
Sibcy La NG24 140 D3
Sibson Dr DE74 203 B2
Sibson Wlk NG5 147 F2
SIBTHORPE 167 E7
Sibthorpe Hill DN22 65 C7
Sibthorpe Rd NG13 167 D5
Sibthorpe St NG18 102 A5
Sidbury Cl NG5 162 E5
Siddalls Dr NG17 100 B3
Side La NG22 106 E8
Side Ley DE74 203 C3
Side Row NG24 140 B8
Sidings La NG8 171 A3
Sidings Rd NG17 115 C7
Sidings The
Aslockton NG13 179 A4
Kimberley NG16 159 A6
Lowdham NG14 164 E8
Mansfield Woodhouse NG19 88 A3
5 Newark-on-Trent NG24 140 B8
Saxilby LN1 57 A3
Sidlaw Rise NG5 147 B2
Sidmouth Cl NG12 197 E4
Sidney Rd NG9 183 E7
Sidney St
Kimberley NG16 158 F6
Long Eaton NG10 193 D6
Sidsaph Hill
Walkeringham DN10 13 F5
Walkeringham DN10 14 A5
Siena Gdn NG19 89 A2
Signal Rd LE14 219 A5
Signal Way NG19 88 B3
Sikorski Cl NG24 124 F1
Silbury Cl NG11 195 D7
Silken Holme DE55 113 B4
Silk St NG17 100 E1
Silver Birch Cl NG6 160 B4
Silverdale NG9 182 E5
Silverdale Ave NG19 88 B4
Silverdale Cl DN22 29 C1
Silverdale Rd NG7 160 F2
Silver Hill Cl NG8 159 D2
Silverhill Cotts NG17 100 A8
Silverhill La NG17 99 F8
Silverhow Cl NG2 186 C6
Silver St
Gainsborough DN21 24 C8
Grassthorpe NG23 81 F4
North Clifton NG23 68 E5
Retford DN22 39 D5
Silverwood Ave NG15 117 A1
Silverwood Rd
Beeston NG9 183 E6
Bottesford NG13 181 A2
Silvey Ave NG25 121 D2
Sime St S80 35 E4
Simkin Ave
Nottingham NG3 162 A1
Porchester NG5 162 A1
Simon Cl DN22 42 B1
Simone Gdns NG7 184 E1
Simons Ct NG9 171 D1
Simpson Cl NG24 140 E3
Simpson Dr NG12 189 B4
Simpson Rd NG19 101 D7
Simpson Wlk 4 DN11 8 F5
Singleton Ave NG18 102 E8
Sir Donald Bailey Academy The
Newark-on-Trent NG24 139 F5
Newark-on-Trent NG24 140 A5
Sir Edmund Hillary Prim Sch S81 36 A4
Sir John Robinson Wy NG5 161 E6
Sir John Sherbrooke Jun Sch NG14 148 E8
Sir Thomas Ave DN21 24 E6
Siskin Cl NG9 183 C6
Siskin Ct S81 35 C7
Siskin Dr LE12 206 A3
Sisley Ave NG9 182 E6
Sitwell Cl S81 36 B4
Sitwell Rd S81 36 C4
Six Hills La LE14 219 A2
Six Hills Rd LE14 219 E3
Sixth Ave
Beeston NG9 184 D6
Clipstone NG21 89 E3
Edwinstowe NG21 75 F1
Edwinstowe NG21 76 A1
Mansfield NG19 103 A8
Skeavington's La DE7 157 E5
SKEGBY 100 E6
Skegby Hall Gdns NG17 100 F6
Skegby Jun Acad NG17 100 D7
Skegby La NG17, NG19 101 C6
Skegby Mount NG19 101 E5
Skegby Rd
Annesley Woodhouse NG17 129 F8
Huthwaite NG17 100 A3
Normanton on T NG23 81 C7
Sutton in Ashfield NG17 101 A4
SKELLINGTHORPE 71 F3
Skellingthorpe Rd
Saxilby LN1 57 D2
Saxilby LN6 71 E8
Skelwith Cl NG2 186 C5
Skerry Hill NG18 102 E7
Skerry La NG13 181 F1
Sketchley Ct 2 NG6 160 A7
Sketchley St NG3 173 F6
Skiddaw Cl NG2 186 D5
Skipper Cl LE12 214 E8
Skipton Cir NG3 174 A5
Skipton Cl DE7 157 D3
Skirbeck Dr LN1 57 A3
Skithorne Rise NG14 164 D8
Skylark Cl
Arnold NG15 132 A8
Bingham NG13 177 F3
Skylark Dr NG6 160 D4
Skylark Hill NG12 188 E2
Skylark Ri NG9 170 E2
Skylarks Nature Reserve★ NG12 175 A3
Skylark Way NG21 89 F4
Sky Wlk NG18 102 E1
Slack Rd DE7 157 A3
Slack's La
Flintham NG23 152 E1
Flintham NG23 166 D8
Kneeton NG13 152 B2
Slack Wlk S80 35 E1
Slade Cl DE55 113 B4
Slade Rd NG9 183 B5
Slaidburn Ave NG11 185 A5
Slake La NG24 124 E6
Slalom Run NG5 162 C1
Slant La NG19 88 B4
Slater St NG17 100 F4
Slaters Way 1 NG5 160 F5
Slaughter House La NG24 124 F1
Slaynes La DN10 11 A8
Sleaford Rd
Beckingham LN5 142 E8
Beckingham NG24 127 B1
Coddington NG24 126 D2
Newark-on-Trent NG24 125 A1
Winthorpe NG24 125 F4
Sleath Dr NG23 110 B2
Sleights La NG16 113 C2
Slim Dr NG4 162 D4
Slingsby Gdns NG13 177 B8
Sloan Dr NG9 171 B3
Sloane Ct NG11 185 C3
Sloswicke Dr DN22 29 C2
Slowthorne Gdns 2 NG5 161 D8
Smalley Cl NG16 129 A1
Small Farm Centre★ NG13 202 E7
Small Gate NG19 88 E6
Small's Croft NG14 149 C4
Smeath La DN22 30 C4
Smeath Rd
Retford DN22 30 A3
Selston NG16 129 A2
Smedley Ave DE7 170 A7
Smedley Cl NG8 160 B2
Smedley's Ave NG10 182 B5
Smeeton St DE75 143 B1
Smew Rd NG4 175 C7
Smite Cl NG13 179 A4
Smite La NG13 179 E7
Smith Dr NG16 143 A3
Smithfield Ave NG9 170 D4
Smiths Cl NG12 189 A4
Smithson Cl NG24 140 C4
Smithson Dr NG8 171 E4
Smith Sq DN11 8 F4
Smith St
Mansfield NG18 102 E6
Newark-on-Trent NG24 140 A8
Smithurst Rd NG16 158 B7
Smithy Cl
Nottingham NG11 184 D2
Woodborough NG14 149 C3
Smithy Cres NG5 161 F8
Smithy La LE12 212 A2
Smithy Row
Nottingham NG1 223 E2
Sutton in Ashfield NG17 100 D2
Smithy View
Calverton NG14 148 E7
Killarney Park NG6 147 B5
Smythson Green LN6 71 C1
Snaefell Ave NG19 89 A2
Snape La
Ranskill DN22 19 A6
Scrooby DN10 18 E7
Styrrup DN11 9 A2
Snape Nook Ct NG6 159 F7
Snape Wood Prim Sch NG6 160 A7
Snape Wood Rd NG6 159 F7
Snead Ct NG5 147 A1
SNEINTON 173 E4
Sneinton Bvd NG2 174 A4
Sneinton Dale NG2 174 A5
Sneinton Hermitage
Nottingham NG2 173 E3
Nottingham NG7 222 F1
Sneinton Hollows NG2 173 F4
Sneinton Rd NG2 173 E4
Sneinton St Stephen's CE Prim Sch NG2 173 F5
Snell Cl NG23 81 E1
Snipe Pk Rd DN11 9 B4
Snowden Dr DN22 40 A3
Snowdon Cl 2 NG5 147 B1
Snowdon Rd NG23 112 A8
Snowdrop Ave NG24 125 E1
Snowdrop Cl NG15 146 D4
Snowdrop Dr NG19 88 F4
Snowdrop Gdns S81 25 F7
Soarbank Cl NG16 158 E7
Soar La
Normanton on S LE12 213 D3
Ratcliffe on Soar NG11 203 F7
Sutton Bonington LE12 212 F8
Sobers Gdns NG5 162 B6
Softwood Cl NG6 159 F7
Softwood Mws NG8 172 A6
Soloman Pk NG16 158 B2
Soloman Rd NG16 158 B2
Solway Cl NG9 183 E5
Somerby Ct NG9 171 B3
Somerby Rd DN21 15 F1
Somerleyton Dr DE7 170 A4
Somersall St NG19 101 E8
Somersby Ct NG18 103 B5
Somersby Rd NG5 162 A5
Somerset Cl NG10 194 A8
Somerton Ave NG11 185 A4
Somerton Rd S81 35 C8
Songthrush Ave NG6 160 D4
Sookholme Cl NG20 72 F3
Sookholme Dr NG20 74 A3
Sookholme La NG20 73 E3
Sookholme Rd
Market Warsop NG20 73 E1
Shirebrook NG20 72 F3
Sophie Rd NG7 222 B4
Sorrel Dr
Bingham NG13 177 C4
Kirkby-in-Ashfield NG17 115 A3
7 Shireoaks S81 35 A7
Sorrell Sq NG21 89 F4
Soss La DN10 7 B2
Sotheby Ave NG17 101 C1
Soudan Dr NG2 173 B1
Sough Rd DE55 113 B7
Southampton St NG3 173 E6
South Ave
Bawtry DN10 10 A8
Radcliffe on Trent NG12 176 B3
Rainworth NG21 104 A1
Shirebrook NG20 72 F3
Worksop S80 36 B1
Southbreck Rise S80 36 B1
Southchurch Dr NG7 184 F2
Southcliffe Rd NG4 174 D7
SOUTH CLIFTON 68 E1
South Cres
Bottesford NG13 181 A1
Clipstone NG21 90 A3
South Croft NG22 51 F2
Southdale Dr NG4 174 D7
Southdale Rd NG4 174 D7
Southdene S81 36 A6
South Devon Ave NG3 162 B2
South Dr NG22 105 F7
South End NG23 111 F7
Southend Ave NG24 139 F7
Southern Wood S80 46 E8
Southey St NG7 222 C4
Southfall Cl DN22 19 B5
Southfield NG24 140 E3
Southfield Dr DE55 113 C5
Southfield Gr NG13 177 E3
Southfield Ind Est S80 45 A4
Southfield La
Beckingham DN10 23 C8
Whitwell S80 45 A4
Southfield Rd NG8 172 D6
Southfields NG10 193 E7
Southfields Ave NG16 113 D4
Southfields Cl NG17 114 E1
Southfields Ct NG9 183 B5
Southfields Rise DN22 42 C8
Southgate DN22 39 E3
Southgate Rd NG20 74 C5
Southglade Food Pk NG5 160 E6
Southglade L Ctr NG5 160 F7
Southglade Prim Sch NG5 161 A7
Southglade Rd NG5 160 F6
Southgore La DN22 42 D8
Southgreen Cl NG18 102 E2
Southgreen Hill NG18 102 E2
South La NG23 81 E5
Southlands NG17 100 E4
Southlands Ave DN21 15 B4
Southlands Dr DN21 15 B4
Southlands Gdns DN21 15 B4
Southlea Rd NG4 174 D7
SOUTH LEVERTON 42 C6
Southmoor La LN1 69 B7
Southmoor Rd
Newton on Trent LN1 55 C1
Newton on Trent LN1 69 A8
Worksop S80 36 B1
South Moor Rd DN10 13 F6
SOUTH MUSKHAM 124 D7
SOUTH NORMANTON 113 A7
South Nottingham Coll
Nottingham NG1 223 E1
Nottingham NG4 223 F1
South Nottinghamshire Acad NG12 176 A3
Southolme DN21 24 D8
South Par
Bawtry DN10 10 A6
Gainsborough DN21 24 F7
Nottingham NG1 223 E2
Saxilby LN1 57 A4
Worksop S81 36 A4
Southpark Ave NG18 102 F2
Southport Terr 4 NG7 172 E7
South Rd
Beeston NG9 184 B4
Nottingham NG5 161 B4
Nottingham, Dunkirk NG7 172 D2
Nottingham, The Park NG7 222 C1
West Bridgford NG2 185 E6
West Burton DN22 32 E7
South Ridge Dr NG18 102 D3
SOUTH SCARLE 98 C5
Southscarle La LN6 83 E2
South Scarle La
North Scarle LN6 83 D1
South Scarle LN6 98 F5
South Scarle Rd NG23 98 B2
South Sherwood St NG1 223 E3
Southside NG5 162 C7
South Snape Cl NG6 159 F7
South St
Bole DN22 23 E2
Eastwood, Bailey Grove NG16 143 E2
Eastwood, Giltbrook NG16 158 C8
Hucknall NG15 146 A7
Long Eaton NG10 193 E7
Loughborough LE11 220 B3
Morton DN21 15 B4
Normanton on T NG23 81 E6
Retford DN22 39 F6
South Normanton DE55 113 B6
South View
Austerfield DN10 3 C1
Whitwell S80 45 A5
Worksop S81 35 F5
South View Dr DN22 30 D3
Southview Gdns NG15 117 A2
South View Rd NG4 162 D1
Southwark Prim Sch NG6 160 E4
Southwark St NG6 160 E3
SOUTHWELL 121 C1
Southwell Cl
East Leake LE12 205 E1
Kirkby-in-Ashfield NG17 115 A6
Worksop S80 36 A2
Southwell Gdns NG18 103 A4
Southwell La NG17 114 F6
Southwell La Ind Est NG17 115 A7
Southwell L Ctr NG25 136 D7
Southwell Minster★ NG25 136 E8
Southwell Rd
Farnsfield NG22 120 A5
Halloughton NG25 135 F3
Halloughton NG25 136 B3
Kirklington NG22 120 F7
Kirklington NG25 121 A5
Lowdham NG14 150 F2
Nottingham NG1 223 F2
Oxton NG25 134 D4
Thurgarton NG14 151 D8
Upton NG25 122 B1
Southwell Rd E
Mansfield NG21 103 E2
Rainworth NG21 118 B8
Southwell Rd W NG18 102 E5
Southwell Rise
Eastwood NG16 158 B7
Giltbrook NG16 158 C8
SOUTH WILFORD ENDOWED CE VA Prim Sch NG11 185 B7
Southwold Dr NG8 172 C5
Southwold Prim Sch & Early Years Centre NG8 172 D5
South Wolds Com Sch NG12 197 E3
Southwood Ave NG17 100 D4
South Yorkshire Aviation Mus★ S81 16 B7
Sovereign Gr NG10 193 B7
Sovereign Gdns NG16 129 A7
Sovereign Way
Mansfield NG18 103 B4
Worksop S81 25 D1
Sowter Ave NG17 100 E4
Spa Cl NG17 114 F8
Spa Common 2 DN22 39 F6
Spafford Cl DN21 44 D8
Spa La
Mansfield Woodhouse NG19 88 F3
Orston NG13 180 B7
Spalding Rd NG3 173 F5
SPALFORD 83 B7
Spalford La LN6 83 D4
Spalford Rd LN6 83 E5
Spalford Warren Nature Reserve★ LN6 83 A5
Spang La NG17 99 F4
Spaniel Row
Nottingham NG1 223 E2
Nottingham NG14 173 C4
Spa Ponds Nature Reserve★ NG19 89 C4
Spa Rd DN22 39 F6
Sparken Cl S80 46 E8
Sparken Dale S80 46 E8
Sparken Hill Acad S80 46 F8
Sparrow Cl DE7 170 A4
Sparrow Gr S81 35 B7
Sparrow Hill 6 LE11 220 B4
Sparrow Lane NG23 68 B1
Spartans Cl NG17 114 E7
Spean Ct 4 NG8 172 A5
Spean Dr NG8 172 B7
Speeds Pingle 1 LE11 220 A4
Speedwell Cl
Bingham NG13 177 C4
Newark-on-Trent NG24 125 E1
Speedwell La NG16 158 E6
Speedwell Pl S80 35 E4
Speight Cl NG24 125 C6
Spencer Ave
Arnold NG3 162 C5
Sandiacre NG10 182 B6
Spencer Cl
Ruddington NG11 196 B7
Saxilby LN1 57 C3
Spencer Cres NG9 182 F8
Spencer Dr NG16 159 C6
Spencer St NG18 102 A6
Sperry Cl NG16 128 F6
Spey Cl NG15 145 D3
Spicer Cl NG9 183 C2
Spicers Ct DN22 39 F6
Spindle Ct NG18 101 E5
Spindle Gdns NG6 160 A7
Spindle View NG14 148 F6
Spinella Rd S80 35 C4
Spinners Cl
Mansfield NG18 101 E5
South Normanton DE55 113 C6
Spinners Way NG24 140 A4
Spinney Cl
Cotgrave NG12 187 F2
Kirkby-in-Ashfield NG17 114 E6
Mansfield Woodhouse NG19 88 E6
Newark-on-Trent NG24 139 E6
West Bridgford NG2 186 C4
Spinney Cres NG9 182 F3
Spinney Dr NG10 182 C2
Spinneymead DN22 19 B5
Spinney Rd
Bingham NG13 177 D4
Keyworth NG12 197 E3
Long Eaton NG10 182 C2
Spinney Rise NG9 182 E3
Spinney The
Arnold NG5 161 E4
Bestwood Village NG6 146 E5
Bulcote NG14 164 B5
Elston NG23 153 D5
Farnsfield NG22 119 E6
14 Gainsborough DN21 15 F2
Mansfield NG18 116 D7
Shirebrook NG20 72 D3
Winthorpe NG24 125 C5
Spinney Way NG11 185 A4
Spinningdale NG5 162 B8
Spinning Dr NG5 161 C5
Spion Pk Mws NG20 73 F2
Spire Cl NG17 129 E8
Spire Gdns NG24 125 B3
Spire Nottingham Hospl (Private) NG12 186 F5
Spire View
Bottesford NG13 181 B3
Long Eaton NG10 193 B4
Spitalfields S81 18 B2
Spital Hill
Gainsborough DN21 15 D1
Gainsborough DN21 15 E1
Retford DN22 39 F7
Spital Rd S81 18 B1
Spital Terr DN21 15 D1
Spitfire Way NG15 145 D3
Spondon St NG5 161 C2
Sporton Cl DE55 113 A7
Sporton La
South Normanton DE55 113 A7
South Normanton DE55 113 B7
Spotlight Gall (Town Hall)★ NG24 139 F8
Spray Cl NG4 174 E5
Spridgeon Cl NG10 182 B2
Springbank Prim Sch NG16 143 E2
Spring Cl
Kimberley NG16 159 A7
1 Kirkby-in-Ashfield NG17 115 A4
West Bridgford NG12 185 D5
Spring Ct NG22 119 E7
Spring Dale Gdns NG9 170 D3
Springdale La NG13 165 E2

Spring Dr NG24 . . . 140 F2
Springfield DE74 . . . 203 B1
Springfield Ave
Eastwood NG16 . . . 144 A2
Long Eaton NG10 . . . 193 F8
Sandiacre NG10 . . . 182 B3
Shirebrook NG20 . . . 72 E5
Springfield Cl
Cropwell Bishop NG12 . . . 189 B4
Gainsborough DN21 . . . 24 E8
Mansfield NG18 . . . 103 A5
Springfield Ct NG9 . . . 170 E1
Springfield Dr NG6 . . . 159 F6
Springfield Gdn DE7 . . . 157 F2
Springfield Pastures
NG14 . . . 173 D8
Springfield Prim Sch
NG6 . . . 146 C1
Springfield Rd
Arnold NG5 . . . 147 E1
Hucknall NG15 . . . 145 D6
Retford DN22 . . . 39 F8
Retford DN22 . . . 40 A8
Southwell NG25 . . . 121 D2
Springfield Ret Pk
NG6 . . . 160 C8
Springfields NG2 . . . 185 D6
Springfield St NG7 . . . 160 F1
Springfield Way NG17 . 115 D6
Spring Gdns
Bawtry DN10 . . . 10 A8
Gainsborough DN21 . . . 24 D8
Newark-on-Trent NG24 . 139 E7
Nottingham NG8 . . . 171 C7
Spring Gdn Terr DE7 . . . 157 F2
Spring Gn NG11 . . . 195 E7
Springhead Ct NG6 . . . 160 A6
Spring Hill
Kimberley NG16 . . . 158 F5
Mansfield Woodhouse
NG19 . . . 88 B3
Southwell NG25 . . . 136 F7
Southwell NG25 . . . 137 A7
Whitwell S80 . . . 45 A6
Springhill Cl NG6 . . . 146 B1
Spring La
Arnold NG3 . . . 162 E6
East Bridgford NG13 . . . 166 B2
Elmton NG20 . . . 58 A7
Farnsfield NG22 . . . 119 E7
Flintham NG13 . . . 166 F7
Lambley NG4 . . . 163 B6
Long Whatton LE12 . . . 212 C2
Rhodesia S80 . . . 35 A3
Shireoaks S80 . . . 34 F5
Sturton le Steeple DN22 . . 32 D4
Warsop Vale NG20 . . . 73 C6
Warsop Vale NG20 . . . 73 D3
Wiseton DN10 . . . 21 B8
Springland Farm Cotts
NG16 . . . 159 D6
Spring Mdw
Cotgrave NG12 . . . 188 A3
Kirkby-in-Ashfield NG17 . 114 D3
Tibshelf DE55 . . . 99 B7
Spring Moor NG2 . . . 174 D5
Spring Rd
Nottingham NG6 . . . 160 C7
Sutton in Ashfield NG17 . 100 E2
Springs Rd DN10 . . . 4 D6
Spring St
Hucknall NG15 . . . 146 A7
Whitwell S80 . . . 45 A6
Spring Terr NG16 . . . 159 D5
Spring The NG10 . . . 193 D5
Springthorpe Rd DN21 . . 24 F8
Springvale Rd DN22 . . . 64 E6
Springwell St
Huthwaite NG17 . . . 99 F2
Huthwaite NG17 . . . 100 A2
Spring Wlk S80 . . . 35 E1
Springwood Dr NG19 . . 88 C2
Springwood Gdns NG5 . 161 F3
Springwood View Cl
NG17 . . . 100 C3
Spruce Ave NG16 . . . 128 D6
Spruce Ct S80 . . . 35 B2
Spruce Gdns NG6 . . . 160 A7
Spruce Gr
Hucknall NG15 . . . 146 B4
Kirkby-in-Ashfield NG17 . 115 C6
Sprydon Wlk NG11 . . . 195 F7
Spur Cres
Worksop S80 . . . 36 B1
Worksop S80 . . . 47 B8
Squares Dr NG6 . . . 147 B5
Square The
Beeston NG9 . . . 183 F6
Bestwood Village NG6 . . 146 E4
Bottesford NG13 . . . 181 A3
Costock LE12 . . . 206 C1
Elmton S80 . . . 58 A7
Gotham NG11 . . . 195 B1
Keyworth NG12 . . . 197 E2
Nottingham NG8 . . . 171 E4
Rainworth NG21 . . . 104 B1
Retford DN22 . . . 39 E7
Squires Ave NG6 . . . 160 B8
Squires Cl NG12 . . . 189 B4
Squires Croft NG21 . . . 90 C5
Squires Gr NG13 . . . 177 D6
Squires La NG21 . . . 90 B6
Squires Way NG2 . . . 185 D6
Squirrel Side Rd S81 . . . 35 B7
Squirrel Way 3 LE11 . . 220 A2
Sta App DN21 . . . 24 D8
Stable Cl
East Bridgford NG13 . . . 165 D3
Worksop S81 . . . 36 A7
Stable Yard LN1 . . . 57 A3
Stacey Ave NG5 . . . 160 F8
Stacey Rd NG19 . . . 87 D2
Stadium Ave NG24 . . . 140 A5
Stadium Cl S81 . . . 35 C6
Stadium Ind Pk NG10 . . 193 F8
Stafford Ave
New Balderton NG24 . . . 140 C4
Nottingham NG6 . . . 160 B6
Stafford Ct NG6 . . . 159 F5
Staffords Acre DE74 . . . 203 C2
Stafford St
Long Eaton NG10 . . . 193 F8
Mansfield NG19 . . . 101 F8
Stagsden Cres NG8 . . . 171 C5
Staindale Dr NG8 . . . 160 D1
Stainforth St NG19 . . . 88 C2
Stainmore Gr NG13 . . . 177 C4
Stainsborough Rd
NG15 . . . 145 C6
Stainsbury Mill* S44 . . 85 D7
STAINSBY . . . 85 B7
Stainsby Dr NG18 . . . 103 A7
Stainsby Gr NG17 . . . 99 F2
Stakeford Ct NG5 . . . 147 F2
Stamford Cl NG10 . . . 193 E4
Stamford Ct 4 NG5 . . . 161 B8
Stamford Rd NG2 . . . 186 A6
Stamford St
Awsworth NG16 . . . 158 C4
Eastwood NG16 . . . 144 C1
2 Ilkeston DE7 . . . 157 E1
Stamper Cres NG17 . . . 100 F6
Stanage Ct NG18 . . . 103 B5
Stancliffe Ave NG6 . . . 160 C7
Standard Hill NG1 . . . 223 D2
Standhill Ave NG4 . . . 174 B8
Standhill Inf Sch NG4 . . 174 B7
Standhill Rd NG4 . . . 174 B8
Stanesby Rise NG7 . . . 184 E1
Stanford Gdns NG12 . . 175 F4
Stanford Hill 1 LE11 . . 220 B6
Stanford La LE12 . . . 220 D7
STANFORD ON SOAR . . 214 D1
Stanford Rd LE12 . . . 213 F1
Stanford St NG1 . . . 223 E2
Stanhome Dr NG2 . . . 185 D4
Stanhome Sq NG2 . . . 185 D4
Stanhope Ave
Newark-on-Trent NG24 . . 125 C3
Nottingham NG5 . . . 161 B1
Stanhope Cl
Newthorpe NG16 . . . 144 B2
Walesby NG22 . . . 64 A2
Stanhope Cres
Arnold NG5 . . . 161 E8
Stoke Bardolph NG14 . . 175 F7
Stanhope Prim Sch
NG4 . . . 162 D3
Stanhope Rd
Arnold NG5 . . . 161 E8
Carlton NG4 . . . 162 D3
Stanhope St
Ilkeston DE7 . . . 170 A6
Long Eaton NG10 . . . 193 D8
Nottingham NG1 . . . 223 F2
Stanhope Way NG13 . . . 177 E4
Stanier Dr NG12 . . . 186 A3
Staniland Cl 3 NG9 . . . 183 C2
STANLEY . . . 85 D1
Stanley Ave 5 NG7 . . . 173 A8
Stanley Cl NG15 . . . 117 A3
Stanley Dr NG9 . . . 171 A1
Stanley La NG17 . . . 85 D2
Stanley Mws NG16 . . . 158 D7
Stanley Pl NG1 . . . 223 D3
Stanley Rd
Mansfield NG18 . . . 102 B4
Mansfield Woodhouse
NG19 . . . 89 B1
Nottingham, Hyson Green
NG7 . . . 173 A8
Nottingham, Portchester
NG3 . . . 162 A1
West Bridgford NG2 . . . 185 F6
Stanley St
Gainsborough DN21 . . . 24 D6
Long Eaton NG10 . . . 193 E7
Loughborough LE11 . . . 220 B2
Newark-on-Trent NG24 . . 125 B1
Retford DN22 . . . 39 F4
Retford DN22 . . . 40 A4
Worksop S81 . . . 35 E5
Stanley Terr NG24 . . . 140 B8
Stanmore Cl NG8 . . . 159 E3
Stanmore Gdns NG5 . . . 161 F6
Stannier Wy NG16 . . . 159 A7
Stansfield St
Nottingham NG7 . . . 222 A3
Nottingham NG8 . . . 172 E4
Stanstead Ave
Nottingham NG5 . . . 146 D1
Tollerton NG12 . . . 186 D1
Stanstead Prim Sch
NG5 . . . 160 E8
Stanthorne Cl NG11 . . . 185 A4
STANTON-BY-DALE . . 170 A1
Stanton Cres NG17 . . . 100 D3
Stanton Gate DE7 . . . 170 C1
STANTON HILL . . . 100 C5
Stanton La NG12 . . . 198 B2
STANTON-ON-THE-WOLDS . . . 198 C1
Stanton Pl
Mansfield NG10 . . . 102 A7
New Houghton NG19 . . . 86 F7
Stanton Rd
Sandiacre NG10 . . . 182 A7
Stapleford NG10 . . . 182 B7
Stanton St NG19 . . . 86 F7
Stanton Vale Sch
NG10 . . . 193 C7
Stanway Cl NG3 . . . 174 C6
Stanwick Cl NG8 . . . 171 E8
STAPLEFORD
Lincs . . . 127 E8
Notts . . . 182 E7
Stapleford Bypass
Stapleford NG9 . . . 182 D4
Stapleford NG9 . . . 183 A8
Stapleford La
Beeston NG9 . . . 182 F3
Brough NG23 . . . 112 E1
Coddington NG24 . . . 126 D3
Stapleford Rd
Stapleford NG9 . . . 170 D3
Trowell NG9 . . . 170 D3
Staplehurst Dr NG5 . . . 161 A4
Staple La NG24 . . . 140 C2
Staples St NG3 . . . 161 E2
Stapleton Rd DE7 . . . 157 E4
Starch Cl LE12 . . . 205 E1
Starch La NG10 . . . 182 C7
Starling Cl NG12 . . . 185 C6
Starnhill Wy NG13 . . . 177 E3
Starr Ave NG17 . . . 100 D3
Starth Wood Rd NG15 . . 145 D4
Star Wlk 3 NG18 . . . 102 E2
Statham Ct S81 . . . 36 B5
STATHERN . . . 202 F3
Stathern La LE14 . . . 202 B2
Stathern Rd LE14 . . . 202 C3
Stathern Wlk NG5 . . . 161 B7
Station App LN1 . . . 57 A3
Station Ave
Carlton NG4 . . . 163 A1
Ranskill DN22 . . . 19 B5
Station Bvd LE11 . . . 220 C6
Station Cl NG23 . . . 112 B7
Station Ct 3 DE7 . . . 157 E1
Station Hill NG19 . . . 88 B3
Station La
Edwinstowe NG21 . . . 76 B1
Farnsfield NG22 . . . 119 E7
Fiskerton NG25 . . . 137 D4
Ironville NG16 . . . 128 A3
Station Rd
Awsworth NG16 . . . 158 C5
Barnby Moor DN22 . . . 28 E5
Bawtry DN10 . . . 10 A7
Beckingham DN10 . . . 23 C8
Beeston NG9 . . . 184 A5
Bleasby NG14 . . . 151 F8
Bottesford NG13 . . . 181 C3
Burton Joyce NG14 . . . 163 F3
Carlton NG4 . . . 174 F7
Clipstone NG21 . . . 89 E2
Collingham NG23 . . . 112 A8
Cotham NG23 . . . 154 F1
Cotham NG23 . . . 155 A1
East Leake LE12 . . . 205 D1
Edingley NG22 . . . 120 E5
Elton NG13 . . . 179 F3
Fiskerton NG25, NG23 . . 137 E4
Gainsborough DN21 . . . 15 D1
Gainsborough DN21 . . . 24 D8
Harby NG23 . . . 70 E3
Heanor NG16 . . . 143 A2
Hucknall NG15 . . . 146 B7
Ilkeston DE7 . . . 157 F1
Kegworth DE74 . . . 203 F2
Keyworth NG12 . . . 197 E6
Kimberley NG16 . . . 158 F6
Kingston on Soar LE12 . . 204 A3
Kirklington NG25 . . . 121 A5
Kirton NG22 . . . 78 B5
Langley Mill NG16 . . . 143 B2
Long Eaton NG10 . . . 193 F8
Lowdham NG14 . . . 150 E1
Mansfield NG18 . . . 102 B6
Misson DN10 . . . 4 B3
Newstead NG15 . . . 130 E6
Nottingham NG6 . . . 160 C6
Old Dalby LE14 . . . 218 F4
Ollerton NG22 . . . 77 A3
Orston NG13 . . . 180 A5
Rainworth NG21 . . . 118 A8
Ranskill DN22 . . . 19 B4
Retford DN22 . . . 39 E5
Rolleston NG23 . . . 138 A6
Sandiacre NG10 . . . 182 C5
Scarcliffe NG20 . . . 72 A6
Scrooby DN10 . . . 10 A2
Selston NG16 . . . 113 E1
Selston NG16 . . . 128 E8
Shirebrook NG20 . . . 72 E6
South Leverton DN22 . . . 42 D8
Southwell NG25 . . . 121 F1
Sturton le Steeple DN22 . . 32 C6
Sutton in Ashfield NG17 . 101 B1
Sutton on Trent NG23 . . . 96 E8
Thurgarton NG14 . . . 151 D6
Torksey LN1 . . . 44 B3
Upper Broughton LE14 . . 218 C8
Walkeringham DN10 . . . 14 A5
Whitwell S80 . . . 45 A5
Widmerpool NG12 . . . 208 E6
Widmerpool NG12 . . . 209 A7
Willoughby-on-the-Wolds
LE14 . . . 217 F7
Station St
Bingham NG13 . . . 177 F5
Cossall DE7 . . . 158 A2
Kirkby-in-Ashfield NG17 . 115 B5
Long Eaton NG10 . . . 193 E7
6 Mansfield NG18 . . . 102 B6
Mansfield Woodhouse
NG19 . . . 88 B3
Misterton DN10 . . . 7 A2
Nottingham NG2 . . . 223 F1
Sutton in Ashfield NG17 . 100 F2
Station Terr
Hucknall NG15 . . . 146 B7
Kingston on Soar DE74 . . 203 F2
Station Terr *continued*
Kingston on Soar DE74 . . 204 A2
Radcliffe on Trent NG12 . 175 F3
Station View NG20 . . . 72 E3
Station Villas NG9 . . . 184 A5
Station Yd NG17 . . . 100 F7
Staunton Dr NG5 . . . 161 C4
Staunton Hall* NG13 . . 169 B3
STAUNTON IN THE VALE . . . 169 B4
Staunton Rd
Cotham NG23 . . . 155 A1
Long Bennington NG13 . . 169 F5
Newark-on-Trent NG24 . . 139 F5
Staunton in the Vale
NG13 . . . 169 A6
Staveley Ct
Farndon NG24 . . . 139 A4
1 Loughborough LE11 . . 220 B5
Stavely Way NG2 . . . 186 C7
Stavely Wy NG2 . . . 186 C7
Staverton Rd NG8 . . . 171 E7
STAYTHORPE . . . 138 D8
Staythorpe Rd
Averham NG23 . . . 123 E1
Rolleston NG23 . . . 138 C7
Steadfold Cl NG6 . . . 160 B6
Steadings The LN6 . . . 83 E3
Steads Cl NG4 . . . 174 F7
Steedman Ave NG3 . . . 162 A4
Steeles Dr NG24 . . . 140 E3
Steeles Way NG4 . . . 163 B7
Steeple Row 3 LE11 . . . 220 B4
Steeples The NG17 . . . 129 E8
Steetley La
Rhodesia S80 . . . 35 A4
Whitwell S80 . . . 34 E4
Steinbeck Rd NG4 . . . 174 C7
Stella Ave NG12 . . . 197 D8
Stella Gr NG12 . . . 197 D8
Stella St NG18 . . . 102 B5
Stenton Cl NG25 . . . 121 E2
Stephenson Rd 1 DE7 . 157 F8
Stephenson Way NG24 125 C3
Stepnall Hts NG22 . . . 77 E6
Stepney Ct NG8 . . . 159 F1
Sterling Cl S81 . . . 35 E8
Sterling Dr NG24 . . . 125 E1
Sterndale Rd NG10 . . . 193 B6
Sternthorpe Cl NG23 . . . 81 E1
Steven Cl NG9 . . . 182 F4
Stevenholme Cres
NG5 . . . 161 A6
Stevenson Cres NG17 . . 100 E2
Stevenson Gdns NG11 . 196 D6
Stevenson Rd S81 . . . 36 B4
Stevens Rd NG10 . . . 182 A5
Stewart Cl S81 . . . 25 E6
Stewarton Cl NG5 . . . 148 B1
Stewart Rd S81 . . . 25 E6
Stewart Way NG15 . . . 130 D7
Stiles Rd NG5 . . . 162 C6
Stillwell Gdns 5 S81 . . . 35 D8
Stinsford Cl 6 NG5 . . . 161 C8
Stinting La
Mansfield Woodhouse
NG19 . . . 88 E2
Shirebrook NG20 . . . 72 D3
Stirling Ave
Bawtry DN10 . . . 10 A8
Mansfield NG19 . . . 101 E5
Stirling Cl DN21 . . . 15 E2
Stirling Dr
Carlton in Lindrick S81 . . 25 E6
Newark-on-Trent NG24 . . 125 E2
Stirling Gdns NG9 . . . 183 B2
Stirling Gr
Kimberley NG16 . . . 158 E7
Nottingham NG11 . . . 195 F8
Stirling Rd DN22 . . . 39 D5
Stirling Way LN6 . . . 71 F4
Stockdale Cl NG5 . . . 147 A2
Stockgill Cl NG2 . . . 186 C6
Stockhill Cir NG8 . . . 160 C2
Stockhill La NG6 . . . 160 C3
Stocking La
Askham DN22 . . . 51 E3
East Leake LE12 . . . 205 D4
Stocks Fold
East Markham NG22 . . . 65 F7
Tuxford NG22 . . . 66 F7
Stocks Rd NG16 . . . 158 E7
Stockton St 4 NG6 . . . 160 B7
Stock Well NG6 . . . 160 B6
Stockwell Gate 8
NG18 . . . 102 B7
Stockwell La NG12 . . . 189 B4
Stockwell The LE12 . . . 216 C3
Stockwith Rd DN10 . . . 14 B8
Stodman Mews NG24 . . 139 F8
Stodman St NG24 . . . 139 F8
Stoke Ave NG24 . . . 139 E4
STOKE BARDOLPH . . . 175 F7
Stoke Ferry La NG12 . . 164 A1
Stokeham Rd
Laneham DN22 . . . 53 F5
Laneham DN22 . . . 54 A5
Stoke La NG14 . . . 163 F2
Stokes Ind Est NG18 . . . 101 E4
Stolle Cl NG5 . . . 162 C7
Stoneacre NG5 . . . 161 B8
Stone Ave DE75 . . . 143 A1
Stone Bank NG18 . . . 102 D1
Stonebridge City Farm*
NG3 . . . 173 E5
Stonebridge Ct Ind Est 9
NG3 . . . 173 E5
Stonebridge Dr LE12 . . . 205 F2
Stonebridge La NG20 . . 74 A4
Stonebridge Rd NG20 . . 74 A4
Stone Bridge Rd NG3 . . 173 E5
Stonebridge Way
NG14 . . . 148 C8
Stonechurch View
NG15 . . . 130 B8
Stone Cres NG19 . . . 101 D7
Stonecroft S80 . . . 45 C6
Stone Cross La NG18 . . 102 B8
Stone Gr NG20 . . . 59 A1
Stonehaven Cl NG5 . . . 148 B1
Stonehill Cl DN22 . . . 19 B5
Stonehills DE74 . . . 203 C2
Stonehills Way NG17 . . . 101 B4
Stonehurst La LE12 . . . 213 D3
Stone La DN22 . . . 31 D8
Stoneleigh Cl NG9 . . . 183 C5
Stone Leigh Cl NG18 . . 102 E5
Stoneleigh St NG7 . . . 222 C3
Stonemasons Mews
NG17 . . . 115 B5
Stone Mdws NG10 . . . 193 E5
Stonepit Cl NG3 . . . 161 F1
Stonepit Wood Access
Gotham NG11 . . . 194 E1
Gotham NG11 . . . 204 E8
Stone Rd End NG23 . . . 80 E7
Stonesby Vale NG2 . . . 185 B3
Stones Cl 3 NG16 . . . 144 A2
Stonesdale Cl NG5 . . . 161 C5
Stoney Bank NG14 . . . 150 D2
Stoneycroft Rd NG6 . . . 160 E5
Stoneyford Rd NG17 . . . 100 E4
Stoney Houghton Gdns
NG6 . . . 159 F8
Stoney La
Brinsley NG16 . . . 143 D6
Selston NG16 . . . 128 E7
Trowell NG9 . . . 170 B5
Stoney St
Beeston NG9 . . . 183 F7
Nottingham NG1 . . . 223 F2
Sutton in Ashfield NG17 . 101 A3
Stoney View NG16 . . . 143 A5
Stonish Hill NG22 . . . 92 C1
Stony Field La NG22 . . . 106 A6
Stoppard Cl DE7 . . . 157 D2
Storcroft Rd DN22 . . . 40 A5
Storey Ave 7 NG4 . . . 162 E2
Stormont Cl DE55 . . . 113 B4
Stornoway Cl NG9 . . . 184 B5
Storth Ave NG15 . . . 146 A6
Storthfield Way DE55 . . 113 B4
Storth La DE55 . . . 113 B4
Stort Sq NG19 . . . 88 D2
Story Gdns NG15 . . . 146 C5
Stotfield Rd NG8 . . . 171 B5
Stourdale Cl NG10 . . . 193 A6
Stow Ct NG19 . . . 88 E3
Stowe Ave NG2 . . . 185 D5
Stow Pk Rd DN21 . . . 44 D8
Strafford St DN21 . . . 24 D6
Stragglethorpe Rd
Cotgrave NG12 . . . 187 D8
Cotgrave NG12 . . . 188 B6
Straggle Thorpe Rd
NG4 . . . 175 C1
Straight Mile DN22 . . . 38 D6
Strand The NG9 . . . 183 D1
Stranraer Cl NG19 . . . 88 C6
Stratford Cl NG4 . . . 174 F5
Stratford Cres DN22 . . . 39 D6
Stratford Rd NG2 . . . 185 F7
Stratford St DE7 . . . 157 F4
Strathavon Rd S81 . . . 25 F6
Strathglen Cl NG16 . . . 158 E7
Strathmore Cl NG15 . . . 145 E5
Strathmore Ct DN11 . . . 9 A5
Strathmore Dr S81 . . . 25 F6
Strathmore Rd NG5 . . . 148 B1
Strawberry Bank NG17 . . 99 E4
Strawberry Fields NG23 . 96 F8
Strawberry Hall La
NG24 . . . 125 B2
Strawberry Rd DN22 . . . 40 A6
Strawberry Way NG19 . . 103 B8
Straws Croft NG13 . . . 165 D3
Straw's La NG13 . . . 165 D3
Street La Rd DN22 . . . 42 E8
STRELLEY . . . 171 B8
Strelley Cl NG15 . . . 130 F2
Strelley La NG8 . . . 171 B7
Strelley Rd NG8 . . . 159 E1
Strelley St NG6 . . . 160 B7
Striding Edge Cl NG10 . 182 B2
Stringer Cl DE7 . . . 157 E2
Stripe Rd
Tickhill DN11 . . . 8 E7
Tickhill DN11 . . . 8 E8
Stripes View NG14 . . . 148 F6
Strome Cl 8 NG2 . . . 173 B2
Strome Ct 1 NG2 . . . 173 C2
Stroud Cl NG13 . . . 181 B3
Stroud Ct NG13 . . . 181 B3
Stroud's Cl LE14 . . . 211 F8
Strutt Cl 5 DE55 . . . 99 A3
Stuart Ave
Mansfield NG18 . . . 102 F8
New Ollerton NG22 . . . 77 D6
Stuart Cl NG5 . . . 162 B8
Stuart St
Mansfield NG18 . . . 102 E7
Sutton in Ashfield NG17 . 100 E1
Stubbing La S80 . . . 35 D3
Stubbins La NG25 . . . 136 C5
Stubbins Wood NG20 . . . 72 E6
Stubbins Wood La NG20 72 E5
Stubbin Wood Sch
NG20 . . . 72 E6
Stubbin Wood Sch (Main Site) NG20 . . . 72 D6
Stubton Rd NG23 . . . 156 F6
Studland Cl NG19 . . . 88 D6
Studland Way NG2 . . . 185 C5
Stukeley Ct NG24 . . . 125 D4
Sturgate Wlk DN21 . . . 24 F7
Sturgeon Ave NG11 . . . 184 F4
Sturmer Way 6 NG8 . . . 172 B7
Sturton CE Prim Sch
DN22 . . . 32 D4
STURTON LE STEEPLE . . 32 D5
Sturton Rd
Bole DN22 . . . 23 D2
North Leverton with
Habblesthorpe DN22 . . . 32 D1
Saxilby LN1 . . . 57 A7
South Wheatley DN22 . . . 31 E7
Sturton le Steeple DN22 . . 32 C8
Sturton St NG7 . . . 173 A8
St.Werburghs View 4
DE55 . . . 99 A3
Styring St NG9 . . . 183 F6
STYRRUP . . . 8 D1
Styrrup Ct DN11 . . . 8 D1
Styrrup La DN11 . . . 8 B1
Styrrup Rd DN11 . . . 8 E3
Sudbury Ave
Ilkeston DE7 . . . 170 A7
Sandiacre NG10 . . . 182 B6
Sudbury Ct NG18 . . . 103 B5
Sudbury Dr NG17 . . . 99 F2
Sudbury Mews NG16 . . . 143 E1
Suez St NG7 . . . 160 F1
Suff La NG16 . . . 113 C3
Suffolk Ave
Beeston NG9 . . . 184 C4
Bircotes DN11 . . . 9 D4
Hucknall NG15 . . . 145 C5
Suffolk Gr DN11 . . . 9 C4
Suffolk Rd DN11 . . . 9 C4
Sulby Cl NG19 . . . 89 B2
Sulis Gdns S81 . . . 35 E8
Sullivan Cl NG3 . . . 174 A6
Sulney Cl LE14 . . . 209 F1
Sumburgh Rd NG11 . . . 185 A1
Summercourt Dr NG15 . 116 F3
Summer Cres NG9 . . . 184 B7
Summerdowns NG19 . . . 89 A1
Summer Dr NG12 . . . 185 D5
Summerfield Cl NG23 . . 156 E2
Summerfield Rd 11
NG17 . . . 114 E7
Summerfields Way
DE7 . . . 157 D3
Summerfields Way S
DE7 . . . 157 D2
Summergangs La DN21 . 24 D5
Summer Hill DN21 . . . 15 E1
Summer Leys La NG2 . . 223 F1
Summer's Rd NG24 . . . 125 A2
Summer Way NG12 . . . 175 E4
Summerwood La NG11 195 E7
Summit Cl NG17 . . . 115 A6
Summit Dr NG20 . . . 72 E4
Sunbeam St NG13 . . . 179 B4
Sunbourne Ct NG7 . . . 222 C4
Sunbury Gdns NG5 . . . 148 A1
Sunderland Farm Cl
DN11 . . . 8 C7
Sunderland Gr
Nottingham NG8 . . . 159 D2
Tickhill DN11 . . . 8 B7
Sunderland Pl DN11 . . . 8 B7
Sunderland St DN11 . . . 8 B7
Sundown Adventureland*
DN22 . . . 42 E3
Sundown Dr NG12 . . . 188 A5
Sundridge Pk Cl NG2 . . 185 C5
Sunfield Ave S81 . . . 36 A4
Sunflower Cl NG20 . . . 72 D3
Sunflower Dr NG12 . . . 186 A2
Sunlea Cres NG9 . . . 182 F5
Sunnindale Dr NG12 . . . 186 E1
Sunningdale DN22 . . . 39 D2
Sunningdale Cl 4
NG17 . . . 114 E7
Sunningdale Dr NG14 . . 149 C5
Sunningdale Rd NG6 . . 160 E6
Sunningdale Way DN21 . 15 E3
Sunninghill Dr NG11 . . . 184 E3
Sunninghill Rise NG5 . . 148 A1
Sunny Bank
Mansfield NG18 . . . 102 C3
Newton DE55 . . . 99 A5
Worksop S81 . . . 36 A4
Sunny Bank Gdns DN10 . 12 F3
Sunnydale Rd NG3 . . . 174 B6
Sunnymede S81 . . . 36 A6
Sunny Row NG9 . . . 171 E5
Sunnyside
Farnsfield NG22 . . . 119 F5
Whitwell S80 . . . 45 A6
Worksop S81 . . . 35 F6
Sunnyside Rd NG9 . . . 183 C6
Sunnyside Spencer Acad
NG9 . . . 183 B6
Sunray Gr NG15 . . . 145 E8
Sunridge Ct NG3 . . . 173 C8
Sunrise Ave NG5 . . . 160 F5
Sunrise Hill Nature Reserve* NG5 . . . 161 A6
Sunset Ave NG14 . . . 149 C6
Sunshine Cl NG16 . . . 113 D1
Sunstone Gr NG17 . . . 114 D8
Superbowl 2000*
NG18 . . . 102 B7
Surbiton Sq NG8 . . . 160 B3
Surfleet Cl NG8 . . . 171 C3
Surgery La NG21 . . . 118 A4
Surgey's La NG5 . . . 148 A2
Surrey Dr NG19 . . . 101 F8

Susan Cl NG15 131 B1
Susan Dr NG6 160 D4
Sussex Cl NG16 158 A8
Sussex Way NG10 182 B5
Sutherland Cl S81 25 F8
Sutherland Dr NG2 186 A4
Sutherland Rd NG3 174 B7
Suthers Rd DE74 203 C2
Suthers Sch The NG24 140 E1
Sutton Ave NG24 139 E5
Sutton Back La NG15 116 B4
SUTTON BONINGTON 213 A7
Sutton Bonington Prim Sch
LE12 213 B6
Sutton Bonington Spinney & Mdws Nature Reserve*
LE12 213 A7
Sutton Cl
Bottesford NG13 181 B3
Sutton Bonington LE12 213 C5
Sutton in Ashfield NG17 101 A6
Sutton Com Acad
NG17 100 F2
Sutton Ct NG16 143 F2
SUTTON CUM LOUND 28 F6
Sutton Cum Lound CE Prim Sch DN22 29 A6
SUTTON FOREST SIDE 101 B3
Sutton Gdns NG11 196 C6
SUTTON IN ASHFIELD 100 B2
Sutton La
Elton NG13 179 F1
Granby NG13 191 D6
Retford DN22 29 A1
Sutton NG13 191 E8
Sutton L Ctr NG17 100 F2
Sutton Mid La NG17 114 F6
SUTTON ON TRENT 96 E7
Sutton-on-Trent Prim Sch
NG23 97 A8
Sutton Parkway Sta
NG17 115 B8
Sutton Passeys Cres
NG8 172 B3
Sutton Pool Complex
NG17 100 E2
Sutton Rd
Arnold NG5 147 F2
Beckingham LN5 142 E6
Huthwaite NG17 99 F3
Kegworth DE74 203 C1
Kirkby-in-Ashfield NG17 114 E6
Mansfield NG18 101 E5
Redmile NG13 192 C5
Sutton in Ashfield NG17 100 A3
Sutton Road Prim Sch
NG18 101 F6
Swab's La
Cropwell Bishop NG12 188 F1
Owthorpe NG12 199 F8
Swain's Ave NG3 174 A6
Swale Cl NG6 160 D7
Swaledale S81 36 A7
Swaledale Cl NG8 160 C1
Swale Dr 5 DN21 15 F2
Swale Gr NG13 177 D3
Swales Cl DN22 39 C8
Swallow Cl
Mansfield NG18 103 B4
Nottingham NG6 160 D3
Swallow Cres NG15 132 A8
Swallow Ct DN10 7 A2
Swallow Dr
Bingham NG13 177 F3
Claypole NG23 156 D7
Swallow Gate LN1 57 A5
Swallow Gdns NG4 162 B1
Swallow Gr S81 35 D7
Swallows Dr LE14 202 F3
Swallowtail Dr S81 25 D1
Swallow Wlk LE12 213 A1
Swan Cl NG21 118 B6
Swan Ct
12 Gainsborough DN21 15 F1
Sutton Bonington LE12 213 B6
Worksop S81 35 C7
Swan La
Mansfield Woodhouse
NG19 88 B3
New Ollerton NG22 77 C6
Swan Mdw NG4 174 F4
Swann Yd NG17 99 F3
Swansdowne Dr NG7 184 F2
Swanson Ave NG17 99 F3
Swans Quay DN22 39 F5
Swan St
Bawtry DN10 10 A6
Loughborough LE11 220 B4
Swanton Cl DN22 29 C2
Swanwick Ave NG20 72 F3
Swanwick Rd DE7 157 F5
Sweeney Ct 3 NG5 161 A8
Sweet Leys Dr LE12 205 E3
Sweet Leys Rd 7 NG2 173 C1
Swenson Ave NG7 222 A1
Sweyn La 6 DN21 15 F2
Swift Ct NG16 143 F2
Swift Dr NG24 140 A4
Swift's Cl LE12 216 C3
Swifts Vw NG17 114 F1
Swigert Cl NG6 159 F5
Swildon Wlk NG5 160 F8
Swinburne Cl NG24 140 D5
Swinburne St 3 NG3 173 F6
Swinburne Way NG5 161 D7
Swindale Cl NG12 186 B7
Swindell Cl NG3 162 B5
Swinderby Cl
Gateford S81 35 C8
Newark-on-Trent NG24 125 D1
Swinderby Rd
Collingham NG23 112 B8
Eagle LN6 84 A1
Eagle LN6 84 D1
North Scarle LN6 83 E2
Swindon Cl NG16 158 B7
Swinecote Rd NG21 76 B4
Swiney Way NG9 183 A2
Swinfen Broun NG18 102 C3
Swingate NG16 159 A5
Swinnow Rd DN11 9 C4
Swinscoe Gdns NG5 160 F8
Swinstead Cl NG8 171 F6
Swinton Copse NG22 77 E6
Swinton Rise NG15 117 A2
Swish La NG22 105 F8
Swithland Dr NG2 185 E4
Swynford Cl LN1 55 B4
Sycamore Acad NG3 223 F4
Sycamore Ave
Glapwell S44 86 B8
Kirkby-in-Ashfield NG17 114 E6
Torksey Lock LN1 44 C1
Sycamore Cl
Bingham NG13 178 A4
Hucknall NG15 145 E5
Newark-on-Trent NG24 139 D3
Pinxton NG16 113 D3
Radcliffe on Trent NG12 175 F2
Rainworth NG21 104 B1
Retford DN22 40 A5
Ruddington NG11 196 D7
Selston NG16 128 D7
Worksop S80 35 E1
Sycamore Cres
Bawtry DN10 9 F7
Sandiacre NG10 182 A7
Sycamore Ct
Beeston NG9 184 A7
Retford DN22 39 E4
Sycamore Dr
Gainsborough DN21 15 E2
Ilkeston DE7 170 B7
Sycamore La NG14 152 B7
Sycamore Pl 2 NG3 173 C8
Sycamore Rd
Awsworth NG16 158 C5
Carlton in Lindrick S81 25 E7
East Leake LE12 214 D8
Long Eaton NG10 193 C5
Mansfield Woodhouse
NG19 88 C5
New Ollerton NG22 77 D4
Sycamore Rise NG6 160 C4
Sycamore St NG20 74 A6
Sycamores The
Eastwood NG16 143 E1
South Normanton DE55 113 A5
Stanton Hill NG17 100 D5
Sycamore Works 1
NG6 160 C8
Sydenham Ct 6 NG7 172 E2
Syderstone Wlk NG5 161 F6
Sydney Cl NG19 88 C6
Sydney Gdns 2 NG24 140 A7
Sydney Gr NG12 175 E3
Sydney Rd NG8 172 B5
Sydney St NG24 125 A1
Sydney Terr 3 NG24 140 A7
SYERSTON 153 B4
Syerston Hall Pk
Syerston NG23 153 A4
Syerston NG25 152 F4
Syerston Rd NG18 103 A2
Syerston Wy NG24 125 D1
Syke Rd NG5 160 F8
Sykes La
Balderton NG24 140 D3
Saxilby LN1 56 E5
Saxilby LN1 56 F4
Sykes Mws LN1 57 A3
Sylvan Ave NG17 115 A3
Sylvan Cres NG17 101 A5
Sylvan Way
Fernwood NG23 156 A7
Fernwood NG24 155 F7
Sylvester Ct NG21 76 D3
Sylvester St NG18 101 F6
Symmetry Dr S81 18 A6
Symmetry Way S81 18 A6
Synge Cl NG11 195 C8
Sywell Cl NG17 100 F5

T

Taft Ave NG10 182 B6
Taft Leys Rd LE12 205 F2
Taiga Pl S80 35 B5
Talbot Ct NG12 175 E3
Talbot Dr NG9 170 D2
Talbot Rd
Bircotes DN11 9 B4
Worksop S80 36 A2
Talbot St
Mansfield NG18 102 B4
Nottingham NG1 223 D3
Pinxton NG16 113 C2
Tales of Robin Hood The*
NG1 223 E2
Tall Gables NG22 54 C1
Tamarix Cl NG4 163 A2
Tambling Cl NG5 162 B6
Tame Cl NG11 184 E4
Tamworth Gr NG7 184 F2
Tamworth Rd
Long Eaton NG10 193 B4
Long Eaton NG10 193 C5
Tangmere Cres NG8 159 E1
Tanner's La LE12 213 A1
Tannery Rd NG16 158 C7
Tannery Wharf NG24 139 E8
Tannin Cres NG6 160 C5
Tansley Heath NG18 103 C5
Tansy Wy NG13 177 C3
Tanwood Rd NG9 183 B1
Tanyard NG22 79 E6
Tapestry Cl NG5 161 E2
Tapton Pk 3 NG18 103 B7
Tarbert Cl NG2 173 B2
Target St NG7 222 A3
Tarmac Way NG20 73 D8
Tarn Cl NG16 143 B4
Tarrat St 2 DE7 157 E2
Tasmania Cl NG14 173 C1
Tatham's La DE7 157 E2
Tathams Orchard
NG25 121 D1
Tatmarsh LE11 220 B5
Tattersall Cl NG21 76 B2
Tattersall Wlk NG19 88 E4
Tattershall Dr
Beeston NG9 184 B7
Nottingham NG7 222 C2
Nottingham NG7 222 D2
Taunton Rd NG2 185 F6
Taunton Way DN22 39 E4
Taupo Dr NG15 145 D5
Taurus Cl NG18 102 E1
Tavern Ave NG8 160 C2
Tavistock Ave NG3 161 C1
Tavistock Cl NG15 145 D5
Tavistock Dr NG3 161 C1
Tavistock Rd NG2 185 F6
Taylor Cl NG2 174 A4
Taylor Cres
Stapleford NG9 182 E8
Sutton in Ashfield NG17 100 F1
Taylor Pl NG14 173 F8
Taylor's Cl NG18 102 E8
Taylors Croft NG14 149 C4
Taylor St DE7 157 F1
Teague Pl S80 35 D3
Teak Cl NG3 173 D7
Teal Ave NG18 103 B4
Tealby Cl NG6 159 F7
Tealby Wlk NG19 88 E4
Teal Cl
Carlton NG4 175 B6
Shirebrook NG20 72 D3
Teal Ct S81 35 D7
Teal Wharf 4 NG2 173 A2
Teasels The NG13 177 D3
Technology Dr NG9 184 A5
Ted Baker Way LN1 57 C3
Tedburn Dr NG18 103 A2
Teddy's Farm Pk* LN5 142 E8
Teesbrook Dr NG8 171 B4
Tees Ct NG13 177 D3
Teesdale Ct NG9 183 A4
Teesdale Rd
Long Eaton NG10 193 A6
Nottingham NG5 161 B2
Teignmouth Ave
Mansfield NG18 102 F6
Mansfield NG18 103 A6
Telford Dr
Eastwood NG16 144 B3
Newark-on-Trent NG24 125 C3
Temperance La
Collingham NG23 111 F8
Collingham NG23 112 A7
Templar Rd NG9 184 B6
Templars Ct NG7 222 A4
Temple Cres NG16 159 D4
Temple Dr NG16 159 E4
Templemans Way
NG25 136 F8
Templemen Cl NG11 196 B7
Templeoak Dr NG8 171 D3
Tenantshall Cl NG8 172 A1
Tenbury Cres NG8 160 C1
Tenby Gr S80 36 A2
Tene Cl NG5 147 F2
Tenman La NG13 166 A2
Tennis Ct Ind Est NG2 174 A3
Tennis Dr NG7 222 C2
Tennis Mews NG7 222 C2
Tennyson Ave
Carlton NG4 162 F1
Carlton NG4 163 A1
Mansfield Woodhouse
NG19 88 C2
Tennyson Ct NG15 145 D6
Tennyson Dr
Beeston NG9 183 D2
Worksop S81 36 C4
Tennyson Rd
Arnold NG5 161 E4
Balderton NG24 140 D4
Tennyson Sq NG16 158 C4
Tennyson St
Gainsborough DN21 15 D1
Ilkeston DE7 157 E3
Kirkby-in-Ashfield NG17 115 B4
10 Mansfield NG18 102 A7
Nottingham NG7 222 C4
Tenter Cl
Long Eaton NG10 193 D5
Nottingham NG5 160 F8
Sutton Forest Side NG17 101 A3
Tenter La NG18 102 A5
Tenters La NG22 92 E1
Tenzing Wlk NG24 140 E4
Terrace La NG19 86 F5
Terrace Rd NG18 102 C8
Terrace St NG7 172 F7
Terrian Cres NG2 185 F7
Terry Ave NG24 125 B3
Terton Rd NG5 160 F8
Tetford Wlk NG19 88 E4
Tethering La DN10 12 A4
Tetney Wlk NG8 172 A6
Tettenbury Rd NG5 160 F3
TEVERSAL 100 C8
Teversal Ave
Nottingham NG7 222 B2
Pleasleyhill NG19 87 B4
Teversal Pastures Nature Reserve* NG17 100 E8
Teversal Visitor Ctr*
NG17 100 B7
Tevery Cl NG9 182 E8
Teviot Rd NG5 160 F5
Tewkesbury Ave NG19 88 D4
Tewkesbury Cl NG2 186 A6
Tewkesbury Dr
Kimberley NG16 158 E7
Nottingham NG6 160 E4
Tewkesbury Rd NG10 193 E4
Thackeray Cl S81 36 B4
Thackeray's La NG5 161 E5
Thackerey St NG7 222 B3
Thales Dr NG5 162 C7
Thames St NG6 160 B7
Thane Rd
Beeston NG9 184 C5
Nottingham NG9 184 E6
Thatcham Cl NG8 172 D7
Thatch Carr Bank DN9 2 A8
Thatchmarsh Cl DE7 157 F6
Thaxted Cl NG8 171 D6
Theaker Ave DN21 15 F1
Theaker La DN10 10 D5
Theatre Sq NG1 223 D3
The Courtyard NG16 158 E8
Thelda Ave NG12 197 E3
Theresa Ct NG24 140 D4
Thetford Cl NG5 162 A6
Thickley Bank NG20 72 F4
Thievesdale Ave S81 35 F7
Thievesdale Cl S81 36 A7
Thievesdale La S81 37 A8
Thieves Wood La
NG15 116 C8
Third Ave
Beeston NG9 184 C6
Carlton, Gedling NG4 162 F1
Carlton, Thorneywood
NG4 174 B8
Clipstone NG21 89 F3
Edwinstowe NG21 76 A1
Mansfield NG21 103 F2
Mansfield Woodhouse
NG19 89 A1
Nottingham NG6 160 B7
Thirlbeck NG12 188 A1
Thirlmere NG2 186 D5
Thirlmere Cl
Long Eaton NG10 182 B2
Nottingham NG3 173 F7
Thirlmere Rd NG10 182 B2
Thirston Cl NG6 159 F7
Thistle Bank
East Leake LE12 205 E3
Mansfield Woodhouse
NG19 88 F4
Thistle Cl NG16 158 B8
Thistledown Rd NG11 195 E7
Thistle Gn Cl DE75 143 B1
Thistle Rd DE7 170 A4
Thomas Ave NG12 176 C3
Thomas Cl NG3 223 F4
Thomas Cook Pl LE11 220 C5
Thomas Parkyn Cl
NG11 206 E7
Thomas Pl NG23 110 F1
Thomas Rd
Kegworth DE74 203 C1
Newark-on-Trent NG24 140 F2
Thomas St DN22 39 F5
Thompson Ave DN11 8 F4
Thompson Cl
Beeston NG9 183 C3
Coddington NG24 125 E2
East Leake LE12 205 E2
Nether Broughton LE14 219 C8
Thompson Cres NG17 100 F1
Thompson Gdns NG5 147 A1
Thompson St NG16 143 B3
Thonock Ave DN21 15 E3
Thonock Dr LN1 56 F4
Thonock Rd DN21 15 E5
Thoresby Ave
Carlton NG4 162 D2
Edwinstowe NG21 76 A2
Kirkby-in-Ashfield NG17 115 D4
Newark-on-Trent NG24 140 A6
Nottingham NG2 173 F3
Shirebrook NG20 72 E4
Thoresby Cl
Harworth DN11 9 B5
Meden Vale NG20 74 D8
Radcliffe on Trent NG12 176 A4
Thoresby Cres NG17 100 C6
Thoresby Ct NG3 173 D8
Thoresby Dale NG15 146 B7
Thoresby Gall (Pierrepont Art Gall)* NG22 62 D3
Thoresby Glade NG22 106 A5
Thoresby Pk NG22 62 F3
Thoresby Rd
Beeston NG9 171 C2
Bingham NG13 177 C4
Clumber and Hardwick
S80 47 F3
Long Eaton NG10 193 C6
Mansfield NG21 103 F1
Mansfield Woodhouse
NG19 88 A3
Thoresby St
3 Mansfield NG18 102 A7
10 Nottingham NG2 173 E4
Sutton in Ashfield NG17 101 A4
Thoresby Way DN22 39 E3
Thoresby Wood NG22 65 F7
Thor Gdns NG5 146 F2
Thorlby Dr S81 35 A7
Thorn Ave NG19 87 F1
Thorn Bank DN9 2 C8
Thornbridge Mws DN11 9 C4
Thornbury Dr NG19 101 D8
Thornbury Hill La S81 16 D8
Thornbury Way NG5 160 F7
Thorncliffe Rd NG3 173 C8
Thorncliffe Rise NG3 173 C8
Thorndale Rd
Calverton NG14 148 F7
Nottingham NG6 160 C2
Thorndike Cl NG9 184 B4
Thorndike Way DN21 24 E7
Thorn Dr NG16 158 B8
Thorner Cl NG6 160 E5
Thorne Rd
Bawtry DN10 10 B8
Harworth DN11 8 D4
THORNEY 69 F7
Thorney Abbey Rd
NG21 118 B5
Thorney Ct 8 NG18 103 A2
Thorney Hill NG3 173 F7
Thorney Rd
Wigsley LN1 69 F1
Wigsley NG23 70 A2
THORNEYWOOD 174 B8
Thorneywood Ave
NG17 129 E8
Thorneywood Mount
NG3 173 F7
Thorneywood Rd NG10 193 F8
Thornfield Ind Est NG3 173 F5
Thornfield Way NG13 178 F5
Thorn Gr NG15 146 B4
Thornham Cres NG17 129 F8
Thornhill Cl NG9 171 B2
Thornhill Dr
Boughton NG22 77 E5
South Normanton DE55 113 B6
Thornhill La DN22 33 C2
Thornhill Rd DN11 8 E4
Thornley St 7 NG7 172 E7
Thornthwaite Cl NG2 186 C6
Thornton Ave NG5 147 D1
Thornton Cl
Bilsthorpe NG22 106 A5
Mansfield NG18 103 B5
Nottingham NG8 171 E4
Thornton Dale S81 36 B7
Thornton Mws NG13 177 D6
Thornton Rd NG23 112 A8
Thorntons Cl NG12 188 A2
Thornton St
Gainsborough DN21 24 D7
Sutton in Ashfield NG17 100 F1
Thorn Tree Gdns NG16 143 F4
Thorold Cl NG7 184 E2
THOROTON 167 E2
Thoroton Ave NG24 140 D3
Thoroton Rd
Hawksworth NG23 167 D2
Thoroton NG13 179 D8
Thoroton NG23 167 E1
Thoroton St NG7 222 C3
Thoroughfare La NG23 125 D7
THORPE 138 F1
Thorpe Cl
Coddington NG24 126 B2
Newark-on-Trent NG24 139 E4
18 Nottingham NG5 161 A8
Stapleford NG9 182 D7
Thorpe Cres NG3 162 A1
Thorpe Farm Cl DN22 52 C6
Thorpe La
Eagle LN6 84 E2
Farndon NG24 139 A3
Shireoaks S80 34 C6
Thorpelands Ave NG19 88 E1
Thorpe Lea NG14 165 A5
Thorpe Leys NG10 193 D5
Thorpe Rd
Eastwood NG16 143 F4
Mansfield NG18 103 A2
Mattersey DN10 20 B8
THORPE SALVIN 34 A6
Thorpe St
Askham DN22 52 C7
Ilkeston DE7 157 E3
Thrapston Ave NG5 147 F2
Threadneedle Way
NG24 140 A4
Three Leys La DN22 32 D3
Three Tuns Rd NG16 144 A2
Threlkeld Cl NG2 186 C6
THRUMPTON 194 C3
Thrumpton Ave NG10 194 A7
Thrumpton Cl DN22 39 F4
Thrumpton Dr NG2 173 B1
Thrumpton Hall*
NG11 194 B3
Thrumpton La DN22 39 F5
Thrumpton Prim Sch
DN22 39 F4
Thurcaton Way DE55 99 A3
THURGARTON 151 D7
Thurgarton Ave 8
NG2 173 F4
Thurgarton La
Thurgarton NG14 151 D5
Thurgarton NG14 151 E3
Thurgarton St NG2 173 F4
Thurgarton Sta NG14 151 D6
Thurland St NG1 223 E2
Thurlby Cl NG12 189 A4
Thurlby Ct NG19 88 E4
Thurlby La
Stanton-on-the-Wolds
NG12 198 C1
Widmerpool NG12 208 D8
Thurlby Rd DN21 24 F8
Thurlestone Dr NG3 162 C6
Thurley Wlk NG18 103 B4
Thurloe Ct NG11 185 C3
Thurman Dr NG12 187 F3
Thurman St
Ilkeston DE7 170 A6
Nottingham NG7 222 B4
Thursby Rd NG11 184 E3
Thymus Wlk NG11 184 C1
Thyra Ct NG3 161 E1
Thyra Gr
Beeston NG9 184 A6
Nottingham NG3 161 D1
Tiberius Gdns NG15 146 C8
TIBSHELF 99 A6
Tibshelf Bsns Pk DE55 99 C6
Tibshelf Inf Sch DE55 99 A7
Tibshelf Rd NG17 100 A7
TICKHILL 8 B8
Tickhill Castle* DN11 8 A6
Tickhill Rd
Bawtry DN10 9 F7
Harworth DN11 8 E5
Tickhill St Mary's CE Prim Sch DN11 8 A7
Tideswell Cl NG15 117 A3
Tideswell Ct NG18 102 D7
Tidworth Cl NG8 172 A6
Tilberthwaite Cl NG2 186 C6
Tilbury Rise NG8 160 B3
Tilford Gdns NG9 182 E6
Till Bridge La DN21 44 F7
Tiln Ct DN22 29 F1
Tiln La DN22 29 F3
Tilstock Ct NG16 159 A8
Tim La NG14 163 F4
Timothy Rd NG22 79 C3
Tindale Bank Rd DN10 6 C7
Tindall Cl NG9 183 B2
Tinker La DN22 27 F6
Tinkers La NG23 82 F1
Tinker's La NG23 97 F8
Tinkers Way NG7 223 D1
Tinsley Cl NG23 156 E6
Tinsley Rd NG16 143 D1
Tintagel Gn NG7 184 E1
Tintagel Green NG11 195 E8
Tintagel Way 9 NG19 87 D1
Tintern Cl NG17 115 C5
Tintern Dr NG8 160 E2
Tippett Ct NG3 173 F6
Tippings La NG22 119 F5
Tip Tree Cl NG16 158 F7
Tiree Cl NG9 170 D2
Tishbite St 7 NG6 160 B7
Tissington Ave NG20 74 C7
Tissington Cl
Beeston NG9 183 C1
3 Nottingham NG7 173 A8
Tissington Rd NG7 173 A8
Titchfield Ave
Mansfield Woodhouse
NG19 88 D3
Sutton in Ashfield NG17 100 E2
Titchfield St
Hucknall NG15 146 A7
Mansfield NG18 102 A8
Market Warsop NG20 74 B3
Titchfield Terr NG15 146 B7
TITHBY 189 E6
Tithby Ct 10 NG18 103 A2
Tithby Dr NG5 161 D4
Tithby Rd
Bingham NG13 177 E2
Cropwell Butler NG12 189 C6
Tithe Barn Ct NG24 125 A1
Tithe Gdns 2 NG5 147 A1
Tithe La NG14 148 F7
Tithes La DN11 8 A7
Tiverton Cl
Hucknall NG15 145 D5
Nottingham NG8 160 B2
Toad La
Elston NG23 153 E4
Epperstone NG14 150 A5
Laxton NG22 79 B2
Tobias Cl NG5 160 F8
Todd Cl NG11 195 C8
Todd Ct NG11 195 C8
Toft Cl NG12 187 E2
Toft Rd NG9 183 A3
Tokenhouse Yd NG1 223 E2
Toll Bar Ave NG13 181 A3
TOLLERTON 186 D1
Tollerton Gn NG6 160 D5
Tollerton La NG12 186 E5
Tollerton Sch NG12 186 E1
Tollhouse Hill NG1 223 D3
Tolney La
Newark-on-Trent NG24 139 D8
Newark-on-Trent NG24 139 E7
Tom Blower Cl NG8 172 A5
Tomlinson Ave NG11 195 A1
Tomlinson Cl DE55 99 A3
Tom Otter's La NG23 70 E8
Tom Stimpson Wy
NG17 101 B3
Tom Wass Rd NG17 114 E8
Tonbridge Mount NG8 171 D2
Tongue Way NG11 196 A7
Ton La NG14 150 D2
Tooley St DN21 24 D7
Toothill Cl NG14 148 C8

Toothill La NG18 102 C7
Toothill Rd
Loughborough LE11 220 B5
7 Mansfield NG18 102 B7
Toot Hill Sch NG13 177 E4
Topaz Cres NG17 114 D8
Topaz Gr NG18 102 C5
Top Cart Gaps NG22 66 A7
Top Gn LE14 210 A1
Top La
Egmanton NG22 79 D7
Mansfield NG19 87 A1
Topliff Rd NG9 183 C2
Top Pasture La
North Wheatley DN22 31 E8
South Wheatley DN22 32 A8
Top Rd
Blidworth NG21 117 F2
Blidworth NG21 118 A2
Misson DN10 4 D3
Ruddington NG11 196 C6
Thorney NG23 69 F5
Top Row
Mansfield NG19 87 F6
Newark-on-Trent NG24 140 C8
Westwood NG16 128 A5
Top Sandy La NG20 74 C3
Top St
Askham NG22 51 F2
Askham NG22 52 A2
Bawtry DN10 10 A7
East Drayton DN22 53 B3
Elston NG23 153 D4
North Wheatley DN22 31 D8
Rainworth NG21 104 B1
Top Valley Dr NG5 160 E8
Top Valley Way NG5 160 E7
Topyard La DN22 30 D6
Torbay Cres NG5 161 B5
Torkard Ct NG15 146 A5
Torkard Dr NG5 160 F8
Torkard Way NG15 146 B7
TORKSEY 44 B2
Torksey Ave
Saxilby LN1 56 F4
Saxilby LN1 57 A4
Torksey Ferry Rd DN22 43 C2
Torksey Mews DN22 39 D2
Torksey St DN22 43 A2
Torksey Wlk NG19 88 E4
Tor La NG22 77 A3
Torr St DN21 24 D8
Torvill Dr
Nottingham NG8 171 E5
Nottingham NG9 171 F5
Torvill Heights NG8 171 E5
TORWORTH 19 B2
Toseland Gdns NG15 145 F4
Toston Dr NG8 172 C4
Totland Dr NG8 160 D2
Totland Rd NG9 171 C2
Totley Cl NG6 146 C2
Totnes Cl NG15 145 D6
Totnes Rd NG3 174 B5
TOTON 182 E2
Toton Bispham Drive Jun Sch NG9 182 E3
Toton Cl NG6 160 D5
Toton La NG9 182 E6
Tottle Gdns 2 NG7 172 D6
Tottle Rd NG11 185 A8
Tow Ct NG24 139 A4
Tower Cres NG16 159 A4
Tower St DN21 15 D1
Towe's Mount NG4 174 E7
Towle St NG10 193 A4
Towlsons Croft NG6 160 D3
Town Cres NG16 113 D4
Town End NG22 79 B3
Town End La NG23 167 B8
Towngate DN10 10 A7
Townhill Sq 3 NG24 140 F2
Town La DE55 99 B3
Town Mill Cl NG25 121 E2
Townroe Dr NG19 101 D7
Townsend Ct NG5 147 A1
Townside Cl NG10 193 B4
Townside La DN22 42 D3
Townside Rd DN22 32 D1
Town St
Askham NG22 52 A3
Beeston NG9 183 B8
Clayworth DN22 21 D5
Cottam DN22 43 D5
Grassthorpe NG23 81 F4
Hawksworth NG13 167 C3
Lound DN22 20 C1
Pinxton NG16 113 E3
Sandiacre NG10 182 B6
South Leverton DN22 42 C7
Sutton DN22 28 F6
Treswell DN22 42 B3
Town View NG16 158 F7
Tow Path Cl LE11 220 C5
Towpath Gdns S80 36 B3
Towson Ave NG16 143 C2
Towson Field LE12 205 E2
Towyn Ct 8 NG5 161 A7
Tracy Cl NG9 171 D1
Trafalgar Cl NG7 222 B4
Trafalgar Ct DN21 24 E4
Trafalgar Rd
Beeston NG9 184 A4
Long Eaton NG10 193 D6
Trafalgar Sq
Long Eaton NG10 193 E7
Sutton on Trent NG23 97 A8
Trafalgar Way NG19 88 C6
Traffic St NG2 223 E1
Trafford Gdns 1 NG8 172 D7
Tranby Gdns NG8 171 F4
Tranker La S81 35 A6
Travell's Hill LE12 214 A7
Travers Rd NG10 182 A6
Treegarth Sq NG5 147 B1
Tree View Cl NG5 147 C1
Trefan Gdns NG5 161 A7
Trefoil Cl NG13 177 D3
Trelawn Cl 1 NG5 161 D2
Tremayne Rd NG8 171 C6
Trenchard Cl NG13 177 C8
Trenchham Gdns NG14 163 D3
Trent Approach DN21 44 B8
Trent Ave NG11 196 C8
Trent Bank NG23 68 D1
Trent Bridge (Nottinghamshire Cty CC) NG2 173 E1
Trent Bridge Rd DN22 39 E4
Trent Bsns Ctr NG10 182 C1
Trent Bvd NG2 174 A1
Trent Cl NG23 110 F2
Trent Coll NG10 193 C8
Trent Cotts NG10 193 F5
Trent Cres NG9 183 E3
Trentdale Rd NG4 174 D6
Trent Dr NG15 145 D3
Trent Gdns
2 Burton Joyce NG14 163 F4
Burton Joyce NG14 164 A4
Trent Gr DN21 14 A5
Trentham Dr NG8 172 C7
Trentham Gdns NG8 172 C7
Trent La
Besthorpe NG23 97 E6
1 Burton Joyce NG14 163 F4
Burton Joyce NG14 164 C4
East Bridgford NG13 165 B4
East Stoke NG23 153 A8
East Stoke NG24 138 A1
East Stoke NG24 138 B1
Fiskerton NG25 137 F2
Girton NG23 82 E2
Gunthorpe NG13 165 A4
Kelham NG23 124 B5
Long Eaton NG10 193 F5
Newark-on-Trent NG24 125 A2
Newark-on-Trent NG24 125 A3
Newton on Trent NG22 54 F1
North Clifton NG23 68 E5
Nottingham NG2 174 A3
South Clifton NG23 68 D1
Trenton Cl NG9 171 A1
Trenton Dr NG10 194 A8
Trent Port Rd DN21 44 B8
Trent Rd
Beeston NG9 184 B4
Kirton NG22 77 F4
Nottingham NG2 173 F4
Wellow NG22 78 A4
Trentside NG14 165 A4
Trent Side NG11 194 D6
Trentside N NG2 173 E1
Trent S Ind Pk NG2 174 A3
Trent St
Gainsborough DN21 24 D7
Long Eaton NG10 193 E8
Nottingham NG1 223 F1
Retford DN22 40 A6
Worksop S80 35 E4
Trentvale Ave 4 DN21 15 F2
Trent Vale Inf Sch NG9 184 B4
Trent Vale Rd NG9 184 A4
Trent Valley Rd NG4 163 C1
Trent Valley View NG3 162 A1
Trent View DN21 44 C8
Trentview Ct NG2 173 F2
Trent View Gdns NG12 176 A5
Trent Way NG24 125 B2
Trent Wlk NG19 88 E4
Tressall Cl DE7 170 A8
TRESWELL 42 C3
Treswell Ct 9 NG18 103 A2
Treswell Rd
Rampton DN22 42 F2
South Leverton DN22 42 C5
Treswell Wood Nature Reserve* DN22 41 E4
Trevelyan Rd NG2 173 F1
Trevino Gdns 10 NG5 147 A1
Trevone Ave NG9 182 E6
Trevor Rd
Beeston NG9 183 F5
West Bridgford NG2 186 A6
Trevose Gdns NG5 161 D3
Treyford Cl NG11 185 A4
Triangle The
Ilkeston DE7 170 A6
Nottingham NG2 173 A1
Nottingham NG8 172 F1
Tricornia Dr NG6 160 B4
Tring Vale NG5 161 A4
Trinity Ave NG7 222 B1
Trinity Catholic Sch The NG8 172 A8
Trinity Cl DE7 157 E3
Trinity Cres
East Markham NG22 66 B7
Lambley NG4 163 C7
Wymeswold LE12 216 B3
Trinity Cres N NG22 66 B7
Trinity Cres S NG22 66 D6
Trinity Fields Rd DN22 29 B1
Trinity Rd
Edwinstowe NG22 75 F2
Newark-on-Trent NG24 140 A4
Retford DN22 29 D1
RETFORD DN22 39 D8
Southwell NG25 136 C8
Trinity Sq NG1 223 E3
Trinity St
Gainsborough DN21 24 D7
Loughborough LE11 220 C3
Trinity View 1 DN21 15 D1
Trinity Wlk NG1 223 E3
Trinstead Way NG5 161 C7
Triumph Cl NG22 106 F8
Triumph Rd
Eakring NG22 106 E8
Nottingham NG7 172 D4
Nottingham NG7 222 A1
Trivett Sq NG1 223 F2
Troon Cl NG16 158 E7
Troon Ct DN22 39 E2
Trough La NG16 158 F8
Trough Rd NG16 159 A8
Troutbeck NG12 188 A3
Troutbeck Cres NG9 183 C8
TROWELL 170 C5
Trowell Ave
Ilkeston DE7 170 A5
Nottingham NG8 171 B5
Trowell CE Prim Sch NG9 170 D4
Trowell Ct 7 NG18 103 A2
Trowell Gr
Long Eaton NG10 182 C1
Stapleford NG9 170 E3
Trowell La LE12 213 E7
Trowell Pk Dr NG9 170 D2
Trowell Rd
Nottingham NG8 171 D5
Stapleford NG9 170 D2
True Lovers Wlk 1 LE11 220 A3
Trueman Ct S81 36 B5
Trueman Gdns NG5 162 B6
Trueman St DE7 157 F4
Truman Cl
Costock LE12 206 D1
Nottingham NG3 223 F4
Truman Dr NG15 146 A6
Truman's Rd NG2 173 D1
Truman St
Cossall DE7 158 A1
Kimberley NG16 158 D7
Truro Cl LE12 205 E1
Truro Cres NG7 172 E7
Trusley Wlk NG19 88 E4
Tryst The NG24 125 A2
Tuckers Cl LE11 220 C2
Tuckers La
Mansfield NG18 102 A7
Mansfield NG19 101 F8
Tuckwood Ct NG12 207 D3
Tudor Ave NG18 102 F8
Tudor Cl
Carlton NG4 174 E5
Long Eaton NG10 182 E1
Newark-on-Trent NG24 140 B8
Tudor Cres NG21 118 A8
Tudor Ct
Arnold NG5 162 B5
Hucknall NG15 145 C5
Tudor Dr
Mansfield NG18 102 C4
Morton DN21 15 B4
Tudor Gr NG1 223 D4
Tudor Oaks NG23 153 D5
Tudor Rd NG2 185 F7
Tudor Sq NG2 185 F7
Tudor St NG17 100 E1
Tudsbury Terr NG17 101 A3
Tudwal Cl NG5 161 A7
Tudwal Wlk 2 NG5 161 A7
Tulip Ave NG3 173 D7
Tulip Cl NG12 188 A5
Tulip Rd NG16 158 B4
Tunnel Rd
Nottingham NG7 222 C2
Retford DN22 39 E5
Tunnicliffe Cl DE7 157 E2
Tunstall Cres NG8 160 A1
Tunstall Dr NG5 160 F4
Tunstall Rd NG5 161 F4
Turnberry S81 36 B5
Turnberry Ave 6 NG17 114 E7
Turnberry Cl
Beeston NG9 183 C6
Ilkeston DE7 157 C2
Turnberry Ct NG12 186 C3
Turnberry Rd NG6 160 D6
Turner Ave
Langley Mill NG16 143 A3
Loughborough LE11 220 A2
Turner Cl
Nottingham NG5 161 C5
Stapleford NG9 182 E6
Turner Dr
Eastwood NG16 158 B7
Worksop S81 35 F4
Turner Gr NG15 145 E3
Turner Rd
Long Eaton NG10 193 C4
Worksop S81 35 E4
Turners Croft DN22 42 C8
Turner St NG15 146 A7
Turneys Ct NG2 173 E1
Turney St NG2 173 D1
Turnley Rd DE55 113 C6
Turnoak Ave DE7 157 F5
Turnpike La NG9 184 A6
Turnpike The NG22 120 F2
Turnstone Cres NG18 103 C4
Turnstone Wharf 1 NG7 172 F2
Turpin Ave NG4 162 D3
Turpin Cl DN21 15 F1
Turton Cl NG16 143 A3
Turton Dr NG5 161 E7
Turvey La LE12 212 D2
Tutt Cl 4 NG24 140 F2
TUXFORD 66 B2
Tuxford Acad NG22 66 B3
Tuxford Ave NG20 74 E8
Tuxford Ct 6 NG18 103 A2
Tuxford Prim Sch and Early Years Centre NG22 65 E2
Tuxford Rd
Boughton NG22 77 E5
East Markham NG22 65 F5
Egmanton NG22 79 E7
Kirton NG22 78 D7
Normanton on T NG23 81 D6
Walesby NG22 64 C2
Tuxford Windmill* NG22 65 E4
Tuxford Wlk NG3 173 F6
Twells Cl NG3 173 E7
Twentylands Dr LE12 205 D1
Twickenham Rd NG17 114 E8
Twin Oaks Dr NG17 100 C2
Twinyards Cl NG17 100 C1
Twistlace Cl NG9 183 F4
Twist Mill Cl NG15 146 C1
Twitchell The
Beeston NG9 183 E4
Newark-on-Trent NG24 139 E5
Sutton in Ashfield NG17 100 F1
Two Acres S81 18 B2
Twycross Rd NG5 161 B7
Twyford Gdns NG11 184 E4
Twyford La DN22 50 C3
Tyburn Cl NG5 147 A1
Tylden Rd S80 35 B5
Tylden Way S80 35 A5
Tyler Dr NG12 197 D2
Tyne Cl NG8 160 C2
Tynedale Cl
Long Eaton NG10 193 A6
Nottingham NG8 160 D1
Tyne Gdns NG15 145 D3
Tyrian St NG16 158 B8

U

Ulgham Cl NG5 147 F2
Ulldale Ct NG9 183 B4
Ullscarf Cl NG2 186 C5
Ullswater Cl
Carlton NG4 162 F2
Gamston NG12 186 D6
Ullswater Cres NG9 183 D8
Ullswater Dr NG15 145 F7
Ulster Rd DN21 15 D2
Underwood Ave DN22 19 B3
Underwood CE Prim Sch NG16 128 F1
Underwood Gdns S80 35 C3
Underwood Mews NG8 159 C1
Union Cl NG15 131 A2
Union Rd
Nottingham NG14 173 C5
Nottingham NG3 223 F3
Union St
Beeston NG9 184 A6
Bingham NG13 177 E4
Long Eaton NG10 193 E8
Loughborough LE11 220 A4
Mansfield NG18 102 A7
Retford DN22 39 F7
Selston NG16 129 A7
Sutton in Ashfield NG17 100 F2
Unity Cres NG3 162 C2
Unity Prim Sch NG7 222 C4
Unity Rd NG17 115 B7
Unity Sq NG2 223 E1
University Bvd NG7 184 C8
Univ of Nottingham
Beeston, Nottingham NG9 184 A8
Nottingham NG7 172 D2
Univ of Nottingham, Centre for Dairy Science Innovation LE12 204 B3
Univ of Nottingham Innovation Pk NG7 172 D4
Univ of Nottingham (Jubilee Campus) NG7 172 D4
Univ of Nottingham (King's Meadow Campus) NG7 172 F1
Univ of Nottingham, (Sutton Bonington Campus) LE12 204 B1
Univ of Nottingham (Univ Park Campus) NG7 171 B1
Unwin Rd NG17 101 B3
Unwin St NG17 100 A3
Uplands Ct NG8 171 F6
Upminster Dr
Arnold NG5 147 F1
Nuthall NG16 159 D3
UPPER BROUGHTON 210 B2
Upper Canaan NG11 196 D8
Upper Coll St NG1 223 D3
Upper Cross La NG20 74 C4
Upper Dunstead Rd NG16 143 B4
Upper Eldon St NG2 173 E4
UPPER LANGWITH 72 D8
Upper Mexborough Rd NG16 129 A7
Upper Mill St NG17 101 B3
Upper Orch St NG9 182 E7
Upper Parliament St NG1 223 E3
Upper Row NG22 54 B2
Upper Wellington St NG10 182 C1
Uppingham Cres NG2 185 D5
Uppingham Gdns NG2 173 D2
UPTON 122 F1
Upton Cl DE75 143 A1
Upton Dr NG5 161 D5
Upton Hill NG22 52 A4
Upton Mount NG19 87 E1
Upton Rd
Askham NG22 52 A4
Southwell NG25 122 A1
Southwell NG25 137 A8
Upton Wlk DN21 24 F7
Urban Rd NG17 115 A5
Urban Road Bsns Pk NG17 115 A4
Utile Gdns 3 NG6 160 A7

V

Vale Ave NG20 74 A4
Valebrook Rd
Nottingham NG5 161 B4
Nottingham NG5 161 C5
Stathern LE14 202 F3
Vale Cl
Aslockton NG13 179 A4
Eastwood NG16 144 B2
Mansfield NG18 102 E4
Vale Cres N NG8 172 D6
Vale Cres S NG8 172 D6
Vale Dr NG20 72 F2
Vale Gdns NG4 174 D5
Valentine Ave NG16 128 E7
Vale Rd
Carlton NG4 174 E5
Mansfield Woodhouse NG19 88 B4
Nottingham NG4 174 D5
Valerian Wy NG13 177 C3
Valeside Gdns NG4 174 E5
Vale The DE7 157 E3
Valetta Rd NG5 162 B7
Vale View
Dry Doddington NG23 156 D1
Newark-on-Trent NG24 139 E5
Vallance St NG19 88 B4
Valley App NG22 105 F7
Valley Dr NG16 144 B1
Valley Farm Ct 16 NG5 161 A8
Valley Gdns NG2 186 C5
Valley La NG23 169 D8
Valley Prospect NG24 139 D5
Valley Rd
Beeston NG9 183 B5
Bilsthorpe NG22 105 F7
Carlton NG4 162 B1
Kimberley NG16 158 D7
Nottingham NG5 161 B4
Radcliffe on Trent NG12 176 A5
Shirebrook NG20 72 E5
West Bridgford NG2 186 B5
Worksop S81 35 E6
Valley View NG24 126 A1
Valley Vw NG18 102 E4
Valmont Ave NG18 103 A6
Valmont Rd
Beeston NG9 183 A7
Nottingham NG5 161 A3
Vancouver Ave NG12 175 E2
Vanessa Dr DN21 15 C3
Vanguard Rd NG10 193 D5
Varden Ave NG9 172 A1
Varley Cl DE75 143 A1
Varney Rd NG11 184 F3
Varsity Gr NG13 177 B7
Vasey Cl LN1 57 C3
Vaughan Ave
Bottesford NG13 181 C2
Hucknall NG15 131 C1
Vaughan Pl NG20 72 E6
Vaughan Rd NG9 183 A4
Vedonis Pk NG15 146 A5
Velerian Gr NG15 146 C8
Vellus Ct NG17 101 B2
Ventnor Rise NG5 160 F4
Ventura Dr NG5 146 C1
Venture Ave DE55 113 F8
Venus Cl NG6 160 E5
Vera Cres NG21 118 B8
Verbena Cl 3 NG3 173 D7
Verder Gr NG5 160 E8
Vere Ave NG17 100 E5
Vere St NG6 160 B7
Verne Cl NG4 174 C7
Verney St NG19 86 F7
Verney Way NG19 86 F7
Vernon Ave
Beeston NG9 183 F6
Carlton NG4 162 F1
Newark-on-Trent NG24 140 B8
Nottingham, Old Basford NG6 160 E3
Nottingham, Wilford NG11 185 B8
Ravenshead NG15 116 F1
Retford DN22 40 A4
Vernon Cres NG15 117 A1
Vernon Ct
Nuthall NG16 159 F3
Shirebrook NG20 73 A4
Vernon Dr NG16 159 F3
Vernon Pk Dr NG6 160 E3
Vernon Pk Trad Est NG5 160 E3
Vernon Rd
Kirkby-in-Ashfield NG17 114 F6
Nottingham NG6 160 E3
Vernon St
Ilkeston DE7 157 F4
Newark-on-Trent NG24 140 B8
Nottingham NG1 223 D3
Shirebrook NG20 73 A4
Verona Ave NG4 174 F6
Verona Ct NG18 103 A3
Veronica Dr
Carlton NG4 162 D1
Eastwood NG16 158 C8
Veronica Wlk NG11 184 C1
Veronne Dr NG17 101 A6
Versailles Gd NG15 146 A5
Vesper Ct NG18 102 F8
Vessey Cl NG24 140 C4
Vessey Rd S81 35 E7
Vesuvius Way S80 35 C4
Vexation La NG22 91 E7
Vicarage Ave DE7 157 D4
Vicarage Cl
Collingham NG23 98 A1
Nottingham, Old Basford NG5 160 F3
Nottingham, St Ann's NG3 223 E4
Shirebrook NG20 72 E3
Vicarage Ct
3 Mansfield NG19 87 E1
Sutton in Ashfield NG17 100 E7
Vicarage Dr
Burton Joyce NG14 163 E4
Clarborough DN22 30 D5
Kirkby-in-Ashfield NG17 114 F7
Vicarage Gdns NG24 140 E4
Vicarage Gn NG12 186 B3
Vicarage La
Beckingham DN10 14 C2
Farnsfield NG22 119 E6
Kneeton NG13 151 F1
North Muskham NG23 110 D4
Radcliffe on Trent NG12 175 E3
Ruddington NG11 196 C7
Scrooby DN11 9 F2
Vicarage Rd
South Clifton NG23 68 F1
Southwell NG25 136 C8
Vicarage St
Beeston NG9 183 E6
Ilkeston DE7 157 D4
Vicarage Way NG17 129 F8
Vicar La
Misson DN10 4 C3
Tibshelf DE55 99 A6
Vicars Ct NG21 89 E2
Vicar's La DN22 43 A2
Vicar's Wlk S80 35 F2
Vicar Water Cl NG21 89 F2
Vicar Water Ctry Pk* NG21 89 E1
Vicar Way NG18 103 B7
Vickers Cl NG5 162 E3
Vickers St
Market Warsop NG20 74 B4
Nottingham NG3 173 D8
Vickers Way NG22 105 F7
Vickery Way NG9 183 B2
Victor Cres NG10 182 C4
Victoria Ave
Lowdham NG14 150 E1
5 Nottingham NG2 173 F4
Victoria Bsns Pk NG4 175 C6
Victoria Cl
Arnold NG5 147 F1
Boughton NG22 77 E5
Gainsborough DN21 24 F6
Victoria Cres NG5 161 D2
Victoria Ct
Ilkeston DE7 157 E1
Mansfield NG18 102 A5
Victoria Emb NG2 185 D8
Victoria Gdns
Newark-on-Trent NG24 140 A8
Watnall NG16 145 A1
Victoria Gr NG15 131 B1
Victoria L Ctr NG1 223 F3
Victoria Pk NG4 175 B6
Victoria Pk L Ctr DE7 157 E2
Victoria Pk Way NG4 175 B6
Victoria Prim Sch NG2 173 B1
Victoria Rd
Bingham NG13 178 A5
Bunny NG11 196 E1
Carlton NG4 175 A6
Kirkby-in-Ashfield NG17 114 F5
Nottingham NG5 161 B3
Pinxton NG16 113 D3
Retford DN22 39 E6
Sandiacre NG10 182 B5
Selston NG16 129 A7
West Bridgford NG2 185 E7
Worksop S80 35 F2
Victoria Ret Pk NG4 175 B6
Victoria Sq S80 35 F3
Victoria St
Carlton NG4 162 F1
Hucknall NG15 146 A8
Ilkeston DE7 157 F3
Kimberley NG16 159 A6
Langley Mill NG16 143 C3
Long Eaton NG10 193 D5
Loughborough LE11 220 B3
Newark-on-Trent NG24 139 E7
Nottingham NG1 223 E2
Radcliffe on Trent NG12 175 F3
Selston NG16 129 A7
Shirebrook NG20 72 F4
South Normanton DE55 113 A6
Stanton Hill NG17 100 C6

Victoria St *continued*
Stapleford NG9 182 D7
Sutton in Ashfield NG17 100 E2
Victoria Terr DE55 99 B7
Victoria Way NG15 146 C4
Victor Terr 6 NG5 161 C2
Victory Cl
1 Eastwood NG16 144 A2
Kirkby-in-Ashfield NG17 115 B6
Long Eaton NG10 193 D5
Mansfield Woodhouse NG19 89 A1
Victory Dr NG19 88 F1
Victory Rd NG9 184 A4
View The NG9 183 B7
Village Cl
Farndon NG24 139 B5
West Bridgford NG12 186 B3
Village Farm Cl
Stanford on Soar LE12 214 C1
West Leake LE12 204 F1
Village Rd
Normanton on S LE12 213 D2
Nottingham NG11 184 D2
Village St
Owthorpe NG12 199 E7
West Bridgford NG12 186 B3
Village Way NG24 139 A5
Villa Rd
Keyworth NG12 197 F4
Nottingham NG3 173 C7
Villa St NG9 183 F7
Villas The NG20 59 A3
Villiers Rd
Arnold NG5 161 D4
Mansfield NG18 102 E7
West Bridgford NG2 186 A6
Vincent Ave NG9 183 F5
Vincent Cl NG15 131 C1
Vincent Gdns 8 NG7 172 E7
Vine Cl NG13 181 A1
Vine Cres NG10 182 B6
Vine Farm Cl NG12 187 E3
Vine Farmyard NG23 98 A1
Vine Rd DN11 8 C7
Vines Cross NG8 171 E2
Vines The NG23 96 F8
Vine Terr NG15 146 B7
Vine Tree Terr LE12 215 C1
Vine Way NG24 140 B8
Vine Wlk NG19 88 C6
Violet Ave
Eastwood NG16 144 B1
Giltbrook NG16 158 B8
Violet Cl
Nottingham NG6 160 D3
Shirebrook NG20 72 D3
Violet Dns NG12 186 A3
Violet Gr
HUCKNALL NG15 146 C7
Newark-on-Trent NG24 139 F4
Violet Hill NG18 103 A8
Violet Rd
Carlton NG4 162 D1
West Bridgford NG2 186 A8
Vision Bsns Pk NG6 146 A1
Vision West Nottinghamshire Coll (Derby Road Campus) NG18 102 C2
Vision West Notts Coll (Vision Apprentices) NG1 223 F1
Vista The NG9 182 E5
Vivian Ave NG5 173 B8
Vixen Cl NG24 139 F4
Viyella Gd NG15 146 A5
Viyella Mws NG15 146 A6
Voce Ct S81 36 B6
Voce Gdns NG15 146 C6
Vulcan Cl NG6 160 E4
Vulcan Gdns NG13 177 B6
Vulcan Pl S80 35 F3
Vyse Dr NG10 193 C6

W

Waddington Dr NG2 185 D4
Waddington La NG23 97 E6
Wade Ave DE7 170 A7
Wade Cl NG18 102 C3
Wades Ave NG7 172 E8
Wadham Rd NG5 161 E5
Wadhurst Gdns NG3 223 F4
Wadhurst Gr NG8 171 D2
Wadnal La NG23 80 F3
Wadsworth Fields Prim Sch NG9 182 F8
Wadsworth Rd NG9 182 F8
Wagstaff La NG16 128 B4
Wagtail Cl NG9 170 E2
Wain Ct S81 36 B7
Waingrove NG11 185 A3
Wainwright Ave
2 Mansfield NG19 87 D1
Mansfield NG19 101 D8
Wainwright Prim Acad NG19 101 F8
Wakefield Ave NG12 176 A4
Wakefield Cl 3 NG2 185 A5
Wakefield Croft DE7 157 C3
Wakeling Cl NG25 136 E8
Walbrook Cl NG8 160 A3
Walcote Dr NG2 185 C4
Walcot Gn NG11 184 D1
Waldeck Rd NG5 161 B1
Waldemar Gr NG9 184 A6
Waldrom Rd NG5 162 E3
Waldron Cl 1 NG2 173 D2
WALESBY 64 A1
Walesby CE Prim Sch NG22 64 A2
Walesby Ct 1 NG18 103 A3
Walesby Dr NG17 115 D5
Walesby La NG22 77 C5
Walford Cl NG13 181 A2
Walgrave Wlk 12 NG5 161 A7
Walkden St NG18 102 B7
Walker Cl
Ilkeston NG9 170 A4
Newark-on-Trent NG24 140 A7
New Ollerton NG22 77 C5
Walker Gr NG9 182 E6
WALKERINGHAM 13 F5
Walkeringham Prim Sch DN10 13 F6
Walkeringham Rd
Beckingham DN10 14 B2
Gringley on the Hill DN10 13 A3
WALKERITH 14 D7
Walkerith Rd
Morton DN21 15 A5
Walkerith DN10 14 D8
Walkers Ave NG16 143 E6
Walkers Cl
Bingham NG13 177 E4
Bottesford NG13 181 D2
Mansfield Woodhouse NG19 89 B1
Walkers Ind Est NG22 65 C3
Walker Sq NG5 160 E3
Walker St
Eastwood NG16 144 A3
Nottingham NG2 173 E4
Walkers Yd NG12 175 F3
Walk Mill Dr NG15 131 B1
Walks of Life Heritage Ctr★ NG22 66 A3
Walk The DN21 24 F7
Wallace Ave NG4 174 F7
Wallace Gdns
Beeston NG9 182 F2
Long Eaton NG9 182 F1
Wallace Rd LE11 220 A2
Wallace St NG11 195 B2
Wallan St NG7 222 A4
Wallet St NG4 175 A7
Wallett Ave NG9 183 F8
Wallingbrook Rise S80 35 B3
WALLINGWELLS 25 C5
Wallingwells La
Wallingwells S81 25 A6
Wallingwells S81 25 C4
Wallingwells S81 25 C5
Wallis Rd NG18 102 C7
Wallis St NG6 160 E4
Wallsend Cl 16 DE7 157 F5
Wall St DN21 24 D7
Walnut Ave
Shireoaks S81 34 F7
Tickhill DN11 8 B7
Walnut Cl
Aslockton NG13 178 F5
Ilkeston DE7 170 A7
Weston NG23 81 B4
Walnut Dr
Beeston NG9 183 B8
Calverton NG14 148 F8
Walnut Gdns LE12 205 D1
Walnut Gr
Cotgrave NG12 187 F3
East Bridgford NG13 165 C2
Radcliffe on Trent NG12 175 F3
Walnut Paddock LE14 202 B3
Walnut Rd NG13 181 A2
Walnut Tree Cres NG19 89 D2
Walnut Tree Gdns NG6 159 F7
Walnut Tree La NG13 165 C2
Walsham Cl NG9 183 C2
Walsingham Rd NG5 162 B5
Walter Halls Prim Sch NG3 161 E2
Walter's Cl NG24 139 A5
Walters Cres NG16 128 D6
Walter St NG7 222 C4
Waltham Cl
Balderton NG24 140 D3
West Bridgford NG2 186 B6
Waltham La
Harby LE14 202 B1
Long Clawson LE14 211 E2
Waltham Rd NG15 117 A2
Walton Ave NG3 173 F5
Walton Cl NG19 103 B8
Walton Cres NG4 174 E7
Walton Dr
Keyworth NG12 197 F3
Sutton in Ashfield NG17 114 D8
Walton Rd NG5 148 A1
Walton's La NG23 110 E3
Walton St
Long Eaton NG10 182 D1
Sutton in Ashfield NG17 101 A3
Wands Cl NG25 136 D8
Wan Gr NG17 114 E7
Wansbeck Cl
Arnold NG5 147 F2
Nottingham NG7 222 C3
Wansford Ave NG5 147 F1
Wanstead Way NG5 146 E1
Wapping La DN21 44 C8
Warbler Cl NG11 196 B6
Warburton St NG24 125 A1
Ward Ave
Hucknall NG15 130 F1
Nottingham NG5 162 A3
Wardle Gr NG5 162 A8
Wardlow Rd DE7 157 E3
Ward Pl NG18 101 E6
Ward Rd NG21 89 F4
Ward's End LE11 220 B3
Ward St 2 NG7 172 F8
Wareham Cl
Nottingham NG8 160 A3
West Bridgford NG2 185 C5
Warkton Cl NG9 183 C5
Warnadene Rd NG17 114 E8
Warner Pl LE11 220 C4
Warners La 9 LE11 220 B4
Warner St NG7 222 A3
Warrands Cl NG25 136 C8
Warren Ave
Annesley NG15 130 C8
Nottingham NG5 161 A2
Stapleford NG9 182 D7
Warren Ave Extension NG9 182 D7
Warren Cl
Gainsborough DN21 15 B2
2 Sutton in Ashfield NG17 100 A2
Warren Ct NG9 182 D7
Warrender Cl NG9 171 C1
Warren Dr S81 36 B8
Warrener Gr NG5 160 E8
Warrenhill Cl NG5 161 C7
Warren La
Kegworth DE74 193 B2
Long Eaton DE74 203 B7
Warren Prim Sch NG5 147 A2
Warren Rd
Annesley Woodhouse NG17 115 B1
Hucknall NG15 145 D5
Warren The NG12 187 F2
Warren Way NG19 103 C8
Warren Wood Specialist Acad DN21 24 E7
Warrington Rd NG6 160 C7
Warser Gate NG1 223 F2
Warsop Cl NG8 159 D2
Warsop Ent Ctr NG20 74 B5
Warsop La NG21 117 F7
Warsop Rd NG19 88 D3
WARSOP VALE 73 D4
Warton Ave NG3 173 F8
Warwick Ave
Arnold NG5 161 E5
Beeston NG9 183 F7
Carlton in Lindrick S81 25 F6
Carlton in Lindrick S81 26 A6
Warwick Brewery (5) NG24 125 A2
Warwick Cl
Kirkby-in-Ashfield NG17 115 D5
Saxilby LN1 56 F5
Saxilby LN1 57 A4
Warwick Dr
Mansfield NG18 102 E7
Shipley DE7 157 C3
Warwick Gdns NG12 187 F1
Warwick Rd
Balderton NG24 140 D4
Long Eaton NG10 194 A7
Nottingham NG3 161 D2
Wasdale Cl NG2 186 C5
Washdyke La
Hucknall NG15 145 E8
Hucknall NG15 145 F8
Washington Dr
Mansfield NG18 101 F5
Stapleford NG9 170 F1
Washington St DN21 24 D6
Wash Pit La
Colston Bassett NG12 200 D8
Hickling LE14 210 C5
Wash Tub La NG23 98 D4
Wasnidge Cl NG3 223 F3
Wasnidge Wlk NG3 223 F4
Watchorn Cl NG23 122 F2
Watchwood Gr NG14 148 F8
Watcombe Cir NG5 161 B1
Watcombe Rd NG5 161 C1
Watendlath Cl NG2 186 C5
Waterdown Cl NG19 88 D6
Waterdown Rd NG11 184 D1
Waterfield Ave NG20 74 A5
Waterfields DN22 39 F8
Waterfield Way
Clipstone NG21 89 F4
Clipstone NG21 90 A4
Mansfield NG21 89 F4
Water Fir Dr 2 DN11 8 F4
Waterford St NG6 160 E3
Waterfront Ctry Pk★ DN10 7 C2
Waterfront The NG24 139 E7
Waterfurrows La NG12 164 D1
Waterhouse La NG4 163 A2
Water La
Carlton in Lindrick S81 26 A6
Long Clawson LE14 211 E4
Mansfield NG19 87 B3
Newark-on-Trent NG24 124 F1
Oxton NG25 134 B3
Radcliffe on Trent NG12 175 E3
Retford DN22 39 F8
Shelford NG12 164 D1
South Normanton DE55 113 B6
Tickhill DN11 8 A6
Waterloo Cl DE55 113 C8
Waterloo Cres NG7 222 C4
Waterloo La NG9 170 F6
Waterloo Prom NG7 222 C4
Waterloo Rd
Beeston NG9 184 A5
Hucknall NG15 131 A2
3 Mansfield NG19 88 B2
Waterloo Rd *continued*
Nottingham NG7 222 C4
Watermark Cl 16 NG5 161 B1
Water Mdws S80 35 D1
Water Mdws Swimming Complex NG18 102 C6
Watermeadows The NG10 193 B8
Water Orton Cl NG9 182 E3
Waters Edge 6 NG24 125 A2
Waterside Cl
2 Loughborough LE11 220 B5
Sandiacre NG10 182 B3
West Bridgford NG2 186 C6
Waterside Gdns NG7 172 E1
Waterside Lound Hall Est DN22 64 E7
Waterside Orchard DN10 6 E1
Waterside Way NG4 174 A2
Waterslack Rd DN11 9 B4
Waterson Ave NG18 102 F3
Waterson Cl NG18 103 A4
Waterson Oaks NG18 102 F4
Waterway St W NG2 173 C2
Waterway St 3 NG2 173 D2
Waterway The NG10 182 C4
Waterworks Dr NG21 90 C5
Waterworks St DN21 24 D6
Watford Rd NG8 160 B2
Watkins La DN22 32 D6
Watkin St NG3 223 E4
WATNALL 159 A8
Watnall Cres NG19 101 E7
Watnall Rd
Hucknall NG15 145 E4
Nuthall NG16 159 C6
Watnall Rd Aerodrome NG15 145 E3
Watson Ave
Mansfield NG18 102 C7
Nottingham NG3 174 B6
Watson Cl NG23 68 E5
Watson Pk DN10 23 C8
Watson Rd
Ilkeston DE7 157 C2
Worksop S80 35 F2
Watson's La LE14 202 B3
Watson St NG20 74 B4
Watts Cl NG5 162 C8
Wavell Cl 2 S81 35 D8
Wavell Cres
Everton DN10 11 A1
Mattersey DN10 20 A8
Waveney Cl NG5 162 A6
Waverley Ave
Beeston NG9 184 A5
Carlton NG4 163 A1
Waverley Pl S80 47 A8
Waverley Rd NG18 102 B4
Waverley St
Long Eaton NG10 193 E8
Nottingham NG7 223 D4
Tibshelf DE55 99 A7
Waverley Terr NG1 223 D3
Waverley Way S80 47 A8
Waverly Cl NG17 115 D5
Waydale LE12 216 C4
Wayford Wlk 6 NG6 160 B8
Wayne Cl NG7 184 E1
Weardale Rd NG5 161 B2
Wearmouth Gdns
5 Nottingham NG5 147 A1
1 Nottingham NG5 147 F1
Weave Cl NG6 160 E4
Weaver Ave NG24 140 A4
Weaver Cl LE11 220 B1
Weavers Cl LE12 205 F3
Weaver's La NG15, NG16 129 F3
Weavers The NG24 139 C6
Weavers Way DE55 113 B6
Weaverthorpe Rd NG5 162 A5
Weaving Gdns NG5 161 C5
Webb Ellis Rd NG17 114 F7
Webb Rd NG8 172 B7
Webb St NG15 130 E6
Webster Ave NG16 143 F1
Webster Cl NG21 104 B1
Webster Rd LE11 220 D3
Wedding Dr S80 47 A3
Weedon Cl NG3 174 A6
Weekday Cross NG1 223 E2
Weetman Ave NG20 74 B6
Weetman Gdns 12 NG5 161 A8
Weighbridge Rd
Mansfield NG18 102 C6
Shirebrook NG20 72 F2
Shirebrook NG20 73 A1
Shirebrook NG20 73 A3
Weightman Ave NG4 162 E4
Weightman Dr NG16 158 B7
Weirside S81 16 F6
Welbeck Abbey★ S80 46 A1
Welbeck Ave
Carlton NG4 162 D2
Newark-on-Trent NG24 125 A1
Welbeck Cl
Nottingham NG3 223 E4
Sutton in Ashfield NG17 100 F5
Welbeck College La
Welbeck S80 45 F1
Welbeck S80 46 A1
Welbeck Dr NG21 75 F2
Welbeck Gdns
Beeston NG9 182 F3
Nottingham NG3 162 A4
Welbeck Gr NG13 177 C4
Welbeck Pl NG22 66 A3
Welbeck Prim Sch NG2 173 C2
Welbeck Rd
3 Harworth DN11 8 F5
Harworth DN11 9 A5
Long Eaton NG10 182 C3
Mansfield Woodhouse NG19 88 C3
Radcliffe on Trent NG12 176 A4
Retford DN22 39 E4
West Bridgford NG2 185 E8
Welbeck Sq NG17 100 C6
Welbeck St
Creswell S80 58 E8
Kirkby-in-Ashfield NG17 115 C5
Mansfield NG18 102 A7
Market Warsop NG20 74 B4
Sutton in Ashfield NG17 100 F2
Whitwell S80 45 A6
Worksop S80 35 F4
Welbeck Wlk NG3 223 E4
Welby Ave NG7 222 B2
Welch Ave NG9 182 E8
Weldbank Cl NG9 183 B4
Welfare Cl NG20 72 E3
Welfitt Gr NG20 59 B2
Welham Cres NG5 162 A7
Welham Gr DN22 40 A8
Welham Rd DN22 40 A8
Welland Cl
Newark-on-Trent NG24 125 B2
Worksop S80 35 E7
Welland Gdns NG13 177 D3
Wellcroft Cl NG18 101 F5
Wellesley Cl S81 35 D8
Wellesley Cres NG8 159 D2
Well Fen La NG23 156 D7
Well Hill Dr DN11 9 A4
Wellin Cl NG12 186 B3
Wellin Ct NG12 186 B3
Wellington Ave NG13 177 B8
Wellington Cir NG1 223 D2
Wellington Cl NG20 74 B3
Wellington Cres NG2 185 F7
Wellington Gr DN10 9 F8
Wellingtonia Cres 8 NG12 186 B2
Wellington Pl NG16 143 F2
Wellington Rd
Burton Joyce NG14 164 A5
1 Newark-on-Trent NG24 140 A8
Wellington Sq
Nottingham NG7 222 C3
Retford DN22 39 F7
Wellington St
Eastwood NG16 143 F3
Gainsborough DN21 24 D7
Long Eaton NG10 182 C2
Loughborough LE11 220 C3
Nottingham NG3 223 E4
Retford DN22 39 F7
Stapleford NG9 182 C6
Wellington Terr NG7 222 C3
Wellington Villas NG7 222 C3
Wellin La NG12 186 B3
Well La
Upper Broughton LE14 210 A1
West Markham NG22 65 C6
WELLOW 77 E1
Wellow Cl NG17, NG19 101 D8
Wellow Gn NG22 77 D2
Wellow House Sch NG22 77 D1
Wellow Rd
Eakring NG22 92 E2
Ollerton NG22 77 A3
Wellow NG22 77 C2
Wells Acad The NG3 161 E2
Wells Cl
Collingham NG23 98 D4
Mansfield Woodhouse NG19 88 D4
North Scarle LN6 83 E3
Wells Ct LN1 57 C3
Wells Gdns NG3 173 F8
Wells La DN22 43 D5
Wellspring Dale NG9 182 E5
Wells Rd
Edwalton NG12 186 A2
West Bridgford NG12 185 F1
Wells Rd Ctr Hospl The NG3 161 F2
Wells Rd The NG3 161 F1
Welshcroft Cl NG17 115 A6
Welstead Ave NG8 160 B2
Welton Gdns NG6 160 A8
Welwyn Ave NG19 88 E4
Welwyn Rd NG8 171 E5
Wembley Gdns NG9 171 B2
Wembley Rd
Arnold NG5 162 B5
Langold S81 16 F3
Wembley St DN21 24 D8
Wemtworth Cl DN21 15 E2
Wemyss Gdns NG8 172 D3
Wendling Gdns NG5 161 B8
Wendover Dr NG8 160 B2
Wenham La NG17 99 F4
Wenlock Cl NG16 158 C8
Wenlock Dr
Hucknall NG15 146 C8
West Bridgford NG2 185 F5
Wensleydale S81 36 B7
Wensleydale Cl
Mansfield NG19 88 E1
Nottingham NG8 160 D1
Wensleydale Rd NG10 193 B6
Wensley Rd NG5 161 E5
Wensor Ave NG9 183 F8
Wentbridge Dr NG18 103 A4
Wentworth Cl NG19 88 F2
Wentworth Cnr NG24 139 E5
Wentworth Croft DE75 143 A3
Wentworth Ct
Bawtry DN10 10 A6
Kimberley NG16 158 E6
Wentworth Gn DN22 39 D3
Wentworth Rd
Beeston NG9 183 C6
Kirkby-in-Ashfield NG17 114 E7
Nottingham NG5 161 B2
Wentworth St DE7 158 A2
Wentworth Way NG12 186 C3
Wesleyan Chapel Wlk NG9 182 D7
Wesley Ave NG9 183 F6
Wesley Cl
Balderton NG24 140 D4
Hathern LE12 213 A1
Wesley Gr 10 NG5 161 B1
Wesley Pl NG9 182 E8
Wesley Rd DN22 39 F7
Wesley St
Annesley Woodhouse NG17 130 A8
Ilkeston DE7 157 E4
Langley Mill NG16 143 C3
12 Nottingham NG5 161 B1
Wesley Way
North Scarle LN6 83 E3
Ruddington NG11 196 D6
Wessex Cl S81 36 A6
Wessex Dr NG16 158 A8
Wessex Rd S81 36 A6
West Ave
Sandiacre NG10 182 A6
Stapleford NG9 182 E8
West Bridgford NG2 185 E7
West Bank LN1 56 F2
West Bank Ave NG18 102 B8
West Bank Lea NG19 88 B1
West Bank Link NG19 88 B1
West Bank Mews DE74 203 C2
West Bank Wynd NG18 102 B8
Westborough La NG23 156 E1
Westbourne Cl
Mansfield Woodhouse NG19 88 E4
Retford DN22 40 A6
Sutton in Ashfield NG17 100 D3
Westbourne Rd
Selston NG16 129 A2
Sutton in Ashfield NG17 100 D3
Westbourne View NG17 100 D3
Westbrecks La DN22 43 A5
WEST BRIDGFORD 186 A7
West Bridgford Inf Sch NG2 185 E7
West Bridgford Jun Sch NG2 185 F6
West Bridgford Sch The NG2 185 D5
Westbrook Ave NG15 116 F3
Westbrook Dr NG21 104 B1
West Brook La NG23 112 A6
West Burton Meadow Nature Reserve★ DN22 32 D7
West Burton Medieval Village of★ DN22 32 F7
Westbury Cl NG9 183 C4
Westbury Mws NG6 160 F2
Westbury Rd NG5 161 A2
Westbury Sch NG8 171 E8
Westby La NG16 158 D3
West Carr Rd DN22 39 D6
West Cl NG12 197 E2
Westcliffe Ave
Carlton NG4 162 D3
Radcliffe on Trent NG12 176 A4
West Cres NG9 184 B4
West Croft Cl DN22 42 F2
Westcroft Dr LN1 57 A5
Westcross Ave NG9 182 E8
West Ct DN22 39 D7
Westdale Ave NG17 101 A5
Westdale Cl NG10 193 A5
Westdale Cres NG4 162 E1
Westdale Ct
Carlton NG4 162 D2
1 Carlton NG5 162 D2
Westdale Inf Sch NG3 162 C3
Westdale Jun Sch NG3 162 B3
Westdale La E NG4 162 E1
Westdale La W NG3 162 A3
Westdale Rd
Mansfield NG19 88 B1
Westwood NG16 128 C4
West Dr NG21 76 A2
WEST DRAYTON 51 A2
West Drayton Ave
Clumber and Hardwick S80 48 F1
West Drayton DN22 50 F2
West End
Beeston NG9 183 F5
Beeston NG9 183 F6
Calverton NG14 148 C7
Farndon NG24 138 F4
Long Clawson LE14 211 C3
Long Whatton LE12 212 A4
Pinxton NG16 113 C4
Sutton in Ashfield NG17 100 E2
West End Arc NG1 223 D2
West End Cl NG13 181 A2
West End St NG9 182 C5
West End Villas 3 NG4 175 E3
Westerdale S81 36 A8
Westerdale Dr NG12 198 A3
Westerfield Way NG11 185 A5
Westerham Cl NG8 171 D7

Westerham Rd NG11 196 B6
Westerhope Cl NG12 186 C4
Westerlands NG9 182 F6
Western Ave
Bingham NG13 177 D5
Kirkby-in-Ashfield NG17 115 B3
Mansfield NG18 101 F5
Saxilby LN1 56 F4
Western Bvd NG8 172 D8
Western Cl NG18 101 E5
Western Fields NG11 196 B6
Western Gdns NG8 172 D8
Western Rd LE14 219 A5
Western St NG1 223 F3
Western Terr NG7 222 C2
Western Wlk DN10 10 A8
Westfield Cl
Mansfield NG19 101 F8
Sutton in Ashfield NG17 100 E2
Westfield Dr
Ilkeston DE7 157 D2
Mansfield NG19 101 E8
Worksop S81 36 A5
Westfield La
Collingham NG23 111 E8
Mansfield NG18, NG19 101 E8
Woodborough NG14 149 A4
Westfield Rd
Annesley Woodhouse NG17 115 B1
Bingham NG13 177 D4
Retford DN22 39 D6
Westfield Way NG24 139 A4
West Furlong
Cotgrave NG12 188 A2
Retford DN22 39 D8
Westgate
Southwell NG25 136 D8
Worksop S80 35 E2
West Gate
Long Eaton NG10 193 E7
1 Mansfield NG18 102 B7
Tickhill DN11 8 A6
Westgate Ms NG25 136 D8
Westgate St NG3 173 E6
Westgate View S80 35 E2
Westglade Prim Sch NG5 160 F8
West Gr Rd DN22 39 F5
WEST HALLAM 157 A1
Westhay Ct NG8 172 C5
West Hill
Mansfield NG18 102 A8
Sutton in Ashfield NG17 100 D6
West Hill Ave NG18 102 B7
West Hill Pk NG19 88 B3
West Hill Rd DN22 39 D3
West Hill Wy NG18 102 B7
Westholme Gdns NG8 172 C6
Westhorpe NG25 136 C8
Westhorpe Ave NG3 173 F5
Westhorpe Dr NG10 193 C8
Westhorpe Mkt Pl NG25 136 C8
Westhouse Rd NG15 146 E5
West La
Edwinstowe NG21 76 A2
Girton NG23 82 E1
Westland Ave NG15 145 D4
Westland Dr NG16 113 C3
West Lawns The NG25 136 C8
WEST LEAKE 205 A1
West Leake Lane NG11 204 D5
West Leake Rd LE12 205 C1
Westleigh NG19 88 D6
Westleigh Rd NG8 159 E2
West Manor Pk NG14 149 F6
WEST MARKHAM 65 B6
Westminster Ave
Kirkby-in-Ashfield NG17 115 C5
Stapleford NG10 182 C5
Westminster Cl
Morton DN21 15 B5
Nottingham NG3 173 E7
Worksop S81 36 A7
Westminster Dr NG12 176 E3
Westminster Way NG15 146 C4
West Moor NG2 174 D4
Westmoore Cl NG3 162 A3
Westmoor La
Kettlethorpe LN1 55 D3
Kettlethorpe LN1 69 D8
Newton on Trent LN1 55 C1
Newton on Trent LN1 69 C8
West Moor Rd DN10 13 E6
Westmoreland Ct 8 NG5 161 B1
Westmorland Ct DN11 9 D4
Westmorland Dr S81 25 F8
Westmorland Way NG16 128 B3
West Nottinghamshire Coll (18) NG18 102 B7
WESTON 81 B4
Weston Ave NG7 173 A7
Weston Cl
Arnold NG5 161 E4
Sutton in Ashfield NG17 115 C8
Weston La NG23 81 D5
Weston Rd NG22, NG23 80 A6
Weston St DE75 157 A8
West Pk Ct NG10 193 D7
West Pk L Ctr DE72 193 B7
West Pk Pl DN22 39 D6
Westray Cl NG9 171 B3
West Rd
Nottingham NG8 172 D2
Thorney NG23 69 F7
West St
Arnold NG5 161 E7
Harworth DN11 9 A5
Hucknall NG15 146 A7
Kimberley NG16 159 A4
Langley Mill NG16 143 B3
Misson DN10 4 B2
Morton DN21 15 B4
Nottingham NG2 173 E4
Retford DN22 39 E6
Shelford NG13 164 C1
Warsop Vale NG20 73 D4
Whaley Thorns NG20 58 F3
Whaley Thorns NG20 59 A3
Worksop S80 35 E2
WEST STOCKWITH 7 D2
West Stockwith Park DN10 7 C1
West Terr
Hucknall NG15 146 A7
6 Ilkeston DE7 157 F1
West Thorpe LE12 217 C7
West View
Carlton in Lindrick S81 25 F8
West Bridgford NG2 185 D5
Westview Ct NG4 174 F8
West View Rd NG4 174 F8
Westville Dr NG15 145 E4
Westville Gdns NG3 173 D7
Westward Ave NG9 184 A5
Westway
Cotgrave NG12 187 F2
Worksop S81 36 A7
West Wells La DN10 12 E2
Westwick Rd
Nottingham NG8 171 C5
Nottingham NG9 171 C5
Westwick St DE7 170 A6
West Wlk
1 Nottingham NG1 173 E4
Retford DN22 39 C8
WESTWOOD 128 C3
Westwood Dr S80 35 B3
West Wood Est DN10 9 F6
Westwood Inf Sch NG16 128 C4
Westwood Rd
Bircotes DN10 9 F6
Nottingham NG2 173 F4
Wetherby Cl
Kimberley NG16 158 E7
Nottingham NG8 160 B1
Wetherlam Cl NG2 173 C2
Wetlands Waterfowl Reserve★ DN22 29 D7
Wetsyke La NG24 140 E4
Wetton La DE55 99 A6
Whaddon Ct LE11 220 C1
WHALEY 58 D4
Whaley Bridge Cl NG18 103 C5
Whaley Comm S44 58 D4
Whaley Common NG20 58 D4
Whaley Rd
Holbeck NG20 58 F5
Holbeck NG20 59 B5
Whaley NG20 58 B3
Whaley Thorns NG20 58 E2
WHALEY THORNS 59 A2
Whaley Thorns Prim Sch NG20 59 A3
Wharfdale Gdns NG18 103 A5
Wharfdale Rd NG10 193 A6
Wharfedale
Nottingham NG8 171 B3
Worksop S81 36 A7
Wharf Gdns NG13 177 C3
Wharf La NG12 175 E3
Wharf Rd
9 Mansfield NG18 102 B6
Misterton DN10 6 F1
Nottingham NG7 223 D1
Pinxton NG16 113 D2
Retford DN22 39 E6
Stanton Hill NG17 100 C6
Wharf St DN10 10 A7
Wharf The
Morton DN21 15 B4
Newark-on-Trent NG24 124 E1
Wharmby Ave NG19 87 D3
Wharncliffe Rd
7 Ilkeston DE7 157 E1
Loughborough LE11 220 C3
Retford DN22 39 E4
Wharton Cres
Beeston NG9 183 F4
Beeston NG9 184 A4
Wharton St DN22 40 A6
Whatten Gdns★ LE12 212 E5
WHATTON 179 A3
Whatton Ct 2 NG18 103 A3
Whatton Dr NG2 185 B3
Whatton Est LE12 212 D4
Whatton Rd
Hathern LE12 212 E2
Kegworth DE74 203 C1
Kegworth DE74 212 B8
Whatton Rise NG5 161 B4
Wheatacre Rd NG7 184 F1
Wheat Cl NG8 171 D5
Wheat Croft S81 36 B7
Wheatcroft Bsns Pk NG12 185 F1
Wheatcroft Dr
5 Edwalton NG12 185 F2
3 Edwalton NG12 186 A2
Wheatcroft View NG11 185 C3
Wheatfield Cres NG19 88 E5
Wheatfield Dr DN11 8 B8
Wheatfields Rd NG3 174 A7
Wheatfield Way NG17 100 E7
Wheatgrass Hill NG25, NG23 122 D4
Wheatgrass Rd NG9 183 B5
Wheatland Dr LE11 220 C2
Wheatley Ave NG17 114 F5
Wheatley Cl
Mansfield Woodhouse NG19 88 F1
Ruddington NG11 196 C5
Wheatley Dr NG4 174 C7
Wheatley Gr NG9 183 F4
Wheatley La NG23 112 B4
Wheatley Rd
Clayworth DN22 21 F3
South Wheatley DN22 31 F7
Sturton le Steeple DN22 32 B6
Wheatsheaf Av 3 NG24 125 B4
Wheatsheaf Ct NG14 163 F4
Wheeldale Cl NG8 171 B4
Wheeldon Cl DE7 157 F6
Wheeldon St DN21 24 D7
Wheeler Ave NG16 144 B1
Wheeler Gate
Nottingham NG1 223 E2
Selston NG16 129 A2
Wheelgate Park★ NG22 119 B7
Wheelwrghts The NG21 76 B2
Wheldon Ave NG4 162 C2
Whernside Rd NG5 161 F5
Whetstone Cl NG8 159 D3
Whickham Ct 4 NG2 173 D1
Whilton Cl NG17 101 B5
Whimpton Medieval Village of★ NG22 67 E8
Whimsey Pk NG4 174 E6
Whinbush La NG14 133 D4
Whinfell Cl NG7 184 F2
Whinlatter Dr NG2 186 C6
Whinleys La DN22 41 B8
Whinleys Rd DN22 31 A2
Whinney Bank NG19 88 D4
Whinney Hill NG19 88 D4
Whinney La
Boughton NG22 63 D1
New Ollerton NG22 77 D5
New Ollerton NG22 77 D7
Whinney La North NG22 77 D7
Whinney Moor Cl DN22 39 F5
Whinney Moor La DN22 39 F5
Whinney Moor Way DN22 39 F5
Whinny Haugh La DN11 8 B4
Whipling Cl NG13 179 B3
Whiston Cl NG5 161 A6
Whitaker Cl DN22 29 C1
Whitakers Farm LE14 202 C3
Whitbread St NG7 172 F8
Whitburn Rd NG9 182 E3
Whitby Cl NG8 171 B4
Whitby Cres NG5 162 A5
Whitby Rd
Eastwood NG16 144 A3
Harworth DN11 9 A5
Whitchurch Cl NG5 160 F8
Whitcliffe Gdns NG12 185 F5
Whitcombe Ct DN22 39 C4
Whitcombe Gdns
11 Nottingham NG5 147 A1
Nottingham NG5 161 A8
White Ave S81 16 E3
Whitebeam Cl 3 NG12 186 A1
Whitebeam Gdns NG6 159 F7
Whitechapel St NG6 160 D2
Whitedale Rd NG14 148 C8
White Furrows NG12 187 E2
Whitegate LE11 220 C5
Whitegate Prim Sch NG11 184 D1
Whitegates Way NG17 99 E2
Whitegate Vale NG11 184 D1
Whitehall Ct
Retford DN22 39 E6
Upper Saxondale NG12 176 E3
Whitehall Gdns DN22 39 F6
Whitehall Rd DN22 39 F6
White Hart La NG23 112 A8
White Hart St NG18 102 B6
White Hart Yd S80 35 E1
Whitehead Cl DE7 157 D2
Whitehead Dr NG16 143 D8
Whitehead La NG17 100 F6
Whitehouse Ave LE11 220 C2
Whitehouse Ct DN11 9 C5
White House Rd DN11 9 C4
White Lady Ct NG15 117 B3
Whitelands NG12 188 A2
White Lodge Gdns NG8 171 D7
Whitely Ave 13 DE7 157 F5
Whitely Cl NG9 182 E7
Whitemoor Ave 5 NG8 172 D8
Whitemoor Ct NG8 172 D8
Whitemoor La NG23 112 A4
Whitemoor Prim Sch NG8 160 D1
Whitemoor Rd NG6 160 D2
Whitemoss Cl NG8 171 E3
White Park Pl DN22 39 C4
White Post Farm Ctr The★ NG22 119 B7
White Rd NG5 160 E3
White Rose Ave NG19 102 D5
White's Ave NG4 174 B6
Whites Farm DN22 42 D7
Whitestone Cl NG18 103 A3
Whitestub La NG22 106 F5
White's Wood Acad 5 DN21 24 F8
Whites Wood La DN21 24 E8
White's Wood La 5 DN21 24 F8
Whitewater Cl NG22 77 C5
Whitewater La
Blyth S81 18 A5
Walesby NG22 63 B1
Whitewater Rd NG22 77 C5
Whitfield Cl NG11 185 B6
Whitfield St NG24 140 A7
Whiting Ave NG9 182 F2
Whitney Cl NG19 89 A1
Whitsun Dale S81 36 B8
Whittaker Rd
Beeston NG9 183 A3
Rainworth NG21 118 A8
Whittier Rd NG2 174 A3
Whittingham Ct NG3 162 A3
Whittingham Rd NG3 162 A3
Whittle Cl NG24 125 C2
Whittle Way NG24 141 A2
Whitton Cl
4 Beeston NG9 183 C2
3 Nottingham NG5 147 B1
Ranskill DN22 19 B4
WHITWELL 45 B6
Whitwell Cl
Ilkeston DE7 157 E6
Nottingham NG8 159 E1
Whitwell Prim Sch S80 45 A5
Whitwell Rd
Nottingham NG8 159 E1
Thorpe Salvin S80 34 A4
Whitwell Sta S80 45 A5
Whitworth Dr
Carlton NG4 163 C2
Radcliffe on Trent NG12 175 F2
Whitworth Rise NG5 160 F8
Whomsley Cl NG24 140 D8
Whyatt Ct NG5 161 D6
Whyburn La NG15 145 D7
Whyburn St NG15 146 C5
Whysall Rd NG10 193 B7
Whyston Ct NG15 145 C5
Wibberley Dr NG11 196 B7
Wichal Cl NG5 161 C5
Wichnor Cl NG11 184 E4
Wickenby Ave NG24 140 F3
Wickens Wlk NG3 173 E6
Wicker Cl NG6 160 E4
Wickerwood Dr NG17 114 E6
Wicket Cl
3 Kirkby-in-Ashfield NG17 115 A3
Loughborough LE11 220 A2
Wicket Gr NG7 222 A2
Wickets The
Bottesford NG13 181 B1
Market Warsop NG20 74 B3
Wickliffe Pk NG23 156 D6
Wickstead Cl NG5 161 F3
Widdington Cl NG5 147 F2
Widdowson Cl NG6 159 F8
Widdowson Rd NG10 193 B5
Widecombe La NG11 195 D8
Wide La
Hathern LE12 213 A1
Wymeswold LE12 217 C3
Wide St LE12 213 A1
WIDMERPOOL 208 B5
Widmerpool La
Keyworth NG12 208 B8
Keyworth NG12 208 D1
Stanton-on-the-Wolds NG12 198 B1
Willoughby-on-the-Wolds LE12 217 D8
Widmerpool Pk NG12 208 B4
Widmerpool Rd
Wysall NG12 207 D3
Wysall NG12 207 E3
Widmerpool St NG16 113 C2
Widnall Dr NG13 177 D6
Widows Row LN1 55 B5
Wighay Rd NG15 131 A2
Wigley Cl NG3 173 E6
Wigman Rd
Nottingham NG8 171 E7
Nottingham NG9 171 D8
Wigsley Rd
Harby NG23 70 C2
North Scarle LN6 83 D5
Thorney NG23 69 F4
Thorney NG23 70 A4
Wigthorpe La S81 26 A4
Wigwam Gr NG15 146 C7
Wigwam La NG15 146 C7
Wilberforce Rd
Mansfield NG19 87 D2
West Bridgford NG2 185 A5
Wilcox Ave NG19 88 B5
Wilcox Dr NG16 129 A1
Wilde Cres NG16 129 A6
Wilden Cres NG7 184 E2
Wilders Way DE74 203 A2
Wildflower Gr NG17 100 D1
Wild Flower Rise NG18 102 C8
Wild Hill
Fackley NG17 100 A7
Huthwaite NG17 99 E7
Wildman St NG7 222 C4
Wildman Villas DN10 14 B1
WILFORD 185 B6
Wilford Ave NG13 177 D6
Wilford Cl NG24 140 B8
Wilford Cres NG11 196 C8
Wilford Cres E NG2 173 D1
Wilford Cres W NG2 173 C1
Wilford Gr
Nottingham NG2 173 C1
West Bridgford NG2 185 D8
Wilford La NG2 185 C7
Wilford Rd
Mansfield NG18 103 A3
Nottingham NG2 223 E1
West Bridgford NG11 185 C2
Wilford Sports Complex NG2 185 D6
Wilford St NG2 223 E1
Wilfred Ave NG24 140 C4
Wilfrid Gr NG2 185 E3
Wilhallow La NG16 128 E2
Wilkins Gdns NG11 184 C1
Wilkinson Ave NG9 183 F6
Wilkinson Cl
Beeston NG9 183 B2
Pleasley NG19 87 A5
Wilkinson St NG7 172 E8
Willam Hall Way NG24 140 E1
Willand Ct DN22 29 E1
Willaston Cl NG6 160 C4
Willbert Rd NG5 148 A1
Willerby Rd NG5 162 A5
Willersley Dr NG2 173 C2
Willesden Gn NG16 159 D3
Willetts Ct NG17 100 F1
Willey La NG16 144 A8
William Ave NG16 143 F2
William Booth Birthplace Mus★ NG2 173 E4
William Booth Primary Sch NG2 173 E4
William Booth Rd NG2 174 A4
William Bradford Cl DN10 3 C1
William Cl NG4 175 B8
William Gdns DN22 29 F1
William Gladstone CE Prim Sch The NG24 139 F6
William & Henry Mews LN6 84 D3
William Lilley Inf Sch NG9 182 D6
William Old Ct 3 NG8 172 A5
William Rd
Stapleford NG9 182 D7
West Bridgford NG2 185 E8
Williams Dr NG14 133 E1
Williams La NG24 140 E2
Williamson Gdns DE75 143 A2
Williamson St NG19 101 E7
Williams Rd NG9 183 B3
Williams St S81 16 E3
William St
Hucknall NG15 146 A7
Long Eaton NG10 182 C2
Loughborough LE11 220 A3
Newark-on-Trent NG24 140 A8
Saxilby LN1 57 A3
William Straw Gdns S80 35 F1
Willingham Rd DN21 24 F2
Willis Rd NG24 139 F6
Willoughby Ave
Long Eaton NG10 182 C3
Nottingham NG7 222 B2
Willoughby Chase DN21 24 E5
Willoughby Cl NG7 184 B8
Willoughby Ct
11 Mansfield NG18 103 A2
Norwell NG23 110 A8
Nottingham NG7 222 B1
Willoughby Gdns NG21 104 B1
Willoughby La NG12 207 F3
WILLOUGHBY-ON-THE-WOLDS 217 D8
Willoughby Prim Sch LE14 217 C7
Willoughby Rd
West Bridgford NG2 185 F6
Widmerpool NG12 208 C3
Willoughby St
Beeston NG9 184 A6
Cossall DE7 158 A2
Gainsborough DN21 24 D7
Nottingham NG7 222 B1
Willoughby Way NG22 64 B2
Willow Ave
Carlton NG4 175 A8
Carlton in Lindrick S81 25 E7
Hucknall NG15 145 D4
Kirkby-in-Ashfield NG17 114 E6
Long Eaton NG10 182 C2
Mansfield Woodhouse NG19 89 A1
Misterton DN10 6 E2
Ranskill DN22 19 C4
Shirebrook NG20 72 D5
Stapleford NG9 182 D6
Willowbridge Cl DN22 39 E6
Willowbridge La NG17 100 D2
Willow Brook NG12 198 A2
Willowbrook Ct 6 NG2 173 C1
Willow Brook Prim Sch NG12 198 A2
Willow Cl
Burton Joyce NG14 163 F5
Calverton NG14 149 C6
East Leake LE12 214 D8
Gainsborough DN21 15 B3
Granby NG13 191 B5
Nottingham NG16 143 B1
Radcliffe on Trent NG12 175 F2
Saxilby LN1 57 B3
Selston NG16 129 B7
South Normanton DE55 113 B5
Worksop S80 35 E1
Willow Cres
Carlton NG4 163 A2
Willow Cres *continued*
Lambley NG4 163 C7
Sutton in Ashfield NG17 100 D3
Willow Ct NG16 129 A1
Willowdene NG12 188 A3
Willow Dr
Annesley Woodhouse NG15 129 F6
North Muskham NG23 110 E2
1 Shireoaks S81 35 A7
Willow Farm Prim Sch NG4 163 A2
Willow Gd NG17 101 B2
Willow Gr
3 Harworth DN11 8 F4
Retford DN22 40 A5
Willow Hill DN10 11 F2
Willow Hill Cl NG6 160 A6
Willow Holt
Lowdham NG14 150 E1
Retford DN22 39 E3
Sutton on Trent NG23 96 F8
Willow La
Beckingham DN10 23 C8
Carlton NG4 163 A2
Langar NG13 190 C2
Maythorne NG25 121 D4
Torksey Lock LN1 44 B1
Willow Mws DN10 23 C8
Willow Poole La LE12 213 C5
Willow Rd
Bingham NG13 178 A4
Carlton NG4 175 A8
Cotgrave NG12 188 A5
New Balderton NG24 140 C5
Nottingham NG7 172 E2
West Bridgford NG2 185 E3
Willow Rise NG10 182 B5
Willow Rundle Dr NG23 153 D5
Willows The
Everton DN10 11 C3
Farndon NG24 139 A4
Nottingham NG8 172 A7
Pleasley NG19 87 A6
Worksop S80 35 E2
Willows Wlk NG24 140 A4
Willow Tree Cl NG19 89 D2
Willow Wong NG14 163 F5
Will Scarlet Cl NG21 118 A4
Willwell Dr NG2 185 C3
Wilmington Ct LE11 220 C2
Wilmington Gdns NG5 161 D6
Wilmore Cl NG9 183 D4
Wilmore Way NG19 101 C5
Wilmot La NG9 183 F5
Wilmot St
Ilkeston DE7 157 E1
Long Eaton NG10 193 A5
Wilmot Way S81 36 C3
Wilne Ave NG10 193 A4
Wilne Rd NG10 193 A4
Wilsic Rd DN11 8 A8
Wilson Ave NG17 114 F5
Wilson Cl
Arnold NG5 162 B5
Mattersey DN10 20 A8
Wilson Rd NG16 143 F1
Wilson's La NG25 137 E4
Wilson St
Gainsborough DN21 15 B1
Newark-on-Trent NG24 124 F1
Pinxton NG16 113 D3
Radmanthwaite NG19 87 D2
Wilsthorpe Com Sch NG10 182 B1
Wilsthorpe Rd DE72 193 A8
Wilton Ave LE11 220 C1
Wilton Pl DE7 157 F1
Wilton Rd NG7 222 A4
Wilton St
5 Ilkeston DE7 157 F1
Nottingham NG6 160 E4
Wilton Terr NG6 160 E4
Wiltshire Ave NG16 128 B4
Wilwell Farm Cutting Nature Reserve★ NG11 185 B2
Wimbishthorpe Cl NG13 181 A3
Wimbledon Dr NG16 159 E3
Wimbledon Rd NG5 161 A3
Wimborne Cl NG2 185 C5
Wimbourne Rd NG7 222 B4
Wimpole Rd NG9 171 D1
Winborne Cl NG19 101 D6
Winchester Ave NG9 183 E7
Winchester Cl
East Leake LE12 205 E1
Mansfield NG18 103 A3
Worksop S81 36 A7
Winchester Cres DE7 170 A8
Winchester Ct NG5 161 E3
Winchester Dr NG19 88 D4
Winchester Mws DN11 9 C5
Winchester St NG5 161 D2
Winchester Terr 7 NG5 161 C3
Winchilsea Ave NG24 140 A7
Winco Bank Way DE55 113 C7
Windermere Ave DN11 8 F4
Windermere Cl
Carlton NG4 162 F2
Mansfield Woodhouse NG19 88 E3
West Bridgford NG2 186 C6
Worksop S81 35 E8

Windermere Gdns
NG10 182 B2
Windermere Rd
Beeston NG9 183 D8
Hucknall NG15 145 F7
Long Eaton NG10 182 A2
Nottingham NG7 173 A8
Windlass Cl LE11 220 D3
Windles Sq NG14 149 A6
Windley Dr DE7 157 D3
Windmill Ave NG15 146 A6
Windmill Cl
Gotham NG11 195 B1
Kirton NG22 78 B6
Nottingham NG3 173 F5
Windmill Cres LE12 214 F8
Windmill Ct NG12 197 F2
Windmill Gr NG15 146 A6
Windmill Hill NG25 134 C5
Windmill La
Mansfield NG18 102 C8
Nottingham NG2 173 F5
Worksop S80 47 B7
Windmill Prim Sch
NG2 174 A4
Windmill Rd LE11 220 D3
Windmill View NG2 174 A4
Windmill Way
Blidworth NG21 117 F4
Kegworth DE74 203 B2
Sutton In Ashfield NG17 100 A2
Windrush Cl
Beeston NG9 171 D1
Sutton in Ashfield NG17 100 E2
Windsmoor Rd NG16 143 D8
Windsor Ave
Newark-on-Trent NG24 139 E6
Sutton in Ashfield NG17 100 B3
Windsor Cl
Collingham NG23 112 A8
Gringley on the Hill DN10 12 E2
Hucknall NG15 146 B8
Nottingham NG8 172 D7
Trowell NG9 170 A5
Windsor Cres
Arnold NG5 162 B5
Stapleford NG9 182 E7
Windsor Ct
Bingham NG13 177 C4
Carlton in Lindrick S81 25 F6
Harworth DN11 9 B5
Sandiacre NG10 182 B4
Windsor Dr NG20 74 A4
Windsor Gdns
Carlton in Lindrick S81 25 E6
Mansfield NG18 102 D5
Windsor Rd
Carlton in Lindrick S81 25 E6
Clipstone NG19 89 D3
Mansfield NG18 102 D5
Newark-on-Trent NG24 139 F6
Retford DN22 29 C1
Selston NG16 129 A8
Worksop S81 35 D7
Windsor St
Beeston NG9 184 A6
Stapleford NG9 182 E7
Windyridge DN10 11 C3
Windy Ridge NG20 74 C3
Winfield's La LE12 216 E2
Wing Alley NG1 223 F2
Wingate Cl NG8 171 F6
Wingbourne Wlk NG6 146 C1
Wingfield Ave S81 36 A6
Wingfield Dr
Beeston NG9 172 A1
Ilkeston DE7 157 D3
Wingfield Rd NG18 103 A4
Wings Dr NG15 145 D3
Winifred Cl 1 NG2 185 A6
Winifred Cres NG14 163 F4
Winifred St
Hucknall NG15 146 B6
Rhodesia S80 35 A4
WINKBURN 108 A1
Winkburn La
Hockerton NG22 121 E7
Winkburn NG22 107 F1
Winkburn NG22 108 A1
Winkburn Rd
Mansfield NG19 101 F7
Maplebeck NG22 107 F5
Maplebeck NG22 108 A6
Winnery Cl DN11 8 A8
Winrow Gdns NG6 160 C3
Winscale Ave NG5 161 A8
Winscale Gdns 13 NG5 161 A8
Winscombe Mount
NG11 195 E7
Winsford Cl NG8 160 B2
Winstanley Dr NG24 140 E8
Winster Ave
Carlton NG4 162 D1
Ravenshead NG15 117 B3
Winster Cl NG9 171 F1
Winster Gr S81 35 F8
Winster Way NG18 103 C5
Winston Cl
Arnold NG3 162 C5
Stapleford NG9 182 E8
Winston Ct NG24 139 E5
Winston Dr NG23 153 E4
Winston Gn
Mattersey DN10 19 F8
Mattersey DN10 20 A8
Winston Gr DN22 30 A1
Winston Green DN10 11 A1
Winterbank Cl NG17 100 D1
Winterbeck Cl NG13 181 A3
Winterbourne Dr NG9 170 E1
Winter Closes NG16 128 F1
Winterdale Cl NG24 125 D1
Wintern Ct DN21 24 D6
Winterton Cl NG5 161 F6
Winterton Gdns NG5 161 B7
Winterton Rise NG5 161 B7
WINTHORPE 125 D6
Winthorpe Prim Sch
NG24 125 D7
Winthorpe Rd
Arnold NG5 162 A7
Gateford S81 35 C8
Newark-on-Trent NG24 125 B3
Winthorpe St NG19 101 D6
Wintringham Cres
NG5 162 A5
Wire La DE55 99 B3
Wisa Terr NG5 161 D2
Wisdom Cl 2 NG24 140 F2
Wiseton Rd DN22 21 C6
Wishford Ave NG7 222 A1
Wisley Cl NG11 185 C3
Wisteria Dr NG12 185 F2
Wisteria Rd NG4 175 C7
Wistow Cl NG8 172 E8
Witch La NG23 96 F8
Witham Cl NG24 125 B2
Withern Rd NG8 159 F1
Withnall Cl NG4 162 E4
Withorn Mews NG19 101 E7
Witney Cl NG5 160 E7
Wittering Cl NG10 193 E5
Wiverton Rd
Bingham NG13 177 E4
Nottingham NG7 173 A8
Woburn Ave NG17 115 C5
Woburn Cl NG2 186 C4
Woburn Croft NG10 182 A4
Woburn Gr DN22 39 E3
Woburn La NG19 87 C4
Woburn Pl NG19 87 C4
Woburn Rd NG19 87 C4
Woburn Rise NG5 162 B5
Wodehouse Ave NG11 195 B2
Wolds Cl LE12 215 E5
Wolds Dr NG12 197 F3
Wolds Farm Bsns Pk
NG12 209 B8
Wolds La NG12 198 B7
Wolds Rise NG12 197 F3
Wolfit Ave NG24 140 E5
Wollacombe Cl NG3 162 D5
WOLLATON 171 E4
Wollaton Ave NG4 162 E2
Wollaton Cl NG18 103 B7
Wollaton Cres NG9 183 E8
Wollaton Ct NG6 160 E6
Wollaton Hall* NG8 172 A3
Wollaton Hall Dr NG8 172 D3
Wollaton Paddocks
NG8 171 C4
Wollaton Pk* NG8 171 F3
Wollaton Rd
Beeston NG9 183 E7
Kirkby-in-Ashfield NG17 115 C5
Nottingham NG8 172 D5
Wollaton Rise
Nottingham NG8 171 E2
Retford DN22 39 E3
Wollaton St NG1 223 D3
Wollaton Vale NG8 171 E2
Wolseley Ct NG17 100 F3
Wolsey Ave NG7 222 B3
Wolsey Cl
Papplewick NG25 136 D8
Southwell NG25 121 D1
Wolsey Dr NG17 115 B7
Wolsey Rd NG24 125 B3
Wolsey Way 2 LE11 220 C4
Wong La DN11 8 A8
Wood Ave
Creswell S80 58 C8
Sandiacre NG10 182 A5
Woodbank Cl NG22 106 A6
Woodbank Dr NG8 171 D2
WOODBECK 53 A8
Woodbeck Rise
Retford DN22 29 E1
Retford DN22 39 E8
WOODBOROUGH 149 C3
Woodborough La NG5 148 C3
Woodborough Rd
Mansfield NG19 87 E1
Nottingham NG3, NG1 161 E2
Woodbridge Ave NG11 184 E3
Woodbridge Cl DE75 143 B1
Woodchurch Rd NG5 147 B1
Wood Cl
Mansfield NG18 102 F8
Ruddington NG11 196 B6
Woodcoates Rd NG22 67 B5
Woodcroft Rd LN1 56 F4
Wood Dr DE74 203 C3
Wooden Beck Hill
DN10 13 C4
Woodend S80 35 B5
Wood End Dr NG15 117 A2
Woodfield Gdns S81 35 E6
Woodfield Rd
Gainsborough DN21 15 F1
Nottingham NG8 159 E1
Pinxton NG16 113 D4
Woodford Cl NG5 146 E1
Woodford Rd
Arnold NG5 162 A5
Hucknall NG15 146 B6
Wood Gate LE11 220 B3
Woodgate Cl NG12 187 E3
Woodgate Ct NG7 222 C3
Woodgate La
Beckingham LN5 142 E8
Cotgrave NG12 187 D3
Woodgate Rd LE12 214 C8
Wood Gr NG14 148 F8
Woodhall Cl
2 Kirkby-in-Ashfield
NG17 114 E7
Mansfield NG18 102 F8
Woodhall Cres
Saxilby LN1 56 F4
Saxilby LN1 57 A4
Woodhall Gdns NG18 102 F8
Woodhall Gn DN22 39 D2
Woodhall Rd NG8 172 B5
Woodhead Cl NG21 76 B1
Woodhedge Dr NG3 174 A8
Wood Hill LE14 218 E3
Woodhill Ave DN21 15 E2
Woodhill Rd NG23 98 A1
Woodhorn Cl NG5 147 F2
Woodhouse Cl S80 35 B5
Woodhouse Ct NG19 88 C2
Woodhouse Gdns
NG11 196 B8
Woodhouse La
Carlton in Lindrick S81 26 A7
Skegby NG17 100 F7
Sutton in Ashfield NG17 101 A7
Woodhouse Mws NG5 161 A2
Woodhouse Pl NG22 66 A2
Woodhouse Rd
Mansfield NG18 102 B8
Norwell NG23 109 E8
Norwell Woodhouse
NG23 95 D1
Woodhouse St NG3 173 F5
Woodhouse Way NG16 159 D3
Woodkirk Rd NG7 184 F2
Wood La
Barkestone-le-Vale
NG13 192 C1
Beckingham DN10 23 B8
Carlton NG4 163 A2
Creswell S80 58 D8
Drakeholes DN10 11 F2
Egmanton NG22 79 F5
Gotham LE12 205 A6
Gringley on the Hill DN10 12 E3
Grove DN22 41 E4
Hucknall NG15 145 F7
Kersall NG22 94 A1
Kingston on Soar NG11 204 F7
Market Warsop NG20 73 F7
Nether Langwith NG20 59 D1
North Wheatley DN22 22 D1
Shirebrook NG19 72 E1
South Scarle NG23 98 E6
Treswell DN22 41 F5
West Markham NG22 65 B4
Wiseton DN10 12 A2
Woodland Ave
Gainsborough DN21 15 B3
Huthwaite NG17 99 E4
Ilkeston DE7 157 D4
Nottingham NG6 160 D5
Worksop S80 36 B1
Woodland Chase DN21 15 E1
Woodland Cl
Clipstone NG21 90 B4
Cotgrave NG12 187 F2
Farnsfield NG22 120 A6
Hodthorpe S80 45 C6
Radcliffe on Trent NG12 176 B3
Woodland Cres NG18 102 F4
Woodland Ct LN1 44 B1
Woodland Dr
Mansfield NG18 102 F4
Nottingham NG3 161 D2
Nuthall NG16 159 F4
Southwell NG25 121 D1
Worksop S81 35 E6
Woodland Gr
Arnold NG5 161 D4
Beeston NG9 183 D5
Carlton NG4 174 F6
Mansfield Woodhouse
NG19 88 C4
Market Warsop NG20 74 B4
Shirebrook NG20 72 D2
Woodland Pk View
NG18 101 F5
Woodland Rd
Mansfield NG18 102 F8
West Bridgford NG2 173 F1
Woodland Rise NG15 117 A2
Woodlands NG24 125 D7
Woodlands Cl
Newark-on-Trent NG24 139 E6
Wymeswold LE12 216 C3
Woodlands Dr LE11 220 A2
Woodlands Farm Cl
NG15 145 D4
Woodlands Gr NG15 145 D4
Woodland Spinney
NG23 152 E2
Woodlands Sch NG8 172 A8
Woodlands The
Blyth S81 18 B6
5 Mansfield NG19 88 B1
Newark-on-Trent NG24 140 E8
4 Radcliffe on Trent
NG4 175 E3
Whaley Thorns NG20 58 F3
Whaley Thorns NG20 59 A3
Woodlands Way NG17 100 C1
Woodlands Wy NG20 73 F1
Woodland View
Southwell NG25 136 D8
Whaley Thorns NG20 59 A3
Woodland Way NG16 143 E2
Woodland Wlk
Collingham NG23 112 B8
Kirkby-in-Ashfield NG17 115 D5
Woodlane Gdns NG3 173 F7
Woodlark Cl
Rainworth NG21 118 A8
Worksop S81 35 D6
Woodleigh NG12 197 E2
Woodleigh Gdns NG5 162 B2
Woodley Sq NG6 146 C2
Woodley St NG11 196 C7
Wood Link NG6 159 E7
Woodlins Gr S81 16 F3
Wood Nook Cl NG16 128 F6
Woodpecker Cl
Bingham NG13 177 F3
East Leake LE12 205 F3
West Bridgford NG12 185 C6
Worksop S81 25 D1
Woodpecker Dr NG21 118 B8
Woodpecker Gr NG17 101 B3
Woodroffe Way LE12 205 E3
Woodrow Av NG8 172 A8
Woodruff La NG22 106 A5
Woodsend NG14 163 F4
Woodsetts La S81 25 A1
Woodsford Gr NG7 184 E2
Wood's Foundation CE Prim
Sch NG14 149 B4
Woods Hill NG17 100 E2
Woodside
Eastwood NG16 143 E3
Farnsfield NG22 120 A6
Retford DN22 39 C8
Sutton in Ashfield NG17 100 E7
Woodside Ave
Mansfield NG18 102 D3
Nuthall NG16 159 B5
Radcliffe on Trent NG12 176 B3
Woodside Cres
Ilkeston DE7 157 D5
Long Eaton NG10 193 B8
Woodside Dr NG5 161 D8
Woodside Rd
Beeston NG9 183 F8
Beeston, Chilwell NG9 183 B3
Burton Joyce NG14 163 D3
Radcliffe on Trent NG12 176 B3
Ravenshead NG15 116 F3
Sandiacre NG10 182 B5
Shirebrook NG20 72 E5
Shireoaks S81 34 F7
Woodside View DN11 9 B4
Woods La NG14 148 E7
Wood's La NG23 153 A1
Wood St
Arnold NG5 161 F8
Eastwood NG16 143 F3
Ilkeston DE7 157 F1
Mansfield NG18 102 A7
Market Warsop NG20 74 B5
Newark-on-Trent NG24 140 B8
Nottingham NG7 222 C3
Woods Terr DN21 15 C2
Woodstock Ave NG7 222 A4
Woodstock Cl NG24 140 C8
Woodstock Rd NG9 182 F3
Woodstock St NG15 146 B6
Woodston Wlk NG5 148 A2
WOODTHORPE 161 E5
Woodthorpe Ave
Arnold NG5 161 E4
Loughborough LE11 220 B1
Woodthorpe Ct NG5 161 E3
Woodthorpe Dr NG3 161 E4
Woodthorpe Gdns
NG5 161 F3
Woodthorpe Hospl
(Private) NG5 161 D4
Woodthorpe Inf Sch
NG5 161 F5
Woodthorpe Rd
Loughborough LE11 220 B1
Nottingham NG3 161 F3
Woodview NG12 188 A2
Wood View NG12 186 B4
Woodview Bsns Ctr 15
NG5 147 A1
Woodview Ct NG4 174 C5
Woodview Gdns NG19 89 C2
Woodville Cl NG9 183 C6
Woodville Dr NG5 161 C3
Woodville Rd 2 NG5 161 C2
Woodward Ave NG9 183 B2
Woodward Gdns NG5 148 E7
Woodward St NG2 173 D1
Woodwards The NG24 140 C6
Woodyard La DN22 40 A1
Wooliscroft Way DE7 157 C2
Woollaton St NG15 146 B7
Woolmer Rd NG2 173 C1
Woolpack La NG1 223 F2
Woolpack St DN22 39 F7
Woolsington Cl NG8 159 D2
Woolsthorpe Cl 2
NG8 172 A6
Wooster Cl NG12 186 A3
Wootton Cl
East Leake LE12 205 E2
Nottingham NG8 171 D7
Worcester Ave NG19 88 C6
Worcester Cl
Lowdham NG14 150 E1
Worksop S81 36 A7
Worcester Gdns NG5 161 E5
Worcester Mews NG19 88 C6
Worcester Rd NG5 161 E5
Wordsworth Ave
Hucknall NG15 145 D6
Mansfield Woodhouse
NG19 88 B4
Wordsworth Ave *continued*
Sutton in Ashfield NG17 100 B3
Wordsworth Dr NG24 140 D5
Wordsworth Rd
Arnold NG5 161 D7
Awsworth NG16 158 C4
Nottingham NG7 222 A4
West Bridgford NG2 185 E6
Workhouse La NG25 122 A1
Workhouse Southwell
The* NG25 122 A1
WORKSOP 35 C5
Worksop Coll S80 47 B7
Worksop College Prep Sch
(Ranby House) DN22 38 B7
Worksop L Ctr S81 35 E6
Worksop Mus* S80 35 F2
Worksop Post 16 Centre
S81 35 E5
Worksop Priory CE Prim
Sch S80 35 F1
Worksop Rd
Babworth DN22 49 C7
Babworth S80 48 F8
Blyth S81 18 A2
Clumber and Hardwick
S80 48 D8
Cuckney NG20 60 A4
Darfoulds S80 34 C1
Edwinstowe NG21, NG22 76 D5
Holbeck S80 45 D1
Holbeck S80 59 E7
Nottingham NG3 173 F5
Ollerton NG22 77 A4
Whitwell S80 45 A7
Whitwell S80 45 A8
Woodsetts S81 25 A2
Worksop S80 36 E1
Worksop S80 47 F8
Worksop S80 48 A8
Worksop S81 36 F1
Worksop Sta S80 35 F4
Worrall Ave
Arnold NG5 161 F7
Long Eaton NG10 182 E1
Worsborough Cl NG18 101 E5
Worthington Rd NG24 140 E3
Worth St NG4 174 E8
Wortley Ave NG9 170 D3
Wortley Cl DE7 170 A8
Wortley Hall Cl NG7 172 C2
Worwood Dr NG2 185 C4
Wossock La LE12 204 F3
Woulds Field NG12 187 F1
Wragby Rd NG7 222 A3
Wray Cl NG3 173 E5
Wren Ct
Long Eaton NG10 193 A4
Worksop S81 35 C7
Wren Dr NG6 146 E3
Wrenthorpe Vale
NG11 195 E8
Wright Dr DN11 9 C5
Wright Gdns DN21 14 A5
Wrightson Cl NG17 101 B3
Wrights Orch NG12 197 E2
Wright St
Carlton NG4 175 A7
Newark-on-Trent NG24 140 B8
Wright Wilson St DN22 39 F6
Wroot Rd
Finningley DN9 1 A5
Finningley DN9 1 B6
Wroughton Ct NG16 144 A2
Wroxham Dr NG8 171 D2
Wycar Rd NG22 106 A4
Wychwood Dr NG9 170 D2
Wychwood Rd NG13 177 C4
Wycliffe Gr NG3 161 E2
Wycliffe St NG7 160 F1
Wycombe Cl NG11 195 D8
Wycombe Grange 1
NG19 88 F2
Wye Gdns NG7 172 D6
Wyggeston Rd NG13 181 B2
Wykeham Rd NG5 162 A5
Wyke La NG24 138 F5
Wykes Ave NG4 162 F2
WYMESWOLD 216 C4
Wymeswold CE Prim Sch
LE12 216 C3
Wymeswold Ind Est
LE12 216 A1
Wymeswold La LE12 216 B1
Wymeswold Meadows
Nature Reserve*
LE12 216 E3
Wymeswold Rd
Hoton LE12 215 E2
Rempstone LE12 215 E5
Thorpe in the Glebe
LE12 216 C8
Wysall NG12 207 C2
Wymondham Cl NG5 162 A6
Wynbreck Dr NG12 197 F3
Wyndale Dr NG18 103 A5
Wyndham Ct NG9 183 B8
Wyndham Mews NG3 173 B7
Wyndham Way NG19 87 B4
Wyndings The NG5 161 F4
Wynhill Ct NG13 177 C5
Wynlea Dr S81 16 F6
Wynndale Dr NG5 161 A3
Wynndale Prim Sch
NG18 103 A5
Wynward Cl DE7 157 C3
Wynwood Cl NG9 183 B2
Wynwood Rd NG9 183 B1
Wyrale Dr NG8 159 E1
WYSALL 207 D3
Wysall Cl NG19 87 E1
Wysall La
Keyworth NG12 197 E1
Keyworth NG12 207 D7
Rempstone LE12 215 F6
Widmerpool NG11 208 B4
Willoughby-on-the-Wolds
LE12 217 B8
Willoughby-on-the-Wolds
NG12 208 A1
Wymeswold LE12 216 D5
Wysall NG12 207 F2
Wysall Rd
Costock LE12 206 E1
Keyworth NG12 197 B1
Wysall NG12 207 A2
Wyton Cl NG5 161 A5
Wyvelle Cres DE74 203 C3
Wyvern Ave NG10 193 D6
Wyvern Cl NG16 158 A8
Wyville Cl NG7 222 A3

Y

Yalding Dr NG8 171 C4
Yalding Gdns NG8 171 C4
Yarnsworth Rd NG24 140 A4
Yarrow Dr NG11 196 E5
Yarwell Cl NG3 174 C7
Yatesbury Cres NG8 171 E8
Yates Croft NG22 119 E7
Yates Gdns 2 NG5 161 A8
Yellowhammer Dr S81 35 D7
Yellowhammer Way
NG5 148 D8
Yeoman Ave NG6 146 F4
Yeoman Cl S80 36 A1
Yeoman Park Sch NG19 88 C4
Yeomans Ct NG7 222 C2
Yeovil Ct 3 NG18 103 A2
Yew Barrow Cl NG2 186 C5
Yew Cl
East Leake LE12 214 D8
Nottingham NG5 161 D2
Yewdale Cl
Nottingham NG11 195 D8
West Bridgford NG2 186 C5
Yews Farm Ct DN11 8 D1
Yews The S81 16 C6
Yew Tree Ave
5 Kirkby-in-Ashfield
NG17 114 F6
Nottingham NG5 161 C1
Yew Tree Cl
Gamston DN22 51 A5
New Ollerton NG22 77 C5
Radcliffe on Trent NG12 175 D3
Yew Tree Dr
Bawtry DN10 9 F7
Huthwaite NG17 99 F2
Shirebrook NG20 72 D5
Yew Tree La
Carlton NG4 163 A2
Nottingham NG11 184 C2
Yew Tree Rd
Cotgrave NG12 188 A5
Elkesley DN22 50 B4
Hucknall NG15 146 B4
New Ollerton NG22 77 C5
Upton DN22 52 B6
Yew Tree Way NG24 125 F2
Yonge Cl NG12 175 E2
York Ave
Beeston NG9 183 F4
Sandiacre NG10 182 A5
Westwood NG16 128 B4
York Cl
Carlton NG4 162 F2
East Leake LE12 205 D1
York Dr NG8 159 D2
Yorke Dr NG24 125 B3
Yorke St
Hucknall NG15 146 A7
Mansfield Woodhouse
NG19 88 B2
York Gr NG17 115 C5
York Mws NG5 161 E8
York Paddock NG22 65 F7
York Pl S81 34 F7
York Rd
Harworth DN11 9 A4
Long Eaton NG10 182 D1
Loughborough LE11 220 A3
Shirebrook NG20 72 E3
Tickhill DN11 8 B7
York St
Carlton NG4 175 A7
East Markham NG22 65 F7
Mansfield NG18 102 A5
Nottingham NG1 223 E4
Sutton in Ashfield NG17 100 E3
York Terr
Market Warsop NG20 74 B4
Misterton DN10 7 A2
Pinxton NG16 113 C1
Young Cl NG6 159 F5
Young Cres NG17 101 B2
Youngs Av NG24 140 E2
Youngs Cl NG24 125 E2
Yvonne Cres NG4 174 F7

Z

Zambra Ct NG12 186 A1
ZOUCH 213 B3
Zouch Rd LE12 213 A3
Zulla Rd NG3 173 C8
Zulu Rd NG7 160 F2